MW00817243

EVIDENCE: COMMON LAW AND FEDERAL RULES OF EVIDENCE

LexisNexis Law School Publishing Advisory Board

Paul Caron
Professor of Law
Pepperdine University School of Law

Bridgette Carr
Clinical Professor of Law
University of Michigan Law School

Steven I. Friedland
Professor of Law and Senior Scholar
Elon University School of Law

Carole Goldberg
Jonathan D. Varat Distinguished Professor of Law
UCLA School of Law

Oliver Goodenough
Professor of Law
Vermont Law School

John Sprankling
Distinguished Professor of Law
McGeorge School of Law

EVIDENCE: COMMON LAW AND FEDERAL RULES OF EVIDENCE

SEVENTH EDITION

Wesley M. Oliver
Professor of Law and Associate Dean for Faculty Research and Scholarship
Duquesne University School of Law

Dale B. Durrer
District Court Judge, 16th Judicial District
Culpeper, Virginia
Adjunct Professor, American University, Washington College of Law,
Washington, D.C.

Kirsha Weyandt Trychta
Teaching Associate Professor and Director of the Academic Excellence Center
West Virginia University College of Law

ISBN: 978-1-6328-0947-6
Looseleaf ISBN: 978-1-6328-0948-3

Library of Congress Cataloging-in-Publication Data

Oliver, Wesley M., author.
Evidence : common law and federal rules of evidence / Wesley Oliver, Associate Professor and Criminal Justice Program Director, Duquesne University School of Law; Dale B. Durrer, District Court Judge, 16th Judicial District, Richmond, Virginia; Kirsha Weyandt Trychta, Assistant Professor of Clinical Legal Skills, Director of Academic Excellence, Duquesne University School of Law. -- Seventh edition.
pages cm.
Includes index.
ISBN 978-1-63280-947-6 (hardbound)
1. Evidence (Law)--United States. I. Durrer, Dale B., author. II. Trychta, Kirsha Weyandt, author. III. Title.
KF8935.R4865 2015
347.73'6--dc23
                                                                                      2015032580

This publication is designed to provide authoritative information in regard to the subject matter covered. It is sold with the understanding that the publisher is not engaged in rendering legal, accounting, or other professional services. If legal advice or other expert assistance is required, the services of a competent professional should be sought.

LexisNexis and the Knowledge Burst logo are registered trademarks of Reed Elsevier Properties Inc., used under license. Matthew Bender and the Matthew Bender Flame Design are registered trademarks of Matthew Bender Properties Inc.

Copyright © 2015 Matthew Bender & Company, Inc., a member of LexisNexis. All Rights Reserved.

No copyright is claimed by LexisNexis or Matthew Bender & Company, Inc., in the text of statutes, regulations, and excerpts from court opinions quoted within this work. Permission to copy material may be licensed for a fee from the Copyright Clearance Center, 222 Rosewood Drive, Danvers, Mass. 01923, telephone (978) 750-8400.

NOTE TO USERS
To ensure that you are using the latest materials available in this area, please be sure to periodically check the LexisNexis Law School web site for downloadable updates and supplements at
www.lexisnexis.com/lawschool.

Editorial Offices
630 Central Ave., New Providence, NJ 07974 (908) 464-6800
201 Mission St., San Francisco, CA 94105-1831 (415) 908-3200
www.lexisnexis.com

MATTHEW◆BENDER

Preface to the Seventh Edition

For decades, Paul Rice's Evidence casebook has been perhaps the most comprehensive text on the market. Professor Rice himself was a giant in the field, and his thorough casebook straddled the line between teaching text and treatise. This version attempts to update the existing text while preserving Professor Rice's effort to produce a book that would be useful for students attempting to learn the subject and provide them with a text thorough enough to serve as a reference for them when they enter practice.

New evidence teachers will find this book somewhat overwhelming in its coverage. Our respect for the dual casebook/treatise role of the book led us to retain its considerable coverage. Teachers should choose the parts they wish to emphasize and make reference to the coverage in the remainder of the book, allowing students to begin to treat the book as a reference text.

Finally, we should note that at this point, the title of the book is somewhat misleading. When Paul Rice produced the first edition of this book, the Federal Rules of Evidence were new. An understanding of the common law rules of evidence provided an essential backdrop for the Federal Rules of Evidence. Decades later, the common law background is rarely needed, and so for the most part has been eliminated. We retain the original name of the book, as this remains the book that Paul Rice first produced with updates to keep it current.

We are honored to be a part of the work Professor Rice started decades ago and hope to do justice to this book on which we have each relied as practitioners and teachers.

Wesley M. Oliver
Dale B. Durrer
Kirsha Weyandt Trychta

Summary Table of Contents

Table of Contents

Table of Contents

Table of Contents

Table of Contents

Table of Contents

Table of Contents

Table of Contents

Table of Contents

Table of Contents

Table of Contents

Table of Contents

Table of Contents

Table of Contents

Table of Contents

Table of Contents

Table of Contents

Chapter 1

STRUCTURE OF THE TRIAL AND PRESENTATION OF EVIDENCE

§ 1.01 INTRODUCTION

Understanding the evidentiary rules that regulate the presentation of evidence in judicial proceedings requires an understanding of the structure within which those rules apply, because their application frequently varies with the circumstances in which the court applies them. This first chapter, therefore, explains the structure, process, and general rules that apply to the presentation of evidence.

§ 1.02 STRUCTURE OF THE TRIAL

In litigation in common-law courts (both civil and criminal), one can visualize the trial as a rectangle divided into four parts.

As illustrated in Diagram 1-1, the first stage of the trial is the plaintiff's case-in-chief. In this part of the trial, the plaintiff must present sufficient evidence from which a reasonable jury could find that the plaintiff has proven all of the elements of the claim upon which its cause of action is based. After the plaintiff completes its presentation by resting its case, the defendant can test whether the plaintiff has satisfied this burden through a motion to the court for a directed verdict. If, at this point, the presiding judge concludes the plaintiff has not presented sufficient evidence from which a jury could find that the plaintiff has established all the elements of its cause of action — a prima facie standard — the judge will grant the defendant's motion for a directed verdict. Granting the motion for a directed verdict ends the action, and the judge will enter a judgment for the defendant before the defendant has even presented any evidence; the trial never advances to the second stage.

Assuming the judge denies the motion for a directed verdict and the defendant wishes to present evidence in response to the plaintiff's case, the defendant may do so in the second stage of the trial: the defendant's case-in-chief or case-in-defense.[1]

The defendant's case may take several different forms:

   (1) the defendant may offer evidence to disprove the facts the plaintiff's witnesses have attempted to establish;

---

[1] If the defendant does not wish to present such evidence, the trial will end after the first stage and the judge will submit the action to the trier of fact for determination.

DIAGRAM 1–1

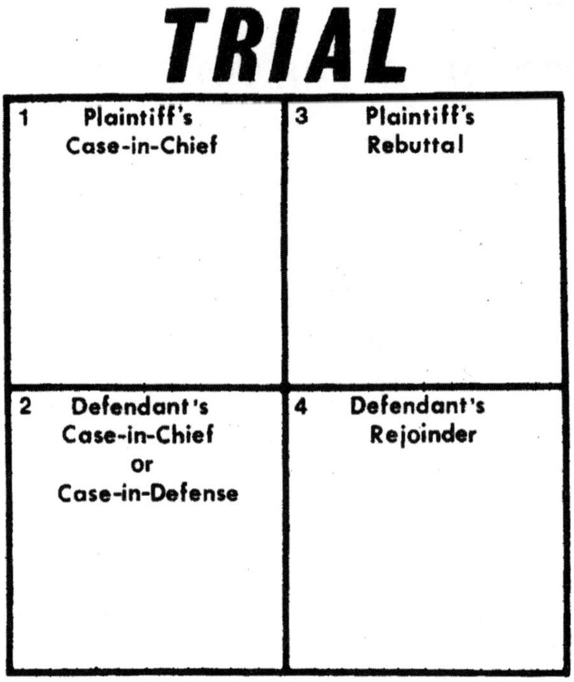

TRIAL

1 Plaintiff's Case-in-Chief	**3 Plaintiff's Rebuttal**
2 Defendant's Case-in-Chief or Case-in-Defense	**4 Defendant's Rejoinder**

    (2)   the defendant may present evidence to establish an affirmative defense that would preclude judgment for the plaintiff even if the jury concluded the plaintiff had proved its case; or

    (3)   the defendant may offer evidence that attacks the credibility of the witnesses on whom the plaintiff relied.

After the defendant has concluded the presentation of its defense, the plaintiff has the opportunity to respond to any affirmative defense the defendant might have presented and to "shore-up" or reinforce its case relative to those issues and facts contested in the defendant's presentation. This third stage of trial is called "rebuttal."

The fourth and last stage of the trial is the rejoinder. In this stage, the defendant has an opportunity to respond to the additional issues raised and the evidence presented in the plaintiff's rebuttal.

Courts at common law and federal courts generally manifest this same trial structure. Rule 611(a) of the Federal Rules of Evidence, however, has codified only the courts' common-law power and responsibility to regulate the order of presenting evidence. It has not codified the structure itself.

[*See* **Fed. R. Evid. 611: Mode and Order of Interrogation and Presentation**]

§ 1.03 PRESENTATION OF TESTIMONY

Within each phase of the trial, the parties will present evidence through the testimony of witnesses. Like the structure of the trial itself, one can visualize the presentation of this testimony as a rectangle divided into four parts (see Diagram 1-2).

The initial presentation of testimony by the party who called the witness — the proponent of the testimony — is denoted "direct examination." During direct examination, to the extent permitted by evidentiary rules, the proponent may elicit firsthand information the witness possesses concerning facts related to the claims or defenses that have been raised in the cause of action, as well as facts that relate to the credibility of any witness who has testified.

DIAGRAM 1–2

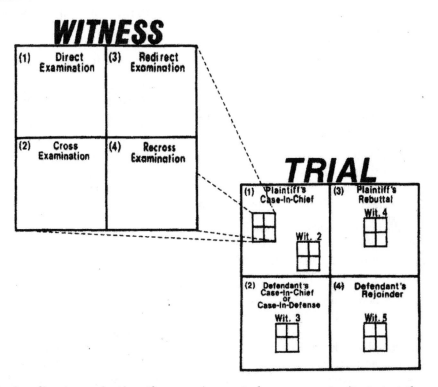

Following direct examination, the opposing party has an opportunity to test the witness' credibility and the reliability of the facts elicited from the witness on direct examination. This second stage of the presentation of testimony — the testing stage — is denoted "cross-examination."

Most jurisdictions limit the scope of cross-examination to those issues the proponent raised directly or by implication during the direct examination, even though the witness might have more relevant information on other issues involved in the cause of action. Courts have adopted this limitation in the belief it contributes to the orderly presentation of evidence. An additional reason for this limitation in criminal cases is the defendant's Fifth Amendment privilege against compelled self-incrimination. A defendant who takes the witness stand can fairly be held to have voluntarily waived the privilege only with regard to the issues addressed in the defendant's direct testimony.

A number of state jurisdictions impose no such limitation on cross-examination and permit wide open cross-examination. Thus, the party conducting the cross-examination can elicit all the relevant information the witness possesses, whether or not, during direct examination, the proponent touched on the issues to which this information relates. The reason for this broad approach is the belief that it facilitates the search for truth by allowing all a witness knows to be brought to light at one time, thereby preventing adversaries from making their cases and misleading the jury through the controlled disclosure of facts. Even in these jurisdictions, however, the Fifth Amendment privilege against compelled self-incrimination limits the breadth of the defendant's cross-examination in criminal cases.

Under the Federal Rules of Evidence, Rule 611(b) limits the scope of cross-examination.

[*See* Fed. R. Evid. 611: Mode and Order of Interrogation and Presentation]

Of course, both at common law and under the Federal Rules, the exploration of facts relevant to the witness' credibility is always appropriate on cross-examination, because courts consider the proponent's presentation of the witness to automatically put the witness' credibility at issue.

If the opposing party is successful in raising questions as to credibility and reliability, and the witness was not given an opportunity to explain during cross-examination, the proponent may elicit those explanations in the third phase of the witness' examination, redirect examination.

The final phase of examination is recross-examination. In this phase the opposing party is given another opportunity to test any new information that the proponent may have brought out during redirect examination.

The presiding judge may propound questions to clarify preceding testimony or to elicit new information at any time during the parties' examination of a witness. This power exists under both the common law and Rule 614 of the Federal Rules of Evidence. The judge must be careful, however, not to assume the role of an advocate and thereby influence the jury's decision. Of course, this concern does not exist if there is no jury because the case is being tried to the court. In this circumstance, there are virtually no restrictions on the judge's power to conduct examinations that will assist in rendering a fair decision.

EXERCISE

Ronald, the defendant, testified on his own behalf at trial. The trial court judge skeptically questioned Ronald at length during Ronald's direct examination, and, after the plaintiff completed his thorough cross-examination, the judge followed up on the plaintiff's questions with more of his own. On redirect, the judge repeatedly interrupted again, challenging Ronald about his assertions and other defense witnesses' testimony. May a trial judge ask the defendant questions during trial? If so, are there any restrictions?

§ 1.04 RULES APPLICABLE TO ELICITATION OF TESTIMONY

[A] Competency of Witnesses

At early common law, there were a number of grounds on which a court could find a witness incompetent to testify. These included lack of a belief in a supreme being who would punish for false swearing (all witnesses were required to take an oath prior to testifying); inability to perceive, remember, and recount accurately because of a mental incapacity resulting from a mental disease or immaturity; having been convicted of certain felonies; and serving as the judge or a juror in the trial in which the testimony was sought. With the exception of incompetency of the witness serving as judge or juror, most jurisdictions have eliminated these testimonial disqualifications in the belief such factors can be brought to the jurors' attention during cross-examination, enabling the jurors to make their own assessment of the proper weight they should give to the testimony.

Rule 601 of the Federal Rules of Evidence reflects this modern trend and creates a presumption that every person is competent to be a witness.

[*See* Fed. R. Evid. 601: General Rule of Competency]

As explained by the U.S. Court of Appeals for the Fourth Circuit, a witness is competent unless shown not to have "personal knowledge of the matter about which he is to testify [required by Rule 602], that he does not have the capacity to recall, or that he does not understand the duty to testify truthfully [does not understand the duty created by the oath that he must take pursuant to Rule 603]." *United States v. Lightly*, 677 F.2d 1027, 1028 (4th Cir. 1982). Although Rule 601 recognizes state rules of incompetency in civil actions and proceedings in which state law supplies the rule of decision,[2] the only explicit grounds of incompetency included in the Federal Rules are contained in Rule 605, which makes the

---

[2] Although Rule 601 makes no provision for the common-law disqualification of parties and interested witnesses from testifying to statements by deceased parties — a limitation that was commonly included in provisions known as "Dead Man's Statutes" — some states still maintain such a provision. Dead Man's Statutes were intended to prevent fraudulent claims against estates. They have been roundly criticized, however, because they often result in the preclusion of legitimate claims. In fact, they may create more injustice than they eliminate. *See* McCORMICK ON EVIDENCE § 65, at 159–61 (3d ed. 1984); 2 WIGMORE ON EVIDENCE § 578, at 821 (Chadbourn rev. 1979). In recognition of this unfairness, many states either have eliminated their Dead Man's Statutes or have modified them in various ways. Some states have made the rule contained in their Dead Man's Statute inapplicable if the deceased party's communication is corroborated. Other states have limited the application of the rule to oral communications. Certain jurisdictions have permitted judges to disregard the rule if, in the exercise of the judge's discretion, he determines that application of the rule would create an injustice. Finally, some states have refused to apply the rule if the representative of the deceased party called the witness in question.

presiding judge incompetent as a witness, and Rule 606, which precludes a juror from testifying in the trial of a case in which he is sitting as a juror.

EXERCISES

1.   The plaintiff's case rests primarily on the testimony of one eyewitness named Chapman. Prior to trial the defense learns that Chapman habitually uses narcotics and has been hospitalized twice previously for anxiety; the latter hospitalization having occurred just one month prior to the events about which Chapman was purporting to testify as an eyewitness. Defense counsel has concerns about Chapman's ability to recall the specific events underlying the lawsuit. What should the defense counsel ask the Judge to do prior to Chapman testifying at trial?

2.   Kerry, a member of the Ute Mountain Ute tribe, was charged with forcibly assaulting a Bureau of Indian Affairs officer with a dangerous weapon. The case proceeded to trial and the jury found Kerry guilty. The day after the jury announced its verdict, one juror — "Juror K.C." — approached defense counsel and claimed that the jury deliberation had been improperly influenced by racist claims about Native Americans. The foreman, according to Juror K.C., told the other jurors that he used to live near an Indian Reservation and that "when Indians get alcohol, they all get drunk, and that when they get drunk, they get violent." Several other jurors then agreed with the foreman and discussed the need to "send a message back to the reservation." Defense counsel immediately filed a post-trial motion seeking a new trial, arguing that several of the jurors obviously lied during voir dire when asked if they harbored any bias or prejudice toward Native Americans. Juror K.C. is willing to testify at this post-trial proceeding. The government opposes the motion on the ground that Kerry's only evidence of misconduct (namely, Juror K.C.'s testimony) is inadmissible under the Rules of Evidence. Is the government correct?

[B]   Personal Knowledge

The court seeks to obtain reliable accounts of facts relevant to the cause of action through examination of witnesses who have personal, firsthand knowledge of such facts. Only if the witness has personal knowledge can the opposing party test the reliability of information elicited by the proponent on direct examination. For example, if the witness testified to an object's condition solely on the basis of statements made to the witness by others who had actually observed the object, the opposing party could not test the accuracy of the description of that condition because the persons whose observations are being related to the court are not present in the courtroom. In such a situation, all that the witness could verify on cross-examination is that he completely and accurately perceived, remembered, and repeated what someone else had told him. The accuracy and reliability of the witness' source of information would be left totally to speculation. This danger is the basis of the hearsay exclusionary rule that will be examined in Chapters 4 and 5. To provide an adequate basis for testing the reliability of a witness' testimony, therefore, courts at common law required that witnesses have personal knowledge of the facts they describe. Congress has perpetuated this requirement of personal knowledge in Rule 602 of the Federal Rules of Evidence.

[*See* Fed. R. Evid. 602: Lack of Personal Knowledge]

The only exceptions to this requirement of firsthand knowledge are the testimony of expert witnesses (*see* Chapter 8) and admissions by party opponents (*see* Chapter 5).

[C]   Focused Questions Calling for Specific Answers

The purpose of the rules of evidence is to ensure the reliability of the evidence on which factual findings will be made and to preserve the impartiality of those who have been called on to make those determinations by conditioning or precluding the introduction of certain evidence.

It is the parties' responsibility to enforce these rules by objecting to questions that call for inadmissible testimony. The success of these evidentiary prohibitions usually turns on the adversaries' ability to exclude such testimony prior to its being given before the jury. Once the jury hears the inadmissible testimony, much of its potential damage has already been done, and the remedy of instructing the jury to disregard it is virtually inconsequential.

Realistically, the opposing party can exclude inadmissible testimony prior to its being heard by the jury only if the proponent gives sufficient notice that it is seeking such testimony. Consequently, courts at common law generally required that questions eliciting testimony be focused, in that they call for specific and limited answers. Questions calling for narrative answers, such as "Could you relate to the jury the things that you experienced after you arrived at the scene of the accident?" would be objectionable because the witness could respond by relating inadmissible statements made by others (hearsay), as well as details that are irrelevant and potentially inflammatory before the opposing party has an opportunity to object.

The narrative form of answer is more consistent with the manner in which individuals commonly communicate outside the courtroom and is usually a more effective means of expression. Therefore, trial judges have tended to relax this restriction, to obtain the perceived overriding benefit of a more natural and spontaneous account from the witnesses of the facts they have personally experienced. This relaxation has been particularly noticeable under the Federal Rules of Evidence relative to testimony of expert witnesses called to assist the jury in understanding complex and difficult concepts and principles and applying them to specific factual situations. Courts have justified this relaxation of the focused question requirement with regard to expert witnesses, as opposed to other types of witnesses, not only because of the nature of expert testimony, but also because the Federal Rules have significantly diminished the number and kinds of potential objections an opposing party can make to expert testimony. Consequently, advance notice of what an expert witness might say is not nearly so important for the purpose of forestalling objectionable testimony from being heard by the jury.

Rule 611(a) of the Federal Rules of Evidence has encouraged this relaxation of the specific question and answer requirement. For the text of Rule 611(a), see § 1.02.

[D] Leading Questions

[1] Leading Questions Prohibited on Direct Examination

It is feared that a witness who is aligned in interest with a party might consciously or unconsciously color testimony according to what he believes a party's lawyer wants to hear. Therefore, courts prohibit that lawyer from using leading questions when examining the witness.

Leading questions suggest the answer the questioner seeks. They are objectionable because they allow the witness to accommodate the party with whom the witness is aligned in interest merely by confirming the story the examiner either is telling or suggesting through his questions. For example, in the following questions and answers, the attorney's questions reveal more of the facts on which the plaintiff's claim is based than do the witness' answers.

Q.   After the accident that resulted in the death of the plaintiff, did you, as the plant engineer, carefully examine the machine that was found lying next to the plaintiff?

A.   Yes.

Q.   Was your purpose in examining the machine to determine whether it was the cause of the plaintiff's injuries, and if so, why?

A.   Yes.

Q.   When you say that you carefully examined the machine, do you mean you opened the machine and examined and tested its contents as well as its exterior?

A.   Yes.

Q.   As you conducted this examination, did you discover anything to suggest the machine was the cause of the plaintiff's injuries?

A.   Yes, I found an indentation on the right front exterior of the machine — the position where the plaintiff's head would have been struck.

Q.   Did you find anything inside the machine, like loose wiring, that could have caused the machine to lunge forward suddenly and unexpectedly, like witnesses have testified that it did?

A.   Yes, I did discover two loose wires.

Q.   Which wires did you find loose?

A.   I found the yellow and red wires leading from the starter to the ignition switch.

Q.   You previously testified you had experienced wiring problems with this machine. Were these the same red and yellow wires involved in those problems?

A.   Yes.

Q.   Was your examination of this machine such that you could feel
            confident that had anything else been the cause of the machine
            lunging forward, you would have found it?

A.   Yes, quite confident.

Q.   Could you describe for the jury how this wiring condition could have
            caused the machine to lunge forward the way that witnesses have
            described?

A.   Yes. . . .

To be leading, questions need not be as blatantly suggestive as those in the
preceding example. Suggestiveness is a matter of degree, and the application of the
rule against it requires the presiding judge to exercise his discretion. An appellate
court will reverse a trial judge's determination of suggestiveness only on a
demonstration of arbitrary abuse. For example, in examining a witness, a lawyer
might ask, "Did you hear anyone talking?" This question is leading to the extent it
suggests someone was talking. Its leading nature probably is harmless, however,
and the trial judge will overlook it because the question is beneficial in that it
expedites the examination by focusing the inquiry.

If the witness gives an affirmative answer to the above question, however, the
follow-up question to elicit the source and nature of the overheard statement should
be neutral in content. For example, the lawyer may not ask if the witness heard the
defendant talking about having shot his partner. To elicit this information properly,
the lawyer might ask, "Could you identify the individual you heard speaking?" If the
answer to this question were "Yes, the defendant," the lawyer might follow up this
answer by asking, "What did you hear him say?"

Many leading questions call for yes or no answers. Consequently, it is not
uncommon for some judges to mistakenly classify all questions calling for such
answers as leading questions. This classification erroneously places form over
substance. Questions are leading because of their suggestive nature, not because of
the brevity of the answers they elicit. The central issue is whether the question
propounded was an inquiry through which substantive information was being
elicited or an assertion of fact for which confirmation was sought.

The following questions illustrate the above point. If a witness had testified that
after hearing what sounded like shots, she ran to the upstairs bedroom, a court
should not consider the question, "Did anyone accompany you when you ran
upstairs?" to be leading merely because the question prompts a one-syllable
answer. Upon an affirmative answer, the follow-up question "Who?" also would not
be leading. However, approaching the same substantive inquiry with a more
factually explicit question, such as, "Did your brother accompany you when you
went upstairs?" could correctly be considered leading.

Closely related to the issue of leading questions is the prohibition against *loaded
questions*. These are questions that assume the truth of unproven facts. For
example, in the question, "Who accompanied you when you went upstairs?" the
questioner is leading the witness to accept the unproved fact that someone actually
did accompany her upstairs by her confirmation of the fact through her answer to

the question. Courts also prohibit the use of loaded questions because they are too suggestive.

The prohibition against the use of leading or loaded questions is applicable only if the witness is aligned in interest with the examining party. Only then is there a significant risk the witness will adopt suggested facts. Because parties usually call witnesses who will testify favorably to their side of the case, the prohibition against leading questions usually will be applicable only during the proponent's direct examination, not during the opponent's cross-examination.

It would be misleading, however, to characterize the prohibition against leading questions as a rule applicable only to direct examination; instances will arise in which a party, by necessity, will have to call a witness aligned with the opposition. This is particularly true in civil litigation in which the parties can call one another as witnesses. In these circumstances, it would be ludicrous to prohibit the proponent from examining its adversary through leading questions, because there is little chance that the proponent will induce the adversary to give misleading or inaccurate testimony through suggestive questioning. It would be even more absurd to permit such questions by the adversary's own lawyer on cross-examination, because in this instance, the risks that the rule was designed to guard against would be at their highest.

[2] Exceptions to Leading Question Prohibition

Courts have recognized a number of exceptions to the prohibition against leading questions in situations where the consequences of leading questions are not significant and the benefits, in terms of efficiency, are great. Courts also have recognized these exceptions when there is a need for leading questions to develop the testimony properly.

The most obvious exception to the prohibition against leading questions, based on reduced risk, efficiency, and possibly an element of need, is cross-examination by a party with whom the witness is not aligned in interest. Another exception is that, during examination by a party with whom the witness *is* aligned in interest, that party may use leading questions in addressing preliminary matters or undisputed facts. For example, in establishing a witness' name, address, age, occupation, place of employment, years of service to the employer, and work schedule, there is little need to consume blocks of time and pages of transcript by eliciting the information through the neutral, and less direct, question-and-answer format. Similarly, in addressing uncontested matters of substance, it is generally agreed that the more efficient and logical approach to matters in which the witness' testimony is important is for the examining attorney to move through the uncontested matters by stating them and having the witness confirm them.

Most exceptions to the leading-question rule are grounded in necessity. This need results either from the nature of the witness' testimony or the status of the witness being examined. If a party's witness surprises the party by giving testimony that is inconsistent with what the witness had previously indicated he would say and with what he previously had said, and if the inconsistent testimony is damaging, the court will allow the proponent to use leading questions to elicit from the witness the fact that in the past he gave an inconsistent account of the facts to a specific person at a particular time in a particular place. The witness also might fail to give needed testimony because of a memory failure, rather than by giving inconsistent testimony. To jog the witness's memory, a court will allow the interrogator to suggest facts to the witness in anticipation that hearing them will revive the witness's memory. Of course, those facts, as stated in the leading questions, will not constitute evidence unless the witness's memory is jogged and the witness adopts them as part of his testimony.

A witness' status can give rise to a need to use leading questions in two particular instances. First, if the witness has limited abilities to testify because of his age, mental infirmity, or unfamiliarity with the English language, leading questions might be the only effective means of obtaining the information the witness possesses.[3] Second, at the other end of the spectrum, a witness may qualify as an expert who can provide particularly helpful information and assistance to the jury, but who may lack knowledge of the facts that are relevant to the case. To take advantage of the expert's expertise, the court will allow the proponent to use leading questions to pose hypothetical questions in which the proponent makes the relevant facts known to the expert.

Despite these exceptions to the leading-question rule, it still must be followed. Continued disregard for the rule can lead to the termination of the direct examination of a witness by order of the court. *See United States v. Clinical Leasing Serv., Inc.*, 982 F.2d 900 (5th Cir. 1992) (ruling that district court did not abuse its discretion by terminating direct examination of witness when court had warned attorney no less than seven times to refrain from using leading questions).

The Federal Rules of Evidence have codified the common law relating to the use of leading questions, permitting leading questions only on cross-examination, or if a witness is identified as a hostile witness.

[*See* Fed. R. Evid. 611: Mode and Order of Interrogation and Presentation]

§ 1.05   PRESENTING AND EXCLUDING EVIDENCE

[A]   Qualifying and Offering Evidence

Before a party may offer any evidence, whether testimonial or tangible, in any of the four stages of trial, that party first must show that the evidence is related to the cause of action. This requires that the proponent authenticate the evidence to be offered. The authentication of evidence entails the laying of a factual foundation through which the proponent identifies the evidence and establishes its relationship to the cause of action in connection with which it is offered.

Although the concept of authentication, in the context of testimonial evidence, is more likely to be referred to as "qualification" of the witness, the purpose of both

---

[3] In this situation, courts will take great care to strike the difficult balance between the risk and benefits of leading questions. On the one hand, these witnesses need assistance to efficiently present a logical and coherent story. On the other hand, they are the most susceptible to manipulation by their questioners.

authentication and qualification is to establish the logical relevance of the evidence before the finder of facts hears it. For testimonial evidence, qualification involves identifying the witness, establishing that his testimony is based on personal knowledge of the facts related, and explaining the origin and context within which the witness perceived those facts, whether the accounts of facts relate directly or indirectly to the incident in question or to questions of credibility. Rule 602 of the Federal Rules of Evidence imposes the personal-knowledge component of authentication on all witnesses except experts. *See* § 1.04[B].

Similarly, a proponent must authenticate tangible evidence prior to its introduction by establishing its relationship to the cause of action, whether it is factually related to the cause of action (real evidence) or offered solely for its illustrative or explanatory purposes (demonstrative evidence). Before authenticating tangible items, however, the proponent first must comply with a procedural requirement. Tangible items, unlike witnesses, do not have distinguishing names or other identifying labels by which they may be referred to in testimony so that the transcript clearly reflects the item or items to which the testimony relates. Accordingly, the proponent first must mark tangible items of evidence for identification. This procedure entails assigning each item an identification letter or number by which it can be referred to throughout the proceedings. The first tangible item presented by the plaintiff, for example, might be marked Plaintiff's Exhibit #1, and all additional exhibits would be marked sequentially. If the plaintiff's exhibits are identified with numbers, the defendant's exhibits will be identified with letters. The court reporter usually will mark each item presented upon a party's request.

Real evidence is comprised of all tangible evidence involved in a cause of action that a party introduces as substantive proof, whether directly or circumstantially relevant. Usually it is the actual item involved in the cause of action. The gun used in the armed robbery, the writing that created a contract, the writing or recording in which a party opponent made an admission, and the broken bicycle frame represent examples of real evidence. Prior to the introduction of an item of real evidence, the proponent first must have a sponsoring witness, who has been properly qualified, establish that the item actually is what the proponent purports it to be. This procedure is known as "authentication."

The most common method of authentication is direct authentication through either testimonial admissions by the party opponent or the testimony of other witnesses with personal knowledge of the exhibit in question and of its relationship to the cause of action. However, there are no limitations on the circumstantial means by which a party can authenticate evidence. Congress codified, in Rules 901 and 902 of the Federal Rules of Evidence, the more common methods of authentication recognized at common law. Because the issue of authentication is pervasive, in addition to the brief discussion included in this section, these methods will be discussed throughout the text as they arise in the context of cases and particular evidentiary issues under discussion.

The process of authenticating real evidence occasionally will involve the necessity of establishing what has been called a *chain of custody*. This entails tracing the custody of the offered item backwards from the time it is offered at trial to the time of the incident that gave rise to the cause of action. Establishing a chain of custody is necessary in two instances: (1) if no single person can identify the item and connect it back to a particular event or person; or (2) if the nature of the item is such that the naked eye cannot detect its alteration and any alteration would significantly affect its relevance.

The first instance would arise if a witness picked up a gun at the scene of a crime, but could not identify the gun at trial as the object he found. To connect the gun to the crime scene, the prosecution would have to call the witness who discovered it and establish through his or her testimony that: (1) he possesses relevant firsthand knowledge of the murder weapon (that he found it); (2) the exhibit in question looks like the weapon the witness found; and (3) the witness gave the gun to a particular police officer. The prosecution also would have to call the officer to whom the first witness gave the weapon and establish through the officer's testimony that the first witness gave him a gun and that the exhibit in question is the gun that he received. The officer's in-court identification of the gun usually will be made possible by the fact that the officer placed an identifying mark on the weapon when he received it, usually on a tag affixed to the item. Of course, if the first witness were able to identify the gun because he had placed his own identifying mark on it, or because of the unique characteristics of the weapon, no chain of custody would be necessary.

The necessity of establishing a chain of custody also would arise in such situations as the above hypothetical if, in addition to connecting the gun back to the crime, the prosecution wished to introduce fingerprint evidence lifted from the gun. The prosecution first would have to establish an additional link in the chain of custody between the officer who initially received the gun and the lab technician who performed the fingerprint tests. The prosecution also would have to establish that, during the interval in which each custodian possessed the gun, the individual whose fingerprints were discovered during the tests did not have access to the gun and therefore could not have placed his prints on it after the crime was committed. The prosecution would have to establish the chain of custody in the same manner, of course, if the exhibit in question were, for instance, a white powder alleged to be a controlled substance. Once again, the prosecution would have to discount the possibility that the substance was altered by those who possessed or had access to it from the time it was obtained from the defendant.

The requirement of establishing a chain of custody is not limited to real evidence. Demonstrative evidence, such as a tape recording of a party's statements, for example, could be tampered with between the time it was made and the time a party offered the recording into evidence. If no one was available to verify, from personal knowledge of what was recorded, that the recording accurately reflected what the recorded individual actually said at the time of the recording, the proponent, after establishing that the tape was accurately made, would have to establish a chain of custody from the time of production to the time of offering; the proponent would have to address and discount the possibility of tampering at each link of the custodial chain.

Although the chain of custody often is important in ensuring the integrity of evidence, it is not a requirement that courts impose so strictly or with such stringency that they exclude evidence unless the proponent discounts all possibilities of tampering. A reasonable assurance of authenticity is all that courts require. This determination is a discretionary one made by the trial judge, whose decision will be reversed on appeal only upon a showing of a clear abuse of discretion. Because of the judgmental nature of the determination, the stringency of the chain of custody requirement varies from one case to the next, depending on the nature of the item in question and the probability of alteration under each particular set of circumstances. The contingent nature of this determination is demonstrated in *United States v. Howard-Arias*, 679 F.2d 363 (4th Cir. 1982), in which the prosecution did not completely establish the chain of custody from the time the authorities seized bales of a substance from the defendant's boat until the time the prosecution offered samples of the substance into evidence at trial. Although the Coast Guard officer who seized and tested the marijuana, the officer to whom he surrendered it, the DEA custodian in Norfolk and the DEA chemist all appeared as witnesses, the special agent who received the marijuana from the second Coast Guard officer for transit to the DEA agent in Norfolk did not. Upholding the trial judge's finding that a sufficient chain of custody had been demonstrated, the appellate court stated:

> The "chain of custody" rule is but a variation of the principle that real evidence must be authenticated prior to its admission into evidence. . . . The purpose of this threshold requirement is to establish that the item to be introduced, *i.e.*, marijuana, is what it purports to be, *i.e.*, marijuana seized from the Don Frank. Therefore, the ultimate question is whether the authentication testimony was sufficiently complete so as to convince the court that it is improbable that the original item had been exchanged with another or otherwise tampered with. . . . Contrary to the appellant's assertion, precision in developing the "chain of custody" is not an ironclad requirement, and the fact of a "missing link does not prevent the admission of real evidence, so long as there is sufficient proof that the evidence is what it purports to be and has not been altered in any material aspect. . . ." Resolution of this question rests with the sound discretion of the trial judge. . . .

Id. at 366.

Demonstrative evidence, as distinguished from real evidence, encompasses all tangible evidence other than those things involved in the cause of action: evidence used to demonstrate, explain, or illustrate the substance of testimony and other tangible evidence, so that the finder of facts can more fully understand and accurately resolve the factual issues in the case. Sponsoring witnesses also are needed for the introduction of demonstrative evidence. Unlike real evidence, however, the foundation for demonstrative evidence requires a showing that the evidence sufficiently reflects and duplicates the critical conditions that existed at the time the cause of action arose, so that it fairly illuminates the testimonial evidence it is offered to support. For example, if the prosecution in a murder case were attempting to demonstrate how the defendant could have concealed the murder weapon in the palm of his hand, it would not need the actual murder weapon to do this. The prosecution could select a handgun that was similar in size, shape, and color to the one used and, if its similarity could be established through the testimony of a witness who saw the actual weapon, the court then would allow the prosecution to physically demonstrate how one could conceal the weapon in the palm of one's hand. Although there is no universal rule that demonstrative evidence must be offered into the record as an exhibit, the better practice, which is imposed as a rule in many courts, is to do so. This is particularly true if the accompanying testimony that appears in the transcript is so intertwined with the object's appearance that the testimony's clarity at the appellate level will be jeopardized unless both the transcript and the exhibit are presented together for appellate review.

The same is true, of course, of scientific experiments and in-court demonstrations. If, for example, a proponent were offering the results of an experiment to prove how a product like the Rely tampon can produce the bacteria that causes the toxic shock syndrome by which the plaintiff claims to have been injured, the proponent of the experiment's results, or of an in-court demonstration recreating the phenomenon, would have to authenticate the evidence through a qualified sponsoring witness (in this instance, probably an expert in bacteriology). This witness would have to establish that the conditions under which the experiment was or is to be conducted sufficiently recreate the physical conditions in a woman's vagina to reflect fairly the potential consequences of the use of the product in question. The level of similarity the proponent must demonstrate, and the degree to which the scientific principles underlying the experiment must be accepted in the relevant scientific discipline, before a court will admit the evidence will be discussed in later sections examining the topics of expert opinions and scientific evidence. *See* §§ 8.02, 8.03.

A proponent who uses technical equipment to produce demonstrative evidence first must prove that the equipment accurately recreated or reproduced an event by presenting evidence showing that the equipment was functioning properly at the time of the recreation and the operator used the equipment correctly. Depending on the kind of evidence produced, a proponent can accomplish this in two ways. First, if the evidence is a photograph or a tape recording of something a witness previously saw or heard, the proponent can have that witness look at the photograph or listen to the tape recording, identify what it recorded (*i.e.*, the individuals or things involved), and testify it is accurate. Second, if the evidence is a record of something that a sponsoring witness with personal knowledge cannot verify is accurate (for example, infrared photographs of activities that took place in the dark), the technical accuracy of the equipment must be established through the testimony of someone who knows how the equipment works and who tested it to ensure that it was functioning accurately at the time the evidence was recorded. The proponent then will have to establish that the operator of the equipment was competent: that he knew how to operate the machine and that he actually did so correctly. The proponent often can establish all of this solely through the operator's testimony.

Once a proponent has laid the foundation for the authentication of tangible evidence, it then must orally offer the tangible exhibit into the record ("Your Honor, at this time the plaintiff offers Plaintiff's Exhibit A into evidence"). The presiding judge must accept the exhibit as substantive evidence before the finder of fact may rely upon it during its deliberations. It is at this point — when the evidence is formally offered — that the opposing party should make whatever objections it might have to the introduction of the evidence. If the opponent makes no objections, usually the court will accept the offer without question. The judge has the inherent power to exclude the evidence, even in the absence of objection, but rarely exercises it, reserving it for those limited instances in which it is clear that an injustice would result from introduction of the evidence.

If the opposing party makes an objection, the proponent is entitled to a ruling and should insist that the judge make this ruling, because the judge's silence does not necessarily reflect consent to the exhibit's introduction. Moreover, if the court does not admit the evidence, the evidence will not become part of the record on which the judgment will be based. If the court admits the evidence over the opponent's objection, the proponent may read from the exhibit if it is a writing, use it while interrogating witnesses and for demonstrative purposes, and give it to the jury for examination.

EXERCISES

1. Pedro, a mid-level drug dealer, agreed to cooperate with the Drug Enforcement Administration's investigation into Ron — a suspected kingpin. The government instructed Pedro to record his telephone conversations with Ron, and Pedro agreed. Several weeks later Pedro hand-delivered three tape recordings to federal agents. Each recording was made outside the presence of the federal agents and contains the voices of two men discussing a large scale drug distribution operation. The government promptly indicted Ron for drug conspiracy and is now preparing for trial. The prosecutor would like to offer the tape recordings as evidence against Ron at trial, but Pedro is not willing to authenticate the tape recordings at trial. Moreover, Ron vehemently denies that he is one of the speakers in the phone conversations. How can the government authenticate the tape recordings at trial?

2. At trial the plaintiff would like to admit emails purportedly drafted and sent by one of the defendants, Ms. Hayward Borders an employee of More Than Enough, Inc. Border denies sending the emails and no one saw Border draft or send the emails. Since there is no testimony from a witness with first-hand knowledge, the plaintiff must authenticate the emails using circumstantial evidence. What type of circumstantial evidence could plaintiff offer to authenticate the emails?

3. At Chaim's criminal trial, the prosecution called as a witness a United States Postal Inspector, who had spent eighty percent of her time over the previous three years investigating the defendant. She testified that during that time she became familiar with Chaim's handwriting by viewing documents such as his passport, driver's license, post-arrest documents, and a check register for an account in his name. She then offered her lay opinion that certain signature and handwriting samples shown to her at trial were written by Chaim. Chaim objects. How should the court rule?

4. Are these in-court demonstrations admissible?

a. The prosecution seeks to show a color photograph of the victim's skeleton to corroborate testimony that the victim passively climbed into his own grave and waited to be executed.

b. On the issue of damages, plaintiff's counsel wants the plaintiff to remove, clean, and replace his artificial eye in front of the jury.

c. The prosecution wants to compel the criminal defendant to participate in an in-court demonstration, by speaking or displaying a unique physical characteristic to the jury.

d. A defendant railroad company in a wrongful death action seeks to demonstrate that a train's headlight would bend around a corner and be visible to an oncoming driver. The demonstration will require extensive jury movement and participation.

e. The government wants to detonate a fake pipe bomb in the courtroom to show how the defendant's bomb would have ignited had he been able to carry out his plot to blow up an office building.

5. John suffered a severe brain injury when the ladder he was using to clean his gutters buckled and collapsed. John filed suit against the ladder's manufacture alleging defective design and negligence. At trial a defense expert illustrated his testimony by using an exemplar of the ladder in question. The exemplar ladder was new but had been built to the exact specifications of the ladder John had been using. John objected to use of the exemplar ladder as substantive evidence, and the trial court allowed its use for solely demonstrative purposes. During jury deliberations, the jury asks to see, touch, and step on the ladder. May the trial judge grant the jury's request?

[B]   Excluding Inadmissible Evidence

[1]   Necessity for Objection

The rules of evidence are not self-executing. Usually a court will enforce them to exclude evidence only if the opposing party properly objects to the introduction of the evidence. The substantive bases on which an opposing party can object to offers of evidence will be the subject of examination over the remainder of this text. One must, therefore, examine and understand the process by which a party makes an objection and some of the basic rules governing the process.

[2]   Timeliness

In our adversarial system of adjudication, it is the responsibility of the parties, not the presiding judge, to enforce the rules of evidence. This is accomplished through *timely objections* to the opponent's offers of evidence. Of course, it is the judge's responsibility to rule correctly on any objections that are interposed. This judicial responsibility, however, only arises after one of the parties has made a timely objection. Failure to make a timely objection waives the objection, and the finder of fact may use the otherwise inadmissible evidence in the resolution of any issue to which the evidence is logically relevant. A timely objection is one that a party makes when the objectionable nature of the evidence being offered first becomes apparent. With testimony, this usually means the party must object contemporaneously with the asking of the opponent's question — after the opponent has asked it, but before the witness has answered it. Occasionally, this is not possible because the witness answers too quickly, fails to stop answering when opposing counsel stands to make an objection, or gives an answer that is not responsive to the question that the opponent asked. Under such circumstances, the court will excuse counsel's delay in making his objection, and the court will often admonish the witness not to respond to any question that the opposing counsel has indicated is objectionable, or to answer only the questions posed by the examining attorney.

With tangible evidence, objections usually are appropriate only after the proponent has called the sponsoring witness, authenticated the exhibit, and formally offered the exhibit into evidence. Objections prior to that time would be premature because the proponent might use the tangible evidence only for demonstrative purposes and never offer the exhibit into evidence.

If a party anticipates that its adversary will attempt to introduce testimony or tangible evidence that is so inflammatory or otherwise sensitive that its mere mention in the jury's presence would be unfairly prejudicial (even if used only for demonstrative purposes), it may forego the normal objection procedures by filing a motion *in limine*, through which it may obtain a preliminary ruling on admissibility or fairness of use. This type of anticipatory objection will, of course, be based on speculation as to what the proponent intends to do. At the hearing on the motion, the court will ask the proponent to confirm or deny the movant's speculation concerning the challenged exhibit. If the proponent confirms the speculation, the court will hear and resolve the substance of the motion. If the proponent denies that it intends to use the challenged exhibit, the issue is moot and the proponent will be bound by this representation.

Does an in limine motion excuse a losing party from making a timely objection when the evidence is later offered at trial? When the substance of an objection has been thoroughly explored prior to trial and the court's ruling permitting introduction of the evidence was explicit and definitive, Rule 103(a) dispenses with contemporaneous objections at trial after a *definitive ruling* has been made on the record.

When would a ruling not be definitive, and therefore require a contemporaneous objection at trial? In *United States v. Küster*, 208 F.3d 227 (10th Cir. 2000) the district court specifically declined to make a definitive pre-trial ruling, electing instead to make individualized decisions throughout trial. This necessitated contemporaneous objections. In *Wright v. Montgomery County*, 2003 U.S. Dist. LEXIS 1080 (E.D. Pa. Jan. 23, 2003) the trial court issued a pretrial ruling excluding testimony proffered by the plaintiff. In its Memorandum Order the court specifically stated that the "witnesses were excluded *absent a renewed offer acceptable to the Court.*" Since the plaintiff chose not to renew his offer of proof, the court held that he was barred from challenging these exclusions as error. In *Kiss v. Kmart*, 2001 U.S. Dist. LEXIS 6744 (E.D. Pa. May 22, 2001) the court expressly declined to rule on a pretrial motion in limine. Therefore, when no objection was made at trial to the testimony the plaintiff previously sought to exclude, the plaintiff waived her right to challenge the admission as error. If the pretrial ruling were clearly not definitive, but the trial judge states that he does not want to hear repetitive arguments, the failure to make a contemporaneous objection may be excused. *United States v. Harrison*, 296 F.3d 994 (10th Cir. 2002).

If the party opposing the introduction of evidence loses in a definitive pretrial ruling, he may not be required to make a contemporaneous objection at trial, but he will waive the right to claim error if he attempts to minimize the sting of the evidence (often referred to as stealing the opposing party's thunder) by introducing the evidence himself. This waives the objection. *United States v. Huerta-Orosco*, 340 F.3d 601 (8th Cir. 2003).

Rule 103(a) raises at least one serious problem. Since many pretrial evidentiary rulings are made by judges who will not be trying the case, erroneous rulings may be foisted on unsuspecting trial judges who may have come to the correct decision had they been given a chance to rule by the making of a contemporaneous objection. This right to stand mute while the evidence is being offered could be used as a tool by guilty criminal defendants to perpetuate errors for appellate review purposes following an inevitable conviction. Bad corporate actors could employ the same tactic. Perhaps the elimination of the contemporaneous objection requirement should have been limited to instances where the same judge will be asked to hear the same issue both before and during trial.

Failure to make a timely objection where required results in a waiver of the error as a ground for appellate review, unless the error constitutes *plain error*. Plain errors are those that should have been obvious to the trial judge and that had a substantial impact on the trial. Plain error also includes unspecified reasons either for offering or objecting to evidence. *See Reese v. Mercury Marine Div. of Brunswick Corp.*, 793 F.2d 1416 (5th Cir. 1986). *See generally* 1 WEINSTEIN'S FEDERAL EVIDENCE, § 103.42[3] (Matthew Bender 2d ed.).

EXERCISE

Randy was permanently blinded when an automobile battery designed and manufactured by Defendant Corporation explodes. Randy filed a products liability suit against Defendant Corporation. During trial Randy offered testimony speculating that the explosion occurred as a result of a manufacturing defect in the battery. At the end of Randy's direct examination, Defendant Corporation moved to strike Randy's speculative testimony. The court declined to strike the testimony. Has this issue been properly preserved for appeal?

[3] Specificity

Objections must be specific, in addition to being timely. An objection should focus the judge's and adversary's attention on the legal infirmity that compels exclusion. This specificity requirement has two dimensions: the basis of the objection must be specific (whether hearsay, privileged material, a violation of the best evidence rule, etc.), and the proponent must identify the evidence or portions of it that allegedly are inadmissible. For example, one inappropriate entry in a 50-page medical record will not render the entire report inadmissible. An appropriate objection should focus on the single inadmissible entry if the entire report is offered.

This specificity requirement naturally follows from the imposition of the responsibility for enforcing the rules of evidence on the adversaries, who have prepared for the trial, as opposed to the presiding judge, who is hearing and seeing the evidence and relating it to the issues in the case for the first time. In recognition of the fact that the judge is not as familiar as the parties with the evidentiary issues presented, appellate review of judicial actions based on unfocused, generalized objections is heavily weighted in the judge's favor. This usually means an appellate court will uphold a trial judge's decisions based on such objections (whether sustaining or overruling them) if there is any reasonable basis to do so. For example, generalized objections that are overruled will not be reversed unless the ground for objection was obvious. Conversely, if a judge sustained such an objection, reversal will not result if there was *any ground* on which the trial court could have properly excluded the evidence. Under Rule 103(a)(1) of the Federal Rules of Evidence, both timeliness and specificity continue to be required of objections.

[*See* **Fed. R. Evid. 103: Rulings on Evidence**]

EXERCISES

Are the following objections specific enough to preserve the issue for appellate review?

    a.   Party objects to the introduction of a document at trial on the grounds that the document is "immaterial, irrelevant, and incompetent." On appeal will Party be permitted to further specify that the documents were not sufficiently authenticated to be admitted in evidence?

    b.   Party objects to a witness's statement at trial on two separate grounds: hearsay and improper character evidence. On appeal can Party also argue that the statement was unfairly prejudicial under Rule 403?

[4] Offers of Proof

A party offers testimonial evidence by asking questions of a witness. Each question constitutes a formal offer of the response it seeks. A party offers tangible evidence, on the other hand, by moving for its introduction after a sponsoring witness has authenticated it. If the opposing party makes an objection after either type of offer is made, the judge's decision is subject to appellate review at the conclusion of the trial. An erroneous decision can result in a reversal of the judgment, but only if the error was harmful; that is to say, if the erroneous decision probably affected the outcome of the case.

The determination of what harm, if any, resulted from the sustaining of an objection can be especially difficult because, having been rejected as evidence, the substance of the excluded evidence will not appear in the record, rendering an assessment of its potential impact difficult, if not impossible. To remedy this, the law requires that the proponent of evidence who wishes to seek appellate reversal based on its erroneous exclusion make an *offer of proof* at the time the objection is sustained. A proponent can make an offer of proof by any of several procedures through which it places that evidence into the record — into the transcript, if the evidence is testimonial, or into the collection of exhibits, if it is a tangible object — so that its substance will be known to the appellate court on review. Because the primary purpose of the offer of proof is to apprise the appellate court of the substance of the party's objection, it is incumbent upon the offering party to ensure that the offer of proof is made on the record and is recorded properly. *See United States v. Clark*, 918 F.2d 843 (9th Cir. 1990).

A residual benefit from the making of an offer of proof is that it places before the trial judge, in more detail, the evidence the court has decided to exclude. This enhanced opportunity to examine the evidence and consider it in context allows the judge a different perspective that could prompt reversal of the decision to exclude.

An offer of proof of tangible evidence is quite simple. After the evidence is formally offered, objected to, and the objection sustained, the proponent merely hands the item to the court reporter, and, referring to it by exhibit number, announces to the court that it is making an offer of proof. The proponent of oral testimony can make an offer of proof in several ways. It is more complicated than an offer of proof of tangible evidence, however, because it involves placing into the record oral communications that should be kept from the hearing of the jury. Consequently, the proponent usually makes these offers of oral testimony outside the jury's presence.

One method of making an offer of proof of oral testimony is to have the lawyer state what the witness would have said had the court allowed the witness to answer the propounded question. This is called a "proffer." Following this statement, either the attorney who made it, the presiding judge, or the opposing counsel likely will ask the witness to confirm the accuracy of what the lawyer represented to the court, although this is not required and occasionally is not done. This confirmation is most often done if the lawyer has made an offer of proof of what an adverse or hostile witness would have stated had examination of the witness not been limited.

A second method of making an offer of proof of oral testimony, which is more accurate than the first method but substantially more time-consuming, is for the lawyer, out of the presence of the jury, to continue the question-and-answer format to elicit the substance of the witness's testimony from the witness. This method ensures that the transcript reflects a complete and precise account of what the court's ruling excluded. A third method is for the proponent to submit the witness's testimony in written form. This has been done through the transcript of a deposition or an affidavit signed by the witness.

Under the Federal Rules of Evidence, Rule 103 governs offers of proof.

[*See* Fed. R. Evid. 103: Rulings on Evidence]

Because the purpose of an offer of proof is to have the record reflect what was excluded and why the exclusion justifies reversal if found to have been erroneous, it also is important for the opposition — the party who prevailed on the objection to the evidence — to take steps to have the record accurately reflect the consequences of the trial court's decision. This may require a counter-offer of proof or the cross-examination of the witnesses through whom the original offer was made so that the true value of the evidence, and therefore its probable effect on the outcome of the case, will be apparent. *See Gilchrist v. Bolger*, 733 F.2d 1551, 1555–1557 n.3 (11th Cir. 1984); *Christensen v. Felton*, 322 F.2d 323, 328 (9th Cir. 1963).

A question that arises concerning offers of proof under Rule 103(a) is how detailed and specific an offer of proof must be. On this issue, the Seventh Circuit has concluded:

> Although Rule 103(a)(2) merely requires the proponent to make the "substance of the evidence" known to the court, an offer of proof generally should state a ground for admissibility, inform the court and opposing counsel what the proponent expected to prove by the excluded evidence and demonstrate the significance of the excluded testimony. . . . This court does not require that a formal offer of proof be made or that grounds of error be precisely specified. . . . "[I]t is enough 'if the record shows . . . what the substance of the proposed evidence is.' "

United States v. Peak, 856 F.2d 825, 832 (7th Cir. 1988).

What if the objection is overruled? What must the opponent do to ensure that this potential ground of error is protected for appellate review? Under the common law, the party had to *take an exception* to the court's ruling. Apparently the theory behind this requirement was that, through such action, the trial judge would be alerted to the seriousness with which the objection had been interposed and, therefore, presumably reassess his decision with greater care for its accuracy. This logic, of course, was perverse. Ethical lawyers would not have made objections without a serious basis, and conscientious judges would have rendered their decisions with care in the first instance. Over time, the requirement came to be seen as the meaningless procedure that it was, and it was eliminated in virtually all jurisdictions. Now, in both state and federal courts, the opposing party need do nothing more to protect the record for appellate review than make a timely objection specifying the nature of the claim raised.

Strategy Note: The trial is not a contest between opposing lawyers who are being tested on who better understands the rules of evidence. Tactically, it is unwise to object to an opponent's attempts to introduce evidence just because such evidence is objectionable. If the substance of the evidence is not harmful, objecting may do far more damage than admission of the evidence in the eyes of the lay jurors, who are likely to perceive the objection as an attempt to conceal from them unfavorable evidence. If the evidence is damaging, but the likelihood of the evidence being excluded is slight, its harm may be accentuated because the objection emphasizes the testimony in question. Finally, a party who objects too frequently (even when the objections are technically correct) is perceived as being unnecessarily disruptive and alienates both the judge and the jury.

In situations involving outrageous conduct by an opposing attorney, however, fear of objecting too frequently can be viewed by the court as an irrelevant concern. When an attorney engages in an extreme abuse of the evidence rules by constantly exposing the jury to clearly inadmissible and inflammatory material, the opposing attorney has a duty to object as often as necessary to alert the trial judge of the potential for mistrial or reversal on appeal. In *Igo v. Coachmen Indus., Inc.*, 938 F.2d 650 (6th Cir. 1991), the circuit court noted that the unprofessional conduct of plaintiff's counsel in repeatedly referring to prejudicial material explicitly excluded by the judge in his *in limine* motion and referring to the defendant in derogatory terms as a "billion dollar corporation" so tainted the trial that it alone could be the basis for reversal. *Id.* at 653. Despite defendant's counsel's contention that persistent objection would place her in a bad light with the jury, the circuit court asserted that counsel's failure to object more frequently compounded the adverse impact of plaintiff's counsel on the trial.

Strategy Note: Jurors tend to perceive objections as attempts to conceal harmful evidence from them. Therefore, it is important for objections to be stated in layman-like terms and for the policies underlying them to be made explicit. For example, if the opponent asked its witness to repeat what another person had said, it might be helpful to state that the objection is being interposed because the witness is being asked to repeat what someone else said, and because that person is not in the courtroom under oath, there is no way the jury can meaningfully evaluate his perception and memory of what he described or the sincerity with which he made the previous statement, rather than objecting simply on the ground of hearsay (which jurors may only vaguely understand).

In summary, the steps in the presentation of tangible evidence are as follows:

1. Call a sponsoring witness, if the evidence is not being presented during the cross-examination of an opposition witness (which, although permissible, is the exception rather than rule).

2. Establish the relationship of the tangible evidence to the cause of action, if this has not already been done through the testimony of other witnesses. For example, elicit testimony that a certain kind of instrumentality was involved in the incident that caused the injuries to the plaintiff. This is *laying* the *general foundation* for the evidence.

3. Have the court reporter mark for identification the specific item that you wish to introduce into evidence.

4. Show the item to opposing counsel.

5. Present the item to the sponsoring witness (referring to it by exhibit number) and ask her if she can identify it. This identification should connect the particular item with the incident giving rise to the cause of action. This lays the *specific foundation* for the introduction of the item that is critical to its relevance to the case.

6. *Move* for the *admission* of the specific exhibit *into evidence.* At this time, the exhibit should be presented to the presiding judge for examination.

Note: It is at this point that the opponent should interpose an objection if he wishes to contest the admissibility of the evidence. If an objection is made, the judge will hear oral argument. This argument may or may not occur in the jury's presence, depending on the nature of the issues that have been raised and on whether one of the parties requests the jury's exclusion.

7. Be sure to *obtain a ruling* from the presiding judge on your motion to admit the evidence and on any objection that has been made. If an objection has been made, the judge may defer ruling until he has had more time to study the briefs (if any were prepared beforehand) and the applicable case law that has been cited.

8(a). If the judge admits the exhibit into evidence (overruling the opponent's objection), the evidence should be *shown to the jury* and may thereafter be used during the examination of other witnesses; *or*

8(b). If the presiding judge does not admit the exhibit into evidence (sustaining the opponent's objection), make an *offer of proof* by handing the evidence to the court clerk, indicating to the judge and on the record (in the transcript) that you are making an offer of proof.

EXERCISES

1. According to the criminal indictment, Ernest conspired to defraud the United States by securing unlawful Medicare payments. At trial the prosecution called several doctors as witnesses to testify as to conversations that they had with Ernest. In his defense Ernest sought to offer his rendition of those same conversations. The government objected on hearsay grounds and the trial court sustained the objection. If you represent Ernest, what must you do to preserve the issue for appeal?

2. An adequate offer of proof not only describes the evidence and what it tends to show, but also identifies the grounds for admitting the evidence. Below are four ways to make an offer of proof. Place these proffers in order from least effective to most effective.

a. Examine the witness before the court and have the answers reported on the record.

b. An oral statement of counsel as to what the testimony would be.

c. A written statement by counsel describing the answers the proposed witness would give if permitted to testify.

d. A written statement of the witness's testimony signed by the witness and offered as part of the record.

§ 1.06 DIVISION OF RESPONSIBILITY WITHIN TRIAL

[A] In General

Responsibility in a trial is divided among the parties, the jury (the finder of facts), and the judge.

[B] Finder of Facts

The finder of facts — the jury, or the presiding judge in a non-jury case — is responsible for determining whether the parties have satisfied their assigned burdens of persuasion; that is, whether they have presented enough evidence to prove the facts they were required to prove. This determination is based on the evidence the presiding judge has admitted into the record, the facts about which the judge has taken judicial notice and instructed the jury to accept as established, and the presumptions that have been imposed by operation of law because of facts that have been accepted as true by operation of law. *See* Chapter 10, *Presumptions and Judicial Notice.*

[C] Parties

[1] Satisfying Burdens of Proof

The parties' responsibility is to present sufficient relevant evidence to convince the finder of facts, by whatever burden of persuasion is applicable, that their claims or defenses are valid. This burden of persuasion is one of two burdens allocated to the parties under the loose heading of burdens of proof. The other is the burden of producing evidence (often referred to as the burden of going forward with evidence).

[2] Burden of Producing Evidence

The trial judge has the power to end the trial prematurely by directing a verdict if the evidence a party presents, in support of the claims that it has been required to prove, is facially deficient. Consequently, the parties bear the burden of presenting sufficient evidence to get by this initial stage of judicial screening. To accomplish this, the parties must present sufficient evidence to make out a *prima facie* case — one from which a reasonable jury *could* find that the necessary facts have been established. Note that in making this determination, the trial judge is assessing only whether a reasonable jury could find the necessary facts to be true, not whether the judge would so find, were she deciding the question herself and assessing the credibility of the witnesses through whom the facts were proved. In practical terms, this means, for example, the plaintiff in a civil action for negligence resulting from injuries received when riding an amusement device must, prior to resting at the end of his case-in-chief, present sufficient evidence from which the jury could find that: (1) he was injured; (2) the injury was caused by the amusement device (proximate cause); and (3) the existence of the condition that caused the injury was the result of the defendant's negligence (breach of a duty of care).

At the end of the plaintiff's case-in-chief, the plaintiff's cause of action will be in one of three stages. First, if the plaintiff has failed to meet its burden of production, the presiding judge will conclude the action by granting a directed verdict for the defendant. Second, if the judge finds that the plaintiff has satisfied its burden of production, the state of the evidence may be such that, even if the defendant presented no evidence at all, reasonable jurors still could differ as to the appropriate resolution of the claim. In this instance the plaintiff has met the burden of producing evidence with no immediate legal consequences for the defendant because the judge still will submit the action to the jury for resolution. Third, the plaintiff may have so convincingly established its case that the judge will grant a directed verdict for the plaintiff unless the defendant comes forward with evidence to refute the plaintiff's case. The defendant's evidence either could contradict the evidence the plaintiff has presented or could establish an affirmative defense that would preclude the plaintiff's claim. In the latter instance, the burden of producing evidence is said to have shifted to the defendant. *See* McCORMICK ON EVIDENCE § 338, at 956 (3d ed. 1984).

If the defendant, in its case-in-defense, attempts to refute the plaintiff's claim through an affirmative defense rather than through a refutation of the facts upon which the plaintiff's claim is based, the defendant usually must bear the same burden of production on the affirmative defense as the plaintiff did on the original claim. At the end of the defendant's case-in-defense, the trial judge can grant a directed verdict for the plaintiff dismissing the affirmative defense issue if the defendant has failed to satisfy his burden of production.

If the defendant meets the burden of production that shifted to it as a result of the plaintiff's having met its initial burden of production, as well as the burden of producing evidence in support of its affirmative defense, the status of defendant's case can be the same as the plaintiff's at the end of plaintiff's case-in-chief: a reasonable jury question may be raised even though the plaintiff presents no further evidence in rebuttal, or the judge may direct a verdict for the defendant on the affirmative defense if the plaintiff presents no further evidence on that issue. In the latter instance, the burden of producing evidence on the affirmative defense would have shifted to the plaintiff, who must satisfy that burden during the rebuttal phase of the trial.

[3] Burden of Persuasion

To avoid decisional stalemates in litigation — situations in which the finder of fact cannot decide who should prevail — the law allocates among the parties burdens of persuasion on every issue raised in the case. The party with this burden must convince the finder of fact that the facts support its position on the issue. If it is unable to convince the jury of the validity of its position on a particular issue (whether they have concluded that the facts support the opposite conclusion or are undecided about what the facts support), it has failed to satisfy its burden and will, therefore, lose on that issue. If the issue is important to the cause of action as a whole, it may also lose on the basic claim itself.

The degree to which a party must persuade the finder of facts on each issue usually is consistent throughout any action. For example, in civil actions, parties generally must establish their positions on particular issues by a preponderance of the evidence. In other words, they must show that the proposition in question is more likely true than not. In criminal actions, the Government must prove each element of its charges against the defendant beyond a reasonable doubt — a standard that is impossible to quantify precisely and, therefore, usually is characterized in terms of a state of conviction on the part of the jurors sufficient to persuade them to act on the more grave transactions in their lives. In all likelihood, the beyond a reasonable doubt standard fluctuates according to the individuals applying it, the gravity of the charge being tried, and the consequences of conviction. Criminal defendants frequently have the burden of persuasion on affirmative defenses. The level of this burden varies significantly. Although usually at a preponderance of the evidence level, some jurisdictions require that the defendant establish certain affirmative defenses by clear and convincing evidence, a standard somewhere between preponderance of the evidence and proof beyond a reasonable doubt. Some jurisdictions even have required defendants to establish the defense of insanity beyond a reasonable doubt.

Occasionally an issue is raised in a civil action that is so disfavored (usually because of the social stigma and legal consequences the issue carries with it) that the law places a higher burden of persuasion on the party with the burden on that issue. For example, in a child support action, if the alleged father defends on the ground that the child is illegitimate, the law requires him to prove this claim by clear and convincing evidence. Courts justify this increased burden because of the injury that will result to an innocent third party (the child) if the alleged father's defense is upheld (*i.e.*, loss of financial support and inheritance rights).

[4] Allocating Burdens

The burdens of persuasion and of going forward with evidence usually are complementary. Although they could be assigned to different parties on the same issue (as in some states that initially require criminal defendants to produce evidence of insanity but impose on the prosecution the ultimate burden of persuading the jury that the defendant is sane), in the overwhelming majority of cases the party to whom the ultimate burden of persuasion is assigned also will be allocated the initial burden of production. Consistent with this alignment of burdens, the party with the burdens of production and persuasion at trial often also will have the initial burden of pleading — raising the issue at the inception of the action. It is not uncommon, however, for the assignment of the burden of pleading and the trial burdens to differ. For example, in some jurisdictions, the defendant is required to plead contributory negligence as a defense, but the plaintiff then is required to disprove that its own negligence contributed to its injuries.

A statute that creates a cause of action often will allocate the burdens of going forward with evidence and of persuasion. As to the burden of persuasion, this allocation would include not only the question of who bears the burden but also the level of persuasion required. If the statute creating a cause of action does not address the issue of burden allocation or, if a cause of action is rooted in the common law, the task of allocating the burdens necessarily is delegated to the courts. On what basis do courts make this determination?

There are several overlapping bases. The most common basis for allocating the burden is assigning it to the party who seeks to change the status quo, usually the party who instituted the action. Usually the court will assign all burdens — the initial burden of pleading, the initial trial burden of going forward with evidence, and the ultimate burden of persuasion — to the plaintiff. In a tort action, for example, the plaintiff usually will have to plead the defendant's negligence, come forward with evidence of the defendant's negligence, and persuade the jury of that contention. All of the other factors on which courts assign trial burdens appear to be considered only to the extent they justify modification of the burden allocation compelled by the "change from the status quo."

Most notable among these other factors is *probability*. The court may assign a party who relies on an improbable fact the responsibility for establishing that fact.

For example, because a child born in wedlock is probably the husband's offspring, the husband likely will bear the burden of establishing a claim that the child is illegitimate. Courts also have cited probability as the reason for requiring the defendant in a negligence action to prove its affirmative defense of contributory negligence. Courts do not agree on this assessment, however, in that some states require the plaintiff to disprove contribution to his own injuries once the defendant has pleaded the claim of contributory negligence, as discussed above.

Convenience and *fairness* are other factors that influence courts in their allocation of burdens at trial. Occasionally, courts will relieve a party of the burden of persuasion if imposition of the burden on that party is unfair in light of the adversary's unique access to exculpatory or inculpatory evidence. For example, where the plaintiff establishes the liability of one of multiple potential tortfeasors but cannot establish the tortfeasor's identity, courts have shifted the burden of persuasion to the defendants to prove their individual innocence. In *Summers v. Tice*, 199 P.2d 1 (Cal. 1948), for example, in which the plaintiff was negligently injured by one of two hunters but could not prove which of the two was responsible, the court imposed joint liability by shifting the burden to both defendants to prove their lack of culpability. More recently, a court reached the same result in an action involving several potential manufacturers of a drug taken by a pregnant woman that had caused injury to her unborn child. *See Sindell v. Abbott Labs.*, 607 P.2d 924 (Cal. 1980). *See also Ybarra v. Spangard*, 154 P.2d 687 (Cal. 1944) (shifting to each person who participated in a medical operation on the unconscious plaintiff the burden of establishing nonresponsibility for the injury to the plaintiff that occurred during the operation).

As previously mentioned, the *nature of the issue* upon which burdens are being assigned also will influence their allocation. The issue of illegitimacy is a primary example. Its potential consequences on an innocent child have resulted not only in the assignment of the burden of persuasion to the alleged father but also in the elevation of that burden to one based on clear and convincing evidence. Similar policy considerations have prompted the United States Supreme Court to conclude that the termination of parental rights by a preponderance of the evidence violates principles of fundamental fairness and, therefore, due process of law. In *Santosky v. Kramer*, 455 U.S. 745 (1982), the Court held that only the standard of clear and convincing evidence strikes a fair balance between the rights of the natural parents and the interests of the State.

[5]   Another Burden of Persuasion: Establishing Admissibility of Evidence

Thus far, discussion of the trial burdens the parties must bear has focused on proving the factual basis for the cause of action and the defenses that have been raised. Throughout the trial, however, there is another burden of persuasion the parties constantly must face relating to the admissibility of the evidence by which these claims and defenses are being proven. Because rules of evidence establish standards for the admissibility of evidence (standards designed to ensure reliability), a proponent of either testimony or tangible exhibits must establish that it has met the applicable standards for the evidence in question. This showing often involves factual issues beyond what is apparent from the general nature of the evidence and from the context in which it is being offered. Thus, it can involve the need for evidentiary hearings at which the proponent must persuade the judge, by a preponderance of the evidence, that it has met the factual prerequisites. The preponderance of the evidence standard for preliminary issues of admissibility is uniformly applicable, even to the determination of the admissibility of evidence against defendants in criminal cases. *See Lego v. Twomey*, 404 U.S. 553 (1972). The scope of the judge's responsibility with regard to determinations of the admissibility of evidence is discussed below.

The allocation of this preliminary burden on evidentiary issues can vary between the proponent and opponent, depending on the nature of the evidentiary rule involved, prevailing policies — whether they favor admission or exclusion — and considerations of fairness and efficiency, i.e., which party has the greatest access to relevant information. Occasionally the burden will be placed on the opponent of the evidence. For example, because it is presumed that all witnesses are competent, the party objecting to the competence of a witness will have the burden of substantiating that claim. More frequently, the burden will be shared. An example of this arises with the use of business records to prove the truth of what was recorded in them.

The hearsay rule excludes out-of-court statements, like business records, if they are offered to prove the truth of the assertions contained in them. Courts, however, consider business records to be inherently reliable if the records were made in the course of a regularly conducted business activity and the continued successful operation of the enterprise depended on their accuracy. Consequently, courts have recognized a "business records exception" to the hearsay rule of exclusion. To qualify under this exception, the *proponent must prove* the records were made in the regular course of business, as a routine matter, based on personal knowledge of the facts recorded, and made at or near the time of the events recorded. Once this has been proved, the records are deemed presumptively trustworthy, and therefore admissible, unless the *opponent can establish* that the source of the information recorded or the methods or circumstances of the record's preparation (like being prepared in anticipation of the litigation in which they are being offered) indicate lack of trustworthiness.[4] The allocation of this burden of persuasion on evidentiary issues will be addressed throughout the text as the various evidentiary rules are examined. For an excellent discussion of the assignment of burdens on the various evidentiary issues that arise during a trial, see Bridge, *Burdens Within Burdens at a Trial Within a Trial*, 23 B.C. L. REV. 927 (1982).

[D] Judge

The presiding judge's responsibilities are to determine the legal principles that will control the cause of action and to supervise, through the enforcement of the rules of evidence and procedure, the parties' presentation of evidence in their attempt to satisfy their assigned burdens under those controlling legal principles. Although the jury is the finder of facts relative to the issues raised by the parties'

---

[4] The hearsay rule and its exceptions are discussed in Chapters 4 and 5.

claims and defenses, the presiding judge also must make a substantial number of factual determinations throughout the trial relative to application of the rules of evidence that the judge is charged with administering. For example, under the best evidence rule, a party proving the content of a writing must use the original writing (as opposed to a copy) at trial, unless the original has been lost or destroyed due to no serious fault of the proponent. If the proponent offers a copy and the opponent makes a best evidence objection, the admissibility of that copy will turn on the presiding judge's resolution of two factual questions: (1) whether the original is lost or destroyed; and (2) whether the proponent is responsible for the loss or destruction. For further discussion of the best evidence rule, see Chapter 7, *Writings*.

The administration of other exclusionary rules, such as the prohibition on the use of hearsay, also involves the resolution of numerous preliminary factual questions by the presiding judge. This is especially true of hearsay because of the numerous exceptions to the rule that courts have recognized. Although courts generally exclude out-of-court statements from evidence under the hearsay rule because their reliability is suspect, courts consider a number of out-of-court statements to be sufficiently reliable to be heard and considered by the finder of fact if the statements were made under circumstances that provided an assurance of accuracy and sincerity. Declarations against interest are an example. A statement against one's own interest made with awareness of that fact carries with it an assurance of reliability, because it is unlikely the declarant would have made the statement insincerely or without having taken some measures to ensure the statement's accuracy. In determining whether a statement falls within the exception for declarations against interest, the presiding judge must resolve two factual issues: (1) whether the statement was against the declarant's interests, and (2) whether the declarant was aware of this fact when uttering the statement.

All of these preliminary factual issues on which the admissibility of evidence depends historically have been considered part of the judicial function. A proponent of evidence that required a preliminary showing of competency to be admissible first had to present sufficient evidence to convince the presiding judge, by a preponderance of the evidence (a "more likely than not" standard), that each of the necessary preliminary facts was true. This was the orthodox rule. The consequence of this orthodox rule was that the judge's fact-finding role often was as great as that of the jury.

The only significant exception recognized to this orthodox rule occurred where the preliminary factual questions on which the admissibility of evidence turned overlapped the factual issues that formed the basis of the cause of action, and therefore were to be decided by the jury. In a will contest, for example, the issue might have been the authenticity of the document submitted for probate. If the jury found the document to be the deceased's authentic will, the defendant would inherit under it. If the jury found the document not to be authentic, the plaintiff would inherit under the law of intestacy. If the defendant/devisee offered into evidence the document upon which he based his claim to the proceeds of the estate, he first had to authenticate it — prove it to be what it purported to be on its face — before it was deemed relevant and therefore admissible. If the judge concluded, by a preponderance of the evidence (the standard by which courts normally make admissibility decisions, as well as the standard by which the jury would determine the central issue in the cause of action), that the will was *not* authentic, the judge effectively decided the case because the admissibility determination necessarily resulted in the elimination of the basis of one party's claim. Although the same result would not necessarily follow from the admission of the document after a finding of authenticity, because theoretically the jury still could come to the opposite conclusion, many courts were concerned that the judicial decision to admit the document would determine the jury's ultimate decision. The legitimacy of this fear, however, was highly debatable because the jury could be influenced by the judge's decision only if it were aware of the basis on which the decision had been made — a finding of authenticity — and, under normal circumstances, the jury would be totally ignorant of the nature and substance of what the judge had previously decided. Nevertheless, the courts often compromised their admissibility decisions in these instances by making their preliminary determinations according to a *prima facie* standard (sufficient evidence from which a reasonable person could find), rather than a preponderance standard. This insured against the exclusion of documents and therefore against judicial resolution of the cause of action, except in those cases in which the evidence was so insubstantial that a directed verdict otherwise would have been compelled. Congress has adopted the orthodox rule in Rule 104(a) of the Federal Rules of Evidence.

[*See* Fed. R. Evid. 104: Preliminary Questions]

The only exceptions to this rule concern issues of conditional relevance, which, under Rule 104(b), the presiding judge delegates to the jury after preliminarily screening them. This concept of conditional relevance is discussed following the examination of the concept of relevance in Chapter 2, § 2.03.

Although the presiding judge makes many preliminary factual determinations relative to questions of admissibility, it is important to understand that the jury often makes these same factual determinations again relative to the question of how much weight it will give to the evidence the judge has decided is admissible. Because determinations of admissibility and assessments of the probative value of evidence both are based on assessments of reliability, it is not uncommon for there to be a substantial, if not complete, overlap in the factual questions that will determine each issue. For example, although the judge might have been convinced the declarant's hearsay statement was sufficiently against his interest, and known by the declarant to have that effect, to be admissible under that exception, a party in closing argument could persuade the jury to give the statement little or no weight because it was not, in fact, against the declarant's interest.

EXERCISES

1. The government charged Joseph with being an alien in the United States after deportation, as well as misrepresenting his identity and citizenship to fraudulently obtain supplemental social security benefits, acquire food stamps, make a claim of citizenship, and apply for a passport. Joseph's primary defense to all of the charges is that he is a citizen of the United States, and his primary evidence in support of his defense is a birth certificate issued by the State of Idaho. Prior to trial, the government asserts that it has three credible witnesses who can establish that the birth certificate is fraudulent. Consequently, the government asks the court to conduct a hearing under Rule 104 to determine if the birth certificate is fraudulent. May the court conduct such a hearing?

2. In a prosecution for possession of cocaine, the Government called the arresting Coast Guard officer to the stand. During direct examination, the Coast Guard officer testified that, while searching the defendant for weapons upon arrest, the officer found a plastic packet in the defendant's jacket containing a white powder of unknown composition. The officer testified that he thought the powder was cocaine, but he was not certain. The Coast Guard officer further testified that he placed an identification mark on the packet and then turned it over to a DEA agent in charge of the investigation. Although he was not certain, the Coast Guard officer also testified that he assumed that the DEA agent, in turn, transferred custody of the packet to the agent in charge of the evidence storage facility in the local DEA office.

Counsel for the Government then showed the Coast Guard officer a plastic packet containing a white powder that had been marked for identification as Government Exhibit #1. The officer identified the exhibit as the packet that he had seized from the defendant, whereupon counsel for the Government moved the packet into evidence.

As its next witness, the Government called the laboratory technician who had tested the white powder contained in the plastic packet. The technician testified, without objection, that the powder was uncut cocaine. On appeal, what issue(s) could, or should, one raise as a basis for overturning the defendant's conviction? *See United States v. Parodi*, 703 F.2d 768 (4th Cir. 1983).

3a. An automobile driven by Dennis Novaha collided in Utah with a motorcycle driven by James Tuntland. Tuntland died as a result of the accident. Tuntland's estate subsequently brought an action against Novaha for wrongful death. In his answer to the complaint, Novaha claimed that the action was barred by the applicable Utah statute of limitations. Alternatively, Novaha alleged that the accident was the result of Tuntland's own negligence and filed a counterclaim against Tuntland for injuries resulting from the accident.

To clarify the presentation of evidence, the parties call upon the presiding judge to allocate the appropriate burdens of proof amongst them. How should the judge rule? *See Aetna Cas. & Sur. Co. v. General Elec. Co.*, 581 F. Supp. 889 (E.D. Mo. 1984).

b. Novaha did not own the car that he was driving when he collided with Tuntland. He also did not have any insurance. Cassidy, a friend of Novaha's, owned the car that Novaha was driving. Cassidy was insured by the Utah Insurance Company. Tuntland was insured by the Dairyland Insurance Company, and his policy contained an uninsured motorist provision. In an unusual action, Utah Insurance Company filed a "Complaint for Interpleader and Declaratory Relief" in the action between Novaha and Tuntland's estate. In its complaint, Utah Insurance Company sought a declaratory judgment that it had no duty under its policy with

Cassidy either to defend Novaha or to indemnify him for any judgment rendered against him. Dairyland Insurance Company was allowed to appear in the action as a defendant in interpleader. How do these additional facts affect the allocation of burdens of proof in this trial? *See Hartford Accident & Indem. Co. v. Shaw,* 273 F.2d 133, 137 (8th Cir. 1959).

Chapter 2

AN INTRODUCTION TO RELEVANCE

§ 2.01 THE GENERAL ADMISSIBILITY OF RELEVANT EVIDENCE

[A] Components of Relevance

Fundamental to a rational system of jurisprudence is the requirement that all evidence offered be relevant to the issues being litigated. The concept of relevancy turns on the relationship of an item of evidence to the proposition a party seeks to prove, and it has two dimensions, both of which must be present for a judge to consider the evidence relevant.

First, the evidence must be *probative* of the proposition it is offered to prove; that is, the evidence must logically tend to make the proposition more or less likely. For example, if a defendant were charged with negligence for failing to maintain control of his automobile, evidence that he learned to drive in Mississippi would not be relevant to prove he failed to maintain control of the car prior to striking the plaintiff. Logically, there is no connection between where one learns to drive and how one subsequently drives under any particular set of circumstances.

Second, the standard of relevance requires the *proposition* that the evidence makes more or less likely to be *of consequence* to the claims or defenses raised, the credibility of witnesses who have testified, the reliability of evidence, or the level of damages suffered. This has often been referred to as a requirement of *materiality*, with courts considering evidence to be immaterial if it has "some probative value upon an issue in the action but of such slight value as not to be worth the time, expense and inconvenience which the process of proving it would require." E. Morgan, Basic Problems of Evidence 183 (1961).

Federal Rules of Evidence 401 and 402 define relevance and the role of relevance in determining the admissibility of evidence.

[*See* Fed. R. Evid. 401, 402]

[B] What Propositions Are Provable?

The following opinion in *State v. Newman* illustrates how determination of the propositions that are provable in a cause of action is dependent on the principles of law brought into play through the pleadings and the courts' interpretation of that law. In *Newman*, a criminal defendant sought to introduce evidence of "sleep driving," the admissibility of which, you will discover, turns on whether proving this fact constitutes a defense to the crime of driving while intoxicated.

STATE v. NEWMAN
Supreme Court of Oregon
302 P.3d 435 (2013)

BALDWIN, J.

Defendant was convicted of felony driving under the influence of intoxicants (DUII), ORS 813.010. At trial, defendant sought to introduce evidence that he suffers from a sleepwalking disorder and was "sleep driving" at the time he was stopped in his vehicle. Defendant argued he did not voluntarily drive his vehicle, an element of proof necessary to establish criminal liability for DUII. The trial court excluded defendant's proffered evidence, concluding it was not relevant because DUII is a strict-liability offense. On appeal, the Court of Appeals agreed that DUII is a strict-liability offense and affirmed. *State v. Newman*, 246 Or. App. 334, 265 P.3d 86 (2011).We allowed defendant's petition for review. For the reasons that follow, we conclude defendant's proffered evidence was relevant to the driving element of the DUII charge. Accordingly, we reverse.

I. BACKGROUND

We take the following facts from the Court of Appeals opinion.

> "Defendant met his friends for dinner one evening and, anticipating that he would drink alcohol at dinner, left his car parked by his apartment and walked to the restaurant. Thereafter, defendant's friends drove him home, and he went to sleep. Later that evening, a police officer followed defendant's car and observed defendant make a left-hand turn without signaling or stopping, run a red light, and drive down the middle of a street, straddling the two traffic lanes. The officer then activated his overhead lights to initiate a traffic stop and, in response, defendant pulled into a parking lot. The officer approached defendant's car, smelled a strong odor of alcohol, and observed defendant's bloodshot, watery eyes and slow, slurred speech. Defendant agreed to perform field sobriety tests and, after failing them, was taken into custody. At the police station, defendant consented to a Breathalyzer test, which revealed that he had a blood alcohol level of 0.15 percent."

Id. at 336, 265 P.3d 86.

Defendant was charged with felony DUII, reckless driving, and recklessly endangering another person. Before trial, the state filed a motion seeking to exclude as irrelevant testimony regarding defendant's sleepwalking disorder and his "sleep driving on the night in question." Defendant argued that evidence of his sleepwalking was relevant to negate the requirements for criminal liability under ORS 161.095 — specifically, proof of a voluntary act with respect to the driving element of DUII. Defendant contended that he was not capable of performing the necessary volitional movements to consciously control his vehicle because he was asleep when the police stopped his vehicle.

As part of his offer of proof, defendant testified that he had sleepwalked within his apartment on a number of occasions in the past, but, to his knowledge, had not left his apartment while sleepwalking before this incident. A friend also provided testimony confirming defendant's sleepwalking behaviors. Defendant further testified that, after he went to sleep that evening, he had no recollection of leaving his apartment, getting behind the wheel of his car, or driving. Also, as part of defendant's offer of proof, Dr. Joshua Ramseyer, a physician certified in neurology and sleep medicine, provided expert testimony about the symptoms associated with parasomnia — a category of unwanted behavior that emerges during sleep. Within that category of sleep phenomenon, Dr. Ramseyer explained, exists somnambulism — which is also known as sleepwalking disorder. As Dr. Ramseyer explained:

> "Sleep driving is thought of as being sort of a subtype of sleepwalking or an extension of sleepwalking. It's a motor behavior that occurs without consciousness * * * that comes out during sleep.
>
> "* * *
>
> "[J]ust as someone's capable of sort of walking around the house, doing goal-directed behavior, such as eating, people can get behind the wheel, start up the car, and drive."

Dr. Ramseyer emphasized that activities performed while sleepwalking, such as "sleep driving," are *unconscious* acts. He further noted that sleepwalking resulting in "sleep driving," while uncommon in the general population, is a well-established phenomenon. If permitted to testify, Dr. Ramseyer would have rendered an expert opinion that defendant was "sleep driving" when stopped by police.

In seeking to exclude defendant's proffered evidence, the state argued that the evidence was irrelevant because the state was required to prove only that defendant drove a vehicle with a blood alcohol content of .08 percent or greater or was otherwise under the influence of an intoxicant. The trial court agreed with the state. It concluded that DUII is a strict-liability offense under *State v. Miller*, 309 Or. 362, 788 P.2d 974 (1990), and excluded defendant's proffered "sleep driving" evidence as irrelevant.[2] The state then dismissed the charges of reckless driving and reckless endangerment and proceeded solely on the charge of felony DUII. Defendant waived his right to a jury and was convicted of the charge.

*   *   *

II. ANALYSIS

The relevant statutory provision defining felony DUII is set forth in the Oregon Vehicle Code as ORS 813.010. At the time that police officers stopped defendant, that statute provided, in pertinent part:

---

[2] In *Miller*, we held that "being under the influence of an intoxicant is a strict liability element" of DUII, and, as such, requires no proof of a culpable mental state as to that element. 309 Or. at 364, 788 P.2d 974. As we explain later in this opinion, *Miller* did not address whether the *driving* element of DUII requires a voluntary act as provided for in ORS 161.095(1).

"(1) A person commits the offense of driving while under the influence of intoxicants if the person drives a vehicle while the person:

"(a) Has 0.08 percent or more by weight of alcohol in the blood of the person as shown by chemical analysis of the breath or blood of the person made under ORS 813.100, 813.140 or 813.150;

"(b) Is under the influence of intoxicating liquor, a controlled substance or an inhalant; or

"(c) Is under the influence of any combination of intoxicating liquor, an inhalant and a controlled substance.

"* * *

"(4) Except as provided in subsection (5) of this section, the offense described in this section, driving while under the influence of intoxicants, is a Class A misdemeanor and is applicable upon any premises open to the public.

"(5)(a) Driving while under the influence of intoxicants is a Class C felony if the current offense was committed in a motor vehicle and the defendant has been convicted, at least three times in the 10 years prior to the date of the current offense, of any of the following offenses * * *:

"(A) Driving while under the influence of intoxicants * * *[.]"

ORS 813.010 (2007).

ORS 813.010 sets forth two essential elements. A person commits the crime of DUII when the person (1) "drives a vehicle" (2) while "under the influence" of an intoxicating substance. *See State v. King*, 316 Or. 437, 446, 852 P.2d 190 (1993) (so stating), *overruled in part on other grounds by Farmers Ins. Co. v. Mowry*, 350 Or. 686, 697, 261 P.3d 1 (2011). As this court recently emphasized, the statute "prohibits *driving* under the influence of intoxicants." *State v. Eumana-Moranchel*, 352 Or. 1, 7, 277 P.3d 549 (2012) (emphasis in original). Thus, the focus of the DUII statute "is on the act of driving, and doing so while impaired." *Id.; see also State v. Clark*, 286 Or. 33, 38 593 P.2d 123 (1979) ("gravamen" of the predecessor statute to ORS 813.010 is driving with a certain blood alcohol level).

As noted, when he was stopped, defendant admitted that he was intoxicated. He did not admit, however, that he had been consciously driving. He now contends, therefore, that he cannot be found criminally liable for *driving* his vehicle unless the voluntary act requirement of ORS 161.095(1) is met in this case. That statute requires a "voluntary act" as a "minimal requirement" for criminal liability:

"The minimal requirement for criminal liability is the performance by a person of conduct which includes a voluntary act or the omission to perform an act which the person is capable of performing."

ORS 161.095(1). Defendant thus contends that he should have been allowed to show that he was not engaged in a volitional act when driving because he was unconscious. The state responds that ORS 161.095(1) does not apply to DUII, or, alternatively, that ORS 161.095(1) nevertheless does not require that the voluntary act be limited to the driving element of DUII. We first address the state's contention that the volitional act requirement of ORS 161.095(1) does not apply to DUII.

* * *

B. *Voluntary Act — ORS 161.095(1)*

We now turn to the legislative determination that a person perform a voluntary act for imposition of criminal liability. Again, ORS 161.095(1) provides that:

"The minimal requirement for criminal liability is the performance by a person of conduct which includes a voluntary act or the omission to perform an act which the person is capable of performing."

The legislature has defined a "voluntary act" as used in ORS 161.095(1) to mean "a bodily movement performed consciously and includes the conscious possession or control of property." ORS 161.085(2). Applying that understanding to this case, defendant is not criminally liable under ORS 161.095(1) if he did not perform a bodily movement consciously.

Although the legislature has defined "voluntary act," it has not further defined what constitutes a "conscious" bodily movement. We have recognized that "conscious" as used in ORS 161.085(2) is a word of common usage. *State v. McDonnell*, 313 Or. 478, 497, 837 P.2d 941 (1992). Accordingly, we turn to the dictionary for further guidance to determine whether defendant's movements, if done while sleepwalking or "sleep driving," would be consciously performed. *See PGE v. Bureau of Labor and Industries*, 317 Or. 606, 611, 859 P.2d 1143 (1993) (stating that words of common usage should be given their plain, natural, and ordinary meaning). The dictionary definition of "conscious" includes:

"2: perceiving, apprehending, or noticing with a degree of controlled thought or observation: recognizing as existent, factual, or true: a: knowing or perceiving something within oneself or a fact about oneself * * * b: recognizing as factual or existent something external * * * 5 a: having rational power: capable of thought, will, design, or perception * * * 7: mentally active: fully possessed of one's mental faculties: having emerged from sleep, faint, or stupor: AWAKE <the patient becoming as the anesthesia wears off>"

Webster's Third New Int'l Dictionary 482 (unabridged ed. 2002) (boldface omitted). That definition associates consciousness with a wakeful state and implies that a person in a state of sleep cannot execute a conscious action.

That understanding is consistent with the pertinent legislative history. The commentary accompanying the 1971 substantive criminal code revisions explains that ORS 161.095(1)

"enunciates the basic principle that, no matter how an offense is defined, the minimal requirement for criminal liability is conduct which includes a 'voluntary' act or omission. This excludes all 'involuntary' acts such as reflex actions, acts committed during hypnosis, epileptic fugue, etc."

Criminal Law Revision Commission Proposed Oregon Criminal Code, Final Draft and Report § 11 Commentary (July 1970) (providing comments to §§ 7, 8). That explanation discloses a legislative intent to exclude from the definition of voluntary acts any acts that are taken when a person is sleeping.

In drafting the criminal code's liability requirements, the legislature looked to analogous provisions of the Model Penal Code. Model Penal Code section 2.01 is the counterpart of ORS 161.095(1), and requires proof of volition to establish criminal liability. Section 2.01 provides examples of what is *not* a voluntary act. Those examples include a reflex or convulsion, a bodily movement during unconsciousness or sleep, conduct during or resulting from hypnosis, and movement that otherwise is not a product of the effort or determination of the actor.[3] The commentary to section 2.01 clarifies that while "unconsciousness" may imply collapse or coma, there are "states of physical activity where self-awareness is grossly impaired or even absent," — *i.e.*, what the commentary refers to as states of active automatism — that are subsumed within the meaning of the term. American Law Institute, Model Penal Code Comments § 2.01, 121 (Tentative Draft No. 4 1955). The commentary explains that sleepwalking activity "should receive the same treatment accorded other active states of true automatism." *Id.* at 122. Thus, as the text and commentary suggest, the drafters of the Model Penal Code understood a person engaged in sleepwalking to lack the level of consciousness necessary for a volitional act.

Furthermore, the commentary to Model Penal Code section 2.01 states that criminal liability must be based on conduct that includes a voluntary act because

> "[t]he law cannot hope to deter involuntary movement or to stimulate action that cannot physically be performed; the sense of personal security would be short-lived in a society where such movement or inactivity could lead to formal social condemnation of the sort that a conviction necessarily entails. People whose involuntary movements threaten harm to others may present a public health or safety problem, calling for therapy or even for custodial commitment; they do not present a problem of correction."

American Law Institute, Model Penal Code Comments § 2.01, 119 (Tentative Draft No. 4 1955). *See also* Wayne R. LaFave, 1 *Substantive Criminal Law* § 6.1(c), 425–26 (2d ed. 2003) ("The deterrent function of the criminal law would not be served by imposing sanctions for involuntary action, as such action cannot be deterred."). In sum, the deterrent function of criminal sanctions and basic fairness are not served by punishing a person whose acts are the result of unconscious movement because the person committed those acts while sleeping. Thus, in enacting ORS 161.095(1), the legislature requires proof of a voluntary act for criminal liability to attach.

---

[3] The American Law Institute, Model Penal Code, section 2.01, 24 (Proposed Official Draft 1962) provides:

"(2)   The following are not voluntary acts within the meaning of this Section:

"(a)   a reflex or convulsion;

"(b)   a bodily movement during unconsciousness or sleep;

"(c)   conduct during hypnosis or resulting from hypnotic suggestion;

"(d)   a bodily movement that otherwise is not a product of the effort or determination of the actor, either conscious or habitual."

*   *   *

We conclude that the text, context, and legislative history of ORS 161.095(1) demonstrate a legislative intent to require that a defendant committed a voluntary act with respect to the driving element of DUII. This court's case law is not to the contrary. Although the courts below cited *Miller*, 309 Or. 362, 788 P.2d 974, in excluding defendant's proffered "sleep driving" evidence, *Miller* did not address the volitional act requirement of ORS 161.095(1). In *Miller*, the court examined how other statutes — namely ORS 161.095(2) and ORS 161.105 — operate with respect to the offense of DUII in determining whether a defendant may be convicted of DUII without proof of a culpable mental state when under the influence of an intoxicant. The court concluded that the "being-under-the influence-of-an-intoxicant element of DUII, ORS 813.010, requires no proof of a culpable mental state." *Id.* at 371, 788 P.2d 974. However, the court did not consider how the voluntary act requirement of ORS 161.095(1) applies to the driving element in a DUII prosecution. *Miller* simply did not address the issue of volitional driving presented in this case.

To summarize: We hold that the minimal voluntary act requirement of ORS 161.095(1) applies to the driving element of DUII in this case. Here, the trial court erred in not allowing defendant to adduce evidence that he was not conscious when he drove on the evening in question. The state was entitled to present evidence that defendant's drinking or other volitional act resulted in defendant driving his vehicle that evening. As noted, the state may also show a voluntary act with evidence that defendant had engaged in "sleep driving" prior to this incident and failed to take adequate precautions to remove access to his car keys. *See State v. Newman*, 353 Ore. 632, [644–45 n. 4,] 302 P.3d 435 (2013).

[C]   Determining Probative Value

Once it is established that a proposition is provable in a cause of action, how does a court determine whether a particular piece of evidence is probative of that proposition? On what does a court rely in making this determination? How does a court determine that evidence that a person learned to drive in Mississippi is not logically related to the proposition that he drove negligently on a particular occasion?

The answer to these questions lies in whether there is any acceptable underlying factual premise or intermediate proposition that connects the evidence and the ultimate proposition to be proven (both as a general truth and as a fact under the unique circumstances of the case at hand). There must be a premise that logically allows the finder of fact to draw the desired inference from the fact proven. Our common experiences and observations, the knowledge we have acquired from them, and the absence of statistical or scientific evidence proving what is not logically apparent inform us there is nothing inherent in the climate or terrain of Mississippi, in the people who teach others to drive there, or in the skills and personalities of those who learn in that state that allows us to draw the rational conclusion that having learned to drive there increases the probability of reacting in a certain way to future stimuli. In contrast, however, evidence that the defendant regularly drove his car without wearing his prescription eyeglasses is relevant to the question of the defendant's alleged negligence on a particular occasion for failing to take measures to avoid hitting the plaintiff. Because humans are creatures of habit, an acceptable underlying premise arises that if one regularly drives without glasses, he probably drove on the occasion in question without them, thereby diminishing his ability to perceive. Of course, if the basis for the claim of negligence were unconnected to the perception of the defendant — for example, if it were claimed that he failed to maintain his tires properly — then the evidence would not be relevant because the proposition that it proves (faulty perception) is neither an issue in the case nor probative of the proposition that is in issue: the operation of the car with faulty equipment.

The less apparent the logical connection between the evidence offered and the proposition to be proved, the greater the burden on the proponent to identify the underlying premises and persuade the judge of their viability through logical analysis or scientific documentation. Establishing this connection often is a test of a trial attorney's ingenuity.

Of course, admissibility is only the first challenge for the litigants. Because the purpose of the trial is not to see who can introduce the most evidence, but rather to prevail in the jury's determination of the factual issues, a party not only must convincingly articulate the inference or series of inferences through which a piece of evidence proves a particular proposition, it also must persuasively explain and argue its point to the jury.

[1]   When Does Evidence Sufficiently Tend to Demonstrate a Provable Proposition?

Only where the evidence is facially without probative value will a court exclude it. *Lombardi* offers a rare example of a court finding evidence to so lack probative value as to be inadmissible.

LOMBARDI v. CITY OF GROTON
Connecticut Court of Appeals
599 A.2d 388 (1991)

HEIMAN, JUDGE.

The defendants, David Bailey, Ronald Jenkins and Cindy Grenier, appeal from a judgment rendered on a verdict against them for compensatory and punitive damages. The action arose out of the plaintiff's allegations of excessive use of force in effecting his arrest, false arrest, extreme and outrageous conduct, a violation of his civil rights. and unlawful restraint.

On appeal, the defendants assert that the trial court improperly . . . refused to admit evidence of the plaintiff's prior criminal record when it was offered to show bias, prejudice, habit or custom, and . . . refused to admit evidence of the plaintiff's prior criminal record on the issue of the plaintiff's claim of emotional damages, mental distress and humiliation. We affirm the judgment of the trial court.

The jury could reasonably have found the following facts. For several years, the plaintiff operated as a catering vendor in the vicinity of the Electric Boat Division of General Dynamics in Groton. On June 9, 1987, at about 7:50 a.m., he was operating a catering truck near Electric Boat.

At that time, Grenier, Bailey and Jenkins were employed by the town of Groton as uniformed police officers and were patrolling the area surrounding Electric Boat. Grenier and Bailey were riding together in a marked police car when they stopped the plaintiff's vehicle. When the plaintiff stopped, he, Grenier and Bailey exited their vehicles. The plaintiff asked Bailey why he was being stopped, and Bailey told him that it was because he was not displaying an emissions sticker.

Bailey then asked the plaintiff to produce his license. When the plaintiff attempted to remove it from his wallet, Bailey slapped the wallet to the ground and shoved the plaintiff against his truck. At that time, Grenier and Jenkins, a third Groton police officer who had arrived at the scene, leaped into the fray and, with Bailey, threw the plaintiff to the ground and landed on top of him. Bailey then handcuffed the plaintiff, pulled him up, and put him in a police car. The plaintiff was then transported to the Groton police station. Upon arrival, Bailey threw the plaintiff against the steel plate of a cell. Later, the plaintiff was given a motor vehicle summons for having an expired emissions sticker. At no time was he advised of his constitutional rights.

As a consequence of the defendants' conduct, the plaintiff suffered bruises and contusions to the lower back and legs and a fracture of the L3 transvere process of the lumbar spine, which caused physical pain and required medical treatment.

The plaintiff was arrested and charged with breach of peace, assault on a police officer, interfering with a police officer and engaging an officer in pursuit. After a jury trial, he was acquitted of all charges. The plaintiff subsequently commenced a civil action against the defendants based on their alleged excessive use of force in effecting his arrest, false arrest, extreme and outrageous conduct, violation of his civil rights and unlawful restraint.

The jury awarded the plaintiff $125,000 in compensatory damages against the defendants, and punitive damages of $400 against Grenier, $2400 against Bailey, and $1200 against Jenkins. In addition, the court awarded the plaintiff attorney's fees of $35,731.25.

*   *   *

The defendants complain that the trial court improperly excluded evidence of the plaintiff's prior criminal record when that evidence was admissible (1) on the issues of bias, prejudice, habit or custom, and (2) on the claim of emotional damages, mental distress and humiliation. We disagree.

The defendants sought to introduce into evidence the fact that the plaintiff had been convicted of breach of the peace on March 25, 1965, May 7, 1966, and January 25, 1977, of assault in the third degree on December 4, 1971, and disorderly conduct on December 21, 1978.[3] The trial court sustained the plaintiff's relevancy objection

---

[3] All of the criminal convictions sought to be introduced were at that time and are now misdemeanors. See General Statutes (1958 Rev.) § 53-174 and General Statutes §§ 53a-181, 53a-182 and 53a-61.

to these questions. The defendants then advised the trial court that they would attempt to reintroduce this evidence when the expert medical witnesses testified, for the purpose of disputing the plaintiff's claim of psychological and emotional injury. When physician Alan J. Greenwald testified on behalf of the plaintiff, the defendants conducted a voir dire examination on the issue of prior arrests and convictions as it related to psychological and emotional injury. Upon completion of the voir dire of Greenwald, the defendants indicated to the trial court that they would not pursue that line of questioning before the jury.

We first note that the defendants did not and could not claim that the plaintiff's prior convictions were admissible for the purposes of impeaching his credibility because all of the convictions were for misdemeanors and, thus, are not crimes punishable by more than one year in prison. General Statutes § 52-145; *Heating Acceptance Corporation v. Patterson*, 152 Conn. 467, 471–72, 208 A.2d 341 (1965); see also *State v. Martin*, 201 Conn. 74, 86, 513 A.2d 116 (1986) (reaffirming *Heating Acceptance Corporation*).

As to the defendants' claims, trial courts are vested with liberal discretion in determining the relevancy of evidence. *Delott v. Roraback*, 179 Conn. 406, 414, 426 A.2d 791 (1980); *Pagani v. BT II, Limited Partnership*, 24 Conn. App. 739, 748, 592 A.2d 397 (1991). Evidence is relevant if "it tends to establish a fact in issue or to corroborate other direct evidence in the case." *Federated Department Stores, Inc. v. Board of Tax Review*, 162 Conn. 77, 82, 291 A.2d 715 (1971). "Because there is no precise and universal test of relevancy, however, the question must ultimately be addressed on a case-by-case basis in accordance with the teachings of reason and judicial experience." (Internal quotation marks omitted.) *Metropolitan District v. Housing Authority*, 12 Conn. App. 499, 508, 531 A.2d 194 (1987). We will set aside rulings on evidentiary matters only upon a clear showing of an abuse of discretion. Id.

The trial court did not abuse its discretion in ruling that the proffered evidence was inadmissible. None of the prior instances of misconduct involved the defendants in this case. Only one of the five instances involved an act directed against a police officer. The acts of misconduct occurred between eleven and twenty-five years prior to this trial, and involved only misdemeanors. In addition, the court noted that to admit the proffered evidence would result in diverting the inquiry from the ultimate issues presented.

In light of these factors, the trial did not abuse its discretion in refusing to admit the proffered evidence. Even if the evidence had been marginally relevant, "[i]t is a reasonable exercise of judicial discretion to exclude . . . evidence the relevancy of which appears to be so slight and inconsequential that to admit it would distract attention which should be concentrated on vital issues of the case." *State v. Moynahan*, 164 Conn. 560, 589, 325 A.2d 199, cert. denied, 414 U.S. 976, 94 S. Ct. 291, 38 L. Ed. 2d 219 (1973); *State v. Plaza*, 23 Conn. App. 543, 549, 583 A.2d 925 (1990), cert. denied, 217 Conn. 811, 587 A.2d 153 (1991).

The defendants' alternative claim of relevance was that the evidence of prior convictions was probative of the extent of emotional damages suffered by the plaintiff. Specifically, the defendant hoped to establish that a person who had been arrested on a number of occasions would be less traumatized by an additional arrest than one who had never been arrested. This attempt, however, died aborning during the defendants' offer of proof, when Greenwald testified that he could not reach such a conclusion because of the number of variables. After failing to establish a factual basis for this testimony, the defendants abandoned their offer of proof on this issue. See *Stephanofsky v. Hill*, 136 Conn. 379, 384–85, 71 A.2d 560 (1950). Thus, we need not decide whether the trial court properly excluded the proffered testimony on the issue of damages, because the defendants have failed to demonstrate that they suffered probable harm as a result of such ruling. See *Starzec v. Kida*, 183 Conn. 41, 49, 438 A.2d 1157 (1981).

The judgment is affirmed.

[2]   When Is Evidence Sufficiently Reliable to Advance a Provable Proposition?

Very rarely (with the exception of scientific evidence that we will take up later) is a proposition so unreliable that it becomes irrelevant. Once the evidence has *some* reliability, it is typically given to the jury and the parties are permitted to argue about its reliability. *Jones* provides an illustration of this basic principle. It would be fairly remarkable for a witness — as in the *Jones* case below — to be able to identify a gray hoodie as the specific one worn by a burglar. As you will see in *Jones*, however, as unlikely as such a positive identification of such a non-descript item may be, the reliability of the identification is a matter for the jury.

STATE v. JONES
North Carolina Court of Appeals
750 S.E.2d 920 (2013)

GEER, JUDGE.

Defendant Rodney Eugene Jones appeals from his conviction of first degree burglary, larceny after a breaking and entering, and being a habitual felon.

Facts

The State's evidence tended to show the following facts. On the evening of 20 October 2008, Tracy Thompson was alone and asleep in her townhome on North Church Street in Charlotte, North Carolina. Before going to bed at around 9:30 p.m., Ms. Thompson had dead-bolted the front door and left the light on in the hallway outside her bedroom. After she had fallen asleep at about 10:00 p.m., Ms. Thompson was awakened by a pounding sound, but she fell back to sleep.

At around 10:30 p.m., Brandon Phillips was a passenger in an automobile parked on North Church Street. Mr. Phillips was talking to a coworker when he noticed two individuals, one wearing a black hoodie and the other wearing a gray hoodie, on the street. Thinking the pair looked suspicious, Mr. Phillips and his coworker sat back in the car and watched them. They saw the two individuals walk up to a townhouse, and the one wearing a gray hoodie, who was taller, kicked the door two or three times until the door came open. Both of the individuals ran into the townhouse.

Sometime after that, Ms. Thompson was awakened by a loud crash, a flash of light, and her bedroom door being flung open. She saw a thin black male in his forties wearing a light-colored hoodie and dark pants. Ms. Thompson could see the intruder's face because the hallway light illuminated his face and he was only three to five feet away from her. Ms. Thompson screamed, told the man she had a gun, and threatened to kill him. The intruder turned and walked back toward the hallway. Ms. Thompson then opened the window, kicked out the screen, screamed out the window for help, and called 911.

Still sitting outside, Mr. Phillips saw Ms. Thompson, heard her scream for help, and watched the two individuals run from her townhouse. The two ran down North Church Street toward Discovery Place with Mr. Phillips and his companion in their car following slowly behind them. Mr. Phillips called 911 while keeping the two intruders in sight. As the two individuals continued down Church Street, the man wearing the gray hoodie took off the hoodie. The two individuals then made a right turn onto 6th Street and crossed that street.

At that point, Officer Marvin Bell, an off-duty officer with the Charlotte-Mecklenburg Police Department, who had heard the call regarding the break-in and gone to the area, saw what he believed to be two men crossing 6th Street. Officer Bell was looking at their backs and could not see either person's face, although he believed them to be the two suspects based upon the descriptions of their clothing that had come over the radio. Officer Bell lost sight of the two as they turned a corner.

Officer Benjamin Roldan and another officer, who were responding to the breaking and entering call, saw two individuals matching the description of the suspects walk across 6th Street and detained them. At that point, Mr. Phillips identified the two people as the individuals who had broken into and fled from Ms. Thompson's townhouse. Mr. Phillips noted that the gray hoodie had disappeared sometime between the time the two intruders had turned the corner and the police had arrived. It turned out that the person wearing a black hoodie was female while the other individual was male. Officer Roldan searched the two suspects and recovered a cell phone, charger, and digital camera.

Meanwhile, Ms. Thompson informed Officer Patrick Mulhall, who arrived at her home, that her cell phone was missing. Officer Mulhall called the cell phone's number, and Officer Roldan answered — the cell phone he had retrieved from the suspects was Ms. Thompson's phone.

Ms. Thompson was then taken to 6th and Poplar Streets where she saw two individuals standing in a parking lot. The area was well lit, and she was taken within 15 feet of the two suspects. She identified defendant as the person who had entered her bedroom. After identifying defendant, Ms. Thompson traveled with police down an alley through which the two suspects had traveled. Ms. Thompson noticed a light colored hoodie sweatshirt in a bush that looked like the one defendant was wearing when he kicked in her bedroom door.

Defendant was indicted for first degree burglary and larceny after breaking and entering. At trial, Ms. Thompson testified that she was 100 percent sure that defendant was the man who had broken into her townhouse and that she had not forgotten his face. The jury convicted defendant of both offenses, and defendant pled guilty to being a habitual felon. The trial court consolidated the offenses into a single judgment and sentenced defendant to a presumptive-range term of 151 to 191 months imprisonment. Defendant timely appealed to this Court.

*　　*　　*

II

Defendant . . . contends that photographs of the light-colored hoodie recovered in the alley near where defendant was apprehended were improperly admitted. At trial, Ms. Thompson was asked about three photographs:

Q.   And what are State's Exhibits Numbers 14 through 16?

A.   Pictures of a sweatshirt and some shrubbery.

Q.   And do you recognize these pictures?

A.   Yes.

Q.   . . . Do these pictures fairly and accurately depict the sweatshirt as you saw it on October 20th, 2008?

A.   Yes.

Q.   And would these pictures help to illustrate your testimony?

A.   Yes.

Although defendant objected that the photographs were duplicitous, the trial court admitted the photographs for illustrative purposes.

Ms. Thompson then testified regarding what the photographs showed:

Q.   Ms. Thompson, I'm showing you what's been marked as State's Exhibit 14. What is this a picture of?

A.   It's a picture of a light-colored hoodie sweatshirt in the shrubbery.

Q.   And where is that shrubbery?

A.   Just off the alley.

Q.   And when you're saying the "alley," is that the same alley that you're referring to in State's Exhibit 13?

A.   Correct, the alley behind Discovery Zone parking between 6th and 7th.

Q.   I'm also showing you what's been marked as State's Exhibit 15. Can you tell me what that is?

A.   The picture of the sweatshirt that was found in the alley.

Q.   And that's the same picture — that's the same sweatshirt that was found in State's Exhibit 14?

A.   Yes.

Q.   And also, I'm showing you what's been marked as State's Exhibit 16.
                Can you tell the jury what that is a picture of?

MR. BUTLER: Objection.

THE COURT: Overruled.

THE WITNESS: It is a picture of the sweatshirt that was found in the alley on
                the evening of 10/20/08.

*   *   *

Ms. Thompson testified that the photographs were an accurate representation of
what she saw when she and the officer found the grey hoodie in a shrub in the alley.
That testimony was sufficient to permit the admission of the photographs for
illustrative purposes. With respect to Ms. Thompson's testimony that the sweatshirt
depicted in the photographs — the sweatshirt found in the alley — was the
sweatshirt that the intruder was wearing in her house, defendant argues that the
testimony was so unreliable that it should have been excluded as irrelevant under
Rule 401 of the Rules of Evidence. Alternatively, defendant argues that the evidence
should have been excluded as more unfairly prejudicial than probative under Rule
403 of the Rules of Evidence.

Defendant's arguments regarding the reliability of Ms. Thompson's testimony
raise questions for the jury. Only the jury may determine whether Ms. Thompson
was credible when she testified that she could recognize the hoodie in the shrub as
being that of the intruder. Moreover, as for defendant's Rule 403 argument, this
Court may not apply plain error analysis to decisions under Rule 403. *See State v.
Cunningham*, 188 N.C.App. 832, 837, 656 S.E.2d 697, 700 (2008) ("The balancing
test of Rule 403 is reviewed by this court for abuse of discretion, and we do not apply
plain error to issues which fall within the realm of the trial court's discretion."
(internal quotation marks omitted)).

[D] Limiting Relevant Evidence by Statute

We considered in the *Newman* case the fact that evidence is limited to that
which is relevant to a proposition that can be proven. Fed. R. Evid. 402 further
provides, however, that even relevant evidence can be excluded by the Constitution,
a statute, other rules of evidence, or a rule of a court. *Egelhoff* takes up this
question of when a statute may exclude relevant evidence. Notice how the
argument between the majority and the dissent is really one of form versus
substance. For the majority, Montana has changed the elements of the crime,
which it is allowed to do. For the dissent, however, the statute improperly excluded
evidence that was relevant to an element the state was required to prove.

MONTANA v. EGELHOFF

Supreme Court of the United States
518 U.S. 37 (1996)

JUSTICE SCALIA announced the judgment of the Court and delivered an opinion, in which THE CHIEF JUSTICE, JUSTICE KENNEDY, and JUSTICE THOMAS join.

We consider in this case whether the Due Process Clause is violated by Montana Code Annotated § 45-2-203, which provides, in relevant part, that voluntary intoxication "may not be taken into consideration in determining the existence of a mental state which is an element of [a criminal] offense."

I

In July 1992, while camping out in the Yaak region of northwestern Montana to pick mushrooms, respondent made friends with Roberta Pavola and John Christenson, who were doing the same. On Sunday, July 12, the three sold the mushrooms they had collected and spent the rest of the day and evening drinking, in bars and at a private party in Troy, Montana. Some time after 9 p.m., they left the party in Christenson's 1974 Ford Galaxy station wagon. The drinking binge apparently continued, as respondent was seen buying beer at 9:20 p.m. and recalled "sitting on a hill or a bank passing a bottle of Black Velvet back and forth" with Christenson. 272 Mont. 114, 118, 900 P.2d 260, 262 (1995).

At about midnight that night, officers of the Lincoln County, Montana, sheriff's department, responding to reports of a possible drunk driver, discovered Christenson's station wagon stuck in a ditch along U.S. Highway 2. In the front seat were Pavola and Christenson, each dead from a single gunshot to the head. In the rear of the car lay respondent, alive and yelling obscenities. His blood-alcohol content measured .36 percent over one hour later. On the floor of the car, near the brake pedal, lay respondent's .38-caliber handgun, with four loaded rounds and two empty casings; respondent had gunshot residue on his hands.

Respondent was charged with two counts of deliberate homicide, a crime defined by Montana law as "purposely" or "knowingly" causing the death of another human being. Mont.Code Ann. § 45-5-102 (1995). A portion of the jury charge, uncontested here, instructed that "[a] person acts purposely when it is his conscious object to engage in conduct of that nature or to cause such a result," and that "[a] person acts knowingly when he is aware of his conduct or when he is aware under the circumstances his conduct constitutes a crime; or, when he is aware there exists the high probability that his conduct will cause a specific result." App. to Pet. for Cert. 28a–29a. Respondent's defense at trial was that an unidentified fourth person must have committed the murders; his own extreme intoxication, he claimed, had rendered him physically incapable of committing the murders, and accounted for his inability to recall the events of the night of July 12. Although respondent was allowed to make this use of the evidence that he was intoxicated, the jury was instructed, pursuant to Mont. Code Ann. § 45-2-203 (1995), that it could not consider respondent's "intoxicated condition . . . in determining the existence of a mental state which is an element of the offense." App. to Pet. for Cert. 29a. The jury found respondent guilty on both counts, and the court sentenced him to 84 years' imprisonment.

The Supreme Court of Montana reversed. It reasoned (1) that respondent "had a due process right to present and have considered by the jury all relevant evidence to rebut the State's evidence on all elements of the offense charged," 272 Mont., at 125, 900 P.2d, at 266, and (2) that evidence of respondent's voluntary intoxication was "clear[ly] . . . relevant to the issue of whether [respondent] acted knowingly and purposely," *id.*, at 122, 900 P.2d, at 265. Because § 45-2-203 prevented the jury from considering that evidence with regard to that issue, the court concluded that the State had been "relieved of part of its burden to prove beyond a reasonable doubt every fact necessary to constitute the crime charged," *id.*, at 124, 900 P.2d, at 266, and that respondent had therefore been denied due process. We granted certiorari. 516 U.S. 1021, 116 S. Ct. 593, 133 L. Ed. 2d 514 (1995).

II

The cornerstone of the Montana Supreme Court's judgment was the proposition that the Due Process Clause guarantees a defendant the right to present and have considered by the jury " *all relevant evidence* to rebut the State's evidence on all elements of the offense charged." 272 Mont., at 125, 900 P.2d, at 266 (emphasis added). Respondent does not defend this categorical rule; he acknowledges that the right to present relevant evidence "has not been viewed as absolute." Brief for Respondent 31. That is a wise concession, since the proposition that the Due Process Clause guarantees the right to introduce all relevant evidence is simply indefensible. As we have said: "The accused does not have an unfettered right to offer [evidence] that is incompetent, privileged, or otherwise inadmissible under standard rules of evidence." *Taylor v. Illinois*, 484 U.S. 400, 410, 108 S. Ct. 646, 653, 98 L. Ed. 2d 798 (1988). Relevant evidence may, for example, be excluded on account of a defendant's failure to comply with procedural requirements. See *Michigan v. Lucas*, 500 U.S. 145, 151, 111 S. Ct. 1743, 1747, 114 L. Ed. 2d 205 (1991). And any number of familiar and unquestionably constitutional evidentiary rules also authorize the exclusion of relevant evidence. For example, Federal (and Montana) Rule of Evidence 403 provides: "*Although relevant,* evidence may be excluded if its probative value is substantially outweighed by the danger of unfair prejudice, confusion of the issues, or misleading the jury, or by considerations of undue delay, waste of time, or needless presentation of cumulative evidence." (Emphasis added.) Hearsay rules, see Fed. Rule Evid. 802, similarly prohibit the introduction of testimony which, though unquestionably relevant, is deemed insufficiently reliable. Of course, to say that the right to introduce relevant evidence is not absolute is not to say that the Due Process Clause places *no* limits upon restriction of that right. But it is to say that the defendant asserting such a limit must sustain the usual heavy burden that a due process claim entails:

Our primary guide in determining whether the principle in question is funda-mental is, of course, historical practice. See *Medina v. California*, 505 U.S. 437, 446, 112 S. Ct. 2572, 2577–2578, 120 L. Ed. 2d 353 (1992). Here that gives respondent little support. By the laws of England, wrote Hale, the intoxicated defendant "shall have no privilege by this voluntary contracted madness, but shall have the same judgment as if he were in his right senses." 1 M. Hale, Pleas of the Crown *32–*33.

* * *

Against this extensive evidence of a lengthy common-law tradition decidedly against him, the best argument available to respondent is the one made by his *amicus* and conceded by the State: Over the course of the 19th century, courts carved out an exception to the common law's traditional across-the-board condemnation of the drunken offender, allowing a jury to consider a defendant's intoxication when assessing whether he possessed the mental state needed to commit the crime charged, where the crime was one requiring a "specific intent." The emergence of this new rule is often traced to an 1819 English case, in which Justice Holroyd is reported to have held that "though voluntary drunkenness cannot excuse from the commission of crime, yet where, as on a charge of murder, the material question is, whether an act was premeditated or done only with sudden heat and impulse, the fact of the party being intoxicated [is] a circumstance proper to be taken into consideration." 1 W. Russell, Crimes and Misdemeanors *8 (citing *King v. Grindley*, Worcester Sum. Assizes 1819, MS).

* * *

On the basis of this historical record, respondent's *amicus* argues that "[t]he old common-law rule . . . was no longer deeply rooted at the time the Fourteenth Amendment was ratified." Brief for National Association of Criminal Defense Lawyers as *Amicus Curiae* 23. That conclusion is questionable, but we need not pursue the point, since the argument of *amicus* mistakes the nature of our inquiry. It is not the State which bears the burden of demonstrating that its rule is "deeply rooted," but rather respondent who must show that the principle of procedure *violated* by the rule (and allegedly required by due process) is " 'so rooted in the traditions and conscience of our people as to be ranked as fundamental.' " *Patterson v. New York*, 432 U.S., at 202, 97 S. Ct., at 2322. Thus, even assuming that when the Fourteenth Amendment was adopted the rule Montana now defends was no longer generally applied . . . [t]he burden remains upon respondent to show that the "new common-law" rule — that intoxication may be considered on the question of intent — was so deeply rooted at the time of the Fourteenth Amendment (or perhaps has become so deeply rooted since) as to be a fundamental principle which that Amendment enshrined.

That showing has not been made. Instead of the uniform and continuing acceptance we would expect for a rule that enjoys "fundamental principle" status, we find that fully one-fifth of the States either never adopted the "new common-law" rule at issue here or have recently abandoned it. . . .

It is not surprising that many States have held fast to or resurrected the common-law rule prohibiting consideration of voluntary intoxication in the determination of *mens rea*, because that rule has considerable justification — which alone casts doubt upon the proposition that the opposite rule is a "fundamental principle." A large number of crimes, especially violent crimes, are committed by intoxicated offenders; modern studies put the numbers as high as half of all homicides, for example. See, *e.g.*, Third Special Report to the U.S. Congress on Alcohol and Health from the Secretary of Health, Education, and Welfare 64 (1978); Note, Alcohol

Abuse and the Law, 94 Harv. L. Rev. 1660, 1681–1682 (1981). Disallowing consideration of voluntary intoxication has the effect of increasing the punishment for all unlawful acts committed in that state, and thereby deters drunkenness or irresponsible behavior while drunk. The rule also serves as a specific deterrent, ensuring that those who prove incapable of controlling violent impulses while voluntarily intoxicated go to prison. And finally, the rule comports with and implements society's moral perception that one who has voluntarily impaired his own faculties should be responsible for the consequences. See, *e.g., McDaniel v. State*, 356 So. 2d 1151, 1160–1161 (Miss. 1978).

There is, in modern times, even more justification for laws such as § 45-2-203 than there used to be. Some recent studies suggest that the connection between drunkenness and crime is as much cultural as pharmacological — that is, that drunks are violent not simply because alcohol makes them that way, but because they are behaving in accord with their learned belief that drunks are violent. See, *e.g.*, Collins, Suggested Explanatory Frameworks to Clarify the Alcohol Use/ Violence Relationship, 15 Contemp. Drug Prob. 107, 115 (1988); Critchlow, The Powers of John Barleycorn, 41 Am. Psychologist 751, 754–755 (July 1986). This not only adds additional support to the traditional view that an intoxicated criminal is not deserving of exoneration, but it suggests that juries — who possess the same learned belief as the intoxicated offender — will be too quick to accept the claim that the defendant was biologically incapable of forming the requisite *mens rea*. Treating the matter as one of excluding misleading evidence therefore makes some sense.

In sum, not every widespread experiment with a procedural rule favorable to criminal defendants establishes a fundamental principle of justice. Although the rule allowing a jury to consider evidence of a defendant's voluntary intoxication where relevant to *mens rea* has gained considerable acceptance, it is of too recent vintage, and has not received sufficiently uniform and permanent allegiance, to qualify as fundamental, especially since it displaces a lengthy common-law tradition which remains supported by valid justifications today.

*   *   *

JUSTICE O'CONNOR, with whom JUSTICE STEVENS, JUSTICE SOUTER, and JUSTICE BREYER join, dissenting.

*   *   *

Due process demands that a criminal defendant be afforded a fair opportunity to defend against the State's accusations. Meaningful adversarial testing of the State's case requires that the defendant not be prevented from raising an effective defense, which must include the right to present relevant, probative evidence. To be sure, the right to present evidence is not limitless; for example, it does not permit the defendant to introduce any and all evidence he believes might work in his favor, *Crane, supra*, at 690, 106 S. Ct., at 2146, nor does it generally invalidate the operation of testimonial privileges, *Washington v. Texas, supra*, at 23, n. 21, 87 S. Ct., at 1925, n. 21. Nevertheless, "an essential component of procedural fairness is an opportunity to be heard. That opportunity would be an empty one if the State were permitted to exclude competent, reliable evidence" that is essential to the accused's defense. *Crane, supra,* at 690, 106 S. Ct., at 2146 (citations omitted). Section 45-2-203 forestalls the defendant's ability to raise an effective defense by placing a blanket exclusion on the presentation of a type of evidence that directly negates an element of the crime, and by doing so, it lightens the prosecution's burden to prove that mental-state element beyond a reasonable doubt.

This latter effect is as important to the due process analysis as the former. A state legislature certainly has the authority to identify the elements of the offenses it wishes to punish, but once its laws are written, a defendant has the right to insist that the State prove beyond a reasonable doubt every element of an offense charged. See *McMillan v. Pennsylvania,* 477 U.S. 79, 85, 106 S. Ct. 2411, 2415–2416, 91 L. Ed. 2d 67 (1986); *Patterson v. New York,* 432 U.S. 197, 211, n. 12, 97 S. Ct. 2319, 2327, n. 12, 53 L. Ed. 2d 281 (1977) ("The applicability of the reasonable-doubt standard, however, has always been dependent on how a State defines the offense that is charged"). "[T]he Due Process Clause protects the accused against conviction except upon proof beyond a reasonable doubt of every fact necessary to constitute the crime with which he is charged." *In re Winship,* 397 U.S. 358, 364, 90 S. Ct. 1068, 1073, 25 L. Ed. 2d 368 (1970); *Patterson, supra,* at 210, 97 S. Ct., at 2327. Because the Montana Legislature has specified that a person commits "deliberate homicide" only if he "purposely or knowingly causes the death of another human being," Mont.Code Ann. § 45-5-102(1)(a) (1995), the prosecution must prove the existence of such mental state in order to convict. That is, unless the defendant is shown to have acted purposely or knowingly, *he is not guilty of the offense of deliberate homicide.* The Montana Supreme Court found that it was inconsistent with the legislature's requirement of the mental state of "purposely" or "knowingly" to prevent the jury from considering evidence of voluntary intoxication, where that category of evidence was relevant to establishment of that mental-state element. 272 Mont., at 122–123, 900 P.2d, at 265–266.

Where the defendant may introduce evidence to negate a subjective mental-state element, the prosecution must work to overcome whatever doubts the defense has raised about the existence of the required mental state. On the other hand, if the defendant may *not* introduce evidence that might create doubt in the factfinder's mind as to whether that element was met, the prosecution will find its job so much the easier. A subjective mental state is generally proved only circumstantially. If a jury may not consider the defendant's evidence of his mental state, the jury may impute to the defendant the culpability of a mental state he did not possess.

EXERCISES

1. Hatch competed with 16 other contestants on a reality television show filmed on a remote island. As the "survivor" of the competition, Hatch won a prize of one million dollars. Hatch failed to report his winnings on his federal income tax return. In his criminal trial for filing false tax returns, Hatch seeks to introduce testimony that (a) he believed that the television show producers were responsible for paying the taxes on his winnings, and (b) that portions of the reality show had been improperly staged by the producers. Is the testimony relevant?

2. Ken and Roger robbed a bank. During pre-trial discovery Ken learns that Roger previously robbed several other banks with Charles. At trial Ken raises a duress defense and claims that Roger forced him to rob the bank by pointing a gun at him and saying, "We're going to rob that bank." Ken also seeks to introduce the evidence that Roger previously robbed several other banks with Charles. Are Roger's prior bank robberies relevant?

3. Police charged Ronald with manufacturing marijuana with the intent to deliver after they discovered a field of marijuana growing near his home. At trial Ronald seeks to call a witness who can testify as to Ronald's finances prior to and at the time of his arrest. The witness will state that Ronald had a wall safe installed in his home, and that that safe only contained $100. Additionally, the witness will authenticate Ronald's tax returns and bank statements. The government objects to the admission of this evidence on relevancy grounds. Is this testimony relevant?

4. John files a medical malpractice suit against his physician, following a back operation from which John awoke with total loss of sight in his left eye. At trial the physician testifies that although he is a licensed surgeon, he is not board certified. John now wants to cross-examine the physician as to the reason he is not board certified, specifically that the physician failed the board certifying examination on four separate occasions. Is John's cross-examination relevant?

5. At Luis' criminal trial for alleging conspiring to possess with intent to distribute cocaine, the government seeks to offer the testimony of Rodriguez, another purported member of the conspiracy, to testify that Luis murdered two other co-conspirators. According to Rodriguez, Luis killed A because A refused to follow Luis' instructions on how to package the drugs. Then Luis killed B because B tried to sell drugs in Luis' neighborhood. Ignoring any other potential evidentiary issues, is Rodriguez's testimony of the two murders relevant under Rule 401 in Luis' drug conspiracy case?

6. Stephen and GasCo, a natural gas company enter into a contract, whereby Stephen granted GasCo the right to drill wells on his property. In exchange for the right to drill, GasCo agreed to pay Stephen using one of two possible payment methods: the "fair market value" of the extracted gas or the "federal government rate" which would be calculated in accordance with complex federal regulations. GasCo opted to pay Stephen using the fair market value method. Stephen filed suit alleging that GasCo failed to properly calculate the fair market value, and, consequently he was underpaid on the contract. At trial Stephen seeks to introduce evidence that a competing gas company, with similar contract language, opted to pay its landowners using the federal government rate. GasCo objects. Is this testimony relevant?

7. Police conducted a traffic stop on William's vehicle. William pulled the vehicle over, but then jumped out of the car and ran. As William — who was dressed all in black — ran from the car, a loaded firearm fell out of his jacket pocket. Police gave chase, caught William, and recovered the firearm from the ground. Police then lawfully searched William's car and found a backpack containing a crow bar, a flashlight, a surgical mask, a winter cap, a can of beer, and a honey dispenser filled with gasoline. Police charged William with unlawful possession of a firearm. At his trial for the gun offense, the government seeks to admit the physical evidence recovered from William's vehicle, and William objects on relevancy grounds. How should the court rule?

§ 2.02 BALANCING PROBATIVE VALUE AGAINST PREJUDICE

[A] A Precursor to the Federal Rules of Evidence

As mentioned in *Lomardi*, questions about the reliability of evidence occasionally are so significant that, if coupled with the inherently convincing or inflammatory nature of the evidence, or jurors' inability to properly assess its value, courts will exclude the evidence, not because it is irrelevant, but because the danger of unfair prejudice substantially outweighs its probative value. This balancing of probative value and prejudice is reflected in *People v. Collins*, in which the court considered the use of evidence of mathematical probability to establish the identity of an individual in a criminal prosecution. As you read *Collins*, consider why exactly the court excluded the evidence. Surely, it is not something inherently problematic about the statistics used, similar statistics are regularly used in DNA cases in courtrooms daily. Yet the court seems troubled about something more than merely the assumptions the prosecution's expert used in his calculations. Ask yourself what exactly the court finds problematic about this evidence.

PEOPLE v. COLLINS
California Supreme Court
68 Cal. 2d 319, 66 Cal. Rptr. 497, 438 P.2d 33 (1968)

SULLIVAN, JUSTICE.

We deal here with the novel question whether evidence of mathematical probability has been properly introduced and used by the prosecution in a criminal case. While we discern no inherent incompatibility between the disciplines of law and mathematics and intend no general disapproval or disparagement of the latter as an auxiliary in the fact-finding processes of the former, we cannot uphold the technique employed in the instant case. As we explain in detail *infra*, the testimony as to mathematical probability infected the case with fatal error and distorted the jury's traditional role of determining guilt or innocence according to long-settled rules. Mathematics, a veritable sorcerer in our computerized society, while assisting the trier of fact in the search for truth, must not cast a spell over him. We conclude that on the record before us defendant should not have had his guilt determined by the odds and that he is entitled to a new trial. We reverse the judgment.

A jury found defendant Malcolm Ricardo Collins and his wife defendant Janet Louise Collins guilty of second degree robbery . . . . Malcolm appeals from the judgment of conviction . . . .

On June 18, 1964, about 11:30 a.m. Mrs. Juanita Brooks, who had been shopping, was walking home along an alley in the San Pedro area of the City of Los Angeles.

She was pulling behind her a wicker basket carryall containing groceries and had her purse on top of the packages. She was using a cane. As she stooped down to pick up an empty carton, she was suddenly pushed to the ground by a person whom she neither saw nor heard approach. She was stunned by the fall and felt some pain. She managed to look up and saw a young woman running from the scene. According to Mrs. Brooks the latter appeared to weigh about 145 pounds, was wearing "something dark," and had hair "between a dark blond and a light blond," but lighter than the color of defendant Janet Collins' hair as it appeared at trial. Immediately after the incident, Mrs. Brooks discovered that her purse, containing between $35 and $40, was missing.

About the same time as the robbery, John Bass, who lived on the street at the end of the alley, was in front of his house watering his lawn. His attention was attracted by "a lot of crying and screaming" coming from the alley. As he looked in that direction, he saw a woman run out of the alley and enter a yellow automobile parked across the street from him. He was unable to give the make of the car. The car started off immediately and pulled wide around another parked vehicle so that in the narrow street it passed within six feet of Bass. The latter then saw that it was being driven by a male Negro, wearing a mustache and beard. At the trial Bass identified defendant as the driver of the yellow automobile. However, an attempt was made to impeach his identification by his admission that at the preliminary hearing he testified to an uncertain identification at the police lineup shortly after the attack on Mrs. Brooks, when defendant was beardless.

In his testimony Bass described the woman who ran from the alley as a Caucasian, slightly over five feet tall, of ordinary build, with her hair in a dark blond ponytail, and wearing dark clothing. He further testified that her ponytail was "just like" one which Janet had in a police photograph taken on June 22, 1964.

On the day of the robbery, Janet was employed as a housemaid in San Pedro. Her employer testified that she had arrived for work at 8:50 a.m. and that defendant had picked her up in a light yellow car about 11:30 a.m. On that day, according to the witness, Janet was wearing her hair in a blonde ponytail but lighter in color than it appeared at trial.[3]

*   *   *

At the seven-day trial the prosecution experienced some difficulty in establishing the identities of the perpetrators of the crime. The victim could not identify Janet and had never seen defendant. The identification by the witness Bass, who observed the girl run out of the alley and get into the automobile, was incomplete as to Janet and may have weakened as to defendant. There was also evidence, introduced by the defense, that Janet had worn light-colored clothing on the day in question, but both the victim and Bass testified that the girl they observed had worn dark clothing.

In an apparent attempt to bolster identifications, the prosecutor called an

---

[3] (Court's original footnote 3.) There are inferences which may be drawn from the evidence that Janet attempted to alter the appearance of her hair after June 18. Janet denies that she cut, colored, or bleached her hair at any time after June 18, and a number of witnesses supported her testimony.

instructor of mathematics at a state college. Through this witness he sought to establish that, assuming the robbery was committed by a Caucasian woman with a blond ponytail who left the scene accompanied by a Negro with a beard and mustache, there was an overwhelming probability that the crime was committed by any couple answering such distinctive characteristics. The witness testified, in substance, to the "product rule," which states that the probability of the joint occurrence of a number of *mutually independent* events is equal to the product of the individual probabilities that each of the events will occur.[4] *Without presenting any statistical evidence whatsoever in support of the probabilities for the factors selected*, the prosecutor then proceeded to have the witness *assume*[5] probability factors for the various characteristics which he deemed to be shared by the guilty couple and all other couples answering to such distinctive characteristics.[6]

Applying the product rule to his own factors the prosecutor arrived at a probability that there was but one chance in 12 million that defendants were innocent and that another equally distinctive couple actually committed the robbery. Expanding on what he had thus purported to suggest as a hypothesis, the prosecutor offered the completely unfounded and improper testimonial assertion that, in his opinion, the factors he had assigned were "conservative estimates" and that, in reality "the chances of anyone else besides these defendants being there, . . . having every similarity, . . . is somewhat like one in a billion."

---

[4] (Court's original footnote 8.) In the example employed for illustrative purposes at the trial, the probability of rolling one die and coming up with a "2" is 1/6, that is, any one of the six faces of a die has one chance in six of landing face up on any particular roll. The probability of rolling two "2's" in succession is 1/6 × 1/6, or 1/36, that is, on only one occasion out of 36 double rolls (or the roll of two dice), will the selected number land face up on each roll or die.

[5] (Court's original footnote 9.) His argument to the jury was based on the same gratuitous assumptions or on similar assumptions which he invited the jury to make.

[6] (Court's original footnote 10.) Although the prosecutor insisted that the factors he used were only for illustrative purposes — to demonstrate how the probability of the occurrence of mutually independent factors affected the probability that they would occur together — he nevertheless attempted to use factors which he personally related to the distinctive characteristics of defendants. In his argument to the jury he invited the jurors to apply their own factors, and asked defense counsel to suggest what the latter would deem as responsible. The prosecutor himself proposed the individual probabilities set out in the table below. Although the transcript of the examination of the mathematics instructor and the information volunteered by the prosecutor at that time create some uncertainty as to precisely which of the characteristics the prosecutor assigned to the individual probabilities, he restated in his argument to the jury that they should be as follows:

	Characteristic	Individual Probability
A.	Partly yellow automobile	1/10
B.	Man with moustache	1/4
C.	Girl with ponytail	1/10
D.	Girl with blond hair	1/3
E.	Negro man with beard	1/10
F.	Interracial couple in car	1/1000

In his brief on appeal defendant agrees that the foregoing appeared on a table presented in the trial court.

Objections were timely made to the mathematician's testimony on the grounds that it was immaterial, that it invaded the province of the jury, and that it was based on unfounded assumptions. The objections were "temporarily overruled" and the evidence admitted subject to a motion to strike. When that motion was made at the conclusion of the direct examination, the court denied it, stating that the testimony had been received only for the "purpose of illustrating the mathematical probabilities of various matters, the possibilities for them occurring or re-occurring."

Both defendants took the stand in their own behalf. They denied any knowledge of or participation in the crime and stated that after Malcolm called for Janet at her employer's house they went directly to a friend's house in Los Angeles where they remained for some time. According to this testimony defendants were not near the scene of the robbery when it occurred. Defendants' friend testified to a visit by them "in the middle of June" although she could not recall the precise date. Janet further testified that certain inducements were held out to her during the July 9 interrogation on condition that she confess her participation.

Defendant [contends] that the introduction of evidence pertaining to the mathematical theory of probability and the use of the same by the prosecution during the trial was error prejudicial to defendant . . . .

As we shall explain, the prosecution's introduction and use of mathematical probability statistics injected two fundamental prejudicial errors into the case: (1) the testimony itself lacked an adequate foundation both in evidence and in statistical theory; and (2) the testimony and the manner in which the prosecution used it distracted the jury from its proper and requisite function of weighing the evidence on the issue of guilt, encouraged the jurors to rely upon an engaging but logically irrelevant expert demonstration, foreclosed the possibility of an effective defense by an attorney apparently unschooled in mathematical refinements, and placed the jurors and defense counsel at a disadvantage in sifting relevant fact from inapplicable theory.

We initially consider the defects in the testimony itself. As we have indicated, the specific technique presented through the mathematician's testimony and advanced by the prosecutor to measure the probabilities in question suffered from two basic and pervasive defects — an inadequate evidentiary foundation and an inadequate proof of statistical independence. First, as to the foundation requirement, we find the record devoid of any evidence relating to any of the six individual probability factors used by the prosecutor and ascribed by him to the six characteristics as we have set them out in footnote 10, *ante*. To put it another way, the prosecution produced no evidence whatsoever showing, or from which it could be in any way inferred, that only one out of every ten cars which might have been at the scene of the robbery was partly yellow, that only one out of every four men who might have been there wore a mustache, that only one out of every ten girls who might have been there wore a ponytail, or that any of the other individual probability factors listed were even roughly accurate.[7]

---

[7] (Court's original footnote 12.) We seriously doubt that such evidence could ever be compiled since no statistician could possibly determine after the fact which cars, or which individuals, "might" have been present at the scene of the robbery; certainly there is no reason to suppose that the human and

The bare, inescapable fact is that the prosecution made no attempt to offer any such evidence. Instead, through leading questions having perfunctorily elicited from the witness the response that the latter could not assign a probability factor for the characteristics involved,[8] the prosecutor himself suggested what the various probabilities should be and these became the basis of the witness' testimony (*see* fn. 10, *ante*). It is a curious circumstance of this adventure in proof that the prosecutor not only made his own assertions of these factors in the hope that they were "conservative" but also in later argument to the jury invited the jurors to substitute their "estimates" should they wish to do so. We can hardly conceive of a more fatal gap in the prosecution's scheme of proof. A foundation for the admissibility of the witness' testimony was never even attempted to be laid, let alone established. His testimony was neither made to rest on his own testimonial knowledge nor presented by proper hypothetical questions based upon valid data in the record. . . . In [*State v. Sneed*, 76 N.M. 349, 414 P.2d 858 (1966)], the court reversed a conviction based on probabilistic evidence, stating: "We hold that mathematical odds are not admissible as evidence to identify a defendant in a criminal proceeding *so long as the odds are based on estimates, the validity of which have [sic] not been demonstrated.*" (emphasis added) (414 P.2d at p. 862).

But, as we have indicated, there was another glaring defect in the prosecution's technique, namely an inadequate proof of the statistical independence of the six factors. No proof was presented that the characteristics selected were mutually independent, even though the witness himself acknowledged that such condition was essential to the proper application of the "product rule" or "multiplication rule . . . ."[9] To the extent that the traits or characteristics were not mutually independent (e.g., Negroes with beards and men with mustaches obviously represent overlapping categories[10]), the "product rule" would inevitably yield a wholly erroneous and exaggerated result even if all of the individual components had been determined with precision . . . .

---

automotive populations of San Pedro, California, include all potential culprits — or, conversely, that all members of these populations are proper candidates for inclusion. Thus the sample from which the relevant probabilities would have to be derived is itself undeterminable. (*See generally*, Yaman, Statistics, An Introductory Analysis (1964), ch. I.).

[8] (Court's original footnote 13.) The prosecutor asked the mathematics instructor: "Now, let me see if you can be of some help to us with some independent factors, and you have some paper you may use. Your specialty does not equip you, I suppose, to give us some probability of such things as a yellow car as contrasted with any other kind of car, does it? . . . I appreciate the fact that you can't assign a probability for a car being yellow as contrasted to some other car, can you? A. No, I couldn't."

[9] (Court's original footnote 14.) It is there stated that: "A trait is said to be independent of a second trait when the occurrence or non-occurrence of one does not affect the probability of the occurrence of the other trait. The multiplication rule cannot be used without some degree of error where the traits are not independent . . . ."

[10] (Court's original footnote 15.) Assuming *arguendo* that factors B and E (*see* fn. 6, *ante*), were correctly estimated, nevertheless it is still arguable that most Negro men with beards *also* have mustaches (exhibit 3 herein, for instance, shows defendant with both a mustache and a beard, indeed in a hirsute continuum); if so, there is no basis for multiplying 1/4 by 1/10 to estimate the proportion of Negroes who wear beards *and* mustaches. Again, the prosecution's technique could *never* be meaningfully applied, since its accurate use would call for information as to the degree of interdependence among the six individual factors. (*See* Yamane, *op. cit. supra.*) Such information cannot be compiled, however, since the relevant sample necessarily remains unknown. (*See* fn. 6, *ante*.)

In the instant case, therefore, because of the aforementioned two defects — the inadequate evidentiary foundation and the inadequate proof of statistical independence — the technique employed by the prosecutor could only lead to wild conjecture without demonstrated relevancy to the issues presented. It acquired no redeeming quality from the prosecutor's statement that it was being used only "for illustrative purposes" since, as we shall point out, the prosecutor's subsequent utilization of the mathematical testimony was not confined within such limits.

We now turn to the second fundamental error caused by the probability testimony. Quite apart from our foregoing objections to the specific technique employed by the prosecution to estimate the probability in question, we think that the entire enterprise upon which the prosecution embarked, and which was directed to the objective of measuring the likelihood of a random couple possessing the characteristics allegedly distinguishing the robbers, was gravely misguided. At best, it might yield an estimate as to how infrequently bearded Negroes drive yellow cars in the company of blonde females with ponytails.

The prosecution's approach, however, could furnish the jury with absolutely no guidance on the crucial issue: *Of the admittedly few such couples, which one, if any, was guilty of committing this robbery?* Probability theory necessarily remains silent on that question, since no mathematical equation can prove beyond a reasonable doubt (1) that the guilty couple *in fact* possessed the characteristics described by the People's witnesses, or even (2) that only *one* couple possessing those distinctive characteristics could be found in the entire Los Angeles area.

As to the first inherent failing we observe that the prosecution's theory of probability rested on the assumption that the witnesses called by the People had conclusively established that the guilty couple possessed the precise characteristics relied upon by the prosecution. But no mathematical formula could ever establish beyond a reasonable doubt that the prosecution's witnesses correctly observed and accurately described the distinctive features which were employed to link defendant to the crime . . . . Conceivably, for example, the guilty couple might have included a light-skinned Negress with bleached hair rather than a Caucasian blonde; or the driver of the car might have been wearing a false beard as a disguise; or the prosecution's witnesses might simply have been unreliable.[11]

The foregoing risks of error permeate the prosecution's circumstantial case. Traditionally, the jury weighs such risks in evaluating the credibility and probative value of trial testimony, but the likelihood of human error or of falsification obviously cannot be quantified; that likelihood must therefore be excluded from any effort to assign a *number* to the probability of guilt or innocence. Confronted with an equation which purports to yield a numerical index of probable guilt, few juries could resist the temptation to accord disproportionate weight to that index; only an exceptional juror, and indeed only a defense attorney schooled in mathematics, could successfully keep in mind the fact that the probability computed by the

---

[11] (Court's original footnote 16.) In the instant case, for instance, the victim could not state whether the girl had a ponytail, although the victim observed the girl as she ran away. The witness Bass, on the other hand, was sure that the girl whom he saw had a ponytail. The demonstration engaged in by the prosecutor also leaves no room for the possibility, although perhaps a small one, that the girl whom the victim and the witness observed was, in fact, the same girl.

prosecution can represent, *at best*, the likelihood that a random couple would share the characteristics testified to by the People's witnesses — *not necessarily the characteristics of the actually guilty couple.*

As to the second inherent failing in the prosecution's approach, even assuming that the first failing could be discounted, the most a mathematical computation could *ever* yield would be a measure of the probability that a random couple would possess the distinctive features in question. In the present case, for example, the prosecution attempted to compute the probability that a random couple would include a bearded Negro, a blonde girl with a ponytail, and a partly yellow car; the prosecution urged that this probability was no more than one in 12 million. Even accepting this conclusion as arithmetically accurate, however, one still could not conclude that the Collinses were probably *the* guilty couple. On the contrary, as we explain in the Appendix, the prosecution's figures actually imply a likelihood of over 40 percent that the Collinses could be "duplicated" by at least *one other couple who might equally have committed the San Pedro robbery.* Urging that the Collinses be convicted on the basis of evidence which logically establishes no more than this seems as indefensible as arguing for the conviction of X on the ground that a witness saw either X or X's twin commit the crime.

Again, few defense attorneys, and certainly few jurors, could be expected to comprehend this basic flaw in the prosecution's analysis. Conceivably even the prosecutor erroneously believed that his equation established a high probability that *no* other bearded Negro in the Los Angeles area drove a yellow car accompanied by a ponytailed blonde. In any event, although his technique could demonstrate no such thing, he solemnly told the jury that he had supplied mathematical proof of guilt.

Sensing the novelty of that notion, the prosecutor told the jurors that the traditional idea of proof beyond a reasonable doubt represented "the most hackneyed, stereotyped, trite, misunderstood concept in criminal law." He sought to reconcile the jury to the risk that, under his "new math" approach to criminal jurisprudence, "on some rare occasion . . . an innocent person may be convicted." "Without taking that risk," the prosecution continued, ". . . there would be immunity for the Collinses, for people who chose not to be employed to go down and push old ladies down and take their money and be immune because how could we ever be sure they are the ones who did it?"

In essence this argument of the prosecutor was calculated to persuade the jury to convict defendants whether or not they were convinced of their guilt to a moral certainty and beyond a reasonable doubt. Undoubtedly the jurors were unduly impressed by the mystique of the mathematical demonstration but were unable to assess its relevancy or value. Although we make no appraisal of the proper applications of mathematical techniques in the proof of facts, . . . we have strong feelings that such applications, particularly in a criminal case, must be critically examined in view of the substantial unfairness to a defendant which may result from ill conceived techniques with which the trier of fact is not technically equipped to cope. We feel that the technique employed in the case before us falls into the latter category.

We conclude that the court erred in admitting over defendant's objection the evidence pertaining to the mathematical theory of probability and in denying defendant's motion to strike such evidence. The case was apparently a close one. The jury began its deliberations at 2:46 p.m. on November 24, 1964, and retired for the night at 7:46 p.m.; the parties stipulated that a juror could be excused for illness and that a verdict could be reached by the remaining 11 jurors; the jury resumed deliberations the next morning at 8:40 a.m. and returned verdicts at 11:58 a.m. after five ballots had been taken. In the light of the closeness of the case, which as we have said was a circumstantial one, there is a reasonable likelihood that the result would have been more favorable to defendant if the prosecution had not urged the jury to render a probabilistic verdict. In any event, we think that under the circumstances the "trial by mathematics" so distorted the role of the jury and so disadvantaged counsel for the defense, as to constitute in itself a miscarriage of justice. After an examination of the entire case, including the evidence, we are of the opinion that it is reasonably probable that a result more favorable to defendant would have been reached in the absence of the above error. The judgment against defendant must therefore be reversed.

[B]   Federal Rule of Evidence 403

Relevance is the first evidentiary hurdle over which all evidence must successfully pass. Relevance, however, does not ensure admissibility; ultimate admissibility will depend on the applicability of other evidentiary rules that will be the focus of the remainder of this evidence text. These rules are based on principles of social policy, the reliability of the evidence, and fairness. Their application turns on such factors as the nature of the evidence in question, the context in which it will be used, which party is attempting to use it, the purpose for which the proponent is offering it, the kind of proceeding, and at what point during the proceeding the proponent is offering it.

In addition to these evidentiary rules, the trial judge has discretionary power to exclude relevant evidence if, in his or her judgment, its probative value is sufficiently outweighed by its cost; *i.e.*, by the danger of confusion, due to the evidence's misleading nature, or by the possibility of unfair prejudice, because of the evidence's inflammatory character. The judge also has discretion to exclude evidence if the probative value of the evidence is so slight that its use will result in undue delay, waste of time, or needless presentation of cumulative evidence. This balancing is occasionally referred to as determining the "legal relevance" of the evidence. Congress has recognized this discretionary power in Rule 403 of the Federal Rules of Evidence.

[*See* Fed. R. Evid. 403: Exclusion of Relevant Evidence on Grounds of Prejudice, Confusion, or Waste of Time]

[C]   Applying 403

The assessment of probative value and the balance of that value against potential prejudice is highly subjective. Both determinations require judgment significantly influenced by the unique facts and circumstances of each case. Because of the trial judge's unique ability to make these assessments, as a result of having heard the evidence on which they will be based, the judge's decision will be reversed on appeal only upon a showing of abuse of discretion. Although broad, the judge's power in this regard is not unlimited. In *United States v. Hitt*, the evidence in question was not cumulative and the defendant did not offer to stipulate to the fact the evidence was offered to prove. In the case that follows *Hitt*, *Old Chief v. United States*, the Supreme Court addresses how the 403 balance plays out when one of the parties offers to stipulate to the fact the evidence is offered to prove.

UNITED STATES v. HITT
United States Court of Appeals, Ninth Circuit
981 F.2d 422 (1992)

KOZINSKI, CIRCUIT JUDGE:

Dale Lee Hitt was convicted of possessing an unregistered machine gun in violation of 26 U.S.C. § 5861(d). The government alleged he had altered a semiautomatic rifle so it would discharge more than one shot per trigger pull — the defining characteristic of a machine gun. 26 U.S.C. § 5845(b). The rifle had indeed been modified in a way consistent with the government's theory, though Hitt's lawyer suggested it had been modified by its previous owner. I RT 49. Some internal parts usable for machine guns (but not themselves illegal) were found in a gun case in Hitt's room, but Hitt's lawyer suggested they too might have come from the rifle's previous owner. *Id.*

The key question, though, was whether the rifle would in fact rapid-fire. The government and Hitt each had their own experts test-fire it: In the government's test, the rifle did fire more than one shot per trigger pull, but when Hitt's expert (witnessed by two police officers) tested it, it didn't. Hitt's expert suggested the gun may have fired automatically in the government's test because of a malfunction, perhaps because the internal parts were dirty, worn or defective. In response, the government introduced a photograph of the rifle which, it argued, showed the rifle was neither dirty, worn nor defective. II RT 95.

Unfortunately, the photograph showed nothing of the gun's interior. All the jury could see was the outside, and not very well at that, as the gun occupied only a small part of the 4" x 6" photograph. The rest was taken up by about a dozen other weapons — nine other guns, including three that looked like assault rifles, and several knives — all belonging to Hitt's housemate. Hitt objected to admission of the photograph under Fed. R. Evid. 403, but the district court overruled his objection.

I

A. Under Fed. R. Evid. 402, "[a]ll relevant evidence is admissible," except as otherwise provided. We let jurors see and hear even marginally relevant evidence, because we trust them to weigh the evidence appropriately. Nonetheless, when the probative value of the evidence is "substantially outweighed by the danger of unfair prejudice . . . or misleading the jury," Fed. R. Evid. 403, the evidence must be kept out.

B. The photograph's probative value was exceedingly small. The defense theory was that the gun fired as an automatic because the *internal* parts were dirty, worn or defective. II RT 70–71. The prosecution understood this too: When the prosecutor cross-examined the defendant's expert, he asked whether there was "exceptional dirt *in*" the rifle, and whether there were "worn or dirty parts *in* that machine." *Id.* at 71–72 (emphasis added).

But the gun's external appearance reveals nothing at all about its internal state. Firearms are designed so the internal parts suffer most of the strain from the discharge. Wear, dirt and defects that afflict the internal mechanism generally have no effect on the firearm's appearance; it's not uncommon for a gun that looks clean and in working order to misfire because of dirt or defects inside. Here there was absolutely no indication that the type of wear, dirt or defect Hitt's expert was talking about could be seen by inspecting the outside of the gun.

Moreover, even if the rifle's inside condition were somehow related to its outside appearance, it's virtually impossible to tell whether the gun is clean or dirty from the photograph, in which the rifle is seen from several feet away. The photograph might well have been excludible under Rule 402 as totally irrelevant, had a Rule 402 objection been made.

C. At the same time, the photograph was fraught with the twin dangers of unfairly prejudicing the defendant and misleading the jury. It showed a dozen nasty-looking weapons, which the jury must have assumed belonged to Hitt. The photograph looked like it was taken at Hitt's residence: The guns were laid out in an obviously residential room; the jury knew Hitt was arrested at home, I RT 23–24; the photograph was talked about in the same breath as two others identified at trial as having been taken in Hitt's bedroom, I RT 36. Moreover, there was no one else the jury could have suspected of owning the guns. Hitt's roommate, who in fact owned all the other weapons, wasn't even mentioned during Hitt's trial. Inferring that all the weapons were Hitt's wasn't just a plausible inference; it was the only plausible inference.

Once the jury was misled into thinking all the weapons were Hitt's, they might well have concluded Hitt was the sort of person who'd illegally own a machine gun, or was so dangerous he should be locked up regardless of whether or not he committed this offense. Rightly or wrongly, many people view weapons, especially guns, with fear and distrust. Like evidence of homosexuality, *see, e.g., United States v. Gillespie*, 852 F.2d 475, 478 (9th Cir. 1988); *Cohn v. Papke*, 655 F.2d 191, 194 (9th Cir. 1981), or of past crimes, *see, e.g., United States v. Bland*, 908 F.2d 471, 473 (9th Cir. 1990), photographs of firearms often have a visceral impact that far exceeds their probative value. *See, e.g., United States v. Green*, 648 F.2d 587, 595 (9th Cir. 1981) (per curiam); *see also United States v. Peltier*, 585 F.2d 314, 327 (9th Cir. 1978) (dictum), *cert. denied*, 440 U.S. 945, 99 S. Ct. 1422, 59 L. Ed. 2d 634 (1979); *United States v. Robinson*, 560 F.2d 507, 513–14 (2d Cir. 1977), *cert. denied*, 435 U.S. 905, 98 S. Ct. 1451, 55 L. Ed. 2d 496 (1978); *United States v. Warledo*, 557 F.2d 721, 724–26 (10th Cir. 1977). The prejudice is even greater when the picture is not of one gun but of many.

But the photograph could do more than arouse irrational fears and prejudices. It could also lead the jury to draw some perfectly logical — though mistaken — inferences. Hitt's main defense was that he had the bad luck of owning a rifle that was defective or dirty, or perhaps had been modified by its previous owner. A jury that thought Hitt owned almost a dozen guns could very reasonably have viewed this argument with skepticism. The jurors could have inferred that a gun enthusiast like Hitt would be able to tell if the gun had been modified by someone else, or be able to make the modifications himself. Or they could have thought that someone that interested in guns would naturally keep them clean and in good working order. Of course, the jury shouldn't have drawn these inferences, because none of the other guns were Hitt's. Yet the inferences were entirely plausible once the jury concluded Hitt owned the whole arsenal.

D. The district judge has wide latitude in making Rule 403 decisions. *United States v. Kinslow*, 860 F.2d 963, 968 (9th Cir. 1988), *cert. denied*, 493 U.S. 829, 110 S. Ct. 96, 107 L.Ed.2d 60 (1989). But this latitude isn't unlimited. Where the evidence is of very slight (if any) probative value, it's an abuse of discretion to admit it if there's even a modest likelihood of unfair prejudice or a small risk of misleading the jury.

The evidence here was not only highly prejudicial and at most marginally probative — it was also misleading. It's bad enough for the jury to be unduly swayed by something a defendant did; it's totally unacceptable for it to be prejudiced by something he seems to have done but in fact did not. Admitting the photograph, with nothing at all to keep the jury from being misled — no limiting instruction, no redaction — violated Rule 403.

II

Having determined there was error, we must next decide whether it was harmless. There's a conflict in our circuit about the standard of review for harmless error. Some cases require that we affirm only if we can say with "fair assurance" that the error was harmless. *See, e.g., United States v. Webbe*, 755 F.2d 1387, 1389 (9th Cir. 1985); *United States v. Felix-Jerez*, 667 F.2d 1297, 1304 (9th Cir. 1982). This standard seems to have the Supreme Court's blessing. *See Kotteakos v. United States*, 328 U.S. 750, 764–65, 66 S. Ct. 1239, 1247–48, 90 L. Ed. 1557 (1946). Other Ninth Circuit cases compel affirmance if it's "more probable than not" that the error was harmless. *See, e.g., United States v. Lui*, 941 F.2d 844, 848 (9th Cir. 1991); *United States v. Browne*, 829 F.2d 760, 766 (9th Cir. 1987), *cert. denied*, 485 U.S. 991, 108 S. Ct. 1298, 99 L. Ed. 2d 508 (1988).[2]

We needn't resolve this conflict here, though, because the error wasn't harmless under either standard. This was a close case: An expert on one side claimed the gun

---

[2] This isn't just wordplay: A 55% likelihood that the error was harmless qualifies as "more probable than not," but it's hardly a "fair assurance" of harmlessness. *Kotteakos* defines "fair assurance" as absence of a "grave doubt," 328 U.S. at 765, 66 S. Ct. at 1248, and a 45% chance that the defendant would have been acquitted but for the error certainly seems like a "grave doubt." While we obviously don't deal in such precise probabilities, "more probable than not" and "fair assurance" can, in some cases, lead to conflicting results.

fired more than one shot per trigger pull; an expert on the other (corroborated by two police officers) said it didn't. The photograph may well have made the difference between acquittal and conviction. We can't say it was more probable than not that Hitt would have been convicted without the photograph. A fortiori, then, we can't say with "fair assurance" that he'd have been convicted without it.

REVERSED.

OLD CHIEF v. UNITED STATES
United States Supreme Court
519 U.S. 172 (1997)

JUSTICE SOUTER delivered the opinion of the Court:

*   *   *

In 1993, petitioner, Old Chief, was arrested after a fracas involving at least one gunshot. The ensuing federal charges included not only assault with a dangerous weapon and using a firearm in relation to a crime of violence but violation of 18 U.S.C. § 922(g)(1). This statute makes it unlawful for anyone "who has been convicted in any court of, a crime punishable by imprisonment for a term exceeding one year" to "possess in or affecting commerce, any firearm. . . . " "[A crime punishable by imprisonment for a term exceeding one year" is defined to exclude "any Federal or State offenses pertaining to antitrust violations, unfair trade practices, restraints of trade, or other similar offenses relating to the regulation of business practices" and "any State offense classified by the laws of the State as a misdemeanor and punishable by a term of imprisonment of two years or less." § 921(a)(20).

The earlier crime charged in the indictment against Old Chief was assault causing serious bodily injury. Before trial, he moved for an order requiring the Government "to refrain from mentioning — by reading the Indictment, during jury selection, in opening statement, or closing argument — and to refrain from offering into evidence or soliciting any testimony from any witness regarding the prior criminal convictions of the Defendant, *except* to state that the Defendant has been convicted of a crime punishable by imprisonment exceeding one (1) year." App. 6. He said that revealing the name and nature of his prior assault conviction would unfairly tax the jury's capacity to hold the Government to its burden of proof beyond a reasonable doubt on current charges of assault, possession, and violence with a firearm, and he offered to "solve the problem here by stipulating, agreeing and requesting the Court to instruct the jury that he has been convicted of a crime punishable by imprisonment exceeding one (1) yea[r]." *Id.*, at 7. He argued that the offer to stipulate to the fact of the prior conviction rendered evidence of the name and nature of the offense inadmissible under Rule 403 of the Federal Rules of Evidence, the danger being that unfair prejudice from that evidence would substantially outweigh its probative value. He also proposed this jury instruction:

"The phrase 'crime punishable by imprisonment for a term exceeding one year' generally means a crime which is a felony. The phrase does not include any state offense classified by the laws of that state as a misdemeanor and punishable by a term of imprisonment of two years or less and certain crimes concerning the regulation of business practices.

> "[I] hereby instruct you that Defendant JOHNNY LYNN OLD CHIEF has been convicted of a crime punishable by imprisonment for a term exceeding one year." *Id.*, at 11.

The Assistant United States Attorney refused to join in a stipulation, insisting on his right to prove his case his own way, and the District Court agreed, ruling orally that, "If he doesn't want to stipulate, he doesn't have to." . . . At trial, over renewed objection, the Government introduced the order of judgment and commitment for Old Chief's prior conviction. This document disclosed that on December 18, 1988, he "did knowingly and unlawfully assault Rory Dean Fenner, said assault resulting in serious bodily injury," for which Old Chief was sentenced to five years' imprisonment. . . . The jury found Old Chief guilty on all counts, and he appealed.

The Ninth Circuit addressed the point with brevity:

> Regardless of the defendant's offer to stipulate, the government is entitled to prove a prior felony offense through introduction of probative evidence. *See United States v. Breitkreutz*, 8 F.3d 688, 690 (9th Cir.1993) (citing *United States v. Gilman*, 684 F.2d 616, 622 (9th Cir.1982)). Under Ninth Circuit law, a stipulation is not proof, and, thus, it has no place in the FRE 403 balancing process. *Breitkreutz*, 8 F.3d at 691–92.

*   *   *

> Thus, we hold that the district court did not abuse its discretion by allowing the prosecution to introduce evidence of Old Chief's prior conviction to prove that element of the unlawful possession charge. . . .

We granted Old Chief's petition for writ of certiorari . . . because the Courts of Appeals have divided sharply in their treatment of defendants' efforts to exclude evidence of the names and natures of prior offenses in cases like this. Compare, *e.g.*, *United States v. Burkhart*, 545 F.2d 14, 15 (C.A.6 1976); *United States v. Smith*, 520 F.2d 544, 548 (C.A.8 1975), cert. denied, 429 U.S. 925, 97 S. Ct. 328, 50 L. Ed. 2d 294 (1976); and *United States v. Breitkreutz*, 8 F.3d 688, 690–692 (C.A.9 1993) (each recognizing a right on the part of the Government to refuse an offered stipulation and proceed with its own evidence of the prior offense), with *United States v. Tavares*, 21 F.3d 1, 3–5 (C.A.1 1994) (en banc); *United States v. Poore*, 594 F.2d 39, 40–43 (C.A.4 1979); *United States v. Wacker*, 72 F.3d 1453, 1472–1473 (C.A.10 1995); and *United States v. Jones*, 67 F.3d 320, 322–325 (C.A.D.C. 1995) (each holding that the defendant's offer to stipulate to or to admit to the prior conviction triggers an obligation of the district court to eliminate the name and nature of the underlying offense from the case by one means or another). We now reverse the judgment of the Ninth Circuit.

II

A

As a threshold matter, there is Old Chief's erroneous argument that the name of his prior offense as contained in the record of conviction is irrelevant to the prior-conviction element, and for that reason inadmissible under Rule 402 of the Federal Rules of Evidence. Rule 401 defines relevant evidence as having "any tendency to make the existence of any fact that is of consequence to the determination of the action more probable or less probable than it would be without the evidence." . . . To be sure, the fact that Old Chief's prior conviction was for assault resulting in serious bodily injury rather than, say, for theft was not itself an ultimate fact, as if the statute had specifically required proof of injurious assault. But its demonstration was a step on one evidentiary route to the ultimate fact, since it served to place Old Chief within a particular sub-class of offenders for whom firearms possession is outlawed by § 922(g)(1). A documentary record of the conviction for that named offense was thus relevant evidence in making Old Chief's § 922(g)(1) status more probable than it would have been without the evidence.

Nor was its evidentiary relevance under Rule 401 affected by the availability of alternative proofs of the element to which it went, such as an admission by Old Chief that he had been convicted of a crime "punishable by imprisonment for a term exceeding one year" within the meaning of the statute. The 1972 Advisory Committee Notes to Rule 401 make this point directly:

> The fact to which the evidence is directed need not be in dispute. While situations will arise which call for the exclusion of evidence offered to prove a point conceded by the opponent, the ruling should be made on the basis of such considerations as waste of time and undue prejudice (see Rule 403), rather than under any general requirement that evidence is admissible only if directed to matters in dispute. . . .

If, then, relevant evidence is inadmissible in the presence of other evidence related to it, its exclusion must rest not on the ground that the other evidence has rendered it "irrelevant," but on its character as unfairly prejudicial, cumulative or the like, its relevance notwithstanding.

B

The principal issue is the scope of a trial judge's discretion under Rule 403, which authorizes exclusion of relevant evidence when its "probative value is substantially outweighed by the danger of unfair prejudice, confusion of the issues, or misleading the jury, or by considerations of undue delay, waste of time, or needless presentation of cumulative evidence." Fed. Rule Evid. 403. Old Chief relies on the danger of unfair prejudice.

1

The term "unfair prejudice," as to a criminal defendant, speaks to the capacity of some concededly relevant evidence to lure the factfinder into declaring guilt on a ground different from proof specific to the offense charged. . . . So, the Committee Notes to Rule 403 explain, " 'Unfair prejudice' within its context means an undue tendency to suggest decision on an improper basis, commonly, though not necessarily, an emotional one.". . . .

Such improper grounds certainly include the one that Old Chief points to here: generalizing a defendant's earlier bad act into bad character and taking that as raising the odds that he did the later bad act now charged (or, worse, as calling for preventive conviction even if he should happen to be innocent momentarily). As then-Judge Breyer put it, "Although . . . 'propensity evidence' is relevant, the risk that a jury will convict for crimes other than those charged — or that, uncertain of guilt, it will convict anyway because a bad person deserves punishment — creates a prejudicial effect that outweighs ordinary relevance." *United States v. Moccia*, 681 F.2d 61, 63 (C.A.1 1982). Justice Jackson described how the law has handled this risk:

> Courts that follow the common-law tradition almost unanimously have come to disallow resort by the prosecution to any kind of evidence of a defendant's evil character to establish a probability of his guilt. Not that the law invests the defendant with a presumption of good character, *Greer v. United States*, 245 U.S. 559, 38 S. Ct. 209, 62 L.Ed. 469, but it simply closes the whole matter of character, disposition and reputation on the prosecution's case-in-chief. The state may not show defendant's prior trouble with the law, specific criminal acts, or ill name among his neighbors, even though such facts might logically be persuasive that he is by propensity a probable perpetrator of the crime. The inquiry is not rejected because character is irrelevant; on the contrary, it is said to weigh too much with the jury and to so overpersuade them as to prejudge one with a bad general record and deny him a fair opportunity to defend against a particular charge. The overriding policy of excluding such evidence, despite its admitted probative value, is the practical experience that its disallowance tends to prevent confusion of issues, unfair surprise and undue prejudice.

Michelson v. United States, 335 U.S. 469, 475–476, 69 S. Ct. 213, 218–219, 93 L. Ed. 168 (1948) Rule of Evidence 404(b) reflects this common-law tradition by addressing propensity reasoning directly: "Evidence of other crimes, wrongs, or acts is not admissible to prove the character of a person in order to show action in conformity therewith." Fed. Rule Evid. 404(b). There is, accordingly, no question that propensity would be an "improper basis" for conviction and that evidence of a prior conviction is subject to analysis under Rule 403 for relative probative value and for prejudicial risk of misuse as propensity evidence. . . .

As for the analytical method to be used in Rule 403 balancing, two basic possibilities present themselves. An item of evidence might be viewed as an island, with estimates of its own probative value and unfairly prejudicial risk the sole reference points in deciding whether the danger substantially outweighs the value and whether the evidence ought to be excluded. Or the question of admissibility might be seen as inviting further comparisons to take account of the full evidentiary context of the case as the court understands it when the ruling must be made. This second approach would start out like the first but be ready to go further. On objection, the court would decide whether a particular item of evidence raised a danger of unfair prejudice. If it did, the judge would go on to evaluate the degrees of probative value and unfair prejudice not only for the item in question but for any actually available substitutes as well. If an alternative were found to have substantially the same or greater probative value but a lower danger of unfair prejudice, sound judicial discretion would discount the value of the item first offered and exclude it if its discounted probative value were substantially outweighed by unfairly prejudicial risk. As we will explain later on, the judge would have to make these calculations with an appreciation of the offering party's need for evidentiary richness and narrative integrity in presenting a case, and the mere fact that two pieces of evidence might go to the same point would not, of course, necessarily mean that only one of them might come in. It would only mean that a judge applying Rule 403 could reasonably apply some discount to the probative value of an item of evidence when faced with less risky alternative proof going to the same point. Even under this second approach, as we explain below, a defendant's Rule 403 objection offering to concede a point generally cannot prevail over the Government's choice to offer evidence showing guilt and all the circumstances surrounding the offense. . . .

The first understanding of the Rule is open to a very telling objection. That reading would leave the party offering evidence with the option to structure a trial in whatever way would produce the maximum unfair prejudice consistent with relevance. He could choose the available alternative carrying the greatest threat of improper influence, despite the availability of less prejudicial but equally probative evidence. The worst he would have to fear would be a ruling sustaining a Rule 403 objection, and if that occurred, he could simply fall back to offering substitute evidence. This would be a strange rule. It would be very odd for the law of evidence to recognize the danger of unfair prejudice only to confer such a degree of autonomy on the party subject to temptation, and the Rules of Evidence are not so odd.

Rather, a reading of the companions to Rule 403, and of the commentaries that went with them to Congress, makes it clear that what counts as the Rule 403 "probative value" of an item of evidence, as distinct from its Rule 401 "relevance," may be calculated by comparing evidentiary alternatives. The Committee Notes to Rule 401 explicitly say that a party's concession is pertinent to the court's discretion to exclude evidence on the point conceded. Such a concession, according to the Notes, will sometimes "call for the exclusion of evidence offered to prove [the] point conceded by the opponent. . . . " As already mentioned, the Notes make it clear that such rulings should be made not on the basis of Rule 401 relevance but on "such considerations as waste of time and undue prejudice (see Rule 403). . . . " The Notes to Rule 403 then take up the point by stating that when a court considers "whether to exclude on grounds of unfair prejudice," the "availability of other means of proof may . . . be an appropriate factor." . . . The point gets a reprise in the Notes to Rule 404(b), dealing with admissibility when a given evidentiary item has the dual nature of legitimate evidence of an element and illegitimate evidence of character: "No mechanical solution is offered. The determination must be made whether the danger of undue prejudice outweighs the probative value of the evidence in view of the availability of other means of proof and other facts appropriate for making decision of this kind under 403." . . . Thus the notes leave no question that when Rule 403 confers discretion by providing that evidence "may" be excluded, the discretionary judgment may be informed not only by assessing an evidentiary item's twin tendencies, but by placing the result of that assessment alongside similar assessments of evidentiary alternatives. . . .

2

In dealing with the specific problem raised by § 922(g)(1) and its prior-conviction element, there can be no question that evidence of the name or nature of the prior offense generally carries a risk of unfair prejudice to the defendant. That risk will vary from case to case, for the reasons already given, but will be substantial whenever the official record offered by the Government would be arresting enough to lure a juror into a sequence of bad character reasoning. Where a prior conviction was for a gun crime or one similar to other charges in a pending case the risk of unfair prejudice would be especially obvious, and Old Chief sensibly worried that the prejudicial effect of his prior assault conviction, significant enough with respect to the current gun charges alone, would take on added weight from the related assault charge against him.

The District Court was also presented with alternative, relevant, admissible evidence of the prior conviction by Old Chief's offer to stipulate, evidence necessarily subject to the District Court's consideration on the motion to exclude the record offered by the Government. Although Old Chief's formal offer to stipulate was, strictly, to enter a formal agreement with the Government to be given to the jury, even without the Government's acceptance his proposal amounted to an offer to admit that the prior-conviction element was satisfied, and a defendant's admission is, of course, good evidence. See Fed. Rule Evid. 801(d)(2)(A). Old Chief's proffered admission would, in fact, have been not merely relevant but seemingly conclusive evidence of the element. The statutory language in which the prior-conviction requirement is couched shows no congressional concern with the specific name or nature of the prior offense beyond what is necessary to place it within the broad category of qualifying felonies, and Old Chief clearly meant to admit that his felony did qualify, by stipulating "that the Government has proven one of the essential elements of the offense." . . . As a consequence, although the name of the prior offense may have been technically relevant, it addressed no detail in the definition of the prior-conviction element that would not have been covered by the stipulation or admission. Logic, then, seems to side with Old Chief.

3

*   *   *

[T]here is something even more to the prosecution's interest in resisting efforts to replace the evidence of its choice with admissions and stipulations, for beyond the power of conventional evidence to support allegations and give life to the moral underpinnings of law's claims, there lies the need for evidence in all its particularity to satisfy the jurors' expectations about what proper proof should be. Some such demands they bring with them to the courthouse, assuming, for example, that a charge of using a firearm to commit an offense will be proven by introducing a gun in evidence. A prosecutor who fails to produce one, or some good reason for his failure, has something to be concerned about. "If [jurors'] expectations are not satisfied, triers of fact may penalize the party who disappoints them by drawing a negative inference against that party." Saltzburg, A Special Aspect of Relevance: Countering Negative Inferences Associated with the Absence of Evidence, 66 Calif. L. Rev. 1011, 1019 (1978) (footnotes omitted). Expectations may also arise in jurors' minds simply from the experience of a trial itself. The use of witnesses to describe a train of events naturally related can raise the prospect of learning about every ingredient of that natural sequence the same way. If suddenly the prosecution presents some occurrence in the series differently, as by announcing a stipulation or admission, the effect may be like saying, "never mind what's behind the door," and jurors may well wonder what they are being kept from knowing. A party seemingly responsible for cloaking something has reason for apprehension, and the prosecution with its burden of proof may prudently demur at a defense request to interrupt the flow of evidence telling the story in the usual way.

In sum, the accepted rule that the prosecution is entitled to prove its case free from a defendant's option to stipulate the evidence away rests on good sense. A syllogism is not a story, and a naked proposition in a courtroom may be no match for the robust evidence that would be used to prove it. People who hear a story interrupted by gaps of abstraction may be puzzled at the missing chapters, and jurors asked to rest a momentous decision on the story's truth can feel put upon at being asked to take responsibility knowing that more could be said than they have heard. A convincing tale can be told with economy, but when economy becomes a break in the natural sequence of narrative evidence, an assurance that the missing link is really there is never more than second best.

4

This recognition that the prosecution with its burden of persuasion needs evidentiary depth to tell a continuous story has, however, virtually no application when the point at issue is a defendant's legal status, dependent on some judgment rendered wholly independently of the concrete events of later criminal behavior charged against him. As in this case, the choice of evidence for such an element is usually not between eventful narrative and abstract proposition, but between propositions of slightly varying abstraction, either a record saying that conviction for some crime occurred at a certain time or a statement admitting the same thing without naming the particular offense. The issue of substituting one statement for the other normally arises only when the record of conviction would not be admissible for any purpose beyond proving status, so that excluding it would not deprive the prosecution of evidence with multiple utility; if, indeed, there were a justification for receiving evidence of the nature of prior acts on some issue other than status (i.e., to prove "motive, opportunity, intent, preparation, plan, knowledge, identity, or absence of mistake or accident," Fed. Rule Evid. 404(b)), Rule 404(b) guarantees the opportunity to seek its admission. Nor can it be argued that the events behind the prior conviction are proper nourishment for the jurors' sense of obligation to vindicate the public interest. The issue is not whether concrete details of the prior crime should come to the jurors' attention but whether the name or general character of that crime is to be disclosed. Congress, however, has made it plain that distinctions among generic felonies do not count for this purpose; the fact of the qualifying conviction is alone what matters under the statute. "A defendant falls within the category simply by virtue of past conviction for any [qualifying] crime ranging from possession of short lobsters, *see* 16 U.S.C. § 3372, to the most aggravated murder." . . . The most the jury needs to know is that the conviction admitted by the defendant falls within the class of crimes that Congress thought should bar a convict from possessing a gun, and this point may be made readily in a defendant's admission and underscored in the court's jury instructions. Finally, the most obvious reason that the general presumption that the prosecution may choose its evidence is so remote from application here is that proof of the defendant's status goes to an element entirely outside the natural sequence of what the defendant is charged with thinking and doing to commit the current offense. Proving status without telling exactly why that status was imposed leaves no gap in the story of a defendant's subsequent criminality, and its demonstration by stipulation or admission neither displaces a chapter from a continuous sequence of conventional evidence nor comes across as an officious substitution, to confuse or offend or provoke reproach.

Given these peculiarities of the element of felony-convict status and of admissions and the like when used to prove it, there is no cognizable difference between the evidentiary significance of an admission and of the legitimately probative component of the official record the prosecution would prefer to place in evidence. For purposes of the Rule 403 weighing of the probative against the prejudicial, the functions of the competing evidence are distinguishable only by the risk inherent in the one and wholly absent from the other. In this case, as in any other in which the prior conviction is for an offense likely to support conviction on some improper ground, the only reasonable conclusion was that the risk of unfair prejudice did substantially outweigh the discounted probative value of the record of conviction, and it was an abuse of discretion to admit the record when an admission was available. What we have said shows why this will be the general rule when proof of convict status is at issue, just as the prosecutor's choice will generally survive a Rule 403 analysis when a defendant seeks to force the substitution of an admission for evidence creating a coherent narrative of his thoughts and actions in perpetrating the offense for which he is being tried.

The judgment is reversed, and the case is remanded to the Ninth Circuit for further proceedings consistent with this opinion.

JUSTICE O'CONNOR dissenting:

Even more fundamentally, in our system of justice, a person is not simply convicted of "a crime" or "a felony." Rather, he is found guilty of a specified offense, almost always because he violated a specific statutory prohibition. For example, in the words of the order that the Government offered to prove petitioner's prior conviction in this case, petitioner "did knowingly and unlawfully assault Rory Dean

Fenner, said assault resulting in serious bodily injury, in violation of Title 18 U.S.C. §§ 1153 and 113(f)." . . . That a variety of crimes would have satisfied the prior conviction element of the § 922(g)(1) offense does not detract from the fact that petitioner committed a specific offense. The name and basic nature of petitioner's crime are inseparable from the fact of his earlier conviction and were therefore admissible to prove petitioner's guilt.

The principle is illustrated by the evidence that was admitted at petitioner's trial to prove the other element of the § 922(g)(1) offense — possession of a "firearm." The Government submitted evidence showing that petitioner possessed a 9-mm. semiautomatic pistol. Although petitioner's possession of any number of weapons would have satisfied the requirements of § 922(g)(1), obviously the Government was entitled to prove with specific evidence that petitioner possessed the weapon he did. In the same vein, consider a murder case. Surely the Government can submit proof establishing the victim's identity, even though, strictly speaking, the jury has no "need" to know the victim's name, and even though the victim might be a particularly well loved public figure. The same logic should govern proof of the prior conviction element of the § 922(g)(1) offense. That is, the Government ought to be able to prove, with specific evidence, that petitioner committed a crime that came within § 922(g)(1)'s coverage.

The Court never explains precisely why it constitutes "unfair" prejudice for the Government to directly prove an essential element of the § 922(g)(1) offense with evidence that reveals the name or basic nature of the defendant's prior conviction. It simply notes that such evidence may lead a jury to conclude that the defendant has a propensity to commit crime, thereby raising the odds that the jury would find that he committed the crime with which he is currently charged. With a nod to the part of Rule 404(b) that says "[e]vidence of other crimes, wrongs, or acts is not admissible to prove the character of a person in order to show action in conformity therewith," the Court writes: "There is, accordingly, no question that propensity would be an 'improper basis' for conviction and that evidence of a prior conviction is subject to analysis under Rule 403 for relative probative value and for prejudicial risk of misuse as propensity evidence." *Ante*, at 651.

A few pages later, it leaps to the conclusion that there can be "no question that evidence of the name or nature of the prior offense generally carries a risk of unfair prejudice to the defendant." . . .

Yes, to be sure, Rule 404(b) provides that "[e]vidence of other crimes, wrongs, or acts is not admissible to prove the character of a person in order to show action in conformity therewith." But Rule 404(b) does not end there. It expressly contemplates the admission of evidence of prior crimes for other purposes, "such as proof of motive, opportunity, intent, preparation, plan, knowledge, identity, or absence of mistake or accident." The list is plainly not exhaustive, and where, as here, a prior conviction is an element of the charged offense, neither Rule 404(b) nor Rule 403 can bar its admission. The reason is simple: In a prosecution brought under 922(g)(1), the Government does not submit evidence of a past crime to prove the defendant's bad character or to "show action in conformity therewith." It tenders the evidence as direct proof of a necessary element of the offense with which it has charged the defendant. To say, as the Court does, that it "unfairly" prejudices the defendant for the Government to establish its § 922(g)(1) case with evidence showing that, in fact, the defendant did commit a prior offense misreads the Rules of Evidence and defies common sense.

Any incremental harm resulting from proving the name or basic nature of the prior felony can be properly mitigated by limiting jury instructions.

EXERCISES

1. Advantage Corporation sued Defendant for tortious conduct. On the issue of damages, Advantage called Expert — who is both a CPA and lawyer — to offer testimony about Advantage's lost profits. On cross-examination Defendant seeks to question Expert about two events: (1) loans Expert had taken from his accounting clients that he did not repay in full because of a subsequent bankruptcy proceeding and (2) Expert's recent disciplinary proceedings before the Bar Association and Institute of Certified Public Accountants where both agencies concluded that there was insufficient evidence to sanction Expert. Advantage's counsel objects to the proposed cross-examination. Applying a 403 balancing test, should the trial judge permit the cross-examination?

2. Alex, a 52 year-old pharmaceutical sales rep, filed suit against his former employer alleging age discrimination following his termination. At trial Alex seeks to offer a company newsletter that attributes the great success of the company's sales force to a policy of recruiting either recent college graduates or proven sales people without experience in pharmaceuticals marketing, and of having them learn and profit from the seasoned, experienced sales people who had been with the company for several years. Alex contends that the article proves that the company was unlawfully pursuing younger employees. The defendant-employer objects to the newsletter's admission. Applying a 403 balancing test, should the trial judge permit the newsletter?

3. At Ray's trial for bank robbery the prosecution wants to offer two pieces of prejudicial testimony. First, the prosecution seeks to establish that Ray stated to his friend (a convicted bank robber himself) that Ray "would like to rob a bank too someday." Second, prosecutors hope to introduce Ray's birth certificate which links Ray to his aunt — who was formerly a senior teller at the bank and who would have known that an armored delivery truck would have been making a delivery to the bank on the day that it was robbed. Ray objects to the proposed testimony. Applying a 403 balancing test, should the trial judge permit (a) Ray's statement or (b) the birth certificate?

4. Cornelius, an African-American employee, brought an employment discrimination suit against his employer, a steel manufacturing plant, alleging that the employer created a racially hostile work environment. At trial Cornelius seeks to call another African-American employee named Danny to testify about racial harassment Danny himself experienced at the plant. Specifically, Danny will state that the supervisors regularly used racial epithets, that racial graffiti commonly appeared in the bathrooms, that black employees were ridiculed on the workplace radio system, that a rubber chicken was "lynched" near a black employee's work area, that he discovered several pictures of monkeys in his work area, and that the Confederate flag was often displayed in the plant, including on Confederate-style "do-rags" sold in the employer's on-site store for employees. None of these events specifically involved the plaintiff, Cornelius. The employer objects arguing that Danny's testimony is both irrelevant under Rule 402 and unfairly prejudicial under Rule 403. Should the trial judge allow Danny to testify?

5. Two men approached Stephen — an undercover FBI agent posing as the leader of a well-established terrorist organization abroad — believing that he could help them carry out their plot to blow up an airport. Instead of helping the men, Stephen arrested them and charged them with conspiracy to commit acts of terrorism. Before trial, the government moved in limine for the admission of a terrorism expert to describe numerous terrorist organizations and their activities abroad, and to define various terms related to terrorism. The defendants object on Rule 403 grounds. What is the government's best argument for admittance and how should the court rule?

6. Ousman worked as a clerk at a gas station for two years. During year one Ousman worked full-time without incident, with an average of 40 hours per week. At the start of year two, the gas station hired a new scheduling supervisor. For the first six months of year two, Ousman continued to work an average of 40 hours per week. Then Ousman was injured in a car accident. The next day Ousman informed his supervisor that he was taking FMLA leave for two months on his doctor's recommendation, due to a back injury sustained in the accident. When Ousman returned to work, he was consistently scheduled to work 30 hours per week — as opposed to the 40 hours he typically worked prior to the accident. Eventually Ousman quit the job and filed a civil claim against the gas station, arguing that the supervisor unlawfully reduced his work hours in retaliation for Ousman taking FMLA leave. At trial Ousman wants to introduce evidence of his work hours for the entire two year period of employment, while the gas station argues that only the hours for year two are relevant. How should the court rule?

7. Lisa was seriously injured in a car accident when the car she was driving collided in an intersection with a van driven by James. Lisa filed a civil suit alleging that James ran his stop sign, causing the accident. At trial Lisa called an eyewitness who testified that they saw James' van run the stop sign. Lisa also wanted to offer additional testimony about James' behavior immediately after the accident, but James objected on relevance grounds. The Judge overruled James' objection and permitted the testimony. The witness then stated that they saw James run towards the woods, throw something into the tree line, and fail to render any assistance to Lisa. Later, in the defense case, James testified on his own behalf that he did not run the stop sign, and asserted that Lisa ran her stop sign. James also explained that he ran away from the van because he thought it was on fire, that he was not impaired at the time of the accident, and that he did not approach Lisa's car because emergency personnel were on the way. Was the Judge correct in admitting Lisa's testimony about James' behavior after the accident?

8. Over a period of 20 years, Gerald successfully filed two civil suits against Credit Reporting Agency alleging that the agency included erroneous entries on Gerald's credit report. After discovering a new inaccuracy related to a cable television account, Gerald filed a third law suit against Credit Reporting Agency. At trial Gerald testified on his own behalf about his long history of issues with the agency. He now seeks to introduce, as documentary evidence, 10 different copies of his credit report covering the entire 20 year period. Credit Reporting Agency objects to the introduction of the reports on relevance grounds. What is Credit Reporting Agency's best argument to support its objection and how should the court rule?

Chapter 3

SPECIFIC EVIDENTIARY RULES BASED ON RELEVANCE, PUBLIC POLICY, AND UNFAIR PREJUDICE

§ 3.01 INTRODUCTION

Chapter Two discussed the fundamental requirement that all evidence offered be relevant to the issues being litigated. This relevancy requirement is applicable to all evidence regardless of its nature or the purpose for which it is offered. Courts have modified the general relevancy requirement, based on considerations of public policy and unfair prejudice, developing rules applicable to particular kinds of evidence that exclude that evidence no matter how probative. The courts have developed these exclusionary rules for several kinds of evidence, including character and habit evidence, evidence of similar happenings, evidence of subsequent repairs, and evidence of offers of compromise. Because the rules that courts have developed concerning each category of evidence listed above differ significantly, each category of evidence is discussed separately below.

We begin this chapter with a general discussion of character evidence, a topic which plays a role in many of the issues discussed in this chapter and then move to specific reasons the rules provide for admission or exclusion of evidence in the following order:

General Inadmissibility of Character Evidence: Fed. R. Evid. 404(a)

Character Evidence to Prove an Element or Defense: Fed. R. Evid. Rule 404(a)

Prior Bad Acts: Fed. R. Evid. Rule 404(b)

    Prior Sexual Acts by Victim of Sexual Assault: Fed. R. Evid. 412

    Prior Sexual Acts by Defendant in Sexual Assault: Fed. R. Evid. 413–415

Habit: Fed. R. Evid. 406

Subsequent Remedial Measures: Fed. R. Evid. 407

Offers of Compromise: Fed. R. Evid. 408

Offers to Pay Medical Expenses: Fed. R. Evid. 409

Pleas, Plea Discussions, and Related Statements: Fed. R. Evid. 410

Liability Insurance: — Fed. R. Evid. 411

79

§ 3.02   CHARACTER EVIDENCE:
Rules 404–405, 412–413

[A]   Admissibility and Use Depends on Context

The use of character evidence is one of the more confusing areas of evidence law because, during a trial, a party may use such evidence in a number of different contexts in which the rules of admissibility differ. Both admissibility and the manner of use can turn on one or more of the following factors: the purpose for which the proponent is offering the evidence, the kind of proceeding in which it is sought to be used (civil or criminal), which party is seeking to introduce the evidence, and the stage of the proceeding in which the evidence is being offered. *The purpose for which the proponent is offering the evidence is the most important of the factors governing the admissibility of character evidence.* The following discussion is organized according to the various purposes for which character evidence may be used.

[1]   Using Character Evidence to Prove Element of Claim, Charge, or Defense

Character evidence is admissible in both civil and criminal litigation in which an individual's character is an element of a claim, charge, or defense. There are no limitations on the form such evidence may take. In such actions, evidence of an individual's reputation, of other persons' opinions concerning the individual's character, and of the individual's prior specific acts are all admissible, depending on the claim. Notice that Rule 404(a) prohibits only the introduction of character evidence to prove "the person acted in accordance with the character or trait." There is no limitation on when, during the trial, a proponent may offer such evidence.

Character evidence is admissible if it is relevant to a claim, charge, or defense. Cases in which an individual's character constitutes an element of a claim, charge, or defense include, among others, defamation actions in which the defense is the truth of the allegedly libelous statement and actions for negligent entrustment and seduction. For example, a person who is sued for defamation for calling another person a thief can introduce in her case-in-defense evidence that the plaintiff possesses a character trait for dishonesty, by offering testimony that the plaintiff has a reputation for being a thief or by offering opinion testimony to the same effect by individuals who know the plaintiff. The defendant also could offer evidence of the plaintiff's prior larcenous acts, through the testimony of those who observed the prior dishonest conduct. Similarly, in an action for negligent entrustment, the plaintiff could introduce evidence that the defendant entrusted a dangerous instrumentality, such as an automobile, to a person who was known or reputed to be incompetent or reckless, to show that such entrustment was negligent. In an action for seduction, if the statute establishing the cause of action requires the victim to have been chaste in order for an action to lie, evidence addressed to the victim's character trait of chastity is admissible.

Schafer offers a fairly typical example of the use of character evidence under Fed. R. Evid. 405, its use in a defamation action.

SCHAFER v. TIME, INC.
United States Court of Appeals for the Eleventh Circuit
142 F.3d 1361 (1998)

BIRCH, CIRCUIT JUDGE:

*   *   *

BACKGROUND

On December 21, 1988, Pan Am Flight 103 exploded in mid-flight over Lockerbie, Scotland, causing the death of everyone on board. A terrorist's bomb was then, and is now, widely suspected to be the source of that explosion. On April 20, 1992, defendant-appellee, Time, Inc. ("Time"), published a cover story entitled "The Untold Story of Pan Am 103." The article purported to debunk the then-prevailing theory that the government of Lybia had sponsored the attack on Pan Am 103. Instead, the article posited that a Palestinian group, with connections to Syrian drug traffickers, had targeted Pan Am 103 to eliminate several of the passengers who were members of a United States counter terrorism team attempting to rescue United States hostages in Lebanon. The article claims that these passengers had discovered an unsavory, covert relationship between the Syrian drug traffickers and a unit of the United States Central Intelligence Agency and intended to expose it upon their return to the United States.

The article further stated that an American agent, David Lovejoy, had become a double agent and had leaked information regarding the team's travel plans to forces hostile to the United States. The article included a photograph of a man identified by the following caption:

> David Lovejoy, a reported double agent for the U.S. and Iran, is alleged to have told Iranian officials that McKee [one of the U.S. agents] was booked on Flight 103.

See Schafer R. Excerpt 1, Exh. A at 31. The article went on to imply that the information Lovejoy disclosed to hostile forces led to the attack on Pan Am 103.

The photograph in question apparently became associated with the Pam Am 103 bombing in connection with a civil case filed by the families of the Pan Am 103 victims. The families' law suit claimed that Pan Am had failed to take adequate security precautions to prevent the bombing. One of Pan Am's lawyers in that case, James Shaughnessy, filed a sworn affidavit that contained a variety of assertions about the attack that he hoped to explore through discovery in the Pan Am litigation. Shaughnessy's affidavit alleged that unnamed sources had identified Lovejoy, the double agent whose treachery facilitated the attack on Pan Am 103, as the man in an attached photograph. The man in the photograph, however, is Michael Schafer, the plaintiff-appellant in this case. Time's article, therefore, erroneously identified Schafer, then working in his family's janitorial business in Austell,

Georgia, both as a traitor to the United States government and a player in the bombing of Pan Am 103.

Upon discovering his picture in the magazine, Schafer demanded and eventually received a retraction from Time. Schafer filed suit against Time, making claims under Georgia's libel laws. A jury returned a verdict in Time's favor, finding no liability for the error.

* * *

Before trial, the district court instructed the parties that Time would not be permitted to introduce and explore a number of specific acts and events in Schafer's life as they were irrelevant to the issues before the jury. At that time, however, the district court warned both parties that the court would revisit the character issue to the extent that particular acts and events were shown to be relevant to the question of damages or how Schafer's picture might have become associated with the Pan Am case. During the course of the trial, the district court made a preliminary ruling permitting Time to explore selective incidents and acts in Schafer's background but excluding evidence of others. Specifically, the district court ruled that Time would be permitted to question Schafer about a felony conviction, a possible violation of his subsequent parole, convictions for driving under the influence, an arrest for writing a bad check, failure to file tax returns, failure to pay alimony and child support, and evidence concerning Schafer's efforts to change his name and social security number. Schafer attacks the district court's ruling and argues that these specific acts were inadmissible.

The Federal Rules of Evidence detail the circumstances under which character evidence is admissible and the methods available for presenting such evidence. In all cases in which character evidence is admissible a party may offer reputation or opinion testimony on the issue of a person's character. *See* Fed. R. Evid. 405(a). Only in cases in which a person's character is "an essential element of a charge, claim or defense," however, may a party offer evidence of specific instances of conduct. *See* Fed. R. Evid. 405(b).

Character evidence does not constitute an "essential element" of a claim or charge unless it alters the rights and liabilities of the parties under the substantive law. *See United States v. Keiser*, 57 F.3d 847, 856 & n. 20 (9th Cir. 1995); *Perrin v. Anderson*, 784 F.2d 1040, 1045 (10th Cir. 1986) (citing *McCormick on Evidence* § 187 at 551 (3d ed. 1984)). Our determination of whether character constitutes an essential element requires us to examine the "authoritative statutory or common law statement of the elements of the prima facie case and defenses." *Keiser,* 57 F.3d at 856 n. 20. The advisory committee's notes to the Federal Rules of Evidence provide two examples in which character evidence constitutes such an essential element: "[1] the chastity of a victim under a statute specifying her chastity as an element of the crime of seduction, or [2] the competency of the driver in an action for negligently entrusting a motor vehicle to an incompetent driver." Fed. R. Evid. 404(a) adv. comm. note (explaining that Rule 404 does not exclude such evidence because it is not offered to prove conduct consistent with character). In addition to these examples, a charge of defamation or libel commonly makes damage to the victim's reputation or character an essential element of the case. *See e.g., Johnson v. Pistilli*, 1996 U.S. Dist. LEXIS 14931, No. 95 C 6424 (N.D. Ill. Oct. 8, 1996) ("It is rare that character is an essential element. The typical example of such a case is defamation where injury to reputation must be proven."); *see also* Michael H. Graham, *Handbook of Federal Evidence* § 405.2 (4th ed.1996). Georgia law confirms that an assertion of damage to reputation in a libel case makes the plaintiff's character an issue under the substantive law. *See Ajouelo v. Auto-Soler Co.*, 61 Ga. App. 216, 6 S.E.2d 415, 419 (1939) ("It is generally held that the foundation of an action for defamation is the injury done to the reputation, that is, injury to character in the opinion of others arising from publication. . . ."); *Redfearn v. Thompson*, 10 Ga. App. 550, 555, 73 S.E. 949 (1912) (permitting the jury to consider plaintiff's bad reputation in mitigation of damages). Since the plaintiff's character is substantively at issue in a libel case under Georgia law, Rule 405(b) permits the admission of evidence regarding specific instances of the plaintiff's conduct on that issue. *See Perrin*, 784 F.2d at 1045; *Government of the Virgin Islands v. Grant*, 775 F.2d 508, 511 n. 4 (3d Cir. 1985); *cf. Longmire v. Alabama State Univ.*, 151 F.R.D. 414, 419 (M.D. Al. 1992) (permitting discovery regarding specific incidents because the libel plaintiff put his character in issue); *accord Ex Parte Healthsouth Corp.*, Nos. 1961758, 1970010, 2–3, [712 So. 2d 1086] (Ala. 1997) (permitting discovery of such evidence in a libel case under a state rule of evidence identical to Fed.R.Evid. 405(b)); *Daniels v. Wal-Mart Stores, Inc.*, 634 So. 2d 88, 93 (Miss.1993) (making a similar observation in dicta). Given the plain language of Rule 405(b), Schafer's arguments that specific acts remain inadmissible to prove character in an action for libel are unpersuasive.

[2]   Using Character Evidence to Establish Propensity from Which Conduct Can Be Inferred

[a]   Use for Propensity Generally Prohibited

Rule 404(a)(1) prohibits "[e]vidence of a person's character or character trait . . . to prove that on a particular occasion the person acted in accordance with the character or trait."

Parties involved in litigation often seek to introduce character evidence in cases in which a person's character is not an element of a claim, charge, or defense. They wish to introduce evidence of a person's reputation, standing in the eyes of a fellow citizen, or past conduct as proof that the person acted, or failed to act, in a particular manner on the occasion in question. Although the desire to use such evidence reflects our regular reliance on propensity evidence in our lives, courts generally have forbidden parties to use this evidence at trial. This next section discusses the rationales underlying parties' desire to use propensity evidence and courts' corresponding refusal to allow its use in most instances.

Ordinarily, we predict a person's actions and decide whether she has committed a particular act by relying on the many forms of behavior that reflect the person's particular character traits and, in sum, compose her personality. We know that some people, for example, are naturally aggressive — always ready to pick a fight — and we are not surprised if they are alleged to have committed an act of aggression, such as an assault and battery. Indeed, we often assume, based on our knowledge of this person's past behavior, the person actually committed the alleged act. We draw similar conclusions about persons we know or believe to be liars or cheaters; we are prepared to believe allegations that these persons have passed bad checks, cheated on their tax returns, or failed to pay their bills.

These conclusions, however, often are inaccurate. No person's behavior is uniformly bad or good, and the information on which we rely in drawing conclusions about an individual's propensity to act in a certain way often is incomplete. Past or current behavior, moreover, does not always indicate a propensity to engage in similar behavior in the future. That a person has been involved in fights in the past, for example, does not necessarily indicate that she will be involved in fights in the future. Similarly, a person's failure to report all of her income to the IRS one year does not necessarily indicate that she will commit the same dishonest act in the future. Frequently, such conduct often is probative of a propensity only in the particular factual context in which it occurred. Some of us might cheat on our income tax returns but would not be dishonest in another context, such as in submitting travel vouchers to our employers. Similarly, a person might exhibit violent behavior only around certain persons or when put in a specific situation. These factors demonstrate the tenuousness of relying on a particular character trait, as evidenced by past behavior, in determining whether a person committed a particular act. In the context of a lifetime of behavior, one incident, or even several, may indicate little about the individual.

Coupled with this problem of reliability is the distinct possibility the jury will accord too much weight to character evidence — that it will allow its resolution of the issues to be influenced more by the character of the parties involved than by the factual evidence presented. This possibility could materialize in either of two ways. First, the jury could assign much greater value to such evidence than is justified. Second, even if the jury properly weighs such evidence, the character evidence could lead the jury to find culpability on a lesser quantity or quality of evidence based on the belief that the defendant is deserving of punishment, whether guilty of the instant charge or not.

In addition to the limited probative value of character evidence and the risk that a jury might give it too much weight, thereby increasing the probability of erroneous decisions, introducing issues of character can significantly lengthen the trial and unfairly surprise the party against whom the character evidence is presented. Depending on the method of proof employed to establish the character trait (reputation, personal opinion, or prior act testimony), the problems of unfair prejudice, delay, and confusion could be compounded.

These three possible problems have caused the courts to adopt a basic rule that excludes character evidence if it is offered solely to prove that a party acted in conformity with a character trait. Courts have strictly enforced this rule, however, only in civil actions. For example, in a civil action for assault and battery in which the defendant pleaded self-defense, the court would not permit either the plaintiff or the defendant, at any phase of the trial, to introduce any form of character evidence on the traits of aggressiveness or peacefulness of either party for the purpose of proving who was the first aggressor. In criminal actions, however, courts have allowed certain limited use of character evidence to establish a party's propensity to act in a particular manner.

[b]　　Exception: Character of Criminal Defendant or Victim

In criminal actions, the courts have allowed the defendant to initiate the use of character evidence about either the victim or himself if the court has found such evidence relevant to the charge or defense asserted. Because application of the exclusionary rule for character evidence in criminal cases primarily benefits the defendant — by keeping out evidence that could unduly prejudice the jury against him — courts allow defendants to decide whether such evidence should be used in the trial. Because allowing the defendant to make this decision eliminates the problem of unfair prejudice to him, courts regard the probative value of character evidence as sufficient to outweigh the other problems associated with its use and thus generally admit it into evidence.

If the defendant initiates the use of such evidence, the court will limit the kind of character evidence the defendant may offer as to the *reputation* of the victim or defendant. Courts will not admit evidence of either personal opinions of an individual's character or specific acts that reflect on character. Courts have adopted this limitation on proof of character for two reasons. First, courts believe reputation evidence is more reliable because it reflects the collective judgment of the community as derived from a history of conduct. Opinion and specific-act evidence, on the other hand, are based only on selected acts of prior conduct. Second, reputation evidence involves less time and confusion for the jury because it entails less exploration into collateral issues.

A witness called to give reputation testimony, of course, must be shown to be familiar with those who know the defendant or victim and, therefore, that the witness has a basis for assessing the collective community judgment about the individual in question. Once qualified, a court will limit a reputation witness' testimony to the character trait that is most pertinent to the charge or defense that justified the use of the evidence. For example, if the charge against the criminal defendant were embezzlement, the pertinent character trait would be honesty, and reputation evidence concerning the defendant's honesty would be admissible. If the charge were assault and the defense raised were self-defense, the pertinent character trait for both the defendant and the victim would be peacefulness or aggressiveness, and reputation evidence concerning either of these traits would be admissible.

Once the defendant has introduced the issue of character, the prosecution has the right to *respond in kind* in its case-in-rebuttal. This means the court will allow the prosecution to put on only reputation testimony addressed to the same character trait of the person who was attacked or supported in the case-in-defense. The defendant does not open his own character for examination by presenting character evidence about the victim, and, conversely, does not open the victim's character by presenting evidence of his own.

The following diagram illustrates the use of reputation evidence in a criminal trial.

DIAGRAM 3–1

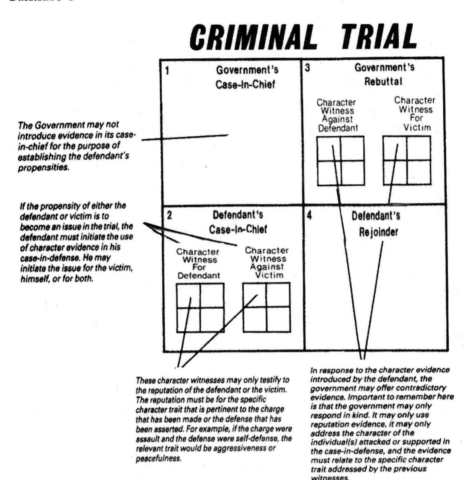

CRIMINAL TRIAL

1 Government's Case-In-Chief

The Government may not introduce evidence in its case-in-chief for the purpose of establishing the defendant's propensities.

3 Government's Rebuttal

Character Witness Against Defendant

Character Witness For Victim

If the propensity of either the defendant or victim is to become an issue in the trial, the defendant must initiate the use of character evidence in his case-in-defense. He may initiate the issue for the victim, himself, or for both.

2 Defendant's Case-In-Chief

Character Witness For Defendant

Character Witness Against Victim

4 Defendant's Rejoinder

These character witnesses may only testify to the reputation of the defendant or the victim. The reputation must be for the specific character trait that is pertinent to the charge that has been made or the defense that has been asserted. For example, if the charge were assault and the defense were self-defense, the relevant trait would be aggressiveness or peacefulness.

In response to the character evidence introduced by the defendant, the government may offer contradictory evidence. Important to remember here is that the government may only respond in kind. It may only use reputation evidence, it may only address the character of the individual(s) attacked or supported in the case-in-defense, and the evidence must relate to the specific character trait addressed by the previous witnesses.

[i]   Character of Defendant Offered by the Defendant

The opinion in *Michelson v. United States* below further illustrates the application of the rules governing use of character evidence in a criminal trial. Though *Michelson* is a bit old, and pre-dated the adoption of the Federal Rules of Evidence by decades, it provides a nice description of the use of evidence of the defendant's character — and the very limited value it has for the defense — with one exception. Rule 405 now allows a character witness to testify to the defendant's reputation as well as the witness's *opinion of the defendant's character*. At the time of *Michelson*, the character witness was only permitted to address the defendant's reputation. The case also reveals another level of complexity in the use of character evidence: the nature of the cross-examination of a reputation witness.

MICHELSON v. UNITED STATES

United States Supreme Court

335 U.S. 469, 69 S. Ct. 213, 93 L. Ed. 168 (1948)

MR. JUSTICE JACKSON delivered the opinion of the Court.

In 1947 Petitioner Michelson was convicted of bribing a federal revenue agent. The Government proved a large payment by accused to the agent for the purpose of influencing his official action. The defendant, as a witness on his own behalf, admitted passing the money but claimed it was done in response to the agent's demands, threats, solicitations, and inducements that amounted to entrapment. It is enough for our purposes to say that determination of the issue turned on whether the jury should believe the agent or the accused.

On direct examination of defendant, his own counsel brought out that, in 1927, he had been convicted of a misdemeanor having to do with trading in counterfeit watch dials. On cross-examination it appeared that in 1930, in executing an application for a license to deal in second-hand jewelry, he answered "No" to the question whether he had theretofore been arrested or summoned for any offense.

Defendant called five witnesses to prove that he enjoyed a good reputation. Two of them testified that their acquaintance with him extended over a period of about thirty years and the others said they had known him at least half that long. A typical examination in chief was as follows:

Q: Do you know the defendant Michelson?

A: Yes.

Q: How long do you know Mr. Michelson?

A: About 30 years.

Q: Do you know other people who know him?

A: Yes.

Q: Have you had occasion to discuss his reputation for honesty and truthfulness and for being a law-abiding citizen?

A: It is very good.

Q: You have talked to others?

A: Yes.

Q: And what is his reputation?

A: Very good.

These are representative of answers by three witnesses; two others replied, in substance, that they never had heard anything against Michelson.

On cross-examination, four of the witnesses were asked, in substance, this question: "Did you ever hear that Mr. Michelson on March 4, 1927, was convicted of a violation of the trademark law in New York City in regard to watches?" This referred to the twenty-year-old conviction about which defendant himself had testified on direct examination. Two of them had heard of it and two had not.

To four of these witnesses the prosecution also addressed the question the allowance of which, over defendant's objection, is claimed to be reversible error:

Did you ever hear that on October 11th, 1920, the defendant, Solomon Michelson, was arrested for receiving stolen goods?

None of the witnesses appears to have heard of this.

The trial court asked counsel for the prosecution, out of presence of the jury, "Is it a fact according to the best information in your possession that Michelson was arrested for receiving stolen goods?" Counsel replied that it was, and to support his good faith exhibited a paper record which defendant's counsel did not challenge.

The judge also on three occasions warned the jury, in terms that are not criticized, of the limited purpose for which this evidence was received.

* * *

Courts that follow the common-law tradition almost unanimously have come to disallow resort by the prosecution to any kind of evidence of a defendant's evil character to establish a probability of his guilt. Not that the law invests the defendant with a presumption of good character, . . . but it simply closes the whole matter of character, disposition and reputation on the prosecution's case-in-chief. The State may not show defendant's prior trouble with the law, specific criminal acts, or ill name among his neighbors, even though such facts might logically be persuasive that he is by propensity a probable perpetrator of the crime. The inquiry is not rejected because character is irrelevant; on the contrary, it is said to weigh too much with the jury and to so over persuade them as to prejudge one with a bad general record and deny him a fair opportunity to defend against a particular charge. The overriding policy of excluding such evidence, despite its admitted probative value, is the practical experience that its disallowance tends to prevent confusion of issues, unfair surprise and undue prejudice.

But this line of inquiry firmly denied to the State is opened to the defendant because character is relevant in resolving probabilities of guilt. He may introduce affirmative testimony that the general estimate of his character is so favorable that the jury may infer that he would not be likely to commit the offense charged. This privilege is sometimes valuable to a defendant for this Court has held that such testimony alone, in some circumstances, may be enough to raise a reasonable doubt of guilt and that in the federal courts a jury in a proper case should be so instructed. . . .

When the defendant elects to initiate a character inquiry, another anomalous rule comes into play. Not only is he permitted to call witnesses to testify from hearsay, but indeed such a witness is not allowed to base his testimony on anything but hearsay. What commonly is called "character evidence" is only such when "character" is employed as a synonym for "reputation." The witness may not testify about defendant's specific acts or courses of conduct or his possession of a particular disposition or of benign mental and moral traits; nor can he testify that his own acquaintance, observation, and knowledge of defendant leads to his own independent opinion that defendant possesses a good general or specific character, inconsistent with commission of acts charged. The witness is, however, allowed to summarize what he had heard in the community, although much of it may have been said by persons less qualified to judge than himself. The evidence which the law permits is not as to the personality of defendant but only as to the shadow his daily life has cast in his neighborhood. This has been well described in a different connection as

> the slow growth of months and years, the resultant picture of forgotten incidents, passing events, habitual and daily conduct, presumably honest because disinterested, and safer to be trusted because prone to suspect. . . . It is for that reason that such general repute is permitted to be proven. It sums up a multitude of trivial details. It compacts into the brief phrase of a verdict the teaching of many incidents and the conduct of years. It is the average intelligence drawing its conclusion.

While courts have recognized logical grounds for criticism of this type of opinion-based-on-hearsay testimony, it is said to be justified by "overwhelming considerations of practical convenience" in avoiding innumerable collateral issues which, if it were attempted to prove character by direct testimony, would complicate and confuse the trial, distract the minds of jury men and befog the chief issues in the litigation. . . .

Another paradox in this branch of the law of evidence is that the delicate and responsible task of compacting reputation hearsay into the "brief phrase of a verdict" is one of the few instances in which conclusions are accepted from a witness on a subject in which he is not an expert. However, the witness must qualify to give an opinion by showing such acquaintance with the defendant, the community in which he has lived and the circles in which he has moved, as to speak with authority of the terms in which generally he is regarded. To require affirmative knowledge of the reputation may seem inconsistent with the latitude given to the witness to testify when all he can say of the reputation is that he has "heard nothing against defendant." This is permitted upon assumption that, if no ill is reported of one, his reputation must be good. But this answer is accepted only from a witness whose knowledge of defendant's habitat and surroundings is intimate enough so that his failure to hear of any relevant ill repute is an assurance that no ugly rumors were about.

Thus the law extends helpful but illogical options to defendant. Experience taught of necessity that they be counterweighted with equally illogical conditions to keep the advantage from becoming an unfair and unreasonable one. The price a defendant must pay for attempting to prove his good name is to throw open the entire subject which the law has kept closed for his benefit and to make himself vulnerable where the law otherwise shields him. The prosecution may pursue the inquiry with contradictory witnesses to show that damaging rumors, whether or not well-grounded, were afloat — for it is not the man that he is, but the name that he has which is put in issue. Another hazard is that his own witness is subject to cross-examination as to the contents and extent of the hearsay on which he bases his conclusions, and he may be required to disclose rumors and reports that are current even if they do not affect his own conclusion.[2] It may test the sufficiency of his

---

[2] (Court's original footnote 16.) A classic example in the books is a character witness in a trial for

knowledge by asking what stories were circulating concerning events, such as one's arrest, about which people normally comment and speculate. Thus, while the law gives defendant the option to show as a fact that his reputation reflects a life and habit incompatible with commission of the offense charged, it subjects his proof to tests of credibility designed to prevent him from profiting by a mere parade of partisans.

* * *

Wide discretion is accompanied by heavy responsibility on trial courts to protect the practice from any misuse. The trial judge was scrupulous to so guard it in the case before us. He took pains to ascertain, out of presence of the jury, that the target of the question was an actual event, which would probably result in some comment among acquaintances if not injury to defendant's reputation. He satisfied himself that counsel was not merely taking a random shot at a reputation imprudently exposed or asking a groundless question to waft an unwarranted innuendo into the jury box.

The question permitted by the trial court, however, involves several features that may be worthy of comment. Its form invited hearsay; it asked about an arrest, not a conviction, and for an offense not closely similar to the one on trial; and it concerned an occurrence many years past.

Since the whole inquiry, as we have pointed out, is calculated to ascertain the general talk of people about defendant, rather than the witness' own knowledge of him, the form of inquiry, "Have you heard?" has general approval, and "Do you know?" is not allowed.

A character witness may be cross-examined as to an arrest whether or not it culminated in a conviction, according to the overwhelming weight of authority. This rule is sometimes confused with that which prohibits cross-examination to credibility by asking a witness whether he himself has been arrested.

Arrest without more does not, in law any more than in reason, impeach the integrity or impair the credibility of a witness. It happens to the innocent as well as the guilty. Only a conviction, therefore, may be inquired about to undermine the trustworthiness of a witness.

Arrest without more may nevertheless impair or cloud one's reputation. False arrest may do that. Even to be acquitted may damage one's good name if the community receives the verdict with a wink and chooses to remember defendant as one who ought to have been convicted. A conviction, on the other hand, may be accepted as a misfortune or an injustice, and even enhance the standing of one who mends his ways and lives it down. Reputation is the net balance of so many debits and credits that the law does not attach the finality to a conviction when the issue

---

murder. She testified she grew up with defendant, knew his reputation for peace and quiet and that it was good. On cross-examination, she was asked if she had heard that the defendant had shot anybody and, if so, how many. She answered, "Three or four," and gave the names of two but could not recall the names of the others. She still insisted, however, that he was of good character. The jury seems to have valued her information more highly than her opinion, and on appeal from conviction, the cross-examination was held proper. . . .

is reputation, that is given to it when the issue is the credibility of the convict.

The inquiry as to an arrest is permissible also because the prosecution has a right to test the qualifications of the witness to bespeak the community opinion. If one never heard the speculations and rumors in which even one's friends indulge upon his arrest, the jury may doubt whether he is capable of giving any very reliable conclusions as to his reputation.

In this case the crime inquired about was receiving stolen goods; the trial was for bribery. The Court of Appeals thought this dissimilarity of offenses too great to sustain the inquiry in logic, though conceding that it is authorized by preponderance of authority. It asks us to substitute [a] rule which allows inquiry about arrest, but only for very closely similar if not identical charges, in place of the rule more generally adhered to in this country and in England. We think the facts of this case show the proposal to be inexpedient.

The good character which the defendant had sought to establish was broader than the crime charged and included the traits of "honesty and truthfulness" and "being a law-abiding citizen." Possession of these characteristics would seem as incompatible with offering a bribe to a revenue agent as with receiving stolen goods. The crimes may be unlike, but both alike proceed from the same defects of character which the witnesses said this defendant was reputed not to exhibit. It is not only by comparison with the crime on trial but by comparison with the reputation asserted that a court may judge whether the prior arrest should be made the subject of inquiry. By this test the inquiry was permissible. It was proper cross-examination because reports of his arrest for receiving stolen goods, if admitted, would tend to weaken the assertion that he was an honest and law-abiding citizen. The cross-examination may take in as much ground as the testimony it is designed to verify. To hold otherwise would give defendant the benefit of testimony that he was honest and law-abiding in reputation when such might not be the fact; the refutation was founded on convictions equally persuasive though not for crimes exactly repeated in the present charge.

The inquiry here concerned an arrest twenty-seven years before the trial. Events a generation old are likely to be lived down and dropped from the present thought and talk of the community and to be absent from the knowledge of younger or more recent acquaintances. The court in its discretion may well exclude inquiry about rumors of an event so remote, unless recent misconduct revived them. But two of these witnesses dated their acquaintance with defendant as commencing thirty years before the trial. Defendant, on direct examination, voluntarily called attention to his conviction twenty years before. While the jury might conclude that a matter so old and indecisive as a 1920 arrest would shed little light on the present reputation and hence propensities of the defendant, we cannot say that, in the context of this evidence and in the absence of objection on this specific ground, its admission was an abuse of discretion.

We do not overlook or minimize the consideration that "the jury almost surely cannot comprehend the Judge's limiting instructions," which disturbed the Court of Appeals. The refinements of the evidentiary rules on this subject are such that even lawyers and judges, after study and reflection, often are confused, and surely jurors in the hurried and unfamiliar movement of a trial must find them almost unintelligible. However, limiting instructions on this subject are no more difficult to comprehend or apply than those upon various other subjects; for example, instructions that admissions of a co-defendant are to be limited to the question of his guilt and are not to be considered as evidence against other defendants, and instructions as to other problems in the trial of conspiracy charges. A defendant in such a case is powerless to prevent his cause from being irretrievably obscured and confused; but, in cases such as the one before us, the law foreclosed this whole confounding line of inquiry, unless defendant thought the net advantage from opening it up would be with him. Given this option, we think defendants in general and this defendant in particular have no valid complaint at the latitude which existing law allows to the prosecution to meet by cross-examination an issue voluntarily tendered by the defense. . . .

We end, as we began, with the observation that the law regulating the offering and testing of character testimony may merit many criticisms. England, and some states have overhauled the practice by statute. But the task of modernizing the longstanding rules on the subject is one of magnitude and difficulty which even those dedicated to law reform do not lightly undertake.

The law of evidence relating to proof of reputation in criminal cases has developed almost entirely at the hands of state courts of last resort, which have such questions frequently before them. This Court, on the other hand, has contributed little to this or to any phase of the law of evidence, for the reason, among others, that it has had extremely rare occasion to decide such issues, as the paucity of citations in this opinion to our own writings attests. It is obvious that a court which can make only infrequent sallies into the field cannot recast the body of case law on this subject in many, many years, even if it were clear what the rules should be.

We concur in the general opinion of courts, textwriters and the profession that much of this law is archaic, paradoxical and full of compromises and compensations by which an irrational advantage to one side is offset by a poorly reasoned counter-privilege to the other. But somehow it has proved a workable even if clumsy system when moderated by discretionary controls in the hands of a wise and strong trial court. To pull one misshapen stone out of the grotesque structure is more likely simply to upset its present balance between adverse interests than to establish a rational edifice.

The present suggestion is that we adopt for all federal courts a new rule as to cross-examination about prior arrest, adhered to by the courts of only one state and rejected elsewhere. The confusion and error it would engender would seem too heavy a price to pay for an almost imperceptible logical improvement, if any, in a system which is justified, if at all, by accumulated judicial experience rather than abstract logic.[4]

---

[4] (Court's original footnote 25.) It must not be overlooked that abuse of cross-examination to test credibility carries its own corrective. Authorities on practice caution the bar of the imprudence as well as the unprofessional nature of attacks on witnesses or defendants which are likely to be resented by the jury. . . .

The judgment is Affirmed.

[The concurring opinion of JUSTICE FRANKFURTER, and the dissenting opinion of JUSTICES RUTLEDGE and MURPHY are omitted.]

[ii] Character Evidence About the Victim's Character for Aggressiveness

COMMONWEALTH v. ADJUTANT
Supreme Judicial Court of Massachusetts
824 N.E.2d 1 (2005)

CORDY, J.

Following a jury trial, Rhonda Adjutant, a woman employed by an escort service, was found guilty of voluntary manslaughter for killing Stephen Whiting, a client of the service. In this appeal, Adjutant argues that evidence of Whiting's violent reputation and past conduct, even though unknown to her at the time of the killing, should have been admitted at her trial because it was relevant to her claim that Whiting was the "first aggressor" in the altercation that resulted in his death, and that she acted in self-defense.

After surveying the state of the law in jurisdictions throughout the country, we are persuaded that evidence of a victim's prior violent conduct may be probative of whether the victim was the first aggressor where a claim of self-defense has been asserted and the identity of the first aggressor is in dispute.[1] Consequently, when such circumstances are present, we hold, as a matter of common-law principle, that trial judges have the discretion to admit in evidence specific incidents of violence that the victim is reasonably alleged to have initiated. While there is potential for confusion and prejudice inherent in the admission of this type of evidence, trial judges are well equipped to decide whether the probative value of the evidence proffered outweighs its prejudicial effect in the context of the facts and issues presented in specific cases.

In the present case, relying on language in past decisions of this court, see, e.g., *Commonwealth v. Graham*, 431 Mass. 282, 291, 727 N.E.2d 51 (2000); *Commonwealth v. Dilone*, 385 Mass. 281, 285–286, 431 N.E.2d 576 (1982), the judge ruled that she lacked the discretion to admit evidence of prior violent acts committed by Whiting but unknown to Adjutant. Because we conclude that the judge's ruling, while understandable, was prejudicial to Adjutant's claim that she acted in self-defense, we reverse the judgment and remand the case for a new trial.

1. *Background.* The evidence at trial was as follows. Adjutant worked as an escort for Newbury Cosmopolitan International Escort Service (Newbury). In the early morning of September 25, 1999, Whiting telephoned Newbury and requested an

---

[1] Indeed, such evidence may be the jury's only means of assessing the likelihood of the defendant's account of the incident in a homicide case.

escort. The Newbury dispatcher told Whiting that he could receive a full body massage and one hour of an escort's company for $175. Whiting agreed to these terms, and arrangements were made for Adjutant to visit Whiting's home in Revere. Shortly thereafter, Adjutant was dropped off there by a driver and the dispatcher's boy friend (drivers). Whiting met her outside his building and accompanied her to his basement apartment.

Once inside, Whiting paid Adjutant, who then telephoned Newbury to report that she had received payment. Adjutant testified that during and after the call Whiting snorted two lines of cocaine. Adjutant then offered to begin a massage. Whiting replied that he wanted intercourse and believed that he had paid for it. Adjutant denied that she was sent to have intercourse with him, and telephoned the Newbury dispatcher on her cellular telephone to inform her that Whiting wanted more than a massage. Adjutant then handed the phone to Whiting, and the dispatcher reminded him of the original terms. Whiting demanded a total refund, which neither the dispatcher nor Adjutant offered. When Whiting returned the telephone to Adjutant, the dispatcher told her to leave and agreed to stay on the line until Adjutant was out of the apartment.

There was conflicting testimony as to when the defendant and the victim armed themselves for their fatal confrontation. Adjutant testified that when she attempted to leave, Whiting pushed her onto his bed and retrieved a crowbar from the kitchen, at which point Adjutant picked up a knife that was lying on the bedside table, next to a plate of cocaine. The dispatcher, on the other hand, testified that while she was talking to Whiting, he said that Adjutant had a knife, and that when Adjutant then got back on the telephone with her, Adjutant said that Whiting was picking up a crowbar.

In any event, after arming himself, Whiting first slammed the crowbar on a counter and then swung it at Adjutant, striking her in the leg. She responded by nicking him in the face with the knife, drawing blood. Adjutant testified that she next tried to avert further confrontation by offering to begin again with a massage, but Whiting refused. Meanwhile, at Adjutant's urging, the dispatcher alerted Adjutant's drivers to return to Whiting's apartment. At this point, Adjutant testified that she attempted to run toward the door, but Whiting tackled her. During the struggle, Adjutant stabbed Whiting in the shoulder with the knife and moved away. Whiting, however, continued to block Adjutant's exit, while Adjutant screamed at him to stay back and threatened to cut him again if he came any closer.[2]

Within minutes, Adjutant's drivers returned to the scene, heard her screams, and kicked in the door to the apartment. According to Adjutant, the moment one of the drivers kicked in the door, Whiting advanced on her with the crowbar raised, at which point she stabbed him in the neck, inflicting the fatal wound. Whiting did not immediately drop the crowbar or move away from the door. When he eventually did, Adjutant fled the apartment with the drivers, throwing down the knife and her

---

[2] Adjutant's telephone was apparently on throughout the incident, and the dispatcher testified that she heard Adjutant say that Whiting was coming toward her and that she "would cut [him] from ear to ear" "if [he came] anywhere near [her]."

telephone.[3] One of the drivers provided a different account of the fatal stabbing. He testified that after the door was kicked open, Whiting turned to face the drivers, at which point he saw Adjutant move toward Whiting and stab him in the neck in a straightforward thrusting motion. The medical examiner's testimony concerning the likely manner in which the fatal knife wound was inflicted was not entirely consistent with the driver's testimony.

Adjutant maintained at trial that all her actions were defensive and intended to help her escape the apartment. The jury's main task was determining whether Adjutant acted in self-defense. That inquiry required the jury to weigh Adjutant's credibility, as well as that of the dispatcher and the driver, and decide who moved first to attack the other during the last moments of the standoff. See *Commonwealth v. Kendrick*, 351 Mass. 203, 210–212, 218 N.E.2d 408 (1966).

In her defense, Adjutant focused on Whiting's intoxication and drug use that evening. The medical examiner testified at trial that Whiting had cocaine in his bloodstream, and that his blood alcohol level reflected his consumption of the equivalent of sixty ounces of beer or five ounces of whiskey. Two of Whiting's neighbors testified that, earlier that evening, Whiting appeared intoxicated and had made unsuccessful sexual advances toward women near the apartment building. Adjutant testified that she became terrified when her initial blows to Whiting did not seem to faze him, apparently because of his drugged condition.

During the trial, Adjutant's counsel sought to cross-examine Whiting's neighbors about his previous violent behavior and reputation for violence. The judge sustained the prosecutor's objections to these questions and also barred testimony about Whiting's behavior while intoxicated, ruling that Whiting's violent past or reputation for violence was only relevant if Adjutant had been aware of them at the time of the stabbing.[4] When the prosecution subsequently elicited testimony that Whiting was "calm," "talked . . . very softly," and "sounded like a nice person" on the night of the incident, defense counsel moved for permission to "impeach" this testimony by evidence of Whiting's prior acts of aggression. The judge denied the motion, except insofar as to permit Adjutant to introduce percipient witness testimony to Whiting's previous use of a crowbar. No such witnesses were called.[5]

---

[3] A neighbor found Whiting's dead body in the doorway of the apartment several hours later and summoned police.

[4] In connection with Adjutant's sentencing, evidence of three violent acts committed by Whiting while he was intoxicated and within three months of his death was presented to the court. In one of the instances, Whiting, while on cocaine, allegedly chased after his neighbor "like a raging bull" when confronted about vandalizing the common yard. In another, he allegedly threatened two neighbors with a butcher knife. And in the third, he allegedly threw boiling water on a friend with whom he was arguing. We leave it to the judge before whom the case will be retried to determine whether these or any other alleged violent acts of the victim are incidents which he likely initiated and are more probative than prejudicial.

[5] According to the transcript of the in limine motion on this evidence, the defendant sought to show that Whiting was involved in a cocaine purchase at some point less than a year before he died in which he let his dealer see that he had much more money than necessary for the transaction. The dealer returned later with another man, both wearing masks and carrying a baseball bat and a pipe. They entered Whiting's apartment and assaulted him, demanding his money. Whiting responded by attacking them with a crowbar, refusing to back down despite being completely outmatched. The assailants seized

PP

At the conclusion of the trial, the jury convicted Adjutant of voluntary man-slaughter. She appealed and the Appeals Court affirmed the conviction. *Commonwealth v. Adjutant*, 60 Mass. App. Ct. 1107, 800 N.E.2d 346 (2003). We granted her application for further appellate review limited to whether the trial judge erred in concluding that she had no discretion to admit Adjutant's proffered evidence and consequently excluding it.

Rule

2. *Discussion.* In almost every American jurisdiction, evidence of a victim's violent character may be admitted to support an accused's claim of self-defense under two distinct theories. First, it may be admitted to prove that at the time of the assault the defendant was reasonably apprehensive for his safety, and used a degree of force that was reasonable in light of the victim's violent tendencies. Because such evidence is relevant to the defendant's state of mind (the subjective reasonableness of his apprehension and actions), a predicate to its admissibility is the defendant's prior knowledge of it. Second, it may be admitted as tending to prove that the victim and not the defendant was likely to have been the "first aggressor," where there is a dispute as to who initiated the attack. Under the first theory, the evidence is not admitted for the purpose of showing that the victim acted in conformance with his character for violence; under the second theory, it is.

Massachusetts has long followed the evidentiary rule that permits the introduction of evidence of the victim's violent character, if known to the defendant, as it bears on the defendant's state of mind and the reasonableness of his actions in claiming to have acted in self-defense. See *Commonwealth v. Edmonds*, 365 Mass. 496, 502, 313 N.E.2d 429 (1974) (victim's reputation as violent person admissible). See also *Commonwealth v. Fontes*, 396 Mass. 733, 735–736, 488 N.E.2d 760 (1986) (instances of victim's prior acts of violence admissible). This court has not, however, had occasion to rule on the second theory, raised in this case, regarding the use of such evidence to prove who was the first aggressor. *Id.* at 736 n. 1, 488 N.E.2d 760 ("It should be recognized that we are not considering here the admission of evidence of general reputation or of specific incidents of violence to show that the victim was, or was likely to have been, the aggressor").

Under Rules 404 and 405 of the Federal Rules of Evidence, all Federal courts now permit the introduction of evidence of the victim's violent character to support a defendant's self-defense claim that the victim was the first aggressor.[7] Similarly, appellate courts in forty-five of the forty-eight State jurisdictions that have

---

the money and left Whiting near death. Whiting eventually filed a police report and gave grand jury testimony, detailing the combat.

[7] The Federal Rules of Evidence make an explicit exception to their general exclusion of character evidence as propensity evidence when "[e]vidence of a pertinent trait of character of the alleged victim of the crime [is] offered by an accused . . . ." Fed. R. Evid. 404(a)(2). The circuit courts of the United States Court of Appeal that have considered the issue are unanimous that Fed. R. Evid. 404(a)(2) allows the introduction of character evidence to show the victim's violent propensity if the identity of the first aggressor is in dispute, regardless whether the defendant knew of the victim's propensity for violence. See *United States v. Emeron Taken Alive*, 262 F.3d 711, 714 (8th Cir. 2001); *United States v. Smith*, 230 F.3d 300, 307 (7th Cir. 2000), cert. denied, 531 U.S. 1176, 121 S. Ct. 1151, 148 L. Ed. 2d 1013 (2001), citing *United States v. Greschner*, 647 F.2d 740, 742 (7th Cir. 1981); *United States v. Bautista*, 145 F.3d 1140, 1152 (10th Cir.), cert. denied, 525 U.S. 911, 119 S. Ct. 255, 142 L. Ed. 2d 210 (1998); *United States v. Keiser*, 57 F.3d 847, 855 (9th Cir.), cert. denied, 516 U.S. 1029, 116 S. Ct. 676, 133 L. Ed. 2d 525 (1995); *United States v. Piche*, 981 F.2d 706, 713 (4th Cir. 1992), cert. denied, 508 U.S. 916, 113 S. Ct. 2356, 124

considered the issue have decided that some form of such evidence is properly admissible on the first aggressor issue, regardless whether the victim's violent character was known to the defendant at the time of the assault.[8] The two States that have not considered the matter have both adopted versions of Federal Rules of Evidence[9] that would appear to permit the introduction of such evidence. Of the three State appellate courts that have declined to follow the modern trend, two did so over vigorous dissents.[10]

L. Ed. 2d 264 (1993); *Lagasse v. Vestal,* 671 F.2d 668, 669 (1st Cir.), cert. denied, 457 U.S. 1122, 102 S. Ct. 2939, 73 L. Ed. 2d 1337 (1982).

[8] Both jurisdictions that have adopted the Federal Rules of Evidence and jurisdictions that have not affirm the admissibility of some form of character evidence to show the likelihood that the victim was the first aggressor. *White v. State,* 294 Ala. 265, 273, 314 So. 2d 857, cert. denied, 423 U.S. 951, 96 S. Ct. 373, 46 L. Ed. 2d 288 (1975); *McCracken v. State,* 914 P.2d 893, 898 (Alaska Ct. App. 1996); *State v. Santanna,* 153 Ariz. 147, 149, 735 P.2d 757 (1987); *McClellan v. State,* 264 Ark. 223, 225–226, 570 S.W.2d 278 (1978); *People v. Wright,* 39 Cal. 3d 576, 587, 217 Cal. Rptr. 212, 703 P.2d 1106 (1985); *People v. Ferguson,* 43 P.3d 705, 710 (Colo. Ct. App. 2001); *State v. Smith,* 222 Conn. 1, 17, 608 A.2d 63, cert. denied, 506 U.S. 942, 113 S. Ct. 383, 121 L. Ed. 2d 293 (1992); *Rawls v. United States,* 539 A.2d 1087, 1089 (D.C. 1988); *Smith v. State,* 606 So. 2d 641, 642–643 (Fla. Dist. Ct. App. 1992); *Chandler v. State,* 261 Ga. 402, 407, 405 S.E.2d 669 (1991); *State v. Basque,* 66 Haw. 510, 513–515, 666 P.2d 599 (1983); *State v. Custodio,* 136 Idaho 197, 203, 30 P.3d 975 (Ct. App. 2001); *People v. Lynch,* 104 Ill. 2d 194, 200, 83 Ill. Dec. 598, 470 N.E.2d 1018 (1984); *Teague v. State,* 269 Ind. 103, 115–116, 379 N.E.2d 418 (1978); *State v. Dunson,* 433 N.W.2d 676, 680 (Iowa 1988); *State v. Deavers,* 252 Kan. 149, 156–157, 843 P.2d 695 (1992), cert. denied, 508 U.S. 978, 113 S. Ct. 2979, 125 L. Ed. 2d 676 (1993); *Boyle v. Commonwealth,* 694 S.W.2d 711, 713 (Ky. Ct. App. 1985); *State v. Edwards,* 420 So.2d 663, 669 (La. 1982); *Thomas v. State,* 301 Md. 294, 306–307, 483 A.2d 6 (1984), cert. denied, 470 U.S. 1088, 105 S. Ct. 1856, 85 L. Ed. 2d 153 (1985); *People v. Stallworth,* 364 Mich. 528, 536, 111 N.W.2d 742 (1961); *State v. Irby,* 368 N.W.2d 19, 23 (Minn. Ct. App. 1985); *Aguilar v. State,* 847 So. 2d 871, 879 (Miss. Ct. App. 2002); *State v. Sattler,* 288 Mont. 79, 95, 956 P.2d 54 (1998); *State v. Lewchuk,* 4 Neb. [Ct.] App. 165, 175, 539 N.W.2d 847 (1995); *Daniel v. State,* 119 Nev. 498, 78 P.3d 890, 901 (2003), cert. denied, 541 U.S. 1045, 124 S. Ct. 2161, 158 L. Ed. 2d 736 (2004); *State v. Newell,* 141 N.H. 199, 201, 679 A.2d 1142 (1996); *State v. Aguiar,* 322 N.J. Super. 175, 183–184, 730 A.2d 463 (1999); *State v. Baca,* 114 N.M. 668, 671–672, 845 P.2d 762 (1992); *State v. Watson,* 338 N.C. 168, 187–188, 449 S.E.2d 694 (1994), cert. denied, 514 U.S. 1071, 115 S. Ct. 1708, 131 L. Ed. 2d 569 (1995); *State v. McIntyre,* 488 N.W.2d 612, 616 (N.D. 1992); *State v. Barnes,* 94 Ohio St. 3d 21, 24, 759 N.E.2d 1240 (2002); *Harris v. State,* 400 P.2d 64, 70 (Okla. Crim. App. 1965); *State v. Lotches,* 331 Or. 455, 489, 17 P.3d 1045 (2000), cert. denied, 534 U.S. 833, 122 S. Ct. 82, 151 L. Ed. 2d 45 (2001); *Commonwealth v. Beck,* 485 Pa. 475, 478, 402 A.2d 1371 (1979); *State v. Dellay,* 687 A.2d 435, 438 (R.I. 1996); *State v. Latham,* 519 N.W.2d 68, 71 (S.D. 1994); *State v. Furlough,* 797 S.W.2d 631, 649 (Tenn. Crim. App. 1990); *Tate v. State,* 981 S.W.2d 189, 192–193 (Tex. Crim. App. 1998); *State v. Howell,* 649 P.2d 91, 96 (Utah 1982); *Jordan v. Commonwealth,* 219 Va. 852, 855, 252 S.E.2d 323 (1979); *State v. Roy,* 151 Vt. 17, 30–31, 557 A.2d 884 (1989); *State v. Kelly,* 102 Wn.2d 188, 193–194, 685 P.2d 564 (1984); *State v. Boggess,* 204 W.Va. 267, 275–276, 512 S.E.2d 189 (1998); *Werner v. State,* 66 Wis. 2d 736, 744 n. 6, 226 N.W.2d 402 (1975); *Edwards v. State,* 973 P.2d 41, 45–46 (Wyo. 1999).

[9] Delaware and South Carolina. See Del. Uniform R. Evid. 404(a)(2) (2005); S.C. R. Evid. 404(a)(2) (1995).

[10] *State v. Johns,* 34 S.W.3d 93, 111 (Mo. 2000), cert. denied, 532 U.S. 1012, 121 S. Ct. 1745, 149 L. Ed. 2d 668 (2001); *State v. Leone,* 581 A.2d 394 (Me. 1990); *Matter of Robert S.,* 52 N.Y.2d 1046, 1048, 438 N.Y.S.2d 509, 420 N.E.2d 390 (1981), citing *People v. Rodawald,* 177 N.Y. 408, 70 N.E. 1 (1904), and *People v. Miller,* 39 N.Y.2d 543, 551, 384 N.Y.S.2d 741, 349 N.E.2d 841 (1976). The dissents in the Maine and New York cases highlighted the relevance of evidence of the victim's violent character and made reference to the modern trend favoring the admission of such evidence. See *State v. Leone, supra* at 402 (Glassman, J., dissenting) (evidence of victim's past aggression "highly probative" and "[i]t was for the jury to determine the credibility of and the weight to be given this evidence in deciding whether [the defendant] was guilty of murder or manslaughter or not guilty because he acted in self-defense"); *Matter of Robert S., supra* at 1049, 438 N.Y.S.2d 509, 420 N.E.2d 390 (Fuchsberg, J., dissenting) (exclusion of victim's long

The basis of the overwhelming trend toward admitting some form of this evidence can be found in the view that evidence reflecting the victim's propensity for violence has substantial probative value and will help the jury identify the first aggressor when the circumstances of the altercation are in dispute . . . .

There can be no doubt that at least some of the proffered evidence in this case was relevant to Adjutant's self-defense claim. Whether Whiting was a violent man, prone to aggression when intoxicated or under the influence of drugs, "throws light" on the crucial question at the heart of Adjutant's self-defense claim — who attacked first in the final moments before the fatal stabbing. *Commonwealth v. Woods*, 414 Mass. 343, 356, 607 N.E.2d 1024, cert. denied, 510 U.S. 815, 114 S. Ct. 65, 126 L. Ed. 2d 35 (1993), quoting *Commonwealth v. Palladino*, 346 Mass. 720, 726, 195 N.E.2d 769 (1964). The evidence, if admitted, would have supported the inference that Whiting, with a history of violent and aggressive behavior while intoxicated, probably acted in conformity with that history by attacking Adjutant, and that the defendant's story of self-defense was truthful. *State v. Miranda*, 176 Conn. 107, 113–114, 405 A.2d 622 (1978).

. . . [W]e are persuaded that some form of evidence tending to show the victim's violent character should be admissible for the limited purpose of supporting the defendant's self-defense claim that the victim was the first aggressor. We now turn to the separate question of the permissible form of such evidence.

The defendant urges the court to allow the admission of evidence both of the victim's violent reputation and of his specific violent acts. The Commonwealth argues that if the court permits character evidence to be admitted, it should be limited to specific acts of violence committed by the victim. All other State jurisdictions that admit character evidence in these circumstances admit reputation evidence. Some of these States also admit evidence of specific violent acts.[15]

The arguments against admitting specific violent acts include (1) the danger of ascribing character traits to a victim with proof of isolated incidents, (2) the worry that jurors will be invited to acquit the defendant on the improper ground that the

---

history of aggressive behavior and violence when intoxicated "deprived [the defendant] of proof which went to the heart of his guilt or innocence"). In addition, the New York rule has been specifically criticized, but found not to transgress a defendant's constitutional right to a fair trial. See *Williams v. Lord*, 996 F.2d 1481, 1484–1485 (2d Cir. 1993) (Cardamone, J., concurring), *cert. denied*, 510 U.S. 1120, 114 S. Ct. 1073, 127 L. Ed. 2d 391 (1994).

[15] Rules 404 and 405 of the Federal Rules of Evidence and similar State rules permit the defendant to introduce reputation and opinion evidence, but not specific acts of violence, to prove the victim's violent character. See, e.g., *United States v. Keiser*, 57 F.3d 847, 857 (9th Cir. 1995); *State v. McIntyre*, 488 N.W.2d 612, 616–617 (N.D. 1992). Despite this dominant interpretation of the Federal Rules of Evidence, some State courts have held that the victim's character is an "essential element" of a defendant's self-defense claim, allowing the use of specific acts evidence under the State equivalent of Fed. R. Evid. 405(b). See, e.g., *State v. Dunson*, 433 N.W.2d 676, 680–681 (Iowa 1988); *State v. Baca*, 114 N.M. 668, 671–673, 845 P.2d 762 (1992). Other States with versions of the Federal Rules of Evidence have crafted a compromise rule allowing evidence of the victim's specific acts only in the form of convictions. See, e.g., *State v. Miranda*, 176 Conn. 107, 113–114, 405 A.2d 622 (1978); *State v. Howell*, 649 P.2d 91, 96 (Utah 1982). Jurisdictions that have not adopted the Federal Rules of Evidence are split on the issue. Compare *People v. Wright*, 39 Cal. 3d 576, 587–588, 217 Cal. Rptr. 212, 703 P.2d 1106 (1985), and *People v. Lynch*, 104 Ill. 2d 194, 200, 470 N.E.2d 1018, 83 Ill. Dec. 598 (1984), with *State v. Waller*, 816 S.W.2d 212, 216 (Mo. 1991), and *Matter of Robert S.*, 52 N.Y.2d 1046, 1048, 438 N.Y.S.2d 509, 420 N.E.2d 390 (1981).

victim deserved to die, (3) the potential for wasting time trying collateral questions surrounding the victim's past conduct, (4) the unfair difficulty of rebuttal by the prosecution, and (5) the strategic imbalance that flows from the inability of prosecutors to introduce similar evidence of the defendant's prior bad acts. See *Chandler v. State*, 261 Ga. 402, 409, 405 S.E.2d 669 (1991) (Benham, J., concurring specially); *Henderson v. State*, 234 Ga. 827, 829, 218 S.E.2d 612 (1975); *State v. Jacoby*, 260 N.W.2d 828, 838 (Iowa 1977); *Williams v. State*, 565 S.W.2d 503, 505 (Tenn. 1978). See also Note, A New Understanding of Specific Act Evidence in Homicide Cases Where the Accused Claims Self-Defense: Striking the Proper Balance Between Competing Policy Goals, 32 Ind. L. Rev. 1437, 1447–1448 (1999). Many courts that follow the Federal Rules of Evidence rely on the Federal Rules advisory committee's note's succinct rationale for exclusion: "Of the three methods of proving character [reputation, opinion, and specific instances of conduct,] evidence of specific instances of conduct is the most convincing. At the same time it possesses the greatest capacity to arouse prejudice, to confuse, to surprise, and to consume time." Advisory Committee's Note, Fed. R. Evid. 405, 56 F.R.D. 183, 222 (1972). See *United States v. Smith*, 230 F.3d 300, 308 (7th Cir. 2000), cert. denied, 531 U.S. 1176, 121 S. Ct. 1151, 148 L. Ed. 2d 1013 (2001); *United States v. Keiser*, 57 F.3d 847, 855 n. 16 (9th Cir. 1995); *Daniel v. State*, 119 Nev. 498, 78 P.3d 890, 901 (2003).

While we acknowledge the validity of these concerns, we disagree that they require an unbending rule excluding all of the victim's specific acts of violence when relevant to the identity of the first aggressor. This court rejected similar arguments in *Commonwealth v. Fontes*, 396 Mass. 733, 736–737, 488 N.E.2d 760 (1986), and approved the admission of such evidence when relevant to the defendant's reasonable apprehension of imminent bodily harm. Testimony about the victim's prior acts of violence can be convincing and reliable evidence of the victim's propensity for violence . . . . Such evidence becomes relevant to the first aggressor issue when the prior acts of violence demonstrate a propensity for initiating violence. "Such instances may be very significant; their number can be controlled by the trial court's discretion; and the prohibitory considerations applicable to an accused's character . . . have here little or no force." 1A J. Wigmore, Evidence § 63.1, at 1382 (Tillers rev. ed. 1983). See Annot., 1 A.L.R.3d 571, 601 (1965).

* * *

We are persuaded that the sound discretion of trial judges to exclude marginally relevant or grossly prejudicial evidence can prevent the undue exploration of collateral issues . . . .

For these reasons, where the identity of the first aggressor is in dispute and the victim has a history of violence, we hold that the trial judge has the discretion to admit evidence of specific acts of prior violent conduct that the victim is reasonably alleged to have initiated, to support the defendant's claim of self-defense.

With respect to the usefulness of reputation evidence in the context of establishing who was the first aggressor, we are presently of a different view. While such evidence may be quite probative in evaluating a defendant's subjective state of mind, and the reasonableness of the actions thereby taken to defend himself, it is far less reliable in the present context. Reputation evidence is often "opinion in disguise."

Advisory Committee's Note, Fed. R. Evid. 405, 56 F.R.D. 183, 222 (1972). We do not allow the admission of the private opinions of individual witnesses as character evidence. See *Commonwealth v. Connolly*, 356 Mass. 617, 626, 255 N.E.2d 191, cert. denied, 400 U.S. 843 (1970). See also *Commonwealth v. Belton*, 352 Mass. 263, 269, 225 N.E.2d 53, cert. denied, 389 U.S. 872, 88 S. Ct. 159, 19 L. Ed. 2d 153 (1967) (defendant prohibited from introducing character evidence of his peacefulness in form of private opinions). Reputations or opinions are often formed based on rumor or other unreliable hearsay sources, without any personal knowledge on the part of the person holding that opinion. See Advisory Committee's Note, Fed. R. Evid. 405, *supra*, quoting 7 J. Wigmore, Evidence § 1986 (describing reputation evidence as "secondhand, irresponsible product of multiplied guesses and gossip"). In this case, had Adjutant offered the testimony of Whiting's neighbors that Whiting was known to be a violent man, without the corroborating details of the victim's specific acts, such evidence would have been little more than a few neighbors' accumulated opinions. Juries should have the ability to draw their own inferences in assessing the bearing of the victim's prior violent conduct on the probability that he was the first aggressor.

Jurisdictions that exclude the victim's specific acts of violence and admit reputation evidence make that choice because reputation evidence is filtered, general in nature, with less potential to inflame or sidetrack the proceedings than evidence of the victim's specific acts — in essence, because such evidence is less "convincing" and thus less controversial. See Advisory Committee's Note, Fed. R. Evid. 405, *supra* ("When character is used circumstantially and hence occupies a lesser status in the case, proof may be only by reputation and opinion"); McCormick, Evidence § 186, at 650 (5th ed. 1999) ("As one moves from the specific to the general in this fashion, the pungency and persuasiveness of the evidence declines . . . "). Given our rationale for allowing the admission of prior acts of violent conduct initiated by the victim, we favor the admission of concrete and relevant evidence of specific acts over more general evidence of the victim's reputation for violence. Evidence of specific acts also lends itself more readily to the necessary weighing of probative value against prejudicial effect in the factual context of particular cases.

While constrained by the trial judge's sound discretion, the defendant's ability to introduce evidence of the victim's prior history as a violent aggressor should also be matched with safeguards for prosecutors. See, e.g., 1A J. Wigmore, Evidence § 63, at 1369–1373 (Tillers rev. ed. 1983); *Chandler v. State*, 261 Ga. 402, 407–408, 405 S.E.2d 669 (1991). A defendant who intends to introduce evidence of the victim's specific acts of violence to support a claim that the victim was the first aggressor must provide notice to the court and the Commonwealth of such intent and of the specific evidence he intends to offer. This notice must come sufficiently prior to trial to permit the Commonwealth to investigate and prepare a rebuttal. The prosecutor, in turn, must provide notice to the court and the defendant of whatever rebuttal evidence he or she intends to offer at trial.[19]

---

[19] We need not decide in this case whether the Commonwealth may introduce evidence of prior violent incidents initiated by the defendant once the defendant has done so with respect to the victim, for the purpose of proving who was the first aggressor. We note that Fed. R. Evid. 404(a)(1) was amended

*   *   *

3. *Conclusion.* This opinion adopts a new common-law rule of evidence. Because the defendant alleged the error and argued for the rule on direct appeal, she should have the benefit of this decision. Otherwise, it shall apply only prospectively. *Commonwealth v. Dagley,* 442 Mass. 713, 721 n. 10, 816 N.E.2d 527 (2004).

The judgment against the defendant is reversed, the verdict is set aside, and the case is remanded to the Superior Court for a new trial and further proceedings consistent with this opinion.

So ordered.

COWIN, J., dissenting.

The court today holds that a "victim's prior violent conduct may be probative in determining whether the victim was the first aggressor where a claim of self-defense has been asserted and the identity of the first aggressor is in dispute." *Ante* at 650, 824 N.E.2d 3. In particular, the court creates a new rule of evidence in which prior acts of violence "reasonably alleged to have [been] initiated" by a victim, and unknown to a defendant, may be admitted to establish a victim's tendency toward violence. *Id.* Because I believe that past acts of violence by a victim, unknown to a defendant, do little to help a jury resolve the issue whether a *defendant* was the first aggressor and have no place in our consideration of a defendant's guilt or innocence, I respectfully dissent.

*   *   *

Even if we assume that such prior acts are sufficiently probative of future behavior, today's rule would be fair only if victims were equally able to explore defendants' violent histories. Instead of creating an even-handed approach, the court today constructs a one-sided rule that is prejudicial to victims. In cases involving two parties with violent pasts (not uncommon in murders and assaults), defendants may now introduce evidence of the victims' violent histories, while the Commonwealth will remain powerless to introduce similar evidence concerning defendants. See *Commonwealth v. Helfant,* 398 Mass. 214, 224, 496 N.E.2d 433 (1986). The court asserts that today's ruling will provide juries with "as complete a picture of the (often fatal) altercation as possible." *Ante* at 658–659, 824 N.E.2d at 9. But by constructing a lopsided rule that permits consideration of only one side of the story, the decision does little to paint a "complete" picture for the jury and much to promote a biased view of the parties. And what of a victim's propensity toward peacefulness? Will prosecutors be able to rebut damaging character evidence with more favorable character evidence?

---

in 2000, opening the door to the admission of such evidence once the accused attacks the character of the victim for this purpose, making clear that the accused cannot simultaneously attack the alleged victim's character and yet remain shielded from the disclosure of equally relevant evidence concerning his own same character trait. 192 F.R.D. 340, 414 (2000). At a minimum, once evidence of the victim's violent conduct is admitted, the prosecutor may introduce evidence of the victim's peaceful propensities. See *Commonwealth v. Lapointe,* 402 Mass. 321, 325, 522 N.E.2d 937 (1988). See, e.g., Fed. R. Evid. 404(a)(2); 1A J. Wigmore, Evidence § 63, at 1369 (Tillers rev. ed. 1983); 2 J. Wigmore, Evidence § 246, at 59–60 (Tillers rev. ed. 1983).

Hoping to neutralize this imbalance, the court notes (one would presume favorably) that Fed. R. Evid. 404(a)(1) now allows the Commonwealth to respond to victim character evidence with evidence of a defendant's violent character. See *ante* at 669 n.19, 824 N.E.2d at 14 n.19. Admittedly, the Federal approach, if adopted by the Commonwealth, would resolve the imbalance cited above. However, the court today does not adopt this more equitable Federal approach. Even if the court or the Legislature were eventually to adopt the Federal approach, this "solution" to the unfairness problem would be more troublesome than the court's decision today. The Federal approach, while equitable, would greatly diminish our traditional evidentiary protections that prevent defendants from being "reconvicted" of their prior acts. See, e.g., *Commonwealth v. Baker, supra; Commonwealth v. Brusgulis*, 406 Mass. 501, 505, 548 N.E.2d 1234 (1990); *Commonwealth v. Triplett*, 398 Mass. 561, 562–564, 500 N.E.2d 262 (1986); *Commonwealth v. Stone, supra*. I believe today's decision, by creating a gross imbalance and necessitating some sort of "fix," sets us on precisely this dangerous course toward the erosion of long-held evidentiary safeguards for defendants. Given this court's valid concern for defendants' rights, see *ante* at 662, 824 N.E.2d at 12, I would reject the court's new rule in favor of our well-balanced traditional approach of excluding most character evidence concerning both victims and defendants.

Today's decision will have other undesirable consequences. First, the admission of character evidence against victims will unduly prejudice juries against victims with violent pasts. See Liacos, *supra* at § 4.4.1, at 131 (rule against use of character evidence for propensity purposes premised on "high risk that such evidence will have a prejudicial impact on the jury and will result in a decision motivated by something other than the particular facts of the incident before the court"). Our new rule unreasonably invites the fact finder to evaluate the relative worth of a deceased victim without logical basis. As the court acknowledges, "[t]he deep tendency of human nature to punish not because [the defendant] is guilty this time but because he is a bad man and may as well be condemned now that he is caught is a tendency that cannot fail to operate with any jury, in or out of court." 1A J. Wigmore, *supra* at § 57, at 1185. While such prejudice raises due process concerns when applied to a defendant, we should be no more willing to allow its application to a victim. If we find it unacceptable to imprison people for their prior bad acts, how is it any more acceptable to punish people for their prior bad acts by sanctioning their deaths?

Second, today's ruling will result in jury distraction and confusion, contribute to judicial delay, and increase litigation costs for the Commonwealth and the defense. Fact finders considering this newly permitted character evidence will be asked to wade through multiple incidents of violence (perhaps having to weigh conflicting evidence concerning several such incidents) before turning to the basis of the prosecution . . . .

[3] Prior-Act Evidence Offered for Purposes Other than Propensity: Rule 404(b)

Although the courts have excluded evidence of prior specific instances of conduct offered for the purpose of proving a defendant's propensity to act in a particular manner, they have consistently admitted such evidence if offered for another purpose not related to the defendant's propensity.

Rule 404(b) governs the admissibility of such evidence. Often the type of evidence admitted under Rule 404(b) is referred to as prior bad act evidence, and this characterization is statistically an accurate description. Most of the time, a party offering evidence under this rule will attempt to introduce evidence of occurrences before the disputed act. The rule itself, however, does not so limit the evidence of other acts. Parties may offer prior, contemporaneous, or subsequent acts under this rule if they are relevant to an issue other than the defendant's propensity to commit crimes.

The following excerpt from McCormick on Evidence discusses the uses of character evidence for purposes other than to establish propensity and the admissibility requirements for such uses. Note that although McCormick speaks of the rule in terms of prior *criminal acts*, and of their *use by the prosecution*, evidence of all prior acts relevant for purposes other than proving propensity is admissible in civil as well as criminal cases, and parties generally may introduce such evidence at any stage of the trial.

McCormick on Evidence
§ 190, at 284–287 (5th ed. 2000)[5]

§ 190 Bad Character as Evidence of Criminal Conduct — Other Crimes

If anything, the rule against using character evidence to prove conduct on a particular occasion applies even more strongly in criminal cases. Unless and until the accused gives evidence of his good character, the prosecution may not introduce evidence of (or otherwise seek to establish) his bad character. The evidence of bad character would not be irrelevant, but particularly in the setting of the jury trial the dangers of prejudice, confusion and time-consumption outweigh the probative value.

This broad prohibition includes the specific and frequently invoked rule that the prosecution may not introduce evidence of other criminal acts of the accused unless the evidence is introduced for some purpose other than to suggest that because the defendant is a person of criminal character, it is more probable that he committed the crime for which he is on trial. As Federal and revised Uniform Rule (1986) 404(b) put it:

> Evidence of other crimes, wrongs, or acts is not admissible to prove the character of a person in order to show that he acted in conformity therewith. It may, however, be admissible for other purposes, such as proof of motive, opportunity, intent, preparation, plan, knowledge, identity or absence of mistake or accident.

As the rule indicates, there are numerous uses to which evidence of criminal acts may be put, and those enumerated are neither mutually exclusive nor collectively exhaustive. Subject to such caveats, examination is in order of the principal

---

[5] Copyright © 2000. Reprinted with the permission of West, a Thompson business.

purposes for which the prosecution may introduce evidence of a defendant's bad character. Following this listing, some general observations will be offered about the use of other crimes evidenced for these purposes. The permissible purposes include the following:

(1) To complete the story of the crime on trial by placing it in the context of nearby and nearly contemporaneous happenings. For example, in a prosecution for the murder of one child, the state was allowed to show that the defendant shot the child along with his other children and his wife while they were asleep. The phrases "same transaction" or, less happily, "res gestae" often are used to denote such evidence. This rationale should be applied only when reference to the other crimes is essential to a coherent and intelligible description of the offense at bar.

(2) To prove the existence of a larger plan, scheme, or conspiracy, of which the crime on trial is a part. For example, when a criminal steals a car to use it in a robbery, the automobile theft can be proved in a prosecution for the robbery. Although some courts construe "common plan" more broadly, each crime should be an integral part of an overarching plan explicitly conceived and executed by the defendant or his confederates. This will be relevant as showing motive, and hence the doing of the criminal act, the identity of the actor, or his intention.

(3) To prove other crimes by the accused so nearly identical in method as to earmark them as the handiwork of the accused. Much more is demanded than the mere repeated commission of crimes of the same class, such as repeated murders, robberies or rapes. The pattern and characteristics of the crimes must be so unusual and distinctive as to be like a signature. For example, in *Rex v. Smith*, the "brides of the bath" case, George Joseph Smith was accused of murdering Bessie Mundy by drowning her in the small bathtub of their quarters in a boarding house. Mundy had left all her property to Smith in a will executed after a bigamous marriage ceremony. The trial court allowed the prosecution to show that Smith "married" several other women whom he drowned in their baths after they too left him their property. In all the drownings, Smith took elaborate steps to make it appear that he was not present during the drownings. The Court of Criminal Appeal affirmed the resulting conviction on the ground that the evidence in connection with Mundy's death alone made out a prima facie case, and the other incidents were properly admitted "for the purpose of shewing the design of the appellant."

(4) To show, by similar acts or incidents, that the act in question was not performed inadvertently, accidentally, involuntarily, or without guilty knowledge. *Rex v. Smith* falls in this category. The death of one bride in the bath might be an accident, but three drownings cannot be explained so innocently. Another classic example of the "improbability" logic is the "baby farming" case of *Makin v. Attorney General of New South Wales*. The remains of thirteen infants were discovered in places where John and Sarah Makin were living or had lived, and the Crown charged the Makins with the murder of two of these children. One was identified by his clothing and hair. His mother testified that the Makins had agreed to adopt her son

in exchange for only three pounds. The jury convicted the Makins of murdering the boy whose remains had been identified. On appeal, the couple argued that all the evidence concerning other missing children should not have been admitted. The Privy Council rejected this argument. Although its opinion did little to explain the basis for this conclusion, counsel for the Crown had stressed that "the recurrence of the unusual phenomenon of bodies of babies having been buried in an unexplained manner in a similar part of premises previously occupied" implied that the deaths were "wilful and not accidental." In these cases, the similarities between the act charged and the extrinsic acts need not be as extensive and striking as is required under purpose (3), and the various acts need not be manifestations of an explicit, unifying plan, as required for purpose (2).

(5) To establish motive. The evidence of motive may be probative of the identity of the criminal or of malice or specific intent. This reasoning commonly is applied in cases in which a husband charged with murdering his wife had previously assaulted or threatened her, evincing not merely a general disposition toward violence, but a virulent hostility toward a specific individual.

An application of this principle to cases in which the defendant is charged with conduct that interferes with the enforcement of the law enables the prosecution to prove that the defendant committed a crime that motivated the interference. Finally, a variation of the reasoning permits proof of a consciousness of guilt as evidenced by criminal acts of the accused that are designed to obstruct justice or to avoid punishment for a crime.

(6) To establish opportunity, in the sense of access to or presence at the scene of the crime or in the sense of possessing distinctive or unusual skills or abilities employed in the commission of the crime charged. For example, a defendant charged with a burglary in which a sophisticated alarm system was deactivated might be shown to have neutralized similar systems in the course of other burglaries.

(7) To show, without considering motive, that defendant acted with malice, deliberation, or the requisite specific intent. Thus, weapons seized in an arrest have been held admissible to show an "intent to promote and protect" a conspiracy to import illicit drugs.

(8) To prove identity. Although this is indisputably one of the ultimate purposes for which evidence of other criminal conduct will be received and frequently is included in the list of permissible purposes for other-crimes evidence, it is rarely a distinct ground for admission. Almost always, identity is the inference that flows from one or more of the theories just listed. The second (larger plan), third (distinctive device), and sixth (motive) seem to be most often relied upon to show identity. Certainly, the need to prove identity should not be, in itself, a ticket to admission. In addition, the courts tend to apply stricter standards when the desired inference pertains to identity as opposed to state of mind.

(9) To show a passion or propensity for unusual and abnormal sexual relations. Initially, proof of other sex crimes was confined to offenses involving the

same parties, but many jurisdictions now admit proof of other sex offenses with other persons, at least as to offenses involving sexual aberrations. Federal Rules of Evidence 413 and 414, added by Congress in 1994, allow the broadest conceivable use of "similar crimes" in sexual assault and child molestation cases, making "evidence of defendant's commission" of other such offenses "admissible . . . for its bearing on any matter to which it is relevant."

Unlike the other purposes for other crimes evidence, the sex-crime exception flaunts the general prohibition of evidence whose only purpose is to invite the inference that a defendant who committed a previous crime is disposed toward committing crimes, and therefore is more likely to have committed the one at bar. Although one can argue for such an exception in sex offense cases in which there is some question as to whether the alleged victim consented (or whether the accused might have thought there was consent), a more sweeping exception is particularly difficult to justify. It rests either on an unsubstantiated empirical claim that one rather broad category of criminals are more likely to be repeat offenders than all others or on a policy of giving the prosecution some extra ammunition in its battle against alleged sex criminals.

(10) To impeach an accused who takes the witness stand by introducing past convictions.

A number of procedural and other substantive considerations also affect the admissibility of other crimes evidence pursuant to these ten exceptions. To begin with, the fact that the defendant is guilty of another relevant crime need not be proved beyond a reasonable doubt. The measure of proof that the defendant is guilty of the other crime has been variously described, ranging from "sufficient . . . to support a finding by the jury," to "preponderance," to "substantial," to "clear and convincing." If the applicable standard is satisfied, then the other crimes evidence should be potentially admissible even if the defendant was acquitted of the other charge.

Second, the connection between the evidence and the permissible purpose should be clear, and the issue on which the other crimes evidence is said to bear should be the subject of a genuine controversy. For example, if the prosecution maintains that the other crime reveals defendant's guilty state of mind, then his intent must be disputed. Thus, if the defendant does not deny that the acts were deliberate, the prosecution may not introduce the evidence merely to show that the acts were not accidental. Likewise, if the accused does not deny performing the acts charged, the exceptions pertaining to identification are unavailing.

Finally, even if one or more of the valid purposes for admitting other crimes evidence is appropriately invoked, there is still the need to balance its probative value against the usual counterweights described in § 185. When the sole purpose of the other crimes evidence is to show some propensity to commit the crime at trial, there is no room for ad hoc balancing. The evidence is then unequivocally inadmissible — this is the meaning of the rule against other crimes evidence. But the fact that there is an accepted logical basis for the evidence other than the forbidden one of showing a proclivity for criminality does not preclude the jury from relying on a defendant's apparent propensity toward criminal behavior. Accordingly, most authority recognizes that the problem is not merely one of pigeonholing, but of classifying and then balancing. In deciding whether the danger of unfair prejudice and the like substantially outweighs the incremental probative value, a variety of matters must be considered, including the strength of the evidence as to the commission of the other crime, the similarities between the crimes, the interval of time that has elapsed between the crimes, the need for the evidence, the efficacy of alternative proof, and the degree to which the evidence probably will rouse the jury to overmastering hostility.

[a]   The Threshold for Admissibility for 404(b) Evidence

It is hornbook law that evidence of other bad acts cannot be admitted to demonstrate a defendant's propensity to commit bad acts. Juries are told that the other evidence can only be considered for the purpose, other than propensity, for which the evidence is offered. There is, of course, a real risk that jurors will decide that because the defendant committed one bad act, that he committed the bad act for which he is presently on trial.

With other act evidence, courts have to decide what sort of evidence can be admitted to demonstrate something other than propensity. Courts must also decide whether there is adequate proof of the other act.

The *Beechum* opinion was one of the earliest opinions decided after the adoption of Federal Rule of Evidence 404(b). It holds, as you will discover, that a trial court may admit evidence of other acts under this rule with only a minimal showing that the other act occurred. At the time *Beechum* was decided, this was the minority view, but the Supreme Court adopted this position in *Huddleston v. United States*, 485 U.S. 681 (1988). Quite logically, the Supreme Court would also later decide that acquittal on a charge would not prevent introducing evidence of the act under 404(b). An acquittal is a finding that there is not proof, beyond a reasonable doubt, that an act occurred. As *Beechum* and then *Huddleston* concluded, nothing close to proof beyond a reasonable doubt is required to admit the prior bad act under 404(b).

As you read the majority and dissenting opinions, notice how they seem to be ships passing in the night. The majority seems to pay only lip service to the dissent's concern about the misuses of this sort of evidence. The dissent, for its part, seems to want to deny the possibility that evidence of other bad acts could be admitted, despite the rule.

UNITED STATES v. BEECHUM
United States Court of Appeals, Fifth Circuit
582 F.2d 898 (1978)

TJOFLAT, CIRCUIT JUDGE.

This case comes before the court *en banc* for reconsideration of the circuit's doctrine on the admissibility of offenses extrinsic to a defendant's indictment to prove his criminal intent.[8] That doctrine, deriving in part from the case of *United States v. Broadway*, 477 F.2d 991 (5th Cir. 1973), requires that the essential physical elements of the extrinsic offense include those of the offense charged and that each of these elements be proved by plain, clear, and convincing evidence. We are here called upon to determine the effect of the recently enacted Federal Rules of Evidence on this doctrine, an issue expressly reserved in a number of our cases decided prior to the panel opinion in this case. The panel hearing this case was of the opinion, Judge Gee dissenting, that *Broadway* and its progeny survived intact the enactment of the rules. *United States v. Beechum*, 555 F.2d 487, 504–08 (5th Cir. 1977). With deference to the panel, we must disagree.

A jury convicted Orange Jell Beechum, a substitute letter carrier for the United States Postal Service, of unlawfully possessing an 1890 silver dollar that he knew to be stolen from the mails. . . . To establish that Beechum intentionally and unlawfully possessed the silver dollar, the Government introduced into evidence two Sears, Roebuck & Co. credit cards found in Beechum's wallet when he was arrested. Neither card was issued to Beechum, and neither was signed. The Government also introduced evidence indicating that the cards had been mailed some ten months prior to Beechum's arrest to two different addresses on routes he had serviced. The propriety of the admission of this evidence is the primary issue in this appeal. Before we reach this issue, however, we must round out the facts and note several additional issues.

* * *

---

[8] (Court's original footnote 1.) We shall use the term "extrinsic offense" to denote an "offense," *see infra* this note, for which the defendant is not charged in the indictment that is the subject of the case sub judice. Commentators and cases have referred to such offenses as "prior" or "similar" offenses. We choose to avoid the connotations carried by these more commonly used terms for the following reasons.

The principles governing extrinsic offense evidence are the same whether that offense occurs before or after the offense charged. . . . The term "prior offense" is therefore unnecessarily restrictive and misleading.

"Similar offense" is a phrase that assumes the conclusion that extrinsic offenses are admissible only if similar to the offense charged. Although in a technical sense that is true, the common connotations of the word are misleading. The meaning and significance of similarity depends on the issue to which the extrinsic offense evidence is addressed. . . . Therefore, to avoid an ambiguous application of the term, we shall speak of similarity only when its meaning is clear in context.

We use the term "offense" to include "other crimes, wrongs, or acts," as set forth in Fed. R. Evid. 404(b). *See* Part III. C. *infra*. Our analysis applies whenever the extrinsic activity reflects adversely on the character of the defendant, regardless of whether that activity might give rise to criminal liability.

C. The Extrinsic Offense

At the time of his arrest, Beechum possessed a silver dollar and two credit cards, none of which belonged to him. The only contested issue concerning the silver dollar was whether Beechum intended to turn it in, as he claimed, or to keep it for himself. Apparently, he had possessed the credit cards for some time, perhaps ten months, prior to his arrest. The obvious question is why would Beechum give up the silver dollar if he kept the credit cards. In this case, the Government was entitled to an answer.

It is derogative to the search for truth to allow a defendant to tell his story of innocence without facing him with evidence impeaching that story. A basic premise of our adversary system of justice is that the truth is best attained by requiring a witness to explain contrary evidence if he can. As we have seen, for this reason the defendant who chooses to testify waives his Fifth Amendment privilege with respect to relevant cross-examination. This is not to say that merely by taking the stand a defendant opens himself to the introduction of evidence that is relevant solely to his propensity to commit bad acts or crimes. But where the defendant testifies to controvert an element of the Government's case, such as intent, to which the extrinsic offense is highly relevant, the integrity of the judicial process commands that the defendant be faced with that offense.

In this case, the jury was entitled to assess the credibility of Beechum's explanation but was deprived of the most effective vehicle for determining the veracity of Beechum's story when the judge erroneously allowed Beechum to invoke the Fifth Amendment and avoid the critical question on cross-examination. The Government was relegated to the inferences the jury might draw from the credit cards themselves and the additional evidence relating to them. The panel held that the cards and this evidence were insufficient to satisfy the strict standards for admissibility of extrinsic offense evidence established by *United States v. Broadway*. . . . We agree that *Broadway* dictates that the credit cards should not have been admitted; because this is so, we must reject the *Broadway* standards.

Broadway established two prerequisites to the admissibility of extrinsic offense evidence. First, it required that the physical elements of the extrinsic offense include the essential physical elements of the offense for which the defendant was indicted. Second, the case mandated that each of the physical elements of the extrinsic offense be established by plain, clear, and convincing evidence. The elements of the offense for which Beechum was convicted, . . . include the following: (1) that the defendant possessed the item, (2) that the item was stolen from the mail, (3) that the defendant knew that the item was stolen from the mail, and (4) that the defendant specifically intended to possess the item unlawfully. . . . The first three elements were not disputed, except to the extent that a denial of the fourth renders the item not stolen for the purposes of the second and third elements. The physical elements of the crime are the first two. The panel held that the Government's proof as to the credit cards failed to establish the second element, that the cards were stolen from the mail, by the plain, clear, and convincing evidence required by the second prong of the *Broadway* test. For the purposes of the following analysis, we accept this conclusion as valid.

We must overrule *Broadway* because a straightforward application of the

Federal Rules of Evidence calls for admission of the cards. The directly applicable rule is Fed. R. Evid. 404(b). . . . The rule follows the venerable principle that evidence of extrinsic offenses should not be admitted solely to demonstrate the defendant's bad character. Even though such evidence is relevant, because a man of bad character is more likely to commit a crime than one not, the principle prohibits such evidence because it is inherently prejudicial. *See, e.g., Michelson v. United States,* 335 U.S. 469, 475–76 (1948). Without an issue other than mere character to which the extrinsic offenses are relevant, the probative value of those offenses is deemed insufficient in all cases to outweigh the inherent prejudice. Where, however, the extrinsic offense evidence is relevant to an issue such as intent, it may well be that the evidence has probative force that is not substantially outweighed by its inherent prejudice. If this is so, the evidence may be admissible.

What the rule calls for is essentially a two-step test. First, it must be determined that the extrinsic offense evidence is relevant to an issue other than the defendant's character. Second, the evidence must possess probative value that is not substantially outweighed by its undue prejudice and must meet the other requirements of rule 403. . . . The test for relevancy under the first step is identical to the one we have already encountered. The standards are established by rule 401, which deems evidence relevant when it has "any tendency to make the existence of any fact that is of consequence to the determination of the action more probable or less probable than it would be without the evidence." Where the evidence sought to be introduced is an extrinsic offense, its relevance is a function of its similarity to the offense charged. In this regard, however, similarity means more than that the extrinsic and charged offense have a common characteristic. For the purposes of determining relevancy, "a fact is similar to another only when the common characteristic is the significant one for the purpose of the inquiry at hand." . . . Therefore, similarity, and hence relevancy, is determined by the inquiry or issue to which the extrinsic offense is addressed.

Where the issue addressed is the defendant's intent to commit the offense charged, the relevancy of the extrinsic offense derives from the defendant's indulging himself in the same state of mind in the perpetration of both the extrinsic and charged offenses. The reasoning is that because the defendant had unlawful intent in the extrinsic offense, it is less likely that he had lawful intent in the present offense.[9] . . . Under *Broadway,* that the defendant had unlawful intent in the

---

[9] (Court's original footnote 15.) It is crucial to distinguish the use of extrinsic offense evidence to prove issues other than intent. In other contexts different standards apply because the inference to be drawn from the extrinsic offense is not based upon the reasoning applicable here. To illustrate this proposition and to place our discussion in the proper context, we digress briefly and examine the use of extrinsic offense evidence in other settings.

Evidence of extrinsic offenses may be admissible to show motive, which has been defined as "the reason that nudges the will and prods the mind to indulge the criminal intent,". . . . For example, the prosecution may establish impecuniousness as a motive for robbery by showing that the defendant had been threatened for nonpayment of a debt incurred in a drug transaction. . . . The only point of similarity between the charged and extrinsic offenses in this instance is that the same individual committed both. Therefore, overall similarity is not required when the offense is introduced to show motive.

Such evidence is admissible to indicate knowledge. Thus, the Government may prove that the defendant knowingly had purchased counterfeit currency on a prior occasion. . . . Again, similarity of

commission of the extrinsic offense is established by requiring the Government to prove each element of that offense by plain, clear, and convincing evidence. And the extrinsic evidence is deemed admissible only if its physical elements include those of the offense charged. We think that *Broadway* runs afoul of the Federal Rules of Evidence by imposing on the Government too strict a standard of proof and by requiring too close an identity of elements.

Obviously, the line of reasoning that deems an extrinsic offense relevant to the issue of intent is valid only if an offense was in fact committed and the defendant in fact committed it. Therefore, as a predicate to a determination that the extrinsic offense is relevant, the Government must offer proof demonstrating that the defendant committed the offense. If the proof is insufficient, the judge must exclude the evidence because it is irrelevant. The issue we must decide is by what standard the trial court is to determine whether the Government has come forward with sufficient proof.

The standard of proof for ruling upon factual conditions to relevancy is supplied by Fed. R. Evid. 104(b). . . . As the rule provides, the task for the trial judge is to determine whether there is sufficient evidence for the jury to find that the defendant in fact committed the extrinsic offense. . . . The judge need not be convinced beyond a reasonable doubt that the defendant committed the extrinsic offense, nor need he require the Government to come forward with clear and convincing proof. The standard for the admissibility of extrinsic offense evidence is that of rule 104(b): "the preliminary fact can be decided by the judge against the proponent only where the jury could not reasonably find the preliminary fact to exist." . . .

Once it is determined that the extrinsic offense requires the same intent as the charged offense and that the jury could find that the defendant committed the extrinsic offense, the evidence satisfies the first step under rule 404(b). The extrinsic offense is relevant (assuming the jury finds the defendant to have committed it) to

---

the physical elements of the crime need not be established. The extrinsic offense need merely be of such a nature that its commission involved the same knowledge required for the offense charged.

The identity of the defendant may be established by evidence of offenses extrinsic to the indictment. In this instance, the likeness of the offenses is the crucial consideration. The physical similarity must be such that it marks the offenses as the handiwork of the accused. In other words, the evidence must demonstrate a modus operandi. . . . Thus, "[a] much greater degree of similarity between the charged crime and the uncharged crime is required when the evidence of the other crime is introduced to prove identity than when it is introduced to prove a state of mind." . . . As an example, a prior conviction for possession of heroin may not in itself establish that in an unrelated prosecution a defendant possessed heroin with intent to distribute. If, however, that conviction and the charged offense involved white heroin, an extremely rare type in the region, a distinctiveness may be established that is sufficient to allow admission of the prior offense to show identity. . . .

Extrinsic offenses may be admitted if part of a common plan, scheme, or design. Although this category encompasses a variety of circumstances, . . . we shall address only one. If the uncharged offense is "so linked together in point of time and circumstances with the crime charged that one cannot be fully shown without proving the other, the general rule of exclusion does not apply." . . . Evidence admitted under this test is termed part of the *res gestae* of the crime charged. . . .

We have taken this opportunity to digress to point out that the meaning and nature of the "similarity" requirement in extrinsic offense doctrine are not fixed quantities. Each case must be decided in its own context, with the issue to which the offense is directed firmly in mind.

an issue other than propensity because it lessens the likelihood that the defendant committed the charged offense with innocent intent. . . . It is not necessary that the physical elements of the charged and extrinsic offenses concur for this inference to be drawn and relevancy established. If the elements do match, the extrinsic offense may have greater probative value, but this is not an issue of relevancy. Evidence is relevant once it appears "to alter the probabilities of a consequential fact." . . . The probative value of the evidence is a matter to be weighed against its potential for undue prejudice, and the similarity of the physical elements of the charged and extrinsic offenses figures in at this stage. Therefore, we turn to the second step of the analysis required by rule 404(b), whether the evidence satisfies rule 403.

As we have stated, the central concern of rule 403 is whether the probative value of the evidence sought to be introduced is "substantially outweighed by the danger of unfair prejudice." *Broadway* would reverse this standard by requiring a high degree of similarity between the extrinsic and charged offenses and a stringent standard of proof. In effect, the case attempts to establish a threshold requirement that the evidence possess great probative value before it can be admitted. This requirement not only contravenes rule 403 but also fails to meet its own declared ends. Demanding that the Government prove by excessive evidence each physical element of the extrinsic offense does not necessarily enhance its probative value and may in fact increase its unfair prejudice. One of the dangers inherent in the admission of extrinsic offense evidence is that the jury may convict the defendant not for the offense charged but for the extrinsic offense. . . . This danger is particularly great where, as here, the extrinsic activity was not the subject of a conviction; the jury may feel that the defendant should be punished for that activity even if he is not guilty of the offense charged. Moreover, "[e]ven if the jury is no more disposed to punish the accused for his unpunished past crimes, 'over-persuasion' may lead them to conclude that, having committed a crime of the type charged, he is likely to repeat it." . . . It is for fear that the jury would draw just this inference that extrinsic offense evidence is excluded when it is relevant solely to the issue of the defendant's character. The touchstone of the trial judge's analysis in this context should be whether the Government has proved the extrinsic offense sufficiently to allow the jury to determine that the defendant possessed the same state of mind at the time he committed the extrinsic offense as he allegedly possessed when he committed the charged offense. Forcing the Government to "overpersuade" the jury that the defendant committed an offense of substantial similarity engenders excessive and unnecessary prejudice.

The task for the court in its ascertainment of probative value and unfair prejudice under rule 403 calls for a common sense assessment of all the circumstances surrounding the extrinsic offense. As the Advisory Committee Notes to rule 404(b) state: "No mechanical solution is offered. The determination must be made whether the danger of undue prejudice outweighs the probative value of the evidence in view of the availability of other means of proof and other facts appropriate for making a decision of this kind under Rule 403." . . .

Probity in this context is not an absolute; its value must be determined with regard to the extent to which the defendant's unlawful intent is established by other evidence, stipulation, or inference. It is the incremental probity of the evidence that is to be balanced against its potential for undue prejudice. . . . Thus, if the Government has a strong case on the intent issue, the extrinsic offense may add little and consequently will be excluded more readily. . . . If the defendant's intent is not contested, then the incremental probative value of the extrinsic offense is inconsequential when compared to its prejudice; therefore, in this circumstance the evidence is uniformly excluded.[10] . . . In measuring the probative value of the evidence, the judge should consider the overall similarity of the extrinsic and charged offenses. If they are dissimilar except for the common element of intent, the extrinsic offense may have little probative value to counterbalance the inherent prejudice of this type of evidence. Of course, equivalence of the elements of the charged and extrinsic offenses is not required. But the probative value of the extrinsic offense correlates positively with its likeness to the offense charged.[11] Whether the extrinsic offense is sufficiently similar in its physical elements so that its probative value is not substantially outweighed by its undue prejudice is a matter within the sound discretion of the trial judge. The judge should also consider how much time separates the extrinsic and charged offenses: temporal remoteness depreciates the probity of the extrinsic offense. . . .

As this case demonstrates, a significant consideration in determining the probative value of extrinsic offense evidence is the posture of the case. If at the commencement of trial it is not certain that the defendant will contest the issue of intent, the judge is in a poor position to weigh the probative value against the prejudice of the evidence because he cannot foresee the nature or extent of either the Government's case or the defendant's response. Whether a mere plea of not guilty justifies the Government in introducing extrinsic offense evidence in its case in chief is an open question in this circuit. . . . We need not now answer it. Although the credit cards in this case were introduced by the Government in its case-in-chief,

---

[10] (Court's original footnote 19.) Although it would seem that the extrinsic offense would be irrelevant if the issue of intent were not contested, the rules apparently deem evidence that has probative force with regard to an uncontested issue to be relevant.

The fact to which the evidence is directed need not be in dispute. While situations will arise which call for the exclusion of evidence offered to prove a point conceded by the opponent, the ruling should be made on the basis of such considerations as waste of time and undue prejudice (see Rule 403), rather than under any general requirement that evidence is admissible only if directed to matters in dispute.

Advisory Committee Notes to Rule 401. Where, however, intent is not an element of the crime charged, extrinsic offense evidence directed to that issue would be irrelevant and therefore subject to exclusion under rule 402. . . .

[11] (Court's original footnote 20.) It is true as well that the more closely the extrinsic offense resembles the charged offense, the greater the prejudice to the defendant. The likelihood that the jury will convict the defendant because he is the kind of person who commits this particular type of crime or because he was not punished for the extrinsic offense increases with the increasing likeness of the offenses. Of course, it is also true that this prejudice is likely to be less when the extrinsic activity is not of a criminal nature. . . .

In any event, the judge must consider the danger of undue prejudice of this type when he determines whether to admit the extrinsic offense evidence. The judge should be mindful that the test under rule 403 is whether the probative value of the evidence is substantially outweighed by its unfair prejudice. As one commentator has put it, "the discretionary policy against undue prejudice would seem to require exclusion only in those instances where the trial judge believes that there is a genuine risk that the emotions of the jury will be excited to irrational behavior, and that this risk is disproportionate to the probative value of the offered evidence." . . .

it was clear before the case went to trial that the crucial issue would be Beechum's intent. In effect all the other elements of the crime for which Beechum was indicted were conceded. . . . Where it is evident that intent will be an issue at trial, we have held the admission of the extrinsic offense as part of the Government's case-in-chief not to be grounds for reversal. . . . In any event, Beechum waived any objection he might have had to the Government's order of proof when he took the stand and professed the innocence of his intent.

We shall now apply the precepts we have set forth to the facts of this case. As we have demonstrated above, the credit card evidence is relevant to Beechum's intent with respect to the silver dollar. That Beechum possessed the credit cards with illicit intent diminishes the likelihood that at the same moment he intended to turn in the silver dollar. If there is sufficient evidence to establish that Beechum wrongfully possessed the credit cards, the requirement of the first step under rule 404(b), that the evidence be relevant to an issue other than propensity, is met. This is so even if the evidence were insufficient for a finding that the cards were stolen from the mail. As we have said, relevancy is established once the identity of the significant state of mind is established. The similarity of the physical elements of the extrinsic and charged offenses is a measure of probity.

The standard for determining whether the evidence is sufficient for a finding that Beechum wrongfully possessed the credit cards is provided by rule 104(b): whether the evidence would support such a finding by the jury. We think the evidence in the record clearly supports a finding that Beechum possessed the credit cards with the intent not to relinquish them to their rightful owners. Beechum possessed the credit cards of two different individuals. Neither card had been signed by the person to whom it was issued. When asked about the cards, Beechum answered first that the only cards he had were his own. When confronted with the credit cards, which were obviously not his own, Beechum responded that they had never been used. He refused to respond further because the inspector "had all the answers." The logical inference from this statement is that Beechum was attempting to mitigate his culpability, having been caught red-handed. The undisputed evidence indicated that he could have possessed the cards for some ten months. The jury would have been wholly justified in finding that Beechum possessed these cards with the intent permanently to deprive the owners of them. This is all the rules require the court to determine to establish the relevancy of the extrinsic offense evidence.

We move now to the second step of the rule 404(b) analysis, the application of rule 403. The incremental probity of the extrinsic offense evidence in this case approaches its intrinsic value. Indeed, the posture of this case and the nature of the Government's proof with respect to the intent issue present perhaps the most compelling circumstance for the admission of extrinsic offense evidence. From the very inception of trial, it was clear that the crucial issue in the case would be Beechum's intent in possessing the silver dollar. He took the stand to proclaim that he intended to surrender the coin to his supervisor. The issue of intent was therefore clearly drawn, and the policies of justice that require a defendant to explain evidence that impugns his exculpatory testimony were in full force. As we have seen, these policies dictate that a defendant waive his Fifth Amendment privilege against self-incrimination as to cross-examination relevant to his testimony. Where a privilege so central to our notions of fairness and justice yields to the search for truth, we should not lightly obstruct that quest. The credit card evidence bore directly on the plausibility of Beechum's story; justice called for its admission.

That the posture of this case demanded the admission of the credit card evidence is reinforced by the nature of the Government's proof on the issue of intent apart from that evidence. This proof consisted of the following. The Government called Cox, Beechum's supervisor, who testified that Beechum had had several opportunities to surrender the coin to him. Beechum denied this, and called two fellow employees who testified that Beechum had asked them if they had seen Cox. Absent the credit card evidence, the issue would have been decided wholly by the jury's assessment of the credibility of these witnesses. The Government, therefore, did not make out such a strong case of criminal intent that the credit card evidence would have been of little incremental probity. In fact, the credit card evidence may have been determinative.

The overall similarity of the extrinsic and charged offenses in this case generates sufficient probity to meet the rule 403 test that the probative value of the evidence not be substantially outweighed by its unfair prejudice. We think this to be true even if it could not be established that the credit cards were stolen from the mail. At the least, there was sufficient evidence for the jury to find that Beechum possessed property belonging to others, with the specific intent to deprive the owners of their rightful possession permanently. That Beechum entertained such intent with respect to the credit cards renders less believable the story that he intended to turn in the coin in this instance. The force of this inference is not appreciably diminished by the failure of the Government to prove that the cards actually were stolen from the mail.

The probity of the credit card evidence in this case is augmented by the lack of temporal remoteness. Although Beechum may have obtained the cards as much as ten months prior to his arrest for the possession of the silver dollar, he kept the cards in his wallet where they would constantly remind him of the wrongfulness of their possession. In effect, Beechum's state of mind with respect to the credit cards continued through his arrest. He maintained contemporaneously the wrongful intent with respect to the cards and the intent as regards the coin. The force of the probity of this circumstance is illustrated by what Beechum would have had to convince the jury in order to avoid it. He would have been forced to argue that his state of mind was schizoid — that he intended at the same time to relinquish the coin but to keep the cards. This situation does not differ significantly from one in which a thief is caught with a bag of loot, is charged with the larceny as to one of the items, but claims that he intended to return that item. Would any reasonable jury believe this story when it is established that he had stolen the rest of the loot?

The remaining considerations under rule 403 do not alter our conclusion as to the admissibility of the extrinsic offense evidence in this case. The extrinsic offense here is not of a heinous nature; it would hardly incite the jury to irrational decision by its force on human emotion. The credit card evidence was no more likely to confuse the issue, mislead the jury, cause undue delay, or waste time than any other type of extrinsic offense evidence. Since the need for the evidence in this case was great, it can hardly be said that the admission of the cards constituted "needless presentation of cumulative evidence."

It is significant that the court was careful to allay, as much as limiting instructions can, the undue prejudice engendered by the credit card evidence. It gave extensive instructions to the jury on the limited use of extrinsic offense evidence employed to prove unlawful intent.

Having examined at length the circumstances of this case, we conclude that the credit card evidence meets the requirements of rule 403. Therefore, the conditions imposed by the second step of the analysis under rule 404(b) have been met, and the extrinsic offense evidence in this case was properly admitted at trial.

Affirmed.

GOLDBERG, CIRCUIT JUDGE, dissenting.

As the lights are being extinguished on *Broadway*, I feel impelled to light a few candles in requiem.

The majority has gone well out of its way to overrule *Broadway*. In the panel opinion, the panel majority explained why the policies and doctrines of *Broadway* are sound. I affirm those views here. But I must add a few comments because the opinion of the en banc majority leaves the law in this area in such a confused state. In this dissent I make two broad arguments. First I show how the majority misinterpreted Rule 404(b) of the Federal Rules of Evidence. Basically the majority's reading of the rule fails because it reads so broadly the second sentence in Rule 404(b), which makes certain evidence admissible, that it allows the second sentence to swallow up the first sentence of Rule 404(b), which explicitly bars the admissibility of certain evidence. In addition, this too broad reading of Rule 404(b)'s second sentence conflicts with explicit language in other related federal evidence rules, such as Rules 609 and 608. Finally I note that no other circuit or legal commentator has seen in Rule 404(b) the same destructive and revolutionary intent that the majority apparently sees. On the contrary, many circuits calmly preserved doctrines similar to *Broadway* in the wake of Rule 404(b)'s passage, often even terming the rule a codification of their law. My second broad argument concerns the test with which the majority replaces *Broadway*. I argue that not only is this test little more than a subjective, difficult to apply version of *Broadway*, but that is even more hostile to extrinsic offense evidence than *Broadway* in some respects.

I. The Majority Misinterprets Rule 404(b)

A. The Majority's Too Broad Reading of the Second Sentence in Rule 404(b) Allows It to Swallow Up the First Sentence.

*   *   *

Rule 404(b) seems to me to identify two conflicting policies and to require the courts to reconcile them. One policy is that extrinsic acts evidence is sometimes probative of material facts. For that reason, the second sentence authorized us to reason from unrelated past acts and states of mind to current states of mind. But at the same time the drafters of the rule were wary of such reasoning. Thus they wrote the first sentence. Its purpose is to caution us that extrinsic acts evidence is fraught with dangers of prejudice — extraordinary dangers not presented by other types of evidence. Had the drafters not thought the dangers were extraordinary, they would never have given us the first sentence; they would have written only the second sentence and the general balancing test of Rule 403. *Broadway* and similar doctrines were designed precisely to deal with such extraordinary dangers.

The majority reads this rule differently. It thinks that so long as the probative value of extrinsic acts evidence is not "substantially outweighed" by its prejudicial effect, Rule 403, the evidence is to be admitted. . . . How does the majority dispose of the first sentence, then? Here is where, to my mind, it seriously misapprehends the rule. The majority reads the rule to establish two watertight compartments: extrinsic acts evidence which relates "solely to . . . the defendant's character," . . . and that which is relevant for other purposes, including state of mind. Thus the majority thinks the rule unequivocally allows us to reason that because a defendant displayed an improper intent in the past, he is more likely to have had an evil intent in the act for which he is tried. . . . How this differs from reasoning that the defendant has a "propensity" to act with evil intent, . . . is beyond reason; but the majority says the rule prohibits references based on propensity. There simply are no such watertight compartments to be found, unless we engage in subtle and sophisticated metaphysical analysis.

* * *

Moreover, the majority's "watertight compartment" view of Rule 404(b) leads to a conclusion that the first sentence of Rule 404(b) is superfluous. Simply, evidence which is probative "solely" of bad character and not of any fact related to the elements of the crime, such as intent, identity, etc., is inadmissible in any event, under Rule 401, because it is irrelevant. . . .

To be sure, I find it nearly impossible to imagine any "extrinsic offense" which would make a jury think that the defendant had a bad character or a criminal propensity, but which did not also have at least some tendency to make it less probable than it would be without the evidence that he had a purely innocent, law-abiding intent in the charged offense. But, more importantly, if such "extrinsic offense" evidence were so purely irrelevant to intent and to the other elements of the charged crime, I cannot see how it could pass the Rule 401 relevancy test even to necessitate the application of the Rule 404(b) bar to its admission.

The "watertight compartment" view of Rule 404(b) could lead to other peculiarities as well. Constrained by the explicit words of Rule 404(b), the majority concedes that extrinsic offense evidence which relates "solely" to a defendant's propensity to commit the charged crime is barred by the first sentence of Rule 404(b), no matter how much its probative value outweighs its prejudicial effect. But when a judge thinks the extrinsic offense also relates to the defendant's propensity to intend to commit the charged crime, then the question leaps over to the second watertight compartment, where the presumption is heavily in favor of admitting the evidence, unless its probative value is substantially outweighed by prejudice. The alchemy of the majority opinion would radically change the rule from a total bar of the evidence regardless of the probative-prejudice balance to a balancing test substantially weighted in favor of admissibility, simply because a judge metaphysically classifies the question as propensity to intend rather than as propensity to commit. Since propensity is largely a concept of a person's psychological bent or frame of mind, it seems extreme to have so much turn on so little, if any, of a distinction. I respectfully refuse to adopt the majority's Dr. Jekyll-Mr. Hyde interpretation of Rule 404(b). It is a horror fantasy that should pass by the boards of *Broadway*.[12]

B. The Majority's Reading of Rule 404(b) Conflicts With the Explicit Language in Rules 609 and 608

Another problem with the majority's interpretation of the vague language in Rule 404(b) is that it conflicts with the specific language in Rules 608 and 609. Suppose, for example, that Beechum had been convicted of fraudulent use of credit cards 10 years before his trial for the coin theft. Under Rule 609, if Beechum took the stand his credibility could be impeached with evidence of the prior conviction only if the probative value of the prior offense substantially outweighed its prejudicial impact on the jury. If the conviction had been more recent than 10 years ago, then the test would be a simple weighing of probativeness and prejudice.

Next, suppose that the evidence of the prior offense were clear and convincing, but that the defendant had never been convicted for it. In this case, Rule 608 would forbid any admission of the evidence of the prior offense except for what could be elicited from the defendant on the stand. If the defendant chose to exercise his Fifth Amendment right of silence, then no evidence of the prior offense could reach the jury.

Now, finally, consider the result under the majority's reading of Rule 404(b). Here the evidence of a prior offense is independently admissible to the jury, as long as its probative value is not substantially outweighed by its prejudicial impact. The prior offense need not be proved beyond a reasonable doubt, as in Rule 609, nor even clearly and convincingly, as might be the case under Rule 608, but rather only to the minimal Rule 104 standard, *i.e.*, where a reasonable jury might find the defendant committed the crime. This leads to a bizarre anomaly. According to the majority, the government under Rule 404(b) can submit with ease prejudicial, flimsy evidence of an extrinsic offense, but under Rule 609, where the crime was proved beyond a reasonable doubt, the admissions standards are much stricter. Under Rule 608, the evidence is inadmissible entirely except from the defendant's own mouth, even if the evidence of the other crime is clear and convincing, or established beyond a reasonable doubt. You might say then that, for purposes of admitting extrinsic offense evidence, the majority of this court may at times presume a defendant guilty

---

[12] (Dissent's original footnote 5.) At worst, of course, the extreme result of the majority position might even be that the first sentence in Rule 404(b) effectively applies only to crimes in which criminal intent is not an element.

Even where intent is not disputed by the defendant, the majority notes extrinsic offense evidence would still be relevant and admissible. Thus, it might be that once intent is an element of the crime — as it is with almost all crimes — then the defendant is left only with the minimal protection afforded by the "substantial prejudice" test in Rule 403. Such a lop-sided reading of Rule 404(b) is sheer illogic. More importantly, it invites a flagrant abuse of the rights of accused citizens.

To escape this unthinkable result, the majority reads into Rule 401 a "same intent" requirement that is little more than a subjective version of *Broadway*, and in some way is even stricter than *Broadway*. This aspect of the majority opinion is discussed in Part II *infra*.

until he is proven guilty beyond a reasonable doubt, at which point the court may begin presuming him innocent.

C. The Majority's View of Rule 404(b) Conflicts with the Views of Other Circuits and with Leading Commentators

The majority is of the opinion that Rule 404(b) demands that *Broadway* be strictly overruled. . . . No other circuit or legal commentator has come close to giving the rule such destructive force or intent. The Eighth Circuit has calmly preserved a doctrine similar to *Broadway*, citing for authority pre-Rule 404(b) cases, post-Rule 404(b) cases, and the rule itself.

The Ninth Circuit, terming the rule a codification of prior case law, continues to apply the same test as the Eighth Circuit, including the "clear and convincing" proof requirement.

The Seventh Circuit has continued its use of the same three-part test used by the Eighth and Ninth Circuits, including the "clear and convincing" evidence requirement, calling the test "well established."

Other circuits also have maintained tests much stricter than the test the majority here feels is required by Rule 404(b). For example, the Sixth circuit still requires a "substantial similarity" between the extrinsic and charged offenses as a "prerequisite to qualify for one of the exceptions" in Rule 404(b). The Second Circuit continues to apply its "well-established" threshold test that evidence of the "similar" extrinsic acts must be *substantially* relevant for a purpose other than merely to show defendant's criminal character or disposition." (Emphasis added.) Even the Third Circuit, which has one of the least rigid Rule 404(b) tests in the country, sees the rule as codifying its requirement that the probative value must outweigh the prejudice, rather than our majority's "substantially outweighed" by prejudice test. Weinstein's Evidence also concludes the rule has little or no impact on the case law.

Even the Advisory Committee Notes cast doubt on the majority's sense that Rule 404(b) compels us to use the "substantially outweighed" test in Rule 403. The Notes say: No mechanical solution is offered. The determination must be made whether the danger of undue prejudice outweighs the probative value of the evidence in view of the availability of other means of proof and other facts appropriate for making decisions of this kind under Rule 403. . . .

Thus, the Notes seem to advise use of a straight-forward prejudice/probativeness balancing test, not the "substantially outweighed" test of Rule 403.[13]

II. The Majority Replaces *Broadway* with a Worse Test

If Rule 404(b) were no more than the intersection of Rules 104, 401 and 403, as the majority at times implies, then the prosecution of any crime in which intent was an element could include evidence of any extrinsic wrong-doing of the defendant

---

[13] (Dissent's original footnote 16.) The Notes' reference to Rule 403 is only to the kinds of facts "appropriate" under Rule 403, not to that rule's "substantially outweighed" test. . . .

which had any tendency to prove that it was less probable he acted with law-abiding intent (Rule 401), and which evidence had a prejudicial effect which might outweigh its probativeness, but not substantially (Rule 403).[14] Instead the majority restricts this hopelessly broad floodgate for extrinsic offense evidence by building into Rule 401 a "similarity" test reminiscent of *Broadway*. Strictly speaking, the relevance test in Rule 401 is no more than a requirement that the evidence have some "tendency" to change the probability of a consequential fact, such as criminal intent. But the majority adds to this simple, albeit grossly overbroad threshold test, the requirement that the intent of the extrinsic crime be the "same" as the intent of the charged crime.

*   *   *

The majority nowhere explains where it gets this additional test. It is no more stated in Rules 401, 403 and 404 than is *Broadway*. Admittedly it does seem to serve the same critical function of preventing the second sentence in Rule 404(b) from swallowing the first. Nevertheless, it is a poor replacement for *Broadway* for two reasons. First, it replaces *Broadway's* objective test of similar physical elements with a subjective, psychological test of determining when a defendant was "indulging . . . in the same state of mind in the perpetration of both the . . . offenses." Second, in some situations it could be even more hostile to the admission of extrinsic offense evidence than *Broadway* was.

A. The Majority's New Similarity Test is a Subjective Version of *Broadway*

The majority's "psychological indulgence" test seems to call on a district judge to decide whether the defendant "indulged himself" in the "same state of mind" in the preparation of two crimes. It totally escapes me how one would go about making this decision. If a person snatches a purse, cheats on his income taxes, and then steals a coin from the mail, is he "indulging himself in the same state of mind in the perpetration" of the offenses? Would a court say, for example, that the defendant is "indulging himself in the same state of mind in the perpetration" of these offenses because, at some point in each offense, he intends to possess property rightfully belonging or owed to another? Moreover, is this Freudian and ill-defined type of psychoanalysis required, or even suggested, by Rule 401's definition of relevance?

It was precisely this impossibility of comparing psychological states of mind that led *Broadway* to settle on a simple comparison of only the physical elements of the two crimes. As is demonstrated in the next section, the issue of the strictness of a test can be kept entirely separate from whether the test turns on subjective or objective factors. Thus I do not see what the majority accomplishes by telling a

---

[14] (Dissent's original footnote 17.) This standard would be as unfair as it is all encompassing, given that criminal defendants invariably tend to live in the real world, which is not inhabited by saints alone. (Even visitors to Broadway must travel a few paces on 42nd Street before reaching the comfort and safety of their loge seats). The plain fact is that many people think there is a criminal "type" who not only has a bad "character," but everything that goes with it — bad intentions, bad motives, bad plans, etc. This kind of thinking is inimical to the principles of due process and presumed innocence that dignify our criminal system. In this country our government simply may not deprive one of its citizens of his freedom unless it charges that he committed a specific crime and proves beyond a reasonable doubt that he committed that specific crime.

district judge to match up psychological indulgences rather than physical elements. The new test seems to add little to the effort except hazy uncertainty. One might even say that the majority did not overrule *Broadway* at all; it simply moved it from Times Square to the Bermuda Triangle.

B. The Majority's "Psychological Indulgence" Test Could Be Even Stricter Than *Broadway*

Needless to say, turning a test of objective facts into a test of subjective facts does not necessarily make it a looser test. In fact, in this case there is a good chance that the majority's "psychological indulgence" test could be even more hostile to extrinsic offense evidence than was *Broadway*. The majority deludes itself on this point by defining *Broadway* too harshly. Specifically, the majority seems to think that *Broadway* requires a one-to-one correspondence between all the physical elements of the two offenses. This is wrong. In fact, in this case the panel opinion even left open the question whether both thefts had to involve the mails. For example, it might be possible that *Broadway* would be satisfied by an extrinsic offense involving a theft of credit cards from a neighbor's wallet, as long as the essential physical elements of theft were shared and there was "some basis for an inference of similarity between the mental elements of the extrinsic and charged offenses." . . . As the panel opinion said,

> we must not demand perfect identity between the prior and charged offenses or impose mechanical requirements that lose sight of the under-lying purpose of the rule. Broadway's requirement that the essential physical elements of the charged offense be matched by physical elements of the prior conduct allows a surprising degree of flexibility to this end. . . .

But in its "psychological indulgence" test, the majority requires much more than "some basis for an inference of similarity between the mental elements." To be specific, the majority requires that the government must prove "the extrinsic offense sufficiently to allow the jury to determine that the defendant possessed the *same state of mind* at the time he committed the extrinsic offense as he allegedly possessed when he committed the charged offense." (emphasis added). . . .

We might easily imagine a situation in which two crimes involved the same essential physical elements and in which there was "some basis for an inference of similarity between the mental elements" of the two crimes, but in which there was not enough evidence to support a jury determination that the defendant possessed the same state of mind in both cases. For example, imagine a defendant who stole two cars, one for a joy ride around the block and one to resell surreptitiously. *Broadway* might allow in evidence of the joy ride, whereas the "psychological indulgence" test might not.

Conclusion

The concepts in this case are not simplistic. But our task is made especially difficult here by the language we use to solve it. We are all guilty to some extent (mea culpa) of indulging in jurisprudential jargon. But the analysis of the majority too often bogs down by trying to solve problems with a few keys words, phrases and clauses, such as "substantially outweighed," "relevance," "probative," "similarity," "prejudicial effect," and the like. To make matters worse, the majority debases these words by trading their established meanings for its own language of semantic subjectivity, such as its "psychological indulgence" test.

At the heart of the majority's error in this case is its mistaken placement of the spotlight on the Federal Rules of Evidence, instead of where it rightfully belongs — on the criminal trial of a human being. The majority places the vague and uninformed stage hands of the drama — the Federal Rules of Evidence — in the center of the stage, and pushes the principles of a fair criminal trial into weak, whispered supporting roles off to the edge of the proscenium wall. This means the death of *Broadway*, the majority admits. But it is also an assault on the legitimacy of our criminal system. The majority was, and is, misdirected. The Federal Rules can be supporting actors, at most. They must be directed one way in a civil trial and another in a criminal trial where human freedom is at stake. Rule 404(b), and most of the other federal rules as well, were designed to be broadly applicable to both criminal and civil trials. But evidence is allowed into a civil trial under a much more flexible, utilitarian standard than in a criminal trial. Due process requires extreme vigilance against the contamination of a criminal trial with cheap and mean character slander, and against the conviction of a citizen for improper reasons. The majority cannot possibly think that Rule 404(b) overrules this central principle of justice, or that it collapses the criminal trial into the utilitarianism of civil litigation.

Broadway may not be stylish, it may not be chic, but its old-fashioned virtues should command our reverence. *Broadway* was one more last bastion of judging a man by the specifics of the charged crime, rather than by a vague, undocumented, unauthenticated record of misbehavior. The protective mantle of presumed innocence is under severe attack in some modern-day jurisprudence, but the majority's Cain marks become almost ineradicable. The majority's opinion goes far in making one slip a noose.

At the heart of this dissent is a concern about the proper level of hostility or hospitality to extrinsic offense evidence. But in this dissent I am even more concerned about the practicality and integrity of the analysis this circuit will employ in making these judgments. In this case the majority has obliterated a venerable, well-reasoned body of law for no good reason at all, and has replaced it with a Freudian, difficult to apply subjective test that, outside this and a few other similar cases, will not even accomplish what the majority wants. It is especially ironic that the majority should justify its evisceration of *Broadway* by declaring that the "revolutionary" drafters of Rule 404(b) wanted the old standards cleared from the stage to make room for the free form, uncontrolled balancing-test discretion of the new Theatre of the Absurd. For no sooner were the objective flats and screen of the legitimate *Broadway* stage pulled aside, than the majority brought in the psychological psychedelics of the Theatre of Indulgence. I can only hope that the majority will soon see the error of its ways and return to the Great White Way of *Broadway* with the appreciation and respect that the grand old boulevard deserves.

I would reverse the judgment of the district court and remand the case for a new trial.

[b]   Using Evidence Under 404(b) to Show Knowledge or Intent

In *Beechum*, the Fifth Circuit was considering whether the defendant intended to return a gold coin in his possession. The Court held that the jury could consider that the defendant had in his possession credit cards belonging to others on his possession for 10 months to evaluate whether he intended to return the gold coin. Some cases, like *Beechum*, are relatively easy, though it is difficult to see how this evidence is not just a specific type of propensity evidence. Other cases for admission under 404(b) are easily imagined. If the defendant previously possessed marijuana, it raises the odds that he knew the item in his possession was marijuana. If the defendant previously distributed marijuana, this raises the odds that he intended to distribute marijuana in his possession. The *Davis* opinion offers a much closer case involving possession of drugs with intent to distribute. The extent to which the other bad act evidence bears on an issue other than propensity is, of course, a question of degree. *Davis* will provide you tools for understanding how to evaluate whether the other bad act evidence is sufficiently probative of an issue other than the defendant's propensity to commit crimes.

UNITED STATES v. DAVIS
United States Court of Appeals, Third Circuit
726 F.3d 434 (2013)

SMITH, CIRCUIT JUDGE.

Police arrested Terrell Davis after finding him in a Jeep with nearly a kilo of cocaine in the backseat. The arrest led to a conviction for possession with intent to distribute. As evidence that Davis recognized the cocaine in the Jeep, the government proved at trial that he had two prior convictions for possessing cocaine. Yet the government never proved that the cocaine from his past was similar in appearance, quantity, or form. We acknowledge that some of our cases admitting prior criminal acts under Federal Rule of Evidence 404(b) have been expansive. But our expansiveness is finite, and this case crosses the line. We will vacate Davis's conviction and remand.

I

The events at issue took place on a wintry afternoon over two years ago. Two Philadelphia police officers were patrolling near 5100 Market Street — roughly four miles west of Independence Hall and the Liberty Bell. This is a dangerous part of the city where drug deals and robberies are commonplace. Officer Clifford Gilliam parked his patrol car, and Officer Shawn Witherspoon joined him on foot. On the opposite side of the street, the officers spotted a black Jeep Grand Cherokee, later determined to be from Enterprise Rent-A-Car. Inside were two men, Terrell Davis and Jamar Blackshear. The Jeep's engine was running but nothing seemed amiss.

After a period of time, Davis and Blackshear began to act suspiciously. They reached toward each other with "body motions [that] were consistent with the exchanging of narcotics in a narcotics transaction." B.A. 8.[2] The officers exited their patrol car and approached the Jeep. Upon noticing the officers, Davis and Blackshear had "expressions of shock on their faces," B.A. 8, and they tossed something into the backseat. They exited the Jeep and quickly walked away — so quickly, in fact, that Blackshear did not bother closing his door. Officer Gilliam stopped Blackshear and patted him down to search for weapons. He instead found a wad of cash in his pocket. In the meantime, Officer Witherspoon stopped Davis and patted him down. He found a similar amount of cash.

Everything indicated to the officers that this was a drug deal: the suspicious movements, the hurried departures, the wads of cash, and the neighborhood itself. Knowing that guns often accompany drug deals, the officers decided to search the Jeep for weapons — and to see if there were any other occupants. Officer Witherspoon tried to look through the tinted rear window, but it was too dark. So he opened the already-ajar driver's door and saw a handgun wedged between the driver's seat and the middle console. At that point, the officers arrested Davis and Blackshear and placed them in the patrol car.

The handgun was not the only item in the Jeep. Officer Witherspoon returned and spotted an opaque shopping bag in the backseat. It was open and contained a white substance. The officers requested a drug-detection dog, which alerted to the presence of drugs. The officers obtained a warrant and recovered ten cell phones, a pair of binoculars, and two shopping bags with roughly 740 grams of cocaine distributed among nine smaller Ziploc bags. The cocaine itself was compressed into the shape of a brick and had a street value over $75,000.

Davis and Blackshear were charged with possessing a controlled substance with intent to distribute under 21 U.S.C. § 841(a)(1) and with possessing a firearm in furtherance of a drug-trafficking crime under 18 U.S.C. § 924(c). They were also charged with aiding and abetting under 18 U.S.C. § 2.

*   *   *

. . . Blackshear pled guilty but reserved the right to appeal the denial of his suppression motion. He received two consecutive sixty-month sentences plus four years of supervised release. Davis opted for a jury trial. As the trial approached, the government asked permission to introduce Davis's two prior convictions for possessing cocaine. The District Court consented, stating that the convictions were admissible under Federal Rule of Evidence 404(b) to show that Davis recognized the drugs in the Jeep. At trial, the jury heard testimony from a range of witnesses, including Officers Gilliam and Witherspoon; Keith Festus, the owner of a nearby cell-phone store; and a narcotics expert. The jury ultimately found Davis guilty of the drug crime but not guilty of the gun crime. He received a seventy-eight-month sentence plus four years of supervised release.

*   *   *

---

[2] The officers did not explain how the "body motions" were inconsistent with lawful behavior, such as sharing a meal or exchanging gifts.

III

Davis's second argument is that the District Court erred in admitting his two prior convictions for possessing cocaine. We review that decision for an abuse of discretion. *United States v. Butch,* 256 F.3d 171, 175 (3d Cir. 2001) (noting that a decision is an abuse of discretion if "clearly contrary to reason and not justified by the evidence" (quotation marks omitted)). Though we have held that some prior drug convictions are admissible under Federal Rule of Evidence of 404(b), we have never held that a *possession* conviction is admissible to show knowledge or intent in a *distribution* trial. We decline to do so today.

A

American courts have long excluded evidence of a person's prior bad acts. This tradition reflects a fear that the jury will place too much weight on past crimes and prior misdeeds. "[I]t is said to weigh too much with the jury and to so overpersuade them as to prejudice one with a bad general record and deny [the accused] a fair opportunity to defend against a particular charge." *Michelson v. United States,* 335 U.S. 469, 476, 69 S. Ct. 213, 93 L. Ed. 168 (1948); *see also* H. Richard Uviller, *Evidence of Character to Prove Conduct: Illusion, Illogic, and Injustice in the Courtroom,* 130 U. Pa. L. Rev. 845, 884 (1982) ("[A]s the special conditions of predictive value coalesce, the potential for prejudice also rises."). The risk is that jurors will focus on evidence of prior acts, believing that someone with a criminal record cannot change and discounting any evidence to the contrary.

Over the past two hundred years, the prior-acts rule has changed much in form but little in function. In the early days of the common law, courts used an inclusionary approach: evidence of prior acts was presumptively admissible unless it was relevant only to the defendant's propensity to commit a crime. *See* Julius Stone, *The Rule of Exclusion of Similar Fact Evidence: America,* 51 Harv. L. Rev. 988, 989–90 (1938). In the nineteenth century, the rule slowly became exclusionary: such evidence was presumptively inadmissible unless the proponent could show that it was relevant to one of several specific purposes, such as motive or intent. *See id.* at 990–93 (concluding that American courts applied this rule on the mistaken belief that the exclusionary approach was part of the English common law). But that trend faded, and courts began to use different approaches — some inclusionary, some exclusionary. *See United States v. Long,* 574 F.2d 761, 765–66 (3d Cir. 1978) (noting the division of authorities). The Federal Rules of Evidence settled the matter in 1975, establishing a uniform inclusionary approach. *Id.; United States v. Green,* 617 F.3d 233, 244 (3d Cir. 2010). Yet this change, "like the nineteenth century switch from the inclusionary to the exclusionary approach, did not give rise to any significant change in the admissibility of such evidence." Kenneth J. Melilli, *The Character Evidence Rule Revisited,* 1998 B.Y.U. L. Rev. 1547, 1560.

The modern approach is set forth in Federal Rule of Evidence 404(b). "Evidence of a crime, wrong, or other act is not admissible to prove a person's character in order to show that on a particular occasion the person acted in accordance with the character." Fed. R. Evid. 404(b)(1). That principle seems strict, but prior-acts evidence "may be admissible for another purpose, such as proving motive, opportunity, intent, preparation, plan, knowledge, identity, absence of mistake, or lack of accident." Fed. R. Evid. 404(b)(2). Uncontroversial at the time of adoption, Rule 404(b) has become the most cited evidentiary rule on appeal. *See* Thomas J. Reed, *Admitting the Accused's Criminal History: The Trouble with Rule 404(b)*, 78 Temp. L. Rev. 201, 211 (2005).

The text of Rule 404(b) has led to a four-part test. Prior-acts evidence is admissible only if it is (1) offered for a proper purpose under Rule 404(b)(2); (2) relevant to that purpose; (3) sufficiently probative under the Rule 403 balancing requirement; and (4) accompanied by a limiting instruction, if requested. *See Green*, 617 F.3d at 249; *see also Huddleston v. United States*, 485 U.S. 681, 691–92, 108 S. Ct. 1496, 99 L. Ed. 2d 771 (1988) (discussing these four requirements). All this really means is that such evidence must have a nonpropensity purpose and satisfy the same relevancy requirements as any other evidence.

And yet the relevancy requirements pose problems of their own in this context. Indeed, the problems are in many cases insurmountable. *See* Uviller, 130 U. Pa. L. Rev. at 878 ("The test of ordinary relevance is often an insuperable barrier."). For starters, the prior-acts evidence must be relevant to a proper purpose, and it must be relevant without requiring the factfinder to make a propensity inference. *See United States v. Sampson*, 980 F.2d 883, 887 (3d Cir. 1992) ("If the government offers prior offense evidence, it must clearly articulate how that evidence fits into a chain of logical inferences, no link of which can be the inference that because the defendant committed drug offenses before, he therefore is more likely to have committed this one."). Consider a defendant who has been convicted of manslaughter. In a later assault prosecution, the government might want to use the conviction, perhaps to prove intent. But that use is off limits if the only reason the conviction is relevant to intent is the inference that because the defendant has committed manslaughter before, he must have committed assault now. *See id.* at 887–88. In addition, the conviction must be relevant based on what the factfinder knows about the prior act. So even if the defendant was convicted of intentional manslaughter, the conviction will be relevant to intent only if the jury knows the act was intentional and not reckless or negligent.

That is why the use of prior-acts evidence requires care from prosecutors and judges alike. In proffering such evidence, the government must explain how it fits into a chain of inferences — a chain that connects the evidence to a proper purpose, no link of which is a forbidden propensity inference. *Id.* at 887. And then the "district court, if it admits the evidence, must in the first instance, rather than the appellate court in retrospect, articulate reasons why the evidence also goes to show something other than character." *Id.* at 888. The reasoning should be detailed and on the record; a mere recitation of the purposes in Rule 404(b)(2) is insufficient.[6] Unfortunately, these requirements are "so often honored in the breach" that they resonate "about as loudly as the proverbial tree that no one heard fall in the forest." *United States v. Givan*, 320 F.3d 452, 466 (3d Cir. 2003) (McKee, J., dissenting).

---

[6] We have affirmed even when a district court's analysis was somewhat flimsy — but only when the government had already established a valid chain of inferences. *See, e.g., United States v. Lopez*, 340 F.3d 169, 173–74 (3d Cir. 2003).

B

With these principles in mind, we conclude that Davis's convictions for possessing cocaine were inadmissible to prove knowledge or intent in his trial for possessing with intent to distribute. The District Court abused its discretion by admitting this evidence, and we will vacate Davis's conviction.

Davis was twice convicted of possessing cocaine under Pennsylvania law — once in 2007 and once in 2008. The government filed a motion to introduce these convictions, advancing a pentad of purposes. J.A. 18 ("This evidence is relevant to prove the defendant's plan to, knowledge of, and intent to distribute and/or possess cocaine, and absence of mistake or accident."). To its credit, the able District Court admitted the convictions as relevant to a single purpose: "Clearly, evidence of his prior convictions for possession of crack cocaine makes it more likely than not that Davis knew that the white substance in the plastic bag on the back seat of the Jeep was cocaine." D.A. 18. The government now argues on appeal that the evidence also was relevant to intent. *See* Appellee Br. at 45.

Knowledge and intent are indeed proper purposes under the first part of our Rule 404(b) test. And "[t]here is no question that, given a proper purpose and reasoning, drug convictions are admissible in a trial where the defendant is charged with a drug offense." *Sampson*, 980 F.2d at 887. We have held, for example, that evidence of past distribution is relevant to prove knowledge of the same or different drug in a later distribution trial. *E.g.*, *Givan*, 320 F.3d at 461 ("The evidence that Givan had been convicted of distribution of cocaine makes Givan's knowledge of the presence of the heroin more probable than it would have been without the evidence."); *United States v. Boone*, 279 F.3d 163, 187 (3d Cir. 2002) (considering the defendant's past cocaine-distribution acts as evidence that he was not "an ignorant 'go-fer' "); *cf. United States v. Vega*, 285 F.3d 256, 263 (3d Cir. 2002) ("[E]vidence of Vega's participation in a prior drug conspiracy is probative of his knowledge of, and relationship with a member of, a later drug conspiracy."). And we have held that evidence of past distribution is relevant to prove intent to distribute in a later distribution trial. *E.g.*, *United States v. Lee*, 573 F.3d 155, 166 (3d Cir. 2009) ("Lee's prior drug trafficking conviction was properly admitted as evidence that Lee intended to distribute any drugs in his possession."); *Givan*, 320 F.3d at 461; *Boone*, 279 F.3d at 187. We have even held that evidence of past distribution is relevant to prove knowledge of a different drug in a later possession trial. *United States v. Lopez*, 340 F.3d 169, 174 (3d Cir. 2003). But we have never held that a possession conviction is relevant to prove either knowledge or intent in a distribution trial, and rightly so.

1. Knowledge. Possession and distribution are different in ways that matter — something that both the District Court and the government failed to appreciate. As to knowledge, one who possesses a drug might not recognize the same drug when prepared for distribution. The packaging or quantity might be different, and objects in greater quantities often have an appearance or smell of their own. Take water, which is transparent by the drop but blue in the ocean, or powdered sugar, which is floury on a donut but dense in a bag. In this case, the jury knew only that Davis had been twice convicted of possessing cocaine. *See* Appellee Br. at 19 n. 3. The jury knew nothing of the packaging or quantity that led to those convictions, so it could not have known whether Davis's past helped him to recognize the nearly one kilogram of cocaine in the Jeep.

Then there is the problem that the cocaine from Davis's past might have been in a different form. Cocaine is consumable either as a powder or as one of several bases, most often crack. *See DePierre v. United States*, — U.S. — , 131 S. Ct. 2225, 2228–29, 180 L. Ed. 2d 114 (2011). Neither form particularly resembles the other. As its name suggests, powder cocaine is a powder — specifically, a salt — that can be compressed or loose. *See* David A. Sklansky, *Cocaine, Race, and Equal Protection*, 47 Stan. L. Rev. 1283, 1290–91 (1995). On the other hand, crack cocaine is hard and waxy and often resembles small rocks or crystals. *See id.* This distinction matters, and the jury did not know which form Davis had possessed back in 2007 and 2008. For all the jury knew, the cocaine could have been a dash of powder on a golden tray. It could have been hidden in the lining of a suitcase. Or it could have been crack cocaine — in crystal form, in liquid form, rolled up in paper, or stuffed in a syringe. In any of those instances, Davis's past would not have helped him to identify the compressed powder in the backseat.

The two prior convictions thus fail the second part of our Rule 404(b) test, the relevancy requirement. *See* Fed. R. Evid. 401 (explaining that evidence is relevant if it is probative of a consequential fact). Based on the bare-bones stipulation before it, the jury had no way of knowing whether Davis's experiences made him any more likely to recognize the cocaine in the backseat. The convictions simply were not probative of Davis's knowledge. *See Givan*, 320 F.3d at 466 (McKee, J., dissenting) (noting the difficulty when "there is absolutely nothing on this record that would allow the jury to make any meaningful or relevant comparison" between past and present drugs). At best, the convictions had such limited probative value that they fail the third part of our test, the balancing requirement. *See* Fed. R. Evid. 403 (allowing courts to "exclude relevant evidence if its probative value is substantially outweighed by a danger of . . . unfair prejudice."). Either way, the convictions are inadmissible to prove Davis's knowledge.

The government nonetheless urges us to follow *Lopez* and *Givan*. In *Lopez*, we held that the defendant's participation in a cocaine-distribution conspiracy was admissible in a possession trial to prove knowledge of heroin, a different drug altogether. *Lopez*, 340 F.3d at 174 ("[The conviction] was admissible for the purpose of rebutting the defendant's anticipated claim of innocent association with, and lack of knowledge of, the heroin found near his bunk."). And in *Givan*, we held that the defendant's conviction for distributing cocaine was likewise admissible to prove knowledge and intent in a heroin-distribution trial. *Givan*, 320 F.3d at 461. These cases are at the outer bounds of admissibility under Rule 404(b). *See* David Culberg, Note, *The Accused's Bad Character: Theory and Practice*, 84 Notre Dame L. Rev. 1343, 1358–59 & n. 83 (2009) (criticizing *Lopez* and *Givan*). At all events, the two cases are distinguishable because the defendants had been convicted of dealing cocaine, and drug dealers presumably have more knowledge of drugs in general. By contrast, a possession conviction does not imply a similar level of knowledge.

2. Intent. Nor does a possession conviction imply an intent to distribute. Possession and distribution are distinct acts — far more people use drugs than sell them — and these acts have different purposes and risks. A prior conviction for possessing drugs by no means suggests that the defendant intends to distribute them in the future. "Acts related to the personal use of a controlled substance are of a wholly different order than acts involving the distribution of a controlled substance. One activity involves the personal abuse of narcotics." *United States v. Ono*, 918 F.2d 1462, 1465 (9th Cir. 1990). The other usually involves "the implementation of a commercial activity for profit." *Id.* As a result of these differences, Davis's convictions again fail the second part of our Rule 404(b) test.

In cases such as this, there is an ever-present danger that jurors will infer that the defendant's character made him more likely to sell the drugs in his possession. But that is precisely the type of inference that Rule 404(b) forbids. Any other conclusion would run the risk of unraveling the prior-acts rule:

> [I]f the act of possessing or using marijuana is to be admissible to prove intent to transport and sell marijuana, or, to go even further, to prove intent to transport and sell a different drug, then there is no reason why participation in any drug-related crime could not be used to prove intent to engage in any other drug-related crime, or why any robbery could not be used to prove the requisite intent with respect to any other robbery. A rule allowing such evidence would eviscerate almost entirely the character evidence rule.

David P. Leonard, *The New Wigmore. A Treatise on Evidence: Evidence of Other Misconduct and Similar Events* § 7.5.2(d); *see also* Charles Alan Wright & Kenneth W. Graham, Jr., 22A *Federal Practice and Procedure: Evidence* § 5242 (2d ed. 2013) ("[T]he routine use of [the intent] exception [under Rule 404(b)] could easily destroy the exclusionary rule.").[7]

We join other circuits in declaring that a possession conviction is inadmissible to prove intent to distribute. The Sixth Circuit, for example, held that "possession of a small quantity of crack cocaine for personal use on one occasion . . . sheds no light on whether [the defendant] intended to distribute crack cocaine in his possession on another occasion nearly five months earlier." *United States v. Haywood*, 280 F.3d 715, 721 (6th Cir. 2002). The Seventh and Ninth Circuits have suggested likewise. *See United States v. Santini*, 656 F.3d 1075, 1078 (9th Cir. 2011) (holding that prior convictions "for simple possession" were "not similar to the importation of marijuana and thus lack[ ] probative value"); *Ono*, 918 F.2d at 1465 (distinguishing between possession and distribution in dicta); *United States v. Monzon*, 869 F.2d 338, 344 (7th Cir. 1989) (concluding that evidence of the defendant's prior marijuana possession was not probative of his intent to distribute cocaine); *United States v. Marques*, 600 F.2d 742, 751 (9th Cir. 1979) (distinguishing between "personal use versus resale"); *cf. Enriquez v. United States*, 314 F.2d 703, 717 (9th Cir. 1963)

---

[7] Some circuits require prior acts under Rule 404(b) to "meet a threshold level of similarity in order to be admissible to prove intent" to commit the charged offense. *United States v. Long*, 328 F.3d 655, 661 (D.C. Cir. 2003); *see also United States v. Foskey*, 636 F.2d 517, 524 (D.C. Cir. 1980) (citing cases in Second, Fifth, and Ninth Circuits for the idea that "[w]hen a prior criminal act is relied upon to prove intent or knowledge, similarity between the two events must be shown" (alteration in original and quotation marks omitted)). We need not adopt that requirement in our Circuit or decide whether cocaine possession and distribution are sufficiently similar. After all, a past intent to possess drugs simply is not probative of a future intent to distribute.

(concluding that a trial was unfair because the court had admitted evidence of marijuana possession to show intent to sell heroin). *But see United States v. Wash*, 231 F.3d 366, 370–71 (7th Cir. 2000) (allowing the admission of a possession conviction in a distribution trial because the conviction involved "distribution amounts"). Other circuits have reached the opposite result, but we are not persuaded. *See, e.g., United States v. Butler*, 102 F.3d 1191, 1196 (11th Cir. 1997); *United States v. Logan*, 121 F.3d 1172, 1178 (8th Cir. 1997); *United States v. Gadison*, 8 F.3d 186, 192 (5th Cir. 1993). We conclude that Davis's convictions should not have been before the jury — not as evidence of knowledge, not as evidence of intent.

[c]   Identity

Identity is a legitimate purpose for admitting evidence of other bad acts under Rule 404(b). Obviously when identity is at issue, the issue is the perpetrator, not the act committed. The proponent of other bad act evidence to show identity is demonstrating that the other bad act, which we know the individual committed, bears such consistency with the act by an unknown perpetrator, that the odds are increased that the same individual committed both acts. A very high degree of similarity is required between the charged act and the prior act when the prior act is offered to show the identity of the perpetrator of the charged act.

GRAVES v. COMMONWEALTH
Supreme Court of Kentucky
384 S.W.3d 144 (2012)

Opinion of the Court by JUSTICE VENTERS.

Appellant, Perry Graves, appeals as a matter of right from a judgment entered upon a jury verdict by the Monroe Circuit Court convicting him of first degree trafficking in a controlled substance, second or subsequent offense, and sentencing him to twenty years imprisonment. On appeal, he asserts . . . the trial court erred during the guilt phase of his trial, by admitting evidence of other acts of drug trafficking . . . .

We reverse the judgment of the Monroe Circuit Court and remand for a new trial because evidence alleging Appellant had committed other acts of drug trafficking was admitted in violation of KRE 404(b) . . .

I. FACTUAL AND PROCEDURAL BACKGROUND

Brett Page was a confidential informant working with Kentucky State Police detectives in Monroe County.[1] As relevant here, Page assisted the detectives with two drug deals targeting Appellant as a trafficker in cocaine. One deal occurred on April 22, 2008; the other deal occurred on May 14, 2008.

---

[1] Page became a confidential informant after being charged with possession of cocaine. Due to working as a confidential informant, his charge was dismissed. Additionally, he received monetary compensation for every felony or misdemeanor case in which he assisted.

On each of the two occasions, Page and his girlfriend, Amanda Murphy, met the detectives at a location specified by the officers. The detectives searched Page and Murphy, as well as their automobile. They placed a hidden recording device on Page, gave him $200.00 in cash, and directed him to purchase ten rocks of cocaine from Appellant. With the detectives following, Page and Murphy drove to the mobile home of Appellant's sister, where Appellant was assumed to reside. The detectives waited at a nearby location from which they could observe the residence when Page went inside. Murphy remained in the car. No one during either transaction, except Page, saw Appellant because the inside of the residence was not visible to the outside observers.

Page testified that on both occasions, he met Appellant inside the residence and exchanged the $200 for ten rocks of cocaine. Page then immediately left the residence and returned with Murphy to the initial location. The detectives followed Page and Murphy and searched them again to retrieve the suspected cocaine and the recording device.

As it turned out, the recordings of the two transactions were of such poor quality that using them to identify Appellant as the person selling the drugs was impossible. The suspected cocaine was submitted to the state crime lab for identification. The crime lab confirmed that the substance procured by Page on both occasions contained cocaine and weighed 1.374 grams and 1.177 grams respectively.

Appellant was indicted for two counts of first degree trafficking in a controlled substance, second or subsequent offense. At the trial, however, the Commonwealth elected to prosecute Appellant only for the May transaction. The jury found Appellant guilty on that count of first degree trafficking in a controlled substance, second or subsequent offense. His sentence was fixed at imprisonment for twenty years and judgment was entered accordingly.

II. THE TRIAL COURT IMPROPERLY ADMITTED EVIDENCE OF PRIOR ACTS OF DRUG DEALING

KRE 404(b) provides:

> Evidence of other crimes, wrongs, or acts is not admissible to prove the character of a person in order to show action in conformity therewith. It may, however, be admissible: (1) If offered for some other purpose, such as proof of motive, opportunity, intent, preparation, plan, knowledge, identity, or absence of mistake or accident[.]

Appellant contends that the trial court erred by admitting into evidence allegations from Page that Appellant had sold drugs on occasions other than the one being tried. We have consistently observed that KRE 404(b) is "exclusionary in nature," and "any exceptions to the general rule that evidence of prior bad acts is inadmissible should be 'closely watched and strictly enforced because of [its] dangerous quality and prejudicial consequences.' " *Clark v. Commonwealth*, 223 S.W.3d 90, 96 (Ky. 2007) (quoting *O'Bryan v. Commonwealth*, 634 S.W.2d 153, 156 (Ky. 1982)).

Appellant's argument is based upon the general prohibition of "other crimes" evidence as set forth in KRE 404(b). Specifically, he claims that the trial court erred by allowing the jury to hear evidence of the April transaction. We have recognized that "it would typically be improper for the Commonwealth or a testifying witness to refer to the undercover buys as Appellant was not being tried for such conduct." *Muncy v. Commonwealth*, 132 S.W.3d 845, 847 (Ky. 2004).[2]

Appellant also contends that the trial court erred by allowing Page to testify that Appellant knew him because they had engaged in other illegal drug transactions. We address these two arguments in separate sections below.

A. Evidence Regarding the April Transaction.

*   *   *

At trial, Page and the detectives testified in detail about the April and May transactions. The jury also heard several non-testimonial references to the April transaction.[4] Appellant contends the evidence of the prior drug transaction falls outside of KRE 404(b) and is unduly prejudicial. The Commonwealth responds that the evidence of the April drug deal fits comfortably within KRE 404(b)(1) exception allowing proof of another crime that is so similar to the crime on trial that it tends to prove the identity of the perpetrator by establishing his *modus operandi.*

We certainly agree with the legal principle relied upon by the Commonwealth. While evidence of prior crimes, wrongs, or acts is inadmissible to prove the propensity of an accused, such evidence may be admissible to prove the identity of a perpetrator when the evidence of other crimes indicates a *modus operandi.* *Woodlee v. Commonwealth*, 306 S.W.3d 461, 463 (Ky. 2010); *Billings v. Commonwealth*, 843 S.W.2d 890, 893 (Ky. 1992). "To indicate *modus operandi*, the two acts must show 'striking similarity' in factual details, such that 'if the act occurred, then the defendant almost certainly was the perpetrator[.]' That is, the facts underlying the prior bad act and the current offense must be 'simultaneously similar and so peculiar or distinct,' that they almost assuredly were committed by the same person." *Woodlee*, 306 S.W.3d at 464 (quoting *Clark v. Commonwealth*, 223 S.W.3d 90, 96 (Ky. 2007)).

However, we disagree with the application of the principle by the trial court in this case. The Commonwealth's evidence of the April drug deal is, indeed, virtually identical to the evidence of the May drug deal. The prosecutor argued at the pretrial hearing, "The transactions are almost identical. Same defendant, same [confidential informant], same officers, same residence, same type of drugs purchased."

---

[2] In *Muncy*, the evidence was deemed to be admissible, however, because the defendant had opened the door to its introduction when he denied any knowledge of the drugs.

[4] The seven occasions on which the jury heard reference and evidence regarding the April transaction were: 1) the trial judge read the count of the indictment relating to the April transaction to the jury; 2) the Prosecutor mentioned the transaction during his opening and closing arguments; 3) Detective Decker testified about the transaction and identified the cocaine purchased during the drug deal; 4) a state crime lab technician testified about testing the procured cocaine; 5) Detective Murphy testified regarding the transaction; 6) Page also testified regarding the transaction and 7) the recording of the transaction was admitted into evidence and played for the jury.

But, the similarities noted by the Commonwealth are not so peculiar or distinctive as to create a method of operation unique to *Appellant*. Rather, they seem to follow the same pattern of facts involved in any routine controlled drug buy arranged by police. In fact, the detective testified at trial, "We do [controlled drug buys] the same way every time." What is established by the evidence is *not* Appellant's *modus operandi*; rather, it is the *modus operandi* of the police unit involved in this investigation. The essential factors that make these two incidents similar were not shown to be the choice of Appellant. It was the detectives who on each occasion wired Page and sent him, along with Murphy, to the mobile home of Appellant's sister, with $200 in cash and instructions to buy ten rocks of cocaine. Therefore, the April drug deal does nothing to identify Appellant as the person inside the residence who conducted the May drug deal.

There is also another fundamental flaw in the Commonwealth's reasoning, and it arises from the fact that the only evidence that identified Appellant as the drug seller in *either* transaction was Page's testimony. No one else saw Appellant or could otherwise identify him as the drug seller. Evidence of the April deal, to the extent it established a unique *modus operandi*, was relevant *only* if it tended "to make the existence of any fact that is of consequence to the determination of the action [here, the identity of the May drug seller] more probable or less probable than it would be without the evidence." KRE 401.

The relevance of *modus operandi* evidence is based upon the simple logical precept that begins with this premise: One can reasonably infer that two strikingly similar crimes were probably committed by the same person. That means that the identity of an unknown perpetrator can be inferred by the striking similarity between his crime and a different crime committed by a known perpetrator. Therefore, if we know the identity of the person who committed one of the crimes, we can infer that *that* person committed the other strikingly similar crime.

Here, the Commonwealth is not inferring the unknown event (that Appellant sold cocaine in May) from a known event (that Appellant sold cocaine in April.) The proof linking Appellant to the April crime is no better than the proof linking him to the crime on trial. In fact, it's the exact same evidence: Page's testimony. The only evidence identifying Appellant as the drug dealer in the April transaction is Page's testimony, which is the exact same evidence that identifies him in the May transaction. Page's testimony that Appellant sold cocaine in April, therefore, adds no credence to the accusation that Appellant also sold cocaine in May. With nothing more than Page to identify Appellant at either event, all that was presented to the jury was a pair of successive accusations, neither of which has any independent probative value that tends to prove the other. Multiple accusations by the same witness against an individual, generated under the same circumstances, do not establish a *modus operandi* that is relevant to prove that one of the accusations is true.

We therefore reject the Commonwealth's argument that Page's testimony that Appellant sold drugs in April is relevant to prove that Appellant committed the May offense. We do not suggest that to be relevant to prove identity under KRE 404(b), the Commonwealth must establish with certainty that the defendant on trial actually committed the "other crimes." Rather, we hold that, in the context of *modus operandi*, that multiple uncorroborated accusations of the same accuser, as here, have no independent probative value that would reasonably permit the inference that the perpetrator of one act also committed the other. Under such circumstance, the only relevance of the "other crimes" evidence is to suggest that the accused has the propensity to commit the offense under review. That of course, is the very thing that KRE 404(b) prohibits.

Therefore, we hold that the evidence regarding the April transaction did not fall within an exception to KRE 404(b) and was improperly admitted during trial . . . .

EXERCISES

1. During a lawful search of Derek's suitcase, police found a kilogram of cocaine. Derek admitted that the suitcase belonged to him, but denied any knowledge that the suitcase contained cocaine. At Derek's criminal trial, the prosecution wants to call a witness who will testify that when Derek was arrested, he was also carrying a notebook which contained a handwritten verse: "Kilo for kilo, rock for rock, pound for pound, I'm the biggest dope dealer around." The defense objects under Rule 404(b). How should the court rule? Would your answer change if the defense can prove that Derek drafted the verse for use in a rap song?

2. Landlord owns a commercial building which he leases to two tenants: a law firm and a clothing store. The lease requires the tenants to abide by all laws, including a local noise ordinance. Shortly after executing the lease agreement, the clothing store begins to play loud music to attract customers, which annoys the workers of the law firm. The law firm files a request for an injunction against the clothing store, demanding that the clothing store turn down its music. At the hearing on whether to grant the injunction, the law firms seeks to offer evidence of prior excessive noise problems in the clothing stores' other retail locations. What argument should the law firm make in support of admitting the proposed testimony and how should the court rule?

3. Laval is alleged to have killed someone to increase his status within his gang. At Laval's murder trial, the prosecution seeks to elicit testimony that Laval's nickname among his fellow gang members is "Murder." Laval acquired the nickname many years before the instant offense. Laval objects to the use of his nickname and offers to concede identification to avoid its use at trial. Applying a Rule 404 analysis, should the trial court allow the prosecution to elicit the nickname? Would your answer change if Laval's nickname was "Big Time" or "Red."

4. Police charged Shariff, a former felon, with possessing cocaine and a firearm after recovering both items during a search of his home. During opening statements at trial, Shariff's counsel argued that the drugs and firearm belonged to another occupant of the house. In its case-in-chief the government plans to call two witnesses. The first witness will testify that she saw Shariff take the same firearm (identified by its dark, rusty grey color) out of his pants and place it on a table approximately two months before his arrest. The second witness will testify that Shariff was convicted of a felony eight years ago, when he possessed cocaine. Sharif objects to both witnesses' testimony. How should the court rule?

5. Alvin — a licensed attorney, realtor, and contractor — defrauded banks into giving him excessive funds during mortgage transactions by forging invoices suggesting that his contracting company had performed extensive renovations on the properties, when it had not. At his criminal trial, the government seeks to offer four witnesses who will testify that Alvin also engaged in fraud when applying for his contractor's license because he forged each of their signatures on the professional references section of his application. Alvin objects under Rule 404. How should the court rule?

6. Mary is accused of using forged and fabricated bank letters and IRS documents to defraud a business investor out of a $250,000. Prior to trial the prosecution gives proper notice that it intends on introducing Mary's prior conviction for attempted escape from federal custody as evidence under Rule 404(b). Fifteen years earlier, while incarcerated in a federal penitentiary, Mary fabricated a court order and used an envelope she stole from the probation office to mail the court order to a case manager at the penitentiary. The court order stated that her sentence had been reduced, and that she should be released immediately. The court order contained the forged signature of a federal judge. Mary objects to the proposed testimony. How should the court rule?

7. Rodney is alleged to have committed three armed robberies in a one week span. In each instance he is suspected of ordering a pizza for delivery, giving the delivery driver the address of a vacant house, and when the delivery driver arrives brandishing a firearm while demanding that the delivery driver produce his money and cell phone, and then stealing the delivery driver's car. Prior to trial, the government gives notice that it intends on introducing evidence at trial that 17 months before the pizza delivery robberies, Rodney pled guilty in a neighboring state to a robbery after he approached a man on a public sidewalk, told the man that he had a gun in his pocket, and demanded the man's property. The government contends that the testimony will help the jury identify Rodney as the robber in the pizza delivery cases. Should the court allow the proposed "other acts" testimony?

[d]   Prior Sexual Misconduct Under Federal Rules of Evidence 413–415

Under the federal rules, as you will see, juries are essentially permitted to consider evidence of prior sex crimes to demonstrate a defendant's propensity to commit such crimes. Judge Arnold in the *LeCompte* case recognizes how differently the rules treat other crimes evidence when the other crime involves sexual assault.

UNITED STATES v. LeCOMPTE
United States Court of Appeals, Eighth Circuit
131 F.3d 767 (1997)

RICHARD S. ARNOLD, CHIEF JUDGE.

Before the trial of Leo LeCompte for the alleged sexual abuse of his wife's 11-year old niece, "C.D.," under 18 U.S.C. §§ 2244(a)(1) and 2246(3) (1994), the defendant moved *in limine* to exclude evidence of prior uncharged sex offenses against another niece by marriage, "T.T." The government argued that the evidence was admissible under Federal Rule of Evidence 414 (Evidence of Similar Crimes in Child Molestation Cases). The District Court excluded the evidence under Rule 403. The government appeals this evidentiary ruling. Such pretrial appeals are authorized by 18 U.S.C. § 3731 (1994). We reverse and hold that the motion *in limine* should not have been granted. We do so in order to give effect to the decision of Congress, expressed in recently enacted Rule 414, to loosen to a substantial degree the restrictions of prior law on the admissibility of such evidence.

I.

LeCompte is charged with child sex offenses allegedly committed in January 1995. According to the victim C.D., prior to January 1995, LeCompte had played games with her at her aunt's trailer and had exposed himself to her on at least one occasion. The actual incidents of molestation allegedly occurred while she was lying on a couch at her aunt's, with her siblings sleeping on the floor next to her. LeCompte allegedly joined her on the couch, forced her to touch his penis, and touched her breasts.

The government offered evidence of sex offenses committed by LeCompte against a niece of his first wife during that marriage, between 1985 and 1987. This niece, T.T., would testify that LeCompte had played games with her at her aunt's house, had exposed himself to her, had forced her to touch his penis, and had touched her private parts.

The admissibility of T.T.'s testimony has been considered by this Court once before. In LeCompte's first trial, the government offered the evidence under Rule 404(b). It was not then able to offer the evidence under Rule 414 because of its failure to provide timely notice of the offer, as required by Rule 414. The District Court admitted the evidence, and the jury convicted LeCompte. On appeal, this Court held that the District Court's admission of the evidence under Rule 404(b) was improper, and reversed LeCompte's conviction. *United States v. LeCompte*, 99 F.3d 274 (8th Cir. 1996). We now consider the admissibility of T.T.'s testimony in LeCompte's retrial, under Rule 414, the government having given timely notice the second time around.

II.

On remand, LeCompte moved *in limine* to exclude the evidence. The District Court ruled that T.T.'s testimony was potentially admissible under Rule 414, but excluded by Rule 403. It noted that although the evidence's only relevance was as to LeCompte's propensity to commit child sexual abuse, Rule 414 expressly allowed its use on that basis. The Court then turned to a Rule 403 analysis of the evidence. As to the evidence's probative value, the Court recognized the similarities between C.D.'s and T.T.'s accounts: they were both young nieces of LeCompte at the time he molested them, he forced them both to touch him, he touched them both in similar places, and he exposed himself to both of them. The Court found that the evidence's probative value was limited, however, by several differences. First, the acts allegedly committed against C.D. occurred with her siblings present, while the acts against T.T. occurred in isolation. Second, LeCompte had not played games with C.D. immediately before molesting her, as he had with T.T. Finally, the acts against C.D. and T.T. were separated by a period of eight years. The District Court concluded that the probative value of T.T.'s testimony was limited.

On the other hand, it found that the risk of unfair prejudice was high, reasoning that "T.T.'s testimony is obviously highly prejudicial evidence against defendant . . . . 'child sexual abuse deservedly carries a unique stigma in our society; such highly prejudicial evidence should therefore carry a very high degree of probative value if it is to be admitted.' " District Court Order at 4 (citation omitted). The Court therefore excluded the evidence under Rule 403.

III.

We first note that no procedural bars prevent the government from offering the evidence under Rule 414 at this time. First, as the District Court reasoned, the law of the case doctrine is inapplicable; this Court's holding that the evidence was inadmissible under Rule 404 at the first trial does not foreclose consideration of admissibility under a different rule of evidence on retrial. Second, LeCompte's retrial will fall after Rule 414's effective date, July 9, 1995. The Rule applies in all trials held after this original effective date. Act of September 30, 1996, Pub. L. No. 104-208, § 120, 110 Stat. 3009–25.

Rule 414 provides in relevant part:

> (a) In a criminal case in which the defendant is accused of an offense of child molestation, evidence of the defendant's commission of another offense or offenses of child molestation is admissible, and may be considered for its bearing on any matter to which it is relevant.

Rule 414 and its companion rules — Rule 413 (Evidence of Similar Crimes in Sexual Assault Cases), and Rule 415 (Evidence of Similar Acts in Civil Cases Concerning Sexual Assault or Molestation) — are "general rules of admissibility in sexual assault and child molestation cases for evidence that the defendant has committed offenses of the same type on other occasions. . . . The new rules will supersede in sex offense cases the restrictive aspects of Federal Rule of Evidence 404(b)." 140 Cong. Rec. H8992 (daily ed. Aug. 21, 1994) (statement of Rep. Molinari).

Evidence offered under Rule 414 is still subject to the requirements of Rule 403. *Id.* This Court has recognized that evidence otherwise admissible under Rule 414 may be excluded under Rule 403's balancing test. *United States v. Sumner,* 119 F.3d 658, 661 (8th Cir. 1997). See also *United States v. Meacham,* 115 F.3d 1488, 1492 (10th Cir. 1997); *United States v. Larson,* 112 F.3d 600, 604–05 (2d Cir. 1997). However, Rule 403 must be applied to allow Rule 414 its intended effect.

We review the District Court's application of Rule 403 for abuse of discretion. *United States v. Johnson,* 56 F.3d 947, 952 (8th Cir. 1995). In light of the strong legislative judgment that evidence of prior sexual offenses should ordinarily be admissible, we think the District Court erred in its assessment that the probative value of T.T.'s testimony was substantially outweighed by the danger of unfair prejudice. The sexual offenses committed against T.T. were substantially similar to those allegedly committed against C.D. By comparison, the differences were small. In particular, the District Court itself acknowledged that the time lapse between incidents "may not be as significant as it appears at first glance, because defendant was imprisoned for a portion of the time between 1987 and 1995, which deprived defendant of the opportunity to abuse any children." District Court Order at 4.

Moreover, the danger of unfair prejudice noted by the District Court was that presented by the "unique stigma" of child sexual abuse, on account of which LeCompte might be convicted not for the charged offense, but for his sexual abuse of T.T. This danger is one that all propensity evidence in such trials presents. It is for this reason that the evidence was previously excluded, and it is precisely such holdings that Congress intended to overrule. Compare *United States v. Fawbush*, 900 F.2d 150 (8th Cir. 1990) (prior acts of child sexual abuse inadmissible to show propensity under Rule 404(b)). On balance, then, we hold that the motion *in limine* should not have been granted.

The order of the District Court is reversed, and the cause remanded for further proceedings not inconsistent with this opinion.

EXERCISE

Police charged Gilbert with sexually assaulting his two nieces, ages 6 and 9. The sexual assaults began with inappropriate touching and escalated to sexual intercourse. Prior to trial, the prosecution files notice that it also intends on calling three other adult female relatives at trial. Each of these adult relatives would testify that Gilbert also inappropriately touched them when they were in elementary school. Gilbert has not been charged with assaulting these other three women due to statute of limitations issues. Should the court permit the prosecution's adult witnesses to testify?

[e]   Limits on Admissibility of Acts of Victims of Sexual Assault

Rules 413–415 have led courts to categorically admit evidence of other sexual misconduct by defendants in criminal and civil cases. The flip side of this rule, the rape shield law, codified in Federal Rule of Evidence 412, has, by contrast, not created a categorical exclusion of sexual conduct by alleged victims. The deeply split *en banc* Sixth Circuit opinion in *Gagne v. Booker* illustrates the difficult issues that can arise as courts attempt to balance a defendant's constitutional right to defend himself against Rule 412 efforts to protect the privacy of alleged victims and encourage other victims to report.

GAGNE v. BOOKER

United States Court of Appeals, Sixth Circuit
680 F.3d 493 (2012)

ALICE M. BATCHELDER, CHIEF JUDGE.

I.

In July 2000, Lewis Gagne and his friend Donald Swathwood (also his codefendant) had decided to move to California. Gagne was unemployed and his turbulent six-month relationship with his former-girlfriend, P.C., had ended approximately three weeks earlier. On the evening of July 3, 2000, Gagne, Swathwood, and another friend, David Stout, were out for a good time.

When their car ran out of gas, they walked to P.C.'s house and found her there. P.C., who had been drinking for most of the day, agreed to get cash from the ATM to buy gas, beer, and crack cocaine. Upon their return, and after smoking, drinking, and showering, P.C. began to have sex with Gagne, whereupon Swathwood joined in. P.C. engaged in fellatio, vaginal intercourse, and anal intercourse with both men. She also engaged in fellatio with Stout, albeit briefly, and during the course of this "escapade," had multiple vibrators and a wine bottle inserted into her vagina and rectum. At approximately 5:00 a.m. the next morning, the three men took P.C.'s ATM card, withdrew $300, bought crack cocaine, and smoked it all themselves.

Later that afternoon, P.C. called the police and accused Gagne and Swathwood of rape. She claimed that, while she had originally begun a consensual sexual encounter with Gagne, she had protested Swathwood's uninvited participation and, rather than relenting when she objected, Swathwood and Gagne had held her down, forcibly raped and sodomized her, mocked her and laughed at her, and tried to force her to perform fellatio on Stout, who was drunk, stoned, and virtually incoherent. Gagne and Swathwood replied that the whole episode was consensual; that P.C. had initiated and directed the "wild orgy" and had given them the ATM card with orders to return with more crack. They claimed that P.C. was the classic "woman scorned," frustrated that Gagne was leaving for California and angry that the men had smoked the crack without her.

The State charged Gagne and Swathwood with three counts each of first-degree criminal sexual misconduct in violation of Michigan law, M.C.L. § 750.520b(1)(f) (sexual penetration through use of force, causing injury to the victim). Both defendants entered not-guilty pleas, and the case was set for a jury trial in a Michigan state court. Stout was to be a witness, but not a defendant.

At the conclusion of a seven-day trial, the jury convicted Swathwood on all counts and Gagne on two (the jury acquitted Gagne of one count of forced fellatio). The court sentenced Swathwood to a prison term of 15 to 30 years, and Gagne to a term of 22 1/2 to 45 years.

II.

The present appeal stems from a pre-trial ruling by a Michigan trial court on the admissibility of two particular pieces of evidence proffered by the two criminal defendants: an allegation that the alleged victim, P.C., and defendant Gagne had, on a certain prior occasion, engaged in group sex with another individual, one Ruben Bermudez; and a separate allegation that P.C. had, on a certain prior occasion, offered to engage in group sex with Gagne and his father. The defendants moved to admit this evidence pursuant to the Michigan Rape Shield Law, M.C.L. § 750.520j, but the trial court denied the motion and excluded the evidence (and any argument regarding it).

*   *   *

A.

Michigan's Rape Shield Law, which lies at the origin of Gagne's constitutional claim, is a rule of evidence particular to criminal sexual-misconduct cases and provides that:

> (1) Evidence of specific instances of the victim's sexual conduct, opinion evidence of the victim's sexual conduct, and reputation evidence of the victim's sexual conduct shall not be admitted under sections 520b to 520g [FN 1] unless and only to the extent that the judge finds that the following proposed evidence is material to a fact at issue in the case and that its inflammatory or prejudicial nature does not outweigh its probative value:
>
> > (a)   Evidence of the victim's past sexual conduct with the actor.
> >
> > (b)   Evidence of specific instances of sexual activity showing the source or origin of semen, pregnancy, or disease.
>
> (2) If the defendant proposes to offer evidence described in subsection (1)(a) or (b), the defendant within 10 days after the arraignment on the information shall file a written motion and offer of proof. The court may order an in camera hearing to determine whether the proposed evidence is admissible under subsection (1). If new information is discovered during the course of the trial that may make the evidence described in subsection (1)(a) or (b) admissible, the judge may order an in camera hearing to determine whether the proposed evidence is admissible under subsection (1).

[FN 1] M.C.L.A. §§ 750.520b to 750.520g.

M.C.L. § 750.520j.

Prior to trial, Gagne identified certain items or instances concerning P.C.'s sexual history that he deemed relevant to his defense and filed a "Motion and Offer of Proof," pursuant to § 750.520j(2), seeking to admit them as "proof of the victim [P.C.]'s past sexual conduct with him for the purpose of establishing consent." Five of those items were argued together:

1. An allegation that P.C., Gagne, and Swathwood had, on a certain prior occasion in June 2000, engaged in group sex, which also included two other women they had met at a bar (i.e., "the Tony's Lounge Incident");

2. An allegation that P.C. and Gagne had, on a certain prior occasion in June 2000, engaged in group sex with another individual, one Ruben Bermudez;

3. An allegation that P.C. and Gagne, during their relationship, had commonly used "sex toys", including vibrators, a wine bottle, and others;

4. An allegation that it was P.C. who had invited Stout (who was not charged as a defendant) to participate in the group sex on the night in question; and

5. An allegation that P.C. had, on a certain prior occasion, offered to engage in group sex with Gagne and his father, Rodney Gagne.

Gagne asserted that these "factual scenarios[,] constituting [his] offer of proof[,] [we]re probative of the issue of the alleged victim [P.C.]'s consent to have sexual relations with multiple partners simultaneously[,] and that the use of objects in connection with sexual activities is not necessarily inconsistent with the existence of consent on the part of the alleged victim [P.C.]."

* * *

In discussing these items, the trial court expressed its concern that, "I just don't have any case law on a situation where somebody other than the victim and the actor, being the defendant, participated in sexual activities," to which Gagne's counsel responded:

> And . . . maybe this will be the case. This is, to put it mildly, an unusual case, and I would only submit [that] to prohibit that evidence [of the group sex with Bermudez and the offer of group sex with Gagne's father] from coming in because there is a third party involved would serve no purpose either under the rape shield statute and it certainly would, I think, violate my client's [constitutional] right to confrontation and right to establish evidence that goes toward the issue of consent.

* * *

The trial court analyzed the items' admissibility under the Rape Shield Law, M.C.L. § 750.520j, and did not address Gagne's constitutional claim (i.e., "right to confrontation") or the State's argument concerning Rule 404 of the Michigan Rules of Evidence. The court explained:

> As to 520j (a), evidence of a victim's past sexual conduct with the actor, the [c]ourt believes that as to [the Tony's Lounge Incident,] that that matter ought to be permitted to come to the jury's attention. I don't find that it is inflammatory or prejudicial in nature, and its probative value outweighs its possible prejudicial value.

> As to [the sex toys], the [c]ourt will permit discussions with the victim, I take it on cross-examination of the victim by [Gagne's counsel] and perhaps [Swathwood's counsel]. [The use of sex toys], it would appear to the [c]ourt, if true, it is not inflammatory or prejudicial to the extent that it outweighs its probative value.

As to the remainder of [Gagne's] motion, [the group sex with Ruben Bermudez] doesn't fit the statute, [the invitation to David Stout] doesn't fit the statute, [another item] is withdrawn, [and the offer of group sex with Gagne's father] doesn't fit the statute. So none of those may be — inquiry may not be made about any of those; only [the Tony's Lounge Incident and the sex toys].

The court granted Gagne's "Motion and Offer of Proof" in part, by admitting the first and third items (the Tony's Lounge Incident and the use of sex toys), and formalized this decision in an order filed January 17, 2001. The court denied the second and fifth items (the group sex with Bermudez and the offer of group sex with Gagne's father), along with some other proposed evidence. The court's basis for excluding each of these items was that it "doesn't fit the statute," meaning that because an item involved a third party (i.e., another *person*), it would not satisfy the § 750.520j(1)(a) exception for "[e]vidence of the victim's past sexual conduct *with the actor.*" The trial court initially excluded the fourth item (the invitation to Stout) based on a misunderstanding of its nature, but then clarified that it would allow that item, as it was limited to events on the night in question.

* * *

B.

On direct appeal to the Michigan Court of Appeals, Gagne challenged the trial court's exclusion of the evidence regarding the group sex with Bermudez and the offer of group sex with Gagne's father, claiming that the court had (1) misinterpreted the Rape Shield Law and (2) misapplied the Rape Shield Law in a way that violated his constitutional rights.

* * *

The Michigan Court of Appeals began its analysis by quoting the Rape Shield Law, M.C.L. § 750.520j(1), but acknowledged that "[i]n certain limited situations, evidence that does not come within the specific exceptions of the statute may be relevant and its admission required to preserve a criminal defendant's Sixth Amendment right of confrontation." *Swathwood*, 2003 Mich. App. LEXIS 922, [at *2].

[T]he Michigan Court of Appeals framed Gagne's argument thus: Gagne and Swathwood "argue that without this evidence that group sex was not foreign to [P.C.], the jury likely would reject a consent defense because the incident involved more than one partner." *Swathwood*, 2003 Mich. App. LEXIS 922, [at *5]. The court rejected this argument, explaining:

[E]vidence of a victim's prior sexual conduct with [a] defendant is only admissible if and to the extent that the judge finds that the evidence is material to a fact at issue in the case and that its inflammatory or prejudicial nature does not outweigh its probative value. [P.C.]'s willing participation in a threesome with Gagne and Bermudez is not probative of whether she consented to a threesome with Gagne and Swathwood on the night of the alleged offense. [T]he threesome involving Bermudez occurred while [P.C.] and Gagne were still dating. The instant offense occurred after they had ended their relationship and it involved Swathwood, not Bermudez. In light of the lack of similarity between the Bermudez threesome and the instant offense, we conclude that the trial court did not abuse its discretion in excluding the evidence.

Id. (quoting M.C.L. § 750.520j(1)) (quotation and editorial marks omitted; other citations omitted).

The Michigan Court of Appeals also rejected Gagne's argument that the trial court erred by excluding testimony of P.C.'s "expressed desire to engage in group sex with Gagne and his father":

> Although the conduct involved defendant Gagne, like the evidence of the threesome with Bermudez, the evidence is not probative of whether [P.C.] consented in the instant matter to engage in sexual relations with Gagne and Swathwood. . . . [T]he evidence was not relevant to the issue of consent, and . . . the trial court did not abuse its discretion in excluding the evidence.

> Moreover, in light of the other evidence of [P.C.]'s past sexual conduct that the trial court did admit, we reject [the] defendants' argument that their [Sixth Amendment] rights of confrontation compelled the admission of this evidence and take note of the evidence that the trial court did admit. The jury heard about 'The Tony's Lounge Incident,' in which [the] defendants, [P.C.], and two other women engaged in group sex, according to [the] defendants' version of the incident. [The] [d]efendants further testified that the incident included [P.C.] performing oral sex on Swathwood. Even [P.C.] testified that[,] after The Tony's Lounge Incident[,] Gagne told her that she had engaged in oral sex with Swathwood, but she was unable to recall whether she had done so because she was intoxicated. Therefore, [the] defendants presented evidence that [P.C.] was not averse to group sexual activity.

Id. at [*7–*9]. The Michigan Court of Appeals also rejected the several other claims, including prosecutorial misconduct and ineffective assistance, and affirmed the convictions and sentences.

Gagne sought leave to appeal to the Michigan Supreme Court, but was denied. *Michigan v. Gagne*, 469 Mich. 982, 673 N.W.2d 755 (2003). That exhausted his possible state remedies.

*   *   *

III.

*   *   *

B.

Gagne contends that the Michigan Court of Appeals unreasonably applied the principles clearly established in *Lucas* and *Crane* when it affirmed the trial court's exclusion of the testimony and questioning about the alleged group sex with Bermudez and the alleged offer of group sex with Gagne's father. *Lucas*, 500 U.S. at 152–53, 111 S. Ct. 1743, stands for the proposition that the trial court must balance a state's interest in excluding certain evidence under the rape shield statute against a defendant's constitutionally protected interest in admitting that evidence, on a case-by-case basis — neither interest is superior *per se*. And *Crane*, 476 U.S. at 690–91, 106 S. Ct. 2142, stands for the general proposition that "the Constitution guarantees criminal defendants a meaningful opportunity to present a complete defense" — such that the court may not "exclude competent, reliable evidence . . . central to the defendant's claim of innocence[,] . . . [i]n the absence of any valid state justification."

The Michigan Court of Appeals did not cite *Lucas* or *Crane* by name, but identified the governing principles nonetheless, stating: "Application of the rape-shield statute must be done on a case-by-case basis, and the balance between the rights of the victim and the defendant must be weighed anew in each case." *Swathwood*, 2003 Mich. App. LEXIS 922, [at *3]. Moreover, "[i]n certain limited situations, evidence that does not come within the specific exceptions of the [rape-shield] statute may be relevant and its admission required to preserve a criminal defendant's Sixth Amendment right of confrontation." *Id.* And, "[i]n exercising its discretion, the trial court should be mindful of the significant legislative purposes underlying the rape-shield statute and should always favor exclusion of evidence of a complainant's sexual conduct where its exclusion would not unconstitutionally abridge the defendant's right to confrontation." *Id.* (quotation marks omitted).

The Michigan Court of Appeals then analyzed this particular evidence by weighing its probative value against its prejudicial effect, and the State's interest against the defendant's:

> The rape-shield statute generally precludes admission of evidence of a victim's past sexual conduct with others, while excepting instances of a victim's past sexual conduct with the defendant to the extent it is relevant and not unfairly [ ]prejudicial. In this case, the prior sexual conduct in question involves both 'others', (i.e., Ruben Bermudez) and defendant Gagne. Defendants argue that the complainant's prior consensual participation in a threesome with Gagne tends to show that the complainant is not averse to such conduct, which is probative of whether she consented in the instant case. The trial court was concerned that although the threesome was indeed prior sexual conduct with defendant, it also involved a nonactor, Bermudez. Defendants argue that the fact that the complainant's and Gagne's sexual history included another person was merely an aspect or characteristic of their sexual relationship. Defendants argue that without this evidence that group sex was not foreign to the complainant, the jury likely would reject a consent defense because the incident involved more than one partner.

We disagree. Even viewing the evidence as defendants urge, as merely an instance of prior sexual conduct with defendant, an aspect of which was the inclusion of other persons, the evidence is not automatically admissible. Rather, evidence of a victim's prior sexual conduct with defendant is only admissible if and to the extent that the judge finds that the evidence is material to a fact at issue in the case and that its inflammatory or prejudicial nature does not outweigh its probative value. Here, the complainant's willing participation in a threesome with Gagne and Bermudez is not probative of whether she consented to a threesome with Gagne and Swathwood on the night of the alleged offense. Notably, the threesome involving Bermudez occurred while the complainant and Gagne were still dating. The instant offense occurred after they had ended their relationship, and it involved Swathwood, not Bermudez. In light of the lack of similarity between the Bermudez threesome and the instant offense, we conclude that the trial court did not abuse its discretion in excluding the evidence.

Defendants also argue that the trial court erred in excluding evidence that the complainant invited Gagne and his father to participate in a threesome. We disagree.

The evidence that the complainant expressed a desire to have a threesome with Gagne and his father is a statement that may also be conduct. . . . Although the conduct involved defendant Gagne, like the evidence of the threesome with Bermudez, the evidence is not probative of whether the complainant consented in the instant matter to engage in sexual relations with Gagne and Swathwood. . . . We conclude that the evidence was not relevant to the issue of consent, and that the trial court did not abuse its discretion in excluding the evidence.

Moreover, in light of the other evidence of the complainant's past sexual conduct that the trial court did admit, we reject defendants' argument that their rights of confrontation compelled the admission of this evidence and take note of the evidence that the trial court did admit. The jury heard about 'The Tony's Lounge Incident,' in which defendants, the complainant, and two other women engaged in group sex, according to defendants' version of the incident. Defendants further testified that the incident included the complainant performing oral sex on Swathwood. Even the complainant testified that after The Tony's Lounge Incident Gagne told her that she had engaged in oral sex with Swathwood, but she was unable to recall whether she had done so because she was intoxicated. Therefore, defendants presented evidence that the complainant was not averse to group sexual activity.

Swathwood, 2003 Mich. App. LEXIS 922, [at *4–*9] (quotation marks and citations omitted).

The Michigan Court of Appeals therefore decided that neither the evidence of group sex with Bermudez nor the offer of group sex with Gagne's father was probative of P.C.'s consent on the night in question because the third participant was different (Swathwood rather than Bermudez or Gagne's father) and the surrounding circumstances were different (i.e., "the threesome involving Bermudez occurred while [P.C.] and Gagne were still dating[, whereas] [t]he instant offense occurred after they had ended their relationship"). Furthermore, the jury did hear evidence of P.C.'s participation in group sex with Gagne and Swathwood during the Tony's Lounge Incident.

The Michigan Court of Appeals accepted that the State has a legitimate interest under its Rape Shield Law in excluding evidence, and considered the probity of the evidence as a measure of Gagne's interest in admitting it. The United States Supreme Court has never held that rape-shield statutes do not represent a legitimate state interest, nor has it ever held that highly probative evidence will necessarily outweigh that interest. Quite to the contrary, the Court held in *Lucas*, 500 U.S. at 152–53, 111 S. Ct. 1743, that the trial court must balance the state's interest against the defendant's interest on a case-by-case basis, and neither interest is superior *per se*. And the Court concluded in *Crane*, 476 U.S. at 690, 106 S. Ct. 2142, that a trial court may even "exclude competent, reliable evidence . . . central to the defendant's claim of innocence," so long as there exists a "valid state justification." The Michigan Court of Appeals properly weighed the competing interests, as Supreme Court precedent requires, and did not misidentify or misapply any clearly established federal law.

C.

Gagne argues here — as he argued to the Michigan Court of Appeals[20]— that evidence of group sex with Bermudez and the offer of group sex with Gagne's father was not merely competent, reliable, and central to his claim of innocence, but was the "most relevant piece of evidence":

> [T]he excluded evidence was the most relevant piece of evidence. It was critical for the defense to show that [P.C.] was willing to engage in sex with Mr. Gagne and another person at the same time. Without such a showing, the jury undoubtedly viewed Mr. Gagne's claim that [P.C.] voluntarily engaged in group sex with him with inherent disbelief. . . .

> The possibility that a woman would consent to have sex with two or more men at the same time strikes most people as bizarre, disgusting, and unlikely. In fact, a recent survey found that only 1% of women found group sex appealing. Thus, a jury may be inclined to view a consent defense with inherent disbelief. In this regard, evidence that the complainant previously consented to group sex with two or more men including one or more of the defendants does have legitimate probative value on the issue of consent, beyond the forbidden yes/yes inference. In any event, courts tend to admit such evidence.

Because Lewis Gagne was not permitted to introduce the evidence of the prior instances of where [P.C.] engaged in or sought to engage in sex with

---

[20] Recall that Gagne had argued to the Michigan Court of Appeals that "[t]he idea that a woman would have sex with two or more men at the same time strikes most people as bizarre and a jury, therefore, [would] be inclined to view a consent defense in a case like this one with inherent disbelief." *See* Section II.B, *supra*.

him and another man, a critical question on the jury's mind — how would anyone consent to this kind of three-way group sexual activity, was left unanswered. Unanswered by evidence, the jury would be likely to conclude that she did not consent to such activity.

Appellee Br. at 16–17 (Sept. 20, 2010) (quotation and editorial marks, and citations omitted).

* * *

It might be that Gagne is correct that, as a matter of his defense, this was the "most relevant evidence" and the state courts were wrong to exclude it, but "whether the trial judge was right or wrong is not the pertinent question under AEDPA," *Renico*, 130 S. Ct. at 1865 n. 3. The question is whether the last state court's decision was "objectively unreasonable," *Williams*, 529 U.S. at 409, 120 S. Ct. 1495. One might disagree with the reasons given by the Michigan Court of Appeals — that the evidence was not sufficiently probative because the third participant(s) in and the surrounding circumstances of these other incidents were different, or that exclusion of the evidence was not particularly prejudicial because the jury heard about the Tony's Lounge Incident — but these are nonetheless legitimate reasons, and certainly not "so lacking in justification" as to be "beyond any possibility for fairminded disagreement," *see Harrington*, 131 S. Ct. at 787.

The "group sex" at issue in this case involved P.C.'s prolonged sex (oral, vaginal, and anal) in various positions with both men concurrently, spankings, and repeated vaginal and anal penetrations with multiple sex toys, vibrators and a wine bottle, resulting in vaginal and rectal bleeding and bruising. To be sure, jurors might find this behavior outlandish, aberrant, abnormal, bizarre, disgusting, or even deviant and, therefore, find it incredible or inherently unbelievable that P.C. would have consented to it. And it is not unreasonable to surmise that those jurors would be more likely to find consent if they were told that she had engaged in — and offered to engage in — group sex at least two other times in the past. But, again, that is not the question. The question is whether the Michigan Court of Appeals was "objectively unreasonable" in rejecting this argument. Considering the general antipathy for propensity evidence, the State's established interest in rape-shield laws, and the Michigan Supreme Court's repeated rejection of this argument, we cannot say that the decision in this case was "beyond any possibility for fairminded disagreement."

IV.

Because Lewis Gagne cannot demonstrate that the decision of the Michigan Court of Appeals was objectively unreasonable, we **REVERSE** the district court and deny the petition.

KAREN NELSON MOORE, CIRCUIT JUDGE, concurring in the judgment only.

I agree that habeas relief is unwarranted under these circumstances. I do not agree, however, with the plurality's explanation of why the district court erred in granting habeas relief in this case.

Clearly established federal law requires that when excluding evidence offered by a criminal defendant, the trial court must balance the interests of the state in excluding the evidence with the infringement upon the weighty interests of the defendant in presenting a complete defense. "Whether rooted directly in the Due Process Clause of the Fourteenth Amendment or in the Compulsory Process or Confrontation clauses of the Sixth Amendment, the Constitution guarantees criminal defendants a meaningful opportunity to present a complete defense." *Crane v. Kentucky*, 476 U.S. 683, 690, 106 S. Ct. 2142, 90 L. Ed. 2d 636 (1986) (internal citations and quotation marks omitted). However, the exclusion of evidence pursuant to evidentiary rules "do [es] not abridge an accused's right to present a defense so long as [the rules] are not 'arbitrary' or 'disproportionate to the purposes they are designed to serve' " and thus do not "infringe[ ] upon a weighty interest of the accused." *United States v. Scheffer*, 523 U.S. 303, 308, 118 S. Ct. 1261, 140 L. Ed. 2d 413 (1998) (quoting *Rock v. Arkansas*, 483 U.S. 44, 56, 107 S. Ct. 2704, 97 L. Ed. 2d 37 (1987)). Rape-shield statutes represent legitimate state interests and may, in some circumstances, preclude the admission of evidence relating to a prior sexual relationship between a victim and a defendant. *Michigan v. Lucas*, 500 U.S. 145, 152–53, 111 S. Ct. 1743, 114 L. Ed. 2d 205 (1991).

The plurality starts off on the right track, correctly explaining that a "trial court must balance a state's interest in excluding certain evidence under the rape shield statute against a defendant's constitutionally protected interest in admitting that evidence, on a case-by-case basis." Plur. Op. at 514. But the plurality then makes no effort to analyze whether the state court reasonably conducted that balancing in Gagne's case. Instead, the plurality concludes that because the Supreme Court has not explicitly held that "highly probative evidence" could ever outweigh the state's interest in a rape-shield statute, the state court's identification of the state's interest in a rape-shield statute alone justifies the exclusion of all related evidence. *Id.* at 516. Even when that evidence is purportedly the "most relevant piece of evidence" to a defense, the plurality's approach would presumptively call a state-court decision excluding such evidence reasonable simply if the state court identified a rape-shield statute as the reason behind the exclusion. *Id.* at 516–17. This is not a correct basis for concluding that the Michigan Court of Appeals in this case — or in any case — did not unreasonably apply clearly established federal law.

* * *

Gagne is not entitled to habeas relief because the Michigan Court of Appeals did not unreasonably apply the clearly established constitutional principles discussed above to the excluded evidence in this case. An examination of the last reasoned state-court decision reveals a not-unreasonable weighing of the probative value of the excluded evidence against the state's interest in its rape-shield statute, resulting in exclusion that was neither arbitrary nor disproportionate. *See People v. Swathwood*, Nos. 235540, 235541, 2003 Mich. App. LEXIS 922, [at *3–*9] (Mich. Ct. App. Apr. 15, 2003) (unpublished opinion). In many ways, the dissent by Judge Kethledge has the better exposition of the general constitutional principles at issue in this case and how they should be considered on habeas. But the dissent, too, errs by grossly exaggerating the application of these principles to the facts of this case in assessing the reasonableness of the state court's application of these principles. I do not agree with the dissent that the evidence excluded from Gagne's trial was "indispensable."

Dissent Op. at 535. Nor would I categorize the state's interest in this case as "minimal." *Id.* At a minimum, reasonable minds could readily differ on these issues, making habeas relief inappropriate.

The dissent of Judge Kethledge boldly claims that "[t]he only evidence with which Gagne could realistically defend himself . . . was the evidence that the trial court excluded." Dissent Op. at 534. I do not find the excluded evidence so compelling. The dissent relies heavily on the defense counsel's proffer that the Bermudez incident was "nearly identical" to the charged events to then conclude that the Bermudez incident was "nearly identical *brutal* sex." Dissent Op. at 533, 536 (emphasis added). This is a significant overstatement of the proffer. Defense counsel told the court that "the events alleged by [Bermudez] is nearly identical in most regards. There are some exceptions, but the general M.O., if you will, the way that event took place is almost identical to the way that the events charged in this case took place." R. 11-2 (1/2/01 State Hr'g Tr. at 19). At no point did defense counsel, either in his papers or at the hearing, characterize the Bermudez incident as "brutal" or "violent" in any way, and the defense certainly did not proffer that the Bermudez incident left the victim bleeding and with bruises all over her body. R. 11-2 (1/2/01 State Hr'g Tr. at 18–19); R. 23-4 (Def.'s Mot. and Offer of Proof at ¶ 4).

The dissent also suggests that the Bermudez incident and the alleged offer regarding Gagne's father were necessary to establish that the victim was willing to consent to simultaneous sex with more than one person. This is another overstatement. Although the admitted testimony regarding the Tony's Lounge incident did not involve *simultaneous* sex with two men, the incident involved allegations that the victim engaged in sexual acts in a group setting with both Gagne and Swathwood. To the extent that any prior sexual conduct by the victim could bear on her consent in the instant offense without resting purely on an inappropriate propensity argument, the Tony's Lounge incident arguably had greater probative value than either of the excluded encounters in that it involved group sexual activity with the two men she accused of rape. The excluded evidence was not so probative of consent in the instant offense as to render its exclusion a violation of Gagne's rights, particularly because the trial court did permit similar testimony relating to the victim's history. It was certainly not unreasonable for the state court to conclude as much.

On the other side of the balancing test, the state's interest in this case is particularly compelling. The state has a valid interest "in encouraging rape victims to come forward and in protecting victims from an embarrassing display of their past sexual history regardless of whether that history includes socially acceptable sexual practices." Resp. Supp. Br. at 11; *see also Lucas*, 500 U.S. at 149–50, 111 S. Ct. 1743 ("The Michigan [rape-shield] statute represents a valid legislative determination that rape victims deserve heightened protection against surprise, harassment, and unnecessary invasions of privacy."). The state also has an interest in preventing irrelevant character evidence in the form of a victim's sexual history from misleading or prejudicing a jury when considering a victim's testimony relating to the charged events. I do not agree with the dissent's view that the state's interest in excluding evidence under a rape-shield statute in this case was "minimal." Dissent Op. at 535, 536. The state's interests are not eviscerated just because a trial court has admitted some evidence of a victim's past sexual practices, as the dissent seems to suggest. Dissent Op. at 534–35.

The dissent's efforts to analogize the enforcement of the state rape-shield statute in this case with the state rules arbitrarily enforced in *Chambers* and *Crane* inappropriately minimizes the state's interest in shielding rape victims and in preventing irrelevant character evidence from biasing a jury. In *Crane*, the state had not "advanced any rational justification for the wholesale exclusion" of evidence relating to the circumstances surrounding a confession when doing so undoubtedly infringed on weighty interests of the defendant. *Crane*, 476 U.S. at 691, 106 S. Ct. 2142. In *Chambers*, the state had a discernible interest in the rule in question — hearsay generally may be excluded to insure fairness and reliability — but the Supreme Court held that "the hearsay rule may not be applied mechanistically to defeat the ends of justice," particularly when the excluded testimony had other indicia of reliability that would protect the state's interests in a fair proceeding. *Chambers v. Mississippi*, 410 U.S. 284, 302, 93 S. Ct. 1038, 35 L. Ed. 2d 297 (1973). Neither case is truly comparable to the state's interest in excluding evidence in this case.

When a state court mechanistically applies a rape-shield statute to exclude indispensable evidence of a victim's sexual history, habeas relief may be warranted. That situation, however, is not before us today. The Michigan Court of Appeals properly stated the relevant constitutional principles and conducted a reasonable review of the trial court's evidentiary rulings in light of these constitutional principles. *Swathwood*, 2003 Mich. App. LEXIS 922, [at *2] (acknowledging need to balance interests protected by rape-shield statute with defendant's right to confrontation). The Michigan Court of Appeals considered the probative value of the excluded evidence and concluded that the trial court did not err in excluding some, but not all, of the victim's past sexual conduct. *Id.* [at *5–*9]. The added probative value of the excluded evidence was indeed questionable, and the state court's application of the rape-shield statute was neither arbitrary nor disproportionate to the state's interests in exclusion in this case. Even assuming that it was a close question whether the excluded evidence should have been admitted, the state court's decision upon balancing these interests was not unreasonable. I therefore concur in the judgment reversing the district court.

KETHLEDGE, CIRCUIT JUDGE, dissenting.

Even the State admitted, in oral argument for this case, that the sexual conduct at issue here — rough, three-way sex involving the complainant, the defendant, and another man — would appear "facially coercive" to a jury. The charged conduct would appear that way, that is, *unless* the jury was told that the complainant had consented to virtually identical conduct with Gagne and another man just four weeks earlier, and had proposed the same thing to Gagne and another man on a third occasion. Viewed in that context, conduct that at first seemed facially coercive to the jury might not have seemed coercive at all, at least not on its face. That is a critical difference in a rape trial in which the only issue was consent and the stakes ran as high as 45 years in prison. Yet the state courts barred Gagne from presenting evidence of these incidents on relevance grounds.

The logic of the State's concession is that, as a practical matter, the burden was on Gagne at trial to prove that the charged conduct was consensual. And so the question presented by Gagne's case is a narrow one: whether, in a trial where the charged conduct is facially coercive and the only issue is consent, evidence that the complainant had consented to the same kind of conduct with the defendant, only a handful of weeks before, is indispensable to his defense. Under the Supreme Court's caselaw — and by any measure of fairness and common sense — the clear answer to that question is yes.

I.

At the outset, it is important to make clear what this case is not about. The State and its amici argued in seeking rehearing, and continue to argue before the court *en banc*, that a decision to affirm the district court's issuance of the writ in this case would "effectively abrogate every rape-shield law in this circuit." Seldom in legal analysis is an assertion so demonstrably false.

Begin with the fact that the State does not even venture to assert that Michigan's rape-shield statute (or any other) actually bars admission of the evidence at issue here. There is a reason for that omission. The core of any rape-shield law is its proscription against evidence of past sexual activity by the victim. But every one of those laws contains an exception for evidence of the victim's prior sexual activity *with the defendant*. And that is precisely the kind of evidence at issue here. Michigan's statute excepts from its proscription "[e]vidence of the victim's past sexual conduct with the actor." Mich. Comp. Laws § 750.520j(1)(a). Ohio's statute does the same. *See* Ohio Rev. Code § 2907.02(D) (excepting evidence of "the victim's past sexual activity with the offender"). So does the Tennessee rule. *See* Tenn. R. Evid. 412(c)(3) (allowing admission of evidence if "sexual behavior was with the accused, on the issue of consent"). The Kentucky rule affirmatively provides that "evidence of specific instances of sexual behavior" between the alleged victim and defendant "*is* admissible" if offered to prove consent and otherwise admissible under the rules. *See* Ky. R. Evid. 412(b)(1)(B) (emphasis added). The federal rule does the same. *See* Fed. R. Evid. 412(b)(1)(B).

* * *

The various arguments offered in support of the State's position on rehearing, in contrast, do not offer anything at all like mathematical proofs. What they offer is scarecrow rhetoric. We are told, for example, that affirmance of the district court's judgment would deal the statutes a "serious blow," and indeed would "call into question the ordinary application of the rape-shield statute" — this, in a case where the statute's bar would not apply in the first place. The arguments' driving impulse, it seems, is that we ought to have a penumbra of inadmissibility around the zone of inadmissibility that the rape-shield statutes actually prescribe — lest anyone ever infer that we undermine those statutes in vindicating a defendant's constitutional rights. The arguments' premise, fundamentally, is that certain statutory values are so important as to trump constitutional ones. The premise is viable only to the extent it remains unstated. There is no rape-defendant exception to the Constitution.

But the conflict the State posits is a false one. The dynamic between a defendant's constitutional rights and the interests served by the rape-shield laws is not a zero-sum game. The laws themselves strike a balance between the important interests they serve, on the one hand, and evidence critical to the defense, on the other. And thus our concern for a defendant's constitutional rights does not amount to a lack of concern for the interests served by the rape-shield laws. We honor these laws when we respect the balance they strike. It is the State's position, and not ours, that imperils these laws, by giving them a scope beyond their terms, and thus bringing them into conflict, needlessly, with constitutional values.

* * *

II.

* * *

A.

During his rape trial, Gagne sought to admit evidence that, "within 30 days of the charged offense," the complainant had engaged in three-way sex with Gagne and another man, Ruben Bermudez, and that "the way that event took place is almost identical to the way that the events charged in this case took place." 1/2/01 Hearing Tr. at 18–19. Gagne's counsel stated that both Bermudez and Gagne himself would testify to that effect. Gagne also sought to admit evidence that, within approximately two months of the charged conduct, the complainant had proposed the same kind of conduct to Gagne and his father. The trial court excluded all this evidence on grounds that it was more prejudicial than probative.

In his direct appeal, Gagne claimed that the exclusion of this evidence violated his procedural due-process right to present a complete defense and his Sixth Amendment right to confront the witnesses against him. The Michigan Court of Appeals held that these claims were meritless. The decisions of the Supreme Court of the United States show otherwise.

B.

"Whether rooted directly in the Due Process Clause of the Fourteenth Amendment or in the Compulsory Process or Confrontation Clauses of the Sixth Amendment, the Constitution guarantees criminal defendants 'a meaningful opportunity to present a complete defense.' " *Holmes v. South Carolina*, 547 U.S. 319, 324, 126 S. Ct. 1727, 164 L. Ed. 2d 503 (2006) (quoting *Crane v. Kentucky*, 476 U.S. 683, 690, 106 S. Ct. 2142, 90 L. Ed. 2d 636 (1986)). At the same time, trial judges must make "dozens, sometimes hundreds" of evidentiary decisions throughout the course of a typical case; and "the Constitution leaves to the judges who must make these decisions 'wide latitude' to exclude evidence that is 'repetitive . . . , only marginally relevant' or poses an undue risk of 'harassment, prejudice, [or] confusion of the issues.' " *Crane*, 476 U.S. at 689–90, 106 S. Ct. 2142 (quoting *Delaware v. Van Arsdall*, 475 U.S. 673, 679, 106 S. Ct. 1431, 89 L. Ed. 2d 674 (1986)) (alterations and omissions in original). The point of cases like *Crane*, however, is not that this latitude exists. The point is that the Constitution places limits upon it.

1.

One case that marks out those limits is *Chambers v. Mississippi*, 410 U.S. 284, 93 S. Ct. 1038, 35 L. Ed. 2d 297 (1973). There, Leon Chambers had been charged in state court with the fatal shooting of a police officer, Aaron Liberty. After Chambers had been charged, another man, Gable McDonald, gave a sworn confession that he had shot the officer. But McDonald repudiated his confession a month later, claiming that he had only made the confession as part of a deal to share the proceeds of a lawsuit that Chambers allegedly planned to bring as a result of Chambers's own injuries in the melee in which the officer was killed. The State proceeded with Chambers's prosecution. His defense was that McDonald shot Officer Liberty. At trial, the court allowed Chambers to admit some evidence in support of that defense, including McDonald's written confession, a witness's testimony that he saw McDonald shoot the officer, another witness's testimony that he saw McDonald with a gun after the shooting, and the testimony of a third witness who contradicted McDonald's alibi. But the trial court excluded testimony from three witnesses to the effect that, in separate conversations with each of them, McDonald had confessed to the killing. The court also refused to allow Chambers to cross-examine McDonald as an adverse witness. The jury eventually convicted Chambers of murdering Officer Liberty.

Chambers argued in the Supreme Court that the trial court's evidentiary decisions had violated his procedural due-process right "to a fair opportunity to defend against the State's accusations." *Id.* at 294, 93 S. Ct. 1038. The State there appeared to respond much as the State does here: trial courts have wide latitude to exclude evidence at trial; the court's decisions were based upon state evidentiary rules that serve important interests; and, given the evidence that the trial court did admit, its decisions adverse to Chambers did not render his trial fundamentally unfair.

The Supreme Court rejected the State's arguments. The Court said that "[t]he rights to confront and cross-examine witnesses and to call witnesses in one's own behalf have long been recognized as essential to due process." *Id.* The Court described these two rights — confrontation and calling witnesses — in similar terms. Although the right to confront and cross-examine is "essential and funda-mental" to a fair trial, the Court said, the right "may, in appropriate cases, bow to accommodate other legitimate interests in the criminal trial process." *Id.* at 295, 93 S. Ct. 1038. But the right's "denial or significant diminution calls into question the ultimate integrity of the fact-finding process and requires that the competing interest be closely examined." *Id.* (internal punctuation omitted). Similarly, the Court said that "[f]ew rights are more fundamental than that of an accused to present witnesses in his own defense." *Id.* at 302, 93 S. Ct. 1038. And so the Court took a close look at the competing interests with respect to that right as well. *Id.*

In gauging these interests, the Court delivered a notably realistic assessment of how Chambers's ability to defend himself was affected by the trial court's decisions in his case. The Court observed that the trial boiled down to a credibility contest between Chambers and McDonald, since, "in the circumstances of this case, McDonald's retraction [of his confession] inculpated Chambers to the same extent that it exculpated McDonald." *Id.* at 297, 93 S. Ct. 1038. And in that contest

Chambers was significantly, though by no means totally, disabled. His "predicament" as a result of the trial court's rulings, the Court said, was that "he was unable either to cross-examine McDonald or to present witnesses in his own behalf who would have discredited McDonald's repudiation and demonstrated his complicity." *Id.* at 294, 93 S. Ct. 1038. It was true, the Court said, that the evidence admitted at trial — McDonald's written confession, testimony from one witness contradicting McDonald's alibi, testimony from another who said he had seen McDonald shoot the officer first-hand — had "chipped away" at McDonald's credibility. *Id.* Thus the State argued in effect — just as the amici States argue here — that the trial court had split the difference, and that the Court ought to leave things where they were. But the Supreme Court chose not to decide the case upon a mere recitation of platitudes. It instead took a careful look at all of the evidence, admitted and excluded alike, and analyzed impartially the effect of the trial court's decisions upon the dynamic at trial. Its conclusion was based upon common sense: "Chambers' defense was far less persuasive than it might have been had he been given an opportunity to subject McDonald's statements to cross-examination or had the other confessions been admitted." *Id.*

Against these interests, the Court weighed the State's interests in support of the trial court's decisions. The trial court had excluded McDonald's confessions to the three witnesses on hearsay grounds. As a generic matter, the Court recognized, the interests supporting that rule are significant: "perhaps no rule of evidence has been more respected or more frequently applied in jury trials than that applicable to the exclusion of hearsay[.]" *Id.* at 302, 93 S. Ct. 1038. But the court did not weigh those interests generically; it weighed them "under the facts and circumstances of this case[.]" *Id.* at 303, 93 S. Ct. 1038. And having done so, the Court determined that the interests supporting exclusion of the three confessions were slight, primarily because the confessions themselves were trustworthy — again in light of the particular facts and circumstances of Chambers's case. *Id.* at 302, 93 S. Ct. 1038.

The Court likewise made short work of the trial court's decision to bar Chambers from examining McDonald as an adverse witness, which had been based on Mississippi's "voucher rule." *Id.* at 295–96, 93 S. Ct. 1038. Again looking at the specific facts of his case, the Court said that "McDonald's testimony was in fact seriously adverse to Chambers[,]" regardless of who put McDonald on the stand. *Id.* at 297, 93 S. Ct. 1038. Thus, the Court held, "[t]he 'voucher' rule, as applied in this case, plainly interfered with Chambers' right to defend against the State's charges." *Id.* at 298, 93 S. Ct. 1038. The Court concluded: "the exclusion of this critical evidence, coupled with the State's refusal to permit Chambers to cross-examine McDonald, denied him a trial in accord with traditional and fundamental standards of due process." *Id.* at 302, 93 S. Ct. 1038.

a.

The parallels here are not hard to discern. This case too boiled down to a credibility contest between the defendant and another witness. In this case too the defendant was allowed to admit some of the evidence he proffered at trial — specifically, testimony concerning the so-called "Tony's Lounge" incident, which was a five-way orgy in which the complainant consensually participated, and which the

State and the Michigan Court of Appeals said was an adequate substitute for the three-way evidence that the trial court excluded. (To be clear, however, the record indicates that this incident was actually a room full of two-way sex, during which the complainant engaged in sex with Gagne and Swathwood sequentially rather than at the same time, *see* Joint App'x at 43–46; and, as shown below, the State itself characterized the incident as sequential two-way sex in its closing argument to the jury.) The issue here, then, is no different from the issue in *Chambers*: Whether the excluded evidence lost its "critical" nature in light of the evidence that the trial court did admit. That, I suggest, is the nub of this appeal.

The issue, in terms specific to this case, is whether the admission of the Tony's Lounge evidence rendered the prior three-way incidents merely "cumulative[,]" as the State now argues, rather than critical. But on this issue the State has virtually made Gagne's case for him. To do more than "chip [ ] away" at the State's case against him, *Chambers*, 410 U.S. at 294, 93 S. Ct. 1038, Gagne had to do more than demonstrate the complainant's willingness to engage in sequential sex with Gagne and another man. Instead, he had to demonstrate the complainant's willingness specifically to engage in the kind of *facially coercive three-way sex* (with Gagne) involved in the charged incident. This distinction has been the prosecution's battering ram throughout this litigation. Consider, for example, how in closing argument the prosecution itself distinguished the Tony's Lounge incident from the charged conduct in this case:

> That situation [the Tony's Lounge incident] did not involve, ladies and gentlemen, *two men*. That situation did not involve penetration of her anus multiple times, her vagina, multiple times, and oral sex multiple times. *It did not involve physical abuse*, which is what is charged here, and what the physical and testimonial evidence show occurred.

2/5/01 Trial Tr. at 12–13 (emphasis added).

To which I would say: Precisely. The Tony's Lounge evidence was not a fair substitute for the excluded evidence precisely because of the very distinctions called out by the prosecution in seeking (and obtaining) a conviction in this case. That the complainant would engage in comparatively benign sequential sex in the Tony's Lounge incident does not come close to refuting the prosecution's argument that she would *not* consent to what the State itself calls the "brutal" three-way sex at issue here. State's Supp. Br. at 12. To offer some bland assurance to the contrary is to ignore reality, and to apply the Constitution's principles to a fairyland trial rather than the trial that actually occurred.

The State makes this point even more emphatically in its supplemental brief to this court — albeit inadvertently. The State argues:

> [T]he dissimilarity between the charged act and the prior excluded acts cannot be emphasized enough *because of the violent nature of the rape*. . . . [T]here is no evidence that the alleged threesome with Bermu-dez involved the type of sexual activity or the type of brutality that the charged incident involved. There was no offer of proof that [the complain-ant] engaged in anal sex, *that she allowed a bottle to be inserted in her rectum and vagina, that she allowed a whip to be used*, or that she allowed

or enjoyed being hit in the buttocks. There is nothing in the excluded evidence that indicates she would consent to the brutal sex that took place on the night of the charged incident. Thus, it is only minimally relevant.

State's Supp. Br. at 12 (emphasis added). The major premise of the State's argument here, as with its closing argument at trial, is that the complainant's participation in *non*-brutal sex — such as the Tony's Lounge incident — is "only minimally relevant" to whether she would have consented to "the brutal sex that took place on the night of the charged incident." (More on that below.) The argument's minor premise is that the Gagne-Bermudez incident was not brutal in the ways that the charged incident was. Thus, the State concludes, the Gagne-Bermudez incident was "only minimally relevant."

The problem with the State's syllogism is that it has its facts wrong. Gagne's counsel stated that Gagne and Bermudez were each ready to testify that their three-way sex with the complainant — less than 30 days before the charged incident — was " *almost identical to the way that the events charged in this case took place.*" *See* 1/2/01 Hearing Tr. at 18–19 (emphasis added); *see also id.* at 19 (noting that the prior incident was "*nearly identical in most regards*") (emphasis added). Non-brutal three-way sex is not "almost identical" or "nearly identical" to brutal three-way sex. And thus it is simply not an accurate reading of the record to say that the Bermudez incident, as described in the proffer, was less brutal than the charged incident.

Moreover, Gagne's counsel stated in a Motion for Reconsideration that, when the excluded testimony is considered "*in conjunction*" with the evidence that the court did admit (including testimony relating to the use of sex objects, such as the whip and blue champagne bottle), the Bermudez incident "establish[es] as clear a pattern as can be imagined *which is similar to what is alleged here as non-consensual conduct.*" R. 23-4 at 20 (emphasis added). The trial court did admit testimony that the complainant had used the whip and bottle during sex generally; but the true power of that testimony comes from its combination (or "conjunction") with the excluded testimony regarding the Bermudez incident — which then could have been shown to have been "almost identical to the events charged in this case." The State simply overlooks these aspects of the record in its brief.

And so the State should reap the whirlwind here. It is undisputed that evidence of the complainant's consent to non-brutal sex was only minimally relevant to Gagne's ability to defend himself at trial. The Tony's Lounge evidence was precisely that. Per the State's own arguments, that evidence was no substitute for the evidence that the trial court excluded in this case.

It follows that the excluded evidence was "critical" to Gagne's defense. *Chambers*, 410 U.S. at 302, 93 S. Ct. 1038. What Gagne faced was a theory of *res ipsa loquitur* as applied to a rape case: the brutal and facially coercive nature of the charged conduct spoke for itself at trial, to the effect that the conduct was not consensual. That undisputed fact severely disadvantaged Gagne in the credibility contest upon which his trial turned. His only chance of defending himself was to admit evidence that the complainant had consented to in one instance, and proposed in another, almost identical conduct with Gagne and another man — and moreover that the complainant had done so just weeks before the charged conduct here.

Absent this evidence, Gagne's "defense was far less persuasive than it might have been had he been given an opportunity" to admit this evidence and then cross-examine the complainant on the basis of it. *Id.* at 294, 93 S. Ct. 1038. That parallel with *Chambers,* I think, cannot be seriously disputed. Indeed I think that Leon Chambers was better off in his trial than Gagne was in his — since in Chambers's credibility contest he at least had McDonald's written confession and a witness's firsthand testimony that McDonald had done the shooting. Gagne, by comparison, had next to nothing at all.

The only evidence with which Gagne could realistically defend himself — evidence, I might add, that suggests a substantial possibility that he is innocent — was the evidence that the trial court excluded. Even when viewed deferentially, the court's decision to strip that evidence out of the case "plainly interfered with [Gagne's] right to defend against the State's charges." *Id.* at 298, 93 S. Ct. 1038. What was left was an empty husk of a trial — at whose conclusion came a prison sentence of up to 45 years.

b.

Chambers instructs that we must look at not only the interests supporting admission of Gagne's evidence, but also the interests supporting its exclusion . . . .

[The State argues that the exclusion of this evidence advances the interests] advanced by Michigan's rape-shield law. As a generic matter, I entirely agree that Michigan's rape-shield law (like the hearsay rule in *Chambers*) protects important state interests in the vast majority of cases in which it is implicated. We cast no aspersion upon that law when we say that a defendant was denied a fair trial in a case in which the law's proscription does not even apply. But more to the point: *Chambers* makes clear, as discussed above, that the interests supporting exclusion of Gagne's evidence must be assessed not generically, but rather in light of "the circumstances of this case." 410 U.S. at 297, 93 S. Ct. 1038.

In this trial, I respectfully submit, there was virtually nothing left for the rape-shield statute to protect. As an initial matter, this case only weakly implicates the interests protected by the statute, since the statute's terms did not even bar the excluded testimony, but instead left its admission to the discretion of the Ingham County Circuit Judge. *See* Mich. Comp. Laws § 750.520j(1)(a). And it is hard to see what was left of those interests, such as they were in this case, given the evidence of sexual activity (albeit non-brutal) and drug use that *was* admitted at trial. The only sense in which Gagne's evidence was "cumulative," I submit, was as to whether its admission in this trial would have diminished those interests any further.

And so we must decide whether the court of appeals's decision in this case reflects an unreasonable application of *Chambers.* For all the reasons described above — the palpably indispensable nature of this evidence to Gagne's defense, the minimal interests supporting its exclusion in the circumstances of this case, and the State's own arguments as to why the Tony's Lounge evidence was no substitute — I do not think that "fairminded jurists" could conclude that the state court's decision here was consistent with *Chambers.* . . .

*   *   *

Gagne's rights were violated on the facts of this case. The Michigan courts unreasonably applied the Supreme Court's precedents in holding the contrary. I respectfully dissent.

EXERCISE

Jonathan is accused of kidnapping and vaginally raping Lisa, a woman whom he met at a college dance. At the trial a medical professional testified that she had seen vaginal injuries like those suffered by Lisa only in cases of forced vaginal penetration, never in cases of consensual sex. Jonathan now seeks to call an eyewitness who would testify that at the dance that preceded the rape he observed Lisa intoxicated and in a state of partial undress in the presence of two other men. Jonathan contends that such testimony tends to show that Lisa engaged in a consensual encounter with these two men, and that they were responsible for Lisa's vaginal injuries. Jonathan also argues that the evidence would show Lisa's state of intoxication and undermine the reliability of her testimony. Should the court allow Jonathan's witness to testify?

[B] Propensity in the Extreme: Admissibility of Habit Evidence

[*See* **Fed. R. Evid. 406**]

Although character evidence generally may not be used to establish a propensity from which the conduct of an individual can be inferred, the same is not true of habit evidence. Testimony as to an individual's habit or an organization's custom or practice, or as to specific instances of prior conduct from which a habit or custom can be inferred, is admissible to prove conduct consistent with that habit or custom on a particular occasion. The rules governing habit evidence, therefore, constitute an exception to the general character evidence rules in several respects: (1) they allow any party to introduce propensity evidence in the form of an individual's habits or routine practices; (2) they allow parties to use such evidence in both civil and criminal cases; and (3) they allow parties to introduce evidence of specific instances of prior conduct as proof of that habit or practice.

"Habit" is the regular response of an individual to, or the customary practice of an organization in, the context of a specific situation. It differs from character in the degree of similarity of situations to which the individual or organization is responding and in the regularity of the response. It is difficult to determine with precision when evidence of an individual's conduct graduates from inadmissible character to admissible habit evidence. It is clear, however, the individual's conduct must be highly predictable as a result of the habit in question. The conduct must be to the point of being virtually automatic — a reflexive response to a particular stimulus. The courts generally have required that it be an invariably regular practice in response to a specific repetitive situation.

DIAGRAM 3-4

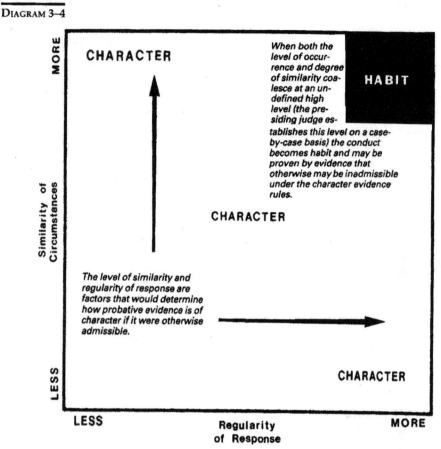

Were the variables of similarity and regularity charted, for the purpose of illustrating the difference between character and habit, habit likely would be limited to the extreme upper right-hand corner of the chart, as reflected in Diagram 3-4, above.

On a more practical plane, Professor McCormick explains the difference between character and habit as follows:

> Character is a generalized description of a person's disposition, or of the disposition in respect to a general trait, such as honesty, temperance or peacefulness. Habit, in the present context, is more specific. It denotes one's regular response to a repeated situation. If we speak of a character for care, we think of the person's tendency to act prudently in all the varying situations of life — in business, at home, in handling automobiles and in walking across the street. A habit on the other hand, is the person's regular practice of responding to a particular kind of situation with a specific type of conduct. Thus, a person may be in the habit of bounding down a certain stairway two or three steps at a time, of patronizing a particular pub after each day's work, or of driving his automobile without using a seatbelt. The doing of the habitual act may become semi-automatic, as with a driver who invariably signals before changing lanes.

McCormick on Evidence, § 195, at 351 (4th ed. 1994).

As with the basic relevancy issue of probative worth, the determination of the point at which conduct becomes so regular that evidence of it is admissible as habit calls for the trial judge's reasoned judgment. As might be expected, the context in which the evidence is offered will often influence the trial judge in this regard. In *Keltner v. Ford Motor Co.*, 748 F.2d 1265 (8th Cir. 1984), for example, the court admitted evidence of the plaintiff's past intemperate behavior (regularly drinking a six-pack of beer four nights a week), which is generally excluded if offered as proof of drunkenness in accident cases. The court admitted this evidence, however, after Ford made an offer of proof that included the expected testimony of the investigating officer and the attending physician that the plaintiff smelled of alcohol after the accident, as well as the expected testimony of a truck driver that, as the plaintiff was driving his van immediately prior to the accident, the van was swerving from one side of the road to the other.

Courts recognize habit evidence as an exception to the general rule excluding character evidence because of the regularity and predictability of the conduct in question. Consequently, the probative value of evidence of an individual's habits is significantly greater than that of the more generalized character propensity evidence. Moreover, because the evidence is so situation-specific, the potential for generalized prejudice from the jurors' emotional reactions to the parties is substantially less.

Despite the increased probative value and decreased potential for prejudice of this particularized evidence of an individual's habits, many jurisdictions have imposed restrictions on its use that commentators have criticized as unnecessary and illogical. One restriction limited the use of habit evidence to instances in which there were no eyewitnesses. Courts applied this restriction regardless of the competency, veracity, or lack of bias of those eyewitnesses whose testimony precluded the use of habit evidence and despite the strength of the habit that a party was seeking to prove. A second restriction limited use of habit evidence to instances in which there was corroboration of the habit or custom. For example, if one were attempting to prove that a letter was properly mailed through evidence of office custom or practice, there would have to be corroboration from an office mail clerk that the custom testified to by a higher official in the organization was actually followed on the day in question. Many commentators cogently argued that such corroboration should be a factor that goes only to the probative sufficiency of the habit or custom and not to its admissibility.

[1] The Policy For and Against Habit Evidence

As you will see in the *Burchett* decision, Kentucky was one of the last states to adopt a rule admitting habit evidence. The dissent presents a very good argument against the admission of this type of evidence and also challenges the sufficiency of the evidence of habit in this case — testimony that the defendant smoked marijuana every morning.

BURCHETT v. COMMONWEALTH
Supreme Court of Kentucky
98 S.W.3d 492 (2003)

Opinion of the Court by JUSTICE JOHNSTONE.

As the result of a fatal automobile collision, Appellant, George Burchett, Jr., was convicted by a Green Circuit Court jury of reckless homicide, for which he received a sentence of five years' imprisonment. Burchett appealed his conviction to the Court of Appeals and that court affirmed. We granted discretionary review to consider the only issue raised on appeal: whether evidence that a defendant smoked marijuana on a daily basis is admissible to prove that he smoked marijuana on the day of the collision. For the reasons discussed below, we hold this evidence to be inadmissible; accordingly, we reverse and remand this case to the circuit court.

On December 12, 1997, Sherman Darnell was killed when his vehicle was struck by Appellant's vehicle. Mr. Darnell, traveling on highway 61 in Green County, Kentucky, had the right of way and was not required to stop at the Bloyds Crossing intersection of highway 569. Appellant, traveling on highway 569, failed to stop at the intersection and caused the collision. Although Appellant initially denied running the stop sign, brake marks conclusively indicate that he skidded through the intersection. At the time of the collision, Appellant was on his way to the Taylor County Hospital to visit his girlfriend, Melissa Grider, who had given birth to their child the previous day. Appellant and Grider worked together on the farm owned by David and Dorothy Scott. On the afternoon of the collision, Grider telephoned the Scott residence and left a message for Appellant to come to the hospital as soon as he finished work. Fearing for the health of his child, Appellant left for the hospital after he received the message. The fatal collision occurred shortly afterward, around 3:40 p.m.

Soon after the collision, police trooper Whitlock began his investigation. Trooper Whitlock found an unopened, one-half gallon bottle of vodka in Appellant's vehicle. When questioned, Appellant denied that he had consumed any alcohol that day. Appellant was then taken to Taylor County Hospital, where he was treated for his minor injuries. During his treatment and evaluation at the hospital, Appellant told the emergency room nurse that he drinks "anywhere from one-half to three-fourths of a gallon a day of vodka" and that he smokes marijuana daily, "one joint in the morning and one at night." To the nurse, Appellant denied smoking marijuana the day of the collision. But Appellant later told a lab tech that he smoked "this morning." The treating physician's notes support the lab tech's version of events. A lab test of Appellant's blood later confirmed that Appellant drank no alcohol before the collision. A drug screen of Appellant's urine sample revealed the presence of three substances: benzodiazepines (*e.g.*, Valium), opiates (*e.g.*, Tylenol 3), and tetrahydrocannabinol (THC) (marijuana). Unfortunately, the blood sample was insufficient to test for these drugs.

Appellant was indicted for second-degree manslaughter. This offense requires proof of a wanton mental state. One way to prove wantonness is to show that the defendant in a vehicle-homicide case was driving while intoxicated. *See Estep v.*

Commonwealth, Ky., 957 S.W.2d 191 (1997). Consequently, the prosecutor intended to show that Appellant was under the influence of marijuana or other drugs at the time of his collision with Mr. Darnell. While Appellant did not contest admission of evidence that he smoked a marijuana cigarette the day before the collision, Appellant did contest the admission of any evidence that he had a habit of drinking alcohol or smoking marijuana everyday. Relying primarily on KRE 404(b) and KRE 403, Appellant made a motion in limine to suppress such habit evidence. Just before trial, the court ruled that evidence concerning Appellant's daily drinking would not be admitted. But the court also ruled that evidence of Appellant's daily use of marijuana was admissible.

This evidence was first introduced during the prosecution's direct examination of the emergency room nurse, who read the notes she took after assessing Appellant in the ER: "Patient states I smoke one joint in the morning and one at night." The nurse later read the physician's notes: "[Patient a]dmits to one joint this morning. Two joints daily." Later, Appellant admitted on direct examination that he told a hospital employee that he usually smoked a "joint" at night and in the morning. Appellant also admitted smoking marijuana the day before the collision and taking Tylenol 3 and Valium the day before, and the day of, the collision. Appellant testified that he has had spinal bifida since he was a child and he uses the Tylenol 3 and Valium — for which he does not have a prescription — to ease the muscle spasms in his leg and the swollen joints in his back. Appellant further admitted that he gave conflicting statements to hospital personnel about whether he smoked marijuana the morning of the collision. But despite his admitted daily marijuana usage, and his conflicting statements at the hospital, at trial he denied that he smoked marijuana the morning of the collision.

Appellant explained that he accompanied his girlfriend to the hospital to induce labor at 5:00 a.m. on December 11. He smoked marijuana while she drove. He stayed at the hospital all day, save one trip to Wal-Mart for baby clothes, and spent the night at the hospital. The next day, the day of the collision, he left the hospital around 6:30 a.m. to go directly to work. He later testified that if he had marijuana that morning, he probably would have smoked it, but he did not. Concerning his inconsistent statements, Appellant testified: "I told somebody that I had smoked some weed earlier [the morning of the collision] but it was the day before. It was on the 11th when I smoked the weed because I didn't have none [on the 12th]." On cross-examination the prosecutor explored Appellant's marijuana use in depth, asking questions like: "[At what age] did you start smoking?" "What's your normal consumption?" The prosecutor finally concluded: "You're just pretty much a one joint morning [sic] and one joint at night, that's just your habit."

The jury was instructed on second-degree manslaughter and reckless homicide. Appellant was convicted of the lesser offense, reckless homicide. He appealed to the Court of Appeals, and now this Court, decrying the admission of evidence of his daily marijuana use. Appellant argues that the evidence was habit evidence, which has been inadmissible in Kentucky courts for at least a century. *See Chesapeake & O. Ry. Co. v. Riddle's Adm'x*, Ky., 72 S.W. 22 (1903).

*   *   *

It is easy to recognize the prejudice to the defendant if the prosecutor is permitted to attach the label of "habit" to his actions. *E.g.*, John Doe has the "habit" of watching pornographic videos after work in front of his minor daughters. Or, John Doe has the "habit" of beating his wife on the weekends. Simply characterizing the defendant's actions as a "habit" attaches excessive significance in the minds of jurors, as Wright and Graham noted: "Even if the court thought that the specific instances of conduct had some probative worth so as to be admissible on another ground, *e.g.*, Rule 404(b), the court may feel that permitting the label 'habit' to be attached to the evidence may tend to unfairly enhance its value in the eyes of the jury." 23 Wright and Graham, *Federal Practice and Procedure: Evidence*, § 5273 (1980). The label becomes a scarlet letter. Because of that, courts have correctly been "reluctant to admit evidence that a person is a 'habitual drunk' or has a habit of reckless driving [or smoking a joint every morning] [because] such evidence may be more prejudicial than probative with respect to the issues in the case." *Id.* In this case, the prosecutor used the term in just this inflammatory manner when he declared: "You're just pretty much a one joint morning [sic] and one joint at night, that's just your habit."

*   *   *

In the present case, even though Appellant testified about his own habit, there were numerous collateral evidentiary issues related to his marijuana use that were not explored, but likely could have been. These issues could easily have involved other witnesses. Appellant testified that he slept at the hospital the night before the collision and he drove directly to work the next morning. Even if he smoked marijuana "every" morning — a statement that is likely not literally true — he could not smoke it if he did not have any. How much evidence could Appellant introduce that he never kept marijuana in his truck but only at his home? Or that when he spent the night away from home, he did not smoke marijuana in the morning? Could Appellant offer evidence that he did not have marijuana when other important family events occurred, like the death of a parent or sibling? Or that he typically ran out of marijuana on a particular day of the week? Or that he met his supplier on a typical day? This is the type of evidence that delays trials and confuses jurors — an exorbitant price to pay for evidence that fails to even address the critical issue.

Another difficulty that plagues the use of habit evidence is the inexorable tendency for courts to require less and less proof of the habit. Appellant testified that he typically smoked marijuana everyday. If this statement were true, it would be simple to calculate the ratio of reactions to situations — one. But few cases are likely to have such a unitary ratio. This begs the question concerning how many instances of a practice and what ratio of reactions to situations is sufficient to establish proof of a habit. Judges and scholars have yet to offer good answers to this question. Perhaps evidence of four instances would be enough to conclude that the defendant had a habit. *See Whittemore v. Lockheed Aircraft Corp.*, 65 Cal. App. 2d 737, 151 P.2d 670, 678 (1944) (evidence that alleged pilot of crashed aircraft was pilot on four previous flights admitted to show habit) (cited with approval in Advisory Committee notes); *see also Chomicki v. Wittekind*, 128 Wis. 2d 188, 381 N.W.2d 561, 565 (Wis. App. 1985) (Testimony of four female tenants that landlord made sexual advances held sufficient to establish habit. Significantly, the court made no determination of how many female tenants landlord dealt with, i.e., no attempt was made to determine the ratio of reactions to situations.); Wright and Graham, § 5273 (". . . the standard of frequency for the admissibility of habit evidence . . . appears to be weakening"). Indeed, one court has even divined a habit from a single act. *See French v. Sorano*, 74 Wis. 2d 460, 247 N.W.2d 182, 186 (Wis. 1976) (one instance of person hiding money in car sufficient to demonstrate a habit). The tendency of courts to go down this judicial slippery slope further attenuates the efficacy of this already dubious evidence.

Of course one of the most compelling reasons to exclude habit evidence is presented by the facts of this case. Appellant stated that, in addition to smoking marijuana daily, it was his normal routine to drink one-half to three-quarters of a gallon of vodka daily. If habit evidence were admissible, Appellant's drinking practice would have been admissible as substantive evidence that Appellant had likely been drinking on the day of the collision. That evidence would undoubtedly weigh heavily on the minds of the jurors. But that evidence would have been utterly false. In fact, Appellant did not drink any alcohol that day, as was confirmed by the blood alcohol test, which was the only reason the evidence of Appellant's drinking "habit" was excluded. Unfortunately for Appellant, his blood sample could not be tested and the drug test results could not corroborate his testimony that he did not smoke marijuana that morning, so evidence of his daily smoking was admitted. This scenario ferrets out the dangerous non sequitur that the habit evidence rule encourages: because a defendant regularly performs a particular act, he also did so on this particular occasion. In light of these difficulties, this Court chooses to avoid the introduction of such specious evidence into the courtrooms of this Commonwealth.

Having no proper basis for admission, the evidence of Appellant's marijuana use should have been excluded. This error by the trial court was not harmless. Accordingly, we reverse and remand this case to the Green Circuit Court for a new trial consistent with this Opinion.

COOPER, JUSTICE, Dissenting.

On December 12, 1997, Appellant George H. Burchett, Jr., drove his vehicle past a stop sign without slackening speed and into the Bloyds Crossing intersection of Kentucky highways 61 and 569 in Green County, Kentucky, and collided with a vehicle being driven by Sherman Darnell. Darnell, who had the right of way at the intersection, was resultantly killed. Appellant was indicted for manslaughter in the second degree and, following a trial by jury, convicted of reckless homicide and sentenced to imprisonment for five years. To prove a criminal *mens rea, i.e.,* wantonness or recklessness, as opposed to mere negligence, the Commonwealth sought to prove that Appellant was operating his vehicle under the influence of drugs and/or alcohol. *See Estep v. Commonwealth, Ky.*, 957 S.W.2d 191, 193 (1997) (wanton murder conviction upheld on evidence of the defendant's ingestion of controlled substances and subsequent erratic operation of a motor vehicle). Specifically, the Commonwealth sought to introduce evidence of Appellant's own statements made at the scene of the collision and/or subsequently at the hospital that he "drinks anywhere from one-half to three-fourths of a gallon a day of vodka" (one-half gallon of vodka was found in Appellant's vehicle) and that "I smoke one joint [marijuana cigarette] in the morning and one at night." He also made conflicting statements at the hospital as to whether he had smoked marijuana on the day of the fatal collision.

A laboratory test of a sample of Appellant's blood was negative for alcohol content. However, a drug screen of Appellant's urine sample was positive for Valium, Tylenol 3, and marijuana. The Commonwealth also had evidence that Appellant "had the giggles" on the day of the collision and had left his work duties (stripping tobacco) on numerous occasions that day for short visits to his automobile; and that the known effects of marijuana consumption include a feeling that everything is fine, a better mood, talkativeness, a lessening of motor control, and altered judgment.

Appellant moved *in limine*, KRE 103(d), to suppress his admissions as to his alcohol and marijuana habits on grounds that the statements were either inadmissible character evidence, KRE 404(a), or inadmissible evidence of other crimes, wrongs, or acts, KRE 404(b). In fact, as correctly noted in the plurality opinion, *ante*, Appellant's admissions constituted neither character evidence nor evidence of other crimes, wrongs, or acts, but evidence of habit. In view of the laboratory test results, the trial judge, in weighing probative value against the danger of undue prejudice, KRE 403, sustained Appellant's motion to suppress the evidence of his admitted alcohol habit but overruled the motion to suppress the evidence of his admitted marijuana habit.

Obviously, Appellant's admission that he smoked two marijuana cigarettes every day, one in the morning and another at night, was probative of the Commonwealth's theory of the case, especially in view of Appellant's conflicting statements to hospital personnel as to whether he had, in fact, smoked marijuana on the morning of the collision. Nevertheless, for various reasons expressed in three separate opinions, a majority of this Court has concluded, at least in this case, that we should retain our 100-year-old rule excluding, under all circumstances, admission of evidence of an individual's habit as circumstantial proof of his/her conforming conduct on a specific occasion and thereby maintain our status as the only jurisdiction in the United States that does so.

I. HABIT EVIDENCE VS. CHARACTER EVIDENCE.

In recommending admission of habit evidence, as opposed to character evidence, the Advisory Committee's Notes to Federal Rule of Evidence (FRE) 406 reiterated the oft-quoted paragraph from McCormick's treatise on the law of evidence:

> Character and habit are close akin. Character is a generalized description of one's disposition, or of one's disposition in respect to a general trait, such as honesty, temperance, or peacefulness. "Habit," in modern usage, both lay and psychological, is more specific. It describes one's regular response to a repeated specific situation. If we speak of character for care, we think of the person's tendency to act prudently in all the varying situations of life, in business, family life, in handling automobiles and in walking across the street. A habit, on the other hand, is the person's regular practice of meeting a particular kind of situation with a specific type of conduct, such as the habit of going down a particular stairway two stairs at a time, or of

giving the hand-signal for a left turn, or of alighting from railway cars while they are moving. The doing of habitual acts may become semi-automatic.

FRE 406 Advisory Committee's Note (1972) (*quoting* McCormick, *Evidence* § 162, at 340 [now see John W. Strong, 1 *McCormick on Evidence* § 195, at 584–85 (5th ed. West 1999)]).

Both character evidence and habit evidence are offered as circumstantial evidence of conforming conduct. The element of habit evidence that distinguishes it from character evidence is the element of specificity, as opposed to mere disposition. Thus, evidence that Appellant is a "drunkard" would be character evidence, whereas evidence that he drinks "one-half to three-quarters of a gallon a day of vodka" is evidence of a habit. *See generally* 29 Am.Jur.2d, *Evidence* § 391 (1994). The Advisory Committee noted that "*[a]greement is general that habit evidence is highly persuasive of conduct on a particular occasion.*" FRE 406 Advisory Committee's Note, *supra* (emphasis added). Again quoting McCormick:

> Character may be thought of as the sum of one's habits though doubtless it is more than this. But unquestionably the uniformity of one's response to habit is far greater than the consistency with which one's conduct conforms to character or disposition. Even though character comes in only excep-tionally as evidence of an act, surely any sensible man in investigating whether X did a particular act would be greatly helped in his inquiry by evidence as to whether he was in the habit of doing it.

Id.

II. PROOF OF HABIT.

The National Conference of Commissioners on Uniform State Laws promulgated the first version of the Uniform Rules of Evidence (URE) in 1953. 13A *Uniform State Laws Annotated* 3 (West 1986). As work progressed on the Federal Rules of Evidence, the Uniform Rules were redrafted with a view to conform to the Federal Rules so far as practicable. *Id.* at 5. The final version of the Uniform Rules was promulgated in August 1974 and recommended for adoption in all states. *Id.* at iii. URE 406 ("Habit; Routine Practice") provides:

> (a) Admissibility. Evidence of the habit of a person or of the routine practice of an organization, whether corroborated or not and regardless of the presence of eyewitnesses, is relevant to prove that the conduct of the person or organization on a particular occasion was in conformity with the habit or routine practice.

> (b) Method of proof. Habit or routine practice may be proved by testimony in the form of an opinion or by specific instances of conduct sufficient in number to warrant a finding that the habit existed or that the practice was routine.

The Federal Rules of Evidence were adopted by Congress in 1975. Pub.L. 93-595, § 1, Jan. 2, 1975, 88 Stat. 1932. FRE 406 is identical to URE 406(a). However, Congress did not adopt URE 406(b) and most jurisdictions that have adopted a version of URE 406 have also omitted subsection (b).[2] *See* Jack B. Weinstein and Margaret A. Berger, 2 *Weinstein's Evidence* ¶ 406[05] (Matthew Bender 1989). In jurisdictions that have adopted URE 406(a), but not URE 406(b), the method of proof of habit or routine practice is determined on a case-by-case basis. Typically, it is established by testimony of a knowledgeable witness that there exists such a habit or practice. John W. Strong, 1 *McCormick on Evidence, supra,* § 195, at n. 20. Of course, here, the proof was even stronger since it consisted of the admission of Appellant, himself, the person most knowledgeable of his own habits.

If proof of habit is by specific instances of conduct,[3] there must be evidence of enough such instances to establish the existence of a habit, and the circumstances under which the habit is followed must be present at the time of the conduct sought to be proved. *Id.* § 195, at n. 22, 23; *see also* John Henry Wigmore, 2 *Evidence* § 375 (3d ed. Little Brown & Co.1940). The elements of a habit are generally said to be (1) regularity, (2) specificity, and (3) an involuntary or semiautomatic response. 29 Am.Jur.2d, *Evidence* § 393 (1994). The last element, however, does not require that the response be reflexive or nonvolitional,[4] but only that it be uniform. *Steinberg v. Arcilla,* 194 Wis.2d 759, 535 N.W.2d 444, 447 (App. 1995) ("a person's 'regular response' need not be 'semi-automatic' or 'virtually unconscious" ' in order to be admissible). "[A]dequacy of sampling and uniformity of response are key factors." FRE 406 Advisory Committee's Note, *supra;* Wright and Graham, *supra,* note 3, § 5233. The requirements for admission of habit evidence were summarized as follows in the frequently cited case of *Wilson v. Volkswagen of America, Inc.,* 561 F.2d 494 (4th Cir. 1977):

> It is only when the examples offered to establish such pattern of conduct or habit are "numerous enough to base an inference of systematic conduct" and to establish "one's regular response to a repeated specific situation" or, to use the language of a leading text, where they are "sufficiently regular or the circumstances sufficiently similar to outweigh the danger, if any, of prejudice and confusion," that they are admissible to establish pattern or habit. In determining whether the examples are "numerous enough" and "sufficiently regular," the key criteria are "adequacy of sampling and uniformity of response," or, as an article cited with approval in the note to Rule 406, *Federal Rules of Evidence,* puts it, on the "adequacy of sampling" and the "ratio of reactions to situations."

> These criteria and this method of balancing naturally follow from the definition of habit itself as stated in the *Model Code of Evidence:* "Habit means a course of behavior of a person regularly repeated in like circumstances."

Id. at 511 (citations omitted). The court went on to explain that "ratio of reactions

---

[2] See note 5, *infra,* for a list of jurisdictions that have adopted a version of URE 406.

[3] One authority notes that "one could reasonably testify to having observed habitual behavior, but character is almost always a matter of opinion." Charles A. Wright & Kenneth W. Graham, Jr., 22 *Federal Practice and Procedure* § 5233, at 354 (West 1978).

[4] *But see Levin v. United States,* 338 F.2d 265 (D.C. Cir. 1964), a case decided before the adoption of the federal rules.

to situations" means a "comparison of the number of instances in which any such conduct occurs with the number in which no such conduct took place." *Id.* at 512.

Thus, in *United States Football League v. National Football League*, 842 F.2d 1335 (2d Cir. 1988), evidence that the National Football League disregarded antitrust advice three or four times over a twenty-year period was insufficient to prove a pattern of behavior amounting to habit, *id.* at 1373; in *Weisenberger v. Senger*, 381 N.W.2d 187 (N.D. 1986), a brother of a deceased motorist was precluded from testifying that the deceased, who was reported to have been driving over the center line at the time of the fatal collision, had a habit of driving on the extreme right side of the road, because the brother was not shown to have observed the decedent's driving habits with sufficient frequency to be able to testify that such conduct was habitual, *id.* at 191; and in *Waldon v. Longview*, 855 S.W.2d 875 (Tex. App. 1993), three prior similar accidents over a six-year period were held insufficient to establish habit. *Id.* at 879.

Specifically with reference to intemperate habits, it was held in *Reyes v. Missouri Pacific R. Co.*, 589 F.2d 791 (5th Cir. 1979), that evidence of four prior convictions of public intoxication was insufficient evidence of habit to be probative of intoxication on a given occasion. *Id.* at 794. However, in *Loughan v. Firestone Tire & Rubber Co.*, 749 F.2d 1519 (11th Cir. 1985), evidence from three sources, including the plaintiff, himself, that he routinely kept a cooler of beer in his truck during working hours, regularly consumed alcohol during working hours, and "normally" had something to drink in the early morning hours was sufficient evidence of habit to be probative of his intoxication at the time of his on-the-job injury. *Id.* at 1524. And in *Keltner v. Ford Motor Co.*, 748 F.2d 1265 (8th Cir. 1984), evidence that the plaintiff regularly drank a six-pack of beer four nights a week was held to be sufficient evidence of habitual conduct to be probative of his intoxication on the occasion of his injury. *Id.* at 1269.

There is authority for the proposition that, in a criminal case, evidence of a "habit" of committing the charged offense is inadmissible because "[e]vidence of these habits would be identical to the kind of evidence that is the target of the general rule against character evidence." *United States v. Mascio*, 774 F.2d 219, 222 n. 5 (7th Cir. 1985) (*quoting* Edward W. Cleary, *McCormick on Evidence* § 195, at 574 (3d ed. West 1984)). As applied to the facts of this case, that would mean that the prosecution could not introduce evidence under the guise of "habit" that Appellant had caused other fatal vehicle collisions in the past. Such evidence would be admissible only if it satisfied the requirements of KRE 404(b)(1) or (2). For other applications of the "habit" rule, *see generally* John P. Ludington, Annotation, *Habit or Routine Practice Evidence Under Uniform Evidence Rule 406*, 64 ALR 4th 567 (1988); George H. Genzel, Annotation, *Admissibility of Evidence of Habit, Customary Behavior, or Reputation as to Care of Motor Vehicle Driver or Occupant, on Question of His Care at Time of Occurrence Giving Rise to His Injury or Death*, 29 ALR 3d 791 (1970).

III. HABIT EVIDENCE IN OTHER JURISDICTIONS.

In addition to the enactment by Congress of FRE 406, forty-three of the fifty states have adopted URE 406(a) either by rule or by statute.[5] Five additional states

---

[5] Alabama: Ala.R.Evid. 406;

Alaska: Alaska.R.Evid. 406;

Arizona: Ariz.R.Evid. 406;

Arkansas: Ark.R.Evid. 406;

California: Cal. Evid.Code § 1105;

Colorado: Colo.R.Evid. 406;

Connecticut: Conn. Code of Evid. § 4–6;

Delaware: Del.R.Evid. 406;

Hawaii: Haw.R.Evid. 406;

Idaho: Idaho.R.Evid. 406;

Indiana: Ind.R.Evid. 406;

Iowa: Iowa Code Ann. Rule 5.406;

Kansas: Kan. Stat. Ann. § 60-449;

Louisiana: La. Code Evid. Ann., Art. 406;

Maine: Me.R.Evid. 406;

Maryland: Md. R. Proc. 5-406;

Michigan: Mich.R.Evid. 406;

Minnesota: 50 Minn. Stat. Ann., R.Evid. 406;

Mississippi: Miss.R.Evid. 406;

Montana: Mont.R.Evid. 406;

Nebraska: Neb. Rev. Stat. § 27-406;

Nevada: Nev. Rev. Stat. § 48.059;

New Hampshire: N.H.R.Evid. 406;

New Jersey: N.J.R.Evid. 406;

New Mexico: N.M.R.Evid. 11-406;

North Carolina: N.C.R.Evid. 406;

North Dakota: N.D.R.Evid. 406;

Ohio: Ohio.R.Evid. 406;

Oklahoma: 12 Okla. Stat. Ann. § 2406;

Oregon: Or. Evid. Code, Rule 406;

Pennsylvania: Pa.R.Evid. 406;

Rhode Island: R.I.R.Ev. 406;

South Carolina: S.C.R.Evid. 406;

South Dakota: S.D.R.Evid. § 19-12-8 (Rule 406);

Tennessee: Tenn.R.Evid. 406;

Texas: Tex.R.Evid. 406;

Utah: Utah.R.Evid. 406;

Vermont: Vt.R.Evid. 406;

Virginia: Va. Code Ann. § 8.01-397.1;

Washington: Wash.R.Ev., ER 406;

have common law rules admitting evidence of habit to prove conduct with some variation. Georgia and New York admit habit evidence by common law under circumstances virtually identical to those described in URE 406(a). *Sams v. Gay*, 161 Ga. App. 31, 288 S.E.2d 822, 824 (1982); *Halloran v. Virginia Chem., Inc.*, 41 N.Y.2d 386, 393 N.Y.S.2d 341, 361 N.E.2d 991, 995 (1977). Florida admits evidence of habit by common law only if the occurrence of the conforming conduct is corroborated by other evidence. *Nationwide Mut. Ins. Co. v. Jones*, 414 So.2d 1169, 1171 (Fla. Ct. App. 1982).[6] (Note that the instant case would satisfy Florida law because the evidence of Appellant's marijuana habit was circumstantially corroborated by the positive drug screen, the evidence of his demeanor and conduct prior to the accident, his statement to a hospital medical technician that "I haven't smoked any pot *since this morning*" (emphasis added), and the treating physician's entry in the medical records that Appellant "[a]dmits to *one joint this morning* (emphasis added).") Illinois admits habit evidence only when there is no eyewitness testimony with respect to the conduct at issue. *Grewe v. West Wash. Cty.*, 303 Ill. App. 3d 299, 707 N.E.2d 739, 744–45, 236 Ill. Dec. 612 (1999).[7] Missouri courts have admitted habit evidence, but the precise boundaries of the rule remain unclear. *Hawkins v. Whittenberg*, 587 S.W.2d 358, 363–64 (Mo.App. 1979) (discussing same). Nevertheless, Missouri follows Illinois (at a minimum) and admits habit evidence in the absence of eyewitness testimony. *Gerhard v. Terminal R. Ass'n of St. Louis*, 299 S.W.2d 866, 872 (Mo. 1957). *See also State v. Hemby*, 63 S.W.3d 265, 269 & n. 2 (Mo.App. 2001) (rejecting habit evidence when based on only two prior experiences and noting that the issue has been addressed rarely in Missouri).

Except for Kentucky, Massachusetts is the only jurisdiction that purports to preclude evidence of habit to prove conforming conduct.

> For the purpose of proving that one has or has not done a particular act, it is not competent to show that he has or has not been in the habit of doing other similar acts.

Figueiredo v. Hamill, 385 Mass. 1003, 431 N.E.2d 231, 232 (1982) (*quoting Davidson v. Massachusetts Cas. Ins. Co.*, 325 Mass. 115, 89 N.E.2d 201, 205 (1949)). Nevertheless, the Massachusetts Supreme Court has clarified that habit evidence is not inadmissible in all circumstances.

> Massachusetts draws a distinction between evidence of personal habit and evidence of business habit or custom. . . . [E]vidence of business habits or customs is admissible to prove that an act was performed in accordance

---

West Virginia: W.Va.R.Evid. 406;

Wisconsin: Wis. Stat. Ann. § 904.06;

Wyoming: Wyo.R.Evid. 406.

[6] URE 406(a) permits evidence of habit to prove conduct "whether corroborated or not." Florida has adopted the "routine practice" provision, but not the "habit" provision, of URE 406(a). Fla. Stat. § 90.406. A leading authority on Florida evidence law has opined that prior cases allowing admission of evidence of the habit of an individual, if corroborated by other evidence of the occurrence of the conforming conduct, were not "displaced" by the adoption of the statutory provision and are "still good law." Charles W. Erhardt, *Florida Evidence* § 406.1, at 158 (2d ed.1984).

[7] URE 406(a) permits evidence of habit "regardless of the presence of eyewitnesses." Note that other than Appellant, there were no surviving eyewitnesses to the fatal collision in this case.

with the habit. For example, this court has upheld the admission of evidence of business habits or customs to prove that a letter had been sent, that an insurance application had not been blank when approved, that the police would have impounded money if found in a fugitive's possession, and that goods unaccompanied with a receipt had not been paid for.

Palinkas v. Bennett, 416 Mass. 273, 620 N.E.2d 775, 777 (1993) (internal citations omitted). And in *O'Connor v. SmithKline Bio-Science Laboratories, Inc.*, 36 Mass. App. Ct. 360, 631 N.E.2d 1018 (1994), the Appeals Court of Massachusetts held that a laboratory technician could testify to her "usual practice" of noting a deviation in a urine sample and the significance of the absence of such a notation on the chain of custody form that she signed, *id.* at 1019, carefully (and somewhat dubiously) characterizing such "usual practice" evidence as admissible evidence of a "business custom" rather than inadmissible evidence of an "individual habit." *Id.* at 1021. Massachusetts also has a statute that admits evidence of a decedent's habits in an action brought against the decedent's personal representative to rebut evidence of statements made or documents drafted by the decedent when living. Mass. Gen. Laws, ch. 233, § 66. Thus, Kentucky is the only jurisdiction that precludes, under all circumstances, admission of evidence of individual habit or of the routine practice of an organization as circumstantial evidence of conforming conduct on a specific occasion.

* * *

VI. ADMISSIBILITY OF HABIT EVIDENCE IN THIS CASE.

Like any evidence, evidence of habit or routine practice is admissible only if relevant to a fact in issue. *Compare Gregory v. State*, 9 Ark. App. 242, 657 S.W.2d 570, 571 (1983) (in a trial for receiving stolen property, marijuana habit of witness who allegedly sold stolen property to defendant was not relevant to prove any issue in the case). Thus, whether Appellant smoked marijuana on the morning of the collision would not have been relevant to prove *that* he drove past the stop sign and into the intersection at Bloyds Crossing without slackening his speed. However, it was relevant to prove the element of a criminal *mens rea* of wantonness or recklessness, *i.e.*, to prove *why* he ran the stop sign and drove into the intersection without slackening his speed. The Commonwealth's theory was that Appellant had smoked marijuana on the morning of December 12, 1997, and that his operation of a motor vehicle under the influence of the combined effects of marijuana, Valium, and Tylenol 3 amounted to wanton or reckless conduct. His admitted habit of smoking two marijuana cigarettes every day, one in the morning and another at night, was highly probative of that theory.

The instances of past conduct ("every morning") were "numerous enough to base an inference of systematic conduct." *Wilson v. Volkswagen of America, Inc.*, 561 F.2d 494, 511 (4th Cir. 1977) (quotation omitted). And since the habit was identified by occurrence, *e.g.*, "every morning," as opposed to circumstance, *e.g.*, "when stripping tobacco," there is no issue here with respect to similarity of circumstances or ratio of reactions to situations. Nor is there any issue here as to either competency or the knowledge of the person reporting the habit. The evidence was in the form of an admission by Appellant, himself, KRE 801A(b)(1), who was the person most knowledgeable of his own habits.

Even if relevant and competent, evidence of a habit or routine practice, like other relevant evidence, is subject to exclusion under KRE 403 if its probative value is substantially outweighed by the danger of undue prejudice.[13] The trial judge concluded that the probative value of the evidence of Appellant's alcohol habit was substantially outweighed by its prejudicial effect (because his blood tested negative for alcohol content) but that such was not the case with respect to the evidence of his marijuana habit (because his urine tested positive for marijuana and because of his prior conflicting statements with respect to whether he had or had not smoked marijuana on the day of the accident). I discern no abuse of discretion with respect to either of these KRE 403 rulings. *English, supra,* note 13, at 945.

Accordingly, I dissent and would affirm the judgment of the Green Circuit Court in all respects.

GRAVES AND WINTERSHEIMER, JJ., join this dissenting opinion.

[2]   The Requirement of Automatism

As the court described in *Weil*, habit is different than recidivism. The mere repetition of an act is not sufficient to make it a habit. There must be an almost unthinking, or automatic quality to the act, such as putting on one's seat belt, to qualify as habit evidence.

WEIL v. SELTZER
United States Court of Appeals, District of Columbia Circuit
873 F.2d 1453 (1989)

FLOYD R. GIBSON, SENIOR CIRCUIT JUDGE.

This is an appeal from a final judgment entered on a jury's verdict in a survival and wrongful death action. This case is now before us after two successive trials. The first trial resulted in a verdict for the defendant/appellant; however, the district court set aside the verdict and ordered a new trial after concluding that a contributory negligence instruction was erroneously submitted to the jury. On retrial before a different judge, the jury returned a verdict in favor of the plaintiff/appellee. The jury awarded $1,080,000 under the wrongful death claim and $3,000,000 under the survival act claim. Final judgment was entered in the district court pursuant to that verdict.

One of the grounds of error raised by the defendant on appeal was whether the district court erred in permitting the testimony of five of the defendant's former

---

[13] The plurality opinion, *ante,* seems to assert that *all* evidence of habit or routine practice is *automatically* excluded under KRE 403. That assertion turns KRE 403 on its head; for the premise of the rule is that evidence that is otherwise relevant and *admissible* can be excluded if the trial judge, *in his/her discretion,* determines that it should be excluded because its prejudicial effect substantially outweighs its probative value. *Commonwealth v. English,* Ky., 993 S.W.2d 941, 945 (1999). Here, the majority of the Court holds that evidence of habit or routine practice is *always inadmissible,* thus, KRE 403 does not come into play.

patients in order to establish the defendant's habit and routine practice of prescribing steroids to his patients. . . .

For the following reasons we vacate the district court's judgment and remand this case for a new trial.

I. Background

This case was filed against Dr. Alvin Seltzer in the district court by Brian Keith Weil, as personal representative of Martin Weil's estate [hereinafter appellee or Weil's estate]. After the case was commenced, Dr. Seltzer died and was replaced by Florence Seltzer, as personal representative of his estate [hereinafter appellant].

On March 27, 1984, Martin Weil died unexpectedly at the age of 54 years. Weil's treating physicians could not explain the cause of his death nor could they account for a series of recent medical problems which he suffered from prior to his death.[21] An autopsy was performed in order to determine the cause of Weil's death. The autopsy and a subsequent investigation into the treatment that Weil received from his allergist, Dr. Seltzer, were very revealing.

Dr. Seltzer had treated Weil for more than twenty years and over the course of this treatment Dr. Seltzer regularly prescribed medication which Weil was led to believe were antihistamines. After Weil's death, however, it was determined that Dr. Seltzer had been prescribing a drug called prednisone, which is a steroid. Suddenly, Weil's treating physicians were able to explain his bizarre medical problems that predominated the last ten years of his life. It became apparent that Weil's illnesses were attributable to his long-term ingestion of steroids prescribed by Dr. Seltzer.

The autopsy, which was consistent with long-term steroid use, determined that Weil's cause of death was a saddle block embolus (a type of blood clot), which contained several bone marrow fragments. The autopsy also revealed significant atrophy in Weil's adrenal glands and severe osteoporosis.

Medical experts testified that Weil's osteoporosis, which was linked to his steroid use, may have caused his bones to crumble thus explaining the presence of bone marrow fragments in the fatal blood clot. Long-term steroid use also may have been the cause of the atrophy in Weil's adrenal glands. This condition reduces the body's ability to ward off infection.

Weil's estate filed suit against Dr. Seltzer and began discovery. Through its discovery efforts, Weil's estate learned that Dr. Seltzer prescribed steroids to Weil on his first visit in 1963 and continued to prescribe steroids over a period of more than twenty years. Indeed, Dr. Seltzer had prescribed steroids just eight days before Weil's death and on at least three other occasions during the three months immediately preceding Weil's death.

---

[21] (Court's original footnote 1.) During the ten years leading up to his death, Weil suffered from severe flu-like symptoms; cysts on his face, neck, and eyelids; a broken hip; a fractured knee; general osteoporosis; a life-threatening drop in blood pressure; an abscess in his groin; pain associated with the collapse of his vertebrae; and a severe infection in his left hand. Many of these illnesses were unusual for a man of Weil's age. Medical experts called to testify on behalf of Weil's estate linked many of these problems to long-term use of steroids.

The most startling fact revealed in the discovery was the frequency with which Dr. Seltzer prescribed steroids to his patients. Dr. Seltzer's purchase orders for medication during the years 1980 through 1984, which were produced during discovery, revealed that he purchased 10,000 tablets of the steroidal drugs. Weil's estate then contacted three of the drug companies named in the purchase orders and learned that Dr. Seltzer had purchased more than 1.7 million tablets containing steroids during the 1980–1984 period alone. Weil's estate then contacted eight of Dr. Seltzer's former patients and learned that each had been treated by Dr. Seltzer for many years and they were prescribed pills which Dr. Seltzer represented to be antihistamines and decongestants. All of the patients later learned that the pills prescribed by Dr. Seltzer were in fact steroids. Finally, a number of boxes and bottles labeled with the names of antihistamines and other non-steroidal medications were found in the possession of Dr. Seltzer, Weil, and several of Dr. Seltzer's former patients. These boxes and bottles were mislabeled because they actually contained cortisone, another type of steroid.

II. DISCUSSION

* * *

B. "Former Patient" Evidence

The next issue concerns the testimony of five of Dr. Seltzer's former patients which was admitted in the second trial, over appellant's objection. The substance of this testimony indicated that Dr. Seltzer had prescribed steroids to other allergy patients while representing the drugs to be antihistamines or decongestants.

The district court admitted the evidence under Federal Rule of Evidence 406 which provides:

> Evidence of the habit of a person or of the routine practice of an organization, whether corroborated or not and regardless of the presence of eyewitnesses, is relevant to prove that the conduct of the person or organization on a particular occasion was in conformity with the habit or routine practice.

FED. R. EVID. 406.

Appellant argues that the district court erred in admitting the "former patient" evidence because its admission is forbidden by Federal Rule of Evidence 404(b) which provides:

> Evidence of other crimes, wrongs, or acts is not admissible to prove the character of a person in order to show action in conformity therewith. It may, however, be admissible for other purposes, such as proof of motive, opportunity, intent, preparation, plan, knowledge, identity, or absence of mistake or accident.

FED. R. EVID. 404(b).

[W]e review the district court's action for an abuse of discretion. . . . For the reasons discussed below we believe that the district court abused its discretion in allowing the former patient evidence under Rule 406.

Rule 406 allows certain evidence which would otherwise be inadmissible if it rises to the level of habit. In this context, habit refers to the type of nonvolitional activity that occurs with invariable regularity. It is the nonvolitional character of habit evidence that makes it probative. *See, e.g., Levin v. United States,* 338 F.2d 265, 272 (D.C. Cir. 1964) (testimony concerning religious practices not admissible because "the very volitional basis of the activity raises serious questions as to its invariable nature, and hence its probative value"), *cert. denied,* 379 U.S. 999, 85 S. Ct. 719, 13 L.Ed.2d 701 (1965). *But see Perrin v. Anderson,* 784 F.2d 1040, 1046 (10th Cir. 1986) (five instances of violent encounters with police sufficient to establish "habit" of reacting violently to uniformed police officers). Thus, habit is a *consistent* method or manner of responding to a particular stimulus. Habits have a reflexive, almost instinctive quality. The advisory committee notes on Rule 406 illustrate this point:

> A habit . . . is the person's regular practice of meeting a particular kind of situation with a specific type of conduct, such as the habit of going down a particular stairway two stairs at a time, or of giving the hand-signal for a left turn, or of alighting from railway cars while they are moving. The doing of the habitual acts may become semiautomatic.

FED. R. EVID. 406. Advisory Committee's Note. . . . *See also United States v. Troutman,* 814 F.2d 1428, 1455 (10th Cir. 1987) (evidence of past conduct not admissible because "[e]xtortion or refraining from extortion is not a semi-automatic act and does not constitute habit"). The former patient evidence in this case certainly does not meet this criteria.

We do not believe the evidence of Dr. Seltzer's treatment of five former patients constitutes habit as envisioned by Rule 406. . . . In deciding whether conduct amounts to "habit" significant factors include the "adequacy of sampling and uniformity of responses." FED. R. EVID. 406 advisory committee's note. Thus, one of the concerns over the reliability of habit testimony is that the conduct at issue may not have occurred with sufficient regularity making it more probable than not that it would be carried out in every instance or in most instances. *Levin,* 338 F.2d at 272. This concern is not allayed by the former patient testimony because none of the former patients had ever observed Dr. Seltzer with another patient. Before the former patient evidence could be properly admitted as habit evidence the witnesses "must have some knowledge of the practice and must demonstrate this knowledge prior to giving testimony concerning the routine practice. Where a witness cannot demonstrate such knowledge, he cannot testify as to the routine nature of the practice." *Laszko v. Cooper Laboratories, Inc.,* 114 Mich. App. 253, 318 N.W.2d 639, 641 (1982). Each witness who testified against Dr. Seltzer only knew of the way Dr. Seltzer treated his own allergies. Although they each saw Dr. Seltzer on more than one occasion, he was treating the same patient (the testifying witness) on each occasion. None of the patients were able to testify concerning Dr. Seltzer's method of treating others. Dr. Seltzer's actions might constitute habit only if he reacted the same way each time he was presented with a new patient with allergies. For the former patient testimony to be at all probative it must show that Dr. Seltzer responded the same way with each patient as he did with the testifying patient. . . .

Weil's estate emphasizes the appellant's failure to contradict the testimony of Dr.

Seltzer's former patients, noting that evidence concerning Dr. Seltzer's treatment of his former patients was within appellant's control. We note, however, that the admissibility of habit evidence under Rule 406 does not hinge on the ability of the party seeking exclusion of the evidence to disprove the habitual character of the evidence. *But see Perrin v. Anderson*, 784 F.2d at 1046. Rather, the burden of establishing the habitual nature of the evidence rests on the proponent of the evidence.

Evidence concerning Dr. Seltzer's treatment of five former patients is not of the nonvolitional, habitual type that ensures its probative value. Rather the former patient evidence is the type of character evidence contemplated under Rule 404(b). This evidence of Dr. Seltzer's treatment of the former patients was clearly an attempt to show that Dr. Seltzer treated Weil in conformity with his treatment of the five testifying patients. *See, e.g., Outley v. City of New York*, 837 F.2d 587, 592–93 (2d Cir. 1988) (evidence of six prior lawsuits filed by litigant improper under Rule 404(b) because it is improper evidence of the character trait of litigiousness). . . . Thus, the evidence was admitted for an improper purpose and was undoubtedly prejudicial to the appellant's defense.

We note that under Rule 404(b) the former patient evidence may have been admissible for other purposes, *i.e.,* to show plan, knowledge, identity, or absence of mistake or accident. Indeed, Judge Oberdorfer ruled in the first trial that the evidence could be introduced for that purpose. We, of course, express no view on the correctness of that ruling since that issue is not before us in this case.

Accordingly, the admission of this prejudicial evidence under the standard of "habit" requires us to vacate the district court's judgment.

* * *

Conclusion

* * *

We reverse the district court's decision in the second trial which allowed the testimony of five of Dr. Seltzer's former patients as it was improperly admitted as evidence of habit under Rule 406. However, we recognize that this type of testimony may be admissible and of probative value under Rule 404(b). . . .

Accordingly, we vacate the judgment and remand this case to the district court for a new trial.

EXERCISE

Joel was run over by a train as he lay on the railroad tracks. Joel filed a civil suit against the railroad company, alleging negligence on the part of the railroad's employees in failing to discover him as he lay on the tracks and failing stop the train in time to avoid the accident. The railroad argued that Joel was contributorily negligent because he was intoxicated on the night of the accident and passed out on the tracks before the train arrived. Joel denies being intoxicated. To support its position that Joel was intoxicated, the railroad company seeks to offer evidence that Joel has been convicted for public intoxication four times within the last three years. Do you think four similar convictions within three years rises to the level of "habit" under Rule 406? Is this evidence admissible under Rule 404(b)?

§ 3.03   SIMILAR OCCURRENCES

[A]   The Character of Inanimate Objects

Evidence of occurrences similar to the event that gave rise to the cause of action can be relevant to the determination of facts in the action because such evidence increases the probability that (1) the event giving rise to the cause of action actually occurred, and (2) the event occurred in the way the proponent of the similar-occurrence evidence alleges. For example, in a tort action for negligent maintenance of a walkway, evidence that several persons other than the plaintiff had fallen in the same spot in the same manner could be probative in establishing that the walkway was poorly maintained and that the defendant should have had notice of that fact. Similarly, a demonstration simulating the plaintiff's fall, a created similar occurrence, could be probative, among other things, of how she incurred her injuries. Unlike character evidence, that addresses the propensity of an individual, this evidence addresses probabilities relating to occurrences and conditions independent of a particular individual's inclinations.

Rules relating to the admissibility of similar occurrence evidence has grown up around the general concept of logical relevance. As under the common law, the Federal Rules of Evidence control the admissibility of this evidence through the concept of logical relevance under Rule 401 balanced against potential unfair prejudice under Rule 403. There is no specific rule in the Federal Rules of Evidence addressing the admissibility of similar occurrences.

Evidence of similar occurrences, both spontaneous and created, is often relevant to material issues in litigation. Consequently, courts both at the common law and under the Federal Rules of Evidence have generally admitted it unless its potential prejudice to the opposing party was unfair and outweighed its probative value. Although the rules for admissibility of both spontaneous and created similar occurrences are essentially the same, courts have phrased the requirements for each kind of similar occurrence differently. Consequently, this section will discuss each kind of similar occurrence separately.

[B]   Spontaneous Similar Occurrences

Spontaneous similar occurrences are those that neither party has caused or instigated for purposes of the present litigation. Spontaneous similar occurrences usually occur prior to the event that gave rise to the cause of action, although this is not always the case. Spontaneous similar occurrences may include such occurrences as a series of accidents similar to the one constituting a tort cause of action or a course of dealing in a contract case. Similar occurrences do not include, of course, any events that reflect solely on an individual's character, because it would violate the prohibition against general propensity evidence in civil cases.

Evidence of spontaneous similar occurrences may be relevant in a trial for a number of reasons. In tort actions, such evidence can assist in establishing: (1) the nature and condition of certain instrumentalities; (2) it may also be probative of causation; or (3) it can help establish notice of a dangerous condition, thereby giving rise to a duty of care on the part of those responsible for the condition. In condemnation proceedings, prior sales of comparable real estate can assist in establishing the value of condemned real property. In contract actions, prior contracts between the parties to the action or between a party and a third party can assist in establishing a course of dealing that can be probative of the terms and conditions of the contract in dispute. For example, in an action over disputed grazing rights, if the defendant, the owner of land on which he claims to have reserved grazing rights under an oral lease agreement, offered to lease the same land to others without reserving grazing rights, evidence of such offers would decrease the probability that he included the reservation in the lease offer to the plaintiff.

The admissibility of evidence of spontaneous similar occurrences is governed solely by general principles of logical relevance. This is true both under the common law and the Federal Rules of Evidence. *See* Fed. R. Evid. 401–403. Although courts have differed as to whether such evidence is sufficiently probative to overcome the perceived risk of misuse by the finder of fact through overemphasis, as explained in the following opinion in *Simon v. Kennebunkport*, a blanket rule that such evidence is inadmissible is illogical, unjustified, and inconsistent with modern principles of evidence.

SIMON v. TOWN OF KENNEBUNKPORT
Supreme Judicial Court of Maine
417 A.2d 982 (1980)

GLASSMAN, JUSTICE.

On the morning of July 22, 1977, the appellant, Irene Simon, sustained a broken hip when she stumbled and fell while walking on a sidewalk along Ocean Avenue in Kennebunkport. The elderly woman filed a complaint . . . against the appellee, Town of Kennebunkport (Town), alleging that her injury was proximately caused by a defect in the design or construction of the sidewalk. Following a trial in the Superior Court, York County, the jury determined by special verdict that no defect in the sidewalk had proximately caused the appellant to fall, and judgment was entered for the appellee. The appellant contends that the presiding Justice erred in excluding evidence, offered to establish the defective condition of the sidewalk, that during the two years prior to the accident many other persons stumbled or fell at the location. We vacate the judgment.

Greg Quevillon and Anthony Cooper both operated businesses in the building in front of which the appellant fell. At trial Quevillon testified that the condition of the uneven, inclined sidewalk had not changed from the time it was constructed in 1974 or 1975 until the time of the accident in 1977. The appellant then attempted to elicit from this witness whether he had observed other persons fall at the location. The presiding Justice sustained the Town's objection, ruling that although the appellant could establish that the condition of the sidewalk had remained unchanged since its construction she could not offer evidence that other persons had fallen during this period. The appellant then represented that "if permitted to testify both Mr. Quevillon and Mr. Cooper would state that they saw nearly one person a day fall on that particular sidewalk, and . . . evidence of prior fall[s] is admissible where it goes to show a defect." Later, referring to the proposed testimony of Cooper, the appellant stated:

> My offer of proof is that if permitted to testify this witness would indicate that on similar conditions of weather, and under conditions where the road was identical to that, the condition of July 22, 1979 [sic], he saw approximately 100 people stumble or fall on that particular portion of the roadway.

*   *   *

In a negligence action, evidence of other similar accidents or occurrences may be relevant circumstantially to show a defective or dangerous condition, notice thereof or causation on the occasion in question. The absence of other accidents or occurrences may also be probative on these issues. . . . Nevertheless, Maine courts, with only rare exceptions, traditionally excluded such evidence on the ground that it "tends to draw away the minds of the jury from the point in issue [negligence of the defendant at the time and place of the accident], and to excite prejudice, and mislead them; and, moreover, the adverse party, having no notice of such a course of evidence, is not prepared to rebut it." . . .

The genesis of an inflexible rule excluding other-accident evidence is commonly believed to be the early Massachusetts case of *Collins v. Inhabitants of Dorchester,* 60 Mass. (6 Cush.) 396 (1850), which reasoned that such evidence was largely irrelevant, involved proof of collateral facts and engendered unfair surprise. Id. at 398. The overwhelming majority of jurisdictions, including Massachusetts, *see Robitaille v. Netoco Community Theatres of North Attleboro, Inc.,* 305 Mass. 265, 267–68, 25 N.E.2d 749, 750 (1940), have since either rejected or abandoned a positive rule of exclusion in favor of a standard of discretion. These courts hold that where the proponent can show that other accidents occurred under circumstances substantially similar to those prevailing at the time of the injury in question such evidence is admissible subject to exclusion by the trial court when the probative value of the evidence on the issues of defect, notice or causation is substantially outweighed by the danger of unfair prejudice or confusion of the issues or by consideration of undue delay. . . .

A blanket rule of irrelevance is manifestly incompatible with modern principles of evidence. Although the introduction of other-accident evidence may carry with it the problems associated with inquiry into collateral matters, such evidence may also be highly probative on material issues of a negligence action, as illustrated by the instant case. Early cases failed to discern that admitting this evidence for its circumstantial force is not inconsistent with the fundamental principle that negligence liability is to be predicated on absence of due care under the circumstances at the time and place of injury. . . . Although not rejecting prior case law, several later decisions of this Court appeared to eschew a per se rule as unnecessarily broad and to recognize that the similarity requirement, together with the trial court's discretion, adequately safeguards the proper use of this evidence. . . .

Whatever the continued vitality following these cases of an absolute prohibition against other-accident evidence, it is clear that such a rule did not survive the adoption of our new Rules of Evidence in 1976.[23] Because the comprehensive reformulation does not specifically bar the use of this evidence, its admissibility must be determined by reference to the general provisions governing the admission of relevant evidence. M.R. Evid. 401 defines relevancy in terms of probative value and materiality. With exceptions not here pertinent, M.R. Evid. 402 provides that all relevant evidence is admissible. Although relevant, evidence may nevertheless be excluded under M.R. Evid. 403 when the danger of unfair prejudice, confusion or undue delay is disproportionate to the value of the evidence. Under this formulation, therefore, when a party seeks to introduce evidence of other accidents over objection on the ground of irrelevance, M.R. Evid. 401 requires the presiding Justice to determine the relevancy of the evidence on the basis of whether there is a substantial similarity in the operative circumstances between the proffer and the case at bar and whether the evidence is probative on a material issue in the case.[24] He must then consider whether the probative value of such evidence is substantially outweighed by the countervailing considerations of M.R. Evid. 403. As with other determinations of admissibility involving the balancing of probative value against prejudicial effect, the admission of other-accident evidence is committed to the sound discretion of the presiding Justice.[25] . . .

In the case at bar, it is readily apparent that the ruling of the presiding Justice constituted an abuse of discretion which rose to the level of prejudicial error. Evidence that in the two years prior to the accident as many as one hundred persons stumbled or fell under similar circumstances at the same location, unchanged in condition, clearly satisfies the substantial-similarity foundational requirement and is highly probative on the material issue whether the sidewalk was in a defective condition at the time of the appellant's fall. . . . As demonstrated by its prepared objection to the introduction of this evidence, the Town was well aware of the evidence before trial and therefore would not have been unfairly surprised by its admission. Because the evidence was to be offered through the personal observations of two witnesses, its introduction would not have consumed an inordinate amount of time or tended to confuse or excite the jury. The excluded evidence was crucial to the case of the appellant. The judgment of the Superior Court cannot stand.

The entry is:

---

[23] The Maine Rules of Evidence are virtually identical to the Federal Rules of Evidence.

[24] (Court's original footnote 4.) As part of this determination, the presiding Justice must examine the temporal relationship between the proffered evidence and the injury in the case at bar. For example, evidence that other accidents occurred after the injury in question may be relevant to show causation but is without probative force on the issue of notice.

[25] (Court's original footnote 5.) At a later stage of the trial, the Town offered evidence that the appellant's husband, who was walking directly in front of the appellant at the time of the accident, did not fall as tending to show the absence of a defect in the sidewalk. Over the appellant's objection, the presiding Justice admitted this evidence, ruling that, unlike the excluded evidence of prior falls, the "non-fall" evidence related to the immediate time frame of the accident. In view of our disposition of this appeal, we need not decide whether this ruling, assigned as an additional ground of error by the appellant, constituted an abuse of discretion and, if so, whether the error was harmless. See M.R. Evid. 103(a).

Appeal sustained. Judgment vacated.

Remanded to the Superior Court for further proceedings consistent with the opinion herein.

Costs allowed to appellant.

All concurring.

[C] Created Similar Occurrences: Experiments and Demonstrations

Experiments and in-court demonstrations are nothing more than manufactured similar occurrences. Consequently, the same principles that govern the admissibility of evidence of spontaneous similar happenings also govern the admissibility of experiments and in-court demonstrations. A party may offer experimental or demonstrative evidence to simulate an actual event or to demonstrate the physical properties of a material involved in the litigation. Such evidence is relevant because it duplicates the circumstances that existed at the time the cause of action arose. To ensure that such evidence is relevant to the purpose for which it is being offered, courts, both at common law and under the Federal Rules of Evidence, have required a party offering such evidence to lay a proper foundation by showing a "sufficient similarity" (usually substantial) between the conditions the experiment or demonstration creates and those that existed at the time the cause of action arose. The following opinion *Jodoin v. Toyota Motor Corp.* discusses the principles governing the admissibility of experimental evidence. These principles also apply to the admissibility of demonstrative evidence.

JODOIN v. TOYOTA MOTOR CORP.
United States Court of Appeals, First Circuit
284 F.3d 272 (2002)

TORRUELLA, CIRCUIT JUDGE.

Shelley Jodoin was injured in a car accident and, with her husband and son, sued Toyota Motor Corporation and Toyota Motor Sales U.S.A., Inc. ("Toyota") alleging a design defect in her vehicle. During trial, the district court excluded all evidence relating to testing done by plaintiffs' expert. After this ruling, plaintiffs conceded that they would be unable to prove defect, an element of their prima facie case, and the district court granted judgment as a matter of law in favor of Toyota. On appeal, plaintiffs challenge the district court's exclusion of the testing evidence. We vacate the judgment in favor of Toyota and remand for a new trial.

I.

On October 6, 1995, plaintiff-appellant Shelley Jodoin was hit from behind as she drove her 1988 Toyota 4x4 pick-up truck. The impact pushed her vehicle into a counter-clockwise turn. She attempted to correct the course of her truck, but as she turned to the right, her truck flipped, rolling over several times. As a result of the accident, Mrs. Jodoin is permanently paralyzed.

Mrs. Jodoin, her husband, and her son brought suit against Toyota alleging a design defect in Mrs. Jodoin's truck which made it prone to rollover. At trial, plaintiffs relied on the testimony of their primary liability expert, Robert Loyd Anderson, to prove this defect. They had employed Mr. Anderson to perform an accident reconstruction and test another 1988 Toyota 4x4 truck to determine its rollover propensity. Mr. Anderson was allowed to testify about his accident reconstruction conclusions. However, when plaintiffs attempted to introduce Mr. Anderson's testimony regarding the testing of the exemplar vehicle, the court refused to allow the testimony for lack of a proper foundation. The court reasoned as follows:

> [Y]ou've got a big problem here that you can't remedy . . . we're not interested in the date of manufacture what these two vehicles were like. What we're interested in is what they were like at the time of the . . . accident, and whether the exemplar was the same. And we don't know what condition the exemplar was or what it went through, what its history was. For example, whether it had been in an accident previously, which weakened some structures and other factors. And this witness can't testify to that. He knows nothing about the history of the vehicle. So you're wasting your time. All of this is irrelevant until you establish that the exemplar was virtually identical in all respects with the subject vehicle. And only then can you get into the question of what tests were run. . . . You can't get there from here, I can tell you now, not with this witness.

The court suggested that plaintiffs could lay a proper foundation by introducing testimony from the people who purchased the car for Mr. Anderson or the people from whom the exemplar vehicle was purchased. Plaintiffs introduced no such testimony. Therefore, Mr. Anderson was not allowed to testify as to how the design of the exemplar vehicle compared with the design of Mrs. Jodoin's vehicle.

Plaintiffs did try to lay a foundation based on Mr. Anderson's testimony. First, Mr. Anderson claimed to have checked the vehicle identification tags to verify that the load ratings and tires were the same. Furthermore, the record reflects that the exemplar and Mrs. Jodoin's vehicle had similar vehicle identification numbers ("VIN"). Second, he testified to performing a structural examination of the steering components, suspension components, tires, and springs, including crawling under the truck to inspect the undercarriage. Third, he said he had looked at the instrumentation and modifications made for the purposes of testing, which he documented. This examination included "[e]verything [Mr. Anderson] thought . . . would be related to the vehicle dynamics and the issues that [he] was evaluating." He testified that he detected no evidence of any modifications or any parts that were not Toyota's original equipment. However, Mr. Anderson had no personal knowledge of where the exemplar vehicle came from or how it was obtained, and he did not testify to that history.

When plaintiffs attempted to question Mr. Anderson regarding the relationship between the design characteristics of Mrs. Jodoin's vehicle and its rollover stability, the court upheld an objection to the testimony, stating, "obviously [Mr. Anderson's testimony is] based on testing; and the results of the testing is not admissible at this point, [sic] it never will be." When plaintiffs had previously attempted to introduce testimony on the general relationship between a vehicle's design features and its propensity to rollover, the court excluded that testimony as irrelevant. Therefore, plaintiffs were unable to introduce any testimony regarding design and rollover propensity.

* * *

III.

Plaintiffs challenge the district court's ruling excluding all evidence relating to the testing of the exemplar vehicle. This evidence consists principally of Mr. Anderson's testimony. The district court deemed the evidence irrelevant unless plaintiffs could show that the exemplar vehicle was "virtually identical" to Mrs. Jodoin's truck. Because we find that the district court employed the wrong legal standard, we conclude that the district court abused its discretion by summarily excluding the evidence relating to the testing of the exemplar vehicle and that this error was not harmless.

The Federal Rules of Evidence establish a low threshold for relevance, generally.[4] However, relevant evidence may be excluded if its probative value is "substantially outweighed" by its likelihood to confuse the issue or mislead the jury. Fed. R. Evid. 403. In this regard, courts have treated with skepticism evidence that seeks to recreate accidents. See, e.g., *Swajian v. Gen. Motors Corp.*, 916 F.2d 31, 36 (1st Cir. 1990) (upholding exclusion of a videotape test which portrayed the consequences of a car's axle fracturing). They have not, however, excluded all such evidence. See, e.g., *Robbins v. Whelan*, 653 F.2d 47, 49–50 (1st Cir. 1981) (overturning district court's exclusion of report documenting stopping distances for various vehicles).

When a party introduces evidence that attempts to reconstruct an accident, that party must show a "substantial similarity in circumstances" between the reconstruction and the original accident. *Fusco v. Gen. Motors Corp.*, 11 F.3d 259, 264 (1st Cir. 1993). In contrast, a party may introduce evidence that simply illustrates general scientific principles. *See id.* Then, we simply inquire whether the test on which the evidence is premised was "properly conducted." *Id.* Differentiating between recreations and illustrations of general scientific principles can be difficult. See *McKnight v. Johnson Controls, Inc.*, 36 F.3d 1396, 1402 (8th Cir. 1994). Generally, we look to whether the evidence "is sufficiently close in appearance to the original accident to create the risk of misunderstanding by the jury, for it is that risk that gives rise to the special requirement to show similar conditions." *Fusco,* 11 F.3d at 264.

Here, Mr. Anderson tested a vehicle of the same make and model year as Mrs. Jodoin's truck. He was also prepared to testify about the rollover propensity of the vehicle based on these tests. Because the two trucks are facially similar, we believe

---

[4] Relevant evidence is defined as any evidence having a "tendency to make the existence of any fact that is of consequence to the determination of the action more probable or less probable than it would be without the evidence." Fed. R. Evid. 401.

that a jury would likely view the testing as a reconstruction of the actual accident, not as simply illustrative of scientific principles. *See McKnight*, 36 F.3d at 1402–03 (holding that tests performed on a battery of the same type and make which were used to explain what happened when the subject battery exploded "clearly were not limited to a demonstration of scientific principles in the abstract"). Therefore, the proper test is the substantial similarity standard. *See Fusco*, 11 F.3d at 264.

When reviewing the district court's application of the substantial similarity test, we accord substantial deference to the trial court, looking only for an abuse of discretion. *See Udemba v. Nicoli*, 237 F.3d 8, 14 (1st Cir. 2001). While this accords the district court considerable latitude, it is not a toothless standard. *See Espeaignnette v. Gene Tierney Co.*, 43 F.3d 1, 5 (1st Cir. 1994). An error of law, underlying the evidentiary ruling, constitutes an abuse of discretion. *See Koon v. United States*, 518 U.S. 81, 100, 116 S. Ct. 2035, 135 L. Ed. 2d 392 (1996) ("A district court by definition abuses its discretion when it makes an error of law."); *see also United States v. Kayser-Roth Corp.*, 272 F.3d 89, 100 (1st Cir. 2001).

Here, the district court never specifically applied the substantial similarity standard. Instead, it announced several times that plaintiffs needed to show that the exemplar vehicle was "virtually identical" to Mrs. Jodoin's vehicle. "Virtually identical" is an incorrect standard. *See Robbins v. Whelan*, 653 F.2d 47, 49 (1st Cir. 1981) (holding that "perfect identity" is incorrect standard); *see also Randall v. Warnaco, Inc., Hirsch-Weis Div.*, 677 F.2d 1226, 1233–34 (8th Cir. 1982) ("Admissibility, however, does not depend on perfect identity between actual and experimental conditions. Ordinarily, dissimilarities affect the weight of the evidence, not its admissibility."); *accord Szeliga v. Gen. Motors Corp.*, 728 F.2d 566, 567 (1st Cir. 1984) (holding that "[d]issimilarities between experimental and actual conditions affect the weight of the evidence, not its admissibility," but not specifically applying the substantial similarity standard). Therefore, the district court abused its discretion when it required plaintiffs to demonstrate that the exemplar vehicle was "virtually identical" to Mrs. Jodoin's truck.

* * *

"Substantial similarity depends upon the underlying theory of the case." *Four Corners Helicopters, Inc. v. Turbomeca, S.A.*, 979 F.2d 1434, 1440 (10th Cir. 1992). We have looked to the specific variables in various accidents when determining whether the recreation is substantially similar to the original accident. *Compare Swajian*, 916 F.2d at 36 (focusing on the fact that the driver during a recreation was a professional driver who knew the axle was going to fracture when driver response to an alleged axle fracture was a key element in the original accident), *with Robbins*, 653 F.2d at 49–50 (reversing exclusion of test data when the only suggested difference between re-enactment and actual accident was the skill level of the drivers and the trial issue revolved solely around using length of skid marks to estimate the car's original speed). When the relevant elements are sufficiently similar, we further emphasize that other differences are for defendants to highlight and the jury to weigh in its deliberations. *Robbins*, 653 F.2d at 50.

Here, plaintiffs alleged a design defect based on the rollover propensity of Mrs. Jodoin's truck. At this point, only the characteristics of the truck are at issue, not the characteristics of the test. The evidence presented shows that the two vehicles were essentially the same at the time of manufacture. The question, then, is whether the exemplar vehicle had suffered alterations or damage which could affect its rollover propensity prior to any testing.

Mr. Anderson testified that he personally inspected the exemplar vehicle for everything that "would be related to the vehicle dynamics and the issues that [he] was evaluating." Based on that examination, he found no evidence of any non-original equipment or modifications. Plaintiffs, in their offer of proof, submitted that Mr. Anderson could further testify that the truck showed no evidence of having been in any accidents, otherwise damaged or modified.

The district court, however, required that plaintiffs introduce evidence of the exemplar vehicle's history. We see no reason such information would need to be presented in order to show substantial similarity. No cases suggest such a requirement. *Bogosian v. Mercedes-Benz of N. Am., Inc.,* 104 F.3d 472, 480 (1st Cir. 1997), on which Toyota relies heavily, is inapposite to the current case. There, the court excluded testing evidence performed on the same car when the parties were unable to show that the car had not been materially changed in the two years since the accident and after that car had been examined by numerous experts in the intervening period. *Id.* Here, plaintiffs' expert testified that he had performed a thorough inspection of the exemplar vehicle and detected no evidence of accidents, damage or modification. If the evidence suggested the exemplar had been altered in some material respect, the district court might legitimately require a more complete vehicle history. However, the district court, *sua sponte,* instituted this requirement even though nothing in the record suggested any alteration to the exemplar.

We are, nonetheless, troubled by Toyota's allegation that undisclosed modifications may have been made to the exemplar vehicle before testing. Assuming that these allegations can be substantiated with competent evidence, any such modifications may preclude a finding of substantial similarity should they impact the rollover propensity of the exemplar. These, however, are questions for the district court to consider on remand.

Because we find that plaintiffs cleared the "substantial similarity" hurdle and because this evidence is admittedly crucial to their case, the exclusion of the testing evidence was reversible error.

IV.

For the foregoing reasons, we vacate the judgment below and remand for a new trial.

Vacated and remanded.

§ 3.04　SUBSEQUENT REPAIRS

[*See* Fed. R. Evid. 407]

Subsequent repairs, or remedial measures that an individual may undertake after an allegedly tortious incident has occurred, may take many forms. Such measures have included changes in a product's design, warnings to consumers on particular dangers in using a product, the imposition of safety procedures, changes in methods of operation, the discontinuation of certain practices, the installation of new or different equipment, the discharge of an old employee or retention of a new one, as well as the repair of a defective condition.

Evidence concerning the corrective measures is often quite persuasive to the finder of facts that the condition being corrected was indeed hazardous and that the defendant should have taken precautions *prior* to the incident in the exercise of due care. Such measures tend to be more persuasive than is logically justified. Frequently such measures are not at all indicative of the defendant's failure to act with reasonable diligence and foresight prior to the injury, because he might have made the repairs to correct conditions that either did not exist or were not apparent until after the accident. In this instance, any inference from the subsequent repairs of an admission of negligence from the act would be unfair to the repairing party.

The introduction of such evidence as an admission of negligence on the part of the repairing party would not only raise questions of relevance and unfair prejudice but also place those responsible for the product or instrumentality involved in the accident in a precarious position immediately after the event. On the one hand, if those responsible for the product or instrumentality did not repair the items or take other remedial measures, they would risk further liability to others for any additional injuries the instrumentality might cause. Moreover, the individual's liability in such a circumstance could be much greater, because punitive damages could be justified if the failure to repair were found to constitute gross negligence. On the other hand, if the individual does repair the condition in order to avoid potential liability, evidence of such repairs increases the probability the individual will be held liable for the injuries that have already occurred. To avoid imposing this dilemma on defendants, and thereby discouraging the correction of dangerous conditions and situations, courts have accorded a privileged status to evidence of subsequent repairs, holding it inadmissible to prove negligence or culpable conduct on the part of the one responsible for the corrective measures.

It is important to note that the scope of the subsequent-repair prohibition is limited. The rule's focus is on the unfair admissions of negligence the finder of fact might infer from the remedial measures. The rule does not, therefore, prohibit the use of such evidence if it is relevant to, and offered on, any controverted issue in the litigation other than the defendant's negligence or culpable conduct. Consequently, if the defendant denied ownership or control of the instrumentality that caused the injuries or the feasibility of remedial measures, a court would not exclude evidence of subsequent repairs as bearing on these issues.

These other issues *must* affirmatively be disputed in the litigation before such evidence may be offered to establish them. Consequently, the fact that an issue such as ownership or control is critical to the defendant's liability does not allow a court to admit such evidence if the defendant concedes the issue either in its pleadings or at trial. The theory for this limitation on the rule's prohibition is apparently that if a party offers evidence of subsequent repairs on issues other than negligence or culpable conduct, the probative value of the evidence is not sufficiently counterbalanced by the public policies that would be furthered by its exclusion.

Another significant limitation on the exclusionary effect of the subsequent-repair rule results from the fact that the rule's policy is only furthered if the party against whom the evidence is offered was responsible for the repairs in question. Consequently, remedial measures taken by third parties that have some relevance to the question of the defendant's negligence may be offered as proof on that issue. For example, if a plaintiff brought a products liability action against the manufacturer of a piece of equipment that had injured him, the remedial-measure rule would not exclude evidence of modifications by the owner of the equipment after the accident in question when offered on the question of the feasibility of precautionary measures. *See Koonce v. Quaker Safety Prod. & Mfg. Co.*, 798 F.2d 700, 720 (5th Cir. 1986); and *Grenada Steel Indus. v. Alabama Oxygen Co.*, 695 F.2d 883, 889 (5th Cir. 1983). More often than not, however, when such cases are tried to a jury, evidence of nonparty design changes will be excluded because it lacks sufficient probative value to overcome the confusion it would create.

[A]   Is Rationale Sound?

One aspect of the rationale for the rule excluding evidence of subsequent repairs is that admission of such evidence would discourage individuals from undertaking such repairs. Is this rationale sound? If evidence of subsequent repairs were admissible, would people be discouraged from making them? Would the public safety be jeopardized because dangerous conditions known to exist would go uncorrected?

It is difficult to conclude that admission of such evidence would compromise public safety, because such a conclusion requires the acceptance of two questionable premises. First, it assumes that the existence of the privilege against the introduction of such evidence is generally known. This is highly unlikely, and if existence of the subsequent-repair rule is not common knowledge, it simply cannot achieve its desired end of encouraging defendants to repair dangerous conditions. Second, the conclusion assumes people will risk future liability through potential injuries to others as a result of the continued existence of the condition, rather than risk the increased possibility of being found liable for the injury that has already occurred by changing that condition. What makes this assumption improbable is that the number of potential injuries an uncorrected condition could cause are unlimited, and the level of damages that could be incurred as a result is significantly increased by the fact that allowing the known condition to go uncorrected may constitute gross negligence, thereby justifying punitive damages.

[B]   Should Evidence of Subsequent Repairs Be Admitted for Impeachment?

Is the goal of encouraging remedial measures jeopardized by permitting the use of this evidence to impeach the defendant if she is called as a witness and testifies to the instrumentality's condition prior to the accident? If the defendant is contesting liability, would not the defendant's testimony always be to the effect that the condition was safe and that she was not negligent in allowing the instrument to remain in the condition it was in at the time of the accident? If subsequent repair of the instrumentality can logically be construed as an admission of the hazardous nature of the condition and of the defendant's negligence in allowing the condition to exist, that act will always be inconsistent with the defendant's testimony, and, therefore, admissible for the limited purpose of impeachment. *See* Chapter 6, *Cross-Examination and Impeachment*, § 6.04, Prior Inconsistent Statements.

Circumventing the subsequent-repair rule through the use of such evidence for the purpose of impeachment would seem to be a particular problem in civil litigation in which the plaintiff can call the defendant as a witness. Because the plaintiff may impeach the defendant as an adverse witness, the plaintiff could always circumvent the subsequent-repair rule by the simple expedient of putting the defendant on the witness stand for the sole purpose of having him deny that the condition of the instrument was dangerous prior to the accident, thereby making his subsequent repairs inconsistent with his testimony, and therefore admissible. Should a court allow this? Should it make a difference whether the testimony that the evidence of subsequent repairs is offered to impeach was volunteered by the defendant or intentionally elicited from the defendant by the plaintiff? In *Probus v. K-Mart, Inc.*, 794 F.2d 1207 (7th Cir. 1986), it was held that, even though the defendant introduced evidence that its product was not inadequate for its intended use, the contradictory evidence of subsequent remedial measures could not be introduced for impeachment purposes, because the recognition of such an exception "would elevate it to the rule." *Id.* at 1210. As explained in § 6.04[C], only if the common-law requirement of "surprise" is imposed as a precondition to a party's impeaching its own witnesses with prior inconsistent statements can this ploy to circumvent the subsequent remedial measures rule be avoided.

As a general rule, however, if a party responsible for an instrumentality volunteers testimony about its condition, courts will not prohibit its opponent from impeaching it through evidence of its subsequent repairs. In *Muzyka v. Remington Arms Co.*, 774 F.2d 1309 (5th Cir. 1985), for example, the defendant in its opening statement contended it would show that its rifle was one of the "safest rifles" on the market. Through the testimony of its expert witness, defendant asserted that its two-position, bolt-lock safety was the best available and that its rifle was the best and safest on the market. The appellate court held it was error to prohibit the plaintiff from presenting evidence of design changes in the gun's safety for the purpose of impeaching the expert who spoke in such superlatives about the weapon.

If the court allows plaintiffs to use evidence of subsequent repairs for the limited purpose of impeachment, the defendant is entitled to a limiting instruction to the jury in which the judge would tell them they cannot consider the evidence for any purpose other than impeachment.

Similarly, in *Petree v. Victor Fluid Power, Inc.*, 887 F.2d 34 (3d Cir. 1989), the defendant's expert offered the opinion that the danger of metal spacers being ejected from the press — the apparent cause of the plaintiff's injuries — had been designed out of the product at the time it was sold to the plaintiff's employer. It was held that the trial judge's exclusion of a warning decal cautioning about ejection hazards that was subsequently placed on the defendant's presses was reversible error, because the use of the decal served to directly contradict the expert's claim. For a further discussion of this exception to Rule 407, see § 6.04[C], Relationship to Other Rules.

[C]   Feasibility of Precautionary Measures

When feasibility of precautionary measures is an issue in the litigation, subsequent remedial measures that are probative of that question are admissible. How does feasibility become an issue? In design defect cases feasibility is often at issue. Many courts consider feasibility of precautionary measures in question unless the defendant is willing to make an explicit admission on the issue of feasibility. *See Anderson v. Malloy*, 700 F.2d 1208, 1213 (8th Cir. 1983) (noting that in a case where feasibility is controverted by the assertion that the precautionary measure would be unhelpful, subsequent remedial measures can be admitted into evidence to refute the feasibility argument. "Whether something is feasible relates not only to actual possibility of operation, and its cost and convenience, but also to its ultimate utility and success in its intended performance."). *But see Rimkus v. Northwest Colorado Ski Corp.*, 706 F.2d 1060, 1065 (10th Cir. 1983) (defendant did not raise issue of feasibility when it asserted that safety measures were not necessary, not that they were impossible). The court in *In re Eastern Dist. & Southern Dist. Asbestos Litig.*, 995 F.2d 343, 345 (2d Cir. 1993), noted that " 'feasibility' is not an open sesame whose mere invocation parts Rule 407 and ushers in evidence of subsequent repairs and remedies. To read it that casually will cause the exception to engulf the rule."

[D]   Application to Strict Liability Products Actions

In *Hyjek v. Anthony Industries*, the majority and dissent disagree over the applicability of the doctrine of subsequent remedial measures to strict liability cases. Perhaps more importantly, the dissent offers a justification for the subsequent change in the product's design not recognized by the majority — to demonstrate the practicality of the plaintiff's proposed design.

HYJEK v. ANTHONY INDUSTRIES
Supreme Court of Washington
944 P.2d 1036 (1997)

MADSEN, JUSTICE.

Plaintiff Gary Hyjek brought an action claiming design defect against Anthony Industries' subsidiary, K2 Corporation (K2), as a result of an injury he sustained while using a K2 snowboard. Plaintiff contends the trial court's decision excluding evidence of subsequent remedial measures relating to the binding retention system of K2's snowboards was error. We affirm.

STATEMENT OF THE CASE

K2 Corporation (K2), a subsidiary of Anthony Industries, designs, manufactures, and markets snowboards and other winter sports equipment. In 1990, K2 marketed a snowboard model called the "Dan Donnelly XTC." Ex. 6. The Dan Donnelly XTC was sold without bindings, allowing customers to affix their bindings of choice. K2 did not pre-drill the snowboard for bindings. Without a pre-set hole pattern, the purchaser could install his choice of any bindings on the market by simply screwing them into the snowboard. Coarse threaded screws were screwed directly into a fiberglass retention plate in the snowboard's core to affix the bindings ultimately chosen by the customer.

Plaintiff purchased a Dan Donnelly XTC and was injured on March 24, 1991, while using the snowboard. He testified that the binding came loose from the snowboard, which then struck his inside left ankle. In 1993, Plaintiff sued Anthony Industries, claiming the snowboard as designed was not reasonably safe in that it provided for the affixing of bindings to the snowboard by means of threaded screws which foreseeably could and did prove to be an inadequate and unsafe binding retention method.

In 1992, K2 began to design a new binding system involving "through-core inserts" molded into the snowboard. Fine threaded screws were then screwed into the inserts to hold the bindings in place. Clerk's Papers (CP) at 34–35. Plaintiff sought to enter into evidence K2's subsequent change in design to support his claim for design defect.

K2 brought a motion in limine to exclude evidence of subsequent remedial measures pursuant to Evidence Rules (ER) 402, 403, and 407 and the motion was granted. A jury returned a special verdict in favor of K2. Plaintiff appealed to Division One of the Court of Appeals, arguing that ER 407 does not apply to strict product liability cases, and the evidence of subsequent measures should have been admitted. We accepted certification from the Court of Appeals.

DISCUSSION

The issue in this case is whether ER 407, which provides that a party may not introduce evidence of subsequent remedial measures to establish culpable conduct or negligence, applies in products liability cases where strict liability is alleged. ER 407 provides:

> When, after an event, measures are taken which, if taken previously, would have made the event less likely to occur, evidence of subsequent measures is not admissible to prove negligence or culpable conduct in connection with the event. This rule does not require the exclusion of evidence of subsequent measures when offered for another purpose, such as proving ownership, control, or feasibility of precautionary measures, if controverted, or impeachment.

Washington's Evidence Rule is identical to former Federal Evidence Rule 407 and codifies the common law doctrine which excludes evidence of subsequent remedial measures as a proof of an admission of fault. Wash. Evid. R. 407 advisory committee note; *see also Cochran v. Harrison Mem'l Hosp.*, 42 Wn.2d 264, 254 P.2d 752 (1953).

Courts justify the exclusion of such evidence because it is not relevant and it may discourage development of safety measures. Regarding relevancy, courts have found that evidence of a subsequent repair is of little probative value, since the repair may not be an admission of fault. . . .

While the historical use of relevancy as the basis for excluding evidence of subsequent remedial measures as evidence of negligence is well established, the more widely accepted basis for exclusion appears to be the social policy rationale of encouraging safety precautions . . . .

Although the rule clearly applies in products liability actions based in negligence, where the claim seeks recovery under theories of strict liability, the applicability of Rule 407 varies from state to state[4] and across the federal circuits. Neither the text of Washington's rule nor the Advisory Committee's Note addresses the issue of whether Rule 407 should apply to strict product liability actions. *See* Wash. Evid. R. 407 advisory committee note. Additionally, Washington courts have not squarely addressed this question. *See Haysom v. Coleman Lantern Co.*, 89 Wn.2d 474, 573 P.2d 785, 93 A.L.R.3d 86 (1978).[5]

In the federal circuits, a solid majority apply Rule 407 in products cases where strict liability is alleged and exclude evidence of subsequent remedial measures only where an exception applies. The First, Second, Third, Fourth, Fifth, Sixth, Seventh,

---

[4] For state courts applying ER 407, or equivalent, to strict products liability actions, *see Davis v. International Harvester Co.*, 167 Ill. App. 3d 814, 521 N.E.2d 1282, 1287, 1289, 118 Ill. Dec. 589, 594, 596 (1988); *Krause v. American Aerolights, Inc.*, 307 Or. 52, 762 P.2d 1011, 1013 (1988); *Kallio v. Ford Motor Co.*, 407 N.W.2d 92, 97–98 (Minn. 1987); *Rix v. General Motors Corp.*, 222 Mont. 318, 723 P.2d 195, 202 (1986); *Voynar v. Butler Mfg. Co.*, 463 So. 2d 409, 411, 413 (Fla. Dist. Ct. App. 1985); *Troja v. Black & Decker Mfg. Co.*, 62 Md. App. 101, 488 A.2d 516, 522 (1985); *Hallmark v. Allied Prods. Corp.*, 132 Ariz. 434, 646 P.2d 319, 325–26 (1982); *Hohlenkamp v. Rheem Mfg. Co.*, 134 Ariz. 208, 655 P.2d 32, 37–39 (1982); *Moldovan v. Allis Chalmers Mfg. Co.*, 83 Mich. App. 373, 268 N.W.2d 656, 660 (1978); *see also Benson v. Tennessee Valley Elec. Coop.*, 868 S.W.2d 630, 642 (Tenn. Ct. App. 1993) (construing statute that explicitly excludes evidence of subsequent remedial measures in strict liability cases). *Cf. Siruta v. Hesston Corp.*, 232 Kan. 654, 659 P.2d 799, 808–09 (1983). For states admitting evidence of subsequent remedial measures, *see Caterpillar Tractor Co. v. Beck*, 624 P.2d 790, 793–94 (Alaska 1981); *Ault v. International Harvester Co.*, 13 Cal.3d 113, 117 Cal. Rptr. 812, 814, 528 P.2d 1148, 1150, 74 A.L.R.3d 986 (1974); *Sanderson v. Steve Snyder Enters.*, 196 Conn. 134, 491 A.2d 389, 396 (1985); *Ford Motor Co. v. Fulkerson*, 812 S.W.2d 119, 126 (Ky. 1991); *Carey v. General Motors Corp.*, 377 Mass. 736, 387 N.E.2d 583, 587–88 (1979); *Pollard v. Ashby*, 793 S.W.2d 394, 402–03 (Mo. Ct. App. 1990); *Jeep Corp. v. Murray*, 101 Nev. 640, 708 P.2d 297, 302 (1985); *Caprara v. Chrysler Corp.*, 52 N.Y.2d 114, 436 N.Y.S.2d 251, 256, 417 N.E.2d 545, 551 (1981); *McFarland v. Bruno Mach. Corp.*, 68 Ohio St. 3d 305, 626 N.E.2d 659, 664 (1994); *Matsko v. Harley Davidson Motor Co.*, 325 Pa. Super. 452, 473 A.2d 155, 159 (1984); *Shaffer v. Honeywell, Inc.*, 249 N.W.2d 251, 257 n. 7 (S.D. 1976); *D.L. v. Huebner*, 110 Wis.2d 581, 329 N.W.2d 890, 905 (1983); *Caldwell v. Yamaha Motor Co.*, 648 P.2d 519, 525 (Wyo. 1982). For statutory schemes that admit evidence of subsequent remedial measures; *see* Alaska R. Evid. 407; Haw. R. Evid. 407; Tex. R. Civ. Evid. 407(a); Me. R. Evid. 407 (Maine also specifically allows the admission of subsequent remedial evidence even in negligence cases).

[5] The court's decision in *Haysom v. Coleman Lantern Co.*, 89 Wn.2d 474, 573 P.2d 785, 93 A.L.R. 3d 86 (1978), is not decisive on the issue presented to this court. The court declined to adopt a rule of "universal admissibility of subsequent remedial measures" in a strict products liability action but did not categorically bar the admission of such evidence in a strict products liability action. *Id.* at 483–84, 573 P.2d 785. The court's decision in *Haysom* was made prior to the adoption of the Washington Rules of Evidence and prior to the passage of the Products Liability Act. Professor Tegland noted "there was no fixed rule of admissibility or inadmissibility in strict liability cases before the adoption of the Evidence Rules." Tegland, 5 Wash. Prac. § 132 at 475 (discussing *Haysom*).

and Ninth Circuits each has applied Rule 407 in strict products liability cases.[6] Only the Eighth and Tenth Circuits allow evidence of subsequent remedial measures to be admitted in strict product liability actions.[7]

The debate in the federal courts, however, has recently been answered. Federal Evidence Rule 407 has been amended, adopting the view of the majority of the federal courts, providing that "evidence of the subsequent measures is not admissible to prove negligence, culpable conduct, *a defect in a product, a defect in a product's design, or a need for a warning or instruction.*" (emphasis added). Amend. Fed. R. Evid. 407. (Westlaw 1997).[8]

Plaintiff asks this court to adopt the reasoning of those courts finding that ER 407 does not apply to strict products liability actions and find that the trial court erred in excluding evidence of subsequent remedial measures. Finding the majority of federal courts holding that ER 407 applies to actions based in strict liability persuasive and considering the recent amendment to the Federal Rule, we decline to reverse the trial court's decision.

Plaintiff relies primarily on the California Supreme Court's decision in *Ault v. International Harvester Co.,* 13 Cal. 3d 113, 117 Cal. Rptr. 812, 528 P.2d 1148, 74 A.L.R. 3d 986 (1974), which was one of the first to admit evidence of subsequent remedial measures in a strict liability action. The *Ault* court reasoned that the public policy considerations underling the rule were not valid in strict products liability cases, and held that a plaintiff may use evidence of a subsequent remedial measure to prove a defect. The court found inapplicable the goal of encouraging repairs in the case of mass produced products. *Id.*, 528 P.2d at 1152, 117 Cal. Rptr. at 816. A mass producer, the court reasoned, would not "risk innumerable additional lawsuits and the attendant adverse effect upon its public image" merely to avoid admission of the evidence in the first lawsuit. *Id.* The threat of future increased

---

[6] *See In re Joint E. Dist. & S. Dist. Asbestos Litig.,* 995 F.2d 343, 345 (2d Cir. 1993); *Kelly v. Crown Equip. Co.,* 970 F.2d 1273, 1275 (3d Cir. 1992); *Raymond v. Raymond Corp.,* 938 F.2d 1518, 1522–24 (1st Cir. 1991); *Chase v. General Motors Corp.,* 856 F.2d 17, 21–22 (4th Cir. 1988); *Gauthier v. AMF, Inc.,* 788 F.2d 634, 637–38 (9th Cir. 1986); *Flaminio v. Honda Motor Co.,* 733 F.2d 463, 469–70 (7th Cir. 1984); *Grenada Steel Indust. Inc. v. Alabama Oxygen Co.,* 695 F.2d 883, 888–89 (5th Cir. 1983); *Josephs v. Harris Corp.,* 677 F.2d 985, 990–91 (3d Cir. 1982); *Hall v. American S.S. Co.,* 688 F.2d 1062, 1066–67 (6th Cir. 1982); *Cann v. Ford Motor Co.,* 658 F.2d 54, 59–60 (2d Cir. 1981); *Werner v. Upjohn Co.,* 628 F.2d 848, 852–58 (4th Cir. 1980); *Bauman v. Volkswagenwerk Aktiengesellschaft,* 621 F.2d 230, 232 (6th Cir. 1980); *Roy v. Star Chopper Co.,* 584 F.2d 1124, 1134 (1st Cir. 1978); *see also Dollar v. Long Mfg.,* 561 F.2d 613, 618 (5th Cir. 1977) (admitting evidence of post-accident warning about backhoe for limited purpose of impeachment). While the District of Columbia has never ruled on the issues, in an unofficial reported district court case the court indicated that it would exclude such evidence in a strict products liability case. *See Dine v. Western Exterminating Co.,* 1988 U.S. Dist. LEXIS 4745, at *2 (D.C.C. Mar. 16, 1988) (stating that "[t]he majority of circuits perceive no distinction between strict liability and negligence cases that renders inapplicable the policy underlying Rule 407 [and] . . . [t]his Court is persuaded by the majority.")

[7] *See Burke v. Deere & Co.,* 6 F.3d 497, 506 (8th Cir. 1993); *Huffman v. Caterpillar Tractor Co.,* 908 F.2d 1470, 1480–81 (10th Cir. 1990); *Donahue v. Phillips Petroleum Co.,* 866 F.2d 1008, 1013 (8th Cir. 1989); *Herndon v. Seven Bar Flying Serv., Inc.,* 716 F.2d 1322, 1331 (10th Cir. 1983); *Unterburger v. Snow Co.,* 630 F.2d 599, 603 (8th Cir. 1980); *Robbins v. Farmers Union Grain Terminal Ass'n.,* 552 F.2d 788, 793 (8th Cir. 1977). These cases have been superseded by amendment to Federal Evidence Rule 407.

[8] The rule is effective Dec. 1, 1997, absent Congressional action. [This provision is part of the current Federal Rules of Evidence. Eds.]

liability for failure to remedy a product defect is a sufficient impetus to encourage the mass producer to take remedial actions. *Id.* Therefore, the court concluded, exclusion of subsequent remedial actions only provides "a shield against potential liability." *Id.*

The *Ault* court also considered whether the phrase "culpable conduct" included the actions of manufacturers who were sued under strict liability. *Id.* at 1151, 117 Cal. Rptr. at 815. If the Legislature had intended to apply the rule to strict liability, the court asserted, a phrase without the connotation of "affirmative fault" would have been used. *Id.*

The *Ault* court's dual rationale, that the additional impetus of exclusion is unnecessary to encourage remedial action in a products liability case and that culpable conduct does not apply to strict liability actions, has been followed by numerous state courts and in early federal court decisions concerning ER 407. *See e.g.*, *Robbins v. Farmers Union Grain Terminal Ass'n*, 552 F.2d 788, 793 (8th Cir. 1977); *Herndon v. Seven Bar Flying Serv., Inc.*, 716 F.2d 1322 (10th Cir. 1983); *Ford Motor Co. v. Fulkerson*, 812 S.W.2d 119, 125 (Ky. 1991); *Sanderson v. Steve Snyder Enter., Inc.*, 196 Conn. 134, 491 A.2d 389, 395 (1985); *McFarland v. Bruno Mach. Corp.*, 68 Ohio St. 3d 305, 626 N.E.2d 659, 663 (1994).

Expanding on the courts' reasoning in *Ault*, the Nevada Supreme Court held that the rule "comes into play only where negligence or other 'culpable' conduct is alleged." *Jeep Corp. v. Murray*, 101 Nev. 640, 708 P.2d 297, 302 (1985). Strict liability, the court stated, does not include either of those issues. *Id.* In a products liability case the focus is on the defect in the product, not on any culpable acts of the manufacturer. *Id.* Because there is no negligent conduct to influence in strict products liability cases the rule does not apply. *Id; see also Caldwell v. Yamaha Motor Co.*, 648 P.2d 519, 524 (Wyo. 1982) (since due care or culpability is not at issue in a strict liability action, the exclusionary rule was not applicable).

We, however, agree with the majority of the federal circuits rejecting these arguments and applying the exclusionary rule to actions brought under a theory of strict products liability. The reasoning employed by the Fourth Circuit in *Werner v. Upjohn Co.*, 628 F.2d 848 (4th Cir. 1980), exemplifies the rationale followed by the majority. In *Werner*, the court found that, regardless of the theory used to require a manufacturer to pay damages, the deterrent to taking remedial measures is the same, namely, the fear that the evidence may ultimately be used against the defendant. *Id.* at 856–57.

Werner acknowledged that ER 407 does not mention the use of remedial measures to prove strict liability and that some courts have used the rule's silence to conclude that strict liability must be an unstated exception. *Id.* at 856. However, keeping in mind the precept that admission could defeat the goal of encouraging repairs, the *Werner* court emphasized that the rules of evidence contain many "gaps" and that where the rules are silent, common law principles should be applied to fill in the gaps and achieve the policy objectives of Congress. *Id.*

With a view towards encouraging development of safety enhancements, the court focused on whether distinctions between negligence and strict liability warrant different treatment under rule 407. *Id.* at 857. The rationale behind the rule, the court explained, is that people generally will not take actions that can be used against them. *Id.* The court recognized the difference between negligence and strict liability: in negligence the focus is on the defendant and in strict liability it is on the product. *Id.* Nevertheless, the *Werner* court found this distinction "hypertechnical" because the suit is against the manufacturer, *not* against the product, "regardless of theory." (Emphasis added). *Id.* Therefore, the court concluded, the policy of encouraging remedial measures by excluding repair evidence will be served as effectively in strict liability as in negligence. In neither case does the manufacturer want to be liable, and the assumption that he will not take steps which can be used against him remains undisturbed. *Id.*

*   *   *

Soon after the Fourth Circuit's decision in *Werner,* other circuits began adopting that court's approach. *See Cann v. Ford Motor Co.*, 658 F.2d 54 (2d Cir. 1981) (court found congressional purpose of not deterring remedial measures applicable to strict liability cases); *Gauthier v. AMF, Inc.*, 805 F.2d 337 (9th Cir.1986) (no practical difference between strict liability and negligence in defective design cases and public policy rationale to encourage remedial measures remains the same); *Flaminio v. Honda Motor Co.*, 733 F.2d 463, 467 (7th Cir. 1984) (Judge Posner notes " 'test for an 'unreasonably dangerous' condition is equivalent to a negligence standard of reasonableness . . . .' ") (quoting *Birchfield v. International Harvester Co.*, 726 F.2d 1131, 1139 (6th Cir. 1984)).

Courts have also emphasized the irrelevance of evidence of subsequent remedial measures and have declined to admit it in a strict products liability action. In *Grenada Steel Indust. Inc., v. Alabama Oxygen Co.*, 695 F.2d 883 (5th Cir. 1983), the Fifth Circuit stated the probative nature of such evidence was "based on little direct evidence of why manufacturers make product changes" and that the decision to apply ER 407 to strict liability actions "rests more firmly on the proposition that evidence of subsequent repair or change has little relevance to whether the product in question was defective at some previous time." *Id.* at 887.

The differences between theories of negligence and strict liability are not significant enough to require different approaches when viewed against the goal of encouraging manufacturers to implement safety measures. Instead, the focus must be on the realistic implications of applying the exclusionary rule in strict products liability cases. From a defendant's point of view, it does not matter what kind of action the plaintiff brings. Rather, the manufacturer's focus will be on the fact that if it makes any repairs or safety improvements to its product, evidence of those repairs may be used at trial to show the product was defectively designed. Thus, failing to apply the exclusionary rule in strict liability actions will have the same deterrent affect on subsequent remedial measures as in a negligence case.

Further, admitting evidence of subsequent remedial measures in strict liability cases while excluding such evidence in negligence actions will, as the court suggested in *Werner,* create "gaps" through which irrelevant and prejudicial evidence may be admitted. The Second Circuit in *Cann* noted that plaintiffs "frequently" bring an action under both negligence and strict liability theories. *See Cann*, 658 F.2d at 60. If a defendant could admit evidence of subsequent remedial measures pursuant to the strict liability count, the beneficial effect of the rule is lost. *Id.*

We are also unpersuaded by the mass producer rationale advocated by a minority of the courts, as this argument could apply equally to actions based in negligence. Moreover, the Washington Rules of Evidence have not made an exception for mass producers in actions brought under a theory of negligence. The fact of mass production does not support a different result in a strict liability setting.

Additionally, the language of Washington's Product Liability Act (WPLA) supports our conclusion that ER 407 applies to strict products liability actions. The proper application of a state's equivalent of Federal Rule 407 to strict liability actions should be consistent with the state's law regarding determination of the point in time for assessing liability for a defective product. To do otherwise could impact the substantive law. *See* Randolph L. Burns, Note, *Subsequent Remedial Measures and Strict Products Liability: A New — Relevant — Answer To An Old Problem,* 81 Va. L. Rev. 1141, 1146 (1995).

If the time of product distribution or manufacture is the point selected by the Legislature for determining liability in strict liability cases, then the substantive law makes any product knowledge acquired after the point of distribution irrelevant. *See id.* By contrast, if the law assigns the time of trial as the point at which to measure the product against the legal standard for defectiveness, subsequent repairs may be relevant to determining liability. *See id.*

> Admitting evidence of subsequent remedial measures when the time of distribution is selected, therefore, means the manufacturer is held responsible for product knowledge outside the ambit of the strict liability scheme. In other words, the evidence rule shapes the substantive law by expanding the scope of liability.

Id.

Washington's Products Liability Act explicitly provides that products are to be evaluated "at the time of manufacture" when examining a design defect or a failure to warn claim.[10] RCW 7.72.030(1)(a) and (b). RCW 7.72.030(1)(a) states:

> A product is not reasonably safe as designed, if, *at the time of manufacture,* the likelihood that the product would cause the claimant's harm or similar harms, and the seriousness of those harms, outweighed the burden on the manufacturer to design a product that would have prevented those harms

---

[10] In its amicus brief before this court, the Washington State Trial Lawyers Association (WSTLA) cites *Ayers v. Johnson & Johnson,* 117 Wash.2d 747, 818 P.2d 1337 (1991) for the proposition that hindsight is used in assessing whether a product is defective under the Product's Liability Act. However, WSTLA's reliance on *Ayers* is misplaced because the court in *Ayers* was addressing an argument that the phrase "likelihood that the product would cause the claimant's harm or similar harms" supported defendant's argument that foreseeability was an element of a failure to warn claim. *Id.* at 764, 818 P.2d 1337 (citing RCW 7.72.030(1)(a)). The court held that "forseeability" of harm was a negligence concept which was not part of the strict liability law of failure to warn. *Id.* Here the court is not concerned with the foreseeability of the harm but with the defective nature of the product which the language of the statute clearly indicates should be assessed "at the time of manufacture." RCW 7.72.030(1)(a).

and the adverse effect that an alternative design that was practical and feasible would have on the usefulness of the product. (Emphasis added). RCW 7.72.030(1)(a).

Thus, the focus in a strict product liability action brought under the WPLA is whether the product was defective at the time it left the manufacturer's control. The introduction of evidence of subsequent remedial modifications may confuse the jury by diverting its attention from whether the product was defective at the time the product was manufactured to some later point in time. For this reason, as well as those discussed above, we find that evidence of subsequent remedial measures should not be admitted in a strict products liability action absent an exception under ER 407.

In this case, none of the exceptions listed in the Rule was offered to support admission of K-2's later modifications. Therefore, evidence of subsequent remedial measures was correctly excluded in this case.

DURHAM, C.J., and DOLLIVER, GUY, ALEXANDER and SANDERS, JJ., concur.

TALMADGE, JUSTICE (dissenting).

Despite the specific language of ER 407 and RCW 7.72.030(1)(a) regarding a plaintiff's burden of proof in a product liability claim involving unsafe product design, the majority determines that changes in the design of a product occurring after a plaintiff's injury may not be introduced in evidence. The majority ignores the specific language of ER 407 and fails to evaluate the elements of a product liability claim for unsafe product design in Washington. For these reasons, I respectfully dissent.

K2, a subsidiary of the defendant Anthony Industries, Inc. (K2), marketed a snowboard model in 1990 called the Dan Donnelly XTC (XTC). K2 used a particular design for bindings on this model of snowboard. In 1991, Hyjek was injured while using the XTC. He later sued K2, claiming the XTC snowboard was unsafe because it had a design defect. In 1992, K2 began using a new binding system for snowboards like the XTC. At trial, Hyjek sought to introduce K2's change in design through the testimony of Gavin Myers, a designer K2 hired in 1992 to prepare the new snowboard design. K2 successfully moved in limine to exclude such evidence, but Hyjek's attorney was permitted to draw pictures of certain aspects of the binding inserts used in the XTC and other snowboards for illustrative purposes. Experts testifying at the request of the parties indicated the new design was feasible at the time K2 originally manufactured the XTC snowboard.

* * *

A. ER 407

The principal grounds for excluding such evidence has been the policy of encouraging safety measures. Karl B. Tegland, 5 Wash. Prac. § 131 at 471 (1989); *Codd v. Stevens Pass, Inc.*, 45 Wash.App. 393, 406, 725 P.2d 1008 (1986). We criticized this rationale in *Haysom:*

> The policy justification for the rule of exclusion appears to have little force in the context of the typical products liability action. Those who urge departure from the traditional rule all argue it is implausible to assume a manufacturer would risk liability in numerous future cases, as well as potential loss of customer goodwill, by failing to alter a defective product because such alterations might be admissible against it in a single action.

89 Wn.2d at 483, 573 P.2d 785. Instead, in *Haysom,* given concerns about relevancy of postaccident remedial measures, we chose to avoid a universal rule in product cases, acknowledging a case-by-case weighing of relevance of such evidence to be preferable. This remains the sounder approach. *See Haysom,* 89 Wn.2d at 483–84, 573 P.2d 785.

* * *

Despite the majority's suggestion that a "solid majority" of federal circuits apply ER 407 to strict liability cases, Majority op. at 1039, the majority's citations of authority in its opinion indicate that, at present, there is a substantial split in the federal and state courts regarding the applicability of ER 407 to actions in product liability. *See* Majority op. at 1038 n. 4, and 1038-1039 nn. 6–7. *See also* Randolph L. Burns, Note, *Subsequent Remedial Measures and Strict Products Liability: A New — Relevant — Answer to an Old Problem,* 81 VA. L. REV. 1141, 1141–43, and nn.5 and 8 (1995) (collecting cases and designating which states and federal circuits allow admission of subsequent remedial measures evidence in products liability actions and which do not). However, we do not need to decide if ER 407 invariably excludes admission of postaccident remedial changes in the product design, even though I believe the better rule is to evaluate such matters in products claims on a case-by-case basis. By its terms, ER 407 permitted introduction of Gavin Myers' testimony here.

B. Postaccident Design Changes Are Relevant in Actions Under WPLA

The more significant flaw in the majority's analysis, however, is that subsequent changes in the design of the product are relevant to the question of whether, at the time of the manufacture of the product, the design of the product was feasible *and* practical. By its terms, ER 407 is not a universal rule of exclusion and permits admission of postaccident product changes where such remedial measures are relevant to such issues as "proving ownership, control, or feasibility or precautionary measures, if controverted, or impeachment." Similarly, RCW 7.72.050(1) makes it clear that subsequent remedial measures may be relevant to the question of the technological feasibility of the product design.

In order to prove a claim for a design defect in a product, the Washington product liability act at RCW 7.72.030(1)(a) states:

> A product is not reasonably safe as designed, if, at the time of manufacture, the likelihood that the product would cause the claimant's harm or similar harms, and the seriousness of those harms, outweighed the burden on the manufacturer to design a product that would have prevented those harms

and the adverse effect that an alternative design that was *practical* and feasible would have on the usefulness of the product[.]

(Emphasis added.) *See also Connor v. Skagit Corp.*, 99 Wn.2d 709, 715, 664 P.2d 1208 (1983) (in a products liability case alleging a defective design, the existence of an alternative, safe design is a factor the jury may consider in determining whether a product is unreasonably dangerous).

In the present case, K2 conceded that the design of the XTC snowboard advocated by the plaintiff was *feasible* in 1990 when it initially began the manufacture of the product. Although K2 conceded the feasibility of the alternative design to the XTC snowboard in 1990, *it never conceded the practicality of such an alternative design.* Hyjek was entitled to introduce evidence of the practicality of the alternative design of the XTC snowboard in 1990 through Gavin Myers. The testimony of K2's own designer of the XTC snowboard was plainly relevant to the practicality and feasibility of the alternative design in 1990. The fact that K2 ultimately decided to use this alternative design in snowboards after 1992 spoke volumes as to its practicality. It was plainly relevant for purposes of ER 401–403, as we held in an analogous setting in *Haysom:*

> Respondents stipulated in their trial brief to the feasibility of putting additional warnings on the stove (presumably for the purpose of precluding testimony as to subsequent changes on this basis), *see Bartlett v. Hantover, supra;* however, they then went on to both argue and present testimony to the effect that more detailed warnings would not be an effective labeling technique and that attaching the contents of the brochure to the stove would not be practical. While this testimony may arguably have been directed to the feasibility of change, it was also directed toward the adequacy of existing warnings. In such a situation it has been held to be within the trial court's discretion to allow evidence of subsequent changes.

Haysom, 89 Wn.2d at 484, 573 P.2d 785.

The introduction of subsequent remedial measures by Hyjek was not intended to establish liability on the part of K2, but was relevant to the question of whether the alternative design to the XTC was both feasible and practical. RCW 7.72.030(1)(a). ER 407, which may not apply to actions under RCW 7.72 by its own terms, permits the introduction of such evidence for the purpose of proving feasibility or practicality. The jury was entitled to hear the evidence of Gavin Myers on this subject and the exclusion of the evidence was prejudicial to Hyjek's case. I would reverse the trial court's judgment and order a new trial.

[E]   Pre-Planned Repairs

Preventing juries from learning of subsequent remedial measures encourages repairs, which advances a socially useful end of preventing subsequent accidents. Informing a jury that repairs were planned *before* the accident, however, would deter repairs to a lesser extent than informing a jury that a repair was both planned and carried out after the accident. *Ranches* considers how this question of timing affects admissibility.

RANCHES v. CITY AND COUNTY OF HONOLULU
Supreme Court of Hawai'i
168 P.3d 592 (2007)

Opinion of the Court by Acoba, J.

*   *   *

I.

Petitioners present the following questions for this court's decision: "(1) [whether] the definition of what constitutes a subsequent remedial measure under Hawai'i law [should be clarified]; and (2) whether actions taken by [Respondent] in preparation to refinish a floor prior to a slip and fall incident can be defined as *subsequent* remedial measures." (Emphasis in original.)

II.

*   *   *

At trial the following evidence was adduced and events transpired, according to Petitioners [as they described in their brief].

> [Petitioners] were occasional users of Ewa Beach Park. . . . The restroom . . . has no roof and the walls were constructed of concrete block. [Jerry] walked past the shower and into the doorway which required him to take an immediate left turn and right turn. As soon as [Jerry] made the left turn his right foot slipped and he fell. [Jerry] noted that the floor under him was smooth and worn. It had previously been painted but the paint had worn off. . . . [H]e was sitting in a puddle after he fell. There were no drains in the floor and walls of the men's restroom.

> . . . [O]n the day of the incident[, Edgar Cabato] . . . entered the men's restroom at approximately 12:00 p.m. Upon entering the men's restroom, Mr. Cabato saw a puddle of water. The floor "had some green moss and mildew." Mr. Cabato authenticated a photograph of the shower pipes without the water "on" and that photograph was admitted as Exhibit P-65. Mr. Cabato testified that the floor felt slippery in the area where he found [Jerry] still on the floor after his fall.

> . . . Stacey Kahue [(Kahue)] . . . had testified at [a] deposition as [Respondent's Hawai'i Rules of Civil Procedure] Rule 30(b)(6) witness regarding "any and all modifications and/or repairs to the men's restroom and adjacent shower area at Ewa Beach Park from May 26, 1998 up to and including the current date." . . . *[Petitioners] made an offer of proof that [Kahue] would testify regarding his work as the project manager for the Department of Design and Construction, City and County of Honolulu, and his prior work as the project manager for Arakaki Contracting which was involved in a floor resurfacing project of the men's restroom . . . which*

began prior to [Jerry's] fall on May 26, 2003. . . . In addition to testifying regarding . . . the resurfacing work which the floor was determined to require because of its worn, weathered and smooth condition, [Kahue] would testify regarding photographs he took of the condition of the restrooms which were submitted to [Respondent] prior to the subject incident.

[Respondent] objected to [Kahue's] testimony as it would lead "directly to the issue of the resurfacing of the mens' restroom floor in Ewa Beach." The [c]ourt sustained [Respondent's] objection . . . and precluded [Kahue] from testifying regarding all aspects of the floor resurfacing project, even those actions taken before the subject fall. The [c]ourt had deemed the post incident resurfacing to be a "subsequent remedial measure" in its ruling on [Respondent's] Motion in Limine No. 1 . . . and it extended that definition to include events which occurred prior to the subject incident.

(Emphases added.)

* * *

IV.

As to their first question, Petitioners cite the following text of HRE Rule 407.

When, *after an event,* measures are taken which, if taken previously, would have made the event less likely to occur, *evidence of the subsequent measures is not admissible to prove negligence or culpable conduct in connection with the event.* This rule does not require the exclusion of evidence of subsequent measures when offered for another purpose, such as proving a dangerous defect in products liability cases, ownership, control, or feasibility of precautionary measures, if controverted, or impeachment.

(Emphases added.) The Commentary to HRE Rule 407 states in pertinent part as follows:

This rule is similar to [Federal Rules of Evidence (FRE)] 407, the Advisory Committee's Note to which points out: "The rule incorporates conventional doctrine which excludes evidence of subsequent remedial measures as proof of an admission of fault. . . . The . . . *ground for exclusion rests on a social policy of encouraging people to take, or at least not discouraging them from taking, steps in furtherance of added safety.* The courts have applied this principle to exclude evidence of subsequent repairs, installation of safety devices, changes in company rules, and discharge of employees, and the language of the present rule is broad enough to encompass all of them."

* * *

V.

. . . The term "subsequent" indicates that the measure in question must have been undertaken "after [the] event," which is "the occurrence that caused the death or injury cited in the current complaint." *Id.* (brackets in original). This rationale tracks interpretations of FRE Rule 407 as in *Moulton v. Rival Co.*, 116 F.3d 22, 27 (1st Cir. 1997) (admitting evidence of prior accidents was not an abuse of discretion); and *Traylor v. Husqvarna Motor*, 988 F.2d 729, 733 (7th Cir. 1993) (stating that "remedial measures were taken before rather than after the 'event,' which in an accident case the courts have invariably and we think correctly understood to mean the accident" (citations omitted)).

HRE Rule 407, entitled "[s]ubsequent *remedial* measures" (emphasis added), provides in relevant part that "[w]hen, after an event, measures are taken which, if taken previously, would have made the event less likely to occur, evidence of the subsequent measures is not admissible to prove negligence or culpable conduct in connection with the event." The word "remedial" means " *intended* for a remedy or for the removal or abatement of a disease or of an evil." *Webster's Third New Int'l Dictionary* 1920 (1993) (emphasis added). Thus, a "measure" is "remedial" if it is intended to address the occurrence of an event by making the event less likely to happen in the future. Therefore, measures that are taken after an event but that are predetermined before the event are not "remedial" under HRE Rule 407, because *they are not intended to address the event. See Schmeck v. City of Shawnee*, 651 P.2d 585, 600 (Kan. 1982) (holding that the city's ordering and installation of traffic signal control devices at an intersection where the plaintiff had been injured were not " remedial" because the city's actions "had been *predetermined . . .* many, many months prior to [the] accident," and the city had "merely *completed* something which had *started* long before the plaintiff's accident" (first emphasis added and following emphases in original)); 23 Charles Alan Wright & Kenneth W. Graham, Jr., *Federal Practice & Procedure* § 5283, at 104–05 & 105 n. 43 (1st ed. 1980) (observing that when FRE Rule 407 is read to require a " causal relationship" between the accident and the measures, "exclusion would not be required where the motivation for the remedial measure was not the prevention of a recurrence of the accident in issue," such as where "the defendant undertook repairs as a result of an earlier accident"). Because such measures are not "remedial," it follows that evidence of such measures is not inadmissible under the plain language of HRE Rule 407.

* * *

VII.

* * *

B.

Petitioners urge this court to adopt the analysis set forth in several cases that support their position that "Rule 407 limits its scope to evidence of measures which were taken 'subsequent' to the date of the incident which gave rise to the litigation."

As set out by Petitioners, in *Raymond v. Raymond Corp.*, 938 F.2d 1518, 1523 (1st Cir. 1991),

> a side loader . . . identified as Model 75 was involved in the subject accident. [*Id.*] at 1523. Subsequent to the sale of Model 75, but prior to [p]laintiff's injury, the defendant made design modifications in its subsequent Model 76, which "were on the drawing board prior to the manufacture of Model 75." *Id.* The trial court did not admit evidence regarding these modifications, but the [first c]ircuit concluded that "[a]ny reliance upon 407 at all, however, was misplaced[.]" *Id.*

They cite the following statement from *Raymond.*

> *Under [FRE] 407, only measures which take place after the "event" are excluded.* The term "event" refers to the accident that precipitated the suit. *Roberts v. Harnischfeger Corp.*, 901 F.2d 42, 44 n. 1 (5th Cir. 1989); *Chase v. [Gen.] Motors Corp.*, 856 F.2d 17, 21 (4th Cir. 1988).

Id. (emphasis added). This is an accurate assessment of the holding in *Raymond* and establishes a clear before and after "event" delineation. In accordance with this rationale, actions taken by Respondent prior to Jerry's fall would not be afforded protection under HRE 407, because the policy considerations behind the statute would not apply as set forth *infra.*

The rationale for this interpretation, Petitioners urge, is in *Cupp v. National Railroad Passenger Corporation*, 138 S.W.3d 766, 776 (Mo. Ct. App. 2004)[:]

> *The public policy rationale for excluding evidence of post-accident remedial measures does not apply if the measures in question were planned, provided for, or undertaken prior to the accident. The purpose of the exclusionary rule is to protect a defendant who has been first alerted to the possibility of danger after an accident* and has been induced by the accident to make the repair to prevent further injury. A defendant who is aware of the problem and has proposed measures for remediation *prior to the accident is not entitled to the same protection.* (emphasis added.)

*   *   *

. . . Actions contemplated and commenced *prior* to the "event" required by HRE Rule 407 cannot be considered "remedial" in the sense contemplated by that rule. Moreover, the exclusion from evidence of post event measures does not serve the policy underlying Rule 407 of removing any detrimental effect that such repairs would have on a defendant in subsequent litigation inasmuch as the repairs were contemplated before the accident.

. . . HRE Rule 407 was designed to encourage defendants who are first notified of a dangerous conditions to make repairs, without fear of prejudicing their defense in ensuing litigation. It was not, however, designed to protect defendants who knew of a condition, had initiated steps to remedy it, but did not finish before an innocent party was injured. *See, Cupp*, 138 S.W.3d at 776 ("The purpose of the exclusionary rule is to protect a defendant who has been first alerted to the possibility of danger after an accident. . . . A defendant who is aware of the problem . . . prior to the accident is not entitled to the same protection.")

VIII.

In sum and based on the foregoing, the measures taken by Respondent in this case that began prior to Jerry's accident and continued thereafter cannot be characterized as either subsequent or remedial and, therefore, cannot be precluded under HRE Rule 407, notwithstanding the fact that they were completed after Jerry's accident. To the extent the court excluded such evidence on HRE Rule 407 grounds, it reversibly erred, and insofar as the ICA premised its judgment on such a ruling, the ICA gravely erred.

[F]   Ownership or Control

Clausen offer an illustration of an exception to the prohibition on admitting evidence of subsequently remedial repairs. In *Clausen*, evidence of the repair was offered to demonstrate that the defendant had control over the area of dock where the plaintiff was injured.

CLAUSEN v. SEA-3, Inc.
United States Court of Appeals, First Circuit
21 F.3d 1181 (1994)

LEVIN H. CAMPBELL, SENIOR CIRCUIT JUDGE.

On February 6, 1989, Eric Clausen ("Clausen"), plaintiff-appellee, slipped, fell, and injured his back while working as a pile driver at a job site at a fuel terminal facility on the Piscataqua River, Portsmouth Harbor, Newington, New Hampshire . . . .

II.

BACKGROUND

Storage Tank owns docking facilities along the Piscataqua River in Newington, New Hampshire. These include a walkway-pier that first extends perpendicularly from the shore line into the water, and then turns ninety degrees to the left and extends upstream. A concrete mooring cell, referred to as Cell Three, is located in the water beyond the end of the walkway-pier.[11] Cell Three, at the time of Clausen's injury, was connected to the end of the walkway-pier by the ramp upon which Clausen slipped and fell. The ramp sloped downward to Cell Three from the walkway-pier. In April 1992, the ramp was replaced by Storage Tank, at Sea-3's request, with a set of steps because the concrete cell cap had settled.

Sea-3 imports and distributes petroleum products throughout New England. At all material times, Sea-3 had a first-priority contractual right, under a so-called Dock Agreement with Storage Tank, to occupy and use the docking facilities. In

---

[11] The mooring cells were filled with gravel and capped with concrete to provide support for the dolphins and bollards upon which vessels attached their mooring lines.

1983, Sea-3 sought to improve the docking facilities by making structural changes to Cell Three. Sea-3 contracted with Goudreau to perform the work. Storage Tank was not a party to that contract.

On February 5, 1989, Goudreau hired Clausen to work on Cell Three as a pile driver. Clausen's first day on the job was February 6, 1989, the day he suffered his injury. When Clausen arrived at the job site at 7:00 a.m. on the morning of February 6, 1989, it was snowing. Between one and two inches of fresh snow had accumulated on the dock. Upon receiving permission to begin work, Clausen and his coworkers, Daniel Woundy, William Burroughs, and Kenneth King, the foreman, proceeded down the walkway-pier towards Cell Three. Prior to the group's arrival at Cell Three, King instructed Clausen to go back and retrieve an air compressor hose that was stored in a guardhouse. Clausen retrieved the air compressor hose and then headed back down the walkway-pier toward the ramp that connected the walkway-pier to Cell Three. Somewhere along the ramp that connected the walkway-pier to Cell Three, Clausen slipped, fell, and injured his back.

*   *   *

III.

Storage Tank contends that the district court made errors both during trial and after trial. Among the former, Storage Tank alleges mistaken evidentiary rulings and jury instructions. It argues that the district court erred in . . . allowing evidence of subsequent remedial measures undertaken on the ramp where Clausen slipped and fell . . . .

A. Alleged Trial Errors

1. *Evidence of Subsequent Remedial Measures*

Storage Tank complains of the allowance of evidence that, in 1992, Storage Tank, at Sea-3's request, replaced the ramp on which Clausen fell with a set of steps. Prior to trial, Storage Tank had filed a motion in limine seeking to exclude evidence of the changes made to the ramp both on the issues of negligence and control. Storage Tank argued in its motion that evidence of subsequent remedial measures is inadmissible under Fed. R. Evid. 407[14] to prove negligent or culpable conduct. It also contended that, although there was an unresolved issue in the case about whether Goudreau, Storage Tank, Sea-3, or some combination of the three controlled the area where Clausen fell, the evidence of the ramp's replacement in

---

[14] Fed. R. Evid. 407 states:

> When, after an event, measures are taken which, if taken previously, would have made the event less likely to occur, evidence of the subsequent measures is not admissible to prove negligence or culpable conduct in connection with the event. *This rule does not require the exclusion of evidence of subsequent measures when offered for another purpose, such as proving ownership, control, or feasibility of precautionary measures, if controverted, or impeachment.*

(emphasis added).

this case carried no probative weight with regard to the control issue. The district court denied Storage Tank's motion in limine, but limited the scope of the evidence to the issue of who had control over the area where Clausen's injury occurred. At the end of the trial, the district court gave the jury a limiting instruction to this effect.

On appeal, Storage Tank insists that the district court should not have allowed Clausen to introduce evidence of the replacement of the ramp under the control exception to Fed. R. Evid. 407.

*   *   *

Although Fed. R. Evid. 407 proscribes the admission of evidence of subsequent remedial measures to "prove negligence or culpable conduct," it allows such evidence, as already noted, "when offered for another purpose, such as proving . . . control." Fed. R. Evid. 407. The parties agree that control of the ramp area where Clausen's injury occurred was a material issue in this case. According to the appellant, one aspect of the control issue arose because both Storage Tank and Sea-3 asserted that Goudreau was in control of the work site and was, therefore, responsible for clearing and sanding the area where the plaintiff fell. Clausen points out that a second aspect of the control issue in this case, not alluded to by Storage Tank, involved whether Storage Tank, Sea-3, or both jointly, controlled the area where Clausen fell if Goudreau, at that time, did not control the ramp.[16]

*   *   *

EXERCISES

1.   Kevin, a train conductor, injured his back when the train he was operating "bottomed out" on the tracks. Kevin filed a negligence suit against the railroad company, alleging that the railroad company failed to properly maintain the tracks, which caused his accident. The railroad company's business records contain numerous notations that this portion of the tracks was in disrepair and unsafe before Kevin's accident, but at no point prior to Kevin's accident were the railroad tracks replaced. Soon after Kevin's accident, the railroad company undertook repairs on the section of track in question. May Kevin tell the jury about the repairs which occurred after his accident? May Kevin tell the jury about the lack of repairs that occurred before his accident?

2.   Roland filed a strict product liability claim against the manufacturer of apiece of construction equipment, after he was injured while operating the equipment at work. Roland contends that the equipment was unreasonably dangerous, and that a protective plate with more substantial welds would have either prevented or mitigated the effect of the accident. At trial, in an attempt to

---

[16] The trial judge's summary of the control issue sheds additional light on the parties' arguments:

> As I understand it, and as I'm putting it, the defendants, one, deny that there was an accident, two, they say if there was an accident, each one denies that it was responsible and maintains that any fault was that either of the plaintiff or Goudreau or both, and to each one there's an issue as to who was in control of the premises. *You're not in agreement on that, although you both say that Goudreau was in control of the premises, but if not, then who was?*

show that the manufacturer had knowledge that the equipment was unreasonably dangerous without these modifications, Roland moves to introduce (a) evidence regarding the addition of a protective plate to a subsequent model which was manufactured prior to Roland's accident and (b) evidence of post-accident modifications consisting of the addition of a protective plate and more secure welding made by Roland's employer to the piece of equipment involved in the dispute. The manufacturer objects, arguing that Rule 407 prohibits the proposed testimony. How should the court rule? Would your answer change if the manufacturer also objected under Rule 403?

§ 3.05 OFFERS OF COMPROMISE

Rule 408 Compromise and Offers to Compromise

Prior to the Federal Rules of Evidence, the common law conferred a privileged status on offers to compromise claims that are disputed as to either validity or amount. Consequently, courts at common law would not admit evidence of such offers as admissions of either the validity of the claim or its amount. Courts have often stated they exclude evidence of offers to compromise as irrelevant, because an offering of a small sum in settlement of a large claim may reflect nothing more than a desire to avoid conflict on the part of the offeror.

This "buying of peace" rationale, however, cannot justify a general rule of exclusion of all compromise offers, because the rationale applies only where the offer is a small one, particularly in relation to the claim. Any offer to pay more than a small fraction of a claim logically implies a belief on the part of the offeror that the claim is valid or its defense is weak.

The only rationale, therefore, that can completely justify the exclusion from evidence of *all* offers of compromise is that the rule is intended to encourage the settlement of disputes. Unless litigants are assured they can make offers of compromise without giving rise to prejudicial evidentiary inference, they will be discouraged from making such offers.

The purpose of the rule is to encourage compromise. Courts at common law, therefore, limited its application to cases in which the parties actually dispute the validity of the claim under negotiation. If the parties do not dispute either the basis for the claim or its amount, public policy requires the defendant to pay the claim. Consequently, courts will allow a litigant to introduce evidence of its opponent's efforts to obtain more time for payment of an undisputed claim, for example, as an admission of the validity of that claim.

Although the rationale for the rule was the encouragement of claim settlement, the early common-law rule did not effectively further this goal because its scope was limited to the settlement offer itself. All statements that were not inextricably part of the offer of compromise, *i.e.*, factual acknowledgments made in the course of discussions or negotiations, *could be used* as admissions unless the acknowledgments were prefaced by such phrases as "assuming, only for the sake of this discussion . . ." or "hypothetically speaking . . . ." Only through such preliminary qualifications could the parties ensure that all statements made during the course of compromise negotiations would be "without prejudice." Over time, courts began to disregard this illogical limitation and offered the same protection to both the settlement discussion and the offer to compromise. The Federal Rules of Evidence reflected this changing interpretation and excludes all statements made during settlement negotiations, giving the same protection to any settlement offers as to any settlement discussions.

Rule 408, however, does not preclude use of such evidence if offered for some purpose other than proving the claim's validity or amount. Permissible uses of compromise evidence have included impeachment of a witness' credibility. Courts have never agreed, however, whether a litigant may use evidence of a witness' previous settlement of a claim between the witness and either of the parties in the litigation to impeach the witness who has given testimony that is inconsistent with his prior settlement. For example, in the three-party accident hypothetical discussed above, assume that C successfully settles his claim with B — *i.e.*, B pays C, and then B calls C to testify at the trial of *A v. B* that A's negligence was the sole cause of the accident. Could A offer the prior settlement, which implies that B was at least partially responsible for the accident, to impeach C? One can make a strong argument for using such evidence because of the need to evaluate C's credibility accurately (it proves both that he makes inconsistent statements and that he may be biased). There is, moreover, an absence of any apparent diminution of the rule's public policy goals because (1) the opposing party called the witness and elicited the inconsistent testimony; and (2) the evidence of settlement is not being used to prove liability, only to impeach. Few courts, however, have accepted this position. *Hernandez* is an example of a court embracing this rationale, though you will observe that there is a strong dissent. The majority of American courts follow the view in the dissent.

HERNANDEZ v. STATE

Supreme Court of Arizona
52 P.3d 765 (2002)

McGregor, Vice Chief Justice.

We granted review to address whether Rule 408, Arizona Rules of Evidence (Ariz. R. Evid.), prohibits admission of evidence contained in a notice of claim filed pursuant to Arizona Revised Statutes (A.R.S.) section 12-821.01 (Supp. 2001) when the evidence is introduced to impeach a party's credibility. We conclude that, assuming Rule 408 applies, the rule would not preclude the use of impeachment materials contained in a notice of claim.

I.

Hernandez and his family arrived at the Patagonia Lake State Park at dusk on Friday, August 29, 1997. Hernandez and his son attempted to buy bait at the Patagonia Lake Camp store. The store employee informed them that only the marina store sold bait.

The camp store was located on a hill above the marina store. Rather than drive to the marina store, Hernandez and his son tried to reach the store by crossing a parking lot area adjacent to the camp store, stepping over a cable fence supported by posts three feet high, and walking down a very steep hill without any path or trail. Unbeknownst to Hernandez, the hill ended at a retaining wall with a fourteen-foot drop-off to the road below. In the approaching darkness, Hernandez stepped off the retaining wall and fell to the road below. The fall knocked out several of Hernandez's front teeth and fractured his left wrist.

Pursuant to A.R.S. section 12-821.01,[1] Hernandez filed a notice of claim with the State on September 15, 1997. The notice described the facts surrounding Hernandez's fall as well as the amount Hernandez claimed for his injuries.

After filing the notice of claim, Hernandez brought a civil action against the State. In their joint pre-trial statement, Hernandez and the State stipulated to the facts underlying Hernandez's claim. At trial, the State introduced portions of the notice of claim to impeach Hernandez's credibility because the facts in the notice differed from Hernandez's deposition and trial testimony. Hernandez objected, arguing that Rule 408[3] barred its use. The trial court overruled Hernandez's objection and admitted the redacted notice of claim for impeachment purposes. At the end of a five-day trial, the jury returned a verdict in favor of the State.

The court of appeals upheld the trial court's evidentiary ruling. In its majority opinion, the court concluded that no disputed claim exists when a party files a notice of claim, and a notice of claim therefore cannot constitute an offer to compromise excluded by Rule 408. *Hernandez v. State*, 201 Ariz. 336, 339–40 ¶¶ 10–16, 35 P.3d 97, 100–01 (App. 2001). Dissenting, Judge Voss urged that Rule 408 always requires exclusion of a notice of claim. *Id.* at 342 ¶¶ 27–28, 35 P.3d at 103 (Voss, J., dissenting).

We accepted review and exercise jurisdiction pursuant to Article VI, Section 5.3 of the Arizona Constitution and Rule 23 of the Arizona Rules of Civil Appellate Procedure.

---

[1] The statute requires that:

> Persons who have claims against a public entity . . . shall file claims with the person or persons authorized to accept service for the public entity. . . . The claim shall contain facts sufficient to permit the public entity . . . to understand the basis upon which liability is claimed. The claim shall also contain a specific amount for which the claim can be settled and the facts supporting that amount. Any claim which is not filed within one hundred eighty days after the cause of action accrues is barred and no action may be maintained thereon.

A.R.S. § 12-821.01.A.

[3] Rule 408 provides:

> Evidence of (1) furnishing or offering or promising to furnish, or (2) accepting or offering or promising to accept, a valuable consideration in compromising or attempting to compromise a claim which was disputed as to either validity or amount, is not admissible to prove liability for or invalidity of the claim or its amount. Evidence of conduct or statements made in compromise negotiations is likewise not admissible. This rule does not require the exclusion of any evidence otherwise discoverable merely because it is presented in the course of compromise negotiations. This rule also does not require exclusion when the evidence is offered for another purpose, such as proving bias or prejudice of a witness, negativing a contention of undue delay, or proving an effort to obstruct a criminal investigation or prosecution.

Ariz. R. Evid. 408.

II.

A.

We begin by assuming, for purposes of this opinion, that a notice of claim constitutes an offer of compromise under Rule 408. The plain language of Rule 408 does not exclude evidence offered for the purpose of impeaching a party's credibility. The rule states, in pertinent part, that offers to compromise are "not admissible to prove liability for or invalidity of the claim or its amount." Ariz. R. Evid. 408. Thus, although evidence originating from compromise negotiations may not be admitted to prove liability for or invalidity of a claim, the rule does not prevent the use of such evidence in all instances.

In fact, Rule 408 expressly "does not require exclusion when the evidence is offered *for another purpose*, such as proving bias or prejudice of a witness." *Id.* (emphasis added). The "such as" language indicates that a party may introduce evidence presented in offers to compromise for purposes other than proving bias or prejudice, so long as the evidence is not used to prove liability for or invalidity of a claim. Evidence admitted to impeach party credibility, like evidence admitted to prove bias or prejudice, does not prove liability for or invalidity of a claim. Thus, the plain language of Rule 408 does not prohibit admission of evidence disclosed in compromise negotiations for impeachment purposes.

Other courts have interpreted the plain language of Rule 408 to permit the admission of impeachment evidence. In interpreting Arizona's evidentiary rules, we look to federal law when our rule is identical to the corresponding federal rule, as is true for Rule 408. *State v. Green*, 200 Ariz. 496, 498 ¶ 10, 29 P.3d 271, 273 (2001) ("When interpreting an evidentiary rule that predominantly echoes its federal counterpart, we often look to the latter for guidance.").

Most federal circuit courts agree that Rule 408 does not bar evidence from compromise negotiations if the evidence will be used for impeachment purposes . . .

State courts, including the Arizona Court of Appeals, also express general agreement that Rule 408 does not preclude the use of impeachment evidence derived from compromise negotiations . . . .

B.

The public policy underlying both the Arizona and the federal rules of evidence favors allowing courts to admit evidence presented during compromise negotiations for impeachment. The purpose of the rules of evidence is to promote the "growth and development of the law of evidence to the end that *the truth may be ascertained* and proceedings justly determined." Fed. R. Evid. 102 (emphasis added); Ariz. R. Evid. 102 (emphasis added). Moreover, "[t]he purpose of Rule 408 is to foster 'complete candor' between parties, not to protect false representations." 23 Charles Alan Wright & Kenneth W. Graham, Jr., *Federal Practice & Procedure: Evidence* § 5314, at 286 (1980).

Excluding evidence offered solely to impeach a party's credibility does not encourage complete candor. To the contrary, that approach fails to hold parties accountable for setting forth one version of the facts to obtain a settlement and describing another version at trial. Claimants should present their claims truthfully. Lawyers should not lie on behalf of clients in presenting a claim. Allowing the use of evidence from compromise negotiations for impeachment facilitates Rule 408's goal of encouraging truthfulness by putting parties on notice that they should not falsely represent claims, either during compromise negotiations or at trial.

* * *

III.

The facts underlying Hernandez's fall as set forth in the notice of claim differed from the facts to which Hernandez testified prior to and during trial. Because Hernandez presented inconsistent versions of the facts surrounding his alleged injuries, the State sought to admit factual portions of the notice of claim to impeach Hernandez's credibility. Significantly, the State did not introduce the notice to prove that it was not liable for Hernandez's fall or to disprove the validity of Hernandez's claim or its amount. Thus, even if we regard the notice of claim as an offer to compromise under Rule 408, the trial court properly admitted portions of the notice of claim to impeach Hernandez's credibility.

IV.

For the foregoing reasons, we vacate the opinion of the Court of Appeals and affirm the judgment of the Superior Court.

CONCURRING: CHARLES E. JONES, CHIEF JUSTICE and REBECCA WHITE BERCH, JUSTICE.

JOSEPH W. HOWARD, JUDGE, dissenting.

* * *

. . . As noted above, statements made in compromise negotiations are not admissible to prove "liability for or invalidity of the claim or its amount." Ariz. R. Evid. 408. But, such statements are admissible for "another purpose, such as proving bias or prejudice of a witness, negativing a contention of undue delay, or proving an effort to obstruct a criminal investigation or prosecution." *Id.*

Impeachment of a party with a prior inconsistent statement concerning the facts of the accident is not necessary to prove bias and prejudice of a witness. A party is obviously biased by self-interest in favor of its own position. No further proof is necessary. And proof of bias and prejudice is different from impeaching credibility. A witness can lack credibility without bias or be credible even though biased. Moreover, the other examples stated in the rule are completely distinct. Accordingly, impeachment of a party does not come within the examples of exceptions given in Rule 408.

Additionally, impeachment of a party with a prior inconsistent statement concerning the facts of the case made during compromise negotiations is not the same type of "another purpose" as the examples listed in Rule 408. The examples in Rule 408 are not exclusive but merely illustrative of the types of other purposes that should be excluded from rule's protection. Each example involves issues collateral to the disputed claim. Thus, impeaching a party with a prior inconsistent statement about the facts of a claim is not the same type of "purpose" as the exceptions listed in Rule 408.

Furthermore, " '[t]he clear import of the Conference Report as well as the general understanding among lawyers is that [inconsistent] conduct or statements [made in connection with compromise negotiations] may not be admitted for impeachment purposes.' " *EEOC v. Gear Petroleum, Inc.*, 948 F.2d 1542, 1545 (10th Cir. 1991) (offer of settlement letters "a thinly veiled attempt to get . . . 'smoking gun' letters before the jury") (quoting M. Graham, *Federal Rules of Evidence* 116 (2d ed. 1987)) (alterations added by court in *EEOC*). The bases for this conclusion are twofold. First, there is a significant danger that a jury will use impeachment evidence substantively, and, in that way, directly contravene Rule 408. *See id.* at 1546. " 'The danger that the evidence will be used substantively as an admission is especially great when the witness sought to be impeached . . . is one of the litigants in the suit being tried.' " *Id.* (ellipses added) (quoting Jack B. Weinstein & Margaret A. Berger, *Weinstein's Evidence* ¶ 408[05] at 408–34 (1991)); *see also Schlossman & Gunkelman, Inc.*, 593 N.W.2d at 380 ("When the witness sought to be impeached is also a litigant, the admissibility of statements made during settlement negotiations increases the risk a jury may use the evidence substantively as an admission of liability."); 2 John W. Strong et al., *McCormick on Evidence* § 266, at 186 (5th ed. 1999) ("Use of statements made in compromise negotiations to impeach the testimony of a party, which is not specifically treated in Rule 408, is fraught with danger of misuse of the statements to prove liability, threatens frank interchange of information during negotiations, and generally should not be permitted.").

In fact, if the credibility of a party is impeached with a prior inconsistent statement concerning the facts of an accident, the only possible relevance of such evidence is to assist the jury in determining "liability for or invalidity of the claim or its amount." Ariz. R. Evid. 408. A party's credibility is not a separate issue required to be proven or disproven to prevail on any particular cause of action. Evidence concerning credibility merely assists the jury in determining which set of facts it should adopt, which will determine liability. Furthermore, a prior inconsistent statement may be considered as substantive evidence of the facts contained in it. *See* Ariz. R. Evid. 801(d); Joseph M. Livermore, *Arizona Practice: Law of Evidence* § 608.3(F) (4th ed. 2000). When the statement is made by a party concerning the facts of the disputed claim, it will necessarily be used by the jury to determine validity of the claim. And, because here the facts were stipulated, the credibility of the plaintiff was only relevant to determine the amount of his damage, another purpose specifically excluded by Rule 408.

The second basis for concluding that statements concerning the facts of the accident made in compromise negotiations are not admissible to impeach a party is that a contrary conclusion undermines the purpose of Rule 408, which is to facilitate settlements by encouraging "free communication between parties." Advisory Committee Notes to Fed. R. Evid. 408. "The philosophy of [Rule 408] is to allow the parties to drop their guard and to talk freely and loosely without fear that a concession made to advance negotiations will be used at trial." Steven A. Saltzburg & Kenneth R. Redden, *Federal Rules of Evidence Manual* 286 (4th ed. 1986); *see also EEOC*, 948 F.2d at 1545–46; Jack B. Weinstein & Margaret A. Berger, *supra* § 408.08[1], at 408–29 (2d ed. 2001) ("[C]are should be taken that an indiscriminate application of this 'exception' to Rule 408 does not result in undermining the rule's public policy objective."); Hjelmeset, 43 Clev. St. L. Rev. at 112. If such statements are admissible to impeach a party, the incentive to make those statements is greatly reduced and the purpose of Rule 408 is undermined.[8] *See EEOC*, 948 F.2d at 1546; Saltzburg, *supra*. The majority opinion undermines the purposes of Rule 408.

* * *

Furthermore, under the majority's construction, attorneys will likely revert to the common law practice of making hypothetical statements during compromise negotiations to avoid any future impeachment. *See* Advisory Committee Notes to Fed. R. Evid. 408. The purpose of the second sentence of Rule 408 is to eliminate this common law practice, which constituted "a preference for the sophisticated, and a trap for the unwary." Advisory Committee Notes. In the alternative, attorneys will severely limit the facts and inflate the demand put in § 12-821.01 notices or claim and response correspondence, thereby frustrating the policies underlying it. And, because attorneys are often the ones to make statements during compromise negotiations, the majority's construction creates a risk of causing the disqualification of a party's attorney of choice so that he or she may be called as a witness to impeach the party or explain why a particular statement was made. *See* Hjelmeset, 43 Clev. St. L. Rev. at 110. Clearly, this would cause more harm than good to our adversarial system.

Finally, even under the majority's construction, statements made in compromise negotiations that are offered to impeach a party's testimony may still be excluded under Rule 403, Ariz. R. Evid. And I hope that trial courts will vigorously exercise their discretion to prevent admissibility of prior inconsistent statements by a party concerning the facts of the accident made in settlement negotiations. In conducting a Rule 403 analysis in this context, a trial court must "carefully balance the probative value of the evidence against the danger it will be used for an improper purpose within the context of the policies encouraging open and frank discussions during settlement negotiations and fostering the truth-finding process through the evaluation of a witness's credibility." *Schlossman & Gunkelman, Inc.*, 593 N.W.2d at 380. The better practice is to exclude this type of impeachment in doubtful cases. *See id.* And, if it is admitted, a trial court must, upon request, and in other cases should offer an appropriate limiting instruction to the jury. *See also* Ariz. R. Evid. 105 ("When evidence which is admissible as to one party or for one purpose but not admissible as to another party or for another purpose is admitted, the court, upon request, shall restrict the evidence to its proper scope and instruct the jury accordingly."). Such instructions are, of course, of limited practical value and the better practice remains exclusion of the evidence.

---

[8] Obviously, a plaintiff cannot avoid filing a notice of claim pursuant to A.R.S. § 12-821.01. But, under the majority's construction, a plaintiff would be encouraged to disclose as little as possible. And, in the broader application of Rule 408, private parties would have less incentive to make full and frank statements during compromise negotiations.

Based on the foregoing reasoning, I believe the better approach is to exclude statements made in settlement negotiations that are offered to impeach a party's testimony. In my view, such a construction of Rule 408 better serves the purposes underlying the rule. Accordingly, I would reverse the trial court's judgment.

Concurring: STANLEY G. FELDMAN, JUSTICE.

EXERCISES

1.   Plaintiff filed a wrongful discharge suit against his former employer on six separate grounds, but only three claims survived summary judgment. Plaintiff proceeded to trial on the remaining three claims. During the trial, the defendant-employer made three settlement offers, including one for $75,000.00, but Plaintiff rejected each of these offers. The jury found for Plaintiff on one of the three claims, and awarded him $12,000 in lost wages and nominal damages. Plaintiff then moved for attorney's fees and costs of $113,000. The defendant objected to plaintiff's fee amount. Under federal law, the trial court must now review the plaintiff attorney's lodestar (invoice) and determine a reasonable fee consistent with "the degree of success obtained" by the attorney. Under Rule 408, is the trial court allowed to consider the parties' settlement negotiations in his determination of the attorney's fees?

2.   A college fraternity suspected that its treasurer, Terry, might be stealing money from the fraternity and suspended him. The fraternity hired a new treasurer, Jimmy, to review the accounting books. Jimmy discovered $29,000 in checks made out to "cash," none of which had been deposited in the fraternity's bank account. Jimmy confronted Terry with the discrepancy, and Terry replied: "Those checks were deposited into the payroll account."

Jimmy: "I'm telling you, I've gone through the records and the money isn't there."

Terry: "Can we just split this $29,000 and make this situation just go away?"

Jimmy: "I think the total loss is in excess of a hundred thousand dollars."

Terry: "I can't afford to pay that amount."

Jimmy: "If you want to negotiate some kind of settlement, you need to talk to our legal counsel or our president."

Shortly thereafter, the fraternity alerted police, and Terry was indicted for theft. At the trial the prosecution seeks to call Jimmy to testify as to his conversation with Terry. Terry objects. How should the court rule?

§ 3.06   RULE 409 — PAYMENT OF MEDICAL AND SIMILAR EXPENSES

For offers of compromise to be privileged under Rule 408, there must be a claim made and an existing dispute with regard to either the validity or amount of the claim. The purpose of the Rule is to encourage the settlement of disputes. If a dispute does not exist, application of the Rule cannot serve its purpose.

Rule 409 gives a similar privileged status to "[e]vidence of furnishing or offering or promising to pay medical, hospital, or similar expenses occasioned by an injury. . . ." Like Rule 408, Rule 409 precludes evidence of offers to pay medical expenses from being used to prove "liability for the injury," but does not preclude its use if relevant for another purpose. Unlike Rule 408, however, Rule 409's prohibition operates regardless of whether a plaintiff has already made a claim or whether an actual dispute exists as to either the validity or amount of that claim. The reason for this difference between Rules 408 and 409 is the fact that offers to pay medical expenses are often made from humane impulses and, therefore, have no necessary relevance to liability, regardless of whether they were made in the context of a disputed claim.

Rule 409 differs from Rule 408 in another respect. Rule 409 does not apply to statements of fact that accompany the offer of payment. It only protects the offer itself. The reason for this limitation on the Rule's exclusionary effect relates back to the humanitarian impulses on which the Rule is based. As explained in the Advisory Committee's Note to Rule 409:

> This difference in treatment arises from fundamental differences in nature. Communication is essential if compromises are to be effected, and consequently broad protection of statements is needed. This is not so in cases of payments of offers or promises to pay medical expenses, where factual statements may be expected to be incidental in nature.

56 F.R.D. 183, 228 (1972).

Is such a specialized "good Samaritan" rule justified? If offers to pay another's medical expenses are protected, why aren't offers to repair another's car or do anything else that would assist the person and make her whole again protected? There is no apparent answer to this question. However, expanding Rule 409 in such a fashion would significantly limit the value of Rule 408, because it would be addressing many of the same statements but requiring a dispute to exist before the statements are protected.

Rule 409, however, only excludes evidence offered to show liability. In *Pennington*, the plaintiff offered that the unfulfilled promise to pay medical expenses increased the plaintiff's damages.

<h2 style="text-align:center">PENNINGTON v. SEARS, ROEBUCK & Co.</h2>

Colorado Court of Appeals
878 P.2d 152 (1994)

Opinion by JUDGE CASEBOLT.

In this action to recover for injuries resulting from a slip and fall, defendant Sears, Roebuck & Company (Sears), appeals from a judgment entered in favor of plaintiff, Dorothy Pennington. We reverse and remand for a new trial.

Pennington alleged in her complaint that, after a large snowfall, she slipped and fell in a puddle of water inside Sears' store. She asserted Sears was negligent and requested recovery for medical expenses, permanent bodily injury, pain and suffering, mental anguish, and loss of earning capacity.

Sears' answer denied negligence and raised, as relevant here, an affirmative defense of failure to mitigate damages. The parties filed disclosure certificates that did not disclose any additional theories of recovery or other applicable defenses.

On the first day of trial before jury selection commenced, Sears became aware that Pennington intended to introduce evidence that Sears had promised to pay for all of Pennington's medical expenses and later reneged on that promise, paying only a small portion. Sears requested the court to exclude such evidence. The trial court initially held that the evidence would be relevant because Sears had asserted a defense of failure to mitigate damages. However, Sears withdrew that defense in order to prevent presentation of such evidence.

During opening statements, Pennington was precluded from discussing any offer or any subsequent refusal by Sears to pay her medical expenses. Following opening statements, the court again considered whether Pennington would be allowed to present such evidence. Pennington asserted that the evidence remained admissible because it was not offered to prove liability of Sears under CRE 409, but rather was offered to demonstrate that she had incurred mental anguish as a result of Sears' breach of its promise. She further contended that this evidence was admissible to show that her damages were exacerbated or aggravated because of her financial inability to obtain care and treatment.

The trial court ruled that the evidence would be admitted for purposes of demonstrating mental anguish. It further held that it was admissible to show whether the damages incurred by Pennington were exacerbated or aggravated because of the lack of care and also to demonstrate why Pennington did not seek care or treatment sooner.

Before the evidence was first admitted, the trial court instructed the jury that it was being admitted "solely as it relates to the issue of damages, losses or injuries sustained by the plaintiff and not for the purpose of showing the negligence, if any, of the defendant."

After trial, the jury awarded Pennington $100,000 in compensatory damages.

Sears contends that the trial court erroneously admitted evidence that it offered and then refused to pay for Pennington's medical expenses. We agree.

Evidence of an offer to pay for medical expenses may not be admitted to establish a defendant's liability. CRE 409. However, under certain circumstances in which the evidence is offered for purposes other than proof of liability, the evidence may be admissible.

Situations in which other courts have admitted such evidence are illustrative. For example, when a defendant questioned at trial whether an accident occurred on its premises, its offer to pay medical bills was admissible. *Great Atlantic & Pacific Tea Co. v. Custin*, 214 Ind. 54, 13 N.E.2d 542 (1938). Also, when a defendant denied ownership of the instrumentality that had allegedly caused the plaintiff's injury, evidence of his promise to pay medical bills was held to be admissible. *Flieg v. Levy*,

148 App. Div. 781, 133 N.Y.S. 249, *aff'd*, 208 N.Y. 564, 101 N.E. 1102 (1912). Also, when an agency relationship was a material issue for determination, such evidence was likewise appropriate. *Brown v. Wood*, 201 N.C. 309, 160 S.E. 281 (1931).

However, we are aware of no case authority that discusses the propriety of introducing such evidence to prove mental anguish or aggravation of an injury. *See* Annotation, *Admissibility of Evidence Showing Payment, or Offer or Promise of Payment, of Medical, Hospital and Similar Expenses of Injured Party by Opposing Party*, 65 A.L.R. 3d 932 (1975). Hence, we must analyze the issue under CRE 401, 402, and 403.

Under CRE 401, the proffered evidence must relate to a fact "that is of consequence to the determination of the action." Stated differently, the proffered evidence is inadmissible unless it is legally material to some factual issue in the case. *See People v. Carlson*, 712 P.2d 1018 (Colo. 1986).

If the proffered evidence is legally material, its admissibility becomes dependent on whether the evidence has any tendency to make the existence of a consequential fact more probable or less probable than it would be without the evidence. This latter inquiry, then, focuses on logical relevance. If the proffered evidence is not logically relevant, the evidence should not be admitted. *See People v. Carlson, supra.*

In analyzing whether the challenged evidence relates to a fact of consequence, the elements of the negligence claim for relief must be examined.

As pertinent here, § 13-21-115(3)(c)(I), C.R.S. (1993 Cum. Supp.) allows recovery to an invitee for "damages caused by the landowner's unreasonable failure to exercise reasonable care to protect against dangers of which he actually knew or should have known." Thus, the evidence of an offer to pay medical expenses and later refusal may bear upon or relate to the injuries and losses sustained by Pennington following the accident because it concerns medical expenses, the reasonableness of those medical expenses, bodily injury, and mental anguish. However, the proffered evidence does not relate to or bear upon damages proximately caused by the *negligence* of Sears; therefore, legal materiality does not exist under the claim presented here.

Pennington asserted that the particular mental anguish for which she sought recovery, in *addition to* that which was caused by Sears' negligence, arose because of Sears' *breach of promise*. Thus, the offer to pay medical expenses does not meet the test of legal materiality in a negligence claim context.

Likewise, the refusal to pay the medical expenses, while it may be a source of mental anguish, does not show that the type of mental anguish requested for breach of Sears' promise resulted from Sears' alleged *negligence* in maintaining or creating the danger. Thus, absent circumstances not present here, the refusal also does not meet the test of legal materiality.

Regarding aggravation of Pennington's injuries, while the refusal to pay the expenses may explain *why* Pennington's injury created a permanent impairment, *i.e.*, by delaying the surgery to a point when the injury could not be repaired, that issue was not of consequence to the determination of the action. The *reasons* Pennington did not obtain medical care earlier were not important to the determination of the action because Sears withdrew its failure to mitigate defense and did not contend at trial that Pennington was precluded or limited in recovery of damages for the permanent impairment she admittedly sustained because she did not undergo immediate surgery. Indeed, the surgeon's testimony that Pennington's permanent impairment existed because she did not undergo surgery earlier, was uncontested. *See generally* J. Weinstein & M. Berger, *Weinstein's Evidence* ¶ 401(03) (1986).

Moreover, the evidence does not satisfy the test of logical relevance. Under the circumstances of this case, the mere offer and later refusal to pay medical expenses do not by themselves have a tendency to prove or disprove the existence or severity of anxiety, sleeplessness, worry, concern, anger, or frustration that would flow from Sears' negligence as opposed to its breach of promise. This evidence neither affords a reasonable inference that mental anguish resulted from Sears' negligence in maintaining the premises, nor sheds light upon that issue. *See People v. Botham*, 629 P.2d 589 (Colo. 1981).

We do not perceive that a reasonable juror could believe that the fact that Sears offered to pay Pennington's medical expenses and later refused to do so makes it more probable that Pennington had mental anguish caused by Sears' negligence, or increases the degree of that anguish flowing from such negligence. *See* J. Weinstein & M. Berger, *Weinstein's Evidence* ¶ 401(08) (1986).

* * *

The judgment is reversed, and the cause is remanded for a new trial.

JUDGE RULAND dissenting.

I respectfully dissent.

In my view, the trial court did not abuse its substantial discretion in determining that evidence of Sears' promise to pay Pennington's medical bills and subsequent *refusal* to do so was relevant and material to the disputed issue of damages in this case. CRE 401; *People v. Fernandez*, 687 P.2d 502 (Colo. App. 1984).

CRE 409 was adopted verbatim from the Federal Rules of Evidence. *See* F.Ed.R.E. 409. The function of the rule is a salutary one:

> Rule 409 is the product of a desire to encourage humanitarianism, which would be discouraged if the humanitarian act of paying expenses were penalized by making it evidence against the payor. In addition, the inference that the conduct means anything other than humanitarianism is unreliable.

P. Rothestein, *Federal Rules of Evidence* at p. 126.9 (1992); *see also* J. Weinstein & M. Berger, *Weinstein's Evidence* ¶ 409[01] (1986).

Here, there was no violation of either the language or the spirit of the rule in this case because, with one exception, Pennington testified that Sears recanted on the adjustor's promise to pay her medical bills and thus any humanitarian considerations are not involved. Further, the evidence was not admitted on the issue of Sears' liability.

Turning then to the issue of relevancy, it was undisputed that Pennington suffered a massive tear to the rotator cuff of her left shoulder as a result of the fall. However, while Sears withdrew its failure to mitigate affirmative defense, it persisted in its denial of Pennington's claim as to the "nature and *extent*" of her injuries and the jury was so instructed.

The opinion of Pennington's surgeon was uncontroverted that had plaintiff obtained the required surgery soon after receiving her injury, the nature and extent of her permanent impairment and pain would have been substantially diminished. The reasons for the failure to obtain that surgery then became highly relevant and material to explain why she ended up with both the degree of permanent impairment that she did as well as the gravity of the pain, suffering, and mental anguish that she claimed.

As a result, in my view, the evidence of Sears' offer and refusal to honor that offer, evidence that Pennington had no private insurance or funds from which to pay for treatment, and the fact that federal medicaid benefits were unavailable to her were all relevant and material to establish the nature and extent of her injuries. *See* CRE 402.

The jury was instructed on two occasions in close sequence that this evidence was being admitted for the limited purpose of plaintiff's damage claim and not as to Sears' liability. There is a presumption that the jury understood and applied that instruction and I find no basis in this record to conclude otherwise. *See Prutch v. Ford Motor Co.*, 618 P.2d 657 (Colo. 1980).

*   *   *

Under these circumstances and because I do not view Sears' other contentions for reversal as having merit, I would affirm the judgment.

§ 3.07   RULE 410 — INADMISSIBILITY OF PLEAS, PLEA DISCUSSIONS, AND RELATED STATEMENTS

Plea-bargaining is the criminal law equivalent of an offer of compromise on a civil claim. As with civil disputes, there is a need to encourage the settlement of criminal actions. Although it could theoretically come within Rule 408, Congress specifically addressed criminal plea-bargaining in Rule 410.

Prosecutors have extraordinary power in the criminal justice system. They select the charges the defendant will face and decide what, if any, offer to make defendants. *Mezzanatto* considers whether defendants can waive the provisions of Rule 410. Of course, the request for waivers are made by prosecutors who hold all the cards in criminal negotiations. As you read *Mezzanatto*, consider (1) whether the potential of such waivers will decrease the number of guilty pleas (Rule 410 was adopted to encourage pleas); (2) whether the criminal justice system benefits from such a rule; (3) how defendants may actually benefit from allowing waivers.

UNITED STATES v. MEZZANATTO

United States Supreme Court
513 U.S. 196 (1995)

JUSTICE THOMAS delivered the opinion of the Court.

Federal Rule of Evidence 410 and Federal Rule of Criminal Procedure 11(e)(6) provide that statements made in the course of plea discussions between a criminal defendant and a prosecutor are inadmissible against the defendant. The court below held that these exclusionary provisions may not be waived by the defendant. We granted certiorari to resolve a conflict among the Courts of Appeals, and we now reverse.

I

On August 1, 1991, San Diego Narcotics Task Force agents arrested Gordon Shuster after discovering a methamphetamine laboratory at his residence in Rainbow, California. Shuster agreed to cooperate with the agents, and a few hours after his arrest he placed a call to respondent's pager. When respondent returned the call, Shuster told him that a friend wanted to purchase a pound of methamphetamine for $13,000. Shuster arranged to meet respondent later that day.

At their meeting, Shuster introduced an undercover officer as his "friend." The officer asked respondent if he had "brought the stuff with him," and respondent told the officer it was in his car. The two proceeded to the car, where respondent produced a brown paper package containing approximately one pound of methamphetamine. Respondent then presented a glass pipe (later found to contain methamphetamine residue) and asked the officer if he wanted to take a "hit." The officer indicated that he would first get respondent the money; as the officer left the car, he gave a prearranged arrest signal. Respondent was arrested and charged with possession of methamphetamine with intent to distribute, in violation of 84 Stat. 1260, as amended, 21 U.S.C. § 841(a)(1).

On October 17, 1991, respondent and his attorney asked to meet with the prosecutor to discuss the possibility of cooperating with the Government. The prosecutor agreed to meet later that day. At the beginning of the meeting, the prosecutor informed respondent that he had no obligation to talk, but that if he wanted to cooperate he would have to be completely truthful. As a condition to proceeding with the discussion, the prosecutor indicated that respondent would have to agree that any statements he made during the meeting could be used to impeach any contradictory testimony he might give at trial if the case proceeded that far. Respondent conferred with his counsel and agreed to proceed under the prosecutor's terms.

Respondent then admitted knowing that the package he had attempted to sell to the undercover police officer contained methamphetamine, but insisted that he had dealt only in "ounce" quantities of methamphetamine prior to his arrest. Initially, respondent also claimed that he was acting merely as a broker for Shuster and did not know that Shuster was manufacturing methamphetamine at his residence, but he later conceded that he knew about Shuster's laboratory. Respondent attempted to minimize his role in Shuster's operation by claiming that he had not visited Shuster's residence for at least a week before his arrest. At this point, the Government confronted respondent with surveillance evidence showing that his car was on Shuster's property the day before the arrest, and terminated the meeting on the basis of respondent's failure to provide completely truthful information.

Respondent eventually was tried on the methamphetamine charge and took the stand in his own defense. He maintained that he was not involved in methamphetamine trafficking and that he had thought Shuster used his home laboratory to manufacture plastic explosives for the CIA. He also denied knowing that the package he delivered to the undercover officer contained methamphetamine. Over defense counsel's objection, the prosecutor cross-examined respondent about the inconsistent statements he had made during the October 17 meeting. Respondent denied having made certain statements, and the prosecutor called one of the agents who had attended the meeting to recount the prior statements. The jury found respondent guilty, and the District Court sentenced him to 170 months in prison.

A panel of the Ninth Circuit reversed, over the dissent of Chief Judge Wallace. 998 F.2d 1452 (1993). The Ninth Circuit held that respondent's agreement to allow admission of his plea statements for purposes of impeachment was unenforceable and that the District Court therefore erred in admitting the statements for that purpose. We granted certiorari because the Ninth Circuit's decision conflicts with the Seventh Circuit's decision in *United States v. Dortch*, 5 F.3d 1056, 1067–1068 (1993).

II

Federal Rule of Evidence 410 and Federal Rule of Criminal Procedure 11(e)(6) (Rules or plea-statement Rules) are substantively identical. Rule 410 provides:

> "Except as otherwise provided in this rule, evidence of the following is not, in any civil or criminal proceeding, admissible against the defendant who . . . was a participant in the plea discussions: . . . (4) any statement made in the course of plea discussions with an attorney for the prosecuting authority which do not result in a plea of guilty. . . ."

The Ninth Circuit noted that these Rules are subject to only two express exceptions,[1] neither of which says anything about waiver, and thus concluded that Congress must have meant to preclude waiver agreements such as respondent's. 998 F.2d, at 1454–1456. In light of the "precision with which these rules are generally phrased," the Ninth Circuit declined to "write in a waiver in a waiverless rule." *Id.*, at 1456.[2]

---

[1] A statement made by a criminal defendant in the course of plea discussions is "admissible (i) in any proceeding wherein another statement made in the course of the same . . . plea discussions has been introduced and the statement ought in fairness be considered contemporaneously with it, or (ii) in a criminal proceeding for perjury or false statement if the statement was made by the defendant under oath, on the record and in the presence of counsel." Fed. Rule Evid. 410. Accord, Fed. Rule Crim. Proc. 11(e)(6).

[2] Respondent also goes to great lengths to establish a proposition that is not at issue in this case: that

* * *

The presumption of waivability has found specific application in the context of evidentiary rules. Absent some "overriding procedural consideration that prevents enforcement of the contract," courts have held that agreements to waive evidentiary rules are generally enforceable even over a party's subsequent objections. 21 C. Wright & K. Graham, Federal Practice and Procedure § 5039, pp. 207–208 (1977) (hereinafter Wright & Graham). Courts have "liberally enforced" agreements to waive various exclusionary rules of evidence. Note, Contracts to Alter the Rules of Evidence, 46 Harv. L. Rev. 138, 139–140 (1933). Thus, at the time of the adoption of the Federal Rules of Evidence, agreements as to the admissibility of documentary evidence were routinely enforced and held to preclude subsequent objections as to authenticity. See, *e.g.*, *Tupman Thurlow Co. v. S.S. Cap Castillo*, 490 F.2d 302, 309 (CA2 1974); *United States v. Wing*, 450 F.2d 806, 811 (CA9 1971). And although hearsay is inadmissible except under certain specific exceptions, we have held that agreements to waive hearsay objections are enforceable. See *Sac and Fox Indians of Miss. in Iowa v. Sac and Fox Indians of Miss. in Okl.*, 220 U.S. 481, 488–489, 31 S. Ct. 473, 476–477, 55 L. Ed. 552 (1911); see also *United States v. Bonnett*, 877 F.2d 1450, 1458–1459 (CA10 1989) (party's stipulation to admissibility of document precluded hearsay objection at trial).

Indeed, evidentiary stipulations are a valuable and integral part of everyday trial practice. Prior to trial, parties often agree in writing to the admission of otherwise objectionable evidence, either in exchange for stipulations from opposing counsel or for other strategic purposes. Both the Federal Rules of Civil Procedure and the Federal Rules of Criminal Procedure appear to contemplate that the parties will enter into evidentiary agreements during a pretrial conference. See Fed. Rule Civ. Proc. 16(c)(3); Fed. Rule Crim. Proc. 17.1. During the course of trial, parties frequently decide to waive evidentiary objections, and such tactics are routinely honored by trial judges. See 21 Wright & Graham § 5032, at 161 ("It is left to the parties, in the first instance, to decide whether or not the rules are to be enforced. . . . It is only in rare cases that the trial judge will . . . exclude evidence they are content to see admitted"); see also *United States v. Coonan*, 938 F.2d 1553, 1561 (CA2 1991) (criminal defendant not entitled "to evade the consequences of an unsuccessful tactical decision" made in welcoming admission of otherwise inadmissible evidence).

III

Because the plea-statement Rules were enacted against a background presumption that legal rights generally, and evidentiary provisions specifically, are subject to waiver by voluntary agreement of the parties, we will not interpret Congress' silence as an implicit rejection of waivability. Respondent bears the responsibility of identifying some affirmative basis for concluding that the plea-statement Rules depart from the presumption of waivability.

---

the plea-statement Rules do not contain a blanket "impeachment" exception. We certainly agree that the Rules give a defendant the right not to be impeached by statements made during plea discussions, but that conclusion says nothing about whether the defendant may relinquish that right by voluntary agreement.

Respondent offers three potential bases for concluding that the Rules should be placed beyond the control of the parties. We find none of them persuasive.

A

Respondent first suggests that the plea-statement Rules establish a "guarantee [to] fair procedure" that cannot be waived. Brief for Respondent 12. We agree with respondent's basic premise: There may be some evidentiary provisions that are so fundamental to the reliability of the factfinding process that they may never be waived without irreparably "discredit[ing] the federal courts." See 21 Wright & Graham § 5039, at 207–208; see also *Wheat v. United States*, 486 U.S. 153, 162, 108 S. Ct. 1692, 1698–1699, 100 L. Ed. 2d 140 (1988) (court may decline a defendant's waiver of his right to conflict-free counsel) . . . . But enforcement of agreements like respondent's plainly will not have that effect. The admission of plea statements for impeachment purposes *enhances* the truth-seeking function of trials and will result in more accurate verdicts. Cf. *Jenkins v. Anderson*, 447 U.S. 231, 238, 100 S. Ct. 2124, 2129, 65 L. Ed. 2d 86 (1980) (once a defendant decides to testify, he may be required to face impeachment on cross-examination, which furthers the " 'function of the courts of justice to ascertain the truth' ") (quoting *Brown v. United States*, 356 U.S. 148, 156, 78 S. Ct. 622, 627, 2 L. Ed. 2d 589 (1958)) . . . .

B

Respondent also contends that waiver is fundamentally inconsistent with the Rules' goal of encouraging voluntary settlement. See Advisory Committee's Notes on Fed. Rule Evid. 410 (purpose of Rule is "promotion of disposition of criminal cases by compromise"). Because the prospect of waiver may make defendants "think twice" before entering into any plea negotiation, respondent suggests that enforcement of waiver agreements acts "as a brake, not as a facilitator, to the plea-bargain process." Brief for Respondent 23, n. 17. The Ninth Circuit expressed similar concerns, noting that Rules 410 and 11(e)(6) "aid in obtaining th[e] cooperation" that is often necessary to identify and prosecute the leaders of a criminal conspiracy and that waiver of the protections of the Rules "could easily have a chilling effect on the entire plea bargaining process." 998 F.2d, at 1455. According to the Ninth Circuit, the plea-statement Rules "permit the plea bargainer to maximize what he has 'to sell' " by preserving "the ability to withdraw from the bargain proposed by the prosecutor without being harmed by any of his statements made in the course of an aborted plea bargaining session." *Ibid.*

We need not decide whether and under what circumstances substantial "public policy" interests may permit the inference that Congress intended to override the presumption of waivability, for in this case there is no basis for concluding that waiver will interfere with the Rules' goal of encouraging plea bargaining. The court below focused entirely on the *defendant's* incentives and completely ignored the other essential party to the transaction: the prosecutor. Thus, although the availability of waiver may discourage some defendants from negotiating, it is also true that prosecutors may be unwilling to proceed without it.

Prosecutors may be especially reluctant to negotiate without a waiver agreement during the early stages of a criminal investigation, when prosecutors are searching for leads and suspects may be willing to offer information in exchange for some form of immunity or leniency in sentencing. In this "cooperation" context, prosecutors face "painfully delicate" choices as to "whether to proceed and prosecute those suspects against whom the already produced evidence makes a case or whether to extend leniency or full immunity to some suspects in order to procure testimony against other, more dangerous suspects against whom existing evidence is flimsy or nonexistent." Hughes, Agreements for Cooperation in Criminal Cases, 45 Vand. L. Rev. 1, 15 (1992). Because prosecutors have limited resources and must be able to answer "sensitive questions about the credibility of the testimony" they receive before entering into any sort of cooperation agreement, *id.*, at 10, prosecutors may condition cooperation discussions on an agreement that the testimony provided may be used for impeachment purposes. See Thompson & Sumner, Structuring Informal Immunity, 8 Crim. Just. 16, 19 (spring 1993). If prosecutors were precluded from securing such agreements, they might well decline to enter into cooperation discussions in the first place and might never take this potential first step toward a plea bargain.

Indeed, as a logical matter, it simply makes no sense to conclude that mutual settlement will be encouraged by precluding negotiation over an issue that may be particularly important to one of the parties to the transaction. A sounder way to encourage settlement is to permit the interested parties to enter into knowing and voluntary negotiations without any arbitrary limits on their bargaining chips. To use the Ninth Circuit's metaphor, if the prosecutor is interested in "buying" the reliability assurance that accompanies a waiver agreement, then precluding waiver can only stifle the market for plea bargains. A defendant can "maximize" what he has to "sell" only if he is permitted to offer what the prosecutor is most interested in buying. And while it is certainly true that prosecutors often need help from the small fish in a conspiracy in order to catch the big ones, that is no reason to preclude waiver altogether. If prosecutors decide that certain crucial information will be gained only by preserving the inadmissibility of plea statements, they will agree to leave intact the exclusionary provisions of the plea-statement Rules.

In sum, there is no reason to believe that allowing negotiation as to waiver of the plea-statement Rules will bring plea bargaining to a grinding halt; it may well have the opposite effect.[6] Respondent's unfounded policy argument thus provides no basis for concluding that Congress intended to prevent criminal defendants from offering to waive the plea-statement Rules during plea negotiation.

---

[6] Respondent has failed to offer any empirical support for his apocalyptic predictions, and data compiled by the Administrative Office of the United States Courts appear to contradict them. Prior to the Ninth Circuit's decision in this case (when, according to the Solicitor General, federal prosecutors in that Circuit used waiver agreements like the one invalidated by the court below, see Pet. for Cert. 10–11), approximately 92.2% of the convictions in the Ninth Circuit were secured through pleas of guilty or *nolo contendere*. Annual Report of the Director, Administrative Office of the United States Courts, Judicial Business of the United States Courts 278 (1992) (Table D-7). During that same period, about 88.8% of the convictions in all federal courts were secured by voluntary pleas. *Id.*, at 276.

C

Finally, respondent contends that waiver agreements should be forbidden because they invite prosecutorial overreaching and abuse. Respondent asserts that there is a "gross disparity" in the relative bargaining power of the parties to a plea agreement and suggests that a waiver agreement is "inherently unfair and coercive." Brief for Respondent 26. Because the prosecutor retains the discretion to "reward defendants for their substantial assistance" under the Sentencing Guidelines, respondent argues that defendants face an " 'incredible dilemma' " when they are asked to accept waiver as the price of entering plea discussions. *Ibid.* (quoting *Green v. United States,* 355 U.S. 184, 193, 78 S. Ct. 221, 226, 2 L. Ed. 2d 199 (1957)).

The dilemma flagged by respondent is indistinguishable from any of a number of difficult choices that criminal defendants face every day. The plea bargaining process necessarily exerts pressure on defendants to plead guilty and to abandon a series of fundamental rights, but we have repeatedly held that the government "may encourage a guilty plea by offering substantial benefits in return for the plea." *Corbitt v. New Jersey,* 439 U.S. 212, 219, 99 S. Ct. 492, 497–498, 58 L. Ed. 2d 466 (1978). "While confronting a defendant with the risk of more severe punishment clearly may have a 'discouraging effect on the defendant's assertion of his trial rights, the imposition of these difficult choices [is] an inevitable'— and permissible — 'attribute of any legitimate system which tolerates and encourages the negotiation of pleas.' " *Bordenkircher v. Hayes,* 434 U.S. 357, 364, 98 S. Ct. 663, 668–669, 54 L.Ed.2d 604 (1978) (quoting *Chaffin v. Stynchcombe,* 412 U.S. 17, 31, 93 S. Ct. 1977, 1985, 36 L. Ed. 2d 714 (1973)).

The mere potential for abuse of prosecutorial bargaining power is an insufficient basis for foreclosing negotiation altogether. "Rather, tradition and experience justify our belief that the great majority of prosecutors will be faithful to their duty." *Newton v. Rumery,* 480 U.S. 386, 397, 107 S. Ct. 1187, 1194, 94 L. Ed. 2d 405 (1987) (plurality opinion); see also *United States v. Chemical Foundation, Inc.,* 272 U.S. 1, 14–15, 47 S. Ct. 1, 6, 71 L. Ed. 131 (1926) ("[I]n the absence of clear evidence to the contrary, courts presume that [public officers] have properly discharged their official duties"). Thus, although some waiver agreements "may not be the product of an informed and voluntary decision," this possibility "does not justify invalidating *all* such agreements." *Newton, supra,* 480 U.S. at 393, 107 S. Ct. at 1192 (majority opinion). Instead, the appropriate response to respondent's predictions of abuse is to permit case-by-case inquiries into whether waiver agreements are the product of fraud or coercion. We hold that absent some affirmative indication that the agreement was entered into unknowingly or involuntarily, an agreement to waive the exclusionary provisions of the plea-statement Rules is valid and enforceable.

IV

Respondent conferred with his lawyer after the prosecutor proposed waiver as a condition of proceeding with the plea discussion, and he has never complained that he entered into the waiver agreement at issue unknowingly or involuntarily. The Ninth Circuit's decision was based on its *per se* rejection of waiver of the plea-statement Rules. Accordingly, the judgment of the Court of Appeals is reversed.

It is so ordered.

Justice Souter, with whom Justice Stevens joins, dissenting.

*   *   *

The majority comes down on the side of waivability through reliance on the general presumption in favor of recognizing waivers of rights, including evidentiary rights. To be sure, the majority recognizes that the presumption does not necessarily resolve the issue before us, and the majority opinion describes some counterexamples of rights that are insulated against waiver, at least when waiver is expressly prohibited or limited in terms that speak of waiver expressly. See *Crosby v. United States,* 506 U.S. 255, 113 S. Ct. 748, 122 L. Ed. 2d 25 (1993); *Smith v. United States,* 360 U.S. 1, 79 S. Ct. 991, 3 L. Ed. 2d 1041 (1959). Still, the majority seems to assume that the express-waiver cases describe the only circumstances in which the recognition of waiver is foreclosed, and since the Rules in question here say nothing about "waiver" as such, the majority finds that fact really to be the end of the matter.

If there were nothing more to go on here, I, too, would join the majority in relying on the fallback rule of permissible waiver. But there is more to go on. There is, indeed, good reason to believe that Congress rejected the general rule of waivability when it passed the Rules in issue here, and once the evidence of such congressional intent is squarely faced, we have no business but to respect it (or deflect it by applying some constitutionally mandated requirement of clear statement). There is, of course, no claim in this case that Congress should be hobbled by any clear statement rule, and the result is that we are bound to respect the intent that the Advisory Committee's Notes to the congressionally enacted Rules reveal. See *Williamson v. United States,* 512 U.S. 594, 614–615, 114 S. Ct. 2431, 2442, 129 L. Ed. 2d 476 (1994) (KENNEDY, J., concurring in judgment) (citing cases in which Advisory Committee's Notes are taken as authoritative evidence of intent).

[T]he federal judicial system could not possibly litigate every civil and criminal case filed in the courts. The consequence of this is that plea bargaining is an accepted feature of the criminal justice system, and, "[p]roperly administered, it is to be encouraged." *Santobello v. New York,* 404 U.S. 257, 260, 92 S. Ct. 495, 498, 30 L. Ed. 2d 427 (1971). Thus the Advisory Committee's Notes on Rule 410 explained that "[e]xclusion of offers to plead guilty or *nolo* has as its purpose the promotion of disposition of criminal cases by compromise." 28 U.S.C. App., p. 750. "As with compromise offers generally, . . . free communication is needed, and security against having an offer of compromise or related statement admitted in evidence effectively encourages it." *Ibid.* The Advisory Committee's Notes on Rule 11(e)(6) drew the same conclusion about the purpose of that Rule and summed up the object of both Rules as being "to permit the unrestrained candor which produces effective plea discussions between the attorney for the government and the attorney for the defendant or the defendant when acting pro se." 18 U.S.C. App., p. 745 (1979 Amendment) (internal quotation marks omitted).

These explanations show with reasonable clarity that Congress probably made two assumptions when it adopted the Rules: pleas and plea discussions are to be encouraged, and conditions of unrestrained candor are the most effective means of encouragement. The provisions protecting a defendant against use of statements made in his plea bargaining are thus meant to create something more than a personal right shielding an individual from his imprudence. Rather, the Rules are meant to serve the interest of the federal judicial system (whose resources are controlled by Congress), by creating the conditions understood by Congress to be effective in promoting reasonable plea agreements. Whether Congress was right or wrong that unrestrained candor is necessary to promote a reasonable number of plea agreements, Congress assumed that there was such a need and meant to satisfy it by these Rules. Since the zone of unrestrained candor is diminished whenever a defendant has to stop to think about the amount of trouble his openness may cause him if the plea negotiations fall through, Congress must have understood that the judicial system's interest in candid plea discussions would be threatened by recognizing waivers under Rules 410 and 11(e)(6). See ABA Standards for Criminal Justice 14-3.4, commentary (2d ed. 1980) (a rule contrary to the one adopted by Congress "would discourage plea negotiations and agreements, for defendants would have to be constantly concerned whether, in light of their plea negotiation activities, they could successfully defend on the merits if a plea ultimately was not entered"). There is, indeed, no indication that Congress intended merely a regime of such limited openness as might happen to survive market forces sufficient to supplant a default rule of inadmissibility. Nor may Congress be presumed to have intended to permit waivers that would undermine the stated policy of its own Rules. *Brooklyn Savings Bank v. O'Neil,* 324 U.S. 697, 704, 65 S. Ct. 895, 900, 89 L. Ed. 1296 (1945) ("Where a private right is granted in the public interest to effectuate a legislative policy, waiver of a right so charged or colored with the public interest will not be allowed where it would thwart the legislative policy which it was designed to effectuate").

* * *

The unlikelihood that Congress intended the modest default rule that the majority sees in Rules 11(e)(6) and 410 looms all the larger when the consequences of the majority position are pursued. The first consequence is that the Rules will probably not even function as default rules, for there is little chance that they will be applied at all. Already, standard forms indicate that many federal prosecutors routinely require waiver of Rules 410 and 11(e)(6) rights before a prosecutor is willing to enter into plea discussions. Pet. for Cert. 10–11. See also *United States v. Stevens,* 935 F.2d 1380, 1396 (CA3 1991) ("Plea agreements . . . commonly contain a provision stating that proffer information that is disclosed during the course of plea negotiations is . . . admissible for purposes of impeachment"). As the Government conceded during oral argument, defendants are generally in no position to challenge demands for these waivers, and the use of waiver provisions as contracts of adhesion has become accepted practice.[1] Today's decision can only

---

[1] The argument that the plea-bargaining system still works even though waiver has become the accepted practice does not answer the question whether Congress intended to permit a waiver rule. The Court's obligation is to interpret criminal procedure and evidentiary rules according to congressional intent. If the Government believes that the better rule is different from what is currently the law, the

speed the heretofore illegitimate process by which the exception has been swallowing the Rules. See, *e.g.*, *Guidry v. Sheet Metal Workers Nat. Pension Fund*, 493 U.S.
365, 377, 110 S. Ct. 680, 687–688, 107 L. Ed. 2d 782 (1990) (no exception should be
made by Court because it would be too difficult to "carve out an exception that
would not swallow the rule"); *United States v. Powell*, 469 U.S. 57, 68, 105 S. Ct. 471,
478–479, 83 L. Ed. 2d 461 (1984) (respondent's suggested exception to the *Dunn*
rule "threatens to swallow the rule"). See also 23 C. Wright & K. Graham, Federal
Practice and Procedure 121–122, n. 7.3 (1994 Supp.) ("It would seem strange if the
prosecutor could undermine the judicial policy, now endorsed by Congress, of
encouraging plea bargaining by announcing a policy that his office will only plea
bargain with defendants who 'waive' the benefits of Rule 410"). Accordingly, it is
probably only a matter of time until the Rules are dead letters.

The second consequence likely to emerge from today's decision is the practical
certainty that the waiver demanded will in time come to function as a waiver of trial
itself. It is true that many (if not all) of the waiver forms now employed go only to
admissibility for impeachment.[2] But although the erosion of the Rules has begun
with this trickle, the majority's reasoning will provide no principled limit to it. The
Rules draw no distinction between use of a statement for impeachment and use in
the Government's case in chief. If objection can be waived for impeachment use, it
can be waived for use as affirmative evidence, and if the Government can effectively
demand waiver in the former instance, there is no reason to believe it will not do so
just as successfully in the latter. When it does, there is nothing this Court will
legitimately be able to do about it. The Court is construing a congressional Rule on
the theory that Congress meant to permit its waiver. Once that point is passed, as
it is today, there is no legitimate limit on admissibility of a defendant's plea
negotiation statements beyond what the Constitution may independently impose or
the traffic may bear. Just what the traffic may bear is an open question, but what
cannot be denied is that the majority opinion sanctions a demand for waiver of such
scope that a defendant who gives it will be unable even to acknowledge his desire to
negotiate a guilty plea without furnishing admissible evidence against himself then
and there. In such cases, the possibility of trial if no agreement is reached will be
reduced to fantasy. The only defendant who will not damage himself by even the
most restrained candor will be the one so desperate that he might as well walk into
court and enter a naked guilty plea. It defies reason to think that Congress intended
to invite such a result, when it adopted a Rule said to promote candid discussion in
the interest of encouraging compromise.

EXERCISES

Government can petition Congress to change it. See *TVA v. Hill*, 437 U.S. 153, 194, 98 S. Ct. 2279,
2301–2302, 57 L. Ed. 2d 117 (1978) ("Our individual appraisal of the wisdom or unwisdom of a particular
course consciously selected by the Congress is to be put aside in the process of interpreting a statute").

[2] Waiver for impeachment use, however, has been applied broadly. For example, plea statements have
been used to impeach a defendant's witnesses even where the defendant has chosen not to testify. See
United States v. Dortch, 5 F.3d 1056, 1069 (CA7 1993) ("[J]ust as the defendant must choose whether to
protect the proffer statements by not taking the stand, the defendant must choose whether to protect the
proffer by carefully determining which lines of questioning to pursue with different witnesses"), cert.
pending *sub nom. Suess v. United States*, No. 93-7218.

1. Mary was the "prime suspect" in a federal crime. Mary feared that she would be indicted and hired an attorney. Mary and her attorney decided to cooperate and speak with the United States Attorney, hoping that by cooperating Mary would either avoid an indictment or receive a substantially lighter sentence if she were to be convicted. At the meeting with the prosecutor Mary confessed that she had, in fact, committed a crime. Mary never signed a formal plea agreement; there was no firm offer to plead to specific charges, nor any discussion of the sentencing guidelines. There was never a deadline placed on accepting or rejecting any offer. After the meeting, the prosecutor filed an indictment against Mary. The prosecutor now seeks to use the statements Mary made during the meeting against her at trial. Are Mary's statements admissible against her at trial?

2. Thomas, the mayor of a small city, agreed to plead guilty to a bribery charge. Thomas, his attorney, and the prosecution all signed a written plea agreement. The plea agreement included a stipulation to the factual basis supporting the charge: "Thomas used his position as mayor to promote certain businesses in the city in exchange for cash and other things of value totaling $22,000." The agreement also contained a waiver clause providing that if Thomas failed to plead guilty, then any information contained in the plea agreement could be used against Thomas in any future prosecution. After signing the plea agreement, Thomas changed his mind and refused to plead guilty. The government now seeks to admit the stipulated factual basis into evidence at trial. Thomas objects, arguing that the admission of his signed factual basis violates Rule 410. Is the stipulated factual basis contained within the written plea agreement admissible?

§ 3.08   LIABILITY INSURANCE — RULE 411

As with most rules, admissibility turns on the reason the proponent of the evidence is offering it. If there is a reason, other than to show liability, for introducing proof of insurance, then the jury may consider the evidence. *Piontkowiski* considers proof of insurance to demonstrate the bias of a witness.

PIONTKOWISKI v. SCOTT
Ohio Court of Appeals
582 N.E.2d 1002 (1989)

KRUPANSKY, JUDGE.

Plaintiffs, Linda and John Piontkowski, filed a complaint in Cuyahoga County Common Pleas Court case 109705 against defendants Susan and Patricia Scott. Plaintiffs' complaint alleges defendant Susan Scott negligently operated a motor vehicle causing her vehicle to strike the vehicle plaintiff John Piontkowski was driving and in which plaintiff Linda Piontkowski was a passenger. Plaintiffs' complaint further alleges as a result thereof Linda Piontkowski incurred injury to various parts of her body including her jaw and teeth.

Plaintiffs' complaint also alleges defendant Patricia Scott negligently entrusted the vehicle to defendant Susan Scott. Plaintiff John Piontkowski's only claim is for the loss of consortium and services of Linda Piontkowski, his alleged spouse. Linda

Piontkowski prayed for $150,000 damages and John Piontkowski prayed for $50,000 in damages.

Plaintiffs voluntarily dismissed the claim against Patricia Scott for negligent entrustment and amended their prayer against Susan Scott to $250,000.

After a trial by jury, the jury found for plaintiffs and awarded Linda Piontkowski $9,500. The jury awarded John Piontkowski $0. Verdict was journalized February 26, 1988. Plaintiffs filed a timely notice of appeal.

The record before the court of appeals contains a partial transcript of the proceedings in the trial court. The record contains the testimony of plaintiffs' expert Dr. Joel M. Salon and the testimony of defense expert Dr. Kenneth Callahan.

Both witnesses qualified as experts in the field of oral surgery. They both testified to (1) whether plaintiff Linda Piontkowski currently suffers from temporal mandibular joint dysfunction ("TMJ") and (2) whether a TMJ condition did or could have occurred to Linda Piontkowski as a result of the automobile accident giving rise to the case *sub judice*. Plaintiffs' expert testified to a reasonable degree of medical and/or dental certainty Linda Piontkowski suffers from TMJ as a result of a whiplash injury which occurred during the auto accident and this condition is likely to continue into the future.

Dr. Callahan testified that based on a reasonable degree of dental certainty Linda Piontkowski suffers from TMJ but that it is probable the condition resulted from Linda Piontkowski's overbite and not from the automobile accident.

On cross-examination of Dr. Callahan, plaintiffs' counsel elicited Dr. Callahan is usually retained to testify by defense firms when he testifies regarding TMJ. Of the past twenty cases involving TMJ in which Dr. Callahan was retained as an expert witness, he was retained by a plaintiff's firm only once. Plaintiffs' counsel further elicited Dr. Callahan had been retained by defense counsel *sub judice* in the past and Dr. Callahan's fee for preparing two expert reports in the case *sub judice* amounted to approximately $700.

The court refused to allow plaintiffs' counsel to inquire into whether Dr. Callahan had ever been retained by State Farm Insurance. During a proffer at side bar, plaintiffs' counsel indicated Dr. Callahan had been retained by State Farm Insurance in the past and the record indicates State Farm Insurance is defendant's insurance carrier.

Plaintiffs' assign one error on appeal. Plaintiffs' sole assignment of error follows:

> "The lower court erred in sustaining the defendants' objection to the plaintiffs' questioning of the defense dental expert witness concerning his repeated past employment with the defendant's insurance liability carrier and his unfailing favorable testimony to his employer in past litigation for the purpose of showing the extreme prejudice such witness has in favor of the defendants and against the plaintiffs." Plaintiffs' assignment of error lacks merit.

Evid. R. 411, Liability Insurance, provides:

"Evidence that a person was or was not insured against liability is not admissible upon the issue whether he acted negligently or otherwise wrongfully. This rule does not require the exclusion of evidence of insurance against liability when offered for another purpose, such as proof of agency, ownership or control, if controverted, or bias or prejudice of a witness."

Evidence of liability insurance may not be offered to establish proof of negligence but may be offered to show bias or prejudice. See *Beck v. Cianchetti* (1982), 1 Ohio St. 3d 231, 439 N.E.2d 417, 1 OBR 253.

"* * * The exclusionary effect of Evid R. 411 is to minimize any unfair prejudice resulting from knowledge of the existence of liability insurance. It is generally recognized that such information may influence juries to decide cases on whether or not money is available from an insurance company to pay a damage award." *Bletsh v. Parma Community Gen. Hosp.* (June 4, 1987), Cuyahoga App. No. 52204, unreported, at 2, 1987 WL 11980. Admissibility of evidence under Evid.R. 411 must satisfy the balancing requirements of Evid.R. 401 and 403. *Id.*

Evid.R. 401 provides:

" 'Relevant evidence' means evidence having any tendency to make the existence of any fact that is of consequence to the determination of the action more probable or less probable than it would be without the evidence."

Evid. R. 403 provides:

"(A) Exclusion Mandatory. Although relevant, evidence is not admissible if its probative value is substantially outweighed by the danger of unfair prejudice, of confusion of the issues, or of misleading the jury.

"(B) Exclusion Discretionary. Although relevant, evidence may be excluded if its probative value is substantially outweighed by considerations of undue delay, or needless presentation of cumulative evidence."

In the case *sub judice*, evidence Dr. Callahan had been retained by State Farm Insurance in the past may have been relevant to show bias or prejudice of the witness. However, although Dr. Callahan had been retained by defendant's insurer in the past, there is no indication in the record in the case *sub judice* Dr. Callahan is presently retained by defendant's insurer who is State Farm or merely retained by defense counsel. Plaintiffs sought to expose Dr. Callahan's continued financial interest in a continuing remunerative relationship with defendant's insurance carrier. Without evidence of current retention by defendant's insurance carrier, the assumption Dr. Callahan would have a financial interest which could be jeopardized by his failure to support defendant's position is remote and speculative. The trial court could have easily determined the unfair prejudice resulting from knowledge of liability insurance substantially outweighed the probative value of this evidence.

In addition, plaintiffs' counsel had already cross-examined Dr. Callahan regarding (1) his tendency to testify for the defense in TMJ cases; (2) his previous retention by the law firm representing defendant along with his previous relationship with defense attorneys in general; and (3) his fee for preparation of two expert witness reports in the case *sub judice*. Therefore, plaintiffs' counsel was permitted inquiry into the area of bias and prejudice due to the witness's possible pecuniary interest in a favorable outcome for the defense, and evidence of Dr. Callahan's prior relationship with State Farm Insurance was, therefore, cumulative. In this regard, the case *sub judice* is distinguishable from *Beck, supra*. There is no indication in *Beck* that the plaintiff was able to establish witness bias through other means. In addition, unlike the case *sub judice,* in *Beck* the record indicated the witness was an employee of the insurance company.

Furthermore, in *Beck,* unlike the case *sub judice,* the witness was a fact witness and not an expert witness. The scope of cross-examination of an expert witness with respect to bias and pecuniary interest is within the discretion of the trial judge. *Calderon v. Sharkey* (1982), 70 Ohio St. 2d 218, 24 O.O.3d 322, 436 N.E.2d 1008.

" * * * In reviewing this issue, we must keep in mind that '[t]he term "abuse of discretion" connotes more than an error of law or of judgment; it implies that the court's attitude is unreasonable, arbitrary or unconscionable.' " (Citations omitted.) *Id.* at 219–220, 24 O.O.3d at 323, 436 N.E.2d at 1010.

It should be remembered the trial judge has broad discretion in permitting or excluding evidence. The duty of the appellate court is neither to substitute its discretion for that of the trial judge nor reverse on an error of judgment.

Under the circumstances *sub judice,* the trial court did not abuse its discretion in prohibiting inquiry into liability insurance to show bias and prejudice on the part of Dr. Callahan since its ruling was not unreasonable, arbitrary or unconscionable. Accordingly, plaintiffs' sole assignment of error is not well taken and is overruled.

Judgment affirmed.

PATTON, PRESIDING JUDGE, dissenting.

I believe the trial judge abused his discretion by prohibiting, rather than limiting, cross-examination seeking to show bias or prejudice on behalf of defendant's expert witness. Therefore, I must respectfully dissent.

The majority tends to cloud the distinctions between what evidence is and what evidence is not admissible under Evid. R. 411. As a general proposition, the majority correctly states that evidence of liability insurance is generally inadmissible when offered to prove negligence. The case for admitting evidence of liability insurance to show bias or prejudice of a witness, however, is somewhat stronger than indicated. As stated in 23 Wright & Graham, Federal Practice and Procedure (1980) 459, Section 5367, citing analogous Fed. R. Evid. 411:

> "When a witness testifies on behalf of an insured party, the opponent on cross-examination is entitled to ask about any economic ties between the witness and the insurance company that might be expected to color his testimony. * * * The paradigm case for use of evidence of insurance to show bias is in the cross-examination of a claims adjuster or insurance company doctor." (Footnotes omitted.)

While evidence of bias or prejudice must satisfy the balancing requirements of

Evid. R. 403, the majority incorrectly states that such evidence must also satisfy threshold requirements of relevancy. Evid. R. 411 presumes relevancy. See *Beck v. Cianchetti* (1982), 1 Ohio St. 3d 231, 439 N.E.2d 417, 1 OBR 253, syllabus ("Evid. R. 411 allows cross-examination on facts which may show bias, interest or prejudice of a witness, even though it may disclose the existence of liability insurance in a personal injury action."). The rule further presumes some prejudice from the disclosure of the existence of liability insurance. See *Beck, supra.* While the admission of such evidence is within the discretion of the trial judge, that discretion should not be exercised to foreclose inquiry simply because the opposing party will be prejudiced. Prejudice should naturally follow from impeachment.

In this case, it is important to note that liability was stipulated prior to trial. In fact, the sole issue at trial concerned plaintiff's damages.

The proffer showed that the expert's economic ties to State Farm were more compelling than the evidence at trial was allowed to show. In the twenty cases in which the expert had rendered an opinion concerning TMJ syndrome, nineteen of these opinions were rendered on behalf of State Farm. Moreover, plaintiff possessed letters from the expert that clearly cast doubt on the objectivity of the expert's opinion. In these letters to defense counsel, the expert proposed monetary figures for compromise in settlement. The import of this compromise was that the expert was attempting to appease the insurer. This conclusion is reinforced by the expert's statement that he was hopeful his conclusions would be "fair to all parties." The expert later recommended a small settlement sum as being fair on the chance that some of plaintiff's injuries were caused by the accident.

In this case, plaintiffs were allowed some inquiry into defendant's expert's background as a defense witness, but were completely prohibited from inquiring into his relationship with the insurance company. That information was crucial, given the divergent view of the expert opinion. Consider also that plaintiffs' expert had been her oral surgeon well before litigation had commenced and therefore had no demonstrable bias as an expert. Finally, the expert's "proposal" of damages inclined far too much in favor of defendants.[1] Accordingly, I would hold that the trial judge abused his discretion in prohibiting cross-examination of defendant's expert on matters of bias and prejudice and remand the case for a new trial.

---

[1] There is an indication in the record that the insurer offered to settle the matter for $25,000. Hence, there is the very real probability that there was some prejudice in the exclusion of cross-examination on bias.

Chapter 4

DEFINITION OF HEARSAY

§ 4.01 COMMON-LAW DEFINITION OF HEARSAY

[A] Definition and Rationale

[1] The Basics Element of Hearsay

Hearsay is defined as evidence of a statement made outside of the proceedings offered to prove the truth of the matter asserted in the statement. Hearsay generally is inadmissible under the common-law prohibition, because the court cannot test it against the four dangers of testimonial evidence: faulty perception, inaccurate memory, insincerity, and ambiguity.

[See Fed. R. Evid. 801]

If offered for the truth of its content, a statement's probative value turns on the credibility of both the out-of-court declarant, who observed the event and made the statement describing it, and the witness, who is testifying about what he or she heard the declarant say. However, only the latter witness — the one who has firsthand knowledge only of the statement's utterance, not of the underlying facts — is present in the courtroom, subject to the searching eyes of the jurors, sworn to tell the truth upon penalty of perjury, and subject to cross-examination, the engine of truth through which the sincerity, clarity, and accuracy of testimony is tested. Consequently, the court can explore only the hearsay witness' perception, clarity, sincerity, and accuracy with regard to whether the witness heard and remembered correctly the statement uttered by the out-of-court declarant, not the basis for the declaration. Because the hearsay witness has no firsthand knowledge of the event that the out-of-court declarant described, there is no way for the court to test the reliability of the out-of-court declarant's description through the hearsay witness' testimony.

To illustrate this point, assume that D shoots X and this act is observed by Witness #1 (the out-of-court declarant), who subsequently states: "D shot X!" Witness #1 makes this statement in the presence of Witness #2, who later is called as a witness in the criminal trial of D to testify to Witness #1's prior statement. The purpose of offering this testimony is to prove that D shot X. Witnesses may testify only to the truth of facts about which they have firsthand knowledge. Therefore, Witness #2 will be allowed only to repeat what Witness #1 said for the limited purpose of proving that Witness #1 uttered the words, not for the truth of the utterance. Therefore, unless the mere utterance of the words "D shot X" by Witness

#1 is relevant to the litigation — that is, if it is not necessary to accept the truth of the message conveyed by them in order for them to have probative value — then Witness #2's testimony will create a hearsay problem. Of course, in the hypothetical, the purpose of offering this testimony is to prove that D actually did shoot X. The relevance of Witness #2's testimony, therefore, turns on the truth of what Witness #1 said. This creates a hearsay problem because the probative value of Witness #1's statement turns on the untestable perception, memory, and sincerity of Witness #1.

The hearsay issue in the above hypothetical also would be no different had Witness #1 written the statement "D shot X!" in a letter to a friend and that letter were being offered into evidence to prove the truth of its contents. The hearsay problem would be the same because the letter, like Witness #2 in the preceding hypothetical, still represents what Witness #1 perceived and remembered, and there is no way to test the reliability of this perception and memory. The fact that Witness #1 wrote down the statement instead of speaking it matters only in that it eliminates the perception, memory, and sincerity problems relative to the in-court account of Witness #1's statement.

The hearsay nature of witnesses' testimony often can be concealed, because they relate facts as if they have firsthand knowledge of them, when, in fact, they are disclosing only what they have been told by someone else. The hearsay aspects of a statement are not dependent on whether the in-court witness prefaces his or her factual account by the statement "Witness #1 told me. . . ."

Williams and *Jardin* each involve claims that a declarant's conduct was intended to communicate an idea.

[2] Communications by Conduct: Seesay

The problem with hearsay is that facts are being proved through communications of individuals who were not under oath, being observed by the jury, and being tested through cross-examination at the time they communicated the facts about which they had firsthand knowledge. Because the hearsay issue centers around communications, the form that the out-of-court statement takes is irrelevant. Hearsay problems can arise through conduct that is observed as well as words that are heard. Therefore, the descriptive label *hearsay* is deceptive because the rule encompasses "*seesay*" as well.

Consider the previous hypothetical in which Witness #1 observed D shoot X. The hearsay implications arising from Witness #2's testimony that Witness #1 stated "D shot X!" would be the same if Witness #2 testified instead that Witness #1 responded to the question, "Who shot X?", by simply pointing to D. The only difference between the two situations is that the latter involved an indirect message with an observer having to interpret the message that Witness #1 intended his gesture to communicate. The observer must translate the conduct into the words that Witness #1 otherwise might have used. This interpretation will invariably increase the hearsay problem of ambiguity or clarity of communication. Whether, by pointing in response to the question, Witness #1 meant that D shot X or simply that D should be the one to answer the question is unclear.

STATE v. WILLIAMS

South Carolina Court of Appeals
285 S.C. 544 (1985)

SANDERS, CHIEF JUDGE:

Appellant Lee M. Williams appeals his conviction for armed robbery, arguing that he is entitled to a new trial because the trial judge erred in allowing certain testimony. We reverse and remand.

I

THE EVIDENCE

The evidence contained in the record before us can be summarized as follows:

A female employee of an apartment complex testified that a man wearing an "army coat" with a stocking cap over his face walked into the rental office of the complex and pointed a rifle at her. She went on to testify that the man threw a pink pocketbook on her desk and, in a soft, "feminine" voice with a "New York" accent, commanded her to put the office money in it. The employee said she put approximately $1,400 in the pocketbook, and the man fled with it. The employee further testified that the man's voice was familiar to her as that of a black man who had been in the office before, and she said she had told an investigating police officer "a name to place with the voice." She also said she had previously spoken to Williams in the office, but she did not say she told the police officer Williams' name. Finally, she identified a pocketbook and a rifle presented to her by the solicitor as being those used in the robbery.

A police officer testified that Williams had an army coat in his possession when he was arrested. The officer identified a coat as being the one Williams had at that time. He went on to testify that he had gone to the rental office following the robbery and was handed the pocketbook identified by the employee in her testimony. The officer further testified that he had gone to the place where Williams' wife was employed and had spoken to her. The solicitor then asked him these critical questions, receiving the answers indicated:

Q.   And did you take that pocketbook with you to show to her?

A.   Yes, I did.

Q.   Could she identify that pocketbook?

            At this point, Williams' lawyer objected to the question. After hearing arguments of counsel, the trial judge overruled the objection and the officer answered by saying:

A.   Yes, she positively identified that pocketbook.

The State then closed its case, presenting no further evidence.

In our opinion, the admission of this testimony was in violation of the rule against hearsay and the Confrontation Clauses of both the United States and South Carolina Constitutions.

II

THE RULE AGAINST HEARSAY

The rule against hearsay prohibits the admission of testimony (or written evidence) of a statement made out of court, offered in court to prove the truth of the matter asserted, unless an exception to the rule is applicable. *Player v. Thompson*, 259 S.C. 600, 193 S.E.2d 531 (1972), *citing*, C. McCormick, *Law of Evidence* § 225 (1954). The reasons for excluding hearsay are succinctly set out in *Jones v. Charleston & W.C. Ry. Co.*, 144 S.C. 212, 142 S.E. 516 (1928).[1]

In our opinion, the testimony of the police officer was hearsay. Even if Mrs. Williams communicated her identification of the pocketbook to him in some way other than by actually saying she had some knowledge of it, her identification would nonetheless be a "statement" within the meaning of the term hearsay, and it does not matter that there was no direct quotation of any words used by her. Wordless conduct, such as a nod of the head or pointed finger, may be hearsay if it is intended as a communication. Where words are used, no direct quotation of the words is necessary. J. Dreher, *A Guide to Evidence Law in South Carolina* 63 (1967). *Cf.*, *State v. Corn*, 215 S.C. 166, 54 S.E.2d 559 (1949); *State v. Pollard*, 260 S.C. 457, 196 S.E.2d 839 (1973) (cases hereafter discussed in greater detail involving unquoted general statements). Mrs. Williams' identification of the pocketbook was obviously made "out of court." It is equally obvious that the police officer's testimony of her identification was offered "in court."

The State does not argue that any exception to the rule against hearsay is applicable here. Instead, the State argues that the testimony as to Mrs. Williams' having identified the pocketbook was not hearsay because it "does not constitute a declaration offered to prove the truth of the matter asserted; rather it was admissible to show (she) made an utterance." In support of its argument, the State cites *State v. Tabory*, 260 S.C. 355, 196 S.E.2d 111 (1973), and *Player v. Thompson*, 193 S.E.2d 531. We reject this argument.

In *Tabory*, a defendant was convicted of possession of marijuana after having been arrested while a passenger in a truck containing a substantial quantity of the drug. There was evidence of his prior knowledge of the marijuana. At trial, a prosecution witness was allowed to testify that the driver of the truck had said, in the defendant's presence, that the van was empty. On appeal the defendant argued that admission of the testimony violated the rule against hearsay. The Supreme Court affirmed the defendant's conviction, holding that the testimony of what the driver had said was properly admitted, not to prove the truth of the matter asserted (*i.e.*, that the truck was empty), but "as evidence of the utterance."

---

[1] Probably the most important reason for excluding hearsay is the absence of the opportunity for cross-examination, which has been characterized as "the greatest engine ever invented for the discovery of truth." Younger, An Irreverent Introduction to Hearsay, 2 (ABA Litigation Monograph No. 3, 1977).

In *Player,* a passenger in an automobile sued three defendants for injuries received in an accident alleged to have been caused by the automobile having defective tires. There was evidence that the tires were defective when examined after the accident. The plaintiff further alleged that two of the defendants had knowledge of the defective tires before the accident occurred. Prior to suit, one of the defendants gave a sworn statement that she had overheard a conversation which had taken place before the accident between a filling station attendant and another defendant. In her statement, she said the filling station attendant had told the other defendant that the tires were defective. At trial, the plaintiff's lawyer attempted to examine the defendant about the conversation described in her statement, in an effort to show both she and the other defendant had notice of the defective tires before the accident. The trial judge sustained an objection on the ground of the rule against hearsay. The Supreme Court reversed a verdict for the defendants, holding that testimony of what the filling station attendant had said should have been admitted, not to prove the truth of the matter asserted (*i.e.,* that the tires were defective), but as evidence that the two defendants had knowledge of the defective tires before the accident.[2]

Unlike the testimony in *Tabory* and *Player,* the testimony in the instant case was offered to prove the truth of the matter asserted (*i.e.,* that Mrs. Williams had some knowledge of the pocketbook). The solicitor, in arguing for the admissibility of her testimony, suggested no other purpose. It is of no consequence that Mrs. Williams is not quoted as saying exactly what her knowledge of the pocketbook was or how she came to have knowledge of it. While it is possible her knowledge of the pocketbook could have come from some source entirely unrelated to her husband (*e.g.,* her having seen it in the possession of someone else), the testimony that she had identified it was obviously intended to imply he had some connection with it and, thus, the robbery. It is obvious that the testimony could not have been offered for any other purpose relevant to the case. The mere fact that Mrs. Williams made an "utterance" obviously had no relevance to any issue in the case. We therefore find the cases of *Tabory* and *Player,* cited by the State, distinguishable on their facts from the instant case.

On the other hand, we find factual situations analagous to this case in *State v. Corn,* 54 S.E.2d 559, and *State v. Pollard,* 196 S.E.2d 839 (decided two months after *Tabory*).

In *Corn,* the defendant was convicted of murder. There was evidence the murder victim had been shot and killed in the warehouse portion of his place of business and his body then carried some distance away and dumped in a creek, where it was later found floating. The trial judge allowed a policeman to testify he had fired a gun in the warehouse and thereafter could find no one in the neighborhood who had heard the shots. The purpose of the testimony was apparently to prove the shooting could

---

[2] Sometimes a statement not offered to prove a fact asserted contains information which must be proven. The statement in *Player* is an example of such a statement because it contains information that the tires were in fact defective and is also evidence that the defendants had notice they were defective. Presumably for this reason, the Court was careful to note that the fact the tires were defective was a fact "proved by other evidence." As more fully discussed hereafter, the record before us in the instant case contains no evidence of Mrs. Williams' identification of the pocketbook, other than the testimony of the police officer.

have taken place in the warehouse without the neighbors' having heard it. The Supreme Court reversed the conviction, holding that the testimony violated the rule against hearsay. The Court reasoned that allowing the testimony was the equivalent of permitting the police officer to testify that people in the neighborhood had told him they did not hear the shots.

In *Pollard*, the defendant was convicted of armed robbery. The victim of the robbery identified the defendant in his testimony. The trial judge allowed a police officer to testify that he signed the warrant for the defendant's arrest "from information he received in the investigation (of the case)." The Supreme Court reversed the conviction, holding the testimony was "clearly hearsay."

Like the testimony in the instant case, the police officers' testimony in *Corn* and *Pollard* amounted to their saying what they had been told outside of court and, even though they did not testify as to exactly what had been said, their testimony had no purpose other than to prove the truth of the matters asserted.

The State argues further that, even if the testimony was hearsay, Williams was not prejudiced by it because "the record contains independent and overwhelming evidence of guilt." We also reject this argument.

The admission of hearsay constitutes reversible error only if its admission is prejudicial to the accused. *State v. Craig*, 267 S.C. 262, 227 S.E.2d 306 (1976). Where hearsay is merely cumulative to other evidence, its admission has been deemed harmless. *See, e.g., State v. Blackburn*, 271 S.C. 324, 247 S.E.2d 334 (1978).

We have carefully examined the record before us and can find no evidence of Mrs. Williams' knowledge of the pocketbook independent from the testimony of the police officer. Neither do we find any other evidence connecting Williams to the robbery. Indeed, the solicitor represented to the trial judge that whether Williams' wife "has knowledge regarding that pocketbook" was "of critical importance to this case." This is apparent from a review of the evidence previously summarized in Part I of this opinion.

The apartment complex employee, who was the victim of the robbery, described the robbery in some detail, but she did not identify Williams in her testimony as the person who had robbed her. She described the voice of the robber in her testimony, and she testified that Williams had previously been in the office of the apartment complex and had spoken to her. But she did not describe Williams' voice as being the same or similar to that of the robber, and she did not testify she had given the police Williams' name as a person whose voice fitted that of the robber. She testified the robber wore an army coat, but she did not identify the coat which the police officer testified Williams had when he was arrested as being the same or similar to that worn by the robber. She identified the rifle presented to her by the solicitor as being the one used in the robbery, but there was no testimony either by her or the police officer connecting the rifle to Williams.

The police officer's testimony as to Mrs. Williams' having identified the pocketbook was obviously material. (As previously noted, the solicitor characterized it as being of "critical importance to this case.") When hearsay is erroneously admitted, prejudice is presumed if the hearsay had some probative value on a material fact in the case. *Cooper Corp. v. Jeffcoat*, 217 S.C. 489, 61 S.E.2d 53 (1950).

Our conclusion that Williams was prejudiced by the testimony of the police officer is further supported by the result reached by our Supreme Court in *Pollard*. There, as here, the State argued there was no prejudice to the defendant by the admission of hearsay. The Court rejected this argument despite the fact that, unlike the instant case, there was testimony by the robbery victim identifying the defendant as the robber.

For these reasons, we hold the testimony by the police officer as to Mrs. Williams' having identified the pocketbook was hearsay, and Williams was prejudiced by it.

PEOPLE v. JARDIN

New York Supreme Court, Bronx County
154 Misc.2d 172 (1992)

GERALD SHEINDLIN, J.

The defendant was indicted for rape in the first degree (Penal Law § 130.35[1]) and related offenses. Two issues arose during the course of the ensuing jury trial which are the subject of the following opinion. First, the defendant moved for a ruling permitting him to introduce into evidence testimony establishing that he agreed to submit to a DNA test. The defendant argued that his submission of a blood sample demonstrated "consciousness of innocence" and was thus probative on the issue of guilt. Second, in an unrelated application, the People moved to introduce into evidence on their direct case the contents of a "911" tape, wherein an unavailable witness described the sexual assault he had just seen the defendant commit upon a woman. The defendant opposed the application on the grounds that the tape was utter hearsay and that he would be deprived of his right to confront the declarant. For the reasons set forth below, the defendant's motion to introduce the "consciousness of innocence" evidence is denied and the People's motion to introduce the "911" tape is granted

FINDINGS OF FACT

On June 26, 1990, the defendant invited his next-door neighbor into his apartment, ostensibly to get her to assist him with his college studies. After several hours of studying, the defendant went into the bathroom, only to emerge naked moments later. The defendant then grabbed his neighbor, and, despite her hysterical screams of protest, ripped off the woman's clothes, pushed her onto his bed, closed the shade of his bedroom window and proceeded to forcibly rape his victim.

Unbeknownst to the defendant, his actions were witnessed through the open bedroom window by Angel Nieves and Valerie Lopez, both of whom lived directly across the street from the defendant. After they heard the victim's screams and together saw the defendant's assault on the woman, Mr. Nieves and Ms. Lopez immediately ran down to a street phone and called the police. Ms. Lopez stood next to her companion and listened as Mr. Nieves described the events they had just observed to the police operator. Ms. Lopez' voice was recorded on the 911 tape when she aided Mr. Nieves in describing the assault.

The police arrived within minutes after receiving the "911" call, and were directed to the defendant's apartment. In response to the police knock, the defendant, naked, partially opened his door and peeked outside, but was suddenly shoved aside by the victim who, screaming and naked, came running out of the apartment into the arms of the police. The still-naked defendant was allowed to dress before he was placed under arrest.

Despite diligent efforts, the People could not ascertain the whereabouts of Mr. Nieves for trial.

After the victim was transported to the hospital, a Vitullo kit was prepared and the presence of sperm was detected from a vaginal swab slide. The defendant subsequently arranged for a DNA test to be performed by Cellmark Diagnostics Laboratory. Both the People and the defendant agree that the test was properly performed, and there is no issue concerning the reliability of the DNA scientific testing procedure. (*See, People v Castro,* 143 Misc 2d 276 [Sup Ct, Bronx County 1989].) However, the test results were inconclusive. That is, although the DNA lanes for the victim matched, the DNA extracted from the recovered sperm was not of sufficient DNA molecular weight to provide a result.

CONCLUSIONS OF LAW

I

Testimony Describing Defendant's Willingness to
Submit to DNA Testing Is Inadmissible

Absent a demonstrated applicable exception, any out-of-court statement offered in court to establish the truth of the facts asserted therein constitutes inadmissible hearsay. (*See, People v Edwards,* 47 NY2d 493, 496 [1979]; *People v Settles,* 46 NY2d 154, 166 [1978]; Richardson, Evidence § 200 [Prince 10th ed].) The rule against hearsay applies equally to verbal statements as well as to assertions by conduct. (*See, e.g., People v Salko,* 47 NY2d 230, 239 [1979].) However, reasoned analysis must be undertaken to determine whether particular conduct is to be categorized as "communicative or testimonial," and hence subject to hearsay restrictions, or whether the conduct is classifiable as "real or physical" evidence, and thus not subject to hearsay exclusions. (*See, People v Thomas,* 46 NY2d 100, 106 [1978].) Simply put, a determination must be made as to whether the nonverbal act is offered to establish a fact. Here, the defendant has admitted that the sole reason he wished to introduce the contested testimony was to demonstrate his "consciousness of innocence."

(1) In other words, the defendant sought to prove the fact of "innocence" by his conduct. Therefore, the nonverbal assertion clearly constitutes hearsay and can be admitted into evidence only if it falls within a recognized exception to the hearsay rule.

The defendant particularizes no exception which would permit the introduction of the nonverbal statement and this court finds no applicable exception. Indeed, the self-serving nature of this proclamation of innocence renders the statement inherently unreliable and hence inadmissible. (*See, e.g., People v Reynoso*, 73 NY2d 816, 819 [1988]; *People v Perez*, 166 AD2d 166, 167 [1st Dept. 1990]; *People v Hentley*, 155 AD2d 392, 394 [1st Dept. 1989].) The statement is also excludable as a prior consistent statement. (*See, e.g., People v Davis*, 44 NY2d 269, 277 [1978]; *People v Sostre*, 51 NY2d 958 [1980]; *People v Cartagena*, 160 AD2d 608, 609 [1st Dept. 1990]; *People v Jimenez*, 102 AD2d 439, 443 [1st Dept 1984].)

Moreover, the defendant's willingness to acquiesce to a DNA test is not truly probative of an innocent conscience since he would have had, in any event, been compelled to provide a blood sample for testing. (*See*, CPL 240.40 [2].) Finally, since the results of the DNA test were inconclusive and, therefore, irrelevant, any agreement to submit to the process would also be irrelevant.

[B] Offered for Truth

[1] Not Hearsay If Not Offered for Truth

For a court to classify an out-of-court statement as hearsay, the statement must be offered to prove the truth of the matter asserted. This requirement lies at the heart of the hearsay rule. If a statement is not offered for its truth, then hearsay dangers are not present. If truth is unimportant, accuracy is not an issue and the quality of the declarant's perception and memory are not important to the value of the statement. Accordingly, only the quality of an in-court witness' perception and memory of what the out-of-court declarant said will affect the probative value of the witness' testimony.

To determine whether the use of an out-of-court statement falls within the hearsay rule, one must first answer the basic question: "*Why is this statement relevant?*" If relevant to the proof of a proposition solely because of the fact that the word was uttered, there is no hearsay problem. The following hypothetical presents a striking illustration of this point. Soon after an automobile accident that resulted in P's subsequent death, P stated: "I am conscious." This statement is offered in a wrongful death action on the issue of damages. It is relevant to this issue because it establishes that the deceased was conscious after the accident and, therefore, that his estate is entitled to greater damages because of pain that he suffered.

The use of P's statement would *not* give rise to a hearsay problem because the statement established P's consciousness by its mere utterance. The fact that the words uttered were identical to that which is being proven is merely coincidental. Had the victim uttered "I am a banana," that statement's probative value relative to the issue on which it was offered would have been the same. The statement's content is not crucial to its relevance.

Similarly, if an individual stated "I am capable of speaking" or "I speak English" the very utterance of those sentences establishes either that the individual can speak or that he or she can communicate in the English language. Neither would be hearsay if repeated at trial by someone who heard them to prove either of those propositions.

A statement falls outside the scope of the hearsay rule whenever it is offered for a purpose that does not depend on the veracity of the out-of-court declarant, because its value does not turn on the truth of its content. For example, in *Long v. Asphalt Paving Co. of Greensboro*, 47 N.C. App. 564, 268 S.E.2d 1 (1980), the principal issue was whether there was sufficient evidence to support a finding that the decedent was on a business trip to Florida in connection with his duties as an employee of the paving company when he met his demise. Part of the evidence on which the finding was based was the testimony of one witness who stated that, as he was driving the deceased and Sam Martin back to their motel, he heard Martin say to Long, as they passed an asphalt processing place, "George, that is where you can get the asphalt." Finding the admission of the evidence to be proper, the appellate court explained:

> It is well recognized that an out-of-court statement which is offered for any purpose other than to prove the truth of the matter asserted in the statement is not hearsay. . . . The reason such statements are admissible is not that they fall under an exception to the rule, but that they simply are not hearsay — they do not come within the legal definition of the term. Viewed in this light, Tuttle's testimony was not hearsay because Martin's statement as to the place Long could obtain his asphalt was not offered to show where Long could find asphalt, but that business was transacted on the trip. Similarly, Week's testimony that "Mr. Long is in the paving business" was not offered to show the business in which Long was engaged. The statement was offered to show that business was transacted during the Florida trip. As such, this testimony was not hearsay. For the same reason, Martin's other inquiries as to the place where asphalt could be obtained were likewise admissible as nonhearsay.

Id. at 4–5.

In *United States. v. Koskerides*, 877 F.2d 1129 (2d Cir. 1989), the court addressed the issue of whether the testimony of an IRS agent's conversation with the deceased father-in-law of appellant, who communicated through an interpreter, was hearsay under Rule 801(c), if introduced to show that the IRS had satisfied its obligation of pursuing leads to nontaxable sources. In ruling that the statement did not constitute hearsay, the court reasoned "the government did not seek to prove the truth of Kiriakides' [the father-in-law's] statements, but rather that the interview took place." *Id.* at 1135.

The court also determined that the role of the interpreter did not amount to a separate hearsay problem, since the interpreter functioned simply as a "language conduit." *Id.* Is this valid reasoning, especially where the witness is relying on the accuracy of the interpreter's comprehension and translation of the declarant's statements? Probably not, but the translator's statements would be admissible anyway under the present sense impression exception, Rule 803(1).

Frequently a statement or conduct may be relevant for more than one reason. For example, if, following the commission of a crime, the defendant is seen running from the building in which the crime occurred, evidence of this conduct could be relevant for at least two reasons, and its hearsay status would depend on the purpose for which it is offered. First, the conduct is relevant because it establishes opportunity by showing that the defendant was in the vicinity at the time the crime was committed and, therefore, could have committed it. If used for this purpose, the conduct observed has probative value independent of any communication one could imply from the actor's conduct. Alternatively, the evidence also would be relevant because a person's flight from the scene of a crime implies an admission of guilt. If offered for the latter purpose, the evidence would be hearsay because its relevance is dependent on the finder of facts accepting as true the implied communication: the admission of guilt.

There is no limit on the purposes (other than the truth) for which out-of-court utterances may be used without giving rise to a hearsay problem. However, statements that are relevant because of their utterance, not because of their truth, frequently fall into three categories: (1) those that are relevant because of their effect on the hearer; (2) those that are relevant because the law attaches rights, duties, and liabilities as a result of their utterance (these statements have been referred to as operative facts and verbal acts); and (3) those that are relevant because they demonstrate the declarant's knowledge at the time the statement was uttered.

[2]   Offered for Effect on Hearer

A statement is not hearsay if the issue is the statement's effect on the hearer. For example, if the reasonableness of a person's conduct is in issue, information brought to that person's attention through the statements of others is relevant, regardless of whether the statements are true. In the original hypothetical involving the shooting of X by D, Witness #1's statement, "D shot X," was reported to the police by Witness #2, resulting in D's arrest. The statement could be nonhearsay if offered in a civil action for malicious prosecution brought by D against Witness #2. Evidence that Witness #1 made the statement to Witness #2 would establish a defense to the action, because Witness #2's conduct would have been reasonable under the circumstances. It would be the fact that the statement was made to Witness #2, rather than the truth of what was uttered, that would be relevant to the proceeding. Although it would be necessary for the jury to believe that Witness #1 actually said "D shot X," Witness #2's testimony to that effect would create no hearsay problem, because Witness #2 had firsthand knowledge of this fact.

In a prosecution for the murder of X, defendant offers to testify that, immediately before the shooting, his friend A warned him: "You should be careful around X because he has a gun and has threatened to blow your head off when he sees you!" Defendant's testimony about A's statement does not constitute hearsay if offered in support of a defense of self-defense. Regardless of whether X actually possessed a gun and made the reported threat, the defendant can claim reasonable apprehension and, therefore, justification in responding as he did to X's actions based on the fear that he reasonably felt after having heard and believed A's statement.

In a negligence action for injuries suffered in a fall on a wet spot on a floor, the defendant offers to prove, through a bystander's testimony, the statement that an usher made to the plaintiff immediately before the fall, "Watch out lady, the floor is wet over there. You should go around the other side." The mere utterance of this statement is relevant in that it constitutes a warning to which the plaintiff should have reacted. Having failed to react, she would be contributorily negligent. Only the actual utterance of the statement is relevant to whether an adequate warning was given. The statement's truth is irrelevant. This statement would not be hearsay because the bystander who is testifying has firsthand knowledge of both the words that were uttered and the circumstances surrounding the utterance.

In cases in which the content of a statement is relevant both because of its mere utterance and because of the truth of its content, there is no violation of the hearsay rule if the statement's use is limited to establishing that the statement was made. For example, if a gas station attendant informed the driver of a car that his front tire was dangerously defective, and a bystander repeated the statement in court, the bystander's testimony would not be hearsay if the sole purpose in introducing the attendant's statement was to establish that the driver had notice of the dangerous condition and should have taken measures to insure against injury by correcting the defect. This statement also would be relevant to establishing the existence of this dangerous condition. However, so long as the existence of this condition, which is critical to the success of the cause of action, is proved through other evidence, such as expert testimony from someone who examined the tire after the accident, the limited use of the statement to establish notice is permissible. To insure that the jury uses the evidence only for this limited purpose, the court may give the jury a limiting instruction when the testimony is introduced.

In *United States v. Cantu*, 876 F.2d 1134 (5th Cir. 1989), the court reversed the trial judge's ruling that statements made to the defendant by a paid confidential informant of the DEA were hearsay when offered to show that the government induced defendant to commit the offense. In holding that the informant's statements were not hearsay, the court declared that the statements were not offered "as an assertion of a fact but, rather, as the fact of an assertion." *Id.* at 1137. In other words, it is the *mere utterance* of the informant's suggestions to defendant that made the statements relevant in this instance, because of the effect the statements had on the defendant's inclination to commit the underlying offense. It was not offered for the truth of the matter asserted.

KENYON v. STATE
Wyoming Supreme Court
986 P.2d 849 (1999)

Macy, Justice.

Appellant Robert Kenyon appeals from the judgment and sentence which was entered after he was convicted of grand larceny.

We reverse and remand.

ISSUES

Kenyon presents the following issues for our review:

ISSUE I:

Whether the district court abused its discretion when it denied the appellant the opportunity to introduce statements made to him by his fiancee regarding consent to use the vehicle.

ISSUE II:

Whether the trial court committed reversible error when it refused to give a properly requested jury instruction on the defense theory of the case.

FACTS

Kenyon and his fiancee, Kelly Crossfield, went on a trip around the United States during the summer of 1997. They were returning to their home in Oregon when their van broke down in Kansas. Kenyon and Crossfield could not afford to repair the van, so they placed it in storage and hitchhiked to Denver, Colorado. They planned to stay with Crossfield's sister, who lived in Denver, but she did not have room for them. Kenyon and Crossfield continued hitchhiking and eventually ended up in Cheyenne.

In early September 1997, Kenyon and Crossfield entered the Southside Furniture store. Kenyon spoke with James Sanchez, who was a store employee, and told him that he and Crossfield were hungry and did not have a place to stay. Sanchez gave Kenyon and Crossfield some money and told them that they could stay in a trailer which was parked next to the house he shared with his fiancee. Sanchez asked the couple to do some odd jobs in exchange for being allowed to use the trailer.

The trailer did not have running water; consequently, Sanchez left the back door to his house unlocked so that Kenyon and Crossfield could use the bathroom. Sanchez also allowed Kenyon and Crossfield to use his truck on several occasions. Kenyon used the truck to run errands, seek employment, and accomplish odd jobs for Sanchez.

On September 28, 1997, Sanchez allowed Kenyon to use the truck to go to his worksite. Crossfield accompanied Kenyon in the truck. A police officer stopped Kenyon for speeding and discovered that Kenyon's driver's license had been suspended. The officer took Kenyon and Crossfield to Sanchez's home and explained the situation to Sanchez. Sanchez was upset because Kenyon had been driving his truck without a valid driver's license, and he told Kenyon that he could not use his truck any longer.

Shortly thereafter, Crossfield spoke with her children, who were living in California with their father. The children told her about a family emergency. On September 30, 1997, Crossfield and Kenyon took Sanchez's truck and went to California to retrieve Crossfield's children. Sanchez reported to the police that his truck had been stolen.

Kenyon and Crossfield were arrested in Oregon on October 12, 1997. Kenyon pleaded guilty in Oregon to one count of unauthorized use of a motor vehicle. He was subsequently extradited to Wyoming and charged with grand larceny. The trial court held a jury trial on May 11, 1998, and the jury found Kenyon guilty of the crime. The trial court entered a judgment and sentence which was consistent with the jury's verdict, and Kenyon appealed to the Wyoming Supreme Court.

DISCUSSION

A. Admissibility of Crossfield's Statements

Kenyon maintains that the trial court abused its discretion when it refused to allow him to testify that Crossfield told him Sanchez had given them permission to use the truck. We agree with Kenyon.

A trial court has discretion in determining the admissibility of evidence, and the Wyoming Supreme Court will not disturb a trial court's evidentiary rulings unless the trial court abused its discretion. *Kolb v. State*, 930 P.2d 1238, 1245 (Wyo. 1996). A court does not abuse its discretion unless it acts in a manner which exceeds the bounds of reason under the circumstances. *Hilterbrand v. State*, 930 P.2d 1248, 1250 (Wyo. 1997). In determining whether there has been an abuse of discretion, we must decide the ultimate issue of whether or not the court could have reasonably concluded as it did. *Clark v. Gale*, 966 P.2d 431, 435 (Wyo. 1998).

Kenyon was tried for the crime of grand larceny as proscribed by Wyo. Stat. Ann. § 6-3-402(a) and (c)(i) (LEXIS 1999). That statute states:

(a) A person who steals, takes and carries, leads or drives away property of another with intent to deprive the owner or lawful possessor is guilty of larceny.

* * *

(c) Except as provided by subsection (e) of this section, larceny is:

(i) A felony punishable by imprisonment for not more than ten (10) years, a fine of not more than ten thousand dollars ($10,000.00), or both, if the value of the property is five hundred dollars ($500.00) or more; . . .

Section 6-3-402(a) and (c)(i). Wyo. Stat. Ann. § 6-3-401(a)(ii) (LEXIS 1999) states that "deprive" means:

(A) To withhold property of another permanently or for so extended a period as to appropriate a major portion of its economic value or with intent to restore only upon payment of reward or other compensation; or

(B) To dispose of the property so as to make it unlikely that the owner will recover it.

Kenyon testified on his own behalf at the trial. He was the only defense witness. The defense attorney sought to elicit testimony from Kenyon that, before they left Cheyenne, Crossfield told him Sanchez had given them permission to use his truck. The following exchange occurred at the trial:

Q.   (BY [DEFENSE ATTORNEY]) Okay. In any event, there was a family emergency. You decided to leave. What actions did you take?

A.   At that time I didn't take any actions. I wasn't sure exactly what to do. I forget what the date was. It was in the morning. We were going to pull the last of the garbage out to the dump with [Sanchez's] trailer. Went over there, found out it didn't have a license plate, so that was off. [Sanchez] was at work. I don't know if [Sanchez's fiancee] had went to work or not.

[Crossfield] and I had the pickup truck. And I was in the trailer, [Crossfield] was doing something in the house. I don't know what. She come out. She said are you ready? I said to do what? She said well, let's go get the girls. She said that she had spoke with [Sanchez], that it was all right—

[PROSECUTOR]:   Objection, Your Honor, irrelevant, relevance, hearsay.

THE COURT: It is technically hearsay, but it isn't offered for the truth of the matter, so go ahead.

[KENYON]:   She asked me if I was ready. I said for what. And she said that she had spoke with [Sanchez], and that it was all right for us to use the truck to go and get her girls.

[PROSECUTOR]:   May I have a continuing objection to conversation with [Sanchez] along these lines if it's not offered for the truth?

THE COURT: I misspoke. I'm sorry.

[DEFENSE ATTORNEY]:   I'll move on.

THE COURT: The jury will be instructed that the testimony that — who did you speak to? What was her name?

[KENYON]:   My fiancee is Kelly Crossfield.

THE COURT: She told you you had permission?

[KENYON]:   Yes, sir.

THE COURT: I see. That will be stricken. Ladies and gentlemen, the fact that his fiancee told him he had permission will be totally disregarded by you. That's not admissible. I shouldn't have let it come before you.

[DEFENSE ATTORNEY]:   Your Honor, I'd offer that as effect on the—

THE COURT: If you wish to argue, we can go over here.

The trial court conducted a bench conference to consider the admissibility of the proffered testimony. During the bench conference, the defense attorney argued that Crossfield's out-of-court statement was admissible under the exception to the hearsay rule set out in W.R.E. 803(3). The trial court ruled that Crossfield's statement did not fall within the purview of W.R.E. 803(3) and, accordingly, refused to admit the evidence under that rationale. Kenyon concedes on appeal that the trial court's ruling concerning W.R.E. 803(3) was correct. He asserts, however, that he also argued that Crossfield's out-of-court statement was admissible to show its effect on the listener — himself — and not to prove the truth of the matter asserted. His defense counsel stated:

I would further add, Your Honor, that it also falls under the exception, the common-law hearsay exception, effect on the hearer, what he thought of it. It's basic evidentiary law we learned in law school where there's four different common-law exceptions that apply as well.

One of those is the effect it has on the hearer. Now, the effect that it had on Mr. Kenyon is that he apparently had consent. So I would offer under those two . . . hearsay [exceptions], both of those as directly relevant to this case. He has to be able to testify he . . . apparently [had] consent. He thought he had. That's why he took this vehicle.

Although the trial court did not expressly rule on this aspect of Kenyon's argument, it obviously did not agree with Kenyon because it did not allow him to testify about Crossfield's statement.

Kenyon claims that the trial court erred by excluding Crossfield's statement because the statement was not offered to prove the truth of the matter asserted — that Sanchez had, in fact, given Crossfield permission to use the truck — but, rather, was offered to show its effect on him. He argues that the testimony would have bolstered his defense that he did not harbor the criminal intent to permanently deprive Sanchez of his truck.

The state does not respond on appeal to the substantive portion of Kenyon's argument. It asserts that Kenyon did not sufficiently notify the trial court that he was offering the evidence to show its effect on the listener rather than to prove the truth of the matter asserted. We do not agree with the state.

Kenyon's argument was sufficiently clear to alert the trial court that he was asserting that Crossfield's out-of-court statement was admissible under two theories: (1) The statement was not hearsay because it was not offered to prove the truth of the matter asserted — it was offered to show the effect of Crossfield's statement on Kenyon; and (2) even if the statement was hearsay, it was admissible under the exception to the hearsay rule set out in W.R.E. 803(3). *See Padilla v. State*, 601 P.2d 189, 194 (Wyo.1979). We will, therefore, address the substantive issue of the admissibility of Crossfield's statement.

"Hearsay" is defined as "a statement, other than one made by the declarant while testifying at the trial or hearing, offered in evidence to prove the truth of the matter asserted." W.R.E. 801(c). In *Armstrong v. State*, 826 P.2d 1106, 1119 (Wyo.1992), this Court recognized that, when an out-of-court statement is not offered to prove the truth of the matter asserted but is, instead, offered for the purpose of showing its effect on the mental or emotional state of the person hearing it, it is not hearsay. Such out-of-court statements are admissible. 826 P.2d at 1119.

The Arkansas Supreme Court quoted from McCormick on Evidence to explain the general principle that an out-of-court statement offered to show its effect on the hearer is not hearsay. *Cole v. State*, 323 Ark. 8, 913 S.W.2d 255, 257 (Ark.1996).

"Some Out-of-Court Utterances Which Are Not Hearsay.

" . . . Utterances and writing[s] offered to show effect on hearer or reader. When it is proved that D made a statement to X, with the purpose of showing the probable state of mind thereby induced in X, such as being put on notice or having knowledge, or motive, or to show the information which X had as bearing on the reasonableness or good faith or voluntariness of the subsequent conduct of X, or anxiety, the evidence is not subject to attack as hearsay . . ." McCormick on Evidence, § 249, pp. 733–34 (3d Ed. 1984).

Id. Similarly, an Arizona Court of Appeals explained: " 'Words offered to prove the effect on the hearer are admissible when they are offered to show their effect on one whose conduct is at issue.' " *State v. Rivers,* 190 Ariz. 56, 945 P.2d 367, 371 (Ct.App.1997) (quoting *State v. Hernandez,* 170 Ariz. 301, 823 P.2d 1309, 1314 (Ct.App.1991)). The general principle that an out-of-court statement offered to show its effect on the hearer is generally admissible because it is not hearsay is widely recognized. *See, e.g., People v. Thomas,* 296 Ill.App.3d 489, 694 N.E.2d 1068, 230 Ill.Dec. 790 (1998); *Hilliard v. Schmidt,* 231 Mich.App. 316, 586 N.W.2d 263 (1998); *State v. Ninci,* 262 Kan. 21, 936 P.2d 1364 (1997); *State v. Lawrence,* 285 Mont. 140, 948 P.2d 186 (1997); *State v. Copeland,* 928 S.W.2d 828 (Mo.1996) (en banc), *cert. denied,* 519 U.S. 1126, 117 S.Ct. 981, 136 L.Ed.2d 864 (1997); *State v. Harrigan,* 662 A.2d 196 (Me.1995); *Atkins v. State,* 523 A.2d 539 (Del.1987); *Mickel v. State,* 602 So.2d 1160 (Miss.1992); *Laird v. State,* 565 S.W.2d 38 (Tenn.Crim.App.1978).

The traditional credibility concerns associated with hearsay statements are not relevant when an out-of-court statement is offered to show its effect on the listener rather than to prove the truth of the matter asserted. "Testimony of out-of-court statements used other than to establish the truth of the matter asserted does not rest for its value on the credibility of the out-of-court declarant but, rather, on the credibility of the witness, who was present in court and subject to cross-examination." *People v. Shoultz,* 289 Ill.App.3d 392, 682 N.E.2d 446, 449, 224 Ill.Dec. 885 (1997); *see also Laird,* 565 S.W.2d at 41.

Other jurisdictions have considered cases with facts that are similar to those in the case at bar. In *State v. Getz,* 250 Kan. 560, 830 P.2d 5, 8 (1992), the Kansas Supreme Court reviewed Getz's conviction for stealing two horses. Getz claimed that the trial court erred when it refused to allow her to testify that Perry Patton told her he owned the horses and asked her to help him sell them. 830 P.2d at 8–10. Getz maintained that the evidence was not offered to prove the truth of the matter asserted — that Patton owned the horses — but was offered to show her state of mind and lack of criminal intent. 830 P.2d at 8–11. The Kansas Supreme Court agreed with Getz and ruled that the trial court committed reversible error when it refused to allow her to testify about Patton's out-of-court statements. 830 P.2d at 12–13; *see also Harrigan,* 662 A.2d at 197–98.

In *People v. Canamore,* 88 Ill. App. 3d 639, 44 Ill. Dec. 323, 411 N.E.2d 292 (1980), Canamore was convicted of "criminal trespass to vehicles." The trial court refused to allow her to testify that the person from whom she borrowed the car had told her that it was "a family car." 44 Ill.Dec. 323, 411 N.E.2d at 293. Canamore claimed on appeal that the statements were not offered to prove the truth of the matters asserted but were offered to show that she did not know the car was stolen. 44 Ill.Dec. 323, 411 N.E.2d at 294. An Illinois appellate court ruled that the trial court erroneously excluded the evidence. *Id.*

In keeping with the general principle, we conclude that the trial court in this case abused its discretion when it refused to allow Kenyon to testify concerning Crossfield's out-of-court statement that Sanchez had given them permission to use the truck. The statement was not offered to prove the truth of the matter asserted. Crossfield's statement was offered, instead, to show its effect on Kenyon's intent and subsequent conduct.

We must now determine whether the trial court's error was prejudicial or harmless. An error concerning the admissibility of evidence is harmless when a defendant's substantial rights were not affected. W.R.Cr.P. 52(a); *Kerns v. State*, 920 P.2d 632, 641 (Wyo.1996). "The proper inquiry is whether a reasonable probability exists that, but for the error, the verdict would have been more favorable to the defendant." *Kerns*, 920 P.2d at 641.

The issue of whether or not Kenyon possessed the criminal intent to permanently deprive Sanchez of his truck was strongly contested at the trial. The fact that Crossfield told Kenyon that Sanchez had given them permission to use the truck was obviously important to the determination of that issue. Although the state did not address the substantive issue, it could have argued that the trial court's refusal to allow Kenyon to testify about Crossfield's statement was not prejudicial because Kenyon was allowed to testify as follows:

Q.   Okay. Did you have any reason to believe that you could not borrow this vehicle?

A.   No, sir.

Q.   What reason did you have in borrowing the vehicle?

A.   At the time I was told by [Crossfield] that everything was cool, so I didn't question it.

This exchange was not sufficient to cure the trial court's error in refusing to allow Kenyon to testify directly about Crossfield's statement to him that Sanchez had given them permission to use the vehicle. Crossfield's statement that "everything was cool" is not equivalent to a statement that Sanchez had granted them permission to use the vehicle. Furthermore, the trial court originally instructed the jury to totally disregard the fact that Crossfield told Kenyon that they had permission to use the truck. This instruction was not revised when Kenyon was allowed to testify that Crossfield said "everything was cool."

The heart of Kenyon's defense was that he did not have the requisite criminal intent to be convicted of grand larceny. Taking the entire record into consideration, we conclude that there is a reasonable probability that the verdict would have been more favorable to Kenyon if the trial court had admitted Crossfield's out-of-court statement. The trial court's refusal to allow Kenyon to testify about Crossfield's out-of-court statement affected Kenyon's substantial rights, and he is, therefore, entitled to have his conviction reversed.

B. Jury Instruction

Kenyon contends that the trial court erred when it refused to instruct the jury on his theory of defense. We assume that, if Kenyon presents evidence supporting a legitimate theory of defense at his next trial, the trial court will instruct the jury in accordance with Wyoming law.

Reversed and remanded.

[3] Operative Facts or Verbal Acts

Statements that have legal significance because of their utterance under designated circumstances do not constitute hearsay if subsequently repeated in a judicial proceeding to establish the occurrence of the legal event brought about by the utterance. These statements are termed "operative facts" of an occurrence or "verbal acts."

ARGUELLES v. STATE
Florida District Court of Appeal, Fourth District
842 So.2d 939 (2003)

WARNER, J.

Appellant contests his conviction and sentence for trafficking in cocaine and conspiracy to traffic in cocaine, raising five issues on appeal. His main contention concerns the trial court's admission of alleged hearsay statements to his co-defendant, Jose Gajate. Because some of the statements constituted non-hearsay verbal acts and those statements, when combined with the other non-hearsay evidence, sufficiently established appellant's participation in a conspiracy to traffic in cocaine, the trial court did not err in admitting Gajate's other co-conspirator hearsay statements. We thus affirm as to that issue and all other issues raised.

While working as a confidential informant ("CI"), Harold Gomez was paged by an old acquaintance, Gajate, who inquired about buying a kilo of cocaine with the possibility of buying nine more. Gomez advised his controlling agent of the page, and they set up a meeting between Gomez and Gajate the next day to conduct the sale.

Gajate and Gomez met as planned in a parking lot. They talked about the quantity, price, and location of the deal. Gajate told Gomez that the money belonged to his "buddy" who would accompany him later when the transaction was conducted. Once Gajate purchased the first kilo, he said the "other people" would then have to approve the purchase of the other nine kilos. During their conversation, Gajate's "buddy" paged him, and Gajate used Gomez's cellular phone to return the page. Gomez overheard Gajate advise the caller that everything was ready for the transaction and that they should all meet at the caller's house to return and complete the deal. After finishing the call, Gajate told Gomez that his "buddy" (appellant) was the middleman (like Gajate) and another guy (Michael Green) was their client who owned the money. A BellSouth records custodian verified that the number Gajate dialed on Gomez's phone belonged to Olga Arguelles at 1001 Northwest 25th Avenue in Miami.

Gajate then traveled to this residence. After twenty minutes inside, Gajate exited the residence with appellant; neither man carried anything. Gajate eventually returned to the previous parking lot with Green in the passenger seat and appellant in the backseat, parking on the right side of Gomez's SUV.

Gajate informed Gomez that he had the money for the deal. Gomez then told Gajate that the others had to remain behind, and Gajate agreed, stating that he could not have brought the money alone. Gajate returned to his car and leaned into the back seat where appellant handed him a bag full of groceries containing an open box with the money inside. It appeared to one of the surveillance agents that Gajate directed appellant to give him the bag.

After Gajate showed Gomez the money, the two men traveled across the street to a different location where the cocaine was located. Meanwhile, Green and appellant drove up and down several aisles in a nearby mall parking lot, passing several open spaces, and then returned to the original parking lot; the whole drive took five to seven minutes. One of the agents opined that "they were checking the area to see if anybody was watching them."

Upon arriving at a residential area close to the parking lot, Gomez and a second CI showed Gajate the kilo of cocaine. After testing the cocaine, Gajate said that it was good, but needed to show the kilo to his "buddy" and Green because they were the ones that had the last word on it. Gajate took possession of the cocaine and began walking back to Gomez's vehicle. Law enforcement agents then moved in, capturing Gajate after he attempted to flee over a wall.

Other agents arrested Green and appellant after receiving word that the transaction had occurred and Gajate was in custody. Without anyone mentioning drugs, appellant said "[w]hy am I being arrested, I don't have anything to do with drugs." The officers found $3,000 in cash on appellant, and at the police station, appellant gave his address as 1001 Northwest 25th Avenue, Miami. While in the holding cell, appellant told Green, "[t]hen why didn't you leave. We should have run." He later asked Green, "Mike, how much do you think they'll give us for conspiracy."

The state charged appellant, Gajate, and Green by collective information with trafficking in cocaine and conspiracy to traffic in cocaine. Gajate was also charged with resisting arrest without violence. After a trial where Gajate did not testify, the jury returned a verdict of guilty on both the trafficking and conspiracy counts. The court then adjudicated appellant guilty and entered a written judgment and written sentence for those two counts only.

If out-of-court statements are offered to prove the making or terms of a conspiratorial agreement, then they are "verbal acts" not excluded under the hearsay rule. *See* Charles W. Ehrhardt, *Florida Evidence* § 801.6 n. 4 (2001 ed.). These verbal acts prove the nature of the act, as opposed to proving the truth of the alleged statements. *See Harris v. State*, 544 So.2d 322, 323 (Fla. 4th DCA 1989) (en banc); *Decile v. State*, 516 So.2d 1139, 1140 (Fla. 4th DCA 1987). For example, the statements "I need eight" followed by the response "[n]o problem, come inside, I get you rocks," were verbal acts because they constituted part of the underlying transaction. *See Decile*, 516 So.2d at 1139–40; *also Stevens v. State*, 642 So.2d 828, 829 (Fla. 2d DCA 1994) ("I need a dime."). On the other hand, a statement to a police officer that a specific person is dealing cocaine at a specific place is not a verbal act because it is not part of the transaction. *See Harris*, 544 So.2d at 323–24.

The supreme court recently addressed the "verbal acts" exception in *Banks v.*

State, 790 So.2d 1094 (Fla. 2001). The court explained:

> One category of extrajudicial statements excluded from the hearsay rule is referred to as "verbal act" evidence. "Verbal act" evidence has been defined as:
>
>> A verbal act is an utterance of an operative fact that gives rise to legal consequences. Verbal acts, also known as statements of legal consequence, are not hearsay, because the statement is admitted merely to show that it was actually made, not to prove the truth of what was asserted in it.
>
> For utterances to be admissible as verbal acts, (1) the conduct to be characterized by the words must be independently material to the issue; (2) the conduct must be equivocal; (3) the words must aid in giving legal significance to the conduct; and (4) the words must accompany the conduct.

Banks, 790 So.2d at 1097–98 (citations omitted). *Banks* discussed *Stevens,* 642 So.2d 828, and noted that the statement "I need a dime" was not offered for its truth or falsity, but rather "to explain the defendant's reaction to the statement, *i.e.,* the defendant promptly acting to provide the illegal drugs to complete the transaction." *Banks,* 790 So.2d at 1098.

Here, some of the admitted hearsay statements were verbal acts, and some were not. Appellant objected on hearsay grounds to Gajate's statements concerning (1) the initial set up of the drug deal at the first meeting with Gomez, (2) the money he had at the second meeting, and (3) the necessity to show the cocaine to Green and appellant before the transaction was completed because they had the last word. These statements were all part of the transaction and thus verbal acts, not inadmissible hearsay. However, some of Gajate's statements were not verbal acts and were offered for the truth of the matter asserted: (1) appellant was the middleman, and (2) the money belonged to appellant or Green and he could not have brought it alone.

* * *

[4] Knowledge

When the out-of-court declarant's knowledge is relevant to the litigation, statements of fact, on their face, reflect knowledge of those facts by the individual uttering the words. These statements are not hearsay because their value is not dependent on belief in the truth of their content.

STATE v. BERNSTEIN
North Dakota Supreme Court
697 N.W.2d 371 (2005)

PER CURIAM.

Loren Bernstein has appealed from an order deferring imposition of sentence upon a conviction for criminal trespass. We reverse and remand for a new trial, concluding that the district court erred in refusing to admit evidence that Loren's father had told him to go to the property to retrieve some personal items.

I

In 1972, LeRoy Bernstein deeded certain land to his daughter, Caroljoy Richard, and her husband. Caroljoy and her husband lived in a house on the property. In 1987, Caroljoy allowed LeRoy to move his house onto the property, and he lived there from 1987 to 2004. Each house had its own driveway. LeRoy's son, Loren, visited him in his house on a daily basis, regularly bringing the mail and newspaper to his father.

In late October 2003, LeRoy was hospitalized. He asked Loren to go to the house and bring certain personal items to him in the hospital. Loren went to the property, but found that LeRoy's house was locked. A key which LeRoy kept in his garage so his children could get into the house had been removed. When Caroljoy noticed Loren was at LeRoy's house, she went over and told him it was her property and he was not allowed to go into LeRoy's house. Caroljoy also posted a no trespassing sign on the driveway leading to LeRoy's house.

Loren claims that LeRoy, after learning of Caroljoy's refusal to allow Loren into the house, again told Loren to go to the house and bring back certain items, and to use whatever means necessary to get in. Loren returned to the property but again found the house locked. During this visit, he removed the no trespassing sign and placed it in LeRoy's garage.

When Caroljoy learned that Loren had been in LeRoy's garage, she signed a criminal complaint against him for trespassing. Loren was charged with criminal trespass in violation of N.D.C.C. § 12.1-22-03(3).

The case was tried to the court without a jury. At trial, Loren argued that he believed he had a license or privilege to be on the property. When Loren was asked on direct examination about the statements made to him by his father at the hospital directing Loren to go to his house, the State objected on hearsay grounds. The trial court reserved ruling on the State's objection, but allowed Loren to testify about the conversations with his father subject to the court's subsequent ruling on admissibility. LeRoy had died prior to the trial, so Loren offered into evidence an affidavit from LeRoy stating that: (1) he had requested Loren to go to his house and bring certain personal items to him in the hospital, and (2) when Loren returned and told him the house was locked and he could not get in, LeRoy told Loren to "go and get the door opened however would be required to bring me what I was in need of." The State objected to admission of the affidavit on hearsay grounds, and the trial court again reserved ruling on the objection.

At the conclusion of the trial, the court ruled that LeRoy's affidavit and Loren's testimony about what his father told him at the hospital were irrelevant, and excluded the evidence. Loren's counsel asked whether the court was excluding the evidence on relevance grounds and not hearsay grounds, and the court answered, "Correct." The court found Loren guilty of criminal trespass and ordered a deferred imposition of sentence.

II

The order deferring imposition of sentence was filed on October 13, 2004. On October 21, 2004, Bernstein filed a notice of appeal "from the Final Judgment entered in this action on October 13, 2004." However, no separate judgment of conviction was ever entered.

An order deferring imposition of sentence is not an appealable order under N.D.C.C. § 29-28-06. *State v. Nelson*, 2005 ND 11, ¶ 5, 691 N.W.2d 218. However, when the order deferring imposition of sentence meets the requirements of N.D.R.Crim.P. 32(b) for criminal judgments and no separate judgment of conviction has been entered, the order serves as the judgment of conviction and is appealable. *Nelson*, at ¶ 5, 691 N.W.2d 218; *State v. Berger*, 2004 ND 151, ¶ 8, 683 N.W.2d 897. The order in this case includes the plea, the verdict, and the sentence imposed, and therefore satisfies the requirements of N.D.R.Crim.P. 32(b). Accordingly, the order deferring imposition of sentence serves as the judgment of conviction and the appeal is properly before us. *See Nelson*, at ¶ 5, 691 N.W.2d 218; *Berger*, at ¶ 8, 683 N.W.2d 897.

III

Loren argues the trial court erred in concluding that evidence of what LeRoy told him at the hospital was irrelevant.

A trial court has broad discretion in evidentiary matters, and its decision to admit or exclude evidence will not be overturned on appeal unless the court abused its discretion. *State v. Jaster*, 2004 ND 223, ¶ 12, 690 N.W.2d 213; *City of Fargo v. Habiger*, 2004 ND 127, ¶ 31, 682 N.W.2d 300. A trial court abuses its discretion if it acts in an arbitrary, unreasonable, or unconscionable manner, if its decision is not the product of a rational mental process leading to a reasoned determination, or if it misinterprets or misapplies the law. *State v. Tupa*, 2005 ND 25, ¶ 3, 691 N.W.2d 579.

Loren was charged with criminal trespass in violation of N.D.C.C. § 12.1-22-03(3), which provides in pertinent part:

A person is guilty of a class B misdemeanor if, knowing that that person is not licensed or privileged to do so, that person enters or remains in any place as to which notice against trespass is given by actual communication to the actor by the person in charge of the premises or other authorized person or by posting in a manner reasonably likely to come to the attention of intruders.

Under the criminal trespass statute, "privilege" is the freedom or authority to act and to use the property. *State v. Morales*, 2004 ND 10, ¶ 10, 673 N.W.2d 250; *State v. Purdy*, 491 N.W.2d 402, 410 (N.D. 1992). A person is privileged if "he may naturally be expected to be on the premises often and in the natural course of his duties or habits." *Morales*, at ¶ 10 (quoting *State v. Ronne*, 458 N.W.2d 294, 297–98 (N.D. 1990)). A person is "licensed" to be on property if the entry was consensual. *See Purdy*, at 410; *Ronne*, at 297–98.

Under N.D.C.C. § 12.1-22-03(3), the State was required to prove beyond a reasonable doubt that Loren knew that he was not licensed or privileged to enter his father's house or garage. *See Heckelsmiller v. State*, 2004 ND 191, ¶¶ 10, 12, 687 N.W.2d 454; *Morales*, 2004 ND 10, ¶¶ 15, 21, 673 N.W.2d 250. The defendant's state of mind is therefore an element of the offense, and evidence tending to show his state of mind would be relevant and admissible. *See* N.D.R.Ev. 401 and 402.

For purposes of N.D.C.C. tit. 12.1, a person engages in conduct "knowingly" if, "when he engages in the conduct, he knows or has a firm belief, unaccompanied by substantial doubt, that he is doing so, whether or not it is his purpose to do so." N.D.C.C. § 12.1-02-02(1)(b); *see Morales*, 2004 ND 10, ¶ 26, 673 N.W.2d 250; *In re J.D.*, 494 N.W.2d 160, 162 (N.D.1992); *State v. Kaufman*, 310 N.W.2d 709, 713 (N.D.1981). Knowledge need not be absolute, but merely a firm belief unaccompanied by substantial doubt. *J.D.*, at 162; *Kaufman*, at 713. Knowledge is a question of fact. *State v. Hammond*, 498 N.W.2d 126, 129 (N.D.1993); *J.D.*, at 162; *Kaufman*, at 713.

The knowledge requirement is a subjective test, and "[t]he factfinder must make its determination based upon whether the facts and circumstances would have caused this particular defendant to 'know' the requisite facts." *Kaufman*, at 714. The finder of fact therefore must consider all of the surrounding facts and circumstances in determining the defendant's knowledge. *Hammond*, 498 N.W.2d at 129; *Kaufman*, at 714. Thus, to satisfy the knowledge element of the offense of criminal trespass under N.D.C.C. § 12.1-22-03(3), the State was required to prove that Loren knew or had a firm belief, unaccompanied by substantial doubt, that he was not licensed or privileged to be on the property.

The trial court appears to have based its conclusion that evidence about LeRoy's statements to Loren in the hospital was irrelevant upon a misinterpretation of the elements of criminal trespass under N.D.C.C. § 12.1-22-03(3). At the conclusion of the trial, the court announced from the bench its decision finding Loren guilty of criminal trespass. The court began its oral decision by stating: "And the way the Court sees this matter is that the basic issue is did Loren Bernstein have license or privilege to be on the property on that particular day, Friday, November 1st, 2003?" The court then concluded that, because Caroljoy was the owner of the property and had told Loren to stay off the property, it was not reasonable for Loren to think that he could be on the property. The court concluded it did not matter what LeRoy told Loren because LeRoy did not have authority over the property, and therefore the evidence was irrelevant.

The court's analysis essentially eliminates the knowledge element of the offense. The crucial inquiry is not, as the trial court stated, whether Loren was actually licensed or privileged to be on the property, but whether Loren subjectively knew he was not licensed or privileged to be there. The fact that a person who is ultimately determined to be in charge of the premises tells the defendant to stay off of the property is only the beginning of the inquiry. The State must also prove that the defendant knew he was not licensed or privileged to be on the property.

In this case, there was evidence which may have suggested to a layperson that LeRoy had the authority to allow persons onto the property. In addition to the excluded evidence detailing LeRoy's statements to Loren, there was evidence of an unrecorded deed purporting to reserve a life estate in LeRoy; LeRoy paid the real estate taxes on the house; Loren had for years gone to the house on a daily basis to visit his father; and Caroljoy admitted LeRoy had authority over his house and could determine its use while he was on the property, but that she exercised control of the house when he was away. The trial court was presented with a disputed factual issue whether Loren knew or had a firm belief, unaccompanied by substantial doubt, that he was not licensed or privileged to enter his father's house and garage. Under the circumstances, evidence of LeRoy's statements instructing Loren to go to the house and bring back certain personal items for LeRoy are directly relevant to the issue of Loren's knowledge or belief that he had a license or privilege to be on the property. If Loren believed that his father had the authority to consent to his entry onto the property, the knowledge element of criminal trespass under N.D.C.C. § 12.1-22-03(3) would be missing.

We conclude the trial court erred in determining evidence of LeRoy's statements to Loren was irrelevant, and the court abused its discretion in excluding the evidence on relevance grounds. *See Hammond*, 498 N.W.2d at 129 (trial court abused its discretion and misapplied the law when it overlooked the issue of whether a post-dated check was "knowingly received").

IV

The State contends that, even if the trial court erred in excluding the evidence on relevance grounds, the evidence is nevertheless inadmissible hearsay. The State objected to the evidence on hearsay grounds, but the court did not address the hearsay objection when it excluded the evidence. When the judgment below is entirely favorable to the appellee, he is entitled to attempt to save the judgment upon any ground asserted in the trial court. *State v. Sabinash*, 1998 ND 32, ¶ 19, 574 N.W.2d 827.

A

We first consider the trial court's refusal to admit Loren's testimony that his father told him to go to the house and bring back to the hospital certain personal items.

Under N.D.R.Ev. 801(c), hearsay is "a statement, other than one made by the declarant while testifying at the trial or hearing, offered in evidence to prove the truth of the matter asserted." If an out-of-court statement is not offered to prove its truth, it is not hearsay. *Moen v. Thomas*, 2001 ND 95, ¶ 11, 627 N.W.2d 146; *Ehrlich v. Backes*, 477 N.W.2d 211, 214 (N.D.1991); *State v. Welch*, 426 N.W.2d 550, 555 (N.D.1988). A statement offered to prove that it was made is not hearsay. *Moen*, at ¶ 11, 627 N.W.2d 146; *Ehrlich*, at 214; *Welch*, at 555.

Accordingly, a statement offered to show its effect upon the state of mind of the listener, rather than the truth of the matter asserted, is not hearsay. *State v. Hart*, 1997 ND 188, ¶ 20, 569 N.W.2d 451. When a person's knowledge or lack of knowledge is at issue, statements affecting the person's state of mind are not hearsay:

Words offered to prove the effect on the hearer are admissible when they are offered to show their effect on one whose conduct is at issue.

When a person's knowledge or state of mind is at issue, evidence that he has heard or read a statement may be relevant, and it lies beyond reach of a hearsay objection. Where reasonableness of a party's conduct is at issue, knowledge of certain statements may have probative value regardless of the truth of the statements. Thus, an out-of-court statement may be offered to explain responsive conduct. . . .

Evidence which would otherwise be hearsay may be admissible, as bearing on the state of mind of the defendant, if it is not offered for the truth of the statement. This nonhearsay use has been invoked with respect to the issue of duress, authorization, volition, motive, good faith, and knowledge or belief, or the absence of knowledge.

29 Am.Jur.2d *Evidence* § 666 (1994) (footnotes omitted).

Loren's testimony was not offered to prove that the statements made by his father were true, but to show their effect on Loren's state of mind and knowledge. The statements are relevant to whether Loren believed he had consent, and therefore a license, to be on the property. The mere fact that the statements were made, regardless of their truth, had independent legal significance. *See Towne v. Dinius*, 1997 ND 125, ¶ 13, 565 N.W.2d 762; *In re Estate of Raketti*, 340 N.W.2d 894, 901 (N.D.1983). We conclude Loren's proffered testimony about the statements made to him by LeRoy at the hospital was not hearsay.

B

The trial court's exclusion of LeRoy's affidavit, in which LeRoy states he told Loren to go to the house to retrieve certain items, presents a somewhat different evidentiary problem. Although LeRoy could clearly have testified as a witness at trial about these statements, the fact that LeRoy died prior to trial and his "testimony" is now available only through his affidavit creates an additional level of potential hearsay. *See* N.D.R.Ev. 805. In effect, the problem is not with LeRoy's original statements made to Loren at the hospital, but with LeRoy's subsequent statement in the affidavit that he had made the earlier statements. LeRoy's subsequent statement in the affidavit is offered to prove the matter asserted, *i.e.*, the fact that he had made the earlier statements.

15 [¶ 26] An affidavit offered at trial, in lieu of live testimony by the witness, is "classic hearsay" and "must be excluded unless it comes within one of the recognized exceptions to the hearsay rule." *Mehus v. Thompson*, 266 N.W.2d 920, 924 (N.D.1978); *see, e.g., Travelers Cas. and Sur. Co. of America v. Wells Fargo Bank N.A.*, 374 F.3d 521, 524 (7th Cir.2004). The parties have not adequately addressed this issue, and we leave it to the parties and the trial court upon retrial to resolve whether LeRoy's affidavit falls within an exception to the hearsay rule under N.D.R.Ev. 803, 804, or 807.

V

We conclude the trial court erred in excluding evidence of LeRoy's statements to Loren on relevance grounds. We reverse the conviction and order deferring imposition of sentence, and remand for a new trial.

[C]   Silence as Hearsay

If a party offers testimony that there had been no complaints about a particular situation as evidence that there was nothing to complain about, is this evidence hearsay because the silence is being offered for the truth of what was impliedly communicated through the failure to speak? This was the conclusion of the court in *Menard v. Cashman*, 55 A.2d 156 (N.H. 1947). In *Menard*, the plaintiff had brought an action to recover for personal injuries she suffered on a common stairway the defendant maintained. She claimed the stairs were negligently maintained. To prove the stairs were safe, the defendant attempted to introduce evidence that no customer had ever complained about the condition of the stairs. The trial judge excluded this evidence. Upholding this decision, the appellate court stated:

> To show the "safety of the stairs," the probative effect of the excluded evidence would rest on the implication that because patrons did not complain of any defects to the tenant, they thereby indicated that they encountered none, and therefore there were none. Coming from a witness having no personal knowledge of what such users did find, the testimony would have the characteristics of hearsay . . . and the opponent would be deprived of the right to cross-examine as to what conditions were in fact encountered.

55 A.2d at 160.

In *Murray v. American Builders Supply, Inc.*, 472 P.2d 738 (Colo. 1970), the court took a very different approach to the use of silence as negative evidence. The plaintiff sued for a salary that he claimed was owed him under an employment contract that he had negotiated with a previous president of the corporation. To disprove the existence of this contract, the vice-president of the corporation testified, over plaintiff's objection, that he had attended all meetings of the board of directors; that this alleged contract was never discussed in any of these meetings; and that all pay raises had been discussed at those meetings before they were granted. The appellate court upheld the introduction of this evidence, concluding it was not hearsay because the evidence did not derive its value from the veracity and competency of someone other than the person testifying. Quoting from an earlier opinion, the court stated:

> The probative force of negative testimony depends largely upon circumstances. In some circumstances, its probative force may be so slight as to reach the vanishing point; in other circumstances, such testimony may be more persuasive than the positive testimony of some witnesses. It is only when it is so clear that such testimony has no probative value whatever that reasonable men would not differ in their conclusions with reference thereto, that courts are justified in disregarding it on the ground that it does not rise to the dignity of evidence. That is not the situation in the case at bar.

Id. at 740.

Similarly, in *St. Louis Southwestern Ry. v. Arkansas & T. Grain Co.*, 95 S.W. 656 (Tex. Civ. App. 1906), the court held that the lack of complaints from other purchasers from the same lot of corn was not hearsay: "The witness simply stated a fact within his own knowledge; that he did sell [the corn] and no complaint was ever made. These are facts and not declarations of third persons." *Id.* at 660.

Summarizing the general status of the case law relative to silence as hearsay, Professor Falknor explains:

> The "silence" cases (those treating silence as hearsay) fall easily into two groups:
>
> > (1) those concerned with the admissibility of evidence of the failure of the buyer of goods to complain, on an issue of quality; or of the failure of one who might have been injured in an alleged accident to give notice of or make claim for injury, on an issue as to the occurrence or severity of the accident; and
> >
> > (2) those concerned with the admissibility of evidence of the failure of one alleged to have made an agreement, executed an instrument or to have been served with process, to mention the disputed act or event to his family or associates, on an issue as to the occurrence of that act or event.
>
> The cases are few, and consequently it is feasible to make some reference to each of them. Preliminarily, it ought to be said that in none of the cases do we find anything like an adequate discussion of the problem presented. In none is apt authority cited, and in nearly all, the result rests on nothing more than the *ipse dixit* of the court that the evidence is or is not hearsay. In a very few of the cases the court has extended itself to the point of assimilating the failure to speak to an assertion of the belief evidenced thereby.
>
> * * *
>
> Now, the inferential process involved in the evidential use of the conduct in both classifications is very evidently the same. In the first group, relevancy of the evidence of conduct depends upon inferences from the failure of the buyer to complain, to his belief that the goods were of good or specified quality, to the fact that they were of that quality; or . . . upon inferences from the failure to make claim, to the individual's belief that he had not been hurt, to the fact that he was not hurt, with an additional inference here to the non-occurrence or insignificance of the accident. Analogously, in the second classification, relevancy depends upon inferences from the failure to speak, to the belief of the silent individual that the disputed act or event did not occur, to the non-occurrence itself. Yet, while the relevancy of this evidence of "silence" rests, in both cases, on the same circumstantial analysis — failure to speak, to belief, to the fact believed — there is reason to suggest that the evidence typified by the cases in the first group is, theoretically, more trustworthy and, quite obviously, of more probative force than that illustrated by the second group of cases.

Falknor, *Silence as Hearsay,* 89 U. PA. L. REV. 192, 209, 214 (1940).

Should silence be evaluated as hearsay or under a simple relevance standard, looking at the nature of the event or occurrence that was not reported, the likelihood that an occurrence would have been mentioned, and the witness' position as it relates to the likelihood that he or she would have been aware of any mention of the event? For a law review article arguing for such a relevance standard, see Note, *"Negative Hearsay" — The Sounds of Silence,* 84 DICK. L. REV. 605 (1980).

[D]　Intended as an Assertion

[1]　Basic Principles

Rule 801(a) defines the term "statement" that is later used in Rule 801(c) in the definition of hearsay. Rule 801(a) provides that a "statement" is "(1) an oral or written assertion or (2) nonverbal conduct of a person, *if it is intended by the person as an assertion."* (Emphasis supplied.)

It is the last clause of this subsection that is significant. The common law theoretically made no distinction between intended and unintended messages of speech and conduct, considering both to be statements for purposes of the hearsay rule. In contrast, Rule 801(a) considers communications to be "statements" only if the declarant intended the declarations to convey a particular thought. This distinction creates a preliminary factual question under Rule 104(a) that the presiding judge must resolve before determining whether the hearsay rule is applicable.

The basis for this distinction is the belief that, absent an intention to communicate, the hearsay danger of insincerity (mendacity) is eliminated. As you read *Zenni* and *Stoddard* consider the various distinctions between the facts and law involved in each of these cases.

UNITED STATES v. ZENNI
District Court for the Eastern District of Kentucky
492 F. Supp. 464 (1980)

BERTELSMAN, DISTRICT JUDGE.

This prosecution for illegal bookmaking activities presents a classic problem in the law of evidence, namely, whether implied assertions are hearsay. The problem was a controversial one at common law, the discussion of which has filled many pages in the treatises and learned journals. Although the answer to the problem is clear under the Federal Rules of Evidence, there has been little judicial treatment of the matter, and many members of the bar are unfamiliar with the marked departure from the common law the Federal Rules have effected on this issue.

The relevant facts are simply stated. While conducting a search of the premises of the defendant, Ruby Humphrey, pursuant to a lawful search warrant which authorized a search for evidence of bookmaking activity, government agents answered the telephone several times. The unknown callers stated directions for the placing of bets on various sporting events. The government proposes to introduce this evidence to show that the callers believed that the premises were used in betting operations. The existence of such belief tends to prove that they were so used. The defendants object on the ground of hearsay.

COMMON LAW BACKGROUND

At common law, the hearsay rule applied "only to evidence of out-of-court statements[13] offered for the purpose of proving that the facts are as asserted in the statement."

On the other hand, not all out-of-court expression is common law hearsay. For instance, an utterance offered to show the publication of a slander, or that a person was given notice of a fact, or orally entered into a contract, is not hearsay.

In the instant case, the utterances of the absent declarants are not offered for the truth of the words,[14] and the mere fact that the words were uttered has no relevance of itself. Rather they are offered to show the declarants' belief in a fact sought to be proved. At common law this situation occupied a controversial no-man's land. It was argued on the one hand that the out-of-court utterance was not hearsay, because the evidence was not offered for any truth stated in it, but for the truth of some other proposition inferred from it. On the other hand, it was also argued that the reasons for excluding hearsay applied, in that the evidence was being offered to show declarant's belief in the implied proposition, and he was not available to be cross-examined. Thus, the latter argument was that there existed strong policy reasons for ruling that such utterances were hearsay.

The classic case, which is discussed in virtually every textbook on evidence, is *Wright v. Tatham.* . . . Described as a "celebrated and hard-fought cause," *Wright v. Tatham* was a will contest, in which the will was sought to be set aside on the grounds of the incompetency of the testator at the time of its execution. The proponents of the will offered to introduce into evidence letters to the testator from certain absent individuals on various business and social matters. The purpose of the offer was to show that the writers of the letters believed the testator was able to make intelligent decisions concerning such matters, and thus was competent.

One of the illustrations advanced in the judicial opinions in *Wright v. Tatham* is perhaps even more famous than the case itself. This is Baron Parke's famous sea captain example. Is it hearsay to offer as proof of the seaworthiness of a vessel that its captain, after thoroughly inspecting it, embarked on an ocean voyage upon it with his family?

---

[13] (Court's original footnote 4.) It should be noted at the outset that the word *statement* as used in the Federal Rules of Evidence has a more restrictive meaning than as used at common law. F.R. Ev. 801(a). . . .

[14] (Court's original footnote 7.) That is, the utterance, "Put $2 to win on Paul Revere in the third at Pimlico," is a direction and not an assertion of any kind, and therefore can be neither true nor false.

The court in *Wright v. Tatham* held that implied assertions[15] of this kind were hearsay. The rationale, as stated by Baron Parke, was as follows:

> The conclusion at which I have arrived is, that proof of a particular fact which is not of itself a matter in issue, but which is relevant only as implying a statement or opinion of a third person on the matter in issue, is inadmissible in all cases where such a statement or opinion not on oath would be of itself inadmissible; and, therefore, in this case the letters which are offered only to prove the competence of the testator, that is the truth of the implied statements therein contained, were properly rejected, as the mere statement or opinion of the writer would certainly have been inadmissible.

This was the prevailing common law view, where the hearsay issue was recognized. But frequently, it was not recognized. Thus, two federal appellate cases involving facts virtually identical to those in the case at bar did not even discuss the hearsay issue, although the evidence admitted in them would have been objectionable hearsay under the common law view.

THE FEDERAL RULES OF EVIDENCE

The common law rule that implied assertions were subject to hearsay treatment was criticized by respected commentators for several reasons. A leading work on the Federal Rules of Evidence, referring to the hotly debated question whether an implied assertion stands on better ground with respect to the hearsay rule than an express assertion, states:

> By the time the federal rules were drafted, a number of eminent scholars and revisers had concluded that it does. Two principal arguments were usually expressed for removing implied assertions from the scope of the hearsay rule. First, when a person acts in a way consistent with a belief but without intending by his act to communicate that belief, one of the principal reasons for the hearsay rule — to exclude declarations whose veracity cannot be tested by cross-examination — does not apply, because the declarant's sincerity is not then involved. In the second place, the underlying belief is in some cases self-verifying:

> There is frequently a guarantee of the trustworthiness of the inference to be drawn . . . because the actor has based his actions on the correctness of his belief, *i.e.* his actions speak louder than words.

> In a frequently cited article the following analysis appears:

> But ought the hearsay rule be deemed applicable to evidence of conduct? As McCormick has observed the problem "has only once received any adequate discussion in any decided case," *i.e.*, in *Wright v. Tatham*, already referred to. And even in that case the court did not pursue its inquiry

---

[15] (Court's original footnote 11.) The problem is the same whether the relevant assertion is implied from verbal expression, such as that of the bettors in the instant case or the letter writers in *Wright*, or from conduct, as in the sea captain example. . . .

beyond the point of concluding that evidence of an "implied" assertion must necessarily be excluded wherever evidence of an "express" assertion would be inadmissible. But as has been pointed out more than once (although I find no *judicial* recognition of the difference), the "implied" assertion is, from the hearsay standpoint, not nearly as vulnerable as an express assertion of the fact which the evidence is offered to establish.

This is on the assumption that the conduct was "nonassertive;" that the passers-by had their umbrellas up for the sake of keeping dry, not for the purpose of telling anyone it was raining; that the truck driver started up for the sake of resuming his journey, not for the purpose of telling anyone that the light had changed; that the vicar wrote the letter to the testator for the purpose of settling the dispute with the latter, rather than with any idea of expressing his opinion of the testator's sanity. And in the typical "conduct as hearsay" case this assumption will be quite justifiable.

On this assumption, it is clear that evidence of conduct must be taken as freed from at least one of the hearsay dangers, *i.e.*, mendacity. A man does not lie to himself. Put otherwise, if in doing what he does a man has no intention of asserting the existence or non-existence of a fact, it would appear that the trustworthiness of evidence of this conduct is the same whether he is an egregious liar or a paragon of veracity. Accordingly, the lack of opportunity for cross-examination in relation to his veracity or lack of it, would seem to be of no substantial importance. Accordingly, the usual judicial disposition to equate the "implied" to the "express" assertion is very questionable.[16]

The drafters of the Federal Rules agreed with the criticisms of the common law rule that implied assertions should be treated as hearsay and expressly abolished it. They did this by providing that no oral or written expression was to be considered hearsay, unless it was an "assertion" concerning the matter sought to be proved and that no nonverbal conduct should be considered hearsay, unless it was intended to be an "assertion" concerning said matter.[17] . . .

"Assertion" is not defined in the rules, but has the connotation of a forceful or positive declaration. The Advisory Committee note concerning this problem states:

The definition of "statement" assumes importance because the term is used in the definition of hearsay in subdivision (c). *The effect of the*

---

[16] (Court's original footnote 16.) [Falknor, *The "Hear-Say" Rule as a "See-do" Rule: Evidence of Conduct*, 33 Rocky-Myn L. Rev. 133, 136 (1961)]. The context makes clear that the author would apply the same analysis "whether the conduct, although 'verbal,' is relevant, not as tending to prove the truth of what was said, but circumstantially, that is, as manifesting a belief in the existence of the fact the evidence is offered to prove." *Id.* at 134.

[17] (Court's original footnote 18.) *See* the sea captain illustration discussed, *below*. In an unpublished ruling this court recently held admissible as non-hearsay the fact that a U.S. mining inspector ate his lunch in an area in a coal mine now alleged to have been unsafe, and that other inspectors who observed operations prior to a disastrous explosion issued no citations, when it would have been their duty to do so, if there had been safety violations. These non-assertive acts would have been hearsay under the rule of *Wright v. Tatham* but are not hearsay under Rule 801 of the Federal Rules of Evidence, because the inspectors did not intend to make assertions under the circumstances. . . .

definition of "statement" is to exclude from the operation of the hearsay rule all evidence of conduct, verbal or nonverbal, not intended as an assertion. The key to the definition is that nothing is an assertion unless intended to be one.

It can scarcely be doubted that an assertion made in words is intended by the declarant to be an assertion. Hence verbal assertions readily fall into the category of "statement." Whether nonverbal conduct should be regarded as a statement for purposes of defining hearsay requires further consideration. Some nonverbal conduct, such as the act of pointing to identify a suspect in a lineup, is clearly the equivalent of words, assertive in nature, and to be regarded as a statement. Other nonverbal conduct, however, may be offered as evidence that the person acted as he did because of his belief in the existence of the condition sought to be proved, from which belief the existence of the condition may be inferred. This sequence is, arguably, in effect an assertion of the existence of the condition and hence properly includable within the hearsay concept. . . . Admittedly evidence of this character is untested with respect to the perception, memory, and narration (or their equivalents) of the actor, *but the Advisory Committee is of the view that these dangers are minimal in the absence of an intent to assert and do not justify the loss of the evidence on hearsay grounds.* No class of evidence is free of the possibility of fabrication, but the likelihood is less with nonverbal than with assertive verbal conduct. The situations giving rise to the nonverbal conduct are such as virtually to eliminate questions of sincerity. Motivation, the nature of the conduct, and the presence or absence of reliance will bear heavily upon the weight to be given the evidence. . . . *Similar considerations govern nonassertive verbal conduct and verbal conduct which is assertive but offered as a basis for inferring something other than the matter asserted,* also excluded from the definition of hearsay by the language of subdivision (c). (Emphasis added.)

This court, therefore, holds that, "Subdivision (a)(2) of Rule 801 removes implied assertions from the definition of statement and consequently from the operation of the hearsay rule."

Applying the principles discussed above to the case at bar, this court holds that the utterances of the bettors telephoning in their bets were nonassertive verbal conduct, offered as relevant for an implied assertion to be inferred from them, namely that bets could be placed at the premises being telephoned. The language is not an assertion on its face, and it is obvious these persons did not intend to make an assertion about the fact sought to be proved or anything else.[18]

---

[18] (Court's original footnote 21.) A somewhat different type of analysis would be required by words non-assertive in form, but which under the circumstances might be intended as an assertion. For example, an inspector at an airport security station might run a metal detector over a passenger and say "go on through." In the absence of the inspector, would testimony of this event be objectionable hearsay, if offered for the proposition that the passenger did not have a gun on him at that time? Although Rule 801(a) does not seem to require a preliminary determination by the trial court whether verbal conduct is intended as an assertion, it is submitted that such a determination would be required in the example given. If an assertion were intended the evidence would be excluded. If not, it would be admissible. This

As an implied assertion, the proffered evidence is expressly excluded from the operation of the hearsay rule by Rule 801 of the Federal Rules of Evidence, and the objection thereto must be overruled. An order to that effect has previously been entered.

STODDARD v. STATE OF MARYLAND
Court of Appeals of Maryland
389 Md. 681, 887 A.2d 564 (2005)

JUDGES: ARGUED BEFORE BELL, C.J.; RAKER, WILNER, CATHELL, HARRELL, BATTAGLIA, GREENE, JJ. Concurring Opinion by WILNER, J., which BATTAGLIA and GREENE, JJ., join.

OPINION BY: WILNER

Erik Stoddard was convicted of second degree murder and child abuse resulting in death. The primary question we must answer in this case is whether the trial court erred in admitting testimony recounting an out-of-court utterance allegedly made by a non-testifying eighteen month old child to the effect of "is Erik going to get me?" The State offered this utterance as evidence that the child had witnessed Stoddard commit the murder. The case requires us to consider the evidentiary question of whether the unintended implications of speech — a particular class of "implied assertions" — may be hearsay. Both the trial court and the Court of Special Appeals ruled that this evidence was not hearsay. We disagree and reverse the judgments.

Three-year-old Calen DiRubbo died on the evening of June 15, 2002. The Grand Jury for Baltimore City indicted Stoddard for the offenses of first degree murder, second degree murder, and child abuse resulting in death. He was convicted by a jury of second degree murder and child abuse resulting in death and acquitted of first degree murder. The court sentenced him to a term of thirty years incarceration for each offense, to be served consecutively.

At trial, Deputy Chief Medical Examiner Mary Ripple testified that she had performed an autopsy on Calen, and had determined the cause of death to be multiple blunt force injuries. Foremost among these injuries was a severed bowel, an injury typically associated with the infliction of "a tremendous amount of force" to the abdomen. Based on laboratory results, Dr. Ripple placed the time of Calen's death between 8:30 and 10:30 p.m., and placed the time of the fatal injury between four and sixteen hours prior to death. On cross-examination, Dr. Ripple admitted that this range was only an estimate, and that the trauma conceivably could have occurred up to twenty-four hours prior to death.

According to this medical opinion, Calen received the fatal blow between 4:00 a.m. and 6:30 p.m. on June 15th, or, at the very earliest, sometime after 8:30 p.m. on June 14th. The evidence suggested that, for at least part of this period, Stoddard

---

result is implicit in the policy of the drafters of the Federal Rules of Evidence that the touchstone for hearsay is the intention to make an assertion. . . .

was the only adult supervising Calen, her older brother Nicholas Jr., and her cousin Jasmine Pritchett, then eighteen months of age.

The central issue in this case arose during the testimony of Jasmine Pritchett's mother Jennifer Pritchett. The prosecutor asked Jennifer Pritchett, "Since that day, since Saturday June 15th have you noticed any behavioral changes in Jasmine?" Defense counsel objected, and the prosecutor explained to the court:

> "I have to prove time frame and I have to prove when the violence occurred, and it obviously happened when this little girl was there. If she's fine when she goes home and nothing happens, then there is a good defense argument that nothing happened during that time period."

The court replied, "You can get the mother to testify as to what the behavior was before and after . . . I don't even want you to ask her if she's discussed it with her. You can ask her about the differences in the behavior."

Despite this ruling by the court, the following exchange then took place:

"[STATE'S ATTORNEY:]   Ma'am, have you noticed any behavioral changes in Jasmine since Saturday June 15th?

[JENNIFER PRITCHETT:]   Yes, I have.

[STATE'S ATTORNEY:]   And would you describe just the behavioral changes for the jury, please?

[JENNIFER PRITCHETT:]   Jasmine has become—

THE COURT: Keep your voice up.

[JENNIFER PRITCHETT:]   Jasmine is very petrified of any strangers introduced to her or if there is any form of loud noise, yelling, anything, she has gotten so upset that she's broken out in hives. She has nightmares and screaming fits.

[STATE'S ATTORNEY:]   Have you ever seen any of these behaviors prior to June 15th?

[JENNIFER PRITCHETT:]   No.

[STATE'S ATTORNEY:]   Has she ever — you have never discussed this case with her, have you?

[JENNIFER PRITCHETT:]   No.

[DEFENSE COUNSEL]:   Object.

THE COURT: Overruled.

[STATE'S ATTORNEY:]   And—

[JENNIFER PRITCHETT:]   No, I have not.

[STATE'S ATTORNEY:]   And has she ever — has she ever asked you any questions about it?

[JENNIFER PRITCHETT:]   She asked me if Erik was going to—

[DEFENSE COUNSEL]:   Object.

THE COURT: No, I'm going to overrule it.

[STATE'S ATTORNEY:] Go ahead, ma'am.

[JENNIFER PRITCHETT:] She asked me if Erik was going to get her."

The following colloquy then took place at the bench:

"[DEFENSE COUNSEL]: Your Honor, not only is that hearsay, but its reliability is tenuous at best. This is far beyond what I believe was the Court's discretion. I'm going to move for a mistrial at this juncture.

"[STATE'S ATTORNEY:] May I be heard?

THE COURT: I'll hear you.

[STATE'S ATTORNEY:] First off, it's not hearsay. It's a question. The child asked a question and by simply in terms of its form, it can't be hearsay. Secondly, it's — it's not — hearsay isn't a question. Hearsay is a statement offered for its truth of the matter asserted. I am not trying to argue that Erik is going to get her. What it does show is the child's fear-

THE COURT: Effects on her, overruled.

[STATE'S ATTORNEY:] Exactly.

THE COURT: Denied.

[DEFENSE COUNSEL]: Thank you. And my motion for mistrial, Your Honor?

THE COURT: Denied."

During the State's closing argument, the prosecutor referred to this evidence as follows:

"And I'm sure you're thinking, 'It's too bad there wasn't an eyewitness. It's a real pity someone didn't see him do this.

* * *

But you know something? There was an eyewitness in this case. Unfortunately, she's just too young to come into court and testify, and that eyewitness was Jasmine, Jennifer's child. Do you remember when Jennifer testified? She said that starting on June 15th, her little girl, Jasmine, had an abrupt personality change. All of a sudden, out of the blue, little Jasmine started to have nightmares. She started to have behavioral problems and she started to ask her mother, 'Is Erik going to get me?' 'Is Erik going to get me?'

Now, you heard Jennifer testify. Jasmine was two years old. There was no way she discussed the events of Calen's murder with Jasmine. You know they're not going to discuss this in front of a two-year-old child and she's not going to tell Jasmine anything about this, but Jasmine asked her, 'Is Erik going to get me?' Why? She was afraid of Erik. She didn't ask, 'Is Nick going to get me?' She didn't ask, 'Is Mark going to get me?' She wasn't afraid of them. She was afraid of Erik. Why? Because she saw. She was the eyewitness. She saw what happened to Calen that day and she was scared to death it was going to happen to her, too."

Stoddard was convicted and noted a timely appeal to the Court of Special Appeals. Before that court, Stoddard argued, *inter alia*, that Jasmine Pritchett's out-of-court question, "Is Erik going to get me," was hearsay when offered to prove the truth of its "implied assertion" that Jasmine was afraid of Erik Stoddard. The State argued that Jasmine's question was not hearsay because it was simply a request for information, spoken without the intent to "assert" anything, and hence not an "assertion" for purposes of Md. Rule 5-801(a). Alternatively, the State argued that even if Jasmine's question contained an implied assertion, that assertion was "Eric is going to get me," and her words were not offered to prove that Eric was in fact going to "get" Jasmine, but rather as circumstantial evidence of her state of mind. The State also argued that any error in admitting the evidence was harmless.

The Court of Special Appeals affirmed. *Stoddard v. State*, 157 Md. App. 247, 850 A.2d 406 (2004). Tracing the history of the implied assertion doctrine from the noted English case of *Wright v. Doe d. Tatham*, 112 Eng. Rep. 488 (Exch. Ch. 1837) and 47 Rev. Rep. 136 (H.L. 1838), the Court of Special Appeals held that Jasmine's question is a "non-assertive verbal utterance," and is not hearsay.

We granted Stoddard's petition for a writ of certiorari to consider the following question:

> Did the Court of Special Appeals, purporting to overrule this Court's longstanding precedent and drastically narrowing the scope of Maryland's hearsay rule so as to remove virtually all implied assertions from the definition of hearsay, err in holding that an out-of-court statement by a non-testifying eighteen-month-old child in which the child implied that she was afraid of Petitioner because she saw him beat the victim was not an implied assertion under Maryland Rule 5-801?

* * *

II.

Before this Court, Stoddard argues that Maryland has retained, and should retain, the common law view of implied assertions as expressed in *Wright v. Tatham*, at least as applied to words rather than nonverbal conduct. He argues that Jasmine's question was offered for the truth of a matter impliedly asserted — namely, that Jasmine was afraid of Stoddard *because she had seen Stoddard assault Calen* — and thus inadmissible hearsay under the *Wright v. Tatham* approach.

The State argues that the evidence was not hearsay under Md. Rule 5-801. First, the State maintains that Rule 5-801 rejected the holding of *Wright v. Tatum* and that, since the adoption of the Rule, that case no longer defines an assertion for purposes of hearsay in Maryland. Specifically, the State argues that the implications of an utterance now constitute assertions only if the declarant *intended* to communicate those implications. It is most unlikely that Jasmine intended to communicate any implied message through her question, the State continues, and therefore neither the question nor any implication of the question qualifies as an assertion. Finally, the State contends that any error was harmless beyond a reasonable doubt.

This case presents one facet of the classic "implied assertion" hearsay puzzle. We must decide whether out-of-court words are hearsay when offered to prove the truth of a factual proposition communicated unintentionally by the declarant.

In Maryland, the admission of evidence is committed ordinarily to the sound discretion of the trial judge. . . . Hearsay is different. Under Md. Rule 5-802, "except as otherwise provided by these rules or permitted by applicable constitutional provisions or statutes, hearsay is not admissible." In other words, the judge has no discretion to admit hearsay unless it falls within a constitutional, statutory or rule exception.

Maryland Rule 5-801 defines "hearsay" as "a statement, other than one made by the declarant while testifying at the trial or hearing, offered in evidence to prove the truth of the matter asserted." The threshold questions when a hearsay objection is raised are (1) whether the declaration at issue is a "statement," and (2) whether it is offered for the truth of the matter asserted. If the declaration is not a statement, or if it is not offered for the truth of the matter asserted, it is not hearsay and it will not be excluded under the hearsay rule.

"Statement" is defined by Md. Rule 5-801 (a) as "(1) an oral or written assertion or (2) nonverbal conduct of a person, if it is intended by the person as an assertion." The Rule does not define "asserted" or "assertion." The Committee note to Rule 5-801 explains as follows:

> "This Rule does not attempt to define 'assertion,' a concept best left to development in the case law. The fact that proffered evidence is in the form of a question or something other than a narrative statement, however, does not necessarily preclude its being an assertion. The Rule also does not attempt to define when an assertion, such as a verbal act, is offered for something other than its truth."

Much verbal evidence may be sorted into hearsay and non-hearsay without too searching an inquiry into the definitions at issue. In a simpler case, Jasmine would have said "I saw Erik hit Calen," and these words would be hearsay if offered through Jennifer Pritchett to prove that Jasmine had in fact seen Erik hit Calen. Or, had the words "is Erik going to get me" been offered through Jennifer to prove that Jasmine was alive, or knew how to speak English, or could speak at all at the time she spoke them, they would be non-hearsay.

In the instant case, the utterances of Jasmine were not offered for the "truth" of the words "Is Erik going to get me?" Nor was Jasmine's mere act of speaking the words relevant in and of itself. Rather, the State offered the words as evidence of a fact the State sought to prove, *i.e.*, that Jasmine had witnessed Erik assault Calen DiRubbo. The words in and of themselves contain no information about an assault or about someone named Calen. The implied assertion doctrine arises in this case because Jasmine's question is relevant only in that, by asking it, Jasmine may have revealed, by implication, a belief that she had witnessed Erik assaulting Calen. The question before us is whether these words are hearsay when offered to prove the truth of that belief.

Contrary to the State's contention, the words are not relevant if offered merely to prove that Jasmine was afraid of Stoddard. Jasmine's fear of Stoddard is irrelevant unless it stems from a belief that she had seen Stoddard assault Calen. Although it is conceivable that Jasmine's fear, taken together with her presence during the relevant time frame, was circumstantial evidence that Jasmine witnessed Stoddard assault Calen, this conceptualization is a distinction without a difference. Jasmine's fear of Stoddard is relevant only if it is rational, *i.e.*, only if it stems from a real-world condition or event. To rationally fear Erik Stoddard is to believe the proposition "I have a reason to fear Erik Stoddard." Jasmine's belief in this proposition is relevant only if the "reason" at issue is her having witnessed Erik assaulting Calen. Thus, in offering Jasmine's fear as evidence, the State implicitly would be offering Jasmine's belief in the proposition "I have a reason to fear Erik Stoddard and that reason is that I saw him assault Calen."

III.

A. *Wright v. Tatham* and the Implied Assertions Doctrine

The implied assertions doctrine focuses on the implications or inferences contained within or drawn from an utterance, as distinguished from the declaration's literal contents. The evidentiary treatment of implied assertions has been the subject of legal debate and controversy for many years, and has been addressed often since the adoption of the Federal Rules of Evidence. Courts around the country are split as to how such evidence should be treated.

The starting point for a discussion of the implied assertion doctrine is the English case of *Wright v. Doe d. Tatham*, 112 Eng. Rep. 488 (Exch. Ch. 1837) and 47 Rev. Rep. 136 (H.L. 1838). The case involved a will and the competency of the testator. The decedent Marsden had left his estate to his steward Wright. Marsden's heir at law, Admiral Tatham, challenged the will on grounds of testamentary incapacity. In defense of the will, before the Court of King's Bench, Wright sought to introduce several letters that Marsden had received from various correspondents. One letter concerned a legal dispute, three concerned business or politics, one thanked Marsden for having appointed the writer to a curateship, and one described a cousin's voyage to America. Wright did not seek to prove the truth of any explicit factual statement within the letters. Wright argued that the letters were composed in such a way as to indicate that their writers believed Marsden sane and of normal intelligence. From the writers' belief in Marsden's competence, Wright argued, one could infer that Marsden was competent. The letters were excluded as hearsay. On appeal in the Exchequer Chamber, Baron Parke explained as follows:

> "Proof of a particular fact . . . implying a statement or opinion of a third party on the matter in issue, is inadmissable in all cases where such a statement or opinion not on oath would be of itself inadmissable; and, therefore, in this case the letters which are offered only to prove the competence of the testator, that is the truth of the implied statements therein contained, were properly rejected, as the mere statement or opinion of the writer would certainly have been inadmissable."

*   *   *

In reaching his conclusion, Baron Parke introduced the oft-quoted discussion of a sea captain, who after examining his ship carefully, left on an ocean voyage with his family aboard. According to Baron Parke, the captain's conduct would constitute hearsay if offered to prove that the ship had been seaworthy. . . .

> "Baron Parke used the illustration to show that such nonverbal conduct would nevertheless constitute hearsay because its value as evidence depended on the belief of the actor. This illustration was important in the court's analysis because the main problem sought to be avoided by the rule against hearsay — an inability to cross — examine the declarant — is the same whether or not the assertion is implied from a verbal statement or implied from nonverbal conduct. Thus, assertions that are relevant only as implying a statement or opinion of the absent declarant on the matter at issue constitute hearsay in the same way the actual statement or opinion of the absent declarant would be inadmissible hearsay."

State v. Dullard, 668 N.W.2d 585, 591 (Iowa 2003) (citations omitted).

For our purposes, Baron Parke's reasoning, and the common-law view, may be expressed as follows: (1) An out-of-court statement is hearsay when offered to establish the truth of a proposition expressed therein; (2) A letter stating "I believe Marsden to be competent" would be hearsay if offered to prove that Marsden was competent; (3) These letters — of which the tone and content imply a belief in Marsden's competence — are being offered as the functional equivalents of letters directly professing a belief in Marsden's competence; (4) Thus, as offered, these letters express the proposition that Marsden is competent; and (5) Therefore,these letters are hearsay if offered to prove Marsden's competence. Stated more generally, the doctrine holds that where a declarant's out-of-court words imply a belief in the truth of X, such words are hearsay if offered to prove that X is true.

In its original *Wright v. Tatham* form, the doctrine did not inquire into the declarant's intent — beliefs communicated accidentally by implication are as much "implied assertions" as beliefs expressed purposefully in an indirect manner. As evidenced by the "sea captain" hypothetical, the doctrine also did not distinguish between words and non-verbal conduct.

B. Federal Rule of Evidence 801(a) and Its Advisory Committee Note

Perhaps the most significant development in the American judicial treatment of implied assertions was the 1973 adoption of the Federal Rules of Evidence, and the subsequent adoption by numerous states — including this State — of substantially similar rules. The drafters of the Federal Rules apparently agreed with commentators' criticisms of the common law rule that implied assertions should be treated as hearsay. They expressly abolished the implied assertions doctrine with respect to non-verbal conduct not intended by the actor as a communication. As to words, the drafters were more equivocal while the Advisory Committee note to Fed. R. Evid. 801 (a) states that "nothing is an assertion unless intended to be one."

Fed. R. Evid. 801 (c) defines "hearsay" as "a statement, other than one made by the declarant while testifying at the trial or hearing, offered in evidence to prove the truth of the matter asserted." Fed. R. Evid. 801(a) defines "statement" as "(1) an oral or written assertion or (2) nonverbal conduct of a person, if it is intended by the person as an assertion."

As to non-verbal conduct, the Rule injects unequivocally an intent requirement into the common-law implied assertion doctrine. Non-verbal conduct is not a "statement" under the Rule — and thus cannot be hearsay — unless the actor intended the conduct to be an assertion. A definition of "assertion" is not necessary to reach this conclusion; part two of the rule contains the word "intended" explicitly.

The part of the Rule governing speech and writing does not contain the word "intended." Rather, words qualify as a "statement" under the Rule if they constitute "an oral or written assertion." The question of whether the Rule incorporates an intent requirement with respect to words depends upon whether "assertion," standing alone, denotes an *intentional* communication.

Although the federal Rule does not define "assertion," the Advisory Committee note to the Rule states that "nothing is an assertion unless intended to be one." 56 F.R.D. 183, 293 (1972). The Advisory Committee's view with respect to words appears to be as follows: If the declarant intended to communicate the factual proposition which the words are offered to prove as true, then the words are hearsay. If the declarant did not intend to communicate that proposition, the words are not hearsay.

The federal Advisory Committee note has been the source of disagreement in the courts and among scholars. Some federal courts construe Fed. R. Evid. 801 (a) in accord with the Advisory Committee note. *See, e.g., United States v. Long*, 905 F.2d 1572, 1579-80, 284 U.S. App. D.C. 405 (D.C. Cir. 1990) (citing Advisory Committee note in holding that telephone conversation testified to by police officer was not hearsay where the caller inquired about drug transaction because no assertion was intended by caller); *United States v. Lewis*, 902 F.2d 1176, 1179 (5th Cir. 1990) (same); *United States v. Perez*, 658 F.2d 654, 659 (9th Cir. 1981) (citing Advisory Committee note in holding use of defendant's name on telephone nonhearsay when offered to prove defendant was on the line; declarant impliedly believed defendant was on the line but did not intend to assert that fact); *United States v. Zenni*, 492 F. Supp. 464, 469 (E.D. Ky. 1980) (citing Advisory Committee in ruling that telephone instructions to place bets were non-hearsay when offered to prove defendant was a bookmaker because callers did not intend to assert that defendant was a bookmaker when placing their bets).

Other courts have interpreted the Rule with a different result. *See, e.g., United States v. Palma-Ruedas*, 121 F.3d 841, 857 (3d Cir. 1997), *rev'd on other grounds*, 526 U.S. 275, 119 S. Ct. 1239, 143 L. Ed. 2d 388 (1999) (holding statement "nice to meet you" hearsay when offered to prove truth of implication that declarant was meeting listener for the first time); *United States v. Reynolds*, 715 F.2d 99, 104 (3d Cir. 1983) (holding phrase "I didn't tell them anything about you" hearsay when offered to prove truth of implication that defendant was participant in crime); *Lyle v. Koehler*, 720 F.2d 426, 432–33 (6th Cir. 1983) (holding letters detailing request for recipient to give false alibi testimony hearsay when offered to prove truth of implication that declarant and co-conspirator defendant were guilty).

C. The Task of Defining "Assertion" Left to the Courts in Maryland

In the testamentary capacity case of *Waters v. Waters*, 35 Md. 531 (1872), this Court considered whether certain letters were admissible to show "the manner in which the testator was treated, in regard to matters of business . . . by one well acquainted with him," in order to establish the letter-writer's opinions "in regard to the sanity of the testator, and his competency to transact business." . . . In excluding the letters, the Court adopted the rule laid down in *Wright v. Tatham*, which had presented substantially the same factual senario. Maryland Rules 5-801(a), 5-801(c), and 5-802 are identical to the federal counterparts, and, as discussed *supra*, many federal courts have rejected the *Wright v. Tatham* proposition that out-of-court words are hearsay when offered to prove facts that the declarant impliedly believed but did not intend to communicate.

When the words of a Maryland rule and federal rule are the same or similar, often we look to interpretations of the federal rule in construing the Maryland Rule. . . . Federal court interpretations of federal rules are considered persuasive, but are not binding on this Court in interpreting a Maryland rule. . . .

The Committee note to Md. Rule 5-801 departs substantially from its federal counterpart. Rather than restricting the definition of "assertion," the note "does not attempt to define 'assertion,' a concept best left to development in the case law." It is clear that in adopting the Maryland Rule, this Court did not intend to adopt the federal Advisory Committee's view that "nothing is an assertion unless intended to be one," but rather intended to leave to case law the viability of the rule of *Wright v. Tatham*.

D. Theory Underlying the Rule Against Hearsay in General

In order to determine whether the unintentional implications of words should remain within the definition of hearsay, we first look to the theory underlying the rule against hearsay in general. In contrast to the intent-based approach of the federal Advisory Committee, scholars have focused on the veracity of the declarant and have identified four factors (sometimes termed "testimonial inferences"): (1) sincerity (the danger of fabrication); (2) narration (the danger of ambiguity); (3) perception (the danger of inaccurate observation); and (4) memory (the danger of faulty recollection). . . .

Each of the four inferences is strengthened by the requirement that testimony be given in court, under oath, and subject to cross-examination. The witness's presence allows the fact finder to observe physical limitations affecting perception, hesitancy or inconsistency suggesting imperfect memory, unclear or idiosyncratic use of language rendering narration ambiguous, or a demeanor suggestive of intentional falsehood. The oath, and with it the threat of prosecution for perjury, increases the likelihood of sincerity.

Most important to the testimonial inferences is the availability of cross-examination, a procedure Professor John Wigmore described as "beyond any doubt the greatest legal engine ever invented for the discovery of truth." Wigmore, *supra*, § 1376, at 32. All four inferences may be called into question by cross-examination.

When, in lieu of in-court, sworn testimony, a fact is presented to the fact finder from an out-of-court declarant, the four inferences are undermined considerably. The declarant's bare words reveal little or nothing about the circumstances under which the declarant came to believe the factual proposition communicated, nor about the accuracy of the declarant's memory. They do not indicate the declarant's tone or demeanor, the circumstances surrounding the utterance, or the motives which might have influenced the declarant to speak falsely. It is cross-examination, combined with the safeguards of presence and oath, that shores up the inferences of perception, memory, narration, and sincerity.

E. Hearsay Theory As It Relates to the Unintended Implications of Words

The State points to the federal Advisory Committee note to Fed. R. Evid. 801 (a), stating that both verbal and nonverbal implied assertions, if unintentional, should be excluded from the definition of hearsay. The Committee note states as follows:

> "Nonverbal conduct . . . may be offered as evidence that the person acted as he did because of his belief in the existence of the condition sought to be proved, from which belief the existence of the condition may be inferred. This sequence is, arguably, in effect an assertion of the existence of the condition and hence properly includable within the hearsay concept. Admittedly evidence of this character is untested with respect to the perception, memory, and narration (or their equivalents) of the actor, but the Advisory Committee is of the view that these dangers are minimal in the absence of an intent to assert and do not justify the loss of the evidence on hearsay grounds. No class of evidence is free of the possibility of fabrication, but the likelihood is less with nonverbal than with assertive verbal conduct. The situations giving rise to the nonverbal conduct are such as virtually to eliminate questions of sincerity. Motivation, the nature of the conduct, and the presence or absence of reliance will bear heavily upon the weight to be given the evidence. Similar considerations govern nonassertive verbal conduct and verbal conduct which is assertive but offered as a basis for inferring something other than the matter asserted, also excluded from the definition of hearsay by the language of subdivision (c)."

56 F.R.D. 183, 293 (1972) (citations omitted).

The view expressed in the federal Committee note has been criticized in court cases and by legal commentators. The notion that evidence "untested with respect to the perception, memory, and narration (or their equivalents) of the actor" poses minimal dangers "in the absence of an intent to assert" has been labeled a *non sequitur* on the grounds that the inferences of perception, memory, and narration are wholly independent from any intention to assert. The fact that a declarant may not have intended to communicate a particular factual proposition reveals nothing about the circumstances under which the declarant came to believe that proposition, nor about the clarity with which the declarant remembers the underlying events. Professor Paul Rice explains the point as follows:

> "Of the four dangers giving rise to the hearsay exclusionary rule — perception, memory, sincerity, and ambiguity — the assertive/nonassertive

distinction addresses only one: the danger of insincerity (*i.e.* intentional misrepresentation). If a declarant possesses no intention of asserting anything, it would seem to follow that he also possesses no intention of misrepresenting anything. It is a *non sequitur* to conclude from this, as the Advisory Committee has, that the remaining dangers of perception, memory, and ambiguity are automatically minimized with this assurance of sincerity. The logical link which the Advisory Committee finds between sincerity and error is simply nonexistent."

Paul R. Rice, *Should Unintended Implications of Speech be Considered Nonhearsay? The Assertive/Nonassertive Distinction Under Rule 801 (a) of the Federal Rules of Evidence*, 65 Temp. L. Rev. 529, 531 (1992).[19] See also David E. Seidelson, *Implied Assertions and Federal Rule of Evidence 801: A Continuing Quandary for Federal Courts*, 16 Miss. C. L. Rev. 33, 34–35 (1995). . . .

The Supreme Court of Iowa echoed these concerns in *State v. Dullard*, 668 N.W.2d 585, 590 (Iowa 2003):

"The persuasiveness of the committee notes on implied assertions is undermined by the clear split of authority among the federal circuit courts, as well as many legal scholars.

*   *   *

The circumstances of this case, as well as other cases, can make it tempting to minimize hearsay dangers when a declaration is assertive but offered as a basis for inferring a belief of the declarant that most likely was not a significant aspect of the communication process at the time the declaration was made. Absent unusual circumstances, the unknown declarant likely would not have thought about communicating the implied belief at issue, and this lack of intent arguably justifies excluding the assertion from the hearsay rule. Nevertheless, we are not convinced that the absence of intent necessarily makes the underlying belief more reliable, especially when the belief is derived from verbal conduct as opposed to nonverbal conduct.

Four dangers are generally identified to justify the exclusion of out-of-court statements under the hearsay rule: erroneous memory, faulty perception, ambiguity, and insincerity or misrepresentation. Yet, the distinction drawn between intended and unintended conduct or speech only implicates the danger of insincerity, based on the assumption that a person

---

[19] Professor Rice reiterated this point recently, noting as follows:

"The definition of hearsay in Rule 801 incorporates the assertive/nonassertive distinction, which admits unintended statements of an out-of-court declarant as non-hearsay. Even though the hearsay problems of perception, memory and ambiguity are still present, the statement is admitted for the truth of its content, and since it was unintended, the statement must be sincere. *This distinction is illogical to the point of being absurd.* The most that a nonassertive statement can guarantee is that it is sincerely erroneous. To make matters worse, courts are interpreting and applying the assertive/nonassertive distinction in different ways."

Paul R. Rice, Symposium: Federal Privileges in the 21st Century: Back to the Future with Privileges Abandon Codification, Not the Common Law, 38 Loy. L.A. L, Rev. 739, 764–765 (2004) (emphasis added).

who lacks an intent to assert something also lacks an intent to misrepresent."

Id. at 593–94 (citations omitted).

With respect to the danger of ambiguous narration, Professor Ronald Bacigal suggests that absence of an intent to communicate actually *increases* the danger of misunderstanding. He explains this theory as follows:

"If there is a distinction in the ambiguity of intended and implied assertions, the distinction indicates that unintended implied assertions are inherently more ambiguous. When a declarant consciously intends to communicate with an observer, he desires his communication to be understood by that observer. . . . With unintentional implied assertions, however, the declarant makes no effort to avoid ambiguity, because there is no intent to convey his message to anyone. Thus, unintentional implied assertions have an inherently greater potential to be more ambiguous than intended assertions. The Federal Rules have it backward by classifying the less ambiguous intended assertions as hearsay, while classifying the more ambiguous unintentional assertions as nonhearsay."

Ronald J. Bacigal, *Implied Hearsay: Defusing the Battle Line Between Pragmatism and Theory*, 11 S. Ill. U. L.J. 1127, 1132 (1987).

The federal Committee Note has been criticized also for conflating its analysis of the dangers posed by words with the dangers posed by nonverbal conduct. In particular, critics argue that language almost always conveys some intended meaning, and that the value of words as evidence of an underlying belief will necessarily depend on the sincerity with which the intentional meaning of those words is communicated.[20] Professor Rice addresses this problem as follows:

"If the justification for the assertive/nonassertive distinction is the absence of the insincerity problem, and through that guarantee of sincerity a reduced level of perception, memory, and ambiguity problems, this justification cannot be applied to implied statements from speech. Speech is a mechanism of communication; it is virtually always used for the purpose of communicating something to someone. It is illogical to conclude that the question of sincerity is eliminated and that the problem of unreliability is reduced for unintended implications of speech if that speech might have been insincere in the first instance, relative to the direct message intentionally communicated. If potential insincerity is injected into the utterance of words that form the basis for the implied communication, the implication from the speech is as untrustworthy as the utterance upon which it is based."

---

[20] The concurring opinion argues that the majority has committed itself to an "antiquated and wholly illogical view" by adhering to the implied assertions doctrine as it relates to assertions implied from out-of-court words. Concurring op. at 2. Despite the claimed illogic of the Court's holding today, the concurring opinion has not even attempted to answer our central argument that, with respect to assertions implied from out-of-court *words*, all four hearsay concerns of sincerity, narration, perception, and memory are still present.

Rice, *supra*, at 534. Professor Michael Graham considers this problem in his *Handbook of Federal Evidence*:

> "The Advisory Committee's apparent attempted rejection of *Wright v. Doe d. Tatham* is as unfortunate as it is incorrect. When a statement is offered to infer the declarant's state of mind from which a given fact is inferred in the form of an opinion or otherwise, since the truth of the matter asserted must be assumed in order for the nonasserted inference to be drawn, the statement is properly classified as hearsay under the language of [Fed. R. Evid] 801 (c). Since the matter asserted in the statement must be true, a reduction in the risk of sincerity is not present. The Advisory Committee's reliance on the analogy to nonverbal nonassertive conduct where a reduction in the risk of fabrication is caused by a lack of intent to assert anything is thus clearly misconceived."

3 Michael H. Graham, HANDBOOK OF FEDERAL EVIDENCE § 801.7, AT 73–77 (5TH ED. 2001) (CITATIONS OMITTED).[21]

The Iowa Supreme Court addressed this issue in *Dullard*, reasoning as follows:

> "Even the danger of insincerity may continue to be present in those instances where the reliability of the direct assertion may be questioned. If the expressed assertion is insincere, such as a fabricated story, the implied assertion derived from the expressed assertion will similarly be unreliable. Implied assertions can be no more reliable than the predicate expressed assertion."

Dullard, 668 N.W.2d at 594.

We conclude that, with respect to the four testimonial inferences, out-of-court

---

[21] The concurring opinion's discussion of the treatment of the implied assertions doctrine in the treatises is incomplete. The discussion leaves the impression that it is presently beyond serious dispute that the Federal Rules of Evidence reject the implied assertion doctrine in total, and rightly so. *See generally* concurring op. at 21–23. For instance, the concurring opinion says the following about Mueller and Kirkpatrick's FEDERAL EVIDENCE:

> "Mueller and Kirkpatrick purport to see some limited lingering value in *Wright's* analysis of the so-called 'two-step inference' (belief from conduct, fact from belief), but they acknowledge that 'FRE 801 rejects the broad proposition endorsed by Baron Parke' and suggest that, 'arguably, it would be wiser to forget *Wright* than continue to discuss it.'"

Concurring op. at 22 (quoting Christopher B. Mueller and Laird C. Kirkpatrick, FEDERAL EVIDENCE § 378 (2d ed. 1994)). The concurring opinion seems to be implying here that Mueller and Kirpatrick believe (1) that the implied assertion doctrine is inconsistent with the Federal Rules of Evidence, and therefore (2) that *Wright* is no longer significant in the law of evidence because the doctrine developed in it has been rejected. Neither of these propositions is actually supported by what Mueller and Kirkpatrick say. The "broad proposition" in *Wright* that Mueller and Kirpatrick say is rejected by Federal Rule of Evidence 801 is that assertions implied from any conduct, verbal or nonverbal, are "statements" for purposes of the hearsay rule. Mueller and Kirkpatrick, *supra* § 378. In fact, Mueller and Kirkpatrick recognize that *Wright* is of continuing significance precisely because the issue of whether assertions implied from *words* are "statements" for purposes of the hearsay rule is an open question under the Federal Rules. Mueller and Kirkpatrick go on to argue that a case can be made that the exclusion of the letters in *Wright* would be the correct result if the case were decided under the Federal Rules because, unlike a case of nonverbal conduct, "the authors of the letters expressed ideas and information." Mueller and Kirkpatrick, *supra* § 378.

words offered for the truth of unintentional implications are not different substantially from out-of-court words offered for the truth of intentional communications. The declarant's lack of intent to communicate the implied proposition does not increase the reliability of the declarant's words in a degree sufficient to justify exemption from the hearsay rule. Said another way, we conclude that a declarant's lack of intent to communicate a belief in the truth of a particular proposition is irrelevant to the determination of whether the words are hearsay when offered to prove the truth of that proposition.

We hold where the probative value of words, as offered, depends on the declarant having communicated a factual proposition,[22] the words constitute an "assertion" of that proposition. The declarant's intent *vel non* to communicate the proposition is irrelevant. If the words are uttered out of court, then offered in court to prove the truth of the proposition — *i.e.* of the "matter asserted" they are hearsay under our rules.

[2] Does the Assertive/Nonassertive Distinction Make Any Sense?

The sole basis for the distinction between assertive and nonassertive conduct (and possibly speech) is the absence of an intent to communicate, which eliminates the hearsay danger of insincerity. Does this alone justify removing the evidence from the definition of hearsay?

The Advisory Committee acknowledged that when evidence of nonassertive conduct is admitted, the perception, memory, and narration of the actor cannot be tested. It concluded, nevertheless, that the hearsay dangers linked to these elements are minimal in the absence of an intent to assert. How does the absence of an intent to assert minimize the dangers of untested perception, memory, and narration? Assume that individuals exercise greater care to ensure the accuracy of their perception before acting than before speaking. Thus, the mere fact that individuals have committed themselves to a course of conduct supports the reliability of the belief on which the conduct was premised. Is it reasonable to accept this as a universal truth? Professor McCormick, one of the early supporters of the assertive/nonassertive distinction, accepted the foregoing proposition as reasonable, but only where it appeared the actor had firsthand knowledge of the matters on which his belief was based and the conduct engaged in was of consequence to the actor.[23]

In response to the possibility that the actor's conduct was predicated on the actor's mistaken perception, the Advisory Committee stated, "[m]otivation, the nature of the conduct, and the presence or absence of reliance will bear heavily upon the *weight* to be given the evidence." Advisory Committee Note to Rule 801, 56 F.R.D. 183, 294 (1973) (emphasis added). Is this a satisfactory answer? If the probative force of the evidence is substantial, how is it possible for the jury to discount its value appropriately by the mere possibility of mistake? Because the

---

[22] A reasonable test is to ask whether the words would remain probative if it could be established that the declarant *did not believe* the factual proposition for which they are offered.

[23] McCormick, *The Borderland of Hearsay,* 39 Yale L.J. 489 (1930).

absence of an opportunity to cross-examine the actor prohibits this possibility of mistake from being given definite dimensions, isn't the fact-finder left to mere speculation about the relative weight of the evidence presented? Isn't this precisely why we have the hearsay rule — to avoid having the jury engage in this kind of guesswork?

Consider further the following law review article on implied assertions:

Meaning, Intention, and the Hearsay Rule
Paul F. Kirgis
43 Wm. & Mary L. Rev. 275 (2001)

A prerequisite to understanding the modern hearsay rule is understanding the historical debate about the scope of the rule. This debate has its origin in the celebrated nineteenth-century case of *Wright v. Tatham*. A Dickensian epic that meandered through England's courts for the better part of a decade, *Wright* was a suit by an heir at law to recover land from a devisee under a will. The case turned on the validity of the will, specifically on the testator's mental capacity. As evidence of the testator's capacity, the defendant offered several letters written to the testator in the years prior to his death. None of the letters expressly commented on the testator's mental capacity, but the content suggested that the letter writers believed the testator was competent. This inference was offered as evidence that the testator was in fact competent. The case went all the way to the House of Lords, and the letters ultimately were declared inadmissible hearsay because their relevance depended on the credibility of the nontestifying letter writers. That is, the letters were hearsay because the factfinder was being asked to trust the memory, perception, narrative capacity, and sincerity of the letter writers without the benefit of cross-examination.

Wright may be known best for a hypothetical suggested in dicta by Baron Parke, the author of the most influential opinion. Parke posited a hypothetical in which the seaworthiness of a vessel is at issue, and as evidence of seaworthiness, a party calls a witness to testify that the captain of the ship inspected it at the dock and then boarded with his family. Parke concluded that the witness's testimony in that situation would be hearsay, because the captain is in effect "testifying" to the seaworthiness of the vessel, and the factfinder is being asked to rely on the captain's perception, memory, and sincerity without the benefit of cross-examination.

For both the letters actually offered in *Wright* and the ship captain hypothetical given in dicta, the factfinder was asked to make what Christopher Mueller has described as a "two-step inference." From the declarant's conduct — writing a letter proposing a business transaction or boarding a ship — the factfinder is asked to infer the declarant's belief about some real-world condition, in this case the competence of the recipient or the seaworthiness of the vessel. Based on that belief, the factfinder is asked to infer that the real-world condition existed. This type of evidence — now packaged under the heading "implied assertions" — is problematic because its validity turns on the un-cross-examined belief of the declarant. Its treatment has informed the debate about the definition of hearsay for over 150 years.

B. Hearsay Definitions Past and Present

Wright apparently represented the common law view of hearsay at least until the beginning of the twentieth century. Courts and commentators of that era typically eschewed formalistic definitions in favor of a loose, conceptual approach to hearsay, focusing on the importance of the cross-examination of any witness whose credibility was at issue. This approach allowed for essentially *ad hoc* judgments based on a range of credibility concerns, freeing courts either to take the hearsay rule to its *Wright*-inspired limits or to apply it more narrowly.

In the twentieth century, the credibility-based approach embodied by *Wright* began to fall out of favor. The reformist trend, with its emphasis on black letter rules, emerged in the law of evidence as in other common law disciplines. Relying on Wigmore, courts found a concise hearsay formulation in the language that now seems so familiar, defining hearsay as "extrajudicial utterances" offered to prove the "truth of the matter asserted."

Over the next half century, the "truth of the matter asserted" definition became internalized in the common law of evidence. With the passage of the Federal Rules of Evidence, it was formally codified. Under Federal Rule of Evidence 801(c), hearsay is defined as "a statement, other than one made by the declarant while testifying at the trial or hearing, offered in evidence to prove the truth of the matter asserted."

The substitution of a single, concise rule for a vague, conceptual principle necessitated some line drawing on the difficult issues presented by *Wright*. Although influential commentators praised *Wright* for its intellectual integrity, few wanted a hearsay rule as broadly exclusionary as *Wright* seemed to require. In addition, courts defining hearsay in "truth of the matter asserted" terms increasingly held that *Wright*-type evidence was not hearsay. These trends forced the codifiers of the Federal Rules of Evidence to decide how evidence offered for the two-step inference should be treated under their definition.

The drafters easily dispensed with the issue of nonassertive conduct (Baron Parke's ship captain hypothetical). They accomplished this by incorporating into Rule 801 the following definition of "statement": "(1) an oral or written assertion or (2) non-verbal conduct of a person, if it is intended by the person as an assertion." By providing that conduct can qualify for hearsay treatment only if it is intended as an assertion, the definition unambiguously removes nonassertive conduct offered for the two-step inference from the scope of the hearsay rule.

The Rule is not as clear with respect to verbal assertions offered for the two-step inference, as in the letters in *Wright*. In the notes following Rule 801, however, the Advisory Committee expressed its intention to treat verbal assertions as not hearsay when offered for the two-step inference. It did so by explaining why nonassertive conduct is not hearsay. Although modern cognitive research teaches that problems of misperception and poor memory are probably much more significant, legal commentators have tended to see the risk of insincerity as the most problematic of the four testimonial infirmities. Following that line of reasoning, the Advisory Committee enunciated a rationale for the exclusion of nonassertive conduct grounded in the reduced risk of insincerity associated with that kind of evidence:

> Admittedly [nonverbal conduct] is untested with respect to the perception, memory, and narration (or their equivalents) of the actor, but the Advisory Committee is of the view that these dangers are minimal in the absence of an intent to assert and do not justify the loss of the evidence on hearsay grounds. No class of evidence is free of the possibility of fabrication, but the likelihood is less with nonverbal than with assertive verbal conduct.

Having spelled out that rationale, the Committee added one more sentence: "Similar considerations govern nonassertive verbal conduct and verbal conduct which is assertive but offered as a basis for inferring something other than the matter asserted, also excluded from the definition of hearsay by the language of subdivision (c)." The Committee concluded that "[t]he effect of the definition of 'statement' is to exclude from the operation of the hearsay rule all evidence of conduct, verbal or nonverbal, not intended as an assertion. The key to the definition is that nothing is an assertion unless intended to be one." The Committee thus enunciated what might be termed an "intent-based" approach to the hearsay rule. The intent-based approach focuses on what the out-of-court declarant intended to assert, and then asks whether that intended assertion has been offered for its truth at trial. If the statement is offered for something other than its intended assertion, it is not hearsay.

Legitimate questions have been raised both about the degree of authority that should be afforded the Advisory Committee's Notes in general and about the validity of the intent-based approach. For example, a leading critic, David Seidelson, has argued that to draw a distinction between express and implied assertions is "to elevate form over substance and amorphous rules of grammar over the realities of the litigation process." Another critic, Paul Rice, has argued that the Advisory Committee's interpretation fails the test of its own logic because it potentially allows evidence bearing the risk of insincerity — an allowance that the approach is designed to prevent. Nevertheless, most leading treatises and recent judicial opinions seem to accept the Advisory Committee's understanding. As a result, under the prevailing view, Rule 801 draws a line between the risk of sincerity and the other testimonial risks. Evidence that implicates the sincerity of an out-of-court declarant is potentially hearsay; evidence that does not implicate the sincerity of an out-of-court declarant is not hearsay. Because evidence offered to prove something other than what the declarant intended to assert — whether the evidence describes verbal assertions or assertive conduct — does not implicate the sincerity of the declarant, it is not hearsay.

Unfortunately, the matter does not end there. Simply saying that only statements offered for their intended assertions can be hearsay does not erase the interpretive issues. Courts must now identify the assertions in a statement. Experience has shown this to be an exceedingly difficult task. To take just one example, assume the police obtain a confession from an injured suspect after getting permission from his doctor to interrogate him. At trial, the prosecution offers the doctor's permission as evidence that the suspect was competent to confess. Is this hearsay? It depends on whether the permission was an assertion about the suspect's capacity. Without a way to recognize assertions that can count as hearsay, there is simply no means of consistently distinguishing hearsay from nonhearsay.

The process of recognizing the assertions in a statement boils down to the determination of meaning. To know what assertions are intended in an utterance, we must know the meaning of the utterance. While most courts and many commentators have been willing to accept that the Federal Rules cover only intended assertions, they have often struggled in the search for the meaning of the statement.

EXERCISES

1. At the time of his arrest, Lewis had in his possession an electronic pager or "beeper." At the police station the pager associated with Lewis began beeping. The Officer called the number displayed on the pager and identified himself as Lewis. The person on the other end asked Officer "Did you get the stuff?" and Officer answered affirmatively. At trial Officer seeks to testify to the questions asked by the unidentified caller. Lewis objects on hearsay grounds. How should the court rule?

2. A foreign diplomat was robbed at gunpoint as she exited a local gas station. A law enforcement agent interviewed the Owner of the gas station. Owner stated that he had received a tip from an informant that the assailant was someone known in the street as "Gemelo," which in Spanish means twin. Owner also explained that a local man, named Defendant, was a twin. Agent immediately arrested Defendant. At Defendant's trial, may the law enforcement agent state what he learned from his interview with Owner?

3. Attorney successfully litigated a discrimination claim against United Parcel Service (UPS), winning a jury verdict in favor of his client. Attorney then requested that his client's legal fees be paid by UPS. The Court, in an effort to determine the appropriate amount of fees to award, asked Attorney to provide the Court with a sworn declaration (or lodestar) of his hours. The Attorney provided the court with a single spreadsheet listing both his hours and the hours of the paralegal who had also worked on the case. The paralegal did not file her own separate declaration swearing to the hours she spent on this case. UPS objects to the joint declaration, arguing that the declaration contains hearsay — namely the hours performed by the paralegal. Is UPS correct?

4. Two police officers responded to a burglar alarm. When they arrived at the home, the officers saw that the front door had been pried open and that a television was lying in the driveway. Officers then entered the home to search for a burglar. Officer Sexson entered first and yelled to Officer Brooks "Come here. We've got something!" At the burglar's trial, Officer Brooks is asked to explain the manner in which the officers conducted their search of the home. Officer Brooks explains that he intended to search a different room, but proceeded to Officer Sexson's location when he heard Officer Sexson yell "Come here. We've got something!" The suspected burglar objects on hearsay grounds. Is the statement hearsay?

5. Geoffrey and Kelly, owners of G&K, a successful medical supply company, developed a scheme to earn additional income. The pair partnered with Jody, who

was in charge of ordering supplies for a local hospital. Jody agreed to buy all of the hospital's supplies from G&K, and in exchange Jody would receive a percentage of the profits. The hospital administration eventually caught on and alerted police. Police uncovered bank statements showing that G&K paid Jody $34,000 over the last year. When questioned, Kelly described the payments as "a loan" to Jody, not proof of any wrongdoing. Police did not believe Kelly and filed charges against both Geoffrey and Kelly. Prior to trial, Kelly died. At Geoffrey's trial, prosecutors seek to admit Kelly's statement to police. Is Kelly's statement admissible against Geoffrey?

§ 4.02   EXCLUSIONS FROM THE DEFINITION OF HEARSAY

[A]   Statements Excluded from Definition of Hearsay by Federal Rules

Rule 801 defines a number of circumstances when statements, which would otherwise appear to be hearsay, are not hearsay. Some of these require the declarant be available in court, others do not. You will learn in the next chapter about exceptions to the hearsay rule. Other than being defined as "non-hearsay" rather than exceptions to the hearsay rule, there is little practical distinction between one of these "non-hearsay" categories and an exception to the hearsay rule.

[1]   Prior Inconsistent Statements: Rule 801(d)(1)(A)

Statements offered outside a particular proceeding are nevertheless admissible if the witness testifies and made a prior inconsistent statement under oath at another trial, hearing, deposition, or other proceeding. Prior inconsistent statements, not made under oath, can be admitted, as you will discover later, but only to impeach a witness, not as substantive evidence.

[a]   Definition of "Inconsistent" Statement

When are statements inconsistent? Obviously if two statements assert that different facts are true, they are inconsistent with one another. Often, however, inconsistencies are much more subtle and courts must decide whether different versions are truly inconsistent.

WASSILIE v. STATE

Alaska Court of Appeals

57 P.3d 719 (2002)

STEWART, JUDGE.

Henry Wassilie was convicted of one count of second-degree assault for assaulting his mother, Mary Wassilie, and one count of fourth-degree assault for assaulting his father, Evan Wassilie. During the trial, Evan was asked if he spoke to the village police about the assaults. He answered that he "didn't see" police officers at his house on night of the assault. Wasillie's attorney interrupted Evan's direct examination by the State to consult with his client. After that consultation, the defense attorney spoke with the prosecutor, and they both told the court that Evan was released. The State later introduced as prior inconsistent statements Evan's statements to Village Police Chief Steven Alexie that Henry Wassilie hit and kicked both him and Mary.

When this case first appeared before us, we remanded for further findings on the circumstances of Evan Wassilie's dismissal as a witness at trial. Superior Court Judge Dale O. Curda found on remand that Wassilie's defense counsel made a tactical decision not to cross-examine Evan and that both parties consented to Evan's dismissal.

The remaining legal issue in this case is whether the trial court properly admitted Evan's out-of-court statement to Chief Alexie as a prior inconsistent statement under Alaska Rule of Evidence 801(d)(1)(A). Evidence Rule 801(d)(1)(A) provides:

A statement is not hearsay if . . . the declarant testifies at the trial or hearing and the statement is inconsistent with the declarant's testimony.

Wassilie argues that Evan's statement to the police should have been excluded because the prosecutor did not lay a sufficient foundation for admissibility under Evidence Rule 801(d)(1)(A). He also claims that the statement should have been excluded because Evan's genuine loss of memory at trial was not inconsistent with his prior statement for purposes of the rule.

Evan's testimony was translated from Yupik to English. During direct examination, the State asked Evan whether his wife, Mary, was injured the previous winter, and Evan testified that she was injured. However, he could not answer how she was injured. He also could not remember when she was injured. Evan said it was hot out and the sun was up at the time of the assault, but the assault actually occurred on January 8, 1998.

Evan also testified that he could not remember the last time Henry Wassilie, the defendant, was at his house. When the State asked him what time of year Wasillie last lived at his house, he answered, "1917. He was a little boy. But he was always out on the tundra hunting." The State then asked when Henry was born, and Evan answered, "I think it was in '67, but I don't think I have it right, it's on the papers." At that point, the following exchange occurred:

Prosecutor: Do you remember talking to Chief Alexie about the last time your wife lived in your home? . . . Do you remember the police coming to your house this winter, Chief Alexie and VPO Jerry Wassilie? Chief Steven Alexie and VPO Jerry Wassilie.

Evan: Yes. I didn't see any of those guys.

Prosecutor: Does Henry Wassilie live at your house any more?

Translator: He just said, "I can't do it."

At this point, Wassilie's attorney consulted with Wassilie and informed the State that Evan could be released from further testimony. The State agreed to end questioning, and the court excused Evan with both parties' consent.

Later in the trial, the State called Chief Alexie and asked him if he interviewed Evan on the night of the alleged assault. Wassilie objected on hearsay grounds. Judge Curda found that Evan had a loss of memory and admitted the statement to Chief Alexie as a prior inconsistent statement under Evidence Rule 801(d)(1)(A).

Chief Alexie testified as follows:

Prosecutor: What did Evan tell you happened that night?

Alexie: That both he and Mary got beat up by Henry.

Prosecutor: Okay. Did he describe it to you at all?

Alexie: Yes. By hitting with his fists and sometimes kicking also.

Chief Alexie also testified that Evan said he kept his eyes closed to try to avoid the beatings, said that Mary was "crying and wailing aloud" during the beatings, and said that during the beatings Henry announced that he was getting fed up with all of them.

We first address Wassilie's claim that the foundation for Evan's prior statement was inadequate. Evidence Rule 801(d)(1)(A) sets out the foundation requirement for prior inconsistent statements:

> Unless the interests of justice otherwise require, the prior statement shall be excluded unless (i) the witness was so examined while testifying as to give the witness an opportunity to explain or to deny the statement or (ii) the witness has not been excused from giving further testimony in the action.

Wassilie argues that Evan was not "so examined while testifying as to give [him] an opportunity to explain or deny the [prior inconsistent] statement."

During its direct examination, the State did not directly confront Evan with his prior statement and ask him to explain or deny it. However, the State did ask Evan if he remembered the police coming to his house (at which time Chief Alexie took Evan's statement) and asked him if he remembered talking to the police about the last time his wife lived in his home. Evan testified that he "did not see" Chief Alexie and Village Police Officer Wassilie at his house. The defense then interrupted the examination and asked the prosecutor to stop questioning Evan, apparently because Wassilie was concerned about Evan's health.

In *McMaster v. State*, the Alaska Supreme Court reviewed the sufficiency of the foundation for a prior inconsistent statement under former Alaska Rule of Civil Procedure 43(g)(11)(c), the predecessor of Evidence Rule 801(d)(1)(A). The court announced that the foundational requirement "should not be mechanically applied in every instance." The witness whose prior statement was admitted in *McMaster* was five years old. The court noted that a trial court must be given wide latitude when a young child is called as a witness. The testimony of the child in question in *McMaster* highlighted the problem of a young witness because the transcript showed that the child gave unresponsive answers to straight-forward questions and inconsistent answers to questions put by both parties. Although the foundation for the child's prior statement did not technically comply with the rule, the court held that the trial court did not abuse its discretion by overruling McMaster's foundational objection.

In this case, Evan was not a child of tender years but was over 90 years old. The State asked Evan if he remember talking with the officers, and Evan responded that he "didn't see" the officers. We note from our examination of the transcript that at points during his examination, Evan was not able to answer straight-forward questions and some of his answers were inconsistent. And because of apparent concerns about Evan's health, the defense urged that Evan be excused during the prosecutor's direct examination. Thus, Evan's advanced age and apparent poor health presented similar challenges for the superior court as did the testimony of the five-year-old in *McMaster.* And there is no question of bad faith on the prosecutor's part by agreeing to Wassilie's request for Evan's discharge. Under these circumstances, we conclude that the superior court did not abuse its discretion when it admitted Evan's prior inconsistent statement with the minimal foundation presented.

Wassilie next argues that Evan's prior statement is not "inconsistent" when, as the trial judge found, Evan had no memory. In *Richards v. State,* the Alaska Supreme Court held that a videotape in which a witness re-enacted the offense was admissible as a prior inconsistent statement after the witness testified that he could not remember much of what happened on the night of the offense. The court stated, "When [the witness] testified at trial that he had forgotten much of what he had seen that night, the tape was admissible as a prior inconsistent statement." The court did not address the distinction between feigned and genuine memory loss.

In *Van Hatten v. State,* we held that feigned memory loss at trial is inconsistent with an earlier statement for purposes of Rule 801. Van Hatten had argued that a witness's prior statement was not inconsistent for purposes of Rule 801, because a witness's feigned inability to remember amounts to a refusal to testify. However, we concluded that the *Richards* decision implicitly adopted "a broad definition of inconsistency" and determined that there was no reason to adopt a stricter standard when a witness feigned a memory loss. And in *Brandon v. State,* [839 P.2d 400 (Alaska App. 1992),] we upheld the admission of a witness's prior statements as inconsistent even though the witness had no memory at trial of those prior statements.

Also, it is noteworthy that most federal circuit courts have not distinguished between actual and feigned memory loss in interpreting Federal Rule of Evidence 801(d)(1)(A) — which is similar to Alaska Rule of Evidence 801(d)(1)(A) but only applies to prior statements made under oath. Three circuits have held that if a witness testifies not to remember the prior statement at trial, the prior statement is inconsistent for purposes of Rule 801(d)(1)(A). Those circuits did not address the distinction between feigned and genuine memory loss. In *United States v. Gajo,* the Seventh Circuit declined to limit Rule 801(d)(1)(A) to cases of turncoat witnesses and held that "[i]n some cases, a witness's genuine lack of memory may be inconsistent with his prior testimony."

Only two circuits have implied that there may be a distinction between cases of feigned and genuine memory loss. The Fifth Circuit has left open the issue of whether Rule 801(d)(1)(A) applies to genuine memory loss. And, the Third Circuit has implied in dicta that a prior statement may not be inconsistent with genuine memory loss at trial. However, the Third Circuit's decision was issued in 1981, and the position it stated in dicta has not been adopted by the court.

Consistent with the majority view of the federal circuits involving cases of memory loss, we confirm that the rule announced in *Richards* extends to cases of genuine as well as cases of feigned memory loss. If a witness claims not to remember the substance of a prior statement at trial, the witness's trial testimony is inconsistent with the prior statement for purposes of Rule 801(d)(1)(A). It is irrelevant for purposes of the rule whether the claimed memory loss is genuine or feigned because the claimed lack of memory at trial (whether genuine or feigned) is inconsistent with the witness's earlier claim to remember. We conclude that the superior court did not abuse its discretion by ruling that Evan Wassilie's prior statements were inconsistent with his genuine lack of memory at trial.

Conclusion

The judgment of the superior court is AFFIRMED.

[b]   Other Proceedings

The exclusion of prior inconsistent statements from the hearsay rule in Rule 801(d)(1)(A) is limited to sworn statements made in previous trials, hearings, depositions, or other proceedings. The most controversial issue arising under the provision has been how broadly courts should interpret the term "other proceedings." As explained in the following opinion, courts have interpreted the term very broadly because of the perceived legislative intent for such an interpretation.

STATE v. SUA
Washington Court of Appeals
60 P.3d 1234 (2003)

Morgan, J.

Elemene Tinie Sua appeals a conviction for indecent liberties by forcible compulsion. He contends in part that the trial court erred by admitting Exhibits 1 and 2, and by denying his motions for mistrial. We reverse and remand for further proceedings.

In early December 2000, Sua, Karen Williams, and Williams' three daughters were all living together in a motel room in Pierce County. Two of the daughters were S.S., age 16, and A.S., age 19.

On December 5, 2000, S.S. told Williams that earlier that day, Sua taken indecent liberties with her by putting his hands down her pants. Williams and her daughters went to the motel office, where A.S. called 911.

Before the police arrived, S.S. told A.S. that Sua had put his hands down the front and back of her pants. She said he also had touched her breasts.

When Deputies Kolp and Unfred arrived, they spoke with Williams, S.S., and Sua. It was apparent that Williams and Sua had been drinking. Williams initially "said she hadn't witnessed anything." Later, however, she said that Sua had been saying he wanted another child, and that he wanted S.S. to bear that child. S.S. said that Sua had kissed her on the mouth, groped her breasts and buttocks, and put his hands down her pants. Like her mother, she said that Sua had been talking about wanting another child, and wanting her (S.S.) to bear that child. Sua denied wrongdoing; he also explained, however, that as he, Williams and S.S. were all lying on the motel-room bed, he might have put his hands down S.S.'s pants in the mistaken belief that she was Williams.

At the deputies' request, S.S. and Williams each wrote a statement on a printed form. S.S. said:

> Tonight my daddy said to my mom that he was going to have a baby by me and my mom stepped and and (sic) said you're not going to have sex with my daughter. Then he got mad but before that he had me against the wall by the bathroom and asked for a hug. I gave him a hug then he started kissing me and he tryed (sic) to force his tounge (sic) in my mouth then he started putting his hands down my pants and rubbed me un-appriopriately (sic). And I said no to him then he said It doesn't matter what I say or do because what he says and does is right even if I don't think so and I don't like it. He put his hands in the back of my pants and inside my panties then he tried to rub my chest and I don't like it.

Williams said:

> [Sua] said he wanted a child by someone before he died. He said he can not have kids by me that that (sic) the only way that he can have a child is with my Daughter. My Daught[er] is only 16 years old. She's too young to even think about a family. He said he didn't care what I thought as long as he was able to have a child by somebody else. There is a no-contact order in affect (sic).

Neither S.S. nor Williams signed her written statement under oath or penalty of perjury.

Each did, however, sign beneath a printed paragraph that read:

> The above is a true and correct statement to the best of my knowledge. No threats or promises have been made to me nor any duress used against me.

On December 6, 2000, the State charged Sua with indecent liberties by forcible compulsion. Before trial, Sua moved to suppress his pretrial statements on the ground that the deputies had unlawfully obtained them. After a hearing held under CrR 3.5, the court denied the motion.

A jury trial was held in March 2001. All the evidence was produced on March 12. The State presented five witnesses and three exhibits. Its witnesses were S.S., Williams, A.S., Deputy Kolp and Deputy Unfred. Its exhibits were S.S.'s pretrial written statement, Williams' pretrial written statement, and a tape recording of A.S.'s call to 911. Sua did not present evidence.

S.S. testified first. She said that Sua had *not* taken indecent liberties with her. Although she admitted making her earlier oral and written statements to the police, she said they were a "cry for attention" and were not true.

At the end of S.S.'s testimony, the State offered her pretrial written statement as Exhibit 1. Sua objected, claiming the statement was inadmissible hearsay. The court admitted the written statement and excused the jury for the morning recess.

After the jury went out, counsel and the court continued to discuss the admissibility of S.S.'s written statement. The prosecutor said:

> Your Honor, State has not admitted any of these prior statements as substantive evidence. State has brought this forth to show that the witness has made prior inconsistent statements. They've been offered for impeachment value. The specific statements that the witnesses made previously, which contradicted with the testimony today, and only the contradicting statements, have been admitted for the purposes of impeachment, not as substantive evidence.
>
> I am not opposing Counsel being allowed a limiting instruction to the jury at the time when all the other instructions are read. I think that is clearly proper under the WPIC and under case law. . . .
>
> Counsel can argue before the jury that these aren't substantive evidence, but on the same hand, I have not argued to the jurors that these are substantive evidence.

Defense counsel requested a limiting instruction, which the court ultimately agreed to give. Thus, when the jury returned, the court instructed as follows:

> Prior to our recess, State's Exhibit No. 1 was admitted into evidence, and that statement is what we refer to as a prior written statement of a witness. I have an instruction that pertains to Exhibit No. 1 and will pertain possibly to other exhibits that are admitted in this case.

This evidence has been and will be introduced in this case on the subject of prior written statements and statements made to police officers for the limited purpose of assisting you in evaluating the credibility of the witnesses. If you find such prior statements were, in fact, made, they are not to be considered by you as proof of the matters recited in such statements.

Williams testified next. She said that she had been "upset" and "drinking that night," and that she had based her pre-trial written statement on what she had been told by S.S. When she had confronted S.S. about the truth of S.S.'s allegations, S.S. had said the allegations were not true.

At the end of Williams' testimony, the State offered her pretrial written statement as Exhibit 2. When defense counsel objected as hearsay, the prosecutor responded, "State is admitting it for purposes of impeachment, Your Honor." The court then instructed the jury:

> As we have explained once before, evidence has been introduced in this case, Exhibit No. 2, on the subject of prior written statements and statements made to police officers. For the limited purpose of assisting you

in evaluating the credibility of the witnesses, if you find such prior statements were, in fact, made, they are not to be considered by you as proof of the matters recited in such statements.

Given that instruction to the jury, Exhibit No. 2 will be admitted.

A.S. testified next. She said that she had been sleeping in the motel room at the time of the alleged incident. She had not seen anything, and her knowledge was limited to what she had heard from her sister and mother. She had been the one to call 911 because her mother "had a few beers that night" and "was very hysterical[.]"

At the end of A.S.'s testimony, the State offered a tape recording of A.S.'s phone call to 911. When defense counsel objected as hearsay, the court told the jury:

Okay. The Court is going to admit Exhibit 3. However, the jury is instructed that this evidence is introduced in this case and it concerns the subject of prior witness statements and statements made to police officers for the limited purpose of assisting you, the jury, in evaluating the credibility of the witnesses. If you find such prior statements were, in fact, made, they are not to be considered by you as proof of the matters recited in such statements.

With that limiting instruction, the Court will admit the tape.

After Deputies Kolp and Unfred had testified, the State rested. It was about 4 p.m. on March 12, and the court excused the jury for the day. Sua then moved to dismiss, arguing:

Essentially, Your Honor, we don't have any substantive evidence in this case. All the evidence that's been presented by the State is impeachment evidence, and that's not substantive evidence and it can't be used, as the court has already instructed the jury, as proof of the matter asserted in the impeachment statements. All the witnesses have testified that this did not occur. The only evidence that said it did is the impeachment evidence. And just as the jury can't use it, the court can't use it, either.

The State claimed the evidence was sufficient to convict. After saying it would rule the next morning, the court adjourned for the day.

The next morning, March 13, the court *sua sponte* invited additional argument on "why Exhibits 1 and 2 should or should not be admitted under 801(d)(1) as substantive evidence and not only for impeachment." Citing ER 801(d)(1)(i), *State v. Smith*, and *State v. Nelson*, the State argued — in stark contrast to the position it had taken earlier — that Exhibits 1 and 2 were admissible not just for impeachment, but also for substantive use. Defense counsel argued that neither exhibit was admissible for substantive use because neither had been made under oath or penalty of perjury. He also stated:

I think there's another issue here. During the course of the trial, the State brought all this in as impeachment evidence. There was no argument, no request that the Court deal with this as substantive evidence. The Court's read a limiting instruction, appropriately so, to the jury several times prior to this impeachment evidence coming in. At this time, if the Court were to expound and change this from impeachment evidence to substantive evidence, we're dealing with major confusion to the jury because we've been reading them these instructions throughout. I think I'd be in a position of asking the Court to declare a mistrial.

After listening to these additional arguments, the court ruled that Exhibits 1 and 2, S.S.'s and Williams' written statements, could be used to prove the truth of the matters asserted therein. Peculiarly however, the court refused to tell the jury about this new ruling. It stated:

> . . . I am not going to give a special limiting or unlimiting instruction to the jury. The case will go to the jury with the appropriate instructions at the end of the trial, which will not single out or try to explain or recreate what's happened. It will simply remain silent on anything pertaining to how this was admitted.

> In that sense, I feel that the defendant will get the benefit of the limiting instruction with the jury and therefore potentially receive a favorable verdict in this case. However, I'm not going to repeat the limiting instruction since I've now ruled that it's not strictly applicable.

When the prosecutor inquired how she should argue in closing, the court responded: "I do not want you to go into any explanation that you've been limited and now you're not[,]" but "you can certainly act as though there was no limiting instruction . . . ."

Defense counsel then made the first of several motions for mistrial. He predicted that the changed ruling "is going to be confusing to the jury [,]"and that Sua would not receive a fair trial as a result. The trial court denied the motion.

Sua opted not to present evidence, so the trial court proceeded to instruct the jury. The court stated in Instruction 5:

> Evidence has been introduced in this case on the subject of witnesses' oral statements to police officers and Audio 911 tape. You must not consider these evidence as for truth of the matters asserted in those statements, but only for determining the credibility of the witness.

The court said nothing about whether the jury could use Exhibits 1 and 2, S.S.'s and Williams' *written* statements, to prove the truth of the matters asserted therein.

In her initial closing argument, the prosecutor argued that Exhibits 1 and 2 could be used to prove the truth of the matters asserted therein, even though the jury had not been so informed. She stated:

> I want to go into the evidence which shows . . . that he is guilty of indecent liberties.

> First of all, there's evidence . . . of the victim's handwritten statement on the night the incident occurred. Exhibit 1. . . . She wrote in her own words what had occurred.

After reading Exhibit 1 aloud, the prosecutor further stated:

When [S.S.] came in to court and said that nothing had happened, that it was all made up, that she lied to the police, what you have to determine, ladies and gentlemen, is was she telling the truth when she wrote this statement or was she telling the truth when she was testifying on the stand.

*   *   *

. . . She told the truth that night because she just wanted him to stop. She didn't like what he did, and she wanted it to stop. So she told her mom, and the police got called.

*   *   *

The bottom line is this. You have to decide, was [S.S.] telling the truth then or was she telling the truth on the stand? If you believe that she was telling the truth when she wrote this statement, then the defendant is guilty. He's guilty as charged.

In his closing argument, defense counsel tried to explain Instruction 5. He stated:

Substantive evidence is the actual testimony of the witnesses, what they said in open court under oath in front of you, the judge, everybody, and exhibits that were admitted. Impeachment evidence is other types of statements that a person or a witness made to some other people when they weren't under oath and they weren't before a formal hearing.

What that instruction says is you can't base any type of decision on the facts that are contained in those other statements. . . . [T]hat's the law, and it's the law because the courts have found that it's prior statements that aren't in court and aren't under oath and under the penalty of perjury and in front of the formal proceeding that we have. They aren't as reliable. They're not as trustworthy as what you hear in open court. And that's why they say that.

In her rebuttal closing argument, the prosecutor again argued that S.S.'s and Williams' written statements could be used to prove the truth of the matters asserted therein. She stated:

What the defendant said to the police, is that substantive evidence? Absolutely. Is it important what the defendant said to the police? Absolutely. . . . Yes, oral statements, verbal statements, made outside of this courtroom are not substantive evidence, but you know what? Written statements are substantive evidence. They were made outside of this courtroom, and you can consider this as substantive evidence. Let's make that clear.

The jury began its deliberations mid-afternoon on March 13. After an hour or so, it sent out a note asking: "Is it true or is it false that State exhibits # 1 and # 2 can only be used for the purpose(s) of evaluating the credibility of the witnesses?" The court did not respond that day.

The next morning, the court held a hearing on how it should respond. At about 10:30 a.m., it sent the jury a note stating: "False. See Instruction 5." Defense counsel again moved for mistrial, but the motion was denied.

At about 1:30 p.m. that day, the jury sent out a note saying it could not reach a verdict. In open court with the parties present, the court asked each juror if the jury was deadlocked. Although eleven jurors said yes, the court ordered that deliberations continue.

At about 4 p.m. that day, the jury again said "that they're hung." The court and the parties convened without the jury, and the defense made another motion for mistrial. After denying that motion, the court instructed the jury to return the next morning and continue deliberating.

During the afternoon of the next day, March 15, the jury returned a verdict of guilty. The court later imposed a sentence of 67 months.

I.

The primary issue on appeal is whether the trial court properly admitted Exhibits 1 and 2. To resolve that issue intelligently, we must examine ER 801(c) and ER 801(d)(1). Each was taken verbatim from the corresponding Federal Rule of Evidence, so its drafters were, in effect, the Advisory Committee that wrote the Federal Rules.

ER 801(c) embodies the basic definition of hearsay. It has three clauses, which we differentiate as follows:

> [1] "Hearsay" is a statement, [2] other than one made by the declarant while testifying at the trial or hearing, [3] offered in evidence to prove the truth of the matter asserted.

The middle clause is the one pertinent here. It provides in effect that the out-of-court statement of an in-court witness is generally hearsay. By hypothesis, an out-of-court statement is not made at the present trial or hearing. Necessarily then, an out-of-court statement is hearsay when offered to prove the truth of the matter asserted — even if it was made by someone who is now an in-court witness (i.e., even if it was made by someone who is presently under oath, observable by the trier of fact, and subject to cross-examination).

This effect can be confirmed by considering how ER 801(c)'s middle clause could have been worded. It could easily have said that hearsay is a statement, "other than one made by a declarant *who testifies* at the trial or hearing," offered in evidence to prove the truth of the matter asserted. Instead, it says that hearsay is a statement, "other than one made by a declarant *while testifying* at the trial or hearing," offered in evidence to prove the truth of the matter asserted. The effect is to bring within the definition of hearsay any out-of-court statement offered to prove its truth, even if made by a witness at the present trial or hearing.

If ER 801(c)'s middle clause provides as just indicated, it must have a purpose that is additional to, and not satisfied by, the declarant's being under oath, observable, and subject to cross. And indeed it does. It is founded, according to the federal Advisory Committee that drafted it, "upon an unwillingness to countenance the general use of prior prepared statements[.]"

An example will illustrate this concern about "the general use of prior prepared statements." Suppose that a woman sees an auto accident. She tells the plaintiff's investigator how the accident happened. The investigator reports back to the plaintiff's attorney, who "carefully prepares" a written statement that favorably describes the accident from his point of view. The attorney meets with the witness in his office, presents the statement, and goes over it with her. She agrees to it and signs it. At trial, the attorney calls the woman to the stand, establishes her identity, and authenticates her written statement. He then offers the written statement to prove how the accident happened. At the same time, he indicates he will not have any further direct examination. If the written statement is not deemed hearsay because the woman is on the stand at trial, the attorney will be entitled to use her "carefully prepared" written statement as a substitute for direct examination in open court. If the written statement is deemed hearsay even though the woman is on the stand, the attorney will not be entitled to use her pretrial statement, and will instead be required to conduct an extemporaneous direct examination in open court. Choosing to require direct examination in open court, the Advisory Committee intentionally crafted ER 801(c)'s middle clause so that "hearsay" includes the out-of-court statement of an in-court witness when offered to prove the truth of the matter asserted.

Although the Advisory Committee sought to preclude "the *general* use of prior prepared statements as substantive evidence," it also recognized that "particular circumstances call for a contrary result." Accordingly, it drafted and proposed a version of FRE 801(d)(1) that would have provided:

(d) A statement is not hearsay if—

(1) The declarant testifies at the trial or hearing and is subject to cross-examination concerning the statement, and the statement is (A) inconsistent with his testimony, or (B) consistent with his testimony and is offered to rebut an express or implied charge against the declarant of recent fabrication or improper influence or motive, or (C) one of identification of a person made after perceiving him.

This proposal enumerated "three situations" (now called exemptions) in which the out-of-court statement of an in-court witness would be deemed nonhearsay despite the wording of ER 801(c)'s middle clause. This case involves only the first of those three. From here on then, we limit our discussion to the exemption described in FRE 801(d)(1)(A), from which Washington's ER 801(d)(1)(i) was later "taken verbatim."

The Advisory Committee submitted its proposed FRE 801(d)(1)(A) to the United States Supreme Court. The Court adopted the proposed rule and submitted it for Congress to review. In Congress, it went first to the House, then to the Senate, and finally to a conference committee.

In the House, the proposal was referred to the House Committee on the Judiciary. That Committee thought it was too broad and should be significantly narrowed. Accordingly, the Committee recommended an amendment consisting of the following italicized words:

(d) A statement is not hearsay if—

(1) the declarant testifies at the trial or hearing and is subject to cross-examination concerning the statement, and the statement is

(A) inconsistent with his testimony *and was given under oath subject to cross-examination, and subject to the penalty of perjury at a trial or hearing or in a deposition* . . . .

The Committee commented:

> Although there was some support expressed for the Court Rule, based largely on the need to counteract the effect of witness intimidation in criminal cases, the Committee decided to adopt a compromise version of the Rule similar to the position of the Second Circuit. The Rule as amended draws a distinction between types of prior inconsistent statements . . . and allows only those made while the declarant was subject to cross-examination at a tr[ia]l or hearing or in a deposition, to be admissible for their truth. . . . The rationale for the Committee's decision is that (1) unlike in most other situations involving unsworn or oral statements, there can be no dispute as to whether the prior statement was made; and (2) the context of a formal proceeding, an oath, and the opportunity for cross-examination provide firm additional assurances of the reliability of the prior statement.

The full House adopted its Committee's recommendation.

In the Senate, the proposed rule was referred to the Senate Committee on the Judiciary. That Committee thought that the House amendment was improvident, and that the proposed rule should be returned to its initial form. The Committee commented:

> The House severely limited the admissibility of prior inconsistent statements by adding a requirement that the prior statement must have been subject to cross-examination, thus precluding even the use of grand jury statements. The requirement that the prior statement must have been subject to cross-examination appears unnecessary since this rule comes into play only when the witness testifies in the present trial. At that time, he is on the stand and can explain an earlier position and be cross-examined as to both.

> The requirement that the statement be under oath also appears unnecessary. Notwithstanding the absence of an oath contemporaneous with the statement, the witness, when on the stand, qualifying or denying the prior statement, is under oath.

The full Senate adopted its Committee's recommendation.

The proposed rule then went to a Conference Committee. That Committee thought that the House amendment should be adopted if it were broadened to cover statements made before a grand jury. Accordingly, the Committee recommended that the proposed rule be amended as follows:

(d) A statement is not hearsay if—

(2) the declarant testifies at the trial or hearing and is subject to cross-examination concerning the statement, and the statement is

(i) inconsistent with the declarant's testimony, *and was given under oath subject to the penalty of perjury at a trial, hearing, or **other proceeding**, or in a deposition.* . . .

The committee commented:

> The Conference adopts the Senate amendment with an amendment, so that the rule now requires that the prior inconsistent statement be given under oath subject to the penalty of perjury at a trial, hearing, or **other proceeding**, or in a deposition. The rule as adopted covers statements before a grand jury.

The Conference Committee's recommendation was enacted into law, effective July 1, 1975. Washington copied it verbatim, effective April 2, 1979, and it became ER 801(d)(1)(i).

Since 1979, the Washington courts have decided two cases on which the State relies here. In 1982, in a case called *State v. Smith,* the Washington Supreme Court addressed the rule's requirement that the offered statement have been "given . . . at a trial, hearing, or other proceeding[.]" A woman voluntarily gave the police a written statement that implicated the defendant in a crime. She signed the statement under oath before a notary public. When she testified inconsistently at the defendant's trial, the trial court admitted her written statement for substantive use. After discussing a 1976 Ninth Circuit case called *United States v. Castro-Ayon,* the Washington Supreme Court noted that in the case presently at bench "the complaining witness-victim voluntarily wrote the statement herself, swore to it under oath with penalty of perjury before a notary, admitted at trial she had made the statement and gave an inconsistent statement at trial where she was subject to cross examination." The court then concluded that the statement had been given in an "other proceeding," and that "under the totality of these circumstances" the statement fell within ER 801(d)(1)(i).

In 1994, in a case called *State v. Nelson,* Division One seems to have addressed the rule's requirement that the offered statement have been "given under oath subject to the penalty of perjury," as well as the rule's requirement that the offered statement have been "given . . . at a trial, hearing, or other proceeding." A woman told police that she was a prostitute and that the defendant was her pimp. An officer reduced her statement to a writing that she signed before a notary public. Although the notary did not administer an oath, the writing apparently recited, pursuant to RCW 9A.72.085, "that it is certified or declared by the person to be true under penalty of perjury[.]" Concluding that the statement could "be regarded as . . . sworn" because RCW 9A.72.085 had been complied with, Division One held that the statement had been given in an "other proceeding," and that the statement fell within the scope of ER 801(d)(1)(i).

Against this backdrop, the State asks us to rule that ER 801(d)(1)(i) permitted the admission of Exhibits 1 and 2, S.S.'s and Williams' out-of-court written statements, to prove the truth of the matters asserted therein. The State acknowledges that neither statement was "given under oath and subject to [the] penalty [of] perjury[,]" and that the "trial court [ ] admittedly broke new ground with [its] ER 801(d)(1) ruling." Citing *Smith* and *Nelson* however, the State asserts that "[t]he written statements of S.S. and Williams carried sufficient guaranties of truthfulness to allow admissibility under ER 801(d)(1)(i)."

We decline this request for several reasons. First, we cannot just ignore ER 801(d)(1)(i)'s requirement that the out-of-court statement of an in-court witness be "given under oath subject to the penalty of perjury." We are obligated to construe ER 801(d)(1)(i) according to its plain meaning, and to give effect to all of its language. To do that, we must hold that Exhibits 1 and 2 do not satisfy ER 801(d)(1)(i), because they were not "given under oath subject to the penalty of perjury."

Second, we cannot just ignore the compromise that Congress reached and that Washington later adopted. That compromise was expressly and carefully crafted, and it is not our function to upset it.

Third, neither *Smith* nor *Nelson* supports the State's request. The declarant in *Smith* gave her statement under oath subject to penalty of perjury, for she actually took an oath from a notary public. The declarant in *Nelson* gave her statement under oath subject to penalty of perjury, for she complied with RCW 9A.72.085. Neither declarant in this case actually took an oath, complied with RCW 9A.72.085, or in any other way gave her statement "under oath subject to the penalty of perjury."

Fourth, we have not found any case anywhere that supports the State's position, although we have found at least one that does not. In *United States v. Day*, the Sixth Circuit ruled that FRE 801(d)(1)(A) did not authorize the admission of a tape-recorded statement that a witness had made before trial to a law enforcement officer, because the statement was not shown to have been made under oath subject to the penalty of perjury.

Finally, we cannot transform ER 801(d)(1)(i) into a catchall provision that would require only a showing of particularized guaranties of trustworthiness for the out-of-court statements of an in-court witness. The federal courts adopted the catchall concept, but Washington expressly declined to do so.

We conclude that Exhibits 1 and 2 were hearsay within the meaning of ER 801(c)'s middle clause; that they were not exempted from the operation of that clause by ER 801(d)(1)(i); and that the trial court erred by admitting them as substantive evidence. Given the lack of other substantive evidence, it cannot reasonably be argued, and neither party attempts to argue, that the error was harmless. Accordingly, we vacate the conviction, reverse the judgment, and remand for further proceedings.

Reversed and remanded for further proceedings.

We concur: BRIDGEWATER, J., and QUINN-BRINTNALL, A.C.J.

[c] Former Testimony as Prior Inconsistent Statement

The requirements of the hearsay exception for former testimony are quite different from those for the exclusion from the hearsay rule for prior inconsistent statements. However, the two rules often complement one another in situations in which the witness either is not available at the second trial or is available and has given inconsistent testimony. If the witness is unavailable at the second trial, the only way that his or her testimony from the first trial can be offered as substantive evidence is through the former testimony exception to the hearsay rule contained in Rule 804(b)(1). That exception requires that: (1) the testimony was given in an adversarial proceeding in which the opponent had an opportunity and similar motive to develop the testimony on direct, cross, or redirect examination, and (2) the party against whom it is subsequently offered is (a) the same party against whom it was initially offered if the second proceeding is a criminal case, or (b) a predecessor-in-interest if it is a civil action. In contrast, when the witness is available, Rule 801(d)(1)(A), like Rule 804(b)(1), requires that the prior statement was given under oath, but does not require that it was given in an adversarial proceeding where it was tested by someone with similar interest to the one against whom it is now being offered.

[d] Prior Identification as Prior Inconsistent Statement

If a witness gives sworn testimony before a grand jury in which he or she identifies the defendant but subsequently recants that identification at the defendant's trial, the prior identification could be admissible either as a prior inconsistent statement under Rule 801(d)(1)(A) or as a prior identification under Rule 801(d)(1)(C). *See United States v. Marchand*, 564 F.2d 983 (2d Cir. 1977).

[e] Balancing Probative Value and Potential Prejudice

If the witness did not make a prior inconsistent statement under oath, its use is limited to impeachment — demonstrating that the witness tells inconsistent stories and therefore is not worthy of belief. The jury may not consider the statement for the truth of its content, and the court will give an instruction to that effect upon the opposing party's request. Fed. R. Evid. 105.

If the use of a prior statement is limited to impeachment, its admissibility is enhanced in one respect because hearsay concerns are avoided. If there is potential unfair prejudice from the use of such evidence, however, its admissibility may be affected negatively. This is because, with the evidence having less value in the trial, the balance of probative value and potential prejudice under Rule 403 could more easily weigh in favor of exclusion. For example, if the court concludes that a witness has given inconsistent stories by being evasive or feigning a loss of memory after having previously given detailed accounts of an incident,[33] the value of those

---

[33] *See United States v. Morgan*, 555 F.2d 238 (9th Cir. 1977); *State v. Green*, 479 P.2d 998 (Cal. 1971).

prior statements is substantial if they are admissible for their truth. If, however, those prior statements were not made under oath, and therefore are not admissible for truth under Rule 801(d)(l)(A), their value for impeachment purposes might be limited, because the witness may have testified to little by way of substance that the jury would need to be convinced to disregard. In addition, the possibility that the jury would ignore the limiting instruction and use the prior statements impermissibly is significant. Consequently, if a prior inconsistent statement is admissible only for impeachment, the balancing of probative value and potential unfair prejudice required in Rule 403 may compel its exclusion.

EXERCISE

Father and Son were charged with arson in state court after their business suspiciously caught fire. Son agreed to cooperate with the state prosecutors and testified against Father at the state trial. Son testified under oath that Father purchased the gasoline and that Son started the fire at Father's request. Son also answered all of the questions posed to him on cross-examination. At the end of the State's case, the judge dismissed the charges due to a procedural error. The federal government then lawfully filed charges against both men in federal court. At the federal trial, Son again agreed to testify against Father. Son again admitted that he started the fire, but now refused to disclose what Father had done or said. In response, the federal prosecutor wants to read aloud the portion of Son's state court testimony in which Son confirmed that Father had asked him to start the fire. Father objects on hearsay grounds. How should the court rule?

[2]   Prior Consistent Statements: Rule 801(d)(1)(B)

[a]   "Before Motive to Fabricate Arose"

Under the common law, a prior consistent statement was generally considered to be relevant, and therefore admissible to rebut a charge of recent fabrication, only if the declarant made the statement prior to the time when his or her alleged motive to fabricate would have arisen. This view, however, was not universally accepted. This conflict continued after the adoption of Rule 801(d)(1)(B). The Supreme Court resolved it in *Tome v. United States*.

TOME v. UNITED STATES
United States Supreme Court
513 U.S. 150, 115 S. Ct. 696, 130 L. Ed. 2d 574 (1995)

JUSTICE KENNEDY delivered the opinion of the Court, except as to Part IIB.

Various federal Courts of Appeals are divided over the evidence question presented by this case. At issue is the interpretation of a provision in the Federal Rules of Evidence bearing upon the admissibility of statements, made by a declarant who testifies as a witness, that are consistent with the testimony and are offered to rebut a charge of a "recent fabrication or improper influence or motive." Fed. Rule Evid. 801(d)(1)(B). The question is whether out-of-court consistent statements made after the alleged fabrication, or after the alleged improper influence or motive arose, are admissible under the Rule.

I

Petitioner Tome was charged in a one-count indictment with the felony of sexual abuse of a child, his own daughter, aged four at the time of the alleged crime. The case having arisen on the Navajo Indian Reservation, Tome was tried by a jury in the United States District Court for the District of New Mexico, where he was found guilty of violating 18 U.S.C. §§ 1153, 2241(c), and 2245(2)(A) and (B).

Tome and the child's mother had been divorced in 1988. A tribal court awarded joint custody of the daughter, A.T., to both parents, but Tome had primary physical custody. In 1989 the mother was unsuccessful in petitioning the tribal court for primary custody of A.T., but was awarded custody for the summer of 1990. Neither parent attended a further custody hearing in August 1990. On August 27, 1990, the mother contacted Colorado authorities with allegations that Tome had committed sexual abuse against A.T.

The prosecution's theory was that Tome committed sexual assaults upon the child while she was in his custody and that the crime was disclosed when the child was spending vacation time with her mother. The defense argued that the allegations were concocted so the child would not be returned to her father. At trial A.T., then six and one half years old, was the Government's first witness. For the most part, her direct testimony consisted of one- and two-word answers to a series of leading questions. Cross-examination took place over two trial days. The defense asked A.T. 348 questions. On the first day A.T. answered all the questions posed to her on general, background subjects.

The next day there was no testimony, and the prosecutor met with A.T. When cross-examination of A.T. resumed, she was questioned about those conversations but was reluctant to discuss them. Defense counsel then began questioning her about the allegations of abuse, and it appears she was reluctant at many points to answer. As the trial judge noted, however, some of the defense questions were imprecise or unclear. The judge expressed his concerns with the examination of A.T., observing there were lapses of as much as 40–55 seconds between some questions and the answers and that on the second day of examination the witness seemed to be losing concentration. The trial judge stated, "We have a very difficult situation here."

After A.T. testified, the Government produced six witnesses who testified about a total of seven statements made by A.T. describing the alleged sexual assaults: A.T.'s babysitter recited A.T.'s statement to her on August 22, 1990, that she did not want to return to her father because he "gets drunk and he thinks I'm his wife"; the babysitter related further details given by A.T. on August 27, 1990, while A.T.'s mother stood outside the room and listened after the mother had been unsuccessful in questioning A.T. herself; the mother recounted what she had heard A.T. tell the babysitter; a social worker recounted details A.T. told her on August 29, 1990 about the assaults; and three pediatricians, Drs. Kuper, Reich and Spiegel, related A.T.'s statements to them describing how and where she had been touched by Tome. All but A.T.'s statement to Dr. Spiegel implicated Tome. (The physicians also testified that their clinical examinations of the child indicated that she had been subjected to vaginal penetrations. That part of the testimony is not at issue here.)

A.T.'s out-of-court statements, recounted by the six witnesses, were offered by the Government under Rule 801(d)(1)(B). The trial court admitted all of the statements over defense counsel's objection, accepting the Government's argument that they rebutted the implicit charge that A.T.'s testimony was motivated by a desire to live with her mother. The court also admitted A.T.'s August 22d statement to her babysitter under Rule 807, and the statements to Dr. Kuper (and apparently also to Dr. Reich) under Rule 803(4) (statements for purposes of medical diagnosis). The Government offered the testimony of the social worker under both Rules 801(d)(1)(B) and 807, but the record does not indicate whether the court ruled on the latter ground. No objection was made to Dr. Spiegel's testimony. Following trial, Tome was convicted and sentenced to 12 years imprisonment.

On appeal, the Court of Appeals for the Tenth Circuit affirmed, adopting the Government's argument that all of A.T.'s out-of-court statements were admissible under Rule 801(d)(1)(B) even though they had been made after A.T.'s alleged motive to fabricate arose. The court reasoned that "the pre-motive requirement is a function of the relevancy rules, not the hearsay rules" and that as a "function of relevance, the pre-motive rule is clearly too broad . . . because it is simply not true that an individual with a motive to lie always will do so." . . . "Rather, the relevance of the prior consistent statement is more accurately determined by evaluating the strength of the motive to lie, the circumstances in which the statement is made, and the declarant's demonstrated propensity to lie." *Ibid.* The court recognized that some Circuits require that the consistent statements, to be admissible under the Rule, must be made before the motive or influence arose . . . but cited the Ninth Circuit's decision in *United States v. Miller*, 874 F.2d 1255, 1272 (1989), in support of its balancing approach. Applying this balancing test to A.T.'s first statement to her babysitter, the Court of Appeals determined that although A.T. might have had "some motive to lie, we do not believe that it is a particularly strong one." . . . The court held that the district judge had not abused his discretion in admitting A.T.'s out-of-court statements. It did not analyze the probative quality of A.T.'s six other out-of-court statements, nor did it reach the admissibility of the statements under any other rule of evidence.

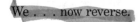 We . . . now reverse.

II

The prevailing common-law rule for more than a century before adoption of the Federal Rules of Evidence was that a prior consistent statement introduced to rebut a charge of recent fabrication or improper influence or motive was admissible if the statement had been made before the alleged fabrication, influence, or motive came into being, but it was inadmissible if made afterwards. As Justice Story explained: "Where the testimony is assailed as a fabrication of a recent date . . . in order to repel such imputation, proof of the antecedent declaration of the party may be admitted." . . .

McCormick and Wigmore stated the rule in a more categorical manner: "[t]he applicable principle is that the prior consistent statement has no relevancy to refute the charge unless the consistent statement was made *before* the source of the bias, interest, influence or incapacity originated." E. Cleary, 4 on Evidence § 47, p. 65 (4th ed. 1994) (hereafter McCormick). *See also* 4 J. Wigmore, Evidence § 1128, p. 268 (J. Chadbourn rev. 1972) (hereafter Wigmore) ("A consistent statement, at a time prior to the existence of a fact said to indicate bias . . . will effectively explain away the force of the impeaching evidence. . . ."). The question is whether Rule 801(d)(1)(B) embodies this temporal requirement. We hold that it does.

A

*   *   *

Rule 801 defines prior consistent statements as nonhearsay only if they are offered to rebut a charge of "recent fabrication or improper influence or motive." Fed. Rule Evid. 801(d)(1)(B). Noting the "troublesome" logic of treating a witness' prior consistent statements as hearsay at all (because the declarant is present in court and subject to cross-examination), the Advisory Committee decided to treat those consistent statements, once the preconditions of the Rule were satisfied, as nonhearsay and admissible as substantive evidence, not just to rebut an attack on the witness's credibility . . . . A consistent statement meeting the requirements of the Rule is thus placed in the same category as a declarant's inconsistent statement made under oath in another proceeding, or prior identification testimony, or admissions by a party opponent. . . .

The Rules do not accord this weighty, nonhearsay status to all prior consistent statements. To the contrary, admissibility under the Rules is confined to those statements offered to rebut a charge of "recent fabrication or improper influence or motive," the same phrase used by the Advisory Committee in its description of the "traditional" common law of evidence, which was the background against which the Rules were drafted. . . . Prior consistent statements may not be admitted to counter all forms of impeachment or to bolster the witness merely because she has been discredited. In the present context, the question is whether A.T.'s out-of-court statements rebutted the alleged link between her desire to be with her mother and her testimony, not whether they suggested that A.T.'s in-court testimony was true. The Rule speaks of a party rebutting an alleged motive, not bolstering the veracity of the story told.

This limitation is instructive, not only to establish the preconditions of admissibility but also to reinforce the significance of the requirement that the consistent statements must have been made before the alleged influence, or motive to fabricate arose. That is to say, the forms of impeachment within the Rule's coverage are the ones in which the temporal requirement makes the most sense. Impeachment by charging that the testimony is a recent fabrication or results from an improper influence or motive is, as a general matter, capable of direct and forceful refutation through introduction of out-of-court consistent statements that predate the alleged fabrication, influence or motive. A consistent statement that predates the motive is a square rebuttal of the charge that the testimony was contrived as a consequence of that motive. By contrast, prior consistent statements carry little rebuttal force when most other types of impeachment are involved. . . .

There may arise instances when out-of-court statements that postdate the alleged fabrication have some probative force in rebutting a charge of fabrication or improper influence or motive, but those statements refute the charged fabrication in a less direct and forceful way. Evidence that a witness made consistent statements after the alleged motive to fabricate arose may suggest in some degree that the in-court testimony is truthful, and thus suggest in some degree that that testimony did not result from some improper influence; but if the drafters of Rule 801(d)(1)(B) intended to countenance rebuttal along that indirect inferential chain, the purpose of confining the types of impeachment that open the door to rebuttal by introducing consistent statements becomes unclear. If consistent statements are admissible without reference to the time frame we find imbedded in the Rule, there appears no sound reason not to admit consistent statements to rebut other forms of impeachment as well. Whatever objections can be leveled against limiting the Rule to this designated form of impeachment and confining the rebuttal to those statements made before the fabrication or improper influence or motive arose, it is clear to us that the drafters of Rule 801(d)(1)(B) were relying upon the common-law temporal requirement.

The underlying theory of the Government's position is that an out-of-court consistent statement, whenever it was made, tends to bolster the testimony of a witness and so tends also to rebut an express or implied charge that the testimony has been the product of an improper influence. Congress could have adopted that rule with ease, providing, for instance, that "a witness' prior consistent statements are admissible whenever relevant to assess the witness's truthfulness or accuracy." The theory would be that, in a broad sense, any prior statement by a witness concerning the disputed issues at trial would have some relevance in assessing the accuracy or truthfulness of the witness's in-court testimony on the same subject. The narrow Rule enacted by Congress, however, cannot be understood to incorporate the Government's theory.

Our analysis is strengthened by the observation that the somewhat peculiar language of the Rule bears close similarity to the language used in many of the common law cases that describe the premotive requirement. "Rule 801(d)(1)(B) employs the precise language — 'rebutting . . . charges . . . of recent fabrication or improper influence or motive' — consistently used in the panoply of pre-1975 decisions." E. O. Ohlbaum, *The Hobgoblin of the Federal Rules of Evidence: An Analysis of Rule 801(d)(1)(B), Prior Consistent Statements and a New Proposal*, 1987 B. Y. U. L. Rev. 231, 245. . . .

The language of the Rule, in its concentration on rebutting charges of recent fabrication, improper influence and motive to the exclusion of other forms of impeachment, as well as in its use of wording which follows the language of the common-law cases, suggests that it was intended to carry over the common-law premotive rule.

B

Our conclusion that Rule 801(d)(1)(B) embodies the common-law premotive requirement is confirmed by an examination of the Advisory Committee Notes to the Federal Rules of Evidence. We have relied on those well-considered Notes as a useful guide in ascertaining the meaning of the Rules. . . . Where, as with Rule 801(d)(1)(B), "Congress did not amend the Advisory Committee's draft in any way . . . the Committee's commentary is particularly relevant in determining the meaning of the document Congress enacted." . . . The Notes are also a respected source of scholarly commentary. Professor Cleary was a distinguished commentator on the law of evidence, and he and members of the Committee consulted and considered the views, criticisms, and suggestions of the academic community in preparing the Notes.

The Notes disclose a purpose to adhere to the common law in the application of evidentiary principles, absent express provisions to the contrary. Where the Rules did depart from their common-law antecedents, in general the Committee said so. . . . The Notes give no indication, however, that Rule 801(d)(1)(B) abandoned the premotive requirement. The entire discussion of Rule 801(d)(1)(B) is limited to the following comment:

> Prior consistent statements traditionally have been admissible to rebut charges of recent fabrication or improper influence or motive but not as substantive evidence. Under the rule they are substantive evidence. The prior statement is consistent with the testimony given on the stand, and, if the opposite party wishes to open the door for its admission in evidence, no sound reason is apparent why it should not be received generally.

Notes on Rule 801(d)(1)(B). . . .

Throughout their discussion of the Rules, the Advisory Committee Notes rely on Wigmore and McCormick as authority for the common-law approach. In light of the categorical manner in which those authors state the premotive requirement . . . it is difficult to imagine that the drafters, who noted the new substantive use of prior consistent statements, would have remained silent if they intended to modify the premotive requirement. As we observed with respect to another provision of the Rules, "with this state of unanimity confronting the drafters of the Federal Rules of Evidence, we think it unlikely that they intended to scuttle entirely [the common-law requirement]." . . . Here, we do not think the drafters of the Rule intended to scuttle the whole premotive requirement and rationale without so much as a whisper of explanation.

*   *   *

Our conclusion is bolstered by the Advisory Committee's stated "unwillingness to countenance the general use of prior prepared statements as substantive evidence." . . . Rule 801(d), which "enumerates three situations in which the statement is excepted from the category of hearsay," . . . was expressly contrasted by the Committee with Uniform Rule of Evidence 63(1) (1953), "which allows any out-of-court statement of a declarant who is present at the trial and available for cross-examination." . . . When a witness presents important testimony damaging to a party, the party will often counter with at least an implicit charge that the witness has been under some influence or motive to fabricate. If Rule 801 were read so that the charge opened the floodgates to any prior consistent statement that satisfied Rule 403, as the Tenth Circuit concluded, the distinction between rejected Uniform Rule 63(1) and Rule 801(d)(1)(B) would all but disappear.

That Rule 801(d)(1)(B) permits prior consistent statements to be used for substantive purposes after the statements are admitted to rebut the existence of an improper influence or motive makes it all the more important to observe the preconditions for admitting the evidence in the first place. The position taken by the Rules reflects a compromise between the views expressed by the "bulk of the case law . . . against allowing prior statements of witnesses to be used generally as substantive evidence" and the views of the majority of "writers . . . [who] had taken the opposite position." . . . That compromise was one that the Committee candidly admitted was a "judgment . . . more of experience than of logic." . . .

"A party contending that legislative action changed settled law has the burden of showing that the legislature intended such a change." . . . Nothing in the Advisory Committee's Notes suggests that it intended to alter the common-law premotive requirement.

C

The Government's final argument in favor of affirmance is that the common-law premotive rule advocated by petitioner is inconsistent with the Federal Rules' liberal approach to relevancy and with strong academic criticism, beginning in the 1940's, directed at the exclusion of out-of-court statements made by a declarant who is present in court and subject to cross-examination. This argument misconceives the design of the Rules' hearsay provisions.

Hearsay evidence is often relevant. "The only way in which the probative force of hearsay differs from the probative force of other testimony is in the absence of oath, demeanor, and cross-examination as aids in determining credibility." . . . That does not resolve the matter, however. Relevance is not the sole criterion of admissibility. Otherwise, it would be difficult to account for the Rules' general proscription of hearsay testimony (absent a specific exception) . . . let alone the traditional analysis of hearsay that the Rules, for the most part, reflect. . . . That certain out-of-court statements may be relevant does not dispose of the question whether they are admissible.

The Government's reliance on academic commentators critical of excluding out-of-court statements by a witness . . . is subject to like criticism. To be sure, certain commentators in the years preceding the adoption of the Rules had been critical of the common-law approach to hearsay, particularly its categorical exclusion of out-of-court statements offered for substantive purposes. . . . General criticism was directed to the exclusion of a declarant's out-of-court statements where the declarant testified at trial. . . . As an alternative, they suggested moving away from the categorical exclusion of hearsay and toward a case-by-case balancing of the probative value of particular statements against their likely prejudicial effect. . . . The Advisory Committee, however, was explicit in rejecting this balancing approach to hearsay:

> The Advisory Committee has rejected this approach to hearsay as involving too great a measure of judicial discretion, minimizing the predictability of rulings, [and] enhancing the difficulties of preparation for trial.

Given the Advisory Committee's rejection of both the general balancing approach to hearsay, and of Uniform Rule 63(1) . . . the Government's reliance on the views of those who advocated these positions is misplaced.

The statement-by-statement balancing approach advocated by the Government and adopted by the Tenth Circuit creates the precise dangers the Advisory Committee noted and sought to avoid: It involves considerable judicial discretion; it reduces predictability; and it enhances the difficulties of trial preparation because parties will have difficulty knowing in advance whether or not particular out-of-court statements will be admitted. . . .

D

The case before us illustrates some of the important considerations supporting the Rule as we interpret it, especially in criminal cases. If the Rule were to permit the introduction of prior statements as substantive evidence to rebut every implicit charge that a witness' in-court testimony results from recent fabrication or improper influence or motive, the whole emphasis of the trial could shift to the out-of-court statements, not the in-court ones. The present case illustrates the point. In response to a rather weak charge that A.T.'s testimony was a fabrication created so the child could remain with her mother, the Government was permitted to present a parade of sympathetic and credible witnesses who did no more than recount A.T.'s detailed out-of-court statements to them. Although those statements might have been probative on the question whether the alleged conduct had occurred, they shed but minimal light on whether A.T. had the charged motive to fabricate. At closing argument before the jury, the Government placed great reliance on the prior statements for substantive purposes but did not once seek to use them to rebut the impact of the alleged motive.

We are aware that in some cases it may be difficult to ascertain when a particular fabrication, influence, or motive arose. Yet, as the Government concedes, a majority of common-law courts were performing this task for well over a century . . . and the Government has presented us with no evidence that those courts, or the judicial circuits that adhere to the rule today, have been unable to make the determination. Even under the Government's hypothesis, moreover, the thing to be rebutted must be identified, so the date of its origin cannot be that much more difficult to ascertain. By contrast, as the Advisory Committee commented . . . the Government's approach, which would require the trial court to weigh all of the circumstances surrounding a statement that suggest its probativeness against the court's assessment of the strength of the alleged motive, would entail more of a burden, with no guidance to attorneys in preparing a case or to appellate courts in reviewing a judgment.

III

Courts must be sensitive to the difficulties attendant upon the prosecution of alleged child abusers. In almost all cases a youth is the prosecution's only eye witness. But "this Court cannot alter evidentiary rules merely because litigants might prefer different rules in a particular class of cases." . . . When a party seeks to introduce out-of-court statements that contain strong circumstantial indicia of reliability, that are highly probative on the material questions at trial, and that are better than other evidence otherwise available, there is no need to distort the requirements of Rule 801(d)(1)(B). If its requirements are met, Rule 807 exists for that eventuality. We intimate no view, however, concerning the admissibility of any of A.T.'s out-of-court statements under that section, or any other evidentiary principle. These matters, and others, are for the Court of Appeals to decide in the first instance.

Our holding is confined to the requirements for admission under Rule 801(d)(1)(B). The Rule permits the introduction of a declarant's consistent out-of-court statements to rebut a charge of recent fabrication or improper influence or motive only when those statements were made before the charged recent fabrication or improper influence or motive. These conditions of admissibility were not established here.

The judgment of the Court of Appeals for the Tenth Circuit is reversed, and the case is remanded for further proceedings consistent with this opinion.

It is so ordered.

[b] Implied Charges of Recent Fabrication or Improper Influence or Motive

Rule 801(d)(1)(B) attempts to accommodate the views that all out-of-court statements offered to prove the truth of the matter asserted are hearsay and that no prior consistent statements should be classified as hearsay if the declarant is testifying and repeating his or her own statement. It excludes consistent statements from the hearsay rule, but only if there had been an express or implied charge of recent fabrication or improper influence or motive and the statements are offered in rebuttal of these charges. The Advisory Committee's rationale was that "if the opposing party wishes to open the door for its admission in evidence, no sound reason is apparent why it should not be received generally." Advisory Committee Note to Rule 801, 56 F.R.D. 183, 296 (1973).

Although an express charge of recent fabrication or improper influence or motive is easily recognizable, what will constitute an implied charge? This is a subject on which common-law courts disagreed, and about which there will be continued disagreement under Rule 801(d)(1)(B) because the Rule offers no guidance on the matter. The most that can be said is that what constitutes an implied charge is a discretionary decision that will vary with the circumstances of each case, and that this decision will be reversed only upon a showing of arbitrary abuse. The following cases are illustrative.

In *United States v. Herring*, 582 F.2d 535 (10th Cir. 1978), defense counsel cross-examined a Government witness about a statement that the witness had previously given to a DEA officer. On redirect examination, the Government offered the statement into evidence and it was admitted as a prior consistent statement. On appeal, the court upheld that ruling under Rule 801(d)(1)(B) because "[t]he questions by the defense to Brown on cross concerning his compensation from the Government for testifying and the questioning which carried the suggestion that his testimony was inconsistent with the statement and was thus fabricated, all justified reception of the prior statement." *Id.* at 541.

In *United States v. Coleman,* 631 F.2d 908 (D.C. Cir. 1980), a detective had identified the defendant as the person from whom heroin had been purchased. His description of the defendant was challenged on cross-examination through an inquiry about the fact that the detective had not mentioned, during his testimony, the medallion the defendant was wearing at the time of the heroin sale. Defense counsel withdrew this question, however, before the detective could answer it. The court held that the mere asking of the question created an inference of a change in description that was necessarily left lingering despite counsel's withdrawal of the question. Consequently, the court held that the detective's prior consistent description of the defendant was admissible as a prior consistent statement.

United States v. Iaconetti, 406 F. Supp. 554 (E.D.N.Y. 1976), offers an extreme example. In that case there was a total variance between the testimony of the defendant, a GSA inspector, and Mr. Lori, the Government witness from whom the defendant was alleged to have solicited a bribe. The conflict involved the defendant's claim that he had not solicited a bribe from Lori, and that Lori, in fact, had attempted to bribe him. The court held that this constituted an implied claim that Mr. Lori had lied because of improper motive — to cover up his own wrongdoing.

The opinion in *United States v. Majors,* 584 F.2d 110 (5th Cir. 1978), offers another extreme example of what a court considered as constituting an implied charge of recent fabrication. In *Majors,* a Government witness had previously entered a guilty plea to narcotics charges resulting from transactions that also constituted the basis of the charges against Majors. This witness was, in the words of the court, "subjected to vigorous and skillful cross-examination designed to discredit his testimony. . . ." The court found that this cross-examination alone constituted an implied charge of recent fabrication and justified the introduction of a prior consistent statement the witness had given to his attorney shortly after he was arrested.

The opinion in *Majors* did not specify the nature or substance of the "vigorous and skillful cross-examination" the prosecution conducted. Conceivably, it may have involved little more than attacks on the quality of the witness' perception and memory. If so, the opinion raises the question whether Congress intended Rule 801(d)(1)(B) to permit the introduction of prior consistent statements to meet a challenge to the accuracy of a witness' memory. A prior consistent statement made closer in time to the event would persuasively rebut such a challenge, but is it authorized under Rule 801(d)(1)(B)? Although there is some case authority for the proposition that attacking the reliability of a witness' memory will serve as a triggering mechanism for the use of consistent statements, the better view, as expressed by Judge Weinstein, is that "[n]ormal usage would argue that the words 'fabrication,' 'influence' and 'motive' are only intended to cover situations where the witness deliberately changes his story." 5 WEINSTEIN'S FEDERAL EVIDENCE, § 801.12[2][b], at 801–31 (Matthew Bender 2d ed.). If courts were to consider mere impeachment of the quality of a witness' memory as justifying the introduction of evidence of prior consistent statements, the exclusionary effect of the hearsay rule would be undermined; any meaningful cross-examination would pave the way for the use of all of a witness' prior consistent statements that would not otherwise be admissible because they did not fall under one of the established exceptions to the hearsay rule.

Merely presenting testimony that contradicts the testimony of a preceding witness has not been considered sufficient to raise an implied charge of recent fabrication. *Breneman v. Kennecott Corp.*, 799 F.2d 470, 472 (9th Cir. 1986). Usually the proponent of the consistent statement must "point to specific questions during his adversary's examination that suggest fabrication or bias." *United States v. Lozada-Rivera*, 177 F.3d 98 (1st Cir. 1999).

EXERCISE

Defendant was arrested and charged with various criminal offenses stemming from his participation in the Latin Kings gang. At trial another gang member, Rios, agreed to testify as a prosecution witness. Rios explained that Defendant had complained about being unsatisfied with his take from a drug robbery. Defendant did not cross-examine Rios about this statement, although he was given an opportunity to do so. Instead, later in the trial, Defendant attempted to impeach Rios by calling a Drug Enforcement Agent to testify about an interview that she conducted with Rios. Agent testified that her report reflects that Rios had actually said that another member of the gang (not Defendant) had been the one expressing dissatisfaction with his take from the robbery. On cross-examination of Agent, the government wants to elicit the fact that Rios had previously mentioned both the Defendant and this other gang member during the interview, even though Agent's report does not reflect that fact. Defendant objects to the cross-examination on hearsay grounds. How should the court rule?

[3]   Statements of Identification: Rule 801(d)(1)(C)

"After Perceiving the Person": Rule 801(d)(1)(C) excludes from the hearsay rule statements of personal identification made after perceiving the person identified. What does perceiving mean? Are only prior corporeal identifications admissible and not photographic identifications? Or is the provision referring only to the declarant's initial perception of the person, rather than the means of making the identification? The court in *United States v. Marchand*, 564 F.2d 983 (2nd Cir. 1977), *cert. denied*, 434 U.S. 1015 (1978), addressed these questions by interpreting Rule 801(d)(1)(C) as allowing witness identifications from photographs and sketches of a person the witness had "initially perceived."

A witness who testifies — and is thus subject to cross-examination — may describe a prior identification of an individual. But is a witness, who previously made an identification, but is not able to recall anything about the identification, available for cross-examination? *Tome* answers this question.

UNITED STATES v. OWENS
United States Supreme Court
484 U.S. 554 (1988)

JUSTICE SCALIA delivered the opinion of the Court.

This case requires us to determine whether either the Confrontation Clause of the Sixth Amendment or Rule 802 of the Federal Rules of Evidence bars testimony concerning a prior, out-of-court identification when the identifying witness is unable, because of memory loss, to explain the basis for the identification.

I

On April 12, 1982, John Foster, a correctional counselor at the federal prison in Lompoc, California, was attacked and brutally beaten with a metal pipe. His skull was fractured, and he remained hospitalized for almost a month. As a result of his injuries, Foster's memory was severely impaired. When Thomas Mansfield, an FBI agent investigating the assault, first attempted to interview Foster, on April 19, he found Foster lethargic and unable to remember his attacker's name. On May 5, Mansfield again spoke to Foster, who was much improved and able to describe the attack. Foster named respondent as his attacker and identified respondent from an array of photographs.

Respondent was tried in Federal District Court for assault with intent to commit murder under 18 U.S.C. § 113(a). At trial, Foster recounted his activities just before the attack, and described feeling the blows to his head and seeing blood on the floor. He testified that he clearly remembered identifying respondent as his assailant during his May 5th interview with Mansfield. On cross-examination, he admitted that he could not remember seeing his assailant. He also admitted that, although there was evidence that he had received numerous visitors in the hospital, he was unable to remember any of them except Mansfield, and could not remember whether any of these visitors had suggested that respondent was the assailant. Defense counsel unsuccessfully sought to refresh his recollection with hospital records, including one indicating that Foster had attributed the assault to someone other than respondent. Respondent was convicted and sentenced to 20 years' imprisonment to be served consecutively to a previous sentence.

On appeal, the United States Court of Appeals for the Ninth Circuit considered challenges based on the Confrontation Clause and Rule 802 of the Federal Rules of Evidence.[1] By divided vote it upheld both challenges (though finding the Rule 802

---

[1] This case has been argued, both here and below, as though Federal Rule of Evidence 801(d)(1)(C) were the basis of the challenge. That is substantially but not technically correct. If respondent's arguments are accepted, it is Rule 802 that would render the out-of-court statement inadmissible as

violation harmless error), and reversed the judgment of the District Court. 789 F.2d 750 (1986). We granted certiorari, 479 U.S. 1084, 107 S.Ct. 1284, 94 L.Ed.2d 143 (1987), to resolve the conflict with other Circuits on the significance of a hearsay declarant's memory loss both with respect to the Confrontation Clause, see, *e.g., United States ex rel. Thomas v. Cuyler,* 548 F.2d 460, 462-463 (CA3 1977), and with respect to Rule 802, see, *e.g., United States v. Lewis,* 565 F.2d 1248, 1252 (CA2 1977), cert. denied, 435 U.S. 973, 98 S.Ct. 1618, 56 L.Ed.2d 66 (1978).

II

The Confrontation Clause of the Sixth Amendment gives the accused the right "to be confronted with the witnesses against him." This has long been read as securing an adequate opportunity to cross-examine adverse witnesses. See, *e.g., Mattox v. United States,* 156 U.S. 237, 242–243, 15 S.Ct. 337, 339, 39 L.Ed. 409 (1895); *Douglas v. Alabama,* 380 U.S. 415, 418, 85 S.Ct. 1074, 1076, 13 L.Ed.2d 934 (1965). This Court has never held that a Confrontation Clause violation can be founded upon a witness' loss of memory, but in two cases has expressly left that possibility open.

In *California v. Green,* 399 U.S. 149, 157–164, 90 S.Ct. 1930, 1934–38, 26 L.Ed.2d 489 (1970), we found no constitutional violation in the admission of testimony that had been given at a preliminary hearing, relying on (as one of two independent grounds) the proposition that the opportunity to cross-examine the witness at trial satisfied the Sixth Amendment's requirements. We declined, however, to decide the admissibility of the same witness' out-of-court statement to a police officer concerning events that at trial he was unable to recall. In remanding on this point, we noted that the state court had not considered, and the parties had not briefed, the possibility that the witness' memory loss so affected the petitioner's right to cross-examine as to violate the Confrontation Clause. *Id.,* at 168–169, 90 S. Ct., at 1940–41. Justice Harlan, in a scholarly concurrence, stated that he would have reached the issue of the out-of-court statement, and would have held that a witness' inability to "recall either the underlying events that are the subject of an extra-judicial statement or previous testimony or recollect the circumstances under which the statement was given, does not have Sixth Amendment consequence." *Id.,* at 188, 90 S.Ct., at 1951.

In *Delaware v. Fensterer,* 474 U.S. 15, 106 S. Ct. 292, 88 L. Ed. 2d 15 (1985) (*per curiam*), we determined that there was no Confrontation Clause violation when an expert witness testified as to what opinion he had formed, but could not recollect the basis on which he had formed it. We said:

> "The Confrontation Clause includes no guarantee that every witness called by the prosecution will refrain from giving testimony that is marred by forgetfulness, confusion, or evasion. To the contrary, the Confrontation Clause is generally satisfied when the defense is given a full and fair opportunity to probe and expose these infirmities through cross-

---

hearsay; but as explained in Part III, it is ultimately Rule 801(d)(1)(C) that determines whether Rule 802 is applicable.

examination, thereby calling to the attention of the factfinder the reasons for giving scant weight to the witness' testimony." *Id.,* at 21–22, 106 S.Ct., at 295.

Our opinion noted that a defendant seeking to discredit a forgetful expert witness is not without ammunition, since the jury may be persuaded that "his opinion is as unreliable as his memory." *Id.,* at 19, 106 S.Ct., at 294. We distinguished, however, the unresolved issue in *Green* on the basis that that involved the introduction of an out-of-court statement. 474 U.S., at 18, 106 S. Ct., at 294. Justice STEVENS, concurring in the judgment, suggested that the question at hand was in fact quite close to the question left open in *Green.* 474 U.S., at 23–24, 106 S.Ct., at 296.

Here that question is squarely presented, and we agree with the answer suggested 18 years ago by Justice Harlan. "[T]he Confrontation Clause guarantees only 'an *opportunity* for effective cross-examination, not cross-examination that is effective in whatever way, and to whatever extent, the defense might wish.'" *Kentucky v. Stincer,* 482 U.S. 730, 739, 107 S.Ct. 2658, 2664, 96 L.Ed.2d 631 (1987), quoting *Fensterer, supra,* 474 U.S., at 20, 106 S.Ct., at 294 (emphasis added); *Delaware v. Van Arsdall,* 475 U.S. 673, 679, 106 S.Ct. 1431, 1435, 89 L.Ed.2d 674 (1986); *Ohio v. Roberts,* 448 U.S. 56, 73, n. 12, 100 S.Ct. 2531, 2543, n. 12, 65 L.Ed.2d 597 (1980). As *Fensterer* demonstrates, that opportunity is not denied when a witness testifies as to his current belief but is unable to recollect the reason for that belief. It is sufficient that the defendant has the opportunity to bring out such matters as the witness' bias, his lack of care and attentiveness, his poor eyesight, and even (what is often a prime objective of cross-examination, see 3A J. Wigmore, Evidence § 995, pp. 931–932 (J. Chadbourn rev. 1970)) the very fact that he has a bad memory. If the ability to inquire into these matters suffices to establish the constitutionally requisite opportunity for cross-examination when a witness testifies as to his current belief, the basis for which he cannot recall, we see no reason why it should not suffice when the witness' past belief is introduced and he is unable to recollect the reason for that past belief. In both cases the foundation for the belief (current or past) cannot effectively be elicited, but other means of impugning the belief are available. Indeed, if there is any difference in persuasive impact between the statement "I believe this to be the man who assaulted me, but can't remember why" and the statement "I don't know whether this is the man who assaulted me, but I told the police I believed so earlier," the former would seem, if anything, more damaging and hence give rise to a greater need for memory-testing, if that is to be considered essential to an opportunity for effective cross-examination. We conclude with respect to this latter example, as we did in *Fensterer* with respect to the former, that it is not. The weapons available to impugn the witness' statement when memory loss is asserted will of course not always achieve success, but successful cross-examination is not the constitutional guarantee. They are, however, realistic weapons, as is demonstrated by defense counsel's summation in this very case, which emphasized Foster's memory loss and argued that his identification of respondent was the result of the suggestions of people who visited him in the hospital.

Our constitutional analysis is not altered by the fact that the testimony here involved an out-of-court identification that would traditionally be categorized as hearsay. See Advisory Committee's Notes on Fed. Rule Evid. 801(d)(1)(C), 28 U.S.C. App., p. 717. This Court has recognized a partial (and somewhat indeterminate) overlap between the requirements of the traditional hearsay rule and the Confrontation Clause. See *Green*, 399 U.S., at 155–156, 90 S.Ct., at 1933–34; *id.*, at 173, 90 S.Ct., at 1943 (Harlan, J., concurring). The dangers associated with hearsay inspired the Court of Appeals in the present case to believe that the Constitution required the testimony to be examined for "indicia of reliability," *Dutton v. Evans*, 400 U.S. 74, 89, 91 S.Ct. 210, 220, 27 L.Ed.2d 213 (1970), or "particularized guarantees of trustworthiness," *Roberts, supra*, at 66, 100 S.Ct., at 2539. We do not think such an inquiry is called for when a hearsay declarant is present at trial and subject to unrestricted cross-examination. In that situation, as the Court recognized in *Green*, the traditional protections of the oath, cross-examination, and opportunity for the jury to observe the witness' demeanor satisfy the constitutional requirements. 399 U.S., at 158–161, 90 S.Ct., at 1935–36. We do not think that a constitutional line drawn by the Confrontation Clause falls between a forgetful witness' live testimony that he once believed this defendant to be the perpetrator of the crime, and the introduction of the witness' earlier statement to that effect.

Respondent has argued that this Court's jurisprudence concerning suggestive identification procedures shows the special dangers of identification testimony, and the special importance of cross-examination when such hearsay is proffered. See, *e.g., Manson v. Brathwaite*, 432 U.S. 98, 97 S.Ct. 2243, 53 L.Ed.2d 140 (1977); *Neil v. Biggers*, 409 U.S. 188, 93 S.Ct. 375, 34 L.Ed.2d 401 (1972). Respondent has not, however, argued that the identification procedure used here was in any way suggestive. There does not appear in our opinions, and we decline to adopt today, the principle that, because of the mere possibility of suggestive procedures, out-of-court statements of identification are inherently less reliable than other out-of-court statements.

III

Respondent urges as an alternative basis for affirmance a violation of Federal Rule of Evidence 802, which generally excludes hearsay. Rule 801(d)(1)(C) defines as not hearsay a prior statement "of identification of a person made after perceiving the person," if the declarant "testifies at the trial or hearing and is subject to cross-examination concerning the statement." The Court of Appeals found that Foster's identification statement did not come within this exclusion because his memory loss prevented his being "subject to cross-examination concerning the statement." Although the Court of Appeals concluded that the violation of the Rules of Evidence was harmless (applying for purposes of that determination a "more-probable-than-not" standard, rather than the "beyond-a-reasonable-doubt" standard applicable to the Confrontation Clause violation, see *Delaware v. Van Arsdall*, 475 U.S., at 684, 106 S.Ct., at 1438), respondent argues to the contrary.

It seems to us that the more natural reading of "subject to cross-examination concerning the statement" includes what was available here. Ordinarily a witness is regarded as "subject to cross-examination" when he is placed on the stand, under oath, and responds willingly to questions. Just as with the constitutional prohibition, limitations on the scope of examination by the trial court or assertions of privilege by the witness may undermine the process to such a degree that meaningful cross-examination within the intent of the Rule no longer exists. But that effect is not produced by the witness' assertion of memory loss-which, as discussed earlier, is often the very result sought to be produced by cross-examination, and can be effective in destroying the force of the prior statement. Rule 801(d)(1)(C), which specifies that the cross-examination need only "concer[n] the statement," does not on its face require more.

This reading seems even more compelling when the Rule is compared with Rule 804(a)(3), which defines "[u]navailability as a witness" to include situations in which a declarant "testifies to a lack of memory of the subject matter of the declarant's statement." Congress plainly was aware of the recurrent evidentiary problem at issue here-witness forgetfulness of an underlying event-but chose not to make it an exception to Rule 801(d)(1)(C).

The reasons for that choice are apparent from the Advisory Committee's Notes on Rule 801 and its legislative history. The premise for Rule 801(d)(1)(C) was that, given adequate safeguards against suggestiveness, out-of-court identifications were generally preferable to courtroom identifications. Advisory Committee's Notes on Rule 801, 28 U.S.C. App., p. 717. Thus, despite the traditional view that such statements were hearsay, the Advisory Committee believed that their use was to be fostered rather than discouraged. Similarly, the House Report on the Rule noted that since, "[a]s time goes by, a witness' memory will fade and his identification will become less reliable," minimizing the barriers to admission of more contemporaneous identification is fairer to defendants and prevents "cases falling through because the witness can no longer recall the identity of the person he saw commit the crime." H.R.Rep. No. 94-355, p. 3 (1975). See also S.Rep. No. 94-199, p. 2 (1975), U.S.Code Cong. & Admin.News, 1975, pp. 1092, 1094. To judge from the House and Senate Reports, Rule 801(d)(1)(C) was in part directed to the very problem here at issue: a memory loss that makes it impossible for the witness to provide an in-court identification or testify about details of the events underlying an earlier identification.

Respondent argues that this reading is impermissible because it creates an internal inconsistency in the Rules, since the forgetful witness who is deemed "subject to cross-examination" under 801(d)(1)(C) is simultaneously deemed "unavailable" under 804(a)(3). This is the position espoused by a prominent commentary on the Rules, see 4 J. Weinstein & M. Berger, Weinstein's Evidence 801-120 to 801-121, 801-178 (1987). It seems to us, however, that this is not a substantive inconsistency, but only a semantic oddity resulting from the fact that Rule 804(a) has for convenience of reference in Rule 804(b) chosen to describe the circumstances necessary in order to admit certain categories of hearsay testimony under the rubric "Unavailability as a witness." These circumstances include not only absence from the hearing, but also claims of privilege, refusals to obey a court's order to testify, and inability to testify based on physical or mental illness or memory loss. Had the rubric instead been "unavailability as a witness, memory loss, and other special circumstances" there would be no apparent inconsistency with Rule 801, which is a definition section excluding certain statements entirely from the category of "hearsay." The semantic inconsistency exists not only with respect to Rule 801(d)(1)(C), but also with respect to the other subparagraphs of Rule 801(d)(1). It would seem strange, for example, to assert that a witness can avoid introduction of testimony from a prior proceeding that is inconsistent with his trial testimony, see Rule 801(d)(1)(A), by simply asserting lack of memory of the facts to which the prior testimony related. See *United States v. Murphy,* 696 F.2d 282, 283–284 (CA4 1982), cert. denied, 461 U.S. 945, 103 S.Ct. 2123, 77 L.Ed.2d 1303 (1983). But that situation, like this one, presents the verbal curiosity that the witness is "subject to cross-examination" under Rule 801 while at the same time "unavailable" under Rule 804(a)(3). Quite obviously, the two characterizations are made for two entirely different purposes and there is no requirement or expectation that they should coincide.

For the reasons stated, we hold that neither the Confrontation Clause nor Federal Rule of Evidence 802 is violated by admission of an identification statement of a witness who is unable, because of a memory loss, to testify concerning the basis for the identification. The decision of the Court of Appeals is reversed, and the case is remanded for proceedings consistent with this opinion.

So ordered.

JUSTICE KENNEDY took no part in the consideration or decision of this case.

JUSTICE BRENNAN, with whom JUSTICE MARSHALL joins, dissenting.

In an interview during his month-long hospitalization, in what was apparently a singular moment of lucid recollection, John Foster selected respondent James Owens' photograph from an array of possible suspects and informed FBI Agent Thomas Mansfield that it was respondent who had attacked him with a metal pipe on the morning of April 12, 1982. Had Foster subsequently died from his injuries, there is no doubt that both the Sixth Amendment and the Federal Rules of Evidence would have barred Mansfield from repeating Foster's out-of-court identification at trial. Fortunately, Foster survived the beating; his memory, however, did not, and by the time of respondent's trial he could no longer recall his assailant or explain why he had previously identified respondent as such. This profound memory loss, therefore, rendered Foster no less a conduit for stale and inscrutable evidence than Mansfield would have been, yet the Court nevertheless concludes that because defense counsel was afforded an unrestricted opportunity to cross-examine him, Foster's unadorned reiteration of his earlier statement did not deprive respondent of his constitutional right to confront the witness against him. In my view, the Court today reduces the right of confrontation to a purely procedural protection, and a markedly hollow one at that. Because I believe the Sixth Amendment guarantees criminal defendants the right to engage in cross-examination sufficient to "affor[d] the trier of fact a satisfactory basis for evaluating the truth of [a] prior statement," *California v. Green,* 399 U.S. 149, 161, 90 S.Ct. 1930, 1936, 26 L.Ed.2d 489 (1970), and because respondent clearly was not afforded such an opportunity here, I dissent.

I

On April 12, 1982, Foster was brutally assaulted while on duty as a correctional counselor at the federal prison in Lompoc, California. His attacker beat him repeatedly about the head and upper body with a metal pipe, inflicting numerous and permanently disabling injuries, one of which was a profound loss of short-term memory. Foster spent nearly a month in the hospital recuperating from his injuries, much of that time in a state of semiconsciousness. Although numerous people visited him, including his wife who visited daily, Foster remembered none except Agent Mansfield. While he had no recollection of Mansfield's first visit on April 19, he testified that his memory of the interview Mansfield conducted on May 5 was "vivid." App. 28. In particular, he recalled telling Mansfield: "[A]fter I was hit I looked down and saw the blood on the floor, and jammed my finger into Owens' chest, and said, 'That's enough of that,' and hit my alarm button." *Id.*, at 31.

Foster testified that at the time he made these statements, he was certain that his memory was accurate. In addition, he recalled choosing respondent's photograph from those Mansfield showed him. There is no dispute, however, that by the time of trial Foster could no longer remember who had assaulted him or even whether he had seen his attacker. Nor could he recall whether any of the prison officials or other persons who visited him in the hospital had ever suggested that respondent had beaten him. A medical expert who testified on behalf of the prosecution explained that Foster's inability to remember most of the details of the assault was attributable to a gradual and selective memory loss caused by his head injuries.

II

The principal witness against respondent was not the John Foster who took the stand in December 1983 — that witness could recall virtually nothing of the events of April 12, 1982, and candidly admitted that he had no idea whether respondent had assaulted him. Instead, respondent's sole accuser was the John Foster who, on May 5, 1982, identified respondent as his attacker. This John Foster, however, did not testify at respondent's trial: the profound memory loss he suffered during the approximately 18 months following his identification prevented him from affirming, explaining, or elaborating upon his out-of-court statement just as surely and completely as his assertion of a testimonial privilege, or his death, would have. Thus, while the Court asserts that defense counsel had "realistic weapons" with which to impugn Foster's prior statement, *ante*, at 843, it does not and cannot claim that cross-examination could have elicited any information that would have enabled a jury to evaluate the trustworthiness or reliability of the identification. Indeed, although the Court suggests that defense counsel was able to explore Foster's "lack of care and attentiveness," his "bad memory," and the possibility that hospital visitors suggested respondent's name to him, *ante*, at 842, 843, Foster's memory loss precluded any such inquiries: he simply could not recall whether he had actually seen his assailant or even whether he had had an opportunity to see him, nor could he remember any of his visitors, let alone whether any of them had suggested that respondent had attacked him. Moreover, by the time of trial, Foster was unable to shed any light on the accuracy of his May 1982 recollection of the assault; the most he could state was that on the day of the interview he felt certain that his statements were true. As the court below found, "[c]learly, two of the three dangers surrounding Foster's out-of-court identifications-misperception and failure of memory-could not be mitigated in any way by the only cross-examination of Foster that was available to [respondent]." 789 F.2d 750, 759 (CA9 1986).

In short, neither Foster nor the prosecution could demonstrate the basis for Foster's prior identification. Nevertheless, the Court concludes that the Sixth Amendment presents no obstacle to the introduction of such an unsubstantiated out-of-court statement, at least not where the declarant testifies under oath at trial and is subjected to unrestricted cross-examination. According to the Court, the Confrontation Clause is simply a procedural trial right that "guarantees only an *opportunity* for effective cross-examination, not cross-examination that is effective in whatever way, and to whatever extent, the defense might wish." *Ante,* at 842 (citations omitted; internal quotation marks omitted; emphasis in original).

Although the Court suggests that the result it reaches today follows naturally from our earlier cases, we have never before held that the Confrontation Clause protects nothing more than a defendant's right to question live witnesses, no matter how futile that questioning might be. On the contrary, as the Court's own recitation of our prior case law reveals, we have repeatedly affirmed that the right of confrontation ensures "an opportunity for *effective* cross-examination." *Delaware v. Fensterer,* 474 U.S. 15, 20, 106 S.Ct. 292, 295, 88 L.Ed.2d 15 (1985) *(per curiam)* (emphasis added); see also *Nelson v. O'Neil,* 402 U.S. 622, 629, 91 S.Ct. 1723, 1727, 29 L.Ed.2d 222 (1971) (Confrontation Clause does not bar admission of out-of-court statement where defendant has "the benefit of full and *effective* cross-examination of [declarant]") (emphasis added); *California v. Green,* 399 U.S., at 159, 90 S.Ct., at 1935 (introduction of out-of-court statement does not violate Confrontation Clause "as long as the defendant is assured of full and *effective* cross-examination at the time of trial") (emphasis added). While we have rejected the notion that effectiveness should be measured in terms of a defendant's ultimate success, we have never, until today, equated effectiveness with the mere opportunity to pose questions. Rather, consistent with the Confrontation Clause's mission of "advanc[ing] a practical concern for the accuracy of the truth-determining process in criminal trials," *Dutton v. Evans,* 400 U.S. 74, 89, 91 S.Ct. 210, 220, 27 L.Ed.2d 213 (1970), we have suggested that the touchstone of effectiveness is whether the cross-examination affords " 'the trier of fact . . . a satisfactory basis for evaluating the truth of the prior statement.' " *Ibid.* (quoting *California v. Green, supra,* at 161, 90 S. Ct. at 1936). See also *Ohio v. Roberts,* 448 U.S. 56, 73, 100 S.Ct. 2531, 2542, 65 L.Ed.2d 597 (1980) (introduction of prior testimony where the declarant was unavailable at trial did not violate Confrontation Clause where previous cross-examination of declarant "afforded the trier of fact a satisfactory basis for evaluating the truth of the prior statement" (citation omitted; internal quotation marks omitted));[1] *Mancusi v. Stubbs,* 408 U.S. 204, 216, 92 S. Ct. 2308, 2315, 33 L.

---

[1] In *Ohio v. Roberts,* the Court indicated that, for purposes of determining the constitutional admissibility of prior testimony where the declarant is unavailable at trial, it is unnecessary to consider whether defense counsel's questioning at the prior hearing "surmount[ed] some inevitably nebulous threshold of 'effectiveness,' " and held that "in all but . . . extraordinary cases, no inquiry into 'effectiveness' is required." 448 U.S., at 73 n. 12. In so ruling, however, the Court did not dispense with

Ed. 2d 293 (1972) (same). Where no opportunity for such cross-examination exists, we have recognized that the Sixth Amendment permits the introduction of out-of-court statements only when they bear sufficient independent "indicia of reliability." *Dutton v. Evans, supra,* 400 U.S. at 89, 91 S.Ct. at 220.

In dispensing with these substantive constitutional requirements today, the Court relies almost exclusively on our decision in *Delaware v. Fensterer, supra,* a case that did not involve the introduction of prior statements. *Fensterer* concerned an expert witness' inability to remember which of three possible scientific theories he had used in formulating his opinion. Although Fensterer contended that the witness' forgetfulness made it impossible to impeach the scientific validity of his conclusions, we noted that "an expert who cannot recall the basis for his opinion invites the jury to find that his opinion is as reliable as his memory." *Id.,* 474 U.S., at 19, 106 S. Ct. at 294. While the witness' endorsement of a given scientific theory might have maximized the effectiveness of cross-examination, the Confrontation Clause guarantees only that level of effectiveness necessary to afford the factfinder a satisfactory basis for assessing the validity of the evidence offered. Thus, because the expert's inability to remember the basis for his opinion was self-impeaching, the constitutional guarantee had clearly been satisfied.

Fensterer, therefore, worked no change in our Confrontation Clause jurisprudence, yet the Court purports to discern in it a principle under which all live testimony as to a witness' past belief is constitutionally admissible, provided the defendant is afforded an opportunity to question the witness. From this the Court derives the corollary that prior statements as to past belief are equally admissible, again given the requisite opportunity for questioning the declarant at trial. Accordingly, the Court asserts, the Confrontation Clause draws no line "between a forgetful witness' live testimony that he once believed this defendant to be the perpetrator of the crime, and the introduction of the witness' earlier statement to that effect." *Ante,* at 843. The obvious shortcoming in this reasoning, of course, is that *Fensterer* announced no such blanket rule: while the expert's memory lapse in that case was self-impeaching, it does not follow-and we have therefore never held-that all forgetfulness may be so characterized. Certainly in the present case, Foster's inability in December 1983 to remember the events of April 1982 in no way impugned or otherwise cast doubt upon the accuracy or trustworthiness of his memory in May 1982, particularly in light of the uncontradicted medical testimony explaining that his forgetfulness was the result of the head injuries he sustained.

---

the Sixth Amendment's substantive minima of effectiveness, but rather rejected the claim that prior testimony should be deemed inherently unreliable where the declarant was cross-examined by an attorney whose performance is subsequently deemed ineffective in collateral habeas corpus proceedings. In this context, therefore, "effectiveness" obviously refers to the attorney's performance, not the impediments to meaningful cross-examination created by a witness' memory loss. Indeed, the footnote in question is appended to a sentence once again affirming the need for affording the factfinder an adequate basis for assessing the truth of prior statements, and the author of *Roberts* has twice since confirmed that the Sixth Amendment guarantees an opportunity for meaningful cross-examination. See *Kentucky v. Stincer,* 482 U.S. 730, 739, n. 9 (1987) (Blackmun, J.) (a state rule precluding access to certain information before trial "may hinder [the] defendant's opportunity for effective cross-examination at trial, and thus . . . may violate the Confrontation Clause"); *Pennsylvania v. Ritchie,* 480 U.S. 39, 63, n. 1 (1987) (Blackmun, J., concurring) (*Fensterer* "[did] not imply that concern about . . . effectiveness [of cross-examination] has no place in analysis under the Confrontation Clause").

Under our prior cases, then, the constitutional admissibility of Foster's prior statement, and the testimony of the Court's hypothetical witness who cannot recall the basis for his past belief, should depend on whether the memory loss so seriously impedes cross-examination that the factfinder lacks an adequate basis upon which to assess the truth of the proffered evidence. Whatever may be said of the Court's hypothetical, it is clear in the case before us that Foster's near total loss of memory precluded any meaningful examination or assessment of his out-of-court statement and thus should have barred the admission of that statement.

To the extent the Court's ruling is motivated by the fear that a contrary result will open the door to countless Confrontation Clause challenges to the admission of out-of-court statements, that fear is groundless. To begin with, cases such as the present one will be rare indeed. More typically, witnesses asserting a memory loss will either not suffer (or claim) a total inability to recollect, or will do so under circumstances that suggest bias or ulterior motive; in either case, given the threshold of "effectiveness" established by our prior decisions, the witness' partial memory or self-interest in claiming a complete memory loss will afford the factfinder an adequate basis upon which to evaluate the reliability and trustworthiness of the out-of-court statement. Even in those relatively few cases where no such basis can be elicited, the prior statement is still admissible if it bears independent "indicia of reliability." Finally, assessments of "effectiveness" for Confrontation Clause purposes are no different than those undertaken by courts in deciding common evidentiary questions, and thus should not prove unduly burdensome.[2] In any event, to the extent such assessments prove inconvenient or troublesome, those burdens flow from our commitment to a Constitution that places a greater value on individual liberty than on efficient judicial administration.

III

I agree with the Court that the Confrontation Clause does not guarantee defendants the right to confront only those witnesses whose testimony is not marred by forgetfulness, confusion, or evasion, and that the right of confrontation " 'is generally satisfied when the defense is given a full and fair opportunity to probe and expose these infirmities through cross-examination.' " *Ante,* at 842 (quoting *Fensterer,* 474 U.S., at 22, 106 S.Ct., at 296). But as we stressed just last Term, this right to cross-examination "is essentially a 'functional' right designed to promote reliability in the truth-finding functions of a criminal trial." *Kentucky v. Stincer,* 482 U.S. 730, 737, 107 S.Ct. 2658, 2663, 96 L.Ed.2d 631 (1987). In the present case,

---

[2] Indeed, in a case such as this one, the inquiry into the constitutional adequacy of defendant's opportunity for cross-examination is identical to that required under Federal Rule of Evidence 804(a)(3), which deems a declarant "unavailable" if, at trial, he or she "testifies to a lack of memory of the subject matter of the declarant's [prior] statement." The Court today, of course, concludes that notwithstanding Rule 804(a)'s definition of unavailability, a prior identification is not hearsay under Rule 801(d)(1)(C), and is therefore admissible, as long as the declarant is subject to cross-examination concerning the statement itself, regardless of whether the declarant can recall the basis for that statement. Because I believe such a construction of Rule 801(d)(1)(C) renders it unconstitutional under the Confrontation Clause, I would require, consistent with Rule 804(a), that the declarant be subject to cross-examination as to the subject matter of the prior statement. See 4 J. Weinstein & M. Berger, Weinstein's Evidence 801-120 to 801-121 (1987) (endorsing such a construction of Rule 801(d)(1)(C)).

respondent Owens was afforded no opportunity to probe and expose the infirmities of Foster's May 5, 1982, recollections, for here cross-examination, the "greatest legal engine ever invented for the discovery of truth," *California v. Green*, 399 U.S., at 158, 90 S.Ct. at 1935, stood as helpless as current medical technology before Foster's profound memory loss. In concluding that respondent's Sixth Amendment rights were satisfied by Foster's mere presence in the courtroom, the Court reduces the right of confrontation to a hollow formalism. Because I believe the Confrontation Clause guarantees more than the right to ask questions of a live witness, no matter how dead that witness' memory proves to be, I dissent.

[B]   Admissions

The Party Admission Doctrine, Fed. R. Evid. 801(d)(2), allows for the introduction for a great deal of statements that would otherwise be excluded. Essentially anything a party to a lawsuit says is admissible. A statement made by the party himself can make the statement, a statement he adopts from another, a statement by one authorized to speak on his behalf, and any statement made by any member of his criminal conspiracy qualifies as admission.

[1]   Who Is a Party Opponent?

HARRIS v. UNITED STATES
District of Columbia Court of Appeals
834 A.2d 106 (2003)

GLICKMAN, ASSOCIATE JUDGE:

Michael Harris was charged with the first degree murder of James Monroe, who was shot to death on July 28, 1995. Harris argued that he acted in self-defense. Harris claimed that James Monroe's nephew Donald Monroe had a grudge against Harris and had ordered James Monroe and another man named Thaddeus Lowe to kill Harris. Harris's first trial ended in a mistrial after the jury deadlocked; after retrial a jury convicted Harris of the lesser-included offense of voluntary manslaughter and related charges of possession of a firearm during a crime of violence and carrying a pistol without a license.

The centerpiece of Harris's self-defense theory was his allegation that James Monroe and Thaddeus Lowe had attempted to kill Harris on July 28, 1995, at Donald Monroe's urging. In confirmation of this theory, Harris claimed that Donald Monroe had tried to have him killed on another occasion by ordering Charles Minnis to shoot Harris on April 23, 1996, an attack that left Harris a paraplegic. To support his self-defense theory, Harris offered his own testimony and attempted to offer two additional pieces of evidence: an application in support of a search warrant for Donald Monroe's residence sworn to by Metropolitan Police Officer James L. Trainum and approved by an Assistant United States Attorney (hereafter "Trainum Affidavit"), which asserted that there was probable cause to believe that Donald Monroe conspired in the April 1996 attempt to murder Harris; and the testimony of Dwayne Drummond, who testified before a grand jury that he saw Donald Monroe's car drive by on the night Harris was shot. Neither piece of evidence was presented to the jury. The trial court ruled that the Trainum Affidavit was inadmissible hearsay, rejecting Harris's contention that the affidavit was a party admission by the government. When Drummond, who was under subpoena, failed to appear to testify, the trial court refused defense counsel's request to send marshals to Drummond's Baltimore residence and rejected defense counsel's alternative proposal to admit Drummond's grand jury testimony under the prior recorded testimony exception to the rule against hearsay.

We hold that the government adopted the conclusions in the Trainum Affidavit regarding probable cause when an Assistant United States Attorney signed and approved the affidavit for submission to the court with an application for a search warrant. The conclusion that probable cause existed to believe that Donald Monroe conspired to kill Harris was, therefore, an adoptive admission by a party that was admissible against the government. It was error to exclude this statement. Whether the government also adopted other statements contained in the Trainum Affidavit is a factual question that should be addressed in the first instance by the trial court on remand. We further hold that the trial court erred by failing to send marshals to secure Drummond's testimony. Because the excluded affidavit and Drummond's testimony would have been the only evidence corroborating Harris's testimony, the trial court's errors were not harmless. We, therefore, reverse Harris's convictions and remand for a new trial.

I.

The government presented the testimony of two witnesses to James Monroe's death, only one of whom claimed to have seen the shooting. Thaddeus Lowe testified that he was with Monroe on July 28, 1995. Both men had been drinking, and Lowe testified that Monroe "looked like he had some PCP."[1] Lowe testified that James Monroe was intoxicated and "fumbling around" to the point that Lowe dropped Monroe off at his house, intending to leave him there. Later, however, Monroe approached Lowe while Lowe was making a call at a phone booth at North Capitol and R Streets, N.E. Monroe asked Lowe to take him down the block so that he could buy PCP. Lowe agreed and drove Monroe to 1st and R Streets, N.E. Monroe exited the car and approached Michael Harris, whom Lowe knew as "Jug." Lowe, still sitting in his car, saw Monroe give Harris some money and saw Harris give Monroe something in return. Lowe testified that Monroe and Harris were "talking and laughing" and that they began walking to Lowe's car. Lowe then heard Monroe challenge Harris by saying, "go head, young 'un, before I slap you" to Harris. *Id.* Lowe urged Harris to ignore Monroe's comment. Monroe began getting in the car when Harris reached behind a nearby wall, picked up a gun, and fired twice at Monroe.

Lowe testified that he drove Monroe to the hospital and left him there without speaking to the police. Lowe went to James and Donald Monroe's home, where he talked to Donald Monroe and other members of James's family before going to his own home. Lowe did not contact the police until he saw several police officers

---

[1] The parties stipulated that James Monroe had PCP in his system at the time of his death.

inspecting his car, at which point he approached the officers and gave a statement. Lowe's statement to the police differed in significant respects from his trial testimony. Lowe told the police that he did not give Monroe a ride, did not know why Monroe was on R Street, and did not know whether Monroe was high on PCP. Most significantly, Lowe said that Monroe was killed by a man named "Chub." Lowe explained this inconsistency at trial by claiming that he was "shaken" and meant to say "Jug."

The government also presented the testimony of Marc Queen, Harris's cousin, who testified that he was with Harris on R Street on July 28, 1995. Queen claimed that he saw Lowe and Monroe drive up the street in Lowe's car and saw Monroe get out and approach Harris. Queen did not see any money or other objects exchanged between Harris and Monroe. According to Queen, Monroe and Harris argued "for a minute." Harris then walked over to Queen and asked him to get Harris's gun from his apartment. Queen initially refused but then complied with the request after Harris asked him again. Queen testified that he retrieved the gun, gave it to Harris, and walked away. Harris and Monroe continued arguing until Harris "pulled [the gun] up." Queen said he closed his eyes and did not see the shooting but "heard like three shots." The defense impeached Queen with his statements to the grand jury that Harris got the gun himself, which Queen admitted were "lies."

Several officers and forensic experts testified that James Monroe was killed by a single gunshot to the back and that one other bullet was retrieved from the door frame of Lowe's car. Detective Donald Bell testified that after Harris was arrested, he denied any involvement in the shooting and tried to place blame on Damion Nicholson, a man who Harris claimed looked just like him.

With the exception of a Howard University Hospital employee called briefly to admit medical records, Michael Harris was the only witness for the defense. Harris testified that a week before he shot James Monroe, Harris won several hundred dollars from Donald Monroe in a dice game. Donald Monroe told Harris "that I [Harris] didn't deserve his money" and punched Harris. Harris knocked Monroe down after a brief fistfight. As Harris left the scene, he heard Donald Monroe say, "I'm gonna get your ass." On July 28, 1995, Harris was hanging around on R Street when a car came up the street. James Monroe was in the car along with Thaddeus Lowe. According to Harris, James Monroe "leaped out and started screaming and shouting at me." Monroe said that "Donald sent him down there to get his money back." Harris said he had no money. Monroe told Harris, "You think I'm playing? I'll slap a cap in your ass." Monroe started walking toward his car. Then, Harris testified, the "[n]ext thing I know I heard a shot come out [of] the car then Mark [sic] Queen handed me his gun and I closed my eyes and I shot back towards the car." Harris later clarified that Lowe was the one shooting at him. Harris testified that he fired because "I was scared for my life, I thought he was about to kill me." He denied ever selling Monroe drugs.

Harris was held in the D.C. Jail until March 17, 1996. Five weeks after his release, on April 23, 1996, Harris was shot several times by Charles Minnis and was left paralyzed. Harris testified that just before he was shot, Donald Monroe's car "rolled past" and Minnis then approached him on foot and shot him. Harris also testified that a friend named Maurice Jackson told him that Donald Monroe was driving and that Minnis emerged from the back seat of the car. (This hearsay was admitted without objection.)

The prosecutor questioned Harris's claim that Donald Monroe was involved in either shooting. She cross-examined Harris about his failure to pick Donald Monroe out of a photo array that Detective Trainum showed Harris after he was shot. The prosecutor also questioned Harris about his failure to mention Donald Monroe when Harris was first arrested for shooting James Monroe in September 1995. The government called Detective Trainum to testify in rebuttal that when he questioned Harris in the hospital, Harris identified Minnis as his assailant and had no reaction to Donald Monroe's photo.

In closing argument, the government contended that Michael Harris's claim that Donald Monroe was involved in shooting him was a recent fabrication:

> What makes sense about what Michael Harris told you? What doesn't? What doesn't make sense is the first photograph in this array [shown to Harris by Trainum] is of Donnie Monroe. And Michael Harris didn't nod, he didn't put an X on the back of it, take it out and take a look. He didn't do anything with respect to Donnie Monroe. In fact, his face didn't even react to Donnie Monroe. . . .

> He didn't say a word about Donnie Monroe. So I'm asking you, ladies and gentlemen, to look when the defendant first says anything about Donnie Monroe. . . .

> I submit to you, ladies and gentlemen, that the name Damion Nicholson did not [sic] and neither does the name Donnie Monroe. Because, ladies and gentlemen, the evidence in this case is not that this cycle of violence started with some silly school yard spat over at the rec center over some craps game. The cycle of violence in this case, ladies and gentlemen, started when Michael Harris picked up a gun and shot a defenseless, unarmed man in the back like a coward.

II.

A.

At both his trials, Harris attempted to introduce the Trainum Affidavit as evidence supporting his self-defense theory. The Trainum Affidavit was submitted on August 27, 1996, to Superior Court Judge Dorsey in support of an application for a search warrant for the residence of Donald Monroe. The affidavit was "subscribed and sworn to" before Judge Dorsey by Detective James Trainum. Before it was submitted to the court, the affidavit was approved by an Assistant United States Attorney, as is the practice in this jurisdiction. *Cf.* 28 C.F.R. § 60.1 (2003) ("[O]nly in the very rare and emergent case is the law enforcement officer permitted to seek a search warrant without the concurrence of the appropriate U.S. Attorney's office."). On each page of the Trainum Affidavit, Clifford T. Keenan wrote the word "approved" and signed his name, identifying himself as an "AUSA."

In his affidavit, Trainum reported information evidencing that Donald Monroe paid Charles Minnis to kill Michael Harris. Trainum reported that one witness saw Donald Monroe's car drive by a few minutes before Minnis shot Harris. This witness saw Minnis driving the car. Trainum also related that several witnesses said that Donald Monroe planned to pay Minnis to kill Harris and that after Minnis was arrested, he asked Monroe to use the money to pay for an attorney. Trainum concluded that he had probable cause to believe that Donald Monroe hired Charles Minnis to kill Harris:

> Based on the above described set of facts and circumstances, the affiant has probable cause to believe that Donald Monroe and Charles Minnis conspired to murder Michael Harris. Donald Monroe's part in the conspiracy was to pay Charles Minnis for the murder and to loan Minnis his car to search for the victim. The payment was to be in the form of money which are [sic] the proceeds of drug sales. Such drug sales take place from Donald Monroe's residence, located at 19 T Street, Northeast, Washington, DC. Since the arrest of Charles Minnis, Donald Monroe has been directed to use the "murder for hire" money to pay Charles Minnis' attorney. The affiant has probable cause to believe that evidence of such criminal activity is currently present inside of 19 T Street, Northeast, and requests a search warrant for that location . . . .

During Harris's first trial, defense counsel argued that the Trainum Affidavit was a party admission that was admissible against the government under *Freeland v. United States*, 631 A.2d 1186 (D.C. 1993), and *United States v. Morgan*, 189 U.S. App. D.C. 155, 581 F.2d 933 (1978). Counsel argued that the affidavit was particularly important as "corroboration evidence" to support Harris's testimony and expressed willingness to redact any inadmissible information from the affidavit. The trial court agreed that the Trainum Affidavit was relevant to Harris's defense because the defense theory that Donald Monroe sent James Monroe to kill Harris was "more likely true if [Donald Monroe] acted consistent with that theory, even after [Harris killed James Monroe]." The court nonetheless ruled that the affidavit would be excluded from evidence. The court reasoned that the hearsay statements of witnesses reported in the affidavit should not be admitted because the government was not "vouching" for the truth of those statements. The court also reasoned from what it perceived to be the purpose of the Trainum Affidavit that the government had endorsed only the "irrelevant" statements in the affidavit regarding drug trafficking at Donald Monroe's residence and not the statements regarding Donald Monroe's participation in a conspiracy to kill Michael Harris:

> The affidavit seeks evidence to prove that Donald Monroe is a drug dealer and not that Donald Monroe conspired to murder Michael Harris.

> Given the purpose — the stated purpose of the warrant affidavit, given the distinction of the warrant affidavit between just a report of what people say and the confirmed and corroborated reports of what others say, it's clear that what the Government was vouching for were the facts that were in support of a finding of probable cause to believe that inside of 19 T Street Northeast, there was evidence of drug trafficking, period, and as a result, the Government should be foreclosed from denying that there is evidence of drug trafficking inside of 19 T Street, which is irrelevant to our case.

To the extent that there is a comment — or even sentences in this affidavit that suggest the detective's opinion that Donnie Monroe had a basis for and an intent to pay for the death or the murder or the shooting of Michael Harris, none of that is corroborated in the warrant affidavit. It is not a statement. These are not statements I can conclude the Government swore were true as opposed to just truly spoken and were basically tangential, or irrelevant, to the purpose for which the warrant affidavit . . . was submitted.

Defense counsel pointed out that Detective Trainum's ultimate conclusion that Donald Monroe had conspired to murder Harris did not include multiple levels of hearsay, but the court reaffirmed its ruling without comment.

At Harris's second trial, defense counsel again argued for the admission of the Trainum Affidavit. The trial court again concluded that the affidavit was inadmissible. The court reasoned that admitting the government's stated views of the facts would invade the province of the jury to determine the facts for itself.

B.

"We have adopted the substance of Federal Rule of Evidence 801(d)(2) on 'admission by party-opponent,' and deem such statements to be admissible into evidence." *Johnson v. Leuthongchak*, 772 A.2d 249, 250 (D.C. 2001). Rule 801(d)(2) applies to out-of-court statements offered against a party that are:

> (A) the party's own statement in either an individual or representative capacity or (B) a statement of which the party has manifested an adoption or belief in its truth, or (C) a statement by a person authorized by the party to make a statement concerning the subject, or (D) a statement by the party's agent or servant concerning a matter within the scope of the agency or employment, made during the existence of the relationship, or (E) a statement by a coconspirator of a party during the course of and in furtherance of the conspiracy.

Party admissions differ from most out-of-court statements in that their admissibility does not require the demonstration of "guarantee[s] of trustworthiness" but is based rather upon the identity of the speaker. FED. R. EVID. 801 advisory committee's note. Therefore, "[p]arty admissions do not require foundations to be admissible as substantive evidence; they need not have been made on personal knowledge and may be in opinion form." *In re M.D.*, 758 A.2d 27, 32 (D.C. 2000). So long as the statement is fairly attributable to the party, "it makes no difference whether the adopting party had any personal knowledge of the truth of the matters mentioned in the statement." 5 WEINSTEIN'S FEDERAL EVIDENCE § 801.31[3][b] (2003); *accord*, 2 MCCORMICK ON EVIDENCE § 255, at 139–40 (5th ed. 1999); 4 WIGMORE, EVIDENCE § 1053(1), at 16 (Chadbourn rev. 1972); FED. R. EVID. 801 advisory committee's note.

One rationale for this "generous treatment" of party admissions, *id.*, is a party's ability to rebut the out-of-court statement by "put[ting] himself on the stand and explain[ing] his former assertion." *Chaabi v. United States*, 544 A.2d 1247, 1248 (D.C. 1988) (quoting 4 WIGMORE, EVIDENCE § 1048, at 5). Another is the sense that in an adversary system a party should be held to its prior statements and should not be able to raise a hearsay objection to statements made by, adopted by, or imputed to that party. *See* Fed. R. Evid. 801 advisory committee's note; *accord*, 2 McCormick on Evidence § 254, at136; *see United States v. GAF Corp.*, 928 F.2d 1253, 1262 (2d Cir. 1991).

As with any other evidence, however, an admission may not be received into evidence if its probative value is substantially outweighed by "countervailing circumstances . . . [such as] prejudice, confusion of the issues, cumulative testimony, [or] undue delay." *Keene v. United States*, 661 A.2d 1073, 1076 (D.C. 1995) (quoting *Johns v. United States*, 434 A.2d 463, 473 (D.C. 1981)); *see United States v. Kattar*, 840 F.2d 118, 131 n. 10 (1st Cir. 1988). The party admission rule does not give parties a license to use an opponent's statement to introduce a "red herring." *United States v. Woo*, 917 F.2d 96, 98 (2d Cir. 1990) (holding that statement that might qualify as an admission was properly excluded on Rule 403 grounds); *see also* 5 Weinstein's Federal Evidence § 801.30[3]; 2 McCormick on Evidence § 254 at 138.

A party may make an admission "by adopting or acquiescing in the statement of another." Fed. R. Evid. 801 advisory committee's note. Whether a party has adopted the statement of another is a preliminary question of fact for the trial judge, *see Foreman v. United States*, 792 A.2d 1043, 1052 (D.C. 2002), which is determined by considering the "context . . . and the surrounding circumstances" of the claimed adoption. *Brown v. United States*, 464 A.2d 120, 124 (D.C. 1983). The rule does not require an explicit statement of adoption; all that is necessary is some "manifestation of a party's intent to adopt another's statements, or evidence of the party's belief in the truth of the statements." *United States v. Rollins*, 862 F.2d 1282, 1296 (7th Cir. 1988); *see United States v. Paulino*, 13 F.3d 20, 24 (1st Cir. 1994). The adoption can be manifested "in any appropriate manner." Fed. R. Evid. 801 advisory committee's note. For example, a criminal defendant can adopt the statements of another as his own admissions "if it clearly appears that the accused understood and unambiguously assented to the statements." *Foreman*, 792 A.2d at 1052 (quoting *Brown*, 464 A.2d at 123); *see Robinson v. United States*, 606 A.2d 1368, 1371 (D.C. 1992). The party seeking to introduce evidence as an adopted admission has the burden to produce "specific proof of such adoption." *United States v. Am. Tel. & Tel. Co.*, 516 F. Supp. 1237, 1239 (D.D.C. 1981).

A party's signature on a document created by another is a circumstance that supports a finding of adoption. *See McQueeney v. Wilmington Trust Co.*, 779 F.2d 916, 930 (3d Cir. 1985) (holding that seaman's signature on Sea Service records prepared by others was "an unequivocal adoption of the contents therein"); *Pillsbury Co. v. Cleaver-Brooks Div. of Aqua-Chem, Inc.*, 646 F.2d 1216, 1218 (8th Cir. 1981) (holding that supervisor adopted contents of employee report by signing each page of the report); *United States v. Ward*, 575 F. Supp. 159, 162 (E.D.N.C. 1983) (holding that signature on food stamp application reduced to writing by another constituted an adoption); 5 Weinstein's Federal Evidence § 801.30[3]; *cf. United States v. Orellana-Blanco*, 294 F.3d 1143, 1148 (9th Cir. 2002) (holding that although defendant's signature "would ordinarily make adoption plain," statement was not adopted where circumstances suggested that Spanish-speaking defendant did not understand contents of statement).

Submission of documents to a court also suggests adoption of the documents. *See Fox v. Taylor Diving & Salvage Co.*, 694 F.2d 1349, 1355–56 (5th Cir. 1983) (holding that party adopted the testimony of his expert witness); *Buckley v. Airshield Corp.*, 116 F. Supp. 2d 658, 664 (D. Md. 2000) (holding that party adopted documents by submitting them as exhibits in a separate case); *see also In re Japanese Elec. Prods. Antitrust Litig.*, 723 F.2d 238, 301 (3d Cir. 1983) (holding that party adopted documents by referring to them in response to interrogatories). One commentator has concluded that documentary evidence submitted to a court should be treated as an adopted admission in most cases, for "[w]hen a party offers in evidence a deposition or an affidavit to prove the matters stated therein, the party knows or should know the contents of the writing so offered and presumably desires that all of the contents be considered on its behalf since only the portion desired could be offered." 2 McCormick on Evidence § 261, at 165–66; *accord*, 4 Wigmore, Evidence § 1075, at 149 n. 2.

Another factor supporting a finding of adoption is "the extent that the adoptive party accepted and acted upon the evidence." *Pilgrim v. Trs. of Tufts Coll.*, 118 F.3d 864, 870 (1st Cir. 1997) (holding that employer who followed recommendations of grievance committee had adopted committee's report); *see Wright-Simmons v. City of Oklahoma City*, 155 F.3d 1264, 1268–69 (10th Cir. 1998) (holding that employer who forced employee to resign based on investigative report and attached witness interview notes had adopted report and notes); 4 Wigmore, Evidence § 1073 at 138 ("The party's use of a document made by a third person will frequently amount to an approval of his statements as correct, and thus it may be received against him as an admission by adoption.").

C.

We have held that, in certain circumstances, statements of Assistant United States Attorneys are party admissions that are admissible against the government in subsequent criminal cases. *See Freeland v. United States*, 631 A.2d 1186 (D.C. 1993). In *Freeland*, the appellant was charged with murdering his wife. Freeland's defense was that his wife was killed by agents of William Hawthorne, who allegedly had been threatening Freeland because he was a potential witness against Hawthorne in a murder trial that was being prosecuted in the Eastern District of Virginia. *See id.* at 1188. In support of his theory Freeland attempted to introduce a motion filed in Hawthorne's murder trial by AUSA Lawrence Leiser, in which Leiser sought to introduce Freeland's grand jury testimony on the ground that Freeland was unavailable. *See id.* at 1191. To demonstrate Freeland's unavailability, Leiser represented in his motion that Freeland had told the government that he was reluctant to testify because he and his family had been threatened with retaliation by Hawthorne. *See id.* The trial court in Freeland's case held that Leiser's motion was not a party admission, in part because of its conclusion that the United States Attorney's offices in Virginia and the District of Columbia could not be considered the same party. *See id.*

We reversed the trial court and held that Leiser's motion was a party admission that should have been admitted. We agreed with the views of the First Circuit, the D.C. Circuit, and then-Judge (now Justice) Stevens that the United States is "bound by the position taken in a formal prosecution . . . [and] cannot escape a view taken in a separate prosecution on the ground that one prosecution simply represents the views of its agents who participate in that particular prosecution." *Id.* at 1192 (citing *United States v. Kattar,* 840 F.2d 118, 130 (1st Cir. 1988); *United States v. Morgan,* 581 F.2d 933, 938, 189 U.S. App. D.C. 155, 160 (1978); *United States v. Powers,* 467 F.2d 1089, 1097–98 (7th Cir. 1972) (Stevens, J., dissenting)). It was immaterial that Leiser's motion was filed by a Virginia AUSA, because the prosecutors in both cases spoke for the same Justice Department.

Our decision in *Freeland* relied in part upon the analysis of the D.C. Circuit in *Morgan,* which we found "persuasive." 631 A.2d at 1194. In *Morgan,* police officers obtained a warrant to search a house based upon the sworn affidavit of a detective who stated that a reliable informant had told him that "Timmy" was selling drugs from inside the house. 189 U.S. App. D.C. at 156, 581 F.2d at 934. When they executed the warrant, the officers arrested Morgan but did not find "Timmy." *Id.* At trial Morgan attempted to introduce the informant's statements contained in the search warrant affidavit as evidence that some of the drugs found in the house belonged to "Timmy." *See* 189 U.S. App. D.C. at 157 n. 5, 581 F.2d at 936 n. 5. The court found that the statements were admissible as adoptive admissions on the part of the government. The court reasoned that "sworn assurances to a judicial officer" in support of a search warrant "represent[ed] the position of the government itself." 189 U.S. App. D.C. at 159 n. 10, 581 F.2d at 937 n. 10 ("[W]hen the government authorizes its agent to present his sworn assurances to a judicial officer that certain matters are true and justify issuance of a warrant, the statements of fact or belief in the officer's affidavit represent the position of the government itself, not merely the views of its agent."). The court concluded that the government's sworn assurance that the informant's statements were "reliable" and sufficient to justify a search warrant manifested the government's adoption of the statements. 189 U.S. App. D.C. at 159, 581 F.2d at 937.

In *United States v. Warren,* 42 F.3d 647, 310 U.S. App. D.C. 1 (1994), the D.C. Circuit reaffirmed its holding that sworn statements of government agents that are presented to a court should be treated as party admissions while clarifying that unsworn statements made during the course of an investigation are not entitled automatically to the same treatment. In *Warren* the defendant attempted to introduce three statements made by police officers: two were statements contained in arrest reports; the third was a sworn statement of facts prepared by a Park Police officer, attached to a criminal complaint, and submitted to a magistrate judge. The court held that the two arrest reports were not party admissions, for having "not [been] sworn before a judicial officer . . . the Government cannot be said to have manifested a belief in their truth." 310 U.S. App. D.C. at 10, 42 F.3d at 656. The third statement, however, was sworn and was submitted to a court; that statement therefore was an adoptive admission. *See* 310 U.S. App. D.C. at 9, 42 F.3d at 656.

Several other courts have held that statements of a prosecutor made in a separate criminal case are party admissions. *See United States v. Salerno,* 937 F.2d 797, 812 (2d Cir. 1991) (holding that closing arguments from other case claiming that defendant was only a "puppet" were party admissions in prosecution where defendant was charged as an active participant); *United States v. GAF Corp.,* 928

F.2d 1253, 1261 (2d Cir. 1991) (holding that prior bill of particulars filed by government was a party admission); *United States v. Kattar*, 840 F.2d 118, 131 (1st Cir. 1988) (holding that brief filed by United States in separate litigation that was inconsistent with its position in this prosecution should have been admitted); *State v. Worthen*, 765 P.2d 839, 847–48 (Utah 1988) (holding that letter written by prosecutor to trial judge was party admission). The party admission rule is "particularly" applicable to statements by government attorneys, who have the power to bind the government. WEINSTEIN'S FEDERAL EVIDENCE § 801.33[3]; *accord*, 2 McCORMICK ON EVIDENCE § 257 at 142 n. 8; *see Giglio v. United States*, 405 U.S. 150, 154, 92 S. Ct. 763, 31 L. Ed. 2d 104 (1972).[4]

The government points out that a few courts have declined to apply the party admission rule to statements made by government employees in criminal cases. In particular, the Seventh Circuit has held that the party admission rule should not be applied against the government in criminal cases because "no individual can bind the sovereign." *United States v. Prevatte*, 16 F.3d 767, 779 n. 9 (7th Cir. 1994) (holding that out-of-court statement by police officer was not a party admission because "no individual can bind the sovereign"); *see United States v. Kampiles*, 609 F.2d 1233, 1246 (7th Cir. 1979). The Seventh Circuit's reasoning reflects that of two cases decided before the adoption of the Federal Rules of Evidence. *See United States v. Pandilidis*, 524 F.2d 644, 650 (6th Cir. 1975) (pre-FRE decision relying on *Santos, infra*, and holding that IRS official's opinion that defendant was only guilty of a civil offense was not admissible); *United States v. Santos*, 372 F.2d 177, 180 (2d Cir. 1967) (pre-FRE decision holding that officer's sworn affidavit identifying an individual other than defendant as an assailant was not a party admission because party admission rule generally did not apply to government in criminal cases). *Santos*'s continuing validity is doubtful in light of later Second Circuit decisions. *See Salerno*, 937 F.2d at 812 (applying party admission rule against government in a criminal case); *GAF Corp.*, 928 F.2d at 1261 (same).

These cases are distinguishable on their facts — as, for instance, where they do not involve statements made or adopted by the government's counsel acting on its behalf but rather simply involve statements made by other government employees in which the government itself has not manifested an adoption. But to the extent these cases may be said to reflect a view that the party admission rule cannot be applied against the government in criminal cases at all, we are not persuaded — nor would precedent in this jurisdiction permit us to adopt that view. The language of the party admission rule provides no basis for creating a prosecutorial exception or an exception where the government is the party opponent. Such an exception is both inconsistent with our decision in *Freeland* and unfair in light of the applicability of the party admission rule to criminal defendants. "[A]t a minimum, the law of evidence regulates the mode of proof impartially for the subject and for the sovereign. The hearsay rule that troubles the former equally vexes the latter; the exceptions to the hearsay rule that ease the latter equally comfort the former."

---

[4] Some courts have gone even further, holding that statements by agents of the government are party admissions regardless of whether they were sworn or presented to a court. *See Garland v. State*, 834 So. 2d 265, 267 (Fla. Dist. Ct. App. 2002) (holding that unsworn forensics report was a party admission); *Allen v. State*, 787 N.E.2d 473, 479 (Ind. Ct. App. 2003) (holding that unsworn pre-arrest statement of police officer was a party admission).

Garland, 834 So. 2d at 267. We reaffirm and adhere to our holding in *Freeland* that the prior statements of an Assistant United States Attorney can be treated as party admissions.

In *Freeland,* the Assistant United States Attorney himself prepared and signed the motion he filed with the court; although we did not specify which provision of the party admission rule applied to that motion, the most applicable provisions are 801(d)(2)(A) for a party's own statement and 801(d)(2)(D) for statements by a party's agent. In the instant case, AUSA Keenan did not author the Trainum Affidavit. He approved and signed it and authorized its submission to the court. Therefore the most appropriate provision is 801(d)(2)(B), which applies to statements in "which the party has manifested an adoption or belief in its truth." To determine whether the adoptive admission rule applies, we must determine whether the context and circumstances surrounding AUSA Keenan's approval of the Trainum Affidavit demonstrate that Keenan manifested an intent to adopt the affidavit. *See Brown v. United States,* 464 A.2d 120, 124 (D.C. 1983).

An affidavit submitted in support of a search or arrest warrant implicates fundamental constitutional rights. The Fourth Amendment mandates that "no Warrants shall issue, but upon Probable Cause, supported by oath or affirmation." The Warrant Clause "surely takes the affiant's good faith as its premise." *Franks v. Delaware,* 438 U.S. 154, 164, 98 S. Ct. 2674, 57 L. Ed. 2d 667 (1978). The ability of a magistrate to evaluate the existence of probable cause depends upon the integrity of the affidavit, which should only contain information that "is believed or appropriately accepted by the affiant as true." *Id.* at 165, 98 S. Ct. 2674. We trust that officers will reflect carefully before asking a magistrate to find probable cause to invade interests protected by the Fourth Amendment. *Cf. Malley v. Briggs,* 475 U.S. 335, 343, 106 S. Ct. 1092, 89 L. Ed. 2d 271 (1986) (holding that officers have only a qualified immunity for their decisions to seek warrants, in part because an affiant should "reflect, before submitting a request for a[n arrest] warrant, upon whether he has a reasonable basis for believing that his affidavit establishes probable cause").

The Warrant Clause encourages such careful reflection by requiring search and arrest warrant applications to be supported by "oath or affirmation." The gravity of an oath or affirmation is an essential "aid to truth in the fact-seeking process." *Beckham v. United States,* 609 A.2d 1122, 1127 (D.C. 1992). "An oath or affirmation reminds both the investigator seeking the search warrant and the magistrate issuing it of the importance and solemnity of the process involved." *State v. Tye,* 248 Wis. 2d 530, 636 N.W.2d 473, 478 (2001). The "deep meaning" of an oath to tell the truth permits magistrates to rely on an officer's good faith in reporting facts when determining whether the facts support probable cause. *Watts v. United States,* 362 A.2d 706, 711 n. 8 (D.C. 1976) (en banc).

Just as we assume that officers will not swear out affidavits without careful reflection, we assume that prosecutors will not give their approval to warrant affidavits and applications lightly. We presume that prosecutors are aware of the significance of truthful affidavits and the gravity of the interests to be invaded. Although a prosecutor may not vouch for the truthfulness of every third party statement reported by the officer in the affidavit, by approving the warrant application the prosecutor certainly endorses the officer's conclusion that probable cause exists to believe that the crime described in the affidavit was committed (and, in the case of a search warrant, that evidence of that crime will be recovered by the search). A prosecutor's signed approval of a warrant application would be meaningless if it did not at least signify agreement that constitutional standards for issuance of the warrant have been met and the warrant should issue.

In light of these considerations, we agree with appellant that AUSA Keenan unambiguously manifested his adoption on behalf of the government of Detective Trainum's conclusions that probable cause existed to believe that "Donald Monroe and Charles Minnis conspired to murder Michael Harris" and that the proposed search of Monroe's residence would recover evidence of that conspiracy. The clearest indication of that adoption is on page 11 of the affidavit, the page that recites Trainum's conclusions that such probable cause existed and describes the items to be seized. AUSA Keenan's signed approval on that page, made with the knowledge that the document would be submitted to the court, can only mean that he agreed in his official capacity with the conclusions set forth there. By giving his signed approval as an AUSA, Keenan informed Judge Dorsey that Detective Trainum's decision to seek a search warrant came with the imprimatur of the United States. AUSA Keenan could not have approved the warrant application in good faith if he had not agreed, at the very least, with the officer's ultimate conclusion regarding the existence of probable cause. Our conclusion is, we think, well nigh inescapable: AUSA Keenan adopted (at a minimum) Detective Trainum's statement that there was "probable cause to believe that Donald Monroe and Charles Minnis conspired to murder Michael Harris," and that statement was admissible in evidence at Harris's behest as an adoptive admission by a party opponent — just as a comparable statement made or adopted by Harris (*e.g.,* "there is reason to believe that Donald Monroe did *not* conspire with Minnis") would have been admissible at the government's behest.

Moreover, we see no reason to think that the revelation of the government's prior admission as to Donald Monroe's involvement in the attempt to murder Harris would have confused the jury so as to justify exclusion of the evidence as substantially more prejudicial than probative. This was not a tangential matter and the government was not placed at any unfair disadvantage in having to address it. The government could have accounted for the discrepancy in its positions by explaining that the information in the affidavit proved to be incorrect (if that was indeed the case) or that it believed that Donald Monroe was indeed the driving force behind the April 1996 attack but was not involved in the July 1995 incident. The fact that materially exculpatory evidence may complicate a trial is no ground to exclude that evidence; some trials are meant to be complicated and juries are capable of dealing with factual complexity.

Although the prosecutor's approval of this search warrant application necessarily implies agreement with the affiant's conclusions as to probable cause, it does not necessarily imply agreement with the entire contents of the affidavit, *i.e.,* with all the subordinate facts set forth in the affidavit. Whether a statement by a third party (or any other fact) that the affiant includes in an affidavit has been adopted is a factual question that must be determined by looking to the context and surrounding circumstances. These circumstances include the essentiality of the third party statement to the determination of probable cause, the extent to which the affiant explicitly vouches for the reliability of the statement or its third party source, whether the statement is based upon the declarant's personal knowledge or hearsay, and any other indicia reasonably bearing on whether the prosecutor who approved the request for a warrant has manifested a belief in the truth of the statement. Where, as in the present case, the warrant application is based on numerous statements from several informants who individually may be more or less trustworthy, and some of the statements incorporate multiple levels of hearsay, it is an open question whether the government has manifested its adoption of any particular facts recited in the affidavit as partial support for the affiant's ultimate conclusion. We leave that fact-specific determination in this case for the trial court to undertake on remand in connection with the new trial that we order.

In this regard, we are not persuaded by the government's argument, *contra Morgan* (among other cases), that third party statements in a warrant affidavit should never be treated as admissions because the affidavit is prepared solely for "investigatory" as opposed to "prosecutorial" purposes. The majority opinion in *State v. Brown*, 170 N.J. 138, 784 A.2d 1244 (2001) drew such a distinction on public policy grounds and held (over a vigorous dissent) that because search warrant affidavits were submitted to judges during the "investigatory stage," any statements of informants contained within the affidavits should not be treated as party admissions, no matter how clearly the prosecutor manifested his belief in the statements. *See id.* at 1257. (The *Brown* majority did not address the principal issue before us in this case, which is whether the affiant's ultimate conclusion of probable cause was a party admission.) But the distinction between "investigatory" and "prosecutorial" stages is an artificial one that is ill-suited to answering the real question of whether the government adopted the statements in question. Whatever might be said regarding other statements made by law enforcement officers and approved by the government's attorneys during investigations, affidavits in support of search or arrest warrants do not deserve to be minimized categorically as "merely" investigative and hence tentative. An application for a warrant is not a mere investigative report or offhand remark. Its contents are not an undigested stew of investigative leads. The warrant affidavit is a sworn statement, reviewed and approved by the government's attorney, that the information known to the affiant and set forth in the application is reliable enough to engender a prudent belief that the subject of the warrant has committed a crime, and reliable enough as well to justify a search or seizure under the Fourth Amendment. We see little reason to exempt sworn, constitutionally required representations to the court from the party admission rule merely because they are made pre-indictment.

*   *   *

After considering the corroborative impact that the government's adoptive admission of statements in the Trainum Affidavit and the proffered testimony of Drummond might have had on the jury's assessment of Harris's self-defense claim, and hence on the verdict, we cannot find that the errors in this case were harmless with the requisite degree of certainty. We conclude that the exclusion of the Trainum Affidavit was not harmless by the measure of *Kotteakos,* and that the refusal to send marshals to locate Drummond was not harmless beyond a reasonable doubt as required by *Chapman.*

V.

For the foregoing reasons, we reverse Harris's convictions and remand for a new trial.

[2] Adoptive Admissions: Rule 801(d)(2)(B)

The probative value of adoptive admissions is often questioned when the statement is not expressly adopted. *Matthews* is a fairly clear case because the defendant is fairly clearly adopting a statement. More problematic cases, such as we will consider in *United States v. Flecha*, find silence in situations similar to *Matthews* to be sufficient for an adoptive admission.

STATE v. MATTHEWS

Supreme Court of Rhode Island

88 A.3d 375 (2014)

JUSTICE GOLDBERG, for the Court.

On the night of May 6, 2009, three men savagely attacked and robbed Cesar Lopez (Lopez or complainant), who had unwittingly arrived at an abandoned house to deliver pizza. The attackers made off with about $20. Several days later, a chance encounter with one of the robbers led to his arrest, and that perpetrator implicated the defendant, Markus Matthews (defendant), in this brutal crime. The defendant was tried and convicted by a jury of a single count of first-degree robbery. He now appeals that conviction, assigning an array of errors to the trial court. For the reasons set forth below, we affirm the conviction.

Facts and Travel

Cesar Lopez was employed by Domino's Pizza (Domino's) as a pizza delivery-person. On May 6, 2009, he drove to 54 Lynch Street in Providence to make a delivery. Upon arriving at that address, Lopez called the phone number associated with the order, and the voice on the other end told him to "go through the back door." Although something about the situation appeared amiss, particularly because the house was dark, Lopez attempted to fulfill the delivery.

As Lopez exited his vehicle, he was struck from behind with "a piece of tubing."[1] As a second attacker grabbed him, he heard someone say "bring him into the house." While Lopez was being moved toward the house, there was one man in front, wearing a blue and white bandana over his nose, and another assailant behind him, with his arm around Lopez's neck. When Lopez tried to turn around, the choke-hold tightened, almost to the point of strangulation. Lopez briefly was able to free himself, but was then struck on the leg with the pipe and dragged up the driveway toward the house.

As the attackers moved Lopez toward the house, the beating continued.

---

[1] It appears from the testimony that the "tubing" was a metal pipe.

According to Lopez, there were three assailants: one with the pipe and two men pummeling with their fists. Lopez testified that he was struck with the pipe on the head and left eye. Approximately $20 was taken from his pocket. As the attackers wrestled him toward the back door of the house, he was able to grab onto the handrail; the attackers repeatedly hit him in an effort to make him let go of the railing. At that point, Lopez fought back. The assailants grabbed his uniform shirt; he slipped out of it and escaped to his car. The assailants were left holding the shirt. After Lopez reached the street, the attackers retreated and, despite his injuries — one eye was completely closed — he was able to drive back to Domino's. When he arrived, he sounded the horn, exited the car, and collapsed. Lopez's co-workers helped him up and called 911. Lopez continues to have problems with his eyesight and suffers from headaches.

On May 10, 2009, Lopez visited Domino's in order to return some items belonging to the store, including his uniform and pizza bag. While driving there with his wife, Lopez saw one of his attackers who was loitering on the street. According to Lopez, when the attacker saw him, he "started doing some suspicious things," such as backing up so that Lopez could not see him. After his wife called the police, they decided to circle the block; when the alleged attacker saw the car again, he went into a driveway and came out onto another street. Lopez directed his wife to drive to another street, where he expected the attacker to appear. Upon seeing Lopez again, the assailant started running with Lopez in pursuit. After a foot chase, Lopez caught the attacker — Michael Long — and held him until the police arrived.

The police arrested Long for the May 6, 2009 robbery and proceeded to interview him. Long initially denied any involvement in the crime, but eventually confessed, and in so doing, he implicated defendant.[2] Based on statements made by Long, defendant was apprehended. Long later pled nolo contendere to charges of robbery and conspiracy to rob.

At trial in this case, the complainant testified about the attack, noting that he could not recall the exact time that he left to deliver the pizza, but that it was after 10 p.m. He also testified about the circumstances that led to Long's arrest. The state also called Long to testify; however, he professed to have no memory of the events, notwithstanding his confession and subsequent plea. Jeannine Labossiere, Michael Long's former fiancee and the mother of his child, also testified at trial, and her memory was intact. She testified that, at about 10:30 p.m. on May 6, 2009, Long borrowed her cell phone and left her apartment. Labossiere testified that he was gone until about 1 a.m. when he returned to her house, accompanied by defendant. She testified that after some prodding, Long disclosed the beating and robbery of a Domino's delivery-person, as defendant stood silent. The defendant neither contested nor denied Long's recital of the events of the evening. Labossiere also testified that her cell phone number matched the one used to call Domino's on May 6, 2009. Because the testimony of both Long and Labossiere are central to the issues in this case, we elaborate upon their testimony in the discussion below.

* * *

---

[2] Long implicated defendant in both versions that he gave to police, including when he denied his own involvement. Long also implicated a third man referred to as "Knowledge" in his recorded statement.

The jury returned verdicts of not guilty on first-degree robbery by means of a dangerous weapon and the conspiracy count. The defendant, however, was found guilty of first-degree robbery resulting in injury. The defendant's motion for a new trial was denied by the trial justice, who subsequently sentenced defendant to twenty years at the Adult Correctional Institutions, with nine years to serve and the remaining eleven years suspended with probation.

The defendant argues that Long's statements to Labossiere should not have been admitted as adoptive admissions by defendant. At trial, Labossiere testified that Long and defendant came to her house at 1 a.m. on May 7, 2009. She noticed that defendant was limping and that Long had a bandana wrapped around his hand; thus, she sensed that something was amiss. After she repeatedly asked them what happened, Long admitted that "they robbed a Domino delivery guy." According to Labossiere, defendant "looked a little mad that Long said something" to her, but he remained silent. Long then provided additional details about the crime, including that he gave Labossiere's cell phone to defendant so that defendant could call Domino's and place an order for delivery to an abandoned house. Long disclosed that, when Lopez approached the house, defendant grabbed him and put him in a choke-hold. At that point, it was defendant who demonstrated the choke-hold to Labossiere. She also testified that Long described Lopez as badly beaten and that he got away a couple of times such that defendant had to put him back in the choke-hold. Shocked at these revelations, Labossiere said to them, "What the hell did you guys do?" She testified that defendant responded, "We just told you what we did." (Emphasis added.) When she inquired about the fruits of the robbery, defendant told Labossiere that he bought her a pack of cigarettes and produced about $15 in cash.

A trial justice's evidentiary rulings are reviewed under an abuse of discretion standard. *McManus*, 990 A.2d at 1234. Rule 801(d)(2)(B) provides that "[a] statement is not hearsay if . . . [t]he statement is offered against a party and is . . . a statement of which the party has manifested his or her adoption or belief in its truth[.]" It is well settled that "silence is sometimes sufficient to signify adoption." *Day*, 925 A.2d at 983. Where an accusatory statement was made within hearing distance of an accused and the accused did not respond to the accusation, this Court has pointed to five factors to consider in deciding whether a purported adoptive admission results:

> "(1) whether the statement was incriminating or accusatory; (2) whether it was one to which an innocent person in the defendant's situation would respond; (3) whether the statement was made within the presence and hearing range of the defendant; (4) whether it was understood by the defendant; and (5) whether the statement was one to which the defendant had an opportunity to respond." *Id.*

We are satisfied that this case represents a use of classic adoptive admissions. Long implicated defendant in a robbery; thus, the statement was clearly incriminating. Furthermore, an innocent person would certainly respond to such a direct suggestion of robbery. Labossiere also testified that Long and defendant were standing side-by-side — clearly within hearing range. The fact that defendant looked annoyed by Long's initial disclosure of the robbery and later demonstrated the choke-hold he applied to subdue Lopez establish that he not only understood the statements, but that he also had an opportunity to respond; additionally, evidence that defendant demonstrated the choke-hold is an admission by conduct. If defendant's silence during Long's initial disclosure was not enough to establish an adoptive admission, defendant later affirmed his participation in the robbery by telling Labossiere, "[w]e just told you what we did." Accordingly, the trial justice did not err by admitting Long's statements to Labossiere in the presence of defendant as adoptive admissions.

Rule 801(d)(2)(B) defines as a party-admission "a statement of which the party has manifested an adoption or belief in its truth." A party may adopt an admission either by affirmatively responding to the statement of another through words or conduct or by failing to object to the assertion of another. If the party expressly adopts the admission of another, the substantive content of the statement by the third party is irrelevant to whether there was an adoption. The statement need not be incriminating or otherwise against the interest of the adopting party; the affirmative statement speaks for itself. This is not true, however, when the party has allegedly adopted the admission by silence. In the latter instance, the rationale for the claimed adoption is that a person ordinarily would respond to the admission with a denial or, at least, with some indication of objection to its truth or accuracy because of its incriminatory or defamatory nature. The application of the concept of admission by silence is illustrated in the following case of *United States v. Flecha*.

UNITED STATES v. FLECHA
United States Court of Appeals, Second Circuit
539 F.2d 874 (1976)

FRIENDLY, CIRCUIT JUDGE:

Appellant was tried before Judge Weinstein and a jury in the District Court for the Eastern District of New York in the spring of 1973 on a three count indictment, along with Jose Pineda-Marin, Hugo Suarez, Ernesto Santo Gonzalez and Moises Banguera. The indictment charged the importation of 287 pounds of marijuana, possession of this with intent to distribute it, and conspiracy to commit these two substantive offenses . . . . The jury returned guilty verdicts against all defendants on all counts, except with respect to Banguera as to whom the court has dismissed the substantive counts at the close of the Government's case. The convictions of Flecha's co-defendants were affirmed by this court on March 7, 1974, without opinion. For reasons unnecessary to detail, Flecha's appeal was delayed in reaching us. Although he raises only a single point with respect to the allegedly erroneous admission of a declaration of his co-defendant Gonzalez, a summary of the facts is necessary for understanding it.

During the morning of March 25, 1973, the Francisco Miguel, a Colombian freighter, arrived in New York and tied up at the State Pier in Brooklyn. As a result of information received from the Customs Service at Galveston, Texas, customs agents set up a surveillance of the vessel that evening. One agent saw Suarez and Pineda-Marin, both crew members, in conversation on the deck. Later the agents observed appellant Flecha, who was not a crew member and was not authorized to be on the ship, in frequent conversations with Suarez and Pineda-Marin between midnight and 1:50 a.m., a time when Suarez was the deck watchman. At times they entered a hatchway at the rear of the ship; at 1:50 a.m., four men, including Pineda-Marin, Flecha, and Gonzalez, who also was not a crew member, came out the hatchway, dragging four large bales to a point amidship on the starboard deck. This was on the seaward side of the vessel and, unlike the similar area on the port side, was not lighted. Five minutes later another agent saw six men enter the pier area through a hole in the fence and scurry to a grain elevator near the bow of the ship. Still another five minutes later two men ran from the grain elevator onto a pier that ran past the bow. One of them slid into the water and swam across the bow; the other, Banguera, remained crouched at the pier's piling.

At this point the agent in charge gave the order to close in. Suarez and Pineda-Marin were found on the port side of the vessel; Flecha and Gonzalez were running on the starboard side from the middle of the ship toward the stern. Agent Cabrera identified himself and ordered them to stop. They did not, Cabrera fell on the slippery deck, and his gun went off. Gonzalez then stopped but Flecha kept running and went down the rear hatchway of the ship. He was apprehended at the entrance to the crew's quarters.

After all the defendants had been arrested, the agents found four bales containing 287 pounds of marijuana in the place where they had been dragged by the four who were aboard ship. The captain of the vessel testified that when he came aboard about 1:45 a.m. Suarez failed to inform him of the presence of unauthorized persons on the ship, although it was part of his duty to do so.

Not satisfied with this compelling case, the prosecutor elicited from Agent Cabrera that, as all five defendants were standing in line, he heard Gonzalez say in Spanish, apparently to Flecha:

Why so much excitement? If we are caught, we are caught.

The three lawyers who represented defendants Banguera, Suarez and Pineda-Marin immediately sought an instruction that this was "not binding" on their clients; the court said "Granted." Counsel for Flecha then joined in the application. Judge Weinstein asked Agent Cabrera how far away Flecha was from Gonzalez; Cabrera answered that Flecha was right next to Gonzalez, only six to twelve inches away. The judge then denied Flecha's application.

Although the judge did not articulate his reasons for granting the applications of Banguera, Suarez and Pineda-Marin but denying Flecha's, it is not difficult to reconstruct what his thought process must have been. To state the matter in terms of the later-enacted Federal Rules of Evidence, which in respects here relevant do not differ from the common law, the judge properly concluded that Gonzalez' declaration was not admissible as "a statement by a co-conspirator of a party during the course and in furtherance of the conspiracy," Rule 801(d)(2)(E), since the conspiracy was over and the statement was not in furtherance of it. He must also have concluded that the declaration was not admissible under Rule 803(2), the hearsay exception for "[a] statement relating to a startling event or condition made while the declarant was under the stress of excitement caused by the event or condition." This was probably right since Gonzalez' plea by its own terms indicated a lack of excitement. His allowing Gonzalez' statement to stand against Flecha although not against the three other objectors must thus have rested on a belief that as to Flecha the case fell within Rule 801(d)(2)(B), allowing receipt, as an admission of the party against whom it is offered, of "a statement of which he has manifested his adoption or belief in its truth."

The brief voir dire demonstrates that the judge fell into the error, against which Dean Wigmore so clearly warned, 4 Wigmore, EVIDENCE § 1071, at 102 (Chadbourn rev. 1972), of jumping from the correct proposition that hearing the statement of a third person is a necessary condition for adoption by silence, . . . to the incorrect conclusion that it is a sufficient one. After quoting the maxim "silence gives consent," Wigmore explains "that the inference of assent may safely be made only when no other explanation is equally consistent with silence; and there is always another possible explanation — namely, ignorance or dissent — *unless the circumstances are such that a dissent would in ordinary experience have been expressed if the communication had not been correct.*" (Emphasis supplied.) However, "the force of the brief maxim has always been such that in practice . . . a sort of working rule grew up that *whatever was said in a party's presence* was receivable against him as an admission, because it was presumably assented to. This working rule became so firmly entrenched in practice that frequent judicial deliverances became necessary in order to dislodge it; for in this simple and comprehensive form it ignored the inherent qualifications of the principle." (Emphasis in original.) Among the judicial deliverances quoted, it suffices to cite Chief Justice Shaw's statements in *Commonwealth v. Kenney*, . . . that before receiving an admission by silence the court must determine, *inter alia*, "whether he [the party] is in such a situation that he is at liberty to make any reply" and "whether the statement is made under such circumstances, and by such persons, as naturally to call for a reply, if he did not intend to admit it"; and Lord Justice Bowen's more succinct statement in *Wiedemann v. Walpole*, . . . :

> Silence is not evidence of an admission, unless there are circumstances which render it more reasonably probable that a man would answer the charge made against him than that he would not.

We find nothing in the Advisory Committee's Note to Rule 801(d)(2)(B) to indicate any intention to depart from these sound principles. To the contrary the Committee noted that difficulties had been raised in criminal cases and that "the inference is a fairly weak one, to begin with."

We find it hard to think of a case where response would have been less expectable than this one. Flecha was under arrest, and although the Government emphasizes that he was not being questioned by the agents, and had not been given *Miranda* warnings, it is clear that many arrested persons know, without benefit of warnings, that silence is usually golden. Beyond that, what was Flecha to say? If the Spanish verb used by Gonzalez has the same vagueness as "caught," it would have been somewhat risible for Flecha, surrounded by customs agents, to have denied that he had been. Of course, Flecha could have said "Speak for yourself" or something like it, but it was far more natural to say nothing.[33]

---

[33] (Court's original footnote 1.) In *United States v. Lo Biondo*, . . . this court held that where two

There is no force in the Government's argument that Gonzalez' statement "was not admitted for its truth, but rather for what it showed about Gonzalez' and Flecha's state of mind," and thus was not hearsay. Of course, it was not hearsay as to Gonzalez but in order to be relevant against Flecha, it would have to be at least a description by Gonzalez of Flecha's state of mind ("You know you are guilty") and that would be hearsay unless Flecha adopted it by silence. There is equally little force in the Government's claim of inadequacy in the objection of counsel. The judge saw the point perfectly well and thought he had met it when it was established that Gonzalez' statement was made in Flecha's presence. In this he was mistaken, as has been shown.

We have thought it desirable to write on this in order to prevent future reliance on the "working rule" so rightly condemned by Wigmore and other eminent jurists, rather than because of the effect of the ruling in this case. For we agree with the Government that the error was harmless. There is no need to restate the damning facts already recounted. It was plain as anything could be that Flecha and Gonzalez were the link between the two crewmen, Suarez and Pineda-Marin, and the men on shore (including the frogman) in what was to be the importation of the four bales of marijuana for distribution. No other credible explanation existed for these antics on a Colombian ship and a Brooklyn pier in the early hours of a rainy morning. Most significantly, although Gonzalez' declaration was not allowed to stand as against the two crew members or Banguera, who had not even been on the ship, the jury convicted them. It seems hard to think of the judge's erroneous admission against Flecha of Gonzalez' statement as having confrontation-clause dimensions; "merely because evidence is admitted in violation of a long-established hearsay rule does not lead to the automatic conclusion that confrontation rights have been denied," *California v. Green*, 399 U.S. 149, 156 (1970). But if there was constitutional error, we have no hesitation in saying it was harmless beyond a reasonable doubt.

Affirmed.

---

defendants are under arrest, and one responds to official questioning with an answer tending to implicate the other, the second need not deny the statement and his failure to deny does not make the statement admissible against him, save perhaps in extraordinary circumstances. Although the parties failed to cite this case to us, the Government did discuss *United States v. Yates* . . . . The facts there were similar to those in *Lo Biondo* except that it is not clear whether the co-defendant's statement alleged to have been adopted by silence was in response to police interrogation. The court held that admission of the statement was precluded by *Miranda v. Arizona*, 384 U.S. 436 (1966). It is the Government's position that *Yates* (and presumably *Lo Biondo*) are inapplicable to a statement "intended to be a private communication."

> The split of opinion regarding whether an admission "adopted" by silence after arrest, especially in the presence of police interrogators, is entirely barred or allowable in proper circumstances, is generally canvassed in 4 *Wigmore, below,* § 1072(4) at 118 and n.11. . . . It is now clear that when *Miranda* warnings have been given, the prosecution cannot constitutionally adduce evidence as to silence at that time. *Doyle v. Ohio*, 426 U.S. 610 (1976). . . . In view of our holding, based on common law rules of evidence, that Flecha's silence could not be considered as having adopted Gonzalez' statement, we have no occasion to consider whether *Miranda* has any application to a case where there was no official interrogation and no warnings had been given.

[3] Authorized and Vicarious Admissions: Rule 801(d)(2)(C), (d)(2)(D)

Rule 801(d)(2)(C) defines as a party-admission "a statement by a person authorized by the party to make a statement concerning the subject." At common law, a principal or employer could be held responsible for the statements of his agents or employees only if the principal authorized those agents or employees, either explicitly or implicitly, through the nature of the work being performed, to speak on a particular subject. The common law drew a clear distinction in this regard between the authority to speak and the authority to act.

Although Rule 801(d)(2)(C) codifies the common law to the extent that an employer still is responsible for statements made by employees who have been authorized to speak for the employer, that provision was rendered meaningless by subsection (D), which eliminates the distinction between employees who were hired to act and employee who were hired to speak. Subsection (d)(2)(D) makes statements by all employees admissible to the extent they "concerned a matter within the scope of the agency or employment." Therefore, subsection (C), which is limited to a particular form of employment, is superfluous.

The *Bonds* case (with which you are no doubt familiar for less legally technical reasons) considers both of these provisions and reveals that a statement satisfying provision (C) also satisfies provision (D). As you will learn in *Bonds*, this provision of evidence law turns on the application of agency law.

UNITED STATES v. BONDS
United States Court of Appeals, Ninth Circuit
608 F.3d 495 (2010)

SCHROEDER, CIRCUIT JUDGE:

In 2001, Barry Bonds hit 73 home runs for the San Francisco Giants. Also in 2001, as well as in prior and succeeding years, BALCO Laboratories, Inc. in San Francisco recorded, under the name "Barry Bonds," positive results of urine and blood tests for performance enhancing drugs. In 2003, Bonds swore under oath he had not taken performance enhancing drugs, so the government is now prosecuting him for perjury. But to succeed it must prove the tested samples BALCO recorded actually came from Barry Bonds. Hence, this appeal.

The government tried to prove the source of the samples with the indisputably admissible testimony of a trainer, Greg Anderson, that Barry Bonds identified the samples as his own before giving them to Anderson, who took them to BALCO for testing. Anderson refused to testify, however, and has been jailed for contempt of court.

The government then went to Plan B, which was to offer the testimony of the BALCO employee, James Valente, to whom Anderson gave the samples. Valente would testify Anderson brought the samples to the lab and said they came from Barry Bonds. But the district court ruled this was hearsay that could not be admitted to establish the truth of what James Valente was told. *See* Fed. R. Evid.

802. Accordingly we have this interlocutory appeal by the United States seeking to establish that the Anderson statements fall within some exception to the hearsay rule.

*   *   *

Admissibility of Anderson's Statements Under 801(d)(2)(C) and (D).

FRE 801(d)(2)(C) provides that a statement is a non-hearsay party admission if it "is offered against a party and is . . . a statement by a person authorized by the[defendant] to make a statement concerning the subject." FRE 801(d)(2)(D) provides that a statement is not hearsay if it "is offered against a party and is . . . a statement by the party's agent or servant concerning a matter within the scope of the agency or employment, made during the existence of the relationship." Subsection (C) thus requires the declarant to have specific authority from a party to make a statement concerning a particular subject. Subsection (D) authorizes admission of any statement against a party, but only provided it is made within the scope of an employment or agency relationship.

*   *   *

We turn first to the government's challenge to the district court ruling that the statements should not be admitted under Subsection (C) because Bonds did not specifically authorize Anderson to make the statements. Both parties agree that if the samples were Bonds', he *could* have authorized Anderson to make the statements. The question is whether the district court was within its discretion in ruling the record failed to establish sufficiently that he did.

The government acknowledges it cannot establish that Bonds explicitly authorized Anderson to identify the samples as his. Bonds was never asked the question during his grand jury testimony and Anderson, of course, is unavailable. The government's position is, in essence, that by authorizing Anderson to act as one of his trainers, Bonds implicitly authorized Anderson to speak to the lab on his behalf. The conclusion does not follow from the premise.

The district court correctly observed that certain relationships do imply an authority to speak on certain occasions. *See e.g., Hanson v. Waller,* 888 F.2d 806, 814 (11th Cir. 1989) (stating that lawyers have implied authority to speak outside of court on matters related to the litigation). Athletic trainers, however, as the district court went on to observe, do not traditionally have such any such implicit authorization to speak. The government suggests that by allowing Anderson to have the samples tested, Bonds impliedly authorized Anderson to identify them to BALCO, citing *United States v. Iaconetti,* 540 F.2d 574, 576–77 (2nd Cir. 1976). In *Iaconetti,* the defendant demanded a bribe from the president of a company. *Id.* The court held that by demanding the bribe, the defendant had provided implicit authorization for the president to discuss the bribe with his business partner. *Id.* Here, Bonds provided the samples after Anderson asked for them and thus *Iaconetti* does not apply. There is no evidence of discussions about how Anderson was to deal with the samples. The district court could have quite reasonably concluded that Bonds was accommodating the wishes of a friend rather than providing Anderson with "the authority to speak" on his behalf.

We cannot agree with the dissent's assertion that the nature of the task of testing blood and urine samples implies that the person who makes the necessary arrangements for the testing and delivers the samples is authorized to identify the samples' origin. Even assuming that Bonds allowed Anderson to have his blood and urine tested in order to obtain medical information rather than to accommodate Anderson's wishes, it was not necessary for Anderson to reveal Bonds' identity to accomplish that purpose. The samples could easily have been identified by a number or a code word. Indeed, there are many legitimate reasons to perform medical testing anonymously. The dissent's conclusion that Anderson was impliedly authorized to identify Bonds depends on the assumption that identifying Bonds by name was the only way to ensure accurate test results. Because we disagree with that assumption, we do not find the dissent's reasoning persuasive.

The district court also expressly found that the government had failed to carry its burden of showing that Bonds had provided Anderson the authority to identify the samples on each particular occasion, because Bonds could not remember how many samples he had provided. ("[Bonds'] equivocal answers about the number of samples he gave Anderson are not sufficiently certain to establish that Anderson had authority to speak with regard to the particular samples at issue here."). The district court thus concluded Bonds' lack of memory about the number of samples militated against his having conferred on Anderson authority to speak for each disputed sample in the case. Contrary to the government's theory, the court was not suggesting Bonds should have had a perfect memory.

*   *   *

There was no abuse of discretion in the court's refusing to admit the statements, under FRE 801(d)(2)(C), as statements authorized by Bonds. We now turn to whether the statements, though not specifically authorized, came within the scope of an agency or employment relationship that permitted their admission under FRE 801(d)(2)(D). That provision makes admissible "a statement by the party's agent or servant concerning a matter within the scope of the agency or employment, made during the existence of the relationship." The district court rejected the government's contention that Anderson's statements to Valente are admissible under this provision. Again, we may reverse only for abuse of discretion. *U.S. v. 4.85 Acres of Land*, 546 F.3d 613, 617 (9th Cir. 2008).

To determine whether Anderson's statements are admissible under Rule 801(d)(2)(D), we must "undertake a fact-based inquiry applying common law principles of agency." *NLRB v. Friendly Cab Co., Inc.*, 512 F.3d 1090, 1096 (9th Cir. 2008). For Anderson's statements to fall under this exception, he would have to have been Bonds' employee or agent.

The government provides two arguments in favor of admissibility of Anderson's statements under Rule 801(d)(2)(D). First, it argues that the district court erred in finding that, as a general matter, Anderson's work as a trainer was not that of an employee or agent. Next, it contends that even if Anderson did not generally act as an employee or agent, he assumed the status of an agent for the purpose of delivering Bonds' blood and urine to BALCO. We cannot accept either argument.

The record supports the district court's conclusion that Anderson was an independent contractor, rather than an employee. The parties briefed this issue under the Second Restatement of Agency, which sets forth ten factors that a court should consider: 1) the control exerted by the employer, 2) whether the one employed is engaged in a distinct occupation, 3) whether the work is normally done under the supervision of an employer, 4) the skill required, 5) whether the employer supplies tools and instrumentalities, 6) the length of time employed, 7) whether payment is by time or by the job, 8) whether the work is in the regular business of the employer, 9) the subjective intent of the parties, and 10) whether the employer is or is not in business. *Restatement (Second) Agency* § 220(2) (1958). Although the parties presented this issue primarily under the Second Restatement, we have independently reviewed the Third Restatement, which abandons the term independent contractor. *See Restatement (Third) Agency* § 1.01 cmt. c. We find nothing in the later Restatement's provisions that would materially change our analysis or cause us to reach a different result than the district court.

In applying the Second Restatement factors, a court will look to the totality of the circumstances, but the "essential ingredient . . . is the extent of control exercised by the employer." *Friendly Cab*, 512 F.3d at 1096 (internal quotation marks and citation omitted). Virtually none of the Second Restatement factors favor the existence of an employment relationship in this case. Most important, there is no evidence that Bonds directed or controlled any of Anderson's activities. To the contrary, the facts on record regarding the Bonds-Anderson relationship evidence a lack of control exercised by Bonds. For example, Anderson seemingly had free reign to provide Bonds whatever muscle creams and supplements he felt appropriate. Bonds took these items without question on the basis of his friendship with Anderson. Rather than exercise control over Anderson's training program, Bonds testified that he had a "Dude, whatever" attitude to Anderson's actions. These facts make it clear that Anderson was, as the district court found, not an employee.

Other elements of the Second Restatement test also point to Anderson's acting as an independent contractor, not an employee. For example, Anderson provided his own "instrumentalities" and "tools" for his work with Bonds. *See Restatement (Second) Agency* § 220(2)(e). All of the aforementioned creams and supplements came from Anderson, not Bonds. There is no evidence that Bonds supplied any type of equipment or material related to Anderson's training regimen. As a trainer, Anderson was engaged in a "distinct occupation." *See id.* § 220(2)(b). He had many different clients and offered his services to others during the same period. Moreover, it is important in this context that Bonds testified that he considered Anderson a friend and not an employee. *See id.* § 220(2)(i) (noting subjective intent of parties relevant to determining whether one is an independent contractor).

The government is correct that certain, but limited, aspects of the Bonds-Anderson relationship may suggest an employer/employee relationship. For example, Bonds conceded that he paid Anderson annually, and not "by the job." *See id.* § 220(2)(g). Yet Bonds paid gratuitously, and not on the basis of any regular employment relationship. There is, thus, sufficient basis in the record to support the district court's conclusion that Anderson acted as an independent contractor rather than an employee.

Unlike employees, independent contractors are not ordinarily agents. *See Dearborn v. Mar Ship Operations, Inc.*, 113 F.3d 995, 998 n. 3 (9th Cir. 1997) (recognizing that "an independent contractor . . . may be an agent" in limited circumstances in which he acts "subject to the principal's overall control and direction"). The district court was therefore correct to conclude that "independent contractors do not qualify as agents for the purposes of Rule 801(d)(2)(D)" in the sense that evidence of an independent contractor relationship is *insufficient* in itself to establish an agency relationship for the purposes of the rule. *See Merrick v. Farmers Ins. Group*, 892 F.2d 1434, 1440 (9th Cir. 1990) (holding that statements of independent contractors were not admissible under Rule 801(d)(2)(D) when there was no showing that the contractors were also agents). However, a finding that a speaker is an independent contractor does not *preclude* a finding that the speaker is also an agent for some purposes.

*   *   *

Accordingly, we must now address the government's argument that even if Anderson was an independent contractor, he acted as an agent in delivering Bonds' blood and urine to BALCO. An agent is one who "act[s] on the principal's behalf and subject to the principal's control." *Restatement (Third) Agency § 1.01*. To form an agency relationship, both the principal and the agent must manifest assent to the principal's right to control the agent. *Id.*

As is clear from the above description of Anderson's and Bonds' relationship, Anderson did not generally act subject to Bonds' control in his capacity as a some-time trainer, nor did he or Bonds manifest assent that Bonds had the right to control Anderson's actions as a trainer. There is no basis in the record to differentiate between Anderson's actions in his capacity as a trainer and his conduct in delivering the samples to BALCO. There is little or no indication that Bonds actually exercised any control over Anderson in determining when the samples were obtained, to whom they were delivered, or what tests were performed on them. Nor, contrary to the dissent's assertion, is there any indication that either Bonds or Anderson manifested assent that Bonds would have the right to instruct Anderson in these respects. It was Anderson who proposed to Bonds that he have his blood and urine tested. Bonds provided samples to Anderson when requested by the latter, and according to Bonds' testimony, "didn't think anything about it" after doing so. It was, further, Anderson who selected BALCO as the location for testing. In short, it was Anderson who defined the scope of the testing. Bonds provided Anderson no guidance or direction in terms of what specific tests BALCO would run on the samples. Bonds did not even inquire into the results of the tests. Rather, Anderson would, apparently on his own initiative, inform Bonds of results. The dissent says that Bonds instructed Anderson to deliver the samples to BALCO within 30 minutes of extraction, but this is not correct. The record shows that it was Anderson who told Bonds about the 30-minute time constraint. Moreover, the samples were taken at Bonds' house not because Bonds so ordered, but because his house was close to BALCO and taking the samples there made it possible for them to be delivered in time. Bonds quite understandably would allow only his own doctor to take the samples, but this does not show that he also had reserved the right to instruct Anderson as to what to do with the samples. *See Restatement (Third) of Agency § 1.01 cmt. f* (stating that the fact that a service recipient imposes some constraints on the provision of services does not itself mean that the recipient has a general right to instruct and control the provider).

While the dissent focuses on whether, as a practical matter, Bonds had the "capacity" to assess Anderson's performance and give Anderson instructions as to how to have the testing performed, it ignores the key question: whether Bonds and Anderson ever agreed that Bonds could do so. These are very different inquiries. Any time one person does something for another, the latter is in all likelihood capable of evaluating and instructing the first. The Restatement provision on which the dissent relies makes it clear, however, that not all service providers and recipients stand in agency relationships. *Restatement (Third) of Agency § 1.01 cmt f.* Rather, as we have seen, an agency relationship exists only if both the provider and the recipient have manifested assent that the provider will act subject to the recipient's control and instruction. *Id.* The question whether Bonds had the ability, in a practical sense, to prevent Anderson from having the testing carried out similarly fails to resolve the question whether Anderson was Bonds' agent. Obviously Bonds could have put an end to the testing by refusing to provide Anderson with samples of his blood and urine, but that does not establish an agency relationship. There is nothing in the record that requires a finding that Bonds actually controlled Anderson with respect to the testing or that Bonds and Anderson had agreed that Anderson would be obligated to follow Bonds' instructions if Bonds chose to provide them. Contrary to the dissent's contention, we do not maintain there needs to be an explicit agreement, but there must be at least some manifestation of assent to the principal's right to control. Here, the testing was performed on Anderson's own initiative and not at the request of Bonds. The dissent incorrectly assumes otherwise. Thus, the district court did not abuse its discretion in finding that Anderson was not an agent for the limited purpose of the drug testing.

BEA, CIRCUIT JUDGE, dissenting:

* * *

C. Anderson's Statements Are Admissible Under Rule 801(d)(2)(D) (statements of an agent concerning a matter within the scope of the agency or employment).[5]

> "A statement by the party's agent or servant concerning a matter within the scope of the agency or employment, made during the existence of the relationship" is not hearsay. Rule 801(d)(2)(D). The district court made two errors of law and one error of fact in deciding Anderson's statements were not admissible into evidence under Rule 801(d)(2)(D). First, the district court erred — and the majority here agrees — as to a matter of law in holding independent contractors could not be agents under Rule 801(d)(2)(D). Second, the district court erred as to a matter of law in holding Anderson's statements were inadmissible because making them was not *within the scope of Anderson's agency,* when the correct legal

---

[5] I begin with Rule 801(d)(2)(D) because it is more broad than Rule 801(d)(2)(C) and our courts have more fully developed what statements are admissible under this rule.

standard is whether an agent's [Anderson] statements *were related to a matter within the scope of his agency* . . . .

The district court erred as to a matter of law in holding: "In the Ninth Circuit, independent contractors do not qualify as agents for the purposes of Rule 801(d)(2)(D)." *United States v. Bonds*, 2009 U.S. Dist. LEXIS 16120, [at *17] (N.D. Cal. Feb.19, 2009) (citing *Merrick v. Farmers Ins. Group*, 892 F.2d 1434 (9th Cir. 1990)). And there the district court stopped its analysis of Rule 801(d)(2)(D). We review de novo the legal issue whether independent contractors may qualify as agents for the purposes of Rule 801(d)(2)(D). *See Hinkson*, 585 F.3d at 1262. The majority correctly holds that finding an independent contractor relationship is not *sufficient* to show agency, but the majority also recognizes that such a finding does not *preclude* the existence of an agency relationship. Majority Op. at 505. The majority is incorrect, therefore, in stating the district court identified the correct legal standard. *See* Majority Op. at 505. On the contrary, based on the law and even on the majority's view of the law, the district court was wrong as a matter of law when it held independent contractors were *categorically* non-agents.

* * *

Because the district court erred as to a matter of law, we should review the record to determine whether its error was harmless; it was not. The evidence is sufficient to support a contrary finding: that Anderson *was* Bonds's agent. More than that, the evidence is compelling that Anderson's statements meet the requirements under Rule 801(d)(2)(D): Bonds's testimony shows that (1) Anderson was Bonds's agent for the Task; (2) Anderson's statements to Valente identifying the samples concerned a matter within the scope of the Task, hence Anderson's agency; and (3) Anderson made his statements during the existence of the agency relationship. Rather than categorically to have eliminated the possibility that Anderson could have been Bonds's agent because Anderson was an independent contractor, the district court should have applied the correct legal standards (see below) to the abundant evidence of Anderson's agency.

(1) *Anderson was Bonds's agent for the Task.* Agency is the fiduciary relationship that arises when one person, the principal, manifests assent to the agent for the agent to act on the principal's behalf and subject to the principal's control, and the agent agrees or otherwise consents. *Batzel v. Smith*, 333 F.3d 1018, 1035 (9th Cir. 2003); *accord* Restatement (Third) of Agency § 1.01 (2006). In short, agency requires (a) the principal's assent; (b) the principal's right to control; (c) the agent acting on the principal's behalf or benefit; and (d) the agent's consent.

(a) *Bonds assented to Anderson's performance of the Task.* Bonds testified that he agreed to have Anderson take his blood and urine samples to BALCO. Moreover, Bonds manifested such assent not only to Anderson, but to BALCO, for Bonds testified he met with Conte, CEO of BALCO, and Anderson at BALCO's facilities. There, Conte, Bonds, and Anderson discussed testing Bonds's bodily fluids and the consequent results as to his nutrient levels. Bonds did not object to Anderson's dealing with BALCO to procure the testing and results discussed. Bonds also asked Anderson to have him tested to check Major League Baseball's tests for errors.

(b) *Bonds had the right to control Anderson's performance of the Task.* "The principal's right of control presupposes that the principal retains the capacity throughout the relationship to assess the agent's performance, provide instructions to the agent, and terminate the agency relationship by revoking the agent's authority." Restatement (Third) of Agency § 1.01 cmt. f (2006). This is a key point of dispute between my analysis and that of the majority; I think the evidence shows Bonds had the capacity to control Anderson's performance of the Task and the panel does not. Admittedly, Bonds testified he did not exercise much supervisory authority over Anderson. But our inquiry is not whether Bonds *exercised* his authority, but only whether Bonds *had* the authority to exercise in the first place. *Id.* cmt. c ("A principal's failure to exercise the right of control does not eliminate it."). For example, just because a movie actor does not exercise his right to reject a screen role through his agent does not mean that he no longer has an agent, or that he can no longer reject roles through the agent.

Here, Bonds had the capacity to assess Anderson's performance. For example, Bonds could have called BALCO to verify Anderson was procuring testing and successfully delivering the samples within 30 minutes of collection. Or, Bonds could have reviewed the test results documents. Bonds's own testimony creates an inference that Bonds could have done so: "So, I never saw the documents. I should have. Now that I think of it with the situation that is now, I should have." The fact that Bonds did not assess and modify or terminate Anderson's performance of the Task does not mean, as a matter of law, that Bonds lacked the *right* to do so.

Bonds also had the right to instruct Anderson. Not only did Bonds have that right, but he exercised it by instructing Anderson when and where Anderson was to collect Bonds's samples and when and where Anderson was to deliver the samples. The majority is correct that Bonds did not instruct Anderson regarding the 30-minute limit, but that limit did provide one measure by which Bonds could evaluate Anderson's actions. The point, however, is that Bonds did instruct Anderson when and where to collect his samples — at his home in San Francisco. The majority seems to argue that the fact that Bonds's house was also a suitable location under the 30-minute requirement is incompatible with Bonds's instructing Anderson, Majority Op. 506–07, but that is illogical. There were many places they could meet that were within 30 minutes of BALCO; Bonds instructed Anderson to come to Bonds's house and not to another location, most likely because it was a private place where Bonds's personal doctor would be comfortable drawing his blood and collecting his urine. Further, Bonds controlled when he could be tested because Anderson could not complete his task without Bonds's samples.

*   *   *

Moreover, the majority completely omits the fact that Bonds met with BALCO's CEO Conte to discuss, in Anderson's presence, the procedure for testing his blood and urine. This fact strongly supports the conclusion that Bonds was intimately familiar with BALCO's testing procedures, and therefore able to assess and instruct Anderson, even if he "didn't think anything about it" after doing so.

Most importantly, Bonds had the right and ability to terminate the agency relationship — a factor essentially ignored by the majority. Were Bonds to decide to terminate the relationship, he could simply have stopped giving samples of his blood and urine to Anderson. Without Bonds's samples, Anderson could not perform the Task. It would be implausible to find Anderson had access to some reserve of Bonds's blood or urine that he could have tested despite Bonds's terminating his agency relationship with Anderson. Besides, any such reserves could not meet the 30-minutes-from-draining "shelf life" requirement. The majority simply asserts, without explanation, that Bonds's right to terminate Anderson's role in dealing with BALCO was not enough to prove Bonds had control over Anderson's actions.

*   *   *

. . . As the Restatement explains:

> If the principal requests another to act on the principal's behalf, indicating that the action should be taken without further communication and the other consents so to act, an agency relationship exists. If the putative agent does the requested act, it is appropriate to infer that the action was taken as agent for the person who requested the action unless the putative agent manifests an intention to the contrary or the circumstances so indicate.

Id. cmt. c. Bonds requested Anderson act on his behalf by taking his samples to BALCO and having them tested. Anderson did so. There is no evidence Anderson manifested an intention to refuse the Task, nor are there circumstances that indicate he did not consent. Therefore, the evidence gives rise to a compelling inference that Anderson acted as Bonds's agent, subject to Bonds's control.

*   *   *

[T]he district court erred as to a matter of law, the majority is wrong to apply a deferential standard of review. Moreover, the majority fails in its attempt to distinguish *Jones* or *Itzhaki*, two cases where the agency relationship at issue was far more attenuated than is the case here. Reviewing the record below to determine only if the district court's misstatements of law caused the government prejudice, the ineluctable conclusion is that the district court's error did prejudice the government and its decision should be reversed.

D. The evidence is also admissible under Rule 801(d)(2)(C) (authorized admissions) because Bonds authorized Anderson to tell BALCO the samples were Bonds's.

"A statement by a person authorized by the party to make a statement concerning the subject" is not hearsay. Rule 801(d)(2)(C). Anderson's statements to Valente identifying blood and urine samples are not hearsay under Rule 801(d)(2)(C) because Bonds impliedly authorized Anderson to make those statements. Bonds's testimony shows he impliedly authorized Anderson to have Bonds's bodily fluids tested by BALCO and to report the results to Bonds so Bonds could know the test results. Anderson's statements identifying Bonds's samples concerned the subject of his Task.

To qualify a statement under this rule, the proffering party must show the declarant had "authority to speak on a particular subject on behalf of someone else." *Precision Piping & Instr., Inc. v. E.I. du Pont de Nemours & Co.*, 951 F.2d 613, 619 (4th Cir. 1991). In practice, courts determine whether the declarant was authorized to speak based on the *nature of the relationship* between the party and the declarant, or based on the *nature of the task* the declarant was to perform. *See* Christopher B. Mueller and Laird C. Kirkpatrick, *Federal Evidence* § 8:50 (2008). The majority errs in stating the applicable law by importing, without citation, the requirement the authority to speak on behalf of the principal be "specific" or done "specifically," whatever that might mean. Majority Op. at 502–04.

*   *   *

Similarly, by asking Anderson to deliver blood samples to BALCO for testing and to report the results back to Bonds, Bonds necessarily authorized Anderson to identify the source of the blood; otherwise, Bonds could not be assured of the accuracy of the results, which was the whole purpose of the Task entrusted by Bonds to Anderson. Without identification of who had supplied the samples, Anderson's Task would have been a fool's errand.

*   *   *

I begin with the district court's most serious error, which pervades its analysis of the admissibility into evidence of Anderson's statements — that it focused solely on whether the nature of Anderson's role *as a trainer* authorized him to speak on Bonds's behalf. In doing so, the district court overlooked the undisputed evidence as to the full nature of Anderson's Task with BALCO. So does the majority. *See* Majority Op. at 502–03. Anderson's formal label as a trainer should not trump the actual function he performed for Bonds. For Anderson to accomplish his Task successfully, it was necessary for Anderson to identify the samples in a manner that would later allow BALCO accurately to report test results back to Anderson and for Anderson to know the results were of Bonds's samples, so he could accurately report to Bonds his BALCO results.

But the district court did not look to the full Task; it stated: "[t]he rationale for Rule 801(d)(2)(C) simply does not apply here. If a party authorizes a declarant to speak on his behalf and the declarant makes an admission, Rule 801(d)(2)(C) provides a mechanism for that admission to be used against the party. Trainers, unlike lawyers, brokers, sales personnel, and those with supervisory responsibilities, are not generally authorized to speak for principals." 2009 U.S. Dist. LEXIS 16120, [at *16]. The district court's standard — that trainers are not generally authorized to speak for their trainees — is correct, but only if read in isolation. The district court does not explain how that *general* standard applies to this particular case. We are left to guess why the district court reached the conclusion that Anderson was not authorized based on this general standard.

*   *   *

Earlier in the district court's opinion, it described the nature of the task Anderson was required to perform as "the delivery of defendant's samples to BALCO." 2009 U.S. Dist. LEXIS 1620, [at *15]. This is a finding of fact, as to what constituted Anderson's task, which we review for clear error. *Hinkson*, 585 F.3d at 1263. But, the district court did clearly err in finding Anderson's task was mere delivery of samples to BALCO because the record shows Anderson's Task included far more — from procuring the vials to reporting the results to Bonds — as discussed earlier in this dissent. *See* discussion *supra* p. 512–13.

*   *   *

If Anderson's sole task were to deliver the samples to BALCO, I would agree with the district court's determination as to lack of authorization of Anderson to speak for Bonds to identify the donor of the samples: couriers and postal workers are not impliedly authorized to make statements as to the parcel's provenance on behalf of the people from whom they take parcels and make deliveries. *See* Restatement (Third) of Agency § 1.01 cmt. h (2006). It is not necessary for a courier to identify the source of a letter or package. Indeed, in most cases the courier has no personal knowledge who delivered the goods to the office for the final delivery. But, as the elements of Anderson's Task reveal — when that Task is at last fully described — Anderson was much more than a courier. He was responsible for *dealing* with BALCO under highly specific conditions of delivery — conditions set by Bonds (samples to be picked up at Bonds's home) and BALCO (samples to be tested within thirty minutes of extraction), but *not* set by Anderson. He was also responsible for reporting back the results of Bonds's tests. Bonds testified: "[Greg Anderson] came in with the vials, my doctor drew the blood, we just gave it to Greg. Greg went down there and *dealt* with it" (emphasis added). The authority to *deal* with a third party is a classic element of authorizing a person to act for another.[16] *See* Restatement (Third) of Agency § 1.01 cmt. c ("Authors, performers, and athletes often retain specialized agents to represent their interests in dealing with third parties . . . . [A] relationship of agency always contemplates three parties — the principal, the agent, and the third party with whom the agent is to *deal*." (internal quotation marks omitted) (emphasis added)).

The district court's errors of law and fact require reversal. In deciding an interlocutory appeal, we will reverse an evidentiary ruling for abuse of discretion only if such nonconstitutional error more likely than not would affect the outcome of the case. *See Hinkson,* 585 F.3d at 1282. A preponderance of the evidence proves Bonds authorized Anderson to perform the task, which impliedly authorized Anderson to identify the origin of the samples he delivered to BALCO. The district court's incorrect reading of the law and clear errors of fact affected and effected its erroneous decision. Therefore, I would reverse the district court's decision not to admit Anderson's statements under Rule 801(d)(2)(C).

[C]   Admissions by Co-Conspirators, Fed. R. Evid. 801(d)(2)(A)

[1]   Establishing the Existence of a Conspiracy

Silverman considers the type of evidence that a trial court may consider in determining whether a conspiracy exists, an obvious pre-requisite to admitting a co-conspirator statement. *Silverman* addresses the question of how a court should respond to the Supreme Court's decision in *Bourjaily v. United States.* The

---

[16] Admittedly, the distinction between an authorized speaker under Rule 801(d)(2)(C) and an agent under Rule 801(d)(2)(D) appears blurry when discussing "authorization." These roles are distinguished, however, by the fact that an authorized speaker under Rule 801(d)(2)(C) is not necessarily subject to the other requirements necessary for agency under Rule 801(d)(2)(D).

Silverman decision is particularly helpful as the drafters of the Federal Rules of Evidence adopted the view from *Silverman*.

UNITED STATES v. SILVERMAN
United States Court of Appeals, Ninth Circuit
861 F.2d 571 (1988)

ALARCON, CIRCUIT JUDGE:

David Silverman appeals from his conviction for conspiracy to distribute a controlled substance (cocaine), possession with intent to distribute a controlled substance (cocaine), interstate travel in aid of racketeering, and aiding and abetting, in violation of 21 U.S.C. §§ 846 and 841(a)(1) and 18 U.S.C. §§ 1952(a)(3) and 2. He seeks reversal on two grounds.

First, he argues that the district court erred in admitting into evidence the extrajudicial statements of an alleged co-conspirator. He claims that apart from the contested statements themselves, insufficient evidence established his connection to the conspiracy.

Second, he contends that the district court erred in instructing the jury that a defendant's concealment of his identity from government agents would support an inference of guilt of the charged offenses. He asserts that because the concealment in this case occurred two months after the last act committed in the course of the alleged conspiracy and because the agents did not disclose the charges against him, no inference of guilt is justified.

In our initial decision on this appeal, we affirmed the judgment of conviction. *United States v. Silverman*, 771 F.2d 1193 (9th Cir. 1985) (2-1). We subsequently granted the petition for rehearing and withdrew our initial decision. *United States v. Silverman*, 796 F.2d 339 (9th Cir. 1986) (2-1). We sent our second opinion in this matter to the clerk's office for filing on June 22, 1987. We were compelled to withdraw that opinion the next day, however, because of the Supreme Court's decision in *Bourjaily v. United States*, 483 U.S. 171, 107 S. Ct. 2775, 97 L. Ed. 2d 144 (1987). *Bourjaily* distinguished decisions we had relied upon in our second opinion on the issue of the admissibility of a co-conspirator's statements.

Having reexamined the record in light of *Bourjaily*, a majority of the court has concluded that the district court erred in admitting the statements of David Silverman's alleged co-conspirator. Because that error was prejudicial, we now reverse.

Reversal based on prejudicial error in the admission of evidence does not bar retrial. *United States v. Harmon*, 632 F.2d 812, 814 (9th Cir. 1980) (per curiam). We, therefore, address David Silverman's contention that the district court erred in instructing the jury on flight, to assist the Government in determining whether retrial of this matter is warranted.

Before presenting the compelling reasons that support our conclusions, we set forth the facts pertinent to a clear understanding of the issues we must resolve in this case.

I. PERTINENT FACTS

A. *Motion in Limine*

Prior to trial, David Silverman, through his attorney Bruce M. Kaufman, filed a motion in limine requesting that the district court exclude certain hearsay statements allegedly uttered by his sister, Pearl Phoenix (Pearl), on the ground that the Government would be unable to demonstrate a preliminary fact upon which admission of the statements depended-David Silverman's connection to the alleged conspiracy. The district court denied the motion "without prejudice to object to the admission of such evidence at the time of trial or to move to strike same."

B. *Testimony of Accomplice Willard*

The Government's principal witness was David Willard (Willard). Willard testified pursuant to a plea agreement in which he promised to assist the Government in exchange for its promise to dismiss certain charges against him.

Willard testified that he purchased cocaine from Pearl and resold it to Robert Zeitziff (Zeitziff). On three occasions, Zeitziff provided a private airplane in which he, Willard, and Pearl flew from Reno, Nevada to Van Nuys, California to obtain cocaine.

The first flight took place on May 13, 1983. After landing in Van Nuys, Willard called Valley Cab Co. to request a cab for Pearl. Willard testified as follows concerning Pearl's conduct and statements at the airport:

Q.   And you called a cab for her?

A.   I called a cab for her and she went outside to a pay phone and at which time—

Q.   Why did she go to a pay phone?

A.   She told me she was going to call somebody.

Q.   Did she tell you who she was going to call?

A.   Yes, she did.

Q.   Who?

A.   Her brother.

The record does not reveal whether Pearl completed this call or, if so, whom she called. The record does show that Pearl had two brothers, Frank Silverman and appellant David Silverman, both of whom resided in the western part of the San Fernando Valley.

Pearl departed in a cab. After having been away for two or three hours, she returned to the airport and gave Willard a package containing about six ounces of cocaine.

Zeitziff, Willard, and Pearl again flew to the Van Nuys Airport on May 31, 1983. Willard again called a cab for Pearl. The transcript contains the following testimony concerning this event:

Q.　　　　　　When you first got there what did you do, what did Bob Zeitziff do?

A.　　　　　　He went to take care of the plane.

Q.　　　　　　What did you do?

A.　　　　　　I went to call the cab.

Q.　　　　　　What did Pearl do?

A.　　　　　　She went to the pay phone.

Q.　　　　　　What did she do?

A.　　　　　　She called somebody.

Q.　　　　　　Who did she call?

A.　　　　　　Said her brother.

MR. KAUFMAN [Silverman's counsel]:　　Objection.

THE COURT:　What is the basis of the objection, please?

MR. KAUFMAN:　It's hearsay. Also calls for a conclusion of this witness.

MR. SULLIVAN [government counsel]:　Your Honor, I submit it's not hearsay. He's basically explaining what the witness did.

THE COURT:　All right, the objection will be overruled.

Again, the record does not show that this call was in fact completed or, if so, which brother was called. On this occasion, Pearl was away from the airport for an hour or two. Upon her return, she gave Willard another package containing approximately six ounces of cocaine.

Pearl, Willard, and Zeitziff flew to the Van Nuys Airport for a third time on June 25, 1983. Willard testified that upon landing they followed the "same procedure." Willard testified as follows:

Q.　　　　　　Where did you go?

A.　　　　　　I went to call a cab.

Q.　　　　　　Same cab company?

A.　　　　　　Same cab company and Mrs. Phoenix went to make a phone call.

Q.　　　　　　Did she tell you who she called?

A.　　　　　　Yes, sir.

Q.　　　　　　Who?

A.　　　　　　Her brother.

MR. KAUFMAN:　Objection, Your Honor.

THE COURT:　All right, is that on the same ground as previously?

MR. KAUFMAN:　Yes, Your Honor.

THE COURT:　Objection will be overruled on the same basis as previously.

This testimony does not establish whether the call was completed. It should also be noted that the court did not articulate the basis for its previous ruling. *See* quoted portion of the transcript concerning the May 31, 1983 extrajudicial statement set forth above. We must assume that the court overruled the objection because it accepted the prosecutor's theory that Willard was "basically explaining what the witness did."

Willard's testimony continued as follows:

Q.   Did she tell you her brother's name?

A.   Yes, sir.

Q.   What was it?

A.   David.

Q.   Did she tell you his last name?

A.   Silverman.

Q.   Did she leave in the cab?

A.   Excuse me, she didn't tell me she called David Silverman at that time. I knew the name was Silverman from before.

Willard further testified that on this occasion, after having been away from the airport for several hours, Pearl returned to the airport in a little blue car driven by a man. Willard made an in-court identification of Silverman, as "look[ing] like the individual" who was driving the car. On redirect examination, Willard stated that the driver "looked very much like him [David Silverman]." Willard testified that he had never met David Silverman, but had seen a photograph of him at Pearl's house prior to June 23, 1983.

Willard was arrested shortly after his return to Nevada following the third trip to Southern California. He promised to cooperate with the Government. As part of the bargain, Willard agreed to record his conversations with Pearl and her husband, David Phoenix.

The Government introduced a tape recording of an August 1, 1983 conversation between Willard and Pearl. The district court overruled David Silverman's objection to the playing of this tape without explanation. During this conversation, Willard asked Pearl, "Is your brother cool?" Pearl responded, "Don't worry." The court indicated that this statement was admissible as "co-conspirators' statements."

Following the playing of these recordings, Government counsel asked Willard whether Pearl or David Phoenix had told him, prior to May 13, 1983, the name of her supplier of cocaine. Mr. Kaufman, Silverman's attorney, objected to this question. The court then heard argument on the objection outside the presence of the jury. Mr. Kaufman argued that the Government had not satisfied its "foundational requirements" for the admission of the extrajudicial statements of a co-conspirator. The court overruled the objection stating that it was "a fairly close, tough question for the court to tackle but nevertheless I think that it does meet the test of [Fed. R. Evid.] 801(d)(2)(E) and so I'm going to permit the question to be answered." The court did not discuss the evidence that it believed satisfied the government's burden of establishing the preliminary fact of Silverman's connection to the conspiracy.

Following the court's ruling, Willard testified as follows:

> Pearl Phoenix. I'm not exactly clear on the dates when she told me, but it was in Floriston at their house, the Phoenixes' house and she explained to me that David Silverman had essentially acquired the cocaine business and that was where she was getting the coke from.

It should be noted that Willard testified that this unrecorded extrajudicial hearsay statement was made by Pearl sometime prior to May 13, 1983. Furthermore, there is no evidence in the record from any witness who saw the person who furnished cocaine to Pearl on May 13, 1983, May 31, 1983, or June 25, 1983.

C. *Evidence of Cab Rides*

In an attempt to connect Silverman to the conspiracy, the Government offered evidence of cab rides taken by some person from the Van Nuys airport on May 13, 1983, May 31, 1983, and June 25, 1983. The general manager of the Valley Cab Co. testified that his business records showed that on May 13, 1983, a passenger was taken from the Van Nuys Airport to the intersection of Louise and Ventura, in Encino, California. The witness stated that this intersection is located in a commercial zone, approximately five miles from the airport. He further testified that his records disclosed that on May 31, 1983, a passenger was transported from the Van Nuys Airport to the intersection of Winnetka and Ventura, also a major commercial area. The witness stated that the distance between Louise and Winnetka on Ventura Boulevard is approximately six or seven miles. No evidence was introduced to prove that Pearl was the passenger in the cab on May 13 or May 31. The record is equally silent regarding whom, if anyone, the passenger contacted after exiting the cab at these two commercial locations.

The cab company's business records also showed that on June 25, 1983, a passenger was transported from Van Nuys Airport to 22601 Waterbury. Other evidence established that David Silverman resided at 22601 Waterbury, Woodland Hills, California. The cab driver made an in-court identification of Pearl as the passenger on this occasion. The Government stipulated, however, that on July 21, 1983, the Government had shown the driver a spread of twelve photographs, from which the driver identified another person as the passenger transported to 22601 Waterbury on June 25.

D. *David Silverman's Concealment of His Identity*

The final piece of evidence relied upon by the Government to connect David Silverman to the conspiracy was his evasive conduct when three agents of the Drug Enforcement Administration (DEA) called at his home. One of the DEA agents testified that on August 23, 1983, at about 4:00 p.m., she and her fellow officers knocked on the door of the residence at 22601 Waterbury, Woodland Hills, California. David Silverman opened the door in response. The officers identified themselves as DEA agents and stated that they wanted to ask David Silverman some questions. Although the DEA agents knew that a warrant for the arrest of David Silverman had been issued, they did not then disclose this information to him. The man at the door replied that David Silverman was not home. The DEA agents left a phone number, requesting that David Silverman be informed that he should contact one of them when he returned.

Soon thereafter, the DEA agents were advised through a radio transmission that someone at 22601 Waterbury had contacted the DEA office. The DEA agents returned to the residence. David Silverman again appeared at the door. He falsely identified himself, claiming to be Jim Walker. The DEA agents then, for the first time, disclosed "that there was a warrant for Mr. Silverman's arrest." The DEA agents then stated that David Silverman should contact the DEA as soon as possible. The record contains no evidence that the DEA agents ever informed David Silverman of the charges contained in the warrant or the relationship of the alleged crimes to his sister or to violations of the narcotics laws.

As the DEA agents were driving away from the area, their supervisor contacted them by radio and stated that an attorney had advised him that David Silverman was willing to turn himself in at a later date. David Silverman surrendered voluntarily two days later. As a result of his voluntary surrender, the district court reduced the bail by two-thirds.

E. *David Silverman's Motion to Strike the Co-Conspirator's Statements*

At the close of the Government's case-in-chief, David Silverman moved to strike the evidence of Pearl's out-of-court statements, "on the grounds that the Government has failed to lay the foundation required by the Court." David Silverman argued, *inter alia*, that the record contained no evidence independent of the statements themselves to connect him to the conspiracy.

The trial judge commented that he had "trouble" with "the proof of the conspiracy so far as David Silverman is concerned." The trial judge pressed the prosecutor to identify the evidence connecting David Silverman to the conspiracy. In response, the prosecutor summarized the evidence discussed above. The trial judge stated that he would consider this "serious question" overnight and announce his ruling in the morning.

The next day, the trial judge denied David Silverman's motion to strike the co-conspirator's statements. The trial judge did not discuss the evidence on which he based his ruling. The trial judge explained: "All that is necessary is that there be independent proof that David Silverman had a slight connection to the conspiracy or some cases say slight evidence of a connection to the conspiracy was offered. By either test there is that much evidence. That is there is a slight connection shown and that's about what it adds up."

II. ANALYSIS

A. *Admission of Co-conspirator's Statements*

Federal Rule of Evidence 801(d)(2)(E) provides: "A statement is not hearsay if . . . [t]he statement is offered against a party and is . . . a statement by a co-conspirator of a party during the course and in furtherance of the conspiracy." Fed. R. Evid. 801(d)(2)(E). An accused's knowledge of and participation in an alleged conspiracy are preliminary facts that must be established before extrajudicial statements of a co-conspirator can be introduced into evidence. *Bourjaily v. United States*, 483 U.S. 171, 107 S. Ct. 2775, 2778, 97 L. Ed. 2d 144 (1987); *United States v. Fleishman*, 684 F.2d 1329, 1337 (9th Cir.), *cert. denied*, 459 U.S. 1044, 103 S. Ct. 464, 74 L. Ed. 2d 614 (1982); *United States v. Weaver*, 594 F.2d 1272, 1274 (9th Cir. 1979); *United States v. Testa*, 548 F.2d 847, 852 (9th Cir. 1977); *United States v. Ledesma*, 499 F.2d 36, 40 (9th Cir.), *cert. denied*, 419 U.S. 1024, 95 S. Ct. 501, 42 L. Ed. 2d 298 (1974). These preliminary facts must be shown by a preponderance of the evidence. *Bourjaily*, 107 S. Ct. at 2779.

Our standard of review is uncertain. Prior to the decision in *Bourjaily*, we reviewed *de novo* a district court's determination that the Government had sufficiently established the factual predicate for admission of a co-conspirator's statement. *See United States v. Smith*, 790 F.2d 789, 794 (9th Cir. 1986) (whether Government has made requisite preliminary showing of conspiracy "is a question of law subject to *de novo* review"); *United States v. Rosales*, 584 F.2d 870, 872 (9th Cir. 1978) (Wallace, J.) (whether Government has made requisite preliminary showing of conspiracy "is a question of law," hence "we are not confined to the 'clearly erroneous' or some other restricted standard of review").

The dissent cites *Bourjaily* for the proposition that "the district court's conclusion that preliminary facts have been established by a preponderance of the evidence is reviewed for clear error." Dissenting op. at 583; *see id.* at 585–586. The *Bourjaily* Court, however, did not address the issue of standard of review, nor did it unequivocally declare which standard is proper. *See United States v. Gordon*, 844 F.2d 1397, 1402 (9th Cir. 1988) ("The appropriate standard of review . . . was not an explicit holding in *Bourjaily*.").

Under the *de novo* standard of review, we do not defer to the lower court's ruling but freely consider the matter anew, as if no decision had been rendered below. *Exner v. FBI*, 612 F.2d 1202, 1209 (9th Cir. 1980). Under the more deferential "clearly erroneous" standard, we must accept the lower court's ruling unless, after reviewing the entire record, we are "left with the definite and firm conviction that a mistake has been committed." *United States v. United States Gypsum Co.*, 333 U.S. 364, 395, 68 S. Ct. 525, 542, 92 L. Ed. 746 (1948), *quoted in Edinburgh Assur. Co. v. R.L. Burns Corp.*, 669 F.2d 1259, 1261 (9th Cir. 1982); *Dollar Rent A Car, Inc. v. Travelers Indem. Co.*, 774 F.2d 1371, 1374 (9th Cir. 1985).

We have carefully reviewed the record in this case. For the reasons discussed herein, we are left with the definite and firm conviction that the admission of the alleged co-conspirator's statements in this case was a serious mistake, one that prejudiced the defendant. Our conviction requires us to reverse the district court's ruling, whether that ruling is reviewed under the *de novo* or the "clearly erroneous" standard. For this reason, we need not, and do not, decide whether *Bourjaily* has effected a change in the standard of review heretofore applied in this circuit.

The Supreme Court ruled in *Bourjaily* that the plain meaning of Fed. R. Evid. 104(a) is that the district courts may consider the contested hearsay statements themselves, along with all other evidence, in determining whether the defendant had knowledge of and participated in the conspiracy. 107 S. Ct. at 2780. The Court explained: "To the extent that [the prohibition against bootstrapping set forth in *Glasser v. United States,* 315 U.S. 60, 62 S. Ct. 457, 86 L. Ed. 680 (1942)] meant that courts could not look to the hearsay statements themselves for any purpose, it has clearly been superseded by Rule 104(a)." *Id.* 107 S. Ct. at 2782.

In *Bourjaily,* the contested hearsay statements offered by the Government to prove the preliminary facts were amply corroborated by other evidence. The co-conspirator in *Bourjaily* told an FBI informant that the defendant was involved in a conspiracy with the co-conspirator, that the defendant had agreed to buy and distribute a kilogram of cocaine, that the defendant would be in his car at a certain hotel parking lot at a certain time, that the co-conspirator would obtain the cocaine from the informant in the parking lot, and that the defendant would accept the cocaine from the co-conspirator. *Id.* at 2781. The co-conspirator's statements were corroborated by defendant's appearance at the designated time and place and by his acceptance of the cocaine. *Id.*

The Supreme Court held in *Bourjaily* that the trial court had not erred in considering the co-conspirator's statements to determine whether the Government had established, by a preponderance of the evidence, the preliminary facts of the defendant's knowledge of and participation in the alleged conspiracy. *Id.* at 2782. Because the contested statements were fully corroborated by evidence of defendant's own actions, the Court found it unnecessary to decide "whether the courts below could have relied *solely* upon [the co-conspirator's] hearsay statements to determine that a conspiracy had been established. . . ." *Id.* at 2781–82 (emphasis added); *see id.* at 2791 (Blackmun, J., joined by Brennan and Marshall, JJ., dissenting) ("It is at least heartening . . . to see that the Court reserves the question whether a co-conspirator's statement alone, without *any* independent evidence, could establish the existence of a conspiracy and a defendant's participation in it.").

This court has answered the question left open in *Bourjaily.* We have ruled that a co-conspirator's out-of-court statement, standing alone, is insufficient to establish that the defendant had knowledge of and participated in a particular conspiracy. *See Gordon,* 844 F.2d at 1402 (for co-conspirator statements to be admissible, "there must be some evidence, aside from the proffered statements, of the existence of the conspiracy and the defendant's involvement"). To abandon the requirement that *some* evidence aside from the proffered co-conspirator's statements be presented to show that the defendant knowingly participated in the alleged conspiracy would be to render all such statements self-validating. Such a ruling would "eliminate one of the few safeguards of reliability that this exemption from the hearsay definition possesses." *Bourjaily,* 107 S. Ct. at 2784 (Blackmun, J., joined by Brennan and Marshall, JJ., dissenting).

Accordingly, in this circuit, when the proponent of the co-conspirator's statement offers *no* additional proof of defendant's knowledge of and participation in the conspiracy, the statement must be excluded from evidence. Where, on the other hand, some additional proof is offered, the court must determine whether such proof, viewed in light of the co-conspirator's statement itself, demonstrates by a preponderance of the evidence that defendant knew of and participated in the conspiracy.

In determining whether the proponent has made a showing sufficient to permit the introduction into evidence of the co-conspirator's statement, the district court must bear in mind that out-of-court statements are presumptively unreliable. *See Bourjaily*, 107 S. Ct. at 2781. When the out-of-court statement is one made by a co-conspirator purporting to implicate others in an unlawful conspiracy, its reliability is doubly suspect. "[C]o-conspirator statements . . . often have been considered to be somewhat unreliable. It has long been understood that such statements in some cases may constitute, at best, nothing more than the 'idle chatter' of a declarant or, at worst, malicious gossip." *Bourjaily*, 107 S. Ct. at 2790 (Blackmun, J., joined by Brennan and Marshall, JJ., dissenting); *accord Wong Sun v. United States*, 371 U.S. 471, 490 n. 17, 83 S. Ct. 407, 419 n. 17, 9 L. Ed. 2d 441 (1963) (quoting Williams, *The Proof of Guilt* 135 (1958)) (" 'Even where . . . the evidence of an accomplice becomes admissible against his fellows, it remains suspect evidence, because of the tainted source from which it comes.' "); Davenport, *The Confrontation Clause and the Co-Conspirator Exception in Criminal Prosecutions: A Functional Analysis*, 85 Harv. L. Rev. 1378, 1386–87 (1972) (statements made by a co-conspirator prior to termination of the conspiracy "may . . . suffer from the same kinds of exclusively self-serving motives and possibly faulty memories that allegedly infect many post-termination statements"); Levie, *Hearsay and Conspiracy: A Reexamination of the Co-Conspirators' Exception to the Hearsay Rule*, 52 Mich. L. Rev. 1159, 1165–66 (1954) ("The conspirator's interest is likely to lie in misleading the listener into believing the conspiracy stronger with more members (and different members) and other aims than in fact it has.").

Although, as *Bourjaily* instructs, Fed. R. Evid. 104(a) permits a trial judge to consider the co-conspirator's out-of-court statement in assessing the statement's admissibility, Rule 104(a) does not diminish the inherent unreliability of such a statement. Because of this presumptive unreliability, a co-conspirator's statement implicating the defendant in the alleged conspiracy must be corroborated by fairly incriminating evidence. Evidence of wholly innocuous conduct or statements by the defendant will rarely be sufficiently corroborative of the co-conspirator's statement to constitute proof, by a preponderance of the evidence, that the defendant knew of and participated in the conspiracy. Evidence of innocent conduct does little, if anything, to enhance the reliability of the co-conspirator's statement. A co-conspirator's statement, which is presumptively unreliable hence inadmissible standing alone, is no more reliable when coupled with evidence of conduct that is completely consistent with defendant's unawareness of the conspiracy.

Bourjaily itself provides one example of the sort of incriminating evidence that sufficiently corroborates a co-conspirator's statement to establish, by a preponderance of the evidence, defendant's connection to the conspiracy. In *Bourjaily*, the evidence showed that the defendant had committed a criminal act that furthered the conspiracy described in the co-conspirator's statement. *See* 107 S. Ct. at 2781. Our own cases provide similar examples. *See, e.g., United States v. Crespo de Llano*, 830 F.2d 1532, 1543 (9th Cir. 1987) (defendant was present during negotiations for sale of cocaine, obtained sample for government undercover agent to taste, translated price of cocaine from Spanish to English, and appeared at prearranged location for the cocaine transaction); *United States v. Paris,* 827 F.2d 395, 400 (9th Cir. 1987) (defendant met with intermediary just before latter provided government under-cover agent with cocaine sample, and defendant arrived with one kilogram of cocaine at prearranged time and location for transaction).

Of course, evidence short of proof of the commission of a substantive offense may also be sufficient to show, by a preponderance of the evidence, the defendant's knowing participation in the alleged conspiracy. *See, e.g., United States v. Stewart,* 770 F.2d 825, 831 (9th Cir. 1985) (defendant was present at seller's house immediately before each of three drug transactions, seller and defendant met immediately after two of the transactions, and defendant's palm print was found on envelope that contained the drug), *cert. denied,* 474 U.S. 1103, 106 S. Ct. 888, 88 L. Ed. 2d 922 (1986); *United States v. Mason,* 658 F.2d 1263, 1269 (9th Cir. 1981) (defendant was the only person to visit seller between time seller telephoned his source to obtain contraband and time seller provided contraband to government undercover agents).

In the present case, by contrast, the evidence aside from the proffered co-conspirator's statements is completely consistent with a conclusion that David Silverman was unaware of the conspiracy. The evidence is insufficiently corrobora-tive of Pearl's out-of-court statements to overcome the presumption of unreliability that makes those statements inadmissible standing alone.

According to Willard, Pearl told him that David Silverman was her cocaine source. In addition, on each trip to the Van Nuys airport, Pearl allegedly told Willard that she was going to call, or had called, an unspecified brother. Pearl also responded "Don't worry" when Willard inquired whether her brother was "cool" concerning payment for cocaine.

Pearl's statements are mutually corroborative only if one assumes, as the dissent apparently does, that each is independently reliable. *See* dissenting op. at 584. We submit that such assumption is erroneous. As explained above, a co-conspirator's out-of-court statements are presumptively unreliable. One presumptively unreliable statement cannot be invoked to corroborate another, particularly when each was allegedly uttered by the same declarant.[1]

The admissibility of the contested statements, therefore, hinges on whether the additional evidence proffered by the Government to demonstrate David Silverman's connection to the conspiracy sufficiently corroborates the statements to overcome their presumed unreliability. We conclude that the additional evidence fails to provide sufficient corroboration.

Evidence that David Silverman drove his sister to the airport on one occasion makes only slightly more probable his connection to the conspiracy than do the hearsay statements alone. Such evidence shows little more than that he was in the presence of a relative who was involved in a conspiracy. That Pearl attempted to visit Silverman during one of her cocaine-buying expeditions is, likewise, only

---

[1] Pearl's statements at the airport that she was going to call "her brother" were admissible to prove Pearl's intent. *See* Fed. R. Evid. 803(3). The fact that such statements were admissible, however, does not make them any more reliable or any more corroborative of Pearl's statement identifying a particular brother-David-as her cocaine source.

marginally probable of his involvement in the conspiracy, hence marginally corroborative of the contested statements. We have consistently recognized that evidence that a defendant merely associated with a member of a conspiracy has little probative value in demonstrating the defendant's connection to that conspiracy. *See, e.g., United States v. Weaver,* 594 F.2d 1272, 1275 (9th Cir. 1979) (evidence that defendant was passenger in truck and that wrapped package of cocaine was found partly under passenger's seat did not constitute even "slight" evidence connecting defendant to alleged conspiracy); *United States v. Griffin,* 434 F.2d 978, 984 (9th Cir. 1970) (quoting with approval *United States v. Ragland,* 375 F.2d 471, 476–77 (2d Cir. 1967), *cert. denied,* 390 U.S. 925, 88 S. Ct. 860, 19 L.Ed.2d 987 (1968)) ("[A]n association with an alleged conspirator, without more, is insufficient to establish the necessary foundation for the admissibility of the incriminating [co-conspirator's] statements."), *cert. denied,* 402 U.S. 995, 91 S. Ct. 2170, 29 L. Ed. 2d 160 (1971).

Although evidence of Pearl's association with her brother David, viewed in light of Willard's statement that Pearl told him that David was her source, makes the hearsay more reliable to some small degree, the evidence is simply too innocent to demonstrate David's connection to the conspiracy by a preponderance of the evidence, *i.e.,* to make the connection more likely than not. It is significant that the Government presented no evidence that David Silverman was aware that Pearl delivered cocaine to Willard after Silverman dropped her off at the airport on June 25, 1983.

Likewise, evidence that David Silverman temporarily concealed his identity from the DEA does not sufficiently corroborate Pearl's statements to prove, by a preponderance of the evidence, that he knew of or participated in the conspiracy with which he was charged. His concealment occurred two months after Pearl's last trip to Van Nuys. As we explain in Part II(B) below, this two-month delay, coupled with the absence of any showing by the Government that David Silverman was aware that he was suspected of involvement in any cocaine-related crime, renders any inference of guilt from such concealment improper.

In summary, we recognize that the Government proffered *some* additional evidence to corroborate Pearl's contested extrajudicial statements. The district court characterized the additional evidence as "slight" but nevertheless found it sufficient to support admission of Pearl's statements under Rule 801(d)(2)(E). We agree that the additional evidence is "slight," if that, but disagree that the evidence supports admission of Pearl's statements. We believe that the additional evidence proffered by the Government was so marginally corroborative that it failed to overcome the presumptive unreliability of Pearl's statements. Thus, even when the additional evidence is assessed in light of those statements, a preponderance of the evidence fails to demonstrate that David Silverman knew of and participated in the alleged conspiracy. Accordingly, the district court erred in admitting Pearl's extrajudicial statements identifying David Silverman as her cocaine source.

An error in the admission of evidence requires reversal only if the error affected a party's substantial rights. *See* 28 U.S.C. § 2111 (1982) (appellate court shall give judgment without regard to errors that do not affect substantial rights of parties); *United States v. Murray,* 751 F.2d 1528, 1533 (9th Cir.) ("An erroneous evidentiary ruling will be reversed if a defendant shows that a substantial right has been affected."), *cert. denied,* 474 U.S. 979, 106 S. Ct. 381, 88 L. Ed. 2d 335 (1985). In the present case, Pearl's contested statements were undoubtedly the bases for the jury's conclusion that David Silverman was guilty of conspiracy. The district court's error in admitting the statements, therefore, was necessarily prejudicial and compels reversal. *See* 11 C. Wright & A. Miller, *Federal Practice and Procedure* § 2885, at 289–90 (1973) ("[I]f the evidence is insufficient to support the verdict without the erroneously admitted evidence, the error must be held prejudicial.") (footnote omitted).

[2]   Made "During the Course of the Conspiracy"

Consistent with the tenuous agency theory that underlies this exclusion, a court will find a co-conspirator's admission to be admissible against all the members of the conspiracy if the statement was made during the existence of the conspiracy. This requirement is comparable to the requirement for the admissibility of a vicarious admission under Rule 801(d)(2)(D), that an employee making a statement about a matter within the scope of his employment must make the statement during the existence of his relationship with the employer. Accordingly, statements made by the co-conspirators before the conspiracy has commenced or after its purpose has been satisfied and the conspiracy, therefore, has ended are not admissible under the Rule.

Courts have held statements made by the initial co-conspirators, however, to be admissible against those who joined the conspiracy after the statements were made. The theory has been that one who joins the conspiracy assumes responsibility for all that preceded. Statements made after the conspiracy has concluded, however, are not admissible against those who previously conspired.

Detection of the illegal scheme and apprehension of the participants usually will result in the court's concluding that the conspiracy has ended, so that statements made after that point are not admissible. Statements made after this point are particularly untrustworthy because of the inclination of those apprehended to point the finger of guilt at others. Conspiracies do not have to come to such a clear end point for the conspiracy to have concluded for the purposes for Rule 801(d)(2)(E).

UNITED STATES v. MAGLUTA
United States Court of Appeals, Eleventh Circuit
418 F.3d 1166 (2005)

CARNES, CIRCUIT JUDGE:

In August of 2002, a jury convicted Salvador Magluta of twelve counts: eight counts of laundering drug proceeds, and one count each of conspiracy to launder drug proceeds, conspiracy to obstruct justice, obstruction of justice by bribing a witness, and obstruction of justice by bribing a juror. The jury also returned a special forfeiture verdict requiring Magluta to forfeit $15 million in currency, and also some real property.

In January of 2003, the district court sentenced Magluta to 2,460 months (205 years) in prison. The total sentence was rang up this way: 240 months on each of the eight substantive drug proceeds laundering counts; 240 months on the conspiracy to launder count; 60 months on the conspiracy to obstruct justice count; 120 months on the obstruction by bribing a juror count; and 120 months on the obstruction by bribing a witness count. Each sentence was made consecutive to every other one.

* * *

III.

Magluta's third major contention is that his conviction for obstruction of justice through juror bribery must be reversed because the district court erred in admitting two out-of-court statements made by Miguel Moya, who had been the jury foreman in the 1996 trial. The government used those statements to prove that Magluta had bribed Moya to produce an acquittal in that earlier case.

The first of the two statements in question was made by Moya to undercover FBI Agent Joaquin Garcia in a recorded conversation that took place in July 1998. In that conversation Garcia told Moya that he had been sent by Magluta (and Magluta's co-defendant in the 1996 trial, Augusto Falcon) to ensure that Moya kept quiet about the bribe he had received two-and-a-half years earlier. After prodding by Garcia, Moya acknowledged having accepted that bribe from Magluta and his co-defendant Falcon.[4] Moya assured Garcia that only his wife and parents knew he had received the bribe money, and he promised Garcia that he would not cooperate with authorities.

The court admitted Moya's statements as non-hearsay statements of a co-conspirator under Fed. R. Evid. 801(d)(2)(E). "We review the district court's evidentiary rulings for an abuse of discretion," *United States v. Hasner*, 340 F.3d 1261, 1274 (11th Cir. 2003), and we may overturn findings of fact only if clearly erroneous, *United States v. Griggs*, 735 F.2d 1318, 1325 (11th Cir. 1984).

"Under Rule 801(d)(2)(E), statements of co-conspirators made during the course and in furtherance of the conspiracy are not hearsay. For evidence to be admissible under Rule 801(d)(2)(E), the government must prove by a preponderance of the evidence these things: (1) a conspiracy existed; (2) the conspiracy included the declarant and the defendant against whom the statement is offered; and (3) the statement was made during the course and in furtherance of the conspiracy. In determining the admissibility of co-conspirator statements, the trial court may consider both the co-conspirator's statements and independent external evidence." *Hasner*, 340 F.3d at 1274. In ruling on the admissibility of the conversation between Moya and Agent Garcia under Rule 801(d)(2)(E), the district court found that:

> [T]his conspiracy continued to exist up through July of 1998, when this statement was made. The Court does find that although Mr. Moya's participation was in just one component, he was a participant in the overall scheme. He would not have known all of the ins and outs of the conspiracy

---

[4] We have no way of knowing exactly how large the bribe was that Moya received. The record does show, however, that although Moya and his family were of modest means, they made $330,000 in cash expenditures and bank deposits in the twenty-seven months following the trial.

that's charged in this Indictment, but . . . in agreeing to . . . accept[ ] the bribe for convincing the other jurors to return a judgment of acquittal, he is still a member of the conspiracy.

He sat and listened to the evidence in the case . . . that Mr. Falcon and Mr. Magluta were participants in a major drug trafficking organization; that the monies that were connected with them were proceeds of a major drug trafficking organization. . . . I find that the government has proved by a preponderance of the evidence that . . . [Moya] knew that the [bribe] money was from a specified unlawful activity and, therefore, he took actions to cover up his sudden found wealth in creating all of the various gifts of funds to his relatives and near relatives and friends . . . . So his participation and his actions continue to evidence efforts to cover up his criminal acts. The law does find that such conduct of covering up the acts are part and parcel of the conspiracy.

Magluta argues that if he and Moya conspired to obstruct justice through juror bribery, the central purpose of that conspiracy ended, at the latest, once the verdict in the earlier case was rendered in February 1996. As a result, according to Magluta, Moya's conversation with the undercover FBI agent, which took place in July 1998, was not made during the course of the juror bribery conspiracy but instead came well after the conspiracy had ended.

In *Grunewald v. United States*, 353 U.S. 391, 77 S. Ct. 963, 1 L. Ed. 2d 931 (1957), the Supreme Court held that: "[A]fter the central criminal purposes of a conspiracy have been attained, a subsidiary conspiracy to conceal may not be implied from circumstantial evidence showing merely that the conspiracy was kept a secret and that the conspirators took care to cover up their crime in order to escape detection and punishment." 353 U.S. at 401–02, 77 S. Ct. at 972. The Court also recognized that "a vital distinction must be made between acts of concealment done in furtherance of the main criminal objectives of the conspiracy, and acts of conceal-ment done after these central objectives have been attained, for the purpose only of covering up after the crime." *Id.* at 405, 77 S. Ct. at 974.

The central purpose of the juror bribery conspiracy between Magluta and Moya was to secure an acquittal for Magluta in return for cash. Once the verdict was rendered, that central purpose was completed. Although it was mutually under-stood that Magluta and Moya would conceal the bribe, in the Supreme Court's words, those "[a]cts of covering up, even though done in the context of a mutually understood need for secrecy, cannot themselves constitute proof that concealment of the crime after its commission was part of the initial agreement among the conspirators." *Id.* at 402, 77 S. Ct. at 972. In light of *Grunewald*, we cannot infer that a subsidiary conspiracy to conceal the bribe Magluta had given Moya existed for almost two-and-a-half-years after the bribery agreement had been made and carried out. *See id.* at 401–02, 77 S. Ct. at 972. As a result, Moya's statement to Agent Garcia was not in furtherance of the conspiracy to obstruct justice through juror bribery.

The government argues, and the district court's findings indicate it believed, that Moya's statements are admissible under Rule 801(d)(2)(E) on the ground that it was in furtherance of another conspiracy. Under this theory, there was a conspiracy between Magluta and Moya to launder drug proceeds in violation of

§ 1956(a)(1)(B)(i). That conspiracy would have begun when Moya accepted the bribe from Magluta, which was paid out of illegal drug proceeds, and it was still ongoing at the time Moya assured Agent Garcia that he would keep quiet about it.[5]

We will assume for the moment that Moya's acceptance of the bribe made him and Magluta participants in a conspiracy to launder drug proceeds under 18 U.S.C. § 1956(a)(1)(B)(i). *Cf. Abbell*, 271 F.3d at 1298 (affirming the defendant lawyers' convictions for violating § 1956(a)(1)(B)(i) where the lawyers gave money to certain inmates while concealing that the money was being paid at the direction of and on behalf of the lawyers' client). Even with that assumption the argument fails under *Grunewald*, because Moya's statements to Agent Garcia were not made during the course of and in furtherance of that money laundering conspiracy.

As we mentioned before, Moya's statements to Agent Garcia occurred two-and-a-half years after Moya accepted the bribe. Assuming Magluta's payment of the bribe to Moya constituted a conspiracy between them to launder drug proceeds in the amount of the bribe, the evidence does not support an inference that the initial conspiracy included a "subsidiary conspiracy to conceal" which was ongoing so long after the bribe — the single act of money laundering — had occurred. *See Grunewald*, 353 U.S. at 401–02, 77 S. Ct. at 972.

Moya's statements to Agent Garcia do constitute an attempt to keep any initial conspiracy secret, but that attempt is not enough by itself to establish the coverup two-and-a-half years later was part of the initial agreement between Magluta and Moya. As the Supreme Court explained: "[E]very conspiracy is by its very nature secret; a case can hardly be supposed where men concert together for crime and advertise their purpose to the world. And again, every conspiracy will inevitably be followed by actions taken to cover the conspirators' traces. Sanctioning the government's theory would for all practical purposes wipe out the statute of limitations in conspiracy cases, as well as extend indefinitely the time within which hearsay declarations will bind co-conspirators." *Id.* at 402, 77 S. Ct. at 972.

That Moya tried to hide the source of the funds he used to make purchases for himself and his family does not bring those acts into any earlier drug laundering conspiracy between Magluta and Moya. Whatever crimes Moya may have committed by concealing the source of the funds that he used to pay for his purchases, there is no evidence to suggest that making them was part of the initial conspiracy between him and Magluta. Otherwise, the government could have charged Magluta with money laundering for every purchase Moya made with the bribe proceeds; that would not be a reasonable interpretation of the conspiracy and money laundering laws. Because the later transactions that Moya engaged in were not part of the "initial agreement" between him and Magluta, *see Grunewald*, 353 U.S. at 402, 77 S. Ct. at 972, they do not extend the life of the money laundering conspiracy that began in January of 1996 to include Moya's July 1998 statements to Agent Garcia. As a result, the district court should not have admitted Moya's statements to Agent Garcia pursuant to Rule 801(d)(2)(E).

---

[5] That this conspiracy was not charged in the indictment in this case does not matter. *United States v. Salisbury*, 662 F.2d 738, 740 (11th Cir. 1981) ("Statements of a coconspirator may be introduced into evidence even though the government has not charged [the coconspirator] with conspiracy as long as the existence of the conspiracy has been properly established.").

[3] Made "In Furtherance of the Conspiracy"

The statement in question, in addition to having been made during the course of the conspiracy, must also serve to further the ends of the illegal partnership; it must be more than mere idle conversation in which the declarant makes casual admissions of culpability. *United States v. Moore*, 522 F.2d 1068 (9th Cir. 1975). The risks of misreporting and fabrication are simply too great in such situations. The declarant must intend his statement to facilitate the conspiracy's goals through preparation, solicitation of business, or the inducement of others to join the venture. *See United States v. Goodman*, 605 F.2d 870 (5th Cir. 1979); Mueller & Kirkpatrick, EVIDENCE PRACTICE UNDER THE RULES § 8.33, at 1141–44 (1999). In *Diez*, because the purpose of the conspiracy was concealment, the court found deceptive statements made after apprehension to be in furtherance of the purpose. Statements made during the course of the conspiracy, but which only discuss the past conduct of the defendant in a context unrelated to the furtherance of the conspiracy, are inadmissible under Rule 801(d)(2)(E). *In re Sunset Bay Assoc.*, 944 F.2d 1503, 1519 (9th Cir. 1991).

The following cases illustrate types of statements that were made in furtherance of a conspiracy: *United States v. Santiago*, 837 F.2d 1545 (11th Cir. 1988) (boasting about exploit in order to gain confidence of others and allay fears of participants); *United States v. Crespo de Llano*, 830 F.2d 1532, 1543 (9th Cir. 1987) (co-conspirator's statement that his apartment was used by defendant as "safe house" to conduct cocaine transactions was made to keep undercover agent abreast of conspirator's activities or to induce him to purchase narcotics); *United States v. Avarza-Garcia*, 819 F.2d 1043, 1050 (11th Cir. 1987) (co-conspirator's false statement to Coast Guard's inquiry when stopped at sea regarding nationality of ship smuggling drugs); *United States v. Andersson*, 813 F.2d 1450, 1456–1457 (9th Cir. 1987) (one co-conspirator's response to another's inquiry during drug transaction whether everything was "going okay" was made to keep conspirator abreast of co-conspirator's activities); *United States v. Gomez*, 810 F.2d 947, 953–954 (10th Cir. 1987) (co-conspirator's statement telling other conspirators that defendant was source of cocaine allayed conspirators' possible suspicions regarding continued availability of cocaine). *But see United States v. Wood*, 834 F.2d 1382, 1385 (8th Cir. 1987) (co-conspirator's statement to his wife that he was working for defendant installing radio equipment in boats "used for marijuana" was not made in furtherance of conspiracy because co-conspirator was not seeking to induce his wife to join conspiracy).

UNITED STATES v. WEAVER
United States Court of Appeals, Third Circuit
507 F.3d 178 (2007)

McKEE, CIRCUIT JUDGE.

The government appeals the district court's grant of Delores Weaver's motion *in limine*. The order precluded the government from introducing a recorded telephone conversation in its case-in-chief. For the following reasons, we will vacate the order and remand.[1]

I. Factual Background and Procedural History

The government's allegations include averments that Faridah Ali, the assistant director of the Sister Clara Mohammed School (the "School"), and Delores Weaver, the director of the Adult Basic Education ("ABE") program at the Community College of Philadelphia ("CCP"), devised a scheme to defraud CCP out of rental payments to the School by representing that they were providing ABE classes that were never taught and then splitting payments CCP sent to compensate the School for those nonexistent classes. To help establish Weaver's involvement in the scheme, the government wanted to introduce a conversation between Faridah Ali and her sister, Zaynah Rasool, that occurred on September 4, 2001 (the "September 4 conversation").

During the September 4 conversation, Ali and Rasool discussed various administrative matters at the School, commented on some of the School's faculty, and talked about the School's arrangement with CCP. Ali also made the following comments about Sayeeda Quaye, a teacher at the School: "[S]he got paid for all summer from [CCP]." This statement prompted Rasool to respond: "[S]he ain't did nothing." Ali continued: "[A]lways people gonna be backbiting us as much as we do for them."

The conversation then turned to Weaver. Ali complained as follows that Weaver had not put her on CCP's payroll: "Delores is . . . just like you said, she does not want me . . . to have more than her. And now that I bought this big car, I'm gonna have to pay for it." The discussion continued:

Ali: [Weaver]'s being a B and I'm so sick of her. I'll be so glad when I won't need her no more. Gonna be asking for half of what the school get. You know what I'm saying?

Rasool: Yeah. It's . . . petty and rotten and illegal.

Ali: Yeah.

Rasool: Cause she's already gettin' other stuff. Uh, so I mean come on now it ain't no sense in just going overboard.

Ali: Right. But I just don't want to do anything right now with Sayeeda and them and jeopardize what we got with the college, you know. Cause you know they be the one's to be calling and saying they ain't nobody here at this time go check the, you know what, I know they'd do that.

App. 134–37.

Weaver filed a motion to exclude the entire September 4 conversation from trial on the grounds that she was not a party to it and Rasool was not a member of the

---

[1] The district court had subject matter jurisdiction pursuant to 18 U.S.C. § 3231. We have jurisdiction pursuant to 18 U.S.C. § 3731. Our review of the district court's interpretation of the Rules of Evidence is plenary. We review the court's findings of fact for clear error. *United States v. Cruz*, 910 F.2d 1072, 1081 (3d Cir. 1990).

conspiracy. The court granted the motion without holding a hearing based on the strength of the briefs and its review of a transcript of the September 4 conversation. The court did not accept either of the grounds for exclusion asserted by Weaver.

Rather, the court reasoned that the September 4 conversation was inadmissible because the statements made therein "cannot be regarded as having been made in furtherance of the alleged conspiracy. . . . "[3] App. 2. The court also concluded that it was difficult to extrapolate any "statement of fact" from the conversation because "the statements seem to constitute derogatory opinions having no conceivable value." *Id.* at 2–3. Accordingly, the court ruled that the statements were not admissible under Federal Rule of Evidence 801(d)(2)(E). The court then granted the government's motion to stay Weaver's trial pending appeal. This appeal followed.

II. Discussion

A. *Rule 801(d)(2)(E)'s "in furtherance" Requirement*

The government argues that the district court erred in ruling that the September 4 conversation was inadmissible hearsay. The government contends that the statements are excepted by the hearsay rule under Rule 801(d)(2)(E). In order for an out-of-court statement to meet the co-conspirator exception:

> the district court must find by a preponderance of the evidence that: (1) a conspiracy existed; (2) the declarant and the party against whom the statement is offered were members of the conspiracy; (3) the statement was made in the course of the conspiracy; and (4) the statement was made in furtherance of the conspiracy.

United States v. Ellis, 156 F.3d 493, 496 (3d Cir. 1998); *United States v. Vega,* 285 F.3d 256, 264 (3d Cir. 2002). Other than finding that the September 4 conversation was not in furtherance of the conspiracy, the district court failed to make any findings in respect to the other foundational requirements of Rule 801(d)(2)(E).

However, Weaver concedes that the district court implicitly found "the existence of a conspiracy, that Ali and Weaver were members of the conspiracy, and that the [September 4 conversation took place] during the course of the conspiracy," Appellee's Br. 8 n. 5, and she does not contest these implied findings. Rather, she argues only that the September 4 conversation is inadmissible because it was not in furtherance of the conspiracy and because the statements are irrelevant, just as the district court concluded. We disagree.

Our analysis is guided by several of our prior decisions addressing this issue. In *United States v. Ammar,* 714 F.2d 238 (3d Cir. 1983), four members of a nine-person conspiracy, Ghassan Ammar, Judith Ammar, Marshall Stillman, and Roger Mc-Fayden, were tried and convicted on several charges stemming from their

---

[3] Rule 801(d)(2)(E) provides: "A statement is not hearsay if — . . . the statement is offered against a party and is . . . a statement by a coconspirator of a party during the course and in furtherance of the conspiracy." Fed. R. Evid. 801(d)(2)(E).

conspiracy to import and distribute heroin. Two of the indicted co-conspirators, Charles Rossi and Michael Dugan, pleaded guilty and testified for the government. The two unindicted co-conspirators, John Welkie and Gilber Bunner, also testified against the defendants at trial. The other three indicted co-conspirators, Ibraham Ammar, Abedeen Ammar, and Naim Dahabi, were fugitives when the trial began. *Id.* at 243. All of the conspirators who went to trial were convicted.

On appeal, Judith and Stillman challenged the admission of certain out-of-court statements made by their co-conspirators on the grounds that the statements were not in furtherance of the conspiracy because they merely "constituted narratives of past events. . . . " *Id.* at 252. Specifically, Judith challenged the admissibility of Ghassan's statements to Welkie and Rossi that when he and Judith returned from a trip to Beirut, Lebanon to purchase heroin they were checked at customs, but their heroin had not been discovered. Stillman challenged the admissibility of Ibraham's statements to Ghassan, Judith, and Welkie that "Stillman owed them a lot of money for the last shipment of heroin and would have to pay up before he could get another package." *Id.*

We rejected the defendants' argument that the foregoing statements were not admissible under Rule 801(d)(2)(E) because they were not made in furtherance of the conspiracy. We explained:

> Statements between conspirators which provide reassurance, serve to maintain trust and cohesiveness among them, or inform each other of the current status of the conspiracy further the ends of the conspiracy and are admissible so long as the other requirements of Rule 801(d)(2)(E) are met. Such statements are more than 'mere narratives' of past events.

Id. at 252. (citations omitted).

We distinguished the admissible out-of-court statements at issue there from the inadmissible out-of-court statements at issue in *United States v. Provenzano*, 620 F.2d 985 (3d Cir. 1980). We explained that the statements in *Provenzano* "had been made to non-members of the conspiracy who had no need to know about the matters disclosed." *Ammar*, 714 F.2d at 252. Provenzano concerned the admissibility of out-of-court statements of the defendants' co-conspirator (and the government's chief witness), Ralph Picardo, about the defendants' involvement in a labor-kickback scheme. Specifically, the defendants argued that statements Picardo had made to his girlfriends, Paulette Compton and Mary Ann Hart, and one of his employees, Alan Abramowitz, concerning (1) the defendants' roles in the scheme, (2) the legitimacy of a corporation central to the scheme, (3) how two other corporations central to the scheme were capitalized and financed, (4) Picardo's high regard for one of the defendants, and (5) the fact that Picardo traveled to Florida on one of the defendant's orders, were inadmissible under Rule 801(d)(2)(E) because those statements were not in furtherance of the conspiracy.

However, we concluded that Picardo's statements to Compton, who had been in charge of one of the businesses at the center of the scheme while Picardo was in jail, were admissible under Rule 801(d)(2)(E) because "[i]f [she] were to run the business, she had to know the details, and therefore, Picardo's telling her the sordid details was in furtherance of the conspiracy." *Id.* at 1001. Picardo's statements to

Hart and Abramowitz were not admissible under the co-conspirator exception. "Only if there was a reason for [them] to know these things about the conspiracy could the statements have been in furtherance of the conspiracy." *Id.* We further reasoned that the statements made to Hart and Abramowitz were not in furtherance of the conspiracy because they were "Picardo's errand runners. The district court made no findings, and the Government has pointed to no evidence indicating anything Picardo told them could have furthered the conspiracy." *Id.*

In *United States v. Gibbs*, 739 F.2d 838 (3d Cir. 1984), we rejected the defendant's contention that the trial court erred in admitting out-of-court statements against him because the statements "were mere narratives of past fact and not made to induce conduct that would further the goals of the conspiracy. . . ." *Id.* at 845. The statements at issue in *Gibbs* involved conversations between Joseph Quintiliano, Charles Bilella, and David White that implicated Stephen Gibbs (also known as "Jake") in a conspiracy to import and distribute marijuana. White and Bilella both testified that Quintiliano told them that he planned to sell the marijuana to a previous customer named "Jake," that "Jake" was getting impatient about receiving the drugs, and that Quintiliano had invited "Jake" to visit him to review plans to import the drugs.

White also testified that he met Gibbs in Philadelphia the day after Quintiliano told him about "Jake's" visit. Gibbs had introduced himself as "Jake," and Gibbs matched the description Quintiliano had given him of "Jake." White further testified that Quintiliano told him that "Jake" wanted to buy the marijuana that was being imported, but needed time to raise the money. Finally, White testified that Quintiliano asked him if he could store the marijuana in his shop until "Jake" could raise the funds to purchase the drugs. *Id.* at 841–42.

In rejecting Gibbs's contention that the foregoing statements were not in furtherance of the conspiracy, we first observed that "[t]he in furtherance requirement is usually given a broad interpretation." *Id.* at 845. We also acknowledged that "statements made to those who are not involved in the conspiracy are not in furtherance of it just as casual conversation between co-conspirators that is not intended to induce continued involvement, or other actions that would not advance the conspiracy, are not in furtherance of a conspiracy." *Id.* (citation omitted). However, we reasoned that this did not apply in *Gibbs* because "[a]s participants in the scheme, it was important for White and Bilella to be kept abreast of developments to induce their continued participation and allay any fear they might have had." *Id.* at 846. We also distinguished the statements that had been at issue in *Gibbs*, from those in *Provenzano*. We reasoned that, unlike in *Provenzano* — where "the statements were made to persons not part of the conspiracy who had no reason to know about the matters disclosed to them" — all of the statements in Gibbs "were made to co-conspirators." *Id.*

Weaver attempts to distinguish *Ammar* and *Gibbs* by stressing that they involve drug conspiracies, which "by their nature and culture are different; many of the conversations are coded or veiled in some way, making it difficult to ascertain the purpose or intent of the statements." Appellee's Br. at 8. Although we agree that drug-conspiracy cases may differ from the fraudulent financial scheme alleged as the object of this conspiracy, the legal principles applicable to evidentiary disputes are the same. Moreover, none of the statements that we ruled admissible in *Ammar* and *Gibbs* were "coded or veiled."

In *Ammar,* the statement Judith challenged was made by her husband to another member of the conspiracy recounting how he and his wife outsmarted customs agents to smuggle drugs into the country. The statement Stillman challenged was made by one co-conspirator to other co-conspirators and informed them that Stillman was delinquent on payments for drugs he had received and that he was not to be sold any more drugs until he cleared his debt. The statements were uncoded and could be understood by someone with no expertise in the drug trade.

In *Gibbs*, Quintiliano's statements to White identified Gibbs as "Jake," kept him current on "Jake's" desire and ability to purchase the marijuana, and arranged to store the marijuana for sale. There is similarly nothing "coded or veiled" about those conversations.

Ironically, Weaver directs our attention to another drug case, *United States v. Reyes,* 798 F.2d 380 (10th Cir. 1986), in arguing that "although there is no 'talismanic formula' for determining the 'in furtherance of' requirement, the statement, at a minimum[,] should advance the object of the conspiracy" to be admissible under Rule 801(d)(2)(E). Appellee's Br. 8. However, her reliance on *Reyes* is unavailing. There, a government informant, William Ayala, was permitted to testify that Raul Reyes's co-conspirator, Roberto Ramirez, told him that Reyes was paying for, and distributing drugs. *Reyes,* 798 F.2d at 384.

Reyes appealed his conviction for conspiring to possess and distribute drugs, in part, on the ground that Ramirez's statement to Ayala did not satisfy Rule 801(d)(2)(E)'s "in furtherance" requirement because the government had not established that Ramirez's statement "both intended to promote the conspiracy and did in fact have the effect of promoting the conspiracy." *Id.* The court of appeals rejected that argument, expressly noting that it "reject[ed] the defendant's proposition that the statements must *actually* further the conspiracy to be admissible." 798 F.2d at 384 (emphasis in original). The court reasoned that "Rule 801(d)(2)(E) . . . says statements need be 'in furtherance of the conspiracy,' not that they 'further the conspiracy.' It is enough that they be *intended* to promote the conspiratorial objectives." *Id.* (emphasis added). The court ultimately concluded that Ramirez's statement to Ayala was in furtherance of the drug conspiracy "[s]ince Ramirez' statements explained events important to the conspiracy to one of its members in order to facilitate the conspiracy. . . . " *Id.*

We understand Weaver to be arguing that Ali's statements did not *actually* facilitate the conspiracy, and therefore should not be admitted under *Reyes*. As an initial matter, we note that we are not bound by *Reyes*. Moreover, insofar as *Reyes* holds that "it is enough" for purposes of Rule 801(d)(2)(E)'s "in furtherance" requirement that statements "be intended to promote the conspiratorial objectives," we agree. However, as *Ammar* makes clear, the "in furtherance" requirement of Rule 801(d)(2)(E) can be satisfied when the declarant merely informs a co-conspirator of the status of the conspiracy.

B. *Statements Informing about the Status of the Conspiracy*

During an important part of the September 4 conversation, Ali told Rasool: "[Weaver's] being a B and I'm so sick of her. I'll be so glad when I won't need her no more. Gonna be asking for half of what the school get. You know what I'm saying?" We believe the district court's analysis of the September 4 conversation, and the court's conclusion that it was inadmissible hearsay that was little more than idle gossip comprised of "derogatory opinions having no conceivable probative value," was unduly influenced by the fact that Ali referred to Weaver as a "B." App. 2–3. However, there is clearly more to the conversation.

If Ali had only stated that "[Weaver's] being a B and I'm so sick of her," we would agree with the district court. But Ali went on to say: "I'll be so glad when I won't need her no more." This statement informs Rasool that Ali was dependent on Weaver for the success of the fraudulent scheme, and Ali is lamenting that dependence. Ali also said about Weaver: "Gonna be asking for half of what the school get." This statement informs Rasool that Weaver is requesting a 50% "kickback" from the rent payments CCP allegedly made to the School.

Since Weaver was the director of the ABE program at CCP, it makes sense that Ali would have been dependent on her to make sure that CCP did not discover that the School was a sham site and that CCP continued to make rental payments to the School. Ali was therefore informing Rasool of the "current status of the conspiracy" when she expressed dissatisfaction with her dependence on Weaver and explained Weaver's request for half of the School's payments.

A declarant's statement explaining the current status of the conspiracy is "in furtherance" of that conspiracy only if the addressee is also a co-conspirator. *See Ammar,* 714 F.2d at 252 ("Statements *between conspirators* which . . . inform each other of the current status of the conspiracy further the ends of the conspiracy . . . .") (emphasis added); *see also Gibbs,* 739 F.2d at 846 (" *As participants in the scheme,* it was important for [the addressees] to be kept abreast of developments to induce their continued participation [in the conspiracy].") (emphasis added). The government argues that Rasool was a co-conspirator. As noted earlier, the district court failed to conduct an evidentiary hearing on Weaver's motion *in limine.* However, we think it clear that, if the government can prove Rasool's involvement in the conspiracy by a preponderance of the evidence, the portion of the September 4 conversation where Ali apprised Rasool of the status of the conspiracy would be admissible because it would then be "in furtherance" of the charged conspiracy.

C. *Statements Concealing the Conspiracy*

In *United States v. Pecora,* 798 F.2d 614 (3d Cir.1986), defendants challenged the admission of a recorded telephone conversation among several unindicted co-conspirators. Their challenge included the argument that the conversations were not in furtherance of the no-show scheme at issue there. *Id.* at 630. The conversations consisted of statements "trying to get their stories straight about what their jobs entailed in anticipation of a government investigation." *Id.* at 625. Defendants argued that the conversations were inadmissible because their purpose was "to conceal the declarants' participation in the conspiracy at a time when the declarants were no longer conspirators, having terminated their involvement." *Id.* at 630.

We rejected that argument explaining:

> "[i]f the acts of concealment amount to nothing more than (1) a criminal conspiracy which is carried out in secrecy; (2) a continuation of the secrecy after the accomplishment of the crime; and (3) desperate attempts to cover up after the crime begins to come to light then declarations made during an agreement to conceal are indeed not made in furtherance of the conspiracy."

Id. (citation and quotation omitted). However, we recognized in Pecora that the Supreme Court has cautioned:

> "[b]y no means does this mean that acts of concealment can never have significance in furthering a criminal conspiracy. But a vital distinction must be made between acts of concealment done in furtherance of the main criminal objectives of the conspiracy, and acts of concealment done after these central objectives have been attained, for the purpose only of covering up after the crime."

Pecora, 798 F.2d at 630 (quoting *Grunewald v. United States,* 353 U.S. 391, 405, 77 S. Ct. 963, 1 L. Ed. 2d 931 (1957)). We concluded that the recorded conversations in *Pecora* were admissible against the defendants because "concealment of the existence of the conspiracy enabled the defendants to continue their illegal payoff scheme for two more years . . . ". *Pecora,* 798 F.2d at 631.

As quoted earlier, here Ali told Rasool:

> I just don't want to do anything right now with Sayeeda and them and jeopardize what we got with the college, you know. Cause you know they be the one's to be calling and saying they ain't nobody there at this time go check the, you know what, I know they'd do that.

App. 134–37. Thus, Ali is cautioning Rasool not to upset a teacher at the School ("Sayeeda") because that teacher might tell CCP ("the college") that there are no ABE classes being taught at the School ("ain't nobody there at this time"). Ali is obviously concerned that if they upset or anger Sayeeda in any way, Sayeeda might report the fact that the School is empty when ABE classes should have been in session, thus revealing the "no show" scheme. Since it is clear that the purpose behind these statements was to conceal that scheme so that it could continue, we conclude that they were made in furtherance of it.

Moreover, our conclusion that Ali's statements to conceal the conspiracy were in furtherance of it is not undermined by the fact that the district court failed to hold an evidentiary hearing on Weaver's motion *in limine.* Even if Rasool was not a member of the conspiracy, Ali's efforts to conceal the scheme were clearly *intended* to further it. *See Reyes,* 798 F.2d at 384.

As we have explained, statements made to inform others of the status of a conspiracy only further the conspiracy if the addressees are also interested in the status of the conspiracy. *See Ammar,* 714 F.2d at 252; *see also Gibbs,* 739 F.2d at

846. Conversely, statements made for the purpose of concealing a conspiracy can further the conspiracy regardless of whether the addressee is a co-conspirator. Although jurors may not interpret this statement as an effort to concealment, the government has at least satisfied the "in furtherance" requirement of Rule 801(d)(2)(E) and is therefore entitled to have the jury consider this portion of the September 4 conversation.

Thus, Weaver's attempt to define the September 4 conversation as merely being Ali's "complaints" about Weaver is not persuasive. Appellee's Br. at 9. Weaver attempts to buttress this argument by relying on the reasoning in *United States v. LiCausi*, 167 F.3d 36 (1st Cir. 1999). *LiCausi* involved a conspiracy to rob several supermarkets and convenience stores. One of the defendants, John LiCausi, argued on appeal that the district court had erred in admitting out-of-court statements of one of his co-conspirators, Bernie Subocz, to a female acquaintance, Lori Munroe, because they were not in furtherance of the conspiracy. *Id.* at 50.

Subocz had returned from a crime spree in Ohio when he told Munroe about several robberies he and his crew had attempted that had been botched for various reasons. The court agreed with LiCausi that the statements were inadmissible because "[a]ll but one were made after the crimes they described took place, and they do not appear to have yielded significant enough information to constitute reports to a coconspirator, assuming Munroe could be considered as such." *Id.* The court also concluded that the statements "appear[ed] . . . to be instances where Subocz was 'merely blowing off steam or venting anxiety'" or simply avoiding an argument with his girlfriend.

Here, even if we were to concede that some of Ali's statements during the September 4 conversation can be fairly characterized as "merely blowing off steam or venting anxiety," the bulk of her statements are qualitatively different than those in *LiCausi*. All but one of the statements in *LiCausi* were made after the crimes were committed, and were obviously not intended to conceal prospective criminal activity. Accordingly, the statements were not in furtherance of a conspiracy. *See id.*

Conversely, as we have explained, Ali's statement to Rasool concerned the need to proceed with caution in order to prevent revelation of the scheme that would result from the discovery of empty classrooms and require an explanation of how the proceeds were being used.

D. *Admissibility of Rasool's Statements*

The government appears primarily interested in admitting Ali's statements during the September 4 conversation. However, if the government intends to introduce Rasool's statements against Weaver under the co-conspirator exception, it must establish by a preponderance of the evidence that Rasool was also a conspirator. As we have noted, the government never had a chance to establish Rasool's membership in the conspiracy. Of course, in addition to establishing Rasool's role in the conspiracy, the government must also satisfy the other requirements of Rule 801(d)(2)(E). *See Ellis*, 156 F.3d at 496.

E. *Relevance of the September 4 Conversation*

The district court also ruled the September 4 conversation irrelevant. Federal Rule of Evidence 401 defines "relevant evidence" as "evidence having any tendency to make the existence of any fact that is of consequence to the determination of the action more probable or less probable than it would be without the evidence." Fed. R. Evid. 401. Here, Ali's statements to Rasool during the September 4 conversation confirm essential elements of the conspiratorial scheme. Specifically, Ali informed Rasool that she was dependent on Weaver for the scheme to continue and that Weaver requested half of the School's proceeds from the scheme. Ali also instructed Rasool not to upset Sayeeda and thereby jeopardize the scheme, as we have just explained.

It is, of course, ultimately for the jury to interpret those statements. However, they are certainly relevant to the charges against Weaver because Ali's statements to Rasool tend to make it more probable than not that Weaver knew about the scheme to defraud CCP and was involved in it. Accordingly, the district court erred in finding the September 4 conversation irrelevant.

In conclusion, we will remand for the district court to provide the government with the opportunity to present evidence in support of its allegation that Rasool was a co-conspirator. We recognize that "the control of the order of proof at trial [for admission of statements under Rule 801(d)(2)(E)] is a matter committed to the discretion of the trial judge," *Ammar,* 714 F.2d at 246, and leave it to the court to decide whether to: (1) conduct a pretrial evidentiary hearing on Weaver's motion *in limine;* or (2) conditionally admit the challenged conversation "subject to the requirement that the government make [its Rule 801(d)(2)(E)] showing by the close of its case," *id.* at 247. *See id.* (noting that the latter procedure should be "carefully considered and sparingly utilized") (quoting *United States v. Continental Group, Inc.,* 603 F.2d 444, 457 (3d Cir. 1979)). After hearing the relevant evidence, whether at a pretrial hearing or during the trial, the district court will then be able to determine whether the government has proven by a preponderance of the evidence that the portion of Ali's statements to Rasool informing her of the status of the conspiracy are admissible under Rule 801(d)(2)(E).

If the evidence shows that Rasool was, as the government claims, a co-conspirator in the charged conspiracy, that portion of the conversation would be admissible under Rule 801(d)(2)(E). If, on the other hand, the evidence shows that Rasool had no involvement in the charged conspiracy, the district court should grant Weaver's motion with respect to that portion of the conversation only. However, regardless of the district court's findings in respect to Rasool's involvement in the conspiracy, Ali's statements to Rasool regarding Sayeeda and concealing the conspiracy are admissible under Rule 801(d)(2)(E).

III.

For the reasons stated above, we will vacate the district court's order granting Weaver's motion *in limine* and remand for further proceedings consistent with this opinion.

EXERCISES

1. Amber filed a products liability action alleging that a hair bleaching product manufactured by Farouk Systems burned her scalp, causing her to suffer physical, mental, and emotional pain. During discovery Amber located Rosemary, a salon owner, who recalled a conversation that she had with Mr. Farouk, the chairman of Farouk Systems. According to Rosemary, Mr. Farouk explained that he was the head of research and development, and that he was aware that the hair bleaching formula occasionally overheated due to an accelerated chemical reaction. Consequently, Farouk Systems was in the process of reformulating the product. Amber wants to call Rosemary to testify at trial, but fears that Farouk Systems will object on hearsay grounds. Will Rosemary's testimony be admissible at trial?

2. Turner wrote a book that instructed readers how to escape federal and state income taxation through the use of "common law trusts." Turner also created a membership organization designed to assist its members in implementing the trusts described in his book. Turner recruited Daniel to join the organization. The two men then placed all of Daniel's assets in a common law trust. Daniel, pleased with the results, agreed to help Turner sell his book in exchange for a portion of the proceeds. The IRS, suspicious of the legitimacy of these "common law trusts," began a criminal investigation. An undercover IRS agent purchased Turner's book and then met with Daniel several times. Daniel encouraged the agent to join the organization and to set up his own trust to avoid taxes. The government then indicted Turner and Daniel for conspiring to defraud the United States government out of tax revenue. At Turner's trial, the government seeks to call the undercover agent to recount the conversations he had with Daniel. Turner objects on hearsay grounds. How should the court rule?

Chapter 5

EXCEPTIONS TO THE HEARSAY RULE

Strict application of the hearsay rule would result in the exclusion of substantial amounts of reliable evidence. It would prevent the finder of fact from considering statements that are inherently trustworthy, either because of their nature (for example, those that are against the interest of the person who made them) or because of the circumstances surrounding their utterance (for example, prior testimony that was given under oath or business records that are routinely kept and upon which a company regularly relies). If the person who made those statements or prepared the records were unavailable to testify, the hearsay rule would result in the total loss of the information contained in the statements. Strictly applied, the rule could result in substantially less accurate findings of fact than would result if there were no exclusion of hearsay evidence and the court admitted all such evidence and the dangers associated with it simply affected its relative weight.

To accommodate this problem, while retaining the hearsay rule, the courts could have made the hearsay rule's application discretionary, with admission of hearsay evidence based on the presiding judge's assessment of its reliability. This approach, however, would not have been practical because it would have led to inconsistencies among the courts, destroyed the rule's predictability and, therefore, encouraged further litigation. Instead, the courts adopted carefully defined and strictly enforced exceptions to the hearsay rule. This chapter will focus on these exceptions and the interpretive problems they have spawned.

Historically, courts and commentators have divided hearsay exceptions into two categories: those exceptions that require a showing that the out-of-court declarant is unavailable to testify, and those that do not. The Federal Rules of Evidence have incorporated this categorization. Rule 803 addresses exceptions for which the declarant's availability is immaterial. Rule 804 addresses those exceptions that require, as a prerequisite to admissibility, a showing that the declarant is unavailable.

The rationale for imposing the requirement of a showing of unavailability on some exceptions and not on others is unclear. If all exceptions were intended to resolve the problem of the hearsay rule's potential exclusion of the only evidence available on a particular point in a trial, one would expect the unavailability requirement to be a prerequisite to the use of all hearsay. Because this is not the case, it might be assumed the decision to predicate the admissibility of some statements on a showing of unavailability and not others was based on the inherent reliability of those statements that are admissible without a showing of unavailability. Under this hypothesis, the finder of fact always would consider those statements that are inherently reliable, regardless of whether the declarant was available and had testified. Conversely, the finder of fact would consider only those statements that were less inherently reliable only if there was a necessity to do so — if the declarant were not available to testify to the facts about which he had firsthand knowledge. A comparison of exceptions from each category, however, fails to support this hypothesis.

An excited utterance, for example, which is admissible regardless of the declarant's availability, offers assurances of sincerity because of the spontaneity with which a declarant makes such a statement and because of the statement's contemporaneity with the incident that caused the declarant to speak. The statement's accuracy, however, is suspect because of the declarant's potentially diminished quality of perception resulting from the extreme circumstances prompting the utterance. Consequently, although inherently sincere, excited utterances are not inherently reliable. Under the above hypothesis, therefore, the admissibility of excited utterances should depend on the proponent's demonstration of the declarant's unavailability. In fact, courts admit such statements regardless of the declarant's availability.

The declaration against interest, on the other hand, provides significant assurances of accuracy because of its nature. Such a statement is, by definition, harmful to the declarant's interests. The declarant, therefore, will likely have taken measures to ensure the statement's accuracy. Despite the great likelihood that the statement is accurate and reliable in this instance, courts have consistently required proponents of a declaration against interest to demonstrate the declarant's unavailability as a prerequisite to the statement's admissibility.

The categorization of hearsay exceptions is at times both illogical and inconsistent. Consequently, one could conclude that the pattern of categorization is little more than the product of historical accident. After first recognizing the exceptions in the factual contexts of particular cases, courts thereafter rigidly defined the exceptions by the contexts in which they were initially created. As McCormick has noted, however, the categorization "has stood the test of time and use, and offers a substantial measure of predictability." McCormick on Evidence § 253, at 444 (4th ed. 1994). Consequently, for purposes of clarity and continuity, this chapter discusses each category of hearsay exceptions separately.

§ 5.01 EXCEPTIONS REQUIRING DECLARANT'S UNAVAILABILITY

Under the Federal Rules of Evidence, there are four recognized hearsay exceptions requiring that the declarant be unavailable as a requisite to admissibility. These are dying declarations, former testimony, declarations against interest, and statements of personal or family history. Unavailability is an element of all of these exceptions and must be established by the proponent before evidence will be admitted under them. This section will discuss the first three exceptions.

In addition to these exceptions, Rule 807 of the Federal Rules of Evidence has added another exception, which has been variously described as the residual, catchall, open-ended, or discretionary exception. It sanctions the admission of statements not specifically covered by any of the other delineated exceptions if the statement has equivalent circumstantial guarantees of trustworthiness and meets certain specified conditions. This discretionary exception is discussed separately in a later section of this chapter.

[A]   Unavailable upon Claim of Privilege

Unavailability based on this exception depends on the existence of a privilege. As you will see in *Basciano*, this criteria depends on the existence of a privilege and its having not been waived.

UNITED STATES v. BASCIANO
United States District Court, Eastern District of New York
430 F. Supp. 2d 87 (2006)

[Vincent Basciano was charged with attempted murder and attempted to have the grand jury testimony of Joseph Filippone admitted under the prior testimony exception, which requires that the declarant be unavailable.]

On April 13, 2006 Basciano submitted a letter brief in support of a motion filed pursuant to Federal Rule of Evidence ("Rule") 804(b)(1). (Basciano Filippone Ltr. of Apr. 13, 2006 ("Basciano Filippone Ltr.") at 1.) Basciano seeks to introduce the grand jury testimony of Joseph Filippone ("Filippone") from December 29, 2005, when Filippone testified before a grand jury of the Eastern District of New York pursuant to a subpoena.[1] (*Id.*) Basciano apparently first sought to have Filippone testify at his trial. In apparent response, Filippone's attorney informed Basciano's counsel, that if called to testify, Filippone intends to invoke his Fifth Amendment right against incrimination and will refuse to testify.[2] (Basciano Filippone Ltr. at 3; Ex. A.) Basciano has filed this motion seeking to introduce Filippone's grand jury testimony pursuant to Rule 804(b)(1).

---

[1] The relevant portion of the transcript is:

Q: Do you have any knowledge, indirect or direct, about the circumstances of Frank Santoro's murder?

A: No, sir.

Q: Has any other person ever told you about anything involving that murder?

A: Right, my brother.

. . .

Q: Did you ever tell anyone besides the police that Frank was a kidnapper?

A: No.

Q: Did you attempt to warn Vincent Basciano that Frank was a kidnapper?

A: No.

Q: Did you pass a message to anyone that Frank perhaps was considering kidnapping Vincent Basciano's children?

A: Not at all.

Q: Were you ever in the drug business with Frank Santoro?

A: No.

(Grand Jury Transcript at 60–62; Basciano Filippone Ltr. at 1–2.)

[2] Filippone is awaiting trial in the Southern District of New York as a defendant in a multi-defendant heroin trafficking prosecution. He has been held in detention since his January 12, 2006 arrest. (Gov't Ltr. of Apr. 14, 2006 ("Gov't Filippone Ltr.") at 2.)

Federal Rule of Evidence 804 provides that subject to the unavailability of the declarant, the following is excluded by the hearsay rule: "[t]estimony given as a witness at another hearing of the same or a different proceeding, . . . if the party against whom the testimony is now offered . . . had an opportunity and similar motive to develop the testimony by direct, cross, or redirect examination." Fed. R. Evid. ("Rule") 804(b)(1). A declarant is unavailable for the purposes of this rule if he or she:

> (1) is exempted by ruling of the court on the ground of privilege from testifying concerning the subject matter of the declarant's statement; or

> (2) persists in refusing to testify concerning the subject matter of the declarant's statement despite an order of the court to do so; . . .

Rule 804(a). A declarant becomes unavailable when he or she successfully invokes the Fifth Amendment privilege against self incrimination. *United States v. Salerno*, 505 U.S. 317, 321, 112 S. Ct. 2503, 120 L. Ed. 2d 255 (1992). *See also United States v. Matthews*, 20 F.3d 538, 545 (2d Cir. 1994); *United States v. Bakhtiar*, 994 F.2d 970, 977 (2d Cir. 1993). A witness need not be physically brought into court to assert the privilege, although it is preferred that the declarant appear before the court to claim the privilege. *See, United States v. Williams*, 927 F.2d 95, 98–99 (2d Cir. 1991).

The Supreme Court has noted that "it is the duty of a court to determine the legitimacy of a witness's reliance upon the Fifth Amendment. A witness may not employ the privilege to avoid giving testimony that he simply would prefer not to give." *Roberts v. United States*, 445 U.S. 552, 560 n. 7, 100 S. Ct. 1358, 63 L. Ed. 2d 622 (1980) (citations omitted). Furthermore, "[a]s to each question to which a claim of privilege is directed, the court must determine whether the answer to that particular question would subject the witness to a 'real danger' of further crimination." *Rogers v. United States*, 340 U.S. 367, 374, 71 S. Ct. 438, 95 L. Ed. 344 (1951); see also *United States v. Zappola*, 646 F.2d 48, 53 (2d Cir. 1981) ("district court simply accepted [ ] [declarant's] blanket assertion of the fifth amendment privilege . . . and did not undertake a particularized inquiry to determine whether the assertion was founded on a reasonable fear of prosecution as to each of the posed questions. This was error.").

Even though witnesses are legally bound to give testimony when called by the grand jury, *United States v. Calandra*, 414 U.S. 338, 343, 94 S. Ct. 613, 38 L. Ed. 2d 561 (1974), the grand jury's authority to compel testimony is conditional on the witness's Fifth Amendment right against self incrimination. *United States v. Mandujano*, 425 U.S. 564, 575, 96 S. Ct. 1768, 48 L. Ed. 2d 212 (1976). If granted immunity to the witness, the witness can be compelled to answer even incriminating questions "on pain of contempt." *Id.* at 575, 96 S. Ct. 1768. Basciano's assertion that Filippone was granted immunity is not supported by any evidence. (*See* Basciano Filippone Ltr. at 3). The grand jury record makes no mention of immunity and the Government proffers that Filippone was not granted such. (*See* Gov't Filippone Ltr. at 1.) Furthermore, it is clear from the grand jury record that Filippone knowingly waived his Fifth Amendment privilege against self-incrimination about certain matters when he voluntarily testified before the grand jury.[3] Under the facts presented, I find that Filippone was not granted immunity for his grand jury testimony of December 29, 2005.

A witness's waiver of privilege may be inferred from his or her course of conduct or prior statements concerning the subject matter of the case, without inquiring into whether or not the witness was aware of the privilege and chose to waive it consciously. *Klein v. Harris*, 667 F.2d 274, 287 (2d Cir. 1981). The privilege against self-incrimination is waived if it is not invoked. *Rogers v. United States*, 340 U.S. 367, 371, 71 S. Ct. 438, 95 L. Ed. 344 (1951) (citations omitted). Furthermore, "[a] witness who fails to invoke the Fifth Amendment against questions as to which he could have claimed it is deemed to have waived his privilege respecting all questions on the same subject matter." *United States v. O'Henry's Film Works, Inc.*, 598 F.2d 313, 317 (2d Cir. 1979). A waiver is found if the witness' prior statements have created a significant likelihood that the finder of fact will be left with and prone to rely on a distorted view of the truth, and the witness had reason to know that his prior statements would be interpreted as a waiver of the fifth amendment's privilege against self-incrimination. *Klein v. Harris*, 667 F.2d 274, 287 (2d Cir. 1981). The second prong requires that the prior statement be testimonial and incriminating. *Id.* at 288.

I find that Filippone cannot find shelter in the Fifth Amendment's privilege against self-incrimination and refuse to testify in Basciano's trial. I first find that Filippone knowingly and voluntarily waived his Fifth Amendment privilege when he testified before the grand jury. He was specifically told about his Fifth Amendment

---

[3] The relevant testimony is:

Q: You are being called as a witness, and like all witnesses, you have the right under the Fifth Amendment of the Constitution to refuse to testify about any information that might implicate you in a crime of your own. Do you understand that?

A: Yes.

Q: You also have the right to have an attorney, and if you can't afford an attorney, one could be appointed for you. I note for the record that you have an attorney for you; is that correct?

A: Yes.

Q: What's his name?

A: I don't even know.

Q: Bennet Epstein?

A: Yes.

Q: And have you spoken with him about today?

A: Yes.

Q: Is he here today?

A: No.

Q: But do you want to continue, anyway?

A: Yes.

Q: But should at any point in this that *[sic]* you want to talk to an attorney, we can arrange for you to speak to an attorney, another attorney, and make him available today, or otherwise adjourn the proceeding, and have you come back another time with that Mr. Epstein, if you want to. Do you understand?

A: Right, Yes.

Grand Jury Transcript at 56–57.

privilege against self incrimination. He was also told that he had a right to have his attorney available at the time of the grand jury proceedings, and that the proceedings could be adjourned until he was provided with his own attorney. I next find that his testimony in reference to these matters does not appear to incriminate him and so he would likely be unable to claim a Fifth Amendment right even if he had not waived the right previously.

Filippone is therefore available for the purposes of Rule 804(a), and his grand jury testimony does not fit the hearsay exception provided by Rule 804(b)(1). Filippone cannot use the Fifth Amendment's privilege against self incrimination to avoid testifying at Basciano's trial. Basciano could subpoena Filippone and compel him to testify to those matters which he testified to at the grand jury. However, if Basciano seeks to question Filippone about a matter outside the scope of the grand jury testimony and Filippone refuses to answer on the basis of his Fifth Amendment right against self-incrimination, I will conduct an in *camera* review to determine Filippone's availability. Basciano's motion to admit Filippone's grand jury testimony under Rule 804(b)(1) is denied.

[B]   Refusal to Testify: Sufficiently Unavailable Only After Ordered to Testify by Court

As a general matter, a declarant must be ordered to testify and refuse to do so before he will be regarded as unavailable. The defendant in *Kitt* attempted to take advantage of an exception to this requirement that a Nebraska court had recognized.

STATE v. KITT
Supreme Court of Nebraska
823 N.W.2d 175 (2012)

[The defendant, Wesley Kitt, was accused of engaging in two episodes of robbery and assault with Joshua Harrington.]

*   *   *

Harrington was called to testify [by the State] and stated that he resided at "OCC" for a crime he committed involving the robbery and assault of Jamie and Jacob, which he believed occurred on June 9, 2007. When asked if there was an individual with him on that occasion, Harrington stated he was advised not to testify by his attorney. Harrington stated that he was refusing to answer any questions regarding allegations against Kitt. The district court then asked Harrington whether he would refuse to testify if the State asked him any questions relating to what happened on June 9 or any events that related to Kitt. Harrington responded affirmatively. The court dismissed Harrington and told the jury that when an incarcerated witness refused to testify, that witness' prior testimony which had been recorded could be read [,] and that the court believed the State intended to proceed by reading into evidence Harrington's prior recorded testimony.

At this point, Kitt's counsel objected [first] to Harrington's being declared unavailable as a witness and to the State's being allowed to read Harrington's deposition into the record. [Second, Kitt] based his objections on Kitt's constitutional right to confront his accusers as well as the constitutional right to cross-examine witnesses testifying against him. The district court overruled Kitt's objection[s], stated that Harrington had been found unavailable based on his refusal to testify, and stated that Harrington's prior recorded testimony would be allowed because case law specifically permitted such testimony to be read into the record without running afoul of the hearsay rule.

The district court explained to the jury that Kitt's attorney had taken Harrington's deposition prior to trial and that this deposition would now be read to the jury. Harrington's deposition testimony was then read into the record.

*   *   *

Kitt claims generally that the Court of Appeals erred when it affirmed the district court's determination that Harrington was unavailable for trial and admitted Harrington's prior deposition testimony. Kitt specifically claims that the determination that Harrington was unavailable and the admission of Harrington's deposition were an abuse of discretion under the exception to the hearsay rule found at rule 804(2)(a). Kitt also specifically claims that the admission of Harrington's deposition is of constitutional magnitude as a violation of the Confrontation Clause. The Confrontation Clause, U.S. Const. amend. VI, provides in relevant part: "In all criminal prosecutions, the accused shall enjoy the right . . . to be confronted with the witnesses against him . . . ." Article I, § 11, of the Nebraska Constitution provides in relevant part: "In all criminal prosecutions the accused shall have the right . . . to meet the witnesses against him face to face . . . ."

We find merit to Kitt's argument to the effect that the district court erred when it determined Harrington was unavailable under rule 804(1)(b) and admitted Harrington's deposition and that thus, the Court of Appeals erred when it endorsed this ruling. However, as explained below, we find that the error was harmless. Further, given the necessity of our harmless error review, we determine that although the Confrontation Clause analysis differs from the hearsay analysis, it is not necessary to engage in the Confrontation Clause analysis in this case because an error for Confrontation Clause purposes would likewise be subject to a harmless error review.

Hearsay

Generally, a hearsay statement is not admissible at trial. See Neb. Evid. R. 802, Neb.Rev.Stat. § 27-802 (Reissue 2008). However, rule 804(2)(a) provides an exception to the hearsay rule if the declarant is unavailable as a witness at trial. In such a case, the declarant's prior statement can be used at trial. Rule 804(2)(a) provides in part that if the declarant is unavailable as a witness, the hearsay rule does not exclude testimony given

> in a deposition taken in compliance with law in the course of the same or a different proceeding, at the instance of or against a party with an opportunity to develop the testimony by direct, cross, or redirect examination, with motive and interest similar to those of the party against whom now offered.

Nebraska's rule 804(2)(a) is similar to rule 804(b)(1)(A) of the Federal Rules of Evidence. At the time of Kitt's trial, Fed. R. Evid. 804(b)(1) provided that if the declarant was unavailable as a witness, the rule against hearsay did not exclude former testimony that was "given as a witness at another hearing of the same or a different proceeding, or in a deposition taken in compliance with law in the course of the same or another proceeding." When a Nebraska Evidence Rule is substantially similar to a corresponding federal rule of evidence, Nebraska courts will look to federal decisions interpreting the corresponding federal rule for guidance in construing the Nebraska rule. *State v. Kibbee*, 284 Neb. 72, 815 N.W.2d 872 (2012).

Nebraska's rule 804(1)(b) sets forth the applicable definition of unavailability, stating that a witness is unavailable if he or she "[p]ersists in refusing to testify concerning the subject matter of his [or her] statement despite an order of the judge to do so." Similarly, at the time of Kitt's trial, federal rule 804 provided in relevant part: "**(a) Definition of Unavailability.** 'Unavailability as a witness' includes situations in which the declarant . . . **(2)** persists in refusing to testify concerning the subject matter of the declarant's statement despite an order of the court to do so. . . ." The advisory committee note to federal rule 804, as proposed in 1972, provides some guidance on the issue of unavailability, and specifically a declarant's refusal to testify: "**Note to Subdivision (a)** . . . **(2)** A witness is rendered unavailable if he simply refuses to testify concerning the subject matter of his statement despite judicial pressures to do so, a position supported by similar considerations of practicality."

*   *   *

As set forth in rule 804(1)(b), unavailability is a term of art. See *People v. Bueno*, 358 Ill.App.3d 143, 829 N.E.2d 402, 293 Ill.Dec. 819 (2005) (commenting on comparable Illinois rule language). Applying the language of rule 804(1)(b), the record shows that Harrington was not unavailable in this case because the judge did not order Harrington to testify before declaring him an unavailable witness. See *Gregory v. Shelby County, Tenn.*, 220 F.3d 433 (6th Cir. 2000). One court has stated: "It is clear . . . that the Rule's requirement of a court order is a necessary prerequisite to a finding of unavailability of a recalcitrant witness under Rule 804. *See United States v. Zappola*, 646 F.2d 48, 54 (2d Cir. 1981) (court order essential component in declaration of unavailability). . . ." *Fowler v. State*, 829 N.E.2d 459, 468 (Ind. 2005), *abrogated in part on other grounds*, *Giles v. California*, 554 U.S. 353, 128 S. Ct. 2678, 171 L. Ed. 2d 488 (2008). It has been observed that where a witness "appears at trial but refuses to respond, [the witness] does not become unavailable until the court orders the witness to answer and the refusal persists." *Id.* at 469.

The unavailability of a witness under rule 804 cannot be fully assessed until the judge orders the witness to testify, because in the absence of an order, it is not known what the witness will do. One court identified the obvious possibilities as follows: "1) [T]he witness decides to avoid contempt and repeats the earlier version; 2) the witness claims loss of memory; 3) the witness comes up with a new version; and 4) the witness persists in refusing to answer." *Fowler v. State*, 829 N.E.2d at 470. In this case, there is no way of knowing how Harrington may have responded to an order to testify. Because the district court did not order Harrington to testify,

Harrington was not unavailable under rule 804(1)(b).

The Court of Appeals relied largely upon *State v. McHenry*, 250 Neb. 614, 550 N.W.2d 364 (1996), when it determined that the district court did not err when it found Harrington unavailable. However, the finding of unavailability in *McHenry* was specific to the facts of that case. In *McHenry*, the district court determined that Frank Ladig, a witness in a murder trial who refused to testify, was unavailable. We affirmed.

The district court in *McHenry* requested Ladig to testify on three separate occasions, but Ladig persistently refused. The district court also asked Ladig if there was any physical safeguard or anything that the court could provide that would change Ladig's mind, and Ladig replied there was not. Furthermore, Ladig refused to take an oath, so he was not competent and could not testify. See Neb. Evid. R. 603, Neb.Rev.Stat. § 27-603 (Reissue 2008). Had the district court threatened to hold Ladig in contempt for refusing to testify, it would have been unavailing because Ladig was already serving a life sentence. See *State v. Ladig*, 248 Neb. 737, 539 N.W.2d 38 (1995). See, also, *Gregory v. Shelby County, Tenn.*, 220 F.3d at 449 (stating that "any pressure of threat applied to the witness by the trial court would undoubtedly have been unavailing as the witness [was] already serving a life sentence"). The specific facts in *McHenry* were tantamount to the district court's ordering Ladig to testify before finding him unavailable, and we affirmed the rule 804 unavailability ruling.

In the present case, however, the district court did not order Harrington to testify before determining he was unavailable; nor are the facts of this case tantamount to an order. Harrington was present in the courtroom, and unlike Ladig, he took the oath and answered a few questions before he stopped answering questions. After Harrington stated upon examination by the State that he would not answer further questions, the judge asked Harrington once if he was going to refuse to testify before allowing Harrington to step down and excusing him as a witness. We agree with the observation that "the unavailability requirement in Rule 804 contemplates more than a brief or minimal examination by the trial court." *State v. Finney*, 358 N.C. 79, 87, 591 S.E.2d 863, 868 (2004). Furthermore, we cannot say that a threat of contempt would have been unavailing, because unlike Ladig, who was serving a life sentence in the *McHenry* case, Harrington, according to his deposition, was serving an 8- to 12-year sentence.

Because there was no district court order for Harrington to testify followed by persistent refusals, we determine the district court erred under rule 804 when it determined that Harrington was unavailable and when it admitted Harrington's deposition. An incorrect unavailability determination and the consequent admission of improper evidence under rule 804 are subject to a harmless error analysis. See, *Gregory v. Shelby County, Tenn.*, 220 F.3d 433 (6th Cir. 2000) (stating that error in finding witness unavailable under rule 804 was harmless); *State v. Perry*, 144 Idaho 266, 159 P.3d 903 (Idaho App. 2007) (stating that incorrect finding of unavailability under rule 804 is subject to harmless error analysis).

[C] Lack of Memory and Physical or Mental Incapacity: A Question of Duration

Absence due to physical or mental incapacity and loss of memory differs from other grounds for unavailability, such as death, and the witness being beyond the jurisdiction and process of the court. Death does not come in degrees and is clearly permanent. The duration of one's absence from the jurisdiction cannot easily be determined with accuracy. If a proponent relies on loss of memory or physical or mental incapacity as indicative of the declarant's unavailability, must the proponent establish that the duration of the declarant's absence probably will be sufficiently long that the need for the evidence contained in the hearsay statement cannot be met by a temporary postponement of the trial? As explained in the following opinion, although there is no absolute requirement that the proponent address the issue of duration, the imposition of the requirement is discretionary with the presiding judge. The judge's determination will turn on a balance of the nature of the unavailability condition on which the proponent relies and on the testimony's importance to the fair resolution of the issues.

UNITED STATES v. AMAYA
United States Court of Appeals, Fifth Circuit
533 F.2d 188 (1976)

RONEY, CIRCUIT JUDGE:

[Amaya was convicted of conspiracy to distribute heroin. This was the second trial for the same offense. The first conviction was reversed because of an improper charge the trial judge gave to the jury. Before the commencement of the second trial, however, Sprouse, a central witness in the Government's case, was injured in an automobile accident that resulted in a loss of memory regarding his prior testimony.]

Amaya first argues that Sprouse was never conclusively shown to be unavailable because it was never established by expert testimony that his lack of memory was permanent. The party offering the prior testimony has the burden of proving the unavailability of the witness. . . . Determination of unavailability is a judicial exercise reviewable by this Court only for abuse of discretion. . . . Defendant alleges that a continuance should have been given to allow expert testimony bearing on the permanence of the loss of memory before establishing unavailability for trial. Although the duration of an illness is a proper element of unavailability, the establishment of permanence as to the particular illness is not an absolute requirement. The duration of the illness need only be in probability long enough so that, with proper regard to the importance of the testimony, the trial cannot be postponed. . . . Defendant relies on our holding in *Peterson v. United States*, 344 F.2d 419 (5th Cir. 1965). The *Peterson* Court stated:

> In criminal prosecutions, according to the weight of authority, the mere temporary illness or disability of a witness is not sufficient to justify the reception of his former testimony . . . .

344 F.2d at 425. Without more, this is a persuasive argument for the defendant; however, the Court further stated:

> . . . it must appear that the witness is in such a state, either mentally or physically, that in reasonable probability he will never be able to attend the trial.

Id. at 425. Pregnancy of the witness in the *Peterson* case was determined to be insufficient "physical disability" to demonstrate that she would not be able to attend trial. Sprouse's loss of memory is different. There was no guarantee that Sprouse's memory would ever return. The trial judge did not abuse his discretion in deciding on the evidence in the record that Sprouse was unavailable for trial . . . .

[D]   Infirmity, Physical Illness, or Mental Illness

A declarant in a coma clearly is suffering from a physical infirmity affecting his ability to testify; a declarant who has developed schizophrenia is similarly clearly experiencing a mental illness affecting his ability to testify. Beyond these paradigm cases, what qualifies as under Fed. R. Evid. 804(a)(4)? *Duncan* takes a very creative, and questionable, approach to defining mental infirmity.

PEOPLE v. DUNCAN
Supreme Court of Michigan
835 N.W.2d 399 (2013)

YOUNG, C.J.

While hearsay is generally inadmissible, the Michigan Rules of Evidence permit certain prior out-of-court statements to be admitted into evidence when a witness is unavailable. MRE 804(a) enumerates five situations when a witness is unavailable, including when the witness is unable to testify because of a then existing physical or mental illness or infirmity. We hold that when a child attempts to testify but, because of her youth, is unable to do so because she lacks the mental ability to overcome her distress, the child has a "then existing . . . mental . . . infirmity" within the meaning of MRE 804(a)(4) and is therefore unavailable as a witness. Accordingly, we reverse the judgment of the Court of Appeals and remand to the trial court for further proceedings consistent with this opinion. On remand, the trial court must determine whether the complainant's preliminary examination testimony satisfies the requirements of MRE 804(b)(1) and, if so, whether admission of that testimony would violate defendants' rights under the Confrontation Clause.

I. FACTS AND PROCEDURAL HISTORY

Defendant Stanley Duncan was charged in the Macomb Circuit Court with five counts of first-degree criminal sexual conduct (CSC-I) and four counts of second-degree criminal sexual conduct (CSC-II). Stanley's wife, defendant Vita Duncan, was charged with two counts of CSC-I, two counts of CSC-II, and with the misdemeanor offense of operating a daycare facility without a license. The alleged victim in this case, RS, is the sole complainant against Vita and one of three complainants against Stanley.

Separate preliminary examinations were held for each defendant. At Stanley Duncan's preliminary examination on October 17, 2011, then three year old RS correctly answered the trial court's questions about her age, her birthday, and her dog's name, among others. The judge then asked RS if she knew the difference between telling the truth and not telling the truth, to which she responded, "Yes." She also affirmed that she would honestly answer the questions of the attorneys. The court therefore qualified RS as competent to testify, determining that she had sufficient mental intelligence to communicate and had a sense of obligation to testify honestly.

RS testified that on at least three occasions, Stanley Duncan touched her "private," indicating her vaginal area, and "blew raspberries" on her vaginal area while her pants and underwear were off. The raspberries hurt "a little bit," and his touching "really hurt." She testified that the acts occurred in the bathroom of defendants' home, where RS attended daycare.

On December 2, 2011, at the preliminary examination concerning the charges against Vita Duncan, RS was qualified as competent after she correctly answered questions about her birthday, her dog's name, and the name of her schoolteacher. RS affirmed her understanding of what telling the truth means, and promised to do so. RS repeated substantially the same answers that she previously gave regarding Stanley Duncan, and also stated that she told Vita more than once that Stanley had touched her. RS also testified that, on at least one occasion while Stanley was touching her, Vita was just outside the bathroom, and that RS could see Vita.

Both defendants were bound over on the charges against them, and a joint trial before a single jury began on September 28, 2012. RS was called to the stand and was first questioned by the court. When asked whether she knew the difference between the truth and a lie, RS responded, "No," and was unable to explain what a promise means. After RS struggled to answer questions similar to those answered at the preliminary examinations, the trial court excused the jury, and met with counsel, RS, and RS's parents in chambers. Afterward, RS was again put on the stand, and again answered, "No" to the questions regarding whether she knew what the truth is, what a lie is, and what a promise is. RS was clearly agitated. Throughout the court's questioning, RS had tears in her eyes and was wringing her hands. RS began crying in earnest just before the court excused her. The court ruled that she was not competent to testify pursuant to MRE 601.

The prosecution immediately asked the court to declare RS unavailable, arguing that RS lacked memory of the events giving rise to the charges, and moved to admit her preliminary examination testimony pursuant to MRE 804(b)(1), a hearsay exception for unavailable witnesses. The trial court considered each of the five situations of unavailability enumerated in MRE 804(a), but held that none of them applied to RS.

After the trial court granted a stay of the trial proceedings, the prosecution sought emergency leave to appeal in the Court of Appeals and moved for immediate consideration of the trial court's ruling that RS was not unavailable. The Court of

Appeals granted the prosecution's motion for immediate consideration, held the applications for leave to appeal in abeyance, and remanded the cases to the trial court with instructions to issue an opinion explaining its decision.

In its opinion on remand, the trial court reiterated its holding that RS was not unavailable because her failure to take the equivalent of the oath did not trigger any of the scenarios enumerated in MRE 804(a). Without much discussion, the court ruled that MRE 804(a)(4), which renders a declarant unavailable if she is dead or has a physical or mental infirmity or illness, did not apply because RS's situation did not include any of these circumstances. The court stressed that RS was even younger at the preliminary examination than at trial and suggested that this fact lent support to its ruling that she was not unavailable at the later trial date.

* * *

. . . [A] witness's unavailability to testify is governed by MRE 804(a), which provides:

Definition of unavailability. "Unavailability as a witness" includes situations in which the declarant—

(1) is exempted by ruling of the court on the ground of privilege from testifying concerning the subject matter of the declarant's statement; or

(2) persists in refusing to testify concerning the subject matter of the declarant's statement despite an order of the court to do so; or

(3) has a lack of memory of the subject matter of the declarant's statement; or

(4) is unable to be present or to testify at the hearing because of death or then existing physical or mental illness or infirmity; or

(5) is absent from the hearing and the proponent of a statement has been unable to procure the declarant's attendance (or in the case of a hearsay exception under subdivision (b)(2), (3), or (4), the declarant's attendance or testimony) by process or other reasonable means, and in a criminal case, due diligence is shown.

A declarant is not unavailable as a witness if exemption, refusal, claim of lack of memory, inability, or absence is due to the procurement or wrongdoing of the proponent of a statement for the purpose of preventing the witness from attending or testifying.

We focus on MRE 804(a)(4), which defines "unavailability" to include a declarant who lacks the physical or mental capability to testify. MRE 804(a)(4) provides that unavailability as a witness includes situations in which the declarant "is unable to be present or to testify at the hearing because of death or then existing physical or mental illness or infirmity [.]" We focus solely on the phrase "then existing . . . mental . . . infirmity," which provides the basis for our decision. First, we address the term "infirmity." "Infirmity" is defined as "the quality or state of being infirm;

lack of strength."[32] In turn, "infirm" is defined as "feeble or weak in body or health, [especially] because of age."[33] Of note, age is specifically designated as a factor that may give rise to an infirmity.

MRE 804(a)(4) contemplates both physical and mental infirmities, though we focus only on whether a mental infirmity existed in this case. The term "mental" modifies "infirmity" and is defined as "1. of or pertaining to the mind. 2. of, pertaining to, or affected by a disorder of the mind [.]" Thus, read together, the phrase "mental infirmity" as used in MRE 804(a)(4) encompasses weakness or feebleness of the mind — one cause of which may be an individual's age.

Furthermore, the language of the rule establishes that the mental infirmity need not be permanent, or even longstanding. The phrase "then existing" specifically limits the temporal scope within which a witness's availability under MRE 804(a)(4) may be assessed; the only relevant reference point is the point at which the witness takes the stand. As a result, the declarant need not suffer from a permanent illness or infirmity. Thus, the fact that RS was competent and available to testify at two preliminary examinations does not affect the determination whether she was mentally capable or infirm for purposes of MRE 804(a)(4) at the time her testimony was sought at trial. Rather, the only relevant inquiry is her condition at the time she was called to testify.

In holding that a child may be mentally infirm in the type of extraordinarily stressful trial situation like the one that existed here, we recognize the obvious truth that children lack the same level of mental maturity as that exhibited by and expected of most adults. Legal and psychological research confirms this uncontroversial proposition.[37] As a result of these limitations, young children are less mentally equipped to cope with severe emotional distress.[38] Testifying in open court can be a harrowing experience for anyone, and young children are much more susceptible to emotional breakdowns than adults.[39] Indeed, testifying in open court "can make some children tearful, ill, or inarticulate in the courtroom. . . . Under the stress of testifying, some children may regress to a more immature level of behavior."[40] When these emotional terrors are severe and a child has not developed the mental capacity to overcome this distress, an emotional breakdown may eliminate any possibility of securing testimony from the young child.

RS was four years old at the time she was called to testify at trial. She demonstrated an inability to overcome her distress when she was unable to answer

---

[32] *Random House Webster's College Dictionary* (1995).

[33] *Id.*

[37] Schuman, Bala & Lee, *Developmentally appropriate questions for child witnesses*, 25 Queen's L. J. 251, 255 (1999) (recognizing that "[c]hildren are not just short adults"). See also *infra* notes 38–40.

[38] Patton, *Viewing child witnesses through a child and adolescent psychiatric lens: How attorneys' ethical duties exacerbate children's psychopathology*, 16 Widener L. R. 369 (2010) ("Many child abuse victims are the most psychologically fragile witnesses in the legal system.").

[39] Schuman, Bala & Lee, at 255, 297 (stating that testifying in court can be "deeply upsetting" for young children and "can cause them considerable anxiety, even terror").

[40] Myers, Saywitz & Goodman, *Psychological research on children as witnesses: Practical implications for forensic interviews and courtroom testimony*, 28 Pac L. J. 3, 70 (1996–1997) (citation and quotation marks omitted).

the trial court's questions. When asked whether she knew the difference between the truth and a lie, RS responded, "No," and was unable to explain what a promise means. Furthermore, she answered, "No" to whether she knew what the truth is, what a lie is, and what a promise is. Importantly, throughout her examination RS had tears in her eyes, was wringing her hands, and ultimately began to cry, rendering her unable to answer counsels' questions. While an older youth or an adult may have been able to suppress the unease of testifying in open court, RS, as a young child, was susceptible to particular challenges that must be taken into consideration when determining whether a witness is mentally infirm under MRE 804(a)(4). As could be expected from a young child, especially in the context of alleged criminal sexual conduct, RS simply did not have the mental maturity to overcome her debilitating emotions while on the stand.

Under the plain language of the rule, and with our recognition of the unique mental and emotional limitations of youth, we hold that RS had a then existing mental infirmity in this case because the facts show that she was unable to sufficiently cope with her significant emotional distress and give testimony at trial, a result of her particularly young age. Therefore, she was unavailable within the plain meaning of MRE 804(a)(4).

We recognize the case-specific nature of the inquiry into whether a witness suffers from a "then existing mental infirmity." In this case, the severity of RS's emotional distress made it impossible for her to testify. This is highlighted by the fact that she had previously been able to give testimony about the alleged sexual contacts at issue in this case. Before trial courts hold that a child has a then existing mental infirmity, we urge them to use, when appropriate, the tools in our court rules and statutes to accommodate young witnesses. For example, MCL 600.2163a enables the use of dolls or mannequins to aid children in their testimony. Moreover, in certain circumstances, the statute allows for witness accompaniment by a "support person," use of videorecorded statements, and testimony via closed-circuit television.

The Court of Appeals concluded that RS did not demonstrate a mental infirmity, characterizing her conduct merely as an inability to provide the trial court with assurances that she was able and willing to testify truthfully. While the Court of Appeals may be correct that she was unable to testify truthfully at the time of trial, this fact does not foreclose the possibility that RS's mental infirmity caused this inability, which ultimately rendered her unavailable. In fact, as discussed, RS clearly demonstrated that, at the time of her trial testimony, she was emotionally overwhelmed and was mentally incapable of overcoming this distress and was therefore unable to affirm that she could testify truthfully. Therefore, the Court of Appeals erred when it failed to examine the reason for RS's inability to testify.

We conclude that the trial court abused its discretion in ruling that RS was not unavailable. As discussed, by using the word "infirmity," MRE 804(a)(4) plainly contemplates that a declarant is unavailable for hearsay purposes when she is unable to overcome severe emotional trouble resulting from the limitations of her young age. Though this is an issue of first impression, the trial court committed a legal error in its interpretation of the rule when it held that RS was not infirm when she was unable to give testimony. The trial court's decision not to admit RS's preliminary examination testimony on the basis of its erroneous legal interpretation necessarily constitutes an abuse of discretion.

MARKMAN, J. (Concurring):

*   *   *

I agree with the majority that the language relevant to analysis under MRE 804(a)(4) is the phrase "then existing . . . mental . . . infirmity[.]" But in my view, a four-year-old child who, so far as we know, does not suffer from any sort of developmental disability, and who appears in all respects to be an entirely normal child of this age, simply cannot be properly categorized as suffering from a mental infirmity.

The majority is correct, of course, that at least one prominent dictionary, *Random House Webster's College Dictionary* (1995), defines "infirmity" as "the quality or state of being infirm; lack of strength." This is the second definition of "infirmity" listed by *Random House Webster's*. Notably, however, the first definition specifies "a physical weakness or ailment: *the infirmities of age.*" *Id.* Of course, in the present case, "mental" modifies infirmity, so that a definition of the term as "mental weakness or ailment," including the contextual example, "the infirmities of age," is appropriate. This first definition of "infirmity" matches up, unsurprisingly, with *Random House Webster's* first definition of "infirm": "feeble or weak in body or health, esp[ecially] because of age." *Id.* . . .

. . . [F]or these reasons, I cannot join in the majority's conclusion that RS was unavailable under MRE 804(a)(4) because of a "mental infirmity," I do conclude that she was in fact unavailable under the general principle of unavailability set forth in MRE 804(a). . . .

. . . [T]he trial court found that RS lacked a sense of obligation to tell the truth. She therefore was not "suitable or ready for use; at hand" as a witness. Repeated good-faith attempts to qualify RS (and thus render her *available*) were unsuccessful. Because the trial court found that RS lacked a sense of obligation to tell the truth, and because good-faith efforts to qualify her as a witness were made yet failed, RS was genuinely "unavailable" under the general principle of unavailability found in MRE 804(a), and I would hold accordingly.

CAVANAGH, J. (dissenting).

I would affirm the result reached by the Court of Appeals. I do not join the majority opinion because, in my view, Justice MARKMAN raises a persuasive point that RS cannot properly be categorized as suffering from an infirmity in this case.

Nevertheless, I disagree with the result reached in Justice MARKMAN's opinion, and in the majority opinion, even accepting for purposes of this appeal Justice MARKMAN'S conclusion that the use of the word "includes" within MRE 804(a) indicates that the definition of "unavailability as a witness" contains a "general principle of unavailability." Given the "importance accorded unavailability in the scheme of hearsay exceptions," 2 McCormick, Evidence (7th ed.), § 253, p. 244, and because "our legal system makes public testimony in front of the fact finder an important element of the truth-seeking process," *People v. Johnson*, 118 Ill. 2d 501, 510, 115 Ill. Dec. 384, 517 N.E.2d 1070 (1987), in my judgment, more rigorous attempts than were made in this case should occur before declaring a child witness unavailable.

In my view, the facts of this case illustrate the tension created in our courts by attempting to apply the rule of evidence to the "unique situation of a child witness in an alleged sexual abuse case." *People v. Straight*, 430 Mich. 418, 422, 424 N.W.2d 257 (1988). Specifically, "[t]he tension originates from the conflict between two underlying policies: a desire to protect the most vulnerable of our citizens from heinous and damaging exploitation, and a need to protect the accused individual against both erroneous conviction and the devastating consequences that can follow." *Id.* at 422–423, 424 N.W.2d 257. Because I question whether our existing rule of evidence was drafted with the unique issues involving child witnesses in mind, I would consider reexamining our rule concerning unavailability, as other jurisdictions have done.

[E]   Procure Through Reasonable Means

In civil cases, unavailability can be satisfied by an inability to serve a subpoena. If witnesses are beyond the subpoena power of the court, or cannot be located after due diligence, then they are unavailable for the purposes of this rule. Due diligence will always be a fact specific question. The *Herrera* case raises a particularly interesting version of the unavailability issue. The government often has unique authority over various types of witnesses, particularly foreign citizens subject to deportation. The government's burden to secure the attendance of such witnesses is greater than it would be for a private citizen and also raises due process concerns about the government's power to detain persons as material witnesses.

PEOPLE v. HERRERA
California Supreme Court
232 P.3d 710 (2010)

BAXTER, J.

Defendant Honorio Moreno Herrera was a member of the criminal street gang known as "Krazy Proud Criminals" or "KPC." In June 2005, he and two fellow KPC members drove into the territory of a rival gang called "Logan," and shot and killed Erick Peralta. In June 2006, Jose Portillo testified at a preliminary hearing that defendant confessed to the shooting. Defendant was then charged by information with one count of first degree murder, with a criminal street gang special circumstance and two gang-related enhancements. He was also charged with one count of street terrorism.

By the time defendant's case was ready for trial in May 2007, Portillo could not be found. The prosecution filed a pretrial motion to admit Portillo's preliminary hearing testimony, contending he was unavailable as a witness. After hearing evidence that Portillo had been deported to El Salvador in September 2006, and that El Salvador and the United States had no treaty providing for his extradition to this country to testify as a witness, the trial court ruled Portillo unavailable and allowed his testimony to be read to the jury. The Court of Appeal reversed, concluding the prosecution had failed to establish Portillo's unavailability as required by the confrontation clauses of the federal and state Constitutions and the Evidence Code. (U.S. Const., 6th Amend.; Cal. Const., art. 1, § 15; Evid.Code, §§ 1290, 1291, 240, subds. (a)(4), (5).)

Consistent with decisions of the United States Supreme Court and our state courts, we hold that the prosecution's showing of Portillo's unavailability, which was based on undisputed testimony, satisfied constitutional and state law requirements. Accordingly, we reverse the judgment of the Court of Appeal, and remand the matter to that court for further proceedings consistent with our opinion.

Factual and Procedural Background

About 10:30 p.m. on June 19, 2005, Erick Peralta and his cousin Efren Enriquez were walking on Spurgeon Street in Santa Ana toward a convenience store. According to Enriquez, a blue four-door car with three people passed them and stopped. A man exited the car and asked where they were from. Enriquez put his hand up and said, "What's up?" as he and Peralta kept walking. A second man with a gun got out of the car and fired at them once. Peralta was shot in the head and killed. The two men got back in the car, someone yelled out "KPC," and the car drove off.

Santa Ana Police Detective Richard Ashby interviewed Enriquez shortly after the shooting. Enriquez was shown photographs of active KPC gang members, but he did not identify anyone as the suspects.

Three months later, on September 17, 2005, Jose Portillo, a former KPC member, was driving a car with defendant as one of the passengers. Portillo sped away when he saw the police. The police gave chase, and Portillo was arrested for felony evading. Defendant was arrested for attempting to flee from Portillo's car.

On September 19, 2005, Portillo told Detective Ashby that defendant had bragged to him about shooting a person who identified himself as a Logan gang member. Defendant had said two people, a guy from "Clown Town" and another "youngster" he did not identify, were with him at the time of the shooting. Portillo also described the car used in the shooting as a dark-purple Chevy Beretta. Portillo had previously seen defendant driving this car and had seen him with Luis Estudillo and Paul Del La Cruz, additional suspects in the case.

On or about November 19, 2005, defendant had a two-hour interview with Detective Ashby after waiving his right to an attorney and right to remain silent. Defendant initially denied knowledge of the shooting, but then admitted witnessing it. He named "Striker," an Anaheim "Clown Town" gang member, as the driver involved in the crime, but refused to name the shooter.

Several months later, on June 19, 2006, Portillo testified at defendant's preliminary hearing. According to Portillo, defendant told Portillo in June of 2005 that defendant was the shooter who killed Peralta. Defendant was bound over for trial and charged by information with one count of first degree murder (Pen.Code, § 187, subd. (a)), with a criminal street gang special circumstance (*id.*, subd. (a)(22)), a gang-benefit enhancement (*id.*, § 186.22, subd. (b)), and an enhancement for gang-member vicarious discharge of a firearm causing death (*id.*, § 12022.53, subds. (d), (e)(1)). Defendant was also charged with one count of street terrorism. (*id.*, § 186.22, subd. (a).)

Trial was scheduled for March 7, 2007, but it was continued two months to May 21 because neither side was ready for trial. On and after May 21, 2007, the trial was trailed three times to May 30.

On May 30, 2007, the prosecution filed a motion to admit Portillo's preliminary hearing testimony. Claiming that Portillo was unavailable to testify at trial, the prosecution requested a hearing on the issue of due diligence. According to the motion, Portillo had been in custody on an unrelated matter at the time of defendant's June 19, 2006, preliminary hearing, and he agreed to provide truthful testimony in exchange for a more lenient sentence. After testifying at the preliminary hearing, Portillo entered a plea in the unrelated matter and was sentenced. Records maintained by the United States Department of Homeland Security indicated that Portillo was later flown to El Salvador, his country of origin, and released.

That same day, May 30, 2007, the trial court held an evidentiary hearing on the prosecution's motion. Investigator Ed Wood of the Orange County District Attorney's Office testified regarding his efforts to secure Portillo's presence for trial and his communications with the Department of Homeland Security concerning Portillo's whereabouts. Wood said he began looking for Portillo the Friday before, on May 25. He started by running Portillo's name through the law enforcement database and discovered two outstanding "no bail" warrants for his arrest. Wood then contacted Detective Ashby and asked him to make out "a BOLO or a wanted flyer" for Portillo. The wanted flyer, which was disseminated at least regionally to all law enforcement, resulted in no helpful information. That afternoon (May 25), Wood went to Portillo's last known residence at an apartment unit in Santa Ana. A woman lived in the unit with her father and daughter, but she did not recognize Portillo when shown his photograph.

Wood also obtained a "Local Arrest Record" printout listing two telephone numbers for Portillo's family members or friends, but he ascertained those numbers had been disconnected or changed. Wood additionally asked Detective Ashby to try contacting Portillo's friends and family, in case Ashby had information in the database that was not accessible to Wood.

Around 3:00 or 3:30 p.m. that same Friday, Wood contacted special agent Mark Johnston of the United States Department of Homeland Security. When asked if Portillo had been deported, Johnston checked and confirmed he had been deported to El Salvador, his country of origin. The deportation had occurred more than eight months earlier, on September 11, 2006. Wood determined that Portillo was released from custody from the Orange County jail on June 24, 2006, and assumed that he "went into" custody of federal immigration authorities around that time.

At 8:30 a.m. on Tuesday, May 29, 2007, Wood spoke with Art Zorilla, an investigator in the foreign prosecution unit of the Orange County District Attorney's Office. At Wood's request, Zorilla contacted INTERPOL, the agency in El Salvador that would search a database for Portillo and send officers out. As of 1:00 p.m. on Wednesday, May 30, Wood had heard nothing from El Salvador about Portillo. Zorilla, however, informed Wood that even if Portillo could be located in El Salvador, that country had no treaty with the United States and would not extradite him.

After Wood concluded his testimony, the prosecution reminded the court that Portillo "entered into an agreement" before testifying at the preliminary hearing. The prosecution offered to stipulate that agreement into evidence, as well as any moral turpitude prior conviction that would have been available to the defense for impeachment purposes had Portillo been present to testify. Finding the prosecution acted with "due diligence" in attempting to secure Portillo's presence, the trial court permitted the use of his preliminary hearing testimony at trial.

A jury convicted defendant of the charged crimes and found true the alleged enhancements and the gang special circumstance allegation. He was sentenced to life in prison without the possibility of parole.

A divided Court of Appeal reversed the judgment, concluding that admission of Portillo's preliminary hearing testimony at trial was reversible error.

Discussion

The central issue is whether admission of Portillo's preliminary hearing testimony was erroneous or in violation of defendant's constitutional right of confrontation.

A criminal defendant has the right, guaranteed by the confrontation clauses of both the federal and state Constitutions, to confront the prosecution's witnesses. (U.S. Const., 6th Amend.; Cal. Const., art. 1, § 15.)

* * *

Although important, the constitutional right of confrontation is not absolute. (*Chambers v. Mississippi, supra,* 410 U.S. at 295, 93 S. Ct. 1038; *Cromer, supra,* 24 Cal.4th at p. 897, 103 Cal.Rptr.2d 23, 15 P.3d 243.) "Traditionally, there has been 'an exception to the confrontation requirement where a witness is unavailable and has given testimony at previous judicial proceedings against the same defendant [and] which was subject to cross-examination . . . .' (*Barber v. Page* [(1968) 390 U.S. 719,] 722 [88 S. Ct. 1318, 20 L. Ed. 2d 255].)" (*Cromer, supra,* at p. 897, 103 Cal.Rptr.2d 23, 15 P.3d 243.) Pursuant to this exception, the preliminary hearing testimony of an unavailable witness may be admitted at trial without violating a defendant's confrontation right. (*People v. Seijas* (2005) 36 Cal.4th 291, 303, 30 Cal.Rptr.3d 493, 114 P.3d 742.)

This traditional exception is codified in the California Evidence Code. (*People v. Friend* (2009) 47 Cal.4th 1, 67, 97 Cal.Rptr.3d 1, 211 P.3d 520.) Section 1291, subdivision (a)(2), provides that "former testimony," such as preliminary hearing testimony, is not made inadmissible by the hearsay rule if "the declarant is unavailable as a witness," and "[t]he party against whom the former testimony is offered was a party to the action or proceeding in which the testimony was given and had the right and opportunity to cross-examine the declarant with an interest and motive similar to that which he has at the hearing." Thus, when the requirements of section 1291 are met, the admission of former testimony in evidence does not violate a defendant's constitutional right of confrontation. (*People v. Friend*, at p. 67, 97 Cal.Rptr.3d 1, 211 P.3d 520.)

There is no dispute that defendant was a party to the action in which Portillo's former testimony was given, and that he actually exercised his right to cross-examine Portillo with the requisite interest and motive. The question is whether Portillo was unavailable as a witness.

A witness who is absent from a trial is not "unavailable" in the constitutional sense unless the prosecution has made a "good faith effort" to obtain the witness's presence at the trial. (*Barber v. Page* (1968) 390 U.S. 719, 724–725, 88 S. Ct. 1318, 20 L. Ed. 2d 255 (*Barber*).) The United States Supreme Court has described the good-faith requirement this way: "The law does not require the doing of a futile act. Thus, if no possibility of procuring the witness exists (as, for example, the witness' intervening death), 'good faith' demands nothing of the prosecution. But if there is a possibility, albeit remote, that affirmative measures might produce the declarant, the obligation of good faith may demand their effectuation. 'The lengths to which the prosecution must go to produce a witness . . . is a question of reasonableness.' [Citation.] The ultimate question is whether the witness is unavailable despite good-faith efforts undertaken prior to trial to locate and present that witness." (*Ohio v. Roberts* (1980) 448 U.S. 56, 74, 100 S. Ct. 2531, 65 L. Ed. 2d 597, *disapproved on another point in Crawford v. Washington* (2004) 541 U.S. 36, 60–68, 124 S. Ct. 1354, 158 L. Ed. 2d 177.)

*   *   *

As indicated, to establish unavailability, the prosecution must show that its efforts to locate and produce a witness for trial were reasonable under the circumstances presented . . . .

In this case, we must consider what prosecutorial efforts will sustain a finding of unavailability when the absent witness was not in this jurisdiction but in another country. We start by consulting two decisions of the United States Supreme Court: *Barber, supra,* 390 U.S. 719, 88 S. Ct. 1318, and *Mancusi v. Stubbs* (1972) 408 U.S. 204, 92 S. Ct. 2308, 33 L. Ed. 2d 293 (*Mancusi*).

In *Barber, supra,* 390 U.S. 719, 88 S. Ct. 1318, the issue was whether the petitioner was deprived of his constitutional right of confrontation at his trial in Oklahoma for armed robbery, in which the principal evidence against him consisted of the preliminary hearing testimony of a witness who at the time of trial was serving a federal prison term in Texas. (*Id.* at p. 720, 88 S. Ct. 1318.)

Barber began by noting the state had made "absolutely no effort to obtain the presence of [the witness] at trial other than to ascertain that he was in a federal prison outside Oklahoma." (*Barber, supra,* 390 U.S. at p. 723, 88 S. Ct. 1318.) Although acknowledging that, at one time, a showing of mere absence from the jurisdiction might have sufficed to demonstrate unavailability, *Barber* observed that times had changed. By 1968, the "increased cooperation between the States themselves and between the States and the Federal Government" in making witnesses available for trial had changed the confrontation clause analysis. *(Ibid.)* As relevant there, a federal statute empowered federal courts to issue appropriate writs at the request of state prosecutorial authorities, and federal prison policy also supported state writ procedures. *(Id.* at p. 724, 88 S. Ct. 1318; *see also id.* at pp. 723–724, fn. 4, 88 S. Ct. 1318 [describing procedures by which a state could secure the attendance of nonincarcerated and state-incarcerated witnesses located in a sister state].)

In light of such developments, *Barber* held the prosecution failed to establish the incarcerated witness's unavailability because it had made absolutely no effort to obtain his attendance by the cooperation of the federal authorities or a federal court. *(Barber, supra,* 390 U.S. at p. 725, 88 S. Ct. 1318.) As *Barber* explained, "So far as this record reveals, the sole reason why [the witness] was not present to testify in person was because the State did not attempt to seek his presence. The right of confrontation may not be dispensed with so lightly." *(Ibid.,* italics added.)

Mancusi, supra, 408 U.S. 204, 92 S. Ct. 2308, decided four years later, discussed and distinguished *Barber, supra,* 390 U.S. 719, 88 S. Ct. 1318, in the context of a nonincarcerated witness residing outside the United States. In *Mancusi,* the petitioner challenged the use of a prior Tennessee murder conviction for sentencing purposes in a New York criminal proceeding, on the ground the Tennessee conviction was obtained in violation of his right of confrontation. *(Mancusi, supra,* 408 U.S. at p. 205, 92 S. Ct. 2308.) At the petitioner's first Tennessee trial, the slain victim's husband, Alex Holm, testified for the prosecution, resulting in a murder conviction. That conviction was reversed, and the petitioner was retried. At the retrial, the prosecution sought to have Holm declared unavailable, based on the testimony of Holm's son that Holm, who was a naturalized American citizen, had left the United States and become a permanent resident of his native Sweden. The trial court permitted Holm's testimony from the first trial to be read to the jury, and the petitioner was again convicted of murder. *(Id.* at pp. 207–209, 92 S. Ct. 2308.)

Mancusi concluded the use of the second Tennessee conviction did not violate the petitioner's right of confrontation. *Mancusi* observed that in *Barber,* the uniform act to secure the attendance of witnesses from without a state, the availability of appropriate federal writs, and the policy of federal prisons to honor writs issued out of state courts, all supported *Barber's* conclusion that "the State had not met its obligations to make a good-faith effort to obtain the presence of the witness merely by showing that [the witness] was beyond the boundaries of the prosecuting State." *(Mancusi, supra,* 408 U.S. at p. 212, 92 S. Ct. 2308.) In *Mancusi,* however, the witness was not simply absent from Tennessee but was a permanent resident of another country. *(Id.* at p. 211, 92 S. Ct. 2308.) *Mancusi* found that distinction significant, emphasizing: "There have been . . . no corresponding developments in the area of obtaining witnesses between this country and foreign nations." *(Id.* at p. 212, 92 S. Ct. 2308.) On this point, *Mancusi* noted that neither the existing case law nor the statutory language of the then effective version of 28 United States Code section 1783(a) would have permitted a federal court to subpoena a United States citizen residing in a foreign country for testimony in a state felony trial. *(Mancusi, supra,* 408 U.S. at pp. 211–212, 92 S. Ct. 2308.)

Under those circumstances, "good faith" did not require additional efforts by the prosecution. As far as the high court was concerned, "[u]pon discovering that Holm resided in a foreign nation, the State of Tennessee, so far as this record shows, was powerless to compel his attendance at the second trial, either through its own process or through established procedures depending on the voluntary assistance of another government." (*Mancusi, supra,* 408 U.S. at p. 212, 92 S. Ct. 2308.) Accordingly, *Mancusi* concluded the state trial court's determination as to Holm's unavailability should stand. (*Mancusi, supra,* 408 U.S. at pp. 212–213, 92 S. Ct. 2308.)

Subsequent to *Mancusi,* the Supreme Court stated in *Ohio v. Roberts, supra,* 448 U.S. 56, 100 S. Ct. 2531, that "if there is a possibility, albeit remote, that affirmative measures might produce the declarant, the obligation of good faith may demand their effectuation." (*Id.* at p. 74, 100 S. Ct. 2531.) This statement did not alter or detract from *Mancusi's* analysis that when the prosecution discovers the desired witness resides in a foreign nation, and the state is powerless to obtain the witness's attendance, either through its own process or through established procedures, the prosecution need do no more to establish the witness's unavailability. Indeed, the Supreme Court cited *Mancusi* as providing "significant support for a conclusion of good-faith effort" in *Ohio v. Roberts.* (*Id.* at p. 76, 100 S. Ct. 2531.)

*   *   *

The foregoing authorities make clear that, when a criminal trial is at issue, unavailability in the constitutional sense does not invariably turn on the inability of the state court to compel the out-of-state witness's attendance through its own process, but also takes into consideration the existence of agreements or established procedures for securing a witness's presence that depend on the voluntary assistance of another government. (*Mancusi, supra,* 408 U.S. at pp. 211–213, 92 S. Ct. 2308.) Where such options exist, the extent to which the prosecution had the opportunity to utilize them and endeavored to do so is relevant in determining whether the obligations to act in good faith and with due diligence have been met. (*Barber, supra,* 390 U.S. at pp. 723–725, 88 S. Ct. 1318; *Sandoval, supra,* 87 Cal.App.4th at p. 1444, 105 Cal.Rptr.2d 504; *St. Germain, supra,* 138 Cal.App.3d at p. 517, 187 Cal. Rptr. 915.)

Mindful of the foregoing authorities, we now consider whether the admission of Portillo's preliminary hearing testimony at trial was erroneous or violated defendant's constitutional right of confrontation. In assessing whether or not Portillo was properly found unavailable, we review the trial court's factual findings under the substantial evidence standard and independently review whether the facts demonstrate prosecutorial good faith and due diligence. (*Cromer, supra,* 24 Cal.4th at pp. 902–903, 103 Cal.Rptr.2d 23, 15 P.3d 243.)

Here, the evidence concerning Portillo's unavailability as a witness was as follows. District Attorney Investigator Ed Wood took the stand on Wednesday, May 30, 2007, and testified that on May 25, the Friday before, he learned from special agent Mark Johnston of the United States Department of Homeland Security that Portillo had been deported to his native El Salvador in September 2006. On Tuesday, May 29, at 8:30 a.m., Wood requested that the foreign prosecution investigator at his office, Art Zorilla, contact law enforcement authorities in El Salvador in an attempt to locate Portillo in that country. Zorilla did so, but Portillo was not found. Zorilla informed Wood that, even if Portillo could be located in El Salvador, there was no treaty between the two countries providing for Portillo's extradition or return to the United States. Wood had made additional efforts to locate Portillo at the residence and in the region where he last lived in California and to track down any information available in the law enforcement database. Wood discovered there were warrants out for Portillo's arrest, but ascertained no information indicating that Portillo had returned to California. Unlike the situation in *Smith*, *supra*, 30 Cal.4th 581, 134 Cal.Rptr.2d 1, 68 P.3d 302, defendant made no hearsay objection to any of Wood's testimony.

After hearing this testimony, the trial court determined that Portillo "certainly was deported." The court further stated that "it would be speculative to come up with further efforts that could be fruitful in obtaining his presence, especially given the testimony we heard with regard to the relationship between El Salvador and this country with regard to extradition." Concluding the prosecution had acted with due diligence, the trial court ruled Portillo's preliminary hearing testimony admissible.

Reviewing the record, we observe that Wood's testimony amply supported the trial court's finding that Portillo had been deported to his native El Salvador in September 2006, about three months after the preliminary hearing and more than eight months before defendant's trial. Wood's testimony also provided substantial support for the court's determination that Portillo was not in California at the time of trial, but was in El Salvador and therefore beyond the court's own process. There was no dispute that attempts to locate Portillo in El Salvador proved unsuccessful. Likewise, there was no dispute that even if Portillo could be found there, the United States and El Salvador had no agreement or treaty providing for an alternative means to compel or facilitate his attendance at defendant's trial. We therefore conclude, consistent with the United States Supreme Court and California decisions discussed above, that the prosecution fulfilled its obligation of good faith and due diligence under the circumstances, that Portillo was unavailable as a witness, and that therefore admission of his preliminary hearing testimony at trial was proper.

[F] Procured Unavailability of Witness — Rule 804(b)(6)

Well before the adoption of the Federal Rules of Evidence, the common law rules held that a declarant's statements could not be excluded if he was unable to come to court because of the actions of the party he was to testify against. *Basciano* discusses the showing that must be made to admit the declarant's statement under such a claim. *Thompson* then considers the admissibility of a statement against a defendant whose co-conspirator caused the declarant's unavailability.

UNITED STATES v. BASCIANO

United States District Court, Eastern District of New York
430 F. Supp. 2d 87 (2006)

The Government has charged that on or around November 14, 1985, Basciano attempted to murder David Nunez. On November 15, 1985, at approximately 6:15 p.m., Basciano was placed in a lineup and was identified by Nunez. (Basciano Nunez

Ltr., dated Apr. 13, 2006, at 1; see also 1987 Wade Tr. at 33 (testimony of Police Officer Keith Garley).) Nunez has since given contradictory accounts of his recollection of his assailant, including (1) in December 1985, when he spoke with Basciano's then-attorneys Elias Martinez and Gary Friedman, and stated that all he remembered was a "man with a moustache" (M & O, dated Jan. 27, 2006, at 6); (2) in May 1986 he informed FBI Special Agents Howard Mette and Randolph Biddle that he made a mistake about the line-up because the person he identified (Basciano) did not have a moustache, and the person who shot him did (*id.*); and (3) he recently reportedly spoke with an investigator working for Basciano, and said that detectives came to his home on November 14, 1985 and showed him photographs of Basciano, which assisted him in identifying Basciano at the line-up. (*Id.* at 6–7.) In the M & O, dated January 27, 2006, in which this court denied Basciano's motion to exclude Nunez's identification of Basciano in the line up, this court rejected Nunez's last account, finding that this account is impossible to reconcile with the fact that hospital records show that he could not have gone home after being discharged and before the line up. *(Id.)*

Basciano now moves *in limine* to exclude the testimony of Officer Keith Garley on Nunez's identification of Basciano in the 1985 line-up as a violation of Basciano's Sixth Amendment Confrontation Clause rights as articulated in *Crawford v. Washington*, 541 U.S. 36, 124 S. Ct. 1354, 158 L. Ed. 2d 177 (2004).

The Confrontation Clause of the Sixth Amendment provides that "In all criminal prosecutions, the accused shall enjoy the right . . . to be confronted with the witnesses against him . . . ." U.S. Const. amend. VI. The Supreme Court in *Crawford v. Washington*, 541 U.S. 36, 124 S. Ct. 1354, 158 L. Ed. 2d 177 (2004) "announced a *per se* bar on the admission of a class of out-of-court statements, denominated 'testimonial,' against an accused who had no prior opportunity to cross-examine the declarant." *United States v. Stewart*, 433 F.3d 273, 290 (2d Cir. 2006).

First, it is clear that the testimony sought, i.e. a police officer's account of Nunez's identification of Basciano in the line-up, is testimonial. "The types of statements cited by the Court as testimonial share certain characteristics; all involve a declarant's knowing responses to structured questioning in an investigative environment or a courtroom setting where the declarant would reasonably expect that his or her responses might be used in future judicial proceedings." *United States v. Stewart*, 433 F.3d 273, 290 (quoting *United States v. Saget*, 377 F.3d 223, 228 (2d Cir. 2004)). Generally, statements made to a law enforcement agent that were not subject to cross-examination are testimonial where, as here, they are offered for their truth. *Id.*

The Government in opposing this motion explains that it is entitled to admit Officer Garley's testimony on the ground that Basciano forfeited his Confrontation Clause rights by tampering with Nunez after the line-up. The Supreme Court in Crawford made clear that "the rule of forfeiture by wrongdoing (which we accept) extinguishes confrontation claims on essentially equitable grounds; it does not purport to be an alternative means of determining reliability." *Crawford*, 124 S. Ct. at 1368. The 'rule of forfeiture' has been articulated by the Supreme Court as follows:

The Constitution gives the accused the right to a trial at which he should be confronted with the witness against him; but if a witness is absent by his own wrongful procurement, he cannot complain if competent evidence is admitted to supply the place of that which he has kept away. The Constitution does not guarantee an accused person against the legitimate consequences of his own wrongful acts.

Reynolds v. United States, 98 U.S. 145, 158, 25 L. Ed. 244 (1878). "Where a defendant has procured the declarant's unavailability 'by chicanery, . . . by threats, . . . or by actual violence or murder,' the defendant is deemed to have 'waived his sixth amendment rights and, a fortiori, his hearsay objection' to the admission of the declarant's statements.' " *United States v. Williams*, 443 F.3d 35, 45 (2d Cir. 2006) (quoting *United States v. Mastrangelo*, 693 F.2d 269, 272–73 (2d Cir. 1982), cert. denied, 467 U.S. 1204, 104 S. Ct. 2385, 81 L. Ed. 2d 343 (1984)). This rule was codified in Fed. R. Evid. 804(b)(6), which provides that evidence of an out-of-court statement by an unavailable declarant is "not excluded by the hearsay rule" when "offered against a party that has engaged or acquiesced in wrongdoing that was intended to, and did, procure the unavailability of the declarant as a witness." Fed. R. Evid. 804(b)(6). "[A]n evidentiary hearing in the absence of the jury is necessary before a finding of waiver may be made." *Mastrangelo*, 693 F.2d at 273. The Government has the burden to show a waiver by the preponderance of the evidence. *Id.*

The Government must therefore show (1) that Basciano tampered with Nunez, and that (2) as a result, Nunez is unavailable. On the first prong, the Government in opposition to Basciano's motion presents to this court evidence in the form of testimony by Tommy Lee, Anthony Bottone, and proffers that it would seek to admit other testimony showing that Basciano intimidated Nunez into denying his original identification of Basciano as the attempted murderer. (See Gov't Nunez Ltr., dated Apr. 14, 2006, at 3–6.) Although there are few post-Crawford cases analyzing the sufficiency of evidence necessary to find that defendant forfeited his Confrontation Clause rights, it is fair to conclude from this evidence that the Government has met its burden to show by a preponderance of the evidence that Basciano threatened Nunez in order to prevent him from testifying truthfully. *See Francis v. Duncan*, 2004 U.S. Dist. LEXIS 16670, at *52–53 (S.D.N.Y. Aug. 23, 2004) (District court sitting in habeas review of New York state conviction held that Government's obligation to show causal link between misconduct and witness's refusal to testify can be met by circumstantial evidence, and judges may use common sense in drawing inference to determine the reasons for the witness's unavailability.); *State v. Hand*, 107 Ohio St. 3d 378, 390, 840 N.E.2d 151 (2006) (considering applicability of analogous Ohio waiver rule, judge found that government's production of witnesses who testified that defendant killed declarant in order to eliminate him as possible witness met prosecution's burden).

However, to properly invoke the forfeiture rule exception to Basciano's Confrontation Clause rights, the Government must show that Nunez is *unavailable* as a result of Basciano's tampering, the second prong of the forfeiture rule. The Government has not yet offered any evidence that Nunez, if called to testify, would not do so. Clearly, if the Government were to call Nunez to the stand, and he refused to testify, e.g. because of fear of retribution, that would satisfy the Government's burden to show that Nunez is unavailable. Similarly, this court could make a determination after an *in camera* interview of Nunez that he is unavailable.

However, until the Government makes the requisite showing that Nunez is unavailable, it has not met its burden under the second prong of the forfeiture rule test and, hence, Officer Garley's testimony would violate Basciano's Confrontation Clause rights under *Crawford.* I hereby reserve judgment on Basciano's motion, subject to any evidence of unavailability presented by the Government on Monday, April 17, 2006.

As you recall from criminal law, a member of a conspiracy is responsible for all the acts of his co-conspirators in furtherance of the conspiracy. *Thompson* raises the question of whether statements made by a declarant, who is made unavailable by one of the defendant's co-conspirators, is admissible against the defendant.

UNITED STATES v. THOMPSON
United States Court of Appeals, Seventh Circuit
286 F.3d 950 (2002)

WILLIAMS, CIRCUIT JUDGE.

In this case, we are presented with former participants in a drug conspiracy who raise a myriad of challenges to their convictions and sentences. We affirm in all respects except we remand for the resentencing of two defendants because the district court erred by applying . . . the drug offense murder cross reference to their sentences. We also, in affirming the district court, adopt the Tenth Circuits's view of waiver, see United States v. Cherry, 217 F.3d 811 (10th Cir. 2000), and approve the admission of the testimony of a murdered co-conspirator when the murder was reasonably foreseeable to other conspirators.

Defendants Willie Boddie, Stephanie Johnson, Dennis Jones, Anthony Spradley, Anthony Thompson, Ellis Walker, and Mark White were charged with crimes arising out of their participation in a large, Indianapolis-based drug conspiracy. The conspiracy reigned from 1992 to 1997 and involved the trafficking of hundreds of kilograms (kilos) of cocaine, the accumulation and laundering of substantial profits, and two short-lived business pursuits. The conspiracy seemed invincible until November 1996, when Marcus Willis, working on behalf of law-enforcement officials, arrived on the scene. He worked for law enforcement for approximately eight months (through June of 1997) until he was murdered in one of the defendant's vehicles. Not long after his murder, charges were filed against each of the defendants and several others not part of this appeal.

* * *

B. Hearsay Statements

Pursuant to Federal Rules of Evidence 804(b)(6), the government sought to admit several hearsay statements made by murdered informant Marcus Willis. Rule

804(b)(6) exempts from the hearsay ban statements made by a declarant whose unavailability the defendant directly or indirectly procured. The government alleged before the district court that some of the defendants (Spradley, White, Boddie, Jones, and Walker) affirmatively participated in Willis's murder or its cover-up. Based on the government's proffer, the district court admitted the hearsay statements against these defendants. The government then argued that the actions of Spradley, White, Boddie, Jones, and Walker should also permit application of Rule 804(b)(6) to the remaining defendants because Willis's murder was within the scope and committed in furtherance of the drug conspiracy, and was reasonably foreseeable to each of the conspirators. Drawing on the conspirator liability rationale first espoused in Pinkerton v. United States (1946), the district court admitted the hearsay statements against those defendant that did not affirmatively participate in the murder or its cover-up.

Both groups of defendants challenge the admission into evidence of Willis's statements. Those defendants alleged by the government to have participated in Willis's murder or its cover-up argue that the district court misapplied Rule 804(b)(6) and violated their confrontation rights pursuant to the Sixth Amendment. Reviewing their Rule 804(b)(6) challenge for abuse of discretion, . . . and Confrontation Clause challenge de novo, . . . we conclude that any error made by the district court was harmless. The second group of defendants, those who did not affirmatively participate in the murder or cover-up, argue that the district court erred by admitting the statements against them based on an extension of Pinkerton. Employing the same standards of review, we reject their challenges as well.

1. Waiver of hearsay and confrontation clause objections

A defendant may waive his right to object on hearsay and Confrontation Clause grounds to the admission of out-of-court statements made by declarant whose unavailability he intentionally procured. . . . The primary reasoning behind this rule is obvious — to deter criminals from intimidating or "taking care of" potential witnesses against them. But the rule is also grounded in principles of equity. . . . Admission of the witness's statements are least partially offsets the benefit the defendant obtained by his misconduct . . . .

*   *   *

b. Coconspirator waiver

For those defendants who did not participate in Willis's murder or its cover-up (Stephanie Johnson and Anthony Thompson), the government urges us to follow *United States v. Cherry*, 217 F.3d 811 (10th Cir. 2000). *Cherry* holds that if a murder is reasonably foreseeable to a conspirator and within the scope and in furtherance of a conspiracy, the conspirator waives his right to confront that witness just as if he killed the witness himself. Although we believe that *Cherry* is well-reasoned, we find that Willis's murder was not reasonably foreseeable to these defendants. But because admission of the statements was harmless, the error does not require reversal.

i. *United States v. Cherry*

The Tenth Circuit's decision in *Cherry* involves three main points. We summarize them briefly and explain why we find them persuasive. First, coconspirator waiver is consistent with waiver-by-misconduct jurisprudence. Several waiver-by-misconduct cases recognize the possibility of imputed waiver, although none ruled explicitly on the question . . . .

Coconspirator waiver fits within the federal rules's codification of the waiver-by-misconduct rule as well. Under Rule 804(b)(6), a defendant who "acquiesces in conduct intended to procure the unavailability of a witness" waives his hearsay objection. We agree with the Tenth Circuit that, by using the term "acquiesce," the drafters of Rule 804(b)(6) expressed an intent to allow for the imputation of waiver. . . . This makes sense because acquiescence itself is an act. . . . And when that act is done intentionally and voluntarily it is no less valid as a means of waiver than the decision to more directly procure the unavailability of a witness by, for example, murdering a witness oneself.

Second, coconspirator waiver strikes the proper balance between protecting a defendant's confrontation rights and preventing witness tampering. . . . Without a rule of coconspirator waiver, the majority of members of a conspiracy could benefit from a few members engaging in misconduct. Such a result is at odds with the waiver-by-misconduct doctrine's equitable underpinning . . . .

Third, as a practical matter, "[i]t would make little sense to limit forfeiture of a defendant's trial rights to a narrower set of facts than would be sufficient to sustain a conviction and corresponding loss of liberty." . . . Pinkerton established the rule that a defendant may be held liable for acts committed by her conspirator that were within the scope and in furtherance of the conspiracy, and were reasonably foreseeable to her. . . . Under this rule, a defendant may be held criminally responsible for any act committed in furtherance of the conspiracy, including acts taken to prevent apprehension. . . . Witness tampering is one example of these sorts of facts . . . and, of course, can constitute waiver-by-misconduct.

. . . The dissent primarily focuses on the idea that mere membership in a conspiracy should not be sufficient to establish waiver. . . . We agree with this proposition and believe that it is inherent in our holding — for waiver to be imputed to a conspirator, the conduct resulting in the witness's unavailability must have been committed in furtherance of the conspiracy, within its scope, and reasonably foreseeable to the conspirator.

To the extent that the Cherry dissent's reliance on the phrase "personal to the accused" communicates a concern that the imputation of waiver will result in the unintentional waiver of defendants' rights . . . we believe that the formulation of the rule we adopt today will insure that the conspirator's waiver meets this constitutional standard. By limiting coconspirator waiver-by-misconduct to those acts that were reasonably foreseeable to each individual defendant, the rule captures only those conspirators that actually acquiesced either explicitly or implicitly to the misconduct.

*   *   *

In sum, a defendant who joins a conspiracy risks many things — e.g. the admission of his conspirator's statements at trial under Federal Rule of Evidence 801(d)(2)(E), the potential conviction for substantive offenses committed in furtherance of the conspiracy, and the inclusion of his conspirator's acts in the computation of his relevant conduct at sentencing. We see no reason why imputed waiver should not be one of these risks, particularly when the waiver results from misconduct designed to benefit the conspiracy's members. For these reasons and the other expressed above, we follow the Tenth Circuit's decision in *Cherry* and hold that the waiver-by-misconduct of one conspirator may be imputed to another conspirator if the misconduct was within the scope and in furtherance of the conspiracy, and was reasonably foreseeable to him.

ii. The *Cherry* rule applied

However, we conclude that Marcus Willis's murder was not reasonably foreseeable to Stephanie Johnson and Anthony Thompson. There is not evidence that these defendants knew or had reason to know that an informant would be murdered. . . . As we noted in our discussion of the First Degree Murder Guideline, there is not evidence that this conspiracy had previously engaged in murder or attempted murder. Therefore, we find that Willis's murder was not reasonably foreseeable to either of these defendants.

If prior experience is the measure of reasonable foreseeability, would the common practice of juvenile gang intimidation and killing of witnesses make incarcerated gang members responsible for the gang's wrongdoing?

Would Rule 804(b)(6) be applicable if a party knew of subpoenaed witness's intention to flee (without coercion from him or his associates) and failed to advise the opposing party?

§ 5.02 HEARSAY EXCEPTIONS REQUIRING DECLARANT'S UNAVAILABILITY — RULE 804

[A] Former Testimony

[1] Scope of Rule 804(b)(1): "Predecessor in Interest"

Rule 804(b)(1) allows a proponent to introduce prior testimony as evidence in a subsequent civil action only if the party against whom it previously was offered was a "predecessor in interest" to the party against whom the proponent now offers it. However, the term "predecessor in interest" is nowhere defined in the Rule.

Courts have disagreed as to the guidance the legislative history provides in this regard. In *In re Master Key Antitrust Litigation*, for example, the court found that the legislative history compelled a narrow interpretation of the term "predecessor in interest" because:

[t]he rule as originally proposed by the Supreme Court would have allowed prior testimony if the earlier party simply shared a "motive and interest similar to those of the party against whom [it is] now offered." The language adopted by Congress severely restricts the evidence which may be offered. The House Report noted:

> The Committee considered that it is generally unfair to impose upon the party against whom the hearsay evidence is being offered responsibility for the manner in which the witness was previously handled by another party.

72 F.R.D. 108, 109 (D. Conn. 1976).

The court in *Master Key* did concede, however, that Congress apparently intended to relax the common law requirement of actual privity between the parties, because the Senate, which accepted the more restrictive language proposed by the House, made statements to that effect in its report accompanying the Federal Rules:

> [W]hile the term "predecessor in interest" is nowhere defined, Congress seems to have intended to relax the common law requirement of actual privity between the parties before prior testimony could be admitted. . . . This is reflected in the Senate Report, which states:
>
>> The House amended the rule to apply only to a party's predecessor-in-interest. Although the committee recognized considerable merit to the rule submitted by the Supreme Court, a position which has been advocated by many scholars and judges, we have concluded that the difference between the two versions is not great and we accept the House amendment.

Id. at 109.

The court concluded that the federal government was a predecessor-in-interest to a private antitrust plaintiff because of the "unique relationship between the Government's antitrust enforcement suits and the private actions which follow," a relationship that Congress had recognized and ratified. *Id.*

In contrast to the opinion in *Master Key*, the Third Circuit in *Lloyd v. American Export Lines, Inc.*, excerpted below, has given a very different interpretation to the legislative history accompanying Rule 804(b)(1).

LLOYD v. AMERICAN EXPORT LINES, INC.
Circuit Court of Appeals, Third Circuit
580 F.2d 1179 (1978)

ALDISERT, CIRCUIT JUDGE.

The major questions presented in the appeal by American Export Lines, Inc., from an adverse Jones Act verdict relate to rulings on evidence. Roland Alvarez, a former third assistant engineer employed by Export in whose favor a verdict was returned below, has cross-appealed from the trial court's refusal to enter judgment n.o.v. on the jury's verdict in favor of Export on an unseaworthiness claim; he also contends the trial court erred in not entering a favorable judgment for maintenance and cure. Because we determine that competent evidence was erroneously excluded, we reverse and remand for a new trial.

I.

This lawsuit emanates from a violent altercation between Alvarez and a fellow crew member, electrician Frank Lloyd, that occurred on September 7, 1974, when their ship, the SS EXPORT COMMERCE, was in the port of Yokohama, Japan. Lloyd filed an action against Export in the district court, alleging negligence under the Jones Act, 46 U.S.C. § 688, and unseaworthiness under general maritime law, seeking redress for the injuries sustained in the fight. Export joined Alvarez as a third-party defendant and Alvarez, in turn, counterclaimed against Export, alleging, as did Lloyd, negligence and unseaworthiness. Lloyd did not proceed in his case as plaintiff, failing to appear on seven occasions for a pretrial deposition, and failing to appear when the case was called for trial on November 18, 1976. Accordingly, his complaint was dismissed by the district court for failure to prosecute, and thereafter trial was had on Alvarez' counterclaim. The jury found that although Export had not breached its warranty of seaworthiness, it was nevertheless negligent, and its negligence contributed to Alvarez' injuries. The jury returned a verdict in favor of Alvarez against Export in the amount of $95,000.

It was Alvarez' theory that Export negligently failed to use reasonable precautions to safeguard him from Lloyd after Export had knowledge of Lloyd's dangerous propensities. Alvarez testified that he suffered from a preexisting heart condition, and that the officers and crew had knowledge of his condition. He further testified to an incident occurring in July 1974 in the port of New York, when he ordered Lloyd to assist in loading electrical stores, and the latter refused. Alvarez maintained that thereafter, until the Yokohama incident, Lloyd "continuously harassed, provoked, and frightened Alvarez as they passed each other amidships," and that he reported these episodes to the captain and other officers who consequently arranged for Alvarez not to work with Lloyd. There was testimony as well that Lloyd had been involved in fights with other individuals prior to the incident at issue.

Alvarez testified that on the day in question he had been ordered to perform electrical work in a resistor house aboard ship after an officer was unable to rouse Lloyd to do it. The court received into evidence a statement by Chief Officer Goslin that, prior to the fight, he went to Lloyd's quarters to inform him of a winch failure and discovered him lying fully clothed in his bunk, apparently intoxicated and unable to perform his duties. The only description of the fight that occurred when Lloyd subsequently entered the resistor house was offered by Alvarez, and is summarized in his brief as follows:

> Lloyd sneaked through the open door unnoticed by Alvarez and without any warning or provocation, Lloyd viciously attacked Alvarez, striking him in the head with an unidentified object while screaming he would "kill him." During this life-threatening struggle, Alvarez was able to pick up a turnbuckle and end the fight by striking Lloyd once.

The jury was not permitted to hear any version of the fight other than that of Alvarez; it was denied the opportunity of hearing the account rendered by Lloyd, who was the other participant in the affray and its only other eyewitness. It is the refusal of the district court to admit a public record of a prior proceeding and excerpts of Lloyd's testimony therein that constitutes the major thrust of Export's appeal. Export contends that this evidence was admissible in the form of transcripts and a final report from a Coast Guard hearing conducted intermittently from January 20, 1975 through January 6, 1976, the purpose of which was to determine whether Lloyd's merchant mariner's document should have been suspended or revoked on the basis of charges of misconduct brought against him for the fight with Alvarez. At that hearing, both Lloyd and Alvarez were represented by counsel and testified under oath.

*   *   *

B.

Our examination of the transcript of Frank Lloyd's testimony at the Coast Guard hearing convinces us that it is highly relevant to the negligence issue raised by Alvarez. Because Lloyd testified not only to the incident of September 1974, but to the history of his relationship with Alvarez as well, his testimony would have been most helpful to the jury in determining the ultimate issue of whether the officers and crew of the SS EXPORT COMMERCE failed to take reasonable precautions to safeguard Alvarez against an attack by Lloyd. Indeed, Lloyd's testimony directly refuted the Alvarez theory . . . .

C.

Alvarez objects to the admission of Lloyd's testimony on two grounds: First, there was insufficient proof that Lloyd was unavailable to testify at trial as contemplated in Rule 804(a)(5), and, second, the Coast Guard proceeding did not qualify under Rule 804(b)(1).

In order for the hearsay exceptions of Rule 804 to apply it is required that the declarant be "unavailable" — in this case, that he be "absent from the hearing and the proponent of his statement [be] unable to procure his attendance . . . by process or other reasonable means." Rule 804(a)(5). In preparation for trial, as has been noted, numerous attempts were made by Export to depose Lloyd, but he repeatedly failed to appear. Finally, on the day set for trial, Export learned that Lloyd would not appear to prosecute his case. Lloyd's counsel represented to the court that extensive efforts had been made to obtain his appearance, but they had failed, due at least in part to his seafaring occupation. We are satisfied that where Export and Lloyd's own counsel were unable to obtain his appearance in an action in which he had a formidable interest as a plaintiff, his unavailability status was sufficient to satisfy the requirement of Rule 804.

D.

We turn now to the more difficult question: did Alvarez or a "predecessor in interest" have the "opportunity and similar motive to develop the testimony by direct, cross or redirect examination" as required by Rule 804(b)(1)? In rejecting the proffered evidence, the district court took a strict view of the new rule, one that we do not share.

We note at the outset that inasmuch as Congress did not define "predecessor in interest," that interpretive task is left to the courts. We find no definitive guidance in the reports accompanying language changes made as the Rules were considered, in turn, by the Supreme Court and the houses of Congress. As originally submitted by the Supreme Court, Rule 804(b)(1) would have allowed prior testimony of an unavailable witness to be received in evidence if the party against whom it was offered, or a person with "motive and interest similar," had an opportunity to examine the witness. The House of Representatives adopted the present language, the Committee on the Judiciary offering this rationale:

> Rule 804(b)(1) as submitted by the Court allowed prior testimony of an unavailable witness to be admissible if the party against whom it is offered or a person "with motive and interest similar" to his had an opportunity to examine the witness. The Committee considered that it is generally unfair to impose upon the party against whom the hearsay evidence is being offered responsibility for the manner in which the witness was previously handled by another party. The sole exception to this, in the Committee's view, is when a party's predecessor in interest in a civil action or proceeding had an opportunity and similar motive to examine the witness. The Committee amended the Rule to reflect these policy determinations.[1]

> The Senate Committee on the Judiciary viewed the import of this change as follows: Former testimony. — Rule 804(b)(1) as submitted by the Court allowed prior testimony of an unavailable witness to be admissible if the party against whom it is offered or a person "with motive and interest similar" to his had an opportunity to examine the witness.

The House amended the rule to apply only to a party's predecessor in interest. Although the committee recognizes considerable merit to the rule submitted by the Supreme Court, a position which has been advocated by many scholars and judges, we have concluded that the difference between the two versions is not great and we accept the House amendment.

We, too, fail to see a compelling difference between the two approaches.

In our analysis of this language change, we are aware of the basic thrust of subdivision (b) of Rule 804. It was originally designed by the Advisory Committee on Rules of Evidence of the Judicial Conference of the United States to strike a proper balance between the recognized risk of introducing testimony of one not physically present on a witness stand and the equally recognized risk of denying to

---

[1] (Court's original footnote 5.) We do not accept the view that this change in wording signalled a return to the common law approach to former testimony, requiring privity or a common property interest between the parties . . . .

the fact-finder important relevant evidence. Even in its slightly amended form as enacted by Congress, Rule 804 still serves the original intention of its drafters: "The rule expresses preferences: testimony given on the stand in person is preferred over hearsay, and hearsay, if of the specified quality, is preferred over complete loss of the evidence of the declarant."

Although Congress did not furnish us with a definition of "predecessor in interest," our analysis of the concept of interests satisfies us that there was a sufficient community of interest shared by the Coast Guard in its hearing and Alvarez in the subsequent civil trial to satisfy Rule 804(b)(1). Roscoe Pound has taught us that interests in law are "the claims or demands or desires which human beings, either individually or in groups or associations or relations, seek to satisfy. . . ." The interest implicated here was a claim or desire or demand which Alvarez as an individual and the Coast Guard as a representative of a larger group, sought to satisfy, and which has been recognized as socially valid by authoritative decision-makers in our society.

Individual interests, like those of Alvarez, are involved immediately in the individual life, in the Pound formulation, and asserted in title of that life. Public interests, like those of the Coast Guard, are involved in the life of a politically organized society, herein the United States, and asserted in title of that entity. Thus, Alvarez sought to vindicate his individual interest in recovering for his injuries; the Coast Guard sought to vindicate the public interest in safe and unimpeded merchant marine service. Irrespective of whether the interest be considered from the individual or public view-points, however, the nucleus of operative facts was the same — the conduct of Frank Lloyd and Roland Alvarez aboard the SS EXPORT COMMERCE. And although the results sought in the two proceedings differed — the Coast Guard contemplated sanctions involving Lloyd's mariner's license, while Alvarez sought private substituted redress, i.e., monetary damages — the basic interest advanced by both was that of determining culpability and, if appropriate, exacting a penalty for the same condemned behavior thought to have occurred.[2] The Coast Guard investigating officer not only preferred charges against Lloyd but functioned as a prosecutor at the subsequent proceeding as well. Thus, he attempted to establish at the Coast Guard hearing what Alvarez attempted to establish at the later trial; Lloyd's intoxication, his role as the aggressor, and his prior hostility toward Alvarez. Dean Pound recognized that there can be such a community of individual and public interests as this: "It must be borne in mind that often we have here different ways of looking at the same claims or same type of claims as they are asserted in different titles."

Moreover, although our precise task is to decide whether the Coast Guard investigating officer was Alvarez' predecessor in interest, it is equally important to respect always the fundamentals that underlie the hearsay rule, and the reasons for

---

[2] (Court's original footnote 12.) In this regard, McCormick takes the position that "insistence upon precise identity of issues, which might have some appropriateness if the question were one of *res judicata* or estoppel by judgment, are out of place with respect to former testimony where the question is not of binding anyone, but merely of the salvaging, for what it may be worth, of the testimony of a witness not now available in person. . . . It follows that neither the form of the proceeding, the theory of the case, nor the nature of the relief sought needs be the same." . . .

the exceptions thereto. Any fact-finding process is ultimately a search for truth and justice, and legal precepts that govern the reception of evidence must always be interpreted in light of this. Whether it be fashioned by rules of decision in cases or controversies, or promulgated by the Supreme Court with the approval of Congress, or designed and adopted by Congress, every rule of evidence is a means to an end, not an end in itself. We strive to avoid interpretations that are wooden or mechanical, like obsolete common law pleadings, and to favor those that facilitate the presentation of a complete picture to the fact-finder. With this approach in mind, we are satisfied that there existed, in the language of Rule 804(b)(1), sufficient "opportunity and similar motive [for the Coast Guard investigating officer] to develop [Lloyd's] testimony" at the former hearing to justify its admission against Alvarez at the later trial.[3]

While we do not endorse an extravagant interpretation of who or what constitutes a "predecessor in interest," we prefer one that is realistically generous over one that is formalistically grudging. We believe that what has been described as "the practical and expedient view" expresses the congressional intention: "if it appears that in the former suit a party having a like motive to cross-examine about the same matters as the present party would have, was accorded an adequate opportunity for such examination, the testimony may be received against the present party." . . . The approach of the Federal Rules of Evidence is to examine proffered former testimony in light of the prior opportunity and motive to develop the testimony, whether in the form of direct, redirect or cross-examination. This less restrictive approach finds support among commentators. . . . Under these circumstances, the previous party having like motive to develop the testimony about the same material facts is, in the final analysis, a predecessor in interest to the present party.

[2] Scope of Rule 804(b)(1): Opportunity and Similar Motive to Develop Prior Testimony

Former testimony meets the requirement of opportunity for cross-examination only if there was a meaningful opportunity to develop the testimony in the prior proceeding. This means that the court in the prior proceeding must not have restricted either the manner or scope of the inquiry beyond what would have been

---

[3] (Court's original footnote 14.) One can discern a confluence between the congressional policy determinations and our view of the interests in this case in an analysis offered by the Fourth Circuit in a case, also involving a prior Coast Guard proceeding, that pre-dated the present rules.

> Chadwick's testimony was presented by use of a portion of the proceedings before the Coast Guard in its investigation of the catastrophe. In those proceedings Chadwick was sworn. There was a presiding officer who conducted the proceedings, ruled on the form of questions and ruled on the admissibility of evidence. The object of the inquiry was to fix responsibility for the fire — the object of these proceedings. Full cross-examination on the facts as then known by counsel for the Trexler estate, counsel for Crown and counsel for the barge and tug was permitted. The interests of those present and represented by counsel were substantially the same as those who are parties in these proceedings, but who did not appear in the Coast Guard proceedings.

Tug Raven v. Trexler, 419 F.2d 536, 542–43 (4th Cir. 1969), *cert. denied sub nom. Crown Central Corp. v. Trexler*, 398 U.S. 938 (1970).

possible and reasonably necessary in the proceeding in which the testimony is subsequently offered. The fact that the party against whom it is now used did not take advantage of that earlier opportunity is irrelevant. If, however, the party against whom the testimony is now being offered was not the same party against whom the testimony was previously offered, a court might not hold against a successor the predecessor's failure to exercise the opportunity to develop the testimony. This decision will turn on the court's assessment of whether the predecessor's motive to cross-examine the testimony was the same as that of its successor.

[a]   Preliminary Hearings

As you will see in *Lopez*, the New Mexico Supreme Court held that defendants have a similar motive to cross-examine prosecution witnesses at preliminary hearings as they have at trial. To say the least, this assumption is overly formalistic. While a preliminary hearing is for the purpose of challenging the state's right to detain a defendant — to consider whether there is probable cause to believe the defendant committed the crimes for which he is charged — the reality is that probable cause is found in nearly all preliminary hearings. Nevertheless, defense lawyers frequently request preliminary hearings. The reason for this disconnect is that the real purpose of the preliminary hearing is to discover the evidence the prosecution intends to use against the defendant. Because probable cause will most often be found, the defense will rarely vigorously cross-examine the state's witnesses at such a hearing so as not to preview the defense for the prosecution. The *Lopez* decision reflects the law on the admissibility of preliminary hearing testimony, but notice how insensitive the reasoning is to the realities of preliminary hearings.

STATE v. LOPEZ
Supreme Court of New Mexico
258 P.3d 458 (2011)

SERNA, JUSTICE.

Defendant Ramon Lopez was convicted by a jury of multiple crimes, including first-degree felony murder, contrary to NMSA 1978, Section 30-2-1(A)(2) (1994), with first-degree criminal sexual penetration (CSP), contrary to NMSA 1978, Section 30-9-11(C)(2) (1995) (amended 2009), as the underlying felony. Defendant invokes this Court's appellate jurisdiction over sentences for life imprisonment, contained in Article VI, Section 2 of the New Mexico Constitution and Rule 12-102(A)(1) NMRA. We address two of the issues Defendant has raised on appeal: whether Defendant's right to confront witnesses who testified against him were violated by the admission of the preliminary hearing testimony of an unavailable witness, and whether the district court erred in allowing the State to impeach its own witness with otherwise inadmissible hearsay. We conclude that the district court committed reversible error by allowing the hearsay to be admitted under the auspices of the State's impeachment of the preliminary hearing testimony of the unavailable witness.

Crystal Calderella (Victim) last was seen alive the night of April 12, 2001, with Defendant, Greg Romero, and others who were consuming drugs and alcohol at Victim's home in Socorro, New Mexico. On April 15, 2001, Victim's body was discovered in her home, her clothes partially removed. There were bruises and contusions on Victim's neck and lower legs, and blood on the back of Victim's head. Semen, later shown to be Defendant's, was found in Victim's vagina. Defendant was charged with Victim's murder after being arrested on an unrelated charge.

At Defendant's preliminary hearing, Romero testified under oath about the events that occurred during the evening of Victim's death. Before trial, the State informed the district court that it was unable to locate Romero, who had absconded from probation in California, and explained the efforts that had been undertaken to locate him. The district court permitted the State to introduce Romero's preliminary hearing testimony via tape under the hearsay exception for unavailable witnesses contained in Rule 11-804(A)(5) and (B)(1) NMRA. Defendant argues that the admission of Romero's preliminary hearing testimony violated the Confrontation Clauses contained in the Sixth Amendment to the United States Constitution and Article II, Section 14 of the New Mexico Constitution.

"We first determine whether the preliminary hearing testimony was properly admitted under the Rules of Evidence." *State v. Henderson*, 2006-NMCA-059, ¶ 8, 139 N.M. 595, 136 P.3d 1005. Only if the preliminary hearing testimony was properly admitted do we address the Confrontation Clause issue. *Id.* Defendant argues that the preliminary hearing testimony was improperly admitted because Defendant did not have an opportunity for a meaningful cross-examination of Romero. We review the admission of evidence pursuant to an exception or an exclusion to the hearsay rule under an abuse of discretion standard. *State v. McClaugherty*, 2003-NMSC-006, ¶ 17, 133 N.M. 459, 64 P.3d 486.

"A hearsay statement consists of an out-of-court statement offered to prove the truth of the matter asserted," and is inadmissible as substantive evidence unless it falls within an exclusion or exception to the hearsay rule. *Id.* Rule 11-804(A)(5) defines as unavailable a witness who "is absent from the hearing and the proponent of a statement has been unable to procure the declarant's attendance . . . by process or other reasonable means." A statement of an unavailable witness is admissible if the unavailable witness's "[t]estimony [was] given as a witness at another hearing of the same or a different proceeding . . . [and] if the party against whom the testimony is now offered . . . had an opportunity and similar motive to develop the testimony by direct, cross or redirect examination." Rule 11-804(B)(1); *see also State v. Gonzales*, 113 N.M. 221, 226, 824 P.2d 1023, 1028 (1992) (stating that the motives for cross-examination at the preliminary hearing and the trial must be similar, but need not be identical).

Whether a party had an opportunity and similar motive to develop testimony must be determined on a case-by-case basis. *Gonzales* addressed a situation where the defendant had an opportunity to cross-examine a witness at a preliminary hearing, but at trial, when the witness was unavailable to testify, the defendant's theory of his defense had changed from self-defense to identification. 113 N.M. at 225–26, 824 P.2d at 1027–28. We noted that the Court of Appeals had set forth a "per se rule that absent extraordinary circumstances preliminary hearing testimony may be admitted at trial if the witness is unavailable because the motive to cross-examine is similar." *Id.* at 226, 824 P.2d at 1028 (citing *State v. Massengill*, 99 N.M. 283, 285, 657 P.2d 139, 141 (Ct. App. 1983)). Despite the change in the defendant's theory, *Gonzales* concluded that because the defendant "was given the opportunity to cross-examine the witness at the preliminary hearing, [the] defendant was not denied the right to confront the witness against him." *Id.* at 227, 824 P.2d at 1029.

In *Henderson*, the preliminary hearing testimony of two unavailable witnesses was admitted at trial. 2006-NMCA-059, ¶ 7, 139 N.M. 595, 136 P.3d 1005. "[T]he trial court acknowledged that [the d]efendant could not have cross-examined [the unavailable witnesses] at the preliminary hearing on all issues that were relevant to his defense because all the issues were not known at that time." *Id.* The Court of Appeals nevertheless concluded that the defendant had an adequate opportunity for cross-examination because he was able to cross-examine the witness "about whether any crime was committed and whether [the d]efendant was involved." *Id.* ¶ 12. The defendant, therefore, "had an 'opportunity and similar motive' to cross-examine [the witness] at the preliminary hearing as he would have at trial." *Id.*

In this case, the purpose of the preliminary hearing was to determine whether "there [was] probable cause to believe that the defendant committed an offense." Rule 5-302(C) NMRA; *see State ex rel. Whitehead v. Vescovi-Dial*, 1997-NMCA-126, ¶ 5, 124 N.M. 375, 950 P.2d 818 ("The primary purpose of the preliminary examination is to provide an independent evaluation of whether the state has met its burden of demonstrating probable cause."). At the preliminary hearing, Defendant questioned Romero about whether Romero witnessed Defendant engage in sexual intercourse with Victim; whether Defendant assaulted Victim, or removed Victim's clothes; and whether Romero witnessed anything "unusual" happen between Victim and Defendant that night. At the preliminary hearing, Defendant argued that there was insufficient evidence to establish probable cause that Defendant committed a crime, and that the case should not be bound over for trial; his motive for cross-examining Romero, therefore, was to show that Defendant did not rape and murder Victim.

Defendant's motive at trial likewise was to demonstrate that he was not guilty of raping and murdering Victim. During both proceedings, Defendant's motive was to discredit the State's case and to argue that the evidence did not establish his guilt. We conclude, therefore, that because Defendant had an opportunity and similar motive to cross-examine Romero at the preliminary hearing as he did at trial, the district court did not abuse its discretion in admitting Romero's preliminary hearing testimony at trial.

[b]   Grand Jury Testimony

The reasoning in the *DiNapoli* case stands in stark contrast with the *Lopez* decision's discussion of the motive of a prosecutor in a prior proceeding. While *Lopez* took a very formal analysis of the motive of defense lawyers at preliminary hearings, *DiNapoli* considers the fact that a prosecutor in a grand jury might refrain from vigorous examination for strategic reasons. Justice Stevens' opinion in this case, described by the Second Circuit, that would use the same sort of analysis for prosecutors in grand jury proceedings as courts use for defense lawyers in preliminary hearings, appears following the Second Circuit's decision in *DiNapoli*.

UNITED STATES v. DiNAPOLI
United States Court of Appeals, Second Circuit
8 F.3d 909 (1993)

JON O. NEWMAN, CHIEF JUDGE:

On this criminal appeal, which is before our Court on remand from the Supreme Court, we have given in banc consideration to a fairly narrow issue of evidence that has potentially broad implications for the administration of criminal justice. The issue concerns Rule 804(b)(1) of the Federal Rules of Evidence, which provides that testimony given by a currently unavailable witness at a prior hearing is not excluded by the hearsay rule if "the party against whom the testimony is now offered . . . had an opportunity and *similar motive to develop the testimony* by direct, cross, or redirect examination." Fed. R. Evid. 804(b)(1) (emphasis added). Our precise issue is whether the prosecution had a "similar motive to develop" the testimony of two grand jury witnesses compared to its motive at a subsequent criminal trial at which the witnesses were unavailable. We hold that the "similar motive" requirement of Rule 804(b)(1) was not met and that the witnesses' grand jury testimony, offered by the defendants, was therefore properly excluded. Having decided the sole issue for which in banc consideration was ordered, we return the appeal to the panel to which it was assigned for consideration of remaining issues.

Background

The facts concerning this case have been recounted in prior decisions of this Court, *see United States v. Salerno*, 974 F.2d 231, 232–37 (2d Cir. 1992); *United States v. Salerno*, 937 F.2d 797, 799–803 (2d Cir. 1991); *United States v. Salerno*, 868 F.2d 524, 527–29 (2d Cir. 1989), and we therefore focus only on the details that concern the pending issue. Briefly, the case concerns conspiracy and substantive charges under the Racketeer Influenced and Corrupt Organizations Act ("RICO"), 18 U.S.C. § 1962(c), (d) (1988), against several defendants accused of participating in a bid-rigging scheme in the concrete construction industry in Manhattan. The trial evidence indicated the existence of a "Club" of six concrete construction companies that during 1980–1985 rigged the bids for concrete superstructure work on nearly every high-rise construction project in Manhattan involving more than $2 million of concrete work. Organized crime figures, notably members of the Genovese Family, orchestrated the scheme and enforced adherence to the bid allocations.

The grand jury investigating the matter returned its first indictment on March 20, 1986. That indictment alleged the essential aspects of the criminal activity and named all of the appellants as defendants. The grand jury continued its investigation in an effort to identify additional participants and additional construction projects that might have been victimized by the bid-rigging scheme. In this subsequent phase of the inquiry, the grand jury called Frederick DeMatteis and Pasquale Bruno as witnesses. They had been principals in Cedar Park Concrete Construction Corporation ("Cedar Park"), a company that other grand jury witnesses had testified had been briefly involved in the scheme. DeMatteis and Bruno, both testifying under grants of immunity, denied awareness of a bid-rigging scheme.

DeMatteis testified in the grand jury on three occasions in 1986 — June 3, June 12, and June 19. His first two appearances primarily concerned background questioning about the construction industry and Cedar Park. At his third appearance, the prosecutor pointedly asked whether DeMatteis had been instructed not to bid on the Javits Convention Center project and whether he was aware of an arrangement whereby the successful bidder paid two percent of the bid price to organized crime figures. DeMatteis denied both the instruction not to bid and awareness of the two percent arrangement. The prosecutor, obviously skeptical of the denials, pressed DeMatteis with a few questions in the nature of cross-examination. However, in order not to reveal the identity of then undisclosed cooperating witnesses or the existence of then undisclosed wiretapped conversations that refuted DeMatteis's denials, the prosecutor refrained from confronting him with the substance of such evidence. Instead, the prosecutor called to DeMatteis's attention the substance of only the one relevant wiretapped conversation that had already become public — a tape played at a prior trial, *United States v. Persico*, 84 Cr. 809 (JFK) (S.D.N.Y. 1984).

Bruno testified at the grand jury on September 11, 1986. Much of the questioning concerned the operations of Cedar Park. Like DeMatteis, Bruno was asked about and denied knowledge of the "Club" and the two percent arrangement for successful bidders. And, like DeMatteis, he was briefly cross-examined and confronted with the contents of the publicly disclosed tape from the *Persico* trial but not with any of the information from undisclosed witnesses or wiretaps. After his denials and after giving an answer that sharply conflicted with an answer given by DeMatteis, Bruno was briefly excused from the grand jury room. Upon his return, after the prosecutor had consulted with the grand jury, he was told by the prosecutor of the grand jury's "strong concern" that his testimony had "not been truthful." Four days later, Bruno's lawyer wrote the prosecutor stating that many of Bruno's answers had been inaccurate. The lawyer suggested that the prosecutor should resubmit his questions to Bruno in writing and that Bruno would respond by affidavit. The prosecutor declined the suggestion.

A thirteen-month trial on a superseding indictment, filed April 7, 1987, commenced April 6, 1987, against eleven defendants, and ended on May 4, 1988, with the convictions of nine defendants, including the six appellants, Vincent DiNapoli, Louis DiNapoli, Nicholas Auletta, Edward J. Halloran, Alvin O. Chattin, and Aniello Migliore. During the trial, the defendants endeavored to call DeMatteis and Bruno as witnesses. Both invoked the privilege against self-incrimination. The defendants then offered the testimony DeMatteis and Bruno had given to the grand jury. After examining sealed affidavits presented by the prosecution, the District Court (Mary Johnson Lowe, Judge) refused to admit the grand jury testimony as prior testimony under Rule 804(b)(1). Judge Lowe appears not to have made specific findings with respect to the grand jury testimony. Instead, she ruled generally that the "motive of a prosecutor . . . in the investigatory stages of a case is far different from the motive of a prosecutor in conducting the trial" and hence the "similar motive" requirement of Rule 804(b)(1) was not satisfied.

On a prior consideration of the appeal, the panel reversed the convictions and ordered a new trial on the ground that it was error to exclude the witnesses' grand jury testimony. *United States v. Salerno*, 937 F.2d 797 (2d Cir. 1991). Though stating that "we agree that the government may have had no motive before the grand jury to impeach the allegedly false testimony of Bruno and DeMatteis," *id.* at 806, the panel ruled that the "similar motive" requirement of Rule 804(b)(1) need not be met because the witnesses were "available" to the prosecution at trial through a grant of immunity, *id.* The panel subsequently denied rehearing after making a slight revision of its opinion, *United States v. Salerno*, 952 F.2d 623 (2d Cir. 1991), and rehearing in banc was denied by a divided vote, *United States v. Salerno*, 952 F.2d 624 (2d Cir. 1991).

Thereafter, the Supreme Court reversed the panel's reversal of the convictions. *United States v. Salerno*, 505 U.S. 317, 112 S. Ct. 2503, 120 L. Ed. 2d 255 (1992). The Supreme Court ruled that all of the requirements of Rule 804(b)(1) must be met, including the "similar motive" requirement. The Court declined to decide whether the "similar motive" requirement was satisfied in this case, believing it "prudent to remand the case for further consideration" of that issue. [*Id.* at 324–327,] 112 S. Ct. at 2509. In dissent, Justice Stevens reached the "similar motive" issue and concluded that a similar motive was present in this case. *Id.* at [324–331, 112 S. Ct. at] 2509–12.

Upon remand, the panel ruled that the "similar motive" requirement was satisfied. *United States v. Salerno*, 974 F.2d 231 (2d Cir. 1992). The panel considered the questioning of the witnesses conducted by an Assistant United States Attorney and concluded that what occurred "was the equivalent of what would have been done if the opportunity to examine them had been presented at trial." *Id.* at 241.

Discussion

Our initial task is to determine how similarity of motive at two proceedings will be determined for purposes of Rule 804(b)(1). In resolving this matter, we do not accept the position, apparently urged by the appellants, that the test of similar motive is simply whether at the two proceedings the questioner takes the same side of the same issue. The test must turn not only on whether the questioner is on the same side of the same issue at both proceedings, but also on whether the questioner had a substantially similar interest in asserting that side of the issue. If a fact is critical to a cause of action at a second proceeding but the same fact was only peripherally related to a different cause of action at a first proceeding, no one would claim that the questioner had a similar motive at both proceedings to show that the fact had been established (or disproved). This is the same principle that holds collateral estoppel inapplicable when a small amount is at stake in a first proceeding and a large amount is at stake in a second proceeding, even though a party took the same side of the same issue at both proceedings. *See, e.g., Hicks v. Quaker Oats Co.*, 662 F.2d 1158, 1171 (5th Cir. Unit A Dec. 1981); *Restatement (Second) of Judgments* § 28, cmt. j (1982). This suggests that the questioner must not only be on the same side of the same issue at both proceedings but must also have a substantially similar degree of interest in prevailing on that issue.

Whether the degree of interest in prevailing on an issue is substantially similar at two proceedings will sometimes be affected by the nature of the proceedings. Where both proceedings are trials and the same matter is seriously disputed at both trials, it will normally be the case that the side opposing the version of a witness at the first trial had a motive to develop that witness's testimony similar to the motive at the second trial. The opponent, whether shouldering a burden of proof or only resisting the adversary's effort to sustain its burden of proof, usually cannot tell how much weight the witness's version will have with the fact-finder in the total mix of all the evidence. Lacking such knowledge, the opponent at the first trial normally has a motive to dispute the version so long as it can be said that disbelief of the witness's version is of some significance to the opponent's side of the case; the motive at the second trial is normally similar.

The situation is not necessarily the same where the two proceedings are different in significant respects, such as their purposes or the applicable burden of proof. The grand jury context, with which we are concerned in this case, well illustrates the point. If a prosecutor is using the grand jury to investigate possible crimes and identify possible criminals, it may be quite unrealistic to characterize the prosecutor as the "opponent" of a witness's version. At a preliminary stage of an investigation, the prosecutor is not trying to prove any side of any issue, but only to develop the facts to determine if an indictment is warranted. Even if the prosecutor displays some skepticism about particular testimony (not an uncommon response from any questioner interested in eliciting the truth), that does not mean the prosecutor has a motive to show the falsity of the testimony, similar to the motive that would exist at trial if an indictment is returned and the witness's testimony is presented by a defendant to rebut the prosecutor's evidence of guilt.

Even in cases like the pending one, where the grand jury proceeding has progressed far beyond the stage of a general inquiry, the motive to develop grand jury testimony that disputes a position already taken by the prosecutor is not necessarily the same as the motive the prosecutor would have if that same testimony was presented at trial. Once the prosecutor has decided to seek an indictment against identified suspects, that prosecutor may fairly be characterized as "opposed" to any testimony that tends to exonerate one of the suspects. But, because of the low burden of proof at the grand jury stage, even the prosecutor's status as an "opponent" of the testimony does not necessarily create a motive to challenge the testimony that is *similar* to the motive at trial. At the grand jury, the prosecutor need establish only probable cause to believe the suspect is guilty. By the time the exonerating testimony is given, such probable cause may already have been established to such an extent that there is no realistic likelihood that the grand jury will fail to indict. That circumstance alone will sometimes leave the prosecutor with slight if any motive to develop the exonerating testimony in order to persuade the grand jurors of its falsity.

Moreover, the grand jury context will sometimes present additional circumstances that render the prosecutor's motive to challenge the exonerating testimony markedly dissimilar to what the prosecutor's motive would be at trial. Frequently the grand jury inquiry will be conducted at a time when an investigation is ongoing. In such circumstances, there is an important public interest in not disclosing prematurely the existence of surveillance techniques such as wiretaps or under-cover operations, or the identity of cooperating witnesses. The results of such techniques and the statements of such witnesses might be powerful ammunition to challenge the grand jury witness's exonerating testimony. By the time of trial, however, the public interest in not disclosing such ammunition will normally have dissipated, and the prosecutor will have a strong motive to confront the witness with all available contradictory evidence.

In recognizing these factors that distinguish the grand jury context from the trial context, we do not accept the position, urged by the Government upon the Supreme Court, that a prosecutor "generally will not have the same motive to develop testimony in grand jury proceedings as he does at trial." *See Salerno*, [505 U.S. at 323–327,] 112 S. Ct. at 2508–09. Though the Supreme Court declined to assess that contention and left its consideration to this Court in the first instance, we discern in its opinion a reluctance to engraft any general exception onto Rule 804(b)(1). "This Court cannot alter evidentiary rules merely because litigants might prefer different rules in a particular class of cases." *Id.* at [321–323, 112 S. Ct. at] 2507. Our point is simply that the inquiry as to similar motive must be fact specific, and the grand jury context will sometimes, but not invariably, present circumstances that demonstrate the prosecutor's lack of a similar motive. We accept neither the Government's view that the prosecutor's motives at the grand jury and at trial are almost always dissimilar, nor the opposing view, apparently held by the District of Columbia Circuit, that the prosecutor's motives in both proceedings are always similar, *see United States v. Miller*, 904 F.2d 65, 68 (D.C. Cir. 1990). *See also United States v. Lester*, 749 F.2d 1288, 1301 (9th Cir. 1984) (upholding trial judge's exercise of discretion to exclude grand jury testimony after finding testimony eligible for admission under Rule 804(b)(1)); *United States v. Young Brothers, Inc.*, 728 F.2d 682, 691 (5th Cir.) (obviating, because of harmless error, the "difficult" question whether grand jury testimony was admissible under Rule 804(b)(1)), *cert. denied*, 469 U.S. 881, 105 S. Ct. 246, 83 L. Ed. 2d 184 (1984); *United States v. Klauber*, 611 F.2d 512, 516–17 (4th Cir. 1979) (suggesting, but not deciding, that grand jury testimony would have been admissible under Rule 804(b)(1)), *cert. denied*, 446 U.S. 908, 100 S. Ct. 1835, 64 L. Ed. 2d 261 (1980).

Nor are we persuaded by the Government's contention that the absence of similar motive is conclusively demonstrated by the availability at the grand jury of some cross-examination opportunities that were forgone. In virtually all subsequent proceedings, examiners will be able to suggest lines of questioning that were not pursued at a prior proceeding. In almost every criminal case, for example, the Government could probably point to some aspect of cross-examination of an exonerating witness that could have been employed at a prior trial and surely at a prior grand jury proceeding. Though the availability of substantial ways of challenging testimony that were not pursued by an examiner is pertinent to the "similar motive" inquiry, especially when such techniques appear far more prom-ising compared to the cross-examination undertaken, the unused methods are only one factor to be considered.

The proper approach, therefore, in assessing similarity of motive under Rule

804(b)(1) must consider whether the party resisting the offered testimony at a pending proceeding had at a prior proceeding an interest of substantially similar intensity to prove (or disprove) the same side of a substantially similar issue. The nature of the two proceedings — both what is at stake and the applicable burden of proof — and, to a lesser extent, the cross-examination at the prior proceeding — both what was undertaken and what was available but forgone — will be relevant though not conclusive on the ultimate issue of similarity of motive.

Having identified the proper approach to the determination of whether a similar motive existed, we might ordinarily remand to the District Court to apply the governing principles to the precise facts of this case. We decline to do so, however, both to avoid further delay in this already long-delayed matter and because this is the unusual case in which it can be shown beyond reasonable dispute that the prosecutor had no interest at the grand jury in proving the falsity of the witnesses' assertion that the "Club" did not exist. Two circumstances independently suffice. First, the defendants had already been indicted, and, as appellants' counsel conceded at argument, there existed no putative defendant as to whom probable cause was in issue. At most the Government had an interest in investigating further to see *whether* there might be additional defendants or additional projects within the criminal activity of the existing defendants. As to these matters, the prosecutor had no interest in showing that the denial of the Club's existence was false. The grand jury had already been persuaded, at least by the low standard of probable cause, to believe that the Club existed and that the defendants had participated in it to commit crimes. It is fanciful to think that the prosecutor would have had any substantial interest in showing the falsity of the witnesses' denial of the Club's existence just to persuade the grand jury to add one more project to the indictment.

Second, the grand jurors had indicated to the prosecutor that they did not believe the denial. The record is clear on this point. After a consultation with the grand jury, the prosecutor told Bruno, in the grand jurors' presence, that there was "strong concern on the part of the grand jury" that his testimony had "not been truthful." A prosecutor has no interest in showing the falsity of testimony that a grand jury already disbelieves.

These two circumstances dispel similarity of motive, and the absence of similar motive is not rebutted by the limited cross-examination undertaken by the prosecutor at the grand jury. A prosecutor may have varied motives for asking a few challenging questions of a grand jury witness who the prosecutor thinks is lying. The prosecutor might want to afford the witness a chance to embellish the lie, thereby strengthening the case for a subsequent perjury prosecution. Or the prosecutor might want to provoke the witness into volunteering some critical new fact in the heat of an emphatic protestation of innocence. In this case, the cross-examination that occurred does not significantly show similarity of motive. Moreover, the strong inference of dissimilarity from the two factors already discussed is powerfully reenforced by the prosecutor's careful limitation of questioning to matters already publicly disclosed, the lack of questioning on the basis of undisclosed wiretaps and reports of cooperating witnesses, and the lack of any follow-up in response to Bruno's generous offer to correct inaccuracies in his testimony.

Since the grand jury as fact-finder had already resolved the issue of the Club's existence in the prosecutor's favor and had announced disbelief of the witnesses' contrary statements, dissimilarity of motive is beyond dispute. The District Court's exclusion of the witnesses' grand jury testimony was therefore entirely correct, and this ground for reversal of the convictions is rejected. We therefore vacate the panel's decision and return the appeal to the panel for further consideration of the appellants' remaining contentions.

GEORGE C. PRATT, CIRCUIT JUDGE, (joined by MINER and ALTIMARI, CIRCUIT JUDGES), dissenting:

My views as to why the grand jury testimony of Bruno and DeMatteis should have been admitted at trial on the issue of whether or not the "Club" existed are set forth at length elsewhere. *See United States v. Salerno*, 974 F.2d 231 (2d Cir. 1991). I write here to highlight what I perceive to be some of the weak points in the position taken by the in banc majority.

Rule 804(b)(1) of the Federal Rules of Evidence would permit receipt of Bruno's and DeMatteis's grand jury testimony if the government's motive to develop the testimony before the grand jury was "similar" to its motive to challenge that testimony at trial.

On remand from the Supreme Court to decide that issue, the panel determined that the government's motive *was* similar, primarily because (1) the government had examined both Bruno and DeMatteis extensively on whether a "Club" existed, (2) the government had vigorously examined both witnesses before the grand jury, and (3) the government was seeking at trial to prove the same issue as before the grand jury — the existence of a "Club" of concrete contractors. 974 F.2d at 240–41. The panel sought to apply the plain meaning of "similar motive" as used in rule 804(b)(1), and sought the administrative ease of determining that issue based on what the prosecutor actually did, on the record, before the grand jury.

The in banc majority, however, now concludes, as a matter of law, that the prosecutor's motive was not "similar". In doing so, it applies a gloss to the language of the rule that would find a similar motive only when the party against whom the testimony is offered had "an interest of substantially similar intensity to prove (or disprove) the same side of a substantially similar issue". Op. at 915. As a practical matter, the gloss effectively rewrites the rule from "similar motive" to "same motive".

Not only is the majority's test more stringent than the rule itself, it could also prove to be extremely difficult to administer, for on its face this test would require the district judge to compare the "intensity of interest" that the prosecutor possessed before the grand jury with his "intensity of interest" at the trial. Careful examination of those two states of the prosecutor's mind would require a district judge to conduct an evidentiary hearing not only into what information was available to the prosecutor at the two different times, but also into what he was thinking about that information at both of those times.

The majority sidesteps the problem in this case, however, by accepting at face value the prosecutor's *post hoc*, self-serving, un-crossexamined statements as to his own motives, and concluding, as a matter of law, that his motives at the two proceedings were not "similar". At the very least, this issue of fact should be decided in the first instance by a district judge, not an in banc appellate court.

One final, troubling aspect of the majority's decision is its acceptance of and reliance on the prosecutor's assertions that he already had an indictment against the defendants, that no new defendants were being contemplated at the time these witnesses were examined, and that, as a result, probable cause was not even an issue before the grand jury when Bruno and DeMatteis were testifying. If all these things were true, then why was the prosecutor using the grand jury at all? Could it have been simply a discovery device to develop more evidence to present at trial on the indictment he already had? If that were the case, however, the prosecutor's continuing use of the grand jury would have been improper. *See United States v. R. Enterprises, Inc.*, 498 U.S. 292, 299, 111 S. Ct. 722, 727, 112 L. Ed. 2d 795 (1991) ("Grand juries are not licensed to engage in arbitrary fishing expeditions, nor may they select targets of investigation out of malice or an intent to harass."); *In re Grand Jury Subpoena Duces Tecum Dated January 2, 1985 (Simels)*, 767 F.2d 26, 29 (2d Cir. 1985) ("The law is settled in this circuit and elsewhere that '[i]t is improper to utilize a Grand Jury for the sole or dominating purpose of preparing an already pending indictment for trial.' ") (quoting *United States v. Dardi*, 330 F.2d 316, 336 (2d Cir.), *cert. denied*, 379 U.S. 845, 85 S. Ct. 50, 13 L. Ed. 2d 50 (1964)); *see also* 8 James W. Moore et al., *Moore's Federal Practice* ¶ 6.04[5], at 6–106 (2d ed. 1993) ("It is not permissible for the prosecutor to subpoena and question potential trial witnesses to an existing criminal proceeding where it is the sole or dominant purpose of such questioning to obtain evidence for use in the upcoming trial. Simply stated, it is not a legitimate function of the grand jury to serve as a substitute for pretrial discovery."); 1 Charles A. Wright, *Federal Practice & Procedure* § 111.1, at 321 (1982).

The effect of the in banc majority's decision will be to leave the determination of whether grand jury testimony may be presented at trial by a defendant entirely in the prosecutor's control, a result that seems at odds with the main objective of going to trial — permitting the jury, not the prosecutor, to determine what is the truth.

Because I agree with the panel's original analysis of "similar motive" in rule 804(b)(1), I respectfully dissent.

———

The Supreme Court affirmed the *DiNapoli* decision in *Salerno*. Justice Stevens' dissent is reproduced below as it offers a very different perspective, one that is consistent with allowing preliminary hearing testimony to be admitted under this exception against a criminal defendant.

UNITED STATES v. SALERNO
United States Supreme Court
505 U.S. 317 (1992)

JUSTICE STEVENS, dissenting.

Because I believe that the Government clearly had an "opportunity and similar motive" to develop by direct or cross-examination the grand jury testimony of Pasquale Bruno and Frederick DeMatteis, I would affirm the judgment of the Court of Appeals on the ground that the transcript of their grand jury testimony was admissible under the plain language of Federal Rule of Evidence 804(b)(1). As the Court explains, *ante*, at 2505–2506, the grand jury testimony of Bruno and DeMatteis was totally inconsistent with the Government's theory of the alleged RICO conspiracy to rig bids on large construction projects in Manhattan. Bruno and DeMatteis were principals in Cedar Park Construction Corporation Cedar Park), which, according to the Government, was a member of the so-called "Club" of concrete companies that submitted rigged bids on construction projects in accordance with the orders of the Genovese Family of La Cosa Nostra. But notwithstanding the fact that they had been given grants of immunity, Bruno and DeMatteis repeatedly testified before the grand jury that they had not participated in either the Club or the alleged bid-rigging conspiracy. As the Court of Appeals explained, Cedar Park was "one of the largest contractors in the metropolitan New York City concrete industry," and it is arguable that without Cedar Park's participation, "there could be no 'club' of concrete contractors." 937 F.2d 797, 808 (CA2 1991). And without the "Club," the allegations of fraud in the construction industry — which "formed the core of the RICO charges" — "simply dissolv[e]." *Ibid.*

It is therefore clear that before the grand jury the Government had precisely the same interest in establishing that Bruno's and DeMatteis' testimony was false as it had at trial. Thus, when the prosecutors doubted Bruno's and DeMatteis' veracity before the grand jury — as they most assuredly did — they unquestionably had an "opportunity and similar motive to develop the testimony by direct, cross, or redirect examination" within the meaning of Rule 804(b)(1).[1]

The Government disagrees, asserting that it "typically does not have the same motive to cross-examine hostile witnesses in the grand jury that it has to cross-examine them at trial." Brief for United States 11. This is so, the Government maintains, because (1) cross-examining the witness might indirectly undermine the secrecy of the grand jury proceedings,[2] (2) the Government might decide to

---

[1] Rule 804(b)(1) provides:

"Hearsay exceptions.— The following are not excluded by the hearsay rule if the declarant is unavailable as a witness:

"(1) Former Testimony.— Testimony given as a witness at another hearing of the same or a different proceeding, or in a deposition taken in compliance with law in the course of the same or another proceeding, if the party against whom the testimony is now offered, or, in a civil action or proceeding, a predecessor in interest, had an opportunity and similar motive to develop the testimony by direct, cross, or redirect examination."

[2] "If the government exposes the extent of its knowledge to an individual who, by his willingness to

discredit the witness through means other than cross-examination, and (3) the issues before the grand jury are typically quite different from those at trial. See *id.,* at 11–14; Reply Brief for United States 9–12. In my view, the first two reasons — even assuming that they are true — do not justify holding that the Government lacks a "similar motive" in the two proceedings. And although the third reason could justify the conclusion that the Government's motives are not "similar," it is not present on the facts of this case.

Even if one does not completely agree with Wigmore's assertion that cross-examination is "beyond any doubt the greatest legal engine ever invented for the discovery of truth,"[3] one must admit that in the Anglo-American legal system cross-examination is the principal means of undermining the credibility of a witness whose testimony is false or inaccurate.[4] For that reason, a party has a motive to cross-examine any witness who, in her estimation, is giving false or inaccurate testimony about a fact that is material to the legal question at issue in the proceeding.

Of course, the party might decide — for tactical reasons or otherwise — not to engage in a rigorous cross-examination, or even in any cross-examination at all.[5] In such a case, however, I do not believe that it is accurate to say that the party lacked a similar motive to cross-examine the witness; instead, it is more accurate to say that the party had a similar motive to cross-examine the witness (*i.e.,* to undermine the false or misleading testimony) but chose not to act on that motive. Although the Rules of Evidence allow a party to make that choice about whether to engage in cross-examination, they also provide that she must accept the consequences of that decision — including the possibility that the testimony might be introduced against her in a subsequent proceeding.[6]

---

commit perjury, has shown himself to be allied with the investigation's targets, the effect may be to provide information to the targets that can be used to threaten witnesses, destroy evidence, fabricate a defense, or otherwise obstruct the investigation." Brief for United States 12.

[3] 5 J. Wigmore, Evidence § 1367, p. 32 (J. Chadbourn rev.1974).

[4] Indeed, the lack of an opportunity to cross-examine the absent declarant has been the principal justification for the Anglo-American tradition of excluding hearsay statements. See, *e.g.,* E. Cleary, McCormick on Evidence § 245, p. 728 (3d ed. 1984); 5 Wigmore, § 1367, at 32. This concern is diminished, however, when the party against whom the hearsay statement is offered had an opportunity to cross-examine the absent declarant at the time the statement was made. Accordingly, the common law developed an exception to the hearsay rule that permitted the introduction of prior testimony if the opponent had an adequate opportunity to cross-examine the declarant. See, *e.g., id.,* § 1386, at 90. Rule 804(b)(1) codified, with a few changes, that common-law rule. See Advisory Committee's Notes on Fed. Rule Evid. 804(b)(1), 28 U.S.C.App., pp. 788–789.

[5] For example, the party might not want to run the risk of appearing to harass or upset a vulnerable witness — such as a young child or the victim of a terrible crime — with rigorous cross-examination if there are other, less confrontational means of undermining the suspect testimony.

[6] As the Advisory Committee explained, the question whether prior testimony should be admitted is, in essence, the question "whether fairness allows imposing, upon the party against whom now offered, the handling of a witness on the earlier occasion." *Id.,* at 788. When, as in this case, the testimony is offered against the party by whom it was previously offered, the party obviously did not have an opportunity to develop the testimony through *cross*-examination. But, the Advisory Committee recognized, the opportunity to engage in "direct and redirect examination of one's own witness [is] the equivalent of cross-examining an opponent's witness." *Id.,* at 789. In either case, as long as the party had a similar motive to develop the testimony in the prior proceeding, there is no unfairness in requiring the

Thus neither the fact that the prosecutors might decline to cross-examine a grand jury witness whom they fear will talk to the target of the investigation nor the fact that they might choose to undermine the witness' credibility other than through rigorous cross-examination alters the fact that they had an opportunity and similar motive to challenge the allegedly false testimony through questioning before the grand jury. Although those might be reasons for declining to take advantage of the opportunity to cross-examine a witness, neither undermines the principal motive for engaging in cross-examination, *i.e.*, to shake the witness' allegedly false or misleading testimony. Indeed, other courts have found the "opportunity and similar motive" requirement of Rule 804(b)(1) satisfied — and hence the prior testimony admissible in a subsequent trial — in many similar situations.[7]

That leaves the Government's third reason, its contention that it lacks a similar motive to question grand jury witnesses because the issues before the grand jury may not be the same issues that are important at trial. If that were true in a particular case, I would agree that the Government lacked a similar motive for developing the witness' grand jury testimony. Because the scope of questioning is necessarily limited by the scope of the legal and factual issues in a given proceeding, a party has little motive, and indeed may not be permitted, to ask questions about other issues. Thus if those other issues become important in a subsequent proceeding, the testimony from the prior proceeding may properly be excluded on the ground that the party against whom it is offered lacked a similar motive for developing the testimony at the prior proceeding.[8]

---

party against whom the testimony is now offered to accept her prior decision to develop or not develop the testimony fully. *Ibid.*

[7] See, *e.g.*, *United States v. Miller*, 284 U.S. App. D.C. 245, 258, 904 F.2d 65, 68 (1990) (prior grand jury testimony admissible against the Government because "as several circuits have recognized, the government had the same motive and opportunity to question [the witness] when it brought him before the grand jury as it does at trial . . . . Before the grand jury and at trial, [the witness'] testimony was to be directed to the same issue — the guilt or innocence of [the defendants]"); *United States v. Pizarro*, 717 F.2d 336, 349–350 (CA7 1983) (initial trial testimony of one defendant which exculpated the second defendant was admissible during the retrial of the second defendant even though the Government may have declined to cross-examine the first defendant about an issue for fear that it would have resulted in a severance of the trials of the two defendants); *United States v. Poland*, 659 F.2d 884, 895–896 (CA9) (identification testimony of witness at suppression hearing admissible in subsequent trial because defendant would have a similar motive at both proceedings to show that the identification was unreliable), cert. denied, 454 U.S. 1059, 102 S. Ct. 611, 70 L. Ed. 2d 598 (1981); *Glenn v. Dallman*, 635 F.2d 1183, 1186–1187 (CA6 1980) (identification testimony of eyewitness at preliminary hearing admissible against defendant at trial even though defendant declined to cross-examine the witness fully), cert. denied, 454 U.S. 843, 102 S. Ct. 155, 70 L. Ed. 2d 128 (1981); *United States v. Zurosky*, 614 F.2d 779, 791–793 (CA1 1979) (suppression hearing testimony of codefendant which inculpated defendant admissible against defendant at trial even though defendant declined to cross-examine codefendant at the hearing), cert. denied, 446 U.S. 967, 100 S. Ct. 2945, 64 L. Ed. 2d 826 (1980).

[8] As Wigmore explained, the common law required identity of issues as a means of ensuring that the cross-examination in the two proceedings would have been directed at the same material points. 5 Wigmore, § 1386, at 90. Rule 804(b)(1) slightly modified the prior testimony exception to the hearsay rule by substituting the "opportunity and similar motive" requirement for the identity-of-issues requirement. The drafters of the Rule reasoned that "[s]ince identity of issues is significant only in that it bears on motive and interest in developing fully the testimony of the witness, expressing the matter in the latter terms is preferable." Advisory Committee's Notes on Rule 804(b)(1), at 789. Nevertheless, for the reasons discussed in the text, "[i]n determining whether a similar motive to develop the testimony existed at the time of the elicitation of the former testimony the courts will search for some substantial identity

That did not occur in this case, however. After reviewing the sealed transcripts of Bruno's and DeMatteis' grand jury testimony, the Court of Appeals concluded that "[v]ery generally stated, their grand jury testimony denied any awareness of, let alone participation in," the "Club" of concrete contractors, the existence of which was crucial to the RICO counts dealing with fraud in the construction industry. 937 F.2d, at 808.[9] Moreover, the transcripts reveal that the prosecutors did challenge some of the witnesses' denials of knowledge of criminal activity by questioning which included probing the basis of their statements and confronting them with contrary statements from other people.

I am therefore satisfied that the Government had an "opportunity and similar motive" to develop the grand jury testimony of witnesses Bruno and DeMatteis; consequently, the transcript of that testimony was admissible against the Government at respondents' trial under Rule 804(b)(1). For that reason, I would affirm the judgment of the Court of Appeals.

[B] Dying Declarations

Federal Rules of Evidence: Rule 804(b)(2)

Rule 804(b)(2) incorporates two significant changes from the common law. First, the Rule expands the applicability of the dying declaration exception to civil cases, although inexplicably, continues to limit its use in criminal cases to homicide prosecutions. Second, although the Rule still requires that the declarant be unavailable pursuant to Rule 804(a), it no longer requires that the declarant be dead. This second change may have caused courts to relax another common law requirement: that for a dying declaration to be admissible, the declarant must have given up all hope of survival at the time he made his statement, as reflected in the following case. *Johnson* raises the question of how certain declarant has to be that he or she is going to die to qualify for the exception.

[1] Degree of Certainty

JOHNSON v. STATE
Supreme Court of Alaska
579 P.2d 20 (1978)

MATTHEWS, JUSTICE.

This petition for review presents questions as to the admissibility of statements made by Elizabeth Johnson, the victim of a beating, who subsequently died as the result of her injuries . . . .

---

of issues." 11 J. Moore & H. Bendix, Moore's Federal Practice § 804.04 [3], p. VIII-266 (2d ed. 1989).

[9] "Indeed," the Court of Appeals explained, "the central importance of the 'club's' existence is probably why the government felt obligated to identify Bruno and DeMatteis as sources of exculpatory testimony under *Brady v. Maryland* [, 373 U.S. 83, 83 S. Ct. 1194, 10 L. Ed. 2d 215 (1963)]." 937 F.2d, at 808.

On December 30, 1975, Mrs. Johnson was taken by ambulance to the emergency room at Mt. Edgecombe Hospital. She was attended by Vera Martin who found Mrs. Johnson having trouble breathing and in considerable pain. Initially, due to the extent of her injuries, Ms. Martin thought that Mrs. Johnson had been run over by an automobile. In answer to inquiries, however, Mrs. Johnson indicated that she had been at a house party and was beaten by another man . . . .

II

DYING DECLARATIONS

On January 2, 1976, Mrs. Johnson's condition worsened, with increased abdominal pain and signs of internal bleeding. It was decided that surgery was required. Because of her critical condition and the possibility that she might not survive surgery, a consulting physician, Dr. George Longenbaugh, called the Sitka Police Department to inform them of the situation. Dr. Longenbaugh told Mrs. Johnson that she might not survive surgery. He testified:

Q: Do you feel that she was in a condition such that she could understand what you were saying to her?

A: I believe so. Her uh — she was (indiscernible) appropriately and seemed clearer mentally than she had at the time of the first examination.

Q: Do you have an opinion as to whether or not at that time following your explanation, Elizabeth Johnson would have been laboring under a sense of impending death?

A: I believe so. I certainly warned her of the gravity of the situation. Yes.

Sgt. Edgar Thornton of the Sitka Police Department interviewed Mrs. Johnson in mid-afternoon on January 2, 1976, shortly before she underwent surgery. Mr. Johnson was present. Sgt. Thornton testified:

A: Well, I asked her who had beaten her up and she stated she didn't know. I then asked her if she and her husband had had an argument and she said I think so. I asked her if she and her husband had had a fight and she said yes. I asked if her husband had hit her and she stated she didn't know or didn't remember. I then asked her if she was married to Elliott Johnson and she stated that they had been married in March 1974. I asked her if Elliott Johnson had beaten her up and she stated he may have, we were alone and started drinking. I also asked her if she knew what her condition was. She said she did.

Q: Did she indicate if she knew whether or not she was hurt if she was hurt slightly or badly?

A: She indicated to me that she knew she was seriously hurt.

The surgery revealed that among other injuries, Mrs. Johnson's pancreas had been ruptured. Upon discovering this, Dr. Longenbaugh believed that it was extremely unlikely that she would survive.

Dr. Longenbaugh told Mrs. Johnson after her surgery that she was gravely ill and that her chances of survival were not good. He testified that he regarded it as generally unsound medical practice to tell a patient he was absolutely certain to die, since that would depress him and further reduce his already small chances of recovery. Dr. Silver agreed with Dr. Longenbaugh that Mrs. Johnson was in very grave condition following surgery, and personally told her that before January 5. She was then, according to Dr. Silver, aware that there was a good possibility that she would die.

On January 5, 1976, three days after the surgery, Sgt. Thornton testified that, prior to the taping of her interview, Mrs. Johnson advised him that she had consulted a priest.

Q: Elizabeth Marie Johnson, do you know the seriousness of your condition?

A: Yes, Dr. Longenbaugh explained it to me.

Q: Dr. Longenbaugh told you how serious it could be?

A: Yah, he told me I was (indiscernible) . . . .

Q: Did your husband, Elliott Johnson, beat you like this?

A: I think so. Like I said before, we were talking the next morning and he told me if I told him where the money was he wouldn't have beat me up. So I guess he did.

Q: Did you hide the money from him?

A: Yes, before we went out drinking, I took just enough to get a car. We had to meet some friends and we went to their place.

Q: And when you got back did you tell me awhile ago that you forgot where you hid the money?

A: Yah.

Q: What was the last thing you remember?

A: That's the only.

Q: You just remember him hitting you?

A: No, after I woke up at 9:00 o'clock the next morning . . . .

Q: Do you remember what morning that was?

A: No I don't. It was the same morning I came over here.

Q: The same morning?

A: Yah.

Q: Did you say anything to him at the time?

A: I kept asking him to take me to the hospital.

Q: Did you know that you had been beaten up then?

A: Yah, I had a black eye and could hardly breathe.

Q: Did he make a statement to you then?

A: No.

Q: Did he tell you that it wouldn't have happened if you had given him the money?

A: Yah, all he said. My mouth is dry, can I take this out for awhile? It sure dries out my throat.

As we have indicated previously, the trial court granted the motion to suppress these two statements.

The admission of dying declarations, under certain conditions, is a well-recognized exception to the rule excluding hearsay testimony. Two basic reasons have been advanced for admission of such testimony: necessity, because of the witness' death, and a belief that the approach of death removes ordinary motives to misstate.[7]

In *Hewitt v. State,* . . . we discussed the subject of dying declarations. The facts in the case revealed that Hicks and Hewitt shot each other in a gunfight. A doctor informed Hicks that he would probably die unless he was operated on, and that he might die anyway. Immediately before surgery, a police officer took a statement from Hicks in which he blamed defendant Hewitt for starting the shooting. Three days after the surgery, Hicks contradicted his previous statement, saying that he, rather than Hewitt, was responsible for starting the shooting. The trial judge admitted the statement taken before surgery as a dying declaration, but refused to admit the subsequent statement in which he took the blame himself. On appeal, four justices participated. Justice Connor, joined by Justice Boochever, held that the statement given to the police officer was not a dying declaration, and indicated that the proper standard required abandonment of all hope of recovery:

To be admissible as a dying declaration, the utterance must be that of a person laboring under a sense of impending death, who has abandoned all hope of recovery.

* * *

Justice Erwin, with whom Justice Rabinowitz joined, held that there was no error in admitting the statement made to the police officer. He indicated no basic disagreement with Justice Connor's statement of the law concerning dying declarations, but expressed the applicable standard as "laboring under a sense of impending death" without also requiring that the declarant abandon all hope of recovery. . . . Justice Erwin stated:

Rarely is medical testimony absolute on the issue of impending death. Further, there is a natural constraint present in such situations which

---

[7] (Court's original footnote 7.) . . . The Advisory Committee on the Federal Rules of Evidence noted, concerning the latter reason:

While the original religious justification for the exception may have lost its conviction for some persons over the years, it can scarcely be doubted that powerful psychological pressures are present.

causes hesitancy in stating to the victim that there is no chance of recovery for fear of destroying whatever fragile hope of survival the will to live will provide.

* * *

It is the state's contention that the trial court erred by applying an incorrect standard. It argues that a requirement that one must abandon all hope of recovery is not realistic because doctors rarely indicate to a patient that there is no hope of recovery.

The recently enacted Federal Rules of Evidence no longer require abandonment of all hope of recovery. . . . The proposed Alaska Rules of Evidence 804(a)(2) similarly demands only that the statement be made "by a declarant while believing that his death was imminent."

We believe that to require that the declarant has abandoned all hope of recovery is overly demanding.[8] In light of modern medical science it is rare indeed that all hope of recovery is abandoned, yet a victim may be aware of the probability that his death is impending to the extent necessary to create sufficient solemnity to give adequate assurance of the trustworthiness of his testimony. What is required for a dying declaration to be admissible is that the declarant have such a belief that he is facing death as to remove ordinary worldly motives for misstatement. In that regard, the court may consider the totality of the circumstances including the presence or absence of motive to falsify and the manner in which the statement was volunteered or elicited.

The trial judge in his decision on the motion to suppress in this case expressed his conclusions in terms of the "abandonment of all hope" standard.

. . . I just can't as a finder of fact establish that first of all . . . that all hope was abandoned

. . . I just do not feel the facts are strong enough to say that she was overwhelmed by the death possibility . . . .

We believe that when the proper standard is used — awareness of impending death — the admission of at least the recorded statement made by Mrs. Johnson on January 5 is required. It was then extremely unlikely that she would survive and she had been advised by two physicians of the gravity of her condition. She was conscious and alert. In the opinion of the only physicians asked to express an opinion, she was laboring under a sense of impending death. She had consulted a priest. Further we find no evidence tending to show that she was not aware that there was a high probability that she would soon die.

---

[8] (Court's original footnote 8.) In adopting a more inclusive dying declaration standard we are influenced in part by those authorities holding that all statements of deceased persons, not merely dying declarations, should generally be excepted from the hearsay rule. . . . This approach was adopted in different forms by the American Law Institute in the Model Code of Evidence, Rule 503(a), and the Commissioners on Uniform State Laws in the Uniform Rules of Evidence, Rule 63(4)(c). The Uniform Rules have been adopted in modified form in Kansas, New Jersey and Utah. . . . Proposed Federal Rule of Evidence 804(b)(2) encompassed the same concept; while this proposed rule was not accepted by Congress, it was adopted by the states of Arkansas, New Mexico and Wisconsin . . . .

Petition for Review granted. Trial court order affirmed in part and reversed in part. Remanded for proceedings consistent with this opinion.

CONNOR, JUSTICE, Concurring.

I concur in the holding that Elizabeth Johnson's statements on January 5, 1976, and afterward were admissible as dying declarations.

However, I think this case can be brought within the traditional criterion of "abandoned hope" which was stated in *Hewitt v. State*. . . . In the case at bar the declarant did not have the same motive to fabricate as did the declarant in *Hewitt*. Moreover, the circumstances here present a much greater probability as to the imminence of death, and from these circumstances we can infer that Elizabeth Johnson was aware of the severity of her injuries and of the great likelihood that she might not survive. In my opinion a sufficient circumstantial showing was made to permit the inference that she spoke "with the consciousness of a swift and certain doom . . . ."

We should not adhere to a rigid formalism in applying the rules of evidence. But it is not because of blind adherence to formalism that the "abandonment of hope" limitation should be retained. Rather, it is that the principles underlying this exception to the hearsay rule should cause us to adhere to traditional requirements.

The dying declaration rule rests upon certain assumptions about human nature which may in themselves be highly questionable. Like many such rules it evolved historically, and it has become considerably ossified within narrow limits. But at least those limits render the rule easy to apply except in a few marginal situations.

The rule assumes that the declarant will be more truthful than others, without reference to the personal characteristics of the declarant. The judicially created limitations on the use of dying declarations have their origins, no doubt, in the inherent danger of giving too much credence to the assumptions underlying the rule. As Professor McCormick observed:

> A belief in the mere probability of impending death would arguably make most men strongly disposed to tell the truth and hence guarantee the needed special reliability. But belief in the certainty of impending death, not its mere likelihood or probability, is the formula insisted on and rigorously applied. Perhaps this limitation reflects some lack of confidence in the reliability of "deathbed" statements generally.

C. McCormick, HANDBOOK OF THE LAW OF EVIDENCE § 310, at 523–24 (4th ed. 1994). Until we substitute by positive enactment a new rule, I see no reason to discard the common law criteria of admissibility. Those criteria reflect a certain accumulated wisdom about the dangers of admitting dying declarations too readily. Until convinced of the desirability of a new rule, I would adhere to all of the elements of the traditional rule.

Boochever, Chief Justice, with whom Rabinowitz, Justice, joins, dissenting. [Opinion omitted.]

[2]   Can Children Appreciate the Meaning of Death?

The *Stamper* case raises a corollary question — are there certain categories of people who are unable to appreciate the fact that they are dying? Specifically, *Stamper* deals with the question of whether children are sufficiently capable to understand death to permit the dying declaration exception to be invoked.

PEOPLE v. STAMPER
Supreme Court of Michigan
742 N.W.2d 607 (2007)

MEMORANDUM OPINION

At issue in this case is whether a four-year-old injured child can be sufficiently aware of his impending death so that a statement given when death was imminent qualifies for admission as evidence under the dying declaration exception to the hearsay rule, MRE 804(b)(2). In lieu of granting leave to appeal, we affirm defendant's convictions and hold that a child may have the capacity to be conscious of his own impending death for purposes of the dying declaration exception.

We adopt the facts as set forth by the Court of Appeals:

> The victim in this case is Jake Logan, the son of defendant's girlfriend, Gloria Ann Logan, who is also the mother of defendant's child. During the late afternoon or evening of September 8, 2004, defendant gave the victim a bath. Gloria heard the victim crying during the bath. After the bath, the victim was "passing out," and defendant put him in the bathtub to revive him. The victim later lay on the bed with Gloria. When Gloria asked him to open his eyes, he responded, "Mom, I can't, I'm dead." Defendant's daughter, Jamie, indicated that the victim stated, "don't bother me, I'm already dead." Gloria called her father, who came over and eventually called 911.

> The victim was admitted to the hospital that evening with bruises on his neck, arms, chest, abdomen, groin, testicles, and legs. Nurse Hillary Hart asked the victim how he got his bruises, and the victim responded, "from 'Mike.'" Nurse Lisa Blanchette asked the victim who Mike was, and the victim responded, "Mom's wife." The victim died shortly thereafter.

> According to Dr. Leigh Hlavaty, an expert in forensic pathology, the victim had 88 bruises on his body as well as anal injuries. Hlavaty testified that the anal injuries were consistent with anal penetration. Hlavaty opined that all of the victim's bruises and injuries were sustained within twenty-four hours of his death and that the victim's internal injuries were likely sustained within the two to six hours preceding the victim's admission into the hospital. He stated that an adult male fist or being struck with a blunt object in the abdomen likely caused the victim's injuries. [Unpublished

opinion per curiam of the Court of Appeals, issued November 16, 2006 (Docket No. 263436), 2006 Mich. App. LEXIS 3397, pp[.] 1–2.]

The trial court admitted Jake's statements implicating defendant under the dying declaration exception. The Court of Appeals affirmed.

Hearsay is an unsworn, out-of-court statement that is offered to establish the truth of the matter asserted. MRE 801(c). It is generally inadmissible unless it falls under one of the hearsay exceptions set forth in the Michigan Rules of Evidence. MRE 802. One of these exceptions is MRE 804(b)(2), commonly known as the dying declaration exception, which provides that a statement by a declarant is admissible if the declarant is unavailable as a witness and the statement was made "while believing that the declarant's death was imminent, concerning the cause or circumstances of what the declarant believed to be impending death." We review a trial court's admission of evidence under a hearsay exception to determine whether there has been an abuse of discretion. *People v. Adair*, 452 Mich. 473, 485, 550 N.W.2d 505 (1996).

Before admitting a statement as a dying declaration, the trial court must make a preliminary investigation of the facts and circumstances surrounding the statement. *People v. Johnson*, 334 Mich. 169, 173–174, 54 N.W.2d 206 (1952); *People v. Fritch*, 210 Mich. 343, 346–347, 178 N.W. 59 (1920). The trial court, in advance of the proof of the declaration itself, may " 'allow evidence as to the circumstances under which the dying declaration was taken to show whether it was really taken when the declarant was under the conviction of approaching and inevitable death . . . .' " *Fritch, supra* at 347, 178 N.W. 59, quoting *People v. Christmas*, 181 Mich. 634, 646, 148 N.W. 369 (1914). If the surrounding circumstances clearly establish that the declarant was *in extremis* and believed that his death was impending, the court may admit statements concerning the cause or circumstances of the declarant's impending death as substantive evidence under MRE 804(b)(2). *Johnson, supra* at 173, 54 N.W.2d 206.

Here, we conclude that the requirements for admissibility have been met. Jake was clearly unavailable as a witness. MRE 804(a)(4). His statement to his mother, "Mom, I can't, I'm dead," when considered along with his injuries, clearly indicated his belief that his death was imminent. *Johnson, supra* at 173, 54 N.W.2d 206. And his statement to the nurses that he received his injuries from "Mike" and that Mike was "Mom's wife" clearly concerned the circumstances of what Jake believed to be his impending death. MRE 804(b)(2).

We reject defendant's argument that a four-year-old child cannot be aware of impending death. Whether a child was conscious of his own impending death must be determined on a case-by-case basis. As with an adult, if the facts show, as they do here, that the child believed that he was about to die, statements he made may be proffered as dying declarations. A declarant's age alone does not preclude the admission of a dying declaration. Therefore, we affirm the Court of Appeals decision to uphold the trial court's admission of the victim's statements.

[C]   Declarations Against Interest

Federal Rules of Evidence: Rule 804(b)(3)

Rule 804 Hearsay Exceptions; Declarant Unavailable

Williamson addresses the question of what exactly constitutes a statement against interest. Rarely are statement simple unambiguous admissions of guilt. *Williamson* deals with a statement that is both inculpatory and exculpatory. As you will see from the multiple opinions of the Supreme Court, there is no clear answer about the admissibility of such complex statements.

WILLIAMSON v. UNITED STATES
United States Supreme Court
512 U.S. 594 (1994)

Justice O'Connor delivered the opinion of the Court, except as to Part II-C.

In this case we clarify the scope of the hearsay exception for statements against penal interest. Fed. Rule Evid. 804(b)(3).

I

A deputy sheriff stopped the rental car driven by Reginald Harris for weaving on the highway. Harris consented to a search of the car, which revealed 19 kilograms of cocaine in two suitcases in the trunk. Harris was promptly arrested.

Shortly after Harris' arrest, Special Agent Donald Walton of the Drug Enforcement Administration (DEA) interviewed him by telephone. During that conversation, Harris said that he got the cocaine from an unidentified Cuban in Fort Lauderdale; that the cocaine belonged to petitioner Williamson; and that it was to be delivered that night to a particular dumpster. Williamson was also connected to Harris by physical evidence: The luggage bore the initials of Williamson's sister, Williamson was listed as an additional driver on the car rental agreement, and an envelope addressed to Williamson and a receipt with Williamson's girlfriend's address were found in the glove compartment.

Several hours later, Agent Walton spoke to Harris in person. During that interview, Harris said he had rented the car a few days earlier and had driven it to Fort Lauderdale to meet Williamson. According to Harris, he had gotten the cocaine from a Cuban who was Williamson's acquaintance, and the Cuban had put the cocaine in the car with a note telling Harris how to deliver the drugs. Harris repeated that he had been instructed to leave the drugs in a certain dumpster, to return to his car, and to leave without waiting for anyone to pick up the drugs.

Agent Walton then took steps to arrange a controlled delivery of the cocaine. But as Walton was preparing to leave the interview room, Harris "got out of [his] chair . . . and . . . took a half step toward [Walton] . . . and . . . said, . . . 'I can't let you do that,' threw his hands up and said 'that's not true, I can't let you go up there for no reason.' " . . . Harris told Walton he had lied about the Cuban, the note, and the dumpster. The real story, Harris said, was that he was transporting the cocaine to Atlanta for Williamson, and that Williamson was traveling in front of him in another rental car. Harris added that after his car was stopped, Williamson turned around and drove past the location of the stop, where he could see Harris' car with its trunk open. . . . Because Williamson had apparently seen the police searching the car, Harris explained that it would be impossible to make a controlled delivery. . . .

Harris told Walton that he had lied about the source of the drugs because he was afraid of Williamson. . . . Though Harris freely implicated himself, he did not want his story to be recorded, and he refused to sign a written version of the statement. . . . Walton testified that he had promised to report any cooperation by Harris to the Assistant United States Attorney. Walton said Harris was not promised any reward or other benefit for cooperating. . . .

Williamson was eventually convicted of possessing cocaine with intent to distribute, conspiring to possess cocaine with intent to distribute, and traveling interstate to promote the distribution of cocaine. . . . When called to testify at Williamson's trial, Harris refused, even though the prosecution gave him use immunity and the court ordered him to testify and eventually held him in contempt. The District Court then ruled that, under Rule 804(b)(3), Agent Walton could relate what Harris had said to him:

> "The ruling of the Court is that the statements . . . are admissible under [Rule 804(b)(3)], which deals with statements against interest.

> "First, defendant Harris' statements clearly implicated himself, and therefore, are against his penal interest.

> "Second, defendant Harris, the declarant, is unavailable.

> "And third, as I found yesterday, there are sufficient corroborating circumstances in this case to ensure the trustworthiness of his testimony. Therefore, under [*United States v. Harrell*, 788 F.2d 1524 (CA11 1986)], these statements by defendant Harris implicating [Williamson] are admissible.". . .

Williamson appealed his conviction, claiming that the admission of Harris' statements violated Rule 804(b)(3) and the Confrontation Clause of the Sixth Amendment. The Court of Appeals for the Eleventh Circuit affirmed without opinion. . . .

II

A

The hearsay rule, Fed. Rule Evid. 802, is premised on the theory that out-of-court statements are subject to particular hazards. The declarant might be lying; he might have misperceived the events which he relates; he might have faulty memory; his words might be misunderstood or taken out of context by the listener. And the ways in which these dangers are minimized for in-court statements — the oath, the witness' awareness of the gravity of the proceedings, the jury's ability to observe the witness' demeanor, and, most importantly, the right of the opponent to cross-examine — are generally absent for things said out of court.

Nonetheless, the Federal Rules of Evidence also recognize that some kinds of out-of-court statements are less subject to these hearsay dangers, and therefore except them from the general rule that hearsay is inadmissible. One such category covers statements that are against the declarant's interest:

> statements which . . . at the time of [their] making . . . so far tended to subject the declarant to . . . criminal liability . . . that a reasonable person in the declarant's position would not have made the statements unless believing [them] to be true." Fed. Rule Evid. 804(b)(3).

To decide whether Harris' confession is made admissible by Rule 804(b)(3), we must first determine what the Rule means by "statement," which Federal Rule of Evidence 801(a)(1) defines as "an oral or written assertion." One possible meaning, "a report or narrative," WEBSTER'S THIRD NEW INTERNATIONAL DICTIONARY 2229, defn. 2(a) (1961), connotes an extended declaration. Under this reading, Harris' entire confession — even if it contains both self-inculpatory and non-self-inculpatory parts — would be admissible so long as in the aggregate the confession sufficiently inculpates him. Another meaning of "statement," "a single declaration or remark," . . . would make Rule 804(b)(3) cover only those declarations or remarks within the confession that are individually self-inculpatory. . . . *See also Id.*, at 131 (defining "assertion" as a "declaration"); *Id.*, at 586 (defining "declaration" as a "statement").

Although the text of the Rule does not directly resolve the matter, the principle behind the Rule, so far as it is discernible from the text, points clearly to the narrower reading. Rule 804(b)(3) is founded on the commonsense notion that reasonable people, even reasonable people who are not especially honest, tend not to make self-inculpatory statements unless they believe them to be true. This notion simply does not extend to the broader definition of "statement." The fact that a person is making a broadly self-inculpatory confession does not make more credible the confession's non-self-inculpatory parts. One of the most effective ways to lie is to mix falsehood with truth, especially truth that seems particularly persuasive because of its self-inculpatory nature.

In this respect, it is telling that the non-self-inculpatory things Harris said in his first statement actually proved to be false, as Harris himself admitted during the second interrogation. And when part of the confession is actually self-exculpatory, the generalization on which Rule 804(b)(3) is founded becomes even less applicable. Self-exculpatory statements are exactly the ones which people are most likely to make even when they are false; and mere proximity to other, self-inculpatory, statements does not increase the plausibility of the self-exculpatory statements.

We therefore cannot agree with Justice Kennedy's suggestion that the Rule can be read as expressing a policy that collateral statements — even ones that are not in any way against the declarant's interest — are admissible. . . . Nothing in the text of Rule 804(b)(3) or the general theory of the hearsay Rules suggests that admissibility should turn on whether a statement is collateral to a self-inculpatory statement. The fact that a statement is self-inculpatory does make it more reliable; but the fact that a statement is collateral to a self-inculpatory statement says nothing at all about the collateral statement's reliability. We see no reason why collateral statements, even ones that are neutral as to interest . . . should be treated any differently from other hearsay statements that are generally excluded.

Congress certainly could, subject to the constraints of the Confrontation Clause, make statements admissible based on their proximity to self-inculpatory statements. But we will not lightly assume that the ambiguous language means anything so inconsistent with the Rule's underlying theory. . . . In our view, the most faithful reading of Rule 804(b)(3) is that it does not allow admission of non-self-inculpatory statements, even if they are made within a broader narrative that is generally self-inculpatory. The district court may not just assume for purposes of Rule 804(b)(3) that a statement is self-inculpatory because it is part of a fuller confession, and this is especially true when the statement implicates someone else. "The arrest statements of a codefendant have traditionally been viewed with special suspicion. Due to his strong motivation to implicate the defendant and to exonerate himself, a codefendant's statements about what the defendant said or did are less credible than ordinary hearsay evidence.". . .

Justice Kennedy suggests that the Advisory Committee Notes to Rule 804(b)(3) should be read as endorsing the position we reject — that an entire narrative, including non-self-inculpatory parts (but excluding the clearly self-serving parts . . .), may be admissible if it is in the aggregate self-inculpatory. . . . The Notes read, in relevant part:

> The third-party confession . . . may include statements implicating [the accused], and under the general theory of declarations against interest they would be admissible as related statements. . . . [*Douglas v. Alabama*, 380 U.S. 415 (1965), and *Bruton v. United States*, 391 U.S. 123 (1968)] . . . by no means require that all statements implicating another person be excluded from the category of declarations against interest. Whether a statement is in fact against interest must be determined from the circumstances of each case. Thus a statement admitting guilt and implicating another person, made while in custody, may well be motivated by a desire to curry favor with the authorities and hence fail to qualify as against interest. . . . On the other hand, the same words spoken under different circumstances, e.g., to an acquaintance, would have no difficulty in qualifying. . . . The balancing of self-serving against dissenting [sic] aspects of a declaration is discussed in McCORMICK § 256.

This language, however, is not particularly clear, and some of it — especially the Advisory Committee's endorsement of the position taken by Dean McCormick's treatise — points the other way:

> A certain latitude as to contextual statements, neutral as to interest, giving meaning to the declaration against interest seems defensible, but bringing in self-serving statements contextually seems questionable. . . . Admitting the disserving parts of the declaration, and excluding the self-serving parts . . . seems the most realistic method of adjusting admissibility to trustworthiness, where the serving and disserving parts can be severed. *See* C. McCORMICK, LAW OF EVIDENCE § 256, pp. 551–553 (1954) (footnotes omitted).

Without deciding exactly how much weight to give the Notes in this particular situation . . . we conclude that the policy expressed in the statutory text points clearly enough in one direction that it outweighs whatever force the Notes may have. And though Justice Kennedy believes that the text can fairly be read as expressing a policy of admitting collateral statements . . . for the reasons given above we disagree.

B

We also do not share Justice Kennedy's fears that our reading of the Rule "eviscerates the against penal interest exception," . . . or makes it lack "meaningful effect," . . . . There are many circumstances in which Rule 804(b)(3) does allow the admission of statements that inculpate a criminal defendant. Even the confessions of arrested accomplices may be admissible if they are truly self-inculpatory, rather than merely attempts to shift blame or curry favor.

For instance, a declarant's squarely self-inculpatory confession — "yes, I killed X" — will likely be admissible under Rule 804(b)(3) against accomplices of his who are being tried under a co-conspirator liability theory. . . . Likewise, by showing that the declarant knew something, a self-inculpatory statement can in some situations help the jury infer that his confederates knew it as well. And when seen with other evidence, an accomplice's self-inculpatory statement can inculpate the defendant directly: "I was robbing the bank on Friday morning," coupled with someone's testimony that the declarant and the defendant drove off together Friday morning, is evidence that the defendant also participated in the robbery.

Moreover, whether a statement is self-inculpatory or not can only be determined by viewing it in context. Even statements that are on their face neutral may actually be against the declarant's interest. "I hid the gun in Joe's apartment" may not be a confession of a crime; but if it is likely to help the police find the murder weapon, then it is certainly self-inculpatory. "Sam and I went to Joe's house" might be against the declarant's interest if a reasonable person in the declarant's shoes would realize that being linked to Joe and Sam would implicate the declarant in Joe and Sam's conspiracy. And other statements that give the police significant details about the crime may also, depending on the situation, be against the declarant's interest. The question under Rule 804(b)(3) is always whether the statement was sufficiently against the declarant's penal interest "that a reasonable person in the declarant's position would not have made the statement unless believing it to be true," and this question can only be answered in light of all the surrounding circumstances.[10]

C

In this case, however, we cannot conclude that all that Harris said was properly admitted. Some of Harris' confession would clearly have been admissible under

---

[10] (Court's original footnote 6.) Of course, an accomplice's statements may also be admissible under other provisions of Rules 801–804. For instance, statements made in furtherance of the conspiracy may be admissible under Rule 801(d)(2)(E), and other statements that bear circumstantial guarantees of trustworthiness may be admissible under Rule 807, the catch-all hearsay exception.

Rule 804(b)(3); for instance, when he said he knew there was cocaine in the suitcase, he essentially forfeited his only possible defense to a charge of cocaine possession, lack of knowledge. But other parts of his confession, especially the parts that implicated Williamson, did little to subject Harris himself to criminal liability. A reasonable person in Harris' position might even think that implicating someone else would decrease his practical exposure to criminal liability, at least so far as sentencing goes. Small fish in a big conspiracy often get shorter sentences than people who are running the whole show, *see, e.g.*, UNITED STATES SENTENCING COMMISSION, GUIDELINES MANUAL § 3B1.2 (Nov. 1993), especially if the small fish are willing to help the authorities catch the big ones, *see, e.g., id.*, at § 5K1.1.

Nothing in the record shows that the District Court or the Court of Appeals inquired whether each of the statements in Harris' confession was truly self-inculpatory. As we explained above, this can be a fact-intensive inquiry, which would require careful examination of all the circumstances surrounding the criminal activity involved; we therefore remand to the Court of Appeals to conduct this inquiry in the first instance.

. . . The judgment of the Court of Appeals is vacated, and the case is remanded for further proceedings consistent with this opinion.

So ordered.

JUSTICE SCALIA, concurring (opinion omitted).

JUSTICE GINSBURG, with whom JUSTICE BLACKMAN, JUSTICE STEVENS, and JUSTICE SOUTER join, concurring in part and concurring in the judgment.

*   *   *

Unlike Justice O'Connor . . . I conclude that Reginald Harris' statements, as recounted by DEA Special Agent Donald E. Walton, do not fit, even in part, within the exception described in Rule 804(b)(3), for Harris' arguably inculpatory statements are too closely intertwined with his self-serving declarations to be ranked as trustworthy. Harris was caught red-handed with 19 kilos of cocaine — enough to subject even a first-time offender to a minimum of 12 1/2 years' imprisonment. *See* UNITED STATES SENTENCING COMMISSION, GUIDELINES MANUAL § 2D1.1(c) (1993); *id.*, ch. 5, pt. A (sentencing table). He could have denied knowing the drugs were in the car's trunk, but that strategy would have brought little prospect of thwarting a criminal prosecution. He therefore admitted involvement, but did so in a way that minimized his own role and shifted blame to petitioner Fredel Williamson (and a Cuban man named Shawn).

Most of Harris' statements to DEA Agent Walton focused on Williamson's, rather than Harris', conduct. Agent Walton testified to the following: During a brief telephone conversation shortly after he was apprehended, Harris said he had obtained 19 kilos of cocaine for Williamson from a Cuban man in Fort Lauderdale, Florida; he stated that the cocaine belonged to Williamson, and was to be delivered to a dumpster in the Atlanta area that evening. . . . Harris repeated this story to Agent Walton when the two spoke in person later in the day. Harris also said that he had rented the car a few days earlier and had included Williamson's name on the rental contract because Williamson was going to be in the Fort Lauderdale area with him. . . . After Agent Walton sought to arrange a controlled delivery, Harris retracted the story about the dumpster, saying it was false.

Harris' second account differed as to collateral details, but he continued to paint Williamson as the "big fish." Harris reported that he was transporting the cocaine to Atlanta for Williamson. When the police stopped Harris' car, Williamson was driving in front of him in another rented car. After Harris was stopped, Williamson turned around and pulled over to the side of the road; from that vantage point, he observed the police officer inspecting the contents of Harris' trunk. . . . And, Harris repeated, "the arrangements for the acquisition and the transportation had been made by Mr. Williamson.". . .

To the extent some of these statements tended to incriminate Harris, they provided only marginal or cumulative evidence of his guilt. They project an image of a person acting not against his penal interest, but striving mightily to shift principal responsibility to someone else. . . .

For these reasons, I would hold that none of Harris' hearsay statements were admissible under Rule 804(b)(3). The trial judge characterized Agent Walton's testimony as "very damning." . . . The prosecutor considered it so prejudicial that she offered to join defense counsel's motion for a mistrial should the trial court determine that the hearsay statements had been erroneously admitted. . . . I concur in the Court's decision to vacate the Court of Appeals' judgment, however, because I have not examined the entire trial court record; I therefore cannot say the Government should be denied an opportunity to argue that the erroneous admission of the hearsay statements, in light of the other evidence introduced at trial, constituted harmless error. . . .

JUSTICE KENNEDY, with whom THE CHIEF JUSTICE and JUSTICE THOMAS join, concurring in the judgment.

I

. . . The rationale of the hearsay exception for statements against interest is that people seldom "make statements which are damaging to themselves unless satisfied for good reason that they are true." . . . Of course, the declarant may make his statement against interest (such as "I shot the bank teller") together with collateral but related declarations (such as "John Doe drove the getaway car"). The admissibility of those collateral statements under Rule 804(b)(3) is the issue we must decide here.

There has been a long-running debate among commentators over the admissibility of collateral statements. Dean Wigmore took the strongest position in favor of admissibility, arguing that "the statement may be accepted, not merely as to the specific fact against interest, but also as to every fact contained in the same statement." . . . According to Wigmore, because "the statement is made under circumstances fairly indicating the declarant's sincerity and accuracy," the entire statement should be admitted. . . . Dean McCormick's approach regarding collateral statements was more guarded. He argued for the admissibility of collateral statements of a neutral character; and for the exclusion of collateral statements of a self-serving character. For example, in the statement "John and I robbed the bank," the words "John and" are neutral (save for the possibility of conspiracy charges). On the other hand, the statement "John, not I, shot the bank teller" is to some extent self-serving and therefore might be inadmissible. . . . Professor Jefferson took the narrowest approach, arguing that the reliability of a statement against interest stems only from the disserving fact stated and so should be confined "to the proof of the fact which is against interest." Jefferson, *Declarations Against Interest: An Exception to the Hearsay Rule*, 58 Harv. L. Rev. 1, 62–63 (1944). Under the Jefferson approach, neither collateral neutral nor collateral self-serving statements would be admissible.

. . . The Court resolves the issue, as I understand its opinion, by adopting the extreme position that no collateral statements are admissible under Rule 804(b)(3). . . . The Court reaches that conclusion by relying on the "principle behind the Rule" that reasonable people do not make statements against their interest unless they are telling the truth, *ante*, at 5, and reasons that this policy "expressed in the statutory text," *ante*, at 8, "simply does not extend" to collateral statements. . . . Though conceding that Congress can "make statements admissible based on their proximity to self-inculpatory statements," the Court says that it cannot "lightly assume that the ambiguous language means anything so inconsistent with the Rule's underlying theory." . . .

With respect, I must disagree with this analysis. All agree that the justification for admission of hearsay statements against interest was, as it still is, that reasonable people do not make those statements unless believing them to be true, but that has not resolved the long-running debate over the admissibility of collateral statements, as to which there is no clear consensus in the authorities. Indeed, to the extent the authorities come close to any consensus, they support admission of some collateral statements. . . . Given that the underlying principle for the hearsay exception has not resolved the debate over collateral statements one way or the other, I submit that we should not assume that the text of Rule 804(b)(3), which is silent about collateral statements, in fact incorporates one of the competing positions. The Rule's silence no more incorporates Jefferson's position respecting collateral statements than it does McCormick's or Wigmore's.

II

Because the text of Rule 804(b)(3) expresses no position regarding the admissibility of collateral statements, we must determine whether there are other authoritative guides on the question. In my view, three sources demonstrate that Rule 804(b)(3) allows the admission of some collateral statements: the Advisory Committee Note, the common law of the hearsay exception for statements against interest, and the general presumption that Congress does not enact statutes that have almost no effect.

First, the Advisory Committee Note establishes that some collateral statements are admissible. In fact, it refers in specific terms to the issue we here confront: "ordinarily the third-party confession is thought of in terms of exculpating the accused, but this is by no means always or necessarily the case: it may include statements implicating him, and under the general theory of declarations against interest they would be admissible as related statements." . . . This language seems a forthright statement that collateral statements are admissible under Rule 804(b)(3), but the Court reasons that "the policy expressed in the statutory text points clearly enough in one direction that it outweighs whatever force the Notes may have." . . . Again, however, that reasoning begs the question: What is the policy expressed in the text on the admissibility of collateral statements? As stated above, the text of the Rule does not answer the question whether collateral statements are admissible. When as here the text of a Rule of Evidence does not answer a question that must be answered in order to apply the Rule, and when the Advisory Committee Note does answer the question, our practice indicates that we should pay attention to the Advisory Committee Note. We have referred often to those Notes in interpreting the Rules of Evidence, and I see no reason to jettison that well-established practice here. . . .

Second, even if the Advisory Committee Note were silent about collateral statements, I would not adopt a rule excluding all statements collateral or related to the specific words against penal interest. Absent contrary indications, we can presume that Congress intended the principles and terms used in the Federal Rules of Evidence to be applied as they were at common law. . . . Application of that interpretive principle indicates that collateral statements should be admissible. "From the very beginning of this exception, it has been held that a declaration against interest is admissible, not only to prove the disserving fact stated, but also to prove other facts contained in collateral statements connected with the disserving statement." . . . Indeed, the Advisory Committee Note itself, in stating that collateral statements would be admissible, referred to the "general theory" that related statements are admissible, an indication of the state of the law at the time the Rule was enacted. Rule 804(b)(3) does not address the issue, but Congress legislated against the common law background allowing admission of some collateral statements, and I would not assume that Congress gave the common law rule a silent burial in Rule 804(b)(3).

There is yet a third reason weighing against the Court's interpretation, one specific to statements against penal interest that inculpate the accused. There is no dispute that the text of Rule 804(b)(3) contemplates the admission of those particular statements. Absent a textual direction to the contrary, therefore, we should assume that Congress intended the penal interest exception for inculpatory statements to have some meaningful effect. . . . That counsels against adopting a rule excluding collateral statements. As commentators have recognized, "the exclusion of collateral statements would cause the exclusion of almost all inculpatory statements." . . . ; *see also* Note, *Inculpatory Statements Against Penal Interest and the Confrontation Clause*, 83 Colum. L. Rev. 159, 163 (1983) ("most statements inculpating a defendant are only collateral to the portion of the declarant's statement that is against his own penal interest. The portion of the statement that specifically implicates the defendant is rarely directly counter to the declarant's penal interest") (footnote omitted); Davenport, *The Confrontation Clause and the Co-Conspirator Exception in Criminal Prosecutions: A Functional Analysis*, 85 Harv. L. Rev. 1378, 1396 (1972) ("the naming of another as a compatriot will almost never be against the declarant's own interest"). Indeed, as one commentator indicated, the conclusion that no collateral statements are admissible — the conclusion reached by the Court today — would "eviscerate the against penal interest exception." Comment, 66 Calif. L. Rev., at 1213.

To be sure, under the approach adopted by the Court, there are some situations where the Rule would still apply. For example, if the declarant said that he stole certain goods, the statement could be admitted in a prosecution of the accused for receipt of stolen goods in order to show that the goods were stolen. . . . But as the commentators have recognized, it is likely to be the rare case where the precise self-inculpatory words of the declarant, without more, also inculpate the defendant. I would not presume that Congress intended the penal interest exception to the Rule to have so little effect with respect to statements that inculpate the accused.

I note finally that the Court's decision applies to statements against penal interest that exculpate the accused as well as to those that inculpate the accused. Thus, if the declarant said, "I robbed the store alone," only the portion of the statement in which the declarant said "I robbed the store" could be introduced by a criminal defendant on trial for the robbery. . . . That seems extraordinary. The Court gives no justification for such a rule and no explanation that Congress intended the exception for exculpatory statements to have this limited effect. . . .

III

Though I would conclude that Rule 804(b)(3) allows admission of statements collateral to the precise words against interest, that conclusion of course does not answer the remaining question whether all collateral statements related to the statement against interest are admissible; and if not, what limiting principles should apply. The Advisory Committee Note suggests that not all collateral statements are admissible. The Note refers, for example, to McCormick's treatise, not to Wigmore's, for guidance as to the "balancing of self-serving against disserving aspects of a declaration." . . . As noted [above], Wigmore's approach would allow the admission of "every fact contained in the same statement," but McCormick's approach is not so expansive. McCormick stated that "[a] certain latitude as to contextual [*i.e.*, collateral] statements, neutral as to interest, giving meaning to the declaration against interest seems defensible, but bringing in self-serving statements contextually seems questionable." MCCORMICK § 256, p. 552. McCormick further stated that, within a declaration containing self-serving and disserving facts, he would "admit the disserving parts of the declaration, and exclude the self-serving parts" at least "where the serving and disserving parts can be severed." *Id.* § 256, p. 553. It thus appears that the Advisory Committee Note, by its reference to (and apparent incorporation of) McCormick, contemplates exclusion of a collateral self-serving statement, but admission of a collateral neutral statement.

In the criminal context, a self-serving statement is one that tends to reduce the charges or mitigate the punishment for which the declarant might be liable. . . . For example, if two masked gunmen robbed a bank and one of them shot and killed the bank teller, a statement by one robber that the other robber was the triggerman may be the kind of self-serving statement that should be inadmissible. . . . By contrast, when two or more people are capable of committing a crime and the declarant simply names the involved parties, that statement often is considered neutral, not self-serving. . . .

Of course, because the declarant is by definition unavailable, see Fed. Rule Evid. 804(a), and therefore cannot be questioned to determine the exact motivation for his statement, courts have been forced to devise categories to determine when this concern is sufficient to justify exclusion of a statement as unreliable. It has been held, for example, that a statement to authorities admitting guilt, made after an explicit promise of dropped charges or of a reduction in prison time in exchange for the admission of guilt, may be so unreliable as to be inadmissible. . . . At the other extreme, when there was no promise of leniency by the government and the declarant was told that he had a right to remain silent and that any statements he made could be used against him, the courts have not required exclusion of the declarant's statement against interest. . . . This kind of line-drawing is appropriate and necessary, lest the limiting principle regarding the declarant's possible desire to obtain leniency lead to the exclusion of all statements against penal interest made to police, a result the Rule and Note do not contemplate.

In sum, I would adhere to the following approach with respect to statements against penal interest that inculpate the accused. A court first should determine whether the declarant made a statement that contained a fact against penal interest. . . . If so, the court should admit all statements related to the precise statement against penal interest, subject to two limits. Consistent with the Advisory Committee Note, the court should exclude a collateral statement that is so self-serving as to render it unreliable (if, for example, it shifts blame to someone else for a crime the defendant could have committed). In addition, in cases where the statement was made under circumstances where it is likely that the declarant had a significant motivation to obtain favorable treatment, as when the government made an explicit offer of leniency in exchange for the declarant's admission of guilt, the entire statement should be inadmissible.

A ruling on the admissibility of evidence under Rule 804(b)(3) is a preliminary question to be determined by the District Judge under Rule 104(a). That determination of necessity calls for an inquiry that depends to a large extent on the circumstances of a particular case. For this reason, application of the general principles here outlined to a particular narrative statement often will require a difficult, factbound determination. District Judges, who are close to the facts and far better able to evaluate the various circumstances than an appellate court, therefore must be given wide discretion to examine a particular statement to determine whether all or part of it should be admitted. Like the Court, then, I would remand this case, but for application of the analysis set forth in this opinion.

[D]   Statements of Personal or Family History: Rule 804(b)(4)

The *Carvalho* case raises the question of the breadth of 804(b)(4). Does a statement "about" one's marriage just relate to the date, or does it contemplate a more expansive context of the family relations?

UNITED STATES v. CARVALHO
United States Court of Appeals, Fourth Circuit
742 F.2d 146 (1984)

MURNAGHAN, CIRCUIT JUDGE:

Martha and Fernando Carvalho appeal from their convictions under 18 U.S.C. § 1426(b)[1] for knowing use of false alien registration receipt cards.

At 6:30 or 7:00 A.M. on January 25, 1983, Larry Valladolid, a criminal investigator with the Immigration and Naturalization Service, appeared at the Carvalhos' house in search of one Fernando Rodriguez. During the course of his questioning, Valladolid demanded identification from the Carvalhos. Mrs. Carvalho produced passports with lawful entry stamps based on the Carvalhos' "green cards" (alien registration receipt cards). Valladolid copied the alien registration numbers, and departed.

Valladolid returned on March 1, 1983, and asked to see Mrs. Carvalho's green card. Instead, she again showed him her passport. Spying a green card in the same zippered bag from which Mrs. Carvalho had drawn the passport, Valladolid demanded to see the green card. He subsequently declared the green card to be counterfeit. Mr. Carvalho then entered the room, and a similar scene transpired. Mr. Carvalho, after some hesitation, produced his green card, later declared to be counterfeit.

The Carvalhos were indicted on May 2, 1983, and were tried before a jury on July 14–15, 1983. Testimony at trial revealed that Mr. Carvalho entered the United States in January, 1971, deserting his ship in February, 1972 and thereafter remaining in the U.S. He married Ramona Cruz in 1973, and applied for permanent residence shortly thereafter. The marriage failed, and Cruz went back to Puerto Rico, withdrawing the petition for Mr. Carvalho's residency in September, 1974. The INS then found Mr. Carvalho deportable. He disappeared, and was ordered deported.

Martha Sanchez Carvalho entered the U.S. in September, 1972. She remained beyond the duration of her temporary work visa. In June, 1973, she married Luiz Hernandez, and applied for permanent residence. The marriage lasted four months, and after its dissolution, Mrs. Carvalho subsequently was found deportable, and granted voluntary departure in lieu of deportation. She, too, disappeared and was ordered deported.

The Carvalhos met each other in New York City and, by then divorced from their

---

[1] § 1426. Reproduction of naturalization or citizenship papers

  (b) Whoever utters, sells, disposes of or uses as true or genuine any false, forged, altered, antedated or counterfeited oath, notice, affidavit, certificate of arrival, declaration of intention to become a citizen, certificate or documentary evidence of naturalization or citizenship, or any order, or proceeding required or authorized by any law relating to naturalization or citizenship or registry of aliens, or any copy thereof, knowing the same to be false, forged, altered, antedated or counterfeited; . . . Shall be fined not more than $5,000 or imprisoned not more than five years, or both.

respective spouses, were married in 1975. Late in that year they had a child, who was a United States citizen by virtue of her birth in the United States. The child's birth also provided a *bona fide* basis for the Carvalho's own lawful permanent residency. A friend of the Carvalho's took them to a lawyer named Garcia, who was to arrange for them to obtain the necessary green cards.[2] The Carvalhos, as they testified, had sought the attorney's assistance in part because of their unfamiliarity with the law and language. They paid $1500 for the services in providing the cards, which, according to their uncontradicted testimony, they believed to be genuine. When Garcia told them that all was in order, they had no apparent reason to suspect that their green cards had been forged. Their belief the cards were genuine had been reinforced by the fact that they had left the United States on numerous occasions, and had been successfully readmitted upon presentation of the cards.

At trial, the government sought to portray the Carvalhos as quite sophisticated regarding the immigration laws, and well aware of what they would need to do to obtain permanent residence. The government, therefore, tried to link the earlier attempts to gain residency through marriage with the obtaining of the green cards. The government contended that the forged green cards comprised merely one of a number of ruses to gain residence, and, over objection, introduced affidavits from the former spouses. Two affidavits were from Cruz, one from Hernandez. All were obtained in 1974 after the initial attempts to gain residency through marriage, when Cruz and Hernandez, following the failure of each marriage, had decided to withdraw the petitions previously filed on behalf of appellants' efforts to obtain permanent residency. All the affidavits were obtained before the Carvalhos' marriage and the birth (and indeed the conception) of the child possessed of United States citizenship.

The Hernandez affidavit in no way suggests that his marriage to Martha Sanchez (later Carvalho) was not genuine, but rather had been entered into to evade the immigration laws. To the contrary, it states: "I married my wife for love . . . ." It concludes, however:

> I wish, on this date, to withdraw the application for permanent residence petition I have filed for my wife because I plan to terminate my marriage to this woman as soon as possible.

The first Cruz affidavit states that she married Mr. Carvalho to spite Joseph Ortiz, the man with whom she had then been living. She adds (in the typewritten portion) that she "married FERNANDO because I felt sorry for him and out of anger because of what had happened to me," after which appears the handwritten addendum "and I wanted to help him get his residence." Other sections of the affidavit state that the marriage was not consummated (a point disputed by an April, 1975 affidavit of Mr. Carvalho), and the marriage "was to do him a favor." The second Cruz affidavit discusses counseling Cruz received prior to the INS hearing regarding the application process, and includes reference to apparent threats to Cruz if she did not cooperate. At the time Cruz rendered the affidavits, she was

---

[2] At trial, seven years later, the Carvalhos were unable to remember Garcia's full name or the precise location of his offices.

pregnant with the child of Joseph Ortiz, the man she sought to spite by marrying Mr. Carvalho.

Although neither Cruz nor Hernandez appeared at trial, the affidavits were admitted over objection. The Carvalhos were each convicted and sentenced to a three-year suspended prison sentence, probation, and a $2,500 fine. On appeal, they contend that the admission of the affidavits was improper under the hearsay rules . . . .

II.

With respect to the hearsay issue, the government contends that the affidavits were admissible . . . under FRE 804(b)(4)[5] as a statement of personal or family history.

*   *   *

B.

The government's [contends] that, since the affidavits related to the respective marriages of Cruz and Hernandez, they were admissible as "statement[s] concerning the declarant's own . . . marriage . . ., or other similar fact of personal or family history," under F.R.E. 804(b)(4). While undoubtedly it is correct that for some purposes a statement regarding one's reasons for entering a marriage might well be a "statement concerning" one's marriage, it is also clear that evidence as to motive or purpose, highly debatable or controversial matters, is simply not within the scope of Rule 804(b)(4).

As Judge Weinstein explains, "the rule rests on the assumption that the type of declarant specified by the rule will not make a statement about the type of fact covered by the rule unless it is trustworthy." 4 Weinstein's Evidence § 804(b)(4)[01] (1981). While the assumption is well-justified where the facts at issue concern, for example, the date of a marriage or existence of a ceremony, the trustworthiness attendant upon the circumstances of utterance is substantially diminished once we confront issues such as motive.

The propriety of a distinction between different types of facts concerning personal or family history relating to marriage is buttressed further by a comparison of marriage to the other items on the non-exhaustive list in Rule 804(b)(4). The list includes, for example, birth, adoption, divorce, legitimacy and ancestry. It is difficult to envision how issues similar to the frame of mind at the time of entering a marital relationship could arise regarding the other items on the list.

---

[5] FRE 804(b)(4) concerns the following statements by unavailable declarants:

    (4) Statement of personal or family history. (A) A statement concerning the declarant's own birth, adoption, marriage, divorce, legitimacy, relationship by blood, adoption, or marriage, ancestry, or other similar fact of personal or family history, even though declarant had no means of acquiring personal knowledge of the matter stated; or (B) a statement concerning the foregoing matters, and death also, of another person, if the declarant was related to the other by blood, adoption, or marriage or was so intimately associated with the other's family as to be likely to have accurate information concerning the matter declared.

More likely, the relevant issues instead would be a date of birth, existence of an adoption, or details of one's ancestry. Since "marriage" appears in Rule 804(b)(4) in the midst of a list of items unlikely to concern complex issues of motive, we conclude that Cruz' or Hernandez' motives for marrying was not a "fact" within the meaning of FRE 804(b)(4), and, accordingly, that the Rule does not provide a basis for admission of the affidavits.

III.

As the foregoing arguments indicate, we conclude that the district court erred in admitting the affidavits over appellant's hearsay objections. Nor can we conclude that the error was harmless. *Kotteakos v. United States*, 328 U.S. 750, 66 S. Ct. 1239, 90 L. Ed. 1557 (1946). The crucial issue at trial was the appellants' *knowledge* of the falsity of the green cards. The crucial argument on knowledge was the Carvalhos' purported familiarity with the intricacies of the immigration system, and the affidavits were tendered in support of the argument that they were intimately familiar. Indeed, the government has never argued that admission of the affidavits, if error, was harmless. We conclude that the convictions must be reversed.

It consequently is unnecessary to resolve the remaining issues on appeal. The affinity between the hearsay rules and the Sixth Amendment's Confrontation Clause has indeed been remarked upon on appropriate occasions. *E.g., Ohio v. Roberts*, 448 U.S. 56, 66, 100 S. Ct. 2531, 2539, 65 L. Ed. 2d 597 (1980).

The two inquiries, however, are not necessarily identical. This court has observed that "the question that arises under the Rules of Evidence is not necessarily the same as that presented under the Confrontation Clause." *United States v. Murphy*, 696 F.2d 282, 286 (4th Cir. 1982). Therefore, we defer, until necessity compels, discussion of the implications of the Confrontation Clause in a situation like the one here presented.

IV.

We decide today not whether there was enough evidence to convict the Carvalhos, but whether they were tried fairly. Although the affidavits contained potentially weighty evidence on the issue of knowledge, it is by no means implausible that, even had they been excluded, the remaining evidence, particularly with respect to the Carvalhos' actions during the "interviews" with Agent Valladolid, would still have been sufficient to sustain a conviction.

The prosecution, however, opted to pursue a strategy of overkill, striving to put before the jury every piece of evidence it could amass, with little regard to countervailing concerns of fairness and undue prejudice.[10] The government not only lessens its chances for retaining convictions on appeal when it offers evidence of

---

[10] The same strategy presumably led the government to persist in linking the Carvalhos to Fernando Rodriguez, the initial object of Agent Valladolid's search, and referring to Fernando Carvalho's efforts to collect unemployment benefits. The government apparently believed it prudent and necessary to paint a general picture of the Carvalhos as people with a propensity to defraud the system and associate with criminals. While we need not decide whether actions such as these amounted to prosecutorial

dubious worth, but, in operating as if the attainment of convictions were desirable at any cost, it ignores the telling words of the Supreme Court in *Brady v. Maryland*, 373 U.S. 83, 87, 83 S. Ct. 1194, 1197, 10 L. Ed. 2d 215 (1963):

> Society wins not only when the guilty are convicted but when criminal trials are fair; our system of the administration of justice suffers when any accused is treated unfairly.

REVERSED.

EXERCISES

1. Officer transported Ray to the police station for questioning on suspicion that Ray was distributing large amounts of methamphetamine. Officer conducted the interview and Ray admitted to selling methamphetamine in exchange for stolen items. Prior to trial Ray's defense counsel filed a pretrial motion asserting that Officer failed to properly advise Ray of his Miranda rights, and thus Ray's statement should be suppressed. Officer testified at the suppression hearing regarding Ray's Miranda waiver and subsequent statement. After the suppression hearing but before trial, Officer was killed by a drunk driver. At trial there is very little evidence against Ray, except for his confession to Officer. The government seeks to admit Officer's former testimony given at the suppression hearing under Rule 804. Defense counsel does not want the damaging testimony admitted at trial. What is defense counsel's best argument against admission and how should the court rule?

2. David and his co-defendant Edward, licensed stock brokers, allegedly engaged in a series of non-competitive trades that defrauded customers out of $2 million. The U.S. Department of Justice (DOJ) filed criminal charges against the duo, while the U.S. Commodity Futures Trading Commission (CFTC) filed a similar civil action. During discovery, the CFTC took lengthy depositions from both David and Edward regarding these trades, during which Edward exculpated David of any wrongdoing. Shortly thereafter, Edward died. At David's criminal trial David seeks to admit Edward's deposition testimony from the CFTC civil hearing under the former testimony exception to the hearsay rule. The DOJ objects. Should the court grant David's request?

3. Three men armed with knives entered a mall jewelry store, demanded Rolex watches from the sales clerk, and then fled. Using video surveillance and eyewitness tips, police arrested Deontaye, Aaron, and Reginald in connection with the robbery. All three men were incarcerated at the same facility pending trial. While awaiting trial Deontaye confessed to his cellmate, Zachary, that he and two friends robbed a mall jewelry store, used knives as weapons, and that they were all now imprisoned in the same jail. The three men proceeded to trial separately. At Reginald's trial, the government seeks to call Zachary (Deontaye's cellmate) as a witness to repeat Deontaye's confession. Reginald objects on hearsay grounds. How should the court rule?

---

misconduct, we decry the prosecution's repeated decision to err on the side of overkill, rather than fairness.

4. In order to establish his own United States citizenship, Randolph has to prove that his Mother was born in the United States and remained in the United States for at least one continuous year before relocating to the Caribbean Islands. At trial Randolph seeks to admit affidavits from Mother and Cousin. Mother's affidavit states: "I was born in Brooklyn in 1929 and moved abroad in 1930 when I was between one year old and two years old." Mother passed away shortly after signing the affidavit. Cousin's affidavit states: "When I was a child, Mother told me that she moved from New York to the Caribbean Islands when she was about one and a half years old. It was common knowledge or reputation among people who knew Mother during her childhood that she left the United States when she was about one and a half years old." Is either affidavit admissible at trial? What are Randolph's strongest arguments for admissibility?

[E]   Constitutional Restrictions on the Use of Hearsay

Constitutionally, the use of hearsay in judicial proceedings is limited by two provisions of the Bill of Rights. First, under the Sixth Amendment a criminal accused is guaranteed the right to confront witnesses against him. Second, under the Fourteenth Amendment all individuals are guaranteed due process of law or fundamental fairness in judicial proceedings.

When a declarant is unavailable for cross-examination in a criminal case, a constitutional provision is at issue — the defendant's Sixth Amendment right to confront his accuser. Recently, the Supreme Court has radically reformed Confrontation Clause doctrines. It is no longer sufficient to show that there was a hearsay exception permitting the use of evidence if the declarant was unavailable.

[1]   Confrontation Clause: The Beginning

Lilly v. Virginia began this revolution which got in full swing with *Crawford v. Washington*. In *Lilly*, the Court held that despite the fact that the declaration against interest is a firmly rooted exception, this aspect of its use is inherently suspicious, and its use against a criminal defendant violates his right to confront witnesses against him, unless particular guarantees of trustworthiness are shown to exist.

LILLY v. VIRGINIA
United States Supreme Court
527 U.S. 116 (1999)

STEVENS, J., . . . delivered the opinion of the Court with respect to Parts I and VI, in which SCALIA, SOUTER, THOMAS, GINSBURG, and BREYER, JJ., joined, the opinion of the Court with respect to Part II, in which SCALIA, SOUTER, GINSBURG, and BREYER, JJ., joined, and an opinion with respect to Parts III, IV, and V, in which SOUTER, GINSBURG, and BREYER, JJ., joined.

The question presented in this case is whether the accused's Sixth Amendment right "to be confronted with the witnesses against him" was violated by admitting into evidence at his trial a nontestifying accomplice's entire confession that contained some statements against the accomplice's penal interest and others that inculpated the accused.

I

On December 4, 1995, three men — Benjamin Lee Lilly (petitioner), his brother Mark, and Mark's roommate, Gary Wayne Barker — broke into a home and stole nine bottles of liquor, three loaded guns, and a safe. The next day, the men drank the stolen liquor, robbed a small country store, and shot at geese with their stolen weapons. After their car broke down, they abducted Alex DeFilippis and used his vehicle to drive to a deserted location. One of them shot and killed DeFilippis. The three men then committed two more robberies before they were apprehended by the police late in the evening of December 5.

After taking them into custody, the police questioned each of the three men separately. Petitioner did not mention the murder to the police and stated that the other two men had forced him to participate in the robberies. Petitioner's brother Mark and Barker told the police somewhat different accounts of the crimes, but both maintained that petitioner masterminded the robberies and was the one who had killed DeFilippis.

A tape recording of Mark's initial oral statement indicates that he was questioned from 1:35 a.m. until 2:12 a.m. on December 6. The police interrogated him again from 2:30 a.m. until 2:53 a.m. During both interviews, Mark continually emphasized how drunk he had been during the entire spree. When asked about his participation in the string of crimes, Mark admitted that he stole liquor during the initial burglary and that he stole a 12-pack of beer during the robbery of the liquor store. Mark also conceded that he had handled a gun earlier that day and that he was present during the more serious thefts and the homicide.

The police told Mark that he would be charged with armed robbery and that, unless he broke "family ties," petitioner "may be dragging you right into a life sentence," . . . . Mark acknowledged that he would be sent away to the penitentiary. He claimed, however, that while he had primarily been drinking, petitioner and Barker had "got some guns or something" during the initial burglary. . . . Mark said that Barker had pulled a gun in one of the robberies. He further insisted that petitioner had instigated the carjacking and that he (Mark) "didn't have nothing to do with the shooting" of DeFilippis. . . . In a brief portion of one of his statements, Mark stated that petitioner was the one who shot DeFilippis.

The Commonwealth of Virginia charged petitioner with several offenses, including the murder of DeFilippis, and tried him separately. At trial, the Commonwealth called Mark as a witness, but he invoked his Fifth Amendment privilege against self-incrimination. The Commonwealth therefore offered to introduce into evidence the statements Mark made to the police after his arrest, arguing that they were admissible as declarations of an unavailable witness against penal interest. Petitioner objected on the ground that the statements were not actually against Mark's penal interest because they shifted responsibility for the crimes to Barker and to petitioner, and that their admission would violate the Sixth Amendment's Confrontation Clause. The trial judge overruled the objection and admitted the tape recordings and written transcripts of the statements in their entirety. The jury found petitioner guilty of robbery, abduction, carjacking, possession of a firearm by a felon, and four charges of illegal use of a firearm, for which offenses he received consecutive prison sentences of two life terms plus 27 years. The jury also convicted petitioner of capital murder and recommended a sentence of death, which the court imposed.

The Supreme Court of Virginia affirmed petitioner's convictions and sentences. As is relevant here, the court first concluded that Mark's statements were declarations of an unavailable witness against penal interest; that the statements' reliability was established by other evidence; and, therefore, that they fell within an exception to the Virginia hearsay rule. The court then turned to petitioner's Confrontation Clause challenge. It began by relying on our opinion in *White v. Illinois*, 502 U.S. 346 (1992), for the proposition that " 'where proffered hearsay has sufficient guarantees of reliability to come within a firmly rooted exception to the hearsay rule, the Confrontation Clause is satisfied.' " . . . The Virginia court also remarked:

> Admissibility into evidence of the statement against penal interest of an unavailable witness is a 'firmly rooted' exception to the hearsay rule in Virginia. Thus, we hold that the trial court did not err in admitting Mark Lilly's statements into evidence. . . .
>
> That Mark Lilly's statements were self-serving, in that they tended to shift principal responsibility to others or to offer claims of mitigating circumstances, goes to the weight the jury could assign to them and not to their admissibility. . . .

Our concern that this decision represented a significant departure from our Confrontation Clause jurisprudence prompted us to grant certiorari. . . .

* * *

III

In all criminal prosecutions, state as well as federal, the accused has a right, guaranteed by the Sixth and Fourteenth Amendments to the United States Constitution, "to be confronted with the witnesses against him." U.S. Const., Amend. 6; *Pointer v. Texas*, 380 U.S. 400, 85 S. Ct. 1065, 13 L. Ed. 2d 923 (1965) (applying Sixth Amendment to the States). "The central concern of the Confrontation Clause is to ensure the reliability of the evidence against a criminal defendant by subjecting it to rigorous testing in the context of an adversary proceeding before the trier of fact." *Maryland v. Craig*, 497 U.S. 836 (1990). When the government seeks to offer a declarant's out-of-court statements against the accused, and, as in this case, the declarant is unavailable,[11] courts must decide whether the Clause

---

[11] (Court's original footnote 7.) Petitioner suggests in his merits brief that Mark was not truly "unavailable" because the Commonwealth could have tried and sentenced him before petitioner's trial, thereby extinguishing Mark's Fifth Amendment privilege. We assume, however, as petitioner did in framing his petition for certiorari, that to the extent it is relevant, Mark was an unavailable witness for Confrontation Clause purposes.

permits the government to deny the accused his usual right to force the declarant "to submit to cross-examination, the 'greatest legal engine ever invented for the discovery of truth.'" . . .

In our most recent case interpreting the Confrontation Clause, *White v. Illinois*, 502 U.S. 346 (1992), we rejected the suggestion that the Clause should be narrowly construed to apply only to practices comparable to "a particular abuse common in 16th- and 17th-century England: prosecuting a defendant through the presentation of ex parte affidavits, without the affiants ever being produced at trial." . . . This abuse included using out-of-court depositions and "confessions of accomplices." . . . Because that restrictive reading of the Clause's term "witnesses" would have virtually eliminated the Clause's role in restricting the admission of hearsay testimony, we considered it foreclosed by our prior cases. Instead, we adhered to our general framework, summarized in *Ohio v. Roberts*, 448 U.S. 56, 100 S. Ct. 2531, 65 L. Ed. 2d 597 (1980), that the veracity of hearsay statements is sufficiently dependable to allow the untested admission of such statements against an accused when (1) "the evidence falls within a firmly rooted hearsay exception" or (2) it contains "particularized guarantees of trustworthiness" such that adversarial testing would be expected to add little, if anything, to the statements' reliability. . . .

Before turning to the dual *Roberts* inquiries, however, we note that the statements taken from petitioner's brother in the early morning of December 6 were obviously obtained for the purpose of creating evidence that would be useful at a future trial. The analogy to the presentation of ex parte affidavits in the early English proceedings thus brings the Confrontation Clause into play no matter how narrowly its gateway might be read.

IV

The Supreme Court of Virginia held that the admission of Mark Lilly's confession was constitutional primarily because, in its view, it was against Mark's penal interest and because "the statement against penal interest of an unavailable witness is a 'firmly rooted' exception to the hearsay rule in Virginia." . . . We assume, as we must, that Mark's statements were against his penal interest as a matter of state law, but the question whether the statements fall within a firmly rooted hearsay exception for Confrontation Clause purposes is a question of federal law. Accordingly, it is appropriate to begin our analysis by examining the "firmly rooted" doctrine and the roots of the "against penal interest" exception.

We have allowed the admission of statements falling within a firmly rooted hearsay exception since the Court's recognition . . . that the Framers of the Sixth Amendment "obviously intended to . . . respect" certain unquestionable rules of evidence in drafting the Confrontation Clause. . . . Justice Brown, writing for the Court in that case, did not question the wisdom of excluding deposition testimony, ex parte affidavits and their equivalents. But he reasoned that an unduly strict and "technical" reading of the Clause would have the effect of excluding other hearsay evidence, such as dying declarations, whose admissibility neither the Framers nor anyone else 100 years later "would have [had] the hardihood . . . to question." . . .

We now describe a hearsay exception as "firmly rooted" if, in light of "longstanding judicial and legislative experience," . . . it "rests [on] such [a] solid foundation that admission of virtually any evidence within [it] comports with the substance of the constitutional protection." . . . This standard is designed to allow the introduction of statements falling within a category of hearsay whose conditions have proven over time "to remove all temptation to falsehood, and to enforce as strict an adherence to the truth as would the obligation of an oath" and cross-examination at a trial. . . . In *White*, for instance, we held that the hearsay exception for spontaneous declarations is firmly rooted because it "is at least two centuries old," currently "widely accepted among the States," and carries "substantial guarantees of . . . trustworthiness . . . [that] cannot be recaptured even by later in-court testimony." . . . Established practice, in short, must confirm that statements falling within a category of hearsay inherently "carry special guarantees of credibility" essentially equivalent to, or greater than, those produced by the Constitution's preference for cross-examined trial testimony. . . .

The "against penal interest" exception to the hearsay rule — unlike other previously recognized firmly rooted exceptions — is not generally based on the maxim that statements made without a motive to reflect on the legal consequences of one's statement, and in situations that are exceptionally conducive to veracity, lack the dangers of inaccuracy that typically accompany hearsay. The exception, rather, is founded on the broad assumption "that a person is unlikely to fabricate a statement against his own interest at the time it is made." . . .

We have previously noted that, due to the sweeping scope of the label, the simple categorization of a statement as a " 'declaration against penal interest' . . . defines too large a class for meaningful Confrontation Clause analysis." . . . In criminal trials, statements against penal interest are offered into evidence in three principal situations: (1) as voluntary admissions against the declarant; (2) as exculpatory evidence offered by a defendant who claims that the declarant committed, or was involved in, the offense; and (3) as evidence offered by the prosecution to establish the guilt of an alleged accomplice of the declarant. It is useful to consider the three categories and their roots separately.

Statements in the first category — voluntary admissions of the declarant — are routinely offered into evidence against the maker of the statement and carry a distinguished heritage confirming their admissibility when so used. . . . Thus, assuming that Mark Lilly's statements were taken in conformance with constitutional prerequisites, they would unquestionably be admissible against him if he were on trial for stealing alcoholic beverages.

If Mark were a codefendant in a joint trial, however, even the use of his confession to prove his guilt might have an adverse impact on the rights of his accomplices. When dealing with admissions against penal interest, we have taken great care to separate using admissions against the declarant (the first category above) from using them against other criminal defendants (the third category).

In *Bruton v. United States*, 391 U.S. 123, 88 S. Ct. 1620, 20 L. Ed. 2d 476 (1968), two codefendants, Evans and Bruton, were tried jointly and convicted of armed postal robbery. A postal inspector testified that Evans had orally confessed that he and Bruton had committed the crime. The jury was instructed that Evans' confession was admissible against him, but could not be considered in assessing Bruton's guilt. Despite that instruction, this Court concluded that the introduction of Evans' confession posed such a serious threat to Bruton's right to confront and cross-examine the witnesses against him that he was entitled to a new trial. The case is relevant to the issue before us today, not because of its principal holding concerning the ability or inability of the jury to follow the judge's instruction, but rather because it was common ground among all of the Justices that the fact that the confession was a statement against the penal interest of Evans did not justify its use against Bruton. As Justice White noted at the outset of his dissent, "nothing in that confession which was relevant and material to Bruton's case was admissible against Bruton." . . .

In the years since *Bruton* was decided, we have reviewed a number of cases in which one defendant's confession has been introduced into evidence in a joint trial pursuant to instructions that it could be used against him but not against his codefendant. Despite frequent disagreement over matters such as the adequacy of the trial judge's instructions, or the sufficiency of the redaction of ambiguous references to the declarant's accomplice, we have consistently either stated or assumed that the mere fact that one accomplice's confession qualified as a statement against his penal interest did not justify its use as evidence against another person. . . .

The second category of statements against penal interest encompasses those offered as exculpatory evidence by a defendant who claims that it was the maker of the statement, rather than he, who committed (or was involved in) the crime in question. In this context, our Court, over the dissent of Justice Holmes, originally followed the 19th-century English rule that categorically refused to recognize any "against penal interest" exception to the hearsay rule, holding instead that under federal law only hearsay statements against pecuniary (and perhaps proprietary) interest were sufficiently reliable to warrant their admission at the trial of someone other than the declarant. . . .

As time passed, however, the precise *Donnelly* rule, which barred the admission of other persons' confessions that exculpated the accused, became the subject of increasing criticism. Professor Wigmore, for example, remarked years after *Donnelly* that:

> The only practical consequences of this unreasoning limitation are shocking to the sense of justice; for, in its commonest application, it requires, in a criminal trial, the rejection of a confession, however well authenticated, of a person deceased or insane or fled from the jurisdiction (and therefore quite unavailable) who has avowed himself to be the true culprit. . . . It is therefore not too late to retrace our steps, and to discard this barbarous doctrine, which would refuse to let an innocent accused vindicate himself even by producing to the tribunal a perfectly authenticated written confession, made on the very gallows, by the true culprit now beyond the reach of justice. . . .

Finally, in 1973, this Court endorsed the more enlightened view in *Chambers*, holding that the Due Process Clause affords criminal defendants the right to introduce into evidence third parties' declarations against penal interest — their confessions — when the circumstances surrounding the statements "provide considerable assurance of their reliability." . . . Not surprisingly, most States have now amended their hearsay rules to allow the admission of such statements under against-penal-interest exceptions. . . . But because hearsay statements of this sort are, by definition, offered by the accused, the admission of such statements does not implicate Confrontation Clause concerns. Thus, there is no need to decide whether the reliability of such statements is so inherently dependable that they would constitute a firmly rooted hearsay exception.

The third category includes cases, like the one before us today, in which the government seeks to introduce "a confession by an accomplice which incriminates a criminal defendant." . . . The practice of admitting statements in this category under an exception to the hearsay rule — to the extent that such a practice exists in certain jurisdictions — is, unlike the first category or even the second, of quite recent vintage. This category also typically includes statements that, when offered in the absence of the declarant, function similarly to those used in the ancient ex parte affidavit system.

Most important, this third category of hearsay encompasses statements that are inherently unreliable. Typical of the groundswell of scholarly and judicial criticism that culminated in the *Chambers* decision, Wigmore's treatise still expressly distinguishes accomplices' confessions that inculpate themselves and the accused as beyond a proper understanding of the against-penal-interest exception because an accomplice often has a considerable interest in "confessing and betraying his cocriminals." . . . Consistent with this scholarship and the assumption that underlies the analysis in our *Bruton* line of cases, we have over the years "spoken with one voice in declaring presumptively unreliable accomplices' confessions that incriminate defendants." . . .

* * *

V

Aside from its conclusion that Mark's statements were admissible under a firmly rooted hearsay exception, the Supreme Court of Virginia also affirmed the trial court's holding that the statements were "reliable . . . in the context of the facts and circumstances under which [they were] given" because (i) "Mark Lilly was cognizant of the import of his statements and that he was implicating himself as a participant in numerous crimes" and (ii) "elements of [his] statements were independently corroborated" by other evidence offered at trial. . . . The Commonwealth contends that . . . these two indicia of reliability, coupled with the facts that the police read Mark his *Miranda* rights and did not promise him leniency in exchange for his statements, demonstrate that the circumstances surrounding his statements bore "particularized guarantees of trustworthiness," . . . sufficient to satisfy the Confrontation Clause's residual admissibility test.[16]

---

[16] (Court's original footnote 12.) Although THE CHIEF JUSTICE contends that we should remand this issue to the Supreme Court of Virginia, see post, at 5–6, it would be inappropriate to do so because we granted certiorari on this issue, see Pet. for Cert. i, and the parties have fully briefed and argued the issue. The "facts and circumstances" formula, recited above, that the Virginia courts already employed

The residual "trustworthiness" test credits the axiom that a rigid application of the Clause's standard for admissibility might in an exceptional case exclude a statement of an unavailable witness that is incontestably probative, competent, and reliable, yet nonetheless outside of any firmly rooted hearsay exception. . . . When a court can be confident — as in the context of hearsay falling within a firmly rooted exception — that "the declarant's truthfulness is so clear from the surrounding circumstances that the test of cross-examination would be of marginal utility," the Sixth Amendment's residual "trustworthiness" test allows the admission of the declarant's statements. . . .

*　　*　　*

The Commonwealth correctly notes that "the presumption of unreliability that attaches to codefendants' confessions . . . may be rebutted." . . . We have held, in fact, that any inherent unreliability that accompanies co-conspirator statements made during the course and in furtherance of the conspiracy is per se rebutted by the circumstances giving rise to the long history of admitting such statements. *See Bourjaily v. United States*, 483 U.S. 171, 182–184 (1987). Nonetheless, the historical underpinnings of the Confrontation Clause and the sweep of our prior confrontation cases offer one cogent reminder: It is highly unlikely that the presumptive unreliability that attaches to accomplices' confessions that shift or spread blame can be effectively rebutted when the statements are given under conditions that implicate the core concerns of the old ex parte affidavit practice — that is, when the government is involved in the statements' production, and when the statements describe past events and have not been subjected to adversarial testing.

Applying these principles, the Commonwealth's asserted guarantees of trustworthiness fail to convince us that Mark's confession was sufficiently reliable as to be admissible without allowing petitioner to cross-examine him. That other evidence at trial corroborated portions of Mark's statements is irrelevant. We have squarely rejected the notion that "evidence corroborating the truth of a hearsay statement may properly support a finding that the statement bears 'particularized guarantees of trustworthiness.' " In *Wright*, we concluded that the admission of hearsay statements by a child declarant violated the Confrontation Clause even though the statements were admissible under an exception to the hearsay rule recognized in Idaho, and even though they were corroborated by other evidence. We recognized that it was theoretically possible for such statements to possess " 'particularized guarantees of trustworthiness' " that would justify their admissibility, but we refused to allow the State to "bootstrap on" the trustworthiness of other evidence. "To be admissible under the Confrontation Clause," we held, "hearsay evidence used to convict a defendant must possess indicia of reliability by virtue of its inherent trustworthiness, not by reference to other evidence at trial." . . .

Nor did the police's informing Mark of his *Miranda* rights render the circumstances surrounding his statements significantly more trustworthy. We noted in

---

in reaching their reliability holdings is virtually identical to the *Roberts* "particularized guarantees" test, which turns as well on the "surrounding circumstances" of the statements. *Idaho v. Wright*, 497 U.S. 805, 820, 110 S. Ct. 3139, 111 L. Ed. 2d 638 (1990). Furthermore, as will become clear, the Commonwealth fails to point to any fact regarding this issue that the Supreme Court of Virginia did not explicitly consider and that requires serious analysis.

rejecting a similar argument in *Lee* that a finding that a confession was "voluntary for Fifth Amendment purposes . . . does not bear on the question of whether the confession was also free from any desire, motive, or impulse [the declarant] may have had either to mitigate the appearance of his own culpability by spreading the blame or to overstate [the defendant's] involvement" in the crimes at issue. By the same token, we believe that a suspect's consciousness of his *Miranda* rights has little, if any, bearing on the likelihood of truthfulness of his statements. When a suspect is in custody for his obvious involvement in serious crimes, his knowledge that anything he says may be used against him militates against depending on his veracity.

The Commonwealth's next proffered basis for reliability — that Mark knew he was exposing himself to criminal liability — merely restates the fact that portions of his statements were technically against penal interest. And as we have explained, such statements are suspect insofar as they inculpate other persons. "That a person is making a broadly self-inculpatory confession does not make more credible the confession's non-self-inculpatory parts." . . . Similarly, the absence of an express promise of leniency to Mark does not enhance his statements' reliability to the level necessary for their untested admission. The police need not tell a person who is in custody that his statements may gain him leniency in order for the suspect to surmise that speaking up, and particularly placing blame on his cohorts, may inure to his advantage.

It is abundantly clear that neither the words that Mark spoke nor the setting in which he was questioned provides any basis for concluding that his comments regarding petitioner's guilt were so reliable that there was no need to subject them to adversarial testing in a trial setting. Mark was in custody for his involvement in, and knowledge of, serious crimes and made his statements under the supervision of governmental authorities. He was primarily responding to the officers' leading questions, which were asked without any contemporaneous cross-examination by adverse parties. Thus, Mark had a natural motive to attempt to exculpate himself as much as possible. . . . Mark also was obviously still under the influence of alcohol. Each of these factors militates against finding that his statements were so inherently reliable that cross-examination would have been superfluous.

VI

The admission of the untested confession of Mark Lilly violated petitioner's Confrontation Clause rights. Adhering to our general custom of allowing state courts initially to assess the effect of erroneously admitted evidence in light of substantive state criminal law, we leave it to the Virginia courts to consider in the first instance whether this Sixth Amendment error was "harmless beyond a reasonable doubt." . . . Accordingly, the judgment of the Supreme Court of Virginia is reversed, and the case is remanded for further proceedings not inconsistent with this opinion.

It is so ordered.

Concurring Opinions by JUSTICES BREYER, SCALIA, THOMAS, and REHNQUIST omitted.

[2] "Testimonial" Statements and Confrontation

Crawford v. Washington fundamentally changed the law regarding the admissibility of hearsay evidence in a criminal trial. The upshot of the rule is that if a statement is "testimonial" then the declarant must be available for cross-examination. The basic rule is develop in *Crawford* and is fleshed out in the subsequent cases.

CRAWFORD v. WASHINGTON
United States Supreme Court
541 U.S. 36 (2004)

JUSTICE SCALIA delivered the opinion of the Court.

Petitioner Michael Crawford stabbed a man who allegedly tried to rape his wife, Sylvia. At his trial, the State played for the jury Sylvia's tape-recorded statement to the police describing the stabbing, even though he had no opportunity for cross-examination. The Washington Supreme Court upheld petitioner's conviction after determining that Sylvia's statement was reliable. The question presented is whether this procedure complied with the Sixth Amendment's guarantee that, "[i]n all criminal prosecutions, the accused shall enjoy the right . . . to be confronted with the witnesses against him."

On August 5, 1999, Kenneth Lee was stabbed at his apartment. Police arrested petitioner later that night. After giving petitioner and his wife *Miranda* warnings, detectives interrogated each of them twice. Petitioner eventually confessed that he and Sylvia had gone in search of Lee because he was upset over an earlier incident in which Lee had tried to rape her. The two had found Lee at his apartment, and a fight ensued in which Lee was stabbed in the torso and petitioner's hand was cut.

Petitioner gave the following account of the fight:

Q.   Okay. Did you ever see anything in [Lee's] hands?

A.   I think so, but I'm not positive.

Q.   Okay, when you think so, what do you mean by that?

A.   I coulda swore I seen him goin' for somethin' before, right before everything happened. He was like reachin', fiddlin' around down here and stuff . . . and I just . . . I don't know, I think, this is just a possibility, but I think, I think that he pulled somethin' out and I grabbed for it and that's how I got cut . . . but I'm not positive. I, I, my mind goes blank when things like this happen. I mean, I just, I remember things wrong, I remember things that just doesn't, don't make sense to me later. App. 155 (punctuation added).

Sylvia generally corroborated petitioner's story about the events leading up to the fight, but her account of the fight itself was arguably different — particularly with respect to whether Lee had drawn a weapon before petitioner assaulted him:

Q.   Did Kenny do anything to fight back from this assault?

A.   (pausing) I know he reached into his pocket . . . or somethin'. . . I don't know what.

Q.   After he was stabbed?

A.   He saw Michael coming up. He lifted his hand . . . his chest open, he might [have] went to go strike his hand out or something and then (inaudible).

Q.   Okay, you, you gotta speak up.

A.   Okay, he lifted his hand over his head maybe to strike Michael's hand down or something and then he put his hands in his . . . put his right hand in his right pocket . . . took a step back . . . Michael proceeded to stab him . . . then his hands were like . . . how do you explain this . . . open arms . . . with his hands open and he fell down . . . and we ran (describing subject holding hands open, palms toward assailant).

Q.   Okay, when he's standing there with his open hands, you're talking about Kenny, correct?

A.   Yeah, after, after the fact, yes.

Q.   Did you see anything in his hands at that point?

A.   (pausing) um um (no). . . . (punctuation added).

The State charged petitioner with assault and attempted murder. At trial, he claimed self-defense. Sylvia did not testify because of the state marital privilege, which generally bars a spouse from testifying without the other spouse's consent. . . . In Washington, this privilege does not extend to a spouse's out-of-court statements admissible under a hearsay exception, . . . so the State sought to introduce Sylvia's tape-recorded statements to the police as evidence that the stabbing was not in self-defense. Noting that Sylvia had admitted she led petitioner to Lee's apartment and thus had facilitated the assault, the State invoked the hearsay exception for statements against penal interest, Wash. Rule Evid. 804(b)(3) (2003).

Petitioner countered that, state law notwithstanding, admitting the evidence would violate his federal constitutional right to be "confronted with the witnesses against him." . . . According to our description of that right in *Ohio v. Roberts*, 448 U.S. 56 (1980), it does not bar admission of an unavailable witness's statement against a criminal defendant if the statement bears "adequate 'indicia of reliability.' " . . . To meet that test, evidence must either fall within a "firmly rooted hearsay exception" or bear "particularized guarantees of trustworthiness." . . . The trial court here admitted the statement on the latter ground, offering several reasons why it was trustworthy: Sylvia was not shifting blame but rather corroborating her husband's story that he acted in self-defense or "justified reprisal"; she had direct knowledge as an eyewitness; she was describing recent events; and she was being questioned by a "neutral" law enforcement officer. . . . The prosecution played the tape for the jury and relied on it in closing, arguing that it was "damning evidence" that "completely refutes [petitioner's] claim of self-defense." . . . The jury convicted petitioner of assault.

The Washington Court of Appeals reversed. It applied a nine-factor test to determine whether Sylvia's statement bore particularized guarantees of trustworthiness, and noted several reasons why it did not: The statement contradicted one she had previously given; it was made in response to specific questions; and at one point she admitted she had shut her eyes during the stabbing. The court considered and rejected the State's argument that Sylvia's statement was reliable because it coincided with petitioner's to such a degree that the two "interlocked." The court determined that, although the two statements agreed about the events leading up to the stabbing, they differed on the issue crucial to petitioner's self-defense claim: "[Petitioner's] version asserts that Lee may have had something in his hand when he stabbed him; but Sylvia's version has Lee grabbing for something only after he has been stabbed." . . .

The Washington Supreme Court reinstated the conviction, unanimously concluding that, although Sylvia's statement did not fall under a firmly rooted hearsay exception, it bore guarantees of trustworthiness: " '[W]hen a codefendant's confession is virtually identical [to, i.e., interlocks with,] that of a defendant, it may be deemed reliable.' " 147 Wash. 2d 424, 437, 54 P. 3d 656, 663 (2002) (quoting *State v. Rice*, 120 Wash. 2d 549, 570, 844 P. 2d 416, 427 (1993)). The court explained:

> Although the Court of Appeals concluded that the statements were contradictory, upon closer inspection they appear to overlap . . . .
>
> [B]oth of the Crawfords' statements indicate that Lee was possibly grabbing for a weapon, but they are equally unsure when this event may have taken place. They are also equally unsure how Michael received the cut on his hand, leading the court to question when, if ever, Lee possessed a weapon. In this respect they overlap.
>
> [N]either Michael nor Sylvia clearly stated that Lee had a weapon in hand from which Michael was simply defending himself. And it is this omission by both that interlocks the statements and makes Sylvia's statement reliable." 147 Wash. 2d, at 438–439, 54 P.3d, at 664 (internal quotation marks omitted).

We granted certiorari to determine whether the State's use of Sylvia's statement violated the Confrontation Clause. 539 U.S. 914 (2003).

II

The Sixth Amendment's Confrontation Clause provides that, "[i]n all criminal prosecutions, the accused shall enjoy the right . . . to be confronted with the witnesses against him." We have held that this bedrock procedural guarantee applies to both federal and state prosecutions. *Pointer* v. *Texas*, 380 U.S. 400, 406 (1965). As noted above, *Roberts* says that an unavailable witness's out-of-court statement may be admitted so long as it has adequate indicia of reliability — i.e., falls within a "firmly rooted hearsay exception" or bears "particularized guarantees of trustworthiness." 448 U.S., at 66. Petitioner argues that this test strays from the original meaning of the Confrontation Clause and urges us to reconsider it.

A

The Constitution's text does not alone resolve this case. One could plausibly read "witnesses against" a defendant to mean those who actually testify at trial, *cf. Woodsides* v. *State*, 3 Miss. 655, 664–665 (1837), those whose statements are offered at trial, *see* 3 J. Wigmore, EVIDENCE § 1397, p. 104 (2d ed. 1923) (hereinafter Wigmore), or something in-between, *see infra*, at 15–16. We must therefore turn to the historical background of the Clause to understand its meaning.

The right to confront one's accusers is a concept that dates back to Roman times. . . . The founding generation's immediate source of the concept, however, was the common law. English common law has long differed from continental civil law in regard to the manner in which witnesses give testimony in criminal trials. The common-law tradition is one of live testimony in court subject to adversarial testing, while the civil law condones examination in private by judicial officers . . . .

Nonetheless, England at times adopted elements of the civil-law practice. Justices of the peace or other officials examined suspects and witnesses before trial. These examinations were sometimes read in court in lieu of live testimony, a practice that "occasioned frequent demands by the prisoner to have his 'accusers,' *i.e.* the witnesses against him, brought before him face to face." . . .

Pretrial examinations became routine under two statutes passed during the reign of Queen Mary in the 16th century, 1 & 2 Phil. & M., c. 13 (1554), and 2 & 3 *id.*, c. 10 (1555). These Marian bail and committal statutes required justices of the peace to examine suspects and witnesses in felony cases and to certify the results to the court. It is doubtful that the original purpose of the examinations was to produce evidence admissible at trial. See J. Langbein, Prosecuting Crime in the Renaissance 21–34 (1974). Whatever the original purpose, however, they came to be used as evidence in some cases . . . resulting in an adoption of continental procedure . . . .

The most notorious instances of civil-law examination occurred in the great political trials of the 16th and 17th centuries. One such was the 1603 trial of Sir Walter Raleigh for treason. Lord Cobham, Raleigh's alleged accomplice, had implicated him in an examination before the Privy Council and in a letter. At Raleigh's trial, these were read to the jury. Raleigh argued that Cobham had lied to save himself: "Cobham is absolutely in the King's mercy; to excuse me cannot avail him; by accusing me he may hope for favour." . . . Suspecting that Cobham would recant, Raleigh demanded that the judges call him to appear, arguing that "[t]he Proof of the Common Law is by witness and jury: let Cobham be here, let him speak it. Call my accuser before my face . . . ." The judges refused . . . and, despite Raleigh's protestations that he was being tried "by the Spanish Inquisition," . . . the jury convicted, and Raleigh was sentenced to death.

One of Raleigh's trial judges later lamented that " 'the justice of England has never been so degraded and injured as by the condemnation of Sir Walter Raleigh.' " . . . Through a series of statutory and judicial reforms, English law developed a right of confrontation that limited these abuses. For example, treason statutes required witnesses to confront the accused "face to face" at his arraignment. . . . Courts, meanwhile, developed relatively strict rules of unavailability, admitting examinations only if the witness was demonstrably unable to testify in person. . . . Several authorities also stated that a suspect's confession could be admitted only against himself, and not against others he implicated . . . .

One recurring question was whether the admissibility of an unavailable witness's pretrial examination depended on whether the defendant had had an opportunity to cross-examine him. In 1696, the Court of King's Bench answered this question in the affirmative, in the widely reported misdemeanor libel case of *King* v. *Paine*, 5 Mod. 163, 87 Eng. Rep. 584. The court ruled that, even though a witness was dead, his examination was not admissible where "the defendant not being present when [it was] taken before the mayor . . . had lost the benefit of a cross-examination." . . . The question was also debated at length during the infamous proceedings against Sir John Fenwick on a bill of attainder. Fenwick's counsel objected to admitting the examination of a witness who had been spirited away, on the ground that Fenwick had had no opportunity to cross-examine. . . . The examination was nonetheless admitted on a closely divided vote after several of those present opined that the common-law rules of procedure did not apply to parliamentary attainder proceedings — one speaker even admitting that the evidence would normally be inadmissible. . . . Fenwick was condemned, but the proceedings "must have burned into the general consciousness the vital importance of the rule securing the right of cross-examination." . . .

Paine had settled the rule requiring a prior opportunity for cross-examination as a matter of common law, but some doubts remained over whether the Marian statutes prescribed an exception to it in felony cases. The statutes did not identify the circumstances under which examinations were admissible, . . . and some inferred that no prior opportunity for cross-examination was required. . . . Many who expressed this view acknowledged that it meant the statutes were in derogation of the common law. . . . Nevertheless, by 1791 (the year the Sixth Amendment was ratified), courts were applying the cross-examination rule even to examinations by justices of the peace in felony cases. . . . When Parliament amended the statutes in 1848 to make the requirement explicit . . . the change merely "introduced in terms" what was already afforded the defendant "by the equitable construction of the law."

B

Controversial examination practices were also used in the Colonies. Early in the 18th century, for example, the Virginia Council protested against the Governor for having "privately issued several commissions to examine witnesses against particular men *ex parte*," complaining that "the person accused is not admitted to be confronted with, or defend himself against his defamers." A Memorial Concerning the Maladministrations of His Excellency Francis Nicholson, reprinted in 9 English Historical Documents 253, 257 (D. Douglas ed. 1955). A decade before the Revolution, England gave jurisdiction over Stamp Act offenses to the admiralty courts, which followed civil-law rather than common-law procedures and thus routinely took testimony by deposition or private judicial examination. . . . Colonial representatives protested that the Act subverted their rights "by extending the jurisdiction of the courts of admiralty beyond its ancient limits." . . . John Adams, defending a merchant in a high-profile admiralty case, argued: "Examinations of witnesses upon Interrogatories, are only by the Civil Law. Interrogatories are unknown at common Law, and Englishmen and common Lawyers have an aversion to them if not an Abhorrence of them." . . .

Many declarations of rights adopted around the time of the Revolution guaranteed a right of confrontation. . . . The proposed Federal Constitution, however, did not. At the Massachusetts ratifying convention, Abraham Holmes objected to this omission precisely on the ground that it would lead to civil-law practices: "The mode of trial is altogether indetermined; . . . whether [the defendant] is to be allowed to confront the witnesses, and have the advantage of cross-examination, we are not yet told. . . . [W]e shall find Congress possessed of powers enabling them to institute judicatories little less inauspicious than a certain tribunal in Spain, . . . the *Inquisition.*" . . . Similarly, a prominent Antifederalist writing under the pseudonym Federal Farmer criticized the use of "written evidence" while objecting to the omission of a vicinage right: "Nothing can be more essential than the cross examining [of] witnesses, and generally before the triers of the facts in question. . . . [W]ritten evidence . . . [is] almost useless; it must be frequently taken ex parte, and but very seldom leads to the proper discovery of truth." . . . The First Congress responded by including the Confrontation Clause in the proposal that became the Sixth Amendment.

Early state decisions shed light upon the original understanding of the common-law right. *State* v. *Webb*, 2 N. C. 103 (1794) *(per curiam)*, decided a mere three years after the adoption of the Sixth Amendment, held that depositions could be read against an accused only if they were taken in his presence. Rejecting a broader reading of the English authorities, the court held: "[I]t is a rule of the common law, founded on natural justice, that no man shall be prejudiced by evidence which he had not the liberty to cross examine." *Id.*, at 104.

Similarly, in *State* v. *Campbell*, 1 S. C. 124 (1844), South Carolina's highest law court excluded a deposition taken by a coroner in the absence of the accused. It held: "[I]f we are to decide the question by the established rules of the common law, there could not be a dissenting voice. For, notwithstanding the death of the witness, and whatever the respectability of the court taking the depositions, the solemnity of the occasion and the weight of the testimony, such depositions are *ex parte*, and, therefore, utterly incompetent." . . . The court said that one of the "indispensable conditions" implicitly guaranteed by the State Constitution was that "prosecutions be carried on to the conviction of the accused, by witnesses confronted by him, and subjected to his personal examination." . . .

*   *   *

III

This history supports two inferences about the meaning of the Sixth Amendment.

A

First, the principal evil at which the Confrontation Clause was directed was the civil-law mode of criminal procedure, and particularly its use of *ex parte* examinations as evidence against the accused. It was these practices that the Crown deployed in notorious treason cases like Raleigh's; that the Marian statutes invited; that English law's assertion of a right to confrontation was meant to prohibit; and that the founding-era rhetoric decried. The Sixth Amendment must be interpreted with this focus in mind.

Accordingly, we once again reject the view that the Confrontation Clause applies of its own force only to in-court testimony, and that its application to out-of-court statements introduced at trial depends upon "the law of Evidence for the time being." 3 Wigmore § 1397, at 101; *accord, Dutton v. Evans*, 400 U.S. 74, 94 (1970) (Harlan, J., concurring in result). Leaving the regulation of out-of-court statements to the law of evidence would render the Confrontation Clause powerless to prevent even the most flagrant inquisitorial practices. Raleigh was, after all, perfectly free to confront those who read Cobham's confession in court.

This focus also suggests that not all hearsay implicates the Sixth Amendment's core concerns. An off-hand, overheard remark might be unreliable evidence and thus a good candidate for exclusion under hearsay rules, but it bears little resemblance to the civil-law abuses the Confrontation Clause targeted. On the other hand, *ex parte* examinations might sometimes be admissible under modern hearsay rules, but the Framers certainly would not have condoned them.

The text of the Confrontation Clause reflects this focus. It applies to "witnesses against the accused" — in other words, those who "bear testimony." 1 N. Webster, An American Dictionary of the English Language (1828). "Testimony," in turn, is typically "[a] solemn declaration or affirmation made for the purpose of establishing or proving some fact." *Ibid.* An accuser who makes a formal statement to government officers bears testimony in a sense that a person who makes a casual remark to an acquaintance does not. The constitutional text, like the history underlying the common-law right of confrontation, thus reflects an especially acute concern with a specific type of out-of-court statement.

Various formulations of this core class of "testimonial" statements exist: "*ex parte* in-court testimony or its functional equivalent — that is, material such as affidavits, custodial examinations, prior testimony that the defendant was unable to cross-examine, or similar pretrial statements that declarants would reasonably expect to be used prosecutorially," Brief for Petitioner 23; "extrajudicial statements . . . contained in formalized testimonial materials, such as affidavits, depositions, prior testimony, or confessions," *White v. Illinois*, 502 U.S. 346, 365 (1992) (*Thomas, J.*, joined by *Scalia, J.*, concurring in part and concurring in judgment); "statements that were made under circumstances which would lead an objective witness reasonably to believe that the statement would be available for use at a later trial," Brief for National Association of Criminal Defense Lawyers et al. as *Amici Curiae* 3. These formulations all share a common nucleus and then define the Clause's coverage at various levels of abstraction around it. Regardless of the precise articulation, some statements qualify under any definition — for example, *ex parte* testimony at a preliminary hearing.

Statements taken by police officers in the course of interrogations are also testimonial under even a narrow standard. Police interrogations bear a striking resemblance to examinations by justices of the peace in England. The statements are not *sworn* testimony, but the absence of oath was not dispositive. Cobham's examination was unsworn . . . yet Raleigh's trial has long been thought a paradigmatic confrontation violation. . . . Under the Marian statutes, witnesses were typically put on oath, but suspects were not. . . . Yet Hawkins and others went out of their way to caution that such unsworn confessions were not admissible against anyone but the confessor.[17]

That interrogators are police officers rather than magistrates does not change the picture either. Justices of the peace conducting examinations under the Marian statutes were not magistrates as we understand that office today, but had an essentially investigative and prosecutorial function. . . . England did not have a professional police force until the 19th century . . . so it is not surprising that other government officers performed the investigative functions now associated primarily with the police. The involvement of government officers in the production of testimonial evidence presents the same risk, whether the officers are police or justices of the peace.

In sum, even if the Sixth Amendment is not solely concerned with testimonial hearsay, that is its primary object, and interrogations by law enforcement officers fall squarely within that class.[18]

B

The historical record also supports a second proposition: that the Framers would not have allowed admission of testimonial statements of a witness who did not appear at trial unless he was unavailable to testify, and the defendant had had a prior opportunity for cross-examination. The text of the Sixth Amendment does not suggest any open-ended exceptions from the confrontation requirement to be

---

[17] (Court's original footnote 3.) These sources — especially Raleigh's trial — refute *The Chief Justice*'s assertion, *post*, at 3 (opinion concurring in judgment), that the right of confrontation was not particularly concerned with unsworn testimonial statements. But even if, as he claims, a general bar on unsworn hearsay made application of the Confrontation Clause to unsworn testimonial statements a moot point, that would merely change our focus from direct evidence of original meaning of the Sixth Amendment to reasonable inference. We find it implausible that a provision which concededly condemned trial by sworn *ex parte* affidavit thought trial by *unsworn ex parte* affidavit perfectly OK. (The claim that unsworn testimony was self-regulating because jurors would disbelieve it, cf. *post*, at 2, n. 1, is belied by the very existence of a general bar on unsworn testimony.) Any attempt to determine the application of a constitutional provision to a phenomenon that did not exist at the time of its adoption (here, allegedly, admissible unsworn testimony) involves some degree of estimation — what *The Chief Justice* calls use of a "proxy," *post*, at 3 — but that is hardly a reason not to make the estimation as accurate as possible. Even if, as *The Chief Justice* mistakenly asserts, there were no direct evidence of how the Sixth Amendment originally applied to unsworn testimony, there is no doubt what its application would have been.

[18] (Court's original footnote 4.) We use the term "interrogation" in its colloquial, rather than any technical legal, sense. Cf. *Rhode Island v. Innis*, 446 U.S. 291, 300–301 (1980). Just as various definitions of "testimonial" exist, one can imagine various definitions of "interrogation," and we need not select among them in this case. Sylvia's recorded statement, knowingly given in response to structured police questioning, qualifies under any conceivable definition.

developed by the courts. Rather, the "right . . . to be confronted with the witnesses against him," . . . is most naturally read as a reference to the right of confrontation at common law, admitting only those exceptions established at the time of the founding. . . . As the English authorities above reveal, the common law in 1791 conditioned admissibility of an absent witness's examination on unavailability and a prior opportunity to cross-examine. The Sixth Amendment therefore incorporates those limitations. The numerous early state decisions applying the same test confirm that these principles were received as part of the common law in this country.[19]

We do not read the historical sources to say that a prior opportunity to cross-examine was merely a sufficient, rather than a necessary, condition for

---

[19] (Court's original footnote 5.) *The Chief Justice* claims that English law's treatment of testimonial statements was inconsistent at the time of the framing, *post*, at 4–5, but the examples he cites relate to examinations under the Marian statutes. As we have explained, to the extent Marian examinations were admissible, it was only because the statutes *derogated* from the common law. See *supra*, at 10. Moreover, by 1791 even the statutory-derogation view had been rejected with respect to justice-of-the-peace examinations — explicitly in *King* v. *Woodcock*, 1 Leach 500, 502–504, 168 Eng. Rep. 352, 353 (1789), and *King* v. *Dingler*, 2 Leach 561, 562–563, 168 Eng. Rep. 383, 383–384 (1791), and by implication in *King* v. *Radbourne*, 1 Leach 457, 459–461, 168 Eng. Rep. 330, 331–332 (1787). None of *The Chief Justice's* citations proves otherwise. *King* v. *Westbeer*, 1 Leach 12, 168 Eng. Rep. 108 (1739), was decided a half-century earlier and cannot be taken as an accurate statement of the law in 1791 given the directly contrary holdings of *Woodcock* and *Dingler*. Hale's treatise is older still, and far more ambiguous on this point, see 1 M. Hale, Pleas of the Crown 585–586 (1736); some who espoused the requirement of a prior opportunity for cross-examination thought it entirely consistent with Hale's views. See *Fenwick's Case*, 13 How. St. Tr. 537, 602 (H. C. 1696) (Musgrave). The only timely authority *The Chief Justice* cites is *King* v. *Eriswell*, 3 T. R. 707, 100 Eng. Rep. 815 (K. B. 1790), but even that decision provides no substantial support. *Eriswell* was not a criminal case at all, but a Crown suit against the inhabitants of a town to charge them with care of an insane pauper. *Id.*, at 707–708, 100 Eng. Rep., at 815–816. It is relevant only because the judges discuss the Marian statutes in dicta. One of them, Buller, J., defended admission of the pauper's statement of residence on the basis of authorities that purportedly held *ex parte* Marian examinations admissible. *Id.*, at 713–714, 100 Eng. Rep., at 819. As evidence writers were quick to point out, however, his authorities said no such thing. *See* Peake, Evidence, at 64, n. *(m)* ("Mr. J. Buller is reported to have said that it was so settled in 1 Lev. 180, and Kel. 55; certainly nothing of the kind appears in those books"); 2 T. Starkie, Evidence 487–488, n. *(c)* (1826) ("Buller, J. . . . refers to *Radbourne's* case . . . ; but in that case the deposition was taken in the hearing of the prisoner, and of course the question did not arise" (citation omitted)). Two other judges, Grose, J., and Kenyon, C. J., responded to Buller's argument by distinguishing Marian examinations as a statutory exception to the common-law rule, but the context and tenor of their remarks suggest they merely *assumed* the accuracy of Buller's premise without independent consideration, at least with respect to examinations by justices of the peace. *See* 3 T. R., at 710, 100 Eng. Rep., at 817 (Grose, J.); *id.*, at 722–723, 100 Eng. Rep., at 823–824 (Kenyon, C. J.). In fact, the case reporter specifically notes in a footnote that their assumption was erroneous. *See id.*, at 710, n. *(c)*, 100 Eng. Rep., at 817, n. *(c)*. Notably, Buller's position on pauper examinations was resoundingly rejected only a decade later in *King* v. *Ferry Frystone*, 2 East 54, 55, 102 Eng. Rep. 289 (K. B. 1801) ("The point . . . has been since considered to be so clear against the admissibility of the evidence . . . that it was abandoned by the counsel . . . without argument"), further suggesting that his views on evidence were not mainstream at the time of the framing. In short, none of *The Chief Justice's* sources shows that the law in 1791 was unsettled *even as to examinations by justices of the peace under the Marian statutes*. More importantly, however, even if the statutory rule in 1791 were in doubt, the numerous early state-court decisions make abundantly clear that the Sixth Amendment incorporated the *common-law* right of confrontation and not any exceptions the Marian statutes supposedly carved out from it. *See supra*, at 13–14; *see also supra*, at 11, n. 2 (coroner statements). The common-law rule had been settled since *Paine* in 1696. See *King* v. *Paine*, 5 Mod. 163, 165, 87 Eng. Rep. 584, 585 (K. B.).

admissibility of testimonial statements. They suggest that this requirement was dispositive, and not merely one of several ways to establish reliability. This is not to deny, as *The Chief Justice* notes, that "[t]here were always exceptions to the general rule of exclusion" of hearsay evidence. . . . Several had become well established by 1791. . . . But there is scant evidence that exceptions were invoked to admit *testimonial* statements against the accused in a *criminal* case.[20] Most of the hearsay exceptions covered statements that by their nature were not testimonial — for example, business records or statements in furtherance of a conspiracy. We do not infer from these that the Framers thought exceptions would apply even to prior testimony. *Cf. Lilly v. Virginia*, 527 U.S. 116, 134 (1999) (plurality opinion) ("[A]ccomplices' confessions that inculpate a criminal defendant are not within a firmly rooted exception to the hearsay rule.").[21]

* * *

V

Although the results of our decisions have generally been faithful to the original meaning of the Confrontation Clause, the same cannot be said of our rationales. *Roberts* conditions the admissibility of all hearsay evidence on whether it falls under a "firmly rooted hearsay exception" or bears "particularized guarantees of trust-worthiness." . . . This test departs from the historical principles identified above in two respects. First, it is too broad: It applies the same mode of analysis whether or not the hearsay consists of *ex parte* testimony. This often results in close constitutional scrutiny in cases that are far removed from the core concerns of the Clause. At the same time, however, the test is too narrow: It admits statements that *do* consist of *ex parte* testimony upon a mere finding of reliability. This malleable standard often fails to protect against paradigmatic confrontation violations.

Members of this Court and academics have suggested that we revise our doctrine to reflect more accurately the original understanding of the Clause. . . . They offer two proposals: First, that we apply the Confrontation Clause only to testimonial statements, leaving the remainder to regulation by hearsay law — thus eliminating the overbreadth referred to above. Second, that we impose an absolute bar to statements that are testimonial, absent a prior opportunity to cross-examine — thus eliminating the excessive narrowness referred to above.

---

[20] (Court's original footnote 6.) The one deviation we have found involves dying declarations. The existence of that exception as a general rule of criminal hearsay law cannot be disputed. . . . Although many dying declarations may not be testimonial, there is authority for admitting even those that clearly are. . . . We need not decide in this case whether the Sixth Amendment incorporates an exception for testimonial dying declarations. If this exception must be accepted on historical grounds, it is *sui generis*.

[21] (Court's original footnote 7.) We cannot agree with *The Chief Justice* that the fact "[t]hat a statement might be testimonial does nothing to undermine the wisdom of one of these [hearsay] exceptions." *Post*, at 6. Involvement of government officers in the production of testimony with an eye toward trial presents unique potential for prosecutorial abuse — a fact borne out time and again throughout a history with which the Framers were keenly familiar. This consideration does not evaporate when testimony happens to fall within some broad, modern hearsay exception, even if that exception might be justifiable in other circumstances.

In *White*, we considered the first proposal and rejected it. . . . Although our analysis in this case casts doubt on that holding, we need not definitively resolve whether it survives our decision today, because Sylvia Crawford's statement is testimonial under any definition. This case does, however, squarely implicate the second proposal.

A

Where testimonial statements are involved, we do not think the Framers meant to leave the Sixth Amendment's protection to the vagaries of the rules of evidence, much less to amorphous notions of "reliability." Certainly none of the authorities discussed above acknowledges any general reliability exception to the common-law rule. Admitting statements deemed reliable by a judge is fundamentally at odds with the right of confrontation. To be sure, the Clause's ultimate goal is to ensure reliability of evidence, but it is a procedural rather than a substantive guarantee. It commands, not that evidence be reliable, but that reliability be assessed in a particular manner: by testing in the crucible of cross-examination. The Clause thus reflects a judgment, not only about the desirability of reliable evidence (a point on which there could be little dissent), but about how reliability can best be determined. *Cf.* 3 Blackstone, Commentaries, at 373 ("This open examination of witnesses . . . is much more conducive to the clearing up of truth."); M. Hale, History and Analysis of the Common Law of England 258 (1713) (adversarial testing "beats and bolts out the Truth much better").

The *Roberts* test allows a jury to hear evidence, untested by the adversary process, based on a mere judicial determination of reliability. It thus replaces the constitutionally prescribed method of assessing reliability with a wholly foreign one. In this respect, it is very different from exceptions to the Confrontation Clause that make no claim to be a surrogate means of assessing reliability. For example, the rule of forfeiture by wrongdoing (which we accept) extinguishes confrontation claims on essentially equitable grounds; it does not purport to be an alternative means of determining reliability. *See Reynolds v. United States*, 98 U.S. 145, 158–159 (1879).

The Raleigh trial itself involved the very sorts of reliability determinations that *Roberts* authorizes. In the face of Raleigh's repeated demands for confrontation, the prosecution responded with many of the arguments a court applying *Roberts* might invoke today: that Cobham's statements were self-inculpatory, . . . that they were not made in the heat of passion, . . . and that they were not "extracted from [him] upon any hopes or promise of Pardon,". . . It is not plausible that the Framers' only objection to the trial was that Raleigh's judges did not properly weigh these factors before sentencing him to death. Rather, the problem was that the judges refused to allow Raleigh to confront Cobham in court, where he could cross-examine him and try to expose his accusation as a lie.

Dispensing with confrontation because testimony is obviously reliable is akin to dispensing with jury trial because a defendant is obviously guilty. This is not what the Sixth Amendment prescribes.

B

The legacy of *Roberts* in other courts vindicates the Framers' wisdom in rejecting a general reliability exception. The framework is so unpredictable that it fails to provide meaningful protection from even core confrontation violations.

Reliability is an amorphous, if not entirely subjective, concept. There are countless factors bearing on whether a statement is reliable; the nine-factor balancing test applied by the Court of Appeals below is representative. . . . Whether a statement is deemed reliable depends heavily on which factors the judge considers and how much weight he accords each of them. Some courts wind up attaching the same significance to opposite facts. For example, the Colorado Supreme Court held a statement more reliable because its inculpation of the defendant was "detailed," . . . , while the Fourth Circuit found a statement more reliable because the portion implicating another was "fleeting," . . . Virginia Court of Appeals found a statement more reliable because the witness was in custody and charged with a crime (thus making the statement more obviously against her penal interest), . . . while the Wisconsin Court of Appeals found a statement more reliable because the witness was *not* in custody and *not* a suspect, ... Finally, the Colorado Supreme Court in one case found a statement more reliable because it was given "immediately after" the events at issue, . . . while that same court, in another case, found a statement more reliable because two years had elapsed . . . .

The unpardonable vice of the *Roberts* test, however, is not its unpredictability, but its demonstrated capacity to admit core testimonial statements that the Confrontation Clause plainly meant to exclude. Despite the plurality's speculation in *Lilly*, 527 U.S., at 137, that it was "highly unlikely" that accomplice confessions implicating the accused could survive *Roberts*, courts continue routinely to admit them. . . . One recent study found that, after *Lilly*, appellate courts admitted accomplice statements to the authorities in 25 out of 70 cases — more than one-third of the time. . . . Courts have invoked *Roberts* to admit other sorts of plainly testimonial statements despite the absence of any opportunity to cross-examine . . . .

To add insult to injury, some of the courts that admit untested testimonial statements find reliability in the very factors that *make* the statements testimonial. As noted earlier, one court relied on the fact that the witness's statement was made to police while in custody on pending charges — the theory being that this made the statement more clearly against penal interest and thus more reliable. . . . Other courts routinely rely on the fact that a prior statement is given under oath in judicial proceedings. . . . That inculpating statements are given in a testimonial setting is not an antidote to the confrontation problem, but rather the trigger that makes the Clause's demands most urgent. It is not enough to point out that most of the usual safeguards of the adversary process attend the statement, when the single safeguard missing is the one the Confrontation Clause demands.

C

Roberts' failings were on full display in the proceedings below. Sylvia Crawford made her statement while in police custody, herself a potential suspect in the case.

Indeed, she had been told that whether she would be released "depend[ed] on how the investigation continues." App. 81. In response to often leading questions from police detectives, she implicated her husband in Lee's stabbing and at least arguably undermined his self-defense claim. Despite all this, the trial court admitted her statement, listing several reasons why it was reliable. In its opinion reversing, the Court of Appeals listed several *other* reasons why the statement was *not* reliable. Finally, the State Supreme Court relied exclusively on the interlocking character of the statement and disregarded every other factor the lower courts had considered. The case is thus a self-contained demonstration of *Roberts'* unpredictable and inconsistent application.

Each of the courts also made assumptions that cross-examination might well have undermined. The trial court, for example, stated that Sylvia Crawford's statement was reliable because she was an eyewitness with direct knowledge of the events. But Sylvia at one point told the police that she had "shut [her] eyes and . . . didn't really watch" part of the fight, and that she was "in shock." . . . The trial court also buttressed its reliability finding by claiming that Sylvia was "being questioned by law enforcement, and, thus, the [questioner] is . . . neutral to her and not someone who would be inclined to advance her interests and shade her version of the truth unfavorably toward the defendant.". . . The Framers would be astounded to learn that *ex parte* testimony could be admitted against a criminal defendant because it was elicited by "neutral" government officers. But even if the court's assessment of the officer's motives was accurate, it says nothing about Sylvia's perception of her situation. Only cross-examination could reveal that.

The State Supreme Court gave dispositive weight to the interlocking nature of the two statements — that they were both ambiguous as to when and whether Lee had a weapon. The court's claim that the two statements were *equally* ambiguous is hard to accept. Petitioner's statement is ambiguous only in the sense that he had lingering doubts about his recollection: "A. I coulda swore I seen him goin' for somethin' before, right before everything happened. . . . [B]ut I'm not positive." . . . Sylvia's statement, on the other hand, is truly inscrutable, since the key timing detail was simply assumed in the leading question she was asked: "Q. Did Kenny do anything to fight back from this assault?" . . . Moreover, Sylvia specifically said Lee had nothing in his hands after he was stabbed, while petitioner was not asked about that.

The prosecutor obviously did not share the court's view that Sylvia's statement was ambiguous — he called it "damning evidence" that "completely refutes [petitioner's] claim of self-defense." . . . We have no way of knowing whether the jury agreed with the prosecutor or the court. Far from obviating the need for cross-examination, the "interlocking" ambiguity of the two statements made it all the more imperative that they be tested to tease out the truth.

We readily concede that we could resolve this case by simply reweighing the "reliability factors" under *Roberts* and finding that Sylvia Crawford's statement falls short. But we view this as one of those rare cases in which the result below is so improbable that it reveals a fundamental failure on our part to interpret the Constitution in a way that secures its intended constraint on judicial discretion. Moreover, to reverse the Washington Supreme Court's decision after conducting our own reliability analysis would perpetuate, not avoid, what the Sixth Amendment condemns. The Constitution prescribes a procedure for determining the reliability of testimony in criminal trials, and we, no less than the state courts, lack authority to replace it with one of our own devising.

We have no doubt that the courts below were acting in utmost good faith when they found reliability. The Framers, however, would not have been content to indulge this assumption. They knew that judges, like other government officers, could not always be trusted to safeguard the rights of the people; the likes of the dread Lord Jeffreys were not yet too distant a memory. They were loath to leave too much discretion in judicial hands. . . . By replacing categorical constitutional guarantees with open-ended balancing tests, we do violence to their design. Vague standards are manipulable, and, while that might be a small concern in run-of-the-mill assault prosecutions like this one, the Framers had an eye toward politically charged cases like Raleigh's — great state trials where the impartiality of even those at the highest levels of the judiciary might not be so clear. It is difficult to imagine *Roberts'* providing any meaningful protection in those circumstances.

Where nontestimonial hearsay is at issue, it is wholly consistent with the Framers' design to afford the States flexibility in their development of hearsay law — as does *Roberts*, and as would an approach that exempted such statements from Confrontation Clause scrutiny altogether. Where testimonial evidence is at issue, however, the Sixth Amendment demands what the common law required: unavailability and a prior opportunity for cross-examination. We leave for another day any effort to spell out a comprehensive definition of "testimonial."[24] Whatever else the term covers, it applies at a minimum to prior testimony at a preliminary hearing, before a grand jury, or at a former trial; and to police interrogations. These are the modern practices with closest kinship to the abuses at which the Confrontation Clause was directed.

In this case, the State admitted Sylvia's testimonial statement against petitioner, despite the fact that he had no opportunity to cross-examine her. That alone is sufficient to make out a violation of the Sixth Amendment. *Roberts* notwithstanding, we decline to mine the record in search of indicia of reliability. Where testimonial statements are at issue, the only indicium of reliability sufficient to satisfy constitutional demands is the one the Constitution actually prescribes: confrontation.

The judgment of the Washington Supreme Court is reversed, and the case is remanded for further proceedings not inconsistent with this opinion.

It is so ordered.

---

[24] (Court's original footnote 10.) We acknowledge *The Chief Justice*'s objection, . . . that our refusal to articulate a comprehensive definition in this case will cause interim uncertainty. But it can hardly be any worse than the status quo. . . . The difference is that the *Roberts* test is *inherently*, and therefore *permanently*, unpredictable.

CHIEF JUSTICE REHNQUIST, with whom JUSTICE O'CONNOR joins, concurring in the judgment.

I dissent from the Court's decision to overrule *Ohio v. Roberts*, 448 U.S. 56 (1980). I believe that the Court's adoption of a new interpretation of the Confrontation Clause is not backed by sufficiently persuasive reasoning to overrule long-established precedent. Its decision casts a mantle of uncertainty over future criminal trials in both federal and state courts, and is by no means necessary to decide the present case.

The Court's distinction between testimonial and nontestimonial statements, contrary to its claim, is no better rooted in history than our current doctrine. Under the common law, although the courts were far from consistent, out-of-court statements made by someone other than the accused and not taken under oath, unlike *ex parte* depositions or affidavits, were generally not considered substantive evidence upon which a conviction could be based.[25] Testimonial statements such as accusatory statements to police officers likely would have been disapproved of in the 18th century, not necessarily because they resembled *ex parte* affidavits or depositions as the Court reasons, but more likely than not because they were not made under oath.[26] . . . Without an oath, one usually did not get to the second step of whether confrontation was required.

Thus, while I agree that the Framers were mainly concerned about sworn affidavits and depositions, it does not follow that they were similarly concerned about the Court's broader category of testimonial statements. *See* 1 N. Webster, An American Dictionary of the English Language (1828) (defining "Testimony" as "[a] solemn declaration or affirmation made for the purpose of establishing or proving some fact. *Such affirmation in judicial proceedings, may be verbal or written, but must be under oath*" (emphasis added)). As far as I can tell, unsworn testimonial statements were treated no differently at common law than were nontestimonial statements, and it seems to me any classification of statements as testimonial

---

[25] (Court's original footnote 1.) Modern scholars have concluded that at the time of the founding the law had yet to fully develop the exclusionary component of the hearsay rule and its attendant exceptions, and thus hearsay was still often heard by the jury. *See* Gallanis, The Rise of Modern Evidence Law, 84 Iowa L. Rev. 499, 534–535 (1999); Mosteller, Remaking Confrontation Clause and Hearsay Doctrine Under the Challenge of Child Sexual Abuse Prosecutions, 1993 U. Ill. L. Rev. 691, 738–746. In many cases, hearsay alone was generally not considered sufficient to support a conviction; rather, it was used to corroborate sworn witness testimony. *See* 5 J. Wigmore, Evidence, § 1364, pp. 17, 19–20, 19, n. 33 (J. Chadbourn rev. 1974) (hereinafter Wigmore) (noting in the 1600's and early 1700's testimonial and nontestimonial hearsay was permissible to corroborate direct testimony); *see also* J. Langbein, Origins of Adversary Criminal Trial 238–239 (2003). Even when unsworn hearsay was proffered as substantive evidence, however, because of the predominance of the oath in society, juries were largely skeptical of it. *See* Landsman, Rise of the Contentious Spirit: Adversary Procedure in Eighteenth Century England, 75 Cornell L. Rev. 497, 506 (1990) (describing late 17th-century sentiments); Langbein, Criminal Trial before the Lawyers, 45 U. Chi. L. Rev. 263, 291–293 (1978). In the 18th century, unsworn hearsay was simply held to be of much lesser value than were sworn affidavits or depositions.

[26] (Court's original footnote 3.) Confessions not taken under oath were admissible against a confessor because "'the most obvious Principles of Justice, Policy, and Humanity'" prohibited an accused from attesting to his statements. 1 G. Gilbert, Evidence 216 (C. Lofft ed. 1791). Still, these unsworn confessions were considered evidence only against the confessor as the Court points out, *see ante*, at 16, and in cases of treason, were insufficient to support even the conviction of the confessor, 2 W. Hawkins, Pleas of the Crown, C. 46, § 4, p. 604, n. 3 (T. Leach 6th ed. 1787).

beyond that of sworn affidavits and depositions will be somewhat arbitrary, merely a proxy for what the Framers might have intended had such evidence been liberally admitted as substantive evidence like it is today.[27]

I therefore see no reason why the distinction the Court draws is preferable to our precedent. Starting with Chief Justice Marshall's interpretation as a Circuit Justice in 1807, 16 years after the ratification of the Sixth Amendment, *United States v. Burr*, 25 F. Cas. 187, 193 (No. 14,694) (CC Va. 1807), continuing with our cases in the late 19th century, *Mattox v. United States*, 156 U.S. 237, 243–244 (1895); *Kirby v. United States*, 174 U.S. 47, 54–57 (1899), and through today, *e.g.*, *White v. Illinois*, 502 U.S. 346, 352–353 (1992), we have never drawn a distinction between testimonial and nontestimonial statements. And for that matter, neither has any other court of which I am aware. I see little value in trading our precedent for an imprecise approximation at this late date.

I am also not convinced that the Confrontation Clause categorically requires the exclusion of testimonial statements. Although many States had their own Confrontation Clauses, they were of recent vintage and were not interpreted with any regularity before 1791. State cases that recently followed the ratification of the Sixth Amendment were not uniform; the Court itself cites state cases from the early 19th century that took a more stringent view of the right to confrontation than does the Court, prohibiting former testimony even if the witness was subjected to cross-examination. . . .

Nor was the English law at the time of the framing entirely consistent in its treatment of testimonial evidence. Generally *ex parte* affidavits and depositions were excluded as the Court notes, but even that proposition was not universal. . . . Wigmore notes that sworn examinations of witnesses before justices of the peace in certain cases would not have been excluded until the end of the 1700's, 5 Wigmore § 1364, at 26–27, and sworn statements of witnesses before coroners became excluded only by statute in the 1800's . . . . With respect to unsworn testimonial statements, there is no indication that once the hearsay rule was developed courts ever excluded these statements if they otherwise fell within a firmly rooted exception . . . .

Between 1700 and 1800 the rules regarding the admissibility of out-of-court statements were still being developed. *See* n. 1, *supra*. There were always exceptions to the general rule of exclusion, and it is not clear to me that the Framers categorically wanted to eliminate further ones. It is one thing to trace the right of confrontation back to the Roman Empire; it is quite another to conclude that such a right absolutely excludes a large category of evidence. It is an odd conclusion indeed to think that the Framers created a cut-and-dried rule with respect to the

---

[27] (Court's original footnote 4.) The fact that the prosecution introduced an unsworn examination in 1603 at Sir Walter Raleigh's trial, as the Court notes, *see ante*, at 16, says little about the Court's distinction between testimonial and nontestimonial statements. Our precedent indicates that unsworn testimonial statements, as do some nontestimonial statements, raise confrontation concerns once admitted into evidence, *see*, *e.g.*, *Lilly v. Virginia*, 527 U.S. 116 (1999); *Lee v. Illinois*, 476 U.S. 530 (1986), and I do not contend otherwise. My point is not that the Confrontation Clause does not reach these statements, but rather that it is far from clear that courts in the late 18th century would have treated unsworn statements, even testimonial ones, the same as sworn statements.

admissibility of testimonial statements when the law during their own time was not fully settled.

To find exceptions to exclusion under the Clause is not to denigrate it as the Court suggests. Chief Justice Marshall stated of the Confrontation Clause: "I know of no principle in the preservation of which all are more concerned. I know none, by undermining which, life, liberty and property, might be more endangered. It is therefore incumbent on courts to be watchful of every inroad on a principle so truly important." . . . Yet, he recognized that such a right was not absolute, acknowledging that exceptions to the exclusionary component of the hearsay rule, which he considered as an "inroad" on the right to confrontation, had been introduced . . . .

Exceptions to confrontation have always been derived from the experience that some out-of-court statements are just as reliable as cross-examined in-court testimony due to the circumstances under which they were made. We have recognized, for example, that co-conspirator statements simply "cannot be replicated, even if the declarant testifies to the same matters in court." *United States v. Inadi*, 475 U.S. 387, 395 (1986). Because the statements are made while the declarant and the accused are partners in an illegal enterprise, the statements are unlikely to be false and their admission "actually furthers the 'Confrontation Clause's very mission' which is to 'advance the accuracy of the truth-determining process in criminal trials.'" . . . Similar reasons justify the introduction of spontaneous declarations, *see White*, 502 U.S., at 356, statements made in the course of procuring medical services, *see ibid.*, dying declarations, *see Kirby, supra*, at 61, and countless other hearsay exceptions. That a statement might be testimonial does nothing to undermine the wisdom of one of these exceptions.

Indeed, cross-examination is a tool used to flesh out the truth, not an empty procedure. . . . "[I]n a given instance [cross-examination may] be superfluous; it may be sufficiently clear, in that instance, that the statement offered is free enough from the risk of inaccuracy and untrustworthiness, so that the test of cross-examination would be a work of supererogation." 5 Wigmore § 1420, at 251. In such a case, as we noted over 100 years ago, "The law in its wisdom declares that the rights of the public shall not be wholly sacrificed in order that an incidental benefit may be preserved to the accused." *Mattox*, 156 U.S., at 243; . . . . By creating an immutable category of excluded evidence, the Court adds little to a trial's truth-finding function and ignores this longstanding guidance.

In choosing the path it does, the Court of course overrules *Ohio v. Roberts*, 448 U.S. 56 (1980), a case decided nearly a quarter of a century ago. *Stare decisis* is not an inexorable command in the area of constitutional law, . . . but by and large, it "is the preferred course because it promotes the evenhanded, predictable, and consistent development of legal principles, fosters reliance on judicial decisions, and contributes to the actual and perceived integrity of the judicial process," . . . And in making this appraisal, doubt that the new rule is indeed the "right" one should surely be weighed in the balance. Though there are no vested interests involved, unresolved questions for the future of everyday criminal trials throughout the country surely counsel the same sort of caution. The Court grandly declares that "[w]e leave for another day any effort to spell out a comprehensive definition of 'testimonial,'" . . . But the thousands of federal prosecutors and the tens of thousands of state prosecutors need answers as to what beyond the specific kinds of "testimony" the Court lists, see *ibid.*, is covered by the new rule. They need them now, not months or years from now. Rules of criminal evidence are applied every day in courts throughout the country, and parties should not be left in the dark in this manner.

To its credit, the Court's analysis of "testimony" excludes at least some hearsay exceptions, such as business records and official records. . . . To hold otherwise would require numerous additional witnesses without any apparent gain in the truth-seeking process. Likewise to the Court's credit is its implicit recognition that the mistaken application of its new rule by courts which guess wrong as to the scope of the rule is subject to harmless-error analysis. . . .

But these are palliatives to what I believe is a mistaken change of course. It is a change of course not in the least necessary to reverse the judgment of the Supreme Court of Washington in this case. The result the Court reaches follows inexorably from *Roberts* and its progeny without any need for overruling that line of cases. In *Idaho v. Wright*, 497 U.S. 805, 820–824 (1990), we held that an out-of-court statement was not admissible simply because the truthfulness of that statement was corroborated by other evidence at trial. As the Court notes, . . . the Supreme Court of Washington gave decisive weight to the "interlocking nature of the two statements." No re-weighing of the "reliability factors," which is hypothesized by the Court . . . is required to reverse the judgment here. A citation to *Idaho* v. *Wright* . . . would suffice. For the reasons stated, I believe that this would be a far preferable course for the Court to take here.

[3] Implications of *Crawford*

[a]   911 Calls

Davis was the Supreme Court's first case to consider the implications of *Crawford*. There were two cases consolidated for decision in *Davis*, each of which considered when statements to the police qualified as "testimonial" under *Crawford* and therefore admissible only if the declarant is available for cross-examination.

DAVIS v. WASHINGTON
United States Supreme Court
547 U.S. 813 (2006)

JUSTICE SCALIA delivered the opinion of the Court.

These cases require us to determine when statements made to law enforcement personnel during a 911 call or at a crime scene are "testimonial" and thus subject to the requirements of the Sixth Amendment's Confrontation Clause.

I

A

The relevant statements in *Davis v. Washington*, No. 05-5224, were made to a 911 emergency operator on February 1, 2001. When the operator answered the initial call, the connection terminated before anyone spoke. She reversed the call, and Michelle McCottry answered. In the ensuing conversation, the operator ascertained that McCottry was involved in a domestic disturbance with her former boyfriend Adrian Davis, the petitioner in this case:

"911 Operator: Hello.

"Complainant: Hello.

"911 Operator: What's going on?

"Complainant: He's here jumpin' on me again.

"911 Operator: Okay. Listen to me carefully. Are you in a house or an apartment?

"Complainant: I'm in a house.

"911 Operator: Are there any weapons?

"Complainant: No. He's usin' his fists.

"911 Operator: Okay. Has he been drinking?

"Complainant: No.

"911 Operator: Okay, sweetie. I've got help started. Stay on the line with me, okay?

"Complainant: I'm on the line.

"911 Operator: Listen to me carefully. Do you know his last name?

"Complainant: It's Davis.

"911 Operator: Davis? Okay, what's his first name?

"Complainant: Adrian

"911 Operator: What is it?

"Complainant: Adrian.

"911 Operator: Adrian?

"Complainant: Yeah.

"911 Operator: Okay. What's his middle initial?

"Complainant: Martell. He's runnin' now." App. in No. 05-5224, pp. 8–9.

As the conversation continued, the operator learned that Davis had "just r [un] out the door" after hitting McCottry, and that he was leaving in a car with someone else. *Id.*, at 9–10. McCottry started talking, but the operator cut her off, saying, "Stop talking and answer my questions." *Id.*, at 10. She then gathered more information about Davis (including his birthday), and learned that Davis had told McCottry that his purpose in coming to the house was "to get his stuff," since McCottry was moving. *Id.*, at 11–12. McCottry described the context of the assault, *id.*, at 12, after which the operator told her that the police were on their way. "They're gonna check the area for him first," the operator said, "and then they're gonna come talk to you." *Id.*, at 12–13.

The police arrived within four minutes of the 911 call and observed McCottry's shaken state, the "fresh injuries on her forearm and her face," and her "frantic efforts to gather her belongings and her children so that they could leave the residence." 154 Wash.2d 291, 296, 111 P.3d 844, 847 (2005) (en banc).

The State charged Davis with felony violation of a domestic no-contact order. "The State's only witnesses were the two police officers who responded to the 911 call. Both officers testified that McCottry exhibited injuries that appeared to be recent, but neither officer could testify as to the cause of the injuries." *Ibid.* McCottry presumably could have testified as to whether Davis was her assailant, but she did not appear. Over Davis's objection, based on the Confrontation Clause of the Sixth Amendment, the trial court admitted the recording of her exchange with the 911 operator, and the jury convicted him. The Washington Court of Appeals affirmed, 116 Wash.App. 81, 64 P.3d 661 (2003). The Supreme Court of Washington, with one dissenting justice, also affirmed, concluding that the portion of the 911 conversation in which McCottry identified Davis was not testimonial, and that if other portions of the conversation were testimonial, admitting them was harmless beyond a reasonable doubt. 154 Wash.2d, at 305, 111 P.3d, at 851. We granted certiorari. 546 U.S. 975, 126 S. Ct. 552, 163 L. Ed. 2d 459 (2005).

B

In *Hammon v. Indiana*, No. 05-5705, police responded late on the night of February 26, 2003, to a "reported domestic disturbance" at the home of Hershel and Amy Hammon. 829 N.E.2d 444, 446 (Ind. 2005). They found Amy alone on the front porch, appearing " 'somewhat frightened,' " but she told them that " 'nothing was the matter,' " *id.*, at 446, 447. She gave them permission to enter the house, where an officer saw "a gas heating unit in the corner of the living room" that had "flames coming out of the . . . partial glass front. There were pieces of glass on the ground in front of it and there was flame emitting from the front of the heating unit." App. in No. 05-5705, p. 16.

Hershel, meanwhile, was in the kitchen. He told the police "that he and his wife had 'been in an argument' but 'everything was fine now' and the argument 'never became physical.' " 829 N.E.2d, at 447. By this point Amy had come back inside. One of the officers remained with Hershel; the other went to the living room to talk with Amy, and "again asked [her] what had occurred." *Ibid.;* App. in No. 05-5705, at 17, 32. Hershel made several attempts to participate in Amy's conversation with the police, see *id.*, at 32, but was rebuffed. The officer later testified that Hershel "became angry when I insisted that [he] stay separated from Mrs. Hammon so that we can investigate what had happened." *Id.*, at 34. After hearing Amy's account, the officer "had her fill out and sign a battery affidavit." *Id.*, at 18. Amy handwrote the following: "Broke our Furnace & shoved me down on the floor into the broken glass. Hit me in the chest and threw me down. Broke our lamps & phone. Tore up my van where I couldn't leave the house. Attacked my daughter." *Id.*, at 2.

The State charged Hershel with domestic battery and with violating his probation. Amy was subpoenaed, but she did not appear at his subsequent bench trial. The State called the officer who had questioned Amy, and asked him to recount what Amy told him and to authenticate the affidavit. Hershel's counsel repeatedly objected to the admission of this evidence. See *id.*, at 11, 12, 13, 17, 19, 20, 21. At one point, after hearing the prosecutor defend the affidavit because it was made "under oath," defense counsel said, "That doesn't give us the opportunity to cross examine [the] person who allegedly drafted it. Makes me mad." *Id.*, at 19. Nonetheless, the trial court admitted the affidavit as a "present sense impression," *id.*, at 20, and Amy's statements as "excited utterances" that "are expressly permitted in these kinds of cases even if the declarant is not available to testify," *id.*, at 40. The officer thus testified that Amy

> "informed me that she and Hershel had been in an argument. That he became irrate [sic] over the fact of their daughter going to a boyfriend's house. The argument became . . . physical after being verbal and she informed me that Mr. Hammon, during the verbal part of the argument was breaking things in the living room and I believe she stated he broke the phone, broke the lamp, broke the front of the heater. When it became physical he threw her down into the glass of the heater.

*   *   *

"She informed me Mr. Hammon had pushed her onto the ground, had shoved her head into the broken glass of the heater and that he had punched her in the chest twice I believe." *Id.*, at 17–18.

The trial judge found Hershel guilty on both charges, *id.*, at 40, and the Indiana Court of Appeals affirmed in relevant part, 809 N.E.2d 945 (2004). The Indiana Supreme Court also affirmed, concluding that Amy's statement was admissible for state-law purposes as an excited utterance, 829 N.E.2d, at 449; that "a 'testimonial' statement is one given or taken in significant part for purposes of preserving it for potential future use in legal proceedings," where "the motivations of the questioner and declarant are the central concerns," *id.*, at 456, 457; and that Amy's oral statement was not "testimonial" under these standards, *id.*, at 458. It also concluded that, although the affidavit was testimonial and thus wrongly admitted, it was harmless beyond a reasonable doubt, largely because the trial was to the bench. *Id.*, at 458–459. We granted certiorari. 546 U.S. 975, 126 S. Ct. 552, 163 L. Ed. 2d 459 (2005).

II

The Confrontation Clause of the Sixth Amendment provides: "In all criminal prosecutions, the accused shall enjoy the right . . . to be confronted with the witnesses against him." In *Crawford v. Washington*, 541 U.S. 36, 53–54, 124 S. Ct. 1354, 158 L. Ed. 2d 177 (2004), we held that this provision bars "admission of testimonial statements of a witness who did not appear at trial unless he was unavailable to testify, and the defendant had had a prior opportunity for cross-examination." A critical portion of this holding, and the portion central to resolution of the two cases now before us, is the phrase "testimonial statements." Only statements of this sort cause the declarant to be a "witness" within the meaning of the Confrontation Clause. See *id.*, at 51, 124 S. Ct. 1354. It is the testimonial character of the statement that separates it from other hearsay that, while subject to traditional limitations upon hearsay evidence, is not subject to the Confrontation Clause.

Our opinion in *Crawford* set forth "[v]arious formulations" of the core class of " 'testimonial' " statements, *ibid.*, but found it unnecessary to endorse any of them, because "some statements qualify under any definition," *id.*, at 52, 124 S. Ct. 1354. Among those, we said, were "[s]tatements taken by police officers in the course of interrogations," *ibid.;* see also *id.*, at 53, 124 S. Ct. 1354. The questioning that generated the deponent's statement in *Crawford* — which was made and recorded while she was in police custody, after having been given *Miranda* warnings as a possible suspect herself — "qualifies under any conceivable definition" of an " 'interrogation,' " 541 U.S., at 53, n. 4, 124 S. Ct. 1354. We therefore did not define that term, except to say that "[w]e use [it] . . . in its colloquial, rather than any technical legal, sense," and that "one can imagine various definitions . . ., and we need not select among them in this case." *Ibid.* The character of the statements in the present cases is not as clear, and these cases require us to determine more precisely which police interrogations produce testimony.

Without attempting to produce an exhaustive classification of all conceivable statements — or even all conceivable statements in response to police interrogation — as either testimonial or nontestimonial, it suffices to decide the present cases to hold as follows: Statements are nontestimonial when made in the course of police interrogation under circumstances objectively indicating that the primary purpose of the interrogation is to enable police assistance to meet an ongoing emergency. They are testimonial when the circumstances objectively indicate that there is no such ongoing emergency, and that the primary purpose of the interrogation is to establish or prove past events potentially relevant to later criminal prosecution.[1]

III

A

In *Crawford*, it sufficed for resolution of the case before us to determine that "even if the Sixth Amendment is not solely concerned with testimonial hearsay, that is its primary object, and interrogations by law enforcement officers fall squarely within that class." *Id.*, at 53, 124 S. Ct. 1354. Moreover, as we have just described, the facts of that case spared us the need to define what we meant by "interroga-

---

[1] Our holding refers to interrogations because, as explained below, the statements in the cases presently before us are the products of interrogations — which in some circumstances tend to generate testimonial responses. This is not to imply, however, that statements made in the absence of any interrogation are necessarily nontestimonial. The Framers were no more willing to exempt from cross-examination volunteered testimony or answers to open-ended questions than they were to exempt answers to detailed interrogation. (Part of the evidence against Sir Walter Raleigh was a letter from Lord Cobham that was plainly *not* the result of sustained questioning. *Raleigh's Case*, 2 How. St. Tr. 1, 27 (1603).) And of course even when interrogation exists, it is in the final analysis the declarant's statements, not the interrogator's questions, that the Confrontation Clause requires us to evaluate.

tions." The *Davis* case today does not permit us this luxury of indecision. The inquiries of a police operator in the course of a 911 call[2] are an interrogation in one sense, but not in a sense that "qualifies under any conceivable definition." We must decide, therefore, whether the Confrontation Clause applies only to testimonial hearsay; and, if so, whether the recording of a 911 call qualifies.

The answer to the first question was suggested in *Crawford,* even if not explicitly held:

> "The text of the Confrontation Clause reflects this focus [on testimonial hearsay]. It applies to 'witnesses' against the accused — in other words, those who 'bear testimony.' 1 N. Webster, An American Dictionary of the English Language (1828). 'Testimony,' in turn, is typically 'a solemn declaration or affirmation made for the purpose of establishing or proving some fact.' *Ibid.* An accuser who makes a formal statement to government officers bears testimony in a sense that a person who makes a casual remark to an acquaintance does not." 541 U.S., at 51, 124 S. Ct. 1354.

A limitation so clearly reflected in the text of the constitutional provision must fairly be said to mark out not merely its "core," but its perimeter.

*   *   *

The question before us in *Davis* . . . is whether, objectively considered, the interrogation that took place in the course of the 911 call produced testimonial statements. When we said in *Crawford, supra,* at 53, 124 S. Ct. 1354, that "interrogations by law enforcement officers fall squarely within [the] class" of testimonial hearsay, we had immediately in mind (for that was the case before us) interrogations solely directed at establishing the facts of a past crime, in order to identify (or provide evidence to convict) the perpetrator. The product of such interrogation, whether reduced to a writing signed by the declarant or embedded in the memory (and perhaps notes) of the interrogating officer, is testimonial. It is, in the terms of the 1828 American dictionary quoted in *Crawford,* " '[a] solemn declaration or affirmation made for the purpose of establishing or proving some fact.' " 541 U.S., at 51, 124 S. Ct. 1354. (The solemnity of even an oral declaration of relevant past fact to an investigating officer is well enough established by the severe consequences that can attend a deliberate falsehood. See, *e.g., United States v. Stewart,* 433 F.3d 273, 288 (C.A.2 2006) (false statements made to federal investigators violate 18 U.S.C. § 1001); *State v. Reed,* 2005 WI 53, ¶ 30, 280 Wis.2d 68, 85, 695 N.W.2d 315, 323 (state criminal offense to "knowingly giv[e] false information to [an] officer with [the] intent to mislead the officer in the performance of his or her duty").) A 911 call, on the other hand, and at least the initial interrogation conducted in connection with a 911 call, is ordinarily not designed primarily to "establis[h] or

---

[2] If 911 operators are not themselves law enforcement officers, they may at least be agents of law enforcement when they conduct interrogations of 911 callers. For purposes of this opinion (and without deciding the point), we consider their acts to be acts of the police. As in *Crawford v. Washington,* 541 U.S. 36, 124 S. Ct. 1354, 158 L. Ed. 2d 177 (2004), therefore, our holding today makes it unnecessary to consider whether and when statements made to someone other than law enforcement personnel are "testimonial."

prov[e]" some past fact, but to describe current circumstances requiring police assistance.

The difference between the interrogation in *Davis* and the one in *Crawford* is apparent on the face of things. In *Davis*, McCottry was speaking about events *as they were actually happening*, rather than "describ[ing] past events," *Lilly v. Virginia*, 527 U.S. 116, 137, 119 S. Ct. 1887, 144 L. Ed. 2d 117 (1999) (plurality opinion). Sylvia Crawford's interrogation, on the other hand, took place hours after the events she described had occurred. Moreover, any reasonable listener would recognize that McCottry (unlike Sylvia Crawford) was facing an ongoing emergency. Although one *might* call 911 to provide a narrative report of a crime absent any imminent danger, McCottry's call was plainly a call for help against bona fide physical threat. Third, the nature of what was asked and answered in *Davis*, again viewed objectively, was such that the elicited statements were necessary to be able to *resolve* the present emergency, rather than simply to learn (as in *Crawford*) what had happened in the past. That is true even of the operator's effort to establish the identity of the assailant, so that the dispatched officers might know whether they would be encountering a violent felon. See, *e.g.*, *Hiibel v. Sixth Judicial Dist. Court of Nev., Humboldt Cty.*, 542 U.S. 177, 186, 124 S. Ct. 2451, 159 L. Ed. 2d 292 (2004). And finally, the difference in the level of formality between the two interviews is striking. Crawford was responding calmly, at the station house, to a series of questions, with the officer-interrogator taping and making notes of her answers; McCottry's frantic answers were provided over the phone, in an environment that was not tranquil, or even (as far as any reasonable 911 operator could make out) safe.

We conclude from all this that the circumstances of McCottry's interrogation objectively indicate its primary purpose was to enable police assistance to meet an ongoing emergency. She simply was not acting as a *witness*; she was not *testifying*. What she said was not "a weaker substitute for live testimony" at trial, *United States v. Inadi*, 475 U.S. 387, 394, 106 S. Ct. 1121, 89 L. Ed. 2d 390 (1986), like Lord Cobham's statements in *Raleigh's Case*, 2 How. St. Tr. 1 (1603), or Jane Dingler's *ex parte* statements against her husband in *King v. Dingler*, 2 Leach 561, 168 Eng. Rep. 383 (1791), or Sylvia Crawford's statement in *Crawford*. In each of those cases, the *ex parte* actors and the evidentiary products of the *ex parte* communication aligned perfectly with their courtroom analogues. McCottry's emergency statement does not. No "witness" goes into court to proclaim an emergency and seek help.

Davis seeks to cast McCottry in the unlikely role of a witness by pointing to English cases. None of them involves statements made during an ongoing emergency. In *King v. Brasier*, 1 Leach 199, 168 Eng. Rep. 202 (1779), for example, a young rape victim, "immediately on her coming home, told all the circumstances of the injury" to her mother. *Id.*, at 200, 168 Eng. Rep., at 202. The case would be helpful to Davis if the relevant statement had been the girl's screams for aid as she was being chased by her assailant. But by the time the victim got home, her story was an account of past events.

This is not to say that a conversation which begins as an interrogation to determine the need for emergency assistance cannot, as the Indiana Supreme Court put it, "evolve into testimonial statements," 829 N.E.2d, at 457, once that purpose has been achieved. In this case, for example, after the operator gained the information needed to address the exigency of the moment, the emergency appears to have ended (when Davis drove away from the premises). The operator then told McCottry to be quiet, and proceeded to pose a battery of questions. It could readily be maintained that, from that point on, McCottry's statements were testimonial, not unlike the "structured police questioning" that occurred in *Crawford*, 541 U.S., at 53, n. 4, 124 S. Ct. 1354. This presents no great problem. Just as, for Fifth Amendment purposes, "police officers can and will distinguish almost instinctively between questions necessary to secure their own safety or the safety of the public and questions designed solely to elicit testimonial evidence from a suspect," *New York v. Quarles*, 467 U.S. 649, 658–659, 104 S. Ct. 2626, 81 L. Ed. 2d 550 (1984), trial courts will recognize the point at which, for Sixth Amendment purposes, statements in response to interrogations become testimonial. Through *in limine* procedure, they should redact or exclude the portions of any statement that have become testimonial, as they do, for example, with unduly prejudicial portions of otherwise admissible evidence. Davis's jury did not hear the *complete* 911 call, although it may well have heard some testimonial portions. We were asked to classify only McCottry's early statements identifying Davis as her assailant, and we agree with the Washington Supreme Court that they were not testimonial. That court also concluded that, even if later parts of the call were testimonial, their admission was harmless beyond a reasonable doubt. Davis does not challenge that holding, and we therefore assume it to be correct.

B

Determining the testimonial or nontestimonial character of the statements that were the product of the interrogation in *Hammon* is a much easier task, since they were not much different from the statements we found to be testimonial in *Crawford*. It is entirely clear from the circumstances that the interrogation was part of an investigation into possibly criminal past conduct — as, indeed, the testifying officer expressly acknowledged, App. in No. 05-5705, at 25, 32, 34. There was no emergency in progress; the interrogating officer testified that he had heard no arguments or crashing and saw no one throw or break anything, *id.*, at 25. When the officers first arrived, Amy told them that things were fine, *id.*, at 14, and there was no immediate threat to her person. When the officer questioned Amy for the second time, and elicited the challenged statements, he was not seeking to determine (as in *Davis*) "what is happening," but rather "what happened." Objectively viewed, the primary, if not indeed the sole, purpose of the interrogation was to investigate a possible crime — which is, of course, precisely what the officer *should* have done.

It is true that the *Crawford* interrogation was more formal. It followed a *Miranda* warning, was tape-recorded, and took place at the station house, see 541 U.S., at 53, n. 4, 124 S. Ct. 1354. While these features certainly strengthened the statements' testimonial aspect — made it more objectively apparent, that is, that the purpose of the exercise was to nail down the truth about past criminal events — none was essential to the point. It was formal enough that Amy's interrogation was conducted in a separate room, away from her husband (who tried to intervene), with the officer receiving her replies for use in his "investigat[ion]." App. in No. 05-5705, at 34. What we called the "striking resemblance" of the *Crawford* statement to civil-law *ex parte* examinations, 541 U.S., at 52, 124 S. Ct. 1354, is shared by Amy's statement here. Both declarants were actively separated from the defendant — officers forcibly prevented Hershel from participating in the interrogation. Both statements deliberately recounted, in response to police questioning, how potentially criminal past events began and progressed. And both took place some time after the events described were over. Such statements under official interrogation are an obvious substitute for live testimony, because they do precisely *what a witness does* on direct examination; they are inherently testimonial.

*   *   *

Both Indiana and the United States as *amicus curiae* argue that this case should be resolved much like *Davis*. For the reasons we find the comparison to *Crawford* compelling, we find the comparison to *Davis* unpersuasive. The statements in *Davis* were taken when McCottry was alone, not only unprotected by police (as Amy Hammon was protected), but apparently in immediate danger from Davis. She was seeking aid, not telling a story about the past. McCottry's present-tense statements showed immediacy; Amy's narrative of past events was delivered at some remove in time from the danger she described. And after Amy answered the officer's questions, he had her execute an affidavit, in order, he testified, "[t]o establish events that have occurred previously." App. in No. 05-5705, at 18.

Although we necessarily reject the Indiana Supreme Court's implication that virtually any "initial inquiries" at the crime scene will not be testimonial, see 829 N.E.2d, at 453, 457, we do not hold the opposite — that *no* questions at the scene will yield nontestimonial answers. We have already observed of domestic disputes that "[o]fficers called to investigate . . . need to know whom they are dealing with in order to assess the situation, the threat to their own safety, and possible danger to the potential victim." *Hiibel*, 542 U.S., at 186, 124 S. Ct. 2451. Such exigencies may *often* mean that "initial inquiries" produce nontestimonial statements. But in cases like this one, where Amy's statements were neither a cry for help nor the provision of information enabling officers immediately to end a threatening situation, the fact that they were given at an alleged crime scene and were "initial inquiries" is immaterial. Cf. *Crawford, supra*, at 52, n. 3, 124 S. Ct. 1354.

IV

Respondents in both cases, joined by a number of their *amici*, contend that the nature of the offenses charged in these two cases — domestic violence — requires greater flexibility in the use of testimonial evidence. This particular type of crime is notoriously susceptible to intimidation or coercion of the victim to ensure that she does not testify at trial. When this occurs, the Confrontation Clause gives the criminal a windfall. We may not, however, vitiate constitutional guarantees when they have the effect of allowing the guilty to go free. Cf. *Kyllo v. United States*, 533 U.S. 27, 121 S. Ct. 2038, 150 L. Ed. 2d 94 (2001) (suppressing evidence from an illegal search). But when defendants seek to undermine the judicial process by procuring or coercing silence from witnesses and victims, the Sixth Amendment does not require courts to acquiesce. While defendants have no duty to assist the State in proving their guilt, they *do* have the duty to refrain from acting in ways that destroy the integrity of the criminal-trial system. We reiterate what we said in

Crawford: that "the rule of forfeiture by wrongdoing . . . extinguishes confrontation claims on essentially equitable grounds." 541 U.S., at 62, 124 S. Ct. 1354 (citing *Reynolds*, 98 U.S., at 158–159). That is, one who obtains the absence of a witness by wrongdoing forfeits the constitutional right to confrontation.

We take no position on the standards necessary to demonstrate such forfeiture, but federal courts using Federal Rule of Evidence 804(b)(6), which codifies the forfeiture doctrine, have generally held the Government to the preponderance-of-the-evidence standard, see, *e.g.*, *United States v. Scott*, 284 F.3d 758, 762 (C.A.7 2002). State courts tend to follow the same practice, see, *e.g.*, *Commonwealth v. Edwards*, 444 Mass. 526, 542, 830 N.E.2d 158, 172 (2005). Moreover, if a hearing on forfeiture is required, *Edwards*, for instance, observed that "hearsay evidence, including the unavailable witness's out-of-court statements, may be considered." *Id.*, at 545, 830 N.E.2d, at 174. The *Roberts* approach to the Confrontation Clause undoubtedly made recourse to this doctrine less necessary, because prosecutors could show the "reliability" of *ex parte* statements more easily than they could show the defendant's procurement of the witness's absence. *Crawford*, in overruling *Roberts*, did not destroy the ability of courts to protect the integrity of their proceedings.

We have determined that, absent a finding of forfeiture by wrongdoing, the Sixth Amendment operates to exclude Amy Hammon's affidavit. The Indiana courts may (if they are asked) determine on remand whether such a claim of forfeiture is properly raised and, if so, whether it is meritorious.

* * *

We affirm the judgment of the Supreme Court of Washington in No. 05-5224. We reverse the judgment of the Supreme Court of Indiana in No. 05-5705, and remand the case to that court for proceedings not inconsistent with this opinion.

[b] Party Causing Declarant to Become Unavailable

Giles was decided as part of the Supreme Court's renewed interest in the Confrontation Clause as source of limitation on hearsay in criminal trials unrelated to the Rules of Evidence. In *Giles*, the Court considers the circumstances under which hearsay becomes admissible as a result of a party causing the declarant to become unavailable. It does not, however, draw on the reasoning of *Crawford* but is included in this section as it also draws upon the Confrontation Clause to interpret the limits of admissible evidence.

GILES v. CALIFORNIA
United States Supreme Court
554 U.S. 353 (2008)

JUSTICE SCALIA delivered the opinion of the Court, except as to Part II-D-2.

We consider whether a defendant forfeits his Sixth Amendment right to confront a witness against him when a judge determines that a wrongful act by the defendant made the witness unavailable to testify at trial.

I

On September 29, 2002, petitioner Dwayne Giles shot his ex-girlfriend, Brenda Avie, outside the garage of his grandmother's house. No witness saw the shooting, but Giles' niece heard what transpired from inside the house. She heard Giles and Avie speaking in conversational tones. Avie then yelled "Granny" several times and a series of gunshots sounded. Giles' niece and grandmother ran outside and saw Giles standing near Avie with a gun in his hand. Avie, who had not been carrying a weapon, had been shot six times. One wound was consistent with Avie's holding her hand up at the time she was shot, another was consistent with her having turned to her side, and a third was consistent with her having been shot while lying on the ground. Giles fled the scene after the shooting. He was apprehended by police about two weeks later and charged with murder.

At trial, Giles testified that he had acted in self-defense. Giles described Avie as jealous, and said he knew that she had once shot a man, that he had seen her threaten people with a knife, and that she had vandalized his home and car on prior occasions. He said that on the day of the shooting, Avie came to his grandmother's house and threatened to kill him and his new girlfriend, who had been at the house earlier. He said that Avie had also threatened to kill his new girlfriend when Giles and Avie spoke on the phone earlier that day. Giles testified that after Avie threatened him at the house, he went into the garage and retrieved a gun, took the safety off, and started walking toward the back door of the house. He said that Avie charged at him, and that he was afraid she had something in her hand. According to Giles, he closed his eyes and fired several shots, but did not intend to kill Avie.

Prosecutors sought to introduce statements that Avie had made to a police officer responding to a domestic-violence report about three weeks before the shooting. Avie, who was crying when she spoke, told the officer that Giles had accused her of having an affair, and that after the two began to argue, Giles grabbed her by the shirt, lifted her off the floor, and began to choke her. According to Avie, when she broke free and fell to the floor, Giles punched her in the face and head, and after she broke free again, he opened a folding knife, held it about three feet away from her, and threatened to kill her if he found her cheating on him. Over Giles' objection, the trial court admitted these statements into evidence under a provision of California law that permits admission of out-of-court statements describing the infliction or threat of physical injury on a declarant when the declarant is unavailable to testify at trial and the prior statements are deemed trustworthy. Cal. Evid.Code Ann. § 1370 (West Supp.2008).

A jury convicted Giles of first-degree murder. He appealed. While his appeal was pending, this Court decided in *Crawford v. Washington,* 541 U.S. 36, 53–54, 124 S. Ct. 1354, 158 L. Ed. 2d 177 (2004), that the Confrontation Clause requires that a defendant have the opportunity to confront the witnesses who give testimony against him, except in cases where an exception to the confrontation right was recognized at the time of the founding. The California Court of Appeal held that the admission of Avie's unconfronted statements at Giles' trial did not violate the Confrontation Clause as construed by *Crawford* because *Crawford* recognized a doctrine of forfeiture by wrongdoing. 19 Cal.Rptr.3d 843, 847 (2004) (officially depublished). It concluded that Giles had forfeited his right to confront Avie because he had committed the murder for which he was on trial, and because his intentional criminal act made Avie unavailable to testify. The California Supreme Court affirmed on the same ground. 40 Cal.4th 833, 837, 55 Cal.Rptr.3d 133, 152 P.3d 433, 435 (2007). We granted certiorari. 552 U.S. 1136, 128 S. Ct. 976, 169 L. Ed. 2d 800 (2008).

II

The Sixth Amendment provides that "[i]n all criminal prosecutions, the accused shall enjoy the right . . . to be confronted with the witnesses against him." The Amendment contemplates that a witness who makes testimonial statements admitted against a defendant will ordinarily be present at trial for cross-examination, and that if the witness is unavailable, his prior testimony will be introduced only if the defendant had a prior opportunity to cross-examine him. *Crawford,* 541 U.S., at 68, 124 S. Ct. 1354. The State does not dispute here, and we accept without deciding, that Avie's statements accusing Giles of assault were testimonial. But it maintains (as did the California Supreme Court) that the Sixth Amendment did not prohibit prosecutors from introducing the statements because an exception to the confrontation guarantee permits the use of a witness's unconfronted testimony if a judge finds, as the judge did in this case, that the defendant committed a wrongful act that rendered the witness unavailable to testify at trial. We held in *Crawford* that the Confrontation Clause is "most naturally read as a reference to the right of confrontation at common law, admitting only those exceptions established at the time of the founding." *Id.,* at 54, 124 S. Ct. 1354. We therefore ask whether the theory of forfeiture by wrongdoing accepted by the California Supreme Court is a founding-era exception to the confrontation right.

A

We have previously acknowledged that two forms of testimonial statements were admitted at common law even though they were unconfronted. See *id.,* at 56, n. 6, 62, 124 S. Ct. 1354. The first of these were declarations made by a speaker who was both on the brink of death and aware that he was dying. See, *e.g., King v. Woodcock,* 1 Leach 500, 501–504, 168 Eng. Rep. 352, 353–354 (1789); *State v. Moody,* 3 N.C. 31 (Super. L. & Eq. 1798); *United States v. Veitch,* 28 F. Cas. 367, 367–368 (No. 16,614) (CC DC 1803); *King v. Commonwealth,* 4 Va. 78, 80–81 (Gen.Ct.1817). Avie did not make the unconfronted statements admitted at Giles' trial when she was dying, so her statements do not fall within this historic exception.

A second common-law doctrine, which we will refer to as forfeiture by wrongdoing, permitted the introduction of statements of a witness who was "detained" or "kept away" by the "means or procurement" of the defendant . . . .

*   *   *

In 1997, this Court approved a Federal Rule of Evidence, entitled "Forfeiture by wrongdoing," which applies only when the defendant "engaged or acquiesced in wrongdoing that was intended to, and did, procure the unavailability of the declarant as a witness." Fed. Rule Evid. 804(b)(6). We have described this as a rule "which codifies the forfeiture doctrine." *Davis v. Washington,* 547 U.S. 813, 833, 126

S. Ct. 2266, 165 L. Ed. 2d 224 (2006). Every commentator we are aware of has concluded the requirement of intent "means that the exception applies only if the defendant has in mind the particular purpose of making the witness unavailable." 5 C. Mueller & L. Kirkpatrick, Federal Evidence § 8:134, p. 235 (3d ed.2007); 5 J. Weinstein & M. Berger, Weinstein's Federal Evidence § 804.03 [7] [b], p. 804–32 (J. McLaughlin ed., 2d ed.2008); 2 K. Broun, McCormick on Evidence 176 (6th ed. 2006).

*   *   *

The state courts in this case did not consider the intent of the defendant because they found that irrelevant to application of the forfeiture doctrine. This view of the law was error, but the court is free to consider evidence of the defendant's intent on remand.

We decline to approve an exception to the Confrontation Clause unheard of at the time of the founding or for 200 years thereafter. The judgment of the California Supreme Court is vacated, and the case is remanded for further proceedings not inconsistent with this opinion.

[c]   Emergency Situations

In *Bryant*, the Court returns to the question of what it means for a statement to be testimonial within the meaning of *Crawford*. The issue in this case is whether statements made in the middle of an emergency situation constitute testimonial statements and whether the situation presented in *Bryant* amounted to an emergency.

MICHIGAN v. BRYANT
United States Supreme Court
562 U.S. 344 (2011)

Justice Sotomayor delivered the opinion of the Court.

At respondent Richard Bryant's trial, the court admitted statements that the victim, Anthony Covington, made to police officers who discovered him mortally wounded in a gas station parking lot. A jury convicted Bryant of, *inter alia*, second-degree murder. 483 Mich. 132, 137, 768 N.W.2d 65, 67–68 (2009). On appeal, the Supreme Court of Michigan held that the Sixth Amendment's Confrontation Clause, as explained in our decisions in *Crawford v. Washington*, 541 U.S. 36, 124 S. Ct. 1354, 158 L. Ed. 2d 177 (2004), and *Davis v. Washington*, 547 U.S. 813, 126 S. Ct. 2266, 165 L. Ed. 2d 224 (2006), rendered Covington's statements inadmissible testimonial hearsay, and the court reversed Bryant's conviction. 483 Mich., at 157, 768 N.W.2d, at 79. We granted the State's petition for a writ of certiorari to consider whether the Confrontation Clause barred the admission at trial of Covington's statements to the police. We hold that the circumstances of the interaction between Covington and the police objectively indicate that the "primary purpose of the interrogation" was "to enable police assistance to meet an ongoing emergency." *Davis*, 547 U.S., at 822, 126 S. Ct. 2266. Therefore, Covington's identification and description of the shooter and the location of the shooting were not testimonial statements, and their admission at Bryant's trial did not violate the Confrontation Clause. We vacate the judgment of the Supreme Court of Michigan and remand.

I

Around 3:25 a.m. on April 29, 2001, Detroit, Michigan police officers responded to a radio dispatch indicating that a man had been shot. At the scene, they found the victim, Anthony Covington, lying on the ground next to his car in a gas station parking lot. Covington had a gunshot wound to his abdomen, appeared to be in great pain, and spoke with difficulty.

The police asked him "what had happened, who had shot him, and where the shooting had occurred." 483 Mich., at 143, 768 N.W.2d, at 71. Covington stated that "Rick" shot him at around 3 a.m. *Id.*, at 136, and n. 1, 768 N.W.2d, at 67, and n. 1. He also indicated that he had a conversation with Bryant, whom he recognized based on his voice, through the back door of Bryant's house. Covington explained that when he turned to leave, he was shot through the door and then drove to the gas station, where police found him.

Covington's conversation with the police ended within 5 to 10 minutes when emergency medical services arrived. Covington was transported to a hospital and died within hours. The police left the gas station after speaking with Covington, called for backup, and traveled to Bryant's house. They did not find Bryant there but did find blood and a bullet on the back porch and an apparent bullet hole in the back door. Police also found Covington's wallet and identification outside the house.

At trial, which occurred prior to our decisions in *Crawford*, 541 U.S. 36, 124 S. Ct. 1354, and *Davis*, 547 U.S. 813, 126 S. Ct. 2266, the police officers who spoke with Covington at the gas station testified about what Covington had told them. The jury returned a guilty verdict on charges of second-degree murder, being a felon in possession of a firearm, and possession of a firearm during the commission of a felony.

II

*   *   *

Deciding this case also requires further explanation of the "ongoing emergency" circumstance addressed in *Davis*. Because *Davis* and *Hammon* arose in the domestic violence context, that was the situation "we had immediately in mind (for that was the case before us)." 547 U.S., at 826, 126 S. Ct. 2266. We now face a new context: a nondomestic dispute, involving a victim found in a public location, suffering from a fatal gunshot wound, and a perpetrator whose location was unknown at the time the police located the victim. Thus, we confront for the first time circumstances in which the "ongoing emergency" discussed in *Davis* extends beyond an initial victim to a potential threat to the responding police and the public at large. This new context requires us to provide additional clarification with regard to what *Davis* meant by "the primary purpose of the interrogation is to enable police assistance to meet an ongoing emergency." *Id.*, at 822, 126 S. Ct. 2266.

III

To determine whether the "primary purpose" of an interrogation is "to enable police assistance to meet an ongoing emergency," *Davis*, 547 U.S., at 822, 126 S. Ct. 2266, which would render the resulting statements nontestimonial, we objectively evaluate the circumstances in which the encounter occurs and the statements and actions of the parties.

A

The Michigan Supreme Court correctly understood that this inquiry is objective. 483 Mich., at 142, 768 N.W.2d, at 70.

B

As our recent Confrontation Clause cases have explained, the existence of an "ongoing emergency" at the time of an encounter between an individual and the police is among the most important circumstances informing the "primary purpose" of an interrogation. See *Davis*, 547 U.S., at 828–830, 126 S. Ct. 2266; *Crawford*, 541 U.S., at 65, 124 S. Ct. 1354. The existence of an ongoing emergency is relevant to determining the primary purpose of the interrogation because an emergency focuses the participants on something other than "prov[ing] past events potentially relevant to later criminal prosecution." *Davis*, 547 U.S., at 822, 126 S. Ct. 2266. Rather, it focuses them on "end[ing] a threatening situation." *Id.*, at 832, 126 S. Ct. 2266. Implicit in *Davis* is the idea that because the prospect of fabrication in statements given for the primary purpose of resolving that emergency is presumably significantly diminished, the Confrontation Clause does not require such statements to be subject to the crucible of cross-examination.

This logic is not unlike that justifying the excited utterance exception in hearsay law. Statements "relating to a startling event or condition made while the declarant was under the stress of excitement caused by the event or condition," Fed. Rule Evid. 803(2); see also Mich. Rule Evid. 803(2) (2010), are considered reliable because the declarant, in the excitement, presumably cannot form a falsehood. See *Idaho v. Wright*, 497 U.S. 805, 820, 110 S. Ct. 3139, 111 L. Ed. 2d 638 (1990) ("The basis for the 'excited utterance' exception . . . is that such statements are given under circumstances that eliminate the possibility of fabrication, coaching, or confabulation . . ."); 5 J. Weinstein & M. Berger, Weinstein's Federal Evidence § 803.04[1] (J. McLaughlin ed., 2d ed. 2010) (same); Advisory Committee's Notes on Fed. Rule Evid. 803(2), 28 U.S.C. App., p. 371 (same). An ongoing emergency has a similar effect of focusing an individual's attention on responding to the emergency.

* * *

C

In addition to the circumstances in which an encounter occurs, the statements and actions of both the declarant and interrogators provide objective evidence of the primary purpose of the interrogation. See, *e.g.*, *Davis*, 547 U.S., at 827, 126 S. Ct.

2266 ("[T]he nature of what was *asked and answered* in *Davis,* again viewed objectively, was such that the elicited statements were necessary to be able to *resolve* the present emergency, rather than simply to learn (as in *Crawford*) what had happened in the past" (first emphasis added)). The Michigan Supreme Court did, at least briefly, conduct this inquiry. 483 Mich., at 144–147, 768 N.W.2d, at 71–73.

As the Michigan Supreme Court correctly recognized, *id.*, at 140, n. 5, 768 N.W.2d, at 69, n. 5, *Davis* requires a combined inquiry that accounts for both the declarant and the interrogator. In many instances, the primary purpose of the interrogation will be most accurately ascertained by looking to the contents of both the questions and the answers. To give an extreme example, if the police say to a victim, "Tell us who did this to you so that we can arrest and prosecute them," the victim's response that "Rick did it," appears purely accusatory because by virtue of the phrasing of the question, the victim necessarily has prosecution in mind when she answers.

The combined approach also ameliorates problems that could arise from looking solely to one participant. Predominant among these is the problem of mixed motives on the part of both interrogators and declarants. Police officers in our society function as both first responders and criminal investigators. Their dual responsibilities may mean that they act with different motives simultaneously or in quick succession. See *New York v. Quarles,* 467 U.S. 649, 656, 104 S. Ct. 2626, 81 L. Ed. 2d 550 (1984) ("Undoubtedly most police officers [deciding whether to give *Miranda* warnings in a possible emergency situation] would act out of a host of different, instinctive, and largely unverifiable motives — their own safety, the safety of others, and perhaps as well the desire to obtain incriminating evidence from the suspect"); see also *Davis,* 547 U.S., at 839, 126 S. Ct. 2266 (Thomas, J., concurring in judgment in part and dissenting in part) ("In many, if not most, cases where police respond to a report of a crime, whether pursuant to a 911 call from the victim or otherwise, the purposes of an interrogation, viewed from the perspective of the police, are *both* to respond to the emergency situation *and* to gather evidence").

Victims are also likely to have mixed motives when they make statements to the police. During an ongoing emergency, a victim is most likely to want the threat to her and to other potential victims to end, but that does not necessarily mean that the victim wants or envisions prosecution of the assailant. A victim may want the attacker to be incapacitated temporarily or rehabilitated. Alternatively, a severely injured victim may have no purpose at all in answering questions posed; the answers may be simply reflexive. The victim's injuries could be so debilitating as to prevent her from thinking sufficiently clearly to understand whether her statements are for the purpose of addressing an ongoing emergency or for the purpose of future prosecution.[12] Taking into account a victim's injuries does not transform

---

[12] In such a situation, the severe injuries of the victim would undoubtedly also weigh on the credibility and reliability that the trier of fact would afford to the statements. Cf. Advisory Committee's Notes on Fed. Rule Evid. 803(2), 28 U.S.C.App., p. 371 (noting that although the "theory" of the excited utterance exception "has been criticized on the ground that excitement impairs [the] accuracy of observation as well as eliminating conscious fabrication," it "finds support in cases without number" (citing 6 J. Wigmore, Evidence § 1750 (J. Chadbourn rev.1976))).

this objective inquiry into a subjective one. The inquiry is still objective because it focuses on the understanding and purpose of a reasonable victim in the circumstances of the actual victim — circumstances that prominently include the victim's physical state.

* * *

IV

As we suggested in *Davis*, when a court must determine whether the Confrontation Clause bars the admission of a statement at trial, it should determine the "primary purpose of the interrogation" by objectively evaluating the statements and actions of the parties to the encounter, in light of the circumstances in which the interrogation occurs. The existence of an emergency or the parties' perception that an emergency is ongoing is among the most important circumstances that courts must take into account in determining whether an interrogation is testimonial because statements made to assist police in addressing an ongoing emergency presumably lack the testimonial purpose that would subject them to the requirement of confrontation. As the context of this case brings into sharp relief, the existence and duration of an emergency depend on the type and scope of danger posed to the victim, the police, and the public.

Applying this analysis to the facts of this case is more difficult than in *Davis* because we do not have the luxury of reviewing a transcript of the conversation between the victim and the police officers. Further complicating our task is the fact that the trial in this case occurred before our decisions in *Crawford* and *Davis*. We therefore review a record that was not developed to ascertain the "primary purpose of the interrogation."

We first examine the circumstances in which the interrogation occurred. The parties disagree over whether there was an emergency when the police arrived at the gas station. Bryant argues, and the Michigan Supreme Court accepted, 483 Mich., at 147, 768 N.W.2d, at 73, that there was no ongoing emergency because "there . . . was no criminal conduct occurring. No shots were being fired, no one was seen in possession of a firearm, nor were any witnesses seen cowering in fear or running from the scene." Brief for Respondent 27. Bryant, while conceding that "a serious or life-threatening injury creates a medical emergency for a victim," *id.*, at 30, 768 N.W.2d 65, further argues that a declarant's medical emergency is not relevant to the ongoing emergency determination.

In contrast, Michigan and the Solicitor General explain that when the police responded to the call that a man had been shot and found Covington bleeding on the gas station parking lot, "they did not know who Covington was, whether the shooting had occurred at the gas station or at a different location, who the assailant was, or whether the assailant posed a continuing threat to Covington or others." Brief for United States as *Amicus Curiae* 15; Brief for Petitioner 16; see also *id.*, at 15, 768 N.W.2d 65 ("[W]hen an officer arrives on the scene and does not know where the perpetrator is, whether he is armed, whether he might have other targets, and whether the violence might continue at the scene or elsewhere, interrogation that has the primary purpose of establishing those facts to assess the situation is designed to meet the ongoing emergency and is nontestimonial").

The Michigan Supreme Court stated that the police asked Covington, "what had happened, who had shot him, and where the shooting had occurred." 483 Mich., at 143, 768 N.W.2d, at 71. The joint appendix contains the transcripts of the preliminary examination, suppression hearing, and trial testimony of five officers who responded to the scene and found Covington. The officers' testimony is essentially consistent but, at the same time, not specific. The officers basically agree on what information they learned from Covington, but not on the order in which they learned it or on whether Covington's statements were in response to general or detailed questions. They all agree that the first question was "what happened?" The answer was either "I was shot" or "Rick shot me."

. . . [T]he scope of an emergency in terms of its threat to individuals other than the initial assailant and victim will often depend on the type of dispute involved. Nothing Covington said to the police indicated that the cause of the shooting was a purely private dispute or that the threat from the shooter had ended. The record reveals little about the motive for the shooting. The police officers who spoke with Covington at the gas station testified that Covington did not tell them what words Covington and Rick had exchanged prior to the shooting. What Covington did tell the officers was that he fled Bryant's back porch, indicating that he perceived an ongoing threat. The police did not know, and Covington did not tell them, whether the threat was limited to him. The potential scope of the dispute and therefore the emergency in this case thus stretches more broadly than those at issue in *Davis* and *Hammon* and encompasses a threat potentially to the police and the public.

This is also the first of our post-*Crawford* Confrontation Clause cases to involve a gun. The physical separation that was sufficient to end the emergency in *Hammon* was not necessarily sufficient to end the threat in this case; Covington was shot through the back door of Bryant's house. Bryant's argument that there was no ongoing emergency because "[n]o shots were being fired," Brief for Respondent 27, surely construes ongoing emergency too narrowly. An emergency does not last only for the time between when the assailant pulls the trigger and the bullet hits the victim. If an out-of-sight sniper pauses between shots, no one would say that the emergency ceases during the pause. That is an extreme example and not the situation here, but it serves to highlight the implausibility, at least as to certain weapons, of construing the emergency to last only precisely as long as the violent act itself, as some have construed our opinion in *Davis*. See Brief for Respondent 23–25.

At no point during the questioning did either Covington or the police know the location of the shooter. In fact, Bryant was not at home by the time the police searched his house at approximately 5:30 a.m. 483 Mich., at 136, 768 N.W.2d, at 67. At some point between 3 a.m. and 5:30 a.m., Bryant left his house. At bottom, there was an ongoing emergency here where an armed shooter, whose motive for and location after the shooting were unknown, had mortally wounded Covington within a few blocks and a few minutes of the location where the police found Covington.

This is not to suggest that the emergency continued until Bryant was arrested in California a year after the shooting. *Id.*, at 137, 768 N.W.2d, at 67. We need not decide precisely when the emergency ended because Covington's encounter with the police and all of the statements he made during that interaction occurred within the first few minutes of the police officers' arrival and well before they secured the scene of the shooting — the shooter's last known location.

We reiterate, moreover, that the existence *vel non* of an ongoing emergency is not the touchstone of the testimonial inquiry; rather, the ultimate inquiry is whether the "primary purpose of the interrogation [was] to enable police assistance to meet [the] ongoing emergency." *Davis*, 547 U.S., at 822, 126 S. Ct. 2266. We turn now to that inquiry, as informed by the circumstances of the ongoing emergency just described. The circumstances of the encounter provide important context for understanding Covington's statements to the police. When the police arrived at Covington's side, their first question to him was "What happened?" Covington's response was either "Rick shot me" or "I was shot," followed very quickly by an identification of "Rick" as the shooter. App. 76. In response to further questions, Covington explained that the shooting occurred through the back door of Bryant's house and provided a physical description of the shooter. When he made the statements, Covington was lying in a gas station parking lot bleeding from a mortal gunshot wound to his abdomen. His answers to the police officers' questions were punctuated with questions about when emergency medical services would arrive. *Id.*, at 56–57 (suppression hearing testimony of Officer Brown). He was obviously in considerable pain and had difficulty breathing and talking. *Id.*, at 75, 83–84 (testimony of Officer McCallister); *id.*, at 101, 110–111 (testimony of Sgt. Wenturine); *id.*, at 126, 137 (testimony of Officer Stuglin). From this description of his condition and report of his statements, we cannot say that a person in Covington's situation would have had a "primary purpose" "to establish or prove past events potentially relevant to later criminal prosecution." *Davis*, 547 U.S., at 822, 126 S. Ct. 2266.

For their part, the police responded to a call that a man had been shot. As discussed above, they did not know why, where, or when the shooting had occurred. Nor did they know the location of the shooter or anything else about the circumstances in which the crime occurred. The questions they asked — "what had happened, who had shot him, and where the shooting occurred," 483 Mich., at 143, 768 N.W.2d, at 71 — were the exact type of questions necessary to allow the police to " 'assess the situation, the threat to their own safety, and possible danger to the potential victim' " and to the public, *Davis*, 547 U.S., at 832, 126 S. Ct. 2266 (quoting *Hiibel v. Sixth Judicial Dist. Court of Nev., Humboldt Cty.*, 542 U.S. 177, 186, 124 S. Ct. 2451, 159 L. Ed. 2d 292 (2004)), including to allow them to ascertain "whether they would be encountering a violent felon," *Davis*, 547 U.S., at 827, 126 S. Ct. 2266. In other words, they solicited the information necessary to enable them "to meet an ongoing emergency." *Id.*, at 822, 126 S. Ct. 2266.

Nothing in Covington's responses indicated to the police that, contrary to their expectation upon responding to a call reporting a shooting, there was no emergency or that a prior emergency had ended. Covington did indicate that he had been shot at another location about 25 minutes earlier, but he did not know the location of the shooter at the time the police arrived and, as far as we can tell from the record, he gave no indication that the shooter, having shot at him twice, would be satisfied that Covington was only wounded. In fact, Covington did not indicate any possible motive for the shooting, and thereby gave no reason to think that the shooter would not shoot again if he arrived on the scene. As we noted in *Davis*, "initial inquiries" may " *often* . . . produce nontestimonial statements." *Id.*, at 832, 126 S. Ct. 2266. The initial inquiries in this case resulted in the type of nontestimonial statements we contemplated in *Davis*.

Finally, we consider the informality of the situation and the interrogation. This situation is more similar, though not identical, to the informal, harried 911 call in *Davis* than to the structured, station-house interview in *Crawford*. As the officers' trial testimony reflects, the situation was fluid and somewhat confused: the officers arrived at different times; apparently each, upon arrival, asked Covington "what happened?"; and, contrary to the dissent's portrayal, *post*, at 1171–1172 (opinion of Scalia, J.), they did not conduct a structured interrogation. App. 84 (testimony of Officer McCallister) (explaining duplicate questioning, especially as to "what happened?"); *id.*, at 101–102 (testimony of Sgt. Wenturine) (same); *id.*, at 126–127 (testimony of Officer Stuglin) (same). The informality suggests that the interrogators' primary purpose was simply to address what they perceived to be an ongoing emergency, and the circumstances lacked any formality that would have alerted Covington to or focused him on the possible future prosecutorial use of his statements.

Because the circumstances of the encounter as well as the statements and actions of Covington and the police objectively indicate that the "primary purpose of the interrogation" was "to enable police assistance to meet an ongoing emergency," *Davis*, 547 U.S., at 822, 126 S. Ct. 2266, Covington's identification and description of the shooter and the location of the shooting were not testimonial hearsay. The Confrontation Clause did not bar their admission at Bryant's trial.

*   *   *

For the foregoing reasons, we hold that Covington's statements were not testimonial and that their admission at Bryant's trial did not violate the Confrontation Clause. We leave for the Michigan courts to decide on remand whether the statements' admission was otherwise permitted by state hearsay rules. The judgment of the Supreme Court of Michigan is vacated, and the case is remanded for further proceedings not inconsistent with this opinion.

JUSTICE SCALIA, dissenting.

*   *   *

. . . The Court invents a world where an ongoing emergency exists whenever "an armed shooter, whose motive for and location after the shooting [are] unknown, . . . mortally wound [s]" one individual "within a few blocks and [25] minutes of the location where the police" ultimately find that victim. *Ante*, at 1164. Breathlessly, it worries that a shooter could leave the scene armed and ready to pull the trigger again. See *ante*, at 1158–1159, 1164, 1166. Nothing suggests the five officers in this case shared the Court's dystopian[4] view of Detroit, where drug dealers hunt their shooting victim down and fire into a crowd of police officers to finish him off, see

---

[4] The opposite of utopian. The word was coined by John Stuart Mill as a caustic description of British

ante, at 1166, or where spree killers shoot through a door and then roam the streets leaving a trail of bodies behind. Because almost 90 percent of murders involve a single victim,[5] it is much more likely — indeed, I think it certain — that the officers viewed their encounter with Covington for what it was: an investigation into a past crime with no ongoing or immediate consequences.

The Court's distorted view creates an expansive exception to the Confrontation Clause for violent crimes. Because Bryant posed a continuing threat to public safety in the Court's imagination, the emergency persisted for confrontation purposes at least until the police learned his "motive for and location after the shooting." *Ante*, at 1164. It may have persisted in this case until the police "secured the scene of the shooting" two-and-a-half hours later. *Ante*, at 1164–1165. (The relevance of securing the scene is unclear so long as the killer is still at large — especially if, as the Court speculates, he may be a spree-killer.) This is a dangerous definition of emergency. Many individuals who testify against a defendant at trial first offer their accounts to police in the hours after a violent act. If the police can plausibly claim that a "potential threat to . . . the public" persisted through those first few hours, *ante*, at 1156 (and if the claim is plausible here it is always plausible) a defendant will have no constitutionally protected right to exclude the uncross-examined testimony of such witnesses. His conviction could rest (as perhaps it did here) solely on the officers' recollection at trial of the witnesses' accusations.

The Framers could not have envisioned such a hollow constitutional guarantee. No framing-era confrontation case that I know of, neither here nor in England, took such an enfeebled view of the right to confrontation. For example, *King v. Brasier*, 1 Leach 199, 200, 168 Eng. Rep. 202, 202–203 (K.B.1779), held inadmissible a mother's account of her young daughter's statements "immediately on her coming home" after being sexually assaulted. The daughter needed to testify herself. But today's majority presumably would hold the daughter's account to her mother a nontestimonial statement made during an ongoing emergency. She could not have known whether her attacker might reappear to attack again or attempt to silence the lone witness against him. Her mother likely listened to the account to assess the threat to her own safety and to decide whether the rapist posed a threat to the community that required the immediate intervention of the local authorities. Cf. *ante*, at 1165–1166. Utter nonsense.

The 16th- and 17th-century English treason trials that helped inspire the Confrontation Clause show that today's decision is a mistake. The Court's expansive definition of an "ongoing emergency" and its willingness to consider the perspective of the interrogator and the declarant cast a more favorable light on those trials than history or our past decisions suggest they deserve. Royal officials conducted many of the *ex parte* examinations introduced against Sir Walter Raleigh and Sir John Fenwick while investigating alleged treasonous conspiracies of unknown scope,

---

policy. See 190 Hansard's Parliamentary Debates, Third Series 1517 (3d Ser.1868); 5 Oxford English Dictionary 13 (2d ed.1989).

5 See Federal Bureau of Investigation, Crime in the United States, 2009: Expanded Homicide Data Table 4, Murder by Victim/Offender Situations, 2009 (Sept.2010), online at http://www2.fbi.gov/ucr/cius2009/offenses/expanded_information/data/shrtable_04.html (as visited Feb. 25, 2011, and available in Clerk of Court's case file).

aimed at killing or overthrowing the King. See Brief for National Association of Criminal Defense Lawyers as *Amicus Curiae* 21–22, and n. 11. Social stability in 16th- and 17th-century England depended mainly on the continuity of the ruling monarch, cf. 1 J. Stephen, A History of the Criminal Law of England 354 (1883), so such a conspiracy posed the most pressing emergency imaginable. Presumably, the royal officials investigating it would have understood the gravity of the situation and would have focused their interrogations primarily on ending the threat, not on generating testimony for trial. I therefore doubt that under the Court's test English officials acted improperly by denying Raleigh and Fenwick the opportunity to confront their accusers "face to face," *id.*, at 326.

Under my approach, in contrast, those English trials remain unquestionably infamous. Lord Cobham did not speak with royal officials to end an ongoing emergency. He was a traitor! He spoke, as Raleigh correctly observed, to establish Raleigh's guilt and to save his own life. See 1 D. Jardine, Criminal Trials 435 (1832). Cobham's statements, when assessed from his perspective, had only a testimonial purpose. The same is true of Covington's statements here.

*   *   *

[d]   Laboratory Tests

Bullcoming is the follow-up to *Melendez-Diaz v. Massachusetts*, which held that an affidavit of a forensic lab test was inadmissible to prove the results of the test. In *Bullcoming*, the Court addressed the question of whether live testimony by a technician in the same laboratory, but not the one who performed the test in question, sufficiently satisfied the requirements of the Confrontation Clause to admit the results of the test.

BULLCOMING v. NEW MEXICO
United States Supreme Court
131 S. Ct. 2705 (2011)

Justice Ginsburg delivered the opinion of the Court, except as to Part IV and footnote 6.*

In *Melendez-Diaz v. Massachusetts*, 557 U.S. 305, 129 S. Ct. 2527, 174 L. Ed. 2d 314 (2009), this Court held that a forensic laboratory report stating that a suspect substance was cocaine ranked as testimonial for purposes of the Sixth Amendment's Confrontation Clause. The report had been created specifically to serve as evidence in a criminal proceeding. Absent stipulation, the Court ruled, the prosecution may not introduce such a report without offering a live witness competent to testify to the truth of the statements made in the report.

In the case before us, petitioner Donald Bullcoming was arrested on charges of driving while intoxicated (DWI). Principal evidence against Bullcoming was a forensic laboratory report certifying that Bullcoming's blood-alcohol concentration

---

* Justice Sotomayor and Justice Kagan join all but Part IV of this opinion. Justice Thomas joins all but Part IV and footnote 6.

was well above the threshold for aggravated DWI. At trial, the prosecution did not call as a witness the analyst who signed the certification. Instead, the State called another analyst who was familiar with the laboratory's testing procedures, but had neither participated in nor observed the test on Bullcoming's blood sample. The New Mexico Supreme Court determined that, although the blood-alcohol analysis was "testimonial," the Confrontation Clause did not require the certifying analyst's in-court testimony. Instead, New Mexico's high court held, live testimony of another analyst satisfied the constitutional requirements.

The question presented is whether the Confrontation Clause permits the prosecution to introduce a forensic laboratory report containing a testimonial certification — made for the purpose of proving a particular fact — through the in-court testimony of a scientist who did not sign the certification or perform or observe the test reported in the certification. We hold that surrogate testimony of that order does not meet the constitutional requirement. The accused's right is to be confronted with the analyst who made the certification, unless that analyst is unavailable at trial, and the accused had an opportunity, pretrial, to cross-examine that particular scientist.

I

A

In August 2005, a vehicle driven by petitioner Donald Bullcoming rear-ended a pick-up truck at an intersection in Farmington, New Mexico. When the truckdriver exited his vehicle and approached Bullcoming to exchange insurance information, he noticed that Bullcoming's eyes were bloodshot. Smelling alcohol on Bullcoming's breath, the truckdriver told his wife to call the police. Bullcoming left the scene before the police arrived, but was soon apprehended by an officer who observed his performance of field sobriety tests. Upon failing the tests, Bullcoming was arrested for driving a vehicle while "under the influence of intoxicating liquor" (DWI), in violation of N.M. Stat. Ann. § 66-8-102 (2004).

Because Bullcoming refused to take a breath test, the police obtained a warrant authorizing a blood-alcohol analysis. Pursuant to the warrant, a sample of Bullcoming's blood was drawn at a local hospital. To determine Bullcoming's blood-alcohol concentration (BAC), the police sent the sample to the New Mexico Department of Health, Scientific Laboratory Division (SLD). In a standard SLD form titled "Report of Blood Alcohol Analysis," participants in the testing were identified, and the forensic analyst certified his finding. App. 62.

SLD's report contained in the top block "information . . . filled in by [the] arresting officer." *Ibid.* (capitalization omitted). This information included the "reason [the] suspect [was] stopped" (the officer checked "Accident"), and the date ("8.14.05") and time ("18:25 PM") the blood sample was drawn. *Ibid.* (capitalization omitted). The arresting officer also affirmed that he had arrested Bullcoming and witnessed the blood draw. *Ibid.* The next two blocks contained certifications by the nurse who drew Bullcoming's blood and the SLD intake employee who received the blood sample sent to the laboratory. *Ibid.*

Following these segments, the report presented the "certificate of analyst," *ibid.* (capitalization omitted), completed and signed by Curtis Caylor, the SLD forensic analyst assigned to test Bullcoming's blood sample. *Id.*, at 62, 64–65. Caylor recorded that the BAC in Bullcoming's sample was 0.21 grams per hundred milliliters, an inordinately high level. *Id.*, at 62. Caylor also affirmed that "[t]he seal of th[e] sample was received intact and broken in the laboratory," that "the statements in [the analyst's block of the report] are correct," and that he had "followed the procedures set out on the reverse of th[e] report." *Ibid.* Those "procedures" instructed analysts, *inter alia*, to "retai[n] the sample container and the raw data from the analysis," and to "not[e] any circumstance or condition which might affect the integrity of the sample or otherwise affect the validity of the analysis." *Id.*, at 65. Finally, in a block headed "certificate of reviewer," the SLD examiner who reviewed Caylor's analysis certified that Caylor was qualified to conduct the BAC test, and that the "established procedure" for handling and analyzing Bullcoming's sample "ha[d] been followed." *Id.*, at 62 (capitalization omitted).

SLD analysts use gas chromatograph machines to determine BAC levels. Operation of the machines requires specialized knowledge and training. Several steps are involved in the gas chromatograph process, and human error can occur at each step.[1]

Although the State presented testimony that obtaining an accurate BAC measurement merely entails "look[ing] at the [gas chromatograph] machine and record[ing] the results," App. 54, authoritative sources reveal that the matter is not so simple or certain. "In order to perform quantitative analyses satisfactorily and . . . support the results under rigorous examination in court, the analyst must be aware of, and adhere to, good analytical practices and understand what is being done and why." Stafford, Chromatography, in Principles of Forensic Toxicology 92, 114 (B. Levine 2d ed.2006). See also McNair 137 ("Errors that occur in any step can invalidate the best chromatographic analysis, so attention must be paid to all steps."); D. Bartell, M. McMurray, & A. ImObersteg, Attacking and Defending Drunk Driving Tests § 16:80 (2d revision 2010) (stating that 93% of errors in laboratory tests for BAC levels are human errors that occur either before or after machines analyze samples). Even after the machine has produced its printed result, a review of the chromatogram may indicate that the test was not valid. See McNair 207–214.

Nor is the risk of human error so remote as to be negligible. *Amici* inform us, for example, that in neighboring Colorado, a single forensic laboratory produced at least 206 flawed blood-alcohol readings over a three-year span, prompting the dismissal of several criminal prosecutions. See Brief for National Association of

---

[1] Gas chromatography is a widely used scientific method of quantitatively analyzing the constituents of a mixture. See generally H. McNair & J. Miller, Basic Gas Chromatography (2d ed.2009) (hereinafter McNair). Under SLD's standard testing protocol, the analyst extracts two blood samples and inserts them into vials containing an "internal standard" — a chemical additive. App. 53. See McNair 141–142. The analyst then "cap[s] the [two] sample[s]," "crimp[s] them with an aluminum top," and places the vials into the gas chromatograph machine. App. 53–54. Within a few hours, this device produces a printed graph — a chromatogram — along with calculations representing a software-generated interpretation of the data. See Brief for State of New Mexico Dept. of Health, SLD as *Amicus Curiae* 16–17.

Criminal Defense Lawyers et al. as *Amici Curiae* 32–33. An analyst had used improper amounts of the internal standard, causing the chromatograph machine systematically to inflate BAC measurements. The analyst's error, a supervisor said, was "fairly complex." Ensslin, Final Tally on Flawed DUI: 206 Errors, 9 Tossed or Reduced, Colorado Springs Gazette, Apr. 19, 2010, p. 1 (internal quotation marks omitted), available at http://www.gazette.com/articles/report-97354-police-discuss.html. (All Internet materials as visited June 21, 2011, and included in Clerk of Court's case file).

Caylor's report that Bullcoming's BAC was 0.21 supported a prosecution for aggravated DWI, the threshold for which is a BAC of 0.16 grams per hundred milliliters, § 66-8-102(D)(1). The State accordingly charged Bullcoming with this more serious crime.

B

The case was tried to a jury in November 2005, after our decision in *Crawford v. Washington*, 541 U.S. 36, 124 S. Ct. 1354, 158 L. Ed. 2d 177 (2004), but before *Melendez-Diaz*. On the day of trial, the State announced that it would not be calling SLD analyst Curtis Caylor as a witness because he had "very recently [been] put on unpaid leave" for a reason not revealed. 2010-NMSC-007, ¶ 8, 147 N.M. 487, 226 P.3d 1, 6 (internal quotation marks omitted); App. 58. A startled defense counsel objected. The prosecution, she complained, had never disclosed, until trial commenced, that the witness "out there . . . [was] not the analyst [of Bullcoming's sample]." *Id.*, at 46. Counsel stated that, "had [she] known that the analyst [who tested Bullcoming's blood] was not available," her opening, indeed, her entire defense "may very well have been dramatically different." *Id.*, at 47. The State, however, proposed to introduce Caylor's finding as a "business record" during the testimony of Gerasimos Razatos, an SLD scientist who had neither observed nor reviewed Caylor's analysis. *Id.*, at 44.

Bullcoming's counsel opposed the State's proposal. *Id.*, at 44–45. Without Caylor's testimony, defense counsel maintained, introduction of the analyst's finding would violate Bullcoming's Sixth Amendment right "to be confronted with the witnesses against him." *Ibid.* The trial court overruled the objection, *id.*, at 46–47, and admitted the SLD report as a business record, *id.*, at 44–46, 57. The jury convicted Bullcoming of aggravated DWI, and the New Mexico Court of Appeals upheld the conviction, concluding that "the blood alcohol report in the present case was non-testimonial and prepared routinely with guarantees of trustworthiness." 2008-NMCA-097, ¶ 17, 144 N.M. 546, 189 P.3d 679, 685.

C

While Bullcoming's appeal was pending before the New Mexico Supreme Court, this Court decided *Melendez-Diaz*. In that case, "[t]he Massachusetts courts [had] admitted into evidence affidavits reporting the results of forensic analysis which showed that material seized by the police and connected to the defendant was cocaine." 557 U.S., at 307, 129 S. Ct., at 2530. Those affidavits, the Court held, were " 'testimonial,' rendering the affiants 'witnesses' subject to the defendant's right of confrontation under the Sixth Amendment." *Ibid.*

In light of *Melendez-Diaz*, the New Mexico Supreme Court acknowledged that the blood-alcohol report introduced at Bullcoming's trial qualified as testimonial evidence. Like the affidavits in *Melendez-Diaz*, the court observed, the report was "functionally identical to live, in-court testimony, doing precisely what a witness does on direct examination." 226 P.3d, at 8 (quoting *Melendez-Diaz*, 557 U.S., at 310, 129 S. Ct., at 2532). Nevertheless, for two reasons, the court held that admission of the report did not violate the Confrontation Clause.

First, the court said certifying analyst Caylor "was a mere scrivener," who "simply transcribed the results generated by the gas chromatograph machine." 226 P.3d, at 8–9. Second, SLD analyst Razatos, although he did not participate in testing Bullcoming's blood, "qualified as an expert witness with respect to the gas chromatograph machine." *Id.*, at 9. "Razatos provided live, in-court testimony," the court stated, "and, thus, was available for cross-examination regarding the operation of the . . . machine, the results of [Bullcoming's] BAC test, and the SLD's established laboratory procedures." *Ibid.* Razatos' testimony was crucial, the court explained, because Bullcoming could not cross-examine the machine or the written report. *Id.*, at 10. But "[Bullcoming's] right of confrontation was preserved," the court concluded, because Razatos was a qualified analyst, able to serve as a surrogate for Caylor. *Ibid.*

We granted certiorari to address this question: Does the Confrontation Clause permit the prosecution to introduce a forensic laboratory report containing a testimonial certification, made in order to prove a fact at a criminal trial, through the in-court testimony of an analyst who did not sign the certification or personally perform or observe the performance of the test reported in the certification. 561 U.S. [1058], 131 S. Ct. 62, 177 L. Ed. 2d 1152 (2010). Our answer is in line with controlling precedent: As a rule, if an out-of-court statement is testimonial in nature, it may not be introduced against the accused at trial unless the witness who made the statement is unavailable and the accused has had a prior opportunity to confront that witness. Because the New Mexico Supreme Court permitted the testimonial statement of one witness, *i.e.*, Caylor, to enter into evidence through the in-court testimony of a second person, *i.e.*, Razatos, we reverse that court's judgment.

II

* * *

The State in the instant case never asserted that the analyst who signed the certification, Curtis Caylor, was unavailable. The record showed only that Caylor was placed on unpaid leave for an undisclosed reason. See *supra*, at 2711–2712. Nor did Bullcoming have an opportunity to cross-examine Caylor. *Crawford* and *Melendez-Diaz*, therefore, weigh heavily in Bullcoming's favor. The New Mexico Supreme Court, however, although recognizing that the SLD report was testimonial for purposes of the Confrontation Clause, considered SLD analyst Razatos an adequate substitute for Caylor. We explain first why Razatos' appearance did not meet the Confrontation Clause requirement. We next address the State's argument that the SLD report ranks as "nontestimonial," and therefore "[was] not subject to the Confrontation Clause" in the first place. Brief for Respondent 7 (capitalization omitted).

A

The New Mexico Supreme Court held surrogate testimony adequate to satisfy the Confrontation Clause in this case because analyst Caylor "simply transcribed the resul[t] generated by the gas chromatograph machine," presenting no interpretation and exercising no independent judgment. 226 P.3d, at 8. Bullcoming's "true 'accuser,' " the court said, was the machine, while testing analyst Caylor's role was that of "mere scrivener." *Id.*, at 9. Caylor's certification, however, reported more than a machine-generated number. See *supra*, at 2710–2711.

Caylor certified that he received Bullcoming's blood sample intact with the seal unbroken, that he checked to make sure that the forensic report number and the sample number "correspond[ed]," and that he performed on Bullcoming's sample a particular test, adhering to a precise protocol. App. 62–65. He further represented, by leaving the "[r]emarks" section of the report blank, that no "circumstance or condition . . . affect[ed] the integrity of the sample or . . . the validity of the analysis." *Id.*, at 62, 65. These representations, relating to past events and human actions not revealed in raw, machine-produced data, are meet for cross-examination.

The potential ramifications of the New Mexico Supreme Court's reasoning, furthermore, raise red flags. Most witnesses, after all, testify to their observations of factual conditions or events, *e.g.*, "the light was green," "the hour was noon." Such witnesses may record, on the spot, what they observed. Suppose a police report recorded an objective fact — Bullcoming's counsel posited the address above the front door of a house or the read-out of a radar gun. See Brief for Petitioner 35. Could an officer other than the one who saw the number on the house or gun present the information in court — so long as that officer was equipped to testify about any technology the observing officer deployed and the police department's standard operating procedures? As our precedent makes plain, the answer is emphatically "No." See *Davis v. Washington*, 547 U.S. 813, 826, 126 S. Ct. 2266, 165 L. Ed. 2d 224 (2006) (Confrontation Clause may not be "evaded by having a note-taking police [officer] recite the . . . testimony of the declarant" (emphasis deleted)); *Melendez-Diaz*, 557 U.S., at 335, 129 S. Ct., at 2546 (Kennedy, J., dissenting) ("The Court made clear in *Davis* that it will not permit the testimonial statement of one witness to enter into evidence through the in-court testimony of a second.").

The New Mexico Supreme Court stated that the number registered by the gas chromatograph machine called for no interpretation or exercise of independent judgment on Caylor's part. 226 P.3d, at 8–9. We have already explained that Caylor certified to more than a machine-generated number. See *supra*, at 2710–2711. In any event, the comparative reliability of an analyst's testimonial report drawn from machine-produced data does not overcome the Sixth Amendment bar. This Court settled in *Crawford* that the "obviou[s] reliab[ility]" of a testimonial statement does not dispense with the Confrontation Clause. 541 U.S., at 62, 124 S. Ct. 1354; see *id.*, at 61, 124 S. Ct. 1354 (Clause "commands, not that evidence be reliable, but that reliability be assessed in a particular manner: by testing [the evidence] in the crucible of cross-examination"). Accordingly, the analysts who write reports that the prosecution introduces must be made available for confrontation even if they possess "the scientific acumen of Mme. Curie and the veracity of Mother Teresa." *Melendez-Diaz*, 557 U.S., at 319, n. 6, 129 S. Ct., at 2537, n. 6.

B

Recognizing that admission of the blood-alcohol analysis depended on "live, in-court testimony [by] a qualified analyst," 226 P.3d, at 10, the New Mexico Supreme Court believed that Razatos could substitute for Caylor because Razatos "qualified as an expert witness with respect to the gas chromatograph machine and the SLD's laboratory procedures," *id.*, at 9. But surrogate testimony of the kind Razatos was equipped to give could not convey what Caylor knew or observed about the events his certification concerned, *i.e.*, the particular test and testing process he employed.[7] Nor could such surrogate testimony expose any lapses or lies on the certifying analyst's part.[8] Significant here, Razatos had no knowledge of the reason why Caylor had been placed on unpaid leave. With Caylor on the stand, Bullcoming's counsel could have asked questions designed to reveal whether incompetence, evasiveness, or dishonesty accounted for Caylor's removal from his work station. Notable in this regard, the State never asserted that Caylor was "unavailable"; the prosecution conveyed only that Caylor was on uncompensated leave. Nor did the State assert that Razatos had any "independent opinion" concerning Bullcoming's BAC. See Brief for Respondent 58, n. 15. In this light, Caylor's live testimony could hardly be typed "a hollow formality," *post*, at 2724.

*   *   *

IV

The State and its *amici* urge that unbending application of the Confrontation Clause to forensic evidence would impose an undue burden on the prosecution. This argument, also advanced in the dissent, *post*, at 2727–2728, largely repeats a refrain rehearsed and rejected in *Melendez-Diaz*. See 557 U.S., at [324–328], 129 S. Ct., at 2540–2542. The constitutional requirement, we reiterate, "may not [be] disregard[ed] . . . at our convenience," *id.*, at [314], 129 S. Ct., at 2540, and the predictions of dire consequences, we again observe, are dubious, see *id.*, at [324–328], 129 S. Ct., at 2540–2541.

New Mexico law, it bears emphasis, requires the laboratory to preserve samples, which can be retested by other analysts, see N.M. Admin. Code § 7.33.2.15(A)(4)-(6)

---

[7] We do not question that analyst Caylor, in common with other analysts employed by SLD, likely would not recall a particular test, given the number of tests each analyst conducts and the standard procedure followed in testing. Even so, Caylor's testimony under oath would have enabled Bullcoming's counsel to raise before a jury questions concerning Caylor's proficiency, the care he took in performing his work, and his veracity. In particular, Bullcoming's counsel likely would have inquired on cross-examination why Caylor had been placed on unpaid leave.

[8] At Bullcoming's trial, Razatos acknowledged that "you don't know unless you actually observe the analysis that someone else conducts, whether they followed th[e] protocol in every instance." App. 59.

(2010), available at http://www.nmcpr.state.nm.us/nmac/_title07/T07C033.htm, and neither party questions SLD's compliance with that requirement. Retesting "is almost always an option . . . in [DWI] cases," Brief for Public Defender Service for District of Columbia et al. as *Amici Curiae* 25 (hereinafter PDS Brief), and the State had that option here: New Mexico could have avoided any Confrontation Clause problem by asking Razatos to retest the sample, and then testify to the results of his retest rather than to the results of a test he did not conduct or observe.

Notably, New Mexico advocates retesting as an effective means to preserve a defendant's confrontation right "when the [out-of-court] statement is raw data or a mere transcription of raw data onto a public record." Brief for Respondent 53–54. But the State would require the defendant to initiate retesting. *Id.*, at 55; *post*, at 2724 (defense "remains free to . . . . call and examine the technician who performed a test"), *post*, at 2727 ("free retesting" is available to defendants). The prosecution, however, bears the burden of proof. *Melendez-Diaz*, 557 U.S., at [324–326], 129 S. Ct., at 2540 ("[T]he Confrontation Clause imposes a burden on the prosecution to present its witnesses, not on the defendant to bring those adverse witnesses into court."). Hence the obligation to propel retesting when the original analyst is unavailable is the State's, not the defendant's. See *Taylor v. Illinois*, 484 U.S. 400, 410, n. 14, 108 S. Ct. 646, 98 L. Ed. 2d 798 (1988) (Confrontation Clause's requirements apply "in every case, whether or not the defendant seeks to rebut the case against him or to present a case of his own").

Furthermore, notice-and-demand procedures, long in effect in many jurisdictions, can reduce burdens on forensic laboratories. Statutes governing these procedures typically "render . . . otherwise hearsay forensic reports admissible[,] while specifically preserving a defendant's right to demand that the prosecution call the author/ analyst of [the] report." PDS Brief 9; see *Melendez-Diaz*, 557 U.S., at [326–328], 129 S. Ct., at 2541 (observing that notice-and-demand statutes "permit the defendant to assert (or forfeit by silence) his Confrontation Clause right after receiving notice of the prosecution's intent to use a forensic analyst's report").

Even before this Court's decision in *Crawford*, moreover, it was common prosecutorial practice to call the forensic analyst to testify. Prosecutors did so "to bolster the persuasive power of [the State's] case[,] . . . [even] when the defense would have preferred that the analyst did *not* testify." PDS Brief 8.

We note also the "small fraction of . . . cases" that "actually proceed to trial." *Melendez-Diaz*, 557 U.S., at [324–331], 129 S. Ct., at 2540 (citing estimate that "nearly 95% of convictions in state and federal courts are obtained via guilty plea"). And, "when cases in which forensic analysis has been conducted [do] go to trial," defendants "regularly . . . [stipulate] to the admission of [the] analysis." PDS Brief 20. "[A]s a result, analysts testify in only a very small percentage of cases," *id.*, at 21, for "[i]t is unlikely that defense counsel will insist on live testimony whose effect will be merely to highlight rather than cast doubt upon the forensic analysis." *Melendez-Diaz*, 557 U.S., at [327–330], 129 S. Ct., at 2542.

Tellingly, in jurisdictions in which "it is the [acknowledged] job of . . . analysts to testify in court . . . about their test results," the sky has not fallen. PDS Brief 23. State and municipal laboratories "make operational and staffing decisions" to facilitate analysts' appearance at trial. *Ibid.* Prosecutors schedule trial dates to accommodate analysts' availability, and trial courts liberally grant continuances when unexpected conflicts arise. *Id.*, at 24–25. In rare cases in which the analyst is no longer employed by the laboratory at the time of trial, "the prosecution makes the effort to bring that analyst . . . to court." *Id.*, at 25. And, as is the practice in New Mexico, see *supra*, at 2717–2718, laboratories ordinarily retain additional samples, enabling them to run tests again when necessary.[10]

*   *   *

For the reasons stated, the judgment of the New Mexico Supreme Court is reversed, and the case is remanded for further proceedings not inconsistent with this opinion.

JUSTICE KENNEDY, with whom THE CHIEF JUSTICE, JUSTICE BREYER, and JUSTICE ALITO join, dissenting.

The Sixth Amendment Confrontation Clause binds the States and the National Government. *Pointer v. Texas*, 380 U.S. 400, 403, 85 S. Ct. 1065, 13 L. Ed. 2d 923 (1965). Two Terms ago, in a case arising from a state criminal prosecution, the Court interpreted the Clause to mandate exclusion of a laboratory report sought to be introduced based on the authority of that report's own sworn statement that a test had been performed yielding the results as shown. *Melendez-Diaz v. Massachusetts*, 557 U.S. 305, 129 S. Ct. 2527, 174 L. Ed. 2d 314 (2009). The Court's opinion in that case held the report inadmissible because no one was present at trial to testify to its contents.

Whether or not one agrees with the reasoning and the result in *Melendez-Diaz*, the Court today takes the new and serious misstep of extending that holding to instances like this one. Here a knowledgeable representative of the laboratory was present to testify and to explain the lab's processes and the details of the report; but because he was not the analyst who filled out part of the form and transcribed onto it the test result from a machine printout, the Court finds a confrontation violation. . . .

I

Before today, the Court had not held that the Confrontation Clause bars admission of scientific findings when an employee of the testing laboratory authenticates the findings, testifies to the laboratory's methods and practices, and is cross-examined at trial. . . .

The procedures followed here, but now invalidated by the Court, make live testimony rather than the "solemnity" of a document the primary reason to credit the laboratory's scientific results. *Id.*, at 838, 126 S. Ct. 2266. Unlike *Melendez-Diaz*,

---

[10] The dissent refers, selectively, to experience in Los Angeles, *post*, at 2727–2728, but overlooks experience documented in Michigan. In that State, post-*Melendez-Diaz*, the increase in in-court analyst testimony has been slight. Compare PDS Brief 21 (in 2006, analysts provided testimony for only 0.7% of all tests), with Michigan State Police, Forensic Science Division, available at http://www.michigan.gov/msp/0,1607,7-123-1593_3800-15901--,00.html (in 2010, analysts provided testimony for approximately 1% of all tests).

where the jury was asked to credit a laboratory's findings based solely on documents that were "quite plainly affidavits," 557 U.S., at [329–332], 129 S. Ct., at 2543 (Thomas, J., concurring) (internal quotation marks omitted), here the signature, heading, or legend on the document were routine authentication elements for a report that would be assessed and explained by in-court testimony subject to full cross-examination. The only sworn statement at issue was that of the witness who was present and who testified.

*   *   *

In the New Mexico scientific laboratory where the blood sample was processed, analyses are run in batches involving 40–60 samples. Each sample is identified by a computer-generated number that is not linked back to the file containing the name of the person from whom the sample came until after all testing is completed. See New Mexico Scientific Laboratory Brief 26. The analysis is mechanically performed by the gas chromatograph, which may operate — as in this case — after all the laboratory employees leave for the day. See *id.*, at 17. And whatever the result, it is reported to both law enforcement and the defense. See *id.*, at 36.

The representative of the testing laboratory whom the prosecution called was a scientific analyst named Mr. Razatos. He testified that he "help[ed] in overseeing the administration of these programs throughout the State," and he was qualified to answer questions concerning each of these steps. App. 49. The Court has held that the government need not produce at trial "everyone who laid hands on the evidence," *Melendez-Diaz, supra*, at [310–312], n. 1, 129 S. Ct., at 2532, n. 1. Here, the defense used the opportunity in cross-examination to highlight the absence at trial of certain laboratory employees. Under questioning by Bullcoming's attorney, Razatos acknowledged that his name did not appear on the report; that he did not receive the sample, perform the analysis, or complete the review; and that he did not know the reason for some personnel decisions. App. 58. After weighing arguments from defense counsel concerning these admissions, and after considering the testimony of Mr. Razatos, who knew the laboratory's protocols and processes, the jury found no reasonable doubt as to the defendant's guilt.

In these circumstances, requiring the State to call the technician who filled out a form and recorded the results of a test is a hollow formality. The defense remains free to challenge any and all forensic evidence. It may call and examine the technician who performed a test. And it may call other expert witnesses to explain that tests are not always reliable or that the technician might have made a mistake. The jury can then decide whether to credit the test, as it did here. The States, furthermore, can assess the progress of scientific testing and enact or adopt statutes and rules to ensure that only reliable evidence is admitted. Rejecting these commonsense arguments and the concept that reliability is a legitimate concern, the Court today takes a different course. It once more assumes for itself a central role in mandating detailed evidentiary rules, thereby extending and confirming *Melendez-Diaz's* "vast potential to disrupt criminal procedures." 557 U.S., at [331–333], 129 S. Ct., at 2544 (Kennedy, J., dissenting).

*   *   *

III

Crawford itself does not compel today's conclusion. It is true, as *Crawford* confirmed, that the Confrontation Clause seeks in part to bar the government from replicating trial procedures outside of public view. See 541 U.S., at 50, 124 S. Ct. 1354; *Bryant, supra,* at 357–360, 131 S. Ct., at 1155–1156. *Crawford* explained that the basic purpose of the Clause was to address the sort of abuses exemplified at the notorious treason trial of Sir Walter Raleigh. 541 U.S., at 51, 124 S. Ct. 1354. On this view the Clause operates to bar admission of out-of-court statements obtained through formal interrogation in preparation for trial. The danger is that innocent defendants may be convicted on the basis of unreliable, untested statements by those who observed — or claimed to have observed — preparation for or commission of the crime. And, of course, those statements might not have been uttered at all or — even if spoken — might not have been true.

A rule that bars testimony of that sort, however, provides neither cause nor necessity to impose a constitutional bar on the admission of impartial lab reports like the instant one, reports prepared by experienced technicians in laboratories that follow professional norms and scientific protocols. In addition to the constitutional right to call witnesses in his own defense, the defendant in this case was already protected by checks on potential prosecutorial abuse such as free retesting for defendants; result-blind issuance of reports; testing by an independent agency; routine processes performed en masse, which reduce opportunities for targeted bias; and labs operating pursuant to scientific and professional norms and oversight. See Brief for Respondent 5, 14–15, 41, 54; New Mexico Scientific Laboratory Brief 2, 26.

*   *   *

Today's opinion repeats an assertion from *Melendez-Diaz* that its decision will not "impose an undue burden on the prosecution." *Ante,* at 2717 (plurality opinion). But evidence to the contrary already has begun to mount. See, *e.g.,* Brief for State of California et al. as *Amici Curiae* 7 (explaining that the 10 toxicologists for the Los Angeles Police Department spent 782 hours at 261 court appearances during a 1-year period); Brief for National District Attorneys Association et al. as *Amici Curiae* 23 (observing that each blood-alcohol analyst in California processes 3,220 cases per year on average). New and more rigorous empirical studies further detailing the unfortunate effects of *Melendez-Diaz* are sure to be forthcoming.

In the meantime, New Mexico's experience exemplifies the problems ahead. From 2008 to 2010, subpoenas requiring New Mexico analysts to testify in impaired-driving cases rose 71%, to 1,600 — or 8 or 9 every workday. New Mexico Scientific Laboratory Brief 2. In a State that is the Nation's fifth largest by area and that employs just 10 total analysts, *id.,* at 3, each analyst in blood alcohol cases recently received 200 subpoenas per year, *id.,* at 33. The analysts now must travel great distances on most working days. The result has been, in the laboratory's words, "chaotic." *Id.,* at 5. And if the defense raises an objection and the analyst is tied up in another court proceeding; or on leave; or absent; or delayed in transit; or no longer employed; or ill; or no longer living, the defense gets a windfall. As a result, good defense attorneys will object in ever-greater numbers to a prosecution failure or inability to produce laboratory analysts at trial. The concomitant increases in subpoenas will further impede the state laboratory's ability to keep pace with its obligations. Scarce state resources could be committed to other urgent needs in the criminal justice system.

*   *   *

Seven years after its initiation, it bears remembering that the *Crawford* approach was not preordained. This Court's missteps have produced an interpretation of the word "witness" at odds with its meaning elsewhere in the Constitution, including elsewhere in the Sixth Amendment, see Amar, Sixth Amendment First Principles, 84 Geo. L.J. 641, 647, 691–696 (1996), and at odds with the sound administration of justice. It is time to return to solid ground. A proper place to begin that return is to decline to extend *Melendez-Diaz* to bar the reliable, commonsense evidentiary framework the State sought to follow in this case.

[F]   Due Process Limits on the Rules of Evidence

[1]   The Renowned Case of *Chambers v. Mississippi*

Hearsay is not always used by the government against criminal defendants. Criminal defendants also find hearsay useful in their defense. The Supreme Court's opinion in *Chambers v. Mississippi*, below, addresses the constitutional limits on evidence rules that prevent criminal defendants from presenting evidence in their defense. Although the Court's opinion addresses the court's refusal to allow the defendant to introduce a third-party's declaration against interest, the Court's analysis casts a constitutional shadow over all evidentiary rules that would preclude the defendant's use of any relevant evidence that possesses strong indicia of reliability.

CHAMBERS v. MISSISSIPPI
United States Supreme Court
410 U.S. 284 (1973)

MR. JUSTICE POWELL delivered the opinion of the Court.

Petitioner, Leon Chambers, was tried by a jury in a Mississippi trial court and convicted of murdering a policeman. The jury assessed punishment at life imprisonment, and the Mississippi Supreme Court affirmed, one justice dissenting. . . . Subsequently, the petition for certiorari was granted . . . to consider whether petitioner's trial was conducted in accord with principles of due process under the Fourteenth Amendment. We conclude that it was not.

I

The events that led to petitioner's prosecution for murder occurred in the small town of Woodville in southern Mississippi. On Saturday evening, June 14, 1969, two Woodville policemen, James Forman and Aaron "Sonny" Liberty, entered a local bar and pool hall to execute a warrant for the arrest of a youth named C.C. Jackson.

Jackson resisted and a hostile crowd of some 50 or 60 persons gathered. The officer's first attempt to handcuff Jackson was frustrated when 20 or 25 men in the crowd intervened and wrestled him free. Forman then radioed for assistance and Liberty removed his riot gun, a 12 gauge sawed-off shotgun, from the car. Three deputy sheriffs arrived shortly thereafter and the officers again attempted to make their arrest. Once more, the officers were attacked by the onlookers and during the commotion five or six pistol shots were fired. Forman was looking in a different direction when the shooting began, but immediately saw that Liberty had been shot several times in the back. Before Liberty died, he turned around and fired both barrels of his riot gun into an alley in the area from which the shots appeared to have come. The first shot was wild and high and scattered the crowd standing at the face of the alley. Liberty appeared, however, to take more deliberate aim before the second shot and hit one of the men in the crowd in the back of the head and neck as he ran down the alley. That man was Leon Chambers.

Officer Forman could not see from his vantage point who shot Liberty or whether Liberty's shots hit anyone. One of the deputy sheriffs testified at trial that he was standing several feet from Liberty and that he saw Chambers shoot him. Another deputy sheriff stated that, although he could not see whether Chambers had a gun in his hand, he did see Chambers "break his arm down" shortly before the shots were fired. The officers who saw Chambers fall testified that they thought he was dead but they made no effort at that time either to examine him or to search for the murder weapon. Instead, they attended to Liberty, who was placed in the police car and taken to a hospital where he was declared dead on arrival. A subsequent autopsy showed that he had been hit with four bullets from a .22-caliber revolver.

Shortly after the shooting, three of Chambers' friends discovered that he was not yet dead. James Williams, Berkley Turner, and Gable McDonald loaded him into a car and transported him to the same hospital. Later that night, when the county sheriff discovered that Chambers was still alive, a guard was placed outside his room. Chambers was subsequently charged with Liberty's murder. He pleaded not guilty and has asserted his innocence throughout.

The story of Leon Chambers is intertwined with the story of another man, Gable McDonald. McDonald, a lifelong resident of Woodville, was in the crowd on the evening of Liberty's death. Sometime shortly after that day, he left his wife in Woodville and moved to Louisiana and found a job at a sugar mill. In November of that same year, he returned to Woodville when his wife informed him that an acquaintance of his, known as Reverend Stokes, wanted to see him. Stokes owned a gas station in Natchez, Mississippi, several miles north of Woodville, and upon his return McDonald went to see him. After talking to Stokes, McDonald agreed to make a statement to Chambers' attorneys, who maintained offices in Natchez. Two days later, he appeared at the attorneys' offices and gave a sworn confession that he shot Officer Liberty. He also stated that he had already told a friend of his, James Williams, that he shot Liberty. He said that he used his own pistol, a nine-shot .22-caliber revolver, which he had discarded shortly after the shooting. In response to questions from Chambers' attorneys, McDonald affirmed that his confession was voluntary and that no one had compelled him to come to them. Once the confession had been transcribed, signed, and witnessed, McDonald was turned over to the local police authorities and was placed in jail.

One month later, at a preliminary hearing, McDonald repudiated his prior sworn confession. He testified that Stokes had persuaded him to confess that he shot Liberty. He claimed that Stokes had promised that he would not go to jail and that he would share in the proceeds of a lawsuit that Chambers would bring against the town of Woodville. On examination by his own attorney and on cross-examination by the State, McDonald swore that he had not been at the scene when Liberty was shot but had been down the street drinking beer in a cafe with a friend, Berkley Turner. When he and Turner heard the shooting, he testified, they walked up the street and found Chambers lying in the alley. He, Turner, and Williams took Chambers to the hospital. McDonald further testified at the preliminary hearing that he did not know what had happened, that there was no discussion about the shooting either going to or coming back from the hospital, and that it was not until the next day that he learned that Chambers had been felled by a blast from Liberty's riot gun. In addition, McDonald stated that while he once owned a .22-caliber pistol he had lost it many months before the shooting and did not own or possess a weapon at that time. The local justice of the peace accepted McDonald's repudiation and released him from custody. The local authorities undertook no further investigation of his possible involvement.

Chambers' case came on for trial in October of the next year. At trial, he endeavored to develop two grounds of defense. He first attempted to show that he did not shoot Liberty. Only one officer testified that he actually saw Chambers fire the shots. Although three officers saw Liberty shoot Chambers and testified that they assumed he was shooting his attacker, none of them examined Chambers to see whether he was still alive or whether he possessed a gun. Indeed, no weapon was ever recovered from the scene and there was no proof that Chambers had ever owned a .22-caliber pistol. One witness testified that he was standing in the street near where Liberty was shot, that he was looking at Chambers when the shooting began, and he was sure that Chambers did not fire the shots.

Petitioner's second defense was that Gable McDonald had shot Officer Liberty. He was only partially successful, however, in his efforts to bring before the jury the testimony supporting this defense. Sam Hardin, a lifelong friend of McDonald's, testified that he saw McDonald shoot Liberty. A second witness, one of Liberty's cousins, testified that he saw McDonald immediately after the shooting with a pistol in his hand. In addition to the testimony of these two witnesses, Chambers endeavored to show the jury that McDonald had repeatedly confessed to the crime. Chambers attempted to prove that McDonald had admitted responsibility for the murder on four separate occasions, once when he gave the sworn statement to Chambers' counsel and three other times prior to that occasion in private conversations with friends.

In large measure, he was thwarted in his attempt to present this portion of his defense by the strict application of certain Mississippi rules of evidence. Chambers asserts in this Court, as he did unsuccessfully in his motion for new trial and on appeal to the State Supreme Court, that the application of these evidentiary rules rendered his trial fundamentally unfair and deprived him of due process of law. It is necessary, therefore, to examine carefully the rulings made during the trial.

II

Chambers filed a pretrial motion requesting the court to order McDonald to appear. Chambers also sought a ruling at that time that, if the State itself chose not to call McDonald, he be allowed to call him as an adverse witness. Attached to the motion were copies of McDonald's sworn confession and of the transcript of his preliminary hearing at which he repudiated that confession. The trial court granted the motion requiring McDonald to appear but reserved ruling on the adverse-witness motion. At trial, after the State failed to put McDonald on the stand, Chambers called McDonald, laid a predicate for the introduction of his sworn out-of-court confession, had it admitted into evidence, and read it to the jury. The State, upon cross-examination, elicited from McDonald the fact that he had repudiated his prior confession. McDonald further testified, as he had at the preliminary hearing, that he did not shoot Liberty, and that he confessed to the crime only on the promise of Reverend Stokes that he would not go to jail and would share in a sizable tort recovery from the town. He also retold his own story of his actions on the evening of the shooting, including his visit to the cafe down the street, his absence from the scene during the critical period, and his subsequent trip to the hospital with Chambers.

At the conclusion of the State's cross-examination, Chambers renewed his motion to examine McDonald as an adverse witness. The trial court denied the motion, stating: "He may be hostile, but he is not adverse in the sense of the word, so your request will be overruled." On appeal, the State Supreme Court upheld the trial court's ruling, finding that "McDonald's testimony was not adverse to appellant" because "[n]owhere did he point the finger at Chambers . . . ."

Defeated in his attempt to challenge directly McDonald's renunciation of his prior confession, Chambers sought to introduce testimony of the three witnesses to whom McDonald had admitted that he shot the officer. The first of these, Sam Hardin, would have testified that, on the night of the shooting, he spent the late evening hours with McDonald at a friend's house after their return from the hospital and that, while driving McDonald home later that night, McDonald stated that he shot Liberty. The State objected to the admission of this testimony on the ground that it was hearsay. The trial court sustained the objection.

Berkley Turner, the friend with whom McDonald said he was drinking beer when the shooting occurred, was then called to testify. In the jury's presence, and without objection, he testified that he had not been in the cafe that Saturday and had not had any beers with McDonald. The jury was then excused. In the absence of the jury, Turner recounted his conversations with McDonald while they were riding with James Williams to take Chambers to the hospital. When asked whether McDonald said anything regarding the shooting of Liberty, Turner testified that McDonald told him that he "shot him." Turner further stated that one week later, when he met McDonald at a friend's house, McDonald reminded him of their prior conversation and urged Turner not to "mess him up." Petitioner argued to the court that, especially where there was other proof in the case that was corroborative of these out-of-court statements, Turner's testimony as to McDonald's self-incriminating remarks should have been admitted as an exception to the hearsay rule. Again, the trial court sustained the State's objection.

The third witness, Albert Carter, was McDonald's neighbor. They had been friends for about 25 years. Although Carter had not been in Woodville on the evening of the shooting, he stated that he learned about it the next morning from McDonald. That same day, he and McDonald walked out to a well near McDonald's house and there McDonald told him that he was the one who shot Officer Liberty. Carter testified that McDonald also told him that he had disposed of the .22-caliber revolver later that night. He further testified that several weeks after the shooting, he accompanied McDonald to Natchez where McDonald purchased another .22 pistol to replace the one he had discarded.[28] The jury was not allowed to hear Carter's testimony. Chambers urged that these statements were admissible, the State objected, and the court sustained the objection. On appeal, the State Supreme Court approved the lower court's exclusion of these witnesses' testimony on hearsay grounds . . . .

In sum, then, this was Chambers' predicament. As a consequence of the combination of Mississippi's "party witness" or "voucher" rule and its hearsay rule, he was unable either to cross-examine McDonald or to present witnesses in his own behalf who would have discredited McDonald's repudiation and demonstrated his complicity. Chambers had, however, chipped away at the fringes of McDonald's story by introducing admissible testimony from other sources indicating that he had not been seen in the cafe where he said he was when the shooting started, that he had not been having beer with Turner, and that he possessed a .22 pistol at the time of the crime. But all that remained from McDonald's own testimony was a single written confession countered by an arguably acceptable renunciation. Chambers' defense was far less persuasive than it might have been had he been given an opportunity to subject McDonald's statements to cross-examination or had the other confessions been admitted.

III

The right of an accused in a criminal trial to due process is, in essence, the right to a fair opportunity to defend against the State's accusations. The rights to confront and cross-examine witnesses and to call witnesses in one's own behalf have long been recognized as essential to due process. Mr. Justice Black, writing for the Court in *In re Oliver*, 333 U.S. 257, 273 (1948), identified these rights as among the minimum essentials of a fair trial:

> A person's right to reasonable notice of a charge against him, and an opportunity to be heard in his defense — a right to his day in court — are basic in our system of jurisprudence; and these rights include, as a minimum, a right to examine the witnesses against him, to offer testimony, and to be represented by counsel.

. . . Both of these elements of a fair trial are implicated in the present case.

---

[28] (Court's original footnote 5.) A gun dealer from Natchez testified that McDonald had made two purchases. The witness' business records indicated that McDonald purchased a nine-shot .22-caliber revolver about a year prior to the murder. He purchased a different style .22 three weeks after Liberty's death.

A

Chambers was denied an opportunity to subject McDonald's damning repudiation and alibi to cross-examination. He was not allowed to test the witness' recollection, to probe into the details of his alibi, or to "sift" his conscience so that the jury might judge for itself whether McDonald's testimony was worthy of belief. . . . The right of cross-examination is more than a desirable rule of trial procedure. It is implicit in the constitutional right of confrontation, and helps assure the "accuracy of the truth-determining process . . . ." It is, indeed, "an essential and fundamental requirement for the kind of fair trial which is this country's constitutional goal . . . ." Of course, the right to confront and to cross-examine is not absolute and may, in appropriate cases, bow to accommodate other legitimate interests in the criminal trial process. . . . But its denial or significant diminution calls into question the ultimate " 'integrity of the fact-finding process' " and requires that the competing interest be closely examined . . . .

In this case, petitioner's request to cross-examine McDonald was denied on the basis of a Mississippi common law rule that a party may not impeach his own witness. The rule rests on the presumption — without regard to the circumstances of the particular case — that a party who calls a witness "vouches for his credibility . . . ." Although the historical origins of the "voucher" rule are uncertain, it appears to be a remnant of primitive English trial practice in which "oath-takers" or "compurgators" were called to stand behind a particular party's position in any controversy. Their assertions were strictly partisan and, quite unlike witnesses in criminal trials today, their role bore little relation to be impartial ascertainment of the facts.

Whatever validity the "voucher" rule may have once enjoyed, and apart from whatever usefulness it retains today in the civil trial process, it bears little present relationship to the realities of the criminal process. It might have been logical for the early common law to require a party to vouch for the credibility of witnesses he brought before the jury to affirm his veracity. Having selected them especially for that purpose, the party might reasonably be expected to stand firmly behind their testimony. But in modern criminal trials, defendants are rarely able to select their witnesses: they must take them where they find them. Moreover, as applied in this case, the "voucher" rule's impact was doubly harmful to Chambers' efforts to develop his defense. Not only was he precluded from cross-examining McDonald, but, as the State conceded at oral argument, he was also restricted in the scope of his direct examination by the rule's corollary requirement that the party calling the witness is bound by anything he might say. He was, therefore, effectively prevented from exploring the circumstances of McDonald's three prior oral confessions and from challenging the renunciation of the written confession.

In this Court, Mississippi has not sought to defend the rule or explain its underlying rationale. Nor has it contended that its rule should override the accused's right of confrontation. Instead, it argues that there is no incompatibility between the rule and Chambers' rights because no right of confrontation exists unless the testifying witness is "adverse" to the accused. The State's brief asserts that the "right of confrontation applies to witnesses *'against'* an accused." Relying on the trial court's determination that McDonald was not "adverse," and on the

State Supreme Court's holding that McDonald did not "point the finger at Chambers," the State contends that Chambers' constitutional right was not involved.

The argument that McDonald's testimony was not "adverse" to, or "against," Chambers is not convincing. The State's proof at trial excluded the theory that more than one person participated in the shooting of Liberty. To the extent that McDonald's sworn confession tended to incriminate him, it tended also to exculpate Chambers. And, in the circumstances of this case, McDonald's retraction inculpated Chambers to the same extent that it exculpated McDonald. It can hardly be disputed that McDonald's testimony was in fact seriously adverse to Chambers. The availability of the right to confront and to cross-examine those who give damaging testimony against the accused has never been held to depend on whether the witness was initially put on the stand by the accused or by the State. We reject the notion that a right of such substance in the criminal process may be governed by that technicality or by any narrow and unrealistic definition of the word "against." The "voucher" rule, as applied in this case, plainly interfered with Chambers' right to defend against the State's charges.

B

We need not decide, however, whether this error alone would occasion reversal since Chambers' claimed denial of due process rests on the ultimate impact of that error when viewed in conjunction with the trial court's refusal to allow him to introduce the testimony of Hardin, Turner, and Carter. Each would have testified to the statements purportedly made by McDonald, on three separate occasions shortly after the crime, naming himself as the murderer. The State Supreme Court approved the exclusion of this evidence on the ground that it was hearsay.

The hearsay rule, which has long been recognized and respected by virtually every State, is based on experience and grounded in the notion that untrustworthy evidence should not be presented to the triers of fact. Out-of-court statements are traditionally excluded because they lack the conventional indicia of reliability: they are usually not made under oath or other circumstances that impress the speaker with the solemnity of his statements; the declarant's word is not subject to cross-examination; and he is not available in order that his demeanor and credibility may be assessed by the jury. . . . A number of exceptions have developed over the years to allow admission of hearsay statements made under circumstances that tend to assure reliability and thereby compensate for the absence of the oath and opportunity for cross-examination. Among the most prevalent of these exceptions is the one applicable to declarations against interest — an exception founded on the assumption that a person is unlikely to fabricate a statement against his own interest at the time it is made. Mississippi recognizes this exception but applies it only to declarations against pecuniary interest. It recognizes no such exception for declarations, like McDonald's in this case, that are against the penal interest of the declarant . . . .

This materialistic limitation on the declaration against interest hearsay exception appears to be accepted by most States in their criminal trial processes, although a number of States have discarded it. Declarations against penal interest have also been excluded in federal courts under the authority of *Donnelly v. United States*, 228 U.S. 243, 272–273, (1913), although exclusion would not be required under the newly proposed Federal Rules of Evidence. Exclusion, where the limitation prevails, is usually premised on the view that admission would lead to the frequent presentation of perjured testimony to the jury. It is believed that confessions of criminal activity are often motivated by extraneous considerations and, therefore, are not as inherently reliable as statements against pecuniary or proprietary interest. While that rationale has been the subject of considerable scholarly criticism, we need not decide in this case whether, under other circumstances, it might serve some valid state purpose by excluding untrustworthy testimony.

The hearsay statements involved in this case were originally made and subsequently offered at trial under circumstances that provided considerable assurance of their reliability. First, each of McDonald's confessions was made spontaneously to a close acquaintance shortly after the murder had occurred. Second, each one was corroborated by some other evidence in the case — McDonald's sworn confession, the testimony of an eyewitness to the shooting, the testimony that McDonald was seen with a gun immediately after the shooting, and proof of his prior ownership of a .22-caliber revolver and subsequent purchase of a new weapon. The sheer number of independent confessions provided additional corroboration for each. Third, whatever may be the parameters of the penal-interest rationale,[29] each confession here was in a very real sense self-incriminatory and unquestionably against interest. . . . McDonald stood to benefit nothing by disclosing his role in the shooting to any of his three friends and he must have been aware of the possibility that disclosure would lead to criminal prosecution. Indeed, after telling Turner of his involvement, he subsequently urged Turner not to "mess him up." Finally, if there was any question about the truthfulness of the extrajudicial statements, McDonald was present in the courtroom and was under oath. He could have been cross-examined by the State, and his demeanor and responses weighed by the jury. . . . The availability of McDonald significantly distinguishes this case from the prior Mississippi precedent, . . . and from the *Donnelly*-type situation, since in both cases the declarant was unavailable at the time of trial.

Few rights are more fundamental than that of an accused to present witnesses in his own defense. . . . In the exercise of this right, the accused, as is required of the State, must comply with established rules of procedure and evidence designed to assure both fairness and reliability in the ascertainment of guilt and innocence. Although perhaps no rule of evidence has been more respected or more frequently applied in jury trials than that applicable to the exclusion of hearsay, exceptions tailored to allow the introduction of evidence which in fact is likely to be trustworthy have long existed. The testimony rejected by the trial court here bore persuasive

---

[29] (Court's original footnote 20.) The Mississippi case which refused to adopt a hearsay exception for declarations against penal interest concerned an out-of-court declarant who purportedly stated that he had committed the murder with which his brother had been charged. The Mississippi Supreme Court believed that the declarant might have been motivated by a desire to free his brother rather than by any compulsion of guilt. The Court also noted that the declarant had fled, was unavailable for cross-examination, and might well have known at the time he made the statement that he would not suffer for it. *Brown v. State*, 99 Miss. 719, 55 So. 961 (1911). There is, in the present case, no such basis for doubting McDonald's statements. *See* Note, 43 Miss. L.J. 122, 127–129 (1972).

assurances of trustworthiness and thus was well within the basic rationale of the exception for declarations against interest. That testimony also was critical to Chambers' defense. In these circumstances, where constitutional rights directly affecting the ascertainment of guilt are implicated, the hearsay rule may not be applied mechanistically to defeat the ends of justice.

We conclude that the exclusion of this critical evidence, coupled with the State's refusal to permit Chambers to cross-examine McDonald, denied him a trial in accord with traditional and fundamental standards of due process. In reaching this judgment, we establish no new principles of constitutional law. Nor does our holding signal any diminution in the respect traditionally accorded to the States in the establishment and implementation of their own criminal trial rules and procedures. Rather, we hold quite simply that under the facts and circumstances of this case the rulings of the trial court deprived Chambers of a fair trial.

The judgment is reversed and the case is remanded to the Supreme Court of Mississippi for further proceedings not inconsistent with this opinion.

[2] The Backstory and Aftermath of *Chambers*

It is probably of little surprise that *Chambers* involves race — this seems to be the pattern of Supreme Court cases involving criminal cases during this era, especially cases coming out of the south. A surprising aspect of *Chambers* is that the story is probably the reverse of what you might expect. The officer was black and the defendant was white. *See* Emily Prifogle, *Law and Local Activism: Uncovering the Civil Rights History of* Chambers v. Mississippi, 101 Calif. L. Rev. 445 (2013).

Chambers v. Mississippi is part of the canon of evidence law. It is taught in virtually every class on the subject and certainly appears in every treatise. Yet the case has not had much impact beyond providing Chambers a new trial. Four justices in *Montana v. Egelhoff*, 518 U.S. 37, 52 (1996), concluded that the opinion had little precedential value as it was "an exercise in highly case-specific error correction." Academic commentators have similarly observed the limited impact of this decision.

The Sixth Amendment's Lost Clause: Unearthing Compulsory Process
Janet C. Hoeffel
2002 Wis. L. Rev. 1275 (2002)

Despite some rhetoric to the contrary, the Court attempts to shrink the right to little more than a right to put on evidence, as long as it comports with the rules of evidence. Extended to its logical conclusion, the constitutional right to present a defense becomes superfluous as a tool of fair process.

Placing Chambers in this camp may surprise some. Chambers has always been hailed as a victory for the accused's right to present a defense. Indeed, the Court used the right to strike down an evidentiary rule, but the holding is so cramped and narrow that Chambers does not allow room for a similar case to recur . . . .

The uniquely compelling facts of Chambers drove the Court's fact-bound analysis. In discussing the hearsay rule preventing the admission of declarations against penal interest, the Court began what appeared to be a Washington-type analysis: it set out the State's overbroad rationale for the rule as the belief that declarations against penal interest would lead to perjured testimony and were unreliable since confessions of criminal activity were often motivated by extraneous considerations. Then, however, the Court abandoned any further broadly applicable analysis and simply explored why the out-of-court statements in this case bore "considerable assurance of their reliability," hence defeating the rationale of the rule . . . .

The Court emphasized, "[i]n reaching this judgment, we establish no new principles of constitutional law . . . [r]ather, we hold quite simply that under the facts and circumstances of this case the rulings of the trial court deprived Chambers of a fair trial." The circumstances of the out-of-court confessions were so peculiar, specific and well-substantiated in Chambers that any court could easily distinguish the facts in its own case. Indeed, one would be hard-pressed to locate a single case that cites Chambers as precedent for its holding.

Chambers also offered no solid advice on the method a court could use for tackling the clash of the Constitution and evidentiary rules. After stating that the "denial or significant diminution [of the defendant's constitutional rights] calls into question the ultimate 'integrity of the fact-finding process' and requires that the competing interest be closely examined," the Court gave no guidance on how to analyze or measure that competing interest.

§ 5.03 HEARSAY EXCEPTIONS FOR WHICH DECLARANT'S UNAVAILABILITY IS IMMATERIAL

[A] Excited Utterances

Federal Rules of Evidence: Rule 803(2)

[1] Excited Utterances Generally

The *Brown* decision considers issues that are crucial to admitting an excited utterance — the degree of the declarant's excitement, spontaneity, and the opportunity to reflect.

BROWN v. UNITED STATES
District of Columbia Court of Appeals
27 A.3d 127 (2011)

OBERLY, ASSOCIATE JUDGE:

A jury convicted appellant Martin "Tony" Brown of second-degree murder while armed, based largely on statements made by the victim, his grandfather. Appellant argues that (1) the trial court erred by admitting the victim's statements under the excited utterance exception to the hearsay rule, (2) admission of the statements violated his rights under the Confrontation Clause, and (3) there was insufficient evidence to prove that appellant was armed with a dangerous weapon. We hold that appellant's claims lack merit and affirm his conviction.

I. Factual Background

Appellant lived with his eighty-nine-year-old grandfather, Howard Brown, who was last seen uninjured in his home on December 7, 2006, sometime between noon and 1:00 p.m. At about 5:00 p.m. on that date, Brown was found lying on the floor in a "massive amount" of his own blood, with his head "busted open" (with three deep gashes), still bleeding from his open wounds, and with his "ear hanging off." He had a telephone receiver in his hand. His initial sounds as he spoke to the first neighbors on the scene (Chris Irby and Malanda Mias) were only grunts. After the neighbors found Brown, the scene became "chaotic" and "frightening," as one neighbor was "screaming pretty violently" and others were yelling hysterically, loud enough to be heard by the 911 operator and in the neighboring house. When neighbor Patricia Johnson, a nursing assistant, arrived on the scene she took Brown's pulse and, finding none, thought he was dead, but he then opened his eyes and she spoke to him, "trying to orient" him. Johnson testified that when she asked Brown how he was feeling, he said, "I'm not doing so good," and that when she asked Brown what had happened, he said he did not know. When she then asked him who had done this to him, Brown "responded with 'Tony' " (appellant's nickname). Mias testified at trial that she, too, "asked [Brown] who did this to him," and that he "sound [ed] like he was trying to catch his breath" and said "Tony." Johnson kept talking to Brown to keep him focused and to prevent him from lapsing into unconsciousness. Asked whether Brown seemed dazed or in shock, Johnson answered that he appeared to be in shock.

Alan Trimble, a paramedic who arrived on the scene within five to ten minutes of the neighbors finding Brown, testified that the blood-drenched carpet in the house squished under his feet as he walked near Brown. Trimble testified that Brown was still bleeding at the time and was coming in and out of consciousness, and that, in the ambulance on the way to the hospital, Brown, who continued to bleed from his head, was "very emotional," "obviously in pain," and "in a lot of distress." Neighbor Shirron Spivey testified at trial that she rode to the hospital in the front of the ambulance and that she heard one of the ambulance staff ask Brown "who did this" and he "told them Tony did it."[1] The trauma surgeon who attended Brown at the hospital had to perform "urgent repair" to keep Brown, who still "had severe bleeding," from "exsanguinating . . . [i]n layman's terms, bleeding to death." Later, when doctors, police, or family members asked him what happened, Brown said he did not know or "did not know him[.]"

Sometime after December 7, 2006, Spivey talked to appellant about visiting his grandfather in the hospital, and appellant told her, "I can't go see my grandfather. How do you think I would feel if he recognized me?" He added, "I'll go if you go with me." In January 2007, appellant told Elsie Spivey, Shirron's sister, that he had killed the person who assaulted his grandfather, and he threatened to "duct tape [her]

---

[1] Trimble confirmed that, in the ambulance, he asked Brown who had assaulted him and that Brown was able to speak, but Trimble could not remember what Brown said in response to the question.

mouth" and "put [her] in the garage," because she had been talking about appellant "doing this to his grandpa."[2] The government also presented evidence that appellant may have believed (mistakenly, it seems) that he would inherit the house in which he and his grandfather lived upon his grandfather's death. On March 28, 2007, Brown died as a result of his injuries.

The court held a hearing prior to appellant's trial to determine whether statements made by the victim were admissible under the excited utterance or dying declaration exceptions to the rule against hearsay and ruled that the statements were admissible as excited utterances.

II. Legal Principles

"Whether a statement constitutes [an excited] utterance depends upon the particular facts of each case." *Smith v. United States*, 666 A.2d 1216, 1222 (D.C. 1995). Where, as here, the issue was preserved for appeal, our review focuses on the different aspects of the trial court's decision-fact — finding, application of the law, and exercise of discretion. *See Dutch v. United States, 997 A.2d 685, 689 (D.C. 2010)* ("We review a trial court's decision to admit hearsay evidence for abuse of discretion; however, the determination of whether a statement falls under an exception to the hearsay rule is a legal conclusion, which we review *de novo*."); *Odemns v. United States*, 901 A.2d 770, 776 (D.C. 2006) ("the underlying factual findings are reviewed under the 'clearly erroneous' standard and . . . the decision whether to admit or exclude the proffered statement, based on those factual findings, is reviewed for abuse of discretion"). In determining whether the trial court abused its discretion, we consider "not only whether the judge erred in the ruling but also whether the error was of a magnitude requiring reversal." *Newman v. United States*, 705 A.2d 246, 257 (D.C. 1997) (citing *(James) Johnson v. United States*, 398 A.2d 354, 366–67 (D.C. 1979)).

Our precedents establish that for a statement to be admissible under the excited utterance exception, "it must be characterized as a spontaneous declaration, not only tending to explain the act or occurrence with which it is connected but also indicating a spontaneous utterance of a thought while under the influence of that act or occurrence, with no opportunity for premeditation or deliberation." *Watts v. Smith*, 226 A.2d 160, 163 (D.C. 1967); *Harris v. United States*, 373 A.2d 590, 593 (D.C. 1977) (concluding that "the trial court did not err in finding that during the time decedent was in the emergency room he was substantially and predominantly under the influence of the trauma which had been inflicted upon him, and that the declarations which he made at the time . . . do qualify as exceptions to the hearsay rule under spontaneous declarations" (quotation marks omitted)). We have said that for the excited utterance exception to apply, there must be "(1) the presence of a serious occurrence which causes a state of nervous excitement *or* physical shock in the declarant, (2) a declaration made within a reasonably short period of time after the occurrence so as to assure that the declarant has not reflected upon his statement or premeditated or constructed it, and (3) the presence of circumstances,

---

[2] Appellant was charged with threatening Elsie Spivey, but the jury was unable to reach a verdict on this count.

which in their totality suggest spontaneity and sincerity of the remark." *Odemns*, 901 A.2d at 776 (emphasis added).

III. Brown's Statements Were Properly Admitted as Excited Utterances

The trial court found that the record showed "a serious occurrence which would cause anyone to be in a state of nervous excitement or physical shock"; that Brown was "barely conscious [and] bleeding profusely on the floor of his home" and that his breathing was "difficult"; and that "Brown was in a state of physical shock, if not also nervous excitement at 5:00 p.m. that afternoon." The court also found that "in the totality of the circumstances, there [was] an indication of spontaneity and sincerity" in Brown's utterance, because he was "barely conscious" when his neighbors arrived, and because he was "still extremely seriously injured, and physically, if not mentally impaired at the time and [his neighbors] were the first persons to whom he had a chance to utter any words after the experience of the assault against him." The court also found "very little in this record to suggest that [Brown] was in any position to do anything by way of premeditation, calculation, construction, or any other fabrication of a falsehood." The court found it "important" that the "first persons [Brown] saw after being beaten, were the ones to whom he made the utterance immediately as soon as he was nudged into consciousness." The testimony summarized above supports each of the court's factual findings, and the record also supports the trial court's legal conclusion that Brown's statements identifying "Tony" as his attacker were admissible as excited utterances.

There is no dispute that there was a serious and startling occurrence that caused Brown to sustain his injuries. There also should be no dispute that Brown, who was bleeding profusely, barely conscious, grunting, and needing to "catch his breath" at the time he uttered "Tony," remained "under the influence of" that serious occurrence when he spoke to his neighbors and to the paramedic. *See* Watts, 226 A.2d at 163. The uncontroverted testimony that Brown "looked like he was in shock" when Johnson roused him (just before he responded to her "who did this" question by answering "Tony"), was "very emotional," "obviously in pain," and "in a lot of distress" when in the ambulance, and had nearly bled to death, establishes that the serious occurrence caused both "nervous excitement" and "physical shock in the declarant."[3] *Odemns*, 901 A.2d at 776. To be sure, Trimble described Brown's demeanor in the ambulance, minutes *after* Brown made the utterance "Tony" to Johnson and to Mias while still lying on the floor. Although our dissenting colleague urges that "[o]ur focus must be on [Brown's] condition 'at the time the statement was uttered' " (*post* at 138 n. 1, quoting *Alston v. United States*, 462 A.2d 1122, 1127 (D.C. 1983)), there is no reason to think that Brown's demeanor was any different a few minutes earlier, and no reason why *Alston* precludes us from relying, in

---

[3] As to "nervous excitement," although Johnson is a nursing assistant, nothing in the record suggests that she intended her comment about Brown looking like he was in shock in a medical sense. She made her statement "I guess you can say he looked like he was in shock" in answer to the inquiry, "He was dazed, right? He looked like he was in shock?" The context suggests that Johnson used the term "shock" according to what the dissenting opinion considers the "general" definition: "sudden agitation or excitement of emotional or mental sensibilities." Websters New Intl. Dict. 2317 (2d ed.1952). Contrary to the dissent's view, on this record we can scarcely call this an "uncritical use" or "rote recitation[]" of the word "shock." *Post* at 138.

appropriate circumstances, on a description of a declarant's mental state moments after he spoke to draw inferences about the declarant's state of mind at the time he spoke. Especially in light of Johnson's testimony about Brown looking like he was in shock, it is reasonable to infer that Brown was rendered nervous and excited upon being nudged into consciousness and oriented to his situation at the same time that his neighbors were screaming hysterically and as he recognized that he was "not doing so good." Further, as noted above, Spivey testified that she heard Brown respond while in the ambulance that "Tony did it" — a response Brown gave at the time when, according to Trimble, he was highly emotional, in distress, and in pain.

Johnson, who testified that she felt no pulse in Brown's neck and thought he was dead, recounted that when he opened his eyes, he "scared the hell" out of her and that she had to "catch up with [her] heart" and get over her "initial shock" before she could speak to Brown. This does not prove that Brown felt the same emotions, but it is an additional factor supporting an inference, that he, too, would have been "scared" and in "shock" as he was nudged into consciousness, heard neighbors screaming, and witnessed Johnson's reaction.

The trial court recognized that an excited utterance must be made "within a reasonably short period of time after the occurrence so as to assure that the declarant has not reflected upon his statement or premeditated or constructed it," *Odemns*, 901 A.2d at 776, but did not make a finding as to the approximate time when the attack occurred.[4] However, "the time element is not controlling." *Alston*, 462 A.2d at 1127; *see also Snowden v. United States*, 2 App. D.C. 89, 94 (D.C. Cir. 1893) ("[N]o inflexible rule as to the length of interval between the act charged against the accused and the declaration of the complaining party, can be laid down as established."). Further, an inference that the attack occurred closer to 5 p.m. (the time when Brown was found) than to noon (the last time he was seen before the attack) would not have been unreasonable. Notably, defense counsel urged the jury to conclude, from the facts that the carpet squished with blood when the paramedic walked on it and that Brown had not bled out despite his gaping wounds, that the attack occurred closer to 5 p.m. than to noon. Although the government could not discount the possibility that five hours passed between the attack and Brown's utterances, for the excited utterance exception to apply, the time between a startling event and an utterance need not be proven beyond a reasonable doubt or even by clear and convincing evidence. *See United States v. Woodfolk*, 656 A.2d 1145, 1150 n. 14 (D.C. 1995) (noting that "preponderance of the evidence is the proper standard of proof for determining the admissibility of an excited utterance").

In any event, we have recognized that even where a startling occurrence happened hours before an utterance was made, the utterance may be admissible under the exception if it was made when an ensuing event made the speaker newly aware of the gravity of the occurrence. *See Price v. United States*, 545 A.2d 1219, 1226 (D.C. 1988) (utterance was admissible even though it was made three hours after declarant witnessed a shooting, because it was made during a phone call in which declarant learned that her lover had been severely injured during the

---

[4] The court recognized that the attack "might have been as recently as five minutes before the arrival of his neighbors. It might have been as early as around noon when he was seen uninjured by a witness. And it might have been anytime in between those two times."

gunfire). The evidence supports our conclusion that Brown's having been nudged into consciousness while his neighbors were screaming hysterically, and his recognition at that time that he was not "doing so good," constituted a startling event. His utterances followed *that* "event"[5] quite closely in time, without his having time for deliberation or fabrication, and, in light of his physical condition, without his having the capacity (as the trial court put it) "to do anything by way of premeditation, calculation, construction, or any other fabrication of a falsehood" before he responded to questioning.[6] *Cf. People v. Robinson*, 41 A.D.3d 1183, 837 N.Y.S.2d 800, 801 (2007) (reasoning that where victim made a statement when he was barely conscious and had difficulty breathing, the evidence established that his statement was "not made under the impetus of studied reflection") (citation and quotation marks omitted); *see also* 2 McCormick, Evidence § 272 at 255 (6th ed. 2006) (noting that the rationale for the excited utterance exception "lies in the special reliability that is furnished when excitement suspends the declarant's powers of reflection and fabrication"). However long Brown might have been conscious and able to deliberate after the attack and before he was found (which apparently was not long enough for him to use the telephone receiver that was in his hand to dial 911 or otherwise call for help), the evidence supports an inference that his utterances when his neighbors found him barely conscious would not likely have resulted from deliberation.[7] *Cf. State v. Ward*, 2001 Wash. App. LEXIS 485, at *23–24 (Wash. Ct. App. Mar. 26, 2001) (reasoning that even though evidence showed that victim had time to fabricate before he placed a 911 call and did actually lie to the 911 operator, his statement to police officer who arrived on the scene was admissible as an excited utterance, because by that time the victim had nearly bled to death, had no pulse, and was barely conscious, such that his statement to the officer "was unlikely to have resulted from the exercise of choice or judgment").

Finally, the trial court did not err by concluding that the circumstances in their totality suggested that Brown's utterances were spontaneous and sincere. The foregoing discussion explains why the utterances appear to have been spontaneous — meaning not "the result of reflective thought" and not "made under the impetus of reflection." *Simmons v. United States*, 945 A.2d 1183, 1189 (D.C. 2008). In addition, the trial court found — and the record supports a finding — that "all [Brown] said over and over" was "Tony." Mindful of the preponderance-of-the-evidence standard that the trial court was required to apply and the "clearly erroneous" standard that applies to our review, we see no reason to disturb the trial

---

[5] The dissent contends that Brown's utterances do not "relate to" this second startling event. *Post* at 139. But Brown uttered "Tony" in response to questioners nudging him back to consciousness as he lay in a pool of his own blood on his living room floor, and asking "who did this to him" as at least one of his neighbors was "screaming . . . violently." "The startling event or condition need not be the principal act underlying the case. For example, a later startling event may trigger associations with an original trauma, recreating the stress earlier produced and causing the person to exclaim spontaneously." *State v. DiBartolo*, 2000 Wash. App. LEXIS 1195, at *41–42 (Wash. Ct. App. July 13, 2000) (citations and quotation marks omitted). That aptly describes the situation here.

[6] Thus, we agree with the government's argument that "because of Mr. Brown's great pain, and because he had just been startled into consciousness by Ms. Johnson, . . . he lacked the opportunity to reflect on his statement."

[7] Such an inference was well within the ken of the trial court, without the need for expert testimony or additional proof.

court's conclusion that although Brown's utterance "Tony" might have been the "product of confusion" or might have indicated "who he wanted to contact," the "most likely interpretation" is that "he meant . . . that Tony is the one who did it." The dissenting opinion cites the evidence (from the portion of the trial transcript that discusses what could be heard on the tape of the 911 call) that, around the time when Brown uttered the word "Tony" in response to Johnson's question "who did this to you," neighbors were asking, "Where's Tony?" and "hollering" up and down the stairs to see whether Tony was in the house. *Post* at 140. Our colleague concludes that this circumstance renders Brown's utterance "Tony" untrustworthy — as if what Brown did was parrot the name he heard called. *Id.* But Mias and Spivey, too, testified that they heard Brown answer "Tony" to the question "who did this?," and there was no evidence that the name "Tony" was being spoken by others at the time when Brown made the utterances that Mias and Spivey heard. In addition, there was testimony that others' names were also spoken to Brown — Johnson testified that she said to Brown, "this is Pat, and Sherrin [sic] is here" — but no evidence was presented that Brown parroted those names.

Finally, we are not troubled by the inconsistent responses to inquiries about the identity of his assailant that Brown provided while in the hospital. For purposes of determining the admissibility of the utterances Brown made immediately after he was discovered, we are not entitled to judge trustworthiness by comparing those utterances to other evidence. "We have held that [when determining whether statements fall within the excited utterance exception] the trial court *should focus on the circumstances ascertainable upon utterance of the statement,* not on other circumstances that might become known at trial or hearing." *Reyes v. United States,* 933 A.2d 785, 790 n. 6 (D.C. 2007) (emphasis added) (citing *Crawford v. Washington,* 541 U.S. 36, 124 S. Ct. 1354, 158 L. Ed. 2d 177 (2004) ("hearsay evidence used to convict a defendant must possess the indicia of reliability by virtue of its inherent trustworthiness, not by reference to other evidence at trial . . . . Thus, we must look to the statement itself and to the circumstances of its delivery for evidence of its inherent reliability.")).[8] Therefore, for purposes of the analysis of the admissibility of Brown's utterance, the trial testimony by Brown's granddaughter — that when she visited Brown at various hospitals after the attack he told her that he did not know who had attacked him — is irrelevant. Nor is it relevant for purposes of the excited utterance analysis that, weeks after the attack, when asked by his doctor at the National Rehabilitation Hospital whether he "knew what had happened," Brown said that "he did not know anything that happened."[9] This evidence was, of course, grist for the defense at trial, but it does not render erroneous the trial court's decision to admit as excited utterances the first utterances Brown made when his neighbors found him bleeding and barely conscious.[10]

---

[8] *Cf. People v. Fratello,* 92 N.Y.2d 565, 572, 684 N.Y.S.2d 149, 706 N.E.2d 1173 (N.Y. 1998) (recognizing the analogous principle that "[g]enerally, the bias of an excited utterance declarant functions as a basis for impeachment of the declaration, thus pertinent to the weight, rather than admissibility of the declaration" (citing 6 Wigmore, Evidence § 1751 at 224 (Chadbourn Rev. 1976))).

[9] This latter evidence was not actually inconsistent with what Brown said to Johnson when he was found: He answered "I don't know" in response to the question "what happened?," but responded with "Tony" when asked "Who did this to you?"

[10] Appellant's argument that Brown's statements were testimonial (and therefore barred by the

* * *

V. Conclusion

Because the trial court did not abuse its discretion by admitting Brown's statements as excited utterances, and appellant's other arguments are meritless, we affirm the judgment of conviction.

So ordered.

FISHER, ASSOCIATE JUDGE, dissenting:

"[T]he excited utterance exception is just that — an *exception* to the hearsay rule, and it should not be construed so broadly that it renders the hearsay rule ineffectual." *State v. Branch*, 182 N.J. 338, 865 A.2d 673, 690 (2005) (emphasis in original). "Over the years, some of our cases have imported a measure of flexibility into the admissibility calculus of spontaneous exclamations and excited utterances, but the fundamentals of the doctrine have remained intact." *Odemns v. United States*, 901 A.2d 770, 778 (D.C. 2006). On this record, I conclude that Mr. Brown's utterances were neither spontaneous nor excited, and they should have been excluded.

I. Governing Principles

To satisfy the spontaneous (or excited) utterance exception, the proponent of the evidence must show:

> (1) the presence of a serious occurrence which causes a state of nervous excitement or physical shock in the declarant, (2) a declaration made within a reasonably short period of time after the occurrence so as to assure that the declarant has not reflected upon his statement or premeditated or constructed it, and (3) the presence of circumstances, which in their totality suggest spontaneity and sincerity of the remark.

In re L.L., 974 A.2d 859, 863 (D.C. 2009) (quoting *Odemns*, 901 A.2d at 776). All "three factors . . . *must* be established before a statement may be admitted" under the exception. *Lewis v. United States*, 938 A.2d 771, 775 (D.C. 2007) (emphasis added); *see Simmons v. United States*, 945 A.2d 1183, 1187 (D.C. 2008) ("the proponent of evidence offered as an excited utterance *must* show" three factors) (emphasis added).

This hearsay exception is premised on the theory that

> under certain external circumstances of physical shock, a stress of nervous excitement may be produced which stills the reflective faculties and

---

Confrontation Clause) is also without merit. Brown's statements were made to his neighbors (and not police), the setting was frantic and informal, he was severely injured, and the "statements and actions of both [Brown] and [his] interrogators" do not indicate that "a person in [Brown's] situation would have had a 'primary purpose' 'to establish or prove past events potentially relevant to later criminal prosecution.'" *Michigan v. Bryant*, 562 U.S. 344, 131 S. Ct. 1143, 1160, 1165, 179 L. Ed. 2d 93 (2011) (quoting *Davis v. Washington*, 547 U.S. 813, 822, 126 S. Ct. 2266, 165 L. Ed. 2d 224 (2006)).

removes their control, so that the utterance which then occurs is a spontaneous and sincere response to the actual sensations and perceptions already produced by the external shock. Since this utterance is made under the immediate and uncontrolled domination of the senses, . . . the utterance may be taken as particularly trustworthy[.]

6 Wigmore, Evidence § 1747 at 195 (Chadbourn Rev. 1976); *Guthrie v. United States*, 92 U.S. App. D.C. 361, 364, 207 F.2d 19, 22 (1953) (same); *Beausoliel v. United States*, 71 App. D.C. 111, 113–14, 107 F.2d 292, 294–95 (1939) (same); *see* 2 McCormick, Evidence § 272 at 255 (6th ed.2006) ("rationale for the exception lies in the special reliability that is furnished when excitement suspends the declarant's powers of reflection and fabrication"); *Odemns*, 901 A.2d at 777 n. 6 (quoting *United States v. Edmonds*, 63 F. Supp. 968, 971 (D.D.C. 1946)) (declarations "made while the spell endures are uncontrolled" and are "practically reflex actions"). Accordingly, we have observed that "the earmarks of an excited utterance [are] spontaneity, lack of reflection or forethought, [and] a reflexive response to a traumatic event[.]" *Clarke v. United States*, 943 A.2d 555, 558 (D.C. 2008).

II. Mr. Brown's Statements Were Not Excited Utterances

A. Lack of Excitement

There is no doubt that this brutal assault was a "serious occurrence." *See generally Lyons v. United States*, 683 A.2d 1080, 1083 (D.C. 1996) (collecting cases). But that is not enough; as noted above, the first element of our test for admissibility has two parts. To satisfy this element, there must also be "evidence that the declarant was highly distraught and in shock at the time the statement was uttered . . . ." *Alston v. United States*, 462 A.2d 1122, 1127 (D.C. 1983); *accord, (Damon) Smith v. United States*, 26 A.3d 248, 258 (D.C. 2011). Here, however, Mr. Brown did not exhibit a "state of nervous excitement as a result of the event." *(Raphael) Smith v. United States*, 666 A.2d 1216, 1222 (D.C. 1995).

None of Mr. Brown's neighbors described him as excited, stunned, surprised, or agitated when he said, "Tony."[1] Indeed, although this was probably his first opportunity to tell anyone what happened, Mr. Brown did not blurt out the name "Tony." Instead, Ms. Johnson first asked Mr. Brown, "are you all right? You okay? How are you feeling?" In response, he told her "very plainly" that "I ain't doing so good."[2] Once Ms. Johnson determined that someone had called an ambulance, she

---

[1] *Cf. Reyes v. United States*, 933 A.2d 785, 790 (D.C. 2007) (declarant, who had escaped a robbery/kidnaping minutes before making challenged statements, was "bleed[ing] profusely" and "very upset, highly agitated, scared" and "was rambling off several things at once in a very agitated tone of voice"); *Price v. United States*, 545 A.2d 1219, 1221 (D.C. 1988) ("Sounding as if she was in tears, [declarant] blurted out [challenged statement] and kept repeating the words.").

The paramedic's trial testimony that Mr. Brown was "emotional," "in pain," and in "distress" in the ambulance described his mental state *after* he made the statements to his neighbors. Our focus must be on his condition "at the time the statement was uttered[,]" *Alston*, 462 A.2d at 1127, and the best evidence of that is the testimony of his neighbors-particularly Ms. Johnson.

[2] *Cf. Bryant v. United States*, 859 A.2d 1093, 1100 (D.C. 2004) ("As soon as [declarant] made eye

told Mr. Brown: "Just keep talking to me," "[e]verything is going to be all right, and the ambulance is on [its] way[.]" Ms. Johnson also asked Mr. Brown, "what happened?" He replied, "I don't know." Then she said, "Who did this to you?" At that point, "he responded with 'Tony.'"

To be sure, our governing case law speaks of "a state of nervous excitement *or* physical shock," and Ms. Johnson, a medical professional, stated that Mr. Brown "looked like he was in shock." However, we have cautioned that the requirements of this hearsay exception "cannot be avoided by rote recitations that the declarant was upset or excited or afraid," *Odemns*, 901 A.2d at 777, and the same may be said about uncritical use of the term "shock." The "medical term 'shock' and the legal concept of an 'excited utterance' are not synonymous. The sheer fact that an individual may medically be in shock when he makes a statement does not demand that his statement be legally recognized as an 'excited utterance.'" *Marquez v. State*, 890 P.2d 980, 984–85 (Okla. Crim. App. 1995); *see also Silver Seal Products Co. v. Owens*, 523 P.2d 1091, 1096 (Okla. 1974) (comparing general and medical definitions of shock and concluding that the "imprecise use of the term has brought confusion into our case law concerning *res gestae* statements").

Shock, in the medical sense, means "a sudden disturbance of mental equilibrium" or "a condition of acute peripheral circulatory failure due to derangement of circulatory control or loss of circulating fluid. It is marked by hypotension [decreased blood pressure], coldness of the skin, usually tachycardia [feeble rapid pulse], and often anxiety." Dorland's Illustrated Medical Dictionary 1197 (26th ed. 1981). Here, of course, the evidence showed that Mr. Brown had lost a massive amount of blood. Dr. Street, the trauma surgeon at the Washington Hospital Center, testified that Mr. Brown was "in shock, meaning he had low blood pressure" — not that he was shocked in the sense contemplated by the excited utterance exception.

B. Time to Reflect

The passage of time is equally, if not more, problematic. This "hearsay exception was . . . intended to apply to situations in which the declarant was so excited by the precipitating event that he or she was still 'under the spell of its effect.'" *Odemns*, 901 A.2d at 777 (quoting *Edmonds*, 63 F. Supp. at 971). Thus, while "the time element is not controlling, it is of great significance," *Alston*, 462 A.2d at 1127, "because it assures that the declarant has not reflected or premeditated or constructed the statement[.]" *Reyes*, 933 A.2d at 790 (citing *Alston*, 462 A.2d at 1127).[3] As the time interval expands, on the other hand, the opportunity for

---

contact with [an officer, she] exclaimed that she had been kidnapped and raped. [The officer] described her as 'crying, shaking, [and] very distraught[.]'"); *Lewis*, 938 A.2d at 773–74 (declarant was bleeding from "multiple lacerations" and "excited," "crying," "agitated," and "very, very upset," when officer saw her within minutes of assault; the "first thing she kept [repeating], even before [he] could [ask] if she needed help or not, [was] he was trying to kill me").

[3] *See Jones v. United States*, 829 A.2d 464, 469 (D.C. 2003) ("[The] hearsay exception for spontaneous exclamations applies where the 'utterance is made under the *immediate* and *uncontrolled* domination of the senses,'" so it "may be taken as particularly trustworthy.") (emphasis added) (quoting *Beausoliel*, 71 App.D.C. at 113–14, 107 F.2d at 294–95); *(Raphael) Smith*, 666 A.2d at 1223 ("The critical factor is that the declaration was made within a reasonably short period of time after the occurrence so as to assure

reflection increases and the likelihood of spontaneity decreases.

Here, the government could not establish that the assault occurred fewer than five hours earlier. Thus, this case is "hardly [one] in which the out-of-court statement was made 'immediately upon the hurt received' " or "so soon after the [serious occurrence] that the victim had no opportunity to reflect." *Odemns*, 901 A.2d at 779 (internal quotation marks and citations omitted).

The majority responds to this problem by positing a different, more recent, startling event — when Mr. Brown was "nudged into consciousness," saw Ms. Johnson staring into his eyes, and heard his neighbors screaming. This reasoning ignores the fact that, to be admissible under the excited utterance exception, the statement must relate to and illuminate the serious occurrence which caused the excitement.[4] Contrary to the majority's suggestion, it is not enough that "a later startling event may trigger associations with an original trauma. . . ." *Ante* at 133 n. 5 (citation omitted). This court has "never held that the declarant's *thinking about* a traumatic event is sufficient to trigger an excited utterance." *In re L.L.*, 974 A.2d at 864 (emphasis in original).

A related, but important, problem is that we have no information about Mr. Brown's mental state from the time of the assault until he made the declarations. We do not know, for example, whether he was unconscious for most of the time, and the government did not present expert testimony about whether such serious injuries would necessarily suspend his capacity for reflection. See *United States v. Kearney*, 136 U.S. App. D.C. 328, 333 n.11, 420 F.2d 170, 175 n.11 (1969) ("[W]hat must be taken into account is not only the length of the intervening time period but also an assessment of the declarant's activities and attitudes in the meanwhile. . . ."); 2 McCormick, Evidence § 272 at 258 ("[W]here the time interval between the event and the statement is long enough to permit reflective thought, the statement will [generally] be excluded in the absence of some proof that the declarant did not in fact engage in a reflective thought process.").

C. Lack of Spontaneity

Finally, the totality of circumstances does not suggest the spontaneity of the remarks.[5] Although the fact that Mr. Brown's "statements . . . were made in response to inquiry is not decisive, . . . that fact is entitled to consideration." *Beausoliel*, 71 App.D.C. at 114, 107 F.2d at 295; *see* 2 McCormick, Evidence § 272

---

that the declarant has not reflected upon his statement or premeditated or constructed it.") (citations and internal quotation marks omitted).

[4] *See (Raphael) Smith*, 666 A.2d at 1223 (trial court properly admitted statement to 911 operator as an excited utterance after determining that victim's "excited state was caused by the shock of being robbed at gunpoint," rather than by discussing the robbery with his mother, who insisted that he call 911).

[5] *Cf. Simmons*, 945 A.2d at 1189–90 ("totality of the circumstances reasonably suggests that the elderly declarant's remarks were 'a spontaneous reaction to the exciting event, rather than the result of reflective thought'" where speaker was "agitated and distressed in the immediate aftermath [about fifteen minutes] of a shocking and frightening shooting, and he blurted out his concerns before the commotion subsided to a total stranger who had only asked him if he was 'okay' ") (quoting *Randolph v. United States*, 882 A.2d 210, 217 (D.C. 2005)).

at 258 ("Although not grounds for automatic exclusion, evidence that the statement was made in response to an inquiry . . . is an indication that [it] was the result of reflective thought. Where the time interval permitted such thought, [these] factors might swing the balance in favor of exclusion."). Moreover, Mr. Brown's response to the question, "who did this to you," came after he answered other questions "very plainly." When we factor into our analysis of the three elements the fact that someone asked about and yelled for "Tony" just before Mr. Brown first uttered that name, the overall "trustworthiness of the utterances was somewhat speculative and marginal, at best." *Alston*, 462 A.2d at 1128 (quotation marks omitted).

The government now claims that "[e]ven if Mr. Brown had been conscious for up to five hours between the assault and his statement," he still "lacked the ability to reflect during the time period, because [he] was undeniably in great pain." This argument is based upon a crucial, but untested, assumption — that pain necessarily deprived Mr. Brown of "the ability to reflect during the time period . . . ." I believe this is a matter to be established, not merely assumed.

Some of our precedents have emphasized that the victim was suffering from great pain at the time of the utterance, but they have treated pain as part of the totality of the circumstances, not as a substitute for more comprehensive analysis. In other words, there is no blanket rule for dealing with pain in this context. In some cases involving "external circumstances of physical shock, a stress of nervous excitement may be produced which stills the reflective faculties and removes their control. . . ." *Beausoliel*, 71 App. D.C. at 113, 107 F.2d at 294. On other occasions, grave and painful injuries may be severely debilitating and have a dulling effect upon the mind.

Two cases involving pain appear to help the government. In *Harris v. United States*, 373 A.2d 590, 593 (D.C. 1977), we upheld the admission of a statement made in the emergency room approximately two hours after a shooting, emphasizing that "there was testimony that [the declarant] was in a great deal of pain, and that it was an effort for him to talk." We held that the trial court had not erred in concluding that the victim "was substantially and predominantly under the influence of the trauma . . ." when he spoke. *Id.*

Because of the brevity of discussion in *Harris*, it is difficult to meaningfully compare that case to ours. Among other things, the court thought it important that there "was little time or opportunity" for the declarant to reflect, as the police arrived "shortly [ ]after" the attack and the victim made the remarks within two hours. We concluded, in light of the circumstances, "that his statement was spontaneous." 373 A.2d at 591, 593. The court also emphasized that the declarant "was supplying raw data for analysis rather than giving any conclusions or pointing a finger at any particular individual[,]" which helped "insure the reliability of the admitted statements." *Id.* at 593 & n. 9 (citing *Kearney*, 136 U.S. App. D.C. at 333, 420 F.2d at 175). Mr. Brown's statements, by contrast, have been treated as an accusation.

In *Guthrie*, 92 U.S. App. D.C. at 363–65, 207 F.2d at 21–23, the victim's statement was admitted although as many as eleven hours may have passed after the initial assault. In that case, the court focused on whether the statement "was made during a period of *nervous stress and shock* caused by physical violence. . . ." *Id.* at 364,

207 F.2d at 22 (emphasis added). There was testimony that the victim was at times incoherent and "in a dazed or semi-conscious condition" and "appeared to be in great pain[.]" *Id.* at 365, 207 F.2d at 23. The victim herself "said she was in terrific pain and screamed as she was carried to an ambulance." *Id.* at 363, 207 F.2d at 21.

Another case involving pain provides an instructive contrast to the present record. In *United States v. Glenn*, 154 U.S. App. D.C. 61, 63–65, 473 F.2d 191, 193–95 (1972), the declarant, who "made her statement only minutes after she was fatally stabbed[,]" was "moan[ing] or groan[ing] as though she were in pain[,]" "gasping for breath, and about to lapse into unconsciousness. . . ." She "appeared as though she was trying to scream but could not get enough breath[,]" and repeated, "Help me. Help me. He did it." *Id.* Another witness stated the declarant "was excited, appeared to be looking for help, and was gasping for breath." *Id.* A doctor testified about when the stabbing probably occurred and "concluded that [she] was in pain from her wounds[.]" *Id.* The circuit court decided that "[h]er situation was not conducive to detached reflection and deliberation; on the contrary the only reasonable conclusion from the uncontradicted proof is that when she spoke she was in the grip of high excitement." *Id.* at 65, 473 F.2d at 195.[6]

Here, neither Mr. Brown's actions, nor his words, nor his tone of voice exhibited the stress of nervous excitement. There was ample time for reflection and no expert testified that Mr. Brown's injuries caused a level of pain that precluded delibera- tion.[7] The statement did not escape his lips as soon as he saw his neighbors. Nor was it even volunteered.

In sum, the trial court erred in admitting the statements as excited utterances. Because the decedent's statements "were the only direct evidence presented which identified appellant as the assailant, we cannot say that the admission [of these utterances] did not substantially sway the judgment of the jury in its deliberations." *Alston*, 462 A.2d at 1129 (citing *Kotteakos v. United States*, 328 U.S. 750, 765, 66 S. Ct. 1239, 90 L. Ed. 1557 (1946)). I respectfully dissent.

[2]   A More Easily Satisfied Standard for Alleged Child Sexual Abuse Victims

As you will see in the *Huntington* dissent, there is frequent criticism of the fact that the excited utterance exception is more readily applied to admit statements when the declarant is a young alleged victim of sexual assault.

---

[6] Although there are additional ways of distinguishing our current case from *Harris, Guthrie,* and *Glenn,* I make no claim that all of our case law can be neatly harmonized.

[7] *See State v. Ruelas*, 174 Ariz. 37, 846 P.2d 850, 852, 854–55 (App. 1992) (victim's statement, made an hour and a half after fatal stabbing was not admissible where victim was "alert and awake, but appeared to be in considerable pain" and "was having some trouble breathing"; "There was no other evidence offered to show the mental state of the victim. Nothing in the record indicates that the victim was nervous, excited, or in shock.").

STATE v. HUNTINGTON
Supreme Court of Wisconsin
575 N.W.2d 268 (1998)

ANN WALSH BRADLEY, JUSTICE.

The defendant, Eugene Huntington, seeks review of an unpublished decision of the court of appeals that affirmed his conviction[1] on three counts of felonious sexual assault of a child under age 13. The defendant challenges testimony concerning the child's statements to others as inadmissible hearsay and argues that an expert witness improperly testified concerning another witness's credibility. Because we determine that the evidence of the child's statements to others falls within recognized hearsay exceptions or constitutes harmless error, and because we conclude that the State's expert witness did not offer an impermissible opinion on the truthfulness of another witness, we affirm the decision of the court of appeals.

At approximately 10:00 p.m. on the evening of August 19, 1994, a hysterical 11-year-old Jeri E. called her mother from a friend's home where she had been planning on staying the night. She told her mother that she had been sexually abused by her stepfather, Eugene Huntington. When Jeri's mother arrived to pick Jeri up ten minutes later, she observed that "her girlfriend's mother was holding her, Jeri was sobbing hysterically and she came running to my arms."

Shortly after returning home, Jeri's sister, Dawn, arrived to find both the mother and child crying and upset. Jeri first told her mother and then her sister that on numerous occasions,[2] while staying overnight with him, the defendant would come into her room and rub her "private parts," both above and below her underwear, insert one of his fingers into her vagina, and make her rub his penis. Jeri also alleged that on one occasion the defendant got on top of her and started moving "up and down." In speaking privately with Dawn, Jeri continued to cry and told Dawn how scared she was and that she thought that it was her own fault that her stepfather did this to her. While the evidence is inconclusive on the issue, the last instance of abuse allegedly occurred two weeks prior to Jeri's disclosure of the abuse to her mother and sister.

Within two hours of first revealing the allegations of abuse to her mother, Jeri was taken to the Spooner Police Department and interviewed by Officer Glau. While she seemed initially shy and fidgeted, Jeri repeated her allegations against the defendant. She remained upset and crying and Officer Glau had to stop the interview and wait for Jeri to regain her composure on several occasions.

Almost three months later, Jeri was also examined by Nurse Diane McCormick to determine the extent of her physical abuse, to evaluate the existence of physical injury, and to develop an appropriate plan of treatment and counseling. McCormick is a pediatric nurse practitioner with a subspecialty in child abuse and neglect. She is on staff with Dr. Carolyn Levitt, the State's expert in this case, at the Midwest Children's Resource Center. Jeri was referred to the center by Lori Carter Bell, the

---

[1] Circuit Court for Washburn County, Warren E. Winton, Judge.

[2] Jeri's statements are inconsistent concerning the number of occurrences of sexual abuse.

tribal therapist working with Jeri, and by the Washburn County Social Services Department. As part of her initial examination of Jeri, McCormick interviewed both Jeri's mother and Bell. Both women repeated Jeri's allegations to McCormick.

Three evidentiary rulings are the focus of the defendant's challenge. First, the defendant filed a pretrial motion in limine asking the circuit court to exclude or limit the testimony of potential witnesses, including that of Jeri's mother, her sister, and Officer Glau.[3] The defendant contended that the child's statements to the mother, sister, and officer constituted impermissible hearsay that did not meet the requirements of the excited utterance exception as applied to child abuse cases and explained in *State v. Gerald L.C.*, 194 Wis.2d 548, 535 N.W.2d 777 (Ct. App. 1995). The circuit court denied the motion.

Second, McCormick testified at trial about her examination of Jeri. McCormick repeated her initial conversations with Bell and Jeri's mother, which included the accusations that Jeri made against the defendant. The defense objected that such statements were double hearsay. The circuit court overruled the objection on the grounds that the testimony fell within the medical diagnosis or treatment exception to the hearsay rule.

Finally, the jury also heard testimony from the State's child sexual abuse accommodation expert, Dr. Carolyn Levitt. The State asked Dr. Levitt to comment concerning whether the facts of Jeri's allegations of abuse, such as her delay in reporting the abuse and her inability to quantify the exact number of instances of abuse, were consistent with the behavior of child abuse victims. Despite defense counsel's objection that the questions called for an inadmissible assessment of Jeri's credibility, the circuit court permitted Dr. Levitt to respond.

The jury found the defendant guilty on three of the six counts of felonious sexual assault of a child under age 13 contrary to Wis. Stat. § 948.02(1).[4] The defendant appealed, and the court of appeals affirmed the conviction.

The court of appeals determined that the circuit court properly admitted the statements of the mother, sister, and Officer Glau as excited utterances. The court also rejected the defendant's interpretation of Dr. Levitt's testimony, declaring that Dr. Levitt did not offer an opinion on Jeri's truthfulness. Finally, the court of appeals found Nurse McCormick's testimony admissible. The appellate court determined that Jeri's statements to her mother were excited utterances and that the mother's recital of such statements to McCormick were made for purposes of medical diagnosis or treatment. The court of appeals also determined that both Jeri's statements to Bell and Bell's recounting of those statements to McCormick fell within the medical diagnosis or treatment exception to the hearsay rule.

---

[3] Bell did not testify in the criminal trial.

[4] Wis. Stat. § 948.02 states:

> Sexual Assault of a child. (1) FIRST DEGREE SEXUAL ASSAULT. Whoever has sexual contact or sexual intercourse with a person who has not attained the age of 13 years is guilty of a Class B felony.

Unless otherwise indicated, all future statutory references are to the 1995–96 volumes.

I. Application of Exceptions to Hearsay Rule.

The admission of out-of-court statements pursuant to an exception to the hearsay rule is a determination left to the discretion of the circuit court. *See State v. Moats*, 156 Wis.2d 74, 96, 457 N.W.2d 299 (1990). Because the circuit court is better able to weigh the reliability of circumstances surrounding out-of-court statements, "we look not to see if we agree with the circuit court's determination, but rather whether the trial court exercised its discretion in accordance with accepted legal standards and in accordance with the facts of record." *Grube v. Daun*, 213 Wis.2d 533, 542, 570 N.W.2d 851 (1997)(internal citations omitted); *see also State v. Martinez*, 150 Wis.2d 62, 71, 440 N.W.2d 783 (1989). If we can discern a reasonable basis for its evidentiary decision, then the circuit court has not committed an erroneous exercise of discretion. *See State v. Sorenson*, 143 Wis.2d 226, 240, 421 N.W.2d 77 (1988).

A. Statements of Mother, Sister, and Officer Glau as Excited Utterances.

The State contended at trial that Jeri's statements to these three parties were admissible either as an excited utterance under Wis. Stat. § 908.03(2), or under the general residual hearsay exception set forth in Wis. Stat. § 908.03(24).[5] The circuit court and court of appeals agreed, and held that the statements to Jeri's mother and sister and Officer Glau fell within the excited utterance exception.

"The excited utterance exception . . . is based upon spontaneity and stress" which, like the bases for all exceptions to the hearsay rule, "endow such statements with sufficient trustworthiness to overcome the reasons for exclusion of hearsay." *Martinez*, 150 Wis.2d at 73, 440 N.W.2d 783 (quoting *Christensen v. Economy Fire & Casualty Co.*, 77 Wis.2d 50, 56–57, 252 N.W.2d 81 (1977)). Accordingly, the excited utterance exception has three requirements. First, there must be a "startling event or condition." *Muller v. State*, 94 Wis.2d 450, 466, 289 N.W.2d 570 (1980). Second, the declarant must make an out-of-court statement that relates to the startling event or condition. Finally, the related statement must be made while the declarant is still "under the stress of excitement caused by the event or condition." *Id.* Essentially, "[i]t must be shown that the statement was made so spontaneously or under such psychological or physical pressure or excitement that the rational mind could not interpose itself between the spontaneous statement or utterance stimulated by the event and the event itself." *Martinez*, 150 Wis.2d at 73, 440 N.W.2d 783 (quoting *Wilder v. Classified Risk Ins. Co.*, 47 Wis.2d 286, 292, 177 N.W.2d 109 (1970)).

---

[5] Wis. Stat. § 908.03 declares:

> Hearsay Exceptions; availability of declarant immaterial. The following are not excluded by the hearsay rule, even though the declarant is available as a witness:
>
> . . .
>
> (2) EXCITED UTTERANCE. A statement relating to a startling event or condition made while the declarant was under the stress of excitement caused by the event or condition.
>
> . . .
>
> (24) OTHER EXCEPTIONS. A statement not specifically covered by any of the foregoing exceptions but having comparable circumstantial guarantees of trustworthiness.

This court has also recognized that "there is a compelling need for admission of hearsay arising from young sexual assault victims' inability or refusal to verbally express themselves in court when the child and the perpetrator are sole witnesses to the crime." *Sorenson*, 143 Wis.2d at 243, 421 N.W.2d 77. Accordingly, in some cases, where a child has made an allegation of sexual abuse that does not immediately follow the incident, Wisconsin appellate courts have liberally construed the excited utterance exception to hold such statements sufficiently contemporaneous and spontaneous to fall within the exception. *See Sorenson*, 143 Wis.2d at 244–45, 421 N.W.2d 77; *Moats*, 156 Wis.2d at 97, 457 N.W.2d 299; *see, e.g., State v. Gilbert*, 109 Wis.2d 501, 515, n. 21, 326 N.W.2d 744 (1982); *State v. Padilla*, 110 Wis.2d 414, 420, 329 N.W.2d 263, 266 (Ct. App. 1982).

This application is consistent with the view that "time is measured by the duration of the condition of excitement rather than mere time elapse from the event or condition described." *Moats*, 156 Wis.2d at 97, 457 N.W.2d 299 (quoting *Muller*, 94 Wis.2d at 467, 289 N.W.2d 570). It is supported by the theory that the immature emotional and psychological characteristics of children extend the time in which statements are likely not the result of "conscious fabrication." *Gerald L.C.*, 194 Wis.2d at 556–57, 535 N.W.2d 777 (citing 2 *McCormick on Evidence* § 272.1, at 224 (John W. Strong ed., 4th ed. 1992)).

Allegations of sexual abuse by children are not, however, pro forma guaranteed admission as excited utterances in proceedings against their abusers. In *Gerald L.C.*, the court of appeals rejected the State's offer of a 14-year-old's statement to a police officer that accused the defendant of sexual assault as neither an excited utterance nor sufficiently trustworthy to invoke the residual hearsay exception. In surveying the law of this state for application of the excited utterance exception to child abuse cases, the *Gerald L.C.* court distilled three common factors arguing for its application: (1) the child is under ten years old; (2) the child reports the sexual abuse within one week of the last abusive incident; and (3) the child first reports the abuse to his or her mother. *See Gerald L.C.*, 194 Wis.2d at 557, 535 N.W.2d 777.

The defendant points to the failure of the facts of this case to comport with the factors enunciated in *Gerald L.C.*, and asks us to apply the factors as a bright-line rule. The victim in this case was nine or ten when the abuse allegedly occurred, but did not report the abuse to her mother until the day after her eleventh birthday. She reported the abuse within two weeks of the last event, not one. Finally, while the victim's hysterical description of the abuse to her mother was the factor initiating this case, the victim had at an undetermined earlier time mentioned the abuse to a cousin and to someone's aunt. Neither prior instance is developed in the record.

Such reliance by the defendant on *Gerald L.C.* is misplaced. As the *Gerald L.C.* court explicitly conceded, "[o]f course, these factors by themselves are not dispositive, and the statements may be admissible if the declarant was still under the stress or excitement caused by the event at the time he or she made the statement." *Gerald L.C.*, 194 Wis.2d at 558–59, 535 N.W.2d 777. Factual scenarios may exist that deviate from the *Gerald L.C.* factors, yet which allow a circuit court to reasonably determine that a child was still under the stress of excitement of the abuse. *See Moats*, 156 Wis.2d at 98, 457 N.W.2d 299 (statement of five-year-old to mother more than one week after incident admissible); *State ex rel. Harris v.*

Schmidt, 69 Wis.2d 668, 230 N.W.2d 890 (1975)(statement of five-year-old child to defendant's probation officer 15 days after incident admissible). Accordingly, we decline to declare the *Gerald L.C.* test a bright-line rule. Even though Jeri's hearsay statements do not fall within the three factors, the statements could still demonstrate sufficient trustworthiness to be admitted under the excited utterance exception.

Jeri first related her allegations of sexual abuse against the defendant to her mother and sister approximately two weeks after the last alleged incident. As noted above, we have allowed an interim period to exist between the abuse and report of abuse in child sexual assault cases. *See Moats*, 156 Wis.2d at 97, 457 N.W.2d 299. At the time of Jeri's statement to her mother and sister relating the abuse, Jeri was alternatively described as "crying," "hysterical," "guilt-ridden," and "scared." While the record is devoid of any information concerning Jeri's conduct in the two weeks after the last incident and preceding her report, there are indications that she had just discovered that she would be spending two weeks alone with the defendant.

After acknowledging familiarity with Wisconsin case law on applying the excited utterance exception to child sexual assault cases, the circuit court found Jeri's statements to her mother, sister, and Officer Glau to be an excited utterance "under all the facts and circumstances in this case." Because we conclude that the circuit court reached a reasonable conclusion concerning the statements to the mother and sister after application of the proper standard of law, we do not believe that the circuit court erroneously exercised its discretion. Because a reasonable basis exists for the admission of the mother and sister's testimony about Jeri's statements under the excited utterance exception, we determine that the circuit court properly exercised its discretion.

The admissibility of Jeri's statement to Officer Glau under the excited utterance exception is a closer call. The statements to Officer Glau were made after telling the mother and sister of the abuse and were made as part of an abuse investigation. Nevertheless, the facts suggest a child "still under the stress or excitement caused by the event at the time he or she made the statement." *Gerald L.C.*, 194 Wis.2d at 558–59, 535 N.W.2d 777.

Shortly after reporting the abuse to her mother, Jeri met with Officer Glau. During that two-hour period she continued to be in a state of emotional distress and was described as "crying," "hysterical," and "scared." Officer Glau stated that during his interview she would cry and he repeatedly had to stop the interview to allow Jeri to regain her composure. Because Jeri continued to exhibit indications of emotional distress relating to her abuse during her interview with Officer Glau, her prior rendition of her abuse to her mother and sister does not defeat application of the excited utterance exception to her statements to Officer Glau. Accordingly, we determine that the circuit court also correctly exercised its discretion when holding Jeri's statement to Officer Glau to be an excited utterance.

JANINE P. GESKE, JUSTICE (dissenting).

Our current case law stretches the excited utterance and the general residual hearsay exceptions in child sexual assault cases to the point that hearsay statements admitted under them no longer possess the inherent trustworthiness justifying admissibility.

The majority correctly applies the holdings in *State v. Gerald L.C.*, 194 Wis.2d 548, 535 N.W.2d 777 (Ct.App.1995), *State v. Moats*, 156 Wis.2d 74, 457 N.W.2d 299 (1990), and other prior cases to the issue of admissibility of Jeri's statements to her mother, her sister, and the police officer under the excited utterance exception, Wis. Stat. § 908.03(2). Under that exception, the majority accurately points out that "the related statement must be made while the declarant is still under the stress of excitement caused by the event or condition." Majority op. at 273. The inherent trustworthiness of a hearsay statement under that exception emanates from the temporary stress of excitement arising from the event and still existing at the time the statement is made. In *Christensen v. Economy Fire & Cas. Co.*, 77 Wis.2d 50, 58, 252 N.W.2d 81 (1977), quoting *Cossette v. Lepp*, 38 Wis.2d 392, 398, 157 N.W.2d 629 (1968), this court stated: "It is the condition of excitement that temporarily stills the capacity for reflection which is the significant factor assuring trustworthiness, assuring that the declarant lacked the capacity to fabricate." Rather than using the traditional analysis for the exception as described in *Christensen*, the majority, consistent with our recent cases, applies what has become a looser test of admissibility under § 908.03(2).

The looseness occurs because this court no longer looks for evidence that the declarant is still under "the condition of excitement" from the event when making the statement. The court looks to see only if the declarant is upset when making the statement. I do not for one moment question that a sexual assault of a child is an extremely stressful event for the child. Nor do I question that a child who has been assaulted may well be under the stress of the event for a prolonged period of time. There is a fundamental difference, however, between a statement "relating to a startling event made while the declarant was under the stress of excitement caused by the event" and a declarant later becoming stressed and upset while describing an earlier event. The latter declaration does not provide the inherent trustworthiness envisioned in the excited utterance exception. Discussing Wisconsin case law, Professor Blinka cautions that "the temporary relationship between the startling event and the making of the statement has been most sorely tested in instances where children have reported sexual or physical abuse long after the event occurred." 7 Daniel D. Blinka, *Wisconsin Practice (Evidence)* § 803.2, at 465 (1991).

Here we know that two weeks after the last alleged incident, Jeri called her mother on the telephone, crying and hysterical. There is nothing in the record about Jeri's emotional condition during the two preceding weeks. In fact, the majority acknowledges that "the record is devoid of any information concerning Jeri's conduct in the two weeks after the last incident and preceding her report. . . ." Majority op. at 274. The circuit court knew only that Jeri was distressed at the time she recounted these alleged incidents two weeks after the last incident. The fact that "there are indications that she had just discovered that she would be spending two weeks alone with the defendant," majority op. at 274, does not establish that Jeri was still under the stress of excitement from an assaultive event two weeks earlier.

EXERCISE

Carl brutally assaulted Jessie, breaking Jessie's jaw and threatening to kill Jessie if Jessie spoke about the assault. One hour after the assault Jessie contacted a police officer and requested medical attention. On the way to the hospital Jessie gave the police officer a detailed statement about the assault, even though Jessie was still in severe pain, had vomited on the floor, and appeared nervous. The police officer arrested Carl for assault. At Carl's assault trial which hearsay exception, if any, would permit the police officer to repeat Jessie's statement about the assault?

[B]   Present Sense Impression

Often statements can be described by more than one exception. The *Hallums* case looks at a situation in which the defendant alleges that the statement looks more like a prior identification under 801(d)(1)(C), but fails to satisfy the criteria for the prior identification.

HALLUMS v. UNITED STATES
District of Columbia Court of Appeals
841 A.2d 1270 (2004)

[A security officer at Lord & Taylor observed a woman taking a purse on a video and said "That's Theresa Hallums." The officer did not testify and the trial court admitted the statement as a present sense impression. The defendant argued that his identification was an identification of a person previously perceived, an out-of-court statement which is admissible only if the declarant is available for cross-examination under Fed. R. Evid. 801(d)(1)(C) and the analogous evidence provision for the District of Columbia.— Eds.]

GLICKMAN, ASSOCIATE JUDGE, concurring:

I would hold that the trial judge did not err, constitutionally or otherwise, in admitting Officer Lee's identification of appellant.

Officer Lee was with Officer Barrick when they saw a woman enter Lord & Taylor and begin removing Coach handbags from a counter top display. According to Officer Barrick, Officer Lee "immediately" declared, "That's Theresa Hallums." In my view, Officer Lee's declaration was a statement of "present sense impression" as defined in Federal Rule of Evidence 803(1): "A statement describing or explaining an event or condition made while the declarant was perceiving the event or condition, or immediately thereafter." The premise of this exception to the rule against hearsay is that "substantial contemporaneity of event and statement negate the likelihood of deliberate or conscious misrepresentation."[1] The requirements of the exception and the conditions of its premise were satisfied here.[2] The triggering

---

[1] Fed. R. Evid. 803(1) & (2) advisory committee's note.

[2] I would adopt the present sense impression exception as it is defined in the Federal Rules of Evidence (together with its implicit requirement of spontaneity, *see infra*), without any of the supposed "safeguards" (corroboration requirements and the like) that Judge Ruiz's opinion for the court notes

event was the shoplifting, and the statement describing the shoplifter was made while it was happening. There is no reason to think that Officer Lee was making a deliberate or conscious misrepresentation. There is every reason to think he was speaking what he believed to be the truth. The present case is not distinguishable in principle from numerous other cases in which courts have held similar statements of identification to be admissible in evidence under the present sense impression exception. *See, e.g., United States v. Murillo*, 288 F.3d 1126, 1137 (9th Cir. 2002) (upholding admission under Rule 803(1) of decedent victim's statement during telephone call that "I'm with Kiane and Rico"); *United States v. Accetturo*, 966 F.2d 631, 633–34 n. 3 (11th Cir. 1992) (holding that where victim pointed to defendant and said to police, "That's Tony," the statement was admissible under Rule 803(1)); *United States v. Delaplane*, 778 F.2d 570, 574 (10th Cir. 1985) (upholding admission of statement in a wiretapped telephone conversation that "Michael's back"); *United States v. Earley*, 657 F.2d 195, 198 (8th Cir. 1981) (holding statement admissible where the declarant said, "That sounded just like Butch" immediately after receiving telephone call; "[t]he spontaneity of the statement in relation to the telephone call attests to its trustworthiness."); *see also Burgess v. United States*, 608 A.2d 733, 737–39 (D.C. 1992) (Rogers, C.J., concurring) (concluding that where the victim of a shooting called his assailant "Tony," the victim's statement was admissible under the present sense impression exception of Rule 803(1)).

I agree that a present sense impression statement must be "spontaneous" as well as contemporaneous with the event being described. A statement that is scripted or planned in advance of the event would not qualify, nor would a statement that is the product of interrogation or deliberation following the event. Spontaneity is a question of fact. In this case the trial court could find that Officer Lee's statement was spontaneous based on Officer Barrick's uncontradicted testimony that Officer Lee identified the shoplifter as Theresa Hallums "immediately" upon seeing her. As the trial court's finding is supported by the evidence, we are not free to disregard it. *See* D.C.Code § 17-305(a) (2001).

The argument is made that Officer Lee's statement identifying the shoplifter as Theresa Hallums was not spontaneous, and hence was not a statement of present sense impression, because it was based on Lee's memory of Hallums from a previous encounter. This argument treats Officer Lee's personal knowledge of Hallums from past contact with her, the *sine qua non* for admitting his identification of her, as the essential basis for excluding that identification. But every valid identification depends on the declarant having a memory of past contact with the person identified. If appellant's argument were sound, it would mean — despite the abundant case law to the contrary — that no valid statement of identification could ever come within the exception for present sense impressions. Appellant's rationale also would mean that statements involving recollection, including statements of identification, could not satisfy the requirements of the closely related spontaneous

have been adopted in a few jurisdictions. See *ante* at 1278–79. For one thing, I doubt the utility of such additional requirements and I think that the presence or absence of corroboration, for example, should go to the weight rather than to the admissibility of the evidence. For another thing, it seems to me that when a statute or other binding authority does not require otherwise, we should strive to align our rules of evidence with the Federal Rules. See, e.g., *Johnson v. United States*, 683 A.2d 1087, 1099–1100 (D.C. 1996) (en banc).

declaration (also known as "excited utterance") exception to the hearsay rule-a conclusion that has been rejected by more cases of this court than one can count. *See, e.g., Jones v. United States*, 829 A.2d 464, 466 (D.C. 2003); *Lyons v. United States*, 683 A.2d 1080, 1082–83 (D.C. 1996); *Smith v. United States*, 666 A.2d 1216, 1222–23 (D.C. 1995); *Young v. United States*, 391 A.2d 248, 250 (D.C. 1978), all cases in which the court upheld the admission as spontaneous declarations of statements in which assault victims identified the persons who had attacked them.

I think that appellant's argument is not sound, however, because it is based on a false dichotomy. Spontaneity and recollection are not opposites. It is a mistake to think that one can restrict the present sense impression exception to statements in which memory plays no role.[3] Indeed, I doubt there is such a thing as a statement of pure perception that is completely unaided or uninfluenced by the declarant's memory. While statements about *past* events are not admissible under Rule 803(1), that Rule does not require that statements of *present* perception be divorced from memory; if it did, the exception would be limited by its terms to pure descriptions and would not encompass as well statements "explaining" an event or condition. Consider, for example, a sports announcer reporting a baseball game as it unfolds. Imagine hearing the announcer say something like this: "Barry Bonds swings at a high fastball, it's going, it's into the right field stands, it's his seventieth home run on the season!" That statement relies in part on the announcer's memory. It is also a statement of present sense impression *par excellence.*

Thus, I am not persuaded by the argument that Officer Lee's statement "That's Theresa Hallums" is equivalent to the typical identification made by a witness to a crime at a subsequent viewing of a suspect. *Ante* at 1273, 1274. When a witness views a photographic array or a lineup, for example, and identifies a suspect as the perpetrator of the crime, the witness's statement is about a past event, the commission of the crime. The statement does not fall within the exception for present sense impressions because it is not made contemporaneously with the event being described or explained. In contrast, Officer Lee's statement "That's Theresa Hallums" was not a statement about a past event. It said nothing about what happened when Officer Lee previously confronted Theresa Hallums. Rather, the statement "That's Theresa Hallums" was purely about the event transpiring as the words were spoken. The event and the statement describing it were contemporaneous, as the present sense impression exception requires.

---

[3] Thus, I am constrained to demur to the statement in Judge Ruiz's opinion for the court that "care must be taken to ensure that this exception is not used to admit statements that circumstances reveal were not truly spontaneous, but instead involved conscious reflection or recall from memory." *Ante* at 1277.

[C]   Declarations of Present State of Mind

[*See* Fed. R. Evid. 803]

[1]   Then-Existing Mental State to Prove Declarant's Future Action

The *Hillmon* case pre-dates the adoption of the Federal Rules of Evidence by almost a century. It has nevertheless remained one of the most important cases in evidence law, standing for the proposition that a person's statement of present intent to do something in the future is admissible, despite the fact that it was made out of court, and regardless of whether the declarant is available. In modern times, this exception is explained as a then-existing mental condition, admissible under Fed. R. Evid. 803(3). *Hillmon* provides the common law origin of this often used application of Rule 803(3).

MUTUAL LIFE INSURANCE CO. v. HILLMON
United States Supreme Court
145 U.S. 285 (1892)

MR. JUSTICE GRAY . . . delivered the opinion of the Court.

[Sallie Hillmon brought this action against the Mutual Life Insurance Co. to recover the value of a policy on her husband's life. The insurance company refused to pay on Mrs. Hillmon's claim, contesting the identity of the man whom Mrs. Hillmon claimed was her deceased husband. The company claimed that the body was that of a Mr. Walters. To support its contention, the company offered into evidence letters that Walters had written to relatives and to his fiancee in which he expressed his intention to go to Crooked Creek, the place where the body was discovered.]

[After finding reversible error on another ground, the Court addressed what it considered to be an important evidentiary question that would likely arise again at the second trial.]

This question is of the admissibility of the letters written by Walters on the first days of March, 1879, which were offered in evidence by the defendants, and excluded by the court. In order to determine the competency of these letters it is important to consider the state of the case when they were offered to be read.

The matter chiefly contested at the trial was the death of John W. Hillmon, the insured; and that depended upon the question whether the body found at Crooked Creek on the night of March 17, 1879, was his body or the body of one Walters.

Much conflicting evidence has been introduced as to the identity of the body. The plaintiff had also introduced evidence that Hillmon and one Brown left Wichita, in Kansas, on or about March 5, 1879, and traveled together through southern Kansas in search of a site for a cattle ranch; and that on the night of March 18th, while they were in camp at Crooked Creek, Hillmon was accidentally killed, and that his body was taken thence and buried. The defendants had introduced evidence, without objection, that Walters left his home and his betrothed in Iowa in March, 1878, and was afterwards in Kansas until March, 1879; that during that time he corresponded regularly with his family and his betrothed; that the letters received from him were one received by his betrothed on March 3d, and postmarked at "Wichita, March 2," and one received by his sister about March 4th or 5th, and dated at Wichita a day or two before; and that he had not been heard from since.

The evidence that Walters was at Wichita on or before March 5th, and had not been heard from since, together with the evidence to identify as his the body found at Crooked Creek on March 18th, tended to show that he went from Wichita to Crooked Creek between those two dates. Evidence that just before March 5th he had the intention of leaving Wichita with Hillmon would tend to corroborate the evidence already admitted, and to show that he went from Wichita to Crooked Creek with Hillmon. Letters from him to his family and his betrothed were the natural, if not the only attainable, evidence of his intention.

The position taken at the bar that the letters were competent evidence . . . as memoranda made in the ordinary course of business, cannot be maintained, for they were clearly not such.

But upon another ground suggested they should have been admitted. A man's state of mind or feeling can only be manifested to others by countenance, attitude, or gesture, or by sounds or words, spoken or written. The nature of the fact to be proved is the same, and evidence of its proper tokens is equally competent to prove it, whether expressed by aspect or conduct, by voice or pen. When the intention to be proved is important only as qualifying an act, its connection with that act must be shown, in order to warrant the admission of declarations of the intention. But whenever the intention is of itself a distinct and material fact in a chain of circumstances, it may be proved by contemporaneous oral or written declarations of the party.

The existence of a particular intention in a certain person at a certain time being a material fact to be proved, evidence that he expressed that intention at that time is as direct evidence of the fact as his own testimony that he then had that intention would be. After his death there can hardly by any other way of proving it, and while he is still alive his own memory of his state of mind at a former time is no more likely to be clear and true than a bystander's recollection of what he then said, and is less trustworthy than letters written by him at the very time and under circumstances precluding a suspicion of misrepresentation.

The letters in question were competent, not as narratives of facts communicated to the writer by others, nor yet as proof that he actually went away from Wichita but as evidence that, shortly before the time when other evidence tended to show that he went away, he had the intention of going, and of going with Hillmon, which made it more probable both that he did go and that he went with Hillmon than if there had been no proof of such intention. In view of the mass of conflicting testimony introduced upon the question whether it was the body of Walters that was found in Hillmon's camp, this evidence might properly influence the jury in determining that question.

The rule applicable to this case has been thus stated by this court: "Wherever the bodily or mental feelings of an individual are material to be proved, the usual expressions of feelings are original and competent evidence. Those expressions are the natural reflexes of what it might be impossible to show by other testimony. If there be such other testimony, this may be necessary to set the facts thus developed in their true light, and to give them their proper effect. As independent, explanatory, or corroborative evidence it is often indispensable to the due administration of justice. Such declarations are regarded as verbal acts, and are as competent as any other testimony, when relevant to the issue. Their truth or falsity is an inquiry for the jury . . . .

* * *

Upon principle and authority, therefore, we are of opinion that the two letters were competent evidence of the intention of Walters at the time of writing them, which was a material fact bearing upon the question in controversy; and that for the exclusion of these letters, as well as for the undue restriction of the defendants' challenges, the verdicts must be set aside, and a new trial had.

As the verdicts and judgments were several, the writ of error sued out by the defendants jointly was superfluous, and may be dismissed without costs; and upon each of the writs of error sued out by the defendants severally, the order will be:

Judgment reversed, and case remanded to the circuit court, with directions to set aside the verdict and to order a new trial.

[2]   Then-Existing Mental State to Prove Other's State of Mind

As we learned in Chapter 2, all evidence must be relevant. The *Shepard* case considers whether a woman's belief that her husband had poisoned her is admissible to show that he had. Of course her present belief qualifies as a then-existing state of mind, but the question is whether her belief is itself relevant. If she believes she is going to die and states as a fact that her husband had poisoned her, then this would be admissible as a dying declaration. The *Shepard* case takes up the question of whether her belief about a fact makes that fact admissible.

SHEPARD v. UNITED STATES
United States Supreme Court
290 U.S. 96 (1933)

Mr. Justice Cardozo delivered the opinion of the Court.

The petitioner, Charles A. Shepard, a major in the medical corps of the United States Army, has been convicted of the murder of his wife, Zenana Shepard, at Fort Riley, Kansas, a United States military reservation . . . .

The crime is charged to have been committed by poisoning the victim with bichloride of mercury. The defendant was in love with another woman, and wished to make her his wife. There is circumstantial evidence to sustain a finding by the jury that to win himself his freedom he turned to poison and murder. Even so, guilt was contested and conflicting inferences are possible. The defendant asks us to hold that by the acceptance of incompetent evidence the scales were weighted to his prejudice and in the end to his undoing.

The evidence complained of was offered by the Government in rebuttal when the trial was nearly over. On May 22, 1929, there was a conversation in the absence of the defendant between Mrs. Shepard, then ill in bed, and Clara Brown, her nurse. The patient asked the nurse to go to the closet in the defendant's room and bring a bottle of whisky that would be found upon a shelf. When the bottle was produced, she said that this was the liquor she had taken just before collapsing. She asked whether enough was left to make a test for the presence of poison, insisting that the smell and taste were strange. Then she added the words, "Dr. Shepard has poisoned me."

The conversation was proved twice. After the first proof of it, the Government asked to strike it out, being doubtful of its competence, and this request was granted. A little later, however, the offer was renewed, the nurse having then testified to statements by Mrs. Shepard as to the prospect of recovery. "She said she was not going to get well; she was going to die." With the aid of this new evidence, the conversation already summarized was proved a second time. There was a timely challenge of the ruling.

She said, "Dr. Shepard has poisoned me." The admission of this declaration, if erroneous, was more than unsubstantial error. As to that the parties are agreed. The voice of the dead wife was heard in accusation of her husband, and the accusation was accepted as evidence of guilt. If the evidence was incompetent, the verdict may not stand.

*   *   *

[The Court first considered the admissibility of the challenged statements as dying declarations, concluding that the statements were not admissible as such.]

2. We pass to the question whether the statements to the nurse, though incompetent as dying declarations, were admissible on other grounds.

The Circuit Court of Appeals determined that they were. Witnesses for the defendant had testified to declarations by Mrs. Shepard which suggested a mind bent upon suicide, or at any rate were thought by the defendant to carry that suggestion. More than once before her illness she had stated in the hearing of these witnesses that she had no wish to live, and had nothing to live for, and on one occasion she added that she expected some day to make an end to her life. This testimony opened the door, so it is argued, to declarations in rebuttal that she had been poisoned by her husband. They were admissible, in that view, not as evidence of the truth of what was said, but as betokening a state of mind inconsistent with the presence of suicidal intent.

(a) The testimony was neither offered nor received for the strained and narrow purpose now suggested as legitimate. It was offered and received as proof of dying declaration. What was said by Mrs. Shepard lying ill upon her deathbed was to be weighed as if a like statement had been made upon the stand. The course of the trial makes this an inescapable conclusion. The Government withdrew the testimony when it was unaccompanied by proof that the declarant expected to die. Only when proof of her expectation had been supplied was the offer renewed and the testimony received again. For the reasons already considered, the proof was inadequate to show a consciousness of impending death and the abandonment of hope; but inadequate though it was, there can be no doubt of the purpose that it was understood to serve. There was no disguise of that purpose by counsel for the Government. They concede in all candor that Mrs. Shepard's accusation of her husband, when it was finally let in, was received upon the footing of a dying declaration, and not merely as indicative of the persistence of a will to live. Beyond question the jury considered it for the broader purpose, as the court intended that they should. A different situation would be here if we could fairly say in the light of the whole record that the purpose had been left at large, without identifying token. There would then be room for argument that demand should have been made for an explanatory ruling. Here the course of the trial put the defendant off his guard. The testimony was received by the judge and offered by the Government with the plain understanding that it was to be used for an illegitimate purpose, gravely prejudicial. A trial becomes unfair if testimony thus accepted may be used in an appellate court as though admitted for a different purpose, unavowed and unsuspected. . . . Such at all events is the result when the purpose in reserve is so obscure and artificial that it would be unlikely to occur to the minds of uninstructed jurors, and even if it did, would be swallowed up and lost in the one that was disclosed.

(b) Aside, however, from this objection, the accusatory declaration must have been rejected as evidence of a state of mind, though the purpose thus to limit it had been brought to light upon the trial. The defendant had tried to show by Mrs. Shepard's declarations to her friends that she had exhibited a weariness of life and a readiness to end it, the testimony giving plausibility to the hypothesis of suicide. . . . By the proof of these declarations evincing an unhappy state of mind the defendant opened the door to the offer by the Government of declarations evincing a different state of mind, declarations consistent with the persistence of a will to live. The defendant would have no grievance if the testimony in rebuttal had been narrowed to that point. What the Government put in evidence, however, was something very different. It did not use the declarations by Mrs. Shepard to prove her present thoughts and feelings, or even her thoughts and feelings in times past. It used the declarations as proof of an act by someone else, as evidence that she was dying of poison given by her husband. This fact, if fact it was, the Government was free to prove, but not by hearsay declarations. It will not do to say that the jury might accept the declarations for any light that they cast upon the existence of a vital urge, and reject them to the extent that they charged the death to someone else. Discrimination so subtle is a feat beyond the compass of ordinary minds. The reverberating clang of those accusatory words would drown all weaker sounds. It is for ordinary minds, and not for psychoanalysts, that our rules of evidence are framed. They have their source very often in considerations of administrative convenience, of practical expediency, and not in rules of logic. When the risk of confusion is so great as to upset the balance of advantage, the evidence goes out . . . .

These precepts of caution are a guide to judgment here. There are times when a state of mind, if relevant, may be proved by contemporaneous declarations of feeling or intent. *Mutual Life Ins. Co. v. Hillmon*, 145 U.S. 285, 296. . . . Thus, in proceedings for the probate of a will, where the issue is undue influence, the declarations of a testator are competent to prove his feelings for his relatives, but are incompetent as evidence of his conduct or of theirs. . . . In suits for the alienation of affections, letters passing between the spouses are admissible in aid of a like purpose. . . . In damage suits for personal injuries, declarations by the patient to bystanders or physicians are evidence of sufferings or symptoms . . . but are not received to prove the acts, the external circumstances, through which the injuries came about. . . . Even statements of past sufferings or symptoms are generally excluded, . . . though an exception is at times allowed when they are made to a physician. . . . So also in suits upon insurance policies, declarations by an insured that he intends to go upon a journey with another, may be evidence of a state of mind lending probability to the conclusion that the purpose was fulfilled. *Mutual Life Ins. Co. v. Hillmon, below.* The ruling in that case marks the high water line beyond which courts have been unwilling to go. It has developed a substantial body of criticism and commentary.[51] Declarations of intention, casting light upon the future, have been sharply distinguished from declarations of memory, pointing backwards to the past. There would be an end, or nearly that, to the rule against hearsay if the distinction were ignored.

The testimony now questioned faced backward and not forward. This at least it did in its most obvious implications. What is even more important, it spoke to a past act, and more than that, to an act by someone not the speaker. Other tendency, if it had any, was a filament too fine to be disentangled by a jury.

The judgment should be reversed and the cause remanded to the District Court for further proceedings in accordance with this opinion.

Reversed.

[3]   Declarant's Then-Existing Mental State to Prove Another's Future Action

Houlihan involves an effort by the prosecution to use the declarant's statement of his intent to meet with another person to show that that meeting actually occurred. To use the *Hillmon* case an analogy, the issue in this case is whether Walter's statement of his intent to go to Crooked Creek with Hillmon would be admissible to prove that Hillmon accompanied him.

---

[51] (Original footnote 1.) Maguire, *The Hillmon Case*, 38 Harvard L. Rev., 709, 721, 727; Seligman, *An Exception to the Hearsay Rule*, 26 Harvard L. Rev. 146; Chafee, *Review of Wigmore's Treatise*, 37 Harvard L. Rev., 513, 519.

UNITED STATES v. HOULIHAN
United States District Court, District of Massachusetts
871 F. Supp. 1495 (1994)

Young, District Judge

I. BACKGROUND

In the early morning hours of Monday, March 2, 1992, James Boyden Jr. was found dead in the vicinity of Spice Street, Charlestown. He had been shot in the back of the head.

On the eve of trial involving federal charges arising out of this and other murders, attempted murders, and allegedly related misconduct, the government moved *in limine* for an Order permitting it to offer, through percipient witnesses, hearsay statements made by James Boyden Jr., James Boyden Sr., and George Sargent, shortly before their respective murders. The Court declined to rule *in limine*, opting instead to await development of the trial record, making only such rulings as ultimately prove necessary and appropriate. Having now admitted one such statement of James Boyden Jr., and the government having withdrawn its proffer of the others, this memorandum addresses only the ruling already made. The admissibility of statements allegedly made by James Boyden Sr. and George Sargent will be addressed when and if necessary.

In its motion *in limine*, the government proffered the following evidence through counsel: Prior to his death, James Boyden Jr. allegedly told his sister, Marie Boyden Connors, that he had had a loud argument with the defendant Jennierose Lynch ("Lynch") in which she warned him that if he did not stop selling cocaine from her corner, she would have the defendant Michael Fitzgerald ("Fitzgerald") "blow [his] head off." James Boyden Jr. allegedly related similar accounts of this event to his mother, Veronica Boyden; his father, James Boyden Sr.; and another witness. His sister and mother each reported seeing him afterwards with a bandage on his face. Both women reported that James Boyden Jr. told them that Fitzgerald had beaten him up. The senior Mr. Boyden and another witness also reported that James Boyden Jr. had told them that he had been hit by Fitzgerald. On the evening before he was found dead, James Boyden Jr. was hanging out in his sister's Charlestown apartment drinking beer, departing at about 8:00 PM. As he was leaving, he allegedly told his sister that he was going out "to meet Billy Herd." William "Billy" Herd ("Herd") is a co-defendant in this case.

As the trial unfolded, the government abandoned its effort to admit most of these hearsay statements. The government did, however, seek to admit the statement of James Boyden Jr. to his sister that he intended to meet Herd as relevant circumstantial evidence that it was Herd who killed him later that evening. The government argued that this statement is admissible because it constitutes a statement of a then existing mental or emotional condition under Federal Rule of Evidence 803(3) ("Rule 803(3)"). Over objection, the Court admitted the statement and Marie Boyden Connors was allowed so to testify. This memorandum explains the Court's reasoning.

*   *   *

II. ANALYSIS

This case presents an issue of first impression in the First Circuit, namely, whether the out-of-court statement of a victim-declarant of an intention to meet with a defendant on the evening of the victim's murder can be admitted at trial as circumstantial evidence of the meeting. Rule 803(3), commonly referred to as the "state of mind exception," excludes from the hearsay rule statements of "the declarant's then existing state of mind, emotion, sensation, or physical condition (such as intent, plan, motive, design, mental feeling, pain, and bodily health) . . . ." Thus, although the statement of James Boyden Jr. that he was going to meet Herd would clearly be admissible, if relevant, as a statement of James Boyden Jr.'s *own* intention, it is unclear whether it can be admitted against others — the defendants here — as evidence that the meeting *actually* took place.

A. The Common Law Prior to Rule 803(3)

Prior to the adoption of the Federal Rules of Evidence, the Supreme Court addressed this issue in the famous case of *Mutual Life Insurance Co. of New York v. Hillmon*, 145 U.S. 285, 12 S. Ct. 909, 36 L. Ed. 706 (1892). In *Hillmon*, an insurance company sought to introduce out-of-court statements by a declarant, Walters, that he intended to travel with the insured, Hillmon. The hearsay statement was used as the principal proof that Hillmon had actually traveled with Walters. In holding this statement admissible, the Supreme Court cited with approval *Hunter v. State*, 11 Vroom (40 N.J.L.) 495, 534, 536–38 (1878), a criminal case which involved facts similar to the case at issue here. In *Hunter*, the Court of Errors and Appeals (now the Supreme Court) of New Jersey held that a victim-declarant's out-of-court statements to his wife and son, just prior to his murder, that he was planning to meet with the defendant were admissible to prove the defendant's subsequent conduct. *See Hillmon*, 145 U.S. at 299, 12 S. Ct. at 914 (paraphrasing the *Hunter* case). The rationale of the New Jersey court was explicitly adopted by the Supreme Court in *Hillmon*. *Id.* Thus, under *Hillmon*, out-of-court statements of a declarant are admissible to prove the subsequent conduct of others.

The analysis, however, does not end here. In 1973, Congress codified *Hillmon* in Federal Rule of Evidence 803(3). The question for this Court, then, is whether in enacting Rule 803(3) Congress codified in full the reasoning of *Hillmon*, or whether it sought to limit the case's application.

B. Rule 803(3) and its Legislative History

Rule 803(3) states that a declarant's out-of-court statement of intent is admissible at trial as an exception to the rule against hearsay. The text of the rule is silent as to whether such statements are admissible against third parties.

Unfortunately, the legislative history of Rule 803(3) only serves to obfuscate the analysis. While the Advisory Committee's Note to Rule 803(3) states that "the rule of *Mutual Life Insurance Co. v. Hillmon*, allowing evidence of intention as tending to prove the doing of the act intended, is, of course, left undisturbed," Fed. R. Evid. 803(3) advisory committee's note, *reprinted in* Eric D. Green & Charles R. Nesson, Federal Rules of Evidence 166 (1992) (citation omitted), the Report of the House Judiciary Committee states that "the committee intends that the rule be construed to limit the doctrine of *Mutual Life Insurance Co. v. Hillmon*, so as to render statements of intent by a declarant admissible only to prove his future conduct, not the future conduct of another person." H.R.Rep. No. 650, 93rd Cong., 1st Sess. (1973) (citation omitted), *reprinted in* 1974 U.S.Code Cong. & Ad.News 7051, 7075, 7087. The Senate Report and the Conference Report are silent on this point.[2]

C. Circuit Split

Courts that have had the opportunity to consider the application of Rule 803(3) are divided. *See Brown v. Tard*, 552 F. Supp. 1341, 1351–52 (D.N.J. 1982) (noting that although under the New Jersey counterpart to Federal Rule 803[3] courts may admit a declarant's statement of intent to prove defendant's subsequent actions, federal courts are split on their interpretation of Rule 803[3]).

1. Second & Fourth Circuit Approach — Requirement of Corroborating Evidence — Some courts have held that a declarant's statement of intent may be admitted against a non-declarant only when there is independent evidence connecting the declarant's statement with the non-declarant's conduct. *See United States v. Jenkins*, 579 F.2d 840, 842–43 (4th Cir.), *cert. denied*, 439 U.S. 967, 99 S. Ct. 458, 58 L. Ed. 2d 427 (1978) (declarant's statement of intent is not admissible to prove subsequent conduct of third party, but is admissible to prove *why* third party acted as he did where there exists independent evidence that third party did in fact engage in the alleged conduct).

Similarly, the Second Circuit has held that "declarations of intentions or future plans are admissible against a nondeclarant when they are linked with independent evidence that corroborates the declaration." *United States v. Nersesian*, 824 F.2d 1294, 1325 (2d Cir.), *cert. denied*, 484 U.S. 958, 108 S. Ct. 357, 98 L. Ed. 2d 382 (1987); *see also United States v. Delvecchio*, 816 F.2d 859, 863 (2d Cir. 1987) (out-of-court statement of an informant that he intended to meet with the defendant was not admissible to prove defendant's actual attendance at the meeting because the government offered no independent evidence of the defendant's presence); *United States v. Badalamenti*, 794 F.2d 821, 826 (2d Cir. 1986) (out-of-court statement by declarant that he was going to meet defendant to obtain heroin was admissible so long as government proffered independent evidence that meeting actually took place); *United States v. Sperling*, 726 F.2d 69, 74 (2d Cir.), *cert. denied*, 467 U.S. 1243, 104 S. Ct. 3516, 82 L. Ed. 2d 824 (1984) (statements concerning declarant's state of mind are admissible against non-declarant when linked with corroborating evidence); *United States v. Cicale*, 691 F.2d 95, 103–104 (2d Cir. 1982), *cert. denied*, 460 U.S. 1082, 103 S. Ct. 1771, 76 L. Ed. 2d 344 (1983) (where defendant's participation in drug transaction was proven by eyewitness testimony,

---

[2] This silence is revealing as it indicates that only one chamber of Congress (indeed, only one committee of that chamber) approved the limitation of the *Hillmon* doctrine urged by the defense.

statements by co-conspirator that he was going to meet the defendant for purposes of engaging in drug transaction were admissible).

A district judge in the Northern District of Illinois has likewise adopted this approach. *See United States v. York*, 1987 U.S. Dist. LEXIS 484, 1987 WL 5938, at *7 (N.D. Ill. Jan. 12, 1987) (hearsay testimony held inadmissible where victim-declarant's statement that she intended to meet with the defendant at a particular time could not be corroborated with particularity). *But cf. Johnson v. Chrans*, 844 F.2d 482, 486 n. 4 (7th Cir.), *cert. denied*, 488 U.S. 835, 109 S. Ct. 95, 102 L. Ed. 2d 71 (1988) (explaining that in some circumstances the Seventh Circuit has been willing to admit a declarant's out-of-court statements to prove conduct of another person, despite opposite result under Illinois state law).

2. Ninth Circuit Approach — No Corroborating Evidence Necessary — To the contrary, the Ninth Circuit has held that statements of a declarant's intent are admissible under Rule 803(3) to prove subsequent conduct of a person other than the declarant without corroborating evidence.[3] *See United States v. Pheaster*, 544 F.2d 353, 374–80 (9th Cir. 1976), *cert. denied sub nom. Inciso v. United States*, 429 U.S. 1099, 97 S. Ct. 1118, 51 L. Ed. 2d 546 (1977) (in kidnapping prosecution, trial court did not err in admitting testimony of a friend of the victim that shortly before the victim disappeared he told his friend that he was going to meet a person with the same name as the defendant). In holding statements of intent admissible against third parties, the *Pheaster* court recognized that such testimony could be unreliable, but rejected this as grounds for its exclusion. The Ninth Circuit explained that

> [t]he inference from a statement of present intention that the act intended was in fact performed is nothing more than an inference . . . . The possible unreliability of the inference to be drawn from the present intention [of the declarant] is a matter going to the weight of the evidence which might be argued to the trier of fact, but it should not be a ground for completely excluding the admittedly relevant evidence.

Id. at 376 n. 14. The court also acknowledged the "theoretical awkwardness" of applying a state of mind exception to prove conduct, but dismissed this objection because of the impressive array of authority favoring such application. *Id.* at 377.

After disposing of these arguments, the Ninth Circuit considered both the California counterpart to Rule 803(3) and the newly enacted Federal Rules of Evidence (which were not in force at the time of the trial below). The Ninth Circuit concluded that the *Hillmon* doctrine (allowing use of such testimony) remains undisturbed (1) because the text of the statute does not explicitly prohibit the use of declarant's statements of intent to prove the conduct of third persons, and (2) because of the contradictory nature of the legislative history of the rule. *Pheaster*, 544 F.2d at 379; *see also Terrovona v. Kincheloe*, 852 F.2d 424, 427 (9th Cir. 1988) (out-of-court statement by victim to his girlfriend that he was leaving to meet the defendant was admissible because it was a statement of declarant's then present

---

[3] According to one commentator, this was the majority position in 1982 among state and federal courts which had considered the issue. *See* Thomas A. Wiseman, III, Note, *Federal Rule 803(3) and the Criminal Defendant: The Limits of the Hillmon Doctrine*, 35 VAND. L. REV. 659, 687, 690 (1982).

intention and because it placed the defendant at the murder scene); *United States v. Astorga-Torres*, 682 F.2d 1331, 1335–36 (9th Cir. 1982), *cert. denied*, 459 U.S. 1040, 103 S. Ct. 455, 74 L. Ed. 2d 608 (1982) (statement of declarant that he intended to bring guards with him to the site of a drug transaction was properly admitted as evidence of declarant's intent to actually bring such individuals, and when appropriate limiting instruction was given, inferences could be drawn by the jury as to whether guards were actually present).

III. GROUND OF DECISION

As the Federal Rules of Evidence were enacted by Congress, this Court must interpret them as it would any statutory mandate. *Daubert v. Merrell Dow Pharmaceuticals, Inc.*, [509 U.S. 579, 585–588,] 113 S. Ct. 2786, 2793, 125 L. Ed. 2d 469 (1993); *Beech Aircraft Corp. v. Rainey*, 488 U.S. 153, 163, 109 S. Ct. 439, 446, 102 L. Ed. 2d 445 (1988). In examining Rule 803(3) as a statute, we begin with the text. The language of Rule 803(3) clearly says that statements of intent are admissible. Thus, because it does not *by its terms* limit the class of persons against whom such statements of intent may be admitted, this Court rules that Rule 803(3) codifies *Hillmon* as written and does not disturb its conclusion or its reasoning.

The Court's holding is supported by examining Rule 803(3) in the context of the rest of the Federal Rules of Evidence. The Rules are replete with examples of Congress' familiarity with the concept of limited admissibility. *Compare* Fed. R. Evid. 803(3) *with* Fed. R. Evid. 404(a) (limiting circumstances in which character evidence may be admitted); Fed. R. Evid. 404(b) (limiting purposes for which evidence of other crimes, wrongs, or acts may be admitted); Fed. R. Evid. 407 (limiting purposes for which subsequent remedial measures may be admitted); Fed. R. Evid. 408 (limiting purposes for which compromises and offers to compromise may be admitted); and Fed. R. Evid. 411 (limiting purposes for which evidence of liability insurance may be admitted). Thus, had Congress intended to limit the admissibility of such statements, it presumably would have done so. This Court will not venture to graft a limitation where none exists.

As Rule 803(3) is unambiguous,[4] this Court is unpersuaded by appeals to legislative history. *See Cabral v. INS*, 15 F.3d 193, 194 (1st Cir. 1994) ("We look to the legislative history only if 'the literal words of the statute create ambiguity or lead to an unreasonable interpretation' "); *United States v. Charles George Trucking Co.*, 823 F.2d 685, 688 (1st Cir. 1987) (if the language of the statute is reasonably definite, it must be regarded as conclusive, and legislative history should not be consulted); *see also* Office of Legal Policy, Report to the Attorney General, Using

---

[4] One might argue that Rule 803(3) is ambiguous because on its face it provides no guidance as to whether it includes statements implicating the conduct of third parties. This, however, is a misunderstanding of the "plain meaning rule." Under this canon of construction, legislative history may only be consulted when the *meaning of the words* is in dispute; questions regarding the *application* of a statute to the facts of a particular case do not render a statute ambiguous. *See* Office of Legal Policy, Report to the Attorney General, Using and Misusing Legislative History: A Re-Evaluation of the Status of Legislative History in Statutory Interpretation iv (1989) (meaning of statute may be plain even where the application of the statute is in dispute). Thus, despite ambiguity in the application of Rule 803(3), the text of the rule is in fact plain and the use of legislative history is therefore unwarranted.

and Misusing Legislative History: A Re-Evaluation of the Status of Legislative History in Statutory Interpretation iii–iv (1989) (it is inappropriate to look at legislative history if the meaning of statutory provision is plain). Even if the Court were properly to engage in an examination of Rule 803(3)'s legislative history, the conflicting nature of that evidence, *see supra*, would nevertheless lead us right back to the text. *See Citizens to Preserve Overton Park, Inc. v. Volpe*, 401 U.S. 402, 412 n. 29, 91 S. Ct. 814, 821 n. 29, 28 L. Ed. 2d 136 (1971) (where the legislative history is ambiguous the Court must consider only the statute itself to discern legislative intent). Therefore, such an inquiry is unnecessary.

Likewise, this Court is not persuaded by the decisions of the Fourth and Second Circuits requiring independent evidence before such testimony can be admitted. Indeed, this requirement is without foundation in either the text or the legislative history of Rule 803(3). Thus, while the approach adopted by the Second and Fourth Circuits may seem practical and fair, it is really little more than judicial policymaking.[5]

This Court finds the decisions of the Ninth Circuit, with their emphasis on text and Supreme Court precedent, more persuasive. *See United States v. Pheaster*, 544 F.2d 353, 374–80 (9th Cir. 1976), *cert. denied sub nom. Incisco v. United States*, 429 U.S. 1099, 97 S. Ct. 1118, 51 L. Ed. 2d 546 (1977); *see also* Glen Weissenberger, *Hearsay Puzzles: An Essay on Federal Evidence Rule 803(3)*, 64 Temp.L.Rev. 145, 164 (1991) (describing assertions by a victim-declarant of intent to meet with defendant as "hybrid" statements of (1) intent to act, and (2) a belief that the other person will show up, that are admissible under Rule 803[3]). *But cf.* Thomas A. Wiseman, III, Note, *Federal Rule 803(3) and the Criminal Defendant: The Limits of the Hillmon Doctrine*, 35 Vand. L. Rev. 659, 705–707 (1982) (arguing that because of potential prejudice to criminal defendants, courts should reconsider their willingness to admit declarant's statement of intent against third parties).

Thus, James Boyden Jr.'s statement that he was going out "to meet Billy Herd" is admissible against Herd under Fed. R. Evid. 803(3). Although it is true that James Boyden Jr.'s statement of intent is only circumstantial evidence that he actually met Herd, this statement will be allowed to function as part of the larger array of evidence before the jury so that they may decide for themselves what weight — if any — to give Ms. Connors' testimony. *See Pheaster*, 544 F.2d at 376 n. 14 (juries should be able to decide what weight to give a victim-declarant's assertion of intent to meet with defendant); *see also Cicale*, 691 F.2d at 104 n. 4 (articulating, but not adopting, the position that statements of intent should be allowed to function as part of a "larger matrix of circumstantial evidence").

IV. CONCLUSION

For the reasons set forth above, on December 14, 1994, during the twenty-third day of trial, Marie Boyden Connors was permitted to testify, over timely objection,

---

[5] It may be that the government will introduce corroborating evidence during the course of the trial. Therefore, the admissibility of the proffered evidence may not depend, as a practical matter, on the approach adopted by this Court. At this middle stage of the trial, however, this Court has admitted Boyden's statement of intent as relevant circumstantial evidence without any corroboration.

that as her brother James Boyden Jr. left her apartment for the last time, he said, he "was going to meet Billy Herd."

EXERCISES

1. Alphonse, a boss within the Colombo Crime Family, was suspected of killing William. At Alphonse's criminal trial, the government seeks to call William's wife as a witness to testify that on the day of the murder William told her that he was going to meet Alphonse at an underpass located at the corner of 92nd Street and Shore Road in Brooklyn. Alphonse objects on hearsay grounds. Is the statement admissible? What if the wife also wants to state that the Brooklyn location is William and Alphonse's routine meeting place because the spot is secluded from the police's view?

2. A bank which operates under the name "First National Bank in Sioux Falls" brought an action against a competitor that uses the name "First National Bank South Dakota," alleging infringement of its common-law service mark. In anticipation of litigation, FNB Sioux Falls established a confusion log on its company intranet site and instructed all its employees to record any confusion on the part of customers, vendors, or delivery services. FNB Sioux Falls seeks to admit the confusion log as evidence at trial, and FNB South Dakota objects on hearsay grounds. How should the court rule?

[D]   Present Physical Condition

[*See* **Fed. R. Evid. 803**]

Rationale

Unlike spontaneous statements of present physical condition, statements to a physician often are in response to questions rather than to the physical or mental sensation for which the declarant is seeking treatment. It is common with many illnesses that the patient is not experiencing the critical symptoms at the time of consultation with the doctor. Although such statements may not be spontaneous, their trustworthiness is not dependent on their spontaneity. Courts believe that an inherent assurance of reliability is present because of the declarant's desire for treatment and the physician's need for accurate information on which to base that treatment. Moreover, when the declarant's responses actually are spontaneous, they provide the best evidence of the true character of the pain the declarant suffered and prove far more probative than any testimony the patient might offer at a later time.

There was considerable confusion in the older cases over the status of statements made by the patient regarding symptoms of the illness for which he was seeking treatment, but which he was not experiencing at the time he was consulting the doctor. Courts commonly precluded doctors from repeating such statements for the purpose of proving the truth of what the patient said, because the courts perceived the statements as constituting "medical history." Medical history was excluded from the exception because it gave rise to memory problems.

Many courts, however, appeared to recognize a distinction between general medical history and past symptoms of the illness for which treatment was sought: treating recent, although past, symptoms of the present illnesses as present symptoms. Consequently, physicians often were allowed to repeat, for the purpose of establishing the truth of what the patient asserted, all of the patient's statements of present and past symptoms of illness.

Primary Purpose Must Be Treatment

A patient will not always consult a physician after an illness or injury solely for the purpose of obtaining treatment. The patient may not even consult a physician until after the patient has seen an attorney for the purpose of obtaining redress for his injuries. This will not preclude a court from admitting for their truth the statements the patient made to the physician in this instance. Progressive courts feel that if the patient's *primary purpose* for consulting the physician is to obtain treatment, then there is adequate assurance of trustworthiness. That the patient was developing the physician's testimony for litigation has no bearing on the statements' admissibility. These courts will regard the patient's other motive for visiting the doctor as a factor to be considered by the fact-finder when assessing the credibility of the statements. Many courts take a more conservative position. They require that the sole purpose of the consultation be for the purpose of obtaining treatment.

Statements of Medical History and Causation

Although logically a patient's motivation for treatment should make his statements about medical history as sincere as his statements about symptoms of the illness, under the common law courts would not admit such statements for their truth. Undoubtedly, the increased memory risk inherent in such statements concerning past medical history prompted this result. Courts at common law also were reluctant to allow a physician to testify to a patient's statements concerning the cause of his injury or illness. In the case of statements of causation, courts emphasized that such information often is not essential to the treatment being sought and that often there is greater likelihood of falsification because of the statement's relationship to the assignment of fault.

Although a patient's statements of medical history and causation were not admissible for their truth, the courts did allow the physician to relate them if they were important to an understanding of the patient's explanation of diagnosis and treatment. Because of the obvious effect that statements of fault could have in litigation over fault, however, courts at common law did not admit these kinds of statements even for explanatory purposes unless they were *crucial* to the doctor's diagnosis or treatment. If the court did admit these statements, it also would instruct the jury that the testimony was being offered solely for the purpose of explanation and, that the jury should not accept the statements as evidence of the truth of what they related.

Statements to Physicians for Purpose of Litigation

Courts consider the enhanced trustworthiness of statements made to a physician for the purpose of obtaining treatment to be lacking if the physician was contacted solely for the purpose of developing testimony for litigation rather than for treatment. In such circumstances, any statement the patient makes to the doctor, even those purportedly relating present pain, are not admissible to prove the statements' truth. The court will allow the doctor to testify only to those symptoms that can be independently verified through clinical observation.

[1]   Statements by Whom?

Clearly Rules 803(3) and 803(4) contemplate statements by patients to doctors, or even by persons expressing their own physical conditions to anyone. It is no great leap to conclude that parents reporting the symptoms of their children would also fit within 803(4) — parents have the same incentive as adult patients to accurately describe medical conditions to doctors. Who else making statements for another's medical treatment should be included in Rule 803(4)? *McKenna v. St. Joseph Hospital* takes up this issue.

McKENNA v. ST. JOSEPH HOSP.
Supreme Court of Rhode Island
557 A.2d 854 (1989)

FAY, CHIEF JUSTICE.

This case comes before us on the plaintiff's appeal and the defendants' cross-appeal of a jury verdict for the defendants. Kathleen M. McKenna, wife of the deceased John W. McKenna, initiated a negligence action, individually and on behalf of all the beneficiaries of John W. McKenna (John), against the physicians and the hospital responsible for the care of her husband on the day of his death. The plaintiff now appeals the favorable ruling on the defendant Dr. Adib Mechrefe's motion in limine and also appeals the restriction of her expert's testimony regarding causation. The defendants cross-appeal the denial of their respective directed-verdict motions and the grant of the plaintiff's motion in limine. The facts relevant to our review are as follows.

On May 9 and 10, 1980, Kathleen M. McKenna noticed that her husband was acting erratically. Because of her concern about confusing statements he was making and the strange behavior he was exhibiting, she suggested that he see a psychiatrist. On May 11 Kathleen called John's father, Jack, as she was very concerned about John's behavior. Early on May 12 when John arrived for work at his father's lumber company, he contacted Dr. Bruno Franek, a psychiatrist, who had treated him in 1972[1] and scheduled an appointment for 8 a.m. of that day.

Doctor Franek testified at trial that at their meeting on the morning of May 12

---

[1] Doctor Franek was a defendant in this lawsuit. The plaintiff's claim against Dr. Franek was settled prior to the commencement of trial.

John told the psychiatrist, "I know that I am God" and "I also know how to go through doors without being seen and without being hurt. I just have to slow my molecules completely down." Doctor Franek determined that the deceased was suffering from "schizophrenic reaction with ideas of reverence-agitation." The doctor prescribed Haldol, which he testified was a major tranquilizer, with five milligrams to be taken immediately. In order to counteract the adverse affects of Haldol, Franek prescribed Artane to be taken in five milligram dosages three times per day. John then took one fivemilligram dosage of Haldol and left saying he would return at 4 p.m., as ordered by Dr. Franek. After John left his office, Dr. Franek called John's father and discussed his diagnosis of John. John returned to the lumberyard at approximately 10 a.m. and remained there until slightly before noon, when he left unattended.

After John left the lumberyard, what his activities were is not entirely clear. It is certain that at 1:15 p.m. Captain Harold Winstanley and Lieutenant Robert Warren of the Cranston Fire Department rescue squad responded to a call and found John on the sidewalk of Park Avenue near his car, which had two wheels on the curb.[2] Lieutenant Warren and Captain Winstanley testified that John was in a "utopic" or "sluggish" state. Captain Winstanley determined that the best course of action would be to transfer John to St. Joseph Hospital for further observation. The officers proceeded to the hospital with John, arriving there at 1:23 p.m.

At St. Joseph Hospital, John was questioned at about 1:30 p.m. by an admitting nurse, Ann McKenna (no relation), who entered on the admitting report that the patient had stated he had taken one five-milligram dosage of Haldol, one five-milligram dosage of Artane and felt dazed. The patient was then examined by defendant Dr. Mechrefe. After examining John and with the knowledge that John had told the admitting nurse that he had taken Artane and Haldol, Dr. Mechrefe determined that when the Cranston Fire Department rescue found John at Park Avenue he was at that time suffering from a medication reaction. He told John to call his doctor, adding that if the medicine or dosage needed to be changed, John's doctor would do it, but in the meantime John should continue taking the medication. The examining-room nurse, Diane LeDoux, repeated these instructions to John.

John walked out of St. Joseph Hospital at about 1:45 p.m. He left without any further assistance or instructions other than to contact his doctor and continue taking the medication. Neither Dr. Franek nor any member of John's family were notified. What John's whereabouts were between 1:45 p.m. and 2:40 p.m. is not ascertainable. What is known is that at approximately 2:40 p.m. John jumped off the Broad Street overpass onto Route 95, thereby causing his own death. A post-mortem examination of the pill vials in John's pockets established that John had not taken any further medication after being examined at St. Joseph Hospital.

Our initial review of the trial court's decision involves the trial justice's exclusion of statements made by unidentified bystanders to the Cranston rescue personnel who attended to John. Before the trial, defendant Dr. Mechrefe made a motion in limine to exclude any of the proffered testimony. The defendant asserted that

---

[2] At the time of the incident, Captain Winstanley was a lieutenant with the Cranston Fire Department and Lieutenant Warren was a private with the same department.

statements made by unidentified bystanders to Captain Winstanley and Lieutenant Warren that John was driving erratically and wandering in the middle of Park Avenue immediately prior to the rescue personnel's arrival at the scene were inadmissible hearsay. The plaintiff's counsel, in opposition to defendant Dr. Mechrefe's motion, stated that Winstanley and Warren would testify that they were informed by unidentified bystanders of John's behavior preceding their arrival. In the alternative, counsel for plaintiff proposed that Winstanley and Warren would testify that upon their arrival at St. Joseph Hospital, they advised the emergency room personnel of the bystanders' statements. The plaintiff's counsel originally argued that although the statements were hearsay within Rule 801 of the Rhode Island Rules of Evidence, they were admissible within the Rule 803(2) or Rule 803(4) exception to Rule 802.

Rule 802, the "hearsay rule," provides a general prohibition against the admissibility of hearsay, except where provided for in the rules. Rule 803(2) is one such exception to Rule 802, removing from the hearsay rule a statement relating to a startling event or condition made while the declarant was under the stress of excitement caused by the event or condition. Another exception to Rule 802 is Rule 803(4), which omits from the hearsay rule statements for purposes of medical diagnosis or treatment.[3]

Failing on the argument to have the statements introduced as exceptions to the hearsay rule, plaintiff's counsel then sought to introduce the statements as nonhearsay admissible evidence. He contended that the proposed testimony was not being offered to prove its truth but rather to indicate that Dr. Mechrefe and the emergency room personnel were aware of the content of the statements. After hearing the arguments of counsel, the trial justice ruled favorably on defendant Dr. Mechrefe's motion in limine, denying introduction of the proffered evidence by any witness.

During trial, plaintiff's counsel sought to make an offer of proof with regard to the testimony of Dr. Mechrefe and Lieutenant Warren. Counsel maintained that if permitted, Lieutenant Warren would testify that upon his arrival at St. Joseph Hospital he informed hospital personnel of the bystanders' remarks. As for Dr. Mechrefe, plaintiff's counsel asserted that if questioned, Dr. Mechrefe would testify that a nurse at the hospital informed him that John had been found wandering in the street. To bolster his contention of admissibility, counsel resuscitated his argument that the introduction of the statement would be only for the purpose of showing knowledge on behalf of Dr. Mechrefe and the personnel at St. Joseph Hospital. The trial justice expeditiously dismissed the offer of proof, analogizing to his earlier refusal to admit the proposed testimony as inadmissible hearsay.

The statements made by the unidentified bystanders to the Cranston rescue

---

[3] Rule 803(4) of the Rhode Island Rules of Evidence states:

> "*Statements for Purposes of Medical Diagnosis or Treatment.* Statements made for purposes of medical diagnosis or treatment and describing medical history, or past or present symptoms, pain, or sensations, or the inception or general character of the cause or external source thereof insofar as reasonably pertinent to diagnosis or treatment, but not including statements made to a physician consulted solely for the purposes of preparing for litigation or obtaining testimony for trial."

personnel and the restatement of these remarks by rescue personnel to emergency room staff of St. Joseph Hospital are both hearsay within Rule 801. Counsel for plaintiff argued clearly that he would use the fact that John had been found wandering in the street to prove a failure by Dr. Mechrefe and St. Joseph Hospital personnel to adhere to the applicable standard of care. As such, the statement that John was wandering in the street before Winstanley and Warren arrived would be hearsay.

Because we determine that both the initial statement and the restatement are hearsay, we focus our inquiry on whether the admissibility requirements for hearsay within hearsay as set forth in Rule 805 are met.[4] Rule 805 provides an exception to the hearsay rule for the unique situation that occurs when a hearsay statement is subsequently restated. Each statement viewed individually must fall within an exception to Rule 802 in order to satisfy the prerequisites of Rule 805.

A preliminary examination of Rule 803(4) would be beneficial to our analysis. Contained within Rule 803 exceptions to the hearsay rule, which make availability of the declarant immaterial, Rule 803(4) was promulgated to allow for the introduction of statements inherently trustworthy because of their nature. The rationale for the exception is "the patient's strong motivation to be truthful about information that will form the basis of his diagnosis and treatment." Rule 803(4) advisory committee's notes. The advisory committee's notes further relate, "The statements do not have to be made to a physician but could be made to any person, such as a *hospital attendant, ambulance driver*, or even a family member, provided they are made for the purpose of diagnosis or treatment." (Emphasis added.) *Id.* The fact that the statement is made to a nonphysician/health-care provider does not detract from its admissibility. As long as the guarantee of trustworthiness inherent in good-faith recitation of symptoms to medical personnel is present, the Rule 803(4) exception to the hearsay rule may be utilized.

Cognizant of the principles embodied in Rule 803(4), we focus our attention on the statements made by unidentified bystanders to Warren and Winstanley. The statement of the symptoms and recent history associated with John W. McKenna on May 12 were given to the rescue personnel with the intent of assisting in his care. At least one observer of Rule 803(4)[5] of the Federal Rules of Evidence has noted, "Nor need the statements refer to the *declarant's* physical condition. Statements relating to someone else's symptoms, pains or sensations would be admissible, provided again, that they were made for purposes of diagnosis or treatment." 4 Weinstein & Berger, *Weinstein's Evidence*, # 803(4) [01] at 803–145 (1985). As factors controlling a court's probative-worth determination of such a statement pursuant to Rule 403, he cites "[the statement's] significance, its contents, by whom it was made, and in what circumstances it was made * * *." *Id.*

---

[4] Rule 805 states: "Hearsay within hearsay.— Hearsay included within hearsay is not excluded under the hearsay rule if each part of the combined statements conforms with an exception to the hearsay rule provided in these rules."

[5] For purposes of this review, Rule 803(4) of the Federal Rules of Evidence is identical to Rhode Island Rule 803(4). The Federal Rule 803(4) does not contain a prohibition on statements made to a physician consulted solely for the purposes of preparing for litigation or obtaining testimony for trial as does our Rule 803(4), a factor not relevant here.

We find that the bystanders' statements come within the exception embodied in Rule 803(4). The statements were made by an individual to emergency personnel with no motive to fabricate or lie, describing with particularity a specific situation. Also, the remarks were made to emergency personnel attending a call for assistance in order to foster treatment. Therefore, the prerequisites of Rule 803(4) have been met, making the statement admissible hearsay.

The next step under Rule 805 is to determine whether the retransmission by Warren to the emergency room staff at St. Joseph Hospital fits within the Rule 803(4) exception to the hearsay rule. As we have stated previously, the fact that the statement does not refer to the declarant's physical condition is not controlling. The crucial factor is that the statement was made to promote the efficient delivery of emergency medical services and was accompanied by indicia of truthfulness. These indicia included the fact that the rescue personnel had no reason to falsify the truth, the fact that they offered the statement to assist in obtaining further medical care, and the fact that they were reciting something recently told to them. Therefore, the statement was admissible under Rule 803(4).

The two-step analysis under Rule 805 requires that we view each of the hearsay statements individually before ruling on the multiple hearsay. In this case both the unidentified bystanders' statements to the Cranston rescue personnel and their restatement to the hospital staff constitute admissible hearsay. The original statement was admissible as an exception to the rule against hearsay under Rule 803(4). The subsequent restatement was also admissible as an exception to Rule 802 under Rule 803(4) and Rule 805. Therefore, we are of the opinion that the exclusion of the proffered evidence was reversible error.

[2] Identifying Causes of Medical Conditions

Statements for medical treatment do not include statements that describe the cause of the declarant's malady unless it is relevant to treatment. If the declarant was in a car accident, it is not relevant to the treatment who was at fault in the accident, for instance. The *Narciso* case considers a case in which the perpetrator of the crime may be relevant to the declarant's treatment. *Dever* then considers a statement from a child victim of sexual assault who identified her attacker. As we have seen previously, different standards often apply to child victims of sexual assault.

UNITED STATES v. NARCISO
United States District Court, Eastern District of Michigan, Southern Division
446 F. Supp. 252 (1977)

Memorandum Opinion and Order Granting Defendant's Motion in Limine PHILIP PRATT, DISTRICT JUDGE.

* * *

[The defendants, nurses at a Michigan hospital, were indicted for the deaths of several patients who died under suspicious circumstances while staying at that hospital.]

*   *   *

The facts, in summary, as they appeared during the evidentiary hearings are: On August 15, 1975, at 4:30 p.m. while a patient in the Ann Arbor Veterans Hospital's cardiac care unit, McCrery suffered a respiratory arrest. Approximately 6:30 p.m. that same day, in response to questions from his attending physician as to whether he had been given an injection and, if so, by whom, McCrery wrote the letters "PIA" on a Doctor's Progress Note form.

*   *   *

Dr. Goodenday stated that her motivation for talking to him was "to find out whether or not he had received any medications" as his chart did not indicate that any had been administered prior to the arrest. She first asked him whether he was aware of what had happened and he nodded "yes." She asked him whether he was awake during the entire resuscitation and he nodded "yes." She then asked him if he had received any medication before it all started and again he indicated he had. She asked him if it was given by mouth or through the vein and he indicated by hand gestures that it was administered through the intravenous tubing. Dr. Goodenday then asked who gave it to him, to which he signified a desire for pencil and paper and used them to make the note which is the subject of this inquiry.

*   *   *

The government . . . asserts that the "PIA" note is admissible under FRE 803(4) — statements made for purposes of medical diagnosis or treatment. . . . The rationale of the rule is that statements made to physicians for purposes of diagnosis and treatment are exceptionally trustworthy since the declarant has a strong motive to tell the truth in order to receive proper care. Moreover, no other way of determining subjective symptoms has yet been devised . . . .

The rule is limited to facts related which are "reasonably pertinent to diagnosis or treatment;" it has never been held to apply to accusations of personal fault, either in a civil or criminal context. Thus, the commentators have said that "a party's statement that he was struck by an automobile would qualify but not his statement that the car was driven through a red light." Adv. Comm. Notes. More relevant to this matter, it is stated that a statement by a patient that he was shot would be admissible, but a statement that he was shot by a white man would not. . . . Each case must, of course, rest on its own facts, but the test is whether a doctor would rely on the facts contained therein solely for treatment of the patient's specific condition . . . .

Although the rule in the abstract is simple enough to grasp, application of that rule to the facts as elucidated above . . . is considerably more difficult. The government argues that these questions were asked of Mr. McCrery for purposes of medical diagnosis and treatment and this argument is certainly supported by the testimony of Dr. Goodenday who indicated that her motivation for questioning McCrery subsequent to his recovery from the arrest was to discover (1) if any medication had been administered to him and (2) if so, who did it. Dr. Goodenday indicated that it would be necessary to find out who administered the medication to find out what it was and thus what further medical treatment would be required.[57]

Yet while the doctor's motive was further diagnosis, the underlying assumption of the rule requires the Court to inquire as to the declarant's motivation for giving the information. If his motive is to disclose the information to aid in his own diagnosis and treatment, this, it is assumed, guarantees the statement's trustworthiness. However, if the declarant makes the statement while under the impression that he is being asked to indicate "who was responsible" for what happened, his response may very well be accusatory in nature and any inherent reliability of such a statement is thereby destroyed. In this instance it is not clear that Dr. Goodenday communicated to McCrery that she wanted to know who had administered the injection to find out what the medication was. Once he indicated that he had indeed been given an injection, she merely asked him who gave it to him. Dr. Goodenday herself admitted that the possibility of someone deliberately injecting a muscle relaxant was being considered by the staff. Moreover, the McCrery arrest was one of the last of a series of arrests which began on July 18 and the record discloses that rumors of these arrests and the possibility that they were deliberately induced were prevalent among both the staff and patients.

Based on the entirety of this record this Court is not convinced that McCrery's response to Dr. Goodenday's questions was motivated solely by a desire to assist her in later diagnosis and treatment. Absent such assurance the government may not rely on the hearsay exception in FRE 803(4).

STATE v. DEVER
Supreme Court of Ohio
596 N.E.2d 436 (1992)

ALICE ROBIE RESNICK, JUSTICE.

This case presents the continuing problem of reaching just results in child abuse cases involving statements made by young children during the course of a medical examination. We must consider the admissibility of the statements at trial pursuant to the hearsay exception contained in Evid.R. 803(4). The principal dilemma arises in attempting to apply to children evidentiary rules which were drafted with adults in mind. In applying these rules of evidence to children, we encounter considerable problems in devising a reasonable and workable application. Nevertheless, we continue to strive for balance in this troublesome area of the law. As was noted in *State v. Boston, supra,* 46 Ohio St.3d at 113, 545 N.E.2d at 1226: " * * * [I]t is the goal of all the members of the judiciary that results are reached that are equitable and fair to both society and defendants who find themselves charged with the crime of child abuse."

In considering the circumstances in the instant case, we . . . address [whether]

---

57 (Court's original footnote 3.) It should be noted, however, that this note was not subsequently placed in McCrery's file nor was any similar recordation of it for filing with his records made. Rather, the note was given to Dr. Goodenday's superiors and ultimately to those administrative officials of the hospital responsible for the investigation then underway.

the trial judge abuse his discretion in allowing Dr. Saluke to repeat at trial statements Kristen made to her during the medical examination as an Evid.R. 803(4) hearsay exception?

* * *

. . . Generally, statements of fault are seen as outside the scope of Evid.R. 803(4) because such statements are usually not relevant to either diagnosis or treatment. See, *e.g.*, *United States v. Iron Shell* (C.A. 8, 1980), 633 F.2d 77, 84. However, in *United States v. Renville, supra*, 779 F.2d at 436–438, the leading case in this area, a federal appellate court found that statements made by a child identifying the perpetrator of the sexual abuse *are* pertinent to both diagnosis and treatment of the child. The *Renville* court made a distinction between statements of fault generally (not admissible pursuant to the medical diagnosis or treatment hearsay exception) and specific statements of *identity* by children in sexual abuse cases (which the court found to be admissible). The *Renville* court found several reasons why the statement of identity is pertinent to treatment or diagnosis. The statement assists the doctor in treating any actual injuries the child may have, in preventing future abuse of the child, and in assessing the emotional and psychological impact of the abuse on the child.[8] *Id.*

[W]e adopt *Renville's* reasoning, and hold that statements made by a child during a medical examination identifying the perpetrator of sexual abuse, if made for purpose of diagnosis and treatment, are admissible pursuant to Evid.R. 803(4), when such statements are made for the purposes enumerated in that rule. This means that a child's statement identifying his or her abuser should be treated the same as any other statement which is made for the purposes set forth in Evid.R. 803(4). We thus find that the trial court did not abuse its discretion in admitting Kristen's statement identifying Dever as her abuser.

[3] Statements to Doctor About Previous Doctor's Diagnosis

Rule 803(4) permits a court to admit a patient's statements of medical history for the truth of the matter asserted. What part of one's history does this include? Does it include the opinion and diagnosis that another doctor has given to the patient? Without calling that prior doctor as a witness or placing that doctor's business records into evidence, can a proponent bring the prior doctor's diagnosis into evidence through the testimony of the second physician?

---

[8] We approve of *Renville's* analysis regarding the child's identification of the perpetrator in sexual abuse prosecutions involving young children. There are several reasons for finding that the identification of the perpetrator is relevant to diagnosis and treatment. As Dr. Saluke testified at trial in this case, questioning of the allegedly abused child is important in determining the extent of contact, if any, the possibility of continued exposure to the perpetrator, and the possibility of sexually transmitted diseases. The identity of the perpetrator is particularly relevant to those inquiries, as well as to the psychological effects on the child.

O'GEE v. DOBBS HOUSES, INC.

United States Court of Appeals, Second Circuit
570 F.2d 1084 (1978)

*   *   *

LUMBARD, CIRCUIT JUDGE

I. FACTS

In 1968, Dobbs and United Air Lines, Inc. [hereafter United] entered into a contract pursuant to which Dobbs agreed to provide the food that United would serve on flights out of Atlanta, Ga. This contract was in effect on April 23, 1972. Part of Dobbs' responsibility in Atlanta was to load food onto a cold buffet belonging to United. The buffet is a large, cabinet-like, four-drawer unit weighing between five and eight hundred pounds when loaded. After being filled, the buffet is raised on the galley section of the aircraft, where it is placed on tracks on the floor and slid into a recessed position.

Dobbs' responsibility ended when the buffet was latched in place. The locking mechanism consisted of a lever/latch on each rail of the track on which the buffet rode. The levers had to be in the "up" position to permit a buffet to be removed; when the buffet was withdrawn, the levers were supposed to drop to the "down" position, permitting a new buffet to be installed. The levers would then remain down, locking the buffet in place, until they were once again raised, manually or by foot. Though this system was designed to work automatically, in that removing a buffet forced the levers down, and a new buffet could not be installed unless the levers were in the locked, "down" position, it was conceded that if the levers were, in fact, in the "up" position while a buffet was in place, the buffet would not be secure, and might slide out into the gallery. Accordingly, the United Ramp Manual, which was binding on Dobbs, required a visual check of the levers, and a physical pull on the buffet, after the buffet was loaded on board, to ensure that the latches were down and that the buffet was locked in place.

On April 23, 1972, O'Gee was a stewardess on United flight #476, a Stretch 727, from Atlanta to New York City. That day Dobbs was late in loading the buffet aboard the plane. O'Gee watched the operation, and noted nothing out of the ordinary either then or when she soon after checked the contents of the buffet. As soon as this check was completed, the galley door was locked to bar entry by passengers during boarding. Since there was an emergency exit in the galley, however, to which access was essential, the galley door was reopened immediately after boarding.

Throughout the period of takeoff, O'Gee faced the galley and observed no one enter the area. Some five minutes after takeoff, she noticed that the buffet had slid two feet out of position, substantially blocking access to the emergency exit. O'Gee immediately sought to push the unit back into position, but failed. At this time, she "felt something pull" in her back. She then braced one foot behind her and tried again, again failing, and feeling a sharper pain in her back. A third try with the help of another stewardess failed, as did an attempt by the flight engineer. Finally, all three acting in concert succeeded in pushing the buffet back; O'Gee stepped on the locking levers to latch the buffet in place, where it remained for the rest of the flight. No report of this incident was made at the conclusion of the flight.

During the remainder of April 23, O'Gee had a "very bad backache," of which she complained to another stewardess and the flight engineer. She returned to work on April 24 and 25, but suffered pain and stiffness throughout both days. On April 26, she reported to a United medical officer, who gave her medication and requested that she return before her next flight. Over the next fourteen months, O'Gee saw several physicians, both in New York City and in Rochester, where her parents lived. Her problem was variously diagnosed as back sprain, a slipped disk, and a herniated disk. Much of this period was spent either in bed or in therapy; attempts to resume work in July and again in October of 1972 were unsuccessful. Finally, in May of 1973, O'Gee underwent a laminectomy for the removal of a herniated disk from her back. After a period of recuperation, she returned to work at United (on smaller planes than formerly) in September of 1973. Thereafter, O'Gee lost no further time from work as a result of the April, 1972, incident, and even received commendations for perfect records in 1975 and 1976.

O'Gee brought suit against Dobbs, alleging that her injury was the result of the defendant's negligence in placing and securing the buffet unit on the plane. Dobbs impleaded United, claiming that any injury sustained resulted from defects in United's equipment. United counterclaimed against Dobbs for costs and counsel fees, citing the indemnity clause of its contract with Dobbs.

At trial, O'Gee did not call to testify any of the doctors she had consulted in the two years immediately following the incident. Rather, she relied for her medical testimony exclusively on Dr. Leo J. Koven, who first saw her in December of 1976, but who was given access to the findings of the Rochester doctors who had recommended and performed the laminectomy, as well as to her hospital records. Dr. Koven was permitted to testify, over strenuous objection, to the opinions of other doctors O'Gee had seen, as he had learned of them through their reports, and through his history he had taken from O'Gee herself.

*   *   *

IV. DR. KOVEN'S TESTIMONY

This allegation of error raises questions of [great] magnitude. Of the doctors O'Gee had consulted in the period immediately following the incident, a number were present right in New York, where the trial was held. Yet instead of calling any of these doctors, who had had a chance to examine her when both the nature of her injuries and the probability of their being sequelae of the incident would have been most apparent, she called only Dr. Koven, a doctor retained for the purposes of the litigation, and who first saw O'Gee in December of 1976, more than four years after the buffet.

It was through the testimony of Dr. Koven that O'Gee presented to the jury the opinions of the doctors she had seen in 1972 and 1973. Judge Weinstein permitted the witness to testify not only to what O'Gee had told him about her condition and its genesis, but also to what O'Gee had told him that the other doctors had told her about her injuries. Thus, Dr. Koven's testimony contained both single and multiple hearsay on crucial issues.

Prior to the adoption of the Federal Rule of Evidence, a non-treating doctor such as Dr. Koven would have been permitted to recite his patient's statements to him, not as proof of the facts stated, but only to show the basis of his opinion. . . . The Federal Rules, however, rejected this distinction as being too esoteric for a jury to recognize. . . . Rule 803(4) clearly permits the admission into evidence of what O'Gee told Dr. Koven about her condition, so long as it was relied on by Dr. Koven in formulating his opinion — a foundation that was properly laid.

Nowhere does the commentary on Rule 803(4) indicate, however, whether the Rule was intended to go so far as to permit a doctor to testify to his patient's version of other doctors' opinions, particularly when no showing is made of those other doctors' unavailability. We need not reach the furthest extent of this issue, however, because Dr. Koven clearly stated that he was not relying solely on O'Gee's recollection of the other doctors' opinions, but actually had before him the reports of at least two of those doctors, and of the hospital where O'Gee's laminectomy was performed. Defendant and third-party defendant were aware of what those reports showed, and should have been prepared to counter them as best they could regardless of how testimony concerning them was introduced. In fact, it appears that portions of the hospital record were used quite effectively against Dr. Koven on cross-examination. Under the circumstances of this case, we do not think it was abuse of discretion for Judge Weinstein to permit Dr. Koven to testify as he did. We observe, however, that while expert witnesses are to be permitted to explain the basis of their opinions, we do not here decide that that leeway extends to the kind of multiple hearsay that would have been present here in the absence of the doctors' reports.

EXERCISE

Mother, fearful that her child had been sexually assaulted, took the child to a hospital. At the hospital a physician conducted a physical examination of the child, including asking the child to explain how she received various bruises and marks on her body. After the physical examination, a social worker interviewed the child again. The interview was videotaped and the physician and a police officer observed the interview through a mirror. Based on the physical exam and interview, criminal charges were filed against defendant. At the trial the defendant seeks to exclude the admission of the social worker's videotaped interview on hearsay grounds. How should the court rule?

[E] Past Recollection Recorded

Federal Rules of Evidence: Rule 803(5)

Rule 803 Hearsay Exceptions; Availability of Declarant Immaterial

The rule regarding recorded recollections permits the declarant's prior statement to be admitted so long as the declarant had knowledge of the matter recorded at the time the matter was recorded. As you will see in the dissent in *Marcy*, this doctrine permits a statement to be admitted contrary to many of the concerns in the hearsay rule.

STATE v. MARCY

Supreme Court of Vermont

680 A.2d 76 (1996)

JOHNSON, JUSTICE.

Defendant appeals his conviction by jury for simple assault. He argues that the trial court erred by (1) admitting the assault victim's tape-recorded statement as past recollection recorded, pursuant to V.R.E. 803(5), and (2) denying defendant's motion for judgment of acquittal pursuant to V.R.Cr.P. 29, because the sole evidence supporting defendant's conviction is past recollection recorded, which defendant argues does not meet the standards for reliability set out by this court in *State v. Robar*, 157 Vt. 387, 395, 601 A.2d 1376, 1380 (1991). We affirm the trial court, holding that the tape-recorded statement of the victim was properly admitted as past recollection recorded and that the victim's statement was sufficiently reliable to support the conviction.

I.

The victim was defendant's wife. Following the assault on December 28, 1992, the victim obtained a restraining order against defendant. On December 29, 1992, the day after the assault, a police officer went to the victim's home in response to her complaint against defendant. The victim told the officer that she had been assaulted by defendant, who had "pounded her head against a door" and "choked her to the point where she nearly blacked out," and that he had damaged several guns. At the time of the interview, the officer observed scratches on the victim's face, which she claimed were the result of the physical confrontation with defendant. The officer also interviewed two other residents of the house. One of those residents stated that he had seen defendant and his wife enter their bedroom, that he had heard shouting, including the victim saying, "Don't do it, please don't do this," and that he had heard noises coming from the bedroom, including a banging against the door. The other resident stated only that he had heard an argument inside the house.

After speaking with these three people, the police officer tape-recorded an interview with the victim, which the officer testified was consistent with what the victim had told him earlier. The officer also testified that the victim appeared to be alert and to understand what she was doing while he was tape-recording the interview, and that she showed no indication that she was having trouble remembering the events of the previous night.

At trial, the victim testified that she did not remember the assault. She maintained that she only could remember visiting a psychiatrist's office with defendant, who left the office without her, returning home afterward, and following defendant into the bedroom to find out what had upset him. She vaguely recalled something about guns being broken, but could not remember the details. She testified that she remembered getting a restraining order on December 28, but she did not remember how she got to the police station. She also remembered that a trooper had come to her home, but she did not remember calling the police, and she did not remember being choked by defendant.

The State then offered the victim's tape-recorded statement pursuant to V.R.E. 803(5), as past recollection recorded. The State called several witnesses (out of the presence of the jury), including the victim, the police officer who took the statement, and a victim advocate with whom the victim had spoken, to lay a foundation for the admission of the statement. The court found that the statement satisfied the requirements of Rule 803(5).

II.

We first consider whether the trial court properly admitted the victim's tape-recorded statement, pursuant to V.R.E. 803(5), as past recollection recorded.[1] Rule 803(5), which is identical to its counterpart in the Federal Rules of Evidence, establishes an exception to the hearsay rule for a previously recorded recollection of an event, when the witness has no present recollection of the event. *State v. Lander*, 155 Vt. 645, 645, 582 A.2d 128, 128 (1990) (mem.). We have previously held that documents admitted pursuant to V.R.E. 803(5) must meet three requirements:

> "(1) The document must pertain to matters about which the declarant once had knowledge; (2) The declarant must now have an insufficient recollection as to such matters; (3) The document must be shown to have been made by the declarant or, if made by one other than the declarant, to have been examined by the declarant and shown to accurately reflect the declarant's knowledge when the matters were fresh in his memory."

State v. Paquette, 146 Vt. 1, 3, 497 A.2d 358, 360 (1985) (quoting *People v. Kubasiak*, 98 Mich.App. 529, 296 N.W.2d 298, 302 (1980)).

Based on the victim's testimony and the circumstances under which the statement was given, the trial court determined that the first two requirements were easily met. As the victim of the assault, the witness once had knowledge of it, and her tape-recorded statement relates that knowledge in detail. Moreover, the court found that it was "clear and without question [ ] that the declarant now has insufficient recollection about any matters contained in that tape or . . . concern-[ing] what did or did not happen to her on [the date of the assault]." As the trial court's findings are supported by the evidence, they are not clearly erroneous and

---

[1] V.R.E. 803(5) provides:

> The following are not excluded by the hearsay rule, even though the declarant is available as a witness:
>
> *   *   *
>
> (5) *Recorded Recollection.* A memorandum or record concerning a matter about which a witness once had knowledge but now has insufficient recollection to enable him to testify fully and accurately, shown to have been made or adopted by the witness when the matter was fresh in his memory and to reflect that knowledge correctly. If admitted, the memorandum or record may be read into evidence but may not itself be received as an exhibit unless offered by an adverse party.

will not be disturbed on appeal. See *State v. Zaccaro*, 154 Vt. 83, 86, 574 A.2d 1256, 1258 (1990) (noting that trial court's findings of fact will not be disturbed "unless they are unsupported by the evidence or clearly erroneous"); see also *Paquette*, 146 Vt. at 4, 497 A.2d at 360 (requirements one and two met under circumstances similar to instant case).

The more difficult question is whether the tape-recorded statement meets the third requirement. To meet this requirement, the statement must pass two separate tests. First, the statement must be shown to have been made by the witness, or if made by another, to have been adopted by the witness. V.R.E. 803(5); see *Paquette*, 146 Vt. at 4, 497 A.2d at 361 (noting that facts "sufficiently show that the statement was *adopted* by the witness") (emphasis added). In this case, the testimony of the police officer who tape-recorded the statement is sufficient to establish that the statement was made by the witness.

Second, the statement must be shown to accurately reflect the witness's knowledge when the matter was fresh in her memory. *Paquette*, 146 Vt. at 3, 497 A.2d at 360. Defendant, arguing that the statement should not have been admitted, emphasizes that the statement was not sworn, and that the witness never affirmed the truth or accuracy of the statement when it was made. Defendant misconstrues the requirements of Rule 803(5). Nothing in the language of the rule indicates that, to be admissible, the prior statement must be sworn, or that the *witness* must affirm the accuracy of the prior statement.

A number of courts have ruled statements inadmissible as past recollection recorded because the statements were not sworn, signed by the witness, or otherwise affirmed by the witness as accurate. Closer examination of those cases reveals, however, that the statements involved were not prepared by the witness, but by another person, usually a law enforcement agent. See, e.g., *United States v. Schoenborn*, 4 F.3d 1424, 1427 (7th Cir. 1993) (noting that witness "did not adopt . . . as his own" report prepared by FBI agent of interview with witness); *People v. Hoffman*, 205 Mich.App. 1, 518 N.W.2d 817, 825 (1994) (holding that denying admission of police officer's typewritten notes of witness's statement was proper where witness never adopted statements as true and accurate); *People v. Kubasiak*, 296 N.W.2d at 302 (holding that police report of witness's statement was inadmissible because witness had not adopted report as accurate when matter was fresh in his memory). Understandably, where a prior statement was prepared by a person other than the witness, courts have relied on or even required evidence that the witness had sworn or otherwise affirmed the accuracy of the prepared statement, to satisfy the requirement that the witness adopted the statement.

Here, there is no dispute that the witness herself gave the tape-recorded statement. The question before us is whether the State presented sufficient evidence to show that the tape-recorded statement accurately reflected the witness's knowledge of the assault. The trial court, in finding the statement admissible, relied upon the following evidence of its accuracy: the statement was given to a police officer within a day of the assault; the tape-recorded statement was made shortly after and was consistent with a prior interview with the police officer; the statement revealed details of the assault; the statement described the events chronologically; the witness spoke coherently, logically, and relatively directly, responding appropriately to questions from the officer; the witness did not appear sleepy or groggy to the officer, despite her later testimony that she was taking prescription drugs at the time the statement was given; and the police officer's interviews with the other residents of the house provided some corroboration. The trial court also emphasized that the witness never recanted the statement, or indicated that the statement was inaccurate or given involuntarily, but rather testified that if she had talked to a police officer she would have tried to be truthful. Specifically, the witness testified that she would not have "intentionally" or "deliberately" lied to the officer.

Defendant points to two elements of the witness's testimony as throwing doubt on the accuracy of the statement. The witness testified that she was using prescription drugs at the time the statement was given, which could have affected her thinking. Also, when asked if she could think of any reason why she might have wanted to tell the police officer something that she did not believe to be true at the time, she replied, "Maybe anger." The trial court judge, who observed the testimony firsthand, found persuasive the police officer's testimony that the witness spoke clearly and did not appear sleepy or groggy at the time of the statement. The judge also found that the witness had not recanted the statement or "given evidence saying that what she said previously is incorrect." Again, the court's findings on these two issues are not clearly erroneous, and will not be disturbed by this Court. See *Zaccaro*, 154 Vt. at 86, 574 A.2d at 1258.

We agree with the court that, taken together, the evidence presented by the State is sufficient to show that the tape-recorded statement of the witness correctly reflects her knowledge of the assault at the time it was made. In so doing, we adopt the reasoning of the Sixth Circuit, which in interpreting the identical federal rule regarding past recollection recorded recently stated:

> Rule 803(5) does not specify any particular method of establishing the knowledge of the declarant nor the accuracy of the statement. It is not a *sine qua non* of admissibility that the witness actually vouch for the accuracy of the written memorandum. Admissibility is, instead, to be determined on a case-by-case basis upon a consideration . . . of factors indicating trustworthiness, or the lack thereof.

United States v. Porter, 986 F.2d 1014, 1017 (6th Cir. 1993). In *Porter*, the defendant was convicted on several charges involving drugs and explosives. Part of the evidence supporting his c onvictions was a detailed written statement given by his girlfriend to the FBI. Portions of the statement were read to the jury after the girlfriend testified that she did not remember much about what she had said in the statement, because "she was confused and on drugs at the time the statement was made." *Id.* at 1016. She did not testify that the statement was accurate. The trial court found "sufficient indicia of trustworthiness," including the details contained in the statement, its internal consistency, and its consistency with other evidence. *Id.* at 1017.[2]

---

[2] The facts in *Porter* are not directly analogous to this case, because the witness in *Porter* had signed the statement under penalty of perjury at the time it was made, and had also initialed the statement several times where she had changed the wording. As in many past recollection recorded cases, the

Here, although the victim did not sign the statement, that factor is much less important because the statement is a tape-recording in the victim's own voice. The other evidence relied on by the trial court is sufficient to establish the accuracy of the statement. The tape-recorded statement of the victim was properly admitted as past recollection recorded and could be relied upon by the jury.

We do not believe that our holding is inconsistent with our memorandum decision in *State v. Lander*, 155 Vt. at 645, 582 A.2d at 128, where we held that a witness's prior statement was not admissible as past recollection recorded. We noted that the witness had not "adopt[ed] his prior statement as his own or aver[red] that the statement accurately reflected his knowledge at the time of its making."[3] *Id. Lander*, however, is a brief memorandum decision which does not provide the relevant facts of the case. The decision does not indicate, for example, whether the statement was prepared by the witness or by a third party, but merely cites to *Kubasiak*, 296 N.W.2d at 302, where the court refused to admit a police officer's report of a witness's prior statement where the witness had not adopted that report as true.

We are not persuaded that our memorandum decision in *Lander* should be interpreted as altering the plain language of V.R.E. 803(5) to add a requirement that the *witness* must testify that the statement accurately reflects the witness's knowledge at the time the statement was made. Had the drafters intended this result, they could easily have accomplished it by changing the language of the rule. Instead, the rule is phrased in the passive voice, requiring only that the memorandum or record be "*shown* to have been made or adopted by the witness." V.R.E. 803(5) (emphasis added). We conclude that the language of the rule contemplates a more flexible case-by-case determination of the admissibility of a statement as past recollection recorded, that evaluates the trustworthiness of the prior statement instead of focusing on hypertechnical evidentiary requirements. See *United States v. Williams*, 571 F.2d 344, 350 (6th Cir. 1978) ("touchstone for admission of evidence as an exception to the hearsay rule has been the existence of circumstances which attest to its trustworthiness"); see also *State v. Discher*, 597 A.2d 1336, 1341 (Me.1991) (past recollection recorded exception does not spell out method for establishing initial knowledge or contemporaneity and accuracy of record, but leaves determination to circumstances of particular case).

ALLEN, CHIEF JUSTICE, concurring.

I agree that the trial court properly admitted the tape recording of the victim's statement and did not err in denying defendant's motion for judgment of acquittal; I therefore join the majority in affirming. I write separately, however, to point out that the disagreement between the majority and the dissent on the foundational

---

statement in *Porter* was prepared by a law enforcement agent, rather than by the witness herself. The reasoning in *Porter* is, however, still applicable. That the witness signed the statement when it was made was not determinative, but was one factor supporting the accuracy of the statement.

[3] The dissent emphasizes this statement as announcing a foundational requirement for admission under Rule 803(5). We note, however, that the statement was based on "a review of the record," *State v. Lander*, 155 Vt. 645, 645, 582 A.2d 128, 128 (1990) (mem.), and may more fairly be read as a recounting of the facts of the case.

requirements of Rule 803(5) need not be resolved to decide this appeal. Even under the dissent's more restrictive interpretation of the rule, the foundational requirements were satisfied in this case.

To ensure that a statement accurately reflects the witness's knowledge, that witness "must either testify (1) that he recalls having made an accurate memorandum or (2) that though he now does not recollect his state of mind when making the record, he would not have made it unless it were correct." 4 Weinstein's Evidence ¶ 803(5)[01], at 803-180 to -181 (1995). Under the second approach, the witness can testify that he would not have written or signed a memorandum unless he had been convinced it was correct. *Id.* at 803–181; 2 McCormick on Evidence § 283, at 259 (4th ed. 1992).

Although this case involved a tape recording rather than a signed statement, the witness's testimony is analogous to the foundational predicate for a written memorandum. See, e.g., *Dennis v. Scarborough*, 360 So.2d 278, 279 (Ala.1978) (the witness testified that "he must have known the recording's veracity (though not whether the statement itself was accurate) because he otherwise would not have written them down."); *Walker v. Larson*, 284 Minn. 99, 169 N.W.2d 737, 742 (1969) (witness "testified that he had never signed any paper which did not contain true facts within his own knowledge."). Referring to statements in a transcript of the tape recording, the state's attorney asked the victim, "[W]ould you have said them if they were not true?" The victim replied, "I don't believe I would have." The state's attorney then asked the victim, "Is there a single thing in those two pages [of the transcript] that you think you would have deliberately said to the police officer if they were not true?" She replied, "No." In its Rule 803(5) analysis, the trial court relied upon this testimony by the witness, saying: "She[ ] further testified that . . . if she had talked to a police officer, and that is now established, about this incident, she would have endeavored to be truthful . . . . She has not given evidence saying that what she said previously is incorrect."[*]

In *United States v. Patterson*, 678 F.2d 774 (9th Cir. 1982), the court concluded that the foundational requirement was satisfied under circumstances similar to this case. In *Patterson*, the government sought to introduce the defendant's grand jury testimony as past recollection recorded. The court concluded that the witness's testimony that "he did not think he had lied to the grand jury" was sufficient to establish that the grand jury testimony accurately reflected the witness's knowledge. *Id.* at 779. In sum, the tape recording of the victim's statements was properly admitted under either the majority or dissent's interpretation of the foundational requirements of Rule 803(5).

I have been authorized to state that JUSTICE GIBSON joins in this concurrence.

---

[*] Although the trial court may have determined the admissibility of the tape recording under the disputed interpretation of Rule 803(5), we can affirm its admissibility determination on any legal ground which would justify the result. *Richards v. Union High Sch. Dist. No. 32*, 137 Vt. 132, 134, 400 A.2d 987, 989 (1979) ("Error will not result in reversal if the record before us discloses any legal ground which would justify the result, even though the ground may not have been raised below and may not be briefed.").

DOOLEY, JUSTICE, dissenting.

The majority opinion represents an unprecedented weakening of the foundational requirements of the hearsay exception for past recollection recorded, V.R.E. 803(5), and an abandonment of the restrictions on the use of such evidence as the sole basis to convict a criminal defendant. The effect is that hearsay evidence, the reliability of which cannot be challenged by normal means, acquires such weight that defendant is stripped of the ability to mount an effective defense. Although I am sympathetic to the majority's goals in this domestic violence case, I cannot agree to the distortion of neutral and essential principles of evidence law and fair play that reaching those goals necessitates. Accordingly, I dissent.

At the outset, I believe that we should be more forthcoming about what is really motivating the decision. This case involves an allegation of spousal abuse in which, as in many such cases, the abused spouse is the only witness to the assault. And too often, after filing a complaint with the police, the abused spouse recants or seeks not to press charges against the abusive spouse. See C. Klein & L. Orloff, *Providing Legal Protection for Battered Women: An Analysis of State Statutes and Case Law*, 21 Hofstra L.Rev. 801, 1187–88 (1993). The reality is that both the trial judge and the majority believe that this is a case of recantation by convenient memory lapse. That is, they are skeptical of the victim's assertion that she remembers neither the assault nor the statement. What the opinion really says is that spousal abusers should not be able to avoid criminal responsibility by such a ploy.

I share the skepticism about the victim's memory failure, but am unwilling to join result-oriented decision-making that eliminates important safeguards on the truth-finding function of trials. In this instance, evidentiary doctrine created to prevent those who feign amnesia from subverting the criminal justice process is equally applicable when the memory lapse is real.[1] The result is to open up the realm of "trial-by-statement" where it is impossible to test the accuracy of the statement or resolve evidentiary conflicts in any reliable way.

I am also troubled that there is an internal inconsistency in the majority's approach to the problem that confronts us. The hearsay rule that allows for the admission of the critical statement is applicable if the declarant "now has insufficient recollection to enable him to testify fully and accurately." V.R.E. 803(5). What the majority is really holding is that because this essential element of the hearsay exception is *not* met, we should broaden the exception to let in *more* hearsay than we would otherwise allow. I fear that we are standing normal evidence analysis on its head to reach the desired result.

I

On the hearsay point, what is in issue is contained in *State v. Lander*, 155 Vt. 645, 582 A.2d 128 (1990) (mem.), where we reversed a criminal conviction because critical

---

[1] By comparison, Rule 801(d)(1)(A), admitting prior inconsistent statements as "not hearsay," can be used when the court finds a witness is feigning a memory loss. See 2 McCormick on Evidence § 251, at 121 (4th ed. 1992). That rule has an additional safeguard that the prior statement must be "given under oath subject to the penalty of perjury." V.R.E. 801(d)(1)(A).

evidence was erroneously admitted under V.R.E. 803(5):

> When a witness has no present recollection of a prior event, a previously recorded recollection of the event is admissible under V.R.E. 803(5) despite the proscription against the use of hearsay, V.R.E. 802, provided that the proponent lays the necessary foundation. . . . Defendant raised a timely objection to the use of the witness's statement based on the inadequacy of the foundation. *A review of the record indicates that the witness did not adopt his prior statement as his own or aver that the statement accurately reflected his knowledge at the time of its making. . . . Therefore, the statement lacked a foundation sufficient to justify its admission into evidence.*

Id. at 645, 582 A.2d at 128 (citations omitted; emphasis supplied). There is no dispute that the foundation required in *Lander* is missing here. The majority has two answers to this obvious obstacle.[2]

The first is to distinguish *Lander* on the basis that the statements involved were prepared by another person rather than by the witness. The majority cites four cases for the significance of this distinction. None state that this distinction is critical so that the evidence would have been admissible if the statement had been prepared by the witness. In *United States v. Schoenborn*, 4 F.3d 1424, 1428 (7th Cir. 1993), for example, the court quoted from its earlier opinion in *United States v. Williams*, 951 F.2d 853, 858 (7th Cir. 1992), that in a third-party-transcription case, the evidentiary foundation must include both testimony to the accuracy of the transcription and testimony by the person whose past recollection is in issue "to the accuracy of his oral report to the person who recorded the statement." What *Schoenborn* holds is that third-party-transcription cases impose an additional foundational requirement beyond that imposed in *Lander*; it clearly does *not* hold that the *Lander* requirements are inapplicable in such cases.

The majority's new distinction is curious because it does not even apply to the facts of this case. V.R.E. 803(5) plainly states that a *"memorandum or record . . .* shown to have been made or adopted by the witness" may be admissible as past recollection recorded. (Emphasis added.) Here, the tape recording was made by the *officer*, not the witness. The police were in possession of the tape until trial. Indeed, we have a copy because the original is lost. Moreover, the officer testified that part of the tape was erased during transcription. The tape recording has pauses and jumps, as the machine was stopped and started during the interview.[3]

The use of the majority's new distinction to distinguish *Lander* is also curious, since there is no indication in that published entry order decision that it is a

---

[2] A footnote suggests a third, that the *Lander* requirements were descriptions of history not law. In the paragraph quoted above, the next to the last statement can and should be taken as a description of what is in the record. The last sentence, commenced with "Therefore," clearly states that the consequence of this history is that the "statement lacked a foundation sufficient to justify its admission." It can be interpreted only as a statement of law, inconsistent with the majority's position here.

[3] I am not suggesting that the tape recording was doctored. I am suggesting that the same issues of accuracy of transcription exist for a tape recording as for written statement which is reduced to writing by a third party.

third-party-transcription case. This the first time I have ever observed that we have guessed at the facts of an appellate precedent in order to distinguish it on grounds never mentioned in the precedent.

In any event, no commentator supports the distinction made by the majority. McCormick comes the closest to the majority by acknowledging that the foundational requirements in issue may be more easily satisfied where there is no third-party-transcription, but is clear that the witness must in some way acknowledge the accuracy of the prior statement. See 2 McCormick on Evidence § 283, at 259–60 (4th ed. 1992). Weinstein states that in any case the witness whose statement is admitted must testify that he now recalls that it was accurate or that he would not have made it if it were not correct. 4 Weinstein's Evidence ¶ 803(5)[01], at 803-180 to -181 (1995).

Nothing in the language of the rule supports the distinction. The rule requires the proponent of admission to show that the statement reflects the witnesses' "*knowledge* correctly." V.R.E. 803(5) (emphasis supplied). If the drafters intended the new majority result, they would have used "statement" not "knowledge."

In short, the majority has created a distinction without a difference in order to distinguish a precedent of this Court which is dead against it. There is no support for the proposition that the difference can eliminate the foundation requirement of *Lander* that the witness "aver that the statement accurately reflected his knowledge at the time of its making." *Lander*, 155 Vt. at 645, 582 A.2d at 128.

The second answer is to ignore the holding of *Lander* as if the inconvenient words within it have somehow disappeared. The majority's view is that *Lander* cannot mean what it says because the plain language of Rule 803(5) does not include the *Lander* requirement. Part of the reason for the brevity of *Lander*, I am sure, is that it restated the widely-accepted requirements of the rule. See 4 Weinstein's Evidence § 803(5)[01], at 803-180 to -181. The rule was drafted to be a codification of the common law hearsay exception, which included the *Lander* requirements. See *id.* at 803-172 (rule is codification of law that was long-favored in the federal courts); 3 Wigmore on Evidence § 747(a) (1970) (hearsay exception for past recollection recorded requires that witness be able to assert that record correctly represented his knowledge and recollection at time of making).

We have said often that our overall aim in construing statutes is to implement the intent of the Legislature. See, e.g., *Lemieux v. Tri-State Lotto Comm'n*, 164 Vt. [110, 113–114], 666 A.2d 1170, 1173 (1995). The same principle applies to construing our rules, but it is our intent that we must follow. Few of our evidence rules have a "plain meaning" when applied to myriad of circumstances that arise in the courtroom. Unlike the Vermont Legislature, we have devices in our rule drafting to explain the intent of the draftspersons. Thus, we have frequently looked to reporter's notes, and other indicia of intent to determine the proper interpretation of rules. See *State v. Bean*, 163 Vt. 457, [463], 658 A.2d 940, 944 (1995). Also in construing a statute or rule, we presume that the common law is not changed except by clear and unambiguous language. See *Estate of Kelley v. Moguls, Inc.*, 160 Vt. 531, 533, 632 A.2d 360, 362 (1993).

The intent behind Rule 803(5) is clear: to codify the common law rule, which contains the *Lander* foundation requirements. The wording of the rule does not clearly and unambiguously modify the common law requirements. It still requires that the past record reflect the declarant's knowledge "correctly," and here, this requirement has not been met. The majority's attempt to find nuances in the drafting of Rule 803(5), while ignoring the statements of intent, only insures that the outcome will not reflect our intent.[4]

I also note that the majority's textual approach explains only part of its rationale. It does not explain, for example, the majority's distinction between statements prepared by the witness and those prepared by third persons. There is no support for this distinction in the text of the rule.

For its new approach, the majority relies on one precedent, *United States v. Porter*, 986 F.2d 1014 (6th Cir. 1993), a decision followed by no other state or federal court. The majority relies primarily on *Porter* for the contention that the accuracy of the statement can be shown according to objective indicia of reliability in lieu of the witness's own attestations. See *id.* at 1017. Although *Porter* contains some broad language, I cannot read it as supporting the majority's conclusion, and the facts are distinguishable from the present case. In *Porter*, the witness admitted making the statement and signing it under penalty of perjury. She testified that she tried to tell the truth to the police officer, but acknowledged that she was high on drugs at the time and could not be certain of what she had told the police. Therefore, she explicitly affirmed that the document reflected her knowledge when the statement was made. *Id.* at 1017.

Porter is, in the words of McCormick, an example of the "extreme, [where] it is even sufficient if the individual testifies to recognizing his or her signature on the statement and believes the statement correct because the witness would not have signed it if he or she had not believed it true at the time."[5] 2 McCormick on Evidence § 283, at 259. Here, the wife, unlike the witness in *Porter*, does not remember meeting the police officer and giving the statement to him. She consistently testified that because of her memory loss, she could not verify the accuracy and truthfulness of the statement. If *Porter* represents the "extreme" case, we have now gone well beyond the extreme and made that normal.

The majority's analysis would render the witness's presence on the witness stand superfluous. See *People v. Simmons*, 123 Cal.App.3d 677, 177 Cal.Rptr. 17, 21 (1981). If third party testimony can establish objective facts indicating the reliability of the statement, then the witness's own attestations to the statement's accuracy become unnecessary. Extending the majority's logic, third party testimony could make admissible a statement that a witness claims is false, inaccurate, or was never made. The majority's holding transforms Rule 803(5) into an exception for prior inconsistent statements not made under oath, see V.R.E. 801(d)(1)(A), and into a "catch-all exception" for hearsay that does not fit within a statutory exception.

---

[4] One of the nuances is that the rule is drafted in the passive voice and should have been stated in the active voice if the draftspersons had intended that the witness testify to the accuracy of the content of the recording. Virtually all of the hearsay exceptions are stated in the passive voice, showing that the real motivation behind the drafting of any exception is parallelism with other exceptions.

[5] The prosecution might have brought this case within the rule by playing the tape for the wife, and eliciting similar responses about it. The prosecution did not do so.

Unlike the federal courts, we specifically decided that we would not adopt a "catch-all" hearsay exception. See Reporter's Notes, V.R.E. 803 (noting that Federal Rule of Evidence 803(24), providing for the catchall hearsay exception, was not adopted in Vermont). If we are to amend V.R.E. 803(5), we should do so by rule amendment and not by decision.

I can find no decision from any court that would allow admission in this case, and the evidence clearly does not meet the foundation requirement set forth in *State v. Lander*. Even if I thought *Porter* would go this far, the majority gives no explanation for overruling *Lander*. I would hold that the evidence did not meet the requirements of V.R.E. 803(5) and is, therefore, inadmissible hearsay. Since the evidence was central to the State's case, indeed was the entirety of the case, I would reverse the conviction on that basis.

II

The concurring opinion has a different theory of admissibility. My main problem is that it is not supported by the facts found by the trial judge.

Through transcript pages of examination and cross-examination, the prosecutor and defense counsel attempted to induce defendant's wife to answer hypothetical statements that might support or oppose admissibility of the tape recording. The result is that she did both. At one point, as the concurring opinion cites, she answered "I don't believe I would have" to a question whether she would have made the statements on the tape if they were not true. At another point, she answered "anger" to a question asking whether there is a reason why she might tell someone something she did not believe was true.

Under V.R.E. 104(a), preliminary fact questions pertaining to admissibility are for the trial court. See Reporter's Notes to V.R.E. 104(a). In this case, the farthest the court went was to find "if she talked to a police officer, and that is now established, she would have endeavored to be truthful." The trial court adopted the theory of admissibility now accepted by the majority; it did not adopt the theory of the concurrence.

The rule requires that the recording be shown "to reflect . . . [the witness's] knowledge correctly." V.R.E. 803(5). I cannot accept that the recording has been shown to have reflected accurately the victim's knowledge when she does not remember making the recording and can state only "she would have endeavored to be truthful." Indeed, if this witness meets the foundation requirement, it is difficult to conceive of a witness who would not.

I can find no case that goes this far. In *United States v. Patterson*, 678 F.2d 774, 779 (9th Cir. 1982), the case relied upon by the concurrence, the witness recalled giving testimony to the grand jury and said "he did not think he had lied to the grand jury" and added that "he recalled the events in question better when he testified before the grand jury." This foundation testimony, which is specific to the prior statement, is far stronger than that here.

As I indicated above, the foundation here is much weaker than what McCormick describes as "the extreme." As McCormick indicates, the more common requirement is that the witness testify to a "habit or practice to record such matters accurately" even though he or she cannot speak to the accuracy of the particular recording at issue. See 2 McCormick, *supra*, § 283, at 259. Here, there is no showing of habit or practice.

I do not agree that we can affirm the trial court by relying on foundational facts not found below. If we accept the fact-finding of the trial court, as we must, the foundation requirements are not met.

*   *   *

IV

One other issue is symbolic of what is going on in this case. Although V.R.E. 803(5) admits past recollection recorded as an exception to the hearsay rule, the use of this evidence is carefully limited. Thus, the record "may be read into evidence but may not itself be received as an exhibit unless offered by an adverse party." The limitation is to "avoid the danger that undue weight might be given to the [record] itself." Reporter's Notes to V.R.E. 803(5). The limitation was ignored in this case. The tape recording was played for the jury, rather than its content being read into evidence. See *State v. Discher*, 597 A.2d 1336, 1339 (Me. 1991) (once tape recording admitted as past recollection recorded, court permitted only transcript of tape recording to be read aloud to jury). It was replayed for the jury during their deliberations, at their request. The point was to give this recording the maximum weight possible because the taped hearsay statement was the primary evidence against defendant. The jury could have convicted defendant because the witness against him "sounded" credible.

The majority's answer to this point demonstrates what went wrong here. They find it "ludicrous to suggest that in this case the jury should hear another person read a transcript of the tape, rather than hear the victim actually making the statement." It is, of course, equally "ludicrous" to have someone read a written statement, rather than giving it to the jury for its perusal. No doubt, the jury will be in a better position to judge reliability if it hears or sees the statement.

Following Federal Rule 803(5), we adopted this "ludicrous" restriction for a reason. Past recollection recorded is evidence of debatable quality, and we did not want excessive reliance placed on it. Unfortunately, this decision is going in the opposite direction. The recorded statement is virtually all of the prosecution's case, and the majority wants the full force of it to get before the jury. As our disagreements on the first two issues demonstrate, the majority has no concerns about the quality of this evidence, and a restriction built on such concerns looks ludicrous.

If this issue had been preserved, I would have voted to reverse also because we cannot say that the jury's verdict was not substantially swayed by the improper playing of the tape. See *United States v. Ray*, 768 F.2d 991, 995 (8th Cir. 1985) (conviction for failure to appear reversed where transcript constituting past recollection was submitted to jury and constituted only evidence of defendant's notice to appear). I raise it now to emphasize that evidence which, at best, is marginally reliable under evidence principles, and impossible to test through cross-examination, became the centerpiece of the prosecution's case and was put in front of the jury in the most damaging way possible. It adds to my firm conclusion that this trial did not meet minimum standards of fairness that allows us to affirm its result.

I dissent.

[F]   Writing Used to Refresh Memory

One should clearly distinguish between the hearsay exception of past recollection recorded, through which a writing is offered into evidence for the truth of the matter asserted therein, and present recollection revived, which involves a proponent's use of that same writing to refresh a witness' exhausted memory but which the proponent does not offer into evidence. Under the concept of present recollection revived, the writing is not used as evidence because the witness who examined it is able to testify to the relevant facts based on the present recollection that the examination of the writing revived. Consequently, a proponent's limited use of a writing to revive a witness' recollection poses no hearsay problem. This limited use of writings, as well as the use that may be made of materials other than writings to refresh recollection, is governed by Fed. R. Evid. 612 and is further explained in the following case of *Baker v. State.*

Rule 612 Writing Used to Refresh Memory

BAKER v. STATE
Maryland Court of Special Appeals
371 A.2d 699 (1977)

MOYLAN, JUDGE.

This appeal addresses the intriguing question of what latitude a judge should permit counsel when a witness takes the stand and says, "I don't remember." What are the available keys that may unlock the testimonial treasure vaults of the subconscious? What are the brushstrokes that may be employed "to retouch the fading daguerreotype of memory?" The subject is that of Present Recollection Revived.[60]

The appellant, Teretha McNeil Baker, was convicted by a Baltimore City jury of both murder in the first degree and robbery. Although she raises two appellate contentions, the only one which we found it necessary to consider is her claim that the trial judge erroneously refused her the opportunity to refresh present recollection of a police witness by showing him a report written by a fellow officer.

The ultimate source of most of the evidence implicating the appellant was the robbery and murder victim himself, Gaither Martin, a now-dead declarant who spoke to the jury through the hearsay conduit of Officer Bolton. When Officer

---

[60] (Court's original footnote 2.) Frequently and alternatively referred to as Present Recollection Refreshed.

Bolton arrived at the crime scene, the victim told him that he had "picked these three ladies up . . . at the New Deal Bar"; that when he took them to their stated destination, a man walked up to the car and pulled him out; that "the other three got out and proceeded to kick him and beat him." It was the assertion made by the victim to the officer that established that his money, wallet and keys had been taken. The critical impasse, for present purposes, occurred when the officer was questioned, on cross-examination, about what happened en route to the hospital. The officer had received a call from Officer Hucke, of the Western District, apparently to the effect that a suspect had been picked up. Before proceeding to the hospital, Officer Bolton took the victim to the place where Officer Hucke was holding the appellant. The appellant, as part of this cross-examination, sought to elicit from the officer the fact that the crime victim confronted the appellant and stated that the appellant was not one of those persons who had attacked and robbed him. To stimulate the present memory of Officer Bolton, appellant's counsel attempted to show him the police report relating to that confrontation and prepared by Officer Hucke.

The record establishes loudly and clearly that appellant's counsel sought to use the report primarily to refresh the recollection of Officer Bolton and that he was consistently and effectively thwarted in that attempt:

BY MR. HARLAN:

Q: Do you have the report filed by Officer Hucke and Officer Saclolo or Saclolo?

A: Right, I have copies.

Q: Okay.

MR. DOORY: I would object to that, Your Honor.

THE COURT: I will sustain the objection. This is not his report.

BY MR. HARLAN:

Q: Can you look at this report and refresh your recollection as to whether or not you ever had the victim in a confrontation with Mrs. Baker?

MR. DOORY: Objection, Your Honor.

MR. HARLAN: He can refresh—

THE COURT: Well, he can refresh his recollection as to his personal knowledge. That's all right.

A: That is what I am saying, I don't know who it was that we confronted really.

BY MR. HARLAN:

Q: All right. Would you consult your report and maybe it will refresh your recollection.

THE COURT: I think the response is he doesn't know who—

MR. HARLAN: He can refresh his recollection if he looks at the report.

THE COURT: He can't refresh his recollection from someone else's report, Mr. Harlan.

MR. HARLAN: I would object, Your Honor. Absolutely he can.

THE COURT: You might object, but—

MR. HARLAN: You are not going to permit the officer to refresh his recollection from the police report?

THE COURT: No. It is not his report.

MR. HARLAN: Your Honor, I think I am absolutely within my rights to have a police officer read a report which mentions his name in it to see if it refreshes his recollection. If it doesn't refresh his recollection, then fine.

THE COURT: Well, he did that.

MR. HARLAN: You have not afforded him the opportunity to do that yet, Your Honor.

THE COURT: He says he does not know who it was before. So, he can't refresh his recollection if he does not know simply because someone else put some name in there.

MR. HARLAN: He has to read it to see if it refreshes his recollection, Your Honor.

THE COURT: We are reading from a report made by two other officers which is not the personal knowledge of this officer.

MR. HARLAN: I don't want him to read from that report. I want him to read it and see if it refreshes his recollection.

On so critical an issue as possible exculpation from the very lips of the crime victim, appellant was entitled to try to refresh the memory of the key police witness. She was erroneously and prejudicially denied that opportunity. The reason for the error is transparent. Because they both arise from the common seedbed of failed memory and because of their hauntingly parallel verbal rhythms and grammatical structures, there is a beguiling temptation to overanalogize Present Recollection Revived and Past Recollection Recorded. It is a temptation, however, that must be resisted. The trial judge in this case erroneously measured the legitimacy of the effort to revive present recollection against the more rigorous standards for the admissibility of a recordation of past memory.

It is, of course, hornbook law that when a party seeks to introduce a record of past recollection, he must establish 1) that the record was made by or adopted by the witness at a time when the witness did have a recollection of the event and 2) that the witness can presently vouch for the fact that when the record was made or adopted by him, he knew that is was accurate . . . .

*   *   *

Had the appellant herein sought to offer the police report as a record of past recollection on the part of Officer Bolton, it is elementary that she would have had to show, *inter alia*, that the report had either been prepared by Officer Bolton himself or had been read by him and that he can now say that at that time he knew it was correct. Absent such a showing, the trial judge would have been correct in declining to receive it in evidence.

When dealing with an instance of Past Recollection Recorded, the reason for the rigorous standards of admissibility is quite clear. Those standards exist to test the competence of the report or document in question. Since the piece of paper itself, in effect, speaks to the jury, the piece of paper must pass muster in terms of its evidentiary competence.

Not so with Present Recollection Revived! By marked contrast to Past Recollection Recorded, no such testimonial competence is demanded of a mere stimulus to present recollection, for the stimulus itself is never evidence. Notwithstanding the surface similarity between the two phenomena, the difference between them could not be more basic.[61] *It is the difference between evidence and non-evidence.* Of such mere stimuli or memory-prods, McCormick says, at 18, "[T]he cardinal rule is that they are not evidence." When we are dealing with an instance of Present Recollection Revived, the only source of evidence is the testimony of the witness himself. The stimulus may have jogged the witness' dormant memory, but the stimulus itself is not received in evidence. Dean McCormick makes it clear that even when the stimulus is a writing, when the witness "speaks from a memory thus revived, his testimony is what he says, not the writing." *Id.* at 15.

* * *

The catalytic agent or memory stimulator is put aside, once it has worked its psychological magic, and the witness then testifies on the basis of the now-refreshed memory. The opposing party, of course, has the right to inspect the memory aid, be it a writing or otherwise, and even to show it to the jury. This examination, however, is not for the purpose of testing the competence of the memory aid (for competence is immaterial where the thing in question is not evidence) but only to test whether the witness' memory has in truth been refreshed. As McCormick warns, "But the witness must swear that he is genuinely refreshed. . . . And he cannot be allowed to read the writing in the guise of refreshment, as a cloak for getting in evidence an inadmissible document." One of the most thorough reviews of this aspect of evidence law is found in *United States v. Riccardi*, 174 F.2d 883 (3rd Cir., 1949), where the court said at 888:

> In the case of present recollection revived, the witness, by hypothesis, relates his present recollection, and under oath and subject to cross-examination asserts that it is true; his capacities for memory and perception may be attacked and tested; his determination to tell the truth investigated and revealed; protestations of lack of memory, which escape criticism and indeed constitute a refuge in the situation of past recollection recorded, merely undermine the probative worth of his testimony.[62]

---

[61] (Court's original footnote 5.) "Under the guidance of Wigmore, we now recognize this as quite a different process. In the one instance, the witness stakes his oath on his present memory; in the other, upon his written recital of things remembered in the past." McCormick, Law of Evidence (1st Ed. 1954), p. 15.

[62] (Court's original footnote 7.) To the same effect, *see* Morgan, *The Relation between Hearsay and*

In solid accord with both the psychological sciences and the general common law of evidence, Maryland has long established it that even when a writing of some sort is the implement used to stir the embers of cooling memory, the writing need not be that of the forgetful witness himself, need not have been adopted by him, need not have been made contemporaneously with or shortly after the incident in question, and need not even be necessarily accurate. The competence of the writing is not in issue for the writing is not offered as evidence but is only used as a memory aid. . . . [The court then offered examples of items courts had allowed proponents to use to refresh the witness' recollection, which included book entries recording the sale of goods; stenographic transcript of a tape recording of telephone conversations; a police officer's note of statements given by the defendant; an unsigned transcript of an oral confession; a typed but unsigned statement of a defendant that had been given to the police (it was used to refresh an officer's recollection); memorandum of sale; and a newspaper.]

When the writing in question is to be utilized simply "to awaken a slumbering recollection of an event" in the mind of the witness, the writing may be a memorandum made by the witness himself — 1)even if it was not made immediately after the event, 2) even if it was not made of firsthand knowledge, and 3) even if the witness cannot now vouch for the fact that it was accurate when made. It may be a memorandum made by one other than the witness, even if never before read by the witness or vouched for by him. It may be an Associated Press account. It may be a highly selective version of the incident at the hands of a Hemingway or an Eliot. All that is required is that it ignite the flash of accurate recall — that it accomplish the revival which is sought.

Not only may the writing fall short of the rigorous standards of competence required of a record of past recollection, the memory aid itself need not even be a writing. What may it be? It may be anything. It may be a line from Kipling or the dolorous refrain of "The Tennessee Waltz"; a whiff of hickory smoke; the running of the fingers across of swatch of corduroy; the sweet carbonation of a chocolate soda; the sight of a faded snapshot in a long-neglected album. All that is required is that it may trigger the Proustian moment.[63] It may be anything which produces the desired testimonial prelude, "It all comes back to me now."[64]

Preserved Memory, 40 Harv.L.Rev. 712, 717–718 (1927):

> [W]here the witnesses, by some stimulus, be it memorandum or other device, has his recollection so revived as to be able to testify entirely from present memory . . . the memory of the witness is actually refreshed. . . . He is not asking the tribunal to believe it because he stated it on a former occasion, but because he is now relating it under oath and subject to cross-examination.

[63] (Court's original footnote 11.) Marcel Proust, in his monumental epic IN REMEMBRANCE OF THINGS PAST, sat, as a middle-aged man, sipping a cup of lime-flavored tea and eating a madeleine, a small French pastry. Through both media, two long-forgotten tastes from childhood were reawakened. By association, long forgotten memories from the same period of childhood came welling and surging back. Once those floodgates of recall were opened, seven volumes followed.

[64] (Court's original footnote 12.) Generally speaking, the process of refurbishing a witness' memory will take place as a part of astute counsel's trial preparation. It is only when memory, through courtroom fear or otherwise, unexpectedly bogs down on the witness stand (or when the witness whose memory needs refreshing is one other than counsel's own) that the courtroom becomes the arena for the refurbishing.

Jerome Frank in *Fanelli v. United States Gypsum Co.*, 141 F.2d 216, 217 (2d Cir. 1944), put it in these terms:

> Common experience, the work of Proust and other keenly observant literary men, and recondite psychological research, all teach us that memory of things long past can be accurately restored in all sorts of ways. The creaking of a hinge, the whistling of a tune, the smell of seaweed, the sight of an old photograph, the taste of nutmeg, the touch of a piece of canvas, may bring vividly to the foreground [of] consciousness the recollection of events that happened years ago and which would otherwise have been forgotten. . . . The memory-prodder may itself lack meaning to other persons as a symbol of the past event, as everyone knows who has ever used a knot in his handkerchief as a reminder. Since the workings of the human memory still remain a major mystery after centuries of study, courts should hesitate before they glibly contrive dogmatic rules concerning the reliability of the ways of provoking it.

Although the use of a memorandum of some sort will continue quantitatively to dominate the field of refreshing recollection, we are better able to grasp the process conceptually if we appreciate that the use of a memorandum as a memory aid is not a legal phenomenon unto itself but only an instance of a far broader phenomenon. In a more conventional mode, the process might proceed, "Your Honor, I am about to show the witness a written report, ask him to read it and then inquire if he can now testify from his own memory thus refreshed." In a far less conventional mode, the process could just as well proceed, "Your Honor, I am pleased to present to the court Miss Rosa Ponselle who will now sing 'Celeste Aida' for the witness, for that is what was playing on the night the burglar came through the window." Whether by conventional or unconventional means, precisely the same end is sought. One is looking for the effective elixir to revitalize dimming memory and make it alive again in the service of the search for truth.

Even in the more conventional mode, it is quite clear that in this case the appropriate effort of the appellant to jog the arguably dormant memory of the key police witness on a vital issue was unduly and prejudicially restricted.

Judgments Reversed; Case remanded for a new trial; costs to be paid by Mayor and City Council of Baltimore.

––––––––––

As the court in *Baker* explained, the kinds of things that a proponent can use to refresh a witness' recollection are limitless. If the proponent uses a writing, however, special rules of disclosure have existed at common law that Congress has codified in Rule 612 of the Federal Rules of Evidence.

EXERCISE

DJ, an eyewitness, begins to testify at trial. In response to a question from counsel, DJ indicates that she cannot remember what happened. Counsel wishes to show DJ a copy of a report describing the incident, written by someone else, to help refresh DJ's memory. May counsel use this report? Must DJ specifically acknowledge that the report helped refresh her recollection before continuing to testify?

[G]   Business Records: Rule 803(6)

[1]   Record Was Regular Part of Activity

Business records are admissible because businesses rely on the records they keep and this reliance means that businesses have an incentive to ensure the accuracy of the records. *Towns* considers whether records that the government requires businesses to keep, but that the business will not use for its own internal affairs, qualifies under the exception.

UNITED STATES v. TOWNS
United States Court of Appeals, Fifth Circuit
718 F.3d 404 (2013)

Edith H. Jones, Circuit Judge:

Melvin Towns ("Towns") challenges his conviction and sentence for conspiracy to manufacture methamphetamine and conspiracy to possess and distribute pseudoephedrine in violation of 21 U.S.C. § 846. He argues primarily that some of the evidence against him — pseudoephedrine purchase logs — was introduced in violation of the business records exception to the hearsay rule. . . Because the purchase transaction logs conform to Federal Rule of Evidence (FRE) 803(6) . . . we **AFFIRM** the conviction. . . .

BACKGROUND

In 2009, James Pieprzica, an officer with the Texas Department of Public Safety, discovered a conspiracy whereby individuals would visit multiple pharmacies to obtain large quantities of pseudoephedrine and use it to manufacture methamphetamine. With the help of cooperating witnesses and informants, Pieprzica compiled a list of alleged conspirators — including Towns — and began submitting requests to various pharmacies to obtain lists of their purchases of pseudoephedrine. Upon receipt of those lists, some of which were in electronic format sent through email and some of which were hard copies that were mailed, Pieprzica and an analyst combined the information into a spreadsheet.

Towns was charged in April of 2011 in a superseding indictment with one count of conspiracy to manufacture 500 grams or more of methamphetamine and to possess and distribute pseudoephedrine knowing that it would be used to manufacture methamphetamine. Towns was charged with furthering the conspiracy by purchasing large quantities of pseudoephedrine to be used in manufacturing methamphetamine. At trial, the Government offered pseudoephedrine purchase logs from various retailers (Walgreens, Wal-Mart, Target, and CVS) to highlight a pattern of movement and purchase implicating Towns in the conspiracy. The log spreadsheets were admitted through Pieprzica, who had received the records and their certifying affidavits from the records custodians of the companies that ran the pharmacies. Towns had filed a motion *in limine* to exclude the records, making the same arguments addressed in this appeal, but the district court denied it. The records were admitted at trial over Towns's objection that they were not kept for business purposes, but as required law enforcement records. He failed to object specifically to the custodian certificates or purchase logs as having an inadequate foundation.

The government then offered several witnesses to prove the existence of the conspiracy. Co-conspirators confirmed Towns's involvement in the plan to manufacture methamphetamine and testified that he acquired pseudoephedrine pills for their operation. He also assisted from time to time in tasks related to the actual "cooking" of the methamphetamine.

Towns testified at trial and admitted to purchasing pseudoephedrine pills in large quantities. He claimed that he took the drug to stay awake in his work as a truck driver, but denied involvement in any illegal drug manufacturing activity. Towns also denied the accuracy of the pseudoephedrine drug purchase logs and denied purchasing pills in excess of the statutorily allowed limit of nine grams per 30 days. During cross examination, the Government asked Towns to read amounts and information contained on the logs, but did not ask about specific store visits or whether he purchased pseudoephedrine with one of his co-conspirators.

Towns was subsequently convicted by a jury. In his motion for a new trial, Towns reurged that the records were both improperly admitted as business records and violated his right to confront the witnesses against him. The motion was denied. Thereafter, the district court found that Towns was ineligible for a safety valve sentence reduction and that the court was required to sentence him to a mandatory sentence of 120 months. He timely appealed both the conviction and the sentence.

* * *

DISCUSSION

I. Pseudoephedrine Purchase Logs

This appeal revolves around the business transaction logs obtained from the pharmacies. If this information is admissible and does not violate the Confrontation Clause, the conviction must be upheld. We hold that the pseudoephedrine purchase logs were business records for the purposes of Federal Rule of Evidence 803(6); admissible under the exception to the hearsay rule via the affidavits certifying their status; and nontestimonial records that do not violate the Sixth Amendment.

A. Business Records

Towns begins by challenging the district court's admission of the purchase logs as an abuse of discretion. This contention focuses on the second and fourth requirements of the business records exception to the rule against hearsay found in

FRE 803(6).[3] First, Towns argues that the logs do not qualify as true business records. He contends they were prepared with a law enforcement purpose in mind and are only kept because of a Texas statute mandates their existence; the pharmacies do not (and actually cannot) use the records for day-to-day business activities. Thus they were not kept in the ordinary course of business. Alternatively, even if the logs are "business records," they were not properly admitted because of their introduction by Officer Pieprzica, not someone with actual knowledge of the records. We reject each of these arguments.

To begin, the undue focus on the law enforcement purpose of the records has little to do with whether they are business records under the Federal Rules of Evidence. What matters is that they were kept in the ordinary course of business. It is not uncommon for a business to perform certain tasks that it would not otherwise undertake in order to fulfill governmental regulations. *See United States v. Veytia-Bravo*, 603 F.2d 1187 (5th Cir. 1979). This does not mean those records are not kept in the ordinary course of business. In *Veytia-Bravo*, this court held that firearm records that gun shops were forced to maintain by law were business records since a company could lose corporate privileges for failing to maintain them properly. *Id.* at 1191. To hold otherwise here would violate precedent and move the inquiry beyond the rule's text. Fed. R. Evid. 803(6)(B) (exempting records "kept in the course of a regularly conducted activity of a business" from the rule against hearsay). The regularly conducted activity here is selling pills containing pseudoephedrine; the purchase logs are kept in the course of that activity. Why they are kept is irrelevant at this stage.[5]

---

[3] There are five requirements for the exemption to be in effect: (A) the records must be made at or near the time of the event by — or from information transmitted by — someone with knowledge of the event; (B) they must be kept in the ordinary course of business; (C) they must be kept regularly; (D) each of these conditions must be proven by the testimony of a qualified witness or by a certification that complies with Rule 902(11) or (12); and (E) neither the source of information nor the circumstances in which the record is prepared can indicate a lack of trustworthiness. Fed. R. Evid. 803(6).

[5] The dissent contends that this court's precedent in *Matthews v. United States*, 217 F.2d 409 (5th Cir. 1954), prevents the transaction logs from being true business records. *United States v. Veytia-Bravo*, 603 F.2d 1187 (5th Cir. 1979), teaches that this is incorrect.

> The documents held inadmissible in *Matthews* were special episodic reports of only certain sales which were, regardless of size or frequency, legal. The IRS used the records to facilitate its enforcement of liquor taxes, not to detect unlawful sales activity by the keeper of the records. The business which recorded the sale had no incentive to keep the records with precision and completeness to show its compliance with any laws prohibiting certain types of transactions.

Id. at 1191. The records in the present case, unlike *Matthews*, are systematic logs of purchases that may or may not be legal. It is imperative that accurate records be kept because, unlike sugar, buyers are limited in pseudoephedrine purchase quantities. Also, retailers are accountable for these records and failure to comply with the regulations renders them subject to penalties. tex. Health & Safety Code Ann. §§ 486.021–486.033 (West 2012).

Veytia-Bravo recognized that external incentives, which cause businesses to accurately record transactions, are what make the records sufficiently trustworthy. Here, stores must show that they have complied "with the regulation's requirement that a complete record of all sales be kept" and they must keep records to assist in restricting those "who c[an]not lawfully purchase" additional pseudoephedrine. *Veytia-Bravo*, 603 F.2d at 1191. The point is that the business records are acceptable under the FRE as long as outside factors ensure they have been systematically checked, regularly and continually made, relied upon for compliance with government regulations, and made according to the duty, under law, to

Next, the purchase records were properly admitted as business records because of the qualifying affidavits offered to the court. For admission, a record of a regularly conducted business activity must be proven by "testimony of the custodian or another qualified witness, *or by a certification* that complies with Rule 902(11)." Fed. R. Evid. 803(6)(D) (emphasis added). According to Rule 902(11), records of regularly conducted business activity — even copies — are self-authenticating if certified as accurate by the custodian. The party against whom the record is offered must also be given notice and opportunity to challenge the records. A proper foundation is laid for business records simply by an affidavit that attests to the requisite elements of FRE 803(6).[7]

This type of attestation aligns with the precedent set forth in *Wilson v. Zapata Off-Shore Co.*, 939 F.2d 260 (5th Cir. 1991). There, a plaintiff objected to the admission of hospital records containing an unfavorable statement about her by her sister. Specifically, the plaintiff complained that a proper foundation was not laid for the admission of business records because there was no statement in the authenticating affidavit verifying the accuracy of a report. This court held, however, that "Rule 803(6) does not require testimony that the record is accurate." *Id.* at 272. It was enough that the affidavit of the record custodian (who did not make the report) "contain[ed] statements that track[ed] the language of Rule 803(6) nearly word for word." *Id.*

Wilson confirms the admissibility of the records in the present case against two primary objections. First, the affidavit of a record custodian is sufficient to lay the foundation for a business record. *Id.* There is therefore no need to have individual cashiers from each of the pharmacies testify. The drug purchases of specific individuals on some date years prior could never be remembered anyway; this is the genesis of the business records exception. What is more important — and actually

---

provide accurate records of such purchases. *See United States v. Wells*, 262 F.3d 455, 462 (5th Cir. 2001); *cf. Palmer v. Hoffman*, 318 U.S. 109, 113, 63 S. Ct. 477, 480, 87 L. Ed. 645 (1943) (approving, as business records, those "typical of entries made systematically or as a matter of routine to record events or occurrences, to reflect transactions with others, or to provide internal controls").

Furthermore, the dissent overlooks the section of *Veytia-Bravo* specifically distinguishing modern record keeping from that in *Matthews*. It would make little sense to treat a case that was to be "read as limited to its facts in their context" as applicable here. *Veytia-Bravo*, 603 F.2d at 1191. The regular and orderly recordation of pseudoephedrine purchases — for which Texas has no minimum amount required, Tex. Health & Safety Code Ann. § 486.014 — is a far cry from the haphazard logging of sugar sales in the 1950s. The guarantees of trustworthiness present today — the requirement of photo identification for purchases and the immediate computerized logging of sales — remove this case from the "limited" facts of *Matthews* and align it with *Veytia-Bravo*, the admitted controlling authority.

[7] The best example of the proper manner in which to present business records can be seen in *O'Connor's Federal Forms*. In this case, each of the pharmacies — Walgreens, Wal-Mart, Target, and CVS — provided affidavits from their respective records custodians that mimic Federal Civil Form 8C:3. O'Connor's Federal Civil Forms 1256 (2012). Its language tracks Rule 803(6) nearly word for word. Contrary to the dissent's assertion in Footnote 7, a party does *not* need to explain the record-keeping system of the organization. It is enough that the 803(6) requirements are certified. A proper foundation was laid in this case by including things such as names, titles, record descriptions, stores, etc. Because the rule does not require anything more for criminal cases than civil ones, we must accept these attestations as authoritative. We are interested in accuracy in a hearsay-type context, a concern identical in both civil and criminal cases, but the Rules of Evidence allow for self-authenticating records to be admitted and then weighed by the jury.

required — is the testimony of the custodian[8] who ensures such records are free from adulteration after the fact. *See United States v. Armstrong*, 619 F.3d 380, 384–85 (5th Cir. 2010). Second, any claim concerning the records' accuracy is not the province of Rule 803(6). *Wilson*, 939 F.2d at 272. The pharmacies' receipts show purchases by one Melvin Towns; his driver's license was recorded for each of the purchases and his signature was obtained in many instances. This is all the identifying information the purchase logs evidenced. Towns was free to make arguments at trial that he was not the actual purchaser of the drugs, but accuracy does not control admissibility.

The purchase logs comprised records of a regularly conducted activity, which were made at or near the time of the purchase by individuals whose job duties entailed making those records. Because this information was certified by the records custodians' affidavits and there was no evidence of untrustworthiness in the record-keeping procedures, the pseudoephedrine purchase logs are admissible business records. *See United States v. Jones*, 554 F.2d 251, 252 (5th Cir. 1977) (per curiam) (holding that a proper foundation was laid for business records by recitation of the facts contained in FRE 803(6)). Once these conditions were met, admission fell within the discretion of the trial court. That discretion was not abused here.

*   *   *

GRAVES, CIRCUIT JUDGE, dissenting.

Because the district court erred in admitting the pseudoephedrine logs as business records and in refusing to consider a safety valve sentence reduction, I would reverse and remand. Therefore, I respectfully dissent.

*   *   *

DISCUSSION

I. Inapplicability of business records exception

The pseudoephedrine logs were entered into evidence under the business records exception to the hearsay rule. Fed. R. Evid. 803(6). The logs are statutorily required to be kept under 21 U.S.C. § 830 and Texas Health and Safety Code § 486.014.

Rule 803(6) creates an exception to the hearsay rule for records kept in the ordinary course of a regularly conducted business activity. The exception applies if:

> (A) the record was made at or near the time by — or from information transmitted by — someone with knowledge;

---

[8] The disjunctive nature of FRE 803(6)(D) eliminates the need to put each custodian on the stand to verify the respective business records. The qualifying information may come through live testimony *or* certification. Agent Pieprzica's introduction of the custodian affidavits was therefore sufficient.

(B) the record was kept in the course of a regularly conducted activity of a business, organization, occupation, or calling, whether or not for profit;

(C) making the record was a regular practice of that activity;

(D) all these conditions are shown by the testimony of the custodian or another qualified witness, or by a certification that complies with Rule 902(11) or (12) or with a statute permitting certification; and

(E) neither the source of information nor the method or circumstances of preparation indicate a lack of trustworthiness.

Fed. R. Evid. 803(6).

As the comment to Rule 803(6) states, while all participants may be acting routinely, if, "however, the supplier of the information does not act in the regular course, an essential link is broken; the assurance of accuracy does not extend to the information itself, and the fact that it may be recorded with scrupulous accuracy is of no avail." Fed. R. Evid. 803(6), n. to para. (6). Despite the majority's statements that "any claim concerning the records' accuracy is not the province of Rule 803(6)" and that "accuracy does not control admissibility." Further, an "illustration is the police report incorporating information obtained from a bystander: the officer qualifies as acting in the regular course but the informant does not." *Id. See also Johnson v. Lutz*, 253 N.Y. 124, 170 N.E. 517 (1930).

*   *   *

This Court has not decided whether pseudoephedrine logs constitute business records for purposes of Rule 803(6). As Towns asserts, the transaction logs at issue here are prepared in accordance with federal and state law. Both the state and federal statutes indicate that the requirements are based on law enforcement purposes. As discussed herein, the majority erroneously finds that the reason the records are kept or their subsequent use has little, if anything, to do with whether the logs are business records.

The majority cites *United States v. Veytia-Bravo*, 603 F.2d 1187 (5th Cir. 1979), for the holding that firearms records that gun shops were required to maintain were business records since a company could lose corporate privileges for failing to maintain them. The majority then concludes that the pseudoephedrine logs are business records because they are kept during the course of the regularly conducted activity of "selling pills containing pseudoephedrine." I disagree with the majority's finding that the logs are business records. However, I agree that *Veytia-Bravo* is controlling authority.

In *Veytia-Bravo*, Judge Charles Clark, writing for the panel, held that the district court did not err in admitting records of firearms and ammunitions sales as business records. After acknowledging that the "primary emphasis of Rule 803(6) is on the reliability or trustworthiness of the records sought to be introduced," the Court then engaged in a thorough analysis of the applicable authority and distinguished prior cases finding records inadmissible.[6] Specifically, this Court

---

[6] *See Palmer v. Hoffman*, 318 U.S. 109, 63 S. Ct. 477, 87 L. Ed. 645 (1943) (Accident report completed

found that Globe, the firearms dealer, "necessarily relied upon these records in the conduct of its own affairs, both to comply with the regulation's requirement that a complete record of all sales be kept and to show that it had not violated 18 U.S.C. § 922 by knowingly selling firearms or ammunition to one who could not lawfully purchase them." *Veytia-Bravo*, 603 F.2d at 1191. This Court also noted that in *Matthews* the "business which recorded the sale had no incentive to keep the records with precision and completeness to show its compliance with any laws prohibiting certain types of transactions." *Id.* In *Matthews*, this Court established the following standard:

> So long as the accuracy and reliability of records sought to be introduced in evidence have been tested by the fact that a business concern carries on its own affairs from day to day in reliance upon such records, there is no departure from the standards of accuracy and trustworthiness that were basic in the historic rule permitting testimony from the shop book or book of account.

Matthews, 217 F.2d at 413–414.[7]

This Court has also said:

> Indeed, the rationale underlying this exception to the rule against hearsay is that the inherent reliability of business records is "supplied by systematic checking, by regularity and continuity which produce habits of precision, by actual experience of business in relying upon them, or by a duty to make an accurate record as part of a continuing job or occupation." Fed. R. Evid. 803(6), Notes of Advisory Committee on Proposed Rules. We have expressly recognized that the " 'primary emphasis of rule 803(6) is on the reliability or trustworthiness of the records sought to be introduced.' " *United States v. Duncan*, 919 F.2d 981, 986 (5th Cir. 1990)(quoting *United States v. Veytia-Bravo*, 603 F.2d 1187, 1189 (5th Cir. 1979)).

United States v. Wells, 262 F.3d 455, 462 (5th Cir. 2001).

---

by railroad employee not admissible under the business records exception to the hearsay rule because it was prepared primarily for use in litigation and not in the conduct of business.); and *Matthews v. United States*, 217 F.2d 409 (5th Cir. 1954) (statutorily required "sugar reports" to detect sales of substances used in the manufacture of distilled spirits were inadmissible as lacking necessary trustworthiness and because they were not used as an integral part of the business in its own interest.)

[7] This case is also factually similar to *Matthews* in that only purchases of sugar in large amounts were required to be reported. Here, pharmacies are only required to log purchases of packages containing in excess of 60 milligrams of pseudoephedrine, contrary to the majority's characterization of these as "systematic logs" of all purchases. *See* 21 U.S.C. § 830(e)(1)(A)(iii). Further, the majority's statement that these purchases "may or may not be legal" is misleading in that retailers are statutorily prohibited from selling pseudoephedrine in illegal amounts in any single transaction and there is absolutely no indication that these records are used "to detect unlawful sales activity by the keeper of the records." Were that the case, then, based on the majority's holding here, the involved pharmacies clearly engaged in unlawful sales activity. To the contrary, a retailer is not maintaining the logs in an attempt to prove it did not sell pseudoephedrine to a purchaser forbidden by law. As evidenced by this case, a retailer is not even maintaining the logs to ensure that it does not sell pseudoephedrine to someone who has already purchased a daily or monthly allotment. Rather, a retailer is merely complying with the requirement of keeping the records, without analyzing or relying on them and with no incentive to ensure accuracy, for the Government to possibly later use for some law enforcement purpose.

Further, to reiterate the comment to Rule 803(6) quoted previously herein, if the supplier of information does not act in the regular course of business, there is no assurance of trustworthiness. Fed. R. Evid. 803(6), n. to para. (6). *See also Broadcast Music, Inc., v. Xanthas, Inc.*, 855 F.2d 233, 238 (5th Cir. 1988); *Johnson v. Lutz*, 253 N.Y. 124, 170 N.E. 517 (1930).

This is consistent with other authority. For example, the Tenth Circuit has said:

> "The essential component of the business records exception is that each actor in the chain of information is under a business duty or compulsion to provide accurate information." *United States v. McIntyre*, 997 F.2d 687, 699 (10th Cir. 1993). "If any person in the process is not acting in the regular course of business, then an essential link in the trustworthiness chain fails . . . ." 2 *McCormick on Evidence* § 290 (Kenneth S. Broun, ed., 6th ed.2006); *McIntyre*, 997 F.2d at 699 (quoting *McCormick* with approval).

United States v. Ary, 518 F.3d 775 (10th Cir. 2008).

These cases clearly support a finding that the pseudoephedrine logs here are not business records. There is no dispute that the pharmacies did not "necessarily rely" upon these records in the conduct of their own affairs. To the contrary, the information in the logs is confidential and subject to non-disclosure with limited exceptions that do not include day-to-day business activities. *See* 21 U.S.C. § 830(c). *See also* Tex. Health & Safety Code § 486.0146. As this Court's finding in *Veytia-Bravo* mandates, mere compliance with the requirement to keep the logs is not sufficient to establish that the pharmacies "necessarily relied upon these records in the conduct of its own affairs." *Veytia-Bravo*, 603 F.2d at 1191.[8] Unlike in *Veytia-Bravo*, there is no indication that the pharmacies had any "incentive to keep the records with precision and completeness to show its compliance with any laws prohibiting certain types of transactions." *Id.*[9] There is no evidence that the

---

[8] In Footnote 5, the majority misapprehends the "section of *Veytia-Bravo* specifically distinguishing modern record keeping from that in *Matthews*." What this Court actually said was:

> To the extent that *Matthews* might be read as concluding that no record required to be kept by law could satisfy the trustworthiness requirement of the business records exception, it would now conflict with the realities of today's business world in which many, if not most, of the records of every business are required to be kept by some government edict.

Veytia-Bravo, 603 F.2d at 1191. This Court said nothing about "haphazard logging of sugar sales in the 1950s" but was merely saying that there are records, like the firearms records, that are required to be kept by law which may satisfy the trustworthiness requirement of the business records exception, unlike the logs here. Further, the majority's statement regarding the "immediate computerized logging of sales" is unsupported by any authority or evidence.

[9] The majority is correct that the Texas Department of State Health Services "may impose an administrative penalty on a person who violates this chapter." Tex. Health & Safety Code § 486.021. However, the Texas statute also provides that a "person is not liable for an act done or omission made in compliance with the requirements of Section 486.014 or 486.0141." Tex. Health & Safety Code § 486.0145. Notably, Section 486.014 is the section providing that a retailer must require a purchaser to display identification, either a driver's license or some other form of identification containing a photograph and indicating the person is over age sixteen (we do not know the form of identification used or required here), sign for the purchase (not provided on all of the logs here nor identified as Towns' signature on the others), and the information required to be recorded by the retailer, i.e., only the name, date, item and number of grams purchased. Tex. Health & Safety Code § 486.014. Thus, any liability for an act or omission in determining a purchaser's identity or in accurately recording the transaction is

accuracy and reliability of the pseudoephedrine logs "have been tested by the fact that a [pharmacy] carries on its own affairs from day to day in reliance upon such records." *Matthews*, 217 F.2d at 413–414. Where, as here, one party seeks to prove a substantive fact by the introduction of evidence that is compiled, not in connection with the pharmacies' own operations, but under sanction of federal statute, "none of the proofs of trustworthiness" is present. *Id.* at 414.

For these reasons, the pseudoephedrine logs are not business records pursuant to Rule 803(6). The evidence in this case included only the pseudoephedrine transaction logs and the testimony of two alleged co-conspirators, admitted "cooks" and convicted drug offenders, offered in exchange for a reduction in sentence. Therefore, it is not evident that the transaction logs did not contribute to the jury's verdict. The district court's error was clearly not harmless beyond a reasonable doubt and I would reverse on this issue.

*   *   *

[2] Incentive to Keep Unbiased Records

Records that businesses create when they are anticipating litigation are different than the records they keep to conduct their business. *T.C.* and *Solomon* consider two types of records that are produced in anticipation of litigation — in *T.C.*, the result of an investigation, in *Solomon*, a report of an incident. Both *T.C.* and *Solomon* involve public agencies and Fed. R. Evid. 803(8) creates a special rule for public records that is, in many ways, redundant of Rule 803(6). Notice, however, that even when public records are involved, the business record exception, Rule 803(6), is often used.

T.C. v. CULLMAN CO. DEPT. OF HUMAN RESOURCES
Alabama Court of Appeals
899 So. 2d 281 (2004)

CRAWLEY, JUDGE.

[The parental rights of T.C. and B.P.B. were terminated on the basis of some very egregious behavior. The court found that, irrespective of the evidentiary challenge presented below, that the juvenile court heard was sufficient to justify its conclusion. The portion of the opinion below addresses the question of whether a report produced by the Department of Human Resources should have been admitted in the proceedings. As you would expect with such a report, it relies on interviews for its findings.]

I.

Citing *Y.M. v. Jefferson County Department of Human Resources*, 890 So.2d 103 (Ala.Civ.App.2003), affirmed, *Ex parte State Department of Human Resources*, 890 So.2d 114 (Ala.2004), the mother and the father contend that the juvenile court

---

specifically limited. *See* Tex. Health & Safety Code § 486.0145.

erred by admitting into evidence a 27-page report entitled "Court Report on Petition for the Termination of Parental Rights" ("the Court Report") prepared by DHR social worker Karen Cowart.

In *Ex parte State Department of Human Resources, supra,* the Alabama Supreme Court affirmed this court's holding that a parental-rights-termination hearing is an adjudicatory proceeding at which hearsay evidence, which is permitted by § 12-15-65(h), Ala.Code 1975, in a dispositional proceeding, is inadmissible. The court stated:

> "[O]nly competent, material, and relevant evidence may be admitted during an adjudicatory proceeding to terminate a parent's rights. See § 12-15-65(f) and § 26-18-7(a), Ala.Code 1975. Additionally, we acknowledge, as did the Court of Civil Appeals, that hearsay evidence is not considered competent evidence in an adjudicatory proceeding, unless it falls within one of the exceptions provided by the Alabama Rules of Evidence, other rules adopted by this Court, or by statute."

Ex parte State Dep't of Human Res., 890 So.2d at 117 (footnote omitted).

The mother and the father objected to the admission of Cowart's report on the basis that it contained hearsay. The court overruled their objections, deciding that the report was admissible, pursuant to Rule 803(6), Ala. R. Evid., as a business-record exception to the hearsay rule. The parents argue that the Court Report does not qualify as a business record under Rule 803(6) because, they say, the report was prepared in anticipation of litigation. Rule 803 states, in pertinent part:

> "The following are not excluded by the hearsay rule, even though the declarant is available as a witness:
>
> ". . . .
>
> "(6) . . . A memorandum, report, record, or data compilation, in any form, of acts, events, conditions, opinions, or diagnoses, made at or near the time by, or from information transmitted by, a person with knowledge, if kept in the course of a regularly conducted business activity, and if it was the regular practice of that business activity to make the memorandum, report, record, or data compilation, all as shown by the testimony of the custodian or other qualified witness, unless the source of information or the method or circumstances of preparation indicate lack of trustworthiness. The term 'business' as used in this paragraph includes business, institution, association, profession, occupation, and calling of every kind, whether or not conducted for profit."

*   *   *

The rationale for the business-records exception to the hearsay rule is that reliability is assured because the maker of the record relies on the record in the regular course of business activities. *See Ex parte Frith*, 526 So.2d 880, 882 (Ala. 1987). The "regular course" of business "must find its meaning in the inherent nature of the business in question and in the methods systematically employed for the conduct of the business as a business." *Palmer v. Hoffman*, 318 U.S. 109, 115, 63 S. Ct. 477, 87 L. Ed. 645 (1943). When an organization does not rely upon particular records for the performance of its functions, those records are not business records within the meaning of the Rule 803(6) exception to the hearsay rule. *See Palmer v. Hoffman*, 318 U.S. at 114, 63 S. Ct. 477 (holding that grade-crossing accident reports prepared by a railroad were not business records because they were not prepared "for the systematic conduct of the enterprise as a railroad business"; rather, "[the] reports are calculated for use essentially in the court, not in the business. Their primary utility is in litigating, not in railroading."). It is not enough to qualify under the business-records exception to show that the records are regularly prepared; instead, a court must evaluate "the character of the records and their earmarks of reliability . . . acquired from their source and origin and the nature of their compilation." *Palmer v. Hoffman*, 318 U.S. at 114, 63 S. Ct. 477.

The issue whether a DHR court report qualifies under the business-records exception to the hearsay rule has not been decided in Alabama. However, the Minnesota Court of Appeals dealt with a similar issue in a termination-of-parental-rights proceeding in *In re Child of Simon*, 662 N.W.2d 155 (Minn. Ct. App. 2003). In that case, the court held that it was error to admit a letter written by a child's therapist " 'to update the district court' on [the therapist's] work with [the child]" because the letter was prepared in anticipation of litigation. 662 N.W.2d at 159. The court stated:

> "[The therapist] wrote the . . . letter expressly to update *the court* on [the child's] progress in therapy and to offer her recommendation for [the child's] placement. [The therapist] noted her understanding that the district court would be making a decision on permanency issues. Thus, [the therapist] clearly prepared the . . . letter in anticipation of litigation, and the district court abused its discretion in admitting the letter."

662 N.W.2d at 161.

Likewise, we conclude that Rule 803(6) was not a basis for admitting the Court Report in this case. Much of the information in the report (which, for the most part, spans a 10-year period, with some information extending as far back as 30 years to the mother's childhood) was not timely recorded. Rule 803(6) states that a business record will be admissible only if it is made "at or near the time" of the events it reports. *See United States v. Kim*, 595 F.2d 755, 760 (D.C. Cir. 1979) (holding that a bank-deposit record, prepared two years after the deposit was allegedly made, was inadmissible under the business-records exception of Rule 803(6), Fed. R. Evid.). The title of Cowart's report, "Court Report on Petition for the Termination of Parental Rights," and the date of the report, six weeks before trial, demonstrate that the document was prepared in anticipation of litigation.

The statutory authority for the preparation and submission of court reports to the juvenile court is found in § 12-15-69(a), Ala. Code 1975, which provides:

> "After a petition alleging . . . dependency has been filed, the court may direct that a predisposition study and report to the court be made by . . . [DHR] when the petition alleges that the child is dependent concerning the child, his family, his environment and other matters *relevant to the need for treatment or disposition of the case.*"

(Emphasis added.) It is clear that the Legislature, by authorizing DHR to prepare and submit reports to the juvenile court on matters that are relevant to the "treatment or disposition" of a dependent child, did not intend to make such reports admissible at an adjudicatory proceeding to terminate a parent's rights. Although hearsay is admissible at the dispositional phase of a parental-rights-termination proceeding, it is not admissible during the adjudicatory phase. *See* § 12-15-65(f) and § 26-18-7(a), Ala. Code 1975; *Y.M. v. Jefferson County Dep't of Human Res.*, 890 So.2d 103, affirmed, *Ex parte State Dep't of Human Res., 890 So.2d 114*. We conclude that the juvenile court erred by admitting the Court Report.

* * *

The judgments of the Cullman Juvenile Court are affirmed.

AFFIRMED.

MURDOCK, JUDGE, concurring specially.

I agree with the conclusion reached in the main opinion that the "Court Report" at issue does not fall within the business records exception to the hearsay rule. The critical nature of what is at issue in a proceeding brought by the state to terminate the rights of a natural parent to his or her child compels me, however, to fully clarify for the sake of future cases my reasons for agreeing with this conclusion.

The main opinion emphasizes the fact that the court report was not admissible as a business record because it was made in anticipation of litigation. I agree. The main opinion also relies on the admittedly valid argument that the court report fails to satisfy the timely recordation requirement for the admission of "business records" under Rule 803(6), Ala. R. Evid. The main opinion also suggests that the court report was not admissible as a business record because its generation was not a regularly conducted activity of DHR. I write separately to explain my view that, because of the unique nature of the "business" of DHR, even if the record in question were one that was timely made and/or regularly generated by DHR, this would not necessarily prevent it from being a record made in anticipation of litigation and therefore from falling outside the intended scope of Rule 803(6), Ala. R. Evid.

In most businesses, a record that is prepared for trial or in anticipation of litigation will not be a record timely and regularly generated by that business; conversely, a record that is timely and regularly generated by a business typically is not one made in anticipation of litigation. The "business" of DHR, however, conflates these two circumstances. The business of DHR, as it relates to dependent children, is one that, by its very nature, anticipates litigation. As a result, the concern reflected in caselaw over the admissibility of records made in anticipation of litigation might exist as to DHR even in a case where the record at issue is one that is routinely and timely prepared. The observations and conclusions placed in such records may not have that "element of unusual reliability" contemplated by Rule 803(6) so as to justify their admission without the ability of an opposing party to confront and cross-examine the declarant. *See* Fed. R. Evid. 803(6), Advisory Committee's Note (also noting "a tendency unduly to emphasize a requirement of routineness and repetitiveness"); *Palmer v. Hoffman*, 318 U.S. 109, 113, 63 S. Ct. 477, 87 L. Ed. 645 (1943) (addressing the admissibility of documents under the precursor to Rule 803(6), Fed. R. Evid., and noting that, although the conduct of a business may commonly entail the necessity of addressing tort claims, "the fact that a company makes a business out of recording its employees' versions of their accidents does not put those statements in the class of records made 'in the regular course' of the business within the meaning of the [rule]. If it did, then any law office in the land could follow the same course."); *United States v. Blackburn*, 992 F.2d 666, 670 (7th Cir. 1993) (noting the difference in motives extant in employees' preparation of normal business records as opposed to employees' preparation of records in anticipation of litigation).

Though focused on the admissibility of an expert report, I find the analysis of the federal district court in *W.D. Rubright Co. v. International Harvester Co.*, 358 F. Supp. 1388 (W.D. Pa. 1973), to be instructive, particularly as it relates to the underlying rationale for the difference in our law's treatment of normal business records and records prepared in anticipation of litigation:

> "The hearsay rule has one basic purpose. When a statement is offered for the truth of that statement, the rule insists that the maker be brought before the jury so that it can evaluate his credibility and thereby gauge the truth of the statement itself. All the exceptions to the hearsay rule are based on the belief that something about the out-of-court statement insures or tends to insure its truthfulness, and therefore the jury need not evaluate the maker's demeanor for signs of credibility. The Business Records exception to the hearsay rule is in keeping with this theory of inherent believability. Giant businesses involve many departments which must interact as well as deal with outsiders over long periods of time. Precise communication and accurate records are extremely important if these interactions are to succeed. *A company cannot lie to itself on a day-to-day basis and survive because business records serve as the corporation's memory.*

> "*So it follows that records made in the ordinary course of a company's business will be truthful. On the other hand, if records are made with the thought of using them at trial, they will not necessarily have the truthfulness inherent in the day-to-day records that are made in the ordinary course of business.* Without this inherent believability, the jury should be permitted to view the demeanor of the maker in order to measure his credibility. The Pittsburgh Testing Laboratory reports do not qualify as business records because they were prepared specially for trial. As in this case, when expert reports are prepared at the behest of a party involved in litigation, it creates the possibility that an overzealous expert might abandon the impartial objectivity that is usually attributed to men of science or specialized learning, and move toward the role of an advocate. The right of cross-examination is the only effective means of dealing with this possibility."

W.D. Rubright Co. v. International Harvester Co., 358 F. Supp. at 1403 (emphasis added). *See generally United States v. Jacoby*, 955 F.2d 1527 (11th Cir. 1992) (noting that "unusual reliability," and not routineness or repetitiveness, is the touchstone of admissibility under the business records exception).

Both the mother and the father also argue that the court report in this case was characterized by what is often referred to as "hearsay within hearsay." In other words, the mother and the father find fault with the fact that much of the information contained in the court report was provided by individuals who were not employees of DHR. In my view, this argument also is well-taken.

The requirement in Rule 803(6) that the document be prepared "by, or from information transmitted by, a person with knowledge" was designed to ensure that the persons providing the information share *the same business purpose and motivation for accuracy* as does the direct preparer of the document. Thus, a report is not admissible under Rule 803(6) if the information at issue has been "supplied by a non-employee or outsider." Charles W. Gamble, *Gamble's Alabama Rules of Evidence* § 803(6) n. 11 (2d ed. Supp. 2003) (citing, inter alia, *James v. State*, 723 So. 2d 776 (Ala. Crim. App. 1998)). As the Ninth Circuit Court of Appeals has aptly put it:

> "[H]earsay statements are admissible only if the observer or participant in furnishing the information to be recorded was 'acting routinely, under a duty of accuracy, with employer reliance on the result, or in short "in the regular course of business." ' "

Clark v. City of Los Angeles, 650 F.2d 1033, 1037 (9th Cir. 1981) (quoting *United States v. Pitman*, 475 F.2d 1335 (9th Cir. 1973)). *See Reeves v. King*, 534 So. 2d 1107, 1111 (Ala. 1988) (noting that, ordinarily, the reports of an investigating police officers are not admissible in evidence and that mere routineness is not a sufficient guarantee of reliability, reasoning that " '[t]he mere fact that recordation of third party statements is routine, taken apart from the source of the information recorded, imports no guaranty of the truth of the statements themselves' " (quoting *Yates v. Bair Transp., Inc.*, 249 F. Supp. 681, 683 (S.D.N.Y. 1965))).

SOLOMON v. SHUELL
Supreme Court of Michigan
457 N.W.2d 669 (1990)

Archer, Justice.

We granted leave to appeal in order to consider two principal questions. The first question is whether four police reports were properly admitted into evidence under either MRE 803(6), the business records exception to the hearsay rule, or MRE 803(8), the public records hearsay exception . . . . We would hold that the police reports were improperly admitted into evidence . . . . We therefore would reverse the judgment of the Court of Appeals and remand the case for a new trial.

I

Plaintiff-appellant Charlotte Solomon, personal representative of the estate of Joseph Solomon, filed this wrongful death action against the City of Detroit and Detroit Police Officers John Shuell, Michael Hall, and Richard Nixon after Officer Shuell shot and killed her husband on March 20, 1981.

Officers Shuell and Nixon were members of the department's Western Surveillance Unit. Sergeant Hall was their supervisor. The three officers were plain clothed and drove separate unmarked automobiles.

On March 19 and 20, 1981, the officers were investigating a series of armed robberies on Detroit's west side. Prior to March 19, four armed men had stolen two cars from two separate automobile dealership salesmen while on test drives. Both robberies were at gunpoint. After reporting the robberies, both salesmen told the police that the perpetrators had driven to their dealerships in a Ford Thunderbird, license plate number SYF-830. The Thunderbird was registered to Claudia Williams, and the police began an undercover surveillance of her home at 18603 Curtis Street in Detroit.

On March 20, at 2:30 p.m., Officers Shuell and Nixon were assigned to the surveillance of Curtis Street in plain clothes and in separate unmarked vehicles. Alvin Solomon, Joseph Solomon's son, and a male passenger arrived in an Oldsmobile at the Curtis Street house and picked up two more men. After informing Sergeant Hall, who was also on duty in his own unmarked car, the officers were ordered to follow the Oldsmobile. They followed it to 20045 Ward, where two of the men got out of the vehicle. The car drove on, and the officers continued to follow the vehicle but lost it in traffic.

Sergeant Hall ordered the officers to return to Ward Street and watch the house. Later that afternoon, the two suspects, who had previously entered 20045 Ward, left the residence. Sergeant Hall and Officers Nixon and Shuell then stopped and questioned the suspects as they walked down the block away from the house.

At approximately the same time as the two suspects were being questioned, another police officer radioed Shuell and Nixon and told them that the Ford Thunderbird used in the armed robberies had returned to the Curtis Street address. Sergeant Hall ordered Shuell and Nixon to return to Curtis Street. Along the way, Nixon spotted the Oldsmobile driven by Alvin Solomon. Alvin, now accompanied by his girl friend, Wynee Green, was driving north on Strathmoor Street. Nixon relayed the information to Shuell and Sergeant Hall and followed the Oldsmobile to 20045 Strathmoor, the Solomon family home. Nixon pulled up behind the Oldsmobile. Shortly thereafter, Shuell stopped in front of the suspect's automobile. The two officers got out and approached the Oldsmobile. The account of what happened next differs according to the trial testimony.

Alvin testified that, after he got out of his car, Nixon rushed him, quickly flashed a badge, threw him toward the car, and confiscated a pellet gun that he carried in his waistband. Shuell ran toward the two, failed to identify himself as a police officer, put his gun to Alvin's head and dragged him to the rear of the car. Alvin told Wynee to get his father, Joseph Solomon, who came outside with a gun, which was pointed down toward the ground. Neither Nixon nor Shuell identified themselves to Alvin's father. Before Joseph Solomon could come off the front porch, Shuell fired his gun, striking him. Joseph Solomon kept approaching Shuell and Alvin and fell dead at the end of the driveway.

Charlotte Solomon, Alvin's mother and Joseph's wife, testified that, at the time of the incident, she and her husband were inside their home watching television.

Joseph got up, briefly left the room and came back in and said, "[s]omebody got my child out there." He went outside with his gun and yelled, "[t]urn my child loose." Charlotte got to the doorway in time to see her husband fall at the end of the driveway.

Nixon testified that, as he approached the Oldsmobile, he showed Alvin his badge and ID card and told him he was a police officer. As Alvin got out of the vehicle, Nixon saw a gun in Alvin's waistband, which he confiscated. At this time, Shuell asked Alvin to put his hands on the car so he could be frisked. Alvin resisted, shouting at his girl friend to get his father. As Nixon walked around the car to restrain the girl, he heard a noise at the doorway of the house. Joseph Solomon ran out of the house and came off the porch holding a gun in both hands, extended in a combat stance. Nixon held his badge up and yelled, "Sir, we're police officers, we're police officers." Nixon heard one shot, turned, and saw Joseph Solomon's hands recoil. He then heard other shots, after which Joseph fell. Nixon also stated that neither Shuell nor he had drawn their guns before Joseph Solomon came out of the house.

Shuell testified that both Nixon and he approached the car, showed Alvin their badges, and told him they were police officers. As Alvin got out of his car, Shuell told Nixon he saw a gun in Alvin's waistband and grabbed Alvin by his left wrist. Shuell told Alvin he was under arrest, and asked him to place his hands on the car. Alvin backed away from the car and told his girl friend to get his father. Shuell told Alvin to go to the rear of the car and put his hands on the trunk. Shuell was frisking Alvin when Nixon yelled, "Police, police, John, look out, he's got a gun." Joseph Solomon assumed a two-hand stance and aimed his gun at Shuell. As Shuell grabbed Alvin, Joseph told Alvin to get down. Alvin shouted, "Daddy, don't do it." Shuell yelled, "Drop the gun. Police." As Shuell fell to the ground with Alvin, his pistol was still in its holster. Joseph fired one shot, which missed Shuell. By this time, Shuell had drawn his weapon and returned Joseph Solomon's fire.

Joseph Solomon fired at least one shot. Shuell fired nine, eight of which hit Solomon, instantly killing him.

Plaintiff-appellant filed the present case in Wayne Circuit Court. She alleged negligence, assault and battery, and the violation of her husband's constitutional rights. Before the case went to the jury, defendant Nixon had been dismissed. In addition, the trial judge granted a directed verdict in favor of defendants Michael Hall and the City of Detroit.

As to defendant Shuell, the jury returned a special verdict, finding that Shuell was negligent and that his negligence was a proximate cause of Joseph Solomon's death. Consequently, the jury found plaintiff's damages to be $100,000. The jury also found, however, that decedent was negligent and that his own negligence was also a proximate cause of his death and assessed this at eighty percent. Accordingly, a judgment was entered in favor of plaintiff for $20,000.[1]

Plaintiff subsequently filed a claim of appeal, alleging that the trial court had

---

[1] The jury also found that Shuell did not commit assault and battery. In addition, the jury did not answer whether decedent's constitutional rights had been violated.

improperly admitted four exhibits into evidence and had improperly instructed the jury. The Court of Appeals panel, one judge dissenting, rejected plaintiff's argument that the trial court improperly admitted into evidence four police reports under MRE 803(6), the business records hearsay exception. Although two members of the panel agreed with plaintiff that the trial court also committed error by giving a modified version of SJI2d 13.07, stating the so-called rescue doctrine, the Court found this error to be harmless.[2] The Court of Appeals, therefore, affirmed the decision of the trial court. 166 Mich.App. 19, 420 N.W.2d 160 (1988).

Plaintiff-appellant subsequently applied for leave to appeal in this Court, which we granted on April 11, 1989, limited to the issues (1) whether the trial court improperly admitted into evidence four police reports prepared during the investigation of decedent's shooting, and (2) whether the trial court properly instructed the jury on the so-called rescue doctrine. 432 Mich. 891, 437 N.W.2d 636 (1989). Subsequently, we ordered the parties to submit supplemental briefs on the applicability of MRE 803(8), the public records hearsay exception, to the four police reports. We also invited amicus curiae briefs to be filed. The order was entered on October 24, 1989.

II

The first question presented is whether four police reports were improperly admitted into evidence. Plaintiff's exhibit 113 and defendant's exhibit 122 are police department homicide witness statements taken during the investigation of decedent's death. Both witness statements are in question and answer form. Plaintiff's exhibit 113 contains Nixon's version of the decedent's shooting, and defendant's exhibit 122 contains Shuell's.

Plaintiff's exhibit 34A and defendant's exhibit 121 are preliminary complaint reports, the initial report an officer writes detailing his actions during a particular assignment. A preliminary complaint report is the starting point for the subsequent interdepartmental investigation of an incident. Plaintiff's exhibit 34A is a supplementary report Sergeant Hall wrote describing in detail his conversation with Officer Shuell immediately following decedent's shooting. Defendant's exhibit 121 is Officer Shuell's report describing his actions during the events leading up to decedent's death.

At various points during the trial, the defense moved to admit each exhibit. The trial court admitted each exhibit over plaintiff's timely objection, and the Court of Appeals affirmed.

Before this Court, the parties concede that the four exhibits are defined as hearsay, MRE 801(c).[3] The exhibits are, therefore, inadmissible under MRE 802,[4] unless subject to an MRE 803 exception.[5] Consequently, we must determine

---

[2] The dissenting judge did not address the jury instruction issue.

[3] "(c) Hearsay. 'Hearsay' is a statement, other than the one made by the declarant while testifying at the trial or hearing, offered in evidence to prove the truth of the matter asserted." MRE 801(c).

[4] "Hearsay is not admissible except as provided by these rules." MRE 802.

[5] Neither party argues that the exhibits are admissible under MRE 804.

whether the Court of Appeals correctly held that the four reports were properly admitted into evidence and that the trial court did not abuse its discretion when it overruled plaintiff's timely objection. *Hadley v. Trio Tool Co.*, 143 Mich.App. 319, 328, 372 N.W.2d 537 (1985). See *People v. Golochowicz*, 413 Mich. 298, 322, 319 N.W.2d 518 (1982).

A

Plaintiff-appellant first argues that the four exhibits are inadmissible under the business records exception to the hearsay rule. MRE 803(6) provides:

> "The following are not excluded by the hearsay rule, even though the declarant is available as a witness:

*   *   *

> "(6) Records of regularly conducted activity. A memorandum, report, record, or data compilation, in any form, of acts, transactions, occurrences, or events, made at or near the time by, or from information transmitted by, a person with knowledge, if kept in the course of a regularly conducted business activity, and if it was the regular practice of that business activity to make the memorandum, report, record, or data compilation, all as shown by the testimony of the custodian or other qualified witness, unless the source of information or the method or circumstances of preparation indicate lack of trustworthiness. The term 'business' as used in this paragraph includes business, institution, association, profession, occupation, and calling of every kind, whether or not conducted for profit."[6]

The defense offered the four exhibits over plaintiff's timely objection. Before the trial court, plaintiff argued that, even if the reports were "records" within the meaning of MRE 803(6), the source of information and the circumstances of preparation lacked trustworthiness. Plaintiff reasoned that the reports and homicide witness statements were untrustworthy because when the documents were prepared, the police officers knew they were the subject of a homicide investigation that could result in criminal prosecution, civil liability, and interdepartmental discipline. In addition, the four documents were prepared following a waiver of *Miranda*[7] rights and in the presence of counsel.[8]

Although the trial court noted the circumstances under which the reports were prepared, it nevertheless rejected plaintiff's argument that the exhibits lacked trustworthiness. As to the motivation to misrepresent, the court acknowledged that the officers could have made their statements in a light most favorable to protect their relationships and avoid interdepartmental sanctions and potential criminal and civil liability. In addition, the court also held, in effect, that the issue of

---

[6] MRE 803(6) is identical to FRE 803(6) except that MRE 803(6) is limited to "acts, transactions, occurrences, or events," while FRE 803(6) applies to "acts, events, conditions, opinions, or diagnoses . . . ."

[7] *Miranda v. Arizona*, 384 U.S. 436, 86 S. Ct. 1602, 16 L. Ed. 2d 694 (1966).

[8] The record reveals that, during oral argument outside the presence of the jury, plaintiff's counsel informed the court that the officers were advised of their constitutional rights and provided counsel.

trustworthiness under MRE 803(6) went to the credibility and weight the jury should assign each exhibit and not to admissibility. Because plaintiff could not point to specific facts on the face of each exhibit indicating a lack of trustworthiness, the court overruled plaintiff's objection and admitted each exhibit into evidence.

*   *   *

It is clear that the traditional business records hearsay exception is justified on grounds of trustworthiness: unintentional mistakes made in the preparation of a record would very likely be detected and corrected. Where, however, the source of information or the person preparing the report has a motivation to misrepresent, trustworthiness can no longer be presumed, and the justification for the business records exception no longer holds true. Wigmore, *supra*, § 1522, pp 442–443, § 1527, p 448; McCormick, Evidence, § 308, pp 875–878. Thus, in *Central Fabricators*, *supra*, we found the leading case of *Palmer v. Hoffman*, 318 U.S. 109, 63 S. Ct. 477, 87 L. Ed. 645 (1943), persuasive authority supporting the proposition that the motivation to misrepresent is a strong indicator of a lack of trustworthiness. In *Palmer*, the United States Supreme Court held that a railroad accident report was not made " 'in the regular course' of the business," a requirement by its nature ensuring trustworthiness, as defined in the federal business records hearsay statute. The Supreme Court reasoned that, although it may have been in the regular course of the railroad's systematic operations to record its employee's version of an accident, the admission of the report into evidence would make the act applicable to any recording system, "though it had little or nothing to do with the management or operation of the business as such." 318 U.S. at 113, 63 S. Ct. at 480. Thus, the Court concluded that the report was not made "for the systematic conduct of the enterprise as a railroad business. . . . [The report's] primary utility is in litigating, not in railroading." 318 U.S. at 114, 63 S. Ct. at 480.

Although in *Palmer* the Supreme Court analyzed the issue in terms of whether the report was made in the regular course of railroad business as defined in the federal act, the motivation for making the report in the first place lies at the very heart of the act's definition of "regular course of business," and, in this respect, the opinion of the United States Court of Appeals for the Second Circuit in *Palmer*[14] analyzed the report from a slightly different perspective while reaching the same result. The Second Circuit panel noted, as did the Supreme Court, that even though the railroad's employee was under a duty to his employer to make the report, the circumstances surrounding the preparation of the report, such as the anticipation of highly probable litigation, took the report outside the special legal meaning of "regular course of business":

> "Each trade has its peculiar jargon and courts rely on that jargon when it finds its way into a statute dealing with that trade.
>
> "And so with 'regular course of business' as applied to records or memoranda in an evidence statute. To a layman, the words might seem to mean any record or paper prepared by an employee in accordance with a rule established in that business by his employer. But according to the

---

[14] 129 F.2d 976 (CA 2, 1942).

jargon of lawyers and judges those words, in discussions of evidence, have always meant writings made in such a way as to afford *some* safeguards against the existence of any *exceptionally* strong bias or *powerful* motive to misrepresent." 129 F.2d 976, 984 (CA 2, 1942) (emphasis in the original).

Thus, the Second Circuit concluded that the document was inadmissible under the federal act not merely because it may have been prepared to "perpetuate evidence" in anticipation of litigation, 129 F.2d at 991, but rather because the looming specter of potential liability supplied a powerful motivation to misrepresent. Because the railroad and its employee were exposed to highly probable litigation and potential liability, any possible errors in the report could no longer be considered mere misstatements. Consequently, the report was "dripping with motivations to misrepresent." 129 F.2d at 991. Although the dissenting panel member noted that "there is hardly a grocer's account book which could not be excluded on that basis," 129 F.2d at 1002 (Clark, J., dissenting), *Palmer* has subsequently been read to stand for the proposition that the trial court, in its discretion, may exclude evidence meeting the literal requirements of the business records exception where the underlying circumstances indicate a lack of the trustworthiness business records are presumed to have. McCormick, *supra*, § 308, p 877.

As *Palmer* indicates, trustworthiness, under the current Rules of Evidence, no longer serves as a mere philosophical justification for the admission of evidence otherwise excluded as hearsay. Rather, under MRE 803(6) and FRE 803(6), trustworthiness is itself an express threshold condition of admissibility. First, the rule on its face provides that evidence otherwise meeting the literal requirements of MRE 803(6) and FRE 803(6) shall not be admissible where "the source of information or the method or circumstances of preparation indicate *lack of trustworthiness*." MRE 803(6), FRE 803(6) (emphasis added).

The trial court improperly concluded that the sources of information and the circumstances under which the four police reports were prepared did not lack trustworthiness as that term is narrowly defined in MRE 803(6). As to the officer's motivation to misrepresent, we agree with dissenting Judge Shepherd, that, in this case, the motivation to misrepresent is obvious and indicates a lack of trustworthiness. Officers Nixon and Shuell's witness statements were taken during the course of the department's homicide investigation, which they knew could result in a criminal prosecution. They, along with Sergeant Hall, would also be subject to the department's internal affairs investigation, which could result in interdepartmental discipline. Finally, it was highly probable that the officers and the city faced civil litigation and potential liability. Although the trial court rejected this potential motivation to misrepresent as too speculative, it did recognize that even Officer Nixon, who did not fire a single shot at decedent, possibly was "anything but totally frank with the homicide investigators."

Rather than reject as speculative plaintiff's argument that the officers had a motivation to misrepresent, we believe that, when the exhibits are viewed under the circumstances of their preparation, the motivation to misrepresent becomes clearer. Although the trial court noted that there is no evidence suggesting an improper motivation to misrepresent on the part of departmental homicide investigators and

that proper departmental procedures were followed, it is these very same procedures that indicate a lack of trustworthiness as that term is defined under MRE
803(6). The homicide witness statements, for example, were taken following a
waiver of *Miranda* rights, which could only heighten the officers' awareness that
anything said could and would be used against them in a court of law.[21] In addition,
the witness statements and the preliminary complaint reports were taken and
prepared with the assistance of counsel, who would, at the very least, advise the
officers not to make any inculpatory statements. The homicide statements were
taken on March 25 and 26, five and six days following decedent's shooting, which
permitted time for reflection and deliberation not contemplated within the meaning
of MRE 803(6). We conclude, therefore, that the homicide investigation reports, as
well as the preliminary complaint reports, lacked trustworthiness and, when made
under these circumstances and in light of the highly probable civil and criminal
litigation and departmental discipline the officers potentially faced, were not the
type of records contemplated by MRE 803(6).

The trial court also incorrectly analyzed the significance of trustworthiness
under MRE 803(6). The trial court held in effect that, under MRE 803(6),
trustworthiness and the presence of a self-serving motivation to misrepresent were
questions for the jury and did not affect admissibility. We agree that the credibility
and weight to be assigned to otherwise admissible evidence is a question for the
trier of fact. We disagree, however, that, under MRE 803(6), trustworthiness is not
also a question of admissibility. As the rule and its theoretical underpinnings
indicate, trustworthiness is, under MRE 803(6), unlike M.C.L. § 600.2146; M.S.A.
§ 27A.2146, an express condition of admissibility. The flaw in the trial court's
reasoning was that its analysis was essentially a strict and literal interpretation of
M.C.L. § 600.2146; M.S.A. § 27A.2146, which preceded MRE 803(6). Unlike the
present rule, § 2146 expressly provided that, once the appropriate foundation had
been established, "[a]ll other circumstances of the making of such writing or record
including lack of personal knowledge by the entrant or maker, may be shown to
affect its weight but not its admissibility." Unlike § 2146, MRE 803(6) now expressly
provides that trustworthiness is a question of admissibility and is not an issue solely
affecting the weight of the evidence.

[3] Recorded During Regularly Conducted Activities

In order to qualify under Fed. R. Evid. 803(6), the record must have been "kept
in the course of a regularly conducted activity of a business." The oil spill case,
dealing with the infamous leak of the BP offshore well in the Gulf Coast, considers
whether emails about a business's activities qualify. The records must not just be
regularly kept, but they must involve "regularly conducted activities." As the
Jackson case then demonstrates, these activities do not have to be legal, so long as

---

[21] "The warning of the right to remain silent must be accompanied by the explanation that anything
said can and will be used against the individual in court. This warning is needed in order to make him
aware not only of the privilege, but also of the consequences of forgoing it. It is only through an
awareness of these consequences that there can be any assurance of real understanding and intelligent
exercise of the privilege. Moreover, this warning may serve to make the individual more acutely aware
that he is faced with a phase of the adversary system — that he is not in the presence of persons acting
solely in his interest." *Miranda v. Arizona*, n. 7 *supra*, 384 U.S. at p. 469, 86 S. Ct. at p. 1625.

they are regularly conducted activities and they were recorded.

IN RE OIL SPILL BY THE OIL RIG DEEPWATER HORIZON IN THE GULF OF MEXICO, ON APRIL 20, 2010

United States District Court, Eastern District of Louisiana
2012 U.S. Dist. LEXIS 3406

CARL BARBIER, DISTRICT JUDGE.

Before the Court are letter briefs from the PSC (Rec. Doc. 4340-1, October 17, 2011; Rec. Doc. 4631, November 16, 2011; Second ltr. dated November 16, 2011; and Ltr. dated November 28, 2011); Transocean (Rec.Doc. 4560, November 10, 2011); Halliburton (Rec.Doc. 4567, November 11, 2011); Cameron (Rec.Doc. 4563, November 11, 2011); and BP (Rec. Doc. 4569, November 14, 2011; Ltr. dated November 23, 2011; and Rec. Doc. 4964, December 2, 2011). The briefs pertain to the first motion set, regarding the issue of admissibility of emails.

BACKGROUND AND PROCEDURAL HISTORY

In order to facilitate a timely resolution of evidentiary issues prior to the upcoming trial in February 2012, Magistrate Judge Shushan ordered the PSC to submit a list of 300 exhibits that would constitute a sample of documents that would present the full range of evidentiary issues to be encountered at trial. The PSC complied, presenting its "List of 300." Accordingly, the Magistrate Judge also issued an order with a schedule for BP's motions *in limine* and responses to PSC issues (Rec.Doc. 4572). The order provides a briefing schedule for 13 categories of evidentiary issues. The first category is described as "BP and others to respond to PSC Letter Regarding 'E-Mail Strings Produced by Defendants.'" Rec. Doc. 4572, at 1. The issues pertain to the admissibility *vel non* of email strings proffered by the PSC.

THE PARTIES' ARGUMENTS

The PSC argues that all of the email communications produced by the defendants are excepted from the hearsay ban by Federal Rule of Evidence 803(6), the "business records" exception. It argues that company email correspondence is created regularly by company employees as part of their business activity. It asserts that courts are increasingly taking a liberal view of emails as business records because email is the modern equivalent of the interoffice memorandum. The PSC cites examples of "mixed recipient" email correspondence (which includes employees of a producing defendant[1] as well as an outside party). It suggests that mixed recipient emails are admissible if they are created regularly, concern a business activity, and an employee of the producing defendant sent or received and maintained the correspondence with an outside employee. The PSC also argues that email correspondence is admissible under other theories: as adoptive admissions,

---

[1] The parties in their letter briefs apparently use the term "producing defendant" to refer to emails that are sent by employees or agents of a party who is a defendant in MDL 2179.

where employees add text to received emails that they then forward to non-employees; as admissions by parties opponent, for all correspondence written by employees of a producing defendant or co-defendant; and as non-hearsay evidence of notice, knowledge, or state of mind of email recipients.

Transocean and Halliburton both responded to the PSC's initial letter brief. They object to the PSC's proposed blanket rule and seek a case-by-case consideration of emails. Transocean argues that the Court must examine whether it was an employee's business duty to make and maintain a particular email as part of his job duties and whether the employee routinely sent or received and maintained such an email. It argues that email from an outsider to a defendant presents multiple levels of hearsay; that merely forwarding an email does not constitute an employee's adoptive admission; and that for the party-admission exception to apply, there must be proof that a given statement falls within the scope of the employee's employment. Halliburton argues that emails should be treated like any other documents in determining their admissibility. It argues that the mere creation and maintenance of emails is not the regularly conducted business activity that triggers the business records exception; but, rather, the email must contain information that is kept in the course of a regularly conducted business activity. Cameron also submitted a letter brief in which it only argues regarding one particular email exchange.

BP, in reply to the PSC's initial letter brief, argues that although some email strings are admissible, others are not. BP argues that the business records exception does not apply to emails prepared primarily in anticipation of litigation and does not apply unless the employer imposed a business duty to make and maintain emails; that the witness required to establish the foundation for the business records exception must be familiar with the records-keeping system of the declarant;[2] and that emails that are excepted from the hearsay prohibition as party admissions are only admissible against the declarant. BP cites several examples of email exhibits that it claims fail to meet the business records exception. For example, an email from a non-party employee to a Halliburton employee concerning what others said is double hearsay. BP argues that even though part of an email may be a business record, this does not make the entire email admissible. It also argues that email statements by party employees are not admissible as admissions of that party if not made concerning a matter within the scope of the employee's employment. It argues that, contrary to the PSC's assertion, there is no increasingly liberal standard with regard to the admissibility of emails as business records.

In rebuttal correspondence, the PSC clarifies that it does not intend to engage in a line-byline analysis of every email, unless requested to do so by the Court; and that argument concerning a particular exhibit does not indicate a concession as to other exhibits. It argues that the imposition of a business duty is not the test under the Fifth Circuit's formulation of the business records exception, but rather whether a document was "retained" and "kept" in the regular course of business. It states that the fact that a document is produced in response to a subpoena does not prevent it from falling under the business records exception.

---

[2] A declarant is a person who makes a statement. Fed. R. Evid. 801(b).

DISCUSSION

A. The Issues

The instant motion set presents the defendants' hearsay objections to email strings that the PSC seeks to introduce. Hearsay is any statement made out of court and offered in evidence to prove the truth of the matter asserted. Fed. R. Evid. 801(c). Hearsay is not admissible except as provided otherwise by federal statute, the Federal Rules of Evidence, or other rules prescribed by the Supreme Court. Fed. R. Evid. 802. The PSC essentially argues that the identified email strings are admissible in their entirety under one or more hearsay exceptions within the federal rules. The defendants advocate a case-by-case inquiry and raise objections as to individual emails and email strings.

B. Each Email Merits Individual Consideration

The Court rejects the PSC's suggestion that all email strings listed in its "List of 300" are categorically admissible, for the following reasons.

1. Problems Under the Business Records Exception

The so-called "business records" exception to the hearsay rule is Federal Rule 803(6).[3] Whether a particular record qualifies for the exception hinges upon the content and preparation of the record. Anthony J. Dreyer, *When the Postman Beeps Twice: The Admissibility of Electronic Mail Under the Business Records Exception of the Federal Rules of Evidence*, 64 FORDHAM L.REV. 2285, 2326 (1996). The rationale for the exception is that business records are reliable due to the qualities of regularity of record-keeping, the fact that they are relied upon in business, and the fact that employees have a duty and incentive to produce reliable records. Advisory Committee's Note, 56 F.R.D. 183, 308 (1973) ("The element of unusual reliability of business records is said variously to be supplied by systematic checking, by regularity and continuity which produce habits of precision, by actual experience of business in relying upon them, or by a duty to make an accurate record as part of a continuing job or occupation.").

---

[3] The 2011 amendment to Rule 803 is only stylistic in nature. The amended formulation of the business records exception clarifies that there are five elements required to trigger the exception:

    (6) Records of a Regularly Conducted Activity. A record of an act, event, condition, opinion, or diagnosis if:

        (A) the record was made at or near the time by-or from information transmitted by-someone with knowledge;

        (B) the record was kept in the course of a regularly conducted activity of a business, organization, occupation, or calling, whether or not for profit;

        (C) making the record was a regular practice of that activity;

        (D) all these conditions are shown by the testimony of the custodian or another qualified witness, or by a certification that complies with Rule 902(11) or (12) or with a statute permitting certification; and

        (E) neither the source of information nor the method or circumstances of preparation indicate a lack of trustworthiness.

Fed. R. Evid. 803(6) (Westlaw 2011). The Fifth Circuit in *Wilander v. McDermott Int'l, Inc.*, 887 F.2d 88 (5th Cir. 1989), *aff'd*, 498 U.S. 337 (1991), described the business records exception as containing five elements, but these elements do not directly correspond with the now re-numbered federal rule. The *Wilander* test is:

> (a) That the document [was] made "at or near" the time of the matters recorded therein; (b) that the document [was] prepared by, or from information transmitted by a person "with knowledge of the matters recorded"; (c) that the person or persons who prepared the document [were] engaged in preparing it, in some undertaking, enterprise or business which can fairly be termed a "regularly conducted business activity"; (d) that it [was] the "regular practice" of that business activity to make documents of that nature; and (e) that the documents [were] retained and kept in the course of that or some other regularly conducted business activity.

Id. at 91 (quotation omitted). Because re-numbered Rule 803(6) contains a more exhaustive list of prerequisites to the exception's application, its structure is used for purposes of the instant motion. Namely, Rule 803(6)'s (A)-(E) list subsumes the (a)-(e) itemization of the *Wilander* test: Rule 803(6)(A) contains *Wilander* parts (a) and (b); Rule 803(6)(B) contains *Wilander* parts (c) and (e); Rule 803(6)(C) contains *Wilander* part (d); and Rule 803(6)(D) and (E) contain no counterparts in the Fifth Circuit's *Wilander* test. Thus, the Court uses the rule's textual framework and merely draws from the *Wilander* elements where necessary to elaborate on the meaning of those rule-enumerated elements.

The individual elements required to trigger the exception's applicability show that there is no categorical rule that emails originating from or received by employees of a producing defendant are admissible under the business records exception. First of all, the email must have been sent or received at or near the time of the event(s) recorded in the email.[4] Thus, one must look at each email's content to determine whether the email was created contemporaneously with the sender's acquisition of the information within the email. Second, the email must have been sent by someone with knowledge of the event(s) documented in the email.[5] This requires a particularized inquiry as to whether the declarant — the composer of the email — possessed personal knowledge of the information in the email. Third, the email must have been sent or received in the course of a regular business activity,[6] which requires a case-by-case analysis of whether the producing defendant had a policy or imposed a business duty on its employee to report or record the information within the email. Fourth, it must be the producing defendant's regular practice to send or receive emails that record the type of event(s) documented in the email.[7] This would require proof of a policy of the producing defendant to use email

---

[4] The record must have been "made at or near the time" of the act, event, condition, opinion, or diagnosis within the record. Fed. R. Evid. 803(6)(A).

[5] *See* Fed. R. Evid. 803(6)(A).

[6] The record must have been kept in the course of a regularly conducted activity of a business. Fed. R. Evid. 803(6)(B).

[7] Making the record must have been a regular practice of the business activity at issue. Fed. R. Evid. 803(6)(C). *See also Canatxx Gas Storage Ltd. v. Silverhawk Capital Partners, LLC*, 2008 U.S. Dist.

to make certain types of reports or to send certain sorts of communications; it is not enough to say that as a general business matter, most companies receive and send emails as part of their business model. Fifth, a custodian or qualified witness must attest that these conditions have been fulfilled — which certainly requires an email-by-email inquiry.[8] Lastly, the objecting defendant is permitted under the rule to argue that the particular email should be excluded due to concerns of lack of trustworthiness, based on the information source underlying the email content or the circumstances under which the email was sent and received.[9] Clearly, there is no across-the-board rule that all emails are admissible as business records.

As to the argument that the defendants regularly receive electronic mail as part of daily business activities and that their regular practice is to receive and retain such emails, if this was sufficient to invoke the business records exception, then all *physical* mail received by a defendant likewise would be a "business record." This cannot be the right result. Many mail items received by a company do not document activities that are routine or otherwise regularly conducted. An analogy to the "interoffice memorandum" may be appropriate, as well.[10] Although interoffice memoranda are indeed regularly sent and received in business practice, the *activity recorded* in such memoranda must regularly occur, for the business records exception to apply. *See* 30B M. Graham, Federal Practice And Procedure: Evidence § 7047 (Interim Edition) (stating that the activity recorded must be the "type which regularly occurs in the course of the business's day-to-day activity"). Thus, courts have excluded memoranda that do not record regularly occurring activities. *See, e.g., Langon v. Dept. of Health and Human Servs.*, 959 F.2d 1053, 1060 (D.C.Cir. 1992) (declining to admit memorandum written to employee by her employer); *U.S. v. Strother*, 49 F.3d 869, 875 (2d Cir. 1995), *cert. denied*, 522 U.S. 1118 (1998) (declining to adopt a rule that would permit the introduction of a memorandum drafted in response to unusual or isolated events); *Standard Oil Co. of Cal. v. Moore*, 251 F.2d 188, 215 (9th Cir. 1958), *cert. denied*, 356 U.S. 975 (1958) (not admitting memoranda and letters where company procedure appeared "nonexisten[t]," many of them were "casual and informal in nature," and many were "written as a result of the exercise of individual judgment and discretion"). Finally, many emails (including many of the informal conversations carried on in the email strings at issue) are essentially substitutes for telephone calls.[11] Telephone calls are routinely made but are not admissible as "business records" because — among other reasons — their individual content does not demonstrate the requisite regularity. In summary, the business records exception does not supply a rule that would render

---

LEXIS 37803, 2008 WL 1999234, at *12 (S.D. Tex. May 8, 2008) (for the business records exception to apply to an email, "the employer [must have] imposed a business duty to make and maintain **such** a record.") (emphasis added); *Wilander*, 887 F.2d at 91 (requiring proof that the person who prepared the document prepared it as part of a regularly conducted business activity).

[8] *See* Fed. R. Evid. 803(6)(D).

[9] *See* Fed. R. Evid. 803(6)(E).

[10] The PSC asserts that "email correspondence is simply the modern equivalent of the interoffice memorandum." Rec. Doc. 4340-1, at 3.

[11] *See* Robert L. Paddock, *Utilizing E-Mail as Business Records Under the Texas Rules of Evidence*, 19 Rev. Litig. 61, 64 (2000) ("Most of these e-mails are likely to be short messages that replace what would otherwise have been conveyed in a telephone call.").

admissible all emails found on a defendant's computer server.

2. Double Hearsay

Many of the emails the PSC seeks to admit present "double hearsay" or "hearsay within hearsay."[12] Namely, not only is the email itself offered for the truth of its contents, and thus hearsay, but also many of the statements within a given email are hearsay. For example, where a producing defendant's employee forwards to a co-worker an email that originated from outside the producing defendant, the forwarding employee (who created the email at issue) has made an out-of-court assertion of what someone outside the ranks of the producing defendant said. This is a situation where "the record is prepared by an employee with information supplied by another person." *U.S. v. Blechman*, 657 F.3d 1052, 1065 (10th Cir. 2011). Although the "outer hearsay" of the email at issue may be admissible under the business records exception, the "inner hearsay" of information provided by an outsider to the business preparing the record must likewise fall under a hearsay exception — the business records exception or some other exception — to be admissible.

3. Direct and Adoptive Admissions

A statement is not hearsay if it was made by a party and is offered against that party. Fed. R. Evid. 801(d)(2). A party can make a statement in one of several ways: for example, through its employee, directly, or by adoption of another person's statement. The PSC argues that many of the emails that were forwarded by employees of the parties are adoptive admissions. This is a plausible argument under Rule 801(d)(2)(B), which makes admissible statements of which a party manifested its adoption or belief. However, the fact that a party's employee forwarded an email originating from outside his employer does not necessarily constitute an adoption of the contents of the forwarded email. *See U.S. v. Safavian*, 435 F. Supp. 2d 36, 43–44 (D.D.C. May 23, 2006) (admitting certain emails where their context and content clearly indicated that the forwarding individual manifested an adoption of or belief in the truth of the statements of other people, but declining to admit other emails that did not clearly demonstrate the forwarder's adoption of the email content). Therefore, a forwarded email is only an adoptive admission if it is clear that the forwarder adopted the content or believed in the truth of the content.

Likewise, although the PSC argues that emails composed by employees of producing defendants are admissions under Rule 801(d)(2)(D), this hearsay exception also requires a case-by-case analysis of such emails. The rule treats as non-hearsay a statement offered against a party and that was made by the party's employee on a "on a matter within the scope of that [employment] relationship and while it existed." Fed. R. Evid. 801(d)(2)(D). The mere fact that a producing defendant's employee sent an email while at work from a work computer to a co-employee does not mean that the email was composed or received concerning a

---

[12] *See* Fed. R. Evid. 805 ("Hearsay within hearsay is not excluded by the rule against hearsay if each part of the combined statements conforms with an exception to the rule.").

matter within the scope of an employee's employment. This "course and scope" inquiry requires a case-by-case analysis to determine whether a particular party employee's statement can be properly admitted as non-hearsay against the party. Therefore, there is no broad rule that all the emails at issue are admissible as party admissions.

C. "Regularly Conducted Activity" Requirements

Concerning the business records exception, the bulk of the parties' arguments concerns the requirements (1) that the emails have been kept in the course of a regularly conducted business activity and (2) that the business's regular practice have been to make the email record. *See* Fed. R. Evid. 803(6)(B)–(C). To assist the parties in resolving hearsay issues regarding emails, the Court notes the following.

First, it must have been the business's regular practice to make the record at issue — the email that the declarant/defendant's employee sends or receives. Fed. R. Evid. 803(6)(B). Therefore, the sending or receiving employee must have been under an obligation imposed by his employer to send or receive the email at issue. The Fifth Circuit in *U.S. v. Robinson*, 700 F.2d 205, 209–10 (5th Cir. 1983), *cert. denied*, 465 U.S. 1008 (1984) held that an employee's handwritten notes that he regularly took during board meetings for his own use in his role as a purchasing clerk were not admissible under the business records exception because there was no showing that the employee regularly compiled notes as part of his official duties. More specifically, applying the *Robinson* rationale to emails, the Southern District of Texas cited to other federal district court decisions in stating that for the business records exception to apply, there must be a showing that the employer imposed a business duty upon the employee to make and maintain the record. *Canatxx Gas Storage Ltd. v. Silverhawk Capital Partners, LLC*, 2008 U.S. Dist. LEXIS 37803, 2008 WL 1999234, at *12 (S.D. Tex. May 8, 2008). Essentially, there must be a showing that the email at issue was not sent or received casually, nor was its creation a mere isolated incident. *See Imperial Trading Co., Inc. v. Travelers Prop. Cas. Co. of Amer.*, 654 F. Supp. 2d 518, 2009 WL 2382787, at *3 (E.D. La. July 31, 2009).

Second, the email itself must have been created as part of the regularly conducted activity of a business. This does not necessarily require the activity to pertain to the business of a producing defendant. For example, Sending Company's employee emails Receiving Company's employee. If Receiving Company is the company whose practice it is to regularly receive and retain emails containing information of this sort, even if the email does not pertain to Sending Company's regular business — but rather, Receiving Company's — the "regularly conducted activity" requirements are fulfilled as to Receiving Company.[13] The key, though, is that the email, as a "record" within the meaning of Rule 803(6), must pertain to a "regularly conducted" business activity. Thus, if the information within an email pertains to a transaction or report of an isolated, sporadic nature that is not within

---

[13] Fed. R. Evid. 803(6)(B)–(C) (requiring the record to be "kept in the course of *a* regularly conducted activity of *a* business," and that "making the record was a regular practice of *that* activity") (emphasis added).

the scope of what the email sender or recipient regularly does to engage in business, the exception does not apply.

The Court does not intend to analyze the multitude of emails for the parties. The permutations of potential admissibility are numerous in the email realm, especially in light of the potential application of the business records exception. In summary, the business records exception does not excuse hearsay unless *the declarant's statement* qualifies as a business record. *See U.S. v. Ismoila*, 100 F.3d 380, 392 (5th Cir. 1996) ("[T]he business records exception 'applies only if the person who makes the statement "is himself acting in the regular course of business." ' "). Every participant in the chain producing a record must be acting in the regular course of business for the business records exception to admit all levels of hearsay within an email or email string. *See id.* It is the parties' responsibility to confer regarding email hearsay issues in light of the above and foregoing. Accordingly,

IT IS ORDERED that the parties confer in a good faith effort to stipulate regarding the admissibility of emails and email strings; and that thereafter if the parties cannot agree as to individual emails, by January 30, 2012 they shall submit briefs to Magistrate Judge Shushan, who will make recommendations to the Court regarding admissibility.

UNITED STATES v. JACKSON
United States Court of Appeals, Fifth Circuit
636 F.3d 687 (2011)

E. Grady Jolly, Circuit Judge:

The petition for rehearing is GRANTED. We WITHDRAW our previous opinion in this matter, *United States v. Jackson*, 625 F.3d 875 (5th Cir. 2010), and substitute the opinion that follows. Although we arrive at the same result as in our earlier opinion, this opinion reflects substantial changes to clarify and further expound that our evidentiary and constitutional analyses are two separate and distinct considerations:

Colin Dalawn Jackson ("Jackson") appeals his conviction and sentence, following a jury trial, for conspiring to possess with intent to distribute more than five kilograms of cocaine, in violation of 21 U.S.C. § 846. Jackson primarily argues that the district court erred in admitting into evidence two notebooks alleged to have been prepared by Jackson's coconspirator. The notebooks were admitted through the testimony of an investigating officer who received them from the coconspirator — without any accompanying statement — during a proffer session that failed to produce a plea bargain. The coconspirator did not testify or otherwise authenticate the notebooks, but they, and the testimony introducing and interpreting them, purportedly show the quantity of cocaine the coconspirator distributed to Jackson. Jackson contends . . . that the notebooks lacked sufficient authentication. We hold that because the notebooks were not adequately authenticated, the government has not met its burden of showing that the notebooks were nontestimonial business records; that the district court erred in admitting the notebooks into evidence at trial; that this error violated Jackson's rights under the Confrontation Clause; and that the error was not harmless. We further hold that the evidence, absent admission of the notebooks, was not constitutionally insufficient under *Jackson v. Virginia*, 443 U.S. 307, 99 S. Ct. 2781, 61 L. Ed. 2d 560 (1979), to sustain Jackson's conviction. We therefore vacate the district court's judgment of conviction and sentencing and remand for further proceedings not inconsistent with this opinion.

I.

A federal grand jury indicted Jackson on April 22, 2008, on a single count of conspiring with Arturo Valdez ("Valdez") and other known and unknown persons, beginning on or about December 1, 2006 and continuing through August 1, 2007, to possess with intent to distribute more than five kilograms of cocaine. The evidence at trial included the following: Officer Christopher Hight, a Dallas police officer and task force officer of the Drug Enforcement Administration (DEA), testified that he was involved in surveillance and interception of communications concerning various drug cartels, including a drug-trafficking organization headed by one Juan Reyes-Mejia. Hight testified that he and other officers had identified a cell operating within this organization, headed by Arturo Valdez. Valdez worked as a cocaine distributor in the larger drug-trafficking organization, collected money from the sale of cocaine that he transferred to couriers for transport to Mexico, had customers of his own, and was a trusted member of the drug-trafficking cartel.

Wiretap surveillance disclosed multiple conversations that Valdez had with an individual identified in the phone conversations as "Cory." Hight testified that he became familiar with Cory's voice over the course of the surveillance and, having subsequently spoken with the defendant, Hight testified that "Cory's" voice was that of the defendant, Mr. Jackson. The jury heard several recordings of the phone conversations between Valdez and "Cory," and Valdez and other persons, which Hight interpreted for the jurors as reflecting plans to engage in various cocaine and other narcotics transactions.

In August 2007, a task force arrested over 30 individuals involved in wide-ranging alleged drug-trafficking conspiracies. Valdez was arrested by DEA agents on August 16, 2007. Apparently seeking to work out a plea agreement and obtain leniency at sentencing, Valdez agreed to a proffer session with law enforcement concerning his knowledge of the drug-trafficking conspiracy. During that session, Valdez and his attorney produced, without comment as far as the record is concerned, two notebooks to Officer Hight containing 78 pages of handwriting, with numbers, notations, and names. Certain lines of text in the notebooks appear to be names or abbreviations for names. The names "Cory," "Corey" and "Cor." appear in several places in the notebooks; Officer Hight testified that these writings identify Jackson. Alongside and beneath several of the alleged references to Jackson are only various numbers. The government's witness testified, and the government asserted in its closing argument, that these numbers reflect payments and amounts of cocaine, totaling approximately 350 kilograms, that were given to Jackson in the course of a conspiracy to possess and distribute cocaine.

The government introduced the notebooks at trial solely through the testimony of Officer Hight, who twice stated that his analysis of them was "based on [his] experience as an officer and nothing from what was obtained from Mr. Valdez."

Officer Hight further testified why drug traffickers often keep ledgers, and he explained the various entries in the ledgers that he interpreted as representing cocaine transactions involving Jackson. He testified that he believed the numbers in the notebooks reflect quantities of cocaine, rather than marijuana, because the numbers are consistent with information the police had gathered through telephone surveillance. Hight also stated that the ledgers' references to "Nove" and "Nov." are likely references to Noe Godines, another participant in the drug conspiracy. Hight testified at length concerning the notebooks' contents, interpreting various numbers and calculations for the jury.

At trial, Jackson objected to admission of the notebooks on Sixth Amendment, hearsay, and authentication grounds. These objections were overruled, and the jury found Jackson guilty of one count of conspiring to possess with intent to distribute more than five kilograms of cocaine. Jackson has timely appealed to this Court, arguing the same ground asserted in his objection to the notebooks before the district court.

A.

Although not in itself determinative in the context of this case, we first address whether the notebooks were properly authenticated as business records.[3] "The requirement of authentication or identification as a condition precedent to admissibility is satisfied by evidence sufficient to support a finding that the matter in question is what its proponent claims." Fed. R. Evid. 901(a). "A proponent may authenticate a document with circumstantial evidence, including the document's own distinctive characteristics and the circumstances surrounding its discovery." *In re McLain*, 516 F.3d 301, 308 (5th Cir. 2008) (internal citations omitted). "[T]his Court does not require conclusive proof of authenticity before allowing the admission of disputed evidence . . . . Rule 901 does not limit the type of evidence allowed to authenticate a document. It merely requires some evidence which is sufficient to support a finding that the evidence in question is what its proponent claims it to be." *Jimenez Lopez*, 873 F.2d at 772. The standard for authentication is not a burdensome one. *United States v. Barlow*, 568 F.3d 215, 220 (5th Cir. 2009). However, the government has failed to meet it in this case.

Although we have not spelled out the precise contours of trustworthiness necessary to authenticate drug ledgers, we have upheld the authenticity of drug

---

[3] Federal Rule of Evidence 803(6) provides an exception to the hearsay rule for

[a] memorandum, report, record, or data compilation, in any form, of acts, events, conditions, opinions, or diagnoses, made at or near the time by, or from information transmitted by, a person with knowledge, if kept in the course of a regularly conducted business activity, and if it was the regular practice of that business activity to make the memorandum, report, record or data compilation, all as shown by the testimony of the custodian or other qualified witness, or by certification that complies with Rule 902(11), Rule 902(12), or a statute permitting certification, unless the source of information or the method or circumstances of preparation indicate lack of trustworthiness. The term "business" as used in this paragraph includes business, institution, association, profession, occupation, and calling of every kind, whether or not conducted for profit.

Fed. R. Evid. 803(6).

ledgers as business records where (1) the ledgers were found in the home of a known drug trafficker, and the government's witness testified (2) that he worked for the drug trafficker who allegedly created the ledgers; (3) that the ledgers resembled those which the drug trafficker maintained; and (4) that the handwriting on the ledgers was similar to the drug trafficker's handwriting. *Arce*, 997 F.2d at 1128.

This case, however, is distinguishable in critical ways. Although there is no dispute that Mr. Valdez is a known drug trafficker, the ledgers were not found in Valdez's home; indeed, they were produced by Valdez at a proffer session, under circumstances that raise questions in and of themselves. Officer Hight conceded that Valdez's motive in turning over the ledgers was to obtain a benefit for himself. We have no information in the record to indicate that Valdez told Officer Hight that he was the recorder of the ledgers. The record thus does not reflect whether the ledgers were prepared by someone with knowledge of the transactions they supposedly record, or whether they record transactions at all. The ledger entries do not include any indication of the term "cocaine" and thus do not facially convey that they are applicable to the conspiracy charged. There are no dates recorded on the ledgers other than a lone reference in each to February 9 (without a year). No handwriting analysis was performed on the notebooks, and no member of the drug-trafficking organization testified relating to their trustworthiness.

For his part, Officer Hight testified that he was not able personally to vouch for the credibility of any entries in the ledgers. Although he testified generally that he believed numbers in the notebooks represent quantities of cocaine because they are consistent with information he gathered from intercepted phone calls, Officer Hight did not connect any specific numbers recorded in the ledgers with amounts of cocaine that he had heard discussed. He even acknowledged that the events recorded in the ledgers could have taken place at times outside the course of the relevant drug-trafficking conspiracy.

We do not overlook that the trial judge exercises broad discretion in ruling on the admissibility of evidence. *United States v. Veytia-Bravo*, 603 F.2d 1187, 1189 (5th Cir. 1979). But here the district court gave no reasons for its decision to admit the notebooks; it simply admitted the ledgers without comment. As the foregoing discussion makes clear, there is very little support for qualifying these ledgers as admissible business records. Indeed, the government has failed to satisfy virtually all of the authentication requirements with respect to the alleged drug ledgers, and the district court has said nothing. Thus satisfied that the district court's assessment of the evidence was incorrect, we conclude that admission of the notebooks under the business records exception was error.

* * *

[H]   Public Records

[*See* Fed. R. Evid. 803(8)]

BEECH AIRCRAFT CORP. v. RAINEY
United States Supreme Court
488 U.S. 153 (1988)

JUSTICE BRENNAN delivered the opinion of the Court.

In this case we address a longstanding conflict among the federal courts of appeal over whether Federal Rule of Evidence 803(8)(C), which provides an exception to the hearsay rule for public investigatory reports containing "factual findings," extends to conclusions and opinions contained in such reports . . . .

I

This litigation stems from the crash of a Navy training aircraft at Middleton Field, Alabama, on July 13, 1982, which took the lives of both pilots on board, Lieutenant Commander Barbara Ann Rainey and Ensign Donald Bruce Knowlton. The accident took place while Rainey, a Navy flight instructor, and Knowlton, her student, were flying "touch-and-go" exercises in a T-34C Turbo-Mentor aircraft, number 3E955. Their aircraft and several others flew in an oval pattern, each plane making successive landing/takeoff maneuvers on the runway. Following its fourth pass at the runway, 3E955 appeared to make a left turn prematurely, cutting out the aircraft ahead of it in the pattern and threatening a collision. After radio warnings from two other pilots, the plane banked sharply to the right in order to avoid the other aircraft. At that point it lost altitude rapidly, crashed, and burned.

Because of the damage to the plane and the lack of any survivors, the cause of the accident could not be determined with certainty. The two pilots' surviving spouses brought a product liability suit against petitioners Beech Aircraft Corporation, the plane's manufacturer, and Beech Aerospace Services, which serviced the plane under contract with the Navy. The plaintiffs alleged that the crash had been caused by a loss of engine power, known as "rollback," due to some defect in the aircraft's fuel control system. The defendants, on the other hand, advanced the theory of pilot error, suggesting that the plane had stalled during the abrupt avoidance maneuver.

At trial, the only seriously disputed question was whether pilot error or equipment malfunction had caused the crash. Both sides relied primarily on expert testimony. One piece of evidence presented by the defense was an investigative report prepared by Lieutenant Commander William Morgan on order of the training squadron's commanding officer and pursuant to authority granted in the Manual of the Judge Advocate General. This "JAG Report," completed during the six weeks following the accident, was organized into sections labeled "finding of fact," "opinions," and "recommendations," and was supported by some 60 attachments. The "finding of fact" included statements like the following:

13. At approximately 1020, while turning crosswind without proper interval, 3E955 crashed, immediately caught fire and burned.

*   *   *

27. At the time of impact, the engine of 3E955 was operating but was operating at reduced power. App. 10–12.

Among his "opinions" Lieutenant Commander Morgan stated, in paragraph five, that due to the deaths of the two pilots and the destruction of the aircraft "it is almost impossible to determine exactly what happened to Navy 3E955 from the time it left the runway on its last touch and go until it impacted the ground." He nonetheless continued with a detailed reconstruction of a possible set of events, based on pilot error, that could have caused the accident.[71]

The next two paragraphs stated a caveat and a conclusion:

6. Although the above sequence of events is the most likely to have occurred, it does not change the possibility that a "rollback" did occur.

7. The most probable cause of the accident was the pilots [*sic*] failure to maintain proper interval . . . .

The trial judge initially determined, at a pretrial conference, that the JAG Report was sufficiently trustworthy to be admissible, but that it "would be admissible only on its factual findings and would not be admissible insofar as any

---

[71] (Court's original footnote 2.) Paragraph five reads in its entirety as follows:

"Because both pilots were killed in the crash and because of the nearly total destruction of the aircraft by fire, it is almost impossible to determine exactly what happened to Navy 3E955 from the time it left the runway on its last touch and go until it impacted the ground. However, from evidence available and the information gained from eyewitnesses, a possible scenario can be constructed as follows:

"a. 3E955 entered the Middleton pattern with ENS Knowlton at the controls attempting to make normal landings.

"b. After two unsuccessful attempts, LCDR Rainey took the aircraft and demonstrated two landings 'on the numbers.' After getting the aircraft safely airborne from the touch and go, LCDR Rainey transferred control to ENS Knowlton.

"c. Due to his physical strength, ENS Knowlton did not trim down elevator as the aircraft accelerated toward 100 knots; in fact, due to his inexperience, he may have trimmed incorrectly, putting in more up elevator.

"d. As ENS Knowlton was climbing to pattern altitude, he did not see the aircraft established on downwind so he began his crosswind turn. Due to ENS Knowlton's large size, LCDR Rainey was unable to see the conflicting traffic.

"e. Hearing the first call, LCDR Rainey probably cautioned ENS Knowlton to check for traffic. Hearing the second call, she took immediate action and told ENS Knowlton she had the aircraft as she initiated a turn toward an upwind heading.

"f. As the aircraft was rolling from a climbing left turn to a climbing right turn, ENS Knowlton released the stick letting the up elevator trim take effect causing the nose of the aircraft to pitch abruptly up.

"g. The large angle of bank used trying to maneuver for aircraft separation coupled with the abrupt pitch up caused the aircraft to stall. As the aircraft stalled and went into a nose low altitude, LCDR Rainey reduced the PCL (power control lever) toward idle. As she was rolling toward wings level, she advanced the PCL to maximum to stop the loss of altitude but due to the 2 to 4 second lag in engine response, the aircraft impacted the ground before power was available." App. 14–15.

opinions or conclusions are concerned . . . ." The day before trial, however, the court reversed itself and ruled, over the plaintiffs' objection, that certain of the conclusions would be admitted. . . . Accordingly, the court admitted most of the report's "opinions," including the first sentence of paragraph five about the impossibility of determining exactly what happened, and paragraph seven, which opined about failure to maintain proper interval as "[t]he most probable cause of the accident . . . ." On the other hand, the remainder of paragraph five was barred as "nothing but a possible scenario," . . . and paragraph six, in which investigator Morgan refused to rule out rollback, was deleted as well.

* * *

Following a two-week trial, the jury returned a verdict for the petitioners. A panel of the Eleventh Circuit reversed and remanded for a new trial. . . . [T]he panel agreed with Rainey's argument that Federal Rule of Evidence 803(8)(C), which excepts investigatory reports from the hearsay rule, did not encompass evaluative conclusions or opinions. Therefore, it held, the "conclusions" contained in the JAG Report should have been excluded . . . .

* * *

II

Federal Rule of Evidence 803 provides that certain types of hearsay statements are not made excludable by the hearsay rule, whether or not the declarant is available to testify. Rule 803(8) defines the "public records and reports" which are not excludable, as follows:

> Records, reports, statements, or data compilations, in any form, of public offices or agencies, setting forth (A) the activities of the office or agency, or (B) matters observed pursuant to duty imposed by law as to which matters there was a duty to report, . . . or (C) in civil actions and proceedings and against the Government in criminal cases, factual findings resulting from an investigation made pursuant to authority granted by law, unless the sources of information or other circumstances indicate lack of trustworthiness.

Controversy over what "public records and reports" are made not excludable by Rule 803(8)(C) has divided the federal courts from the beginning. In the present case, the Court of Appeals followed the "narrow" interpretation of *Smith v. Ithaca Corp.*, 612 F.2d 215, 220–23 (CA5 1980), which held that the term "factual findings" did not encompass "opinions" or "conclusions." Courts of appeal other than those of the Fifth and Eleventh Circuits, however, have generally adopted a broader interpretation. For example, the Court of Appeals for the Sixth Circuit, in *Baker v. Elcona Homes Corp.*, 588 F.2d 551, 557–58 (1978), *cert. denied*, 441 U.S. 933, 99 S. Ct. 2054, 60 L. Ed. 2d 661 (1979), held that "factual findings admissible under Rule 803(8)(C) may be those which are made by the preparer of the report from disputed evidence . . . ."[72] The other courts of appeal that have squarely confronted the

---

[72] (Court's original footnote 6.) *Baker* involved a police officer's report on an automobile accident. While there was no direct witness as to the color of the traffic lights at the moment of the accident, the

issue have also adopted the broader interpretation.[73] We agree and hold that factually based conclusions or opinions are not on that account excluded from the scope of Rule 803(8)(C).

Because the Federal Rules of Evidence are a legislative enactment, we turn to the "traditional tools of statutory construction," . . . in order to construe their provisions. We begin with the language of the Rule itself. Proponents of the narrow view have generally relied heavily on a perceived dichotomy between "fact" and "opinion" in arguing for the limited scope of the phrase "factual findings." *Smith v. Ithaca Corp., below,* contrasted the term "factual findings" in Rule 803(8)(C) with the language of Rule 803(6) (records of regularly conducted activity), which expressly refers to "opinions" and "diagnoses." "Factual findings," the court opined, must be something other than opinions. *Smith, below,* at 221–22.[74]

For several reasons, we do not agree. In the first place, it is not apparent that the term "factual findings" should be read to mean simply "facts" (as opposed to "opinions" or "conclusions"). A common definition of "finding of fact" is, for example, "[a] conclusion by way of reasonable inference from the evidence." BLACK'S LAW DICTIONARY 569 (5th ed. 1979). To say the least, the language of the Rule does not compel us to reject the interpretation that "factual findings" includes conclusions or opinions that flow from a factual investigation. Second, we note that, contrary to what is often assumed, the language of the Rule does not state that "factual findings" are admissible, but that "*reports* . . . setting forth . . . factual findings" (emphasis added) are admissible. On this reading, the language of the Rules does not create a distinction between "fact" and "opinion" contained in such reports.

Turning next to the legislative history of Rule 803(8)(C), we find no clear answer to the question of how the Rule's language should be interpreted. Indeed, in this case the legislative history may well be at the origin of the dispute. Rather than the

---

court held admissible the officer's conclusion on the basis of his investigations at the accident scene and an interview with one of the drivers that "apparently unit #2 . . . entered the intersection against a red light." 588 F.2d at 555.

[73] (Court's original footnote 7.) *See Melville v. American Home Assurance Co.,* 584 F.2d 1306, 1315–16 (CA3 1978); *Ellis v. International Playtex, Inc.,* 745 F.2d 292, 300–01 (CA4 1984); *Kehm v. Proctor & Gamble Mfg. Co.,* 724 F.2d 613, 618 (CA8 1983); *Jenkins v. Whittaker Corp.,* 785 F.2d 720, 726 (CA9), *cert. denied,* 479 U.S. 918, 107 S. Ct. 324, 93 L. Ed. 2d 296 (1986); *Perrin v. Anderson,* 784 F.2d 1040, 1046–47 (CA10 1986) . . . .

[74] (Court's original footnote 8.) The court in *Smith* found it significant that different language was used in Rules 803(6) and 803(8)(C): "Since these terms are used in similar context within the same Rule, it is logical to assume that Congress intended that the terms have different and distinct meanings." 612 F.2d at 222. The Advisory Committee notes to Rule 903(6) make it clear, however, that the Committee was motivated by a particular concern in drafting the language of that Rule. While opinions were rarely found in traditional "business records," the expansion of that category to encompass documents such as medical diagnoses and opinions, in addition to acts, events and conditions, as proper subjects of admissible entries." Advisory Committee's Notes on Fed. Rule Evid. 803(6), 28 U.S.C.App., p. 723. Since that specific concern was not present in the context of Rule 803(8)(C), the absence of identical language should not be accorded much significance. *See Rainey v. Beech Aircraft Corp.,* 827 F.2d 1498, 1511–12 (CA11 1987) (en banc) (Tjoflat, J., concurring). What is more, the Committee's report on Rule 803(8)(C) strongly suggests that that Rule has the same scope of admissibility as does Rule 803(6): "Hence the rule, as in *Exception [paragraph] (6),* assumes admissibility in the first instance but with ample provision for escape if sufficiently negative factors are present." Advisory Committees's Notes on Fed. Rule Evid. 803(8), 28 U.S.C.App., p. 725 (emphasis added).

more usual situation where a court must attempt to glean meaning from ambiguous comments of legislators who did not focus directly on the problem at hand, here the Committees in both Houses of Congress clearly recognized and expressed their opinions on the precise question at issue. Unfortunately, however, they took diametrically opposite positions. Moreover, the two Houses made no effort to reconcile their views, either through changes in the Rule's language or through a statement in the Report of the Conference Committee.

The House Judiciary Committee, which dealt first with the proposed rules after they had been transmitted to Congress by this Court, included in its Report but one brief paragraph on Rule 803(8):

> The Committee approved Rule 803(8) without substantive change from the form in which it was submitted by the Court. The Committee intends that the phrase 'factual findings' be strictly construed and that evaluations or opinions contained in public reports shall not be admissible under this Rule. H.R. Rep. No. 93-650, p. 14 (1973), U.S. Code Cong. & Admin. News 1974, pp. 7051, 7088.

The Senate Committee responded at somewhat greater length, but equally emphatically:

> "The House Judiciary Committee report contained a statement of intent that "the phrase 'factual findings' in subdivision (c) be strictly construed and that evaluations or opinions contained in public reports shall not be admissible under this rule." The committee takes strong exception to this limiting understanding of the application of the rule. We do not think it reflects an understanding of the intended operation of the rule as explained in the Advisory Committee notes to this subsection. . . . We think the restrictive interpretation of the House overlooks the fact that while the Advisory Committee assumes admissibility in the first instance of evaluative reports, they are not admissible if, as the rule states, "the sources of information or other circumstances indicate lack of trustworthiness."
>
> *   *   *
>
> The committee concludes that the language of the rule together with the explanation provided by the Advisory Committee furnish sufficient guidance on the admissibility of evaluative reports. S. Rep. No. 93-1277, p. 18 (1974), U.S. Code Cong. & Admin. News 1974, p. 7064.

Clearly this legislative history reveals a difference of view between the Senate and House that affords no definitive guide to the congressional understanding. It seems clear however that the Senate understanding is more in accord with the wording of the Rule and with the comments of the Advisory Committee.[75]

The Advisory Committee's comments are notable, first, in that they contain no

---

[75] (Court's original footnote 9.) See Advisory Committee's Notes on Fed. Rule Evid. 803(8), 28 U.S.C. App., pp. 724–25. As Congress did not amend the Advisory Committee's draft in any way that touches on the question before us, the Committee's commentary is particularly relevant in determining the meaning of the document Congress enacted.

mention of any dichotomy between statements of "fact" and "opinions" or "conclusions." What was on the Committee's mind was simply whether what it called "evaluative reports" should be admissible. Illustrating the previous division among the courts on this subject, the Committee cited numerous cases in which the admissibility of such reports had been both sustained and denied. It also took note of various federal statutes that made certain kinds of evaluative reports admissible in evidence. What is striking about all of these examples is that these were *reports that stated conclusions. E.g., Moran v. Pittsburgh-Des Moines Steel Co.*, 183 F.2d 467, 472–73 (CA3 1950) (report of Bureau of Mines concerning the cause of a gas tank explosion admissible); *Franklin v. Skelly Oil Co.*, 141 F.2d 568, 571–72 (CA10 1944) (report of state fire marshal on the cause of a gas explosion inadmissible); 42 U.S.C. § 269(b) (bill of health by appropriate official admissible as prima facie evidence of vessel's sanitary history and condition). The Committee's concern was clearly whether reports of this kind should be admissible. Nowhere in its comments is there the slightest indication that it even considered the solution of admitting only "factual" statements from such reports.[76] Rather, the Committee referred throughout to "reports," without any such differentiation regarding the statements they contained. What the Committee referred to in the Rule's language as "reports . . . setting forth . . . factual findings" is surely nothing more or less than what in its commentary it called "evaluative reports." Its solution as to their admissibility is clearly stated in the final paragraph of its report on this Rule. That solution consists of two principles: First, "the rule . . . assumes admissibility in the first instance . . . ." Second, it provides "ample provision for escape if sufficient negative factors are present."

That "provision for escape" is contained in the final clause of the Rule: evaluative reports are admissible "unless the sources of information or other circumstances indicate lack of trustworthiness." This trustworthiness inquiry — and not an arbitrary distinction between "fact" and "opinion" — was the Committee's primary safeguard against the admission of unreliable evidence, and it is important to note that it applies to all elements of the report. Thus, a trial judge has the discretion, and indeed the obligation, to exclude an entire report or portions thereof — whether narrow "factual" statements or broader "conclusions" — that she determines to be untrustworthy. Moreover, safeguards built in to other portions of the Federal Rules, such as those dealing with relevance and prejudice, provide the court with additional means of scrutinizing and, where appropriate, excluding evaluative reports or portions of them. And of course it goes without saying that the admission of a report containing "conclusions" is subject to the ultimate safeguard

---

[76] (Court's original footnote 10.) Our conclusion that the Committee was concerned only about the question of admissibility *vel non* of "evaluative reports," without any distinction between statements of "fact" and "conclusions," draws support from the fact that this was the focus of scholarly debate on the official reports question prior to adoption of the Federal Rules. Indeed, the problem was often phrased as one of whether official reports could be admitted *in view of the fact that they contained the investigator's conclusions.* Thus Professor McCormick, in an influential article relied upon by the Committee, stated his position as follows: "that evaluative reports of official investigators, though partly based upon statements of others, *and though embracing conclusions*, are admissible as evidence of the facts reported." McCormick, Can the Courts Make Wider Use of Reports of Official Investigations?, 42 Iowa L. Rev. 363, 365 (1957) (emphasis added).

— the opponent's right to present evidence tending to contradict or diminish the weight of those conclusions.

Our conclusion that neither the language of the Rule nor the intent of its framers calls for a distinction between "fact" and "opinion" is strengthened by the analytical difficulty of drawing such a line. It has frequently been remarked that the distinction between statements of fact and opinion is, at best, one of degree:

> All statements in language are statements of opinion, *i.e.*, statements of mental processes or perceptions. So-called 'statements of fact' are only more specific statements of opinion. What the judge means to say, when he asks the witness to state the facts, is: "The nature of this case requires that you be more specific, if you can, in your description of what you saw."

W. King and D. Pillinger, Opinion Evidence In Illinois 4 (1942) (footnote omitted). . . .

In the present case, the trial court had no difficulty in admitting as a factual finding the statement in the JAG Report that "[a]t the time of impact, the engine of 3E955 was operating but was operating at reduced power." Surely this "factual finding" could also be characterized as an opinion, which the investigator presumably arrived at on the basis of clues contained in the airplane wreckage. Rather than requiring that we draw some inevitably arbitrary line between the various shades of fact/opinion that invariably will be present in investigatory reports, we believe the Rule instructs us — as its plain language states — to admit "reports . . . setting forth . . . factual findings." The Rule's limitations and safeguards lie elsewhere: First, the requirement that reports contain factual findings bars the admission of statements not based on factual investigation. Second, the trustworthiness provision requires the court to make a determination as to whether the report, or any portion thereof, is sufficiently trustworthy to be admitted.

A broad approach to admissibility under Rule 803(8)(C), as we have outlined it, is also consistent with the Federal Rules' general approach of relaxing the traditional barriers to "opinion" testimony. Rules 702–705 permit experts to testify in the form of an opinion, and without any exclusion of opinions on "ultimate issues." And Rule 701 permits even a lay witness to testify in the form of opinions or inferences drawn from her observations when testimony in that form will be helpful to the trier of fact. We see no reason to strain to reach an interpretation of Rule 803(8)(C) that is contrary to the liberal thrust of the Federal Rules.

We hold, therefore, that portions of investigatory reports otherwise admissible under Rule 803(8)(C) are not inadmissible merely because they state a conclusion or opinion. As long as the conclusion is based on a factual investigation and satisfies the Rule's trustworthiness requirement, it should be admissible along with other portions of the report.[77] As the trial judge in this case determined that certain of the JAG Report's conclusions were trustworthy, he rightly allowed them to be admitted

---

[77] (Court's original footnote 13.) We emphasize that the issue in this case is whether Rule 803(8)(C) recognizes any difference between statements of "fact" and "opinion." There is no question in this case of any distinction between "fact" and "law." We thus express no opinion on whether legal conclusions contained in an official report are admissible as "findings of fact" under Rule 803(8)(C).

into evidence. We therefore reverse the judgment of the Court of Appeals in respect of the Rule 803(8)(C) issue.

* * *

IV

We hold . . . that statements in the form of opinions or conclusions are not by that fact excluded from the scope of Federal Rule of Evidence 803(8)(C). We therefore reverse the judgment of the Court of Appeals in that respect. . . . The case is remanded for further proceedings consistent with this opinion.

It is so ordered.

CHIEF JUSTICE REHNQUIST, with whom JUSTICE O'CONNOR joins, dissenting in part.

[The dissenting opinion agreed with the majority's resolution of the question regarding the scope of Rule 803(8)(C).]

[I]   Absence of Public Record: Rule 803(10)

The *Williams* case illustrates that an absence of a public record showing that an individual owned real property can be used to show that he did not, in fact, own that property.

STATE v. WILLIAMS
Supreme Court of South Dakota
710 N.W.2d 427 (2006)

MEIERHENRY, JUSTICE.

Defendant Gary Dean Williams (Williams) appeals from his conviction for three counts of grand theft by deception. Williams asserts that evidence was improperly admitted at his trial. He also asserts that his thirty-year sentence, with nine years suspended, constitutes cruel and unusual punishment. We affirm.

FACTS

The three counts of which Williams was convicted involved three different victims: Michael Crago (Crago), Michael and Cheryl Brimmer (the Brimmers), and Gerald Heck (Heck). Crago and Williams, both hearing impaired, first became acquainted while attending the South Dakota School for the Deaf. In early 2002, the two met by chance at a gas station. Prior to their encounter at the gas station, the two had not seen each other for a long time. Williams, who worked as a carpenter, convinced Crago to pay him $2,050 to repair Crago's roof. Williams also told Crago that he had $150,000 in the bank and wanted to invest in real estate. Crago agreed to join Williams in the real estate venture, and thereafter wrote Williams a series of personal checks over a period of time. Williams represented to Crago that he used the money to invest in twelve separate properties. By June 2002, Crago had paid

Williams close to $75,000. Although Crago asked Williams for proof of the transactions, Williams cleverly kept stalling with promises of providing it later, all the while taking advantage of Crago's trust and friendship. Crago eventually ran out of cash and began providing additional funds to Williams by borrowing from his credit card. Williams' scheme consisted of a litany of excuses and lies.

In May 2002, Crago introduced Williams to the Brimmers, who were also members of the deaf community. Williams represented himself as a licensed real estate agent who could sell the Brimmers' home. He never produced his license as the Brimmers requested. Nevertheless, the Brimmers agreed to Williams' services. At Williams' request, they also wrote him several personal checks that Williams said he would invest at Great Western Bank. Williams never provided proof to the Brimmers of what he did with the money. Again, his alleged business relationship with the Brimmers was fraught with misrepresentations and conversion of funds for his personal use.

During the same time, Williams met Heck, who was not a member of the deaf community. Heck told Williams that he was an independent investor. Williams lied to Heck by claiming to have purchased the Brimmers' home, and he asked Heck to invest $5,000 in the improvement of the home so that Williams could sell it for a profit. Heck agreed and paid Williams accordingly. Heck drafted a contract to reflect the transaction. Upon the sale of the Brimmers' home, Williams claimed that Brimmers took all the proceeds with no valid explanation of why Heck was not reimbursed. Subsequently, Heck also gave Williams additional money, none of which was returned.

Williams eventually reimbursed Crago for approximately $10,000. Crago, however, never received proof of any other interest in the items in which Williams claimed to have invested. Further, the Brimmers never received statements for their investments at Great Western Bank, and Williams never reimbursed them for the money. The Brimmers' home eventually was sold, but upon sale they discovered that items such as appliances had been removed from the home without the Brimmers' knowledge. Because Williams never owned the Brimmers' home, Heck received no reimbursement from Williams upon the sale of the house.

In early 2004, Williams was indicted on three counts of Grand Theft by Deception, a crime punishable by up to ten years in the penitentiary and/or a $10,000 fine. The indictment alleged that Williams intended to deprive each of his victims-Crago, the Brimmers, and Heck-of property exceeding $500 in value by creating the false impression that he was using their property for investments. Subsequent to the indictment, the State and Williams reached a plea agreement that required Williams to plead guilty to one count of the indictment. In exchange, the State agreed to dismiss the other two counts and recommend a suspended execution of a penitentiary sentence with six months in the county jail and restitution of $169,948 for all three counts. The plea agreement was rejected twice by the circuit court. It later indicated it would accept the plea agreement only if Williams pleaded guilty to two counts of the indictment so that a fifteen-year suspended sentence could be imposed. Williams chose not to plead guilty to two of the counts and withdrew his guilty plea. Subsequently, a jury found Williams guilty of all three counts of grand theft by deception. Judge Lieberman ultimately sentenced Williams to 30 years in the penitentiary, with nine years suspended. Williams appeals and raises the following issues:

ISSUES

1. Whether the trial court erred by admitting testimony concerning the contents of public records.

2. Whether Williams' sentence is cruel and unusual in violation of the Eighth Amendment to the United States Constitution.

DECISION

Admissibility of Testimony Concerning the Contents of Public Records.

At trial, Gayland Schmidt, a detective with the Sioux Falls Police Department, testified about his investigation of the allegations against Williams. Specifically, Schmidt testified that he received a list of the properties in which Williams allegedly invested. The jury then heard the following exchange between the prosecutor and Schmidt:

Q: With that information did you make any attempt to discover if there was any corroboration for representations made to [Crago] that those properties had been purchased by Mr. Williams and [Crago]?

A: Yes, I did.

Q: And how did you go about seeing if there was any corroboration to the fact?

A: I went to the Minnehaha County Register of Deeds Office, which is public records and they allowed me to look up on their computer base the ownership of those properties.

Q: Did you know how to use that system when you got there?

A: They taught me how to use that.

Q: Was it complicated?

A: No.

Q: Did you then go through each of those properties individually to determine if there was any corroboration for [Crago]'s belief that they had been transferred to Mr. Williams and himself?

A: I looked up each property.

Q: And did you find any corroboration of any of those properties being transferred to Mr. Williams or [the victim]?

       . . .

A: No, I could not.

Williams objected to the admission of this testimony, but his objection was overruled. He now appeals that evidentiary ruling. Williams argues that Schmidt's testimony regarding the contents of the deed records constituted inadmissible hearsay. Williams admits that the contents of public records are admissible under the public records exception to the hearsay exclusion rule, SDCL 19-16-12 (Rule 803(8)), which allows the admission of public records kept by public offices or agencies under a duty to report. Williams argues, however, that the best evidence rule, SDCL 19-18-2 (Rule 1002), requires the production of certified copies of those records. Williams claims that without that evidence the State failed to establish that he defrauded Crago.

We review a trial court's ruling on the admissibility of evidence under an abuse of discretion standard. *State v. Mattson*, 2005 SD 71, ¶ 13, 698 N.W.2d 538, 544. Even if error is found, however, "it must be prejudicial in nature before this Court will overturn the trial court's evidentiary ruling." *Id.* (citation omitted). Under the rules of evidence, hearsay is an out-of-court assertion, either oral or written, which is "offered in evidence to prove the truth of the matter asserted." SDCL 19-16-1 (Rule 801(a) to (c)). Hearsay is generally inadmissible. SDCL 19-16-4 (Rule 802).

In this case, the evidence concerning the public records was offered to show that Williams never owned the properties he purported to own when soliciting investments from the victims. While not specifically cited by the trial court, Rule 803(10) explicitly allows the type of testimony at issue here. That rule, known as the negative records rule, provides:

> To prove the absence of a record . . . or the nonoccurrence or nonexistence of a matter of which a record . . . was regularly made and preserved by a public office or agency, evidence in the form of . . . *testimony*, that diligent search failed to disclose the record . . . is not excluded by [SDCL] 19-16-4, even though the declarant is available as a witness.

SDCL 19-16-14 (Rule 803(10)) (emphasis added). Under the federal counterpart to Rule 803(10), the Eighth Circuit Court of Appeals has admitted similar evidence in a criminal case. *United States v. Hale*, 978 F.2d 1016, 1020–21 (8th Cir. 1992). The defendant in *Hale* was charged with possession of unregistered firearms. *Id.* at 1017. To prove the lack of registration, the government introduced two affidavits by specialists from the Bureau of Alcohol, Tobacco and Firearms, which stated that after a diligent search of firearms registration records, no record was located that showed any application by the defendant to register his weapons. *Id.* at 1020. On appeal, the Eighth Circuit held that the evidence was admissible hearsay under the federal "negative records" rule[1] and that such evidence did not violate the constitutional right to confrontation. *Id.* at 1021.

Here, confrontation was not an issue because Schmidt testified at trial and was subject to cross-examination. Consequently, Rule 803(10) renders Schmidt's testimony admissible hearsay. Pursuant to the rule, the State was able to offer proof

---

[1] As noted in *Hale*, Federal Rule of Evidence 803(10) provides an exception to the hearsay rule " '[t]o prove the absence of a record . . . or the nonoccurrence or nonexistence of a matter of which a record . . . was regularly made and preserved by a public office or agency, evidence in the form of . . . testimony, that diligent search failed to disclose the record.' " 978 F.2d at 1020–21 (quoting Fed. R. Evid. 803(10)).

through Schmidt's testimony that Williams had no ownership in the investment properties as he had claimed, that is, proof of the absence of a record of ownership. Even though SDCL 19-16-14 (Rule 803(10)) was not specifically cited, the trial court correctly concluded that the testimony was not inadmissible hearsay.

EXERCISE

At trial, in an effort to establish that Baltazar is not a United States citizen, counsel seeks to offer the testimony of an Immigration and Customs Enforcement Agent. If permitted to testify, the Agent would state that he searched a nationwide database, which archives records of entry documents — such as permanent resident cards, border crossing cards, or certificates of naturalization — for any record of Baltazar. The Agent could not find a match, suggesting that Baltazar had not entered the country legally. Baltazar objects to the proposed testimony on hearsay grounds. How should the court rule?

[J] Family and Religious Record: Rule 803(11)

As the court in *Keate* makes clear, a religious organization does not have to be traditional, well-established, or respected to qualify for this exception, it just has to regularly maintain records.

KEATE v. STATE

Texas Court of Appeals at Austin
2012 Tex. App. LEXIS 2117

J. WOODFIN JONES, CHIEF JUSTICE.

Appellant Allan Eugene Keate and nine other members of the Fundamentalist Church of Jesus Christ of Latter Day Saints (FLDS), living at the YFZ (Yearning for Zion) Ranch in Schleicher County, Texas, were indicted for sexual assault of a child. *See* Tex. Penal Code Ann. § 22.011(a)(2)(A) (West 2011). Subsequently, a jury convicted appellant and assessed his punishment at confinement for thirty-three years in the Institutional Division of the Texas Department of Criminal Justice. *See id.* §§ 12.32, 22.011(a)(2)(A), 22.011(f) (West 2011). This appeal followed . . . .

* * *

II. CHURCH RECORDS

. . . [A]ppellant argues that the trial judge erred in admitting documentary evidence seized from the vaults of the temple and temple annex of the YFZ Ranch. Appellant asserts the trial court abused its discretion by admitting this documentary evidence because the evidence was not properly authenticated under Rule 901 of the Texas Rules of Evidence and, further, because such evidence constituted inadmissible hearsay.

* * *

At trial, Rebecca Musser, a former FLDS member and one of the sister-wives of the former "prophet," testified, based upon her personal experience and training as an FLDS member for twenty-six years, about the process and purpose of maintaining accurate church records relating to FLDS members. In addition, several law enforcement officers testified about recovering the documents from the locked vaults of the temple and temple annex. Based on the appearance, content, and substance of the various documents, taken in conjunction with where the records were located — reflecting how they were maintained and stored — and the testimony of the purpose and importance of making and keeping these records, the trial court could have reasonably concluded that the State satisfied its burden of presenting a prima facie case. In other words, on this record the trial court could have reasonably concluded that the testimony concerning the various documents, together with the documents themselves, was sufficient for a reasonable jury to conclude that the documents were in fact church and family records relating to the family and personal history of the FLDS members. Thus, we discern no abuse of discretion on the part of the trial court in admitting the complained-of documents. We overrule appellant's fourth point of error as it relates to authentication.

Appellant also asserts . . . that the complained-of documents are hearsay and do not fall within one of the hearsay exceptions.

Hearsay is an out-of-court statement "offered in evidence to prove the truth of the matter asserted." Tex.R. Evid. 801(d). Generally, hearsay statements are not admissible unless the statement falls within a recognized exception to the hearsay rule. *Pena*, 353 S.W.3d at 814; *see* Tex.R. Evid. 802. Two exceptions, applicable regardless of whether the declarant is available to testify, are records of religious organizations and family records. Texas Rule of Evidence 803(11) excludes from the hearsay rule "[s]tatements of births, marriages, divorces, deaths, legitimacy, ancestry, relationship by blood or marriage, or other similar facts of personal or family history, contained in a regularly kept record of a religious organization." Tex.R. Evid. 803(11). Similarly, Texas Rule of Evidence 803(13) excludes "[s]tatements of fact concerning personal or family history contained in family Bibles, genealogies, charts, engravings on rings, inscriptions on family portraits, engravings on urns, crypts, or tombstones, or the like." Tex.R. Evid. 803(13). The State offered the complained-of documents under these exceptions to the hearsay rule.

In his argument against admissibility, appellant characterizes FLDS as an extreme breakaway sect of the Mormon church and appears to argue that because the church and the views of its leader (the prophet) are not mainstream, these documents should not be included in the hearsay exception for religious organizations. However, Rule 803(11) does not depend on the popularity or acceptance of the religious organization. Hearsay evidence need only be consistent with the provisions of the exception to be admissible. Here, the documents about which appellant complains were various documents relating to marriages, births, family relationships, personal history, and family history of FLDS members.[12] Further, the

---

[12] For example, documents titled "marriage record" were in fact documents recording the marriage of two individuals: listing the names of the husband, wife, witnesses present, and who performed the ceremony, as well as documenting when and where the ceremony took place. Similarly, documents titled "family group sheet" were documents recording the various members of the family: names, dates and places of birth, gender, and family relationship. Documents titled "personal record" were documents

evidence at trial demonstrated that these documents were regularly maintained by the FLDS as part of the religious organization of the church.[13]

EXERCISE

In order to establish his own United States citizenship, Randolph has to prove that his Mother was born in the United States and remained in the United States for at least one continuous year before relocating to the Caribbean Islands. At trial Randolph seeks to admit affidavits from Mother and Cousin. Mother's affidavit states: "I was born in Brooklyn in 1929 and moved abroad in 1930 when I was between one year old and two years old." Mother passed away shortly after signing the affidavit. Cousin's affidavit states: "When I was a child, Mother told me that she moved from New York to the Caribbean Islands when she was about one and a half years old. It was common knowledge or reputation among people who knew Mother during her childhood that she left the United States when she was about one and a half years old." Is either affidavit admissible at trial? What are Randolph's strongest arguments for admissibility? Do you recognize this exercise from earlier in the chapter? Why is it repeated here?

[K]   Ancient Documents: Rule 803(16)

The admission of statements within ancient documents, such as newspapers more than 20 years old, raises a host of concerns about the unknown biases of the writer as well as problems of double hearsay. The dissent in *Rehm* addresses a number of these issues.

REHM v. FORD MOTOR CO.
Kentucky Court of Appeals
365 S.W.3d 570 (2011)

COMBS, JUDGE:

Debbie Ellen Rehm, individually and as Executrix of the Estate of James David Rehm; Nicholas James Rehm; and Christina Marie Rehm (the Rehms) appeal from the judgment of the Jefferson Circuit Court following a jury verdict in favor of Ford Motor Company in a premises liability lawsuit. Ford Motor Company cross-appeals. Following our review of the extensive record, the facts, and the law, we affirm both as to the appeal and as to the cross-appeal.

James Rehm was the late husband of Debbie and the father of Nicholas James and Christina Marie Rehm. In January 2001, James was diagnosed with malignant

---

describing the personal history of the individual, including the person's name, parents' names, date and place of birth, gender, and the dates and places of significant religious events such as baptism, blessing, and confirmation.

[13] Appellant's expert acknowledged that FLDS uses a standardized system of record keeping for church records-including bishops' records documenting marriages, births, priesthood ordinations, advancement, and community organization as well as marriage records, personal records, and family group records — that were stored in the church archives, though he disagreed that the particular documents offered in this case were part of such a system.

mesothelioma, a form of cancer that is caused by asbestos. He had worked as a millwright (an industrial construction worker) in the late 1970s until 1981 as an employee of Rapid Installations (Rapid). After leaving Rapid sometime in 1981, he went to work as an elevator mechanic at some point in 1981. Critical to the case was the fact that the exact dates of James's employment were highly disputed at trial. James testified that he had been a millwright at Rapid from 1975 through 1982. Ford presented documentation (Social Security records) that indicated James began working at Rapid in 1977 but had stopped by March 10, 1981, the last entry for Social Security withholding listing Rapid Installations as his employer. He began as an elevator mechanic for A-1 Elevator on March 12, 1981, the starting date of employment which he listed on his application for union membership as a millwright in Local 2209.

Rapid manufactured and installed conveyer systems for other companies. Before installing new systems in manufacturing plants, Rapid's millwrights tore out the old systems. The process of removing the old systems often exposed millwrights to asbestos contained in components such as pipe insulation and boiler systems. Rapid performed this work at Ford Motor Company's Louisville Assembly Plant (LAP).

Shortly after his diagnosis of malignant mesothelioma, James Rehm and his wife and children filed the underlying lawsuit in Jefferson Circuit Court. Numerous defendants were named, including Rapid and many companies that had hired Rapid to remove their manufacturing equipment. Ford was one of the original defendants.[1] James Rehm passed away on July 5, 2002, while the lawsuit was still in the discovery phase.

After a long procedural history that is not relevant to this appeal, the Rehms and Ford[2] proceeded to trial on August 3, 2009. On August 17, 2009, the jury rendered its verdict in favor of Ford. The Rehms filed this appeal on October 6, 2009, and Ford filed a cross-appeal on October 20, 2009.

The Rehms first argue that the trial court erred by admitting old newspaper articles into evidence. The Rehms' case was based on the allegation that James Rehm was working at Ford LAP when it converted its facilities in preparation for manufacturing the Ford Ranger and Bronco and after it discontinued manufacturing the LTD. Ford's defense was that James Rehm was no longer employed as a millwright during the time of the changeover and the tear-out process; therefore, he could not have been involved. The Rehms presented witnesses who testified that James Rehm was working during the changeover. In response, Ford presented employment records showing that James had left Rapid in March 1981. It then produced two newspaper articles that reported that the last LTD manufactured in Louisville rolled off the line in June of 1981. Therefore, Ford contended that James could not have been involved in the changeover work that occurred after June 1981.

Our standard of review for evidentiary issues is whether the trial court abused its

---

[1] The judgment from which this appeal is taken was also entered against Garlock Sealing Technologies, which has filed for bankruptcy. Therefore, Garlock is subject to the automatic stay provisions of the United States Bankruptcy Code. This appeal involves only Ford.

[2] The other defendants either had been granted summary judgment or had reached settlements with the Rehms.

discretion. *Partin v. Commonwealth*, 918 S.W.2d 219, 222 (Ky. 1996) (*overruled on other grounds by Chestnut v. Commonwealth*, 250 S.W.3d 288 (Ky. 2008)). Our Supreme Court has defined abuse of discretion as a court's acting arbitrarily, unreasonably, unfairly, or in a manner "unsupported by sound legal principles." *Commonwealth v. English*, 993 S.W.2d 941, 945 (Ky. 1999).

The Rehms contend that the newspaper articles should not have been admitted because they are hearsay. In fact, the court admitted on the record that newspaper articles are "the most specious form of hearsay." However, the judge decided to admit the articles pursuant to the ancient-documents exception to the hearsay rule. Kentucky Rule(s) of Evidence (KRE) 803(16) provides that even if they are hearsay, "[s]tatements in ancient documents . . . in existence twenty (20) years or more the authenticity of which is established" may be admitted into evidence.

The articles at issue were twenty-eight years of age. The Rehms argue that they were not properly authenticated. However, according to KRE 902(6), newspaper articles are self-authenticating. Although no published Kentucky cases have applied the ancient-document exception, Professor Lawson acknowledges that the rule is applicable to newspaper articles. Robert G. Lawson, *The Kentucky Evidence Law Handbook*, § 8.85(4), at 730 (4th Ed.2003).

We have reviewed the cases that the Rehms submitted to support their argument that the articles were inadmissible hearsay. All of them are distinguishable from the facts before us because none of them involved newspaper articles old enough to qualify as eligible for the ancient-document exception. They were contemporaneous with the proceedings for which they were offered. *See Bowling v. Lexington-Fayette Urban Cnty. Gov't*, 172 S.W.3d 333, 342 (Ky. 2005); *Shirley v. Commonwealth*, 378 S.W.2d 816, 818 (Ky. 1964); *Turner v. City of Taylor*, 412 F.3d 629, 651 (6th Cir. 2005); *Barbo v. Kroger Co.*, 2007 U.S. Dist. LEXIS 59883, 2007 WL 2350183, at *2 (W.D. Ky. Aug. 13, 2007); *Gantt v. Whitaker*, 57 Fed. Appx. 141, 149 (4th Cir. 2003); *Spotts v. U.S.*, 562 F. Supp. 2d 46, 54–55 (D.D.C. 2008); *Eisenstadt v. Allen*, 113 F.3d 1240 (9th Cir. 1997).

Additionally, we note that neither the Rehms nor Ford could produce any other written documentation pertaining to the actual dates involving the plant change-over. Each produced witnesses who were asked to recall events of nearly thirty years ago regarding dates that were a mere two months apart. James provided detailed testimony of working at Ford during the changeover; he testified that for several months during that period he had worked in the Ford plant seven days per week — including holidays and Saturdays. Ford presented written evidence that James had left Rapid in March 1981 — prior to the changeover date of June 1981 recounted in the newspaper articles. Bolstering the pertinence of the articles was the testimony of one of Ford's witnesses, who related that the plant would not have retained records relating to the changeover beyond five or six years. The evidence was undeniably tenuous. But we are persuaded that the newspaper articles were more probative than prejudicial in aiding the jury in its finding of fact concerning whether James could have participated in the changeover.

The Rehms argued that the tearing out of equipment *could have begun before* the last LTD rolled off the assembly line (June 1981). They presented testimony to that effect and reiterated that theory in closing argument. The trial court admonished the jury that the articles were not necessarily true, leaving to the jury the ultimate task of fact-finding based on conflicting evidence derived from the newspaper articles *versus* witness recollection. Based on the lengthy passage of time in this case involving some thirty years, the trial court did not abuse its discretion in admitting the newspaper articles under the ancient-documents exception to the hearsay rule.

*   *   *

CAPERTON, JUDGE, Concurring in Part and Dissenting in Part:

I concur with the learned majority on the cross-claim of Ford Motor Company concerning the denial of its summary judgment motion. Otherwise, I dissent.

First, I address the testimony of Dr. Morgan on the theory of household exposure to asbestos which supported Ford's theory that Rehm's father could have been exposed to asbestos because of his occupation and, in turn, exposed Rehm to asbestos. Rehm's father provided the only testimony on this issue and testified that he had not been exposed to asbestos. Since there was no evidence to the contrary, the introduction of testimony from Dr. Morgan on the household exposure theory was error because it was without basis, irrelevant and prejudicial. Additionally, this evidence affected the substantial right of Rehm to a fair trial and is not harmless. I would reverse the trial court and remand for a new trial.

Secondly, I address the admission into evidence of the newspaper article under KRE 803(16). Initially, I note that this evidentiary exception to the hearsay rule is not frequently used and, as a result, only a limited number of cases discuss it. Additionally, this exception is not a wide open door but a narrow crevice, as shall be apparent from the following analysis.

Of the several cases that discuss such an exception, only two will be discussed: *Columbus-America Discovery Group, Inc. v. Unidentified, Wrecked and Abandoned Sailing Vessel*, 742 F. Supp. 1327 (E.D. Va. 1990), and *Hicks v. Charles Pfizer & Co., Inc.*, 466 F. Supp. 2d 799 (E.D. Texas 2005). True, they discuss the Federal Rules of Evidence (Fed. R. Evid.), but, for our purposes, Fed. R. Evid. 803(16) and Fed. R. Evid. 805 are essentially the same as our Kentucky Rules of Evidence. I quote the two cases at length and in detail in hopes that the reasoning therein and the cases they cite will provide for robust debate of the confines of KRE 803(16), and caution that my analysis is not meant to be an exhaustive dissertation.

In *Columbus-America Discovery Group* the court stated:

First, the Court must consider whether the newspaper accounts are subject to the hearsay objection raised at trial.

Rule 802 of the Federal Rules of Evidence provides:

Hearsay is not admissible except as provided by these rules or by other rules prescribed by the Supreme Court pursuant to statutory authority or by act of Congress.

Rule 803 of said rules provides:

That the following are not excluded by the hearsay rule[:]

(16) Statements in ancient documents. Statements in a document in existence twenty years or more the authenticity of which is established.

In a discussion of the admissibility of hearsay, we begin with the established principle that cross-examination is of vital importance in establishing the value and trustworthiness of such evidence. The requirement the witness be sworn, testify in the presence and hearing of the trier and be subject to cross[-]examination is lost in most instances of hearsay. The restriction in the admissibility of ancient documents is "the authenticity of which is established." *The purpose of the admission and exactly what is sought to be established by the item will often determine its admissibility.* For instance, in *Dallas County v. Commercial Union Assurance Co.,* 286 F.2d 388 (5th Cir. 1961), a 58[-]year[-]old newspaper story was admitted to prove the occurrence of a fire in a public building. However, the same Court in *Poretto v. United States,* 196 F.2d 392, 395 (5th Cir. 1952) ruled that newspaper articles are not admissible to prove facts stated therein. In *Montana Power Co. v. Federal Power Commission,* 185 F.2d 491 (D.C. Cir. 1950), *cert. denied,* 340 U.S. 947, 71 S. Ct. 532, 95 L. Ed. 683 [(1951)], old newspaper accounts on the question of navigability of the Mississippi River during the 19th century were admitted to prove navigability at that earlier date. The question often arises as to whether assertive statements in the article are admissible. In *Wathen v. United States,* 527 F.2d 1191, 1199 (Ct. Cl. 1975), the Court in considering a newspaper account of a shooting, held it hearsay, but said "that insofar as they reported the fact of the shooting, resulting in death observed by witnesses, they provided reliable and substantial evidence."

Columbus-America Discovery Group at 1342 (emphasis supplied.)

In *Hicks* the court stated:

The Hicks assert that the ancient documents exception should be applied to render the newspaper articles admissible. This exception provides that "[s]tatements in a document in existence twenty years or more the authenticity of which is established" are admissible. *Fed. R. Evid. 803(16).* Under the Federal Rules of Evidence, newspaper articles are self-authenticating. *See Fed. R. Evid. 902(6); Woolsey v. National Transp. Safety Bd.,* 993 F.2d 516, 520 (5th Cir. 1993), *cert. denied,* 511 U.S. 1081, 114 S. Ct. 1829, 128 L. Ed. 2d 459 (1994); *Perez v. Alcoa Fujikura, Ltd.,* 969 F. Supp. 991, 998 (W.D.Tex.1997).

The dangers of hearsay relate to flaws in perception, memory, narration, and sincerity. *See Park v. Huff,* 506 F.2d 849, 865 (5th Cir.), *cert. denied,* 423 U.S. 824, 96 S. Ct. 38, 46 L. Ed. 2d 40 (1975) (citing Morgan, *Hearsay Dangers & the Application of the Hearsay Concept,* 62 Harv. L. Rev. 177, 218 (1948)); *John W. Strong Et Al., McCormick on Evidence § 245 (5th ed.2003).* An assertive statement found in an ancient document is more likely to be truthful because "age affords assurance that the writing antedates the present controversy," as such a document must have been written before the current motive to fabricate arose. *See United States v. Stelmokas*, No. 92-3440, 1995 U.S. Dist. LEXIS 11240, 1995 WL 464264, at *6 (E.D. Pa. Aug. 2, 1995), *aff'd*, 100 F.3d 302 (3d Cir. 1996), *cert. denied*, 520 U.S. 1242, 117 S. Ct. 1847, 137 L. Ed. 2d 1050 (1997); *John W. Strong Et Al., McCormick on Evidence § 323 (5th ed.2003); Fed. R. Evid. 803(16)* Notes of Advisory Committee on 1972 Proposed Rules. Moreover, the requirement that an ancient document be written protects against the danger of inaccurate narration. *See Stelmokas*, 1995 U.S. Dist. LEXIS 11240, 1995 WL 464264, at *6; *John W. Strong Et Al., McCormick on Evidence § 323 (5th ed.2003)*. Finally, an ancient document is more likely to be accurate than the memory of a person after the passing of a lengthy period of time. *See Dallas County*, 286 F.2d at 396–97; *Stelmokas*, 1995 U.S. Dist. LEXIS 11240, 1995 WL 464264, at *6; *John W. Strong Et Al., MCormick on Evidence § 323 (5th ed.2003)*. Thus, if the author of the ancient document had personal knowledge of the substance underlying the relevant assertive statements, then Rule 803(16) clearly applies.

The crucial issue, however, is whether Rule 803(16) inoculates all assertive statements contained within an ancient document, including double hearsay, against application of the general prohibition against hearsay contained in *Rule 802. The rationale of* Rule 803(16) *in permitting the admission of statements in ancient documents where the author is the declarant does not justify the admission of double hearsay merely because of its presence in an ancient document. The danger of faulty perception persists unabated because a narrator, such as a reporter, may not properly record the remarks of the speaker. See Stelmokas*, 1995 U.S. Dist. LEXIS 11240, 1995 WL 464264, at *6; Greg Kettles, *Ancient Documents & the Rule Against Multiple Hearsay*, 39 Santa Clara L.Rev. 719, 735 (1999). More generally, the risk of deception or mistake is compounded with each additional layer of hearsay, as any error will inevitably be passed on regardless of the accuracy or sincerity of the author of the ancient document or prior relators. *See id.*

Courts are divided as to the proper application of Rule 803(16) to ancient documents involving double hearsay. One position is that a separate hearsay exception must apply to each layer of hearsay contained within the ancient document to warrant admission of the specific statement into evidence. *See United States v. Bronislaw Hajda*, 135 F.3d 439, 444 (7th Cir. 1998) (holding that "if the [ancient] document contains more than one level of hearsay, an appropriate exception must be found for each level") (citing *Fed. R. Evid.* 805); *Columbia First Bank, FSB v. United States*, 58 Fed.Cl. 333, 338 (Fed.Cl.2003) (noting that if Rule 803(16) were read so as to inoculate multiple levels of hearsay, " *Rule 805* would be superfluous") (citing *Stelmokas*, 1995 U.S. Dist. LEXIS 11240, 1995 WL 464264, at *5–6). Analogously, the Fifth Circuit requires that a separate hearsay exception be applicable to each level of hearsay in a business record to render the document admissible. *See United States v. Ismoila*, 100 F.3d 380, 392–93 (5th Cir. 1996), *cert. denied*, 520 U.S. 1219, 117 S. Ct. 1712, 137 L. Ed. 2d

836 (1997), 520 U.S. 1247, 117 S. Ct. 1858, 137 L. Ed. 2d 1060 (1997) (explaining that double hearsay is admissible only when each layer is excused by a hearsay exception) (citing *United States v. Baker*, 693 F.2d 183, 188 (D.C. Cir. 1982)).

Some courts have implied that multiple levels of otherwise inadmissible hearsay may be admitted under Rule 803(16). *See Murray v. Sevier*, 50 F. Supp. 2d 1257, 1265 n. 6 (M.D. Ala. 1999) (permitting statements made in an interview in a newspaper article to be used under Rule 803(16), *vacated on other grounds*, *Murray v. Scott*, 253 F.3d 1308 (11th Cir. 2001); *Gonzales v. North Twp. of Lake County*, 800 F. Supp. 676, 681 (N.D. Ind. 1992), *rev'd on other grounds*, 4 F.3d 1412 (7th Cir. 1993)) ("As the newspaper articles in Exhibit C are well more than twenty-years old, the statements contained within are admissible into evidence . . . .") (citing *Ammons v. Dade City*, 594 F. Supp. 1274, 1280 n. 8 (M.D. Fla. 1984), *aff'd*, 783 F.2d 982 (11th Cir. 1986) (admitting newspaper articles to prove the existence of a street paving program in 1925 without inquiry into the double hearsay issue); *Bell v. Combined Registry Co.*, 397 F. Supp. 1241, 1246–47 (N.D. Ill. 1975), *aff'd*, 536 F.2d 164, 166–67 (7th Cir. 1976) (receiving into evidence newspaper articles detailing the use of a poem to further good works and announcing the poet's death)); *John W. Strong Et Al., McCormick on Evidence § 323 (5th ed. 2003)* ("The more common tendency appears to be to admit newspaper articles over 20 years old without the proper inquiry.").

Better reasoned authority indicates that the ancient documents exception permits the introduction of statements only where the declarant is the author of the document. Even if a document qualifies as ancient under Rule 803(16), *other hearsay exceptions must be used to render each individual layer of hearsay admissible. This interpretation best reconciles the underlying justifications of* Rule 803(16) *with the limitations of Rule 805. See Columbia First Bank, FSB, 58 Fed.Cl. at 338; Stelmokas, 1995* U.S. Dist. LEXIS 11240, 1995 WL 464264, at *6. *Rule 805* provides that "[h]earsay included within hearsay is not excluded under the hearsay rule if each part of the combined statements conforms with an exception to the hearsay rule . . . ." *Fed. R. Evid. 805.* "[A]s long as there is no 'positive repugnancy' between two laws . . . a court must give effect to both." *Connecticut Nat'l Bank v. Germain*, 503 U.S. 249, 253, 112 S. Ct. 1146, 117 L. Ed. 2d 391 (1992) (citing *Wood v. United States*, 41 U.S. 342, 10 L. Ed. 987, 16 Pet. 342, 363 (1842)). *Rule 805* would be superfluous if the explicit hearsay exceptions excused double hearsay. Therefore, the canons of statutory interpretation compel this court to give effect to *Rule 805* as well as Rule 803(16), rendering the newspaper articles inadmissible under the ancient documents exception to the hearsay rule.

Hicks at 804–807 (emphasis supplied).

A reading of both *Columbus-America Discovery Group* and *Hicks* leaves me with multiple conclusions: (1) We must, in applying any exception, remember that cross-examination is vital in establishing the value and trustworthiness of evidence and that when a hearsay exception is applied, the benefits of a sworn witness, testifying in the presence of the trier of fact and subject to cross-examination, are often lost; (2) The purpose of the evidence will often determine its admissibility under KRE 803(16); (3) A newspaper may avoid the pitfalls of recent fabrication, inaccurate narration and faded memory; and lastly, (4) The rationale of Rule 803(16) does not justify the admission of multiple levels of hearsay merely because they are present in an ancient document.

I would align with the reasoning of *Hicks* and find that the ancient-documents exception found in KRE 803(16) permits the introduction of statements only where the declarant is the author of the document. If multiple levels of hearsay exist, then each level must meet a hearsay exception to be admissible because this interpretation of KRE 803(16) reconciles it with KRE 805 and avoids the faulty interpretation or perception an author may have of another's statements.

In applying these conclusions to the newspaper admitted into evidence *sub judice*, which stated that the last Ford LTD rolled off the line on a particular date, I conclude it was admissible for the purpose of showing that a Ford LTD did roll off the line on that date but would require a showing that, either the author-declarant knew it was the last LTD through his personal knowledge, or, that the hearsay upon which he relied in determining it to be the last LTD met a hearsay exception pursuant to KRE 805. Because there was no showing of the author-declarant's knowledge that the LTD was the last LTD or that the hearsay upon which he relied met an exception to KRE 805, it should have been excluded. This evidence was of importance, detrimental to Rehm's case, and affected his substantial right to a fair trial. Therefore, I would reverse the decision of the trial court admitting the evidence and remand for a new trial.

Last, I address the consortium claim asserted by Rehm. I agree with *Capital Holding Corporation v. Bailey*, 873 S.W.2d 187 (Ky. 1994) that a cause of action does not accrue until the exposure to asbestos causes the injury that produces the loss or damage. A plain reading of Kentucky Revised Statutes (KRS) 411.145 would allow the claim to be asserted by Rehm against Ford. Therefore, I would reverse the trial court on this issue.

EXERCISE

Albert wrote and copyrighted a hit gospel song. Following Albert's death several potential heirs filed suit to determine who should inherit the copyright. Central to the court's determination is whether Albert created the song as a "work for hire" while working at Hartford Music. One party seeks to offer into evidence an article appearing in the Music City News and another article appearing in Bluegrass Unlimited magazine. Both articles were published more than 20 years ago and claim that Albert was a salaried employee of Hartford Music at the time that he wrote the song. The opposing party objects on hearsay and authentication grounds. How should the court rule?

[L]   Market Reports: Rule 803(17)

STATE v. BATISTE
Louisiana Court of Appeals
764 So. 2d 1038 (2000)

FOIL, JUDGE.

The defendant, Charles Batiste, was charged by bill of information with illegal possession of stolen things valued over $500, in violation of La. R.S. 14:69. He pled not guilty and, after trial by jury, was found guilty as charged. Thereafter, the state filed an habitual offender bill of information and, during the hearing, the defendant stipulated to being a second felony habitual offender. He received a sentence of twelve years at hard labor.

The defendant appealed, alleging as his only assignment of error that the trial court erred in allowing the state to introduce, over defense objection, the NADA Blue Book to establish the value of the stolen property.

FACTS

The victim, Douglas Schmidt, an employee of Glazer Wholesale, had the use of a 1995 Jeep Cherokee owned by Glazer. On July 14, 1997, he discovered that the vehicle had been stolen from the parking space in front of his apartment in Metairie, Louisiana. He also found broken glass scattered on the ground in the space where the vehicle had been parked. He reported the missing vehicle to the police. On July 16, 1997, the St. Tammany Parish Sheriff's Office received an anonymous tip that there was a stolen vehicle behind a residence on Martin Luther King Drive in Lacombe, Louisiana.

When deputies arrived, they found a trailer next to the driveway. In the driveway was a Cadillac. As they approached the end of the driveway, the deputies saw a red 1995 Jeep Cherokee parked over a trash heap in high weeds behind the trailer. They determined that this was the vehicle that had been stolen from the victim.

The deputies found the defendant inside the trailer. When they arrested him, he asked to remove some of his things from the Jeep before it was towed. The deputies apparently retrieved a radio, some clothes, and a duffel bag from the Jeep. A woman living at the trailer identified these items as belonging to the defendant.

Later, at the Parish Jail, the defendant gave a statement. He explained that he had given Eddie Jones $75 in exchange for the use of the Jeep "for a couple of days." This transaction allegedly took place in New Orleans.

ASSIGNMENT OF ERROR

In his sole assignment of error, the defendant contends that the trial court erred in allowing the state to introduce, over defense objection, the NADA Blue Book to establish the value of the stolen property.

The victim, Mr. Schmidt, testified that the vehicle had been purchased new in 1995 for just over $18,000 and "was in pretty good condition" when it was stolen from him in July of 1997. When the vehicle was recovered, apparently there was some minor damage to it. However, when the prosecutor asked if there was significant damage which would, in his opinion, reduce the vehicle's value to less than $500, Mr. Schmidt replied in the negative.

Thereafter, when the prosecutor offered State Exhibit 2, a copy of the relevant page from the NADA Blue Book containing the retail, trade-in, and loan values for a 1995 Jeep Cherokee, defense counsel objected on the grounds of hearsay. The prosecutor responded that the business records exception applied. The trial court overruled the defense objection. The court did not accept the business records exception, but it noted that the exhibit fell under the market quotations provision of La.Code Evid. art. 803(17). Thereafter, the exhibit, which indicated that a base model 1995 Jeep Cherokee had a retail value of $9,275, a trade-in value of $7,275, and a loan value of $6,550, was admitted into evidence.

La.Code Evid. art. 803(17) provides:

> The following are not excluded by the hearsay rule, even though the declarant is available as a witness:
>
> *   *   *
>
> (17) . . . Market quotations, tabulations, lists, directories, or other published compilations, generally used and relied upon by the public or by persons in particular occupations.

In his brief to this court, the defendant asserts that State Exhibit 2 was inadmissible hearsay. He contends that the supporting testimony of an expert appraiser should have accompanied the NADA Blue Book. He further contends that the error cannot be harmless because the exhibit was used to establish the value of the stolen vehicle, an essential element of the offense. We disagree.

In our view, the NADA Blue Book, containing the relative commercial values of used vehicles, constitutes the exact type of publication contemplated by La.Code Evid. art. 803(17). This article does not condition the admissibility of such publications on the accompanying testimony of an expert appraiser, as the defendant suggests. We find that the trial court correctly overruled the defense objection. In any event, even assuming that the trial court erred in allowing this exhibit to be admitted into evidence, any error was harmless beyond a reasonable doubt. The values contained in this exhibit were merely cumulative and corroborative of the previously admitted testimony by the victim regarding the purchase price, and the condition and value of the vehicle both at the time it was stolen and when it was recovered from the defendant. Even without State Exhibit 2, there can be no doubt that the State established this stolen 1995 Jeep Cherokee was worth far in excess of $500, not only at the time it was stolen, but also when it was recovered from the defendant. *See* La. Code Crim. P. art. 921; *State v. Byrd*, 540 So.2d 1110, 1114 (La. App. 1st Cir.), *writ denied*, 546 So.2d 169 (La.1989). In fact, in his closing argument, trial counsel even conceded that the value of the vehicle was not an issue.

This assignment of error is meritless.

[M] Learned Treatises: Rule 803(18)

[1] Introducing a Learned Treatise

Although the exception works to admit automatically any document that fulfills the requirements set forth in the rule, proponents often encounter significant problems in establishing that the document in question adequately meets those requirements. The following case of *Markiewicz v. Salt River Valley Water Users' Ass'n*, illustrates the difficulties inherent in attempting to introduce a document under this exception.

MARKIEWICZ v. SALT RIVER VALLEY WATER USERS' ASS'N
Arizona Court of Appeals
576 P.2d 517 (1978)

HAIRE, PRESIDING JUDGE.

[Plaintiffs, a group of homeowners, brought an action to recover for damage to their homes caused by water escaping from the defendant's canal. Plaintiffs alleged that the defendant had inadequately designed the canal by failing to accommodate the design to the known rainfall levels in the area. To establish these rainfall levels, the plaintiffs offered into evidence a two-page document that they had obtained from the defendant. The trial court sustained an objection to the document's introduction on hearsay grounds. This ruling was one of the grounds of error that the plaintiffs alleged on appeal.]

Appellants first assert that Exhibit 76 was admissible as an ancient document. A document which is (1) approximately 30 years old or more, (2) unsuspicious in appearance or otherwise, and (3) produced from natural and proper custody, is admissible without further proof of authenticity. . . . In some jurisdictions statements in ancient documents may be received as proof of the facts recited therein provided the writer would have been competent to testify to those facts. . . . However, despite these two aspects of ancient documents — a rule of authentication and an exception to the hearsay rule — an ancient document is not automatically admissible. . . . The document must also be relevant and material to the inquiry.

In some circumstances, Exhibit 76 might arguably qualify for admission as an ancient document. We do not find, however, that the trial judge abused his discretion under the circumstances presented in this case by refusing to admit Exhibit 76. . . . Several factors justified the judge's exclusion of this evidence.

There is no date on the document. The Association's Manager of Water Operations, Mr. Friar, testified that Exhibit 76 was found either with a report on the 1939 storm or with the 1943 storm report. Mr. Friar could not say who prepared the document, or for what purpose. He testified that the Association keeps some documents that are not its own. Normally, the Association identifies its own records, but there is no identification on Exhibit 76. Mr. Friar said he could not identify any of the rain-measuring stations as being in the Cudia City Wash area.

Clearly, there is uncertainty as to whether Exhibit 76 could satisfy the requirements for being an ancient document. No one knows exactly when it was prepared. And since the author and purpose of the document are unknown, it becomes difficult to decide whether Exhibit 76 was found in proper custody — in a place that gives circumstantial evidence that the document is genuine. Even if it is an ancient document, there is no indication that the unidentified author would have been competent to testify to the facts recited in the document.[80] Finally, the probative value of Exhibit 76 is slight, because it is not shown to be an Association document, and it does not relate directly to the rainfall that has been experienced in the Cudia City Wash area.

[2] Learned Treatises as Substantive Evidence

Rule 803(18) established a totally new hearsay exception encompassing materials that in the past were used exclusively in connection with the impeachment of witnesses. Some judges, like old dogs trying to learn new tricks, have had difficulty making necessary adjustments.

TART v. McGANN
United States Court of Appeals, Second Circuit
697 F.2d 75 (1982)

FEINBERG, CHIEF JUDGE:

Plaintiffs William D. Tart and Marion Tart appeal from a judgment for defendants entered in the United States District Court for the Southern District of New York after a jury trial before Judge Edmund L. Palmieri on plaintiffs' medical malpractice claims. On appeal, plaintiffs contend . . . that the judge erroneously excluded evidence admissible under Rule 803(18) of the Federal Rules of Evidence, the "learned treatises" exception to the hearsay rule. For reasons set forth below, we reverse the judgment of the district court, and remand for further proceedings in accordance with this opinion.

I. Background

Prior to the events at issue in this case, plaintiff William D. Tart was employed by the Celanese Corporation as an Assistant Chief Pilot. His employer required him to take an annual physical exam, which included a stress test. During the course of a stress test of the type at issue here, a patient walks or jogs at varying speeds and varying inclines on a treadmill while the physician monitors various lead systems attached to the patient's chest. Since 1973, plaintiff had been taking stress tests at the Life Extension Institute, a partnership of defendants Dr. John P. McGann and Dr. Ronald E. Costin. In September 1979, plaintiff took another such test there, administered by defendant Dr. Robert Mooney. Fifteen to twenty minutes after

---

[80] (Court's original footnote 8.) We take no position on whether Rule 803(16), Arizona Rules of Evidence, has expanded the common law hearsay exception to admit statements in ancient documents which give no indication that the declarant had personal knowledge of the facts.

completing the test, while still at the Life Extension Institute, plaintiff suffered a heart attack. He was subsequently hospitalized for over a week. As a result of the heart attack, the plaintiff lost his pilot license, and could therefore no longer continue to serve as a pilot for his employer.

According to plaintiffs, defendants failed to monitor and administer the stress test properly, in violation of good medical practice. Among other things, plaintiffs allege that Dr. Mooney should have stopped the test during the fourth stage, when Tart complained of "heavy fatigue." Instead, Dr. Mooney continued the test for several minutes, until the fourth stage of the test was completed. The jury found for defendants . . . .

*　　*　　*

III. Learned Treatise Evidence

Plaintiff's . . . argument on appeal concerns the admissibility of so-called learned treatise evidence. During the course of the trial, plaintiffs attempted to bolster the testimony of their expert witness by introducing into evidence an article entitled "Maximal Exercise Testing." The article was written by Dr. Robert A. Bruce, who devised the Bruce-Protocol, which was used as the basis for the stress test taken by plaintiff William Tart. A stress test protocol is a set of directions that describes how a treadmill stress test should be conducted. It indicates, for example, the proper speed and incline of the treadmill at various stages of the test. The district court refused to allow plaintiffs to introduce the Bruce article into evidence as an exhibit or to quote from it on the direct examination of their expert.

The district court also severely restricted plaintiffs' use of learned treatise evidence on the cross-examination of defendants' expert. Plaintiffs sought to cross-examine defendants' expert by asking him whether he agreed with statements and figures contained in a booklet on exercise testing published by the American Heart Association. In particular, plaintiff wished to quote from a table on recommended target heart rates. Judge Palmieri refused to admit the table into evidence, and also refused to allow plaintiffs to quote from it. Judge Palmieri also instructed plaintiffs not to quote from the Bruce article, except to the extent it contradicted defendants' expert.

Judge Palmieri's evidentiary rulings on this issue evidently were based at least in part on a misunderstanding of the status of learned treatise evidence under the current Federal Rules. Judge Palmieri stated in explanation of his decision to prohibit use of the Bruce article as substantive evidence his belief that medical literature can only be used "as a cross-examination tool." But Rule 803(18) . . . explicitly permits the admission of medical literature as substantive evidence "to the extent called to the attention of an expert witness upon cross-examination or relied upon by him in direct examination, . . ." as long as it is established that such literature is authoritative. The admissibility of such evidence is amply confirmed by the relevant case law, . . . and by the commentators . . . .

Prior to the enactment of Rule 803(18), learned treatises were generally usable only on cross-examination, and then only for impeachment purposes. . . . Most commentators found the hearsay objections to learned treatise evidence unconvincing, and recommended that treatises be admitted as substantive evidence. Some commentators went so far as to suggest that treatises be admitted independently of an expert's testimony. . . . The Advisory Committee rejected this position, noting that a treatise might be "misunderstood and misapplied without expert assistance and supervision." Fed. R. Evid. 803(18) Advisory Committee Notes. Accordingly, the Rule permits the admission of learned treatises as substantive evidence, but only when "an expert is on the stand and available to explain and assist in the application of the treatise . . . ." *Id.*

Nonetheless, it may not have been improper for Judge Palmieri to exclude the evidence at issue in this case. First, there was some dispute over the relevancy of the challenged evidence, particularly the chart on recommended target heart rates. Second, it does not appear that the evidence was properly proffered under Rule 803(18); the only rule explicitly referred to by plaintiffs was Rule 703, which deals with the bases of opinion testimony by experts. . . . Finally, it appears that the substance of much of the disputed evidence was made available to the jury. Thus, the exclusion of the evidence at issue may have been harmless error. . . . We need not decide whether exclusion of the evidence at issue was reversible error. We hold only that if on remand the disputed medical literature is shown to be relevant and authoritative, it may be read into evidence if properly proffered under Rule 803(18).

[N] Residual Exception: Rule 807

[1] Declarant's Unavailability Immaterial

Under the Federal Rules of Evidence, the residual exceptions to the hearsay rule formerly codified under Rule 803(24), where the declarant's unavailability was immaterial, and 804(b)(5), where the declarant's unavailability was required, have been consolidated into Rule 807. This rule has codified the inherent power that courts at common law claimed as a basis for admitting otherwise inadmissible yet inherently reliable statements. Rule 807 provides that the hearsay rule does not exclude certain evidence regardless of whether the declarant is available or unavailable as a witness.

The residual exception requires that the statement be more probative on the point for which it is offered than any other reasonably obtainable evidence. It stands to reason, therefore, that declarant's unavailability should be a prerequisite to admission of evidence under this exception. Otherwise, if the declarant is available, her testimony, and not the hearsay statement, would be the most probative evidence on the point. *See Southern Stone Company, Inc. v. Sam Singer*, 665 F.2d 698 (5th Cir. 1982), and *United States v. Mathis*, 559 F.2d 294 (5th Cir. 1977), asserting that, notwithstanding the lack of an unavailability requirement in 807, witness availability re-enters the analysis when considering whether the statement sought to be admitted is more probative than any other reasonably procurable evidence. Notwithstanding this unavailability requirement stemming from the text of the exception, courts have not found it to be a prerequisite to the use of the exception. This may have been due, in substantial part, to the fact that the exception previously was included in Rule 803 (where unavailability is immaterial) as well as 804 (where unavailability is an explicit prerequisite).

While the inclusion of a single residual exception under Rule 807 (*i.e.*, outside of Rule 803) could signal a recognition by the Advisory Committee of the need for a showing of the declarant's unavailability as a prerequisite to admission, the Committee's Notes reflect otherwise. They explicitly state that the change to the residual exceptions is merely technical (*i.e.*, a renumbering) with no change of meaning intended.

[2] Equivalent Circumstantial Guarantees of Trustworthiness

For statements to fall within this exception, Rule 807 requires that the statements in question have "equivalent" guarantees of trustworthiness. Equivalent to what? Presumably, Congress intended to require that such statements have guarantees of trustworthiness equivalent to statements admissible under those traditional exceptions to the hearsay rule codified in the Federal Rules. But which ones? Inasmuch as the traditional exceptions vary significantly in their trustworthiness, should courts measure this equivalency standard against the exception under which the statement would most likely have had to qualify without the residual provision, or against a more generalized standard of trustworthiness? Although courts have not explicitly answered this question in the cases, they appear to be interpreting the provision as requiring "substantial" guarantees of trustworthiness regardless of what any analogous exception may require. Moreover, as reflected in the following opinion in *United States v. Medico* and accompanying trial transcript excerpts, courts frequently make this determination of trustworthiness by considering those factors that courts traditionally considered as demonstrating reliability and trustworthiness, including the declarant's motivation in making the statement, inferential or actual corroboration of the statement, the declarant's availability for cross-examination, and the circumstances under which the statement was made. *See* Note, *The Residual Exceptions to the Hearsay Rule in the Federal Rules of Evidence: A Critical Examination*, 31 RUTGERS L. REV. 687 (1978).

UNITED STATES v. MEDICO
United States Court of Appeals, Second Circuit
557 F.2d 309 (1977)

ROBERT L. CARTER, DISTRICT JUDGE:

On May 27, 1976, there was an armed robbery of the Chemical Bank at 23-98 Bell Boulevard, Queens, New York by two masked men. While one of the men held a shotgun to the assistant bank manager, the other came into the tellers' area, and took almost $23,000 in cash from the tellers' drawers. The two then left the bank. Rosario Frisina, the branch manager, and Barbara Balzarini, a teller, were in the tellers' area. Appellant was indicted and convicted for the crime. He appeals on the grounds that errors at a pre-trial suppression hearing and errors at trial warrant reversal.

* * *

Claimed Errors at The Trial

*   *   *

William Carmody, a bank employee, testified that about five minutes after the robbers had fled with the bank funds and while he was locking the entrance door, a bank customer knocked on the door. Carmody had seen this customer monthly at the bank for the past five years, but he did not know his name and had not seen him since the robbery. A young man about 20 years old whom Carmody did not know was sitting outside in a car giving the customer the make and license plate number of the getaway car. The customer relayed the information through the door to Carmody who took it down on his check book. Carmody could not hear what the young man was saying to the customer, although he could see the youth's lips move as the customer was telling him what was being said. Carmody took down the description of the getaway car as a "tan Dodge Valiant" with license plate number "700 CQA." Judge Weinstein allowed the testimony in under Rule 807, Fed. R. Ev. The judge offered appellant a five-day adjournment to meet the testimony or make his own investigation. Appellant declined the invitation asserting that the government had indicated that it had made serious attempts to locate the two witnesses without success. On admitting the testimony the district judge advised the jury that it was hearsay, that since the two witnesses were not present, the statement was not subject to cross examination; that the probative value of the statement was for the jury to determine, bearing in mind that the two missing witnesses were not subject to cross examination and their testimony was not under oath.

*   *   *

Determination

The admission of the hearsay statements of the bystanders concerning the getaway car raises at first blush serious problems.[81] Those difficulties become even more acute if the hearsay issue is not kept separate and apart from the refusal of the district court to allow the government to question [William] Cariola [a government witness who connected Medico to the getaway car] more closely about the Dodge with license plate 700 CQA being registered in Cariola's name.

------

[81] (Court's original footnote 4.) We would have little difficulty in upholding Judge Weinstein's ruling as a proper exercise of discretion had this been a civil case. We are faced here, however, with the Sixth Amendment's mandate that in "all criminal prosecutions, the accused shall enjoy the right to be confronted with the witnesses against him." This has created some confusion as to whether the reach of the hearsay rules and the confrontation clause are coterminous. *See* Younger, *Confrontation and Hearsay: A Look Backward, A Peek Forward*, 1 Hofstra L. Rev. 32 (1973); Note, *Confrontation and the Hearsay Rule*, 75 Yale L.J. 1434 (1966). The Supreme Court, however, has made clear that while the hearsay rule and the confrontation clause "stem from the same roots," *Dutton v. Evans*, 400 U.S. 74, 96 (1970), and "are generally designed to protect similar values," *California v. Green*, 399 U.S. 149, 155 (1970), their reach is not coextensive. . . . The Sixth Amendment guarantee of confrontation, therefore, should not blind us to the reality that the question of the admission of the hearsay statements, whether in a criminal or civil case, turns on due process considerations of fairness, reliability and trustworthiness. Experience has taught that the stated exceptions now codified in the Federal Rules of Evidence meet these conditions.

The testimony was admitted under the overall residual hearsay exception as provided in Rule 807, Fed. R. Ev. . . .

This court has not yet had occasion to define the proper scope of Rule 807 in a criminal trial. However, in *United States v. Iaconetti,* . . . in upholding the admission of hearsay statements in reliance on Rule 807, this court found the "statements in question possessed sufficient indicia of reliability, and were the best evidence to corroborate" the account of one of the government's witnesses as to what took place. It was also pointed out that "the statements were relevant to a material proposition of fact . . . ."

Rule 804 deals, among others, with situations in which the proponent of a witness' statement has sought by process or other means to procure the attendance of the witness at the trial to testify in person. This situation was present here. Defense counsel readily conceded that the government had made serious efforts to locate the two witnesses so that they could testify in person.

Indeed the testimony meets all the specific requirements for admission as a present sense impression under Rule 803(1) under which a hearsay statement will not be excluded even though the declarant is available. As the Advisory Committee Note to Rule 803(1) indicates, the theory for this exception is that the "contemporaneity of event and statement negate the likelihood of deliberate or conscious misrepresentation." Precise contemporaneity is not required, thus a "slight lapse is allowable . . . ." The Committee Advisory Note points out that the cases reveal a hesitancy to admit the statement without more when the bystander's identity is unknown. . . . This may well be the reason Judge Weinstein decided to rely on Rule 807. That fact, however, that the statement meets all the specific standards for admissions under 803(1) but fails to meet all the criteria set forth in the supportive judicial rationale surely brings it within the grant of discretion which 807 accords to a trial judge, consonant with the legislative purposes which the residual exception was designed to achieve.

Moreover, several factors contribute to the reliability of Carmody's testimony. The two unavailable witnesses were at the scene of the crime. One was in position to perceive and describe the car and license plate number the robbers used to effect their escape; and while the other did not claim to have himself observed the car or the license plate, he relayed to Carmody that information just told him by the first bystander who personally had seen the robbers drive away in the getaway car. The time frame in which the information was passed from the eyewitness to the bank customer and then from the customer to Carmody was very brief and followed the actual getaway so closely, that the likelihood of inaccuracies is small and the possibility that truth was undercut by speculation or fabrication reduced. The probability that the information was accurate is enhanced by the fact that Carmody transcribed it onto his checkbook as it was being told to him.

Carmody's testimony was highly relevant, clearly material, and the need for that evidence was great. No other evidence providing the same information or being more probative of the fact for which the statement was offered was available to the government. It would have been preferable, certainly, to have had the youth and/or the bank customer testify. However, the government made serious efforts to locate these witnesses to no avail, and the defense was offered an adjournment to prepare to meet this evidence or make investigations of its own. The offer was declined.[82] In light of these circumstances, the admission of Carmody's testimony was proper under Rule 807. Clearly the trustworthiness and necessity for the admission of the statement and the specific facts and circumstances warranting allowing the testimony to come before the jury are on par with those which justify the enumerated exceptions.

What in fact makes the admission of Carmody's testimony problematic is not the likelihood of its unreliability or untrustworthiness but the testimony of William Cariola linking Medico to the getaway car described in Carmody's testimony. Cariola testified that for about two months he and Medico were employed by the same taxicab company and that he had seen Medico driving "an off-white 1965 Dodge, license plate 700 CQA."

While it strains credulity that a person could remember the exact number of his co-worker's license plate, when he apparently had known his co-worker only casually and had seen him regularly over a short span of time, that is an issue of credibility for the jury. A crucial fact affecting Cariola's credibility was never told to the jury, however — the fact that the Dodge, license plate 700 CQA, which Cariola, under oath, denied he owned, was in fact registered to him. At a sidebar conference, the U.S. Attorney revealed the highly unusual story that Cariola had lost his identification, wallet, and subsequently it was found, and he said that there was in the car in the wallet information, identification for a car that had been registered, not by him but by another individual, and that was given over to the State Department of Motor Vehicles.

The government asked to bring out this information but defense counsel stated, "I think we ought to leave that out." The court agreed. We recognize that the hindsight nuances which make us believe the testimony should have been allowed may not have been as evident at trial. It certainly was not evident to defense counsel. Both he and the court were concerned that pursuit of Cariola's testimony might lead to matters far removed from the issues at hand. We think, however, that the jury should have had this information to evaluate Cariola's credibility. Because the defense acquiesced in the trial court's decision to exclude these facts, however, we cannot now find that decision constituted plain error.

*   *   *

MANSFIELD, CIRCUIT JUDGE (dissenting):

I respectfully dissent on the ground that the double hearsay identification of the getaway car admitted by the trial court lacked any guarantee of trustworthiness entitling it to admission under the residual hearsay exception, FRE 807, relied upon by the majority. In the absence of any such guarantee or of an opportunity to test the reliability of the proof through cross-examination, the admission of this evidence in my view constituted an abuse of discretion and the error was not "harmless." . . . I would therefore reverse and remand for a new trial.

---

[82] (Court's original footnote 7.) The rule requires prior notice to the adverse party, but this omission was cured by the court's offer to grant the defense a five-day adjournment.

The sole issue in this trial was the identification of appellant as one of two robbers of a Chemical Bank branch in Queens, New York. On this issue the license plate number and description of the alleged getaway car was a critical element, which the government sought to prove through William Carmody, a bank employee. Carmody, however, did not see the car himself. He obtained the information from a man he recognized as a bank customer, but who was neither identified by name nor located for trial. Nor did the customer, according to Carmody, see the getaway car. He, in turn, had obtained the license number and description some five minutes after the robbery from a "young man" seated in a car outside the bank, who also could not be identified or located for the trial. Carmody testified that the young man relayed the license number and description to the customer who shouted through the closed bank door to Carmody, who wrote the information down on his checkbook. Carmody furnished the description after referring to the checkbook to refresh his recollection.

Serious problems are presented as to the trustworthiness of this hearsay, which indicate that it should not qualify as falling within any exception to the hearsay rule.[83] Since the license number and identification were obtained during the armed robbers' hurried flight from the scene of the crime, the young man in the car may well have erred due to excitement, poor eyesight, poor lighting conditions or visual obstructions. Indeed it is possible that the young man may have been sufficiently confused or frightened to have identified a car that was not the getaway vehicle at all. This type of eyewitness identification has long been considered peculiarly riddled with innumerable dangers and variable factors which might seriously, even crucially derogate from a fair trial. The vagaries of eyewitness identification are well-known; the annals of criminal law are rife with instances of mistaken identification . . . .

Yet, because the evidence was admitted from Carmody rather than from the out-of-court declarant himself, the defendant was deprived of the opportunity to cross-examine the declarant, which might have significantly reduced the reliability of the evidence in the eyes of the jury.

It is further evident that some of the same factors which might have interfered with the young man's direct identification of the vehicle might well have prevented the bank customer from correctly relaying the young man's description, including faulty hearing, background noise, excitement, and similar circumstances. Yet, because the bank customer was also unavailable to be cross-examined, the accuracy of his statement could not be tested.

The record in the present case reveals that fears of distortion in this crucial identification testimony are not unjustified. Carmody testified, for instance, that the getaway car was a "Brown Valiant," which would indicate a Plymouth. His checkbook, which was admitted into evidence, noted that the car was not brown, but "tan," and was a "Dodge Valiant," a non-existent model. William Cariola, a corroborating witness, testified that the car driven to and from his job by Medico

---

[83] (Court's original footnote 1.) The foundation for all hearsay exceptions is circumstantial trustworthiness in the absence of cross-examination. *See* 5 Wigmore, EVIDENCE §§ 1420–22 (Chadbourne rev. 1974); Advisory Committee Notes, *Introductory Note: The Hearsay Problem.*

was an "off white Dodge." Thus significant errors in perception or communication found their way into the evidence, even without the presence of the out-of-court declarants for cross-examination.

The unreliability of the hearsay testimony identifying the getaway car was increased by the government's disclosure of a bizarre circumstance. The key witness relied upon by the government to link appellant to the getaway car was Cariola, appellant's former co-worker. Even though the two were only casual acquaintances, Cariola, in testimony which, according to the majority, "strains credulity," was able to remember the exact license number of the car which appellant had driven to work on occasion. This number turned out to be the same as that of the getaway car, as identified by Carmody's double hearsay testimony.[84] More important, in offering this testimony the government advised the trial judge in a side bar conference of the extraordinary fact that the automobile had actually been registered in the name of Cariola himself rather than that of appellant. Although appellant's counsel apparently failed to grasp and exploit the implications of this disclosure, it raises a serious question, particularly in view of Cariola's criminal record, as to whether the failure of the young man or the bank customer (who had been seen frequently at the bank before the robbery but not thereafter) to come forward and testify may not have been attributable to efforts by the conspirators or others to protect against full disclosure of the robbers' identity. Since neither the young man nor the bank customer was produced for cross-examination, their motives, biases and possible connections with appellant or Cariola could not be explored. Neither, therefore, could be compelled to "stand face to face with the jury in order that they may look at him and judge by his demeanor upon the stand and the manner in which he gives his testimony whether he is worthy of belief . . . ."

It is to guard against just such possible consequences that the hearsay rule evolved, with exceptions for hearsay only where there are unusual guarantees of trustworthiness in lieu of cross-examination. In my view it was a serious error for the trial judge to resort to the residual hearsay exception found in FRE 807 as the basis for admitting the double hearsay in the present case.[85] The effect is to emasculate the hearsay rule and violate the fundamental purposes underlying it. In formulating the residual exception, the drafters of the Federal Rules of Evidence cautioned that it should be used sparingly:

> It is intended that the residual hearsay exceptions will be used very rarely, and only in exceptional circumstances. The committee does not intend to

---

[84] (Court's original footnote 2.) By separately resolving the issues raised by Cariola's connection with the alleged getaway vehicle and the admission of Carmody's testimony, the majority conveniently ignores the serious effect of the revelations concerning Cariola on the probative value and trustworthiness of the identification testimony.

[85] (Court's original footnote 3.) At best, the majority's conclusion that Carmody's testimony would be admissible under the exception for present sense impressions, FRE 803(1), would only cover the first stage of the double hearsay, the statement from the "young man" to the bank customer, because only the "young man" was perceiving the startling event he was describing, i.e., the getaway of the robbers. Moreover, it is difficult to conclude that the license number and description of the vehicle would be a description or explanation of the "event," within the meaning and common usage of FRE 803(1).

establish a broad license for trial judges to admit hearsay statements that do not fall within one of the other exceptions contained in rules 803 and 804(b) . . . .

The admission of the double hearsay identification of the getaway car in the present case violated both the spirit and purpose of FRE 807 as thus expressed, since the evidence failed to satisfy any of the basic conditions for exceptions to the hearsay rule. It lacked any circumstantial guarantee of trustworthiness, it was hardly "more probative on the point for which it is offered than any other evidence which the proponent can procure," and its admission did not serve "the interests of justice." Not only was there danger of serious error in perception on the part of the young man and the bank customer but Cariola's testimony purporting to provide the essential link to the appellant was far from being free of doubt and suspicion. As the Supreme Court said in [*United States v. Wade*, 388 U.S. 218 (1967)], a criminal defendant's "most basic right" is that of a "fair trial at which the witnesses against him might be meaningfully cross-examined . . . ."

> For two centuries past, the policy of the Anglo-American system of evidence has been to regard the necessity of testing by cross-examination as a vital feature of the law. The belief that no safeguard for testing the value of human statements is comparable to that furnished by cross-examination, and the conviction that no statement (unless by general exception) should be used as testimony until it has been probed and sublimated by that test, has found increasing strength in lengthening experience. . . . [I]t is beyond doubt the greatest legal engine for the discovery of truth.

5 WIGMORE ON EVIDENCE § 1367.

No authority supports the application of the 807 residual hearsay exception in a case like the present one when serious questions of reliability have been raised in the absence of cross-examination. On the contrary, one circuit has refused to apply the exception because it poses serious constitutional problems . . . .

The cases relied on by the majority are readily distinguishable. In *United States v. Iaconetti*, 540 F.2d 574 (2d Cir. 1976), we found support in the residual hearsay exception for admission of rebuttal testimony by two witnesses (Stern and Goodman) as to statements of a previous witness (Lioi) regarding the defendant Iaconetti's request for money. But the significant difference is that there the declarants (Stern, Goodman, Lioi, and Iaconetti) were all available for cross-examination and the jury was allowed to resolve a conflict in credibility among witnesses who were present and whose demeanor could be judged. In admitting statements similar to those in *Iaconetti*, it has often been stated that where the declarant is present and on the witness stand, present cross-examination provides a sufficient protection against unreliable out-of-court statements. . . . No such protection was available in this case.

The availability of the out-of-court declarants for cross-examination at the trial was expressly relied upon in *United States v. Leslie*, 542 F.2d 285, 288 (5th Cir. 1976), the only other criminal case to uphold the introduction of testimony under the residual hearsay exceptions. There, FBI agents corroborated written statements by the defendants which were recorded by the agents and introduced at trial, after the defendants had taken the stand and denied the truth of those statements. Thus, in that case both the defendants and the agents, whose credibility had to be determined by the jury, were available and present at the trial.[86]

In the present case neither of the out-of-court declarants upon whose reliability and accuracy the identification of the getaway car was based was available, with the result that their credibility could not be tested by appellant. Moreover, not only were there indications that distortions had occurred in the substance of the visual identification, but the linking evidence supplied by Cariola was so suspicious as to undermine the entire theory of the identification.

For these reasons I would reverse.

[3] Evidence of Material Fact and Generally Serving Purposes of Rules and Interests of Justice

These two elements of the residual exceptions appear to be superfluous in light of Rules 401 and 402, which require that evidence be logically relevant to be admissible, and of Rule 102, which states that the "rules shall be construed to secure fairness in . . . promotion of growth and development of the law of evidence to the end that the truth may be ascertained and proceedings justly determined." Courts have not considered these requirements significant limitations on the application of the residual exceptions, generally limiting their textual discussion of the requirements to brief statements, or relegating treatment of them to the footnotes. *See United States v. AT&T Co.*, 516 F. Supp. 1237, 1239 n.3 (D.D.C. 1981).

[4] More Probative than Other Reasonably Procurable Evidence

This requirement appears to create a necessity standard that has two aspects. First, as previously discussed, because the proponent must use reasonable efforts to procure the most probative evidence on the points sought to be proved, Rule 807 seems to have a built-in requirement that the declarant be shown to be unavailable. The second aspect of this necessity requirement is a demonstration that *other sources* of the same evidence are also unavailable. This is illustrated in the following case.

---

[86] (Court's original footnote 4.) In other cases which have applied the residual hearsay exceptions the reliability of the evidence admitted was not in question. *Muncie Aviation Corp. v. Party Doll Fleet*, 519 F.2d 11978, 1184 (5th Cir. 1974) (admitting national air safety codes and recommendations); *Ark-Mo Frams v. United States*, 530 F.2d 1384, 1386–87 (Ct. Cl. 1976) (admitting Corps of Engineers' hydrological study).

DE MARS v. EQUITABLE LIFE ASSURANCE SOCIETY

United States Court of Appeals, First Circuit
610 F.2d 55 (1979)

BOWNES, CIRCUIT JUDGE.

[This case involved an action to recover benefits under an accidental death provision of a life insurance policy. During the trial, the court permitted the plaintiff to read to the jury a portion of a letter from a deceased physician which included the physician's opinion as to the cause of death of the plaintiff's deceased spouse.]

Dr. Rattigan was retained by plaintiff's counsel prior to trial to render an opinion as to the cause of death, which he did on December 19, 1972. Sometime thereafter and prior to trial, Dr. Rattigan died. His report was made available to defendant during discovery procedure on June 15, 1976, well in advance of trial. At the start of the trial, defendant moved *in limine* to have the letter excluded from evidence. The motion was granted "without prejudice." During the cross-examination of one of defendant's experts, Dr. Christian, plaintiff's counsel brought out that defendant had furnished Dr. Christian the Rattigan letter as part of the material to be examined preparatory to giving his opinion as to the cause of death. Plaintiff's counsel then attempted to introduce the letter, or at least cross-examine Dr. Christian as to its contents, pursuant to Federal Rule of Evidence 703. The court refused to allow the letter in evidence at this time, although indicating that Federal Rule of Evidence 804 might apply. After the cross-examination of Dr. Christian was completed, the court had second thoughts about the Rattigan letter and held a bench conference to further discuss its admissibility. He then ruled that, except for the last two paragraphs, the letter could be read to the jury.

Although not explicitly so stating, the statements of the court during the three bench conferences on this issue make it clear that it based its ruling on Federal Rule of Evidence 807 . . . .

The rule's requirement of notice was met: defendant obtained a copy of the letter during discovery, it furnished a copy to Dr. Christian for use in preparing his opinion as to the cause of death, and it brought a motion *in limine* to exclude the letter.

Neither the court nor the parties addressed directly part (B) of the rule, although defendant did assert that plaintiff had plenty of time prior to trial to obtain the services of another expert after Dr. Rattigan died. Plaintiff offered no evidence or explanation as to why another expert was not obtained and the record is silent as to the date of Dr. Rattigan's death. Since Dr. Rattigan's opinion was based solely on his examination of the decedent's medical and hospital records, the death certificate and the report of the postmortem examination, any other physician could have been obtained to render an opinion on fairly short notice. This is not a situation where the treating physician suddenly dies just prior to trial. The following comment in Weinstein's Evidence on the identical provision in Federal Rule of Evidence 807 is instructive on how part (B) is to be construed.

The statement must be "more probative on the point for which it is offered than any other evidence which the proponent can procure through reasonable efforts." What is "reasonable" depends upon such matters as the importance of the evidence, the means at the command of the proponent and the amount in controversy. The good sense of the trial judge must be relied upon. It should not be necessary to scale the highest mountains of Tibet to obtain a deposition for use in a $500 damage claim arising from an accident with a postal truck. Even though the evidence may be somewhat cumulative, it may be important in evaluating other evidence and arriving at the truth so that the "more probative" requirement cannot be interpreted with cast iron rigidity.

4 WEINSTEIN'S EVIDENCE § 103(24)[01] at 803–243 (1977). Since the trial judge never discussed this requirement, we are without the benefit of his thinking. Plaintiff, at least as far as the record shows, made no effort at all to obtain the opinion of another doctor so we do not have to determine whether a reasonable effort was made. The amount at stake here was $160,000, which normally should produce some kind of an effort to take up the slack caused by the death of an important witness.

Congress "intended that the residual hearsay exceptions will be used very rarely, and only in exceptional circumstances." . . . The requirements of part (B) of the rule cannot be ignored . . . .

We find that the requirements of Fed. R. Evid. 807(B) were not complied with and, therefore, the district court erred in admitting the letter.

[5] Pretrial Notice

Although courts generally enforce the requirement of pretrial notice, they occasionally relax or excuse it. Most courts have interpreted the pretrial notice requirement flexibly, in light of its express policy of providing a party with a fair opportunity to meet the proffered evidence. The failure to give pretrial notice has been excused if the proffering party was not at fault (because he could not have anticipated the need to use the evidence) and if the adverse party was deemed to have had sufficient opportunity to prepare for and contest the use of the evidence (for example, because he was offered a continuance, did not request a continuance, or had the statement in advance). *See, e.g., United States v. Obayagbona*, 627 F. Supp. 329, 340 (E.D.N.Y. 1985) (by declining to accept a continuance in order to prepare to meet the evidence, the party waived any objection to a lack of notice); *Furtado v. Bishop*, 604 F.2d 80, 92 (1st Cir. 1979) (because the opposing party had been in possession of the deceased attorney's affidavit for years, the court concluded that lack of pretrial notice was harmless).

[6] Scope of Residual Exception

Will the residual exception become an open-ended provision through which many statements nearly missing the elements of the traditional exception will become admissible? Although the language of the exception itself indicates this result, the legislative history indicates that Congress intended the scope of the residual exceptions to be very narrow and their use infrequent.

When originally proposed to Congress, the residual exceptions provided for the introduction of any statements "not specifically covered by any of the foregoing exceptions but having comparable circumstantial guarantees of trustworthiness." The House Judiciary Committee rejected this broad formulation of the exceptions and recommended their deletion. It did so on the belief that such broad discretionary exceptions to the hearsay rule would inject "too much uncertainty into the law of evidence" and would impair "the ability of practitioners to prepare for trial."[87] In addition, the House Judiciary Committee concluded that Rule 102, which directs courts to construe the rules of evidence so as to promote "growth and development," provided judges with sufficient flexibility to admit "good" hearsay that did not qualify for admission under the traditional rules.

The Senate Judiciary Committee had a different view. Although it acknowledged that Rule 102 gave judges authority to admit otherwise inadmissible hearsay, the Committee concluded that the discretion that the rule provided was too narrow. The Committee feared that without an explicit grant of authority to admit reliable hearsay evidence, judges would resort to tortured interpretations of the enumerated hearsay exceptions to deal with the reliable hearsay that would otherwise be inadmissible.[88] The Senate commented that as a consequence, courts would distort the enumerated exceptions beyond recognition, thereby creating the same uncertainty that the House Committee feared would result from inclusion of a discretionary exception in the rules. The Senate Committee acknowledged that an overly broad residual exception could emasculate the hearsay rule and the recognized exceptions or vitiate the rationale behind codification of the rules — consistency and predictability. The Senate Committee, therefore, reinstated the exception but attempted to limit its scope by adding the requirements that the statements be offered as evidence of a material fact, "be more probative on the point for which it is offered than other reasonably available evidence," and that the "admission of the evidence serve the general purpose of the rules and be in the interest of justice." In so doing, the Senate Committee emphasized that it intended courts to use the exception sparingly:

> It is intended that the residual hearsay exceptions will be used very rarely, and only in exceptional circumstances. The committee does not intend to establish a broad license for trial judges to admit hearsay statements that do not fall within one of the other exceptions contained in rules 803 and 804(b). The residual exceptions are not meant to authorize major judicial revisions of the hearsay rule, including its present exceptions. Such major revisions are best accomplished by legislative actions. It is intended that in any case in which evidence is sought to be admitted under these subsections, the trial judge will exercise no less care, reflection and caution than the courts did under the common law in establishing the now-recognized exceptions to the hearsay rule. S. REP. NO. 1277, 93d Cong., 2d Sess. 20 (1977).

---

[87] H.R. Rep. No. 650, 93d Cong., 1st Sess. 4, 5–6 (1973).

[88] S. Rep. No. 1277, 93d Cong., 2d Sess. 19 (1973).

Thereafter, the House-Senate Conference Committee adopted the Senate Committee view with the addition of the requirement that the proponent give pretrial notice to the adverse party, and Congress enacted the rule in this recommended form.

The inconsistency between the language of the rule and its legislative history has led to a debate over the scope of the exception among courts. This is reflected in the following opinions in *United States v. AT&T*, and *United States v. American Cyanamid Co.*

UNITED STATES v. AT & T
United States District Court, District of Columbia
516 F. Supp. 1237 (1981)

MEMORANDUM

HAROLD H. GREENE, DISTRICT JUDGE.

On May 11, 1981, defendants raised the issue of the admissibility of certain so-called "third party" documents, that is, documents which either were authored by employees or agents of companies that are in competition with defendants or purport to recount statements made by such employees or agents. The statements contained in these documents would, of course, be admissible in evidence as "admissions" under Rule 801(d)(2) of the Federal Rules of Evidence were these companies themselves parties to this action, and the question examined in this Memorandum is whether they should be admitted here even though the companies are not parties herein.

In response to the Court's request to the parties to brief this issue, defendants have proposed two possible routes for the admissibility of these statements: first, that the documents be received in evidence as admissions of a party opponent under Rule 801(d)(2); and second, that they be received under the residual exception to the hearsay rule, [Rule 807].

After having considered the memoranda filed by both parties, the Court has determined that it has sufficient authority to admit most of these documents pursuant to the residual exceptions to the hearsay rule. However, an additional procedure is being established for the admission of these documents, in order to avoid any possibility of unfairness to the government or to nonparties, and to ensure that all documents will be presented to the Court in their most useful and meaningful context.

I.

Defendants argue that the government has adopted, and purports to believe in, the statements made by companies such as MCI, Litton, and others upon whose active assistance it appears to have relied in presenting its case, and that these statements should therefore be admitted as "adoptive admissions" by the government under Rule 801(2)(B).

In order to demonstrate that the government has "adopted" the statement of a third party, defendants must show that it somehow "has manifested [its] adoption or belief in [the statement's] truth." . . . To meet this burden, defendants have primarily pointed to statements by the government to the effect that these third parties and the government are "aligned in interest" with regard to this case.

It is no doubt true that the government shares many common interests with the competitors of AT&T in this suit. This circumstance alone does not, however, entail the automatic adoption by the government of every relevant document originating in the files of these competitors. As stated by the Court of Appeals of this Circuit:

The Government has the same entitlement as any other party to assistance from those sharing common interests, whatever their motives. This is clearly true in antitrust cases, where Congress has established a policy of private enforcement to supplement governmental action against offenders. This policy should not be thwarted by allowing an alleged antitrust offender to acquire the trial preparations of his private adversaries when they cooperate with Government lawyers in a related suit by the Justice Department. *United States v. American Telephone and Telegraph Company*, 642 F.2d 1285 at 1300 (D.C. Cir. 1980).

This congressional policy would similarly be thwarted were the Court to allow the alleged antritrust offender to introduce statements by private parties as admissions against the government merely because these parties have cooperated with the government's lawyers in the preparations for this suit. The government cannot be held to have adopted the contents of documents in the files of others, no matter how aligned in interest they might be, without specific proof of such adoption — proof that, as the Court understands it, is not present here.

II.

Defendants have also proposed the admission of these third party documents under Rule [807].[89] . . . At the Court's request, defendants have submitted a sampling of third party documents for consideration under these rules. These documents are organized into seven broad categories: (1) contemporaneous memoranda reflecting discussions in meetings or telephone conversations with or by adverse third parties;[90] (2) internal memoranda of adverse third parties; (3) diaries and calendars of adverse third parties; (4) correspondence (letters from adverse third parties); (5) public statements by adverse third parties; (6) deposition testimony in other cases; and (7) consultants' reports supplied to adverse third parties.

No case law has been brought to the Court's attention either supporting or prohibiting admissibility of third-party documents of these types pursuant to Subsection 24, and indeed both sides have candidly conceded that no direct precedent exists to sustain their respective positions. The Court accordingly is writing on a more or less of a clean slate in considering the advisability of admitting

---

[89] (Court's original footnote 1.) For purposes of clarity and simplicity, these two Rules will hereinafter generally be referred to as Subsection 24.

[90] (Court's original footnote 2.) That is, AT&T's competitors.

such documents under this rubric. For a number of interrelated reasons, the Court has concluded that it has sufficient authority and it will admit these documents under Subsection 24 if there are circumstantial guarantees of their trustworthiness.[91]

First. There obviously is a need for the Court to have a detailed picture of the circumstances surrounding the grievances of AT&T's competitors with the Bell System from the defendant's point of view, just as the Court has received such a picture from the government's point of view. Thus, the admission of these documents would contribute to the ultimate goal of the determination of the truth through the adversary process, and would thereby serve the interests of justice. . . . Second. The laying of a foundation for an extremely large number of documents by means of live testimony would be cumbersome, unnecessarily time-consuming, and would no doubt interfere with the orderly presentation of an already complicated case.[92] Third. Subsection 24 does not represent a mere surplusage or useless appendage to the Rules; it has a significant purpose and substantial vitality of its own, and that is "to encourage the progressive growth and development of federal evidentiary law by giving courts the flexibility to deal with new evidentiary situations which may not be pigeon-holed elsewhere." *United States v. Mathis*, 559 F.2d 294, 299 (5th Cir. 1977). . . . If the subsection is not to be applied to the present situation in the general fashion in which the Court proposes to apply it (*see below*), it is difficult to see where and to what purpose it might ever be applied. Fourth. Although, as noted *above*, the companies which originated the documents are not sufficiently synonymous with the plaintiff in this case to permit their receipt in evidence under Rule 801(d)(2)(B), the fact is that this plaintiff (the government) has largely built its case around charges made and records supplied, directly or indirectly, by these companies. That fact both tends to sustain the trustworthiness of the documents and to supply a significant additional element of fairness to use of the Subsection 24 procedure. Fifth. This case is both vast and complex and there is, certainly, a public interest in proceeding with and concluding it without the distractions of a pursuit of technical byways which add nothing substantive to the reliability of the evidence being presented. In such a case, in short, the Court would not be fulfilling its responsibility if it were not to pursue the goal of procedural fairness with a modicum of innovation . . . .

On these various bases, the Court has concluded that, assuming trustworthiness (*see below*), fairness to the government can be achieved without requiring defendants to produce hundreds upon hundreds of additional witnesses solely for the purpose of effecting the admission of documents the authenticity of which has not been questioned.

---

[91] (Court's original footnote 3.) As for the requirements of materiality and relative probativeness of subparagraphs (A) and (B) of Subsection 24, the Court finds the documents in the sampling clearly to be material to issues that have been raised in the government's case and that are expected to be raised in the defendant's case. The Court also finds that the efforts which defendants would have to expend in order to obtain other evidence of probativeness comparable to these third party documents would be unreasonable in light of the flexibility the Court has shown to the government in allowing various documents and depositions into evidence without specific, technical foundation.

[92] (Court's original footnote 4.) The Court expresses no opinion on the question whether a procedure similar to that adopted here would be appropriate in a less massive case.

III.

In order to determine whether adequate guarantees of trustworthiness exist, the Court has examined the sampling of documents submitted by defendants to determine whether indications of reliability recognized in some manner by the drafters of the Federal Rules of Evidence are present.

In this regard, for the documents in category (1) (contemporaneous memoranda reflecting discussions in meetings or telephone conversations), two questions must be answered — first, do these memorandum reliably represent what was said at the meeting or conversation? Second, are the substantive statements made in the course of the meeting or conversation themselves trustworthy?

Relevant to the reliability of the memoranda themselves is Rule 803(1), which excepts from the hearsay rule statements "describing or explaining an event or condition made while the declarant was perceiving the event or condition, or immediately thereafter." The rationale behind this exception, as stated in the Notes of the Advisory Committee on the Proposed Rules, is that the "substantial contemporaneity of event and statement negate the likelihood of deliberate or conscious misrepresentation." The contemporaneity of these memoranda and the meetings or conversations which they represent appears to be a guarantee of reliability of similar magnitude for the purposes of Subsection 24.

Rule 804(b)(3) excepts from the hearsay rule a statement which "at the time of its making . . . so far tended . . . to render invalid a claim by him against another, that a reasonable man in his position would not have made the statement unless he believed it to be true." Although the substantive statements recorded in these memoranda probably would not fall within the letter of this exception, the theory which underlies is nevertheless instructive. The Advisory Committee stated that "the circumstantial guaranty of reliability for declarations against interest is the assumption that persons do not make statements which are damaging to themselves unless satisfied for good reason that they are true." The substance of these statements contained in the three types of documents within defendants' category (1) — informal notes of conversations or meetings internal to adverse third parties, formal minutes of meetings between employees of adverse parties, and "external" memoranda by neutral third parties pertaining to their meetings with adverse third parties (to the extent these memoranda recount statements by the adverse third parties) — are all circumstantially reliable under the "declaration against interest" theory of the Advisory Committee. . . . In sum, the documents in question appear reliably to represent what was said in the conversations they record and the statements made in the course of these conversations are also sufficiently trustworthy for admissibility.[93]

While the parallels are not exact, the basic theory which underlies the admissibility under Subsection 24 of the documents in category (1) is also applicable to the following additional categories of documents: the internal memoranda of adverse third parties (category (2)); diaries and calendars of adverse third parties (category

---

[93] (Court's original footnote 8.) The government is, of course, free to contradict these statements by evidence of its own on rebuttal.

(3));[94] correspondence (category (4));[95] and public statements made by adverse third parties (category (5)). With respect to all of these categories, similar circumstantial guarantees of trustworthiness for admissibility under the residual exceptions to the hearsay rule are present, and documents in these categories will accordingly be likewise received in evidence. The sixth category, deposition testimony by employees of adverse third parties taken in conjunction with other litigation, contains additional circumstantial guarantees of trustworthiness in that it was taken under oath subject to penalties for perjury, and such depositions will also be admitted.

Only one of the seven categories of documents lacks similar guarantees of trustworthiness under Subsection 24: the consultants' reports supplied to third parties (category 7). The Court has no way of evaluating the reliability of the studies performed by these consultants unless the authors of the studies are subject to direct and cross examination. Accordingly, it will not admit such documents under the residual exceptions to the hearsay rule.

UNITED STATES v. AMERICAN CYANAMID CO.

United States District Court, Southern District of New York
427 F. Supp. 859 (1977)

MEMORANDUM AND ORDER

BRIEANT, DISTRICT JUDGE.

The United States seeks an order pursuant to Rule 42(b), F. R. Crim. P., adjudging American Cyanamid Company ("Cyanamid") in criminal contempt for the willful violation of a Consent Decree, and the Final Judgment filed pursuant thereto on August 4, 1964, and of the Supplemental Order amending this Final Judgment, filed on May 27, 1969.

Cyanamid is alleged to have committed a criminal contempt by manufacturing and/or importing in excess of thirty million (30,000,000) pounds of melanine during a period when the production capacity of nonconspiratorial melanine producers had not increased by the required twenty-five million pounds, all in violation of the amended decree. . . . The cause was tried before me on May 3 and 6, 1976. Defendant waived a jury.

At the close of the trial the Government moved to strike a great number of Cyanamid's exhibits which were introduced into evidence subject to the Government's motion. As a result, the trial record was left open pending a decision from

---

[94] (Court's original footnote 9.) These also contain some additional measure of reliability in that they are similar to business records, exempted from the hearsay rule under Rule 803(6). Among the elements of "unusual reliability" of business records found by the Advisory Committee include "regularity and continuity which produce habits of precision" and "actual experience of business in relying on them." These elements would be present to some degree in diaries and calendars.

[95] (Court's original footnote 10.) But only to the extent that the letters were authored by an employee or agent of an adverse third party.

this Court as to the admissibility of these exhibits. It was agreed that in the event any of the contested exhibits were admitted, the Government would be allowed, if it wished, the opportunity to rebut the material contained therein. If, however, all of the documents are excluded, then the trial record will be closed when this ruling is issued.

The Court is therefore constrained to decide the admissibility issue prior to and separately from its decision as to whether the guilt of the defendant has been proved beyond a reasonable doubt. Since Cyanamid offered its evidence in eight individual and distinct groups, it is reasonable to rule separately with respect to each group.

*   *   *

[After considering various objections to the admissibility of the first five groups of evidence, the court went on to consider the admissibility of Group 6 under Rule [807.]]

[T]he exhibits of Group 6 [consist] of correspondence between the various melamine producers and the Department of Justice. This group contains seventeen documents of which two were received without objection. Cyanamid offers these exhibits as tending to establish the absence of any industry-wide definition of the term "production capacity." The majority of these exhibits are letters to the Department of Justice, by melamine producers, in response to a Departmental inquiry as to the accepted industry use of the term "production capacity." Defendant contends that these exhibits tend to prove that no industry-wide definition of the term "production capacity" existed in 1972.

The Government has objected to the receipt of these exhibits on the ground of hearsay and best evidence. If Cyanamid desired to prove the lack of an accepted industry definition of "production capacity," the Government argues, it could call its competitors' employees as witnesses and question them concerning their use of this term. The Government also objects to the admission of these exhibits on the ground of relevance.

The Government's objections are overruled and the motion to strike the exhibits of Group 6 is denied. I find that these exhibits do contain hearsay, but are admissible under Rule [807] of the Federal Rules of Evidence, 28 U.S.C. Rule [807], which is the catch-all exception to the hearsay rule. This exception is applicable when an exhibit contains hearsay and is not admissible under any of the specified exceptions to the Rule. Rule [807] provides that such evidence is admissible it if has equivalent circumstantial guarantees of trustworthiness (as required by all exceptions to the Rule), and if it meets four specified requirements:

(A) the statement is offered as evidence of a material fact;

(B) the statement is more probative on the point for which it is offered than any other evidence which the proponent can procure through reasonable efforts; and

(C) the general purpose of these rules and the interests of justice will best be served by the admission of the statement into evidence. In addition, the proponent must give his adversary notice, sufficiently in advance of trial, of his intention to offer the evidence.

The exhibits of Group 6 meet the trustworthiness requirement since they are copies of letters written to the Department of Justice. These exhibits also meet the standards of relevancy in that they tend to prove or disprove a material factual proposition, namely, whether the defendant willfully violated the terms of the Final Judgment as amended. Since these exhibits may tend to establish that there was no accepted industry-wide definition of the term "production capacity," they may lend weight to Cyanamid's denial of a *willful* violation of the Final Judgment as amended. It would be unnecessarily expensive and time-consuming to call witnesses, from various remote places to come here to testify as to what they thought in 1972. The most accurate reflection of their thoughts in 1972 are their contemporaneous letters. Finally, the Government does not dispute the adequacy of notices as to Cyanamid's intention to offer these exhibits in evidence . . . .

The Government argued at the trial, that the hearsay exception of Rule [807] was meant to apply only in exceptional cases. This argument is based on a reading of the Senate Judiciary Committee Report which limits the application of this section to exceptional cases. Neither the Rule, nor the cases in this Circuit interpreting the Rule, however, impose any express limitation concerning exceptional cases. To every criminal defendant, his own case is exceptional. Rule 807 establishes sufficient express criteria which must be satisfied before an item of hearsay will be admissible. Since the exhibits listed above conform to these criteria, they should be received. There is no requirement that the Court find a case to be "exceptional," whatever that means, in order to receive any evidence. To imply such a provision, as suggested by the Judicial Committee, *above*, would negate the requirement of Rule 102, F.R.Evid. that "[t]hese rules shall be construed to secure fairness in administration, elimination of unjustifiable expense and delay, and promotion of growth and development of the law of evidence to the end that the truth may be ascertained and proceedings justly determined." And it would bring into each trial, the foot of the Chancellor, an historical enemy of our liberties.[96]

EXERCISES

1. Investor secured a loan from Bank to purchase an undeveloped parcel of land and turn it into a residential subdivision. Investor knew that the parcel lacked dedicated access to any public road, but planned to obtain an easement from one of the adjoining property owners. Investor was unsuccessful in securing an easement, and thus was unable to develop the land. Investor then filed a claim under his insurance policy covering financial loss incurred due to a "lack of right of access to and from the land." The insurance company refused the claim, and the parties proceeded to trial. The central issue at trial is whether Bank knew at the time that it made the loan to Investor that the parcel did not abut a public road and thus Bank knowingly assumed the risk that the parcel could not be developed. The insurance

---

[96] (Court's original footnote 4.) As long ago as 1818, Lord Chancellor Eldon wrote that . . . .

"I cannot agree that the doctrines of this Court are to be changed with every succeeding Judge. Nothing would inflict on me greater pain in quitting this place, than the recollection that I had done anything to justify the reproach that the equity of this Court varies like the Chancellor's foot."

company seeks to offer a sworn affidavit from the Bank's president (who is now deceased) declaring "I was aware that the tract appeared to be landlocked, but I was told by Investor that he was pursuing and expected to obtain an easement to the highway." Both parties agree that there is no other witness or documentary evidence to establish Bank's knowledge. Investor objects to the affidavit on hearsay grounds. Should the Bank president's affidavit be admissible under the residual exception?

2. Albert wrote and copyrighted a hit gospel song, entitled "I'll Fly Away." Following Albert's death, several potential heirs filed suit to determine who should inherit the copyright. The court must now determine whether Albert created the song as a "work for hire" while working at Hartford Music. One party seeks to offer into evidence a recording of a phone conversation between Albert and his son several years after the creation of the song, in which Albert stated: "I got started at Hartford Music, which is defunct now. I sold some songs to Hartford including 'I'll Fly Away' and two others." All parties agree that the statement by Albert is hearsay. The trial judge however wants to admit the recording under the residual exception to hearsay. Draft a one-paragraph memorandum in support of the judge's decision.

Chapter 6

CROSS-EXAMINATION AND IMPEACHMENT

§ 6.01 INTRODUCTION

Cross-examination is the second stage in the examination of witnesses. It provides the opponent the opportunity to further explore and clarify those matters that the proponent has raised during the direct examination of the witness, and to plant the seeds of doubt in the fact finder's mind regarding the witness' credibility and the reliability of the witness' testimony. This chapter will explore the purposes and general approaches to cross-examination. We will first examine the restrictions that courts have imposed on impeachment through the use of character evidence (a topic that was examined in Chapter 3 in conjunction with the discussion on proving the past conduct of parties to the litigation). This chapter explores the expanded means by which character can be proved for impeachment purposes through reputation, opinion, and prior specific conduct evidence (both in the form of specific acts and convictions for those acts). Thereafter we will examine the most common means of witness impeachment: prior inconsistent statements, bias, and psychiatric conditions.

[A] Rule 611(b) — Scope of Cross-Examination

Under Rule 611(b), courts generally limit the scope of cross-examination to the scope of direct. Only subjects that a proponent raises explicitly or by implication on direct can be explored on cross. This rule does not apply to the issue of a witness' credibility. Consistent with the common law, Rule 611(b) provides: "Cross-examination should be limited to the subject matter of the direct examination and matters affecting credibility of the witness."

[B] Rule 607 — Who May Impeach?

Under Rule 607, a party may impeach any witness. Unlike the common law, parties no longer vouch for the credibility of the witnesses they call. Under the common law, a party could impeach her own witness only if the witness' testimony surprised her (if the party reasonably believed that the witness would have testified differently) and was damaging (as opposed to being just disappointing). These requirements served to preclude a party from calling a witness knowing that the witness would deny the prior statement and testify inconsistently, solely for the purpose of placing before the jury the prior statement, with the expectation that the jury would improperly use it as substantive evidence in violation of the hearsay rule. Inasmuch as neither Rules 607 nor 613 explicitly require surprise and damage as prerequisites to the use of prior inconsistent statements to impeach one's own witness, does this mean that the federal rules have abolished those requirements and protections? The answer is not clear.

This interpretive problem exists because Congress promulgated Rules 607 and 613 to complement Rule 801(d)(1)(A) as originally proposed, which excluded *all* prior inconsistent statements from the definition of hearsay, not just those made under oath in a prior proceeding. If all prior inconsistent statements were admissible for their substantive truth, there would be no need for protection against their substantive use. With the amendment of Rule 801(d)(1)(A), however, Congress recognized the need for protection against improper use of prior inconsistent statements against one's own witnesses. Congress did not, however, resurrect such protections by amending Rules 607 and 613 to include them, at least not explicitly.

Professor Graham persuasively argues that the court should incorporate the common law and read the requirements of surprise and damage into Rule 607. Alternatively, he argues that the courts could impose such requirements through Rule 403, balancing the probative value and potential prejudicial effect of prior inconsistent statements. *See* Graham, *Examination of a Party's Own Witness Under the Federal Rules of Evidence: A Promise Unfulfilled*, 54 TEX. L. REV. 917, 977–83 (1976). In a later clarification of his position, Professor Graham criticized the use of the case-by-case approach under Rule 403 because it would lead to inconsistent results. See Graham, *The Relationship Among Federal Rules of Evidence 607, 801(d)(1)(A), and 403: A Reply to Weinstein's Evidence*, 55 TEX. L. REV. 573 (1977). For a helpful student note in which three approaches to the resolution of this problem are examined, see *Impeachment with an Unsworn Prior Inconsistent Statement as Subterfuge*, 28 WM. & MARY L. REV. 295 (1987).

As explained in *United States v. Webster*, in lieu of imposing a requirement of surprise on parties seeking to impeach their own witnesses, the courts have adopted a good-faith standard.

UNITED STATES v. WEBSTER
United States Court of Appeals, Seventh Circuit
734 F.2d 1191 (1984)

POSNER, CIRCUIT JUDGE.

The defendant, Webster, was convicted of aiding and abetting the robbery of a federally insured bank and receiving stolen bank funds, was sentenced to nine years in prison, and appeals. Only one issue need be discussed. The government called the bank robber, King (who had pleaded guilty and been given a long prison term), as a witness against Webster. King gave testimony that if believed would have exculpated the defendant, whereupon the government introduced prior inconsistent statements that King had given the FBI inculpating Webster. Although the court instructed the jury that it could consider the statements only for purposes of impeachment, Webster argues that this was not good enough, that the government should not be allowed to get inadmissible evidence before the jury by calling a hostile witness and then using his out-of-court statements, which would otherwise be inadmissible hearsay, to impeach him.

Rule 607 of the Federal Rules of Evidence provides: "The credibility of a witness may be attacked by any party, including the party calling him." But it would be an abuse of the rule, in a criminal case, for the prosecution to call a witness that it knew would not give it useful evidence, just so it could introduce hearsay evidence against the defendant in the hope that the jury would miss the subtle distinction between impeachment and substantive evidence — or, if it didn't miss it, would ignore it. The purpose would not be to impeach the witness but to put in hearsay as substantive evidence against the defendant, which Rule 607 does not contemplate or authorize. We thus agree that "impeachment by prior inconsistent statement may not be permitted where employed as a mere subterfuge to get before the jury evidence not otherwise admissible." *United States v. Morlang*, 531 F.2d 183, 190 (4th Cir. 1975). Although *Morlang* was decided before the Federal Rules of Evidence became effective, the limitation that we have quoted on the prosecutor's rights under Rule 607 has been accepted in all circuits that have considered the issue. . . .

But it is quite plain that there was no bad faith here. Before the prosecutor called King to the stand she asked the judge to allow her to examine him outside the presence of the jury, because she did not know what he would say. The defendant's counsel objected and the voir dire was not held. We do not see how in these circumstances it can be thought that the prosecutor put King on the stand knowing he would give no useful evidence. If she had known that, she would not have offered to voir dire him, as the voir dire would have provided a foundation for defense counsel to object, under *Morlang*, to the admission of King's prior inconsistent statements.

Webster urges us, on the authority of GRAHAM, HANDBOOK OF FEDERAL EVIDENCE § 607.3 (1981 and Supp. 1983), to go beyond the good-faith standard and hold that the government may not impeach a witness with his prior inconsistent statements unless it is surprised and harmed by the witness's testimony. But we think it would be a mistake to graft such a requirement to Rule 607, even if such a graft would be within the power of judicial interpretation of the rule. Suppose the government called an adverse witness that it thought would give evidence both helpful and harmful to it, but it also thought that the harmful aspect could be nullified by introducing the witness's prior inconsistent statement. As there would be no element of surprise, Professor Graham would forbid the introduction of the prior statement; yet we are at a loss to understand why the government should be put to the choice between the Scylla of forgoing impeachment and the Charybdis of not calling at all a witness from whom it expects to elicit genuinely helpful evidence. The good-faith standard strikes a better balance; and it is always open to the defendant to argue that the probative value of the evidence offered to impeach the witness is clearly outweighed by the prejudicial impact it might have on the jury, because the jury would have difficulty confining use of the evidence to impeachment. See Fed. R. Evid. 403.

The judgment of conviction is

Affirmed.

Other circuits have agreed with *Webster. See United States v. Gomez-Gallardo*, 915 F.2d 553 (9th Cir. 1990); *United States v. Peterman*, 841 F.2d 1474 (10th Cir. 1988). *United States v. Johnson*, 802 F.2d 1459 (D.C. Cir. 1986); *United States v. Miller*, 664 F.2d 94, 97 (5th Cir. 1981), cert. denied, 459 U.S. 854 (1982); *United States v. DeLillo*, 620 F.2d 939, 946 (2d Cir.), *cert. denied*, 449 U.S. 835 (1980); *Whitehurst v. Wright*, 592 F.2d 834, 839–840 (5th Cir. 1979); *United States v. Morlang*, 531 F.2d 183, 190 (4th Cir. 1975).

Illustrative of when the primary purpose in calling the witness will be found to be a subterfuge for getting inadmissible evidence before the jury is *United States v. Hogan*, 763 F.2d 697 (5th Cir. 1985). The court concluded that the Government was not entitled to assume that the witness called by it would give favorable testimony that was consistent with his prior statement because he had already testified inconsistently three times while under oath and had been convicted of perjury.

The government, like all other parties in litigation, may impeach its own witnesses. This possibility can give rise to a special problem when the witness is a codefendant who previously has been convicted of the offense for which the defendant is being tried. Although this most recent conviction may be admissible under Rule 609 for impeachment purposes, it is possible that when used for that limited purpose the jury will give it a broader use — construing it as evidence of the defendant's guilt. Accordingly, every circuit has adopted the rule that evidence that is inadmissible for substantive purposes may not be purposely introduced under the pretense of impeachment. *See United States v. Peterman*, 841 F.2d 1474, 1479 n.3 (10th Cir. 1988). As one court has observed:

> [I]t would be an abuse of [Rule 607], in a criminal case, for the prosecution to call a witness that it knew would not give it useful evidence, just so it could introduce hearsay evidence against the defendant in the hope that the jury would miss the subtle distinction between impeachment and substantive evidence — or, if it didn't miss it, would ignore it.

United States v. Webster, 734 F.2d 1191, 1192 (7th Cir. 1984) (case excerpted above). The rule adopted by the *Peterman* court was that the prosecution "may not introduce evidence 'under the guise of impeachment for the *primary* purpose of placing before the jury substantive evidence which is not otherwise admissible.' " 841 F.2d at 1479.

§ 6.02   IMPEACHMENT: CHARACTER EVIDENCE

[A]   The Common Law

[1]   Admissibility of Character Evidence for Impeachment Purposes

As discussed in Chapter Three on Character Evidence, the common law prohibits the use of evidence of an individual's character (whether in the form of reputation, opinion, or prior act testimony) to prove that the individual acted in conformity with that character. Parties cannot use character evidence to establish an individual's propensity from which the individual's conduct can be inferred. For example, one could not prove that the defendant had a good character trait for peacefulness or law-abidingness to convince the finder of facts that the defendant did not damage the plaintiff's property. The reasons for this prohibition are twofold. First, courts believe that character evidence has limited probative value. Second, courts do not believe that the limited probative value of character evidence justifies the risk that the jury will improperly use it.

Impeaching the witnesses' credibility with character evidence is an exception to this general prohibition. In all litigation, the parties can attack or support the witnesses' credibility — their propensity to tell the truth — through the introduction of reputation evidence addressed to the witnesses' character trait for truth and veracity. Courts do not limit the use of character evidence that impeaches a witness' credibility, however, to reputation testimony. Subject to limitations, a party may also attack or support a witness' credibility through evidence of specific instances of conduct.

Courts have justified this impeachment exception to the general inadmissibility of character evidence on two grounds. First, the focus of the character impeachment evidence is on the witness' *present conduct* — whether the witness is telling the truth while testifying under oath — as opposed to the witness' conduct in the past. Because such evidence relates to conduct occurring in the presence of the finder of facts, demeanor during testimony enhances the evidence's probative value. Second, the potential for prejudice from the finder of facts' improper use of character impeachment evidence (for example, using such evidence as evidence of the defendant's present culpability) is less because the evidence is generally offered against witnesses and not the accused. Of course, this potential for prejudice will be lessened only if the witness against whom the character impeachment evidence is used is not the defendant testifying in her own defense.

[2] Reputation Testimony

[a]   Limitations on Timing and Manner of Presentation

Parties may call character witnesses to challenge or reinforce the credibility of all witnesses, including that of other character witnesses. There are, however, several limitations on the timing and manner of presentation of this kind of evidence. First, before the proponent may call character witnesses to bolster a witness' credibility, the opponent must first attack that witness' credibility. This attack can be through the testimony of unfavorable character witnesses or other kinds of attacks, such as vigorous cross-examination, that suggest that the witness is lying. Second, courts limit the testimony of character witnesses to reputation evidence. Courts will not permit a character witness to offer her personal opinion about the credibility of a preceding witness. Despite this prevailing limitation, it has been the common, albeit illogical, practice in many courts, to allow the character/credibility witness to respond to the question, "Would you believe this person under oath?" *See, e.g., United States v. Lollar*, 606 F.2d 587, 588–589 (5th

Cir. 1979). Third, the reputation testimony that a character/credibility witness offers must be limited to the preceding witness' character trait for truth and veracity because that is the specific trait that is relevant to credibility. Diagram 6-1 illustrates these rules as well as limitations on when and how parties can introduce character evidence to impeach or reinforce witnesses' credibility during the various stages of a trial.

[b]   Cross-Examining the Reputation Witness

An individual's reputation represents the community's collective opinion or judgment of that individual. The community establishes an individual's reputation through the statements that particular members of that community make about that individual. Consequently, if a person is a qualified and credible reputation witness, the witness will not only know the people who know the individual in question, but she will also be familiar with what those people are saying about that individual. Therefore, on cross-examination, a party may ask a reputation witness whether the witness "has heard" of certain things that the individual has done or is reputed as having done. If the witness has not heard of these things, her credibility as a reputation witness is diminished.

Courts have placed two limitations on this method of cross-examining reputation witnesses. First, the cross-examiner must have a good-faith basis for believing that the conduct about which she asks has a basis in fact. Second, the conduct about which the cross-examiner inquires must be relevant to the character trait to which the reputation witness has testified. If the reputation witness has testified concerning a prior witness' credibility, of course, the relevant character trait would be truth and veracity. Diagram 6-2 illustrates the application of these two limitations on the cross-examination of reputation witnesses.

DIAGRAM 6–1

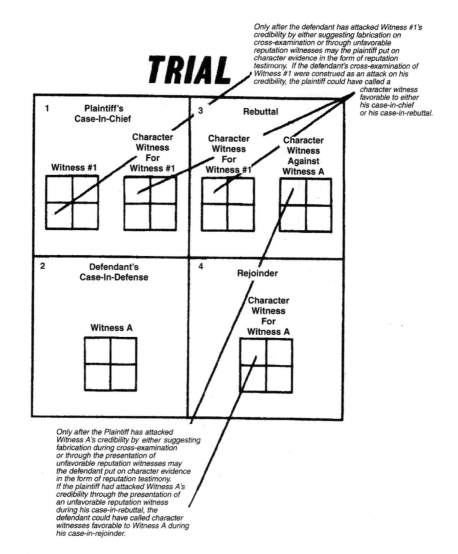

Only after the defendant has attacked Witness #1's credibility by either suggesting fabrication on cross-examination or through unfavorable reputation witnesses may the plaintiff put on character evidence in the form of reputation testimony. If the defendant's cross-examination of Witness #1 were construed as an attack on his credibility, the plaintiff could have called a character witness favorable to either his case-in-chief or his case-in-rebuttal.

TRIAL

1 **Plaintiff's Case-In-Chief**

Character Witness For Witness #1

Witness #1

3 **Rebuttal**

Character Witness For Witness #1

Character Witness Against Witness A

2 **Defendant's Case-In-Defense**

Witness A

4 **Rejoinder**

Character Witness For Witness A

Only after the Plaintiff has attacked Witness A's credibility by either suggesting fabrication during cross-examination or through the presentation of unfavorable reputation witnesses may the defendant put on character evidence in the form of reputation testimony. If the plaintiff had attacked Witness A's credibility through the presentation of an unfavorable reputation witness during his case-in-rebuttal, the defendant could have called character witnesses favorable to Witness A during his case-in-rejoinder.

DIAGRAM 6–2

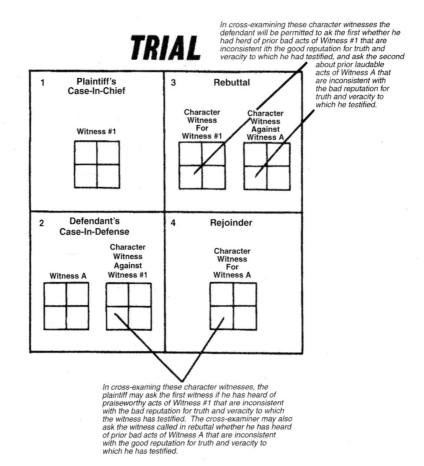

In cross-examining these character witnesses the defendant will be permitted to ak the first whether he had herd of prior bad acts of Witness #1 that are inconsistent ith the good reputation for truth and veracity to which he had testified, and ask the second about prior laudable acts of Witness A that are inconsistent with the bad reputation for truth and veracity to which he testified.

In cross-examing these character witnesses, the plaintiff may ask the first witness if he has heard of praiseworthy acts of Witness #1 that are inconsistent with the bad reputation for truth and veracity to which the witness has testified. The cross-examiner may also ask the witness called in rebuttal whether he has heard of prior bad acts of Witness A that are inconsistent with the good reputation for truth and veracity to which he has testified.

Note: In each instance where the character witness is being cross-examined, and being asked about prior specific acts that are inconsistent with the character trait for truth and veracity, the exploration of these acts will be limited to the cross-examination. Extrinsic evidence to prove their actual occurence will not be allowed unless, of course, evidence of those acts is admissible under some other theory, and therefore under some other rule.

Two assumptions underlie this line of questioning. One is that the community is aware of the conduct in which the cross-examiner alleges that the preceding witness has engaged. The more important assumption is that the community will have been talking about this conduct. If neither of these assumptions is true, then the reputation witness' failure to have heard of the conduct would not diminish the witness' credibility as a reputation witness. Despite the importance of these two assumptions, courts seldom, if ever, inquire about a basis beyond the factual accuracy of the alleged conduct when determining the admissibility of the line of inquiry. Trial judges virtually never ask what basis the attorney has for believing that the community has been aware of and is talking about the conduct.

[3]   Specific Instances of Conduct

[a]   Admissibility of Prior Specific Instances of Conduct for Impeachment Purposes

As previously mentioned, outside of the impeachment context, if character/propensity evidence is admissible in criminal proceedings, it can be proved only through reputation testimony. Evidence of prior specific instances of conduct to establish a defendant's propensity to act in a particular manner, as evidence of the defendant's past conduct, is inadmissible. This is not true, however, if a party offers character/propensity evidence for impeachment purposes — to prove that a witness is *presently not credible* as she appears before the finder of facts because of her propensity to fabricate or exaggerate. Consequently, a party may offer evidence of a *witness'* prior conduct that reflects on the witness' character trait for truth and veracity to demonstrate that witness' propensity to lie. A party may elicit such evidence during the cross-examination of the witness in question with some limitations (to be discussed below) or through independent testimony from other witnesses when that conduct has resulted in a conviction.

[b]   Inquiries During the Witness' Cross-Examination

The majority of common law jurisdictions permit the cross-examiner to inquire about a testifying witness' prior acts that negatively reflect on the witness' credibility. For example, the cross-examiner could ask a witness, "Is it true that you have failed to report all of your income on your tax returns for the past two years?" Courts limit the cross-examiner, however, to this inquiry. Although the cross-examiner may pursue the matter further with other questions on cross-examination, the cross-examiner cannot present extrinsic evidence to prove that the witness actually did falsify her returns. Consequently, if the witness denies the prior act, the cross-examiner ultimately must "take the witness' answer." Even if the witness' denial is perjurious, courts will not permit the cross-examiner to prove the perjury by calling additional witnesses to the stand. The reason for this limitation is the need to avoid the delay and confusion that would result if the court were to permit the parties to pursue all such matters. Each witness' credibility could give rise to multiple minitrials in order to resolve ancillary factual questions.

Diagram 6-3 illustrates this limitation on inquiries into prior bad acts of witnesses that reflect on credibility.

A strong minority of common law jurisdictions, and most federal courts prior to the adoption of the Federal Rules of Evidence, prohibited any inquiry on cross-examination into a witness' prior conduct if the sole purpose of such an inquiry was to establish that the witness had a bad character trait for truth and veracity. In these jurisdictions, the only exceptions to this prohibition were prior acts that had resulted in the witness' convictions. Providing evidence of prior convictions is a method of challenging a witness' character trait for truth and veracity that is recognized in all jurisdictions.

DIAGRAM 6–3

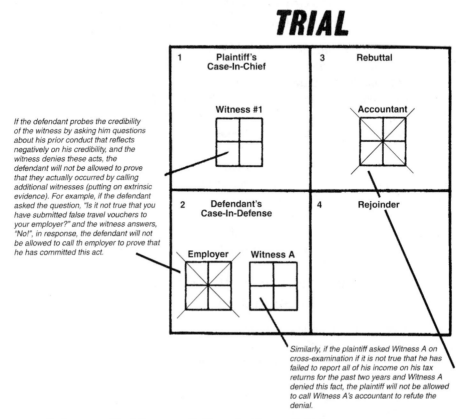

TRIAL

| 1 Plaintiff's Case-In-Chief | 3 Rebuttal |

Witness #1

Accountant

If the defendant probes the credibility of the witness by asking him questions about his prior conduct that reflects negatively on his credibility, and the witness denies these acts, the defendant will not be allowed to prove that they actually occurred by calling additional witnesses (putting on extrinsic evidence). For example, if the defendant asked the question, "Is it not true that you have submitted false travel vouchers to your employer?" and the witness answers, "No!", in response, the defendant will not be allowed to call th employer to prove that he has committed this act.

| 2 Defendant's Case-In-Defense | 4 Rejoinder |

Employer   Witness A

Similarly, if the plaintiff asked Witness A on cross-examination if it is not true that he has failed to report all of his income on his tax returns for the past two years and Witness A denied this fact, the plaintiff will not be allowed to call Witness A's accountant to refute the denial.

[c]   Evidence of Conviction of Crime

If a witness were convicted of a felony grade offense (one involving a potential penalty of death or over one-year imprisonment) or a misdemeanor offense involving moral turpitude (a standard so vague and ambiguous that it can theoretically include all kinds of antisocial conduct), the cross-examiner can ask the witness about these convictions on cross-examination. The cross-examiner can make these inquiries concerning a witness' prior convictions regardless of whether the acts giving rise to the felony convictions have any relevance to the witness' character trait for truth and veracity. Courts believed that merely being convicted of such a serious offense reflected negatively on the witness' willingness to disregard her oath. Not only do courts permit cross-examiners to inquire into a witness' prior felony convictions and convictions involving moral turpitude, but if the witness denies the convictions, the cross-examiner can then prove the prior convictions through extrinsic evidence. Diagram 6-4 illustrates how a witness' prior convictions are used to impeach that witness' credibility.

The topic of prior convictions is explored in greater detail following the materials on specific instances of conduct and Rule 608 of the Federal Rules of Evidence.

DIAGRAM 6-4

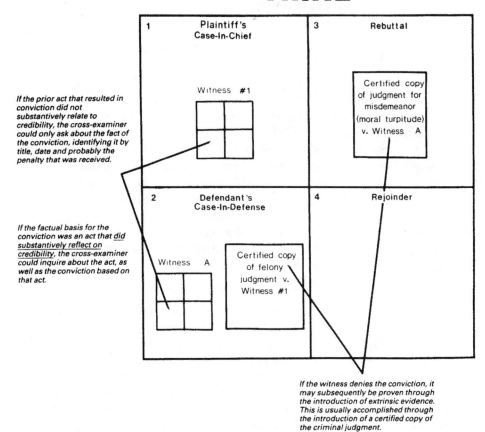

TRIAL

[B]   Rule 608: Evidence of Character and Conduct of Witness

[1]   Reputation or Opinion Character Evidence

A party may offer character evidence under Rule 608(a) in the form of either reputation or opinion testimony. This is consistent with Rule 405, which controls the manner in which character may be proved if it is offered pursuant to Rule 404(a) as circumstantial evidence of past conduct. Both provisions expand the common law that permitted a party to prove character for the purpose of establishing a propensity, regardless of whether it related to past conduct or the present credibility of a witness, only through the use of reputation testimony.

The cross-examination of character witnesses under Rule 608(a) is identical to the examination of character witnesses under Rules 404(a) and 405. Thus, the cross-examiner may ask the reputation witness whether she "has heard" of specific instances of the preceding witness' past conduct that are inconsistent with the direct testimony that the present witness has given about the previous witness' character. The cross-examiner may ask the opinion witness, on the other hand, whether "she knows" about the same prior acts. The only limitation on the cross-examination of either a reputation or an opinion character witness in this regard is that the examiner must have a good faith factual basis for inquiring about the incident, and each incident must be relevant to the character trait to which the character witness has testified — truth and veracity.

[2] Bolstering Credibility After Attack

Rule 608(a)(2) permits a party to bolster a witness' credibility through testimony of character witnesses only after the opponent has attacked the witness' character trait for truthfulness. What kind of "attack" will trigger this use of character evidence to bolster a witness' credibility? Because the rule specifies that an attack "by opinion or reputation evidence *or otherwise*" (emphasis added) will suffice, presumably other attacks authorized by that rule, specifically inquiries on cross-examination about prior specific acts, will be sufficient. It is unclear, however, whether attacks by methods outside of the scope of Rule 608 — for example, through evidence of prior convictions under Rule 609, prior inconsistent statements under Rules 613 and 801(d)(1)(A), or bias — will also suffice as attacks on a witness' credibility for purposes of bolstering her testimony. What is the standard by which this triggering mechanism should be gauged?

The Advisory Committee's Note to Rule 608(a) states:

> Character evidence in support of credibility is admissible under the rule only after the witness' character has first been attacked, as has been the case at common law. . . . The enormous needless consumption of time which a contrary practice would entail justifies the limitation. Opinion or reputation that the witness is untruthful specifically qualifies as an attack under the rule, and evidence of misconduct, including conviction of crime, and of corruption also fall within this category. *Evidence of bias or interest does not.* Whether evidence in the form of contradiction is an attack upon the character of the witness must depend upon the circumstances.

Advisory Committee Note to Rule 608, 56 F.R.D. 183, 268 (1972) (emphasis added).

Why should evidence of a witness' bias not be sufficient as an attack to allow a party to bolster the impugned witness' testimony? Why should courts treat evidence of bias differently than any other contradictory evidence? *Renda v. King*, 347 F.3d 550 (3d Cir. 2003) addresses these questions.

RENDA v. KING
United States Court of Appeals, Third Circuit
347 F.3d 550 (2003)

ROTH, CIRCUIT JUDGE.

In this appeal, defendant Trooper Paul King contends that the District Court abused its discretion in excluding evidence of his good character for truthfulness

. . . . As discussed below, we conclude that the District Court abused its discretion in excluding evidence of King's good character for truthfulness because Renda opened the door for such evidence when she argued that King was corrupt in his conduct of an official police investigation. . . .

*   *   *

I. Facts and Procedural History

This case began with a domestic dispute between Renda and her boyfriend Joe Sonafelt, a Pennsylvania State Trooper . . . . Corporal Kelsey assigned the matter [for investigation] to defendant King, [another] Pennsylvania State Police Trooper.

Trooper King contacted Renda by telephone on the night of [the alleged incident,] May 15. She told him that Sonafelt had slammed her into a wall at their residence earlier that day during an argument. Renda also indicated that she did not want to give a statement or file charges and that she wanted to be left alone. . . .

. . . [O]n May 16, Trooper King and Corporal Kelsey conducted an in-person interview of Renda . . . . They did not provide *Miranda* warnings to Renda, but she gave them a written statement. The statement did not mention the assault of May 15 that she had reported earlier that evening. King and Kelsey both testified at trial that, when they asked Renda why she did not mention the incident, she responded that she did not include the allegation in the written statement because she had lied about it earlier on the telephone. Renda on the other hand testified at trial that the alleged May 15 assault did occur and that she never told King and Kelsey that she had lied. She testified that she did not mention the May 15 incident in the written statement because she did not want to file a complaint against Sonafelt nor did she want him to go to prison. She stated that she provided the written statement because King and Kelsey threatened her.

On June 7, 1995, Trooper King filed a charge of giving false reports to law enforcement authorities against Renda and obtained an arrest warrant. The local police in Altoona, Pennsylvania, arrested Renda at her place of employment. She was arraigned and bond was set at $10,000. She was incarcerated at Westmoreland County Jail until June 20, at which point she was released on her own recognizance. On August 28, 1996, the Court of Common Pleas, Westmoreland County, suppressed any statements from the morning of May 16, 1995, because defendants had not provided plaintiff *Miranda* warnings prior to the custodial interrogation. The case was nolle prossed by the District Attorney of Westmoreland County because of the evidence problems.

Renda then filed this § 1983 civil action alleging that King and Kelsey violated her constitutional rights under the First, Fourth, Fifth, and Fourteenth Amendments when they subjected her to a coercive interrogation; she also claimed that she was interrogated without *Miranda* warnings and subjected to an unlawful search, arrest, imprisonment, and malicious prosecution. Defendants moved for summary judgment on all of Renda's claims, except the allegation of coercive interrogation. On May 14, 1999, the District Court granted the motion on Renda's First Amendment, false arrest, false imprisonment, and *Miranda* warnings claims but denied the motion as to the rest. A jury trial followed on plaintiff's malicious prosecution and coerced interrogation claims. During the trial, the District Court dismissed the coerced interrogation claim. The jury returned a verdict on the malicious prosecution claim, finding against Trooper King and in favor of Renda in the amount of $80,000, and against Renda and in favor of Corporal Kelsey.

*   *   *

III. Discussion

1. *Exclusion of Evidence Regarding Trooper King's Good Character for Truthfulness:*

Generally, evidence of a person's character is not admissible for the purpose of proving action in conformity therewith. *See* Fed. R. Evid. 404(a). However, evidence of a witness's good character for truthfulness is admissible under some circumstances to show that the witness is acting in conformity with that character for truthfulness when testifying in the particular case. *See id.* Those circumstances are that

> (1) the evidence may refer only to character for truthfulness or untruthfulness, and (2) evidence of truthful character is admissible only after the character of the witness for truthfulness has been attacked by opinion or reputation evidence or otherwise.

Fed. R. Evid. 608(a). Evidence of a witness's good character for truthfulness is not admissible absent an attack on the witness's character for truthfulness due to the cost of engaging in a fruitless "swearing match," particularly in light of the fact that a witness is presumed to tell the truth until his character for truthfulness is attacked. *See* 3 Christopher B. Mueller and Laird C. Kirkpatrick, *Federal Evidence* § 269 (2d ed. 1994); 4 John Henry Wigmore, *Evidence in Trials at Common Law* § 1104 (Chadbourn rev. 1972).

Under Rule 608(a), whether a witness's credibility has been attacked depends on the nature of the opponent's impeaching evidence. *See United States v. Dring*, 930 F.2d 687, 690–91 (9th Cir. 1991); 4 Wigmore § 1104. Direct attacks on a witness's veracity in the particular case do not open the door for evidence of the witness's good character. *See Dring*, 930 F.2d at 690. For example, evidence of bias or prior inconsistent statements generally does not open the door for evidence of good character for truthfulness. *See Dring*, 930 F.2d at 691; 4 Wigmore §§ 1104, 1105. The reason that evidence of bias does not open the door for evidence of good character for truthfulness is because evidence of bias only relates to a motive to lie in the particular case, not a general predisposition to lie. *See United States v. Medical Therapy Sciences, Inc.*, 583 F.2d 36, 41 (2d Cir. 1978); 3 Mueller and Kirkpatrick § 270; 4 Wigmore § 1107. . . .

In addition to direct attacks on a witness's general character for truthfulness, indirect attacks also open the door for evidence of a witness's good character for truthfulness. *See Dring*, 930 F.2d at 691. "[I]ndirect attacks on truthfulness include opinion evidence, reputation evidence, and evidence of corruption, which require the jury to infer that the witness is lying at present simply because he has lied often in the past." *Id.* As the Advisory Committee Notes for Rule 608(a) state, "[o]pinion or reputation that the witness is untruthful specifically qualifies as an attack under the rule, and evidence of misconduct, including conviction of crime, and of corruption also fall within this category. Evidence of bias or interest does not." Fed. R. Evid. 608 Advisory Committee Notes to the 1972 Proposed Rules. The reason that an indirect attack on a witness's character for truthfulness opens the door for testimony about the witness's good character for truthfulness is because such attacks directly call into question the witness's moral character for truthfulness. *See id.* at § 1107; 3 Mueller and Kirkpatrick § 270. Likewise, "[a]n act of corruption directly affects moral character; and the corroboration should therefore depend upon the rule for acts involving character." 4 Wigmore § 1107; *see also* 3 Mueller and Kirkpatrick § 270. As the Court of Appeals for the Second Circuit held in *Medical Therapy Sciences, Inc.*:

> Some types of bias, for example bias stemming from a relationship with a party, do not necessarily involve any issue relating to the moral character of the witness, but suggest only that the witness' testimony may perhaps unwittingly be slanted for reasons unrelated to general propensity for untruthfulness. As such, character evidence is not relevant to meet such an attack. On the other hand, *alleged partiality based on hostility or self-interest may assume greater significance if it is sought to be proven by conduct rising to the level of corruption.*

583 F.2d at 41 (emphasis added).

In the present case, the District Court abused its discretion in excluding evidence of Trooper King's good character for truthfulness. Renda clearly engaged in an indirect attack on Trooper King's character for truthfulness by arguing during her opening statement that the jury should not believe Trooper King when he claimed that Renda had told him that she lied — not because of bias in this case but because he was being corrupt in his conduct of his official duties as a police officer. *See United States v. Jones*, 763 F.2d 518, 522 (2d Cir. 1985) (holding that attacks on a witness's character for truthfulness in opening statements may qualify under the "otherwise" portion of Rule 608(a)). Renda's counsel made the following comments in the opening statement:

> So I'm here to tell you a little bit about the Plaintiff's version of the case. And, basically, what I'm here to tell you is that, in a nutshell, Valerie Krah Renda, who is the Plaintiff in this case, is basically claiming that *during the course of a police investigation*, a State Police investigation about an incident between her and a state trooper, who was at the time her boyfriend, *that these officers, these Defendants, misconducted themselves; that they maliciously harassed her; that they attempted to coerce her into making false confessions; and that when she would not do so, they filed false charges against her.* They caused her to be arrested and incarcerated and caused her to hire a lawyer and fight a criminal case against her. . . .

* * *

. . . And after all the evidence is in, we're going to ask that you conclude from your deliberations and from the evidence presented to you that *this young woman* was not only unfairly treated, but she *was maliciously and willfully mistreated by these officers in an attempt to help Joe Sonafelt; that they used illegal investigative techniques;* that they coerced her into talking to them on the morning of the 16th at two o'clock in the morning; they barged into her friend's house; *that they terrorized her;* that they lied about the statements that she gave; *that they caused her to be prosecuted illegally;* and that she has suffered significant damages because of that.

App. 138, 162 (emphasis added).

This argument that Trooper King would lie and engage in illegal police investigative techniques and frame an innocent person in order to help a fellow Trooper goes beyond alleging that Trooper King is biased in his testimony. It suggests that he is corrupt and improperly performed his official duties. *See Sutkiewicz v. Monroe Co. Sheriff*, 110 F.3d 352, 361 (6th Cir. 1997) (holding that it was proper for a District Court to permit a defendant to introduce evidence of good character for truthfulness in response to allegations that the defendant withheld exculpatory information in an attempt to frame the plaintiff). Since this impeachment went beyond a claim of a simple interest in the outcome of the case and rose to the level of corruption, "counterproof of good character should no doubt be admitted." 3 Mueller and Kirkpatrick § 270.

* * *

IV. Conclusion

For the reasons stated above, the judgment of the District Court will be vacated as to the judgment against defendant King on the malicious prosecution claim and the case remanded to the District Court for a new trial on that claim against him. The remainder of the judgment of the District Court will be affirmed.

[3] Rule 608(b): Inquiries into Specific Instances of a Witness' Conduct for the Purpose of Attacking Credibility

Like the common law, Rule 608(b) provides that a party may cross-examine a witness about prior conduct that is inconsistent with the witness' credibility. The conduct must be probative of the witness' character for truthfulness and its probative value must not be substantially outweighed by the danger of unfair prejudice. *See* Fed. R. Evid. 403. The decision in *United States v. Hill*, 550 F. Supp. 983, 989–990 (E.D. Pa. 1982), illustrates the scope of this limitation.

Hill was convicted of distributing heroin. On appeal, the Third Circuit reversed his conviction and remanded for a new trial. At this retrial, during the cross-examination of an agent of the Drug Enforcement Administration (DEA), the court did not allow the defendant to inquire about certain of the agent's prior acts of misconduct. These acts related to a previous investigation of another person, after which the agent had intra-agency charges of unprofessional conduct and criminal charges of disorderly conduct, trespass, and false imprisonment lodged against him. The trial court concluded that the nature of the charges was unrelated to the agent's character trait for truthfulness. In addition, inasmuch as the DEA dropped intra-agency charges against the agent, the agent was acquitted of the criminal charges against him, and the Merit Systems Protection Board found that the DEA had improperly prosecuted the agent, the court found that the probative value of the prior act evidence was substantially outweighed by its prejudice to the Government.

Did an acquittal of the criminal charges necessarily compel the conclusion that the agent did not commit the alleged acts? Does "acquittal" mean "innocent"? What if the agent had been acquitted because of a legal technicality because the trial court suppressed critical evidence?

It is inappropriate to limit this kind of cross-examination to prior acts that resulted in convictions or arrests if the acts are otherwise probative of credibility. In *United States v. Leake*, 642 F.2d 715 (4th Cir. 1981), the court held that such a limitation constituted reversible error. In *Leake* the trial court prohibited the defendant from asking the prosecution's central witness about his indictment for obtaining money by false pretenses, a warrant for his arrest for defrauding an innkeeper, bad checks passed over a period of time, default judgments entered against him for his failure to repay loans, and his failure to complete work on contracts for which he had received payment. The Fourth Circuit reversed, stating that the trial court erroneously prohibited cross-examination on these matters, because they established a pattern of fraudulent activity that called into question testimony that was crucial to the prosecution's case.

In determining whether prior conduct is probative of credibility, courts examine the specific nature and character of that conduct. A defense witness' past failure to file income tax returns in an action charging the defendant with tax evasion was open to exploration by the prosecution on cross-examination for the purpose of probing the defense witness' character for truthfulness. *United States v. Hatchett*, 918 F.2d 631 (6th Cir. 1990). Similarly, a witness' admission at a former hearing that he had submitted an inflated invoice for fees earned as an expert witness has been determined to be probative of credibility. *Navarro de Cosme v. Hospital Pavia*, 922 F.2d 926 (1st Cir. 1991). Cross-examining a witness regarding a previous admission of receiving stolen property has also been ruled probative of credibility. Although stealing does not necessarily involve false statements, and therefore does not go directly to a witness' propensity to lie, people generally regard such acts as reflecting adversely on a person's honesty and integrity. In *Varhol v. National R.R. Passenger Corp.*, 909 F.2d 1557 (7th Cir. 1990), the court recognized that stealing falls in the gray area between acts of violence, which are not independently probative of credibility, and perjury. The plaintiff in *Varhol*, a civil action, was cross-examined about his suspension from work for purchasing stolen train tickets from his employer. The fact that Varhol admitted guilt and paid restitution fairly imputed his knowledge that the tickets were stolen. The Court of Appeals upheld the District Court's ruling allowing the cross-examination, holding:

> The question whether to allow questioning about acts such as receiving stolen property under Rule 608(b) is a close one. But we think the connection between such acts and honesty and integrity, and between

honesty and integrity and credibility, is sufficient to allow admission, subject to the district court judge's sound exercise of discretion. In this case, Varhol's credibility was a key issue. The stolen ticket evidence did arguably reflect upon his honesty, and Varhol's counsel had the opportunity to minimize any adverse inference on redirect examination.

Varhol v. National R.R. Passenger Corp., 909 F.2d 1557, 1567 (7th Cir. 1990). While seeking discharge in bankruptcy does not show a disregard for truth, *United States v. Lanza*, 790 F.2d 1015, 1020 (2d Cir. 1986), *cert. denied sub nom. Lyubarsky v. United States*, 479 U.S. 861 (1986), making fraudulent statements in a bankruptcy application does. *United States v. Cusmano*, 729 F.2d 380, 383 (6th Cir. 1984), *cert. denied*, 467 U.S. 1252 (1984).

The Eleventh Circuit in *Ad-Vantage Telephone Directory Consultants, Inc. v. GTE Directories Corp.*, 37 F.3d 1460, 1464 (11th Cir. 1994), found error in the district judge's allowing a party to cross-examine the opposing party's expert witness, a CPA, about his prior bankruptcy filing. The Eleventh Circuit also went on to find error in the trial judge's allowing questioning about accusations of forgery by the expert — accusations for which no sanctions were brought, and about 15-year-old sanctions that had been levied against the expert by the Board of Accountancy for over-reliance on his partner's work. "To the extent that the evidence was probative at all, it was relevant to either Anton's [the expert's] truthfulness or professional competency. . . . Given the absence of any sanctions from the 1990 accusation and the temporal remoteness of the 1969 sanction, we doubt the evidence's relevance. Nonetheless, the evidence — even if relevant — was certainly too weakly probative to survive Rule 403's balancing test." *Id.*

As despicable as some acts may be, they may not be asked about unless they are probative of the character for truthfulness. In fact, the more despicable, the greater the need for their exclusion because their use could inflame the passions of jurors. In *United States v. McMillon*, 14 F.3d 948 (4th Cir. 1994), the court precluded one co-conspirator from asking another who had turned state's evidence about his past practice of using drugs to manipulate addicts in order to force them to engage in sexual acts with him.

[4] "Taking the Answer" — A Codification of the "Collateral Evidence" Rule

[a] Use of Extrinsic Evidence Restricted

If a party brings out a witness' specific instances of conduct during cross-examination, the cross-examiner must "take the witness' answer" if the witness denies the truth of the alleged instances of conduct. This means that the cross-examiner is precluded from subsequently proving, through extrinsic evidence (evidence from outside sources), that the witness' denial was false. It does not mean that the examiner may not press those matters further during cross-examination in hopes of ultimately getting an admission from the witness concerning the alleged instances of conduct. The court explored the logic of this restriction and the scope of the concept of "extrinsic evidence" in *Carter v. Hewitt*.

CARTER v. HEWITT

United States Court of Appeals, Third Circuit
617 F.2d 961 (1980)

GARTH, CIRCUIT JUDGE:

We are called upon to determine whether a letter written by the plaintiff Reginald Carter, a prison inmate, violated the Federal Rules of Evidence when it was read and admitted into evidence at the trial of a § 1983 action brought by Carter against prison authorities. We determine that it did not, and therefore affirm the judgment of the district court in favor of the defendant.

I.

Reginald Carter is an inmate at the Pennsylvania State Correctional Institution at Huntington. He claims that he was severely beaten in the course of a routine "shakedown," or search, of his cell on September 22, 1977, by three prison guards, defendants John Fuiek, Duane Pyles, and Gilbert Levi. On the date of the incident, Carter was housed in Huntingdon's maximum security block as a result of his role in an escape attempt a week earlier in which a guard was seriously injured. Carter brought suit against the three guards and against Lowell Hewitt, superintendent of the prison, under 42 U.S.C. § 1983.

The defendants moved to dismiss the complaint, or, in the alternative, for summary judgment. Supporting affidavits were filed with their motion. The action was referred to a U.S. Magistrate under 28 U.S.C. § 636 (1976). The Magistrate directed Carter to file responsive affidavits, but Carter claimed that he was unable to do so due to the restrictions he was subject to as a maximum security prisoner. Faced with this circumstance, the Magistrate scheduled an evidentiary hearing at the prison, at which time Carter's factual contentions were fully tried.

At the hearing, conducted without a jury on July 24, 1978, Carter presented three witnesses and also testified himself. The three witnesses were inmates housed in cells adjacent to or near Carter's at the time of the alleged beating. They all testified that Fuiek, Pyles, and Levi, the three defendant guards, came to Carter's cell shortly after 2:00 in the afternoon of September 22, 1977, ordered him out of the cell, and proceeded to beat him with batons, flashlights, fists, and feet. They all testified they could not actually see the beating, due to the restricted visibility from their cells, but they could hear the blows being landed. Two testified that they never noticed any bruises on Carter as a result of the beating; one testified he noticed some swelling of Carter's face.

Carter testified to the beating in greater detail. He stated that he was hit on the head three or four times with a flashlight and hit 30–35 times with a baton. He also claimed he was kneed in the face, causing his mouth to bleed. He testified, however, that the only visible signs of the beating as early as a day or two later were a swollen lip and some bruises on the back of his neck; all other injuries, he claimed, were covered by his clothes.

The defense called as witnesses the three defendant guards. They testified that they went to Carter's cell on the day in question for a routine shakedown. Fuiek entered the cell, ordered Carter out, and commenced the search. When Carter left the cell, he grabbed Officer Levi's baton and a struggle ensued. Pyles tried to pull Carter off Levi, Fuiek heard the commotion, left the cell, and demanded that Carter release the baton with the words, "turn it loose or I'll run this [flashlight] through your face." Carter then released the baton, and Fuiek completed his search. All three guards claimed that Carter had not been hit by anyone in any way.

The defense also put in the testimony of prison infirmary supervisor Morgan, that Carter would have shown more extensive injuries if he had been beaten as badly as he claimed, or in the manner that he described.

The incident giving rise to this appeal occurred during Carter's cross-examination. Carter was shown a letter written by one "Abdullah" to a fellow inmate at Huntingdon. Carter admitted that he had written the letter, and also admitted that he had denied writing this same letter when he had been questioned as to its authorship in an earlier prison disciplinary proceeding. Defense counsel asked Carter to read the letter. Carter objected on the grounds of relevance, claiming that the letter had been written six months after the alleged beating. The Magistrate then ordered Carter to read the letter but expressly reserved ruling on whether the letter was admissible. Complying with the Magistrate's direction, Carter read the letter aloud. The letter which was undated, generally described to its unidentified recipient how to file a complaint charging prison guard brutality. In its most significant portion, the letter reads:

> This is a set up my brother — compile complaints to be used for bullshit courts, possibly news media, and a radio program in Pittsburg [sic] & W.D.A.S. down Philly. We want to establish a pattern of barbaric brutal harassment [sic] and turn it on these chumps to the max.

Defense counsel suggested that this letter was a direction to file a false brutality complaint. Carter claimed that he was only encouraging the filing of a legitimate complaint.

Shortly after the hearing, the Magistrate submitted proposed findings of fact and conclusions of law to the district court. Resolving the matter that had been expressly reserved, the Magistrate admitted the letter in evidence as reflecting on Carter's credibility and demonstrating a modus operandi on Carter's part of filing false brutality complaints. Relying in part on the letter, the Magistrate recommended that the district court find that no beating had occurred and that judgment be entered in favor of the defendant guards. As to Superintendent Hewitt, the Magistrate recommended that his motion for summary judgment be granted since Carter had neither alleged nor proved that Hewitt had directed or encouraged the beating in any way. The district court adopted the Magistrate's recommendations and entered judgment for the defendants.

Carter now appeals, challenging admission of the letter. . . . He claims that the letter is extrinsic evidence used to prove bad acts to impeach his credibility, and is therefore inadmissible under F.R.Evid. 608(b). Finally, he contends that, even if otherwise admissible, the letter should have been excluded under F.R. Evid. 403 because "its probative value is substantially outweighed by the danger of unfair prejudice."

The defendants meet none of these contentions in their brief. Rather, in what we must regard as a questionable litigation strategy, they do not argue that the letter is admissible; they argue, instead, that even if admission of the letter constituted error, the error was harmless. If the letter was inadmissible, as Carter contends, we would find it difficult to hold that its admission was harmless. Both the Magistrate and the district court expressly relied, and relied heavily, on the letter in their opinions. Since, however, on our own analysis, we cannot agree with Carter that the letter was inadmissible, we do not reach the defendant's claim that any such error was harmless.

*　　*　　*

B. The Rule 608(b) Claim

The Magistrate and the district court found the letter admissible in part because it bore on Carter's credibility in testifying that he had suffered a beating at the hands of the defendants. Carter claims this use of the letter violates the limitations on impeachment set forth in F.R.Evid. 608(b). We disagree.

*　　*　　*

The principal concern of the rule is to prohibit impeachment of a witness through extrinsic evidence of his bad acts when this evidence is to be introduced by calling other witnesses to testify. Thus, Weinstein and Berger describe the extrinsic evidence ban as follows:

> Courts often summarize the no extrinsic evidence rule by stating that "the examiner must take his [the witness's] answer." This phrase is descriptive of federal practice in the sense that the cross-examiner cannot call other witnesses to prove the misconduct after the witness' denial; it is misleading insofar as it suggests that the cross-examiner cannot continue pressing for an admission — a procedure specifically authorized by the second sentence of Rule 608(b).

Similarly, McCormick writes:[4]

> In jurisdictions which permit character-impeachment by proof of misconduct for which no conviction has been had, an important curb is the accepted rule that proof is limited to what can be brought out on cross-examination. Thus, if the witness stands his ground and denies the alleged misconduct, the examiner must "take his answer," not that he may not further cross-examine to extract an admission, but in the sense that he may not call other witnesses to prove the discrediting acts.

Thus, the great majority of the decisions finding violations of Rule 608(b) do so when the extrinsic evidence that is challenged is obtained from a witness other than the one whose credibility is under attack. When, however, the extrinsic evidence is

---

[4] (Court's original footnote 8.) McCormick's statement does not describe Rule 608(b) but rather current practice at common law. This portion of the rule, however, simply codifies the common law practice in those jurisdictions that permit bad act impeachment. . . . Thus, McCormick's description of the rule at common law may be used as an aid in interpreting rule 608(b).

obtained from and through examination of the very witness whose credibility is under attack, as is the case here, we must recognize that the rule's core concerns are not implicated. There is, however, an even more significant reason for finding no violation of the extrinsic evidence rule here: Carter did not deny having written the letter; rather, he conceded his authorship but claimed that the letter was not an effort to encourage the filing of false complaints.

Carter's adoption of the letter, and thus his admission of the act used to impeach him, distinguishes this case from every case where the witness, whose credibility is under attack, has denied the evidence which had been obtained from or through him, thus leading to a holding that the extrinsic evidence rule has been violated. In those cases, the witness has denied, rather than admitted, the acts used to impeach him. The impeachment process thus would have required the examiner to produce additional evidence to refute the witness's denial of the acts charged. Such a process makes apparent the basis for the rule against extrinsic evidence: if refutation of the witness's denial were permitted through extrinsic evidence, these collateral matters would assume a prominence at trial out of proportion to their significance. In such cases, then, extrinsic evidence may not be used to refute the denial, even if this evidence might be obtained from the very witness sought to be impeached. But, as we have observed, Carter's case does not present such a situation.

*   *   *

The distinction noted here between our case and those cases in which the extrinsic evidence ban was found to be violated by evidence brought forth during cross-examination of the witness under attack — that Carter admitted the conduct charged while all other witnesses denied it — provides a sound basis for allowing admission of Carter's letter. The purpose of Rule 608(b)'s extrinsic evidence ban, as noted, is "to avoid minitrials on wholly collateral matters which tend to distract and confuse the jury." . . . Wigmore similarly described the rationale behind the common law ban on extrinsic evidence: to prevent confusion of issues through proliferation of testimony on minor matters; and to prevent unfair surprise arising from false allegations of improper conduct. 3A WIGMORE ON EVIDENCE § 979, at 826–27 (Chadbourn rev. ed. 1970). These reasons for barring extrinsic evidence lose their force when the witness whose credibility is challenged concedes the alleged acts. No issues are confused or time wasted through a trial of a collateral matter: no trial is needed since the matter is conceded. The trial judge may exercise control over the degree to which the conceded matters are explored through his power to bar irrelevant or cumulative evidence. F.R.Evid. 402, 403. Nor is there any danger of unfair surprise through false charges of bad conduct. If the witness concedes the matter, we may be confident that the charges were not false.

Thus, there is no need in such a case to invoke Rule 608(b)'s ban on extrinsic evidence, particularly where, as here, credibility is the critical issue. We conclude, then, that the use of Carter's letter for impeachment purposes on cross-examination, and its admission, did not offend Rule 608(b).

C. The Rule 403 Claim

Carter finally contends that the letter should have been excluded under F.R.Evid. 403. Again, we are constrained to disagree.

*　　*　　*

[Rule 403] cannot help Carter. It does not offer protection against evidence that is merely prejudicial, in the sense of being detrimental to a party's case. Rather, the rule only protects against evidence that is *unfairly* prejudicial. Evidence is unfairly prejudicial only if it has "an undue tendency to suggest decision on an improper basis, commonly, though not necessarily, an emotional one." Advisory Committee's Note, F.R.Evid. 403. It is unfairly prejudicial if it "appeals to the jury's sympathies, arouses its sense of horror, provokes its instinct to punish," or otherwise "may cause a jury to base its decision on something other than the established propositions in the case." . . . A classic example of unfair prejudice is a jury's conclusion, after hearing a recitation of a defendant's prior criminal record, that, since the defendant committed so many other crimes, he must have committed this one too. This is an improper basis of decision, and the law accordingly prohibits introduction of prior convictions to demonstrate a propensity to commit crime, F.R.Evid. 404.

Carter's letter, while undoubtedly prejudicial to his case in that it resulted in the district court ruling against him, presents no danger of *unfair* prejudice. The letter was offered by the defendants to suggest that no beating occurred on September 22, 1977 and that Carter was lying when he testified to the contrary. This, of course, was the central issue at trial. In a case such as the one here where the witnesses on each side take diametrically opposed positions, the factfinder's task is to determine which witnesses are more credible. If the Magistrate, after hearing the letter read, drew the inference that Carter was lying, it cannot be claimed that this was an improper basis of decision. It was, rather, a use of properly admitted evidence which, together with other evidence in the case, resulted in a decision on a proper basis. Thus, Carter has made no showing of unfair prejudice: he cannot demand exclusion of the letter under Rule 403.

*　　*　　*

IV

We conclude that all [the] grounds urged by Carter on this appeal, whereby he would have us hold that the district court erred in considering his letter as a matter of evidence, are without merit. We will therefore affirm the October 31, 1978 judgment entered for the defendants and against Carter. Costs will be taxed against the appellant Carter.

The prohibition in Rule 608(b) of introducing "extrinsic evidence" to prove the prior acts inquired about on cross-examination is designed to eliminate the mini-trials that may prove to be necessary on many of these questions. Such inquiries can be both time-consuming and distracting to the jury. Because those problems do not exist when the witness acknowledges the authenticity of a document that disproves what he previously asserted, the court in *Carter v. Hewitt* construed the term "extrinsic evidence" to mean evidence that required the calling of an additional witness. There is some confusion and disagreement about the meaning of "extrinsic" among the courts. Some courts have allowed a witness to be cross-examined with an acknowledged document so long as it was not offered into evidence as an exhibit. *United States v. Shinderman*, 515 F.3d 5, 16–18 (1st Cir. 2008); *United States v. Jackson*, 882 F.2d 1444, 1448 (9th Cir. 1989). The court in *Shinderman* undertook the task of differentiating between extrinsic documents which are inadmissible for impeachment purposes and documents which may be used (but not admitted into evidence) to help refresh a witness' recollection about their past conduct.

UNITED STATES v. SHINDERMAN
United States Court of Appeals, First Circuit
515 F.3d 5 (2008)

SELYA, SENIOR CIRCUIT JUDGE.

The admonition "physician, heal thyself" is a biblical proverb, *Luke* 4:23 (King James), suggesting that people should address their own failings. In the case at hand, this admonition has both literal and figurative application. The tale follows.

Mark S. Shinderman, M.D., is a physician specializing in psychiatry and the treatment of addiction. The federal government indicted him on a gallimaufry of criminal charges stemming from his unauthorized use of another doctor's name and Drug Enforcement Administration (DEA) registration number. A jury convicted him on many of those charges.

* * *

II. ANALYSIS

* * *

C. *Cross-Examination.*

The defendant further complains that the district court violated Rules 403 and 608(b) of the Federal Rules of Evidence when it allowed the government to cross-examine him, over objection, about his responses to certain questions when applying for medical licensure in Maine. We review the disputed ruling for abuse of discretion. *See, e.g., United States v. Brown*, 500 F.3d 48, 58 (1st Cir. 2007); *United States v. Winchenbach*, 197 F.3d 548, 557 (1st Cir. 1999).

We set the stage. The defendant applied for a Maine medical license in 2001 and again in 2002. As part of each application, he answered "no" to the following question: "have you EVER been charged, summonsed, indicted, arrested or convicted of any criminal offense, including motor vehicle offenses, but not including minor traffic or parking violations?" Evidence available to the government suggested that the defendant had been arrested in 1965 and again in 1970 for drug-related offenses (although neither arrest culminated in a conviction).

At trial, the defendant testified in his own behalf. The government sought to cross-examine him about these answers, seeking to cast doubt upon his credibility. The defendant objected and moved in limine to exclude any such inquiry. While he admitted that he had been arrested, he asserted that the arrests had been expunged and that, therefore, he had answered the questions truthfully and in line with the advice of counsel. In support of this assertion, he submitted an affidavit from his Illinois lawyer attesting that, to the best of the lawyer's recollection, the arrests had been expunged. The defendant also argued, in the alternative, that any probative value that might be derived from the cross-examination would pale in comparison to the prejudice that would accrue.

The district court concluded that the carefully worded affidavit provided "no convincing ground" to support the defendant's professed belief that the arrests had vanished and did not have to be revealed on the license applications. Then, in the exercise of its discretion, the court ruled that the government could cross-examine the defendant about his arrest-related answers. Withal, the court precluded the government from introducing the arrest records themselves into evidence. The defendant ascribes error to the former ruling.

The touchstone of our analysis is Federal Rule of Evidence 608(b), which pretermits the use of extrinsic evidence of specific instances of a witness's conduct for the purpose of bolstering or attacking the witness's credibility. Despite this general proscription, the rule explicitly grants district courts discretion to allow cross-examination of a witness about specific instances of misconduct as long as those instances are probative of his "character for truthfulness or untruthfulness."

Typically, a trial court's discretion to determine the scope and extent of cross-examination is broad. *See, e.g., Delaware v. Van Arsdall*, 475 U.S. 673, 679, 106 S. Ct. 1431, 89 L. Ed. 2d 674 (1986); *United States v. Beltrán*, 761 F.2d 1, 11 (1st Cir. 1985). That discretion is nonetheless subject to the overarching need to balance probative worth against prejudicial impact. *See United States v. Simonelli*, 237 F.3d 19, 23 (1st Cir. 2001); Fed. R. Evid. 608(b) advisory committee notes. That balancing function is spelled out in Federal Rule of Evidence 403, which states in pertinent part that relevant evidence "may be excluded if its probative value is substantially outweighed by the danger of unfair prejudice, confusion of the issues, or misleading the jury."

Rule 403 judgments are typically battlefield determinations, and great deference is owed to the trial court's superior coign of vantage. "Only rarely-and in extraordinarily compelling circumstances-will we, from the vista of a cold appellate record, reverse a district court's on-the-spot judgment concerning the relative weighing of probative value and unfair effect." *Freeman v. Package Mach. Co.*, 865 F.2d 1331, 1340 (1st Cir. 1988).

In this instance, we discern no abuse of discretion. After all, a witness's willingness to lie to the government in an application for a license is highly probative of his character for truthfulness. *See, e.g., United States v. Carlin*, 698 F.2d 1133, 1137 (11th Cir. 1983); *see also United States v. Tse*, 375 F.3d 148, 166 (1st Cir. 2004) (discussing false statements in employment application).

Here, moreover, temporal considerations favored use of the evidence; the defendant's answers were not remote in time but, rather, were roughly contemporaneous with the criminal conduct with which he had been charged. *See Simonelli*, 237 F.3d at 23. And, finally, the central factual issue at trial revolved around the defendant's intent. Hence, his credibility was highly relevant to the outcome of the case. *See United States v. Mateos-Sanchez*, 864 F.2d 232, 237 (1st Cir. 1988). Taking all of these factors into account, the district court's determination that the defendant's untruthful answers in his license applications were fair game for cross-examination falls comfortably within the encincture of judicial discretion.

This brings us to the question of prejudice. While we agree with the defendant that the revelation of his prior arrests carried with it some potential for untoward effect, we do not believe that effect was so stark as to compel the exclusion of the evidence. We long have recognized that "all evidence is meant to be prejudicial; it is only *unfair* prejudice which must be avoided." *United States v. Rodríguez-Estrada*, 877 F.2d 153, 156 (1st Cir. 1989) (emphasis in original). Thus, the court appropriately could discount whatever prejudice flowed from the impeaching effect of the answers. Beyond that, the answers themselves were not particularly inflammatory, and the court did not permit the government to elicit any tawdry details.

It is also noteworthy that the court took affirmative steps to minimize any risk of unfair prejudice. For example, it allowed the defendant to tell the jury about the ultimate disposition of the arrests and about his belief that they had been expunged. Furthermore, the court offered to give a limiting instruction; that the defendant eschewed this course does not minimize the value of the court's offer. Given the totality of the circumstances, we find unconvincing the argument that the court committed a palpable error in judgment in allowing the cross-examination to proceed.

The defendant cites our decision in *United States v. Tse* for the proposition that cross-examining a witness about responses to questions included in an employment application violated Rule 608(b). This argument misreads *Tse*, in which the court *permitted* the defendant to cross-examine a government witness regarding his answers in an employment application. 375 F.3d at 166.

Tse also upheld the trial court's discretion to deny the defendant the opportunity to refresh the witness's recollection by showing him the application, itself excludable as extrinsic evidence under Rule 608(b). *See id.* From this portion of the opinion, the defendant selectively quotes out of context dicta to the effect that "[u]sing the employment application [to impeach the witness] would be a clear violation of Rule 608(b)." *Id.* (dictum).

The defendant misreads this as suggesting a barrier to any and all use of evidence deemed "extrinsic" under Rule 608(b) to refresh a witness's recollection. The statement can equally as well be read to articulate the less controversial proposition that introducing such extrinsic evidence for the purpose of proving the witness's truthfulness (as opposed to using it merely to refresh the witness's memory) would violate the express prohibition of Rule 608(b).

We believe the latter reading is sounder and correctly captures the meaning of the *Tse* court. For one thing, Rule 612, rather than rule 608(b), governs the use of evidence to refresh a witness's recollection. That rule never has been construed to require that a writing used to refresh a witness's recollection must be independently admissible into evidence. The case law holds to the contrary. *See, e.g., United States v. Kusek*, 844 F.2d 942, 949 (2d Cir. 1988); *United States v. Scott*, 701 F.2d 1340, 1346 (11th Cir. 1983). The commentators agree. *See, e.g.*, Jack B. Weinstein & Margaret A. Berger, 4 *Weinstein's Federal Evidence* § 612.03[3][b], at 612–14 (2d ed. 2007).

For another thing, as stated in a leading treatise, "[w]hile extrinsic evidence in the form of documents may not be admitted under Rule 608(b) to impeach, nothing in that rule prohibits the use of documents merely to refresh the recollection of a witness who is the target of impeachment." 28 Charles Alan Wright & Victor James Gold, *Federal Practice & Procedure: Evidence* § 6117, at 12 (1993 & Supp. 2007) (citing *United States v. Chevalier*, 1 F.3d 581, 584 n. 2 (7th Cir. 1993)). Thus, *Tse* does not help the defendant here.

*   *   *

III. CONCLUSION

We need go no further. For aught that appears, the defendant was fairly tried, fairly convicted, and fairly sentenced.

Affirmed.

[b]   Inapplicability of Rule 608(b) When Evidence of Prior Conduct Is Admissible for Other Purposes

Rule 608's ban on the use of extrinsic evidence to contradict witnesses who have denied prior conduct during cross-examination represents a codification of a long standing doctrine that forbids the introduction of extrinsic evidence to impeach witnesses on *collateral matters*. Under this doctrine, courts considered prior bad acts not resulting in the witness' conviction "collateral" because they *are relevant only because of their impeachment value*. These bad acts, therefore, are not the proper subject of proof beyond cross-examination. If, however, the impeachment evidence also has relevance to a material issue in the litigation, courts do not consider it collateral. The opinion in *United States v. Blum*, 62 F.3d 63 (2d Cir. 1995), illustrates this point.

In *Blum*, the defendant was charged with obstructing an Environmental Protection Agency investigation for providing a fake logbook to EPA Agents. At trial Blum's former employee, Borovsky, testified that Blum instructed him to fake entries into the logbook. Blum then sought to discredit's Borovsky's testimony by introducing another witness to testify that many supplies and materials went missing from the company during Borovsky's employment, thus providing Borovsky — not Blum — with an incentive to falsify the logbook to hide his own theft. The government objected to Blum's witness, arguing that Rule 608 prohibited introduction of extrinsic evidence of Borovsky's misconduct. The court found that although the evidence certainly reflected on Borovsky's credibility, its intended purpose was to demonstrate that Borovsky — not Blum — had a personal motive to fabricate the production logbook. Thus, the testimony was related to a noncollateral matter, making Rule 608 inapplicable.

Similarly, in *Carson v. Polley*, 689 F.2d 562 (5th Cir. 1982), the court held that the trial court should have admitted a performance evaluation report revealing that the defendant, a deputy sheriff, had problems controlling his temper and that he engaged in arguments with the inmates, to rebut the defendant's claim that it would have been impossible for him to have lost his temper and have used excessive force on the plaintiff. The defendant made this claim during his cross-examination, at which time the following exchange took place:

Q: And you're not testifying under oath today that it's impossible that you used excessive force and lost your temper while helping book in Mr. Carson, are you?

A: It's impossible that I lost my temper, sir.

Q: Well, you have had problems in the past with other prisoners; isn't that correct, learning to control your temper?

A: No, sir.

Ms. Lagarde: Your honor, I object to this. I think that's improper, and I would object to it. I think he should restrict his questions to what happened in this case; those are the issues before the Jury.

The Court: Sustain the objection.

Carson v. Polley, 689 F.2d 562, 574 (5th Cir. 1982).

After this exchange, the plaintiff attempted to admit the performance evaluation report as extrinsic evidence that contradicted the deputy sheriff on a material issue. The court refused to admit the evidence. The appellate court found this to be error, stating: "[T]he likelihood that Ellis [the deputy sheriff] would lose his temper and overreact to a prisoner was a material issue in the case. Ellis' flat denial that it would be possible for him to lose his temper spoke to that issue. The district court should have allowed Carson to introduce contradictory extrinsic evidence on that point to impeach Ellis." *Id.* at 575.

In *United States v. Calle*, 822 F.2d 1016 (11th Cir. 1987), the government's key witness, Garcia, was asked on cross-examination about his plea agreement. He acknowledged the existence of the agreement and that it required him to identify all assets that he had obtained from illegal narcotics activities. Garcia, however, claimed not to have any such assets because he was only an intermediary for the defendant. The court held that it was error to preclude the defendant from proving that the witness' answer was not true and that contrary to its implication he was a major trafficker in cocaine, because that fact supported the inference that Garcia was the true source of the cocaine in the transaction in question rather than the defendant. Therefore, it was relevant to show Garcia's motive to falsify his testimony. As the court stated: "The self-interest of a witness, as opposed to the witness' general character for veracity, is not a collateral issue. . . . Therefore, evidence that happens to include prior misconduct still may be admissible. . . ." *Id.* at 1021.

Aside from the elements of the cause of action or defense, other issues to which prior conduct evidence may be relevant and admissible even if it contradicts a witness' cross-examination testimony, are the reliability of the witness' recitation of facts independent of her credibility and propensity to be inaccurate. Whenever a witness testifies, the witness automatically raises the issues of her ability to have perceived accurately, remembered correctly, and recounted sincerely. Regardless of whether a party asks a witness about prior conduct probative of these matters, or, if asked, regardless of whether the witness denied the acts, the opponent may present evidence addressed to these matters. Addressing the question of perception, such evidence might include: the amount of alcohol the witness had consumed prior to the event observed, where the witness was standing, whether the witness had turned on a light so that the event in question was clearly illuminated, whether the witness was wearing glasses, and whether the witness looked away from the event if another event was occurring simultaneously that might have distracted her. The fact most probative of a witness' ability to remember accurately might be the fact that the witness has made inconsistent statements about what she has observed.

Other evidence probative of these three issues (perception, memory, and sincerity) will also be relevant and admissible. Such evidence would include, for example, evidence: of the witness' mental disorders; that the witness' view was obstructed; of the length of time since the witness perceived the event; of the apparent insignificance of the event and therefore the witness' lack of interest in remembering it completely and correctly; and of the witness' interest in the outcome of the litigation.

[c] Inapplicability of Rule 608(b) to Volunteered Testimony on Direct or Cross-Examination

If a party offers impeachment evidence solely for the purpose of contradicting a witness on a matter that is concededly collateral to the litigation, the rationale behind Rule 608(b), in principle, compels the exclusion of such evidence. Courts have not, however, applied Rule 608(b) in a manner that is consistent with its rationale. Courts at both common law and under the Federal Rules of Evidence have distinguished between collateral matters that the opponent elicited or *invited* on cross-examination and matters that the witness *volunteered* on either direct or cross-examination. Although the rationale (avoiding delay and confusion) is applicable in either situation, courts have found it unfair to prohibit the opponent from countering any advantage that a proponent may have gained through the use of perjured or erroneous testimony. As explained in *United States v. Fleming*, 19 F.3d 1325, 1331 (10th Cir. 1994), "The [extrinsic evidence] rule does not apply . . . when extrinsic evidence is used to show that a statement made by a defendant on direct examination is false, even if the statement is about a collateral issue. . . . A defendant may not make false statements on direct examination and rely on the government's inability to challenge his credibility as to the truth of those statements." As further explained in *United States v. Costillo*, 181 F.3d 1129, 1132 (9th Cir. 1999):

> Rule 608(b) prohibits the use of extrinsic evidence of conduct to impeach a witness' credibility in terms of his general veracity. In contrast, the

concept of impeachment by contradiction permits courts to admit extrinsic evidence that specific testimony is false, because contradicted by other evidence:

> Direct-examination testimony containing a broad disclaimer of misconduct sometimes can open the door for extrinsic evidence to contradict even though the contradictory evidence is otherwise admissible under Rules 404 and 608(b) and is, thus, collateral. This approach has been justified on the grounds that the witness should not be permitted to engage in perjury, mislead the trier of fact, and then shield himself from impeachment by asserting the collateral-fact doctrine.

See Moss, *The Sweeping-Claims Exception and the Federal Rules of Evidence,* 1982 DUKE L.J. 61. The application of the collateral evidence doctrine in Rule 608(b) is further illustrated in the following cases.

In *United States v. Benedetto,* 571 F.2d 1246 (2d Cir. 1978), the defendant was charged with accepting a bribe in the performance of his duties as a government meat inspector. At his trial he stated during his direct examination that he had never taken bribes from anyone — making what Professor Moss would call a "sweeping claim" of innocence or a "sweeping denial" of previous wrongdoing. The court held that "[o]nce a witness (especially a defendant-witness) testifies as to any specific fact on direct testimony, the trial judge has broad discretion to admit extrinsic evidence tending to contradict the specific statement, even if such statement concerns a collateral matter in the case." *Id.* at 1250.

In *United States v. Green,* 648 F.2d 587 (9th Cir. 1981), in response to specific questions on cross-examination, the defendant disclaimed knowledge of or involvement in the making of LSD. Acknowledging that the exclusion of extrinsic evidence under Rule 608(b) gives witnesses a greater opportunity to commit perjury without fear or rebuttal, the court concluded that effective cross-examination was the only solution, albeit a limited one, and held that it was error for the trial court to allow the prosecution to prove that witness' denials were untruthful through the testimony of other witnesses. The Ninth Circuit reached a similar result in *United States v. Bosley,* 615 F.2d 1274 (9th Cir. 1980). After examining the transcript of the trial and concluding that the defendant's denials during cross-examination of involvement in cocaine trafficking were not broader than called for by the questions (therefore not a volunteered sweeping denial), the court held that it was error for the trial court to have admitted extrinsic evidence of the defendant's participation in a cocaine transaction.

If credibility is not a collateral issue, and therefore parties may explore a witness' credibility during the trial through extrinsic evidence establishing bias, prior inconsistent statements, psychiatric condition, and prior convictions, how is it logical to consider as collateral evidence that the witness has perjured himself while testifying? Obviously it is not. So why then do courts exclude what possibly may be the most probative evidence available of the witness' credibility while under oath? The answer, as explained in the preceding cases, is simply one of perceived necessity. If parties could explore all such issues concerning a witness' credibility, numerous mini-trials would result that would distract and confuse the jury.

Is the courts' perceived threat of confusion and delay resulting from concededly relevant inquiries into witness' credibility justified? Will the dangers of such inquiries always outweigh the probative value of the contradicting evidence sufficiently to distinguish it from the other forms of impeachment that parties can explore through extrinsic evidence if the witness denies the truth of matters relating to her credibility? Apparently, Congress did not believe that the dangers of such inquiries would always outweigh their probative value because, aside from Rule 608, which is limited to inquiries into prior bad acts relating to credibility, Congress did not incorporate into the Federal Rules of Evidence a general provision excluding collateral matters. Because there is no explicit "collateral matters" rule in the Federal Rules of Evidence, courts will judge those forms of impeachment outside of Rule 608 (for example, prior inconsistent statements offered solely for the purpose of impeachment and not for truth under Rule 801(d)(1)(A)) according to the standard of logical relevance under Rule 402 and to considerations of prejudice, confusion, and waste of time under Rule 403.

How meaningful is the limitation in Rule 608(b) on extrinsic evidence to prove the truth of prior bad acts that a witness has denied? Rule 608(a) allows witnesses to be called to give their opinions about the credibility of another witness. Consequently, one can easily circumvent Rule 608(b)'s limitation by calling the witness who, but for Rule 608(b), would have contradicted the preceding witness on her denial of the prior bad act. Rather than asking the second witness directly about the prior act, one can ask the second witness to give her opinion about the prior witness' credibility. In all likelihood this opinion will be consistent with the nature of the prior act. Then, to establish the reliability of that opinion, one could ask the second witness to explain the basis for her opinion of the preceding witness' credibility. This would result in the elicitation of the same evidence that Congress intended Rule 608(b) to exclude. For example, if the cross-examiner had asked the initial witness whether she had been fired from her last job because she had submitted false travel vouchers to her employer, and the witness perjured herself by denying it, Rule 608(b) precludes the cross-examiner from calling the former employer as a witness to establish that the initial witness had, in fact, submitted false vouchers. *See* Diagram 6-3, § 6.03[A][3][b]. The cross-examiner could ask that same former employer, however, to give her opinion of the former employee's credibility pursuant to Rule 608(a), which presumably would be negative. The cross-examiner could then ask the employer to explain the basis for her opinion, which, of course, would result in the introduction of evidence of the employee's submission of false travel vouchers. Diagram 6-5 illustrates this manner of elicitation of extrinsic evidence of a witness' prior bad acts.

This elicitation of extrinsic evidence of a witness' prior bad acts is possible only because Rule 608(a) has expanded the common law and allowed the parties to challenge witness' character trait for credibility or truth and veracity through opinion as well as reputation testimony. Whether the courts will allow parties to circumvent Rule 608(b)'s limitation on the use of extrinsic character evidence to prove a witness' prior bad acts in this fashion is yet to be determined.

DIAGRAM 6–5

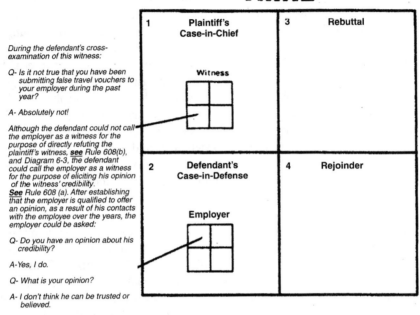

TRIAL

During the defendant's cross-examination of this witness:

Q- Is it not true that you have been submitting false travel vouchers to your employer during the past year?

A- Absolutely not!

Although the defendant could not call the employer as a witness for the purpose of directly refuting the plaintiff's witness, **see** Rule 608(b), and Diagram 6-3, the defendant could call the employer as a witness for the purpose of eliciting his opinion of the witness' credibility. **See** Rule 608 (a). After establishing that the employer is qualified to offer an opinion, as a result of his contacts with the employee over the years, the employer could be asked:

Q- Do you have an opinion about his credibility?

A- Yes, I do.

Q- What is your opinion?

A- I don't think he can be trusted or believed.

Q- On what do you base this opinion?

A- On the fact that for the past year he has been filing false travel vouchers with me.

To preclude such circumvention while still allowing opinion testimony under Rule 608(a), courts would have to restrict the proponent of opinion evidence from eliciting the basis for the character witness' opinion. One court has already done this relative to opinion character evidence under Rules 404 and 405. *See Government of Virgin Islands v. Petersen*, 553 F.2d 324, 328–329 (3d Cir. 1977). The reasonableness of this result, however, is questionable because the character witness' opinion can only be helpful to the jury if the jury has some understanding of the witness' basis for it. Such a result would be unfair if, during the character witness' cross-examination, the cross-examiner challenged the character witness' basis for his opinion through "do you know" questions in which the cross-examiner posed to the testifying witness prior acts favorable to the previous witness' credibility. Should the cross-examiner challenge a character witness' opinion in this manner, it would be untenable to preclude the proponent from reinforcing the character witness' opinion testimony by eliciting the witness' basis for her opinion on redirect examination.

Aside from the possibility of circumventing Rule 608(b)'s limitation through Rule 608(a)'s recognition of opinion character testimony, there are other ways in which a party may place before the jury evidence that Rule 608(b) excludes. First, if the preceding witness' prior conduct is relevant to an issue in the action, such as knowledge or intent, evidence of the prior conduct is independently admissible under Rule 404(b). Second, if the prior act demonstrates the preceding witness' bias, in addition to being generally probative of credibility, it may be proved, once denied. Third, if the cross-examiner attacks the preceding witness' credibility and the party who called the prior witness puts on character evidence to bolster the preceding witness' credibility, the cross-examiner may ask that character witness on cross-examination whether the character witness "has heard" or "knows" of the preceding witness' prior conduct that the preceding witness previously denied. The form of these questions will depend upon whether the character witness gives reputation or opinion testimony.

EXERCISES

1. Police lawfully searched Pamela's home and found several items associated with methamphetamine manufacturing. At Pamela's trial she testified on her own behalf. On direct examination, Pamela stated that the items seized at her house, which had been identified by the government as commonly used for methamphetamine manufacturing, belonged to her neighbor. On cross-examination the government seeks to question Pamela about her prior methamphetamine use, including two positive methamphetamine drug test results. Pamela's attorney objects, arguing that the proposed cross-examination is improper impeachment. How should the court rule?

2. Terrence filed a § 1983 civil rights claim against two police officers, alleging that the police beat him during his arrest. The police officers, however, claim that Terrence was intoxicated and fell down causing his own injury. At trial Terrence testified on direct examination that he never drinks. The police officers now want to cross-examine Terrance about an arrest, which did not result in a conviction, for public intoxication. Should the trial court allow the proposed cross-examination?

§ 6.03 IMPEACHMENT: CONVICTIONS OF CRIME

[A] The Common Law

[1] Prior Conviction as Impeaching Credibility

Courts at early common law deemed an incompetent witness any person who had been convicted of an "infamous" crime — a crime that was either of a felony level (involving death or imprisonment of more than one year as a potential penalty) or involved the element of falsehood (*crimen falsi*). Although no jurisdiction still considers witnesses incompetent on this ground, courts will admit the fact of conviction to impeach the credibility of those who testify. After abolishing this ground for incompetency, some jurisdictions continued to employ the "infamous" crime distinction for determining which convictions were relevant for impeachment purposes. Other jurisdictions permitted impeachment with all prior convictions except for designated minor offenses.

Most jurisdictions have limited admissibility to convictions for *all felonies* or *other crimes* (misdemeanors) *involving moral turpitude*. Crimes involving moral turpitude theoretically could include almost any crime because courts have defined them as including "conduct contrary to justice, honesty, modesty, or good morals" or "an act of baseness, vileness, or depravity in the private and social duties which a man owes to his fellow man or to society in general." *See* Black's Law Dictionary (5th ed. 1979). Consequently, if a witness testifies, the cross-examiner may ask the witness about almost any prior convictions on cross-examination, and, unlike the inquiries about prior bad acts that also may be made on cross-examination, if the witness denies these convictions, the cross-examiner may prove them through extrinsic evidence.

What is the logic behind this distinction between prior bad acts and prior convictions for the purpose of attacking a witness' credibility through extrinsic evidence? Why are acts that have not resulted in convictions but that substantively relate to a witness' credibility not provable through extrinsic evidence should the witness deny them, while convictions for acts that do not reflect on credibility are provable through such evidence? The answer to these questions is both historical and practical.

Courts once believed that a conviction for any crime indicated a witness' general evil disposition and readiness to lie. This is reflected in the following excerpt from the opinion in *Gertz v. Fitchburg Railroad Co.*, 137 Mass. 77, 78 (1884):

> [W]hen it is proved that a witness has been convicted of a crime, the only ground for disbelieving him which such proof affords is the general readiness to do evil which the conviction may be supposed to show. It is from that general disposition alone that the jury is asked to infer a readiness to lie in the particular case, and thence that he has lied in fact. The evidence has no tendency to prove that he was mistaken, but only that he has perjured himself and it reaches that conclusion solely through the general proposition that he is of bad character and unworthy of credit.

Because convictions established the commission of the allegedly relevant acts with certainty and did so without delaying the trial or complicating or confusing the issues for resolution, it made sense to admit extrinsic evidence of those adjudicated acts. Although courts rejected this notion about the relevance of all convictions long ago, they only partially changed the impeachment rule that was premised upon it.

[2] The Felony/Misdemeanor Distinction

Certain jurisdictions only permit parties to impeach witnesses with felony convictions or with convictions of crimes involving moral turpitude. Jurisdictions following this rule base the felony/misdemeanor distinction on the potential penalties these jurisdictions provide for the particular crime involved. If a criminal statute provides for a potential penalty of over one year, the crime is a felony, regardless of the nature of the conduct addressed or the actual sentence imposed. Because various jurisdictions may consider the antisocial nature of the same conduct differently and, therefore, punish such conduct differently, the use of the felony/misdemeanor distinction as a basis for determining which convictions are admissible for impeachment purposes creates the anomalous result of convictions for the same conduct being admissible against some witnesses but not against others, depending solely on where the witnesses were previously convicted.

[3] Between a Rock and a Hard Place: The Dilemma of Criminal Defendants

A criminal defendant controls the general admissibility of character evidence for the purpose of proving her past conduct, because the criminal defendant must initiate the use of such evidence before the Government can offer it against her. The defendant, however, has no control over the admissibility of character evidence for impeachment purposes, other than by refusing to testify. Consequently, a criminal defendant who has a prior criminal record, or whose past conduct raises questions about her credibility, is placed between a rock and a hard place. On the one hand, if the defendant fails to testify, the jury will likely infer guilt from this silence, even though the judge will instruct it not to do so, because jurors perceive it as unnatural to stand mute in the face of ill-founded charges. On the other hand, if the defendant testifies, her prior conduct and convictions will be revealed and the jury will likely consider them on the question of culpability, again, even though instructed otherwise, particularly if the prior offenses are similar to the crime for which the defendant is being tried. Even if the jury doesn't employ the prior bad acts and prior convictions as character evidence establishing the defendant's propensity to commit the charged offense, it is likely that the jury will be prone to convict the defendant on a lesser quantum of proof because of a reduced fear of convicting an "innocent" person.

Is it logical or fair to draw conclusions about one's general credibility from a single act or conviction? Is the probative value of evidence of prior bad acts and convictions that are relevant to credibility sufficient to overcome the dangers that its use will entail? In light of the scope and kinds of convictions and conduct that courts admit under the prior conviction rule, it has been persuasively argued that such conclusions are neither logical nor fair. Ladd, *Credibility Tests — Current Trends*, 89 U. Pa. L. Rev. 166, 176–182 (1940).

In an effort to address the dangers for criminal defendants in the use of prior conviction evidence, the courts resorted to a discretionary balancing test that looked to the circumstances of each case. As the court explained in the leading case of *Luck v. United States*, 348 F.2d 763 (D.C. Cir. 1965):

> There may well be cases where the trial judge might think that the cause of truth would be helped more by letting the jury hear the defendant's story than by the defendant's foregoing that opportunity because of the fear of prejudice founded upon a prior conviction. There may well be other cases where the trial judge believes the prejudicial effect of impeachment far outweighs the probative relevance of the prior conviction to the issue of credibility. This last is, of course, a standard which trial judges apply every day in other contexts; and we think it has both utility and applicability in this field.

> In exercising discretion in this respect, a number of factors might be relevant, such as the nature of the prior crimes, the length of the criminal record, the age and circumstances of the defendant, and, above all, the extent to which it is more important to the search for truth in a particular

case for the jury to hear the defendant's story than to know of a prior conviction.

Luck v. United States, 348 F.2d 763, 768–769 (D.C. Cir. 1965).

The court subsequently refined these considerations in the balancing test in *Gordon v. United States*.

GORDON v. UNITED STATES
United States Court of Appeals, District of Columbia Circuit
383 F.2d 936 (1967)

BURGER, CIRCUIT JUDGE.

Appellant was convicted of robbery and assault with a dangerous weapon. On appeal this Court remanded the case to the District Court without considering the merits when it appeared that the District Court had indicated willingness to grant a new trial because of newly discovered evidence. The new evidence was that the complaining witness, the sole government witness at the first trial, had been convicted of larceny, a factor relevant to his credibility and which was unknown at the time of trial. A new trial followed our remand, and the second trial also resulted in conviction.

On this appeal only one issue raised by Appellant bears comment. Appellant claims that the District Court Judge abused the discretion vested in him by *Luck v. United States*, . . . when he permitted the government to impeach Appellant's testimony by showing prior convictions. However, the record reveals that Appellant did not present the issue to the trial judge in the manner contemplated by *Luck*, although on the whole record we are satisfied that the trial judge did consider the point and exercise his discretion concerning the prior convictions which Appellant now argues should be excluded; as we have said before, absent plain error we will not find an abuse of discretion where there has been no meaningful invocation of that discretion. . . . Nonetheless, we are moved by the arguments of counsel here as well as by the need for clarification relating to the problem of prior-crimes impeachment, . . . to set forth some observations about our decision in *Luck*.

Because of the direct conflict in the evidence the verdict necessarily turned on how the jury resolved the credibility contest between the complainant and the defendant. Appellant's argument now is that while it was appropriate for him to impeach the complaining witness with a prior criminal record, it was improper to allow impeachment of his own credibility by asking him about his criminal convictions, notwithstanding his failure to raise the issue.

The rationale of our *Luck* opinion is important; it recognized that a showing of prior convictions can have genuine probative value on the issue of credibility, but that because of the potential for prejudice, the receiving of such convictions as impeachment was discretionary. The defendant who has a criminal record may ask the court to weigh the probative value of the convictions as to the credibility against the degree of prejudice which the revelation of his past crimes would cause; and he may ask the court to consider whether it is more important for the jury to hear his story than to know about prior convictions in relation to his credibility. We contemplated the possibility of allowing some convictions to be shown and some excluded; examples are to be found in those which are remote and those which have no direct bearing on veracity, and those which because of the peculiar circumstances at hand might better be excluded. The *Luck* opinion contemplated an on-the-record consideration by the trial judge whose action would be reviewable only for abuse of discretion, and that once the exercise of discretion appeared, the trial court's action be "accorded a respect appropriately reflective of the inescapable remoteness of appellate review." This is a recognition that the cold record on appeal cannot present all facets and elements which the trial judge must weigh in striking the balance.

Luck also contemplated that it was for the defendant to present to the trial court sufficient reasons for withholding past convictions from the jury in the face of a statute which makes such convictions admissible. . . . The underlying assumption was that prior convictions would ordinarily be admissible unless this burden is met. "The trial court is not *required* to allow impeachment by prior conviction every time a defendant takes the stand in his own defense."

The standard to be applied by the District Judge was stated in terms of whether he "believes the prejudicial effect of impeachment far outweighs the probative relevance of the prior conviction to the issue of credibility." The impact of criminal convictions will often be damaging to an accused and it is admittedly difficult to restrict its impact, by cautionary instructions, to the issue of credibility. The test of *Luck*, however, is that to bar them as impeachment the court must find that the prejudice must "far outweigh" the probative relevance to credibility, or that even if relevant the "cause of truth would be helped more by letting the jury hear the defendant's story than by the defendant's foregoing that opportunity because of the fear of prejudice founded upon a prior conviction."

The burden of persuasion in this regard is on the accused; and, once the issue is raised, the District Court should make an inquiry, allowing the accused an opportunity to show why judicial discretion should be exercised in favor of exclusion of the criminal record.[6] This, admittedly, places a very difficult burden on trial judges and some added guidelines are needed even at risk of adding to the burdens of the trial courts.

In considering how the District Court is to exercise the discretionary power we granted, we must look to the legitimate purpose of impeachment which is, of course, not to show that the accused who takes the stand is a "bad" person but rather to show background facts which bear directly on whether jurors ought to believe him rather than other and conflicting witnesses. In common human experience acts of deceit, fraud, cheating, or stealing, for example, are universally regarded as conduct

---

[6] (Court's original footnote 8.) It must be remembered that the prior conviction involved in *Luck* was a guilty plea. The relevance of prior convictions to credibility may well be different as between a case where the conviction of the accused was by admission of guilt by a plea and on the other hand a case where the accused affirmatively contested the charge and testified, for example, that he was not present and did not commit the acts charged. In the latter situation the accused affirmatively puts his own veracity in issue when he testifies so that the jury's verdict amounted to rejection of his testimony; the verdict is in a sense a *de facto* finding that the accused did not tell the truth when sworn to do so. Exploration of this area risks a diversion which may well be time consuming; hence use of this inquiry should be limited.

which reflect adversely on a man's honesty and integrity. Acts of violence on the other hand, which may result from a short temper, a combative nature, extreme provocation, or other causes, generally have little or no direct bearing on honesty and veracity. A "rule of thumb" thus should be that convictions which rest on dishonest conduct relate to credibility whereas those of violent or assaultive crimes generally do not; traffic violations, however serious, are in the same category. The nearness or remoteness of the prior conviction is also a factor of no small importance. Even one involving fraud or stealing, for example, if it occurred long before and has been followed by a legally blameless life, should generally be excluded on the ground of remoteness.

A special and even more difficult problem arises when the prior conviction is for the same or substantially the same conduct for which the accused is on trial.[7] Where multiple convictions of various kinds can be shown, strong reasons arise for excluding those which are for the same crime because of the inevitable pressure on lay jurors to believe that "if he did it before he probably did so this time." As a general guide, those convictions which are for the same crime should be admitted sparingly; one solution might well be that discretion be exercised to limit the impeachment by way of a similar crime to a single conviction and then only when the circumstances indicate strong reasons for disclosure, and where the conviction directly relates to veracity.

Of course, there are many other factors that may be relevant in deciding whether or not to exclude prior convictions in a particular case. . . . One important consideration is what the effect will be if the defendant does not testify out of fear of being prejudiced because of impeachment by prior convictions. Even though a judge might find that the prior convictions are relevant to credibility and the risk of prejudice to the defendant does not warrant their exclusion, he may nevertheless conclude that it is more important that the jury have the benefit of the defendant's version of the case than to have the defendant remain silent out of fear of impeachment.[8] . . .

We recognize the undesirability of prolonging the trial unduly when the court is already confronted with requirements which work to that end, but in many cases the best way for the District Judge to evaluate the situation is to have the accused take the stand in a non-jury hearing and elicit his testimony and allow cross examination before resolving the *Luck* issue. Not only the trial judge, but both

---

[7] (Court's original footnote 10.) Neither *Luck* nor this opinion places any limitations on established rules which permit evidence of prior criminality to show a "pattern" of offenses. . . .

[8] (Court's original footnote 11.) This weighing process would occur only where it has been determined that the prior convictions are otherwise admissible. Having made that determination, the judge would then consider whether the defendant's testimony is so important that he should not be forced to elect between staying silent — risking prejudice due to the jury's going without one version of the facts — and testifying — risking prejudice through exposure of his criminal past. In this regard, the judge may want to evaluate just how relevant to credibility the prior convictions are; for example, a recent perjury conviction would be difficult to ignore even where the defendant's testimony would be of great importance. This could well be true as to a multiplicity of convictions for crimes of dishonesty referred to earlier. On the other hand, where an instruction relative to inferences arising from unexplained possession of recently stolen property is permissible, the importance of the defendant's testimony becomes more acute. . . .

counsel, would then be in a better position to make decisions concerning the impeachment issue. Of course, the defendant could not be compelled to give testimony in the non-jury hearing and his testimony taken at the non-jury hearing would not be admissible in evidence except for impeachment. . . .

We are well aware that these are not firm guidelines which can be applied readily as though they were part of the structure of the Federal Rules of Criminal Procedure; the very nature of judicial discretion precludes rigid standards for its exercise; we seek to give some assistance to the trial judge to whom we have assigned the extremely difficult task of weighing and balancing these elusive concepts. Surely, it would be much simpler if prior convictions of an accused were totally admissible or totally excludable as impeachment; but in the face of an explicit, unambiguous statute allowing use of prior convictions and the holding in *Luck* we have little choice. The lesser step has been taken in *Luck* saying that the statute is to be read as permitting a discretion in the trial judge.

Even though we need not go beyond Appellant's failure to raise the issue he now relies on, we note that the admission of Appellant's criminal record here, along with the criminal record of the complaining witness, was not in a vindictive or "eye for an eye" sense, as Appellant argues. Rather it was received because the case had narrowed to the credibility of two persons — the accused and his accuser — and in those circumstances there was greater, not less, compelling reason for exploring all avenues which would shed light on which of the two witnesses was to be believed. The jurors saw and heard both and we are able to see and hear neither. None of the other contentions urged by Appellant affords a basis for disturbing the judgment.

Affirmed.

[B]   Rule 609. Impeachment by Evidence of a Criminal Conviction

[1]   Discretionary Balancing Under Rule 609(a)(1): The Five Factors of *Gordon*

The balancing test incorporated in Rule 609(a)(1) is the same balance employed by the courts under the common law. Professor Surratt explains:

**Prior-Conviction Impeachment Under
The Federal Rules of Evidence:
A Suggested Approach to Applying the
"Balancing" Provision of Rule 609(a)**
Roderick Surratt
31 Syracuse L. Rev. 907, 928–939 (1980)[10]

* * *

---

[10] Copyright © 1980. Reprinted with permission of the Syracuse Law Review.

IV. The "Substance" of Decisionmaking Under Rule 609(a)(1):
The Five Factors Considered by the Courts

The "substantive" aspect of judicial decisionmaking under Rule 609(a)(1) — the question of what *factors* a trial court should consider in determining whether probative value outweighs prejudicial effect, and how those factors should be utilized — has proved troublesome for the courts. Difficulties in this area are not surprising, for inherent in the balancing approach embodied in the rule is an inevitable tension between two concepts that are not readily reconcilable. It should be recalled that the congressional compromise that produced rule 609(a) was one between two sharply conflicting objectives. Those who supported the House version of the proposed rule wished to protect the defendant's interest "in relating his side of the story without being convicted on the basis of his prior record." Conversely, those who supported the Senate version of the proposed rule desired to preserve "the interest of society in assuring that the twelve people it impanels to ascertain the truth in a criminal trial are not deprived of one of the traditional devices for assessing credibility." As one court commented shortly after the adoption of the Federal Rules, "[i]t is incumbent upon the courts, in administering rule 609(a), to reconcile these competing goals to the extent possible."

Reconciling the irreconcilable is not an easy task; consequently, deciding what factors should properly be taken into account in balancing probative value against prejudicial effect under rule 609(a)(1) is fraught with difficulty. Moreover, courts faced with this difficulty can find virtually no guidance in the rule itself or in the legislative history of the rule. In this situation, courts deciding cases under rule 609(a)(1) have often turned, almost by default, to the factors enunciated by Judge Burger under the *Luck* doctrine.

A. Judge Burger's Five Factors

When Judge Burger expounded upon the *Luck* doctrine in his 1967 opinion in *Gordon v. United States*, he identified and discussed five factors that a trial judge could properly consider in balancing probative value against prejudicial effect under *Luck*. Since the adoption of the Federal Rules of Evidence, several courts have identified those five factors as the factors to be considered in balancing probative value against prejudicial effect under rule 609(a)(1).

The first case to embrace explicitly Judge Burger's factors after the adoption of the Federal Rules was *United States v. Mahone*, in which the Seventh Circuit, citing *Gordon*, set out the five factors as follows:

(1) The impeachment value of the prior crime.

(2) The point in time of the conviction and the witness' subsequent history.

(3) The similarity between the past crime and the charged crime.

(4) The importance of the defendant's testimony.

(5) The centrality of the credibility issue.

The factors set out in *Mahone* have been cited with approval in several subsequent cases. Although carefully reasoned opinions evidence a recognition of the fact that the factors must be considered together, it is nevertheless helpful for purposes of analysis to isolate the factors and examine them individually.

1. The Impeachment Value of the Prior Crime

The first factor listed by the courts is the impeachment value of the prior crime. This factor relates to probative value; the higher a crime ranks on "the scale of veracity-related crimes," the more probative value it has on the issue of the defendant's credibility as a witness. . . .

Under Rule 609(a), those crimes that rank highest on the scale of veracity-related crimes — crimes such as perjury, forgery, and embezzlement — are removed from the balancing process and admitted automatically under the provision of Rule 609(a)(2). Courts applying the balancing approach embodied in Rule 609(a)(1), however, have perceived significant differences in probative value among various types of general felony-level crimes.

At one end of the spectrum are crimes of physical violence, which the courts have characterized as having little probative value on the issue of witness credibility. For example, in *United States v. Jackson* the prior crime was assault. The court made the observation that "prior assaultive conduct would seem to have little bearing on the likelihood that one will tell the truth." Other cases decided under rule 609(a)(1) have taken a similar view regarding the crimes of assault, aggravated assault, assault with a deadly weapon, kidnaping, rape, and child molesting.

At the other end of the spectrum are crimes involving participation in the wrongful taking of the property of others. For example, in *United States v. Paige* the prior crime was possession of stolen goods. The court regarded this crime as ranking high on the scale of veracity-related crimes, stating that "the defendant's prior crime reflects adversely on his honesty and integrity." In *United States v. Field* the court took a similar approach, stating that the crime of receiving stolen property "suggests a lack of veracity on the part of [the defendant]." And in *United States v. Hawley* the court apparently gave a high ranking to the crime of attempted burglary.

> Somewhere in between are narcotics offenses, which have been characterized in different ways by different courts. Perhaps the most prevalent view is that "a narcotics conviction is [not] particularly relevant to in-court veracity." In *United States v. Hayes*, however, the court took the position that not all narcotics offenses should be treated alike. The prior conviction in *Hayes* was for the illegal importation of cocaine. For purposes of weighing the prior crime, the court characterized the type of crime involved as "smuggling." The court stated that such a conviction has more probative value on credibility than a conviction for narcotics possession, and in a footnote the court expressed the view that a conviction for sale of narcotics "may fall somewhere between a conviction for narcotics smuggling and one for narcotics possession."[11]

---

[11] (Original footnote 125.) . . . One other case involving a narcotics offense deserves comment, because the court was clearly wrong in its approach to assessing the probative value of the prior crime.

2. The Point in Time of the Conviction and the Witness's Subsequent History

The second factor listed by the courts is the point in time of the conviction and the subsequent history of the witness. This factor relates to probative value in the following manner: on the issue of the defendant's present credibility as a witness, the probative value of the prior conviction decreases as the conviction becomes more remote in time or as rehabilitation is demonstrated.

* * *

In cases decided under rule 609(a)(1), several courts have made mention of the nearness or remoteness of the time of the conviction.[12] Three Second Circuit cases provide examples of the reaction of courts to convictions that are relatively recent. In *United States v. Hayes* the prior conviction occurred approximately two months prior to trial. The court, in upholding the admission of evidence of the prior conviction, stated that "the conviction was a very recent one . . . and . . . convictions have more probative value as they become more recent." In *United States v. Hawley* the prior conviction occurred approximately four months prior to trial. The court mentioned, as a factor favoring admission, the fact that the prior conviction was "recent." In *United States v. Ortiz* the prior conviction was substantially less recent, having occurred approximately four years prior to trial. *Ortiz* produced a split decision, with the majority upholding the admission of the prior- conviction evidence over the dissent of Judge Mansfield. In a thoughtful and well-reasoned dissenting opinion, Judge Mansfield took the position that the four-year time factor should be regarded as substantially reducing the probative value of the prior conviction.

As prior convictions become even more remote in time, their probative value is further decreased. Carefully reasoned opinions, however, recognize the fact that the issue of probative value involves not only the passage of time since the prior

---

In *United States v. Ortiz*, 553 F.2d 782 (2d Cir.), *cert. denied*, 434 U.S. 897 (1977), the prior conviction was for the sale of heroin. The majority of the appellate court, in upholding the trial court's admission of the prior conviction for impeachment purposes, made the following statement:

> Here, the District Judge in his discretion was entitled to recognize that a narcotics trafficker lives a life of secrecy and dissembling in the course of that activity, being prepared to say whatever is required by the demands of the moment, whether the truth or a lie. From this he could rationally conclude that such activity in a witness' past is probative on the issue of credibility.

. . . As the dissenting opinion noted, such a broad view of the impeachment value of the prior crime could be applied to almost any crime: "[I]t could be said of almost any criminal, regardless of his crime, that he lives a 'life of secrecy and dissembling.'" . . . The dissenting opinion, in accord with the prevailing view, took the position that narcotics offenses have relatively little probative value on the veracity of a witness. . . . The broad view espoused in the majority opinion in *Ortiz* has apparently not been followed in other cases.

[12] (Original footnote 127.) It should be noted that some prior convictions will be so remote in time that they will be governed by the provisions of Rule 609(b) rather than Rule 609(a). Under Rule 609(b), "if a period of more than ten years has elapsed since the date of the conviction or of the release of the witness from the confinement imposed for that conviction, whichever is the later date," then evidence of the conviction is not admissible unless the proponent of the evidence gives advance notice of intent to use the evidence and "the court determines, in the interests of justice, that the probative value of the conviction supported by specific facts and circumstances outweighs its prejudicial effect." . . .

conviction, but also the rehabilitation, or lack thereof, of the defendant.[13] Two district court opinions illustrate this concept. In *United States v. Paige* the date of the prior conviction was approximately eight years prior to trial. In analyzing the time-and-rehabilitation factor, the court first made mention of "the length of time between [the prior] conviction and the present trial." The court further stated that at the time of the defendant's prior conviction he "received a five year sentence which term was suspended but for one month" and "[s]ince that time, he has not been convicted of any other crimes." On the basis of these facts, the court concluded that "the defendant's subsequent criminal history and the prior conviction's age diminish its probative value."

A very different fact situation was considered by the court in *United States v. Brewer.* In *Brewer* four prior convictions were considered by the court; the earliest conviction occurred approximately seventeen years prior to trial, while the three more recent convictions all occurred approximately ten years prior to trial. The court began its consideration of the time-and-rehabilitation factor by stating that, although the convictions were remote in time, "the defendant's conduct following release from custody has been less than would be expected of a rehabilitated individual." The court then recounted facts showing that each time the defendant had been released from custody on parole, he had rather quickly been convicted of another crime. The court thus concluded that, because of "the defendant's continued conflict with the law" between the time of the earliest conviction and the time of trial, the probative value of the prior convictions was not reduced by their remoteness in time.

3. The Similarity Between the Past Crime and the Charged Crime

The third factor listed by the courts is the degree of similarity between the past crime and the charged crime.[14] This factor relates to prejudicial effect: with regard to any prior conviction, there is a danger that the jury, despite a limiting instruction, will regard the impeaching evidence as being probative of the defendant's guilt of the charged crime; when the prior crime and the charged crime are similar in nature, the danger obviously increases.

*   *   *

The importance of this factor has often been noted in cases decided under Rule 609(a)(1). The most obvious application of this factor is in situations where the prior crime is exactly the same as the charged crime. In *United States v. Brewer*, for example, the charged crimes were kidnaping and interstate transportation of a

---

[13] (Original Footnote 134.) It should be noted that if rehabilitation has been formally found to exist, by "pardon, annulment, certificate of rehabilitation, or other equivalent procedure," the prior conviction may be excluded under Rule 609(c). . . .

[14] (Original footnote 144.) As the discussion in the text will indicate, the fact that the prior crime is similar to the charged crime will tend, in general, to make it less likely that evidence of the prior conviction will be admissible for impeachment purposes under Rule 609(a). It should be noted, however, that the fact that the prior crime is similar to the charged crime will tend, in general, to make it more likely that evidence of the prior crime will be admissible for purposes other than impeachment under Rule 404(b). . . .

stolen motor vehicle. There were four prior crimes: kidnaping, rape, aggravated assault, and assault with a deadly weapon. Although the court allowed three of the prior convictions to be used for impeachment purposes, the prior conviction for kidnaping was excluded. Citing *Gordon*, the court explained its decision to exclude the kidnaping conviction in terms of its prejudicial effect: "[T]he fact that the [kidnaping] conviction was for the same crime as one of [the charged crimes] would substantially increase the possible prejudicial effect such testimony might have on the jury, in spite of any limiting instruction the Court would give contemporaneously with the admission." Similarly, in *United States v. Seamster*, where the prior crime was second degree burglary and the charged crime was second degree burglary on a military reservation, the appellate court noted the problem caused by the virtual identity of the two crimes: "We recognize that proof of prior convictions of a defendant for crimes identical or similar to the [charged crime] should be carefully scrutinized by the trial court in determining whether the probative value of such evidence outweighs the prejudice to the defendant."

The similarity factor, however, is not limited to situations in which the prior crime and the charged crime are exactly the same. This factor has also been applied in situations involving two crimes that are of the same general type, most often in cases involving narcotics offenses. *United States v. Brown* is a good example of such a case. In *Brown* the charged crime was distribution of heroin; the prior crime was possession of a narcotic drug. The court, implicitly recognizing the reality that the jury would regard both crimes as being in the general category of narcotics offenses, excluded the prior conviction primarily on the basis of the similarity factor: "When, as in this instance, the prior crimes parallels [the charged crime], the quantum of prejudice to the defendant is magnified. . . ."

The same principle has been applied in cases involving crimes other than narcotics offenses. In *United States v. Paige*, for example, the charged crime was receipt and concealment of stolen securities with knowledge that they were stolen. The prior crime was possession of goods of a value in excess of one hundred dollars stolen from a foreign shipment, with knowledge that the goods were stolen. The court, in excluding evidence of the prior conviction, stated that "the prior conviction's effect on the jury is likely to be extremely prejudicial" because "[t]he prior crime and the presently charged crime are similar, sharing the common element of possession of stolen goods."

4. The Importance of the Defendant's Testimony

* * *

In analyzing [the importance of the defendant's testimony], it should be noted that the underlying concept embodied in this factor — the "need" of the defendant to be able to testify without being subjected to prior-conviction impeachment — exists to some degree in every case involving a defendant with a "record." Thus, this factor should be interpreted as applying only where the special circumstances of a particular case give rise to a more-than-average need on the part of the defendant to be able to tell his story to the jury.

Only a few reported cases decided under rule 609(a)(1) have discussed and applied this factor. One of those cases, *United States v. Paige*, offers an excellent illustration of a trial court's utilization of this factor. In *Paige* the defendant was being tried for receipt and concealment of stolen securities with knowledge that they were stolen. The court, in considering this factor, stated that it was "especially important that the defendant feel free to testify" in this case because of the nature of the charged crime and the jury instruction that could be expected to be given:

> The government is likely to ask the Court to instruct the jury that it may infer guilt from proof of the defendant's recent possession of stolen goods, if the defendant has failed to explain such possession to the jury's satisfaction. This instruction is usually given, and it practically shifts the burden to defendant to explain his possession of the goods. For the defendant to do so, he probably will have to testify.

Given the defendant's "special" need to be able to testify in the circumstances of this case, the court concluded that"his defense will be prejudiced severely if he is deterred from testifying from fear that he will be convicted on the bias of a prior crime."

5. The Centrality of the Credibility Issue

The fifth factor listed by the courts is the centrality of the credibility issue. In the *Gordon* case, Judge Burger stated that the trial court had acted properly in permitting the government to use prior-conviction evidence to impeach the defendant

> because the case had narrowed to the credibility of two persons — the accused and his accuser — and in those circumstances there was greater, not less, compelling reason for exploring all avenues which shed light on which of the two witnesses was to be believed.

In analyzing this factor, a similarity to the fourth factor should be noted: the underlying concept embodied in this factor — the "need" of the government to be able to use prior-conviction evidence for impeachment purposes if the defendant takes the stand — exists to some degree in every case involving a defendant with a "record." Thus, this factor should be interpreted as applying only where the special circumstances of a particular case give rise to a more-than-average need on the part of the government to be able to impeach the credibility of the defendant by the use of prior- conviction evidence.

Several cases decided under rule 609(a)(1) have discussed and applied this factor. An example is *United States v. Ortiz*, in which the defendant was tried for distributing cocaine, possessing cocaine with intent to distribute it, and conspiring to distribute. The government's only eyewitness, one Louis Lopez, testified that he went to the defendant's apartment on the day in question and purchased a quantity of cocaine. It is clear from the opinion that the defendant, had he taken the stand, would have testified that no such transaction took place. In other words, the case would have become a classic "swearing match" between the defendant and the witness Lopez. The defendant did not take the stand, however, because the trial court ruled that, should the defendant testify, the government would be allowed to impeach his credibility by using evidence of his prior conviction for the sale of heroin. In upholding the trial court's ruling, the majority of the appellate court, citing *Gordon*, noted that this was a case in which the credibility of the defendant was a central issue. . . .

Courts often experience great difficulty in applying the standards discussed above, not only because of the inherent problems of quantifying the value of each factor in any given context, but also because of the factors' frequently conflicting nature. *See United States v. Jimenez*, 214 F.3d 1095 (9th Cir. 2000) (set forth below). For example, if a conviction's probative value decreases with age, so does its prejudicial effect. Conversely, the more recent the conviction is, the more probative it is of credibility (assuming that it has some probative value to begin with), but simultaneously, the more prejudicial its effect will probably be on the jurors' determination of culpability. Similarly, the more important the defendant's testimony is to the litigation, thereby compelling the exclusion of evidence of her prior convictions, the more central the credibility issue is, thereby compelling the use of the convictions.

[2]   Crimes Involving Dishonesty or False Statement: Is This a Factual Standard or One That Turns Solely on the Elements of the Offense?

When first enacted Rule 609 only referred to crime involving dishonest of false statement. It was believed by many courts that even though the title of an offense would not bring it within the automatic admissibility provision of Rule 609(a)(2), if the prosecutor could demonstrate to the court that the conviction "rested on facts warranting the dishonesty or false statement description," it could still be automatically admissible. Subsequent courts have had varied reactions to this suggestion.

In *United States v. Hayes*, 553 F.2d 824 (2d Cir. 1977), for example, the court expressed a willingness to consider whether the crime of importing cocaine fell under Rule 609(a)(2) but found insufficient evidence of dishonesty or false statement in the manner in which the crime was committed to warrant a conclusion that it did.

> Appellant's conviction was for the importation of cocaine, a crime in the uncertain middle category — neither clearly covered nor clearly excluded by the second prong test — and thus one as to which the Government must present specific facts relating to dishonesty or false statement. If this importation involved nothing more than stealth, the conviction could not be introduced under the second prong. If, on the other hand, the importation involved false written or oral statements, for example on customs forms, the conviction would be automatically admissible. Because nothing more than the bare fact of conviction is before us, we must conclude that the prosecution has failed to carry its burden of justifying the admission of appellant's conviction under the second prong of Rule 609(a).

United States v. Hayes, 553 F.2d 824, 827–828 (2d Cir. 1977). A different court reached the opposite result, however, relative to a similar kind of offense, the distribution of heroin. In *United States v. Lewis*, 626 F.2d 940 (D.C. Cir. 1980), the court concluded that it is the *elements* of the offense, not the manner in which it was committed, that controls whether a court should classify it as a Rule 609(a)(2) crime:

(1) *Crime Involving Dishonesty or False Statement.*

The Government contended at trial that Lewis' prior conviction was admissible under both Rule 609(a)(1) and (a)(2). The trial judge first rejected, as we do here reject, the Government's contention that the crime of heroin distribution involves dishonesty or false statement. It was argued that he who lives by surreptitiously selling drugs on the street to innocent members of the community engages in a crime involving "dishonesty." The argument is ingenious, but it does not comport with the plain meaning of dishonesty, and we have rejected the same contention previously. *United States v. Millings*, 535 F.2d 121, 123 (D.C. Cir. 1976). While *Millings* involved a conviction for simple possession of a narcotic drug, we do not discern that a conviction for distributing heroin is any more indicative of dishonesty or false statement.

Contrary to the Government's construction, we do not perceive that it is the *manner* in which the offense is committed that determines its admissibility. Rather we interpret Rule 609(a)(2) to require that the crime "involved dishonesty or false statement" as an *element* of the statutory offense. While narcotics may be sold in a manner that is "deceitful," which is one synonym for "dishonest," the statutory elements of offenses under the Controlled Substance Act do not require that the drug be sold or possessed in a manner that involves deceit, fraud or breach of trust. If a narcotics pusher misrepresents the strength or quality of his heroin, as frequently happens, he may be defrauding his purchaser, but the *statutory crime* concerns itself only with the sale, not the fraud. Therefore, Lewis' prior felony conviction, involving as it did only "unlawful distribution of a controlled substance," did not involve "dishonesty or false statement" within the meaning of Rule 609(a)(2).

United States v. Lewis, 626 F.2d 940, 946 (D.C. Cir. 1980).

Most courts that addressed this issue favored the position taken in *Hayes* — looking at the actual facts underlying the conviction. *See* ABA LITIGATION SECTION, EMERGING PROBLEMS UNDER THE FEDERAL RULES OF EVIDENCE 163 n.171 (1983). This determination will be made after a hearing outside the presence of the jury. Circuits favoring the *Hayes* (2d Circuit) position include: *United States v. Cathey*, 591 F.2d 268 (5th Cir. 1979); *United States v. Barb*, 20 F.3d 694, 695 (6th Cir. 1994); *United States v. Papia*, 560 F.2d 827 (7th Cir. 1977); *United States v. Hastings*, 577 F.2d 38 (8th Cir. 1978); *United States v. Mehrmanesh*, 689 F.2d 822 (9th Cir. 1982); *United States v. Whitman*, 665 F.2d 313 (10th Cir. 1981). Only the Third Circuit has adopted the *Lewis* (D.C. Circuit) position: *Cree v. Hatcher*, 969 F.2d 34 (3d Cir. 1992). However, in 2006 the Rule was amended to adopt the *Lewis* position. Mandatory admissibility was limited to crimes for which the government had to prove an act of dishonesty or false statement to obtain the conviction.

[3] On-the-Record Findings

Relative to Rule 609(a)(1), the appellate courts have either encouraged or required the lower courts to make explicit on-the-record findings and provide explanations for these findings, even though the rule does not expressly require such findings and explanations. In *United States v. Mahone*, 537 F.2d 922 (7th Cir. 1976), for example, in which the court had to search for implicit indications in the trial record that the judge had exercised his discretion and weighed the prejudicial effect against probative value, the appellate court concluded:

> In the future, to avoid the unnecessary raising of the issue of whether the judge has meaningfully invoked his discretion under Rule 609, we urge trial judges to make such determinations after a hearing on the record, as the trial judge did in the instant case, and to explicitly find that the prejudicial effect of the evidence to the defendant will be outweighed by its probative value. When such a hearing on the record is held and such an explicit finding is made, the appellate court easily will be able to determine whether the judge followed the strictures of Rule 609 in reaching his decision. . . .

> The hearing need not be extensive. Bearing in mind that Rule 609 places the burden of proof on the government, . . . the judge should require a brief recital by the government of the circumstances surrounding the admission of the evidence, and a statement of the date, nature and place of the conviction. The defendant should be permitted to rebut the government's presentation, pointing out to the court the possible prejudicial effect to the defendant if the evidence is admitted.

United States v. Mahone, 537 F.2d 922, 929 (7th Cir. 1976).

Appellate courts have not uniformly imposed an absolute requirement of an explicit finding, the nonperformance of which would mandate reversal. As the court stated in *United States v. Jackson*, 627 F.2d 1198, 1209 (D.C. Cir. 1980):

> The express terms of the Rule require the trial judge to make a determination that the probative value of the prior conviction outweighs its prejudicial effect. The record in this case indicates that the trial court was fully informed of the determination it had to make and of the facts and considerations relevant to that determination. That it did not specifically incant the litany of probative-value-versus-prejudicial effect in its ruling that evidence of the prior conviction would be admissible does not constitute reversible error in the context of the consideration given the issue in the case.

In contrast to Rule 609(a), Rule 609(b) clearly requires on-the-record findings for the admission of convictions that are over ten years old. Rule 609(b) requires that the determination that the probative value substantially outweighs the prejudicial effect of a conviction over ten years old be "supported by specific facts and circumstances." *See United States v. Cavender*, 578 F.2d 528, 530 (4th Cir. 1978). The factors that have proven to be most important to rebutting the presumption that the probative value of convictions decreases over time are the number, type, and frequency of convictions in the ten-year period immediately preceding the last incarceration. Specifically declining to follow *Cavender* is *United States v. Holmes*, 822 F.2d 802 (8th Cir. 1987).

In *United States v. Jimenez*, 214 F.3d 1095, 1098 the Ninth Circuit Court of Appeals found that the district court's on-the-record analysis "was less than optimum" and offered a stern reminder to trial judge's to be "vigilant about seeing to it that the record supports [their] ruling."

UNITED STATES v. JIMENEZ
Court of Appeals, Ninth Circuit
214 F.3d 1095 (2000)

SILVERMAN, CIRCUIT JUDGE:

Defendant Sandro Jimenez was charged with possession of a firearm by a felon in violation of 18 U.S.C. §§ 922(g)(1) & 924(a)(2). At trial, he testified that he neither owned nor possessed the firearm in question. The government sought to impeach Jimenez with his prior convictions for assault with a deadly weapon and burglary. Recognizing the possible prejudice of such impeachment, the district court attempted to "sanitize" the assault prior by directing the prosecution to refer to it only as a "felony involving a firearm." Instead of mitigating the prejudice, this ruling inadvertently exacerbated it by gratuitously informing the jury that the "deadly weapon" involved in the defendant's prior conviction was, indeed, a firearm. Since the main issue in the present case was whether or not the defendant possessed a firearm, the district court's ruling was reversible error.

I. Facts

In the early morning hours of November 21, 1997, Las Vegas Metropolitan Police Officer David Smith was dispatched to an apartment complex in response to a report of a burglary alarm. Upon arriving at the complex, Officer Smith observed two men, Alberto Solis and Defendant Sandro Jimenez, walking near the apartment where Smith believed the burglary alarm had originated. Smith asked the two men to stop and talk to him; Solis complied, but Jimenez continued on, and walked behind a parked pickup truck.

It is at this point that two very different versions of the facts emerge. The jury's verdict would hinge on which version it believed, and therefore, on the credibility of the witnesses. Officer Smith testified for the government that when Jimenez walked behind the truck, Jimenez's arms "from probably the elbow, maybe lower down" were obscured from Smith's view. While Jimenez's hands were concealed behind the truck, Smith heard "a loud metallic sound hit the ground" which Smith believed was the sound of a gun being dropped on the asphalt parking surface. Smith drew his weapon and ordered Jimenez and Solis to raise their hands. Smith then ordered Jimenez out from behind the truck, and had Jimenez and Solis lay prone on the ground. Officer Smith then called for backup.

When Smith's backup arrived, the officers took Jimenez and Solis into custody. Officer Smith then walked behind the pickup truck to where Jimenez had been standing, and discovered a black semiautomatic handgun. The handgun was never checked for fingerprints.

After Jimenez was taken into custody, Officer Warren Gray read him his *Miranda* rights. Officer Gray testified at trial that after he read Jimenez his rights, Jimenez admitted that the gun belonged to him, and that he had thrown it under the truck because he had become scared when he saw Officer Smith.

The defense witnesses testified quite differently. First, Solis testified that after he and Jimenez were taken into custody, both of them had *denied* that the gun belonged to them. Solis also testified that he had not seen Jimenez with a gun that night, that Jimenez never told him he had a gun, and that he had not seen Jimenez drop a gun that night.

Defendant Jimenez testified in his own behalf that when Officer Smith first called out to him as he and Solis were walking in the apartment complex, Jimenez had not realized that Smith was a police officer, so he had continued walking toward the pickup truck. Jimenez testified that he eventually realized Smith was a police officer when Smith asked him to stop again. At this point, Jimenez testified:

> Well, [Officer Smith] asked for me to stop again. When I reached behind the white truck my foot hit something or kicked something which made a metallic sound and he asked me to raise my hands and for Alberto Solis to raise his hands and step out where he could see us.

Jimenez also denied ever telling Officer Gray that the gun belonged to him.

Anticipating that Jimenez might choose to testify, the government sought leave of the court to impeach him with his prior felony convictions for burglary and assault with a deadly weapon. Although the parties previously had entered into a stipulation that Jimenez was a felon, satisfying that element of the felon in possession of a firearm statute, the government wanted to introduce the specific convictions by name in order to impeach Jimenez's testimony under Federal Rule of Evidence 609(a)(1). The issue was whether the probative value of the impeachment outweighed the danger of unfair prejudice. The district judge agreed to allow the government to introduce Jimenez's prior felonies, but ordered that the assault with a deadly weapon conviction be referred to as a "felony involving a firearm." Although the district judge obviously was attempting to minimize any prejudice to the defendant, he made no specific reference to the five factor inquiry set forth in *United States v. Cook*, 608 F.2d 1175, 1185 n. 8 (9th Cir. 1979) (en banc). The first two questions the government asked Jimenez on cross-examination were whether he had been convicted of the two felonies, including the "felony involving a firearm." The district judge gave a limiting instruction to the jury that they were to consider Jimenez's previous felony convictions only as they might bear on his believability as a witness, and the government did not mention the convictions again.

II. Analysis

A. Rule 609(a)(1)

Jimenez contends that the district court erred by failing to make an adequate record of the factors that contributed to the court's decision to admit evidence under Rule 609(a)(1), and by incorrectly weighing the probative value of the evidence against its prejudicial effect. The district court's evidentiary rulings under Rule 609(a) are reviewed for an abuse of discretion. *See United States v. Alexander*, 48 F.3d 1477, 1488 (9th Cir. 1995); *United States v. Browne*, 829 F.2d 760, 762 (9th Cir. 1987).

When impeaching the testimony of a criminal defendant, Rule 609(a)(1) provides in pertinent part, "evidence that an accused has been convicted of [a crime punishable by death or imprisonment in excess of one year] shall be admitted if the court determines that the probative value of admitting this evidence outweighs its prejudicial effect to the accused." This court has outlined five factors that should guide the district court's decision whether to admit evidence under Rule 609(a)(1):

1. the impeachment value of the prior crime

2. the point in time of the conviction and the witness' subsequent history

3. the similarity between the past crime and the charged crime

4. the importance of the defendant's testimony

5. the centrality of the credibility issue

See United States v. Cook, 608 F.2d 1175, 1185 n. 8 (9th Cir. 1979) (en banc); *see also United States v. Wallace*, 848 F.2d 1464, 1473 n. 12 (9th Cir. 1988). Although the trial judge is not required to state his or her analysis of each of the five factors with special precision, "the record should reveal, at a minimum, that the trial judge 'was aware of the requirements of Rule 609(a)(1).' " *Wallace*, 848 F.2d at 1473 (*quoting United States v. Givens*, 767 F.2d 574, 579–80 (9th Cir. 1985)).

The correct procedure is for a district judge to ensure that the record reflects a consideration of the five *Cook* factors, as well as a weighing of the probative value of the conviction being offered against its prejudicial effect. Likewise, as proponents of the impeachment evidence, prosecutors should be vigilant about seeing to it that the record supports the judge's ruling.

We have had previous occasion to consider situations in which the record on the admissibility of the prior conviction was less than optimum. In this case, although the record is less than perfect, it nonetheless compels an inference that the district judge was, "at a minimum . . . aware of the requirements of Rule 609(a)(1)" as required by *Wallace*. This is demonstrated by the fact that the judge recognized the possible prejudicial effect of the assault with a deadly weapon conviction, and attempted, albeit unsuccessfully, to ameliorate that prejudice. The record shows that the judge recognized the centrality of the credibility issue and the defendant's testimony, but also attempted to protect Jimenez to the extent that his assault conviction would unfairly prejudice the jury. Under these particular circumstances, we believe the district judge demonstrated that he was, "at a minimum . . . aware of the requirements of Rule 609(a)(1)."

The real problem in this case is that in the district judge's well-meaning attempt to mitigate the prejudice to the defendant, he inadvertently made it worse. The district judge took Jimenez's assault with a deadly weapon conviction and ordered it referred to as a "felony involving a *firearm*" — this in a trial where the only issue in dispute was whether the defendant had, in fact, possessed a firearm. By altering the nature of Jimenez's previous assault conviction to include the reference to the firearm, the judge increased, rather than decreased, the risk that the jury would "draw a conclusion that is impermissible in law: because he did it before he must have done it again." *Bagley*, 772 F.2d at 488. The limiting instruction the judge later offered could not fully eliminate this danger.

B. Harmless Error

An error in admitting a prior conviction may be considered harmless if the government can show that it is more likely than not that there is "a 'fair assurance' that the error did not substantially sway the verdict." *United States v. Alviso*, 152 F.3d 1195, 1199 (9th Cir. 1998). The government can provide no such "fair assurance" in this case. The central issue in this case, whether Jimenez had possessed a gun the night he was arrested, came down to a question of witness credibility. The defendant offered a not implausible explanation of how the gun came to be found near the spot in the apartment parking lot where he was standing. When presented with the two plausible but conflicting stories, the jury may well have given weight to the fact that Jimenez had been convicted of a firearm felony before, and therefore, was more likely to have had a gun when Officer Smith confronted him at the apartment complex. As such, the government cannot meet its burden of demonstrating that the error was harmless in this case.

III. Conclusion

The district court *should* have engaged in a more extensive Rule 609(a)(1) analysis on the record, noting and discussing the five *Cook* factors. Taken as a whole, however, the district judge's actions reveal a sufficient awareness of the requirements of Rule 609(a)(1) under *Wallace*. However, the district judge's attempt to ameliorate the prejudice of the assault with a deadly weapon conviction had the reverse effect. Because the error was not harmless, the defendant's conviction is REVERSED, and the case remanded to the district court for a new trial.

[4] If Convictions Are Established for Impeachment Purposes, What Information May One Elicit About Them?

In eliciting evidence of prior convictions, courts have allowed parties to elicit the *name* of the *crime* for which the witness was convicted, the *time* and *place* of the conviction, and the *punishment* that the witness received. *See United States v. Boyce*, 611 F.2d 530 (4th Cir. 1979); *United States v. Wolf*, 561 F.2d 1376, 1381 (10th Cir. 1977). The parties may not inquire into the details of the crimes underlying the convictions in question. *See United States v. Callison*, 577 F.2d 53 (8th Cir. 1978).

Aside from the conviction's age, what relevance do the name and the punishment of the crime have to the conviction's impeachment value? Is not the mere fact that the defendant had been convicted sufficient to cast doubt on the defendant's believability? For many decades, the Supreme Court of Florida has believed that it is:

> It was erroneous and unnecessary to press the inquiry [during cross-examination of the defendant] as to the conviction of crime to the point where the particular offense was named; because such course seemed to be for a purpose different from that on which the question is allowable as to a witness' former conviction of crime. It is to discredit him as a witness, but to press the inquiry as to the character of the particular crime that it may be shown to be of a similar character to that for which he is being tried is to use the rule for an improper purpose. . . . *Washington v. State*, 86 Fla. 519, 98 So. 603, 604 (1923).

> The reason for not permitting questioning as to the nature of previous convictions of a criminal defendant for the purpose of impeaching him as a witness is simply that any additional light on his credibility which might be produced by the information would not compensate for the possible prejudicial effect on the minds of the jurors. The jury would almost certainly make inferences which went beyond the question whether or not the witness was worthy of belief. The jurors might conclude in the case at bar, for example, that because the accused had previously been guilty of robbery, he was probably guilty of the robbery with which he was presently charged. Such inferences do not share the dignity of proofs nor of circumstantial evidence and are to be avoided.

Goodman v. State, 336 So.2d 1264, 1266 (Fla. 1976).

A court will allow the Government to introduce the name of the crime into the trial under the "mere fact" approach only if the defendant denied the conviction and the Government introduces the certified copy of the conviction, which will contain the name of the prior offense, into evidence to rebut the defendant's denial.

The facts of the prior crimes are irrelevant to the impeachment purpose for which the convictions are used. Consequently, it is technically inappropriate for the court to allow the defendant to offer an explanation in order to mitigate the conviction's effect. Subject to the limitation of Rule 403, however, which requires the exclusion of evidence that will lead to confusion or delay, judges often exercise discretion and allow the witness to make a brief explanatory statement in response to the introduction of evidence of the defendant's prior conviction.

If the defendant attempts to minimize her guilt by explaining away the significance of her prior conviction, may the Government respond by presenting rebuttal evidence? The answer is no, but it has been held that if the defendant on redirect examination attempts to explain away the conviction and thereby minimize her guilt, the Government, during recross, may examine the defendant about the facts denied or explained. *United States v. Wolf*, 561 F.2d 1376, 1381 (10th Cir. 1977).

[5] Impeachment with Convictions on Direct Examination

In the past, Rule 609(a) provided that "evidence that [a witness] has been convicted of a crime shall be admitted *if elicited* from him or established by public record *during cross-examination*." (Emphasis added.) Literally translated, this rule would allow courts to admit evidence of convictions of crime only during cross-examination. To resolve the conflict that this limitation created, see *United States v. Dixon*, 547 F.2d 1079 (9th Cir. 1976), Rule 609(a) was revised to eliminate any reference to when and how the conviction may be proven. Therefore, a party who, under Rule 607, may impeach her own witness, may establish the existence of a prior conviction during that witness' direct examination.

[6] Balancing Under Rule 609(b): Probative Value Must Substantially Outweigh Potential Prejudice Only When Ten-Year-Old Conviction Is Used to Attack Credibility

Under Rule 609(b) a ten-year-old conviction may be used to attack a witness' credibility only if the court finds that the probative value of the conviction substantially outweighs its prejudicial effect. If, however, the conviction is introduced to "contradict specific statements made by a witness on direct examination," rather than to attack the witness' credibility by proof that she has done bad things and therefore "is not to be trusted to tell the truth," it has been held that Rule 609(b) is inapplicable. *United States v. Leavis*, 853 F.2d 215, 220 (4th Cir. 1988). In *Leavis* the testimony at trial revealed that the conspirators often used the word "dancing" as code for "smuggling." When the defendant elected to testify, he was asked during his direct examination if he had "ever use[d] the phrase, going dancing in connection with this case?" He immediately replied, "I've gone dancing but not this kind of dancing." At a later point in his direct examination he stated:

> I've worked on airplanes off and on for more than fifteen years and I'd never found myself in a situation like I was in, being confronted by some people like this [drug dealers] and having to try to get away from them and the fear that they instilled; the way they made me feel; I just wanted to get away from them.

The court held that it was within the district court's discretion to conclude "that by these statements Leavis implied that he had had no prior contact with drugs or drug dealers, and to admit the evidence of Leavis' [fourteen-year-old] felony drug conviction to contradict his direct examination." Without demonstrating that the probative value substantially outweighed its prejudicial effect, the Court concluded that the prosecution "was entitled . . . to rebut the false impression Leavis was creating by this testimony."

In *Stutzman v. CRST, Inc.*, 997 F.2d 291 (7th Cir. 1993), a defense expert had falsely testified at his deposition that he had never been convicted of a crime. Despite the fact that the conviction was over 10 years old, the court held that the witness' false statement under oath was quite probative of credibility and, because false testimony could not be discussed without mentioning the underlying conviction, the conviction should be let in.

[C] How Rules 608 & 609 Work Together

Courts and students alike have noted that the interplay between Rules 608 and 609 is "most complex and confusing." *See United States v. Cudlitz*, 72 F.3d 992, 995 (1st Cir. 1996) ("The rules governing this subject-cross-examining a criminal defendant about prior wrongs-are among the most complex and confusing in the entire law of evidence."). The Court in *United States v. Osazuwa*, 564 F.3d 1169 (9th Cir. 2009) attempted to clarify the relationship between these two rules.

UNITED STATES v. OSAZUWA
Court of Appeal, Ninth Circuit
564 F.3d 1169 (2009)

GRABER, CIRCUIT JUDGE:

Defendant Daniel Osazuwa was convicted of assaulting a federal prison guard while he was incarcerated for failing to pay restitution associated with a bank fraud conviction. Defendant and the guard, who were the only two eyewitnesses, unsurprisingly offered different accounts of the events. The government cross-examined Defendant concerning his veracity. Defendant challenges the government's use, as impeachment evidence, of the facts underlying his bank fraud conviction. We hold that the district court abused its discretion in admitting that evidence and, accordingly, reverse and remand for a new trial.

FACTUAL AND PROCEDURAL HISTORY

Defendant was convicted of bank fraud in 2003. He was sentenced to one day in jail, restitution, and a period of supervised release. His supervised release was revoked in 2007 for failure to pay restitution and, consequently, he was sentenced to 90 days of incarceration at the Metropolitan Detention Center ("MDC") in Los Angeles.

The incident in question occurred three weeks before Defendant's scheduled release date. Defendant had been transferred to a transitional unit for inmates whose releases were imminent. Officer Oscar Medina testified at trial that, sometime in the morning, he saw Defendant wearing green prison clothing, rather than the khaki clothing that inmates in the transitional unit are required to wear. Medina asked Defendant to change into khaki clothes. The next time Medina saw Defendant, he was still wearing green clothing, so Medina again asked him to change. Shortly thereafter, Medina saw Defendant grab a loaf of bread from the kitchen, which was against MDC's rules. Medina shouted at Defendant to drop the bread, which Defendant did. Medina testified that Defendant cursed at him, but Defendant denied swearing at Medina. Medina called MDC's Activities Lieutenant, who instructed Medina to secure Defendant in his cell so that the Lieutenant could question him about the incident. Another lieutenant checked Defendant's disciplinary record and reported to Medina that Defendant was a "moderate inmate without any prior incidents." When the Activities Lieutenant did not arrive, the second lieutenant gave Medina permission to unlock Defendant's cell and explain to him that he would be placed in official lockdown status if he refused to change his clothing.

From this point on, Defendant's and Medina's versions of the events diverge considerably. Medina testified that when he entered the cell, Defendant stood up and clenched his fists in a fighting position, prompting Medina to activate his body alarm to call for assistance. Medina stated that Defendant "launched" forward and threw two punches, the second of which hit Medina in the back of the head when he turned his face to avoid being hit. Medina responded with a "bear hug" to stop the punches, but Defendant moved forward and Medina lost his footing, causing both men to fall. Medina hit his head on the cell floor and blacked out for a few seconds. When he came to, he testified, Defendant was spitting on him. Medina got up, pinned Defendant to the cell wall, and let the officer who arrived to assist Medina in removing Defendant from the cell. Medina suffered a bruised rib, a swollen hand, and a cut behind his ear.

By contrast, Defendant testified that Medina was frowning when he entered the cell, so Defendant walked toward him. Medina was talking fast, so Defendant patted him and told him to relax. Medina responded to the patting by hitting Defendant's hand back. In Defendant's version, Medina wobbled while pushing Defendant's hands away and grabbed Defendant's shirt for balance, causing both men to fall. Defendant denied ever punching Medina, "launching" forward at him, or spitting in his face.

On direct examination, Defendant was asked what sentence of incarceration he had received for his 2003 bank fraud conviction. Defendant truthfully answered that he was sentenced to, and served, one day in jail. On cross-examination, the government asked a series of questions related to the dishonest conduct that led to Defendant's bank fraud conviction:

Q: Mr. [Osazuwa,] you have been convicted of lying before, haven't you?

A: Lying?

Q: Yes. Lying.

A: I wouldn't — I don't understand. Could you—

Q: Lying means you don't tell the truth.

A: I can't — I pled — I plead [sic] to fraud, yes, but not lying.

Q: Well, weren't you lying as part of your bank fraud?

A: To whom?

Q: Well, you tell us.

A: Tell you?

Q: To anyone. Who were you lying to as part of your bank fraud, sir?

A: Oh, to the bank, yes.

Q: To the bank?

A: Yes.

Q: So you did lie to the bank?

A: Yes. To—

Q: To get some money; right?

A: Yes.

Q: In fact, you lied about who you were to the bank to get some money; right?

A: Yes.

Q: You presented a bank in Ohio with a Visa card in another person's name; correct?

[DEFENSE COUNSEL]:   Your Honor, I am going to object to the extent of this. I think the prosecutor can ask the fact of the conviction, but nothing more.

THE COURT: Well, no. I will allow a few more questions.

Q: You presented a Visa card in someone else's name to a bank in Ohio; right?

A: Yes.

. . . .

Q: In fact, you had taken over that person's credit card account by lying—

[DEFENSE COUNSEL]:   Your Honor, again, I am going to object to the particulars of the conviction.

THE COURT: Overruled.

Q: In fact, you had taken over that person's credit card account by lying to the credit card company that you were, in fact, that person; isn't that right?

A: Yes, sir.

Q: And that's how you got the money; right?

A: Yes, sir.

Q: You had that person's mail delivered to your address, pretending that that was the other person's address. That's a lie, too, isn't it, sir?

A: Yes. We are talking about 1997; right?

Q: That's correct.

. . . .

Q: In fact, you even admitted to your probation officer, didn't you, that you had a fake identification in another person's name; right?

. . . .

[DEFENSE COUNSEL]:   Your Honor, again I am going to object.

THE COURT: Sustained. Why don't you move on, [Prosecutor].

Q: In fact, you also, as part of your bank fraud — you also lied to get office space in someone else's name; isn't that correct?

[DEFENSE COUNSEL]:   Again, I am going to object to the prosecutor going into all the details of the conviction. [Defendant] has admitted that he was convicted, and I don't think the prosecutor can inquire further than what he has already. I don't believe that the purpose of cross is to go through everything that happened in 1997.

At this point, the district court called for a sidebar conference and acknowledged that it did not know the full contours of the law regarding whether the underlying facts of the conviction could properly be used for impeachment. The court asked the parties to submit briefing on this point and dismissed the jury for the day. The next morning, before the jury returned, the court decided that the government should be allowed to use specific instances of untruthfulness as impeachment because Defendant had "opened the door" to this line of questioning by attempting to minimize the seriousness of his conduct. This minimization occurred, in the court's view, when Defendant (truthfully) stated that he had served only one day in custody for the bank fraud conviction. Therefore, the court held that Defendant had opened the door to the evidence of prior acts that otherwise would have been inadmissible as beyond the limits of Federal Rule of Evidence 609.

The court also ruled that the evidence was admissible under Federal Rule of Evidence 608 as past specific instances probative of untruthfulness. The court stated that Rule 608 "clearly allows specific instances of untruthfulness to be introduced but not to be proved by extrinsic evidence." The court further held that the extent of the questioning was not improper because it had taken only a few minutes, but that the issue whether Defendant had lied to his probation officer was irrelevant and could not be mentioned again. After the jury returned, the court gave a limiting instruction about the proper use of the impeachment evidence. The prosecutor continued cross-examination, asking Defendant whether he had given a false name on two specific occasions, and then moved on to another topic. The government did not mention bank fraud in its closing argument.

The jury returned a guilty verdict. Defendant timely appeals, arguing that the court impermissibly allowed the government to elicit the facts underlying his bank fraud conviction.

STANDARD OF REVIEW

We review for abuse of discretion the district court's admission of specific acts as impeachment evidence. *United States v. Geston*, 299 F.3d 1130, 1137 (9th Cir. 2002). We also review for abuse of discretion the district court's ruling that the defense opened the door to the introduction of evidence. *United States v. Tory*, 52 F.3d 207, 210 (9th Cir. 1995).

DISCUSSION

A. *Rule 608*

Defendant first argues that the district court erred in holding that the admission of the facts underlying his bank fraud conviction was warranted under Rule 608. Rule 608 provides, in relevant part:

> Specific instances of the conduct of a witness, for the purpose of attacking or supporting the witness' character for truthfulness, *other than conviction of crime as provided in rule 609*, may not be proved by extrinsic evidence. They may, however, in the discretion of the court, if probative of truthfulness or untruthfulness, be inquired into on cross-examination of the witness. . . .

Fed. R. Evid. 608(b) (emphasis added).

The crux of Defendant's argument is that Rule 608 applies only to specific instances of conduct that were *not* the basis of a criminal conviction. Evidence relating to a conviction, he argues, is treated solely under Rule 609. For the following reasons, we agree.

We begin by noting, as one of our sister circuits has, that the interplay between Rules 608 and 609 is complex. *See United States v. Cudlitz*, 72 F.3d 992, 995 (1st Cir. 1996) ("The rules governing this subject-cross-examining a criminal defendant about prior wrongs-are among the most complex and confusing in the entire law of evidence."). We attempt here to clarify the relationship between these two rules.

"We interpret the legislatively enacted Federal Rules of Evidence as we would any statute." *Daubert v. Merrell Dow Pharms., Inc.*, 509 U.S. 579, 587, 113 S. Ct. 2786, 125 L. Ed. 2d 469 (1993). We begin with the text of Rule 608, which we recognize is ambiguous. Defendant argues that Rule 608 exempts from its coverage a witness' prior criminal convictions and instead delegates to Rule 609 any questions relating to such convictions. The government advances a different construction of Rule 608, arguing that the rule is concerned solely with the admissibility of extrinsic evidence. In the government's view, Rule 608 provides only that, while specific instances of the conduct of a witness may not be proved by extrinsic evidence, extrinsic evidence is admissible to prove criminal convictions. Both Defendant's and the government's constructions are plausible. *See* H. Richard Uviller, *Credence, Character, and the Rules of Evidence: Seeing Through the Liar's Tale*, 42 Duke L.J. 776, 804–05, 822 (1993) (advocating for the "extrinsic evidence" reading of the rule but noting that, in a questionnaire sent to 300 federal district judges, the responding group was "almost evenly divided" between the two readings).

Because the plain meaning of the rule is not apparent from its text alone, we turn to legislative history. The 1972 advisory committee's notes to Rule 608(b) support Defendant's "delegation" construction of the rule. The notes provide that "[p]articular instances of conduct, *though not the subject of criminal conviction*, may be inquired into on cross-examination" and "[c]*onviction of crime* as a technique of impeachment *is treated in detail in Rule 609, and here is merely recognized as an exception to the general rule excluding evidence* of specific incidents for impeachment purposes." Fed. R. Evid. 608 advisory committee's notes (1972) (emphases added). Those comments suggest that evidence relating to convictions falls within the exclusive purview of Rule 609.

Several of our sister circuits have also adopted Defendant's proposed construction. *See United States v. Lightfoot*, 483 F.3d 876, 881 (8th Cir.) ("Rule 608(b) . . . confers upon district courts discretion to permit witness-credibility questioning on specific bad acts *not resulting in a felony conviction*." (emphasis added)), *cert. denied*, [552] U.S. [1053], 128 S. Ct. 682, 169 L. Ed. 2d 534 (2007); *United States v. Parker*, 133 F.3d 322, 327 (5th Cir. 1998) ("Prior bad acts that have *not resulted in a conviction* are admissible under [Rule] 608(b) if relevant to the witness's character for truthfulness or untruthfulness." (emphasis added)); *Mason v. Texaco, Inc.*, 948 F.2d 1546, 1556 (10th Cir. 1991) ("Under [Rule] 608(b), a defendant may impeach a Government witness by cross-examining him about specific instances of conduct *not resulting in conviction* if such conduct is probative of the witness' character for truthfulness or untruthfulness." (emphasis added) (internal quotation marks omitted)).

We further recognize the unfairness that would result if evidence relating to a conviction is prohibited by Rule 609 but admitted through the "back door" of Rule 608. *See* Donald H. Ziegler, *Harmonizing Rules 609 and 608(b) of the Federal Rules of Evidence*, 2003 Utah L. Rev. 635, 677 (2003) ("[I]t plainly seems unfair to forbid impeachment under Rule 609[ ] but allow the defendant to be questioned about the underlying acts under Rule 608(b).").

The government's citation to *United States v. Hurst*, 951 F.2d 1490, 1500–01 (6th Cir. 1991), is unavailing. In *Hurst*, the court permitted brief questioning under Rule 608(b) about the conduct leading to the conviction because the name of the offense, subornation of perjury, did not convey enough information to the jury to assess how the conviction related to the witness' credibility. *Id.* at 1501. Bank fraud, the name of the offense at issue here, is more self-explanatory than subornation of perjury. Moreover, the dishonesty aspect of the crime was covered adequately by the initial questioning, to which Defendant did not object. Therefore, *Hurst* is not particularly persuasive.

The government also argues on policy grounds that it does not make sense to bar inquiry into dishonest acts just because a witness was eventually convicted for them. But that argument ignores that evidence of a prior conviction for dishonest acts can be far more prejudicial to a defendant than evidence of dishonest acts that have not been held to violate the law. Under the government's interpretation, a bad act resulting in a conviction would be, in a sense, counted twice-once by presenting the bad act itself and once by presenting the conviction that flowed from it. The risk of unfair prejudice or undue emphasis is the reason why Rule 609 and its related case law carefully guide the admission of prior convictions and their underlying facts.

Echoing the observations of the Fifth, Eighth, and Tenth Circuits, we hold that Rule 608(b) permits impeachment only by specific acts that have not resulted in a criminal conviction. Evidence relating to impeachment by way of criminal conviction is treated exclusively under Rule 609, to which we now turn.

B. *Rule 609*

The next question is whether the impeachment evidence was properly admitted under Rule 609, which provides in part: "[E]vidence that any witness has been convicted of a crime shall be admitted regardless of the punishment, if it readily can be determined that establishing the elements of the crime required proof or admission of an act of dishonesty or false statement by the witness." Fed. R. Evid. 609(a)(2).

It is undisputed that bank fraud is an act of dishonesty, so the offense falls under Rule 609(a)(2). But the scope of inquiry into prior convictions is limited. " '[A]bsent exceptional circumstances, evidence of a prior conviction admitted for impeachment purposes may not include collateral details and circumstances attendant upon the conviction.' " *United States v. Sine*, 493 F.3d 1021, 1036 n. 14 (9th Cir. 2007) (quoting *United States v. Rubio*, 727 F.2d 786, 797 n. 5 (9th Cir. 1983)). Generally, "only the prior conviction, its general nature, and punishment of felony range [are] fair game for testing the defendant's credibility." *United States v. Albers*, 93 F.3d 1469, 1480 (10th Cir. 1996); *see also United States v. Gordon*, 780 F.2d 1165, 1176 (5th Cir. 1986) (limiting cross-examination to "the number of convictions, the nature of the crimes and the dates and times of the convictions" and excluding "the particular facts of [the defendant's] previous offenses").

The scope of the inquiry is limited because of the unfair prejudice and confusion that could result from eliciting details of the prior crime. *See United States v. Robinson*, 8 F.3d 398, 410 (7th Cir. 1993) (holding that the impeaching party is not "entitled to harp on the witness's crime, parade it lovingly before the jury in all its gruesome details, and thereby shift the focus of attention from the events at issue in the present case to the witness's conviction in a previous case") (internal quotations marks omitted); *United States v. Roenigk*, 810 F.2d 809, 815 (8th Cir. 1987) ("The problem with excessive references to the details of prior criminal conduct is that the jury is likely to infer that the defendant is more likely to have committed the offense for which he is being tried than if he had previously led a blameless life.").

The government does not argue in this case that its cross-examination of Defendant stayed within the established bounds of inquiry under Rule 609. It instead asserts that Defendant "opened the door" to questions about his specific dishonest acts because his testimony about serving only one day in prison minimized the seriousness of his bank fraud offense. We disagree.

In a criminal prosecution, the government may introduce otherwise inadmissible evidence when the defendant "opens the door" by introducing potentially misleading testimony. *United States v. Beltran-Rios*, 878 F.2d 1208, 1212 (9th Cir. 1989). A defendant may open the door by minimizing, or attempting to explain away, a prior conviction. *See, e.g., United States v. Baylor*, 97 F.3d 542, 545 (D.C. Cir. 1996) (noting that "a witness may 'open the door' to more extensive cross-examination by attempting to minimize the conduct for which he was convicted"). If a defendant opens the door, the prosecution may "introduce evidence on the same issue to rebut any *false* impression that might have resulted from the earlier admission." *Sine*, 493 F.3d at 1037 (internal quotation marks omitted).

In *Sine*, we held that a defendant's accurate testimony did not open the door to the introduction of otherwise inadmissible evidence by the government. *Id.* The defendant had stated in his direct testimony that a judge " 'wrote up some bad things about [him]' " in an order from a prior criminal contempt proceeding that was inadmissible in his criminal fraud trial. *Id.* On cross-examination, the government questioned the defendant using specific phrases that appeared in the judge's order, such as "chicanery," "mendacity," and "rife with deceit." *Id.* at 1029. We held that the defendant's "limited" *accurate* testimony about the judge's order "was insufficient to open the door to the government's otherwise impermissible references to the order, as [the defendant] did not introduce an inaccurate portrait of the order itself." *Id.* at 1037. We rejected the government's argument that the defendant's testimony had painted a picture of " 'selflessness and hope,' " thereby opening the door to use of the inadmissible order. *Id.* "Presenting a theory of the case that can be effectively rebutted by otherwise-inadmissible evidence," we held, "does not by itself open the door to using such evidence; only partial, misleading use of the evidence can do so." *Id.* at 1038.

Sine controls here. Defendant was asked how much time he had spent in prison for bank fraud, and he accurately answered "one day." Defendant did not attempt to explain away or otherwise minimize his conviction, as did the defendants in the cases cited by the government. *See, e.g., United States v. Jackson*, 310 F.3d 1053, 1053–54 (8th Cir. 2002) (per curiam) (holding that where a defendant testified that he was previously convicted for attempted capital murder because " '[t]here's no self-defense law in Arkansas,' " the prosecution could elicit, on cross-examination, several details of the crime that were inconsistent with the implication that the defendant had acted in self-defense (alteration in original)); *United States v. Perry*, 857 F.2d 1346, 1352 (9th Cir. 1988) (holding that the defendant opened the door when he attempted to "explain away" his prior convictions "by offering his own version of the underlying facts" (internal quotation marks omitted)). Defendant did not testify about the underlying facts of, or create a false impression about, his conviction; he truthfully answered the question asked. Under *Sine*, that answer was insufficient to open the door to questions about the details of his offense. If the government believed that Defendant's answer about incarceration risked minimizing his crime in the eyes of the jury, it could have questioned Defendant further about the sentence, such as by inquiring how much restitution he had to pay, rather than asking several collateral and prejudicial questions about the underlying dishonest acts.

The government also argues that, even if it was error to admit the evidence, any error was harmless for three reasons: (1) the cross-examination consisted of only 9 of 68 pages of Defendant's trial testimony; (2) the judge gave a limiting instruction; and (3) the prosecutor did not mention the prior bad acts in closing argument. We are not persuaded. The prosecutor hammered Defendant about several specific instances in which he lied to perpetrate bank fraud. The limiting instruction was not given when the government first began its inquiry into the bank fraud acts; rather, it was given the next morning, after Defendant had already been asked about most of the dishonest acts and the jurors had had an evening to assimilate the damaging information. Even though the prosecutor did not mention these acts in its closing argument, the repeated questions about the lies Defendant told in the course of the bank fraud were likely to have influenced the jury's view of Defendant's credibility. Credibility was critical in this case because Defendant's account of the events was pitted against that of the only other eyewitness, Medina. Allowing the prosecution to repeatedly question Osazuwa about his lack of truthfulness in the course of the bank fraud prejudicially tipped the scales against Osazuwa's defense.

CONCLUSION

In short, evidence relating to a prior conviction is not admissible under Rule 608. Evidence of a prior conviction of a crime that involves dishonesty may be admissible under Rule 609. But evidence admissible under Rule 609 for impeachment purposes may not include collateral details of the crime of conviction. A defendant does not "open the door" to otherwise inadmissible evidence by doing no more than providing a truthful answer to a direct question. Here, the improperly admitted testimony prejudiced his case.

For these reasons, we hold that the district court abused its discretion in admitting evidence of the acts underlying Defendant's conviction for bank fraud and that the error was not harmless.

REVERSED and REMANDED.

EXERCISE

Prior to his criminal trial, the government provides Evgeuni written notice that if he takes the stand on his own behalf, the government will seek to impeach his testimony with his 20 year old conviction for larceny. The conviction arose from Evgeuni's theft of multiple pieces of gold over several months from his then-employer, a jewelry company. Evgeuni objects and the Judge withholds a ruling, pending Evgeuni's testimony at trial. At trial Evgeuni takes the stated in his own defense. In an attempt to establish that he is a dutiful worker, Evgeuni testifies that he previously worked at a jewelry store for five months, and that he had left that job and eventually found another position. Evgeuni does not mention the reason for his departure from the jewelry company. Evgeuni also testifies regarding several other jobs he has held in his lifetime. Based on Evgeuni's testimony, should the trial judge now allow the government to ask the defendant about his larceny conviction?

§ 6.04 IMPEACHMENT: PRIOR INCONSISTENT STATEMENTS

[A] The Common Law

Some Observations on Credibility: Impeachment of Witnesses
52 Cornell L.Q. 239, 245–49 (1967)[21]
Mason Ladd

*   *   *

Impeachment by Prior Inconsistent Statement

The impeachment by proof of prior inconsistent statements occurs when the attempt to refresh recollection fails because the witness denies making the out-of-court statement and extrinsic evidence is admitted to prove that he did in fact make it. Ordinarily, the party who calls the witness endeavors to refresh his memory by inquiry concerning his past contradictory statements. When impeachment by prior inconsistent statement is used by the adverse party in cross-examination, the primary objective is to destroy the testimony given in court; there is little hope that the witness will ever admit, much less acknowledge the correctness of, the out-of-court statement. Truth testing through this process involves a somewhat complicated combination of rules, skills, and techniques.

Preliminary analysis of what is known as the Rule of *The Queen's Case* is required for comprehensive understanding of the use of inconsistent statements for impeachment. This 1820 English decision was widely followed in this country, although repudiated in England by legislation. However, its complete elimination is certain in the future development of the law in this country.

The Rule of *The Queen's Case* confused the principles applicable to the best evidence rule with principles applicable to cross-examination concerning the terms of a writing of the witness, when he is being examined about the writing only for the purpose of discrediting his testimony given in court. Under the best evidence rule, where the writing itself is the subject of inquiry, the proof of the contents of the writing is the document itself. Inquiry through secondary sources as to its content cannot be made until it is shown by acceptable proof that the original document is unavailable. If, however, the purpose of the examination into the content of the document is to discredit the witness about matters stated therein, cross-examination as to whether he wrote it and what he said in it may be a most effective method of determining his credibility if he denies making the writing or states its content to be something different than in fact it is. The Rule of *The Queen's Case* required that the writing be shown to the witness before permitting interrogation upon its content, thus eliminating what may be an effective part of the impeachment. Likewise, in reference to an oral statement made out of court, counsel on

---

[21] Copyright © 1967. Reprinted with permission of the Cornell Law Quarterly.

cross-examination may prefer, for the purpose of impeachment, first to ask the witness what he had said, if anything, rather than confront him initially with the statement. In the situation either of a writing or an oral statement, if the witness were asked what he said before being confronted with the statement, he might give a different story, thus disclosing his desire to evade the effect of what he had said previously. Whatever the effect of the divergent answers on his credibility may be, there have been strong protests against restraints on this type of cross-examination.

The elimination of the Rule of *The Queen's Case* would be misleading if it were interpreted as meaning that it is no longer desirable in most situations to inform a witness of the content of his prior allegedly inconsistent statement before offering extrinsic proof that the statement was made. The modern trend is to leave this question to the court's discretion, but in most jurisdictions the rule is that, before proof of the statement or introduction of the writing, the statement must be made known or the writing shown to the declarant so that he will have the opportunity to identify and explain or deny it. *The Queen's Case*, however, dealt only with the question of timing when the content of the alleged contradictory declaration should be made known to the declarant; the question of when proof of the statement should be offered was not involved in that case. The currently favored procedures make it possible to make the impeaching testimony more meaningful should the witness deny making the statement or claim that its contents were different than they in fact are.

A common practice is to proceed as though attempting to refresh the recollection of the witness, making the content of the statement known to him; then, if he denies making the statement, proof by extrinsic evidence may be offered. The detailed steps for impeachment by proof of prior statements of a witness contradictory to the testimony given in court fit into a simple formula, easy to follow and more effective in truth testing than in attempting to do less. A foundation should be laid, identifying the time, place, occasion, and the person to whom it is claimed the declaration in question was made. The witness should then be informed of the statement and asked if he made it. Only if he denies making the statement may those to whom the statement was made be called to present the impeaching testimony. They, too, will be examined in a similar manner to establish the making of the statement. If the alleged statement was in writing, it would be shown to the declarant with opportunity to admit or deny it as his. In event of denial, the writing should be authenticated and offered in evidence.

The Uniform Rules of Evidence have not made the above procedure a rigid requirement, but leave it to the discretion of the judge to determine whether all of the protection afforded through bringing the prior contradictory statements to the attention of the witness while testifying is necessary in the particular case. A significant exception applies when the witness is a party and has made an out-of-court declaration inconsistent with his testimony. The statement would be used by the adverse party only if disserving to the declarant and, therefore, is admissible as an admission. It is substantive evidence requiring no foundation other than proof of the fact that the statement was made by the party against whom it is offered.

As a practical trial technique to gain the most from impeaching testimony through the proof of prior inconsistent statements, it is preferable to follow the procedure of laying the full foundation with a denial by the witness that he made the statement. If the triers of fact conclude that the statement was in fact made, the impeachment value is enhanced. The triers may look upon the denial as an intentional falsification rather than a failure to remember. The principle of *falsa in uno, falsa in omnibus* may become applicable if there is other evidence indicating intention to falsify.

[B]   The Federal Rules of Evidence: Rule 613

[1]   Changes from the Common Law

Prior to the adoption of the Federal Rules of Evidence, most jurisdictions had already abolished the Rule of *The Queen's Case.* Consequently, the abolition of this rule in Rule 613(a) represents a codification of that common law trend. Rule 613(b), on the other hand, significantly modifies the common law foundation requirement, as the court explained in *United States v. Barrett.*

UNITED STATES v. BARRETT

United States Court of Appeals, First Circuit
539 F.2d 244 (1976)

Levin H. Campbell, Circuit Judge.

Arthur Barrett appeals from his conviction after a jury trial for crimes arising from the theft and sale of a collection of postage stamps from the Cardinal Spellman Philatelic Museum in Weston, Massachusetts. Barrett and seven others were charged in a three-count indictment with the interstate transportation of stolen postage stamps, . . . the receipt, concealment, sale, barter, and disposal of stolen postage stamps, . . . and conspiracy. . . . Of the eight indicted, Barrett alone went to trial.

*   *   *

Adams, an admitted and convicted burglar and thief, testified for the Government in exchange for protection for himself and his family. He testified that he was introduced to Barrett by Ben Tilley in early 1972 for the purpose of discussing alarms, and that Barrett displayed knowledge of the use of an ohmmeter to identify alarm wires. Adams also testified that right after being arrested Barrett described his involvement, along with Kirzner, in the Cardinal Spellman stamp theft. He characterized Barrett as "a little familiar with stamps" and as having spoken of collections and stamps, specifically "'Zeplins'" (which the Cardinal Spellman Collection included).

After the Government rested, the defense unsuccessfully sought to introduce testimony from three witnesses under circumstances discussed below; otherwise it presented no testimony of consequence. The defense urged in closing argument that Barrett had been deliberately misidentified by Kirzner for ulterior purposes; that Bass's identification of Barrett was as unreliable as his identification of Tilley, and that "Buzzy" Adams was fingering "Bucky" Barrett to cover his own participation in the stamp theft.

*   *   *

III

We turn next to the court's exclusion of the testimony of the defense's two remaining witnesses, Thomas J. Delaney and Jeanne Kelley. We hold such exclusion to have been error.

Delaney stated that he met with Buzzy Adams in or around November, 1974, in a Boston area restaurant. He was then asked to relate their conversation. The Government objected and Barrett offered to prove that "Adams said that he had heard that Barrett had been indicted, or had gotten into trouble on this matter, and that it was too bad because he, Buzzy, knew that Barrett was not involved." Kelley, a waitress, was prepared to testify that, while waiting on Adams and Delaney at the same restaurant, she overheard Adams say "it was a shame that Bucky got arrested on this matter" because he (Adams) "knew that Bucky didn't have anything to do with it."

Conceding that this evidence was hearsay, Fed.R.Evid. 801(d)(1), and so inadmissible to prove the truth of the matter asserted, Barrett argues that it was admissible as a prior inconsistent statement to impeach Adams' credibility. Adams had earlier testified that Barrett admitted to him shortly after his arrest that he had been involved in the stamp transaction. Barrett contends that Adams' subsequent statement to Delaney in November, 1974, that Barrett was not involved, was contradictory and so admissible to impeach his credibility.

We believe the court erred in excluding this testimony. Counsel for Barrett advised the court, albeit rather succinctly, that the testimony went to the credibility of Adams who had testified. The court ruled it out on the ground that it was a "hearsay opinion by Mr. Adams, that this guy is innocent. That is all this amounts to." The Government now argues, in the same vein, that Adams' purported opinion was too vague and unsupported to be useful. However, the clear purport of Adams' direct testimony was that in late October, 1974, after Barrett's arrest, Adams acquired first-hand knowledge of Barrett's involvement in the stamp affair, and the jury could have inferred from this and other testimony that at all times thereafter Adams remained of the impression that Barrett was involved. The statement to Delaney, therefore, made supposedly in November, 1974, was clearly inconsistent. To be received as a prior inconsistent statement, the contradiction need not be "in plain terms. It is enough if the proffered testimony, taken as a whole, either by what it says or by what it omits to say, affords some indication that the fact was different from the testimony of the witness whom it is sought to contradict." . . . Furthermore, the fact that Adams's belief that Bucky was not involved might be called an "opinion" is immaterial. . . . The important point is the clear incompatibility between Adams' direct testimony and the alleged statement.

The Government also argues that Delaney's memory of the timing of the statement was uncertain, as well as his memory as to other details. And it may well be that Delaney's testimony would have turned out to be inadequate and thin in various respects. But this possibility is not a ground for keeping the evidence from the jury, which is the principal judge of the credibility of witnesses and the weight to be given to otherwise competent testimony.

A more serious argument pressed by the Government is that Barrett failed during cross-examination to lay a foundation for introducing extrinsic evidence of the statement by first directing Adams' attention to the occasion of the alleged contradictory statement and asking him if he made it. Such is the procedure laid down in *Queen Caroline's Case*, 2 Brod. & Bing. 284, 313, 129 Eng. Rep. 976 (1820), and required in many jurisdictions (though not in Massachusetts). It is clear, however, that Fed.R.Evid. 613(b) has relaxed any absolute requirement that this practice be observed, only requiring instead that the witness be afforded at some time an opportunity to explain or deny, and for further interrogation. The purpose of the wording of the new rule is fully explained by the Reporter of the Committee on Rules of Practice and Procedure, of the Judicial Conference of the United States, and we reproduce his relevant commentary in full:

> The traditional practice in most jurisdictions, when it is sought to impeach a witness by proof of a prior inconsistent statement, has been to require that a foundation be laid during the cross-examination of the witness. This foundation consists of directing the attention of the witness to the time when, place where, and person to whom the alleged statement was made, and asking the witness whether under those circumstances he made substantially that statement. In the absence of this preliminary routine, extrinsic evidence to prove the prior statement is held inadmissible.

> The objectives of the procedure are: (1) to save time, since the witness may admit having made the statement and thus make the extrinsic proof unnecessary; (2) to avoid unfair surprise to the opposite party by affording him an opportunity to draw a denial or explanation from the witness; and (3) to give the witness himself, in fairness, a chance to deny or to explain the apparent discrepancy. These are desirable objectives. The second and third can, however, be achieved by affording an opportunity to explain at any time during the trial, and no particular time sequence is required. Only the first of the objectives named above, saving time, points in the direction of the traditional foundation requirement on cross-examination, and even here countervailing factors are present: the time saved is not great; the laying of the foundation may inadvertently have been overlooked; the impeaching statement may not have been discovered until later; and premature disclosure may on occasion frustrate the effective impeachment of collusive witnesses. The argument may be made that the recalling of a witness for further cross-examination will afford an adequate solution for these difficulties and hence that the traditional procedure should be retained. The argument is not a sound one. In the first place, recall for cross-examination has traditionally been very much within the discretion of the judge and seems likely to continue so. And secondly, the admissibility of prior inconsistent statements ought not to be enmeshed in the technicalities of cross-examination when all that is being sought is the presentation of an opportunity to deny or explain.

In view of these considerations, the Advisory Committee concluded that the objectives could better be achieved by allowing the opportunity to deny or explain to occur at any time during the trial, rather than limiting it to cross-examination.

Moreover, occasionally situations may arise where the interests of justice will warrant dispensing entirely with the opportunity to explain or deny. Thus if a witness becomes unavailable through absence or death, the judge ought to have discretion to allow the impeaching statement.

In my view, the existing practice would continue in general to be followed under the rule. It is convenient and effective to raise the matter on cross-examination, and doing so would avoid problems that might ultimately arise if witnesses become unavailable before the end of the trial. The rule ought, however, to remain as drawn, leaving the practical approach to the good sense of the practitioner.

* * *

The foregoing indicates that while good practice still calls for the laying a foundation, one is not absolutely required. It would have been desirable for defense counsel to have asked Adams on cross-examination if he had made the purported statement to Delaney. And where this was not done, if Adams had later become unavailable to explain or deny, the court might properly in its discretion have refused to receive the testimony in question. Here, however, the court dismissed the evidence out of hand and made no inquiry into Adams' availability. On the present record, we have no basis for assuming that he was not available, or even that judicial economy and convenience would have justified the court in ruling as it did. We hold, therefore, that it was error to exclude the testimony.

* * *

EXCERPT FROM TRIAL TRANSCRIPT

NARRATOR: This is a criminal action arising out of the theft and sale of a collection of postage stamps from the Cardinal Spellman Philatelic Museum in Weston, Massachusetts, on March 29, 1973.

Defendant Arthur Barrett and seven other individuals were indicted for criminal conspiracy, interstate transportation of stolen postage stamps, and concealment, sale, barter, and disposal of stolen postage stamps. Of the eight indicted, Barrett was the only defendant to go to trial. Two of Barrett's co-defendants pleaded guilty to one count of interstate transportation of stolen postage stamps. The charges against the remaining five defendants were dismissed.

On the third day of Barrett's jury trial before the United States District Court for the District of Massachusetts, we are still in the Government's case- in-chief. Through its counsel, Mr. Collera, it has called Mr. Robert (a/k/a Buzzy) Adams, a convicted thief and burglar who agreed to testify for the Government in exchange for protection for himself and his family.

DIRECT EXAMINATION — BY MR. COLLERA

Q: Mr. Adams, do you know the defendant, Arthur Barrett?

A: Yes, I do.

Q: Can you tell the Court how and when you were introduced to him?

A: Ben Tilley introduced me to Barrett, oh, I guess some time in early '72.

Q: What was the purpose of that meeting with Tilley and Barrett?

A: The purpose was to talk about alarms. We told him about the stamp score coming down. We asked him if he would be interested in taking a look at the alarm at the museum to find out if the alarm could possibly be by-passed. Barrett said he didn't know. He wanted to know what kind of alarm it was, you know, ADT or whatever.

Q: Did you tell him about the alarm, Mr. Adams?

A: Well, I told him I thought it might be a RIEP, but I wasn't positive.

Q: Was that the end of the conversation?

A: No. He said he could not tell anything from what I told him, and he would have to go down and take a look at it and do what you call a "reading" with an ohmmeter on the telephone lines in order to determine what the voltage was and what you could do about it.

Q: Mr. Adams, is this the only contact you had with the defendant?

A: No, there were other times, too.

Q: Do you recall having any conversations with Barrett that gave you any indication that he was involved in the Cardinal Spellman theft?

A: Yeah.

Q: Do you recall when that was?

A: Yes, right after he was arrested for this wrap. October, late October '74, I think.

Q: Will you recount that conversation for the Court, Mr. Adams?

A: Uh-huh. I asked him what was the story and how did they come down to his house and arrest him. He said that he didn't know too much about that. I said, "How bad is it; how bad have they got you?" He said, "Well, they got me. I bartered with the people that bought the stuff. They can identify me with no problem." He said he was worried about this other fellow, the dealer, Michael Kirzner.

Q: He said he was worried about Mike Kirzner?

A: Right.

Q: Why was he worried about him?

A: Because that is who he dealt with, and the other guys.

Q: Did Barrett at any time mention anything else specifically about the theft?

A: He told me about the stuff — the collection, you know. Like, uh — "zeplins," you know, the stamps, you know — that's a specific kind of stamp. He seemed to know a little about stamps.

NARRATOR: After the close of the Government's case-in-chief, the defendant, Barrett, through his counsel, Ms. Smith, attempted to introduce testimony from two defense witnesses. Ms. Smith called Thomas Delaney. After he has identified himself and given other background information, the questioning of him continues.

DIRECT EXAMINATION — BY MS. SMITH

Q: Mr. Delaney, do you know Robert Adams, also known as "Buzzy" Adams?

A: Yes, sir, I do.

Q: How long have you known him?

A: About three years.

Q: At some time in about October or November 1974, Mr. Delaney, did you ever have a conversation with Mr. Adams at a bar or tavern?

A: Yes, sir, I did.

Q: And in what bar did this conversation occur?

A: The Red Carpet Restaurant.

Q: Where is the "Red Carpet," is that it? Where is the Red Carpet Restaurant located?

A: In Quincy.

Q: Can you tell the Court when that conversation occurred — October or November 1974 — or when it was?

A: I think it was November.

Q: So it might have been after that — in December 1974 or even after that?

A: I thought it was November, but I am not sure.

Q: All right. Mr. Delaney, will you tell the Court what conversation you had with Mr. Adams that day at the Red Carpet Restaurant?

MR. COLLERA: I am going to object, Your Honor.

THE COURT: Counsel approach the bench.

(Conference at the bench.)

THE COURT: Ms. Smith, what is the expected testimony of this witness?

MS. SMITH: Your Honor, the witness will testify that he had a conversation with Buzzy Adams in which Adams stated that he had heard that Barrett had been indicted, or had gotten into trouble on this matter, and that it was too bad because he, Buzzy, knew that Bucky Barrett was not involved with the score.

MR. COLLERA: And how would Delaney know that?

MS. SMITH: He asked Adams.

THE COURT: Is that the end of the conversation?

MS. SMITH: To my knowledge, Your Honor, that is it.

THE COURT: Now, Ms. Smith, that would be out on hearsay grounds.

MS. SMITH: How about the credibility of Buzzy Adams who testified earlier, Your Honor?

THE COURT: I am going to take a look at one section of the code, counsel, but that is a hearsay opinion by Mr. Adams — that this guy, Barrett, is innocent. That's all that this amounts to — a hearsay opinion. From what you said to Ms. Smith, I will treat it as an offer of proof.

Wait just a minute; I am going to look at the code. There is one section of the code I want to check, but what you said as far as I am concerned — where you said the witness would testify that Adams made a statement that in his opinion—

MS. SMITH: No, that he knew.

THE COURT: All right. He knew. All right.

MS. SMITH: Your Honor, that would indicate that he was involved in the incident and he knew Barrett was not — that Barrett was not involved.

MR. COLLERA: Involved in what?

MS. SMITH: In the crimes he was indicted for.

MR. COLLERA: You don't even know—

THE COURT: Let's not quibble; let me see the code. (Pause) All right. I am making a ruling that this is an offer of proof, and I am excluding it.

(End of bench conference.)

THE COURT: You are excused, Mr. Delaney.

NARRATOR: Defendant, through his counsel, called Jeanne Kelley.

MS. SMITH: May we approach the bench, Your Honor?

THE COURT: Yes.

(Conference at the bench.)

THE COURT: Who is she?

MS. SMITH: Her name is Jeanne Kelley, Your Honor, of 85 Old Harbor Street, Boston — South Boston. She would testify that at the time of the incident about which Mr. Delaney would testify that she was the waitress and that Mr. Adams came into the bar and sat down with Mr. Delaney. That she overheard Adams say something to the effect that it was a shame that Bucky had been arrested on this matter and that he, Adams, knew that Bucky did not have anything to do with it.

THE COURT: All right. I'll treat this as an offer of proof.

MS. SMITH: May the record reflect that the defendant was prepared to elicit this testimony from Ms. Kelley?

THE COURT: Oh, yes.

MS. SMITH: The defendant rests, Your Honor.

THE COURT: All right, but you had better announce that.

(End of bench conference.)

THE COURT: Ms. Kelley, you are excused.

MS. SMITH: The defendant rests, if Your Honor please.

THE COURT: All right.

NARRATOR: Barrett was convicted on all counts. This conviction was overturned by the United States Court of Appeals for the First Circuit after concluding that the trial court had committed reversible error in refusing to admit the prior inconsistent statements of the prosecution witness, Buzzy Adams.

[2] What Constitutes an Inconsistency?

When are statements inconsistent? Obviously, if two statements assert that opposing facts are true, they are inconsistent with one another. In *Barrett* Adam's testimony was that Barrett had acknowledged to him his involvement in the stamp theft, while his previous statement was that it was too bad that Barrett had gotten into trouble because Adams knew that Barrett was not involved. Often, however, variations in assertions are much more subtle. For example, if a witness gives an account of a transaction with detail and precision on one occasion and then is either evasive or selectively forgetful on another, is the witness' subsequent incomplete statement "inconsistent"? In *United States v. Morgan*, 555 F.2d 238 (9th Cir. 1977), the court declared that it was.

Morgan involved witnesses who had given precise information to the grand jury on the names of persons who were involved in a particular transaction and how much money was paid to certain individuals. When those witnesses gave indefinite, uncertain, and incomplete answers at trial on the same issues, the prosecution read the testimony that the witnesses had given to the grand jury. In response to the claim that the prior statements were not inconsistent, the court stated:

> We certainly do not wish to encourage the indiscriminate use of prior-prepared statements. We feel, nevertheless, that trial judges must retain a high degree of flexibility in deciding the exact point at which a prior statement is sufficiently inconsistent with a witness's trial testimony to permit its use in evidence. While the rule itself contains no guidelines as to how we are to determine "inconsistency," we find guidance in Judge Weinstein's Treatise on Evidence [4 WEINSTEIN'S EVIDENCE, Matthew Bender, pp. 801-76 to 801-76.1 (1976)]:

. . . Rule 801(d)(1)(A) is silent on whether the impeachment case law test of "inconsistency" should be read into this new rule giving prior inconsistent statements substantive effect. Fortunately, this presents far less of a problem than it would in some jurisdictions which take the highly technical view of finding an inconsistency only when this is apparent on the face of the two statements and the only possible inference. The better view, urged by Wigmore, McCormick, and others, and followed by the federal courts, allows the prior statement whenever a reasonable man could infer on comparing the whole effect of the two statements that they had been produced by inconsistent beliefs. In other words, the keystone for impeachment use is relevancy — would the prior statement of the witness help the trier of fact evaluate the credibility of the witness. . . . The approach under Rule 801 should be the same. Here the question is not whether the statement is helpful in evaluating credibility, but whether it is helpful in resolving a material, consequential fact in issue. . . ."

United States v. Morgan, 555 F.2d 238, 242 (9th Cir. 1977).

As the Supreme Court of California further explained:

Inconsistency in effect, rather than contradiction in express terms, is the test for admitting a witness' prior statement, . . . and the same principle governs the case of the forgetful witness. . . . [H]ere Porter [the Government's witness] admittedly remembered the events both leading up to and following the crucial moment when the marijuana came into his possession, and as to that moment his testimony was equivocal. . . . We conclude that Porter's deliberate evasion of the latter point in his trial testimony must be deemed to constitute an implied denial that defendant did in fact furnish him with the marijuana as charged. His testimony was thus materially inconsistent with his preliminary hearing testimony and his extra-judicial declaration to Officer Wade, in both of which he specifically named defendant as his supplier.

State v. Green, 3 Cal. 3d 981, 985, 92 Cal. Rptr. 494, 479 P.2d 989 (1971). Federal courts have adopted the position of *Green* that feigned memory loss or deliberate evasiveness is a form of inconsistent statement. *See United States v. Shoupe*, 548 F.2d 636, 643 (6th Cir. 1977); *United States v. Insana*, 423 F.2d 1165, 1170 (2d Cir. 1970).

[3] Using Illegally Obtained Statements in Criminal Cases for Impeachment Purposes

If the Government obtained the prior inconsistent statement as a result of a violation of the defendant's Fourth Amendment protection against unreasonable searches and seizures or of his Fifth Amendment privilege against compelled self-incrimination, the exclusionary rule prohibits the Government from using the statement in establishing the defendant's guilt. Is the Government also prohibited from using the prior statement to impeach the defendant if the defendant takes the witness stand at her trial and gives testimony that is inconsistent with the prior statement? If the statement is reliable, because it was not the product of coercion, the Supreme Court has held that the Government may use a defendant's prior inconsistent statement to impeach, and the impeachment may be by way of contradicting testimony that the defendant has given on either direct or cross-examination, so long as the cross-examination is within the scope of the subject matter that the defendant voluntarily opened in her direct testimony. As the Court explained:

> There is no gainsaying that arriving at the truth is a fundamental goal of our legal system. . . . We have repeatedly insisted that when defendants testify, they must testify truthfully or suffer the consequences. This is true even though a defendant is compelled to testify against his will. . . . It is essential, therefore, to the proper functioning of the adversary system that when a defendant takes the stand, the government be permitted proper and effective cross-examination in an attempt to elicit the truth. The defendant's obligation to testify truthfully is fully binding on him when he is cross-examined. His privilege against self-incrimination does not shield him from proper questioning. . . . He would unquestionably be subject to a perjury prosecution if he knowingly lies on cross-examination. . . . In terms of impeaching a defendant's seemingly false statements with his prior inconsistent utterances or with other reliable evidence available to the government, we see no difference of constitutional magnitude between the defendant's statements on direct examination and his answers to questions put to him on cross-examination that are plainly within the scope of the defendant's direct examination. Without this opportunity, the normal function of cross-examination would be severely impeded.

> We also think that the policies of the exclusionary rule no more bar impeachment here than they did in *Walder, Harris,* and *Hass* [previous cases in which the Supreme Court held such statements to be admissible.] In those cases, the ends of the exclusionary rules were thought adequately implemented by denying the government the use of the challenged evidence to make out its case in chief. The incremental furthering of those ends by forbidding impeachment of the defendant who testifies was deemed insufficient to permit or require that false testimony go unchallenged, with the resulting impairment of the integrity of the factfinding goals of the criminal trial. We reaffirm this assessment of the competing interests, and hold that a defendant's statements made in response to proper cross-examination reasonably suggested by the defendant's direct examination are subject to otherwise proper impeachment by the government, albeit by evidence that has been illegally obtained and that is inadmissible on the government's direct case, or otherwise, as substantive evidence of guilt.

United States v. Havens, 446 U.S. 620, 626–628 (1980).

[4]   Conduct as a Prior Inconsistent Statement

One can communicate through conduct as well as speech. The most obvious example is an affirmative or negative nod of the head in response to a question. It would be logical to conclude that if prior conduct is relevant because the message that it conveys is inconsistent with testimony, the conduct would be subject to Rule

613 to the same extent as verbal utterances. The Advisory Committee's Note to Rule 613, however, expressly excludes conduct from the rule: "Under principles of *expression unius* the rule does not apply to impeachment by evidence of prior inconsistent conduct." Advisory Committee's Note to Rule 613, 56 F.R.D. 183, 279 (1972). *See also United States v. Smith*, 605 F.2d 839 (5th Cir. 1979).

Rule 801(a), which defines hearsay for purposes of the hearsay rule's prohibition, defines a "statement" as an oral or written assertion or *non-verbal conduct* that the declarant *intended as an assertion*. In light of the purpose of Rule 613, would it not be preferable to similarly construe "statements" for purposes of Rule 613 as encompassing conduct that the declarant intended as a communication and as a substitute for words?

[5] "[P]rovision Does Not Apply to Admissions"

Rule 613(b) explicitly states that "this provision does not apply to admissions of a party opponent." Why are only admissions excluded? The Advisory Committee's Notes to Rule 613 provide no answer. If admissions are excluded from the rule because they are otherwise admissible for their substantive truth, does this mean that all inconsistent statements that are otherwise admissible for their truth (either excluded from the definition of hearsay, like the admission, or admissible under an exception in Rules 803 or 804) are also impliedly excluded from Rule 613? The common understanding seems to be that if there is an independent basis for admissibility, Rule 613 is inapplicable. *See United States v. IBM*, 432 F. Supp. 138, 139 (S.D.N.Y. 1977).

§ 6.05   IMPEACHMENT: BIAS

[A]   Demonstrating Bias

Of all the factors that a party may examine in evaluating a witness' credibility, the mind-set that the witness brings into the litigation is possibly the most probative. A witness who is biased for or against a party, for whatever reason, may either deliberately distort her testimony or unconsciously color it in order to accommodate the biases or interests that she holds. Therefore, the fairness of the adjudication is dependent upon the witness' potential bias being fully open to exploration on cross-examination and through the introduction of extrinsic evidence.

A party can demonstrate a witness' bias in a number of different ways. The party can show bias through the *statements* of the witness herself. The witness may directly express a bias toward someone, or the witness may indirectly reveal biases and prejudices by the use of racial or ethnic slurs. The *witness' conduct* is also evidence of biases that the witness holds, and the *conduct of others* toward the witness or the witness' friends and associates establishes a basis upon which the witness may have formed biases. For example, slashing the tires of a neighbor or painting a swastika on a synagogue indicate the actor's potential bias or prejudice toward an individual or group of individuals. The commission of these acts is also evidence of bias or animosity that the victims, and those who align themselves with the victims, might harbor toward the actor. *Circumstances, conditions, and relationships* are also probative of a witness' biases. The witness may have a familial, economic, emotional, or litigious relationship to one of the parties. She may have an interest in the outcome of the action as a party, insuror, future claimant, expert witness, or codefendant who has turned government witness in exchange for plea concessions.

The range of facts is infinite from which one can infer bias, prejudice, interest, or partiality of any kind. Litigants' right to establish those facts is limited only by the facts' relevance to the issue. The total preclusion of evidence that is relevant to a question of bias is error. Once a party has fairly raised the issue of bias, however, limitation on proof is within the trial court's discretion, balancing probative value and need against the delay, confusion, and waste of time that further proof of bias will entail. Both the relevance of facts to the question of bias and the adequacy of proof that a court has allowed can be matters about which reasonable minds will differ, as illustrated in the following opinion.

UNITED STATES v. GAMBLER
United States Court of Appeals, District of Columbia Circuit
662 F.2d 834 (1981)

TAMM, CIRCUIT JUDGE:

[Gambler was convicted for wire fraud, false pretenses, and larceny after trust. He was the manager of an interior decorating business. In this business he recommended to, and purchased for, his clients furnishings for the places being decorated. These offenses arose from the defendant having accepted advance payment from Stanley Pottinger and Richard and Barbara Cohen for recommended furniture, using the money for other purposes, and failing to deliver or even order the goods purchased.]

. . . [On appeal] appellant submits that the district court committed reversible error by limiting cross-examination of a complaining witness.

* * *

He argues that he was inappropriately limited in his attempt to probe the accuracy and veracity of statements made by the Government's chief witness Pottinger. In particular, appellant objects to the district court's refusal to allow him to cross-examine Pottinger regarding two civil suits instituted by Pottinger against appellant. Appellant contends that, on the basis of the rationale articulated by this court in *Villaroman v. United States*, 184 F.2d 261 (D.C. Cir. 1950), this refusal to allow cross-examination for bias constituted prejudicial error.

In *Villaroman*, this court reversed a conviction where the district court had refused to allow cross-examination of the complaining witness on the subject of that witness's pending civil suit against the defendant arising out of the same circumstances as the crime with which the defendant was charged. A general rule has evolved from this case and others to the effect that the trial court should allow cross-examination and the airing of evidence with respect to a witness's pending, or even contemplated, suit against the defendant. . . . By allowing a probe into the circumstances of a pending or contemplated lawsuit, it is believed that a defendant may bring to light two factors reflecting the possible bias of the witness: his pecuniary interest in the outcome of the criminal trial and the existence and degree of animosity he may harbor against the defendant.

In this case, however, we are not presented with a situation in which defense counsel sought to probe the subject of pending or contemplated litigation by a witness against the defendant, but one in which counsel attempted to elicit information regarding past litigation. Counsel attempted to extract such information solely to suggest to the jury that Pottinger possessed "considerable hostility" against the defendant that could color his testimony. . . . We cannot assume, as appellant apparently has, the automatic application of *Villaroman* to the case at hand. Here appellant apparently has made no attempt to argue that Pottinger possessed, in this context, any pecuniary interest in the outcome of the trial, a substantial reason for the decision in *Villaroman*. Moreover, we have discovered very little authority discussing the discretion of trial courts to limit cross-examination in similar circumstances, wherein the defendant would have the jury infer hostility, and thereby a motive to falsify testimony, from attempts, now terminated, by a victim to recover compensation for harm perpetrated by the defendant. A state appellate court addressed an analogous situation in a fraud case in which a trial court had foreclosed an inquiry by the defense into the knowledge of the complaining witness before he filed a complaint that the defendant had instituted bankruptcy proceedings. The court affirmed the conviction, noting that the witness,

> as a victim of a crime, stands in the same position as any other victim of a crime and his motive, whether it was outrage due to the crime or a desire for revenge because of the crime, has no relevance to the question of the guilt or innocence of the defendant or the truth or falsity of the testimony.

. . . Neither these sentiments nor the rationale of *Villaroman* readily suggests the resolution of the issue here presented. Absent controlling precedent, we must examine closely the particular circumstances of this case to determine whether the district court exceeded the bounds of its discretion. We are certainly aware that trial courts should give great latitude to defense counsel upon cross-examination of Government witnesses, especially in the area of bias and interest. . . .

The circumstances into which defense counsel sought to inquire cannot be set forth in any summary fashion. Pottinger apparently filed two civil suits against Gambler in an attempt to recover the monies paid out, one suit in New York on May 25, 1979, and another in the District of Columbia approximately three weeks later. . . . The amount requested in each suit was $109,000, including $30,000 for loss of business opportunities and $50,000 for pain and suffering. Gambler filed for bankruptcy on June 29, 1979. . . . Pottinger then filed papers in that proceeding seeking to disallow the discharge of claims he possessed against Gambler. In October of 1979 Gambler filed a lawsuit for defamation against Pottinger. This law suit was settled, however, in a complex agreement in which, among other things, Gambler acknowledged that his suit was groundless and executed a promissory note to Pottinger in the amount of $5,000. In return, Pottinger agreed not to pursue the claims of fraud in the bankruptcy proceeding. . . . Pottinger received no money from that proceeding, however, because no assets were discovered. . . .

At trial, defense counsel attempted to introduce these past proceedings, stating to Pottinger, "I believe you indicated that you initiated a civil suit?" . . . Upon objection, defense counsel explained the necessity for his proposed inquiry:

> it is a matter of showing his hostility toward Mr. Gambler in connection with the type of claims he asserted and his bias against Mr. Gambler, which in turn I think is legitimate for the jury to consider in evaluating his testimony. *This is what he thought he was entitled to, this is what he sued for and he has not received a penny.*

. . . Although noting "some relevance" of the inquiry to bias, the judge ruled that "its relevance is outweighed by confusion of the issues, particularly now that we have to get into the question of bankruptcy, what happened to the bankruptcy proceeding, why it was discharged, and so on." Describing the inquiry as "too far removed," the judge sustained the prosecutor's objection.

In attempting to explore the concluded litigation, defense counsel appeared most intent, at trial and in this court, upon having the jury learn of the amount of damages sought by the complainant in the three different contexts, perhaps to reflect the large measure of animosity allegedly possessed by the witness against the defendant. Were this information introduced, however, the prosecution might well have sought to reexamine Pottinger, and other lawyers employed by him, to establish the validity of the damages sought in the complaint. Balancing the questionable probative value of this amount as indicative of the witness's hostility versus the delay and confusion of the issues resulting from such an extended inquiry, the district court did not abuse its discretion in excluding this evidence. . . .

We believe, however, that the district court did err in sustaining an objection to the initial inquiry made by defense counsel on the subject of Pottinger's lawsuits against the defendant. In so ruling we do not stray from our belief that this case is not controlled by *Villaroman.* Rather, the rationale for our decision is the same as in any other case where the defendant seeks to establish the hostility, and thereby possible bias, of a witness for the prosecution: the defendant must be allowed, either through cross-examination or admission of extrinsic evidence, to set out for the jury the basic facts from which the jury may infer hostility. Pottinger's initiation of legal action may be profitably compared with the existence of a quarrel between him and Gambler. . . . That hostility may be inferred from such a "quarrel" seems to us a reasonable possibility; the exclusion of such discrediting evidence from the view of the jury was therefore erroneous.

We are not unsympathetic to the position in which the district court found itself. Defense counsel sought to explore much more than the bare facts of the litigation between Pottinger and Gambler. . . . The court thus believed itself forced either to allow defense counsel to plunge ahead with his involved exploratory cross-examination or to halt the inquiry ab initio. Although we are loathe to second-guess district courts on such evidentiary matters, we believe that a proper balancing of the defendant's right of cross-examination with the factors of delay and confusion, factors properly considered by the district court, would have resulted in the allowance of a limited examination on this point. As this court has previously stated:

> Our decisions reflect great solicitude for an endeavor by the accused to establish bias on the part of a prosecution witness. They establish the propriety of the showing either by cross-examination or by extrinsic evidence, and indicate the broad range over which the inquiry may extend. We have admonished, however, that when the accused has been afforded a reasonable opportunity to make the point, the trial judge has discretionary authority to limit the scope of the proof. And courts have traditionally exercised their inherent power to confine the impeaching effort to evidentiary items possessing a potential for connoting bias. . . .

This case does not present a question of the trial judge's control over the testimonial scope of cross-examination. . . . Instead, the trial judge here foreclosed any inquiry into Pottinger's unsuccessful litigation against Gambler. Our finding of error does not, however, mandate reversal of appellant's conviction. In this case the district court's failure to allow defense counsel to establish the existence of the witness's prior lawsuits did not affect the substantial rights of the accused and was harmless error beyond a reasonable doubt. . . . Here the jury was fully aware that Pottinger had not received either any of the furnishings ordered or any return of the deposits placed with the defendant. . . . The jury may even have been aware that Pottinger had sued Gambler, through a reference by Pottinger himself and, more readily, because of explicit comments made by the defendant. . . .

Moreover, the defendant was able to present to the jury evidence of Pottinger's pecuniary interest in the outcome of the trial. The district court, recognizing that the possible financial stake of a witness in the outcome of a case is an appropriate subject for cross-examination, . . . allowed defense counsel to inquire into possible tax deductions available to Pottinger for the losses incurred through transactions with the defendant and the effect of the defendant's conviction upon that availability. The jury was thus given reason to question the disinterested nature of Pottinger's testimony, especially in light of the court's explicit instruction on that testimony. Under these circumstances, we believe that the relevance and probative force of the excluded evidence was insufficient to require reversal of appellant's conviction. . . .

*   *   *

We do not apply the doctrine of harmless error lightly. In most cases, it may well be that an erroneous initial limitation upon cross-examination of an appropriate area could not be found harmless. In this case, however, we believe, beyond a reasonable doubt, that no juror would have been swayed by whatever suggestions of hostility and consequent implications of bias might have arisen from the knowledge that the witness had undertaken profitless civil litigation against the defendant on the matter in question. The jury's knowledge of the witness's pecuniary interest in the outcome of the trial, as made explicit by the court in its instruction, provides further support for this conclusion.

Appellant, received a fair trial; the trial court's rulings to which he takes exception give us no cause to overturn his convictions. . . .

Affirmed.

MIKVA, CIRCUIT JUDGE, dissenting:

A trial court cannot permit the government to shield its complaining witness from the probing cross-examination that our system of justice accords a criminal defendant. The right to cross-examine is particularly imperative when an articulate and determined witness, whose testimony is the only real evidence that a crime has in fact occurred, has shown a potential bias by filing a lawsuit against the defendant. I believe that the trial judge's error in curtailing inquiry into Pottinger's effort to bring a $100,000 damage suit against Gambler deprived the jury of evidence that could have seriously diminished Pottinger's credibility. Accordingly, I cannot agree that this error was harmless, and I must respectfully dissent.

The facts underlying this prosecution are amply stated in the majority opinion, and there is no need to recount them here. The opposing positions at trial, however, may bear some repetition. Gambler's defense was that he had no intention to defraud. He claimed that he had merely postponed ordering the merchandise, and that he would have paid the manufacturers and accomplished the delivery in the spring if he had not run out of money. Gambler also denied making false representations.

The government's only witnesses in its case in chief on the Pottinger counts were Pottinger himself and an FBI agent who testified about Gambler's bank account and other financial records. Only Pottinger's testimony related to the possibility of fraudulent representations by Gambler, and there were no documents reflecting a statement by Gambler that the merchandise had been ordered. . . .

In these circumstances, Pottinger's credibility was crucial to the outcome of the case. If the jury believed Pottinger, Gambler would be found guilty. Accordingly, Gambler's counsel made clear to the trial court at a pretrial hearing that he would seek to introduce evidence that Pottinger was improperly motivated in testifying. For that purpose, counsel attempted to question Pottinger about his $109,000 lawsuit, in order to demonstrate to the jury "his antagonism and animosity toward Mr. Gambler, [which] bear on the issue of his bias in connection with his testimony." . . .

Evidence of this character has long been regarded as highly probative in impeaching a complaining witness, and its exclusion has routinely been considered reversible error. Nonetheless, the trial court forbade this line of questioning, believing that its probative force was outweighed by the confusion likely to result if the court was forced to explain to the jury how Pottinger's lawsuit became intertwined with Gambler's bankruptcy. . . . The majority opinion acknowledges that this ruling was legal error, and I cannot support its attempts to rescue the trial court's ruling by invoking the harmless error doctrine and by speculating about how the trial court might have exercised its discretion after permitting counsel to ask his first question. Accordingly, I believe that Gambler's conviction on the Pottinger counts must be reversed.

*   *   *

II. Prejudicial Error

A. Pottinger's Testimony

J. Stanley Pottinger emerges from the transcript of the trial as a very impressive witness. The prosecution lost no time in informing the jury of his credentials:

Q.   Would you please give us your full name?

A.   J. Stanley Pottinger.

Q.   Where are you employed at the present time?

A.   With the law firm of Troy, Mallen and Pottinger, Washington, D.C.

Q.   What did you do prior to that?

A.   I was an Assistant Attorney General of the Civil Rights Division in the Department of Justice.

. . . As Pottinger pointed out in his testimony, even while pressuring Gambler for the return of his money he scrupulously observed the ethics of his profession:

> He said that he had sold 2 of his sconces already for $1500 to a women client of his in New York and was ready to send that check to me right away and he asked me how he should do it, should he simply endorse her check over to me or should [he] put it in his account and write a check over to me. I said it didn't make any difference to me, but we were in an adversary position at that time and if there were any implications about the best way to proceed, he should ask someone other than me. He was asking me as a lawyer on that point.

*   *   *

Pottinger also portrayed himself as sympathetic and understanding in his dealings with Gambler once he discovered that Gambler had been evading him, and had not ordered his furniture.

> I said, Grant, isn't it true that you really didn't order the furniture at all, and he said, no, that is not true, I did order it. I pressed him again on the point, I said Grant, if you are honest with me, we can work out the problem, whatever it is. If you are sick, broke or whatever the problem is, tell me what happened and we'll work it out, we are months overdue, we had all these stories and it should be obvious to you as me, it had not been ordered and he said, I can't remember, I can't remember, I am feeling bad and I can't remember what I did. I said Grant, just tell me the truth, you did not order it, did you? There was a long pause and he said no, I did not. He then said, what do you want and I said I would just like my money back and I will pick it up from here and take care of it. I am sorry things have gone this way for you, but I would like to get my money back.

Against this background, Gambler's counsel had the unenviable task of attacking Pottinger's credibility, of convincing the jury that Pottinger had ulterior motives for remembering conversations the way he did and that despite appearances Pottinger was capable of yielding to this temptation. There was no written evidence of

Gambler's false representations, and the difference between simple breach of contract and criminal fraud lay entirely in whether the jury believed Pottinger's explanation of the past dialogue between them.

Gambler's counsel tried two routes to accomplish this result. The court allowed him one of these: the argument that Pottinger was financially interested in the outcome of the case, because Gambler's conviction would assist Pottinger in deducting for income tax purposes any loss he incurred in their dealings. The trial court instructed the jury that this theory did make sense legally, and that, "[a]ccordingly, he does have a financial interest in the outcome and you may consider that fact in your consideration and weighing of his testimony just as you consider any interest anybody else may have in the outcome of this case weighing their testimony." . . .

Counsel's attempt to confront Pottinger with this theoretical interest was less successful. Pottinger responded on cross-examination as though he were unconcerned with the character of the deduction and unaware of the details:

Q. Is it true, Mr. Pottinger, that your basis for claiming that deduction is on the basis that Mr. Gambler committed larceny, committed a crime in connection with the transaction?

A. I am honestly not sure. It is my understanding, that it is in the nature of a bad debt that could be claimed whether he is convicted or not. In other words, because it is a bad debt and perhaps a condition precedent to that is it is a bad debt through fraud. This was turned over to Tigar and Buffone, with whom you are familiar. The basis for that agreement was worked out, I believe, with agreement with yourself.

* * *

Q. It is not your claim, is it, that this was a loss incurred in your trade or business, is it?

A. I don't know the answer to that. Carolyn Dye of my office, who is a tax attorney in my office, and Tigar and Buffone who handle the suit with your office, provided the memos and information to Beers and Cutler. It is my intention to the extent that the law permits, to take deductions for money I never got from Mr. Gambler, or part of it, not all bec[au]se he provided some service as I testified yesterday.

. . . This testimony did not provide dramatic support for the argument that Pottinger cared so much about his tax deduction that he would depart from the truth to secure it.

The most crucial ammunition in counsel's campaign to convince the jury that Pottinger might be induced to distort his testimony by the same influences that sway less respectable witnesses was the $100,000 damage suit. That litigation not only suggested the degree of Pottinger's hostility toward Gambler — it also specifically contradicted the picture Pottinger had painted of himself as a kind and forgiving victim who "would just like [his] money back." Counsel expressed his disappointment when that evidence was ruled inadmissible, . . . and announced for the record before closing argument that, because he had been deprived of that evidence, his address to the jury would be significantly different than he had planned:

> As a result of the Court's rulings I find myself in a position where I do not have the evidence before the jury to effectively challenge Mr. Pottinger's testimony with respect to it being biased, with respect to his animosity toward Mr. Gambler, and his motive to seek punishment in one form or another, whether financial or if not financial with criminal conviction. As a result my closing address to the jury would be significantly different than otherwise.

. . . I believe that a reading of the record makes it clear that counsel was quite accurate in his assessment of the gap left in his case by the court's exclusion of the impeachment evidence. Gambler's defense was crippled by this ruling. This fact is especially clear when the ruling is viewed in the light of the full evidence of Pottinger's damage claims — and, as I shall explain, this court has no basis for assuming that the district court would have excluded that evidence once the basic fact that Pottinger had sued Gambler had been admitted. But even the admission of the mere fact that Pottinger had brought suit could have made a tremendous difference to Gambler's defense.

B. The Nature of the Lawsuit

The most probative aspect of Pottinger's suit against Gambler is Pottinger's theory of damages. The total amount of money received by Gambler from Pottinger was $17,715.20. Nonetheless, the amount claimed by Pottinger in his civil suit was more than six times that sum — $108,915.70. Pottinger viewed himself as entitled to compensation for 112 hours he had spent with Gambler shopping for his furnishings, and billed the time at $100 per hour, yielding $11,200. Pottinger claimed a further $30,000 as compensation for lost business opportunities caused by his inability to entertain professional acquaintances in his new home, and $50,000 for his pain and suffering.

Pottinger's lawsuit might be thought vindictive. If this evidence had been before the jury, it might have contradicted the impression of the witness as a sympathetic and objective victim recounting the events of his deception. Furthermore, as evidence of Pottinger's actual conduct in response to his dealings with Gambler, these facts might have led the jury to reject an assumption that this impressively respectable witness would be capable of rising above an $18,000 loss and testifying with objectivity.

The majority opinion brushes this evidence aside by speculating that the trial judge might have found some reason to exclude it:

> In attempting to explore the concluded litigation, defense counsel appeared most intent, at trial and in this court, upon having the jury learn of the *amount* of damages sought by the complainant in the three different contexts, perhaps to reflect the large measure of animosity allegedly possessed by the witness against the defendant. Were this information introduced, however, the prosecution might well have sought to reexamine

Pottinger, and other lawyers employed by him, to establish the validity of the damages sought in the complaint. Balancing the questionable probative value of this amount as indicative of the witness' hostility versus the delay and confusion of the issues resulting from such an extended inquiry, the district court did not abuse its discretion in excluding this evidence. . . .

. . . But it is apparent from the record that the district court never exercised any discretion to exclude the evidence for such reasons. Rather, the district court excluded *all reference* to the lawsuit, in order to avoid confusing the jury with an explanation of Gambler's *bankruptcy* proceedings. Once the fact of the lawsuit had been admitted, and any necessary discussion of the bankruptcy process had taken place, cross-examination concerning the nature of the lawsuit would not have created any need for further discussion of the bankruptcy. We have, therefore, no reason to believe that the district court would have sustained an objection to further questioning about Pottinger's lawsuit.

No one questions the trial court's considerable discretion to limit the extent of detail that counsel may elicit on cross-examination. For precisely this reason, however, it is unrealistic to conjuncture that once the magnitude of Pottinger's lawsuit was revealed, the district court would lose control over the progress of the trial, and that confusion and delay, including testimony by Pottinger's attorneys, would result. The trial court never expressed insecurity over its ability to manage this issue.

Nor does the case law suggest that there would be any *impropriety* in asking a complaining witness the extent of the injury he has claimed in a civil suit. The majority opinion cites, and my own research has found, only cases declining to find an abuse of discretion in a trial court's limitation of cross-examination concerning damages. These cases provide no warrant for assuming that inquiry into damage claims will ordinarily be refused.

Rather, the limits of the inquiry will normally be set by common sense. "Without a knowledge of the details, we cannot well know the extent of the ill-feeling and the allowance to be made against the testimony." . . . The surest indication of the "extent of the ill-feeling" in the present case is the extravagant assessment Pottinger made of the value of his own time and suffering. This evidence is available in the damage claim, and is duplicated nowhere else. Accordingly, unless there is some good reason for excluding it, it should be admitted, and we have no reason to assume that the district court would have done otherwise.

C. The Fact of the Lawsuit

After relying on speculation to determine that the jury would never have learned of the peculiar nature of Pottinger's lawsuit, the majority goes on to conclude that the mere fact that suit had been brought would not have been sufficient to change the jury's evaluation of Pottinger's credibility. Even if the majority's conjecture that the trial court would have excluded evidence on the damage claims were proper, I believe it is mistaken in concluding "beyond a reasonable doubt, that no juror would have been swayed by whatever suggestions of hostility and consequent implication of bias might have arisen from the knowledge that the witness had undertaken profitless civil litigation against the defendant on the matter in question." . . . I would conclude that the prejudice resulting from the trial court's error was clear and substantial.

*   *   *

[B] Foundation Requirement

Is the admissibility of extrinsic evidence of bias treated like prior inconsistent statements — admissible only after the impeaching party has laid a foundation? If a witness gives testimony that is inconsistent with statements that he previously made, the common law required the proponent of the prior contradictory statement to confront the witness with it, and obtain a denial from him, before the proponent could offer extrinsic evidence to prove that the witness actually made the prior statement in question. A similar opportunity to deny or explain is required under Rule 613 of the Federal Rules of Evidence. Must an impeaching party give the witness a similar opportunity to admit and explain the evidence of bias?

The rationale for the foundation requirement for prior inconsistent statements is fairness and judicial efficiency. It is unfair to the party who called the witness to allow the impeaching party to introduce extrinsic evidence of such statements without having given the witness an opportunity to admit and explain them on cross-examination. This unfairness arises from the possibility that after the witness has been excused, she may not be available to be recalled for the purpose of explaining the apparent inconsistency. The foundation requirement serves the end of judicial efficiency because if, after being confronted with the statement, the witness admits that she made it (regardless of whether the witness offers a reason to explain it), no further evidence would be necessary to establish it. These same considerations are equally applicable to evidence of bias, particularly bias proven through the witness' prior statements. Consequently, many courts have adopted a foundation requirement for evidence of bias that is similar to that for prior inconsistent statements. In these jurisdictions, extrinsic evidence of bias is admissible only after a necessity for it has been created by the witness' denial of both its existence and of the evidence that proves it.

Would it be logical to limit the foundation requirement to instances in which the bias is to be proven through the witness' statements? Is it not equally unfair and inefficient to present other evidence of bias — prior conduct, for example — without having first confronted the witness with it? Just as there had been a split of authority in the state courts over whether a foundation requirement should be imposed at all, those that have adopted the requirement have similarly split over whether it applies to evidence of bias other than the witness' own statements. In the federal system, courts have generally adopted the foundation requirement, but, as illustrated in the following opinion, the scope of the requirement is unclear. *See United States v. Leslie*, 759 F.2d 366, 380 (5th Cir. 1985) (imposing the requirement); *United States v. Diggs*, 522 F.2d 1310, 1331 (D.C. Cir. 1975) (not imposing the requirement for racial bias).

UNITED STATES v. HARVEY

United States Court of Appeals, Second Circuit
547 F.2d 720 (1976)

KELLEHER, DISTRICT JUDGE.

Defendant appeals from a judgment of conviction after a jury trial in which a verdict of guilty was found as to each of the two counts of the indictment, the first charging the appellant with bank robbery and the second with bank larceny.

The sole question presented on appeal is whether the trial court committed reversible error in excluding evidence proffered by the defendant as to possible bias on the part of the government's chief identification witness. The question presented is of a type likely to occur with some frequency under the Federal Rules of Evidence, which are still rather new, and which at the time of the trial below had been in effect for approximately five months.

On the afternoon of April 22, 1975, the Main-High branch of the Marine Midland Bank-Western was robbed by a man dressed as a woman. Mrs. Florida Strickland, a teller at the bank, described the robber as a medium complexioned black male in his early twenties, 5'11" to 6' in height, 160 lbs., slender build with broad shoulders, five o'clock shadow and a prominent Adam's apple. According to Mrs. Strickland, the robber was wearing a straight-haired wig pulled back into a bun, a blue denim hat, which did not obstruct a full view of the robber's face, gold wire framed dark glasses, lipstick, rouge, a dark coat, and was carrying a 10" wide red print cloth shoulder bag.

Mrs. Strickland was not able to make a positive identification of the robber, and much of the evidence against appellant at the trial consisted of her description of the robber's personal features and bank surveillance photos which the jury was asked to compare to appellant. The sole identification witness at the trial was a Priscilla Martin who testified that on the afternoon of April 22, while passing by on a bus, she observed a man she identified as appellant walk down the steps of the Salvation Army and touch one of the two doors of the Main-High branch of the Marine Midland Bank. Mrs. Martin described the man as wearing red pants, a black coat, black platform shoes and a black floppy hat whose brim obstructed a view of his face from the nose up. She described his hair style as a frizzled bush, "an afro," but could not say whether it was a wig. Mrs. Martin stated that the man was not wearing glasses and she could not recall lipstick but did remember seeing rouge.

Mrs. Martin first learned of the robbery of the Main-High branch on the six o'clock news the evening of the 22nd. A week and a half later, she telephoned the bank to find out the time of the bank robbery, but did not leave her name or reveal any information about the robbery. She eventually spoke about the robbery with the Federal Bureau of Investigation, which had learned of her involvement through a friend of Mrs. Martin's husband.

Mrs. Martin had been acquainted with appellant for a number of years. She testified that she knew the appellant for nineteen years and at one time had lived in the same house with him. On cross-examination, defense counsel questioned Mrs. Martin on whether she had ever had any trouble with appellant or ever had any arguments or disagreements with him, and specifically whether she ever accused appellant of fathering her child and then failing to support this child. Mrs. Martin denied these charges and further denied that appellant visited her in the hospital after birth of the child. Mrs. Martin also denied that she confided in appellant's mother, Mrs. Catherine Harvey, that appellant was the father of the child or that she stated that she would "take revenge" on appellant for not "owning up" to this child.

Following Mrs. Martin's testimony, appellant sought to introduce testimony of Mrs. Harvey which would have shown that Mrs. Harvey was a long-time acquaintance of Mrs. Martin, and that while Mrs. Harvey was on duty as a nurse in a Buffalo hospital, she encountered Mrs. Martin, who was there for treatment of a broken leg. Mrs. Harvey would have testified that during this encounter Mrs. Martin accused appellant of fathering her child and refusing to support it, and that Mrs. Martin further explained that when her husband learned of that he beat her and broke her leg, necessitating the hospital treatment. The trial judge refused this proffer of testimony, considering it "collateral" and inadmissible under Federal Rule of Evidence 613(b). It is this ruling which appellant maintains was error and which requires our consideration.

The law is well settled in this Circuit, as in others, that bias of a witness is not a collateral issue and extrinsic evidence is admissible to prove that a witness has a motive to testify falsely. . . . The law of evidence has long recognized that a cross-examiner is not required to "take the answer" of a witness concerning possible bias, but may proffer extrinsic evidence, including the testimony of other witnesses, to prove the facts showing a bias in favor of or against a party. . . . Special treatment is accorded evidence which is probative of a special motive to lie "for if believed it colors every bit of testimony given by the witness whose motives are bared." . . . This Circuit follows the rule, applicable in a number of other Circuits, that a proper foundation must be laid before extrinsic evidence of bias may be introduced. . . . Prior to the proffer of extrinsic evidence, a witness must be provided an opportunity to explain the circumstances suggesting bias. . . . Federal Rule of Evidence 613(b), which applies to extrinsic evidence of prior inconsistent statements, similarly requires that a witness be "afforded an opportunity to explain or deny" the prior inconsistent statement. Because the testimony of Mrs. Harvey would have impeached Mrs. Martin's credibility by bringing before the jury prior inconsistent statements as well as demonstrate[d] a possible bias on Mrs. Martin's part, Rule 613(b), in effect at the time of trial, required that a proper foundation be laid by appellant's counsel. Rule 613(b) however, relaxes the traditional foundation requirement that a witness's attention on cross-examination be directed specifically to the time and place of the statement and the person to whom made. . . . The Rule provides, as has this Court in prior decisions concerning extrinsic bias testimony, that the witness be provided an "opportunity to explain or deny a prior inconsistent statement." Fed. R.Evid. 613(b). . . . In cross-examining Mrs. Martin, defense counsel clearly asked her whether she had ever accused defendant of fathering her child, whether she had ever stated she would "take revenge" on the defendant and whether she had confided in Mrs. Harvey that defendant was the father of her child. To each of the questions, Mrs. Martin answered no. Thus, on at least three occasions, the witness was afforded an opportunity to explain or deny circumstances suggesting prejudice. Since Mrs. Harvey would have testified that all statements heard by her were made at the same identifiable time and identified place, the reference to Mrs. Harvey as the other party to the conversation should have obviated any surprise to the government as to the when and where of the proffered testimony. . . . While defense counsel could have been more expansive in establishing his foundation, we find that it was sufficiently established.

Although the scope of a defendant's right to introduce evidence of bias is not limitless, and may be restricted as the trial court in its sound discretion deems proper, . . . it is rarely proper to cut off completely a probative inquiry that bears on a feasible defense. . . . "(A) defendant should be afforded the opportunity to present facts which, if believed, could lead to the conclusion that a witness who has testified against him either favored the prosecution or was hostile to the defendant. Evidence of all facts and circumstances which 'tend to show that a witness may shade his testimony for the purpose of helping to establish one side of a cause only,' should be received. . . . Although we are mindful that it is within the sound discretion of the trial judge to determine the extent to which he will receive independent evidence for the purpose of proving a witness' hostility, we do not believe that he may as was done below, exclude all such evidence for that purpose." . . . Since Mrs. Martin was the sole identification witness at the trial, we cannot say that her testimony was not critical to the government's case against appellant. With identity as a principal issue in the trial, appellant was denied an important opportunity to raise a reasonable doubt about his participation in the bank robbery by undermining the credibility of Mrs. Martin. Although Federal Rule of Evidence 403 vests trial courts with discretion to exclude evidence if its probative value is substantially outweighed by the danger of prejudice, confusion, or delay, the trial court apparently did not exclude Mrs. Harvey's testimony on the basis of this consideration. There is no indication in the record that Mrs. Harvey's testimony posed a realistic possibility of confusion or prejudice, . . . or would have caused a significant delay in the proceedings. Indeed, given the importance of the bias testimony to the defense, whatever confusion or delay that may have resulted from its admission would have to have been overwhelming to satisfy Rule 403's balancing test.

We now must consider whether the trial court's error in refusing to admit the testimony of Mrs. Harvey was so prejudicial as to require reversal of appellant's conviction. The right to "place the witness in his proper setting and put the weight of his testimony and his credibility to a test" is an essential safeguard to a fair trial. . . . Exercise of this right is particularly crucial where the witness offers damaging identification testimony, for in the absence of independent contrary evidence, a defendant must rely upon impeachment of the witness's credibility. The record reveals that appellant's conviction rests on the testimony of Mrs. Strickland as to a description of the robber, bank surveillance photos which the jury had an opportunity to review and compare to appellant's appearance, and the identification of Mrs. Martin. We are not convinced that Mrs. Martin's testimony was an insignificant part of the case against appellant and therefore find that denial of the opportunity to raise a reasonable doubt as to identification by showing possible bias was prejudicial to appellant's right to a fair trial.

Accordingly, we reverse appellant's conviction and remand for a new trial.

[C] Demonstrating Bias: A Right of Confrontation

The importance to the fairness of litigation of being given an opportunity to demonstrate witnesses' biases is reflected in the fact that the Sixth Amendment to the U.S. Constitution guarantees the right of confrontation to defendants in criminal prosecutions. In *Davis v. Alaska*, 415 U.S. 308 (1974), the Supreme Court elaborated on the relationship of the Sixth Amendment right of confrontation to the right to demonstrate witnesses' biases, finding that the right of confrontation is paramount to the state's policy of protecting the confidentiality of a juvenile offender's record. The facts in *Davis* are as follows.

A safe was stolen from a local bar, its contents removed, and then abandoned near the home of Richard Green. Green, a minor at the time of the crime who subsequently reached the age of majority by the time of the trial, was a crucial witness for the prosecution. Green informed police on the day of the burglary that he had seen and spoken with two men standing alongside a blue Chevrolet near the area where the safe was eventually discovered. Green identified the defendant from a series of six photographs and subsequently identified defendant in a lineup.

At trial, the prosecutor moved for, and was granted, a protective order to prevent any reference to Green's juvenile record in the course of cross-examination. Defense counsel opposed the protective order, explaining that Green's juvenile adjudication would be revealed only as necessary to probe Green for bias and prejudice and not generally to call Green's good character into question. Defense counsel sought to show specifically that at the time Green was assisting the police in identifying defendant as one of the burglars, Green himself was on probation for burglary. Defense counsel would then argue that Green may have made a faulty identification of defendant to shift suspicion away from himself or that Green's identification may have been subject to undue police pressure under threat of possible probation revocation, which in turn could have affected his later in-court identification of defendant. Agreeing with the claim that the trial judge's restriction on Davis' opportunity to impeach Green violated Davis' right to confrontation, the Court stated:

> Cross-examination is the principal means by which the believability of a witness and the truth of his testimony are tested. Subject always to the broad discretion of a trial judge to preclude repetitive and unduly harassing interrogation, the cross-examiner is not only permitted to delve into the witness' story to test the witness' perceptions and memory, but the cross-examiner has traditionally been allowed to impeach, *i.e.*, discredit, the witness. One way of discrediting the witness is to introduce evidence of a prior criminal conviction of that witness. By so doing the cross-examiner intends to afford the jury a basis to infer that the witness' character is such that he would be less likely than the average trustworthy citizen to be truthful in his testimony. The introduction of evidence of a prior crime is thus a general attack on the credibility of the witness. A more particular attack on the witness' credibility is effected by means of cross-examination directed toward revealing possible biases, prejudices, or ulterior motives of the witness as they may relate directly to issues or personalities in the case at hand. The partiality of a witness is subject to exploration at trial, and is

"always relevant as discrediting the witness and affecting the weight of his testimony." 3A J. Wigmore, EVIDENCE § 940, p. 775 (Chadbourn rev. 1970). We have recognized that the exposure of a witness' motivation in testifying is a proper and important function of the constitutionally protected right of cross-examination. *Greene v. McElroy*, 360 U.S. 474, 496 (1959).

Davis v. Alaska, 415 U.S. 308, 316 (1974).

The Court reversed the defendant's conviction and remanded to the lower court, finding that defendant's right of confrontation — the right to probe through cross-examination to detect the presence of any bias that might influence the testimony of a crucial identification witness — had been violated. Courts have subsequently interpreted the opinion in *Davis* as severely limiting the right of trial courts to prohibit the exploration of matters that arguably reflect a witness' partiality. The case of *Chipman v. Mercer* is illustrative of this point.

CHIPMAN v. MERCER
United States Court of Appeals, Ninth Circuit
628 F.2d 528 (1980)

KENNEDY, CIRCUIT JUDGE:

Herbert Chipman was convicted of burglary in state court. Chipman's conviction was upheld by the Third District Court of Appeal of the State of California, and a petition for hearing was denied by the California Supreme Court. Chipman then filed a petition for writ of habeas corpus in the United States District Court for the Eastern District of California. The district court granted the petition on the ground that Chipman's sixth amendment right to confront witnesses was violated by the state trial court's refusal to permit cross-examination of a witness for bias. We affirm.

The name of the witness in question was Mrs. Ketchum. She testified that Chipman was near the scene of the burglary under suspicious circumstances. There was no other eye witness testimony. Circumstantial evidence linked Chipman to the burglary, but Mrs. Ketchum's testimony contributed significant additional information. She testified that she lived in the neighborhood and that on the night of the burglary she heard footsteps proceeding to and, later, from the victim's house. She said she recognized them as Chipman's because of the noise made by the platform shoes he often wore. She testified further that from her bedroom window she recognized Chipman clearly and saw him running while carrying a guitar case. A valuable guitar in its case was one of the items stolen from the victim's house.

Counsel for the defense undertook an extensive cross-examination of Mrs. Ketchum to test her credibility bias, and memory. During the examination, counsel asked Mrs. Ketchum if she had ever conversed with a neighbor named Mrs. Ford. A relevance objection being interposed, there was an extensive offer of proof. Defendant's counsel said the question bore upon possible bias and prejudice that Mrs. Ketchum entertained. Counsel initially stated he wanted to show bias because Mrs. Ketchum disliked Mrs. Ford, who was Chipman's aunt. There was a later and more elaborate offer of proof permitted by the trial court, however, both with reference to the first question about Mrs. Ford and other questions pertaining to events involving Mrs. Ford, the defendant, and the witness Ketchum. The defense offered to show that Mrs. Ford operated a residential care facility for mentally ill and retarded persons. The facility was located across the street from Mrs. Ketchum's house. Counsel offered to prove that Ketchum knew Chipman had lived in the facility, that Ketchum had previously accused residents of possessing stolen property, and that Ketchum had complained to the neighbors and circulated a petition to city officials in order to close the facility because it was not proper for the neighborhood and had undesirable occupants. It was the defense theory that by reason of her attitude and her former actions, Mrs. Ketchum might be hostile to or prejudiced against persons who had occupied the Ford house, including the defendant Chipman, and, moreover, that she stood to benefit if a former resident of the facility were convicted of burglary. The trial court rejected this more extensive offer of proof as well, stating the evidence would be excluded . . . on the ground that it was not probative of any personal hostility towards the defendant. The court did, however, permit defendant's counsel to cross-examine Ketchum about her possible general racial bias.

The Sixth Amendment guarantees the right of a defendant to confront the witnesses against him or her. *Davis v. Alaska*, 415 U.S. 308 (1974). . . . This right to confrontation is embodied substantially by the right to cross-examine adverse witnesses. *See Davis, above*, 415 U.S. at 315–16. . . . As this court said in *Burr v. Sullivan*, 618 F.2d 583, 586 (9th Cir. 1980), "The right to confront witnesses guaranteed by the sixth and fourteenth amendments includes the right to cross-examine witnesses to show their possible bias or self-interest in testifying." Although, a trial court normally has broad discretion concerning the scope of cross-examination, *see below*, a certain threshold level of cross-examination is constitutionally required, and in such cases the discretion of the trial judge is obviously circumscribed. As the court in *United States v. Elliott*, 571 F.2d 880 (5th Cir.), *cert. denied*, 439 U.S. 953 (1978), said:

> While the scope of cross-examination is within the discretion of the trial judge, this discretionary authority to limit cross-examination comes into play only after there has been permitted as a matter of right sufficient cross-examination to satisfy the Sixth Amendment.

. . . When the cross-examination relates to impeachment evidence, the test as to whether the trial court's ruling violates the sixth amendment is "whether the jury had in its possession sufficient information to appraise the biases and motivations of the witness. . . ."

Confrontation questions must be resolved on a case-by-case basis based on examination of all circumstances and evidence. . . . Neither the confrontation clause nor the case-by-case approach to resolving confrontation questions should be interpreted to permit persons convicted in state proceedings to use putative sixth and fourteenth amendment claims as a vehicle for obtaining federal review of evidentiary questions properly left to resolution by the state courts. Two limiting principles can be identified, and others may be elaborated in appropriate cases. First, the confrontation clause applies to the essentials of cross-examination, not to all the details of its implementation. The provision should not become the source of a vast and precise body of constitutional common law controlling the particulars of cross-examination. From this follows a second, related concept: trial courts have broad discretion concerning the proper extent of cross-examination, to which appellate courts owe deference. . . .

We have recognized that "some topics may be of such minimal relevance that the trial court would be justified either in totally prohibiting cross-examination about them or in allowing only limited questioning." . . . *Davis v. Alaska* and our own precedents do not require a trial court to permit cross-examination on topics of very slight or marginal relevance simply upon the theory that bias or prejudice might be disclosed. Although it tips the scales in favor of permitting cross-examination, the confrontation clause does not prevent the trial court from weighing the offer of proof to determine its probative value to the trier of fact and its probable effect on fair and efficient conduct of the trial. Here, the ruling of the trial court no doubt was intended both to expedite the case and to avoid introduction of collateral issues that might distract the jury or commit its members to one side or the other of an emotional and potentially an extraneous issue, *i.e.*, the desirability of having an ordinary home in a residential neighborhood used as a facility for the retarded. The relevance of the proposed line of examination on the grounds of bias and prejudice was such, however, that we find the ruling did violate the defendant's right to confront witnesses.

Some kinds of animosities are so unlikely to color a witness' testimony that the trial judge might properly exclude testimony regarding them. For example, the sole ground for attempting to show bias may be that the witness dislikes a relative of the defendant for reasons unrelated to the defendant, such as an ordinary neighborhood dispute. Absent further facts justifying questioning, the confrontation clause arguably might not require cross-examination on this subject. Here, the grounds for a suspicion of bias were considerably more extensive and better founded.

The present case involves a potential bias different from that in some other decisions, where the bias sought to be proved was that the witness favored the prosecution in hopes of better treatment for his own crimes. *See, e.g., Davis v. Alaska, above; Burr v. Sullivan, above.* These instances of potential bias appear with such frequency that the necessity to permit cross-examination should be readily apparent to the trial court. We concede that the instant case may not have presented such a routine application of the confrontation clause. Counsel have not directed us to, and we have not discovered, a case with facts resembling this one. Nevertheless, we think cross-examination here was required under principles sufficiently well established that it was a constitutional error to overlook them. . . .

It is true, as the state trial court pointed out, that the case does not involve allegations of particular enmity between the witness and the defendant. . . . On the other hand, that a witness harbors a general bias against a group or class of which the defendant is a member, or an institution with which the defendant has some past or present association, does not make cross-examination concerning that possible bias irrelevant. . . . Bias of a general or pervasive sort is not, at least necessarily, less dangerous to objectivity than hostility to one individual. It is the potential for bias of either kind, and, if established, its value to the trier of fact, which determines if cross-examination is necessary in a given case. Examination for bias and prejudice must be permitted if it is reasonable to assume that animosity to a group might prejudice the witness, either consciously or unconsciously, against a defendant who shares the characteristics of that class.

Cross-examination of Mrs. Ketchum for possible bias and prejudice was especially important because her testimony was very significant to the case. The circumstantial evidence to prove the crime was not overwhelming, and Mrs. Ketchum was the only eyewitness whose testimony could place the defendant at the scene. Her testimony, moreover, was not given in terms of a general description which happened to fit this defendant. Instead, she claimed to know precisely who the defendant was from having observed him on earlier occasions. Counsel should have been permitted to probe the circumstances in which Mrs. Ketchum had previously acquired her knowledge of the defendant when it was alleged that those circumstances affected her attitude and motives towards him. The witness had identified the defendant as someone who had resided in Mrs. Ford's home. Defense counsel requested permission to inquire whether Mrs. Ketchum harbored a bias against Mrs. Ford and the residents of the facility, and in that connection to inquire whether she had sought to have the facility closed. Given this offer of proof, it was required that the defendant be permitted to examine the witness to determine if she harbored a bias or prejudice against the class composed of residents of the home.

There was a further possible source of bias which defense counsel had the right to explore, at least briefly. Defense counsel made an offer of proof, which all concede was in good faith, to show that Mrs. Ketchum had made statements accusing residents of the Ford home of possessing stolen property. The truth of that allegation, and the extent to which it might have affected Mrs. Ketchum's views about the defendant, was also within the zone of potential bias or prejudice upon which inquiry by defense counsel should have been permitted.[22]

Cross-examination for bias or prejudice is generally required only to the extent of exploring the subject with the witness, first in a preliminary way to determine if further inquiry is justified, and then more extensively if the witness' responses or attitude appear to justify it. The argument of the state that this line of examination necessarily would require time-consuming extrinsic evidence from other witnesses to rebut the inference of prejudice is without merit. The trial court retains discretion to control the length and extent of the examination, and, in appropriate cases, to confine examination to the witness who is being tested. . . . The automatic reversal rule is not, therefore, entirely divorced from considerations of prejudicial error in its ultimate operation, even if it is so in its bare statement.

We hold that the denial of cross-examination for bias or prejudice in this case violated the confrontation clause.

The district court's order granting the writ is *Affirmed.*

---

[22] (Court's original footnote 3.) Some trial attorneys might decide to refrain from such questioning to avoid suggesting guilt, but those tactical decisions are for counsel. Once the defense has chosen to enter the area in this case, the confrontation clause requires that some inquiry be allowed.

EXCERPT FROM TRIAL TRANSCRIPT

NARRATOR: Herbert Chipman is accused of burglary. At this point in the trial, the evidence connecting him to the crime has been circumstantial. The prosecution is offering the testimony of Mrs. Ellen Ketchum, a neighbor of the victim. She is the only eyewitness who can place Chipman at the scene of the burglary. On direct examination, Mrs. Ketchum has testified that on the night of the burglary she heard footsteps that she recognized as the defendant's — because he always wore platform shoes — proceeding to and from the victim's house. She has also testified that she looked out her bedroom window and clearly saw Chipman running while carrying a guitar case, one of the items stolen from the neighbor's house.

During the cross-examination of Mrs. Ketchum by defense counsel, Mr. Manning, the factual details surrounding her claimed observation of Mr. Chipman were explored. We join this cross-examination as its focus shifts to another issue.

CROSS-EXAMINATION — BY MR. MANNING

Q: You indicated you had seen Mr. Chipman before in that neighborhood, correct?

A: Yes, I did.

Q: Do you know where Mr. Chipman was living?

A: Yes, I do.

Q: Where was he residing at that time?

A: Well, let me see. I don't know the house number, but he was living with several other people. Let's see; there is a vacant lot between me and the neighbors, and a two-story house, a duplex, and a little yellow house on the south side of the street.

Q: And is the small yellow house the one where he was residing?

A: Yes.

Q: Do you recall approximately what month that you would have first become aware Mr. Chipman was residing in your neighborhood?

A: No, I couldn't tell you that either. When I first saw him, he was living across the street from me.

Q: That is directly across the street from you?

A: Yes, at the Ford residence.

Q: And what kind of residence is the Ford residence?

A: She takes in mentally-retarded men.

Q: It is a home care facility, is it not?

A: Yes, for mentally retarded.

Q: Do you know Mrs. Ford?

A: By sight, yes.

Q: Have you ever had a conversation with Mrs. Ford?

MR. WHITE: I will object to this without an offer of proof for relevancy.

THE COURT: I will sustain the objection.

MR. MANNING: Your Honor—

THE COURT: If you are going to make an offer, you will do it outside the presence of the jury.

MR. MANNING: All right, Your Honor, fine.

THE COURT: You wish to make the offer?

MR. MANNING: Yes.

NARRATOR: The jury and alternates were excused from the courtroom, and the following proceedings were had in open court.

THE COURT: I will hear the offer of proof.

MR. MANNING: Your Honor, at this time I am offering testimony on Mrs. Ketchum's relationship to a Mrs. Amie Ford, an aunt of the defendant, for the purpose of showing a bias and prejudice on the part of Mrs. Ketchum that could significantly affect her testimony today.

THE COURT: Counsel.

MR. WHITE: Your Honor, as counsel knows, Mrs. Ketchum has already testified that she didn't even know of the relationship until after she had testified at the preliminary hearing. I think it is just smoke to confuse the jury, and I would object to it as not being relevant to her identification of the defendant. She has identified this man twice without even knowing he was related to Mrs. Ford.

THE COURT: Have you known prior to March 6, 1976, of there being any relationship between Mrs. Ford and the defendant?

MRS. KETCHUM: No, I did not, Your Honor. When I first saw the defendant, he was living at Mrs. Ford's. She was taking in mentally retarded. There is no reflection on him, but I thought he was one of her patients. I had no idea until the day of the hearing when it was thrown at me then, and I did not know.

THE COURT: I will sustain the objection.

MR. MANNING: Your Honor, may I be heard?

THE COURT: Yes.

MR. MANNING: I am not offering this simply for the purpose that Mr. Chipman is the nephew of Mrs. Ford. I am not offering this to show a bias and prejudice simply because Mr. Chipman is related to Mrs. Ford. Mrs. Ketchum is biased against the residential care facility. That is what I am trying to establish by this line of questioning.

THE COURT: I will exclude it.

MR. WHITE: Thank you, Your Honor.

THE COURT: You may bring the jury back.

CROSS-EXAMINATION — BY MR. MANNING

Q: Mrs. Ketchum, you indicated you do not recall specifically when you first saw Mr. Chipman in the area, is that right?

A: No, I cannot.

Q: Now, you indicated that Mr. Chipman had been going by constantly with platform shoes on, making a disturbance, I believe; is that right?

A: Yes.

Q: When did he first start doing this?

A: Ever since he lived in the neighborhood.

Q: And you are unable to tell us—

MR. WHITE: Objection, asked and answered and argumentative.

THE COURT: I will sustain the objection.

Q: Now, Mrs. Ketchum, you weren't very happy with Mr. Chipman being in your neighborhood, were you?

A: It didn't make any difference to me.

Q: His constant walking past your house with his loud shoes was annoying to you, was it not?

A: Not particularly, no.

Q: That didn't disturb you at all?

A: Not really; I never complained of it.

Q: Could you estimate approximately how old Mr. Chipman is?

A: No; I have no idea.

Q: Mrs. Ketchum, do you have any bias or prejudice against persons of the black race?

A: No, I don't.

Q: Do you know that the term "boy" to black person is—

MR. WHITE: I will object to this and ask for an offer of proof. Counsel is misconducting himself here, and I would like to see it stopped.

THE COURT: I will sustain the objection.

MR. MANNING: Your Honor, I would like to speak to Mr. White.

THE COURT: All right.

NARRATOR: The jury was excused, and the following proceedings were had in open court.

MR. MANNING: Your Honor, I believe from the investigations that we have made that there is evidence of bias and prejudice on the part of Mrs. Ketchum.

In regard to the home care facility where Mrs. Ketchum first saw Mr. Chipman, she has had a running battle, so to speak, trying to get that home out of that neighborhood. I intend to present evidence that she has had a petition circulated in the neighborhood for the purpose of getting neighbors to voice their opposition to the home. In that regard she has made allegations of persons going into that home with stolen property. She has, in fact, had several hearings in front of the City Council on the continued licensing of that home. This shows a bias and prejudice and is vital for the defense for impeachment purposes, and I think it is a proper line of impeachment.

MR. WHITE: Your Honor, first of all, that offer of proof has nothing to do with the question he just asked the witness. Secondly, I think the Court ruled in this area, and it is an area that involves Mrs. Ketchum exercising her civic rights and duty. Going to the City Council or whatever, for a matter unrelated to the defendant is not something that should be used in this courtroom to besmirch Mrs. Ketchum and get an acquittal for the defendant. It is a collateral matter. If he can come in here with a parade of witnesses to show she attempted to have this license pulled, then we will be here two weeks with me showing she has the right to do this and without prejudice to the black race. That concludes my remarks.

THE COURT: You may respond.

MR. MANNING: Your Honor, in regard to my specific question in the preliminary hearing transcript, the District Attorney asked, "Can you identify the person that you observed that night," and Mrs. Ketchum pointed to the defendant and said, "That black boy over there." Now, if Mrs. Ketchum is aware of what "boy" means to a black, I believe that is a prejudicial statement. A statement which shows her prejudice, and I think that we are entitled to show a bias and prejudice on the part of the witness in this case.

MR. WHITE: Then is counsel going to bring in semantics in the case and then psychologists or psychiatrists to tell us first of all what it would mean to somebody of the black race, and secondly, what Mrs. Ketchum meant. Is this how we are going to proceed?

MR. MANNING: I think we can ask Mrs. Ketchum what she meant by it — she is the witness—

MR. WHITE: She told you she is not biased.

MRS. KETCHUM: May I say something?

THE COURT: Just a moment, ma'am. Number one, this reference to the operation of the facility across the street from the witness' home seemingly has no relevancy to these proceedings. There isn't anything to indicate that in any way is directly tied into the defendant here so as to indicate a bias, even if one were assumed as against the operation of the facility as related to the defendant here—

MR. MANNING: Your Honor, may I speak to that?

THE COURT: Counsel, the Court has afforded you every courtesy to be heard. I would assume that you would in turn extend that same courtesy back to the Court.

MR. MANNING: I apologize, Your Honor.

THE COURT: Secondly, your offer did not at the outset relate in any way to the defendant with reference to the precise question you put to the witness. I can see from your offer that it may present a question with reference to her designating individuals in the course of preliminary proceedings.

For that reason, I would permit you to pursue that, but I should make it patently clear, certainly under 352 of the Evidence Code, I will exclude any evidence relating to the operation of the place across the street from this witness and her activity in conjunction therewith. Now I will hear from you.

MR. MANNING: Your Honor, the residents in this facility are black. In the beginning, Mrs. Ketchum felt Mr. Chipman was a resident of that facility. At a later time, it was discovered he is a nephew of the lady that runs that facility. I feel that facility and her understanding of his connection with that facility is relevant to this proceeding. It shows a continuing bias and prejudice. Mrs. Ketchum's interest in the facility has been a continuing one. The petition to have it closed down or limited is quite relevant inasmuch as Mrs. Ketchum believed that Mr. Chipman was a resident. By connecting him to the facility, she furthers her hand of getting rid of it. I think that Mrs. Ketchum is being less than candid when she states she doesn't recall when Mr. Chipman arrived in that area. I think she can answer whether he had been there two weeks before that proceeding or six months before that proceeding. I believe that she is showing her prejudice right here today.

THE COURT: Have you concluded?

MR. MANNING: Yes, Your Honor.

THE COURT: Well, your offer does not indicate that this witness possesses any felling of hostility against the defendant, and that is the primary question. The charge here is one of burglary on the part of the defendant. The hostility has to be in some way connected. I will exclude this line of questioning.

I will, however, permit you to pursue the question of your seeking to attach some feeling of hostility towards the defendant as the result of the language that she may have employed in the sense you may make some inquiry as to whether she had intended any derogation of the defendant as the result of the statement she made.

MR. MANNING: Your Honor, I would feel that a person could have a bias or prejudice against a black—

THE COURT: Counsel, I heard you fully. I am satisfied with the Court's ruling. Your exception is noted.

MR. MANNING: Thank you, Your Honor.

NARRATOR: A short recess was taken. The jury panel returned to the courtroom, and the following proceedings were then had in open court.

CROSS-EXAMINATION — BY MR. MANNING

Q: I believe the question I had just asked you was, "Do you know how persons of the black race feel to the term 'boy'?' "

A: No, I do not. I'm sorry if they misunderstood the word "boy." I didn't mean it in a malicious way.

Q: You never — how old are you, Mrs. Ketchum?

A: Fifty-three.

Q: Have you always resided in California?

A: No.

Q: Where is your home?

A: South Dakota.

Q: How long have you resided in California?

A: Twenty years.

Q: South Dakota doesn't have many persons of the black race?

A: Oh, yes.

Q: What area; do you recall?

A: No, not any special area. They have black people there, yes.

Q: In fact, let me ask you this. Did you have persons of the black race living in the area that you resided in?

MR. WHITE: I will object to this again. He failed to show any foundation at this point.

THE COURT: I will sustain the objection.

Q: And again, how long have you lived in California?

A: Twenty years.

Q: During that period of time have you ever read newspapers?

MR. WHITE: Objection.

MRS. KETCHUM: Oh, yes.

MR. WHITE: Argumentative and not relevant.

THE COURT: I will sustain the objection.

Q:　　　　　In that twenty years you have never heard that the term "boy" is anathema to a person of the black race?

A:　　　　　No, I never have.

MR. WHITE:　Objection on lack of foundation.

THE COURT:　I will sustain it on the basis of argumentative.

NARRATOR:　This ended the questioning on the issue of Mrs. Ketchum's possible bias or prejudice towards Mr. Chipman. He was convicted of burglary. After his conviction was upheld on appeal, Chipman filed a writ of habeas corpus in federal district court. The district court granted the petition, holding that Chipman's Sixth Amendment right of confrontation was violated by the trial court's limitation of the cross-examination of Mrs. Ketchum.

The degree to which *Davis* requires that a criminal defendant be allowed to explore facts relevant to the issue of bias will turn on a number of factors. Two of the more important are the probative value of the facts and the importance of the witness to the prosecution's case. *See United States v. Summers*, 598 F.2d 450, 460 (5th Cir. 1979). The reasonableness of any limitation on the examination will be evaluated on the basis of the extent to which permitted examination allowed the exposure and development of sufficient facts to allow reasonable inferences to be drawn about credibility. *United States v. Calle*, 822 F.2d 1016 (11th Cir. 1987).

§ 6.06　IMPEACHMENT: PSYCHIATRIC CONDITION

Theoretical Relevance

Lack of mental capacity, resulting from insanity, mental disease or defect, or intoxication, caused by drug or alcohol use, is similar to bias in the significance of its probative value relative to a witness' credibility. To be logically relevant, however, the mental condition must affect the quality of a person's perception, memory, or ability to relate observations. Once the theoretical relevance of a witness' mental condition is established, a party may explore the witness' mental condition to demonstrate its practical relevance to the witness' testimony, by establishing that it existed either at the time the witness perceived the facts related in the witness' testimony (thereby distorting the witness' perception), or at the time of testimony (thereby distorting the witness' memory and ability to recite). As the court explained in *United States v. Lindstrom*, preclusion of the opportunity to explore these conditions constitutes a denial of effective confrontation.

UNITED STATES v. LINDSTROM
United States Court of Appeals, Eleventh Circuit
698 F.2d 1154 (1982)

VANCE, CIRCUIT JUDGE.

*　*　*

Dennis Slater and Joanne Lindstrom appeal convictions and sentences for mail fraud, . . . and conspiracy to commit mail fraud, ...

*   *   *

Because we find that the trial court's restrictions on access to documents and on cross-examination denied appellants the right to confront their accusers, we reverse.

The convictions centered around the activities of Bay Therapy, Inc., a Florida corporation purporting to provide physical therapy treatment to injured persons pursuant to doctors' prescriptions. Joanne Lindstrom was a legal secretary employed by Dennis Slater, who was a senior trial attorney with a Tampa law firm. Slater, Lindstrom and David Webster, also an attorney, formed Bay Therapy, Inc. in the summer of 1976, each owning a one-third interest. The three agreed that Lindstrom would oversee the clinic's operation. She leased a building, acquired the necessary equipment and employed Rosamond Sloan, a licensed practical nurse, to operate the clinic. In October 1976, Sloan was replaced by the person who became the government's star witness at trial.

After she had been operating Bay Therapy for about nine months, Sloan's replacement contacted her brother, a former FBI agent who was then employed by the Fraud Division of the Florida Insurance Commissioner's office. At the suggestion of the investigators, she began attempting to learn incriminating information from Lindstrom, Slater and Webster. She also initiated meetings with federal investigators.

Eventually, she became the key witness at the Bay Therapy trial. During 1978, 1979 and 1980, two successive federal grand juries heard extensive evidence on the operations of Bay Therapy before handing down an indictment. The indictment charged that the appellants, as part of a scheme to inflate medical costs and defraud insurance companies, caused patients to be sent to Bay Therapy for treatment they did not need and often did not even receive. The trial lasted for three weeks and involved the testimony of eighty-six witnesses.

The government's key witness testified that during the period when she was overseeing operations at Bay Therapy, she, Lindstrom and Slater had discussed alteration of records, that she and Lindstrom had in fact changed records, that Slater and Lindstrom had ordered her to duplicate billing cards and that patients signed up for treatments they did not receive. Other witnesses testified about Slater's attempts to secure business for the clinic, and a number of former patients related their divergent experiences with Bay Therapy. Insurance claims managers debated whether increased therapy bills would in fact result in higher settlements, and an attorney outlined the factors he customarily considered in settling personal injury cases. Both appellants testified at the trial, denying all charges.

The jury found Slater and Lindstrom guilty of conspiracy to commit mail fraud and seventeen substantive counts of mail fraud. The district court sentenced Slater to concurrent sentences of five years imprisonment on all counts, but the court suspended all but six months of the sentence and placed Slater on four years probation. Lindstrom was placed on three years probation.

*   *   *

Restrictions on Cross-Examination

Appellants contend that the district court improperly (1) placed limitations on defense questioning of the government's chief witness relating to her prior psychiatric treatment and confinement, and (2) denied the defense access to medical records suggesting that the government's witness suffered from psychiatric illnesses, including delusions. In the alternative, appellants assert error in the district court's refusal to order an independent psychiatric examination of the witness. Because we agree that the district court erroneously restricted cross-examination and defense access to documents pertaining to the psychiatric history of the government's witness, we need not reach appellants' alternative argument.

The sixth amendment to the United States Constitution mandates that a criminal defendant has the right "to be confronted with the witnesses against him." The Supreme Court has repeatedly emphasized that its "cases construing the [confrontation] clause hold that a primary interest secured by it is the right of cross-examination." *Davis v. Alaska*, 415 U.S. 308 (1974) quoting *Douglas v. Alabama*, 380 U.S. 415, 418 (1965); *Ohio v. Roberts*, 448 U.S. 56, 63 (1980). The right of cross-examination is an essential safeguard of factfinding accuracy in an adversary system of justice and "the principal means by which the believability of a witness and the truth of his testimony are tested," *Davis v. Alaska*, 415 U.S. at 316.

In its brief and during oral argument, the government urged that the scope of cross-examination is a matter within the discretion of the district court. We have repeatedly held, however, that "this discretionary authority . . . comes into play only after there has been permitted as a matter of right sufficient cross-examination to satisfy the Sixth Amendment." . . . The Supreme Court stated in *Alford v. United States*, 282 U.S. 687, 691 (1931) that "it is the essence of a fair trial that reasonable latitude be given the cross examiner."

One goal of effective cross-examination is to impeach the credibility of opposing witnesses. In *Davis v. Alaska*, 415 U.S. at 316, the Court observed that "the cross-examiner is not only permitted to delve into the witness' story to test the witness' perceptions and memory, but the cross-examiner has traditionally been allowed to impeach, *i.e.*, discredit, the witness." Similarly, in *United States v. Williams*, 592 F.2d 1277, 1281 (5th Cir. 1979), we noted that cross-examination in "matters relevant to credibility ought to be given wide scope."

Certain forms of mental disorder have high probative value on the issue of credibility. Although the debate over the proper legal role of mental health professionals continues to rage,[23] even those who would limit the availability of psychiatric evidence acknowledge that many types of "emotional or mental defect may materially affect the accuracy of testimony; a conservative list of such defects would have to include the psychoses, most or all of the neuroses, defects in the

---

[23] (Court's original footnote 3.) For sophisticated and spirited treatments of the debate from commentators in opposing camps *compare* Bonnie, *The Role of Mental Health Professionals in the Criminal Process: The Case for Informed Speculation*, 66 Va. L. Rev. 427 (1980), *with* Morse, *Failed Expectations and Criminal Responsibility: Experts and the Unconscious*, 68 Va. L. Rev. 971 (1982); Morse, *Crazy Behavior, Morals and Science: An Analysis of Mental Health Law*, 51 So. Cal. L. Rev. 527 (1978).

structure of the nervous system, mental deficiency, alcoholism, drug addiction and psychopathic personality." Juviler, *Psychiatric Opinions as to Credibility of Witnesses: A Suggested Approach*, 48 Cal. L. Rev. 648, 648 (1960). Mental illness may tend to produce bias in a witness' testimony. A psychotic's veracity may be impaired by lack of capacity to observe, correlate or recollect actual events. A paranoid person may interpret a reality skewed by suspicions, antipathies or fantasies. A schizophrenic may have difficulty distinguishing fact from fantasy and may have his memory distorted by delusions, hallucinations and paranoid thinking. A paranoid schizophrenic, though he may appear normal and his judgment on matters outside his delusional system may remain intact, may harbor delusions of grandeur or persecution that grossly distort his reactions to events. As one commentator succinctly summarized the interplay between mental disorders and legal issues of credibility:

> [T]he delusions of the litigious paranoiac make him believe he has grievances, which he feels can be corrected only through the courts. His career as a litigant is frequently touched off by a lawsuit or legal controversy whose outcome left him dissatisfied. Often he will insist on conducting his own case, quoting voluminously from cases and statutes. Because he is likely to be of better-than-average intelligence, he may mislead a jury that is uninformed about his paranoiac career and actually convince them that his cause is just.

> Trivial incidents and casual remarks may be interpreted in a markedly biased way, as eloquent proof of conspiracy or injustice. In his telling them, these trivial incidents may by retrospective falsification be given a grossly distorted and sinister significance. Even incidents of a decade or more ago may now suddenly be remembered as supporting his suspicions, and narrated in minute detail.

> On the other hand, so far as the power of observation is concerned, the paranoid witness may be quite as competent as anyone, and perhaps more than most; his suspiciousness may make him more alert and keen-eyed in watching what goes on.

> Delusions of persecution may evoke intense hatred. This may lead to counter-accusations resting on false memory, which may be very real to the accuser and be narrated by him with strong and convincing feeling. And indeed they may have a kernel of truth; because of his personality and his behavior, many people probably do dislike him. As Freud said, a paranoid does not project into a vacuum. Such a person not infrequently feels the need for vengeance.

Weihofen, *Testimonial Competence and Credibility*, 34 G. Wash. L. Rev. 53, 82 (1965) (footnotes omitted).

The government in this case contends that psychiatric evidence merely raises a collateral issue. But such labels cannot substitute for analysis. Whether called "collateral'" or not, the issue of a witness' credibility is committed to the providence of the jury. Although the use of psychiatric evidence "does not fall within the traditional pattern of impeachment, the law should be flexible enough to make use of new resources." Weihofen, *above* at 68. By this late date, use of this kind of evidence can hardly be termed "new."

At trial the defense sought to show that the key witness for the government was not credible, arguing that her motive for initiating and pursuing the investigation of Bay Therapy was based on hatred of the appellants. Lindstrom and Slater argued to the district court that this witness was carrying out a vendetta against them because she had not received a promised percentage of Bay Therapy when the business was sold. Appellants further sought to impeach the witness' credibility by demonstrating that her alleged vendetta resulted from a continuing mental illness, for which she had been periodically treated and confined. From public sources and from psychiatric records which the district court permitted defense counsel to review, the defense gathered material suggesting that in 1971 the witness was hospitalized following a serious suicide attempt; that in 1977 the witness, while she was running Bay Therapy, offered a patient of Bay Therapy $3,000 to murder the wife of the witness' alleged lover; that in 1978 she was involuntarily committed under Florida's Baker Act after taking an overdose of drugs; that in 1980 she was arrested and charged with aggravated assault for having allegedly fired a shotgun through the window of her purported lover's house; that following this incident she was briefly placed in a stockade until, at the urging of her psychiatrist, she was transferred to Hillsborough County Hospital where she was involuntarily committed under the Baker Act; that during this confinement she was diagnosed "schizophrenic reaction, chronic undifferentiated type" and described by the Chief of Psychology at Hillsborough as being "immature, egocentric, [and] manipulative," having superficial relationships causing "marital problems and sexual conflicts in general" and seeing authority as something to be manipulated for self gratification and as an obstacle; that an unsigned chart entry noted that the patient had a "history of hallucinations" and was "suicidal — homicidal and delusional." Through effective questioning in these areas, appellants contend that they could have shown the witness' past pattern of aggressive and manipulative conduct toward persons close to her and that they could have demonstrated the witness' motivation and determination in pursuing a vendetta.

The trial court, fearing that the defense would attempt to put the witness herself on trial, stated:

> I think we should discuss, too, the extent of the cross-examination of this witness in regard to these activities. I am trying to think this through. I am not fully convinced it's a 608-B question, although I think it's akin to that. But any questions along this line probably would go further than what seems to be envisioned by 608-B, because you're testing the witness's credibility is what you're attempting to do, I would suppose.[24] So, within

---

[24] (Court's original footnote 6.) We agree with the trial court that Federal Rule of Evidence 608 is not controlling:

> The credibility of a witness can always be attacked by showing that his capacity to observe, remember or narrate is impaired. Consequently, the witness' capacity at the time of the event, as well as at the time of trial, are significant. Defects of this nature reflect on mental capacity for truth-telling rather than on moral inducements for truth-telling, and consequently Rule 608 does not apply.

reason, there are two or three properly framed questions I'm going to allow you to at least let this jury know about the fact that this witness has had some mental and emotional problems in the past.

I'm not going to allow the defense to try this witness, so to speak.

Three examples suffice to illustrate the extremely narrow limits within which the district judge permitted cross-examination of the witness.[25] First, the court refused

---

J. Weinstein, WEINSTEIN'S EVIDENCE ¶ 607[4] (1981) (footnotes omitted).

[25] (Court's original footnote 7.) The district court did allow some cross-examination on the witness' psychiatric history. The defense was permitted to ask whether the witness had ever been committed under the Baker Act. Counsel elicited that she had been committed for three weeks in January, 1980, first at Hillsborough County and then at St. Joseph's Hospital. Further, the defense elicited that the witness had been involuntarily committed in 1978.

    Q. On occasion of November 1978, when you were committed under the Baker Act, was that voluntary or involuntary?

    A. It started out as involuntary and turned into voluntary.

    Q. And where were you treated on that ocassion [sic]?

    A. Tampa General Hospital.

    Q. And was that initial commitment as the result of an overdosage of drugs?

    A. Yes.

    Q. Specifically what, if you recall?

    A. Oh, I recall. You want me to name the drug?

    Q. Yes ma'am.

    A. Lithium, Tofranill and one other that I can't recall.

    Q. Transine?

    A. Yes.

    Q. About how many tablets?

    A. I don't recall that.

MR. ATKINSON: Objection, Your Honor.

THE COURT: Objection sustained. That's not necessary. Mr. Devault.

    Q. During, how long did you stay on that occasion?

    A. Just a few days.

    Q. Where were you located?

    A. 4 north.

    Q. 4 north at Tampa General?

    A. Un-hum.

    Q. On the occasion when you were there in Tampa General in November of 1978, did you tell any of the staff at the hospital—

MR. ATKINSON: Objection, Your Honor.

THE COURT: [Following a side-bar conference] The objection is sustained.

    Q. How long was it that you stayed at 4 north on the occassion [sic] in November of'78?

    A. I remember it as being several days.

    Q. I'm sorry?

    A. Several days.

    Q. Were you admitted to Tampa General Hospital psychiatric unit on any other occasions?

MR. ATKINSON: I would ask for a time frame, Your Honor, so we can establish remoteness.

THE COURT: All right, let's do that.

to allow the defense to question the witness about the murder contract that she allegedly offered to a Bay Therapy patient. The defense proffered testimony by the patient to the effect that the witness had approached him and offered him $3,000 to shoot the wife of the witness' purported lover. The court sustained the government's objection to the questions, and also denied a defense request to ask the witness the questions out of the hearing of the jury. Secondly, the district court denied appellants the opportunity to cross-examine the witness about her own alleged attempt to shoot a shotgun through the window of her purported lover's house, after which she was committed under the Baker Act. Thirdly, the judge sustained the government's objection to defense questions focusing on whether, during her commitment, the witness had told hospital personnel that she had attempted suicide for the purpose of manipulating and punishing her boyfriend. Defense counsel proffered hospital records showing that the witness had in fact made such statements. During the ensuing side bar conference, defense counsel stated that the witness' history of manipulation was "the whole point of our defense. It's those people that cross her, Dennis Slater, Joanne Lindstrom, [or her alleged lover], she goes out to get them with a vendetta. She manipulated them. She did it to him on numerous occasions. She's doing the same thing to him. She's told two people that I have a witness for that she's out to get Dennis Slater."

These rulings by the district court constituted an abuse of discretion contradicting Supreme Court and former Fifth Circuit authority on the right of confrontation in general and the right to examine the psychiatric history of adverse witnesses in particular. In *Greene v. Wainwright*, 634 F.2d 272 (5th Cir. 1981), the district court

---

Following a brief digression the cross-examination on the issue of the witness' psychological condition concluded:

Q. Other than the three occasions about which I've just asked you, have you been admitted to any psychiatric facility for care or treatment on any other occasions?

MR. ATKINSON: Again, Your Honor, can I have a time frame?

THE COURT: During '75, from the period of from 1975, was that the question?

MR. DEVAULT: No, I asked at any time, Your Honor.

THE COURT: Well, I sustain the objection.

MR. ATKINSON: Thank you.

Q. Have there been other occasions of treatment during the last six years?

A. Yes.

Q. And would you tell us when those occurred?

A. There was one last May, I think, May of '80.

Q. And where was that?

A. Memorial.

Q. Any others?

A. No.

Q. Are you under any psychiatric care at the present time?

A. I'm on a PRN basis, Mr. Devault.

Q. I'm sorry?

A. Whenever necessary basis.

Q. And on that basis, have you received care in the last month?

A. Yes. [name omitted].

dismissed a petition for habeas corpus claiming a violation of the right to confrontation. The state trial judge had prohibited the defendant from questioning the state's chief witness about his "mental condition and about certain bizarre criminal actions.". . . "His credibility was crucial to the state's case.". . . The Fifth Circuit reversed, holding that the denial of an opportunity to present evidence regarding the "alleged recent history of mental instability . . . exceed[ed] any possible trial court discretion." . . .

We find *Greene* controls this issue. The restrictions on cross-examination in this case are even more egregious than those recently condemned in *Greene*, because the disputed medical records suggested a history of psychiatric disorders, manifesting themselves in violent threats and manipulative and destructive conduct having specific relevance to the facts at issue. As in *Greene*, the witness in question was the chief witness for the prosecution. She initiated and pursued the investigation of Bay Therapy. She was an insider to the fraud scheme, she testified in detail about the operation and about the activities of Slater and Lindstrom. . . . We find the district court committed reversible error in unconstitutionally depriving appellants of their sixth amendment guarantee of the right to confrontation and cross-examination.

*   *   *

Reversed and Remanded.

A party who wishes to explore a witness' psychiatric condition on cross-examination must first show that the condition, if proved, would affect the witness' communicative facilities. In *Lindstrom*, excerpted in [A], *above*, the court discussed the kinds of conditions that are relevant to credibility. Some conditions that courts have found to be insufficiently connected to credibility are depression, *United States v. Brumbaugh*, 471 F.2d 1128, 1129 (6th Cir. 1973), and a "nervous breakdown." *United States v. Honneus*, 508 F.2d 566, 573 (1st Cir. 1974), see discussion of Rule 103(a)(2) at [1] *above*.

The relevance of a psychiatric condition will be influenced by a number of factors. The court in *United States v. Sasso*, 59 F.3d 341, 347–348 (2d Cir. 1995) explains:

> Evidence of a witness's psychological history may be admissible when it goes to her credibility. . . . In assessing the probative value of such evidence, the court should consider such factors as the nature of the psychological problem, *see, e.g., Chnapkova v. Koh*, 985 F.2d 79, 81 (2d Cir. 1993) (paranoid and delusional condition likely to be probative), the temporal recency or remoteness of the history, . . . (paranoid delusions five years earlier not too remote) . . . (more than 10 years too remote) . . . (12 years too remote), and whether the witness suffered from the problem at the time of the events to which she is to testify, so that it may have affected her "ability to perceive or to recall events or to testify accurately." . . .

> The trial court[, however,] has discretion to limit such evidence if it determines that the probative value of the evidence is outweighed by its potential for unfair prejudice, confusion of the issues, or waste of

time. . . . Its decisions on these questions will not be overturned in the absence of an abuse of discretion.

Although credibility and competency are closely related and overlapping concepts that rely upon the same factors, there is an important distinction between them. As explained below, a witness' competency relates to his ability to observe, remember, relate and be truthful, and is determined by the presiding judge. The witness' credibility, on the other hand, relates to the degree to which the witness can perform the four functions that the presiding judge will have determined the witness must be capable of performing in the capacity of witness, and is determined by the jury.

Psychiatric Opinions as to Credibility of Witnesses: A Suggested Approach
Michael Juviler
48 Cal. L. Rev. 648, 648–651 (1960)

*   *   *

The term "competency" refers to qualification as a witness. At common law the mentally deranged and defective were incompetent, thoroughly disqualified as witnesses and excluded from testifying. This restriction was relaxed in 1851 by the English Court of Criminal Appeals, which ruled that a hallucinated mental patient could testify in his own defense in a prosecution for manslaughter, on the theory that the strict rule against deluded people "would have excluded Socrates." Thenceforth, freedom from derangement has not been a requirement of testifying. The test of competency under the modern rule is whether the person has sufficient capacity to observe, recollect and communicate the subject of the testimony. The requisite capacity to communicate includes the ability to understand and answer intelligently the questions of counsel, as well as a sense of moral responsibility to tell the truth; most courts also require that the witness "have sufficient understanding to apprehend the obligation of the oath."

The issue of competency is decided by the court, usually with the jury excused. Generally the hearing is limited to a voir dire examination of the prospective witness by the judge, but the trend is to admit extrinsic evidence as well, and courts have recently gone so far as to permit psychiatric opinions. At the hearing there is a presumption in favor of competency, and this is seldom overcome. The tendency is to qualify the witness if he can cast any light on the events in issue. Review on appeal is restricted to the issue of abuse of discretion, and a trial judge's decision that a challenged witness is competent is rarely reversed. Appellate courts have affirmed the competency of "lunatics," inmates of mental hospitals, narcotic addicts, epileptics, idiots and other mental defectives, and persons judged incapable of managing their affairs or business. Women who are too deranged to consent to intercourse have uniformly been held competent as complaining witnesses in rape cases where the trial judge has so ruled.

The failure of the rules of competency to exclude pathological witnesses imposes heavy responsibility upon the weigher of credibility, usually a jury. After the judge rules that a mentally abnormal person is a competent witness, in other words, that he has the required capacities to observe, recollect and communicate truthfully and intelligently, the jury must determine the extent to which the witness had these capacities, for they also affect credibility. The term "credibilty" includes not only honesty, which the layman equates with credibility, but also other capacities for testifying. Thus, a nearsighted bishop may be less credible than a "psychopathic liar" with perfect vision; the psychopath lacks a sense of responsibility to tell the truth, but the clergyman has a defective capacity to observe.

§ 6.07   IMPEACHMENT: RELIGIOUS BELIEFS

Rule 610 — Religious Beliefs or Opinions

Evidence of the beliefs or opinions of a witness on matters of religion is not admissible for the purpose of showing that by reason of their nature the witness' credibility is impaired or enhanced.

Although the cross-examiner can *inquire into* character evidence in the form of a witness' prior conduct during that witness' cross-examination for the purpose of challenging her character trait for truth and veracity, Rule 610 precludes even inquiry into religious beliefs or opinions. Although such evidence *may* be relevant to the witness' credibility, its use is perceived as potentially too prejudicial. Similarly, a witness may not be cross-examined about her reasons for deciding to affirm her testimony rather than swear on the Koran, pursuant to Rule 603, as that cross-examination would have amounted to impermissible inquiry into firmness of the witness' religious beliefs. *United States v. Kalaydjian*, 784 F.2d 53 (2d Cir. 1986).

Nevertheless, the witness' affiliation with a particular church may be admissible as evidence of his bias if, for example, that church were a party to the litigation. As the Advisory Committee explicitly stated: "an inquiry [into a witness' religious beliefs] for the purpose of showing interest or bias because of them is not within the prohibition." Advisory Committee Note to Rule 610, 56 F.R.D. 183, 272 (1972).

EXERCISE

Plaintiffs, who are Hasidic Jews, commenced a civil action to recover the proceeds of a fire policy after the insurance company rejected their claims. To rebut the insurance company's contention that they had a financial motive to set fire to the premises, the plaintiffs called an accountant to testify as to their financial stability. During cross examination of the accountant, the insurance company's attorney asks the accountant "Isn't it true that you act as an accountant for many members of the Hasidic Jew community?" The plaintiffs object. How should the court rule?

§ 6.08   IMPEACHMENT: RELATIONSHIP TO OTHER RULES

[A]   Rule 103(a)(2) — Offer of Proof

Rule 103(a)(2) provides that if a court erroneously excludes evidence and this exclusion is shown to have affected a substantial right of the objecting party, the exclusion will constitute reversible error only if the substance of the excluded evidence was made known to the court by an offer of proof or was apparent from the context within which the excluded question was asked. If the defendant, through a motion *in limine* prior to testifying, objects to the introduction of her prior conviction for impeachment purposes, and the court overrules this objection and admits the conviction, it is imperative that the defendant place her testimony on the record. This will allow both the trial and appellate courts to meaningfully balance the challenged conviction's probative value against the potential prejudice that its use will create for the defendant. Would an offer of proof through either a proffer by defense counsel or through the defendant's actual examination outside the presence of the jury adequately make this showing if a court required the defendant to make it?

Until fairly recently there was a split of authority among the circuits over whether an offer of proof was even required to establish a basis for the prejudice/probative balance. Needless to say, courts did not envision that such an offer, if made, would be inadequate to preserve the defendants' objection to the introduction of the prior conviction. In *Luce v. United States*, 469 U.S. 38 (1984), however, the Supreme Court held that a defendant who did not testify at trial because the trial court had determined that the defendant's prior convictions were admissible for impeachment purposes was not entitled to appellate review of the trial court's determination admitting the conviction even if the defense made an offer of proof concerning the defendant's testimony.

[B]   Rule 105 — Limited Admissibility

If evidence is offered for a limited purpose, and is inadmissible if used for another, the opponent is entitled to have the jury instructed regarding the proper and improper use of that evidence. Rule 105 provides that "[w]hen evidence which is admissible as to one party or for one purpose but not admissible as to another party or for another purpose is admitted, the court, upon request, shall restrict the evidence to its proper scope and instruct the jury accordingly." With the use of character evidence, for example, if a party/witness is asked about her prior bad acts which reflect on her credibility, or if a reputation character witness for a party/witness is asked "have you heard?" questions by the cross-examiner for the purpose of testing the reliability of the witness' reputation testimony, the court could instruct the jury that neither the questions nor the answers should be construed as evidence of the party's propensity to have committed the past act with which she has been charged. The jury may use the evidence only to the extent that it reflects on the party's credibility as a witness in the proceedings.

Similarly, if a criminal defendant testifies and the prosecution offers evidence of the defendant's prior convictions for impeachment purposes, it is appropriate for the court, either on request or *sua sponte*, to instruct the jury that it is not to use the convictions as substantive evidence of the defendant's guilt in the present proceeding. *See United States v. Diaz*, 585 F.2d 116, 118 (5th Cir. 1978). This is particularly true if the defendant's prior crimes are similar to the one for which the defendant is currently being tried.

[C]   Rule 701 — Opinion Testimony by Lay Witnesses

Rule 608(a) allows a witness to give an opinion about the credibility of another witness (stating whether she would believe the other witness under oath), and imposes no prerequisite that the witnesses be long acquainted or that the testifying witness be aware of any recent information on the other witness. Rule 608(a), however, must be read in conjunction with Rule 701, the lay witness opinion rule. For lay opinions to be admissible under Rule 701, the opinion must rationally be based on the perception of the witness and helpful to a clear understanding of the evidence and the determination of a fact in issue. In *United States v. Dotson*, 799 F.2d 189, 193 (5th Cir. 1986), the testimony of eight police officers that in their opinion the defendant and his witnesses were not truthful was held to be inadmissible because the only basis shown for their opinions was the fact that the officers had taken part in an investigation of the defendant.

Reputation testimony is the reputation witness' personal opinion of what others in the community believe about a particular individual. Courts require this reputation evidence to be based on interactions with people in the community. The basis of reputation evidence under Rule 405 is usually personal acquaintance with those who know the individual whose character is being proven. It is unnecessary that such knowledge be acquired informally and fortuitously. It has been held that knowledge of what others believe can be admissible if it was acquired from surveys conducted for the purpose of the litigation where the testimony is offered. *See United States v. Pacione*, 950 F.2d 1348 (7th Cir. 1991) (holding that reputation witness who spoke with approximately 400 of defendant's former customers had an adequate foundation to present reputation testimony). Knowledge of an individual acquired in this manner is not an adequate basis for the witness to give her personal opinion of the individual's character. It would be inadequate because the witness has no personal knowledge of the individual.

[D]   Rule 702 — Testimony by Experts

The decision whether to admit expert testimony ordinarily lies within the discretion of the trial court. The standard for admissibility under Rule 702 is whether the specialized knowledge "will assist the trier of fact to understand the evidence or to determine a fact in issue. . . . " Courts generally have responded negatively to such testimony because of the fear that the expert opinions on the issue of a particular witness' credibility will be more persuasive than probative, and that the jurors will relegate their responsibility in weighing testimony. *See United States v. Barnard*, § 8.02[C].

In *United States v. Azure*, 801 F.2d 336 (8th Cir. 1986), the admission of the testimony of an expert in child sexual abuse that the alleged victim was telling the truth was found to be reversible error. The pediatrician was permitted to state that he "could see no reason why [Wendy, the alleged victim] would not be telling the truth." The court stated:

> Dr. ten Bensel might have aided the jurors without usurping their exclusive function by generally testifying about a child's ability to separate truth from fantasy, by summarizing the medical evidence and expressing his opinion as to whether it was consistent with Wendy's story that she was sexually abused, or perhaps by discussing various patterns of consistency in the stories of child sexual abuse victims and comparing those patterns with patterns in Wendy's story. However, by going further and putting his stamp of believability on Wendy's story, Dr. ten Bensel essentially told the jury that Wendy was truthful in saying that Azure was the person who sexually abused her. No reliable test for truthfulness exists and Dr. ten Bensel was not qualified to judge the truthfulness of that part of Wendy's story. The jurors may well have relied on his opinion and "surrender[ed] their own common sense in weighing testimony. . . . "

United States v. Barnard, 490 F.2d 907, 912 (9th Cir. 1974).

Some state and federal courts have even excluded expert testimony that is based only on the alleged victim's statements about sexual abuse, because such testimony is merely "vouching for the credibility of the alleged victim." *United States v. Charley*, 176 F.3d 1265, 1279 (10th Cir. 1999). *See generally United States v. Birdsall*, 47 M.J. 404, 409–410 (C.A.A.F. 1998); *United States v. Whitted*, 11 F.3d 782, 785–786 (8th Cir. 1993); *Commonwealth v. Colin C.*, 643 N.E.2d 10, 22–23 (Mass. 1994); *State v. Batangan*, 799 P.2d 48, 52 (Haw. 1990). *But see Johnson v. State*, 970 S.W.2d 716, 721 (Tex. App. 1998) and *State v. Figured*, 446 S.E.2d 838, 842–843 (N.C. Ct. App. 1994).

Similarly, in *Talbott v. Bowen*, 832 F.2d 111 (8th Cir. 1987), the appellate court found it to be reversible error to admit the testimony of a trial judge who previously had heard the testimony of certain police officers and had found them not to be credible. "Judge Flynn was not testifying about the existence of some objective fact as to which he had personal knowledge; but rather, gave his opinion based upon his own assessment of the witnesses' credibility. Such opinion testimony, unless rendered by an expert upon matters of scientific, technical, or other specialized knowledge, . . . is inadmissible." For a further discussion of *Barnard, Azure,* and other cases excluding expert testimony on the credibility of particular witnesses, see Author Commentary following *Barnard*, § 8.02[C].

In substance, these courts are saying that the assistance provided by the testimony is slight because there is little if any need for it and, in balancing its probative value against the potential prejudice, the prejudice substantially out-weighs it. *See* Rule 403.

Judicial decisions on the admissibility of the results of a polygraph test have been mixed. In *United States v. Earley*, 505 F. Supp. 117, 120 (S.D. Iowa 1981), *aff'd on other grounds*, 657 F.2d 195, 198 (8th Cir. 1981), the court held that such results are not admissible because such opinions are not based on the subjects' character. *See also United States v. Thomas*, 768 F.2d 611, 618 (5th Cir. 1985).

The Eleventh Circuit has taken a different view. In *United States v. Padilla*, 908 F. Supp. 923 (S.D. Fla. 1995), the district court reiterated the Eleventh Circuit's prior holding in *United States v. Piccinonna*, 885 F.2d 1529 (11th Cir. 1989), to the effect that polygraph evidence may be admissible for purposes of rehabilitating a witness's credibility under Fed. R. Evid. 608(a). Thus in *Padilla*, where the government introduced the accused's confession of involvement in narcotics traf-ficking, and the accused countered that she had originally denied the charges and only gave the confession due to coercion by the police, the court held that polygraph evidence would be admissible to corroborate the accused's trait for truthfulness, once her credibility had been attacked by the introduction of her confession. *Padilla*, 908 F. Supp at 929. The *Padilla* court made clear that polygraph evidence would not automatically be admissible under the foregoing circumstances, but rather, would still be subject to a Rule 403 analysis, *id.*, and a Rule 702 analysis to determine if the evidence "will help the trier of fact to resolve the issues." *United States v. Padilla*, 908 F. Supp. 923, 929 (S.D. Fla. 1995).

With regard to the Rule 702 analysis and the scientific validity of polygraph results, recent relaxations in the approach to handling the admissibility of scientific evidence (discussed in Chapter 8), as well as technological advances in the discipline of polygraphic examinations, have led some courts to reconsider their prior stance of prohibiting such evidence. In *United States v. Posado*, 57 F.3d 428 (5th Cir. 1995), the Fifth Circuit indicated that a district court would have to reconsider its per se prohibition of polygraph evidence, in light of these evidentiary and scientific developments. The U.S. Supreme Court disagreed. In *United States v. Scheffer*, 523 U.S. 303 (1998), the Court overruled the Sixth Circuit Court of Appeals and held that an evidence rule that makes polygraph evidence inadmissible in court-martial proceedings did not unconstitutionally abridge the accused's right to present evidence in his own defense. "A defendant's right to present relevant evidence is not unlimited, but rather is subject to reasonable restrictions. . . . As a result state and federal rulemakers have broad latitude under the Constitution to establish rules excluding evidence from criminal trial. Such rules do not abridge an accused's right to present a defense so long as they are not 'arbitrary' or 'disproportionate to the purposes they are designed to serve.' " *Id.* at 308. The Court went on to note that the evidence rules in question served three interests: "ensuring that only reliable evidence is introduced at trial, preserving the jury's role in determining credibility, and avoiding litigation that is collateral to the primary purpose of the trial." *Id.* at 309. The Court found two things controlling in its determination. The first, was the fact that there is "simply no consensus that polygraph evidence is reliable." *Id.* at 309. The second was the fact that the rule did not preclude the accused from introducing any factual evidence — it only barred him from introducing expert opinion testimony to bolster his credibility. Justice Stevens dissented on the ground that this categorical rule of exclusion is inconsistent with the Courts decision in *Daubert v. Merrell Dow Pharmaceuticals, Inc., below,* § 6.03[C][9], that requires each admissibility determination to be made by the trial judge based on the reliability of the evidence being presented.

Chapter 7

WRITINGS

§ 7.01 BEST EVIDENCE OR ORIGINAL WRITING RULE

[A] Preference for Original Writing

Courts have accorded writings a special position in our jurisprudence through the Statute of Frauds, which requires certain transactions to be in writing, and the Parol Evidence Rule, which protects the integrity of written instruments whether the transaction is required to be in writing or not. There is a need for precision in transmitting the terms of these instruments. Accordingly, the courts have created what has been called the "best evidence" rule. This rule requires a party to use the original of a writing to prove the writing's contents if the writing is material to the litigation. Secondary evidence (that is, evidence other than the original) is admissible only after the proponent has demonstrated that the original is unavailable due to no serious fault on the proponent's part.

The Best Evidence Rule represents a judicial recognition of the increased risk of error that is created when a party attempts to prove a writing's contents solely through a witness' recollection of the writing or through copies, rather than using the original writing itself. The rule's purpose is to guard against fraud, inaccuracy, and incompleteness in the presentation of the contents of those documents to the finder of facts.

Inasmuch as all testimony can be fabricated and recollection can be faulty, the logic of the best evidence rule could apply to descriptions of any object other than a writing. The rule is applicable only to writings, however, because of what is perceived to be a greater danger of fabrication with writings than with objects, and because fraudulent or inaccurate writings are more likely to affect legal rights and obligations than are objects. The best evidence rule, therefore, is *not* a general "better evidence" rule that would exclude any type of evidence when the source of the facts upon which testimony is based is otherwise available, or because better, more authoritative, or more persuasive evidence can be obtained.

The best evidence principle, the breadth and implications of its logic, the limited scope rule that has evolved, and the rationalization of the existing rule have been examined in great detail by Professor Nance, in *The Best Evidence Principle*, 73 Iowa L. Rev. 227 (1988).

[See Fed. R. Evid. 1001–1008]

The best evidence rule applies only to writings. This rule naturally has caused courts to question what constitutes a "writing." Surprisingly, no definitive answer exists. If constrained by the rule's rationale, courts could limit the definition of writing to those written instruments that create rights and obligations, in other words, those writings addressed under the statute of frauds and the Parol Evidence Rule. Courts, however, have construed the best evidence rule much more broadly. Courts have interpreted a writing as including any chattel (tangible thing) containing an inscription that a party is attempting to prove at trial that is material to the litigation. This definition conceivably could include everything from identification numbers on badges, license plates, and buildings, to inscriptions on tombstones, windows, and panel trucks. Should the best evidence rule apply to all of these things, or, should courts classify chattels as writings according to the degree to which the chattel's written content predominates? McCormick favors neither approach:

> It is here clearly unwise to adopt a purely semantic approach and to classify the object according to whether its written component predominates sufficiently to alter the label attached to it in common parlance. At the same time, however, it would seem also unnecessary to classify as writings . . . any object which carries an inscription of any sort whatsoever. In the final analysis, it is perhaps impossible to improve upon Wigmore's suggestion, followed by a number of courts, that the judge shall have discretion to apply the present rule to inscribed chattels or not in light of such factors as the need for precise information as to the exact inscription, the ease or difficulty of production, and the simplicity or complexity of the inscription.

MCCORMICK ON EVIDENCE § 232, at 413 (4th ed. 1994).

[1]   Inscriptions on Chattels

The approach that *McCormick* advocates, which most courts have adopted, is illustrated in the following opinion.

UNITED STATES v. BUCHANAN
United States Court of Appeals, Eighth Circuit
604 F.3d 517 (2010)

SMITH, CIRCUIT JUDGE.

Ronald Andrew Buchanan was charged in a four-count indictment with possession with the intent to distribute at least 50 grams or more of a mixture and substance containing cocaine base, in violation of 21 U.S.C. §§ 841(a)(1) and (b)(1)(A)(iii) ("Count 1"); possession with intent to distribute a mixture and substance containing cocaine, in violation of 21 U.S.C. §§ 841(a)(1) and (b)(1)(C) ("Count 2"); being a felon in possession of a firearm, in violation of 18 U.S.C. §§ 922(g)(1) and 924(a)(2) ("Count 3"); and notice of forfeiture of all the firearms and ammunition involved in the commission of the foregoing offenses pursuant to 18 U.S.C. § 924(d), 21 U.S.C. § 853, and 28 U.S.C. § 2461(c) ("Count 4"). The jury convicted Buchanan on Counts 1 and 2, but acquitted him on Count 3. The district court sentenced Buchanan to 300 months' imprisonment. On appeal, Buchanan argues that the district court erred in (1) admitting testimony regarding the numeric inscription on a safe where the narcotics were found, in violation of the rule against hearsay and the best evidence rule; (2) denying his objections to the unnoticed expert testimony of latent fingerprint expert John Kilgore, in violation of Federal Rule of Criminal Procedure 16(a)(1)(g); and (3) denying his motion for judgment of acquittal, as there was insufficient evidence to support his conviction. We affirm.

I. Background

As part of a narcotics investigation, law enforcement observed Buchanan at two residences-930 65th Street, Windsor Heights, Iowa ("the 65th Street residence") and 1933 East 33rd Street, Des Moines, Iowa ("the 33rd Street residence") in the fall of 2007. Law enforcement believed that the 65th Street residence was a "stash house"-a place in which drug dealers store money, drugs, and firearms. Law enforcement officials saw Buchanan in three separate vehicles at both addresses-a Chevy Tahoe, a Ford Explorer, and a Chevy Blazer.

Law enforcement executed search warrants for the two residences, the Chevy Blazer, and Buchanan's person on November 2, 2007, at 10 a.m. At that time, officers observed Buchanan leaving the 33rd Street residence in the Chevy Blazer, proceeding to the 65th Street residence, entering that residence, and departing a short time later. Officers stopped the Chevy Blazer. A drug dog at the scene did not alert on the vehicle. Officers read Buchanan his Miranda rights and informed him of the search warrants. Buchanan told the officers that he did not live at the 65th Street residence and that it was his girlfriend's home. According to Buchanan, he had been living at the 33rd Street residence for the previous four to five months.

Officers executed the search warrant on the Chevy Blazer and Buchanan's person. Officers discovered drug notes and a set of keys-including one key bearing the number "2010" upon it-on Buchanan's person. They also found a knotted baggie top on the Chevy Blazer's floorboard, which they considered to be drug-packaging related.

Further investigation determined that the "2010" key matched a large safe under the stairs in the basement of the 65th Street residence. This safe also bore the number "2010" on it and contained within it a manual bearing the same number. The large safe also contained a lease agreement for the 65th Street residence, signed in September 2007, listing Buchanan and Traci Smith, Buchanan's girlfriend, as tenants, a photo of Buchanan, and an Iowa vehicle title for the Chevy Blazer in Buchanan's name. Officers did not seize the safe. Buchanan also had the key to another safe in his wallet, which matched a small personal document safe also under the stairs at the 65th Street residence.

Traci Smith was at the 65th Street residence when law enforcement executed the search warrant. Smith had a previous conviction for possession of crack with intent to distribute. Officers discovered the keys to the small document safe in Smith's bedroom. Smith's documents were in that safe. The keys found in Smith's bedroom did not fit the large safe. A mattress was located on the floor at the foot of the stairs to the basement. The area under the stairs had been finished off to include a storage room. A drug dog "indicated" to the rear of this storage area under the stairs near the large safe. The large safe contained 199.52 grams of cocaine, 176.05 grams of cocaine base, $18,000 in currency, and two digital scales. The quantities of drugs seized were consistent with distribution. The safe also contained other items consistent with distribution-the currency, the digital scales, baggies, red and black rubber bands for bundling currency, and razor blades for shaving larger rocks of crack to smaller rocks for distribution. In the kitchen, officers found a digital scale with three boxes of baggies. One of the digital scales from the large safe was submitted for fingerprint analysis. Latent fingerprints were lifted from the scale that matched Buchanan. Those latent prints were found on the surface of the scale where items would be weighed.

Officers also found surveillance camera equipment on a shelf; a box of Remington nine-millimeter ammunition under the stairs; a loaded Cobray-11 nine-millimeter semi-automatic pistol in the basement under a mattress; a pair of size 44 men's blue jeans on the kitchen table; and jean shorts also in size 44 in a bag in the basement. According to a deputy jailer, Buchanan's personal effects at the jail included size 42 blue jeans.

Based upon the items seized, law enforcement determined that the 65th Street residence was actually a stash house. Buchanan was subsequently charged in the four-count indictment.

Prior to trial, Buchanan moved to exclude the identifying features of the safe on the grounds that testimony describing the safe's interior inscription would be hearsay and not the "best evidence." The district court denied Buchanan's motion.

Buchanan moved for judgment of acquittal at the conclusion of the government's case and renewed it at the close of all the evidence. The district court denied Buchanan's motion.

The jury convicted Buchanan of Counts 1 and 2 and acquitted him on Count 3. Thereafter, Buchanan filed a motion for a new trial, arguing that (1) the district court erroneously permitted testimony regarding the identifying features of the safe and allowed law enforcement to testify that the key allegedly found in Buchanan's possession matched the safe; (2) admission of the testimony regarding the identifying features of the safe violated Buchanan's substantial rights, specifically his right to a fair trial under the Sixth and Fourteenth Amendments to the United States Constitution; and (3) insufficient evidence existed that Buchanan possessed the narcotics because no drugs were found on his person and no evidence established his unrestricted access to the 65th Street residence. The district court denied Buchanan's motion for a new trial.

II. Discussion

On appeal, Buchanan argues that the district court erred in (1) admitting testimony regarding the numeric inscription on the safe where the narcotics were found, in violation of the rule against hearsay and the best evidence rule; . . . .

A. Admission of Testimony Concerning Numeric Inscription on the Safe

According to Buchanan, the district court erroneously permitted law enforcement officers to testify regarding the writings contained within the safe. Buchanan characterizes the government's case as asserting that these writings provided the number of the key that allegedly matched the safe. The government contended the key, purportedly discovered on Buchanan's person, had an inscription matching the key number inscribed in the interior of the safe. The government also alleged that the key matched the safe in which the drugs were discovered. Buchanan contends that the admission of such testimony is inadmissible hearsay and violates the best evidence rule.

> "We review a district court's evidentiary rulings for clear abuse of discretion, reversing only when an improper evidentiary ruling affected [a party's] substantial rights or had more than a slight influence on the verdict." *United States v. Two Shields*, 497 F.3d 789, 792 (8th Cir. 2007) (citation omitted). We will not reverse if the error was harmless. See Fed. R. Civ. P. 61.

United States v. Missouri, 535 F.3d 844, 848 (8th Cir. 2008).

*   *   *

2. Best Evidence

Buchanan next maintains that even if the writings inscribed on the safe's interior did not constitute hearsay, the government's witnesses could not testify as to the contents of the writing without the required foundation and authentication being laid and the writing being introduced into evidence. According to Buchanan, the assertion within the interior of the safe that it was a "2010" model and that the key with the inscription "2010" belonged to the safe is clearly a "writing" or "recording" under Federal Rule of Evidence 1002; therefore, the safe itself-which officers admittedly did not seize-should have been introduced into evidence.

In response, the government asserts that the best evidence rule is inapplicable because the safe was not a "writing" but instead a "chattel."

Federal Rule of Evidence 1002, known as the "best evidence rule," provides that "[t]o prove the content of a writing, recording, or photograph, the original writing, recording, or photograph is required, except as otherwise provided in these rules or by Act of Congress."

The 'Rule' as it exists today, may be stated as follows: [I]n proving the terms of a writing, where such terms are material, the original writing must be produced, unless it is shown to be unavailable for some reason other than the serious fault of the proponent. *United States v. Duffy*, 454 F.2d 809, 811 (5th Cir. 1972) (quoting McCormack, Evidence 409 (1954)) (emphasis added in *Duffy*). The best evidence rule "is applicable only to the proof of the contents of a writing," even though it "is frequently used in general terms." *Id.* The policy-justifications for preferring the original writing include:(1) . . . precision in presenting to the court the exact words of the writing is of more than average importance, particularly as respects operative or dispositive instruments, such as deeds, wills and contracts, since a slight variation in words may mean a great difference in rights, (2) . . . there is a substantial hazard of inaccuracy in the human process of making a copy by handwriting or typewriting, and (3) as respects oral testimony purporting to give from memory the terms of a writing, there is a special risk of error, greater than in the case of attempts at describing other situations generally. In the light of these dangers of mistransmission, accompanying the use of written copies or of recollection, largely avoided through proving the terms by presenting the writing itself, the preference for the original writing is justified. *Id.* at 812 (quoting McCormack, Evidence 410 (1954)).

In *Duffy*, law enforcement officials testified that the trunk of a stolen car contained two suitcases. *Id.* at 811. According to the witnesses, inside one of the suitcases was a white shirt imprinted with a laundry mark reading "D-U-F." *Id.* The defendant, charged with transporting a motor vehicle in interstate commerce knowing it to have been stolen, objected to the admission of the testimony about the shirt and requested that the government produce the shirt. *Id.* The district court overruled the objection and admitted the testimony. *Id.* On appeal, the defendant argued that such testimony violated the best evidence rule. *Id.* The Fifth Circuit rejected the defendant's argument, holding:

> The "Rule" is not, by its terms or because of the policies underlying it, applicable to the instant case. The shirt with a laundry mark would not, under ordinary understanding, be considered a writing and would not, therefore, be covered by the "Best Evidence Rule[."] When the disputed evidence, such as the shirt in this case, is an object bearing a mark or inscription, and is, therefore, a chattel and a writing, the trial judge has discretion to treat the evidence as a chattel or as a writing. See 4 Wigmore, Evidence § 1182 and cases cited therein; McCormack, Evidence 411–412 and cases cited therein. In reaching his decision, the trial judge should consider the policy-consideration behind the "Rule[."] In the instant case, the trial judge was correct in allowing testimony about the shirt without requiring the production of the shirt. Because the writing involved in this case was simple, the inscription "D-U-F[,"] there was little danger that the witness would inaccurately remember the terms of the "writing[."] Also, the terms of the "writing" were by no means central or critical to the case against Duffy. The crime charged was not possession of a certain article, where the failure to produce the article might prejudice the defense. The shirt was collateral evidence of the crime. Furthermore, it was only one piece of evidence in a substantial case against Duffy.

Id. at 812 (emphasis added).

Following *Duffy*, a defendant convicted on various counts related to trafficking in counterfeit watches appealed his conviction, arguing that the district court plainly erred in not requiring the government to produce the actual watches sold as the best evidence that he had trafficked in counterfeit goods. *United States v. Yamin*, 868 F.2d 130, 132 (5th Cir. 1989). The court rejected the defendant's argument, explaining:

This novel argument appears plausible because it is, at least in part, the writing on the watch that makes it a counterfeit. Thus it may be argued that it is the content of that writing that must be proved. The purpose of the best evidence rule, however, is to prevent inaccuracy and fraud when attempting to prove the contents of a writing. Neither of those purposes was violated here. The viewing of a simple and recognized trademark is not likely to be inaccurately remembered. While the mark is in writing, it is more like a picture or a symbol than a written document. In addition, an object bearing a mark is both a chattel and a writing, and the trial judge has discretion to treat it as a chattel, to which the best evidence rule does not apply.

Id. at 134 (internal footnotes omitted).

Here, the district court appropriately treated the safe as chattel. The policy considerations behind the best evidence rule, as in *Duffy* and *Yamin*, are not implicated. The writing — "2010" — was simple, meaning that little danger existed that the witness would inaccurately remember the terms of the "writing" on the safe. And, as the district court noted, the likelihood of fraud was small because the government also admitted into evidence the safe's instructional manual, which was found inside the safe and also bore the number "2010."

Moreover, as the district court explained, "the testimony regarding the inscription on the safe was only a small part of the substantial evidence presented against Buchanan." See infra Part II.C. The numeric inscription was not "critical" to the case against Buchanan; instead, the safe was merely collateral evidence of the crime.

III. Conclusion

Accordingly, we affirm the judgment of the district court.

The best evidence rule applies only to writings, as you will see in the case of *Brown v. Commonwealth.*

[2]   Video Recordings

Consider whether the best evidence rule applied to a video of a purported shoplifting incident. In the following case, the court limited the rule to writings only.

BROWN v. COMMONWEALTH
Virginia Court of Appeals
676 S.E.2d 326 (2009)

Petty, Judge.

On June 11, 2007, Maurice Meade Brown was convicted of grand larceny in violation of Code § 18.2-95. On appeal Brown argues that the trial court erroneously allowed a witness to testify to events he viewed on a video surveillance tape without requiring admission of the tape itself in violation of the best evidence rule.1 In addition, Brown argues that the evidence was insufficient to prove beyond a reasonable doubt that Brown committed grand larceny. For the following reasons, we disagree with Brown and affirm his conviction.

I. BACKGROUND

On appeal, we review the evidence in the "light most favorable" to the prevailing party below, the Commonwealth, *Commonwealth v. Hudson*, 265 Va. 505, 514, 578 S.E.2d 781, 786 (2003), and we grant to that party all fair inferences flowing therefrom. *Coleman v. Commonwealth*, 52 Va. App. 19, 21, 660 S.E.2d 687, 688 (2008).

On October 4, 2006, Brown entered a Giant Foods store in Albemarle County with three other individuals: two males and one female. After all four individuals walked in, they separated and two walked through the beer aisle and two walked through the produce aisle. The group met back at the frozen food section and the three men — including Brown — grabbed twelve bags of crab legs. The men walked in a row, one behind the other, toward the bathroom in the back of the store. They went into the men's bathroom with the bags of crab legs in hand. When they walked out of the bathroom, "they had nothing" in their hands. They walked through the pharmacy toward the front of the store, never stopping to pay for anything at the checkout register. Once they were outside, they ran toward their car. Their female companion was already at the car, and the three men "jumped in" and drove away.

The store florist, Connie Wallace, observed the entire sequence of events. She testified that she saw the group walk into the store, separate, and reassemble at the frozen food section and grab the crab legs. Wallace informed the store security guard of what she believed to be suspicious behavior and followed the group to keep an eye on them. She saw the men take the crab legs into the men's bathroom and come out of the bathroom with nothing. She followed the group out of the store and saw them jump into their car. Before the car could drive out of sight, Wallace wrote down the license plate number and gave that information to the security guard. Wallace testified that, to her knowledge, the crab legs were never recovered.

Greg Moubray, who was employed by Giant Foods Asset Protection Division, testified that Wallace told him about the suspicious group. Moubray personally observed the group of three men — including Brown — run out of the store and jump into a gray Ford Taurus, which sped away. The woman was already at the car.

Moubray went upstairs to observe the store's video surveillance system that "record[s] things that are happening . . . at the time they are happening." Brown objected to Moubray testifying about what he saw on the video recording on two bases: hearsay and best evidence rule. The assistant Commonwealth's attorney replied that "[i]t's not hearsay — it's an image." Brown chose to rely on his argument that Moubray's testimony would violate the best evidence rule. The trial judge then stated that "the best evidence rule applies to writing [sic] and therefore," she overruled the objection.

Moubray testified that on the security video, he saw the three men in the frozen seafood department taking bags of crab legs. There was no one else in the frozen seafood department at the time the three men took the bags of crab legs. Because the store has a video camera directly pointed at the crab legs and shrimp, Moubray was able to count a total of twelve bags of crab legs between the three men. After the group took the bags, Moubray saw them walk into the bathroom corridor at which time he could no longer see their actions on the video. Then, Moubray saw an empty cart and all the crab legs were gone. The bags of crab legs were not found in the bathroom and, in fact, they were never recovered.

Moubray testified that on October 4, 2006, each bag of crab legs cost thirty-nine dollars and ninety-nine cents. However, if a customer had a Giant card, then a bag of crab legs cost twenty-nine dollars and ninety-nine cents. Thus, the total value of the bags of crab legs was at least three hundred and fifty-nine dollars and eighty-eight cents.

Based on this evidence, Brown was convicted of grand larceny and sentenced to ten years imprisonment with eight years and two months suspended. From this judgment, Brown appeals.

II. ANALYSIS

Brown claims the trial court erred by (1) admitting the testimony of Greg Moubray regarding what he observed on the surveillance video because that testimony violated the best evidence rule, and (2) finding the evidence sufficient to convict him of grand larceny in violation of Code § 18.2–95.3

A. The Admissibility of Evidence

Ordinarily, we review questions regarding admissibility of evidence for an abuse of discretion, *Michels v. Commonwealth*, 47 Va. App. 461, 465, 624 S.E.2d 675, 678 (2006), and "[o]nly when reasonable jurists could not differ can we say an abuse of discretion has occurred," *Tynes v. Commonwealth*, 49 Va. App. 17, 21, 635 S.E.2d 688, 689 (2006) (citation and internal quotation marks omitted). However, "when the trial court makes an error of law" in the admission of evidence, "an abuse of discretion occurs." *Bass v. Commonwealth*, 31 Va. App. 373, 382, 523 S.E.2d 534, 539 (2000). "Furthermore, such evidentiary issues presenting a 'question of law' are 'reviewed de novo by this Court.' " *Abney v. Commonwealth*, 51 Va. App. 337, 345, 657 S.E.2d 796, 800 (2008) (quoting Michels, 47 Va. App. at 465, 624 S.E.2d at 678).

Brown contends that the trial court erred in allowing Moubray to testify as to what he observed from the surveillance video recording because his testimony violated the best evidence rule. Brown, without citing any authority, argues that the best evidence rule "controls the proof of the contents of writings, recordings and photographs." (Emphasis added). We disagree with Brown's characterization of the rule because we conclude that in Virginia, the best evidence rule applies only to writings. *Butts v. Commonwealth*, 145 Va. 800, 816, 133 S.E. 764, 769 (1926); *Randolph v. Commonwealth*, 145 Va. 883, 889, 134 S.E. 544, 546 (1926); *Folson v. Commonwealth*, 23 Va. App. 521, 478 S.E.2d 316 (1996); *Bradshaw v. Commonwealth*, 16 Va. App. 374, 379, 429 S.E.2d 881, 884 (1993); *Myrick v. Commonwealth*, 13 Va. App. 333, 339, 412 S.E.2d 176, 179 (1991). *See also* Charles E. Friend, The Law of Evidence in Virginia § 16.1 (6th ed. 2003).

* * *

The best evidence rule began as a broad, short, and convenient phrase that described a conglomerate of auxiliary probative rules "applicable to specific classes of evidential material, and designed to strengthen . . . the evidential fabric and to secure it against dangers and weaknesses pointed out by experience." 4 John Henry Wigmore, Wigmore on Evidence §§ 1171 & 1174 (James H. Chadbourn rev.1972) (emphasis in original). The phrase did not create these rules "by deduction from the principle implied in the phrase; but the phrase came to be used as descriptive of the rules already existing." *Id.* § 1174. Lord Hardwicke, sitting as chancellor, said that "[t]he judges and sages of the law have laid it down that there is but one general rule of evidence, the best that the nature of the case will allow." *Omychund v. Barker*, 26 Eng. Rep. 15, 1 ATK 22, 49 (1744). Even post American Revolution, we can trace opinions describing the rule as "[t]he best evidence which the nature of the case admits of, ought to be produced, and if it may be produced, inferior testimony is inadmissible." *Lee v. Tapscott*, 2 Va. (2 Wash.) 276, 280–81 (1796). Thus, the rule was merely a "general observation that when one sets out to prove something, one ought to prove it by the most reliable evidence available." Friend, *supra*, § 16-1.

The phrase "best evidence" initially included the original document rule, the hearsay rule, witness competency rules, and other rules that prefer reliable evidence to other, less reliable, evidence. Wigmore, *supra*, § 1172. However, almost all of the evidentiary rules that were originally encompassed in the "best evidence" phrase have been eliminated from the modern use of the term and are generally recognized as distinct rules in and of themselves except for one — the original document rule. *Id.* § 1173. Indeed, the phrase " 'would probably have dropped naturally out of use long ago, if it had not come to be a convenient, short description of the rule as to proving the contents of a writing.' " *Id.* § 1173 (quoting James Bradley Thayer, Preliminary Treatise on Evidence 489 (1898)). *See also* Friend, supra, § 16-1 (stating that "many authorities prefer to avoid the term 'best evidence rule' entirely, and describe the modern principle governing the admission of writings by the term 'original document rule' or some similar term"). Since "the first quarter of the 1700s[,]" the original document rule was "regularly acknowledged in practice, and applied to all kinds of writings." Wigmore, supra, § 1177.

In Virginia, the best evidence rule is a legal term of art. *Bell v. Dorey Elec. Co.*, 248 Va. 378, 382, 448 S.E.2d 622, 624 (1994) (citing Black's Law Dictionary 160 (6th ed. 1990)); *see also* Black's Law Dictionary 153 (7th ed.1999). As a legal term of art, "the best evidence rule requires that 'where the contents of a writing are desired to be proved, the writing itself must be produced or its absence sufficiently accounted for before other evidence of its contents can be admitted.' " *Bradshaw*, 16 Va. App. at 379, 429 S.E.2d at 885 (emphasis added) (quoting *Randolph*, 145 Va. at 889, 134 S.E. at 546; *Butts*, 145 Va. at 816, 133 S.E. at 769*); see also Myrick*, 13 Va. App. at 339, 412 S.E.2d at 179 (stating that the best evidence rule excludes secondary evidence only "when the terms of a writing or document are material"). Our Supreme Court even characterized this principle as "elementary law." *Butts*, 145 Va. at 816, 133 S.E. at 769. We have, on at least one occasion, referred to the best evidence rule synonymously with the original document rule, which only applies to writings. *Myrick*, 13 Va. App. at 339, 412 S.E.2d at 179. Further, the original document rule is identical to our Supreme Court's definition of the best evidence rule. *Id.*; *Butts*, 145 Va. at 816, 133 S.E. at 769.

* * *

Moreover, our General Assembly has defined a writing as

> any representation of words, letters, symbols, numbers, or figures whether (i) printed or inscribed on a tangible medium or (ii) stored in an electronic or other medium and retrievable in a perceivable form and whether an electronic signature authorized by Chapter 42.1 (§ 59.1–479 et seq.) of Title 59.1 is or is not affixed.

Code § 1-257.

From this we conclude that the best evidence rule in Virginia applies only to writings and, clearly, a videotape is not a writing as understood at common law and as defined by Code § 1-257. Brown argues, however, that the essential purpose behind the best evidence rule — the preference for the original document rather than the memory of a witness as to its contents — should be applied to videotapes. In other words, he argues, when a party attempts to offer evidence of events recorded on a videotape, the original videotape is the best and most reliable evidence and must be produced. Brown would, therefore, have us expand the best evidence rule to apply to videotapes as well as writings.

In this case, Brown asks us to reverse a trial court for correctly applying the law as it existed at the time of trial. We decline to do so. We believe that when a party seeks to abrogate or significantly limit, modify, or expand a common law rule of evidence that has been so venerably accepted that "the memory of man runneth not to the contrary," 1 William Blackstone, Commentaries on the Laws of England 67 (1765), the responsibility for doing so is primarily a function for the legislature, *Williamson v. The Old Brogue, Inc.*, 232 Va. 350, 354, 350 S.E.2d 621, 624 (1986) (stating that "a decision . . . to abrogate such a fundamental rule as the one under consideration is the function of the legislative, not the judicial, branch of government"). This is because

> [a] legislative change in the law is initiated by introduction of a bill which serves as public notice to all concerned. The legislature serves as a forum for witnesses representing interests directly affected by the decision. The issue is tried and tested in the crucible of public debate. The decision reached by the chosen representatives of the people reflects the will of the body politic. And when the decision is likely to disrupt the historic balance of competing values, its effective date can be postponed to give the public time to make necessary adjustments.

Bruce Farms v. Coupe, 219 Va. 287, 293, 247 S.E.2d 400, 404 (1978).

Because we decline to expand the scope of the best evidence rule, we hold that the trial court did not abuse its discretion by admitting Moubray's testimony describing the contents of the surveillance videotape.

[B]   Intentional Destruction of Original

Is the proponent who has intentionally destroyed the original precluded from using any secondary evidence to prove the writing's content? At early common law, the proponent was precluded, but, as the court explained in *In re Sol Bergman*, the answer now depends on the reason for the destruction and whether the act was free from suspicion of intent to defraud and consistent with an honest purpose.

IN RE SOL BERGMAN
United States Bankruptcy Panel for the
Sixth Circuit Court of Appeals
225 B.R. 896 (1998)

OPINION

This appeal presents two issues: (1) whether the bankruptcy court abused its discretion by admitting secondary evidence of business records which had been lost or destroyed prior to trial; . . . .

Admissibility of Trustee's Exhibits U, V, X, and Y Where the Original Inventory Cards and Computer Records Were Unavailable. Merely establishing the admissibility of the original data from which Trustee's Exhibits U, V, X, and Y were derived is insufficient to establish the admissibility of the exhibits themselves. The "best evidence" rule ordinarily requires the proponent of documentary evidence to produce the original of such evidence for the court: "To prove the content of a writing, recording, or photograph, the original writing, recording, or photograph is required[.]" Fed. R. Evid. 1002. Although the Trustee was unable to produce the original inventory cards and computer records, the bankruptcy court admitted the Trustee's exhibits into evidence based upon the interplay between two exceptions to the best evidence rule — Rule 1006, which permits the introduction of summaries of voluminous evidence, and Rule 1004, which allows the use of secondary evidence where the original evidence has been lost or destroyed. These Rules provide:

Rule 1006. Summaries.

The contents of voluminous writings, recordings, or photographs which cannot conveniently be examined in court may be presented in the form of a chart, summary, or calculation. The originals, or duplicates, shall be made available for examination or copying, or both, by other parties at reasonable time and place. The court may order that they be produced in court.

Rule 1004. Admissibility of Other Evidence of Contents.

The original is not required, and other evidence of the contents of a writing, recording, or photograph is admissible if—

(1) Originals lost or destroyed. All originals are lost or have been destroyed, unless the proponent lost or destroyed them in bad faith[.]

Fed. R. Evid. 1006; Fed. R. Evid. 1004(1).

The unavailability of the lost inventory cards and computer records left the Trustee unable to comply with Rule 1006's requirement that the evidence underlying a summary be made available to other parties. Rule 1004, however, allows the proponent to introduce secondary evidence where original evidence is unavailable, unless the unavailability is the result of the proponent's bad faith. Fed. R. Evid. 1004(1); *Vodusek v. Bayliner Marine Corp.*, 71 F.3d 148, 156 (4th Cir. 1995) ("When a proponent cannot produce original evidence of a fact because of loss or destruction of evidence, the court may permit proof by secondary evidence."); *Neier v. United States*, 127 B.R. 669, 674–675 (D. Kan. 1991). "Once the terms of Rule 1004 are satisfied, the party seeking to prove the contents of the [original evidence] may do so by any kind of secondary evidence." *United States v. Ross*, 33 F.3d 1507, 1513 (11th Cir. 1994) (citation omitted), cert. denied, 515 U.S. 1132, 115 S. Ct. 2558, 132 L. Ed. 2d 812 (1995). *See also Maxwell Macmillan Realization Liquidating Trust v. Aboff (In re Macmillan, Inc.)*, 186 B.R. 35, 47 (Bankr. S.D.N.Y. 1995) ("Rule 1004 recognizes no degrees of secondary evidence."). " '[T]he opponent . . . may attack the sufficiency of the secondary evidence including the credibility of the witness. This attack, however, goes not to the admissibility but to the weight of the evidence and is a matter for the trier of fact to decide.' " *Remington Arms Co. v. Liberty Mut. Ins. Co.*, 810 F. Supp. 1420, 1422–23 (D. Del. 1992) (citation omitted). *See also* Fed. R. Evid. 1008 ("[W]hen an issue is raised . . . whether other evidence of contents correctly reflects the contents, the issue is for the trier of fact to determine as in the case of other issues of fact."); *United States v. Matta-Ballesteros*, [1995 U.S. App. LEXIS 36965, 13] (9th Cir. Dec. 15, 1995) ("Secondary evidence used in place of original evidence need meet no threshold standard of quality or reliability; those questions go to weight, not admissibility."), *cert. denied*, 519 U.S. 1118, 117 S. Ct. 965, 136 L. Ed. 2d 850 (1997).

To establish the admissibility of evidence pursuant to Rule 1004(1), the court must determine whether the original evidence was lost or destroyed and whether the proponent of the secondary evidence has acted in bad faith. Fed. R. Evid. 1004(1); *Cross v. United States*, [1998 U.S. App. LEXIS 10160, 24] (10th Cir. May 19, 1998) (citations omitted). The mere negligent destruction of original evidence is insufficient to establish bad faith on the part of the proponent. Cross, [1998 U.S. App. LEXIS 10160, 13] (citation omitted). "[T]he party against whom the secondary evidence is being offered bears the burden of challenging its admissibility." *Ross*, 33 F.3d at 1513 (citation omitted).

Diamoncut does not dispute that the inventory cards and computer records were irretrievably lost in the course of the administration of the estate, nor does Diamoncut assert that the loss of the original evidence is the result of the Trustee's bad faith. Accordingly, Trustee's Exhibits U, V, X, and Y are admissible pursuant to Federal Rule of Evidence 1004(1) as secondary evidence of the contents of the lost inventory cards and computer records. *Americhem Corp. v. St. Paul Fire and Marine Ins. Co.*, 942 F. Supp. 1143, 1145 (W.D. Mich. 1995).

This result is supported by the Sixth Circuit's recent decision in *United States v. Bray*, 139 F.3d 1104 (6th Cir.1998). The Circuit explained there are three kinds of summary evidence: (1) primary-evidence summaries; (2) pedagogical-device summaries; and (3) secondary-evidence summaries. *Bray*, 139 F.3d at 1112. Primary-evidence summaries are those contemplated by Rule 1006 which summarize the contents of voluminous writings, recordings, or photographs which cannot conveniently be examined in court. *Id.* This type of summary is admitted in lieu of the original evidence, so "the summary, and not the underlying documents, is the evidence to be considered by the factfinder." *Id.* Pedagogical-device summaries are illustrative tools such as chalkboard drawings, graphs, calculations, or data compilations which are used only as an aid to the presentation and understanding of the evidence. *Id.* Pedagogical-device summaries are not themselves admitted into evidence and may be used by the factfinder only to clarify the evidence which has been admitted. *Id.*

Secondary-evidence summaries are a combination of primary-evidence and pedagogical-device summaries. These summaries "are not prepared entirely in compliance with Rule 1006 and yet are more than mere pedagogical devices designed to simplify and clarify other evidence in the case." *Id.* "[S]econdary-evidence summaries are admitted in evidence not in lieu of the evidence they summarize but in addition thereto, because in the judgment of the trial court such summaries so accurately and reliably summarize complex or difficult evidence that is received in the case as to materially assist the [factfinder] in better understanding the evidence." *Id.* A secondary-evidence summary "is not independent evidence of its subject matter, and is only as valid and reliable as the underlying evidence it summarizes." *Id.*

Trustee's Exhibits U, V, X, and Y are closely akin to secondary-evidence summaries as discussed in *Bray* because these exhibits do not comply with Rule 1006 and yet are more than mere pedagogical devices; however, in *Bray* the original evidence was available, but counsel chose not to present original evidence and instead presented only summaries. In this case, the original evidence no longer exists; however, other applicable evidence rules address such circumstances. While a secondary-evidence summary cannot be admitted in lieu of the original evidence under *Bray*, Rule 1004(1) excuses this requirement where the original evidence is unavailable. Rule 1004(1) further permits the secondary-evidence summary to be relied upon as "independent evidence of its subject matter" because of the unavailability of the original evidence. Fed. R. Evid. 1004(1); *Bray*, 139 F.3d at 1112. *See also United States v. Hathaway*, 798 F.2d 902, 907 (6th Cir. 1986) (holding that where records are incomplete or missing, "[o]nce a foundation is laid, in the absence of specific and credible evidence of untrustworthiness, the proper approach is to admit the evidence and permit the jury to determine the weight to be given the records."); *White Indus., Inc. v. Cessna Aircraft Co.*, 611 F. Supp. 1049 (W.D. Mo. 1985) ("[I]f the underlying materials are unavailable (as by loss or destruction), the requirements of Rule 1006 itself cannot be met. . . . [H]owever, the summary can still be admitted as 'secondary evidence' of the underlying materials if the requirements of Rule 1004 . . . are satisfied.").

The Panel further notes Trustee's Exhibit U — a hand-written ledger sheet stating $53,825.75 worth of merchandise had been returned to Diamoncut — was also admitted as a recorded recollection of Mrs. Cahen pursuant to Federal Rule of Evidence 803(5). Diamoncut has not contested this determination on appeal, thus waiving its right to do so. *Kocsis v. Multi-Care Management, Inc.*, 97 F.3d 876, 881 (6th Cir. 1996) (citation omitted).

In admitting the testimony of Mrs. Cahen and Trustee's Exhibits U, V, X, and Y, the bankruptcy court did not rely upon clearly erroneous findings of fact, improperly apply the law, or use an erroneous legal standard. See *Downs*, 103 F.3d at 480–481. Trustee's Exhibits U, V, X, and Y were properly admitted by the bankruptcy court as secondary evidence of the contents of the lost inventory cards and computer records, and Diamoncut has waived its right to contest the admission of Trustee's Exhibit U on the alternative basis of qualifying as a recorded recollection of Mrs. Cahen. Accordingly, the Panel finds no abuse of discretion.

V. CONCLUSION

The order of the bankruptcy court determining that the merchandise returns are avoidable by the Trustee in the amount of $53,825.75 is AFFIRMED.

[C]   Absence of Entry in Public Record

Filing documents, whether of a public or private nature, as public records is authorized so that they will be available for public examination. The production of recorded documents in court could result in their damage or loss, would defeat the purpose of making them public records while they were absent, and would be inconvenient for the official public custodian. Consequently, courts have always excused parties from producing original public records at trial. In the place of original public records, the courts have required that parties establish the contents of the public records either through a copy that the custodian has certified as true and accurate or through a copy compared to the original and authenticated through the testimony of the comparing witness. The absence of a public entry is also significant, but obviously the absence of a record cannot be demonstrated by the record itself.

UNITED STATES v. VALDOVINOS-MENDEZ
United States Court of Appeals, Ninth Circuit
641 F.3d 1031 (2011)

JARVEY, DISTRICT JUDGE:

Francisco Valdovinos-Mendez appeals his conviction for illegally re-entering the United States following removal, in violation of 8 U.S.C. § 1326. Valdovinos-Mendez contends that the admission into evidence of a certificate of non-existence of record ("CNR") and certain documents from his Alien Registration File ("A-file") violated his rights under the Sixth Amendment's Confrontation Clause. Citing the best evidence rule, he also contests the admission of testimony from an A-file custodian regarding the absence of any record of Valdovinos-Mendez applying for permission to re-enter the United States. In addition, he challenges a sixteen-level enhancement to his Sentencing Guideline base offense level imposed for a prior conviction of assault with a deadly weapon under California Penal Code § 245(a), arguing that it does not qualify as a "crime of violence" within the meaning of U.S.S.G.

§ 2L1.2(b)(1)(A)(ii). Finally, Valdovinos-Mendez asserts that *Nijhawan v. Holder*, [557 U.S. 29], 129 S. Ct. 2294, 174 L. Ed. 2d 22 (2009), overruled *Almendarez-Torres v. United States*, 523 U.S. 224, 118 S. Ct. 1219, 140 L. Ed. 2d 350 (1998), requiring that his prior felony conviction be found by the jury before subjecting him to a greater maximum sentence under § 1326(b).

We affirm Valdovinos-Mendez's conviction and sentence.

I. FACTUAL AND PROCEDURAL BACKGROUND

On July 15, 2008, a police officer encountered Valdovinos-Mendez driving erratically in the city of Vista, California. The officer pursued Valdovinos-Mendez as he exited the vehicle and ran into a nearby alleyway. Valdovinos-Mendez gave the officer the false name of Juan Manuel Torres Quintero. He also gave the officer a Mexican driver's license in the name of Juan Manuel Torres Quintero with Valdovinos-Mendez's photograph on it. The officer arrested Valdovinos-Mendez for driving under the influence of alcohol.

A federal grand jury indicted Valdovinos-Mendez for being found illegally in the United States following removal, in violation of 8 U.S.C. § 1326. The indictment alleged that Valdovinos-Mendez had been previously deported and removed to Mexico. Prior to trial, Valdovinos-Mendez moved in limine to exclude the CNR and other documents from his A-file. The district court denied Valdovinos-Mendez's motion.

The jury heard the testimony of Agent Deven Wooddy, custodian of Valdovinos-Mendez's A-file. She described a typical A-file as a physical folder containing records of an alien's immigration status, such as fingerprints, photographs, removal documents, and applications for re-entry into the United States. Agent Wooddy testified that her review of Valdovinos-Mendez's A-file, as well as her search of two immigration databases,1 revealed no documentation that Valdovinos-Mendez had ever applied for permission to re-enter the United States.

The jury found Valdovinos-Mendez guilty of violating § 1326. At sentencing, the court determined that he had a base offense level of 8 and the district court imposed a 16-level enhancement pursuant to U.S.S.G. § 2L1.2(b)(1)(A), because Valdovinos-Mendez had been deported following his conviction for a crime of violence. The resulting total offense level of 24, with a criminal history category V, suggested a range of imprisonment from 92 to 115 months. The court sentenced Valdovinos-Mendez to 48 months in prison, followed by three years of supervised release.

II. DISCUSSION

B.

Valdovinos-Mendez urges us to find that the district court erred under the best evidence rule when it admitted the testimony of Agent Wooddy as to her search of the databases and the absence of any record of Valdovinos-Mendez applying for permission to re-enter the United States. We rejected these arguments in *United States v. Diaz-Lopez*, 625 F.3d 1198, 1200, 1202–03 (9th Cir. 2010) (holding that the agent's testimony about databases "laid a sufficient foundation for this relevant evidence to be admissible" and the best evidence rule does not apply to an agent's testimony about his search of databases).

The best evidence rule applies when the contents of a writing are sought to be proved, not when records are searched "and found not to contain any reference to the designated matter." Fed. R. Evid. 1002 Advisory Committee's Note. Here, Agent Wooddy testified only to the absence of records, not to the contents of records sought to be proved. Moreover, public records are an exception to the hearsay rule and testimony from a qualified agent is permitted to show "that diligent search failed to disclose the record, report, statement, or data compilation, or entry." Fed. R. Evid. 803(10). As public records, the C.I.S. and C.L.A.I.M.S. databases are self-authenticating. *See United States v. Loyola-Dominguez*, 125 F.3d 1315, 1318 (9th Cir. 1997). We reject Valdovinos-Mendez's arguments on this issue.

III. CONCLUSION

The district court did not err in admitting into evidence documents from and testimony about Valdovinos-Mendez's A-file, or in the calculation of his sentence. His conviction and sentence are AFFIRMED.

[D]   Duplicates and Degrees of Secondary Evidence

Since duplicates generally are treated as originals for best evidence purposes, when showing originals to be unavailable under Rule 1004, must the proponent also show the duplicates to be unavailable before he can get other evidence admitted? This question is explored in Mueller & Kirkpatrick, Evidence Practice Under the Rules, § 10.10, at 1533–35 (1999). Professors Mueller and Kirkpatrick conclude that only the originals have to be shown to be unavailable. After the proponent has made that initial demonstration, duplicates and other evidence are equally admissible — there are no degrees of secondary evidence. As the following case indicates, after the proponent has made the initial demonstration of unavailability, duplicates and other evidence are equally admissible — there are no degrees of secondary evidence.

UNITED STATES v. McGEE
United States Court of Appeals for the Eleventh Circuit
2011 U.S. App. LEXIS 18183 (2011)

Per Curiam:

Bernard McGee, a.k.a. Pete Smith, appeals his conviction for production and possession of child pornography, in violation of 18 U.S.C. §§ 2251(a) and 2252A(a)(5)(B). The sole issue on appeal is whether the district court erred in admitting McGee's prior conviction as a self-authenticated document. After thorough review, we affirm.

We review a district court's evidentiary ruling for abuse of discretion. *United States v. Smith*, 459 F.3d 1276, 1295 (11th Cir. 2006). "An abuse of discretion arises when the district court's decision rests upon a clearly erroneous finding of fact, an errant conclusion of law, or improper application of law to fact." *United States v. Baker*, 432 F.3d 1189, 1202 (11th Cir. 2005). We review preserved evidentiary objections for harmless error. *United States v. Hands*, 184 F.3d 1322, 1329 (11th Cir. 1999). Reversible error occurs only when the evidentiary ruling is not harmless, meaning that there is a reasonable likelihood that the error affected the defendant's substantial rights. *Id.* We determine whether error was harmless "by weighing the record as a whole . . . examining the facts, the trial context of the error, and the prejudice created thereby as juxtaposed against the strength of the evidence of [the] defendant's guilt." *Id.* (citation and quotation omitted).

Federal Rule of Evidence 902(4) states that extrinsic evidence of authenticity is not required with respect to "[a] copy of an official record or report or entry therein, or of a document authorized by law to be recorded or filed and actually recorded or filed in a public office . . . certified as correct by the custodian or other person authorized to make the certification, by certificate complying with paragraph (1), (2) or (3) of this rule." Fed. R. Evid. 902(4). Rule 902(1) states that extrinsic evidence of authenticity is not required for a document bearing a seal of any state, "or of a political subdivision, department, officer, or agency thereof, and a signature purporting to be an attestation or execution." Fed. R. Evid. 902(1). We have held that to satisfy the requirements of Rule 902(4), a certification need only identify the legal custodian's position of authority, and that the copy is true and correct. *United States v. Stone*, 604 F.2d 922, 925 (5th Cir. 1979).

The Alabama Board of Corrections is required by law upon receipt of a convict into a penitentiary to record, among other things, a convict's name, date of birth, the county in which he was convicted, the nature of the crime, and the period of imprisonment. Ala. Code § 14-3-35 (1975). All this information must be entered into a permanent record. Id.

Here, the Conviction Report states that "Peter McGhee," with the same date of birth as appellant McGee, was arrested for child molestation, and plead guilty. The record is certified and signed by the clerk of court. This appears to be a copy of an official record authorized by Alabama law to be recorded by the Board of Corrections, and as such is an official record. Additionally, the copy of the record was certified by its legal custodian in a notarized letter, which explained that she was the legal custodian of the record, what her official position was, and that the copy was a true and correct copy of the original. The letter was under the seal of the State of Alabama, signed by the custodian, and notarized. This comports with the requirements of Rule 902(4) and 902(1). Also, under Stone, the certification identified the legal custodian, the custodian's official position, and that the copy is true and correct. As a result, the conviction was properly admitted as a self-authenticating public record.

But even if the district court had erred in admitting this evidence, that error would be harmless. There was a great deal of evidence demonstrating McGee's guilt aside from his prior conviction. The prior conviction, taken in the trial context, was but a minor component of the government's case, while the testimony of a detective and a victim, together with the photographs contained in the trial exhibits, were the linchpins of the government's case. While there may be serious prejudicial effect in the admission of a prior conviction for child molestation, when weighed against the great weight of the evidence indicating McGee's guilt, and in light of the minimal use of the prior conviction at trial, that error, if any, was harmless.

AFFIRMED.

[1]   Conditions Under Which Duplicates Will Not Be Treated as Originals

Rule 1003 precludes parties from using duplicates interchangeably with the original in only two situations: (1) if the opponent raises a genuine question as to the original's authenticity, or (2) if circumstances would make it unfair for the proponent to use the duplicate.

[2]   "Genuine Questions" as to Authenticity

When the original's authenticity is questionable, the proponent of a duplicate will be required to produce the original or account for its absence. Questions about the duplicate's authenticity do not require the original to be produced. The authenticity of the duplicate is simply a factual matter that the jury must resolve pursuant to Rules 104(b) and 1008.

The question that the opponent raises about the original's authenticity must be a "genuine" one. This means that the opponent will have to do more than simply contest authenticity. The opponent must produce some evidence to bring into question whether what the duplicate (assuming it was properly authenticated) actually reflects the original writing.

Precisely how much of a burden this places on the opponent is unclear. Rule 56(c) of the Federal Rules of Civil Procedure establishes this same standard in connection with summary judgment motions. That rule directs that a court should grant the motion only if there is "no genuine issue as to any material fact. . . ." Under that standard, courts have held that if the slightest doubt as to a fact has been raised, the court should deny the summary judgment motion. *See* F. JAMES & G. HAZARD, CIVIL PROCEDURE § 6.18, at 221 (3d ed. 1977).

Is it reasonable to cast the duplicate aside if the slightest question is raised about the original's authenticity? Remember, the court would only be requiring the proponent to account for the original's absence for the duplicate to become admissible secondary evidence. Thus, the ban on a duplicate's introduction may be only temporary. Courts have confronted the issue of electronic mail messages and the authentication of messages sent through social media websites. Consider the court's reasoning in admitting the messages in the following case.

PEOPLE v. CLEVENSTINE

Supreme Court, Appellate Division, Third Department, New York
68 A.D.3d 1448 (2009)

LAHTINEN, J.

Appeal from a judgment of the County Court of Albany County (Breslin, J.), rendered August 28, 2008, upon a verdict convicting defendant of the crimes of rape in the second degree (two counts), rape in the third degree (three counts), criminal sexual act in the third degree, attempted criminal sexual act in the third degree, sexual abuse in the third degree and endangering the welfare of a child (three counts).

Defendant, who was in his late 50s, befriended a family and used that relationship as a means to acquire access to the family's two teenage daughters (born in 1990 and 1992), whom he allegedly subjected to various sex-related activity from January 2006 to August 2007. His conduct was discovered when his wife accidentally found, on their computer in defendant's MySpace account, saved instant message communications between defendant and the younger victim revealing sexually explicit discussions and indicating that the two had engaged in sexual intercourse. She separately confronted the younger victim and defendant, both of whom made comments consistent with confirming the sexual activity. About a week later, defendant's wife notified the State Police, and the ensuing investigation eventually resulted in an 11-count superseding indictment, charging six felonies and five misdemeanors for various acts allegedly perpetrated by defendant against the two girls. He was convicted of all 11 counts following a jury trial and sentenced to an aggregate minimum prison term of 24 ⅔ years (which was adjusted as per Penal Law § 70.30), plus postrelease supervision. Defendant appeals.

Next, we consider defendant's contention that the computer disk containing the electronic communications that occurred between him and the victims via instant message were improperly admitted into evidence. Defendant objected to this evidence at trial upon the ground that it had not been properly authenticated. "[A]uthenticity is established by proof that the offered evidence is genuine and that there has been no tampering with it," and "[t]he foundation necessary to establish these elements may differ according to the nature of the evidence sought to be admitted" (*People v. McGee*, 49 N.Y.2d 48, 59, 424 N.Y.S.2d 157, 399 N.E.2d 1177 [1979]; see Prince, Richardson on Evidence § 4-203 [Farrell 11th ed.]). Here, both victims testified that they had engaged in instant messaging about sexual activities with defendant through the social networking site MySpace, an investigator from the computer crime unit of the State Police related that he had retrieved such conversations from the hard drive of the computer used by the victims, a legal compliance officer for MySpace explained that the messages on the computer disk had been exchanged by users of accounts created by defendant and the victims, and defendant's wife recalled the sexually explicit conversations she viewed in defendant's MySpace account while on their computer. Such testimony provided ample authentication for admission of this evidence (see *People v. Lynes*, 49 N.Y.2d 286, 291–293, 425 N.Y.S.2d 295, 401 N.E.2d 405 [1980]; *People v. Pierre*, 41 A.D.3d 289, 291, 838 N.Y.S.2d 546 [2007], lv. denied 9 N.Y.3d 880, 842 N.Y.S.2d 792, 874 N.E.2d

759 [2007]; *see generally* Zitter, Annotation, Authentication of Electronically Stored Evidence, Including Text Messages and E-mail, 34 ALR 6th 253 [2008]). Although, as defendant suggested at trial, it was possible that someone else accessed his MySpace account and sent messages under his user name, County Court properly concluded that, under the facts of this case, the likelihood of such a scenario presented a factual issue for the jury (see *People v. Lynes*, 49 N.Y.2d at 293, 425 N.Y.S.2d 295, 401 N.E.2d 405). To the extent that defendant asserts on appeal another evidentiary ground for not admitting this evidence, that ground was not preserved since it was not asserted at trial (*see e.g. People v. Bertone*, 16 A.D.3d 710, 712, 790 N.Y.S.2d 311 [2005], lv. denied 5 N.Y.3d 759, 801 N.Y.S.2d 253, 834 N.E.2d 1263 [2005]), and our examination of the record fails to persuade us to exercise our interest of justice jurisdiction as to such issue.

ORDERED that the judgment is modified, on the law, by reversing defendant's conviction of rape in the second degree under count 1 of the superseding indictment; said count dismissed and the sentence imposed thereon vacated; and, as so modified, affirmed.

CARDONA, P.J., MERCURE, SPAIN AND KANE, JJ., concur.

[3] Unfairness

Questions about the duplicate's accuracy, completeness, or adequacy go to the ground of unfairness as a basis for requiring the proponent to produce the original. As with the requirement of a "genuine" question as to authenticity discussed above, courts generally require the opponent to establish a real and substantial possibility that unfairness will result before the court will use its discretionary power to exclude a duplicate on this ground. In *United States v. Enstam*, 622 F.2d 857 (5th Cir. 1980), for example, the court rejected the claim that it was inappropriate for the trial court to have admitted a Xerox duplicate of blank letterhead stationery because the copy did not show the original's colorings. In *Federal Deposit Insurance Corp. v. Rodenberg*, 571 F. Supp. 455 (D. Md. 1983), photocopies of documents did not include portions of the originals. Margins on one photocopy were missing and portions of the other photocopy were illegible. Despite their inaccuracies, the duplicates' admission was upheld by the trial court, which stated:

> The decision as to whether the offered documents constitute accurate duplicates and can be accepted in evidence is "addressed to the sound discretion of the trial court, and in any case considerations of trustworthiness and fairness are paramount." . . . Applying these standards, the Court finds that the submitted documents are accurate copies of the originals. Despite the missing margins and deleted portions, the terms of the continuing guaranty are clear, since only one, two, or at most three of the letters of the starting word on each line are omitted, and, in every relevant line, only one reasonable interpretation can be given to the language used. The promissory note (exhibit 7) is legible at every important point, save part of the signature of the defendant and the name of the witness. Since Rodenberg does not deny signing the documents and the

relevant terms of the promissory note and the guaranty age are clear, the exhibits submitted by the plaintiff are admissible as duplicates.

Id. at 458. Similarly, in *United States v. Balzano*, 687 F.2d 6 (1st Cir. 1982), the court upheld the admission of copies of tape recordings, commenting that they cannot be rendered inadmissible merely because the opponent can conjure up hypothetical possibilities that tampering occurred.

[4]   Rule 1006 — Summaries of Voluminous Writings

[a]   Requirements for Admission of Summaries

Sometimes the documents involved in an action are so voluminous that the only practical means of making them available to and usable by the judge and jury is through a summary of their contents. In such cases, the presiding judge may allow the proponent to use the summaries instead of the original documents, so long as the underlying documents are made available to the opponent for examination. Courts have long recognized this principle. *See* 4 WIGMORE, EVIDENCE, § 1230, at 535 (Chadbourn rev. 1972). Rule 1006 has codified this exception to the best evidence requirement.

As the following case explains, before these summaries can be admitted, the proponent must establish that the summarized materials are admissible and that the summaries accurately reflect the content of those materials.

LINDE v. ARAB BANK, PLC
United States District Court for the Eastern District of New York
922 F. Supp. 2d 316 (2013)

NINA GERSHON, DISTRICT JUDGE.

A. Hamas and Charitable Organization Experts

Plaintiffs claim that defendant Arab Bank provided material support not only to Hamas or Hamas leadership but also to twelve charitable organizations that were fronts for Hamas, and that its provision of banking and administrative services to the Saudi Committee provide further evidence of the Bank's material support to terrorists. The experts addressed below are proffered on one or more of these subjects.

1. Mr. Arieh Dan Spitzen

Defendant moves to exclude the expert testimony of Arieh Dan Spitzen. Mr. Spitzen formerly headed the Palestinian Affairs Department ("PAD") of the Israel Ministry of Defense's Coordinator of Governmental Activities in the Palestinian Territories. He has also conducted independent research and provided expert testimony in Israeli criminal terrorism prosecutions. He is fluent in Arabic.

Before addressing defendant's objections to Mr. Spitzen's proposed testimony, it is important to note that defendant does not challenge Mr. Spitzen's opinions regarding payments from the Bank to senior Hamas leaders; his Arabic naming methodology used to determine whether Bank accountholders and wire transfer beneficiaries were in fact identifiable terrorists; and the identification of individual terrorists or their relatives who received funds through Arab Bank.

What defendant does challenge are those portions of Mr. Spitzen's report which opine on the establishment and organization of Hamas; whether certain charities were under the control of Hamas between 2000 and 2004; or whether certain individuals named on transactions processed by Arab Bank on behalf of Yousef Al-Hayek and others are leaders, members, or relatives of leaders or members, of Hamas. It also challenges Mr. Spitzen's expert opinions as to the Saudi Committee, the Al-Shahid Foundation, and the Al Ansar Society. . . .D. Summary Witness: Mr. Wayne Geisser

Defendant also moves to exclude the report and testimony of Wayne Geisser. Mr. Geisser is a CPA and former Branch Chief in the Securities and Exchange Commission's Division of Enforcement. He has conducted or supervised hundreds of financial investigations that have involved the analysis of banking/financial transactions. He was hired by the plaintiffs to review and analyze bank records, including Arab Bank's New York branch transactions (approximately 3,100 transactions in total) and a subset of transactions involving the Saudi Committee (approximately 16,000 of a total of approximately 200,000 transactions). The New York branch transactions include transactions from Yousef El Hayek to individuals that plaintiffs allege are known Hamas activists or to Hamas front organizations.

Defendant argues, and plaintiffs acknowledge, that Mr. Geisser is more appropriately described as a summary witness than an expert witness. Indeed, Mr. Geisser offers no expert opinions whatsoever. Pursuant to Rule 1006 of the Federal Rules of Evidence, "[t]he contents of voluminous writings . . . which cannot conveniently be examined in court may be presented in the form of a chart, summary, or calculation." Where, as here, a party introduces summary charts, "the court must ascertain with certainty that they are based upon and fairly represent competent evidence already before the jury." *United States v. Conlin*, 551 F.2d 534, 538 (2d Cir.1977) (internal quotation marks omitted).

Defendant argues that Mr. Geisser's proposed testimony will be misleading and confusing because plaintiffs have cherry-picked a subset of transactions that will show a skewed picture of the Saudi Committee's transactions. But "[a] summary may include only evidence favoring one party, so long as the witness does not represent to the jury that he is summarizing all the evidence in the case." *United States v. Bishop, III*, 264 F.3d 535, 547 (5th Cir. 2001); *see also Fagiola v. National Gypsum Co. AC & S, Inc.*, 906 F.2d 53, 57–58 (2d Cir. 1990). The parties agree that Mr. Geisser need not summarize the entire universe of transactions made by the Saudi Committee, and plaintiffs acknowledge that Mr. Geisser's summary excludes payments under $300 processed by Arab Bank on behalf of the Saudi Committee. They represent, however, that his summary includes every transaction in excess of $300, regardless of the recipient, and defendant does not challenge that representation. So long as Mr. Geisser's testimony accurately describes the limits of his analysis, defendant will be able to explore the scope of his work on cross-examination, present its own summary of the evidence it considers relevant, and direct the jury's attention to other evidence in the record.

Moreover, although defendant moves to strike the entirety of Mr. Geisser's report and testimony, it makes no argument with respect to his summary of the New York branch transactions, including the Yousef El Hayek transactions, nor does it argue that any of the summaries, including the Saudi Committee transactions, are inaccurate. In addition, I will instruct the jury on the appropriate use of summary evidence. See *Fagiola*, 906 F.2d at 58.

Defendant's reliance on *Consorti v. Armstrong World Industries, Inc.*, 72 F.3d 1003 (2d Cir.1995), vacated on other grounds, 518 U.S. 1031, 116 S. Ct. 2576, 135 L. Ed. 2d 1091 (1996), is misplaced. Although the district court held in that case that summary evidence could not be introduced because it "may not have comprised the universe of [relevant] documents," the Second Circuit did not rule that summary evidence must summarize all of the documents at issue. *Consorti*, 72 F.3d at 1016–17. Rather, the evidence was excluded because no information about the preparation of the summary evidence was either introduced or made available in court or to opposing counsel. Id. There are no such concerns in this case, where each side has full access to all of the documents being summarized and the opportunity to evaluate the information underlying the summary.

Plaintiffs state that they have no intention of introducing the portion of Mr. Geisser's report which summarizes the allegations in the complaint. That summary is obviously inadmissible. In all other respects, defendant's motion is denied.

SO ORDERED.

[b]   Evidentiary Status of Summaries

The only issue relative to summaries over which courts have disagreed concerns their evidentiary status. Some courts have held that the summaries are not evidence. These courts have restricted the summaries' use to assisting the jury in understanding and using the underlying facts and data that are already in the records. *See United States v. Atchley*, 699 F.2d 1055 (11th Cir. 1983) (restricting use of charts analyzing telephone toll records); *United States v. Nathan*, 536 F.2d 988 (2d Cir. 1976) (restricting use of charts summarizing evidence concerning number and amount of various allegedly fraudulent checks). The court in *United States v. Stephens* on the other hand, interpreted the evidentiary status of summaries differently.

UNITED STATES v. STEPHENS
United States Court of Appeals for the Fifth Circuit
779 F.2d 232 (1985)

JERRE S. WILLIAMS, CIRCUIT JUDGE.

Columbus Schalah Stephens, Jr. appeals his conviction on one count of falsifying information on a Farmers' Home Administration (FmHA) loan application, 18

U.S.C. § 1014, and five counts of mail fraud, 18 U.S.C. § 1341. He contends on appeal: (1) the evidence is insufficient to sustain his conviction, (2) testimony was erroneously excluded, (3) the jury charge was incorrect, (4) government summary exhibits were erroneously admitted into evidence, and (5) the government varied its proof and argument from the bill of particulars. We reject the defendant's arguments and affirm his convictions.

I. FACTS

Columbus Schalah Stephens, Jr. is one of two shareholders in CMW Land Company, Inc., a 5,051 acre cattle farm in Choctaw, Montgomery, and Webster Counties in Mississippi. Stephens and Eph Wiygul purchased CMW from Staple Cotton Discount Corporation in December of 1973 for $300,000 in cash, assumption of debt to SCDC, and assumption of a first mortgage to Equitable of Iowa. Stephens handled the finances of CMW, and Wiygul supervised the actual farming operation. CMW lost money and Stephens applied for an "EM" Farmers' Home Administration (FmHA) loan in 1976 primarily for the purpose of refinancing the Staple Cotton indebtedness. A loan for $2,141,000 was approved. $1,381,700 of the loan proceeds was paid to Staple Cotton in exchange for Staple Cotton releasing its second mortgage lien against CMW's assets.

CMW continued to lose money and FmHA approved additional loans in 1977, 1978, and 1979. The 1979 loan is the subject of the indictment. As one of CMW's principal shareholders, Stephens submitted his application to FmHA together with CMW's application. The Stephens and CMW applications both stated that the purpose of the loan was to "provide for operating requirements and debt service of CMW Land Company." FmHA's application form is a one page document printed on both sides. The back side is a financial statement and it is headed in one-eighth inch high capital letters: "FINANCIAL STATEMENT AS OF DATE OF APPLICA-TION". Stephens' application was dated May 22, 1979. Stephens attached a one page financial statement dated December 31, 1978, to his application. He stated on his application that he owed no judgments yet there was a $7,608 judgment outstanding against him. His application also omitted mention of a $100,000 debt to the Barnett Bank and a $320,000 debt in relation to the "Chambless property." Both of these loans were taken out after December 31, 1978, and prior to May 22, 1979. On the basis of the applications of Stephens and CMW, FmHA approved a $2,960,920 loan.

CMW maintained two accounts in Mississippi, a general account and an operating account. Stephens maintained another account in Florida in the name of CMW Land Company. The address for this account was the same as his residence in Orlando, Florida. Neither Mr. Herrod, the FmHA agent with whom Stephens dealt, nor Mrs. Olmy, CMW's secretary and bookkeeper, had any knowledge of this CMW Florida account. Virtually all of the FmHA loan funds were deposited to either the CMW Mississippi accounts or the CMW Florida account. The evidence shows that Stephens paid $1,122,786.29 out of the CMW Florida account to himself, his creditors, his corporations, his relatives, and others. None of these debt payments or fund disbursements were authorized by FmHA. None of the debts repaid with these funds were listed with CMW's application as debts for which

CMW was seeking funds for "debt services." None of the debts repaid with these funds were listed in the Farm and Home Plan (FHP) debt repayment schedule as debts which were to be repaid from the loan funds, nor were any of these disbursements listed in the FHP operating expenses schedule as expenses which were to paid with loan funds. None of these disbursements were reported in monthly cash flow reports as projected expenses, nor were they reported as actual expenses after they were paid. In short, none of these disbursements were ever discussed with or reported to FmHA orally or otherwise.

On May 17, 1984, a Federal Grand Jury in the Northern District of Mississippi indicted Stephens on the one count of filing a false financial statement to obtain a FmHA loan and the five counts of using the mails to defraud the FmHA. The trial lasted eight days. Stephens was convicted on all counts after jury deliberation of approximately one hour. Stephens was sentenced to concurrent three year terms of imprisonment on Counts 2–6, and a concurrent sentence of one year imprisonment on Count 1. Stephens appeals.

III. SUMMARY CHARTS

Stephens complains that the district court erred in admitting into evidence on the government's proffer certain charts which constituted summaries of evidence already received. He asserts the charts did not qualify for admission under Fed. R. Evid. 1006 and that he was further severely prejudiced when the court allowed the charts to accompany the jury into the jury room.

This contention involves six summary charts which the government introduced in evidence through a witness who was a special agent with the office of the Inspector General of the United States Department of Agriculture. The witness had prepared them. A separate chart illustrated each of the five counts of mail fraud, and the sixth chart summarized the disposition of the entire loan funds. The charts were approximately three feet by five feet in size and consisted of simple flow charts tracing Stephens' use of the loan proceeds. The sixth chart categorized Stephens' expenditures as either "questioned" or "not questioned." The witness defined "questioned" to mean that as an investigator he questioned the particular use of the loan funds. It is clear that all the records upon which the charts were based were also in evidence.

The trial court overruled Stephens' objections to the admission of the charts in evidence. The court expressly found that the charts were a summaries of "voluminous writings and records which have been introduced into evidence and which cannot be conveniently examined in court by this jury" and thus were properly admitted under Rule 1006. As each chart was introduced, the court instructed the jury that the summary charts did not in themselves constitute evidence in the case, the real evidence was the underlying documents. The judge repeated this instruction in his general charge to the jury, and then the court allowed the summary charts to go into the jury room with the jury. The defendant also had introduced a summary chart, and it as well accompanied the jury into the jury room.

Stephens attacks on two fronts the introduction of the charts into evidence under Fed. R. Evid. 1006. First, he argues that the charts were merely pedagogical devices, not proper Rule 1006 summaries, and second, the charts were argumentative. This Court has noted the importance of distinguishing between charts or summaries as evidence pursuant to Rule 1006, *United States v. Smyth*, 556 F.2d 1179, 1184 (5th Cir.), *cert. denied* 434 U.S. 862, 98 S. Ct. 190, 54 L. Ed. 2d 135 (1977) (summaries admitted pursuant to Rule 1006 are evidence) and charts or summaries as pedagogical devices. In *Pierce v. Ramsey Winch Co.*, 753 F.2d 416, 431 (5th Cir. 1985), we recognized that pedagogical charts are not themselves evidence, and, absent the consent of all parties, they should not be sent to the jury room with the other exhibits. Relying on Pierce, Stephens argues that the charts were pedagogical because they summarize and organize data already in evidence. It is his contention that Rule 1006 is restricted to summaries of writings that cannot feasibly be admitted into evidence.

We reject Stephens' reading of Rule 1006. The language of Rule 1006 is not so restrictive. Rule 1006 does not require that "it be literally impossible to examine the underlying records" before a summary chart may be introduced. *United States v. Scales*, 594 F.2d 558, 562 (6th Cir. 1978), *cert. denied*, 441 U.S. 946, 99 S. Ct. 2168, 60 L. Ed. 2d 1049 (1979). The fact that the underlying documents are already in evidence does not mean that they can be "conveniently examined in court." *United States v. Lemire*, 720 F.2d 1327, 1347 (D.C. Cir. 1983), *cert. denied*, 467 U.S. 1226, 104 S. Ct. 2678, 81 L. Ed. 2d 874 (1984). Stephens' reading of Rule 1006 is also clearly inconsistent with one proper method of laying a foundation for admission of summary charts — admitting the documentation on which the summary is based. 5 J. Weinstein & M. Berger, Weinstein's Evidence ¶ 1006 [03], p. 1006–7 (1983).

Stephens' reliance on Pierce is misplaced. Pierce did not hold that charts based upon documents already in evidence are always pedagogical charts and ineligible under Rule 1006. The party in Pierce seeking to admit the charts into evidence did not offer the charts pursuant to Rule 1006, so Rule 1006 was not even an issue in the case. Stephens' position runs counter to our decisions that do deal with Rule 1006 charts. In *United States v. Means*, 695 F.2d 811 (5th Cir.1983), we held that a chart based on documents in evidence was properly admitted under Rule 1006. To the same effect are *United States v. Evans*, 572 F.2d 455 (5th Cir.1978), *cert. denied*, 439 U.S. 870, 99 S. Ct. 200, 58 L. Ed. 2d 182 (1979) and *United States v. Smyth*, 556 F.2d 1179 (5th Cir.), *cert. denied*, 434 U.S. 862, 98 S. Ct. 190, 54 L. Ed. 2d 135 (1977).

Rule 1006 requires (1) the underlying writings be voluminous and (2) in-court examination not be convenient. *Scales*, 594 F.2d at 562. The decision of the trial judge to admit the charts is subject only to an abuse of discretion standard of review. *United States v. Means*, 695 F.2d 811, 817 (5th Cir. 1983). There is no abuse of discretion in this case. The evidence was undisputably complex as it involved hundreds of exhibits. Stephens does not question that the underlying documentation was voluminous. Examination of the underlying materials would have been inconvenient without the charts utilized by the government. *See United States v. Evans*, 572 F.2d at 491; *United States v. Howard*, 774 F.2d 838, 844 (7th Cir. 1985).

We also find no merit to Stephens' contention that the charts were argumentative. Stephens objects to the "questioned" and "unquestioned" characterization used in the sixth chart. He claims that the word "questioned" appeared to establish conclusively that the use of the loan funds was questioned. The use of the term, he maintains, improperly shifted the burden of proof to him.

This case is similar to *United States v. Smyth*, 556 F.2d 1179 (5th Cir.), *cert. denied*, 434 U.S. 862, 98 S. Ct. 190, 54 L. Ed. 2d 135 (1977). The government introduced computer printout summaries that contained "original data", "classified data", "falsified data summarized" and "difference between original/false" headings to illustrate how the defendant used forged time cards to overbill the government. The trial court admitted the computer printout into evidence and instructed the jury that the underlying documents were the evidence and that the computer printout summaries were not evidence. We stated, "[I]n light of appellants' objections to the characterizations the Government utilized in the summary headings the cautionary instruction given by the trial judge was entirely appropriate, if not necessary, for it neutralized their possible prejudicial effect." 556 F.2d at 1184.

Like the court in *Smyth*, the court admitted the summary charts into evidence and instructed the jury that the charts were not to be considered as the evidence in the case, and thus, neutralized the possible prejudicial effect of the headings. Moreover, "questioned" falls far short of being as argumentative as "falsified". The use of the term "questioned" is no more than accurate in a case dealing with alleged conversion of loan proceeds. In sum, we find that the judge properly admitted the summary charts into evidence under Rule 1006, and consequently there was no error in allowing the charts to go into the jury room with the jury.

[5]   Rule 803(7) — Absence of Entry in Business Record; Rule 803(10) — Absence of Public Record or Entry

If a proponent proves an original's unavailability through negative evidence demonstrating the proponent's inability to find the original despite a diligent search of a collection of documents where the original would have been found were it still in existence, courts will not interpret this situation as one that creates another best evidence problem relative to the collection. Courts do not view the absence of something as proving the content of what is present as indicated in the *Bowers* decision below that dealt with the absence of records in an income tax evasion prosecution.

UNITED STATES v. BOWERS

United States Court of Appeals for the Fourth Circuit
920 F.2d 220 (1990)

K.K. HALL, CIRCUIT JUDGE:

Donald and Janet Bowers appeal their convictions for income tax evasion, in violation of 26 U.S.C. § 7201. We affirm.

I.

In this case, we are not burdened by sharp factual disputes. The Bowers presented no evidence at trial, and instead relied wholly on legal arguments that were rejected by the district court and are now renewed.

Through 1979, the appellants filed income tax returns and paid income taxes. In 1980, however, they stopped filing returns and began listing themselves as "exempt" on their W-4s, so that their employers would not withhold tax. The two apparently believe, or at least believed, that taxation is unconstitutional.

In 1982 the Bowers were audited, and taxes were assessed. They responded by instituting a series of Tax Court proceedings in which they challenged the proposed tax assessments under a variety of bizarre legal theories, including that they are not "persons" within the meaning of the Internal Revenue Code and that wage income is non-taxable. The Tax Court upheld the assessments and imposed penalties of $6,500 for the Bowers' frivolous arguments.

Undaunted, the Bowers continued to file "exempt" W-4s and to abstain from filing returns. In March 1984 the IRS levied on their bank accounts, at which time they began a concerted effort to conceal their assets from the government. They closed their checking accounts four days after the levy, and have not since had any account in their own names. In order to pay their bills, they used postal money orders and accounts under their minor sons' names. They transferred title to their mobile home and vehicles to Mrs. Bowers' mother.

The pair were eventually indicted for failing to file income taxes, Donald from 1983 to 1986 and Janet from 1984 to 1986. Over that period, Donald Bowers evaded taxes of $8,069, and Janet Bowers $12,758. They filed a pretrial motion to dismiss for lack of jurisdiction, arguing that the IRS had not complied with the publication requirements of 5 U.S.C. § 552, and they could therefore not be prosecuted for failing to comply with unpublished agency directives. The district court deferred its ruling until after a bench trial, when it denied the motion, and found both guilty. The court sentenced Donald Bowers to 4 consecutive 3-year terms and Janet Bowers to 3 consecutive 4-year terms of imprisonment.

On appeal, the Bowers renew their "lack of publication" defense and challenge the admission of several government exhibits.

* * *

III.

The majority of the facts of this case were stipulated, but the Bowers put the government to its proof on whether they had in fact not paid their taxes.

To prove this essential element, the government offered Exhibit 28 and Exhibits 102–108. The former is a compilation of "Certificates of Assessments and Payments" showing no record of returns filed by the Bowers. Each individual document has a sealed cover certificate authenticating it pursuant to Fed. R. Evid. 902. Exhibits 102–108 are the computer data from the Martinsburg, West Virginia, computer center that were used to construct Exhibit 28.

Appellants argue that these exhibits are hearsay and do not satisfy any hearsay exception. They busy themselves arguing that the exhibits are not "business records" admissible under Rule 803(6) or "official records" admissible under 803(8).

Though the government does not concede the point as to those two exceptions, *see United States v. Hayes*, 861 F.2d 1225, 1230 (10th Cir.1988) (IRS computer records properly admitted under Rule 803(6)), it argues that the exhibits are clearly admissible as "certificates of lack of official record" under Rule 803(10). *E.g., United States v. Neff*, 615 F.2d 1235 (9th Cir. 1980).

All of the exhibits were sponsored by employees at the IRS' Philadelphia Service Center. Appellants' primary argument is that these employees are not the "custodians" of the data stored in the mainframe computer in Martinsburg.

> Rule 803(10) reads: Absence of public record or entry. To prove the absence of a record, report, statement, or data compilation, in any form, or the nonoccurrence or nonexistence of a matter of which a record, report, statement, or data compilation, in any form, was regularly made and preserved by a public office or agency, evidence in the form of a certification in accordance with rule 902, or testimony, that diligent search failed to disclose the record, report, statement, or data compilation, or entry.

The challenged exhibits satisfy this exception to hearsay. The IRS regularly makes and preserves computer "data compilations" about taxpayers. The certificates disclose the "nonoccurrence . . . of a matter" which would have been included in the data compilation.

Appellants' arguments about the "custodian" of the record are weak. Rule 803(10) simply requires a "diligent search." The persons in Philadelphia had access to the computer data stored in Martinsburg. Traditional notions of physical "custody" in hearsay rules make little sense when applied to computer data. We will not impose on a public agency a requirement to send a witness from the physical location of the agency's mainframe computer every time data from that computer must be presented in court. The real custodian is the agency, and those who signed the certifications had the agency's authority to search the records. So long as the sponsoring witness has full access and authority to search the public agency's computer data, conducts the search diligently, and is available for cross-examination about his access, authority, and diligence, the concern for trustworthiness embedded in the rules of evidence is satisfied. The Bowers' anxieties about the reliability of such data are grist for the trier of fact's mill. In a case where a defendant contests the computer-generated evidence, and attacks its reliability, he may succeed in creating a reasonable doubt of his guilt. Nonetheless, we will not make the presentation of such evidence a compulsory dog-and-pony show just because some defendant may someday successfully refute it.

District court rulings on evidence must be affirmed unless they constitute an abuse of discretion. The admission of the challenged exhibits was proper and well within the court's sound discretion.

The judgment of the district court is affirmed.

AFFIRMED.

EXERCISES

1. The central issue at trial is whether a bank was, in fact, federally insured by the Federal Deposit Insurance Corporation. At trial one party is prepared to call as a witness a teller of the bank: (a) to testify that a photocopy of the FDIC certificate of insurance hangs on the wall of the bank, (b) to testify that to teller's knowledge the bank was insured on the date in question, and (c) to authenticate and offer into evidence a photocopy of the bank's certificate of insurance. The proponent does not intend on offering the original and it is unclear whether the teller has ever seen the original certificate of insurance. Will this presentation survive a best evidence challenge?

2. Plaintiff and Defendant are both surgical implant manufactures. Both companies filed cross-claims against each other alleging a breach of the terms of their no-compete contract. At trial the president of Defendant wants to testify regarding buy-out clauses in contracts Defendant has with other third-party companies to prove that he requested and secured a buy-out clause from Plaintiff, a contention which Plaintiff disputes. If Defendant's testimony about the third-party contracts is accurate, then Defendant will be entitled to compensation from Plaintiff. Must Defendant produce the other third-party contracts at trial?

3. Waterloo manufactures computer keyboards. Haworth manufactures an adjustable desk component which allows a keyboard to swing out from under the desk. The two companies entered into a mutually beneficial and exclusive business agreement for a period of ten years. Sometime around the end of year ten, Haworth entered into a similar agreement with SoftView. Waterloo then filed suit against Haworth, alleging that Haworth entered into the new agreement with SoftView before the contract with Waterloo expired. At trial Haworth's president, who personally participated in the contract negotiations with SoftView, seeks to testify that the agreement with SoftView was not finalized until after the Waterloo contract expired. Must Haworth also enter into evidence the original (or suitable copy) of the Haworth/SoftView Agreement as the best evidence of Haworth's president's assertion?

4. The government indicted Phillip, an immigration lawyer, for forging clients' signatures on both work permits and applications for asylum. At trial numerous clients testified that they never signed the work permits or requests for asylum, and had not authorized Phillip to sign on their behalf. The government now seeks to authenticate and offer photocopies of the disputed documents, as opposed to the originals. The government is unable to produce the original documents because the originals were accidently misfiled in a massive storage unit known as the "black hole" and can no longer be located despite reasonable efforts. Should the trial judge allow the government to enter the photocopies?

§ 7.02   AUTHENTICATION

[A]   Direct Methods of Authentication — Rules 901, 902, 903

[1]   Witness with Personal Knowledge

Direct methods of authentication rely on witnesses' personal knowledge, either of the instrument in question or of those who executed it. One could authenticate a document in such a way, for example, by calling an individual who has knowledge of the document's authenticity as a result of having witnessed the document's execution. Alternatively, a document can be authenticated by the testimony of an individual who, due to familiarity with another's signature or handwriting style, can establish that that individual executed the document.

If the opposing party admits the genuineness of a document, its authenticity is also directly established. Under the Federal Rules of Civil Procedure, as well as many state procedural codes, a party can submit documents to his adversary prior to trial for the purpose of obtaining admissions as to the genuineness. If authenticated through such a procedure, their authenticity is conclusively established for that litigation unless the court allows the opponent to withdraw the admission. If the adversary denies a document's genuineness prior to trial and the proponent later proves the genuineness at trial, the court may assess the adversary the costs of establishing that authenticity. *See* Fed. R. Civ. Proc. 36. Similarly, a party can obtain admissions of authenticity through interrogatories under Rule 33 of the Federal Rules of Civil Procedure and by allegations of authenticity in pleadings with the documents attached pursuant to Rule 10(c).

[2]   Handwriting Identification

Handwriting identification can be made either by a lay witness or an expert witness. A lay person who claims no special expertise may authenticate handwriting if he is familiar with a particular individual's handwriting style. A properly qualified expert in handwriting analysis may identify a handwriting by comparing the contested document with a handwriting sample or exemplar. However, the use of an exemplar for comparison purposes creates an additional authentication problem. The proponent must establish that the exemplar is genuine before it can be used as a basis for determining the authenticity of another writing. Under the orthodox common-law rule, the presiding judge made the determination of the exemplar's authenticity as part of a preliminary inquiry as to admissibility. *See United States v. White*, 444 F.2d 1274, 1280 (5th Cir. 1971). Certain jurisdictions, however, allocated both authentication issues to the jury after the proponent's *prima facie* showing of the authenticity of both documents to the presiding judge. In those jurisdictions the judge gave appropriate instructions to the jury, to the effect that the jury should compare the two handwritings and use the comparison testimony of the expert witness only if they first found the exemplar to be genuine.

Lay witnesses — witnesses claiming no expertise in handwriting analysis — were not permitted to testify to comparisons that they had made between the contested document and an exemplar. Because lay witnesses' comparisons could not provide any special assistance that would ensure more accurate jury determinations, their testimony in this regard would constitute little more than a choosing up of sides.

[B] Circumstantial Methods of Authentication

[1] Authenticating Evidence Limited Only by Admissibility

If direct evidence of authenticity is not available through a credible witness with personal knowledge, the proponent must use circumstantial evidence to establish that the document is what the proponent claims it to be. There are no inherent limitations on the means by which one can circumstantially authenticate a piece of evidence. Indeed, to authenticate a document, a proponent can use any evidence relevant to the document's identity, provided that the evidence is not otherwise inadmissible. Often, counsel must demonstrate a great deal of ingenuity in the circumstantial methods of authentication employed. The particular methods of authentication that this section focuses on have been singled out because of the frequency of their use by litigants. These popular methods of authentication have given rise to a considerable body of law that reflects the issues and problems that generally arise with all circumstantial methods of authentication.

[2] The Reply Doctrine

The reply doctrine illustrates the importance of the circumstances surrounding the production and receipt of a document in identifying the document's source or author. The doctrine is premised on the logical inference that one can draw from the timely receipt of a reply to a prior communication. If X writes a letter or sends a telegram to Y, and, by return mail or subsequent telegram, receives what is purportedly Y's response to the prior communication, courts will consider the response to be sufficiently authenticated to be admissible.

For the reply doctrine to be applicable, courts usually impose two conditions. First, the reply in question must refer to the prior communication and claim to be in response to it. Second, the reply must be received without undue delay (measured from the date the original communication was sent). Where the mail is both regular and reliable, the reply refers to the former communication, and there is no delay beyond what one would reasonably expect because of the nature of the communication, courts will consider the possibility of fraud to be minimal.

As Professors Mueller and Kirkpatrick explain, however, the "reply doctrine" is nothing more than a variation of the method of authenticating through contents (the author's expression of knowledge that only a few possess), the application of which is not dependent upon either the use of the mails or the form of the reply:

> The reply letter doctrine, long recognized at common law, represents but a particular application of the more general method of authentication [through apparent knowledge]. If it can be shown that an inquiry was directed to a particular person, and that in due course an apparent reply was received, which expressly refers to or seems implicitly to acknowledge

the earlier inquiry, these facts suffice as the basis for concluding that the reply was sent by the person to whom the inquiry was directed. Only he was likely to have received the inquiry; hence only he was likely to know of it, and to respond. In the typical case, both inquiry and reply are by means of letters sent through the mail, whence comes the name "reply letter doctrine". But there is nothing magic in form, and the principle applies equally to a written reply to an oral inquiry, to a telephonic response to an oral or written inquiry, to a reply by e-mail, and so forth, regardless of whether the mails are involved. The essentials are to establish by evidence independent of the reply that the original inquiry was put, and to find in the reply itself (or for that matter in surrounding circumstances) some indication that the author was indeed responding to the inquiry, for these points are the necessary predicate underlying the inference that the author of the reply is the person to whom the inquiry was put.

In principle, the reply letter doctrine applies as well to reply telegrams, and better reasoned cases so hold. Some authority balking at this extension is reported in Wigmore, who agreed that the principle should apply. Apparently the reason for drawing the line is that intermediaries in the mechanics of transmission reduce confidentiality and lessen the possibility that mistake or fraud would appear on the face of the document. However, these rather small risks seem an insufficient basis for refusing to apply the doctrine.

C. MUELLER & L. KIRKPATRICK, FEDERAL EVIDENCE, § 9:7 (3d ed. 2007).

It is often the case in correspondence with business entities that a person other than the addressee will reply to the communication. For example, Z, who claims to be Y's agent, responds to X's letter to Y. How does one authenticate Z's agency and authority to speak for Y? The reply doctrine authenticates this authority as well.

The reply doctrine does not authenticate the initial communication from X to Y. Anyone can sign someone else's name to a letter. If Y were to use X's letter in litigation against X, Y would have to establish its genuineness by a means other than the reply doctrine, such as: handwriting, typewriter or psycholinguistic comparisons; the communication's unique contents (facts only known to X); or other unique circumstances, such as the stationery upon which the letter was written.

A theory similar to the one behind the reply doctrine operates to authenticate telephone conversations when one person testifies to having looked up an individual or business telephone number in the telephone directory and having properly dialed that number. Courts at common law considered this testimony sufficient authentication of the identity of the individual answering the call, if the individual answering identified himself, herself, or the business. For example, if she answered the telephone, "Hello, Jill Jenkins speaking," this response would suffice. Less persuasive, but in all likelihood still adequate, would be the answer, "Hello, Jenkin's residence," and in response to the caller's question, "May I speak with Jill Jenkins?" Jill's reply, "Speaking." Least sufficient would be the most common kind of answer in which the individual answering the telephone merely responds, "Hello," and then acknowledges her identity when the caller asks to speak to her. Because anyone can claim to be someone else over the telephone, the possibilities of fraud are substantially enhanced in the latter situation. Therefore, under such circumstances, adequate authentication of the speaker may require additional evidence. Such evidence could include the caller's testimony that he recognized the voice of the person with whom he was speaking or that the person who answered possessed a body of knowledge that was held only by a particular individual.

Proving an individual's authority to speak for another poses an issue for telephone conversations the same as it does for reply letters that are signed by someone other than the one to whom the original letter was sent. Courts have considered conversations with those who answer the telephones of business establishments in much the same way they have considered reply letters. Businesses hold themselves out as doing business via the telephone and invite business by listing their numbers in the telephone directory. Courts, therefore, will assume that anyone who transacts business over that telephone line, claiming to have the authority to do so either explicitly or implicitly, has that authority. It is the business and not the customer that takes the risk that the business' employees will exceed the scope of their agency. This assumes, of course, that the kind of business that the parties transacted over the telephone was reasonable under the circumstances and, therefore, would not have alerted the customer to the answering party's lack of authority. Whether this method of authentication will convince the jury will depend on the credibility of the individual who claims to have made the call and to have had the conversation with the individual who answered. The underlying assumption is that the jury will believe the caller.

As with the original letter that X wrote to Y, one cannot authenticate the caller's identity through the caller's self-identification. Anyone can call and identify himself as another. As with the letter from X, the proponent of the contents of the telephone call (other than the caller himself) will have to authenticate any caller's identity through other means, such as: voice identification; speech patterns; the content of the message conveyed (e.g., facts were related that were uniquely known by the person in question); corroborating circumstances; the fact that it was a return call; or, as illustrated in the following opinion in *United States v. Espinoza*, a combination of all these circumstances.

UNITED STATES v. ESPINOZA
United States Court of Appeals, Fourth Circuit
641 F.2d 153 (1981)

STAKER, DISTRICT JUDGE (sitting by designation):

Joseph Jesse Espinoza, appellant here, and J-E Enterprises, Inc., a California corporation (J-E), were jointly indicted and tried, and each was found guilty and convicted, in the United States District Court for the Southern District of West Virginia, at Charleston, upon each of two counts, the first charging that in violation of 18 U.S.C. § 371, they conspired with each other and others to transport in interstate commerce from California to Charleston, West Virginia, obscene films and magazines concerning and involving children, commonly called "kiddie porn," in violation of 18 U.S.C. § 1465.

* * *

Clifford J. Holdren, Jr., owner-operator of Kip's Discount, a retail outlet dealing in sexually explicit matter in Charleston, West Virginia, testified that in response to an order for kiddie porn placed by him in a telephone conversation with "Joe," at J-E's place of business in California, the items of kiddie porn mentioned in the indictment, consisting of magazines and films, were shipped from J-E in California, to Kip's Discount in Charleston, by Greyhound Bus, and that in March, 1977, he delivered to Special Agent Robert Sylvester, of the Federal Bureau of Investigation (FBI), those items of kiddie porn and invoices, cancelled checks and other documents pertaining to that transaction.

Espinoza's defense was that he could not be guilty of the charges, because throughout the period from the fall of 1976 to the spring of 1977, that being the period in which the violations were charged to have occurred, he was not involved in or with J-E's business operations to the extent he could have been implicated in, or even aware of, those violations if they did, in fact, occur. He testified that he caused J-E to be incorporated in April, 1974, for the purpose of wholesaling and distributing adult-oriented, sexually explicit matter from a building housing J-E's warehouses and Espinoza's office, located at 1032 South Gerhart Avenue, Commerce, California (warehouse), and then became J-E's president; that during the ensuing year, he commenced several other businesses; that sometime during the year 1975, he resigned as the president and an officer of J-E, but continued to maintain his office in the warehouse, from which he managed and attended to those other businesses; and that upon his resignation, he was succeeded by Manuel Lopez, who commenced to manage and operate J-E as its president, after which he, Espinoza, no longer helped or assisted J-E at all, though Espinoza admitted in other testimony that from time to time he did assist J-E as aid might be needed in J-E's rubber department, talked on the "phone" about certain aspects of J-E's business in terms of goods ordered and shipped, and occasionally handled invoices of J-E. He further testified that in about March, 1977, Manuel Lopez disappeared and ceased his affiliation with J-E, whereupon he, Espinoza, resumed its management and operations.

* * *

Espinoza claims the court erred by permitting witness Holdren to testify to his telephone conversations with Espinoza, arguing that since Holdren had never met him, Holdren could not identify him as the person with whom Holdren spoke at J-E.

Holdren testified that he communicated by telephone with J-E on at least four occasions, always speaking with "Joe," concerning ordering, pricing and shipping adult materials and kiddie porn, some of those conversations having been initiated by him and some by J-E; that two of those conversations dealt with kiddie porn; that when Holdren called J-E, a lady would answer the telephone, Holdren would ask for "Joe" and a man would get on the telephone and say, "This is 'Joe;' " and that in one of those conversations with Joe, he ordered kiddie porn from J-E as a result of which kiddie porn was shipped to Kip's Discount from J-E by Greyhound Bus.

Holdren could not pinpoint the exact dates upon which he talked with Joe, however, a telephone company statement rendered to Kip's Discount was admitted into evidence and showed changes for calls made from Kip's Discount to a California telephone number shown to be that of J-E on J-E's invoices rendered to Kip's Discount. Two of those invoices bore Espinoza's fingerprints, as testified to by an expert witness. One of the two, invoice 4002, listed several items as having been sold and shipped by J-E to Kip's Discount, including the item "bulbs," which Holdren testified "checked out [as against the merchandise actually received by Kip's Discount from J-E under that invoice] to be kiddie porn."

Also admitted into evidence was Kip's Discount's cancelled check, signed by Holdren, written to J-E in payment of invoice 4002 and identifying that invoice on the face of the check.

Holdren further testified that he had never met "Joe," and that if he saw him at trial he would not know him. On direct examination, the government asked, and Holdren answered:

Q: *Did* you know Joe by any other name or any further names?" (emphasis added).

A: I *know* Joe by Joe Espinoza. (emphasis added).

The differences in the verb tenses of the question and answer were not further explored to ascertain just what Holdren's answer meant.

Witness Ganley, a member of the Los Angeles Police Department Administrative Division, Pornography Unit, identified Espinoza at trial and testified that he had J-E's warehouse under surveillance for two months during the period from the fall of 1976 to and including the spring of 1977, during which he saw Espinoza enter and leave that warehouse regularly.

FBI Agent Dauwalder testified that at the time of the search of J-E's premises on August 13, 1976, he saw a sign on the door of Espinoza's office in J-E's warehouse reading "Joe Espinoza," and saw on a desk in that office business cards reading "J-E Enterprises, Joe Espinoza," and that Espinoza received several telephone calls over that telephone and had a catalog of J-E Enterprises with prices written in it on his desk there and requested Dauwalder not to seize that catalog, because he needed it to transact business.

The admissibility of Holdren's testimony identifying Espinoza as the person with whom he spoke by telephone is governed to some extent by Rules 901(a) and 104(b) of the Federal Rules of Evidence. Under the provisions thereof, it was not requisite to the admissibility of Holdren's testimony that it be sufficient itself to support a finding that it was Espinoza to whom Holdren spoke by telephone; Holdren's testimony was properly admissible, under the provisions of Rule 104(b), "upon, or subject to, the introduction of [other] evidence sufficient to support a finding of the fulfillment of the condition," that is, other evidence which would be sufficient to support a finding that Espinoza was the person to whom Holdren spoke by telephone, the establishment of the identity of Espinoza as that person being requisite to the relevancy of Holdren's testimony.

Testimony of a telephone conversation had between a witness and another person may be conditionally admitted, regardless of which of them initiated or answered the call, even though the witness cannot certainly identify the person with whom he spoke by voice identification, and the identity of the person with whom the witness is alleged to have had the conversation may be established by circumstantial evidence. . . .

Here the circumstantial evidence tending to identify Espinoza as the person with whom Holdren spoke in the telephone conversation in which he communicated his order for kiddie porn to J-E is strong and compelling.

Furthermore, establishing the identity of a person by evidence that he made a reply or response in a manner that was expected to be evoked by a communication made to him by another who cannot identify him is well-recognized and time-honored. In *Van Riper v. United States*, 13 F.2d 961, 968 (2d Cir. 1926), Judge Learned Hand writing for the court said:

> If, for example, a man were to write a letter properly addressed to another, and were to receive a telephone call in answer, professing to come from the addressee, and showing acquaintance with the contents of the letter, it would in our judgment be a good enough identification of the speaker to allow in the proof, though in the end, or course, the issue of identity would be for the jury. This is the reasoning on which a complete correspondence is admitted, once its origin is established, so long as it continues to be consecutive in substance.

Here, the evidence of Espinoza's response to Holdren's telephoned order to J-E for kiddie porn almost certainly identifies Espinoza as the "Joe" to whom Holdren spoke in that conversation: Holdren communicated to J-E, by speaking with "Joe," Holdren's order for kiddie porn, in response to which kiddie porn was shipped from J-E to Holdren (Kip's Discount) along with J-E's invoice therefor listing the kiddie porn thereon as "bulbs," per Holdren's testimony, and Holdren paid J-E the amount of that invoice by his check. These facts, standing alone, perhaps would not be sufficiently probative of Espinoza's identity, as the "Joe" to whom Holdren communicated the order and as a person involved in J-E's response to that order, to permit Holdren's testimony to the telephone conversation to be sufficiently relevant to remain before the jury as to Espinoza. But given the additional evidentiary fact that the invoice rendered by J-E to Holdren for the kiddie porn *bore the fingerprint of Espinoza*, then compelling evidence existed tending not only to establish that Espinoza had a personal role in the making of J-E's response to Holdren's order, thereby sufficiently identifying him as the "Joe" to whom Holdren spoke in the telephone conversation in which he made that order and rendering Holdren's testimony with regard thereto relevant, but also to establish independently that Espinoza was a member of the alleged conspiracy.

[C]　Authenticating Tape Recordings

UNITED STATES v. COLLINS

United States Court of Appeals, Seventh Circuit
715 F.3d 1032 (2013)

BAUER, CIRCUIT JUDGE.

Ron "Ron Ron" Collins participated in a drug-distribution conspiracy stretching from Mexico to Milwaukee that involved mass amounts of cocaine. For his role, Collins was found guilty of conspiracy to possess with intent to distribute and to distribute five kilograms or more of cocaine, in violation of 21 U.S.C. § 846, and sentenced to a prison term of 360 months. Collins challenges both his conviction and the sentence imposed. He contends, first, that the district court improperly admitted into evidence certain tape recordings at trial, and second, that the district court erred in allowing an expert to testify regarding "coded drug-dealing language" on the tapes. He also argues that the district court erred in applying the "manager or supervisor" enhancement pursuant to U.S.S.G. § 3B1.1. Finding all of Collins' contentions unpersuasive, we affirm.

I. BACKGROUND

From at least 2005 to November 2008, Collins acted as a linchpin in a large drug-distribution conspiracy based in Mexico. Collins had two connections in Mexico — the Flores twins, Pedro and Margarito — who were his sources for his drug of choice, cocaine. Whenever Collins needed cocaine to deal, he contacted the Flores twins, who contacted their drug couriers, who in turn would deliver the necessary drugs to Collins in the Chicagoland area. A given delivery to Collins sometimes included 20 to 50 kilograms of cocaine, and the Flores twins often "fronted" the drugs or had them delivered to Collins on "credit."

Upon receipt of the cocaine, Collins would sell it to the members of his "crew." Collins made a profit of approximately $1,500 per kilogram sold; that is how he made the money needed to pay back the Flores twins. The members of Collins' crew sold the cocaine to other lower-level buyers on the streets. This cycle repeated as fast as the cocaine could be sold.

One crew member to whom Collins repeatedly sold cocaine was Robert Gregory, a Milwaukee, Wisconsin native. Collins first met Gregory in early 2006 at Lee's Auto Shop in Chicago, Illinois. It was then that Collins asked Gregory about selling cocaine and whether he would purchase cocaine from Collins to sell to other buyers in Milwaukee; Gregory agreed to do so because Collins offered "a good price." This solidified their relationship, and for the next three years, Collins provided Gregory with cocaine to sell in Milwaukee. However, all of their transactions occurred in the Chicagoland area and at Collins' direction. By the end of the conspiracy, Collins was providing Gregory with four kilograms of cocaine approximately every two to three weeks.

In the fall of 2008, Pedro and Margarito Flores agreed to cooperate with the

Drug Enforcement Administration's (DEA's) investigation of drug trafficking between Mexico and the United States. DEA Special Agent Eric Durante was the lead case agent in the relevant investigation. That put him in contact with Pedro, to whom he periodically spoke with on the phone from August to November 2008.

On November 6, 2008, Agent Durante had a meeting with Pedro in Mexico. At that time Agent Durante instructed Pedro to record his telephone conversations with "drug suppliers and drug customers" when it was safe to do so. Shortly thereafter, Pedro provided the government with numerous tape recordings, some of which included conversations between him and Collins (as we discuss in more detail below).

On August 6, 2009, Collins was indicted on one count of conspiracy to possess with intent to distribute and to distribute five kilograms or more of cocaine and one kilogram or more of heroin, in violation of 21 U.S.C. §§ 841(a)(1) and 846. The reference to heroin was stricken on May 26, 2011, and the case proceeded to trial.

At trial, the government moved to admit three of Pedro Flores' November 2008 taped conversations with Collins. The district court granted the government's request over Collins' objection that the tapes lacked an adequate foundation. With the tapes admitted into evidence, the government called Officer Robert Coleman to testify regarding the "coded drug-dealing language" on the tapes. Collins did not object to the testimony's admissibility at the time but now contends the testimony was improper.

The jury returned a verdict of guilty, and on September 7, 2011, the district judge sentenced Collins to 360 months' imprisonment, followed by five years of supervised release. This sentence was at the lower end of the U.S. Sentencing Guidelines, which called for a term of 360 months to life. The Guidelines range the judge applied included an enhancement under U.S.S.G. § 3B1.1 because the judge determined that Collins' conduct in the conspiracy qualified him as a "manage or supervisor." Collins objected to the enhancement.

II. DISCUSSION

Collins' appeal focuses on three errors he believes the district court made: (1) admitting into evidence the November 2008 taped conversations between him and Pedro Flores; (2) allowing the government expert to testify regarding the "coded drug-dealing language" on the tapes; and (3) determining he was a "manager or supervisor" pursuant to U.S.S.G. § 3B1.1 and increasing the applicable Sentencing Guidelines range. We address each argument in turn.

A. Tape Recordings

The district court admitted into evidence three tape recordings of calls that were purportedly between Pedro Flores and Collins. (Collins contended he was not on the recording.)1 One recording was made on November 25, 2008, at 12:23 p.m.; the second on November 29, 2008, at 1:59 p.m.; and the third on November 30, 2008, at 12:13 p.m. On each of the recordings, Pedro discussed various information regarding the cocaine-distribution scheme with the "speaker," including prices, quantities, quality of drugs, and the use of other people to distribute the goods. Each recording was made outside the presence of government agents.

Collins contends the tape recordings were improperly admitted because the government failed to lay a proper foundation under Federal Rule of Evidence 901. Rule 901(a) requires a party seeking to admit an item into evidence at trial to "produce evidence sufficient to support a finding that the item is what the proponent claims it is." For tape recordings, this can be done in two ways: (1) a chain of custody demonstrating the tapes are in the same condition as when they were recorded, or (2) testimony demonstrating the accuracy and trustworthiness of the tapes. *United States v. Thomas*, 294 F.3d 899, 904 (7th Cir. 2002); *see United States v. Eberhart*, 467 F.3d 659, 667 (7th Cir. 2006). District courts are given wide latitude in determining whether the burden has been met, so we review this determination for an abuse of discretion. *Id.*

In this case, the government satisfied its burden under both methods of proof. Beginning with the chain of custody: Agent Durante, who was stationed in Chicago, and Agent Jake Galvan, who was stationed in Guadalajara, Mexico, testified at length regarding the tapes' history and how Agent Galvan shipped the tapes to Agent Durante once he received them and the tape recorder from Pedro. They described their communications with Pedro in November and December 2008 and their instructions to him regarding when and how to record his conversations with "drug suppliers and drug customers" and to deliver the tapes to the government. They testified that upon receiving the tapes, they labeled them, copied them, and downloaded their contents. They also testified that the tapes never left the government's possession after the moment of receipt. See *Thomas*, 294 F.3d at 905 ("[I]f the tapes were in official custody at all times, a presumption arises that the tapes were handled properly.").

Collins argues this evidence was insufficient to establish a proper chain of custody because the agents' testimony "[did] nothing to answer the lingering questions of the whereabouts of the [recording] device while it was in Mexico." It is this argument, however, that lacks an adequate foundation. We acknowledge that Flores did not testify at trial and that no government agents were present when Flores made the recordings, but merely raising the possibility of tampering is not sufficient to render evidence inadmissible. *Id.*; *see United States v. Wilson*, 973 F.2d 577, 580 (7th Cir. 1992) (explaining that a defendant's contention that certain tape recordings were not authentic because they did not remain "in the sole custody of the government" was meritless). The government is only required to demonstrate that it took "reasonable precautions" in preserving the evidence; it is not required to "exclude all possibilities of tampering." *United States v. Moore*, 425 F.3d 1061, 1071–72 (7th Cir. 2005). We think the government's procedures in obtaining the tape recordings and preserving their accuracy were reasonable in light of the circumstances surrounding this case — it would be an impossible standard to always require agents to be present when a tape recording is made, especially in foreign countries. See *United States v. Fuentes*, 563 F.2d 527, 532 (2nd Cir. 1977) ("There is no requirement that the tapes be put in evidence through the person wearing the recorder, or for that matter, through a contemporaneous witness to the recorded conversations."). Any possible, however hypothetical, gap in the chain of custody goes to the weight of the evidence, not its admissibility. *See, e.g., United States v.*

Tatum, 548 F.3d 584, 587–88 (7th Cir. 2008) ("The government does not need to prove a 'perfect' chain of custody, and any gaps in the chain 'go to the weight of the evidence and not its admissibility.'" (quoting *United States v. Scott*, 19 F.3d 1238, 1245 (7th Cir. 1994))).

Moreover, the government provided ample circumstantial evidence supporting the tapes' accuracy and trustworthiness. One example is voice identification. Federal Rule of Evidence 901(b)(5) permits a witness to identify a person's voice on a recording "based on hearing the voice at any time under circumstances that connect it with the alleged speaker." This is not a very high bar. *See United States v. Mendiola*, 707 F.3d 735, 740 (7th Cir. 2013). Agent Durante testified that he became familiar with Collins' voice during a forty-five minute interview with Collins, and because of that, he was able to identify Collins as one of the speakers on the November 2008 recordings. Likewise, Agent Patrick Bagley testified that he became familiar with Collins' voice after listening to over twenty recordings of Collins speaking at the McHenry County jail and was able to use that familiarity to authenticate Collins' voice on the tapes. Both agents confirmed that the person on the tapes was in fact who the government said it was: Collins.

The government proffered additional information showing that a timestamp on each of the November 2008 recordings coincided with three calls included in the cell phone records of Pedro's phone, which were admitted as evidence at trial. The date, time of day, and duration of each of the three calls matched those of the three recordings. And the three calls were made between Flores and a "773" Chicago area code number that was programmed in Pedro's phone under the name "Ron Ron." Cell phone records obtained later from that "773" number revealed that the three calls matching the dates, times of day, and durations of the three recordings were all with the same Mexico-based phone number. The calls were also made in conformance with the timeframe Flores and the speaker discussed on the recordings. For instance, on the first recording, Pedro told the speaker to give him until Friday or Saturday; the speaker called him back on Saturday, November 29, on the same day and at the same time as the second recording. On the second recording, Pedro told the speaker he would call him right back. That did not occur, and on the third recording — the next day, Sunday, November 30 — Pedro acknowledged forgetting to call the speaker back the previous day, to which the speaker responded, "I'm waiting on y'all." We are satisfied that this information also provided the district court with adequate justification to admit the tape recordings.

III. CONCLUSION

We Affirm Collins' conviction and sentence.

[D] Authenticating Handwriting

Consider the issue in *Van Wyk* concerning the expert's ability to testify as to similarities between defendant's known writings and unknown writings. The court ruled, however, that the expert could not testify as to authorship of unknown writings

UNITED STATES v. VAN WYK
United States District Court, D. New Jersey
83 F. Supp. 2d 515 (2000)

BASSLER, DISTRICT JUDGE.

This opinion addresses the question whether an agent of the FBI can testify as a forensic stylistic expert and whether forensic stylistics is a reliable technique to allow the expert to identify Defendant as the author of unidentified threatening letters.

This matter comes before the Court on the Defendant's in limine motion to exclude the testimony of the Government's expert witness FBI Special Agent James R. Fitzgerald ("Fitzgerald" or "Agent Fitzgerald"). For the reasons set forth below, the Court grants in part Defendant's motion to exclude Fitzgerald's testimony by limiting his testimony to the comparison of characteristics or "markers" between handwritten and typed writings, in which Defendant is known to be the author ("known writings") and the handwritten and typed writings, in which authorship is "questioned" or unknown ("questioned writings"). Fitzgerald's testimony regarding any "external" or extrinsic factors and his conclusion as to the author of the "questioned" writings are barred.

I. BACKGROUND

Defendant Roy Van Wyk ("Defendant") has been charged with a four count Superseding Indictment. Count One alleges that from January 1993 through December 1998, Defendant conspired to make threatening communications in violation of 18 U.S.C. § 875. Counts Two and Three allege two specific instances of threatening communications made to victims "MJ" and "GW." Count Four charges Defendant with possession of a firearm by a convicted felon in violation of Title 18 U.S.C. § 922(g)(1) and (2).

Defendant seeks to exclude the proposed expert testimony of Agent Fitzgerald. Fitzgerald testified at a F.R.E. Rule 104 evidentiary hearing on February 3, 2000. The Government presents Agent Fitzgerald as an expert in forensic stylistics, an area of scientific expertise which the Government has conceded is novel. (February 3, 2000 Hearing Transcript ("Hearing Tr."), at 179.) Forensic stylistics is the examination of writing style "for the express purpose of resolving litigated questions related to disputed authorship or meaning." McMenamin, G. Forensic Stylistics, 58 Forensic Science Int'l, 1, 45 (1993) (hereinafter "McMenamin article"). More specifically, "[i]n cases of disputed authorship, the linguist analyzes and describes the style of writing of a document of questioned authorship and compares and contrasts its language to that of documents known to be written by a given author." *Id.* at 3.

For purposes of this motion, it is helpful to divide Fitzgerald's opinion into three components: (1) internal evidence, which is actual comparisons of similarities or "markers" within the "four corners" of the known and questioned writings; (2) external or extratextual evidence, such as "known dates of composition, date and location of mailing, DNA evidence, and the like"; and (3) opinion that the author of all the questioned writings is the same individual and that Defendant is that author.

Defendant argues that Agent Fitzgerald is not qualified to testify as a forensic stylistics expert. Defendant notes that no expert has yet testified in the area of linguistic stylistics, indicating its lack of reliability. Moreover, the jury is capable of comparing samples of writings without Fitzgerald's testimony. ii. Internal Evidence Testimony

As the Government states, there can be no question that evidence of the known writings and unknown writings is admissible; courts uniformly have admitted evidence of known writings, recognizing that the particular or peculiar use of grammar and spelling, for example, can be observed and identified to establish authorship. See *Clifford*, 704 F.2d 86 (reversing trial court's decision and permitting evidence of the defendant's correspondence to show stylistic similarities between the correspondence known to belong to the defendant and the threatening letters, in order to show that defendant authored the threatening letters); *United States v. Campbell*, 732 F.2d 1017 (1st Cir. 1984) (noting that misspelling a common word can be so much of a testimonial message that defendant's Fifth Amendment rights against self incrimination are triggered); *United States v. Pheaster*, 544 F.2d 353, 372 (9th Cir.1976), *cert. denied*, 429 U.S. 1099, 97 S. Ct. 1118, 51 L. Ed. 2d 546 (1977) ("The manner of spelling a word is no less an identifying characteristic than the manner of crossing a 't' or looping an 'o'. All may tend to identify a defendant as the author of a writing without involving the content or message of what is written"); *United States v. Matos*, 990 F. Supp. 141, 144 (E.D.N.Y. 1998) (holding Fifth Amendment privilege applies because requiring someone to state how he spells a word "may well serve to identify the person as the perpetrator of a crime.")

The question here is whether the Court may properly allow Agent Fitzgerald to testify as an expert regarding the comparisons of markers between the known writings and questioned writings. Defendant argues that Agent Fitzgerald's expert testimony will not be helpful in assisting the trier of fact. He argues that comparisons between the known and questioned writings could easily be drawn by the jurors and that such expert testimony would only overwhelm, confuse or mislead the jury. Unlike his opinion on authorship, Fitzgerald's expertise in text analysis can be helpful to the jury by facilitating the comparison of the documents, making distinctions, and sharing his experience as to how common or unique a particular "marker" or pattern is. See *Hines*, 55 F. Supp. 2d at 69. Therefore, the Court is satisfied that Fitzgerald's testimony as to the specific similarities and idiosyncracies between the known writings and questioned writings, as well as testimony regarding, for example, how frequently or infrequently in his experience, he has seen a particular idiosyncrasy, will aid the jury in determining the authorship of the unknown writings. The internal evidence related to the "four corners" of the writings is admissible.

IT IS FURTHER ORDERED that Agent Fitzgerald may testify to the comparison of characteristics or "markers" between the handwritten and typed writings, of which Defendant is known to be the author, and the handwritten and typed writings, of which authorship is "questioned" or unknown . . . .

[E] Authentication Images

Rule 901(b)(4) is clearly the broadest of all the illustrative methods by which a party can authenticate documentary evidence. This rule allows a party to identify a document, photograph, or tape recording through "[a]ppearance, content, substance, internal patterns, or other characteristics, taken in conjunction with circumstances." Illustrative of the breadth of evidence courts will consider admissible under Rule 901(b)(4) is *United States v. McNealy.*

UNITED STATES v. McNEALY
United States Court of Appeals, Fifth Circuit
625 F.3d 858 (2010)

Owen, Circuit Judge:

Joseph McNealy appeals his conviction for possession and receipt of child pornography in violation of 18 U.S.C. § 2252(a)(2), (a)(4)(B). He raises a number of issues, including whether the Speedy Trial Act was violated, the pornographic depictions of children were properly authenticated as images of actual children, and the destruction of his computer's hard drives was in bad faith. We affirm.

I

A nationwide investigation of commercial child-pornography websites revealed evidence that Joseph McNealy had purchased memberships to a number of such sites. Federal agents interviewed McNealy at his residence, and he consented to a search of his computer. That initial search discovered pornographic images of children on a hard drive. McNealy then consented in writing to the seizure of the computer for further examination.

More than 9,000 pornographic images of children were found. These images had been downloaded from commercial websites and other internet sources. Federal agents created "forensic image" copies of the three hard drives in McNealy's computer; however, his computer and its hard drives were subsequently destroyed. McNealy was indicted for knowing possession and receipt of child pornography in violation of 18 U.S.C. § 2252(a). Before trial, the district court granted continuances at the requests of both McNealy and the Government. At trial, the Government introduced print-outs of some of the images found on McNealy's computer, using the forensic image copies of two of the hard drives. McNealy was found guilty on all charges and sentenced to 70 months of imprisonment, followed by a life term of supervised release. This appeal followed.

III

McNealy contends that images retrieved from his computer and alleged to be child pornography were improperly admitted because they were not authenticated under Federal Rule of Evidence 901 and did not comport with the best-evidence principles embodied in Federal Rule of Evidence 1002. "We review a district court's evidentiary rulings for an abuse of discretion." McNealy preserved the authentication issue, so we apply the harmless error standard of review. He did not preserve his best-evidence contention, so our review is for plain error.

Federal Rule of Evidence 901 provides that "[t]he requirement of authentication or identification as a condition precedent to admissibility is satisfied by evidence sufficient to support a finding that the matter in question is what its proponent claims." Evidence may be authenticated by testimony of a witness with knowledge that a matter is what it is claimed to be. The images at issue are photographs within the meaning of Rule 1001(2).

McNealy asserts that because no witness testified that the printed images of child pornography the Government introduced were "unaltered images of actual minors actually engaged in the conduct depicted," the evidence should have been excluded. He asserts that the jurors were incapable of determining if the images depicted real minors or instead depicted virtual images of minors engaged in sexually explicit activity, the latter of which, the Supreme Court has held, are constitutionally protected speech.

A government witness, Richard Kaplan, testified regarding the images retrieved from McNealy's computer that were admitted into evidence over McNealy's objections. During voir dire of Kaplan regarding the admissibility of the images, McNealy's counsel elicited testimony that Kaplan was not present when the images were taken and had no personal knowledge of how the images were taken. When asked if one of the images depicted a real person, Kaplan responded, "It looks like a real person to me," but that he had never met her. The image looked to him to be a ten- or twelve-year-old girl. When asked if it was in "the realm of possibility that this is a fake image," "a completely fake image that just looks like a real person," the witness answered, "I don't know . . . ." During cross-examination, in the presence of the jury, Kaplan similarly testified that he was not the photographer and was not present when the images were taken, but he believed the images to be those of "real girls" and "real minors." He conceded that he did not "have the ability to look at these images and tell this jury if they've been altered or not," although there was no discussion of what "altered" meant and no context from which its meaning was clear.

Based on this testimony, McNealy contends that the government did not satisfy its burden of authenticating the images. Our court and other circuit courts have considered and rejected similar arguments post-*Free Speech Coalition*. We held in *United States v. Slanina* that expert testimony or additional evidence, other than the images themselves, "was not required." As in the present case, we noted that the defendant did not contend that any of the downloaded images "were virtual children, and not real children." We concluded that "*Free Speech Coalition* did not establish a broad requirement that the Government must present expert testimony to establish that the unlawful image depicts a real child." We agreed with the Tenth Circuit that " '[j]uries are still capable of distinguishing between real and virtual images; and admissibility remains within the province of the sound discretion of the trial judge.' " We reasoned that "[t]he district court, as the trier of fact in this case, was capable of reviewing the evidence to determine whether the Government met its burden to show that the images depicted real children."

McNealy points to two exchanges in the record that he contends establish that neither the jurors nor the district court were capable of determining whether the images admitted at trial were of actual rather than virtual children. The first exchange was during voir dire of the venire when McNealy's counsel asked prospective jurors whether they had "the ability from past skill, training, experience, whatever, to look at a digital image and [] tell which ones have been changed, things have been altered, red eyes removed, you can figure that out by looking." No juror responded affirmatively. This question, by its own terms, inquires only about relatively minor alterations to images of actual individuals. Even if it were proper to voir dire the venire regarding expertise in discerning whether images are of actual or virtual children, an issue we do not broach today, the voir dire in this case did not elicit that information.

The second exchange on which McNealy relies occurred in chambers when McNealy argued that the question he posed to the venire, discussed above, established that the jury was incapable of distinguishing images of virtual children from images of actual children. The district court rejected this argument, but in doing so, made remarks that are quoted in the margin. Later during the trial, counsel for McNealy referred to these remarks regarding the ability of jurors to discern whether the images were of actual children, arguing, "the court's already ruled on the record that it doesn't believe the jury can know that [the images were of actual minors] by looking at these images, that an expert can know that." The district court interrupted, stating, "I didn't say that, now counselor. I think you misunderstood me. I said that — initially, in one of our conferences I believe I stated it would be a jury issue. I can see how it would be difficult, but I didn't say the jury could not do that." The district court admitted the challenged exhibits, overruling McNealy's objections to their authenticity. When the case was submitted to the jury, the district court gave a written instruction regarding the allegation that McNealy possessed a visual depiction of minors engaging in sexually explicit conduct. The written instruction directed the jury that it "must be convinced that the Government has proved . . . beyond a reasonable doubt . . . [t]hat an actual minor was the subject of the visual depiction." This same instruction was repeated three more times in connection with the other counts in the indictment.

The district court complied with the law prevailing in this and other circuits. The court admitted the challenged exhibits, which appear to be what they purported to be, images of actual prepubescent girls and young teen girls (not fully matured), engaging in various forms of sexually explicit conduct. The district court permitted the jury to determine whether the images were of actual rather than virtual children. Nothing in the record, including the images themselves, suggests that they are anything other than images of actual pre-pubescent children and young teenage girls engaged in what McNealy concedes is lewd and lascivious conduct. Moreover, there is no evidence in the record before us that the state of technology is such that images of this nature could have been generated using virtual children. While it remains the Government's burden to show that actual children were depicted, the images themselves sufficed to authenticate them in this regard.

We note that after the Supreme Court's decision in *Ashcroft v. Free Speech Coalition*, Congress amended the Child Pornography Prevention Act of 1996 and made certain findings. Congress found in 2003 that "[t]here is no substantial evidence that any of the child pornography images being trafficked today were made other than by the abuse of real children," and [l]eading experts agree that, to the extent that the technology exists to computer generate realistic images of child pornography, the cost in terms of time, money, and expertise is — and for the foreseeable future will remain — prohibitively expensive. As a result, for the foreseeable future, it will be more cost-effective to produce child pornography using real children.

These findings are not evidence in a criminal trial. They do not indicate, however, a need to revisit our prior decision in *Slanina*, even if a panel of this court had authority to do so. The district court did not abuse its discretion in concluding that the child pornography images were authenticated under Federal Rule of Evidence 901. We similarly conclude that the district court did not plainly err, if it erred at all, in overruling McNealy's argument that admission of the child pornography images violated Federal Rule of Evidence 1002. Rule 1002 provides that "[t]o prove the content of a writing, recording, or photograph, the original writing, recording, or photograph is required, except as otherwise provided in these rules." Rule 1003 states that a "duplicate is admissible to the same extent as an original unless (1) a genuine question is raised as to the authenticity of the original or (2) in the circumstances it would be unfair to admit the duplicate in lieu of the original." McNealy asserts that the Government did not establish that the images were either originals or duplicates.

This argument is unavailing. The forensic imaging process produced an exact copy of the digital files on McNealy's computer, these files were then captured on DVDs, and the exhibits were printed from the DVDs. The Government presented evidence establishing the chain of custody and the technology utilized. McNealy does not argue that the printouts were not accurate representations of the photos on his hard drive. Rather, his argument appears to be that the Government failed to prove that the images depict actual children, an argument we rejected above and that is not pertinent to the Rule 1002 inquiry. The district court's admission of the photographic evidence did not violate Federal Rule of Evidence 1002.

VII

Finally, McNealy argues that the district court erred in denying his motion for a directed verdict because the Government failed to authenticate its image evidence and the Government failed to prove that McNealy knew that the images depicted actual minors. As discussed above, these arguments fail. The district court did not err in denying McNealy's motion for a directed verdict.

*   *   *

For the foregoing reasons, the district court's judgment is AFFIRMED.

EXERCISES

You saw these exercises in Chapter 1, when you were introduced to the concept of authentication. Try them again here. Do you have a better understanding now?

1. At Chaim's criminal trial, the prosecution called as a witness a United States Postal Inspector, who had spent 80% of her time over the previous three years investigating the defendant. She testified that during that time she became familiar with Chaim's handwriting by viewing documents such as his passport, driver's license, post-arrest documents, and a check register for an account in his name. She then offered her lay opinion that certain signature and handwriting samples shown to her at trial were written by Chaim. Chaim objects. How should the court rule?

2. At trial the plaintiff would like to admit emails purportedly drafted and sent by one of the defendants, Ms. Hayward Borders an employee of More Than Enough, Inc. Border denies sending the emails and no one saw Border draft or send the emails. Since there is no testimony from a witness with first-hand knowledge, the plaintiff must authenticate the emails using circumstantial evidence. What type of circumstantial evidence could plaintiff offer to authenticate the emails?

Chapter 8

OPINION TESTIMONY

§ 8.01 DISTINGUISHING BETWEEN LAY AND EXPERT OPINIONS

Lay opinions can typically be described as shorthand for the description of matters that would be difficult, if not impossible, to otherwise describe. Descriptions of emotion, i.e., someone appeared angry or happy, would be very difficult if witnesses had to describe all the characteristics that went into that evaluation. Other lay opinions are commonly made without any way to scientifically validate the conclusions. Assessments of speed, weight, and height are commonly made by ordinary people no formal training. These lay opinion, however, are only useful when the individual offering the opinion has witnessed the matter he or she is describing.

Specialized knowledge or training does, however, occasionally add to a jury's ability to understand a particular matter. While an ordinary person may be able to observe that an individual is out of breath, a pulmonologist may be able to provide insight on the cause of the individual's short-windedness — and may be able to do without actually observing the individual. The pulmonologist would qualify as an expert and special rules would apply to his testimony, giving him or her greater leeway to testify.

Federal Rules of Evidence 701 and 702 describe the admissibility of lay and expert opinion evidence. *United States v. Perkins* discusses the sometimes difficult line to parse between whether testimony amounts to lay or expert evidence.

UNITED STATES v. PERKINS
United States Court of Appeals for the Fourth Circuit
470 F.3d 150 (2006)

WILLIAMS, CIRCUIT JUDGE:

Michael Perkins, a Petersburg, Virginia city police officer, was convicted by a jury of kicking and causing bodily injury under color of law to Lamont Koonce, a motorist stopped for a traffic violation who fled from the police, thus willfully depriving Koonce of his constitutional right to be free from unreasonable force, a felony under 18 U.S.C.A. § 242 (West 2000). Perkins challenges both the admission of opinion evidence at trial and the sufficiency of the evidence. Finding no reversible error, we affirm.

Shortly before midnight on October 13, 2003, Petersburg police officers Michael

829

Tweedy and David House observed a car traveling with no headlights on and damage to its front end. The officers, in separate vehicles, followed the car, pulled it over, and approached the driver to issue a warning or ticket for driving at night without lights. After the officers assisted the driver, Lamont Koonce, out of his car, Koonce broke loose from their hold and fled on foot. House and Tweedy gave chase.

During the chase, Koonce leaped over a fence "like a Superman" and fell on his right side. (J.A. at 236.) Koonce quickly gathered himself and kept running until finally, after a lengthy pursuit, Tweedy caught him and forced him face-down onto the ground, with both of his arms pinned beneath his body. At some point, Tweedy also used pepper spray on Koonce.

After Tweedy moved away from Koonce, House approached Koonce's left side to handcuff him. House attempted to remove Koonce's left arm from under his body, but Koonce resisted. When Koonce finally released his left arm, Koonce grabbed House's ankle. House responded by striking Koonce with a closed fist twice on the arm and once in the underarm to try to free his ankle, but Koonce maintained his hold. Tweedy then forcefully stomped on Koonce's head three times. When Koonce continued to resist, Tweedy stomped on his head three more times. After this second round of stomps, Koonce said, "[a]ll right, man, all right," and allowed House to pull his left arm out from under him and place a handcuff on his wrist. (J.A. at 248, 278.)

Tweedy made a radio call stating that he had a subject in custody. Sergeant John Waldron responded by making a radio call for backup. At this point, House believed that he and Tweedy did not need assistance because Koonce's left wrist was in a handcuff. House radioed Sergeant Waldron and told him that the situation was under control. Waldron responded by telling all officers to disregard his earlier call for backup.

Despite this call, Officer Benjamin Fisher responded to Tweedy's earlier call and arrived at the scene soon thereafter. House asked Fisher to help him secure Koonce's right arm. Tweedy then walked over and kicked Koonce two or three times in the side and stomped on Koonce's head three more times.

A few moments later Perkins, an off-duty Petersburg police officer, arrived at the scene. By the time Perkins arrived, both House and Fisher believed that Koonce was under control, as the bloodied, motionless Koonce was lying face-down on the ground and was not "going anywhere." (J.A. at 300, 403.) Without consulting or speaking with any of the officers standing nearby, Perkins immediately ran up to Koonce and delivered a running kick to Koonce's side. Perkins then kicked Koonce a second time, with slightly less force. Immediately after Perkins's second kick, Tweedy stomped on Koonce's head two more times before Perkins grabbed Tweedy and pulled him away from Koonce. Fisher then helped House place a handcuff on Koonce's right wrist.

Koonce sustained a number of life-threatening injuries, including multiple skull fractures, multiple facial fractures, a pneumothorax (puncture) to his right lung, bleeding in and contusions on the brain, and bruising on his left lung. At the time he was admitted to the Southside Regional Medical Center, Koonce was unconscious; he remained so for several hours.

At the hospital, Koonce was tested on the Glasgow coma scale, a clinical scale that assesses impaired consciousness. Koonce received a score of 1 for mental status, indicating that he did not open his eyes; a score of 1 for verbal response, indicating that he was not speaking; and a score of 3 for motor response, indicating that he moved away in response to pain. Due to the severity of his injuries, the still-unconscious Koonce was transferred to the Medical College of Virginia (MCV) hospital later that night.

On November 16, 2004, a grand jury indicted Perkins. The indictment charged that Perkins, while acting under color of state law, kicked and caused bodily injury to Koonce, thus willfully depriving Koonce of his right to be free from unreasonable force, a felony under 18 U.S.C.A. § 242. The case proceeded to a jury trial.

At trial, Perkins argued that his kicks to Koonce were reasonable under the circumstances. In response to this argument, the Government offered opinion testimony from several officers regarding the reasonableness of Perkins's use of force against Koonce. Of the officers that testified, the Government offered only Inspector Carter Burnett as an expert under Federal Rule of Evidence 702.

Officers House and Fisher — both eyewitnesses to Perkins's kicks to Koonce — testified about their departmental training in defensive tactics and the use of force. Using a use-of-force dummy, they both demonstrated the kicks that they witnessed Perkins deliver to Koonce. The Government asked House whether, based on his experience and his assessment of the situation, he saw "any law enforcement reason for those kicks[.]" (J.A. at 258.) Perkins objected to this question on the ground of "ultimate issue." (J.A. at 259.) The district court overruled the objection, and House answered that he did not see any reason for the kicks. Likewise, in response to the Government's question whether, based on his experience and his assessment of the scene, Perkins's kicks to Koonce were "reasonable," Fisher answered, "No." (J.A. at 376.) Fisher also testified that, in his opinion, the kicks were not necessary and that there were other techniques he was trained to use that would have been appropriate. Perkins did not object to any of Fisher's testimony.

Other officers who had not witnessed Perkins's kicks to Koonce also testified about the reasonableness of the kicks. In response to the Government's question whether it would have been appropriate for an officer to "deliver a hard kick into the side of [a motionless] individual lying on the ground," Corporal Stan Allen, Perkins's defensive tactics instructor, replied, "[n]ot unless [the individual] was armed with a weapon and w[as] threatening the officer." (J.A. at 571.) Perkins only made a general objection to Allen's testimony that reasonable officers would not disagree with Allen's conclusion that Perkins's kicks were inappropriate. Similarly, Sergeant Philip Jones testified that kicks like those Perkins delivered to Koonce were "not appropriate." (J.A. at 591.) He also testified that reasonable officers would not disagree with his opinion. Sergeant Waldron testified that kicking a motionless person on the ground was not "reasonable" under the General Orders of the Petersburg Police Department. (J.A. at 614.) Perkins did not object to Jones's or Waldron's testimony.

Inspector Burnett, the Government's "force expert," testified regarding the classes he taught in defensive tactics and controlling suspects. Burnett stated that he saw no "legitimate" law enforcement reason for Perkins to kick Koonce. (J.A. at

526.) In response to a number of hypotheticals positing a suspect lying motionless on the ground with one arm in a handcuff, Burnett testified that it was inappropriate for an officer to kick a suspect in that posture. Burnett also testified that reasonable officers would not disagree with his conclusions. Perkins's sole objection was to the Government's use of the term "legitimate" in its question to Burnett.

The Government also introduced expert medical testimony about the cause of Koonce's injuries. Dr. Jamal Farran, Koonce's attending physician at MCV and one of the Government's medical experts, testified that the likely cause of Koonce's punctured right lung and bruised left lung was blunt force trauma. When asked about Koonce's Glasgow coma test, Dr. Farran testified that an individual can react to painful stimuli while unconscious.

Both at the conclusion of the Government's case-in-chief and after the Government rested, Perkins moved for acquittal under Federal Rule of Criminal Procedure 29 on the ground that the Government had failed to show that it was Perkins's kicks, as contrasted with Tweedy's kicks, that caused Koonce "bodily injury" under 18 U.S.C.A. § 242.6 The court twice denied Perkins's motion, stating that "[u]nder the case law, . . . just the kicking alone, the infliction of pain, is a bodily injury." (J.A. at 603.) In its instructions to the jury, the court defined "bodily injury" as a "cut, abrasion, bruise, fracture, or other disfigurement, or mere physical pain, or any other injury to the body . . . [even if not] significant, severe or permanent." (J.A. at 685–86.)

On February 17, 2005, after a three-day trial, the jury convicted Perkins of a felony under 18 U.S.C.A. § 242, and he was sentenced to 51 months' imprisonment. Perkins timely noted an appeal. We have jurisdiction pursuant to 28 U.S.C.A. § 1291 (West 2006).

II.

Perkins argues on appeal that the district court erred in admitting expert testimony without a proper foundation, in admitting lay and expert opinion testimony that improperly stated a legal conclusion, and that the evidence was insufficient to prove that Perkins caused "bodily injury" to Koonce. We address each of these arguments in turn.

We typically review for abuse of discretion a district court's evidentiary rulings. *United States v. Gray*, 405 F.3d 227, 238 (4th Cir. 2005). When a party fails to object to the admission of evidence, however, we review the admission for plain error. *United States v. Chin*, 83 F.3d 83, 87 (4th Cir. 1996). Perkins first contends that the district court erred in admitting without a proper foundation the opinion testimony of Officers House and Fisher, Sergeants Jones and Waldron, and Corporal Allen, none of whom were qualified as expert witnesses. Because Perkins did not object at trial to any of the testimony on this ground, we review for plain error.

Federal Rule of Evidence 701 permits a lay witness to give opinion testimony that is "(a) rationally based on the perception of the witness, (b) helpful to a clear understanding of the witness' testimony or the determination of a fact in issue, and (c) not based on scientific, technical, or other specialized knowledge within the scope of Rule 702." Fed. R. Evid. 701. Because Rule 701 "does not distinguish between expert and lay witnesses, but rather between expert and lay testimony," Fed. R. Evid. 701 advisory committee's note, the line between lay opinion testimony under Rule 701 and expert testimony under Rule 702 "is a fine one," 3 Stephen A. Saltzburg, Michael M. Martin & Daniel J. Capra, Federal Rules of Evidence Manual 701–14 (9th ed. 2006). See also United States v. Ayala-Pizarro, 407 F.3d, 25, 28 (1st Cir. 2005) (noting that "[t]he line between expert testimony under Fed. R. Evid. 702 . . . and lay opinion testimony under Fed. R. Evid. 701 . . . is not easy to draw") (internal quotation marks omitted). As an example of the kinds of distinctions that Rule 701 makes, the Committee instructs that the rule would permit a lay witness with personal experience to testify that a substance appeared to be blood, but that it would not allow a lay witness to testify that bruising around the eyes is indicative of skull trauma. Fed. R. Evid. 701 advisory committee's note.

As helpful as this example may be to our interpretive cause, the fine line remains. While we have noted that "[a] critical distinction between Rule 701 and Rule 702 testimony is that an expert witness must possess some specialized knowledge or skill or education that is not in possession of the jurors," *Certain Underwriters at Lloyd's, London v. Sinkovich*, 232 F.3d 200, 203 (4th Cir. 2000) (internal quotation marks omitted), we also have acknowledged that the "subject matter of Rule 702 testimony need not be arcane or even especially difficult to comprehend," *Kopf v. Skyrm*, 993 F.2d 374, 377 (4th Cir. 1993). The interpretive waters are muddier still: while lay opinion testimony must be based on personal knowledge, see Fed.R.Evid. 701, "expert opinions may [also] be based on firsthand observation and experience." 29 Charles Wright & Victor Gold, Federal Practice and Procedure: Evidence § 6253 (1997 & Supp. 2006). At bottom, then, Rule 701 forbids the admission of expert testimony dressed in lay witness clothing, but it "does not interdict all inference drawing by lay witnesses." *United States v. Santos*, 201 F.3d 953, 963 (7th Cir. 2000).

Where opinion testimony focuses on the standard of the objectively reasonable officer, "it is more likely that Rule 702's line between common and specialized knowledge has been crossed." *Kopf*, 993 F.2d at 378. In Perkins's case we conclude that the district court, although close to crossing that line, properly admitted the challenged testimony given by Officers House and Fisher. Both officers observed Perkins kick Koonce and thus testified based on their contemporaneous perceptions; as such, their testimony satisfies Rule 701's personal knowledge requirement. See Fed. R. Evid. 701. Moreover, their observations were "common enough and require[d] such a limited amount of expertise . . . that they can, indeed, be deemed lay witness opinion [s]." *United States v. VonWillie*, 59 F.3d 922, 929 (9th Cir. 1995). Because their testimony was framed in terms of their eyewitness observations and particularized experience as police officers, we have no trouble finding that their opinions were admissible under Rule 701.

On the other hand, the "reasonableness" testimony given by Sergeants Waldron and Jones and Corporal Allen crossed the line between Rules 701 and 702. None of those officers observed Perkins's use of force on Koonce. Their opinions that Perkins's use of force was inappropriate were elicited in response to hypothetical questions based on second-hand accounts, making their testimony similar, if not indistinguishable, from the properly qualified expert testimony admitted at Perkins's trial and admitted in other excessive force cases. *See, e.g., United States v. Mohr*, 318 F.3d 613, 623–24 (4th Cir. 2003) (admitting expert testimony on the reasonableness of the defendant's use of force when the expert did not observe the defendant's actions but instead gave his opinion in response to abstract questions). Such opinion testimony does not satisfy Rule 701's personal knowledge requirement. *See United States v. Glenn*, 312 F.3d 58, 67 (2nd Cir. 2002) (drug dealer's testimony that the defendant must have been carrying a gun was erroneously admitted under Rule 701 because the witness lacked first-hand knowledge); *Washington v. Dep't of Transp.*, 8 F.3d 296, 300 (5th Cir. 1993) ("Under the Federal Rules of Evidence, speculative opinion testimony by lay witnesses — i.e., testimony not based upon the witness's perception-is generally considered inadmissible."). Accordingly, the district court erred in admitting Jones's, Waldron's, and Allen's opinion testimony without a proper foundation.

Nevertheless, we are confident that this error did not affect the outcome of Perkins's trial. Sergeant Jones's brief "reasonableness" testimony came on the heels of his clearly admissible and extensive testimony about a conversation he had with Perkins during which Perkins admitted to kicking Koonce and demonstrated for Jones how he had kicked him. Furthermore, both Sergeant Waldron, who recounted that his fourteen years of experience included time as a training officer, corporal, and sergeant, and Corporal Allen, whose experience and training was enough to cause the district court to assume his expert status, could have been offered as expert police witnesses in the first instance. *See Kopf*, 993 F.2d at 376 (a "witness' qualifications to render an expert opinion are . . . liberally judged by Rule 702"); *United States v. Figueroa-Lopez*, 125 F.3d 1241, 1246–47 (9th Cir. 1997) (holding that, although it was error for the district court to admit opinion testimony under 701, the error was harmless because the witnesses could have been qualified as experts under 702). Therefore, under plain error review, Perkins's challenge fails.

III.

Perkins also argues that the district court erred in admitting both expert and non-expert testimony regarding the reasonableness of Perkins's use of force because such testimony impermissibly stated a legal conclusion. During House's testimony, Perkins objected on the ground that the testimony went to the "ultimate issue" of the reasonableness of Perkins's use of force. Likewise, during Inspector Burnett's testimony, Perkins objected to the Government's question asking whether Burnett saw any "legitimate" reason for Perkins's kicks. Therefore, we review the admission of the challenged portions of House's and Burnett's testimony for abuse of discretion. We review the admission of all other opinion testimony about the reasonableness of Perkins's kicks Federal Rule of Evidence 704(a) provides that, with exceptions not relevant here, "testimony in the form of an opinion or inference otherwise admissible is not objectionable because it embraces an ultimate issue to be decided by the trier of fact." Although this rule officially abolished the so-called "ultimate issue" rule, *see* Fed. R. Evid. 704 advisory committee's notes, it did not lower the bar "so as to admit all opinions." *Id.* Testimony on ultimate issues still "must be otherwise admissible under the Rules of Evidence." Weinstein's Federal Evidence § 704.03[1] (2d ed. 2002). This means that the testimony must be helpful to the trier of fact, in accordance with Rules 701 and 702, and must not waste time, in accordance with Rule 403. "These provisions afford ample assurances against the admission of opinions which would merely tell the jury what result to reach, somewhat in the manner of the oath-helpers of an earlier day." *United States v. Barile*, 286 F.3d 749, 759–60 (4th Cir. 2002) (quoting Fed. R. Evid. 704 advisory committee's notes). The touchstone of admissibility of testimony that goes to the ultimate issue, then, is helpfulness to the jury. *Kopf*, 993 F.2d at 377–78 (stating that while "[a]n opinion is not objectionable simply because it embraces an ultimate issue to be decided by the trier of fact, . . . such an opinion may be excluded if it is not helpful to the trier of fact")(internal quotation marks omitted); Weinstein's Federal Evidence § 704.04[2][a] ("The most common reason for excluding opinion testimony that gives a legal conclusion is lack of helpfulness . . . ."). Thus, the district court's task "is to distinguish [helpful] opinion testimony that embraces an ultimate fact from [unhelpful] opinion testimony that states a legal conclusion," a task that we have acknowledged "is not an easy one." *Barile*, 286 F.3d at 760.

We have stated that "[t]he best way to determine whether opinion testimony [is unhelpful because it merely states] legal conclusions, 'is to determine whether the terms used by the witness have a separate, distinct and specialized meaning in the law different from that present in the vernacular.' " *Id.* (quoting *Torres v. County of Oakland*, 758 F.2d 147, 150 (6th Cir. 1985)). The district court should first consider whether the question tracks the language of the legal principle at issue or of the applicable statute; then, the court should consider whether any terms employed have a specialized legal meaning. *Barile*, 286 F.3d at 760.

To state the general rule, however, "is not to decide the far more complicated and measured question of when there is a transgression of the rule." *Nieves-Villanueva v. Soto-Rivera*, 133 F.3d 92, 99 (1st Cir. 1997). The rule makes ultra-fine distinctions, with admissibility often turning on word choice: the question "Did T have capacity to make a will?" impermissibly asks for a legal conclusion, while the question "Did T have sufficient mental capacity to know the nature and extent of his property?" does not. Fed. R. Evid. 704 advisory committee's notes.

On the one hand, conclusory testimony that a company engaged in "discrimination," that a landlord was "negligent," or that an investment house engaged in a "fraudulent and manipulative scheme" involves the use of terms with considerable legal baggage; such testimony nearly always invades the province of the jury. *See, e.g., Andrews v. Metro N. Commuter R.R. Co.*, 882 F.2d 705, 709–10 (2nd Cir. 1989) (testimony that defendant was "negligent" stated a legal conclusion); *United States v. Scop*, 846 F.2d 135, 140 (2nd Cir. 1988) (testimony that defendants had engaged in a "fraudulent and manipulative scheme" stated a legal conclusion); *Torres*, 758 F.2d at 151 (testimony that county engaged in "discrimination" violated Rule 704). On the other hand, the legal meaning of some terms is not so distinctive from the colloquial meaning, if a distinction exists at all, making it difficult to gauge the helpfulness, and thus admissibility, of the testimony under Rule 704. *See, e.g., United States v. Sheffey*, 57 F.3d 1419, 1426 (6th Cir. 1995) (testimony that the defendant had driven "recklessly, in extreme disregard for human life," did not state a legal conclusion because the terms "recklessly" and "extreme disregard for human life" do not have a legal meaning distinct from everyday usage).

At Perkins's trial, the Government asked House whether, based on his assessment of the situation, he saw "any law enforcement reason for [Perkins's] kicks[.]" (J.A. at 258.) Similarly, the Government asked Burnett whether there was "any legitimate reason for [Perkins to kick] Mr. Koonce[.]" (J.A. at 525–26.) Under 18 U.S.C.A. § 242, courts employ an "objective reasonableness" standard to assess an officer's use of force. *See Mohr*, 318 F.3d 613, 623 (4th Cir.2003). This standard requires the jury to determine "whether a reasonable officer in the same circumstances would have concluded that a threat existed justifying the particular use of force." *Elliott v. Leavitt*, 99 F.3d 640, 642 (4th Cir. 1996). Clearly, then, the word "reasonable" in the § 242 context has a specific legal meaning, but the distinction between its legal and common meaning is not as clear as with other more technical terms like "negligence" or "fraud," i.e., terms that had their common vernacular stem from their legalistic roots.

In *Kopf*, a § 1983 excessive force case involving the use of slapjacks and a police dog, we stated that the facts of every case should determine whether testimony would be helpful to the jury and suggested that "[w]here force is reduced to its most primitive form — the bare hands — expert testimony might not be helpful." *Kopf*, 993 F.2d at 378. We declined to decide whether the experts in that case could have given their opinion on the "ultimate issue" of whether the force used was "reasonable"; indeed, we acknowledged that such testimony might have been inadmissible. *Id.* n. 3.

Later in *Mohr*, a § 242 case also involving a police dog, we held that an expert's rebuttal testimony that an officer "violated 'prevailing police practices nationwide in 1995,' " that the officer's use of the dog was "inappropriate," and that there was "no reason" for the officer's failure to give a canine warning was admissible under Rule 704(a). *Mohr*, 318 F.3d at 624. We attached particular importance to the fact that the testimony was delivered during rebuttal, after the defendant's experts had testified to the reasonableness of the defendant's use of the police dog. *Id.*

Mohr suggests that the challenged testimony in this case did not transgress Rule 704(a). Like in Mohr, the officers here testified that they saw "no reason" for Perkins's use of force. Cf. *id.* Taking helpfulness to the jury as our guiding principle, we conclude that the district court did not err in admitting the challenged portions of Officer House's and Inspector Burnett's testimony. While a very close question, we conclude that the Government's questions were phrased in such a manner so as to avoid the baseline legal conclusion of reasonableness. *See Torres*, 758 F.2d at 151. The officers' responses that they personally saw no reason for Perkins's kicks provided the jury with concrete examples against which to consider the more abstract question of whether an "objectively reasonable officer" would have employed the same force. The Government's questions were not couched in terms of objective reasonableness; instead, they honed in on Officer House's and Inspector Burnett's personal assessments of Perkins's use of force. We recognize that this distinction is a fine one. When the common and legal meanings of a term are not easily unfurled from each other, however, as is certainly the case with "reasonable," it is difficult for us to conclude that testimony was unhelpful to the jury unless the testimony actually framed the term in its traditional legal context. In this case, then, Rule 704 justifies differentiating between the officers' testimony that they saw no "law enforcement" or "legitimate" reason for Perkins's kicks and testimony that Perkins's actions were "objectively unreasonable." To be sure, this distinction must be measured in inches, not feet. Nevertheless, we cannot hold that the officers' testimony was necessarily unhelpful, nor can we say that it merely told the jury what verdict to reach or "supplant[ed] [the] jury's independent exercise of common sense." *Kopf*, 993 F.2d at 377.

Perkins also challenges the admission of Fisher's, Waldron's, Jones's, and Allen's testimony about the reasonableness of his use of force. As noted above, because Perkins did not object at trial, we review the admission of this opinion testimony for plain error. Given our conclusion that the district court did not err in admitting the objected-to portions of House's and Burnett's testimony, we easily conclude that the district court did not commit reversible plain error in admitting these officers' opinions about the reasonableness of Perkins's use of force. *See Olano*, 507 U.S. at 732–34, 113 S. Ct. 1770.

V.

In sum, the district court did not commit reversible error in admitting the officers' opinion testimony that centered on the reasonableness of Perkins's use of force. Moreover, viewing the evidence in the light most favorable to the Government, a reasonable jury unquestionably could have found that Perkins caused "bodily injury" to Koonce. Accordingly, we affirm Perkins's felony conviction.

AFFIRMED

§ 8.02   LAY OPINIONS

[A]   Breadth of Rule 701

The language of Rule 701 indicates that Congress intended the rule to be very broad in scope, allowing courts to admit any opinion that is "helpful" to the finder of facts. As reflected in the following opinion, courts interpreting Rule 701 have construed the provision broadly.

UNITED STATES v. MORELAND

United States Court of Appeals, Seventh Circuit
703 F.3d 976 (2012)

POSNER, CIRCUIT JUDGE.

The nine defendants were charged with conspiracy to distribute large quantities of methamphetamine and marijuana (two of them were charged in addition with being felons in possession of firearms). All were convicted by a jury and given long prison sentences: Moreland 110 months, Smith 151, Bailey 216, Pitts 420, and the others life. Only one defendant, Shelton, was charged with a substantive drug offense; this is a further illustration, if any is needed, that conspiracy is indeed the prosecutors' darling. We listed the reasons in *United States v. Nunez*, 673 F.3d 661, 662–64 (7th Cir. 2012); *see also Krulewitch v. United States*, 336 U.S. 440, 449, 457, 69 S. Ct. 716, 93 L. Ed. 790 (1949) (Jackson, J., concurring); *United States v. Jones*, 674 F.3d 88, 91 and n. 1 (1st Cir. 2012); *United States v. Boidi*, 568 F.3d 24, 29 (1st Cir. 2009); 2 Wayne R. LaFave, Substantive Criminal Law § 12.1(b), pp. 256–65 (2d ed. 2003) — though we add that a prosecutor's putting all his eggs in the conspiracy basket can be a risky tactic, as we'll see.

The details of the conspiracy are not important, so we can proceed to the issues raised by the appellants. We begin with the issues common to all of them. The first concerns the government's use of wiretap evidence. That is permissible only if the government can show that wiretapping was necessary to its investigation because (so far as relates to this case) other investigative methods, such as the use of undercover agents and informants, telephone records, pen registers, trap-and-trace devices, the grand jury, physical searches, and physical surveillance, would not yield essential evidence. 18 U.S.C. § 2518(1)(c). The government argues that without the wiretaps the extent of the conspiracy — 28 persons were charged ultimately — could not have been proved and the leaders, who did not deal face to face with the government's informants or with the members of the conspiracy whom the government was able to identify, could not have been identified. *See United States v. Ceballos*, 302 F.3d 679, 683–84 (7th Cir. 2002); *United States v. Zambrana*, 841 F.2d 1320, 1331 (7th Cir.1988); *United States v. Foy*, 641 F.3d 455, 464–65 (10th Cir. 2011); *United States v. Becton*, 601 F.3d 588, 596 (D.C. Cir. 2010); *United States v. Jackson*, 345 F.3d 638, 644–45 (8th Cir. 2003); *United States v. Rivera-Rosario*, 300 F.3d 1, 19 (1st Cir. 2002). The government supported its argument with detailed affidavits. The defendants asked for an evidentiary hearing, but the judge properly refused because they were unable to specify any assertion in the government's affidavits that they could contest with evidence.

*   *   *

The defendants argue that the jury may have been overawed by the agent's testimony about his long experience investigating drug conspiracies. The party sponsoring an expert witness is entitled to lay his credentials before the jury, but there is a danger that "the jury might be smitten by an expert's 'aura of special reliability' and therefore give his factual testimony undue weight." *United States v. York*, 572 F.3d 415, 425 (7th Cir. 2009); *see also United States v. Upton*, 512 F.3d 394, 401 (7th Cir. 2008); *United States v. Flores-De-Jesus*, 569 F.3d 8, 20–21 (1st Cir. 2009). That was not a realistic danger in this case. Had the agent been testifying exclusively as a lay witness about the code words he had learned the meaning of in the course of his investigation of the defendants' conspiracy, it would not have been improper to introduce him to the jury as an experienced investigator, rather than a novice listening to taped conversations of drug conspirators for the first time, any more than it is improper to ask an eyewitness whether he has good vision.

"Seamlessly switching back-and-forth between expert and fact testimony does little to stem the risks associated with dual-role witnesses." *United States v. York, supra*, 572 F.3d at 426. Telling the jury that a witness is both a lay witness and an expert witness and will be alternating between the two roles is potentially confusing — and unnecessary. The lawyer examining the witness need only ask him the basis for his answer to a question, and the witness will then explain whether it was his investigation of the defendants' conspiracy or his general experience in decoding drug code. That tells the jury what it needs to know in order to determine how much weight to give the testimony and tells opposing counsel what he needs to know in order to be able to cross-examine the witness effectively. Using terms like "lay witness" and "expert witness" and trying to explain to the jury the difference between the two types of witness is inessential and, it seems to us, ill advised.

The judge, while allowing the prosecutor to elicit the fact that the agent had been determined in previous trials to be an expert on drug codes, told the jury that "when you hear a witness give an opinion about matters requiring special knowledge or skill, you should judge this testimony in the same way that you judge the testimony of any other witness. The fact that such a person has given an opinion does not mean you are required to accept it. Give the testimony whatever weight you think it deserves, consider the reasons for the opinion, the witness's qualifications, and all of the other evidence in the case." That was an appropriate instruction.

*   *   *

Nevertheless his conviction must stand. The jury heard evidence that he indeed sold as well as consumed meth that he bought from the drug ring in quantity on credit. He was recorded asking his supplier for multiple ounces of meth on credit and seeking to assuage the supplier's fears about his creditworthiness by assuring him that he could resell it quickly to his customers, and he mentioned having done so in the past. At trial he testified that this was a ruse to obtain a large quantity of meth for his personal use, but the jury didn't have to believe him.

The judgments are AFFIRMED.

[B]   "Rationally Based on the Perception of the Witness"

As the court explained in *Moreland*, there must be a "connection between the opinion or inference and the observed factual basis from which it derives." The court in *United States v. Cox*, 633 F.2d 871 (9th Cir. 1980), found a lay opinion deficient in this regard. During the trial, the court allowed a Government witness to testify that she was under the impression that the defendant was involved with certain bombings. She had based her conclusions on the fact that on two occasions the defendant had told her that he knew someone who would blow up cars for five dollars, and that on one of these occasions he had shown her a newspaper article concerning the bombing. On appeal, the court held that the facts underlying her impression did not rationally lead to the conclusion she made.

[C]   Opinion Must Help Jury Either to Understand Witness' Testimony or to Determine Fact in Issue

What limitation, if any, does the requirement of helpfulness place on the use of lay opinions? If, as Rule 701 also requires, the opinion is based on the witness' own perceptions, when would that witness' inferences, conclusions, or opinions not be helpful? As the court explained in *United States v. Skeet*, 665 F.2d 983 (9th Cir. 1982), such evidence would not be helpful "[i]f the jury can be put into a position of equal vantage with the witness for drawing the opinion. . . . " *Id.* at 985. Similarly, in *United States v. Dicker*, 853 F.2d 1103 (3d Cir. 1988), the court explained that although Rules 701 and 702 "allow the interpretation by a lay witness of coded or 'code-like' conversations, . . . interpretation of clear or straightforward conversations is not helpful to the jury and thus is not admissible under either rule." *Id.* at 1108. As explained in the Advisory Committee's Note on Rule 701, what Congress attempted to exclude with the helpfulness requirement were opinions that add nothing beyond what the witness has already provided to the finder of facts, and which, therefore, amount to little more than "choosing up sides." *See* Advisory Committee's Note to Rule 701, 56 F.R.D. 183, 281 (1972).

Lay witness opinion testimony can also fail to meet the helpfulness requirement when it is couched in terms that have a "separate, distinct, and special legal meaning." *Hogan v. AT&T*, 812 F.2d 409, 411 (8th Cir. 1987). *See also United States v. Baskes*, 649 F.2d 471, 478 (7th Cir. 1980) (upholding district court's exclusion of questioning which required lay witness to answer whether in his opinion he "conspired" in a "lawful" or "willful" manner with the defendant). At common law, such testimony would be excluded because it was likely that it would address an ultimate issue in the case. Although such evidence would be admissible under Rule 704(a), which abolishes the common law restriction on opinion testimony on ultimate issues, Rule 701 would preclude the use of lay witness testimony expressed as a legal conclusion because it is not helpful to the factfinder. *See* § 8.02[B][4][b][ii] (discussing residual aspect of ultimate issue rule).

Because of the nature of opinions that are inadmissible under the helpfulness standard, their introduction should be of little consequence to the trial. Consequently, if the presiding judge does admit such opinions, their admission should seldom result in prejudice that would constitute reversible error. The opinion in *United States v. Burnette*, 698 F.2d 1038 (9th Cir. 1983) is illustrative. In *Burnette*, the trial court permitted a police officer to testify that in his opinion one of the defendants removed the rear license plate from a particular car. The officer offered this opinion after testifying that the license plate was affixed to the car when he arrived at the place where the car was parked; that the defendant was at the rear of the car and was holding what appeared to be a screw driver; that shortly thereafter the rear license plate was missing; and, that no one else had approached the vehicle. The appellate court concluded that, "[w]hile it would have perhaps been better had the District Court limited [the officer] to statement of the underlying facts, we find no abuse of discretion in the admission of [his] opinion testimony." *Id.* at 1051.

As Judge Pratt explains, because the admission of unhelpful lay opinions will rarely result in reversible error, trial courts often freely admit such evidence because "[i]t is frequently quicker and less confusing to permit the witness to express such an opinion than to hear argument upon an objection, a process that always engenders confusion in the minds of the jury. Thus, permitting such an opinion is usually not only harmless but also a timesaver." Pratt, *A Judicial Perspective on Opinion Evidence Under the Federal Rules*, 39 Wash. & Lee L. Rev. 313, 315 (1982).

[D]   Special Topics of Lay Opinion

[1]   Identification from Surveillance Photographs

A number of cases have dealt with the problem of individuals who were not witnesses to bank robberies being asked to identify the defendant from surveillance photographs. Courts have consistently approved of this testimony, particularly in instances in which the defendant's appearance at trial is different from when the surveillance photographs were taken. *See United States v. Barrett*, 703 F.2d 1076, 1086 (9th Cir. 1983). The only issue that has arisen concerning the admissibility of such identifications over which courts have disagreed has been whether the prosecution can use parole officers to make such identifications. Is their use unfairly prejudicial to the defendant because of the strong implication that the defendant has a prior criminal record? In *United States v. Calhoun*, 544 F.2d 291 (6th Cir. 1976), the court found that permitting such witnesses was a *per se* abuse of discretion. Although disagreeing with that conclusion, the court in *United States v. Farnsworth*, 729 F.2d 1158 (8th Cir. 1984), did disapprove of the practice. But *see United States v. Wright*, 904 F.2d 403 (8th Cir. 1990) (court upheld identifications by parole officer, bail bondsman, and police officers when their connection with law enforcement was not revealed); *United States v. Allen*, 787 F.2d 933 (4th Cir. 1986) (government was allowed to call a parole officer to identify the defendant in surveillance photographs on the condition that the officer's occupation was not revealed). In both *Wright* and *Allen*, the defendants claimed that the use of these individuals caused unfair prejudice by discouraging effective cross-examination that might reveal their prior criminal activities. The court held that the admission of this testimony was within the discretion of the trial judge and found no abuse.

In the following case, the court held that a witness could testify as to the identity of the defendant on a surveillance videotape not introduced into evidence.

BOWMAN v. COMMONWEALTH
Virginia Court of Appeals
516 S.E.2d 705 (1999)

LEMONS, JUDGE.

Henry Bowman was convicted in a bench trial of three counts of statutory burglary, three counts of grand larceny and three counts of property damage. On appeal, Bowman argues that the court erred by allowing a witness to identify him as the man depicted in video surveillance tapes. We disagree and affirm the convictions.

I. BACKGROUND

In the summer of 1997, three convenience stores in Campbell County were burglarized. On June 7, 1997, Lester's Market was burglarized, and a safe containing approximately $2,600 was stolen from the store. On July 26, 1997, Miles Market was burglarized, and approximately $6,400 in cash, twenty-five cartons of cigarettes, and several cases of beer were taken from the store. On July 26, 1997, Moore's Country Store was burglarized, and a safe containing $3,000 in cash and checks was stolen.

The evidence revealed that a breaking occurred in the back of Miles Market, approximately nine feet off the ground. The perpetrator of the burglaries at Lester's Market and Moore's Country Store was captured on tape by video surveillance equipment. At trial, Carl Smith testified that Henry Bowman was the person seen on both video surveillance tapes. Smith stated that he was the grandfather of Bowman's children. Smith stated that although he was not present during the commission of any of the charged burglaries, he could positively identify Bowman as the person on the tapes. On cross-examination, Smith testified that he did not like Bowman because Bowman was unemployed.

Smith also identified Bowman as the person in Commonwealth's Exhibits 6 and 7, still photographs taken from the videotapes. Bowman's counsel objected to Smith's testimony, arguing that his statements constituted "non-verbal hearsay," improper lay testimony, and opinion testimony offered to prove an ultimate issue of fact.

Bowman moved to strike at the close of the Commonwealth's case-in-chief and at the close of all evidence. The court denied both motions. The court stated that although the videotapes themselves were insufficient to allow an identification of Bowman, when looking at one of the still photos from the videotape the court itself could identify Bowman as "the burglar."

On appeal, Bowman argues that the court erred in overruling his objection to the admission of Smith's testimony regarding his identity as the perpetrator of the burglaries that were depicted on the two videotapes.

II. IDENTIFICATION OF BOWMAN

Bowman argues that the court erred in allowing Smith to testify about the identity of the perpetrator shown on the videotapes and the still photographs made from the tapes. Bowman contends the Commonwealth "failed to establish Mr. Smith's familiarity with [Bowman] in order to qualify Smith to express an opinion regarding [Bowman's] identity." Bowman argues that Smith's lack of familiarity with Bowman's appearance, coupled with his bad feelings toward Bowman, undermine the credibility of his testimony.

A. Ability of Witness to Identify Appellant

Bowman did not raise at trial the issue of Smith's ability to identify him on the videotape. "In order to be considered on appeal, an objection must be timely made and the grounds stated with specificity. To be timely, an objection must be made when the occasion arises-at the time the evidence is offered or the statement made." *Marlowe v. Commonwealth*, 2 Va. App. 619, 621, 347 S.E.2d 167, 168 (1986); *see* Rule 5A:18. Because Bowman did not raise this objection at trial, we will not consider it for the first time on appeal.

B. Lay Testimony

Bowman also argues that Smith was prohibited from making an identification of the person on the videotape because he was a lay witness testifying about matters that require the testimony of an expert. We disagree. "The admissibility of evidence is within the broad discretion of the trial court, and a ruling will not be disturbed on appeal in the absence of an abuse of discretion." *Brown v. Commonwealth*, 21 Va. App. 552, 555, 466 S.E.2d 116, 117 (1996). "Evidence which tends to cast any light upon the subject of the inquiry is relevant." *Cash v. Commonwealth*, 5 Va. App. 506, 510, 364 S.E.2d 769, 771 (1988). "Relevant evidence which has the tendency to add force and effect to a party's defense is admissible, unless excluded by a specific rule or policy consideration." *Evans v. Commonwealth*, 14 Va. App. 118, 122, 415 S.E.2d 851, 853–54 (1992).

In *Jordan v. Commonwealth*, 66 Va. (25 Gratt.) 943 (1874), the Supreme Court of Virginia considered whether a witness who had been given a description of two men alleged to have recently committed a robbery could testify at their trial. At trial, the witness testified that the men matched the description he had been given. On appeal, the Court held that "upon questions of identity a witness is competent to give his opinion." *Id.* at 945.

"A lay witness may offer an opinion as to the identity of a person." Charles E. Friend, The Law of Evidence in Virginia § 17.10, at 21 (4th ed. 1993). Here, Smith was Bowman's father-in-law and the grandfather of Bowman's children. Smith testified that he had known Bowman for two years and that he recognized Bowman not only in the videotapes but also in the Commonwealth's still photographs of the perpetrator made from the videotape. "The scarcity of case law on the point [of whether a witness may identify a person] is probably due to a general failure to regard identification as an opinion problem, it being considered a matter of 'fact.' " Friend, *supra*, at 21.

C. "Ultimate Issue of Fact"

Bowman also argues that the court erred in allowing Smith's testimony because "[o]pinion testimony on ultimate issues of fact is not admissible in criminal proceedings." Bowman contends that Smith's testimony "goes directly to the ultimate issue: the identity of the culprit." We disagree.

Smith's identification of Bowman did not implicate an "ultimate issue of fact." "Ultimate issues of fact" for purposes of the conviction of a crime are the statutory elements of that offense. *See Llamera v. Commonwealth*, 243 Va. 262, 414 S.E.2d 597 (1992) (in prosecution for possession of cocaine with intent to distribute, the Commonwealth is required to prove the element of possession and the intent to distribute which are both ultimate issues of fact); *Bond v. Commonwealth*, 226 Va. 534, 539, 311 S.E.2d 769, 772 (1984) (where "the crucial issue was whether death was brought about by criminal agency . . . [t]he ultimate question was whether the decedent jumped intentionally, fell accidentally, or was thrown to her death"). The court did not err in allowing Smith to identify Bowman as the person shown on the videotape and the still photos.

[2] Another Person's State of Mind

Lay opinions are frequently offered under Rule 701 concerning another person's state of mind. The courts have consistently held that such opinions are admissible if the witnesses have rationally based their opinions on conduct that the witness personally observed. In *John Hancock Mutual Life Ins. v. Dutton*, 585 F.2d 1289 (5th Cir. 1978), the court allowed a witness to testify that her stepfather did not believe that his wife, the witness' mother, would kill him. The insurance company argued that this testimony violated Rule 602, which requires first-hand knowledge, and Rule 701, because no one can experience first-hand the feelings or state of mind of another. In rejecting this argument, the court quoted from WIGMORE:

> The argument has been made that, because we cannot directly see, hear, or feel the state of another person's mind, therefore testimony to another person's state of mind is based on merely conjectural and therefore inadequate data. This argument is finical enough; and it proves too much, for if valid it would forbid the jury to find a verdict upon the supposed state of a person's mind. If they are required and allowed to find such a fact, it is not too much to hear such testimony from a witness who has observed the person exhibiting in his conduct the operations of his mind.

2 J. WIGMORE, WIGMORE ON EVIDENCE, § 661 at 773–774 (3d ed. 1940). *Id.* at 1294.

In *Bohannon v. Pegelow*, 652 F.2d 729 (7th Cir. 1981), the court allowed a witness to give her opinion of the defendant police officer's racist motivation in arresting the plaintiff. Because the witness observed the officer's conduct at the time of the arrest in question, the court concluded that her testimony would be helpful to the jury's clear understanding and determination of the facts in issue. A different result was reached in *United States v. Hoffner*, 777 F.2d 1423 (10th Cir. 1985). There, the court excluded the lay opinion testimony of defendant's employees who were prepared to testify that defendant, a doctor accused of prescribing drugs for an illegitimate purpose, did not have an illegitimate purpose when she issued the prescriptions. Exclusion of this lay opinion testimony was justified because "none of the witnesses had been present in the examining room when any of the patients who had received the improper prescriptions were with Dr. Hoftner, [and therefore] the court concluded that their opinions as to the doctor's intent were not based on any rational perceptions or observations." *Id.* at 1426.

Courts have also held that sanity is a proper subject of lay opinion under the Federal Rules of Evidence. In *United States v. Lawson*, 653 F.2d 299 (7th Cir. 1981), *cert. denied*, 454 U.S. 1150 (1982), for example, when charged with extortion and assault of a federal officer, the defendant raised an insanity defense. To meet this defense, the Government not only presented the testimony of a psychiatrist, but also introduced the opinions of three officers about the defendant's sanity. In rejecting the defendant's claim that this testimony was inadmissible because the witnesses did not have a sufficient basis for an opinion as to the defendant's sanity, the court stated:

> Lawson contends also that lay testimony on the issue of sanity was improperly admitted. Three FBI agents, including Hirtz, testified over objection that they believed Lawson was sane at the time of the commission

of the offenses. There is no question that the Government (or the defense, for that matter) may introduce lay testimony on the issue of sanity. Rule 701 of the Federal Rules of Evidence expressly permits opinion testimony by lay witnesses. Although the Government here presented Dr. Sheldon as an expert witness, it may, in rebutting an insanity defense, present only lay testimony. . . . Lawson's only argument is that in this case the Government did not lay the proper foundation because the three agents did not observe him for a long enough period of time.

To support this contention, Lawson cites only cases that were decided before the Federal Rules of Evidence became effective. These cases hold that while a lay witness may testify about the conduct, assertions, appearance, and manner of speech of the defendant, they may only state an opinion on an ultimate issue such as sanity when "the witness has been qualified by sufficient association with an opportunity to observe the subject." *United States v. Alden*, 476 F.2d 378, 385 (7th Cir. 1973). The adoption of the Federal Rules, however, modified this requirement. The rules permit the introduction of substantially more evidence than was formerly admissible. They place great reliance on cross-examination, for much evidence is now admissible subject to cross-examination as a means of verification. It is then up to the fact finder to determine the weight to be attached to that evidence. No more foundation was necessary in this case to admit the opinion testimony of the FBI agents. On cross-examination of each of them, defense counsel pointed out that each had had the opportunity to observe Lawson on only one occasion. The jury was free to give that testimony, particularly in light of the expert testimony that was also heard, whatever weight it felt appropriate.

Id. at 303.

[3] Lay Opinions on Ultimate Issues

Revisions to Rule 704, however, have reinstated the ultimate issue restriction on expert witness opinions as to the defendant's mental state or condition in a criminal case. Moreover, even though a lay opinion may not be excluded under Rule 704 because it addresses an ultimate issue in the case, it can still be rendered inadmissible under Rule 701 if it is not "helpful to a clear understanding of [the witness'] testimony or the determination of a fact in issue."

The Sixth Circuit has come to the questionable conclusion that "[a]lthough testimony which embraces an ultimate issue is not objectionable . . . , seldom will be the case when a lay opinion on an ultimate issue will meet the test of being helpful to the trier of fact since the jury's opinion is as good as the witness' and the witness turns into little more than an 'oath helper.' " *Mitroff v. Xomox Corp.*, 797 F.2d 271, 276 (6th Cir. 1986). The degree to which a layperson's opinion will be helpful to the finder of facts has nothing to do with the ultimate nature of the issue upon which it is offered. The "helpfulness" of any opinion necessarily turns on such factors as the quality of the witness' perception, the complexity of the issues being resolved, and the obviousness of the witness' conclusions. The practical effect of the court's conclusion in *Mitroff* is to recreate the ultimate issue rule for lay opinions.

This reasoning has not been embraced by other courts. *See, e.g., Becton v. Starbucks Corp.*, 2007 U.S. Dist. LEXIS 65803, at *5 (S.D. Ohio Sept. 6, 2007) (rejecting *Mitroff* and holding that "this is one of those cases in which the ultimate issue does meet the test of being helpful to the trier of fact.").

Because the question of admissibility of opinions of ultimate issues relates to both lay and expert witnesses, further examination of this issue will be deferred to the next section of this chapter, concerning the admissibility of expert opinions.

EXERCISES

1. Is this lay opinion testimony admissible under Rule 701?

    a. A member of the Gambino Crime Family opines about the meaning of comments made by two other Gambinos during an intercepted phone conversation.

    b. The defendant's sister and ex-girlfriend both opine that the defendant is the individual in a still photograph taken from the surveillance video of a bank robbery.

    c. A local drug dealer, who has never interacted with the defendant, interprets drug lingo used in taped phone calls between the government and the defendant.

    d. A neighbor who is familiar with the plaintiff's voice is called as a witness at trial to identify plaintiff's voice on a taped phone recording.

2. Is the police officer's testimony lay opinion under Rule 701 or expert testimony under Rule 702?

    a. A drug enforcement officer opines about the meaning of slang terms used for heroin in wiretapped conversations.

    b. A police officer testifies that during a search of a home he found a wallet with defendant's identification on the dresser and clothes that fit defendant's build in the master bedroom. The officer also observed bunk beds in the second bedroom and a guest sleeping on the air mattress in the living room. He then opined that the defendant resided in the master bedroom.

    c. A Customs and Border Protection Officer testifies how the float on the outside of a vehicle's gas tank works and why a gas gauge will register zero to empty when drugs are placed inside the gas tank.

3. Matt, a quadriplegic who is confined to a wheelchair, filed suit against a pizza restaurant, alleging that the pizza restaurant's construction violates the Americans with Disabilities Act. At trial Matt is prepared to testify that he personally encountered: (1) disabled parking spaces that have slopes exceeding 2.0%; (2) access aisles next to those spaces that have slopes exceeding 2.0%; (3) no International Symbol of Accessibility on those spaces; (4) sidewalk slopes exceeding 2.0%; (5) no accessible seating designated for the disabled; (6) no handle mounted below the lock of the water closet stall door; (7) insufficient clear floor space in front of the water closet; (8) pipes underneath the lavatory that were improperly and/or incompletely wrapped; and (9) insufficient strike side clearance when exiting the restroom. The restaurant objects, arguing that Matt should not be permitted to testify as a lay

witness; rather such testimony must come from an expert. Is the restaurant correct?

§ 8.03   EXPERT OPINIONS

[A]   Role of Expert Witness

[1]   Guidance

While the principal role of lay witnesses in judicial proceedings is to establish the relevant facts through testimony based on first-hand knowledge, the expert witness' role is to help the jury understand those facts along with their causes and implications. Although experts, as witnesses, could give factual testimony that was based on personal knowledge, their primary role is that of advisor to the finder of facts. They provide guidance on the proper interpretation and application of the facts that other witnesses' testimony establishes. Consequently, at common law, the opinion rule does not apply to expert witness testimony.

Expert guidance is admissible when the jurors are *unable* to properly perform their fact-finding role in the litigation without the assistance of someone who has acquired special expertise through knowledge, skill, or experience. The expert's testimony is admissible if there is a *necessity* for it, namely, when the subject matter is beyond the ken of the average lay juror. Initially, courts did not allow experts to give guidance to jurors on matters about which the jurors had some knowledge and a working understanding. However, over time courts have significantly relaxed this limitation.

The expert's special expertise often included knowledge of, or experience with, technical and scientific principles. But experience with common matters could also qualify as necessary expertise where it provided the witness with substantially more knowledge than the average juror possessed, thereby enabling the witness to provide the jurors with the understanding essential for making an informed decision. For example, experienced fishermen might be qualified to testify as experts on the art of bass casting, or an experienced farmer might be qualified to testify about the effect of certain weather conditions on certain agricultural products. Of course, the need for this experiential expertise will be contingent on the situations in which a party seeks to introduce it. For example, a jury in Iowa may not need the same guidance on the effect of hail on corn as a jury in New York City might. The same would be true of the technique of bass casting in rural lake regions of the country as opposed to metropolitan areas.

As the proponent establishes an expert witness' qualifications, the court will allow the opponent to conduct a limited inquiry of the expert on relevant issues. This preliminary examination of an expert's qualifications is called "voir dire."

If the court accepts the witness as an expert, an exception to the opinion rule applies to the expert's testimony. Thus, the court will permit the expert to offer assistance or guidance to the jury after the proponent establishes that the expert has reviewed the relevant facts of the case, has applied her expertise to them, and has arrived at a conclusion. Courts at common law require this showing to ensure that the expert's testimony will be relevant to the case and helpful to the jurors, who ultimately have the responsibility of making a determination based on the same facts.

Experts who have personal knowledge of the facts of the case can testify to them and then explain how they applied their expertise to those facts in arriving at a conclusion. If the experts do not have first-hand knowledge of the relevant facts, the facts must be made known to the expert and the jury. Sometimes, facts have been made known to an expert from sources that qualify for admission under an exception to the hearsay rule (as they might, for example, if the expert were a physician and a patient seeking treatment had conveyed the relevant information during an examination). Often, the proponent has to present these facts to the expert during the expert's testimony through a device that is unique to the examination of expert witnesses: a hypothetical question that assumes the truth of the facts upon which the proponent seeks the expert's opinion. This device allows the jurors to have the benefit of the expert's advice on those assumed facts in the event they find such facts to be true. In these hypothetical questions, evidence in the record must support each of the proposed facts directly or circumstantially, or the proponent must represent to the court that evidence supporting the facts will be presented later in the trial. This requirement ensures that the expert's opinion is relevant to the case and to the decision that the jury will make. Otherwise, experts could base opinions on facts on which the jury could not base its decision, rendering the expert's opinion irrelevant.

Another method of informing experts of the relevant facts is to have them listen to the testimony of each of the preceding witnesses and tell the experts to assume that what was said is true. This is a particularly advantageous way of eliciting expert advice for two reasons. First, it ensures that the experts will base their opinion only on facts upon which the jury could render a decision. Second, it places the expert in much the same position as the jurors in evaluating the facts as they are presented through testimony.

The use of this method, however, is restricted in two ways. First, the proponent cannot use it if the evidence is conflicting, because the proponent could not then reasonably ask the expert to assume that all the previous testimony is true. Second, it is often impossible to use this method at all, because courts frequently sequester witnesses (that is, exclude them from the courtroom during the trial so that they cannot conform their testimony to the statements made by other witnesses). In such cases, courts often refuse to make an exception for expert witnesses, even though these witnesses will not be testifying to the facts of the case and therefore have no other testimony to which to conform their own testimony. The Federal Rules of Evidence address this issue of sequestration in Rule 615.

[2] The Hypothetical Question

The hypothetical question is a necessity of the system; it permits expert testimony by witnesses who do not have first-hand knowledge of the underlying facts, and seeks to ensure the relevance and helpfulness of experts' opinions by requiring that the facts upon which they base their opinions be delineated beforehand and proven by independent evidence. Nevertheless, commentators have widely criticized the hypothetical question because of the abusive practices that have accompanied its use. The following opinion illustrates some of the issues that arise in hypothetical questions posed to witnesses.

STATE v. ANTHONY

Supreme Court of North Carolina
354 N.C. 372 (2001)

EDMUNDS, JUSTICE.

On 7 July 1997, defendant William Todd Anthony was indicted for first-degree murder of Semantha Belk Anthony and for assault with a deadly weapon with intent to kill inflicting serious injury on John Edward Belk. Defendant was tried capitally before a jury at the 3 May 1999 Criminal Session of Superior Court, Gaston County. On 27 May 1999, the jury found defendant guilty of first-degree murder on the basis of malice, premeditation, and deliberation, but not on the basis of felony murder. The jury also returned a verdict of guilty of assault with a deadly weapon with intent to kill inflicting serious injury. Following a capital sentencing proceeding, the jury recommended a sentence of death for the murder. On 3 June 1999, the trial court sentenced defendant to death for the first-degree murder conviction and seventy-three to ninety-seven months' imprisonment for the assault conviction. Defendant appeals his conviction for first-degree murder and his sentence of death to this Court as a matter of right. On 3 August 2000, we allowed defendant's motion to bypass the Court of Appeals as to his appeal of the assault conviction. For the reasons that follow, we conclude that defendant's trial and capital sentencing proceeding were free from prejudicial error and that defendant's sentence of death is not disproportionate.

At defendant's trial, the State presented evidence that defendant and Semantha Belk Anthony were married on 26 October 1985 and that two children were born of the marriage. Defendant and Semantha separated for several months in 1992. During this separation, defendant wrecked Semantha's vehicle with his truck and grabbed her after allegedly seeing her with another man. Defendant was charged with communicating a threat and with assault on a female as a result of this incident, but the charges were subsequently dropped. Defendant and Semantha temporarily reconciled but separated again in March 1997, as detailed below. Semantha told her mother, Martha Belk, that she was leaving defendant because her sons "were being abused" and "she was scared of [defendant]." Similarly, she told her father, John Edward Belk, that she was separating from defendant because "she was afraid he was going to kill her and the boys."

On 15 March 1997, Semantha met with attorney Jay Stroud, who prepared a separation agreement. This agreement, which defendant and Semantha signed on 19 March 1997, gave Semantha primary custody of the children and entitled defendant, in part, to visitation with the children twice a week and on alternate weekends. Thereafter, Semantha and the children left the marital residence. Semantha stayed with her parents briefly, then moved into an apartment. The children slept at the Belks' home.

A week after signing the separation agreement, defendant contacted Susan Russell, a legal assistant for attorney Stroud, to complain about Semantha's failure to remove the remainder of her property from the marital residence. Ms. Russell contacted Semantha, who responded that defendant had been harassing her since they signed the separation agreement. She further explained that she had not yet acted because she was afraid of defendant and was trying to find someone to accompany her when she retrieved her property. In fact, on 16 March 1997, the day after Semantha visited attorney Stroud, the Gaston County Police Department had been dispatched to the marital residence in response to a domestic dispute. Defendant told the responding officer that he had a gun but had thrown it in the woods behind the house at Semantha's request.

On 9 April 1997, Semantha filed a "Complaint and Motion for a Domestic Violence Protective Order" against defendant in which she stated, "4-8-97. Has threatened to kill me, constantly follows me at different times, carries a gun. I fear for my life." That same day, a judge signed an "Ex Parte Domestic Violence Protective Order" and set a hearing in the matter for 16 April 1997.

On the morning of Tuesday, 15 April 1997, defendant arrived at the Belks' home to visit his children. Although in the past defendant had been welcome do to so whenever he wanted, Semantha instructed her parents no longer to allow defendant to see the children before school because his visits upset them. However, when Mr. Belk told defendant that he could not see his children, defendant pushed him aside and entered the house. Defendant was crying at the time, and his children became agitated while talking to him. After defendant left, Mr. Belk reported the incident to the police, and J.T. Welch, an officer with the Mount Holly Police Department, responded. He testified that Mr. Belk described the incident to him and stated that defendant had at some point made threats that he would kill the whole family. Mr. Belk appeared troubled and said that he did not know what defendant was capable of doing. He added that he thought his daughter had obtained a restraining order against defendant.

Officer Welch advised Scott Wright, an officer with the Mount Holly Police Department, of the incident and of a possible restraining order against defendant. Officer Wright went to the Belks' home to speak with Semantha, who told him about the incident that morning and added that defendant had been following her and threatening to "blow her f___ing head off." After speaking with Semantha, Officer Wright confirmed that an "Ex Parte Domestic Violence Protection Order" had been issued.

Officer Wright saw Semantha later that day at a hair salon. While speaking with her, she exclaimed, "There he is, there he is," and she and the officer watched as defendant drove slowly past the salon. Afterwards, Officer Wright visited Semantha at her residence, where she told him that defendant was supposed to bring the children to her parents' home later that day. She requested that a police officer come by during that time because she thought there would be trouble and added, "He'll kill me if he gets a chance."

That same day, Semantha also called legal assistant Russell to report that defendant had hired an attorney who was going to attempt to have the 16 April 1997 domestic violence hearing postponed because defendant was scheduled to undergo surgery. During their conversation, Semantha told Ms. Russell that she recently had purchased a gun because she was afraid to stay in her residence without protection and that her children were sleeping at her parents' home because she was fearful something would happen.

Defendant went back to the Belks' home on the afternoon of 15 April 1997, bringing flowers for Semantha and steaks for the Belks as an apology for the encounter that morning. Although defendant left after several minutes, events rapidly took an ominous turn. Defendant's stepfather, Johnny Kendall, testified that he later told Mount Holly Police Officer Barry Colvard that he thought he had talked defendant out of doing something he would regret but that when defendant grabbed several shotgun shells and ran out of the house, Mr. Kendall called 911. He told the operator that defendant had left his home with a gun to shoot Semantha. Randy Carter, a neighbor of the Kendalls, testified that Mrs. Kendall came to his house on 15 April 1997 just prior to the shootings and asked him to calm defendant. Defendant told Mr. Carter that he could not take it anymore and was going to kill Semantha. While Mr. Carter was speaking with defendant, defendant was searching for something in three rooms and the attic of the Kendalls' house. When defendant left, Mr. Carter observed a shotgun in the back of defendant's truck.

Approximately one hour after leaving the Belks' home, defendant returned. Semantha, who was there waiting for defendant to drop off the children, ran outside when she heard defendant blow his horn. Mr. Belk, who had seen defendant drive down the street, was outside talking with his neighbor James Fitcher. Several minutes later, Mr. Belk heard someone yell, "Todd's got Sandy, dragging Sandy out front, he's got a gun." Mr. Belk ran inside his home to find something with which to defend himself. When he emerged, he saw that defendant was wielding a shotgun while holding the crouching or kneeling Semantha by her hair. Defendant told Semantha, "Hold still, b____. I'm going to kill you," while she pleaded with defendant to let her go. When Mr. Belk told defendant not to hurt his daughter, defendant became distracted and Semantha was able to break free and run. Defendant chased her and shot her in the back. He then reloaded his shotgun and, as the wounded Semantha lay on the ground begging for her life, flipped her over with his foot; said, "Hold still, b____"; and shot her again. Defendant reloaded; aimed his shotgun at Mr. Belk; said, "You're next, old man"; and shot Mr. Belk in the shoulder. Defendant next aimed at Mrs. Belk, who was standing on her front porch. Although defendant apparently pulled the trigger, his weapon failed to fire. Defendant threw the shotgun in the back of his truck; said, "Now I can go to jail"; then sped away, scattering gravel. Several neighbors, including James Fitcher, Kimberly Fitcher, Brenda Cagle, Bobbie Auten, and Gloria Jenkins, witnessed the shootings and corroborated the testimony of Mr. and Mrs. Belk.

After shooting Semantha and Mr. Belk, defendant drove to his parents' house. Defendant told Mr. Carter that he had shot Semantha and asked Mr. Carter to drive him to the jail. As Mr. Carter was driving, defendant repeatedly stated, "Why did she do this to me? Why? Why? Why?" Mr. Carter saw several patrol vehicles and flagged down Mount Holly Police Officer B.G. Summey. As Officer Summey approached, defendant spontaneously stated, "I did it. I shot them. I couldn't take it anymore." Defendant identified himself and while being handcuffed said, "I shot her twice. Is she all right?" After advising defendant of his Miranda rights, Officer

Summey searched defendant and found several Xanax tablets in defendant's pocket. Defendant then told Officer Summey that the murder weapon was in the back of his truck at his parents' home.

Defendant was taken to the Mount Holly Police Department, where he consented to a search of his truck and his parents' home. When asked to sign a waiver of rights form, defendant responded, "Yes, I'm guilty. I'll sign whatever." Defendant said that he had not slept in three to four weeks and that he had taken several Xanax pills before the shootings. When Officer Summey informed defendant that his wife had died and that he was under arrest for her murder, defendant responded, "I know I'm guilty." Thereafter, defendant was transported to the Gaston County Police Department to be fingerprinted and photographed. While entering the patrol vehicle, defendant responded to an officer's caution to watch his head by saying, "I just killed my wife. My head's the last of my worries." While en route, defendant asked, "Is she still alive?" and "Can I get the death penalty for this?"

Once at the Gaston County Police Department, defendant explained that he killed his wife because she was seeing other men and was not going to let him visit his children. He stated that Semantha had called his mother that day and told her she was never going to let defendant see his children again, she wished defendant was dead, and she would not even visit defendant's grave if he died. Defendant was then taken to the magistrate's office. On the way, defendant commented, "One of the bullets was meant for me, and the old man confronted me so I shot him too," and "I pulled the trigger. I'm guilty. Go ahead and give me the death penalty." Defendant told the magistrate, "I didn't mean to do it but she kept using the kids against me."

Several witnesses testified as to statements defendant made prior to the murder indicating his intention to kill his wife. Benny Hale, owner of Benny's Fishing Lake, testified that defendant was a frequent customer. He noticed a change in defendant in February 1997. Approximately two weeks before Semantha's murder, defendant told Mr. Hale that he was experiencing problems with his wife because she would not let him see his children as often as he wanted. During this conversation, defendant became upset; began to cry; and stated to Mr. Hale, "Benny, I'm thinking about killing the b____." On 10 April 1997, defendant told Kimberly Fitcher, the Belks' neighbor, that Semantha had served papers at his place of employment and was opposing his efforts to obtain joint custody of their children. Ms. Fitcher testified that defendant said "he would hurt anyone who stood in his way of him being with his kids." Gordon Arnold, manager of Mount Holly Farm Supply, testified that defendant entered his store on 14 April 1997. When Mr. Arnold asked defendant, "Can I help you?" defendant, who was visibly upset, responded, "You can't help me with my problems. . . . My wife left me. She is running around on me. She won't let me see my kids. I am going to kill her and if her old man gets in my way, I'm going to kill him, too." Finally, Carl Barker, who had been defendant's supervisor at work for approximately ten years, testified that defendant had not been himself for six months prior to Semantha's murder. On several occasions, including 15 April 1997, defendant told him that "he was going to kill the b____."

Dr. Peter Wittenberg, the pathologist at Gaston Memorial Hospital who autopsied Semantha, testified that her death was caused by bleeding from the lungs and wounds in her chest. He described her death as not immediate and "very painful."

Dr. Timothy Carr, an emergency physician at Gaston Memorial Hospital, treated Mr. Belk on 15 April 1997 and described his injuries as life-threatening. Ronald Marrs, a special agent with the North Carolina State Bureau of Investigation, was accepted as an expert in firearms and tool-mark examinations and identifications. He identified the twenty-gauge shotgun retrieved from defendant's truck as the weapon used in the shootings and determined from examination of Semantha's clothing that defendant was twelve to twenty-one feet away from her when he fired the first shot and six to twelve feet away from her when he fired the second shot.

Defendant presented evidence at the guilt-innocence phase of his trial to establish a history of tension in his relationship with Semantha. He testified that various individuals told him that she was having affairs and that he had seen her kiss another man during their first separation. He claimed that after their March 1997 separation Semantha attempted to prevent him from seeing his children.

On the day of the shootings, defendant was upset about his separation from Semantha and his inability to see his children. He consumed beer, vodka, and Xanax to deal with this distress, and as a result could not remember what happened at the Belks' home and thereafter. Numerous witnesses corroborated defendant's claim to have consumed intoxicants, including defendant's father, Tony Anthony; his mother, Diane Kendall; and his stepfather, Johnny Kendall. Vivian Daley, a nurse at the Gaston County jail, testified that when she saw defendant on 16 April 1997, less than twenty-four hours after the shootings, he "was staring straight ahead and he was crying. . . . [I]n my professional opinion, he did not seem to know where he was." She noted that defendant's eyes were dilated and that he smelled of alcohol. Terry Wellman, a nurse at the Gaston County Police Department, observed defendant on 16 April 1997 shortly after his apparent attempt to commit suicide in jail. Because defendant was crying incoherently and his eyes were dilated, she requested a drug test. The results were positive for Xanax even though the test was administered twenty hours after the murder.

Dr. Roy J. Mathew, who was tendered and accepted as an expert in psychiatry specializing in the fields of addiction medicine and addiction psychiatry, testified as to the effects of Xanax and alcohol on the human brain. Dr. Mathew was of the opinion that defendant's claimed memory loss of the murder was valid, and characterized what happened to defendant as a "black-out." He also believed that defendant's suicide attempt in the Gaston County jail was consistent with ingestion of Xanax. As to defendant's mental condition on the day of the murder, Dr. Mathew stated, "I think he was significantly impaired. He was significantly intoxicated at the time of the alleged crime with alcohol and Xanax. It's very difficult to separate one from the other because, as I indicated earlier, they do more or less the same thing in the brain." When asked whether defendant's mind and reason were so completely intoxicated and impaired that he could not form a specific intent to kill, Dr. Mathew responded, "I feel that he was significantly intoxicated by Xanax, alcohol, and both; that it would have been difficult for him to think rationally and clearly."

Additional evidence was presented during the capital sentencing proceeding. This evidence will be discussed below as necessary to address sentencing issues.

* * *

In his next assignment of error, defendant argues that the State's questions to one of its rebuttal witnesses, Dr. Robert Rollins, "included an assumption that the jury found one or the other State witness[es] credible regarding certain facts[ ] to determine whether that affected [Dr. Rollins'] opinion as to the Defendant's 'ability to form specific intent on April 15th.'" Defendant contends that the State's questions were impermissible because hypothetical questions can be posed only to an expert who has not examined defendant, that Dr. Rollins' responses were too equivocal to have probative value, and that Dr. Rollins' responses impermissibly embraced legal terms.

Examples of questions asked of Dr. Rollins to which defendant objects include:

Q: Now assuming, Dr. Rollins, that the jury believes an officer that testified that the Defendant said immediately after this incident, "One of the bullets was meant for me and the old man confronted me, so I shot him, too," does that affect your opinion as to Mr. Anthony's ability to form specific intent on April 15th?

* * *

Q: Let's assume the jury finds that a police officer is credible when he states that he handcuffed Mr. Anthony and heard him say, "I shot her twice, is she all right"; and then Mr. Anthony was advised of his rights and asked, "You shot your wife, also," and he replied, "Yes, sir," how, if at all, does that affect your opinion as to whether or not Mr. Anthony had the specific intent and ability to plan on April 15th, 1997?

* * *

Q: Dr. Rollins, assume the jury finds that approximately three weeks before the murder that he states to a friend of his who owns a fishing establishment that, "I am going to kill her," how, if at all, does that affect your opinion that Mr. Anthony was able to form specific intent and have the ability to plan on April 15th, 1997?

Throughout this questioning, defendant made general objections, which the trial court overruled.

"[A]n expert witness may express an opinion based on facts within his own knowledge or based on facts not within his knowledge but incorporated into hypothetical questions." *State v. Young*, 312 N.C. 669, 679, 325 S.E.2d 181, 188 (1985). Hypothetical questions "should include only those facts supported by the evidence already introduced or those facts which a jury might logically infer from the evidence." *State v. Boone*, 302 N.C. 561, 566, 276 S.E.2d 354, 358 (1981). Such questions "should not contain repetitions, slanted or argumentative words or phrases." *Id.* In addition, a hypothetical question must be "sufficiently explicit for the witness to give an intelligent and safe opinion." *State v. Dilliard*, 223 N.C. 446, 448, 27 S.E.2d 85, 87 (1943).

Defendant does not allege that the facts were misstated in the hypothetical questions posed to Dr. Rollins. Instead, he argues that hypothetical questions should not be asked to an expert who has interviewed a defendant. However, we find no authority for defendant's contention, and defendant points us to none. *See State v. Boone*, 302 N.C. at 566, 276 S.E.2d at 358 (hypothetical questions posed to expert who had interviewed criminal defendant). After a review of the ten hypothetical questions posed to Dr. Rollins, we conclude that they were based upon facts supported by the evidence. In addition, we conclude that Dr. Rollins' answers were not so equivocal as to render them without probative value. In fact, all of his answers were certain and consistently reflected his opinion "that Mr. Anthony was able to make plans and carry out actions." In addition, these responses did not improperly embrace legal terms. *State v. Hedgepeth*, 330 N.C. 38, 46, 409 S.E.2d 309, 314 (1991) (no error in admission of Dr. Rollins' testimony that defendant was capable of forming the specific intent to kill).

This assignment of error is overruled. Defendant received a fair trial and capital sentencing proceeding, free from prejudicial error.

NO ERROR.

[B]   Expert Testimony on Purported Scientific Evidence

The use of expert testimony often gives rise to questions about the scientific principles and techniques that the experts employed in arriving at the opinions that they offer. Through the testimony of these expert witnesses, the parties often seek to introduce the results of scientific tests that the experts have conducted. Occasionally, the scientific principles or techniques that the experts employed are new or unproven. This raises the question of the burdens that the proponent of such evidence must bear before the courts will admit it. The Supreme Court, however, in *Daubert v. Merrell Dow Pharmaceuticals, Inc.*, rejected "general acceptance" as the exclusive test of admissibility.

DAUBERT v. MERRELL DOW PHARMACEUTICALS, INC.
United States Supreme Court
509 U.S. 579 (1993)

JUSTICE BLACKMUN delivered the opinion of the Court.

In this case we are called upon to determine the standard for admitting expert scientific testimony in a federal trial.

Petitioners Jason Daubert and Eric Schuller are minor children born with serious birth defects. They and their parents sued respondent in California state court, alleging that the birth defects had been caused by the mothers' ingestion of Bendectin, a prescription anti-nausea drug marketed by respondent. Respondent removed the suits to federal court on diversity grounds.

After extensive discovery, respondent moved for summary judgment, contending that Bendectin does not cause birth defects in humans and that petitioners would be unable to come forward with any admissible evidence that it does. In support of its motion, respondent submitted an affidavit of Steven H. Lamm, physician and epidemiologist, who is a well-credentialed expert on the risks from exposure to various chemical substances.

Doctor Lamm stated that he had reviewed all the literature on Bendectin and human birth defects — more than 30 published studies involving over 130,000 patients. No study had found Bendectin to be a human teratogen (i.e., a substance capable of causing malformations in fetuses). On the basis of this review, Doctor Lamm concluded that maternal use of Bendectin during the first trimester of pregnancy has not been shown to be a risk factor for human birth defects.

Petitioners did not (and do not) contest this characterization of the published record regarding Bendectin. Instead, they responded to respondent's motion with the testimony of eight experts of their own, each of whom also possessed impressive credentials. These experts had concluded that Bendectin can cause birth defects. Their conclusions were based upon "in vitro" (test tube) and "in vivo" (live) animal studies that found a link between Bendectin and malformations; pharmacological studies of the chemical structure of Bendectin that purported to show similarities between the structure of the drug and that of other substances known to cause birth defects; and the "reanalysis" of previously published epidemiological (human statistical) studies.

The District Court granted respondent's motion for summary judgment. The court stated that scientific evidence is admissible only if the principle upon which it is based is " 'sufficiently established to have general acceptance in the field to which it belongs.' " . . . The court concluded that petitioners' evidence did not meet this standard. Given the vast body of epidemiological data concerning Bendectin, the court held, expert opinion which is not based on epidemiological evidence is not admissible to establish causation. . . . Thus, the animal-cell studies, live-animal studies, and chemical-structure analyses on which petitioners had relied could not raise by themselves a reasonably disputable jury issue regarding causation. Petitioners' epidemiological analyses, based as they were on recalculations of data in previously published studies that had found no causal link between the drug and birth defects, were ruled to be inadmissible because they had not been published or subjected to peer review . . . .

The United States Court of Appeals for the Ninth Circuit affirmed . . . [c]iting *Frye v. United States*, 293 F. 1013, 1014, 54 App. D.C. 46, 47 (1923)[.] The court stated that expert opinion based on a scientific technique is inadmissible unless the technique is "generally accepted" as reliable in the relevant scientific community. . . . The court declared that expert opinion based on a methodology that diverges "significantly from the procedures accepted by recognized authorities in the field . . . cannot be shown to be 'generally accepted as a reliable technique.' "

The court emphasized that other Courts of Appeals considering the risks of Bendectin had refused to admit reanalyses of epidemiological studies that had been neither published nor subjected to peer review. . . . Those courts had found unpublished reanalyses "particularly problematic in light of the massive weight of the original published studies supporting [respondent's] position, all of which had undergone full scrutiny from the scientific community." . . . Contending that reanalysis is generally accepted by the scientific community only when it is subjected to verification and scrutiny by others in the field, the Court of Appeals rejected petitioners' reanalyses as "unpublished, not subjected to the normal peer review process and generated solely for use in litigation." . . . The court concluded that petitioners' evidence provided an insufficient foundation to allow admission of expert testimony that Bendectin caused their injuries and, accordingly, that petitioners could not satisfy their burden of proving causation at trial.

We granted certiorari . . . in light of sharp divisions among the courts regarding the proper standard for the admission of expert testimony. *Compare, e.g., United States v. Shorter*, 809 F.2d 54, 59–60, 257 U.S. App. D.C. 358, 363–364, *cert. denied*, 484 U.S. 817 (1987), with *DeLuca v. Merrell Dow Pharmaceuticals, Inc.*, 911 F.2d 941, 955 (CA3 1990) (rejecting the "general acceptance" standard).

II

A

In the 70 years since its formulation in the Frye case, the "general acceptance" test has been the dominant standard for determining the admissibility of novel scientific evidence at trial. . . . Although under increasing attack of late, the rule continues to be followed by a majority of courts, including the Ninth Circuit.

The *Frye* test has its origin in a short and citation-free 1923 decision concerning the admissibility of evidence derived from a systolic blood pressure deception test, a crude precursor to the polygraph machine. In what has become a famous (perhaps infamous) passage, the then Court of Appeals for the District of Columbia described the device and its operation and declared:

> Just when a scientific principle or discovery crosses the line between the experimental and demonstrable stages is difficult to define. Somewhere in this twilight zone the evidential force of the principle must be recognized, and while courts will go a long way in admitting expert testimony deduced from a well-recognized scientific principle or discovery, the thing from which the deduction is made must be sufficiently established to have gained general acceptance in the particular field in which it belongs.

54 App. D.C., at 47, 293 F., at 1014 (emphasis added). Because the deception test had "not yet gained such standing and scientific recognition among physiological and psychological authorities as would justify the courts in admitting expert testimony deduced from the discovery, development, and experiments thus far made," evidence of its results was ruled inadmissible.

The merits of the *Frye* test have been much debated, and scholarship on its proper scope and application is legion. Petitioners' primary attack, however, is not on the content but on the continuing authority of the rule. They contend that the *Frye* test was superseded by the adoption of the Federal Rules of Evidence. We agree.

We interpret the legislatively-enacted Federal Rules of Evidence as we would any statute. . . . Rule 402 provides the baseline:

> All relevant evidence is admissible, except as otherwise provided by the Constitution of the United States, by Act of Congress, by these rules, or by

other rules prescribed by the Supreme Court pursuant to statutory authority. Evidence which is not relevant is not admissible.

"Relevant evidence" is defined as that which has "any tendency to make the existence of any fact that is of consequence to the determination of the action more probable or less probable than it would be without the evidence." Rule 401. The Rule's basic standard of relevance thus is a liberal one. *Frye*, of course, predated the Rules by half a century. In *United States v. Abel*, 469 U.S. 45 (1984), we considered the pertinence of background common law in interpreting the Rules of Evidence. We noted that the Rules occupy the field, . . . but, quoting Professor Cleary, the Reporter explained that the common law nevertheless could serve as an aid to their application:

> In principle, under the Federal Rules no common law of evidence remains. "All relevant evidence is admissible, except as otherwise provided. . . . " In reality, of course, the body of common law knowledge continues to exist, though in the somewhat altered form of a source of guidance in the exercise of delegated powers.

We found the common-law precept at issue in the *Abel* case entirely consistent with Rule 402's general requirement of admissibility, and considered it unlikely that the drafters had intended to change the rule. . . . In *Bourjaily v. United States*, 483 U.S. 171 (1987), on the other hand, the Court was unable to find a particular common-law doctrine in the Rules, and so held it superseded.

Here there is a specific Rule that speaks to the contested issue. Rule 702, governing expert testimony, provides:

> If scientific, technical, or other specialized knowledge will assist the trier of fact to understand the evidence or to determine a fact in issue, a witness qualified as an expert by knowledge, skill, experience, training, or education, may testify thereto in the form of an opinion or otherwise.

Nothing in the text of this Rule establishes "general acceptance" as an absolute prerequisite to admissibility. Nor does respondent present any clear indication that Rule 702 or the Rules as a whole were intended to incorporate a "general acceptance" standard. The drafting history makes no mention of *Frye*, and a rigid "general acceptance" requirement would be at odds with the "liberal thrust" of the Federal Rules and their "general approach of relaxing the traditional barriers to 'opinion' testimony." *Beech Aircraft Corp. v. Rainey*, 488 U.S., at 169 (citing Rules 701 to 705). . . . Given the Rules' permissive backdrop and their inclusion of a specific rule on expert testimony that does not mention "general acceptance," the assertion that the Rules somehow assimilated Frye is unconvincing. *Frye* made "general acceptance" the exclusive test for admitting expert scientific testimony. That austere standard, absent from and incompatible with the Federal Rules of Evidence, should not be applied in federal trials.

That the *Frye* test was displaced by the Rules of Evidence does not mean, however, that the Rules themselves place no limits on the admissibility of purportedly scientific evidence. Nor is the trial judge disabled from screening such evidence. To the contrary, under the Rules the trial judge must ensure that any and all scientific testimony or evidence admitted is not only relevant, but reliable.

The primary locus of this obligation is Rule 702, which clearly contemplates some degree of regulation of the subjects and theories about which an expert may testify. "If scientific, technical, or other specialized knowledge will assist the trier of fact to understand the evidence or to determine a fact in issue" an expert "may testify thereto." The subject of an expert's testimony must be "scientific . . . knowledge." The adjective "scientific" implies a grounding in the methods and procedures of science. Similarly, the word "knowledge" connotes more than subjective belief or unsupported speculation. The term "applies to any body of known facts or to any body of ideas inferred from such facts or accepted as truths on good grounds." Webster's Third New International Dictionary 1252 (1986). Of course, it would be unreasonable to conclude that the subject of scientific testimony must be "known" to a certainty; arguably, there are no certainties in science. . . . But, in order to qualify as "scientific knowledge," an inference or assertion must be derived by the scientific method. Proposed testimony must be supported by appropriate validation, i.e., "good grounds," based on what is known. In short, the requirement that an expert's testimony pertain to "scientific knowledge" establishes a standard of evidentiary reliability. Rule 702 further requires that the evidence or testimony "assist the trier of fact to understand the evidence or to determine a fact in issue." This condition goes primarily to relevance. "Expert testimony which does not relate to any issue in the case is not relevant and, ergo, non-helpful." . . . The consideration has been aptly described by Judge Becker as one of "fit." . . . "Fit" is not always obvious, and scientific validity for one purpose is not necessarily scientific validity for other, unrelated purposes. . . . The study of the phases of the moon, for example, may provide valid scientific "knowledge" about whether a certain night was dark, and if darkness is a fact in issue, the knowledge will assist the trier of fact. However (absent creditable grounds supporting such a link), evidence that the moon was full on a certain night will not assist the trier of fact in determining whether an individual was unusually likely to have behaved irrationally on that night. Rule 702's "helpfulness" standard requires a valid scientific connection to the pertinent inquiry as a precondition to admissibility.

That these requirements are embodied in Rule 702 is not surprising. Unlike an ordinary witness, see Rule 701, an expert is permitted wide latitude to offer opinions, including those that are not based on first-hand knowledge or observation. See Rules 702 and 703. Presumably, this relaxation of the usual requirement of first-hand knowledge — a rule which represents "a 'most pervasive manifestation' of the common law insistence upon 'the most reliable sources of information,'" Advisory Committee's Notes on Fed. Rule Evid., 602 (citation omitted) — is premised on an assumption that the expert's opinion will have a reliable, basis in the knowledge and experience of his discipline.

C

Faced with a proffer of expert scientific testimony, then, the trial judge must determine at the outset, pursuant to Rule 104(a), whether the expert is proposing to testify to (1) scientific knowledge that (2) will assist the trier of fact to understand or determine a fact in issue. This entails a preliminary assessment of whether the reasoning or methodology underlying the testimony is scientifically valid and of whether that reasoning or methodology properly can be applied to the facts in issue.

We are confident that federal judges possess the capacity to undertake this review. Many factors will bear on the inquiry, and we do not presume to set out a definitive checklist or test. But some general observations are appropriate.

Ordinarily, a key question to be answered in determining whether a theory or technique is scientific knowledge that will assist the trier of fact will be whether it can be (and has been) tested. "Scientific methodology today is based on generating hypotheses and testing them to see if they can be falsified; indeed, this methodology is what distinguishes science from other fields of human inquiry." . . .

Another pertinent consideration is whether the theory or technique has been subjected to peer review and publication. Publication (which is but one element of peer review) is not a sine qua non of admissibility; it does not necessarily correlate with reliability, . . . and in some instances well-grounded but innovative theories will not have been published. . . . Some propositions, moreover, are too particular, too new, or of too limited interest to be published. But submission to the scrutiny of the scientific community is a component of "good science," in part because it increases the likelihood that substantive flaws in methodology will be detected. The fact of publication (or lack thereof) in a peer-reviewed journal thus will be a relevant, though not dispositive, consideration in assessing the scientific validity of a particular technique or methodology on which an opinion is premised.

Additionally, in the case of a particular scientific technique, the court ordinarily should consider the known or potential rate of error, *see, e.g., United States v. Smith*, 869 F.2d 348, 353–354 (CA7 1989) (surveying studies of the error rate of spectrographic voice identification technique), and the existence and maintenance of standards controlling the technique's operation. *See United States v. Williams*, 583 F.2d 1194, 1198 (CA2 1978), *cert. denied*, 439 U.S. 1117 (1979).

Finally, "general acceptance" can yet have a bearing on the inquiry. A "reliability assessment does not require, although it does permit, explicit identification of a relevant scientific community and an express determination of a particular degree of acceptance within that community." *United States v. Downing*, 753 F.2d, at 1238. . . . Widespread acceptance can be an important factor in ruling particular evidence admissible, and "a known technique that has been able to attract only minimal support within the community," *Downing*, above, at 1238, may properly be viewed with skepticism.

The inquiry envisioned by Rule 702 is, we emphasize, a flexible one. Its overarching subject is the scientific validity and thus the evidentiary relevance and reliability — of the principles that underlie a proposed submission. The focus, of course, must be solely on principles and methodology, not on the conclusions that they generate.

Throughout, a judge assessing a proffer of expert scientific testimony under Rule 702 should also be mindful of other applicable rules. Rule 703 provides that expert opinions based on otherwise inadmissible hearsay are to be admitted only if the facts or data are "of a type reasonably relied upon by experts in the particular field in forming opinions or inferences upon the subject." Rule 706 allows the court at its discretion to procure the assistance of an expert of its own choosing. Finally, Rule 403 permits the exclusion of relevant evidence "if its probative value is substantially outweighed by the danger of unfair prejudice, confusion of the issues, or misleading the jury. . . . " Judge Weinstein has explained: "Expert evidence can be both powerful and quite misleading because of the difficulty in evaluating it. Because of this risk, the judge in weighing possible prejudice against probative force under Rule 403 of the present rules exercises more control over experts than over lay witnesses." Weinstein, 138 F.R.D. at 632.

III

We conclude by briefly addressing what appear to be two underlying concerns of the parties and amici in this case. Respondent expresses apprehension that abandonment of "general acceptance" as the exclusive requirement for admission will result in a "free-for-all" in which befuddled juries are confounded by absurd and irrational pseudoscientific assertions. In this regard respondent seems to us to be overly pessimistic about the capabilities of the jury, and of the adversary system generally. Vigorous cross-examination, presentation of contrary evidence, and careful instruction on the burden of proof are the traditional and appropriate means of attacking shaky but admissible evidence. . . . Additionally, in the event the trial court concludes that the scintilla of evidence presented supporting a position is insufficient to allow a reasonable juror to conclude that the position more likely than not is true, the court remains free to direct a judgment, Fed. Rule Civ. Proc. 50(a), and likewise to grant summary judgment, Fed, Rule Civ. Proc. 56. These conventional devices, rather than wholesale exclusion under an uncompromising "general acceptance" test, are the appropriate safeguards where the basis of scientific testimony meets the standards of Rule 702.

Petitioners and, to a greater extent, their amici exhibit a different concern. They suggest that recognition of a screening role for the judge that allows for the exclusion of "invalid" evidence will sanction a stifling and repressive scientific orthodoxy and will be inimical to the search for truth. . . . It is true that open debate is an essential part of both legal and scientific analyses. Yet there are important differences between the quest for truth in the courtroom and the quest for truth in the laboratory. Scientific conclusions are subject to perpetual revision. Law, on the other hand, must resolve disputes finally and quickly. The scientific project is advanced by broad and wide-ranging consideration of a multitude of hypotheses, for those that are incorrect will eventually be shown to be so, and that in itself is an advance. Conjectures that are probably wrong are of little use, however, in the project of reaching a quick, final, and binding legal judgment — often of great consequence — about a particular set of events in the past. We recognize that in practice, a gatekeeping role for the judge, no matter how flexible, inevitably on occasion will prevent the jury from learning of authentic insights and innovations. That, nevertheless, is the balance that is struck by Rules of Evidence designed not for the exhaustive search for cosmic understanding but for the particularized resolution of legal disputes.

IV

To summarize: "general acceptance" is not a necessary precondition to the admissibility of scientific evidence under the Federal Rules of Evidence, but the

Rules of Evidence — especially Rule 702 — do assign to the trial judge the task of ensuring that an expert's testimony both rests on a reliable foundation and is relevant to the task at hand. Pertinent evidence based on scientifically valid principles will satisfy those demands.

The inquiries of the District Court and the Court of Appeals focused almost exclusively on "general acceptance," as gauged by publication and the decisions of other courts. Accordingly, the judgment of the Court of Appeals is vacated and the case is remanded for further proceedings consistent with this opinion.

It is so ordered,

CHIEF JUSTICE REHNQUIST, with whom JUSTICE STEVENS joins, concurring in part and dissenting in part.

The petition for certiorari in this case presents two questions: first, whether the rule of *Frye v. United States* . . . remains good law after the enactment of the Federal Rules of Evidence; and second, if Frye remains valid, whether it requires expert scientific testimony to have been subjected to a peer-review process in order to be admissible. The Court concludes, correctly in my view, that the Frye rule did not survive the enactment of the Federal Rules of Evidence, and I therefore join Parts I and II-A of its opinion. The second question presented in the petition for certiorari necessarily is mooted by this holding, but the Court nonetheless proceeds to construe Rules 702 and 703 very much in the abstract, and then offers some "general observations." . . .

"General observations" by this Court customarily carry great weight with lower federal courts, but the ones offered here suffer from the flaw common to most such observations — they are not applied to deciding whether or not particular testimony was or was not admissible, and therefore they tend to be not only general, but vague and abstract. This is particularly unfortunate in a case such as this, where the ultimate legal question depends on an appreciation of one or more bodies of knowledge not judicially noticeable, and subject to different interpretations in the briefs of the parties and their amici. Twenty-two amicus briefs have been filed in the case, and indeed the Court's opinion contains no less than 37 citations to amicus briefs and other secondary sources.

The various briefs filed in this case are markedly different from typical briefs, in that large parts of them do not deal with decided cases or statutory language — the sort of material we customarily interpret. Instead, they deal with definitions of scientific knowledge, scientific method, scientific validity, and peer review — in short, matters far afield from the expertise of judges. This is not to say that such materials are not useful or even necessary in deciding how Rule 703 should be applied; but it is to say that the unusual subject matter should cause us to proceed with great caution in deciding more than we have to, because our reach can so easily exceed our grasp.

But even if it were desirable to make "general observations" not necessary to decide the questions presented, I cannot subscribe to some of the observations made by the Court. In Part II-B, the Court concludes that reliability and relevancy are the touchstones of the admissibility of expert testimony. . . . Federal Rule of

Evidence 402 provides, as the Court points out, that "[e]vidence which is not relevant is not admissible." But there is no similar reference in the Rule to "reliability." The Court constructs its argument by parsing the language "[i]f scientific, technical, or other specialized knowledge will assist the trier of fact to understand the evidence or to determine a fact in issue . . . an expert . . . may testify thereto. . . . " Fed. Rule Evid. 702. It stresses that the subject of the expert's testimony must be "scientific . . . knowledge," and points out that "scientific" "implies a grounding in the methods and procedures of science," and that the word "knowledge" "connotes more than subjective belief or unsupported speculation." . . . From this it concludes that "scientific knowledge" must be "derived by the scientific method." . . . Proposed testimony, we are told, must be supported by "appropriate validation." . . . Indeed, in footnote 9, the Court decides that "[i]n a case involving scientific evidence, *evidentiary reliability* will be based upon *scientific validity*." . . . (emphasis in original).

Questions arise simply from reading this part of the Court's opinion, and countless more questions will surely arise when hundreds of district judges try to apply its teaching to particular offers of expert testimony. Does all of this dicta apply to an expert seeking to testify on the basis of "technical or other specialized knowledge" — the other types of expert knowledge to which Rule 702 applies — or are the "general observations" limited only to "scientific knowledge"? What is the difference between scientific knowledge and technical knowledge; does Rule 702 actually contemplate that the phrase "scientific, technical, or other specialized knowledge" be broken down into numerous subspecies of expertise, or did its authors simply pick general descriptive language covering the sort of expert testimony which courts have customarily received? The Court speaks of its confidence that federal judges can make a "preliminary assessment of whether the reasoning or methodology underlying the testimony is scientifically valid and of whether that reasoning or methodology properly can be applied to the facts in issue." . . . The Court then states that a "key question" to be answered in deciding whether something is "scientific knowledge" "will be whether it can be (and has been) tested." . . . Following this sentence are three quotations from treatises, which speak not only of empirical testing, but one of which states that "the criterion of the scientific status of a theory is its falsifiability, or refutability, or testability," . . . .

I defer to no one in my confidence in federal judges; but I am at a loss to know what is meant when it is said that the scientific status of a theory depends on its "falsifiability," and I suspect some of them will be, too. I do not doubt that Rule 702 confides to the judge some gatekeeping responsibility in deciding questions of the admissibility of proffered expert testimony. But I do not think it imposes on them either the obligation or the authority to become amateur scientists in order to perform that role. I think the Court would be far better advised in this case to decide only the questions presented, and to leave the further development of this important area of the law to future cases.

IMPACT OF *DAUBERT*

What did *Daubert* really change with respect to a trial judge's role in assessing the admissibility of purported scientific expert evidence? To be sure, *Daubert's* text announced a new legal standard, wherein reliance on general acceptance in the scientific community was no longer the "litmus test" for admissibility of such evidence. In practice, however, pragmatic application of *Daubert* likely requires judges to defer to the members of the scientific community to determine whether the remaining factors announced in *Daubert* (*i.e.*, testability, error rate, and peer review) have been satisfied. As one commentator has noted:

> The very factors delineated by the Court in *Daubert* require input from the same professional communities that judges looked to for approval of the scientific principles, methodologies, or applications under the *Frye* test. Their necessary input into an intelligent application of the factors delineated by the Court is so great that courts are doing indirectly under *Daubert* what they did directly under *Frye* — relying exclusively on the scientific and technological communities.

> When contested evidence involves the application of a scientific principle, for example, the Court has directed the trial judge to consider whether the community has tested the scientific or technological principles. If such testing has taken place, how does the trial judge determine whether the tests were adequate? Variations in the ways in which the tests were administered can skew the results. How is the judge to know what variations are significant, and what consequences each may have on the results that were achieved? . . . By necessity, therefore, most judges are compelled to go back to the most relevant scientific community for assistance — likely the very community that the judge previously relied upon under *Frye*.

P. Rice, Electronic Evidence: Law and Practice, Ch. 8, n.20 (ABA 2d ed. 2008).

Because non-scientists are ill-suited to sort out what is "good science," *Daubert's* rendition of a four-step yardstick, in the guise of its independent factors, does little to advance the judge's task. Almost by default, lay judges will and do turn to experts in the field in order to assess the propriety of the purported scientific evidence being proffered. The almost foregone conclusion is that all of *Daubert's* weighing factors collapse into the single test of acceptance by the relevant scientific community, as described in the following law review article:

> For example, most judges employing these factors will have no independent basis for evaluating the tests that were employed to assess the validity and reliability of the scientific principles and methodologies in question. . . . They will not have the expertise to determine an acceptable error rate, or to measure that the principles and methodologies that were employed produced accurate results. If people in relevant scientific communities had conducted peer reviews and reported negatively, it is highly improbable the judges would ignore those reviews based on their own assessment of the science.

By the time most courts begin considering the fourth factor, general acceptance, the answer is a foregone conclusion because the relevant community has already been consulted repeatedly in the first three factors. As a consequence, more often than not, in its practical application, *Daubert* will be little more than *Frye* in drag.

P. Rice, *Peer Dialogue: The Quagmire of Scientific Expert Testimony: Crumping the Supreme Court's Style*, 68 Mo. L. Rev. 53, 62 (2003).

[C] "Will Assist the Trier of Fact" — Relaxed Standard for Expert Opinion Testimony

Daubert requires courts to evaluate the legitimacy of scientific testimony, at least theoretically, under a more permissive standard than the old *Frye* test. In reality, *Daubert* transfers the assessment of the qualification of the expert from the community from which his expertise is drawn to the judge considering whether to admit the expert's testimony. In the case that follows, the court followed the flexible standard afforded trial courts after *Daubert*.

KOLBE v. O'MALLEY
United States District Court, District of Maryland
42 F. Supp. 3d 768 (2014)

AMENDED MEMORANDUM

CATHERINE C. BLAKE, DISTRICT JUDGE.

BACKGROUND

The Firearm Safety Act of 2013 provides in general that, after October 1, 2013, a person may not possess, sell, offer to sell, transfer, purchase, or receive "assault pistols," "assault long guns," and "copycat weapons" (together, "assault weapons"). Md. Code Ann., Crim. Law ("CR") §§ 4-301(d), 4-303(a)(2). In addition, the Act states that a person "may not manufacture, sell, offer for sale, purchase, receive, or transfer a detachable magazine that has a capacity of more than 10 rounds of ammunition for a firearm." *Id.* § 4-305(b). A person who violates the Act "is guilty of a misdemeanor and on conviction is subject to imprisonment not exceeding 3 years or a fine not exceeding $5,000 or both," although different penalties are provided for a person who uses an assault weapon or LCM in the commission of a felony or a crime of violence. *Id.* § 4-306.

The Act exempts from the ban the transfer of an assault weapon from a law enforcement agency to a retired law enforcement officer as long as: (1) it is sold or transferred on retirement or (2) it "was purchased or obtained by the person for official use with the law enforcement agency before retirement." *Id.* § 4-302(7). The Act also exempts retired law enforcement officers from the ban on LCMs. *Id.* § 4-305(a)(2), (b).

Just days before the Firearm Safety Act was to go into effect, on September 26, 2013, the plaintiffs filed their complaint, followed the next day by a motion for a temporary restraining order ("TRO"), challenging the law's constitutionality with respect to its ban on assault long guns, copycat weapons, and LCMs. The court heard argument on the TRO on October 1, 2013, and decided that the plaintiffs did not show they were entitled to the extraordinary relief. Following the hearing on the TRO, the parties agreed that, instead of considering a preliminary injunction request, the court should proceed to consider this matter on the merits.

Accordingly, the court will now consider the plaintiffs' claims that the Firearm Safety Act (1) infringes their Second Amendment rights, (2) violates the Equal Protection Clause of the Fourteenth Amendment, and (3) is void for vagueness.

ANALYSIS

* * *

II. Motion to Exclude Testimony

The plaintiffs ask the court to exclude various expert and fact testimony offered by the defendants. Rule 702 of the Federal Rules of Evidence, which governs the admissibility of expert testimony, states:

A witness who is qualified as an expert by knowledge, skill, experience, training, or education may testify in the form of an opinion or otherwise if: (a) the expert's scientific, technical, or other specialized knowledge will help the trier of fact to understand the evidence or to determine a fact in issue; (b) the testimony is based on sufficient facts or data; (c) the testimony is the product of reliable principles and methods; and (d) the expert has reliably applied the principles and methods to the facts of the case.

The party seeking to introduce expert testimony has the burden of establishing its admissibility by a preponderance of the evidence. *Daubert v. Merrell Dow Pharm.*, 509 U.S. 579, 592 n. 10, 113 S. Ct. 2786, 125 L. Ed. 2d 469 (1993). A district court is afforded "great deference . . . to admit or exclude expert testimony under *Daubert.*" *TFWS, Inc. v. Schaefer*, 325 F.3d 234, 240 (4th Cir. 2003) (citations and internal quotation marks omitted); *see also Daubert*, 509 U.S. at 594, 113 S. Ct. 2786 ("The inquiry envisioned by Rule 702 is . . . a flexible one . . . ."). "In applying *Daubert*, a court evaluates the methodology or reasoning that the proffered scientific or technical expert uses to reach his conclusion; the court does not evaluate the conclusion itself," Schaefer, 325 F.3d at 240, although "conclusions and methodology are not entirely distinct from one another," *General Elec. Co. v. Joiner*, 522 U.S. 136, 146, 118 S. Ct. 512, 139 L. Ed. 2d 508 (1997). In essence, the court acts as gatekeeper, only admitting expert testimony where the underlying methodology satisfies a two-pronged test for (1) reliability and (2) relevance. *See Daubert*, 509 U.S. at 589, 113 S. Ct. 2786.

Rule 701 of the Federal Rules of Evidence, which governs the admissibility of lay testimony, states:

If a witness is not testifying as an expert, testimony in the form of an opinion is limited to one that is: (a) rationally based on the witness's perception; (b) helpful to clearly understanding the witness's testimony or to determining a fact in issue; and (c) not based on scientific, technical, or other specialized knowledge within the scope of Rule 702.

"[L]ay opinion testimony must be based on personal knowledge . . . ." *United States v. Perkins*, 470 F.3d 150, 155–56 (4th Cir. 2006) (emphasis in original). "At bottom, . . . Rule 701 forbids the admission of expert testimony dressed in lay witness clothing . . . ." Id. at 156 (quoting *United States v. Santos*, 201 F.3d 953, 963 (7th Cir. 2000)).

A. Koper

Dr. Christopher Koper, as the plaintiffs admit, is the only social scientist to have studied the effects of the federal assault weapons ban that was in place from 1994 to 2004. (See Koper Decl., ECF No. 44–7, ¶ 5.) In addition, he has studied issues related to firearms policy for twenty years, publishing numerous studies in peer-reviewed journals on topics related to crime and firearms. (Id. ¶¶ 3, 6–7.) The plaintiffs ask the court to exclude Koper's expert testimony on two grounds, neither of which is persuasive.

First, the plaintiffs claim that Koper's opinion that the Firearm Safety Act is likely to advance Maryland's interest in protecting public safety is not based on sufficient data, as required by Rule 702, because his study of the federal ban found that the ban did not decrease firearms-related crimes, the lethality and injuriousness of gun crimes, or the criminal use of banned LCMs. (Pls.' Mot. to Exclude, ECF No. 65, at 3–4.) Further, the plaintiffs claim, his previous research revealed that state-level bans did not result in any reduction in crime. (*Id.* at 4.) The plaintiffs also allege that many of Koper's opinions regarding the efficacy of the Firearm Safety Act contradict deposition testimony. (*Id.* at 7.)

As an initial matter, the plaintiffs often mischaracterize Koper's statements and his research, cherry-picking items and presenting them out of context. For example, they cite Koper's acknowledgment in 2004 that a few studies suggest state-level assault weapons bans did not reduce crime as inconsistent with his conclusions regarding the Firearm Safety Act. (Compare Koper Decl., Ex. B, at 81 n. 95 ("[A] few studies suggest that state-level AW bans have not reduced crime . . . ."), with Koper Decl. ¶¶ 77–86 (opining that the Firearm Safety Act is likely to, inter alia, limit the number of long guns in Maryland, limit the number of LCMs in circulation, reduce the number and lethality of gunshot victimizations, and reduce the use of assault weapons and LCMs in crime).) But the plaintiffs omit Koper's numerous qualifications of those state studies. (See Koper Decl., Ex. B, at 81 n. 95 ("[I]t is hard to draw definitive conclusions from these studies . . . : there is little evidence on how state AW bans affect the availability and use of AWs . . . ; studies have not always examined the effects of these laws on gun homicides and shootings . . . ; and the state AW bans that were passed prior to the federal ban . . . were in effect for only three months to five years . . . before the imposition of the federal ban, after which they became largely redundant with the federal legislation and their effects more difficult to predict and estimate.").) Even ignoring the context in which Koper's 2004 statement was made, there is nothing necessarily inconsistent about a 2004 statement that a few state-level bans were not shown to reduce overall crime and Koper's opinion that a different state-level ban, enacted in 2013, likely will reduce the negative effects of gun violence.

To the extent Koper's prior research concluded the federal ban was not effective in various ways, his opinions in the current case are based on several other pieces of data, which the plaintiffs entirely ignore in arguing his testimony should be excluded. (See, e.g., Koper Decl. ¶¶ 13–43.) Further, Koper is clear in noting that the federal weapons ban had several features that may have limited its efficacy that are not present with Maryland's ban. (Id. at ¶¶ 79–81.)

The plaintiffs also challenge Koper's testimony on the basis that he is unable to conclude the Firearm Safety Act will have the desired effects to a "reasonable degree of scientific certainty." It appears the plaintiffs are claiming that expert opinions may not be considered in determining the constitutionality of the bans at issue here unless they are stated with such scientific certainty. In making their argument, however, the plaintiffs fail to recognize that the inquiry under Rule 702, as noted above, is flexible, *see Daubert*, 509 U.S. at 594, 113 S. Ct. 2786, and that, although a reasonable degree of scientific certainty is required for the admission of expert testimony to prove causation in medical malpractice cases — the types of cases the plaintiffs cite to support their position — applying such a standard here would misapprehend the court's inquiry. In attempting to further the state's important interests, the legislature is not required to refrain from acting until it has evidence demonstrating proposed legislation will certainly have the desired effects. It is allowed to make predictions. *See Turner Broadcasting Sys., Inc. v. F.C.C. (Turner I)*, 512 U.S. 622, 665, 114 S. Ct. 2445, 129 L. Ed. 2d 497 (1994) ("Sound policymaking often requires legislators to forecast future events and to anticipate the likely impact of these events based on deductions and inferences for which empirical support may be unavailable."). The court will defer to those predictions as long as they are the result of reasonable inferences and deductions based on substantial evidence. *See Heller v. District of Columbia (Heller III)*, 45 F. Supp. 3d 35, 2014 U.S. Dist. LEXIS 66569, 2014 WL 1978073, at *8 (D.D.C. May 15, 2014) (citing *Turner Broadcasting Sys., Inc. v. F.C.C. (Turner II)*, 520 U.S. 180, 211, 117 S. Ct. 1174, 137 L. Ed. 2d 369 (1997)). Koper's testimony is well-suited to answer the question facing the court and is precisely the kind of evidence upon which other courts have relied in assessing similar assault weapon and LCM bans. *See Heller v. District of Columbia (Heller II)*, 670 F.3d 1244, 1263 (D.C. Cir. 2011); *Fyock v. City of Sunnyvale*, 25 F. Supp. 3d 1267, 2014 U.S. Dist. LEXIS 29722, 2014 WL 984162, at *8–9 (N.D. Cal. Mar. 5, 2014); *San Francisco Veteran Police Officers Ass'n v. San Francisco*, 18 F. Supp. 3d 997, 2014 U.S. Dist. LEXIS 21370, 2014 WL 644395, at *5, *7 (N.D. Cal. Feb. 19, 2014); *Shew v. Malloy*, 994 F. Supp. 2d 234, 249 n.50 (D. Conn. 2014); NYSRPA, 990 F.Supp.2d at 368–72. The court will not, therefore, exclude Koper's testimony.

B. Webster

The plaintiffs argue that Dr. Daniel Webster's testimony should be excluded because he has not conducted any original research but rather has relied on the work of Koper and the data he acquired from the Mother Jones publication. It is acceptable for an expert to rely on the studies of other experts in reaching his own opinions, although courts have excluded testimony where the expert failed to conduct any independent examination or research to ensure the reliability of the information on which he relies. *See Doe v. Ortho-Clinical Diagnostics, Inc.*, 440 F. Supp. 2d 465, 470 (M.D.N.C. 2006) (citation and internal quotation marks omitted) ("Where proffered expert testimony is not based on independent research, but instead on such a literature review, the party proffering such testimony must come forward with other objective, verifiable evidence that the testimony is based on scientifically valid principles. One means of showing this is by proof that the research and analysis supporting the proffered conclusions have been subjected to normal scientific scrutiny through peer review and publication."); *Berlyn, Inc. v. Gazette Newspapers, Inc.*, 214 F. Supp. 2d 530, 539–40 (D. Md. 2002) (excluding an expert because his methods were "wholly lacking in independent research," and there was no evidence that his opinion was "the product of reliable principles and methods, and [was] based upon sufficient facts or data").

Here, over a nearly thirty-year career, Webster has devoted most of his research to gun-related injuries and violence, has directed numerous studies related to gun violence and its prevention, and has published seventy-nine articles in scientific, peer-reviewed journals. (*See* Webster Decl., ECF No. 44-6, ¶¶ 2–5.) Although it is true he relies on Koper's research in his declaration, Webster served as editor of the book that included Koper's 2013 report and, as editor, he subjected Koper's 2013 report to a peer review process. (*See* Koper Decl., Ex. A; Webster Dep., ECF No. 70-4, at 57:11-18.) Likewise, Webster relies on data from the Mother Jones publication, but the data were subject to independent analysis by Koper and his graduate student. (See Koper Decl. ¶¶ 25–28.) In any event, the plaintiffs have offered nothing to suggest the Mother Jones data are unreliable or inaccurate. Accordingly, the court is satisfied that the information on which Webster relies in forming his expert opinion is reliable, and will not exclude his testimony.

C. Vince and Law Enforcement Officers

The plaintiffs argue that the "ballistics opinions" of Joseph Vince and executive law enforcement officers should be excluded, as the opinions are outside the scope of their expertise. They do not, however, identify the paragraphs of Vince's declaration to which they take objection. As the court neither relies on nor refers to any testimony by Vince on "ballistics," the court need not resolve this issue. Turning to the disputed testimony offered by Baltimore County Police Department Chief James Johnson, Baltimore City Police Department Commissioner Anthony Batts, and Prince George's County Police Department Deputy Chief Henry Stawinski, the court agrees with the defendants that none of this testimony contains expert opinions on ballistics. Johnson merely acknowledges that some shots that may be loaded into a shotgun have a risk of over-penetration; Batts offers testimony about research he directed and which was reported to him in connection with his official duties; and Stawinksi testifies on his personal observations of assault weapons piercing soft body armor. (*See* Johnson Decl., ECF No. 44-3, ¶ 35 (opining that "[a] shotgun would . . . be a superior self-defense weapon to an assault weapon, at least if it is loaded with [an] appropriate shot that does not give rise to too great a risk of over penetration"); Batts Decl., ECF No. 44-4, ¶ 21 (testifying about research he personally directed regarding various rounds fired by officers under his command); Stawinski Decl., ECF No. 44-5, ¶ 30 (stating that "[m]ost assault weapons have significant penetration capabilities that are especially dangerous to both law enforcement officers and civilians alike").) The officers' testimony, based on their personal knowledge and experiences, is properly admissible.

D. Allen

The plaintiffs claim that the court should exclude Lucy Allen's expert opinions related to the frequency with which the banned weapons are used defensively for two reasons. First, they claim that her conclusions are based on the coding of stories she did not independently verify. The court notes, however, that the database which Allen studied is maintained by the NRA, suggesting, if anything, that her study may have a bias in favor of finding more instances of the defensive use of firearms. Moreover, the plaintiffs proffer nothing to suggest the stories collected by the NRA are unreliable or inaccurate. Second, they argue that she cannot base her opinions on stories, which, they claim, are inappropriate anecdotal evidence. In light of the apparent dearth of other evidence demonstrating that the firearms at issue here are used for self-defense, Allen's use of the NRA database is appropriate and acceptable. Not only do the cases to which the plaintiffs cite for the opposite conclusion not stand for the proposition that an expert can never rely on anecdotal evidence, they expressly contemplate the use of such evidence. *See Allison v. McGhan Med. Corp.*, 184 F.3d 1300, 1316 (11th Cir. 1999) (acknowledging that case reports do not provide reliable scientific proof of causation, but recognizing their importance for "raising questions and comparing clinicians' findings").

CONCLUSION

In summary, the Firearm Safety Act of 2013, which represents the considered judgment of this State's legislature and its governor, seeks to address a serious risk of harm to law enforcement officers and the public from the greater power to injure and kill presented by assault weapons and large capacity magazines. The Act substantially serves the government's interest in protecting public safety, and it does so without significantly burdening what the Supreme Court has now explained is the core Second Amendment right of "law-abiding, responsible citizens to use arms in defense of hearth and home." Accordingly, the law is constitutional and will be upheld.

A separate order follows.

[D] Subjects of Expert Testimony

[1] Any Appropriate Topic, in Court's Discretion

The subjects upon which courts have held expert testimony to be appropriate under Rule 702 have varied significantly. They range from the highly technical, requiring expertise based on special training and education, to the simple but unusual, requiring expertise gained through experience. These subjects include drug dealers' furtive characteristics, how burglars use certain kinds of tools, elevator safety standards, product defects, trade usage in contract language, vehicles' speed at the time of a collision, professional standards of care, the practice of telephone solicitation, the accuracy of eyewitness identification or voice identification, burglars' modus operandi, and the value of one's own property.

The subjects that courts have found to be inappropriate for expert testimony have been quite limited. Generally they have been subjects upon which the jurors are inherently capable of understanding the evidence presented and of resolving the questions posed. In *United States v. Schmidt*, 711 F.2d 595 (5th Cir. 1983), for example, the defendant was convicted of having committed perjury while testifying before a grand jury. At his trial the defendant offered the testimony of a linguistics expert to show that the defendant did not knowingly and wilfully utter the false statements that he was alleged to have made during the five and one-half hours of questioning before the grand jury. The expert proposed to establish this proposition by explaining that certain answers to certain questions, which on their face might appear to be false, could be interpreted otherwise if placed in the discussion's total context. The Fifth Circuit upheld the trial court's exclusion of this testimony, noting that, although Rule 702 "broadens the range of admissibility, it by no means mandates admission of such testimony." *Id.* at 598–599. The court concluded that the issue presented was not "complex" and that "the jury was more than capable of considering the context in which the defendant had testified" without the aid of an expert witness. *Id.*

Chesebrough-Pond's, Inc. v. Faberge, Inc., 666 F.2d 393 (9th Cir. 1982), offers another example of a subject that courts have considered inappropriate for expert testimony. This case involved a trade infringement action concerning the similarity of two product names, "Match" and "Macho." The plaintiff attempted to present expert testimony on the similarity between these two names. The court excluded this testimony because the jury was as capable as the expert in assessing the names' similarity. The court noted, however, that the expert could properly have testified about the results of opinion polls indicating general consumer recognition and the ability to differentiate between the two product names, because such results might be clarified, and thereby made more meaningful to a jury, through expert interpretation. For related reasons, appellate courts have also upheld the exclusion of expert testimony on the issue of a particular witness' credibility. *See United States v. Awkard*, 597 F.2d 667 (9th Cir. 1979).

One should be careful in interpreting the above decisions. In each case, it is likely that the appellate courts would have upheld the rulings even if the trial courts had ruled the topics to be the proper subject of expert testimony. This is because decisions concerning the appropriateness of proposed subjects of expert testimony are discretionary ones that an appellate court will reverse only if the trial court clearly abuses its discretion. In *United States v. Benveniste*, 564 F.2d 335 (9th Cir. 1977), for example, the defendant was convicted of conspiracy to distribute cocaine and possession with intent to distribute. He raised the defense of entrapment and offered expert testimony on his lack of predisposition and on his psychological susceptibility to the inducements that the Government used to entrap him. The trial judge excluded this evidence and the appellate court upheld this decision on appeal.

The appellate court noted, however, that the admission of this evidence also would not have been error.

The breadth of knowledge necessary to intelligently resolve some issues makes the availability of expert testimony essential. In these instances the exclusion of such testimony will constitute reversible error. Churning, the excessive trading of securities by investment agents to generate commissions and fees, is such an issue for the following reasons:

> Churning consists of the conjunction of three complex factors. The first is excessive trading in view of investment objectives. Excessive trading is analyzed by examining risk, comparative suitability, and trading patterns. Suitability is apparent only by comparison with other possible investments. To determine whether the investments are suitable, one must know the spectrum of possible investments to which the ones in issue are compared. The significance of statistical measurements of account activity, such as the turnover rate, is apparent only in comparison to activity in other accounts. If an expert is not allowed to testify that given statistics evidence excessive trading, the jury is left with meaningless numbers from which they cannot judge the appropriateness of the transactions.

> The second element of churning, control of the accounts, is somewhat more comprehensible to a jury for two reasons. First, it is in part based upon considerations such as the access of the client to the account executive and to the data. Second, the jury generally needs no special expertise to imagine itself in the position of a person of average experience and intelligence. However, this element is so inextricably involved with the other elements that an expert should be permitted to express an opinion to the jury.

> Finally the account executive's scienter, defined as intent to defraud or reckless disregard, must be established. Scienter usually will not be established by direct evidence, but rather will be inferred from a finding of excessive trading and control. The reasons for allowing expert testimony regarding control and excess trading are equally applicable to scienter.

Shad v. Dean Witter Reynolds, Inc., 799 F.2d 525, 530 (9th Cir. 1986).

[2]   Expert's Opinion About Inherent Dangers of Eyewitness Identification

Eyewitness testimony, once believed to be irrefutable proof of guilt, has been shown to be quite unreliable. The *Smith* case demonstrates how *Daubert* empowers trial courts to admit experts on the problems with eyewitness testimony.

UNITED STATES v. SMITH

United States District Court for the Middle District of Alabama
621 F.Supp.2d 1207 (2009)

MYRON H. THOMPSON, DISTRICT JUDGE.

At trial, the United States moved to exclude the testimony of Dr. Sol Fulero, whom defendant Andreas JeJuan Smith offered as an expert on eyewitness identifications generally and cross-racial identifications in particular. The government relied on two evidentiary rules to exclude this testimony. First, it asserted that the testimony violated Fed. R. Evid. 702. Second, it argued that this testimony violated Fed. R. Evid. 403 because its prejudicial value substantially outweighed its probative value. The government's motion was denied in part (allowing Fulero to give his opinion about the science of eyewitness-identifications) and granted in part (not permitting Fulero to testify about specific witnesses in this case). The court promised that a written opinion setting forth its reasoning in more detail would follow, and this is that opinion.

I. BACKGROUND

On June 22, 2007, Montgomery Police responded to a report of a bank robbery at Compass Bank. After several weeks, police identified the robber as Smith and a warrant was issued for his arrest. When a United States Marshal Service task force went to arrest Smith at a friend's home, two shots were fired at arresting officers from inside. Fortunately, neither officer at the door was harmed.

Based on the above events, Smith was charged with armed robbery; assault of a federal officer; carrying a firearm during a crime of violence (the assault of a federal officer); and being a felon in possession of a firearm. A jury found Smith guilty of bank robbery and illegally possessing a firearm, but acquitted him of assaulting a federal officer and carrying a firearm during a crime of violence.

Dr. Fulero's expert testimony went principally to the reliability of witness identifications of Smith as the bank robber. While Smith was found guilty of the robbery after the court allowed Fulero's expert testimony, the court believes that an opinion setting forth its reasoning for allowing the testimony is still warranted.

II. DISCUSSION

The issue before the court is a pressing one. Eyewitness testimony has long been recognized as one of the most persuasive forms of evidence in criminal cases. "[T]here is almost nothing more convincing than a live human being who takes the stand, points a finger at the defendant, and says 'That's the one!'" *Watkins v. Sowders*, 449 U.S. 341, 352, 101 S. Ct. 654, 66 L. Ed. 2d 549 (1981) (Brennan, J., dissenting) (internal citation and emphasis omitted); Henry F. Fradella, *Why Judges Should Admit Expert Testimony on the Unreliability of Eyewitness Testimony*, 2 Fed. Cts. L. Rev. 2 (2007) ("'[S]eeing is believing' is not only ubiquitous common parlance but also appears to be gospel to jurors."); *see also Manson v. Brathwaite*, 432 U.S. 98, 120, 97 S. Ct. 2243, 53 L. Ed. 2d 140 (1977)

(Marshall, J., dissenting) (stating that "juries unfortunately are often unduly receptive to [identification] evidence").

Despite eyewitness testimony's persuasive nature, mounting evidence has suggested that it is not as reliable as has often been assumed. *See* Hon. D. Duff McKee, *Challenge to Eyewitness Identification Through Expert Testimony*, 35 Am.Jur. Proof of Facts 3d 1, § 1 (1996) ("Eyewitness testimony may be the least reliable, and yet the most compelling.") By some estimates, roughly 84% of convicts who have been exonerated by DNA testing were convicted on the basis of mistaken eyewitness testimony. Barry Scheck, et al., *Actual Innocence Five Days To Execution, and Other Dispatches From the Wrongly Convicted* (2000) (finding mistaken eyewitnesses as a factor in 84% of 67 wrongful convictions), *as cited in* Fradella, 2 Fed. Cts. L. Rev. at 2 n. 2; *see also* Edward Connors, et al., *Convicted by Juries, Exonerated by Science: Case Studies in the Use of DNA Evidence to Establish Innocence after Trial* (Dept. of Justice 1996) (examining 28 cases in which DNA evidence exonerated a defendant and stating that, "In all 28 cases, without the benefit of DNA evidence, the triers of fact had to rely on eyewitness testimony, which turned out to be inaccurate"), *available at* http://www.ncjrs.gov/txtfiles/dnaevid.txt (last visited May 21, 2009). There is, then, a vast lacuna between jurors' perceptions of the power of eyewitness testimony and this testimony's accuracy.

Still, despite this gap, courts have sometimes looked askance at expert testimony on the factors that can influence eyewitnesses' perceptions . . . .

*   *   *

It has been over a decade since the Eleventh Circuit last addressed the admissibility of eyewitness-identification expert testimony in a published opinion. In *United States v. Smith*, 122 F.3d 1355, 1358 (11th Cir. 1997), the Eleventh Circuit held that "a district court does not abuse its discretion when it excludes expert testimony on eyewitness identification." Before that decision, the "established rule" of the Eleventh Circuit was apparently that such testimony was not admissible. *Holloway*, 971 F.2d at 679; *see also United States v. Benitez*, 741 F.2d 1312, 1315 (11th Cir. 1984) ("[Defendant's] contention that the district court incorrectly excluded expert testimony concerning identification also lacks merit because such testimony is not admissible in this circuit.").

While *Smith* acknowledged that eyewitness-identification expert testimony has been looked upon "unfavorably" in the Eleventh Circuit, 122 F.3d at 1357, the court explicitly declined to decide at that time whether the "per se inadmissibility rule" remained in effect. *Id.* at 1358. The court also emphasized that the decision whether to admit expert testimony rests within the discretion of the trial court. *Id.* at 1359. 1 A per se proscription against all eyewitness-identification expert testimony is irreconcilable with the United States Supreme Court's decision in *Daubert v. Merrell Dow Pharms., Inc.*, 509 U.S. 579, 113 S. Ct. 2786, 125 L. Ed. 2d 469 (1993). There, the Court eschewed such categorical prohibitions of entire classes of expert *conclusions*; in determining whether to admit testimony, the Court stated, the focus "must be solely on principles and methodology, not on the conclusions that they generate." *Daubert*, 509 U.S. at 595, 113 S. Ct. 2786. The Court emphasized that this inquiry is "a flexible one," *id.* at 594, 113 S. Ct. 2786, and provided a non-exhaustive list of factors for lower courts to consider when determining whether to admit proposed expert testimony as reliable and helpful under Fed. R. Evid. 702. *Id.* at 593–94, 113 S. Ct. 2786.

Heeding the Supreme Court's command, this court at trial examined whether the proposed expert testimony complied with the strictures outlined in *Daubert. See United States v. Frazier*, 387 F.3d 1244, 1260 (11th Cir. 2004) ("[T]he Supreme Court made abundantly clear in *Daubert* [that] Rule 702 compels the district courts to perform the critical 'gatekeeping' function concerning the admissibility of expert scientific evidence.") (citing *Daubert*, 509 U.S. at 589 n. 7, 113 S. Ct. 2786).

A. Rule 702

Fed. R. Evid. 702 provides:

> "If scientific, technical, or other specialized knowledge will assist the trier of fact to understand the evidence or to determine a fact in issue, a witness qualified as an expert by knowledge, skill, experience, training, or education, may testify thereto in the form of an opinion or otherwise, if (1) the testimony is based upon sufficient facts or data, (2) the testimony is the product of reliable principles and methods, and (3) the witness has applied the principles and methods reliably to the facts of the case."

In *Daubert*, the Supreme Court urged lower courts, first, to examine whether reliable methodology undergirds proposed expert testimony. That is, courts are to consider: whether the theory or technique "can be (and has been tested)," "whether the theory or technique has been subjected to peer review and publication," whether there is a known or potential error rate in the scientific technique, and whether the theory or technique has achieved general acceptance in the particular scientific community. 509 U.S. at 593–94, 113 S. Ct. 2786. Second, if the opinion testimony is reliable, the court must determine whether the testimony would aid the trier of fact. *Id.* at 589, 113 S. Ct. 2786. This, essentially, is nothing more than a restatement of the general rule that the trial judge ensure the evidence is "relevant to the task at hand." *Id.* at 597, 113 S. Ct. 2786. To answer this second question, courts should look to whether the reliable scientific methods "fit" the case before a court, *id.* at 591, 113 S. Ct. 2786, an inquiry that typically involves scrutinizing the particular testimony offered and matching that testimony to the specific factual context of a case. The government challenges the admission of Fulero's testimony at each of these stages.

1. Reliability

The government argues that Dr. Fulero's opinion does not constitute reliable scientific or technical knowledge. In support of this position, the government cites a host of cases from other circuits in which eyewitness-identification expert testimony has been rejected as unscientific. However, the purported experts in those cases failed to provide sufficient articles or data demonstrating the reliability of the methods employed by those experts. *E.g., United States v. Kime*, 99 F.3d 870, 883 (8th Cir. 1996) (finding that two articles on the topic of eyewitness identification in lineups were "utterly deficient in regard to determining whether [the expert's] views constitute 'scientific knowledge' within the meaning of *Daubert*"); *United States v. Rincon*, 28 F.3d 921, 923–25 (9th Cir. 1994) (affirming the district court's exclusion of proffered eyewitness-identification expert testimony under *Daubert* and noting that, "while the article identified the research on some of the topics, it did not discuss the research in sufficient detail that the district court could determine if the research was scientifically valid"); *United States v. Brien*, 59 F.3d 274, 277 (1st Cir. 1995) (affirming the inadmissibility of expert testimony on the reliability of eyewitness identification, noting that the defendant failed to provide "data or literature underlying" the expert's opinion).

On the other hand, other courts have specifically reviewed Dr. Fulero's methods and found that they "easily" satisfy the first *Daubert* inquiry. *United States v. Moonda*, No. 1:06CR0395, [2007 U.S. Dist. LEXIS 46950] (N.D. Ohio June 28, 2007) (Dowd, J.). Indeed, in *United States v. Langan*, 263 F.3d 613 (6th Cir. 2001), the Sixth Circuit Court of Appeals refers to Fulero as the expert "whose 'qualifications and scientific methods' [have] already been 'praised' by the Sixth Circuit." *Id.* at 623 (citing *Smithers*, 212 F.3d at 315).

This court concurred at trial with the cases and thus concluded that Fulero's methods satisfied the reliability prong of *Daubert*. In compliance with *Daubert*, the theories underlying Fulero's testimony have been well-tested in peer-reviewed publications, including in articles authored by Fulero. *See, e.g.*, Nancy Steblay, Jennifer Dysart, Sol Fulero, & R.C.L. Lindsay, *A Meta-Analytic Comparison of Showup and Lineup Identification Accuracy*, 27 Law & Hum. Behav. 523 (2003); Nancy Steblay, R.C.L. Lindsay, Sol Fulero, & Jennifer Dysart, *Eyewitness Accuracy Rates in Sequential and Simultaneous Lineup Presentations: A Meta-analytic Review*, 25 Law & Hum. Behav. 459–474 (2001); *see also* R.C.L. Lindsay & Gary L. Wells, *Improving Eyewitness Identification from Lineups: Simultaneous Versus Sequential Lineup Presentations*, 70 J. Applied Psychol. 556 (1985).

Furthermore, Fulero testified that the methods he relies upon are generally accepted, and this representation accords with this court's own findings. *See Frazier*, 387 F.3d at 1261 ("[T]he trial court's gatekeeping function requires more than simply taking the expert's word for it.") (internal quotations omitted). Numerous studies have been done under controlled conditions assessing the factors that influence eyewitnesses "in accordance with generally accepted practice in the behavioral science community" done independent of any litigation. Hon. Robert P. Murrian, *The Admissibility of Expert Eyewitness Testimony Under the Federal Rules*, 29 Cumb. L. Rev. 379, 384–85 (1999) (collecting studies).

* * *

Also of note is that Fulero holds a Ph.D. in psychology and now teaches the subject at the university-level. He has additionally demonstrated extensive knowledge of the ongoing, most recent developments in the field of eyewitness identification. Indeed, Fulero has authored or co-authored roughly 60 publications, primarily addressing how psychological factors affect the administration of criminal justice. Further, he is a reviewer for several major journals, including, among others, Law & Hum. Behav., J. of Forensic Psychol. & Prac., and Psychol. Pub. Pol'y & Law. *See generally City of Tuscaloosa v. Harcros Chems., Inc.*, 158 F.3d 548, 562 (11th Cir. 1998) (requiring that experts be "qualified to testify competently" on a given subject matter); *see also* Michael R. Leippe, *The Case for Expert Testimony about Eyewitness Memory*, 1 Psychol. Pub. Pol'y & L. 909, 951 (1995) (encouraging courts to consider, prior to admitting an eyewitness-identification expert, whether he or she has: "(a) a PhD degree in psychology; (b) documentable extensive graduate-level training in cognitive, social, and other areas of experimental psychology; and (c) evidence of recent and ongoing comprehensive, cutting-edge contact with the eyewitness literature (e.g., research and publication, university-level teaching, reviewing for major journals)." These facts satisfied the court that Fulero is qualified in the field and equipped to provide the jury with reliable expert testimony on eyewitness identifications.

2. Assistance to the Jury

The United States contended that Fulero's proposed testimony would not aid the jury because Fulero's proffered testimony presented no analysis from Fulero tailored to this case. *See Daubert*, 509 U.S. at 591, 113 S. Ct. 2786 (stating that testimony must "fit" the facts of a case to satisfy Fed. R. Evid. 702). Instead, Fulero's testimony would discuss only general problems associated with eyewitness identifications. Such testimony, the government argued, would not aid the jury because problems with eyewitness identification are within the "ordinary knowledge of most lay jurors." *See Langan*, 263 F.3d at 624. In addition to the lack of support for the proposition that juries commonly understand the unnamed (but likely myriad) problems with eyewitness testimony or the ways in which those problems interact with each other and in different factual settings, a further problem with the government's argument was that Fulero's expert testimony actually fitted quite well to Smith's case . . .

[3] Testimony About Memory

Individuals have poor memories just as they have a poor ability to identify individuals they previously encountered. The *Libby* case raises the question of whether experts on memory can be admitted just like experts on eyewitness testimony.

UNITED STATES v. LIBBY
United States District Court, District of Columbia
461 F. Supp. 2d 3 (2006)

I. Background

. . . All of these charges arise from a criminal investigation into the possible unauthorized disclosure of classified information — Valerie Plame Wilson's affiliation with the Central Intelligence Agency ("CIA") — to several journalists. Indictment at 8, ¶ 25. Specifically, the charges against the defendant are predicated upon statements that the defendant allegedly made to Special Agents of the Federal Bureau of Investigation ("FBI") in October and November, 2003, *id.* at 9, ¶ 26, and testimony he provided to a grand jury in March 2004, *id.* at 11, ¶ 30. The alleged false statements occurred when the defendant recounted conversations he had in June and July 2003, with news reporters Tim Russert, Judith Miller, and Matthew Cooper to the FBI Agents and to the grand jury. *See generally* Indictment at 11–22.

The defendant has made clear that in his effort to rebut these charges he will argue, in part, (1) that it is the government's witnesses, and not him, who misremembered the facts and the substance of the various conversations detailed in the indictment and (2) that any errors he may have made in describing the events were occasioned by confusion or faulty memory, not any wilful intent to misrepresent the truth. Def.'s Mot. at 1–2; see *Libby*, 429 F.Supp.2d at 12 (noting that the defendant may assert as his defense that any false statements were the result of confusion, mistake, or a faulty memory). This Court has acknowledged that this "faulty memory defense" is a viable defense to the charges. *Libby*, 429 F. Supp. 2d at 12 (recognizing that "the charges could possibly be defeated by the defendant demonstrating that the alleged misstatements were not made intentionally, but were merely the result of confusion, mistake, faulty memory, or another innocent reason."). Accordingly, the memory and recollection of the principal players will undoubtedly play a substantial role in the assessment of the defendant's culpability in the upcoming trial.

To support his faulty memory defense, the defendant seeks to introduce at trial the testimony of Dr. Bjork "to show that it is entirely plausible, given how memory has been found to function, that Mr. Libby or the government witnesses-or both-have innocently confused or misremembered the conversations on which this case turns." Def.'s Mot. at 2. Specifically, Dr. Bjork would testify about thirteen scientific principles concerning human memory, including the process by which memory is encoded, stored, retained, and retrieved and various scientific bases for memory errors including "content borrowing," source misattribution, subsequent recall, divided attention, and "retroactive interference." Def.'s Mot., Ex. A (listing thirteen opinions Dr. Bjork's testimony would encompass). According to the defendant, Dr. Bjork's expert testimony "will assist the jury by providing information about the findings of memory research that are not already known to the jurors." Def.'s Mot. at 2. It is the admissibility of Dr. Bjork's testimony under Federal Rule of Evidence 702 that is the subject of this opinion.

II. Federal Rule of Evidence 702

The admissibility of expert testimony is governed by Federal Rule of Evidence 702 Central to the court's determination of whether expert testimony is admissible under Rule 702, and consistent with the Rule's purpose, is the two-prong test enunciated by the Supreme Court in *Daubert v. Merrell Dow Pharm.*, 509 U.S. 579, 113 S. Ct. 2786, 125 L. Ed. 2d 469 (1993). Under this test, a court determining the admissibility of purported expert testimony must first determine "[1] whether the reasoning or methodology underlying the testimony is scientifically valid and [2] whether that reasoning or methodology properly can be applied to the facts in issue." *Id.* at 592–93, 113 S. Ct. 2786. When analyzing whether expert testimony is admissible under this test, the Court plays the role of a "gatekeeper" with the responsibility to ensure that the proposed testimony is both reliable and relevant. *Ambrosini v. Labarraque*, 101 F.3d 129, 133 (D.C.Cir.1996); see *Daubert*, 509 U.S. at 589, 113 S. Ct. 2786. The burden is on the proponent of the testimony to establish its admissibility by a "preponderance of proof." *Meister v. Med. Eng'g Corp.*, 267 F.3d 1123, 1127 n. 9 (D.C. Cir. 2001) (citing *Daubert*, 509 U.S. at 592 n. 10, 113 S. Ct. 2786).

This first prong of the *Daubert* test "establishes a standard of evidentiary reliability." Daubert, 509 U.S. at 590, 113 S. Ct. 2786. Although the subject of the scientific testimony need not be "known to a certainty," it must be "ground[ed] in the methods and procedures of science." Id. at 590, 113 S. Ct. 2786. When examining this part of the test, the "court must focus 'solely on principles and methodology, not on the conclusions that they generate.' " *Ambrosini*, 101 F.3d at 133 (citing *Daubert*, 509 U.S. at 595, 113 S. Ct. 2786). The Supreme Court has provided a non-exhaustive, flexible list of factors to help courts determine whether the proffered testimony satisfies the first prong of the *Daubert* test. This list includes: (1) whether the subject of the expert's testimony "can be (and has been) tested"; (2) whether it has been "subjected to peer review and publication"; (3) "the known or potential rate of error" of the relevant scientific technique; (4) "the existence and maintenance of standards controlling the technique's operation"; and (5) whether it is "generally accepted" in the relevant scientific community. *Daubert*, 509 U.S. at 593–94, 113 S. Ct. 2786. It is important to note, however, that

> nothing in either *Daubert* or the Federal Rules of Evidence requires a district court to admit opinion evidence that is connected to existing data only by the ipse dixit of the expert. A court may conclude that there is simply too great an analytical gap between the data and the opinion proffered.

Gen. Elec. Co. v. Joiner, 522 U.S. 136, 146, 118 S. Ct. 512, 139 L. Ed. 2d 508 (1997).

Even if the Court concludes that the proponent of expert testimony has satisfied the first prong of the *Daubert* test, the testimony will only be admissible if it "will assist the trier of fact to understand the evidence or to determine a fact in issue." Fed. R. Evid. 702. This prong of the *Daubert* test "goes primarily to relevance." *Daubert*, 509 U.S. at 591, 113 S. Ct. 2786. Thus, "[e]xpert testimony which does not relate to any issue in the case is not relevant and, ergo, non-helpful." *Id.* (citation and internal quotation marks omitted). As the Supreme Court in *Daubert* explained, the proposed testimony must be a "fit" to assist the jury in resolving an issue relevant to a case, *id.*, which "entails a preliminary assessment of whether . . . scientifically valid . . . reasoning or methodology properly can be applied to the facts in issue," *id.* at 593, 113 S. Ct. 2786. An expert need not offer an opinion on a specific issue to satisfy this "fit" requirement; rather, the expert can testify about general scientific principles. *See, e.g., United States v. Mulder*, 273 F.3d 91, 101–02 (2d Cir. 2001). The Supreme Court has cautioned, however, that " '[f]it' is not always obvious, and scientific validity for one purpose is not necessarily scientific validity for other, unrelated purposes." *Daubert*, 509 U.S. at 591, 113 S. Ct. 2786.

In determining whether proposed scientific evidence has a proper fit, courts have looked to a variety of factors, including: "(1) whether the testimony is relevant; (2) whether it is within the juror's common knowledge and experience; and (3) whether it will usurp the juror's role of evaluating a witness's credibility." *United States v. Rodriguez-Felix*, 450 F.3d 1117, 1123 (10th Cir. 2006) (internal footnotes and citations omitted). Thus, expert testimony concerning matters beyond the understanding of the average juror is often admissible, while expert testimony concerning knowledge within the province of the average juror is not. Compare *United States v. Long*, 328 F.3d 655, 666 (D.C. Cir. 2003) (concluding that "experts may testify regarding the modus operandi of a certain category of criminals where those criminals' behavior is not ordinarily familiar to the average layperson") and *United States v. Moore*, 104 F.3d 377, 384 (D.C. Cir. 1997) (holding that expert testimony concerning practices of persons involved in drug dealing in using duct tape assisted jury in determining whether the defendant intended to distribute drugs), with *Stromback v. New Line Cinema*, 384 F.3d 283, 295 (6th Cir. 2004) (holding that expert testimony was not necessary in a copyright infringement case, as a jury could compare two works to determine if they were substantially similar) and *United States v. Mitchell*, 49 F.3d 769, 780 (D.C. Cir. 1995) (concluding that the district court did not err in preventing a linguistics expert from testifying about taped conversations, as the tapes were before the jury and they could be properly evaluated by the jury). Expert testimony will also be precluded if would usurp the jury's role as the final arbiter of the facts, such as testimony on witness credibility and state of mind. *See, e.g., Nimely v. City of New York*, 414 F.3d 381, 398 (2d Cir. 2005) (holding "that expert opinions that constitute evaluations of witness credibility, even when such evaluations are rooted in scientific or technical expertise, are inadmissible under Rule 702"); *United States v. Boney*, 977 F.2d 624, 630 (D.C. Cir. 1992) (concluding that expert testimony on the guilt or innocence of a defendant in a criminal case invaded the province of the jury and was improper under Rule 702); *Salas v. Carpenter*, 980 F.2d 299, 305 (5th Cir. 1992) (excluding expert testimony on whether the defendant had the requisite state of mind to commit the charged offense).

Admittedly, there is no bright line that separates issues that are considered within the comprehension of juries and those that are not. 4 J. McLaughlin, J. Weinstein, & M. Berger, Federal Evidence § 702.03[2][b] (2d ed. 2006). And some courts have concluded that when a court is presented with a close question of whether an expert's proposed testimony falls within the competence of the jury's apprehension, the court should resolve the question in favor of admitting the testimony. *See, e.g., United States v. Jakobetz*, 955 F.2d 786, 796–97 (2d Cir. 1992) (concluding that courts should resolve doubts about the admissibility of expert testimony in favor of the proponent of the testimony); *Larabee v. M M & L Int'l Corp.*, 896 F.2d 1112, 1116 n. 6 (8th Cir. 1990) (noting that while "the district court ordinarily has broad discretion to admit or exclude expert testimony, . . . doubts about whether an expert's testimony will be useful should generally be resolved in favor of admissibility.") (citation and internal quotation marks omitted). These courts have reasoned that since the Federal Rules of Evidence adopt a liberal approach to the admissibility of expert testimony, close questions should be resolved in favor of admissibility. *Jakobetz*, 955 F.2d at 797. However, although the Federal Rules of Evidence embody a "general approach of relaxing the traditional barriers to 'opinion' testimony," *Daubert*, 509 U.S. at 588, 113 S. Ct. 2786, before expert testimony may be admitted at trial, the Court must first conclude that the proponent of the expert testimony satisfies the two-prong *Daubert* test, *id.* at 589, 113 S. Ct. 2786. And even if this *Daubert* test is satisfied, expert testimony can still be precluded under Rule 403 "if its probative value is substantially outweighed by the danger of unfair prejudice, confusion of the issues, or misleading the jury, or by considerations of undue delay, waste of time, or needless presentation of cumulative evidence." *United States v. Gatling*, 96 F.3d 1511, 1523 (D.C. Cir. 1996) ("If a court determines that expert testimony might be helpful to the jury, it should allow the testimony unless it finds that under Rule 403 the unfair prejudice caused by the testimony outweighs its probative value."); *see Daubert*, 509 U.S. at 594, 113 S. Ct. 2786. In discussing the interplay between Rule 403 and Rule 702, the Supreme Court recognized that " '[e]xpert evidence can be both powerful and quite misleading because of the difficulty in evaluating it. Because of this risk, the judge in weighing possible prejudice against probative force under Rule 403 of the present rules exercises more control over experts than over lay witnesses.' " *Daubert*, 509 U.S. at 595, 113 S. Ct. 2786 (quoting Jack B. Weinstein, Rule 702 of the Federal Rules of Evidence is Sound; It Should Not Be Amended, 138 F.R.D. 631, 632 (1991)).

III. Legal Analysis

A. Daubert Analysis

The government does not challenge the proposed testimony of Dr. Bjork on the grounds that his testimony fails to satisfy the first prong of *Daubert*, noting that it "does not quibble with Dr. Bjork's expertise concerning research into memory, particularly with respect to the reliability of eyewitness identification." Gov't's Opp'n at 1. Rather, the government contends that the defendant "cannot meet his burden as the proponent of the evidence of establishing that the testimony will assist the jury in understanding or determining any of the facts at issue in this case." *Id.* Thus, this is the only question the Court must resolve. For the reasons that follow, this Court agrees with the government. Therefore, Dr. Bjork will not be permitted to testify at trial.

In support of his position that Dr. Bjork's testimony will be helpful to the jury, the defendant asserts that "[r]esearch has shown that jurors are generally unaware of the frequency and causes of honest errors of recollection, and they underestimate the fallibility of memory." Def.'s Mem. at 8. Thus, the defendant claims that Dr. Bjork's testimony about general principles concerning the field of memory research will assist the jurors in understanding the memory issues that will be presented to them in the case. Id. In opposing Dr. Bjork's testimony, the government contends that (1) expert testimony on memory issues is permissible only under special circumstances not at issue here, Gov't's Opp'n at 7–11, (2) the proposed testimony is within the knowledge and experience of an average juror, *id.* at 12–17, (3) the testimony cannot be applied to the facts of this case, *id.* at 17–18, and (4) under Rule 403, the proposed testimony is likely to confuse, mislead, or unduly influence the jury, *id.* at 18–20.

There is no clear case authority, or absolute rule, on when an expert should be permitted to testify on issues regarding memory and perception. Courts have permitted such testimony when the testimony related to eyewitness identifications, repressed memory, and medical conditions that may affect memory. *See, e.g., Rock v. Arkansas*, 483 U.S. 44, 57–62, 107 S. Ct. 2704, 97 L. Ed. 2d 37 (1987) (concluding that Arkansas Supreme Court's conclusion that expert testimony on repressed memory was per se inadmissible was in error); *United States v. Brownlee*, 454 F.3d 131, 140–44 (3d Cir. 2006) (district court erred in excluding expert testimony on memory errors of eyewitnesses related to cross-racial identifications and identifications made under stress in the absence of other inculpatory evidence); *United*

States v. Shay, 57 F.3d 126, 131–34 (1st Cir. 1995) (district court erred in excluding expert testimony concerning defendant's mental disorder that may have impacted his inculpatory statements). And other courts have excluded such testimony when it related to eyewitness identifications and recollection of past events. *See, e.g.*, *United States v. Carter*, 410 F.3d 942, 950–51 (7th Cir. 2005) (excluding expert testimony concerning the reliability of eyewitness identifications); *Robertson v. McCloskey*, 676 F.Supp. 351, 354–55 (D.D.C. 1988) (excluding testimony of an expert in the field of "psychodynamics of memory and perception."). In addition, expert testimony relating to memory and perception has been excluded when, for example, effective cross-examination was employed to challenge the credibility and memory of the witnesses. *Carter*, 410 F.3d at 950–51; *Rodriguez-Felix*, 450 F.3d at 1125. Contrary to the government's position, these cases do not demonstrate that expert testimony on memory and perception is only admissible in certain "special circumstances." Gov't's Opp'n at 7–11. Rather, these cases simply stand for the proposition that there is no per se rule for or against the admissibility of such testimony. And a court presented with a proffer of expert testimony must determine its admissibility on a case-by-case basis. *See, e.g.*, *Brownlee*, 454 F.3d at 144 (examining the facts of the case to determine whether the trial court erred in precluding the expert testimony); *Shay*, 57 F.3d at 133–34 (same). Accordingly, this Court must apply the second prong of the *Daubert* test to determine whether the proffered testimony will be helpful to the jury. For the reasons that follow, it will not be helpful.

To support his argument that Dr. Bjork's testimony will be helpful to the jury, the defendant relies on various studies, which he avers stand for the proposition that "jurors are generally unaware of the frequency and causes of honest errors of recollection, and that they underestimate the fallibility of memory." Def.'s Mem. at 8. As further support for his position, the defendant offered the testimony of Dr. Elizabeth Loftus, who detailed her belief, based upon her research and the research of others, that many of the principles which Dr. Bjork would testify to are not commonly understood by jurors. After carefully reviewing the studies provided by the defendant and the testimony of Dr. Loftus, this Court must conclude that those studies are inapposite to what the jurors will have to decide in this case because: (1) the studies examine issues of memory and cognition under substantially different factual situations than the situation here; (2) the research does not demonstrate that jurors will underestimate the fallibility of memory when the matter is addressed in the trial setting though voir dire, cross-examination, closing arguments, and jury instructions; and (3) insofar as the studies relied on by Dr. Loftus purport to demonstrate the failure of jurors to sufficiently understand factors that impact the accuracy of memory, the scientific value of the studies themselves is suspect.

The studies relied upon by the defendant were based upon research that examined prospective juror understanding of factors that could impact the reliability of eyewitness identifications. *See, e.g.*, R. Schmechel, T. O'Toole, C. Easterly, & E. Loftus, Beyond the Ken? Testing Jurors' Understanding of Eyewitness Reliability Evidence, 46 Jurimetrics J. 177–214 (2006) ("Beyond the Ken") (noting that this survey "would discern what potential District of Columbia jurors understood about memory in general and the reliability of eyewitness identification evidence in particular.") (emphasis added); R. Wise & M. Safer, A Survey of Judges' Knowledge and Beliefs About Eyewitness Testimony, 40 Court Review, Spring 2003, at 6–16 ("A Survey of Judges' Knowledge"); K. Deffenbacher & E. Loftus, Do Jurors Share a Common Understanding Concerning Eyewitness Behavior?, 6 L. and Human Behavior 15–30 (1982) ("Do Jurors Share a Common Understanding"). This Court cannot accept the proposition that the research findings concerning juror knowledge of factors impacting the reliability of eyewitness identification applies equally to juror knowledge of the factors that impact memory and cognition in other contexts, such as the memory and recall of conversations. Thus, while the defendant has proffered numerous scientific studies describing how memory functions, the research showing that jurors do not understand these concepts is limited to the application of the concepts in the discrete area of eyewitness identification and its findings have limited, if any, applicability in other respects. See *Robertson*, 676 F. Supp. at 353.

*   *   *

Moreover, the value of these studies is further diminished by the factual basis that would underscore an expert's testimony on eyewitness identification issues and the expert testimony on the principles of memory and cognition that the defendant seeks to introduce. Under the former category, there can be little doubt that the average juror is not regularly, if at all, presented with issues of eyewitness identification of an alleged perpetrator of a criminal offense. Thus, it is highly probable that the average juror would be less familiar with concepts that may impact a witness's identification such as weapons focus, mug-shot-induced bias, or lineup format. *See, e.g.*, A Survey of Judges' Knowledge at 12. However, on a daily basis the average juror is personally faced with innumerable questions of memory and cognition, as everyone in their daily lives is called upon to store, encode, and retrieve information he or she has been subjected to. Although the average juror may not understand the scientific basis and labels attached to causes for memory errors, jurors inevitably encounter the frailties of memory as a commonplace matter of course. *See, e.g., United States v. Welch*, 368 F.3d 970, 973–75 (7th Cir. 2004) ("[a]lthough the average person may not know what the term 'clothing bias' means, it is common knowledge that one may mistake a person for someone else who is similarly dressed. Moreover, the typical juror would know that two people who are structurally similar are more likely to be confused for each other than are dissimilar individuals. Finally, it does not require an expert witness to point out that memory decreases over time."); *United States v. Labansat*, 94 F.3d 527, 530 (9th Cir. 1996) ("[i]t is common knowledge that memory fades with time").

[4] Credibility of Particular Witnesses

Courts are quite reluctant to admit expert evidence on the credibility of individual witnesses as this invades the role of the fact finder as the *Hill* case demonstrates.

UNITED STATES v. HILL

United States Court of Appeals, Tenth Circuit

749 F.3d 1250 (2014)

LUCERO, CIRCUIT JUDGE.

Stanley Hill appeals following his conviction on several charges related to the robbery of a bank. During trial, Charles Jones, a special agent with the Federal Bureau of Investigation ("FBI"), testified as an expert. Agent Jones stated that he was trained in "special tactics and ways to identify[] deception in statements and truths in statements" and that in his opinion, many of Stanley's1 answers were not worthy of credence and "[did] not make sense." Jones claimed that Stanley displayed evasive behaviors "common among the criminal element to keep law enforcement at bay" during an interrogation. When asked about Stanley's statement that he would rather die than face charges, Jones testified, "Never in my career have I seen that with an innocent person." And when the prosecutor asked about Stanley's repeated invocations of God in support of his truthfulness, Jones stated, "My training has shown me, and more[]so my experience in all these interviews, when people start bringing faith into validating [] their statements, that they're deceptive. Those are deceptive statements."

Stanley did not contemporaneously object to the admission of this evidence. Nevertheless, we conclude the court plainly erred in admitting this testimony and, in light of the relative weakness of the government's overall case, that it affected Stanley's substantial rights. We further conclude that this is one of the exceptional cases in which we exercise our discretion to notice the plain error because failing to do so would seriously undermine the fairness, integrity, or public reputation of judicial proceedings. Exercising jurisdiction under 28 U.S.C. § 1291, we reverse.

I

Stanley Hill and his brother, Vernon Hill, were charged with bank robbery with a dangerous weapon and use of a firearm during and in relation to a crime of violence following the November 5, 2011, robbery of an Arvest Bank in Tulsa, Oklahoma. Stanley was also charged with being a felon in possession of a firearm. Following a jury trial, Vernon was convicted of both charges against him. The jury deadlocked on the charges against Stanley, and the district court declared a mistrial.

The government proceeded at the first trial upon the theory that Vernon and Stanley were the two men who physically entered and robbed the bank. After discovering additional evidence, however, the government came to believe that Vernon and another Hill brother, Dejuan, were the two individuals who entered the bank while Stanley acted as a getaway driver. Stanley and Dejuan were charged by superseding indictment with a Hobbs Act violation, bank robbery with a dangerous weapon, and use of a firearm during and in relation to a crime of violence. Stanley was also charged a second time with being a felon in possession of a firearm.

A

At the second trial, the government adduced testimony from several individuals who witnessed the robbery. A customer of the bank testified that she observed two men wearing hoodies and gloves standing near the bank just before the robbery, one of whom was talking on a cell phone. Bank employees testified that two masked men entered the bank shortly after it opened, ordered the occupants to the floor, and demanded money. One of the robbers brandished a firearm, identified by one of the employees as a 9mm. The thieves put money into a tan-colored pillow case and fled west on foot. A witness who lived near the bank testified that he saw two men running down the street carrying a white bag shortly after the robbery.

The stolen cash included "bait bills" containing a GPS tracking device. This device automatically activated upon being removed from a teller's drawer and sent a notification to a Tulsa police sergeant at 8:30 or 8:31 a.m. The speed of the tracking device indicated it was being transported in a vehicle. Within a few minutes, it came to a stop in the vicinity of 1100 East Pine in Tulsa. A Tulsa police officer testified that within five to ten minutes of being notified by dispatch of the bank robbery, he arrived in that area and focused on a residence at 1107 East Pine (the "East Pine residence"). Shortly after he arrived on the scene, the officer reported that a black Nissan Altima left the driveway of that home. The driver was later identified as Dejuan. No other person entered or exited the home during the officer's surveillance. The tracking device indicated that it was located within the East Pine residence.

After approximately two hours, officers observed Stanley exiting the home and took him into custody. A short time later, Vernon came outside and was also detained. The brothers were transported separately to a Tulsa police station. Stanley identified himself as Daniel Hill and provided a birth date and social security number. After pulling up a picture of Daniel Hill and noticing the absence of a tattoo on Stanley's arm, a detective confronted Stanley about his identity. Stanley began crying and asked to speak with the detective in a room out of Vernon's earshot. After being moved to a separate interview room, Stanley identified himself truthfully.

Tulsa Police Corporal Christopher Stout and Agent Jones conducted a videotaped interview with Stanley, which was played for the jury. In his interview, Stanley stated that he woke up at his girlfriend Whitney Landrum's home although he claimed not to know her address. He said that after waking up he went to the home at 1107 East Pine, which Stanley identified as belonging to his father, Stanley Battle. He claimed that no one was present when he arrived at roughly 6:00 a.m., and that he watched television and fell asleep in the living room shortly thereafter. Stanley said that he planned to watch his stepsister, who was going to be dropped off at the home by her mother sometime that morning. He was unsure of the step-sister's exact age, stating that she was about 11, and said he did not know the name of her mother. Stanley did not know the exact time she was going to be dropped off.

Stanley claimed he was awoken by the house phone several hours later and was informed there were police outside. He went outside and was taken into custody. Stanley claimed that an officer told him that another man had left the house, and said that he did not hear anyone come or go while he was sleeping. He stated in the interview that he was not sleeping very deeply, and would have known if anyone else was in the home.

After hearing Stanley's story, the interviewers challenged his version of the facts. They explained that a bank has been robbed and that material from the bank was found in the East Pine residence. They suggested that if he was the only one in the house, he was likely the bank robber. Stanley then acknowledged that his brother exited the home after he did, but said he did not know anyone else was in the home. He denied involvement in the bank robbery. When officers expressed disbelief, he repeatedly stated that he would swear on the Bible, and swore to God that he was telling the truth. He also stated that he did not want to live and that he would rather die than face charges.

Meanwhile, Tulsa Police obtained a search warrant for the East Pine residence. Officers discovered a tan-colored pillowcase full of cash in the bottom drawer of the oven, including the tracking device taken from the Arvest Bank. An officer testified that "the drawer was very full of pots and pans" and that he could hear officers "struggling to get that drawer open with pots and pans in the way" from the living room. The living room was located fifteen to eighteen feet from the kitchen. Officers also found a Glock .45 caliber pistol, a pair of black pants, a black ski mask, and two pairs of black gloves in a bedroom of the house. They discovered mail addressed to Vernon and Battle.

Corporal Stout testified about the difficulties he encountered attempting to contact Landrum. He stated that Landrum repeatedly hung up on him, and that Landrum resisted contact when served with a subpoena. He also learned that Landrum drove a black 2004 Nissan Maxima. Landrum was subpoenaed, asserted her Fifth Amendment rights, and was granted immunity. She testified that Stanley is her boyfriend and the father of two of her children. Landrum further testified that Stanley left her home early in the morning on the day of the robbery and that she went to the East Pine residence sometime around 8:00 or 9:00 a.m. to pick him up. By the time she arrived in her Nissan, police were already on the scene.

The prosecution also introduced two phone calls made by Stanley from jail. In a discussion between Stanley and Landrum about bond money, Landrum relays that Vernon referred to Stanley as "the weak link of the group" and that he suggested Stanley be bailed out first if possible. In another call between Stanley and his father, Battle warns Stanley not to say "nothing to do with what they holding y'all for . . . don't say where you was." Battle notes that the police might suggest other people had provided information, and says, "you know we're family, we stick together, so you don't have to worry about the police talking about who told what."

*   *   *

C

Jones also testified about the interrogation of Stanley. He stated that he had attended "two specialized courses in interrogation and interviews, including the Reid school, which is a higher-level school of interrogation and interviewing." He explained:

[T]he Reid school is designed to — as an interview process and interrogation process; part of that is psychological as well. It's much like your five-year-old children and how you can break down a story or you understand what's going on during the process of that interview.

In the Reid school, you're trained on some special tactics and ways to identify on deception in statements and truths in statements. That school is a sought-after school for investigators and interviewers because of the caliber of that training you do get towards that endeavor.

Jones further stated that he had conducted over a thousand interviews as an FBI agent.

The prosecution asked, "in reference to [his] earlier testimony regarding [his] training and experience in interrogating and interviewing," what Jones "based on [his] training and experience" took from the interrogation "as to [Stanley's] truthfulness." Jones responded:

[T]he most difficult thing to tell the difference in is partial truths, . . . something that's partly true, that's a lot harder to detect than a flat-out lie or a convicting [sic] truth.

So during the course of that interview, we were able to, as trained eyes, pick out that this isn't — these are partial truths, at best. And several of those are — they're shown through things that are not purposely said or done by the interviewee. They are responses that occur naturally, that's a psychological thing that happens, that we don't control.

For example, in this case, and I've seen it in other interviews, a mumbling of something that they don't want to talk about. You may say, I was at the grocery store at three or whatever or whatever, and you will go away from the question and just discount that as something you don't need to know, Mr. Police Officer. And there was much of that going on throughout the interview, for whatever, or whatever, and whatever with Mr. Stanley Hill's interview, occurred on a continuous basis, just avoiding — it's a way to avoid the question without just flat out saying, I'm not going to talk to you.

The prosecutor then asked, "In reference to the substance of the responses that were provided . . . how does that factor into your observations of whether he's being truthful or not?" She provided Stanley's claim that he planned to babysit his step-sister at the East Pine home as an example of "the substance of responses." Jones answered that Stanley's version of events "does not connect [the] dots," "does not make sense," and was "not something that [he] viewed as reasonable." Specifically, Jones doubted that if Stanley was going to be "responsible for a child," he would immediately fall asleep "and never w[a]ke up while somehow bank robbery money got stuffed in the oven drawer of your house, and then the bank robbers ran away before the police could get there, and you didn't hear anything, but you were waiting on somebody to arrive in this unlocked house in north Tulsa."

Jones then identified several factors that contributed to his opinion that Stanley was being untruthful during the interview. He noted that after Stanley was told that police found items connected to the bank robbery in the East Pine residence, Stanley's

> story ha[d] to change a little bit. And prior to that, I wasn't sleeping that hard. After that, "to my knowledge," "to my knowledge."

> I can't question his knowledge. I cannot say, I know what you knew. But he could evade the question by saying, "well, to my knowledge," because that's something I cannot corroborate. That is a move that is common among the criminal element to keep law enforcement at bay and not be able to determine the actual facts of what happened.

Jones also stated that Stanley's assertions that he "had no will to live" were indicative of guilt, testifying: "I have not seen, in my experience, an innocent person willing to die because they were talking with police officers and FBI agents. Never in my career have I seen that with an innocent person." He continued: "I also don't reasonably believe an innocent person would want to die because they were being talked to by police officers. It doesn't make sense to me." The prosecutor asked if, "in [Jones'] experience, has it been a demonstration of consciousness of guilt that an individual will want to die rather than tell the truth." Jones responded, "In my experience, sometimes people believe death would be better than a long-term prison sentence."

The prosecution also asked how Jones viewed Stanley's "call on his faith or swearing to God" during the course of the interview. Jones testified:

> Beyond my own religious feelings towards what he was saying, the training that I've received, that is a common way that somebody with guilt will want to validate the story they're telling you. They can't validate it with facts, so they hope they can get you to believe them, because they're trying to validate their story through a supposed belief.

> He may be a God-fearing man, I do not know that, but the truth is the truth. You do not have to back the truth. When I'm asked a question, is the car blue, the car is blue. I don't have to swear to God. I do not have to bring religion into that statement. The truth is the truth.

> My training has shown me, and more[ ]so my experience in all these interviews, when people start bringing faith into validating of their statements, that they're deceptive. Those are deceptive statements.

Defense counsel did not make any objections during Jones' testimony about the truthfulness of Stanley's statements. Jones was the final witness at trial. During closing argument, the prosecutor referred the jury back to Jones' testimony, stating that Jones "in scrutinizing this interview with Stanley Hill . . . has to figure out what's truthful in this interview, what's he trying to hide."

D

*   *   *

As a general matter, expert opinion testimony may be introduced at trial if it "will help the trier of fact to understand the evidence or to determine a fact in issue." Fed. R. Evid. 702(a). An expert may provide opinion testimony if: "the testimony is based upon sufficient facts or data" and "is the product of reliable principles and methods," and "the expert has reliably applied the principles and methods to the facts of the case." Fed. R. Evid. 702(b)–(d). "The touchstone of admissibility under Rule 702 is the helpfulness of the evidence to the trier of fact." *United States v. Rangel-Arreola*, 991 F.2d 1519, 1524 (10th Cir. 1993).

Stanley does not argue that Jones was unqualified to offer the opinion he provided, but instead that the subject matter of his testimony — the credibility of another person — may not be addressed by an expert testifying under Rule 702. We agree. As this court made clear in *United States v. Toledo*, 985 F.2d 1462 (10th Cir. 1993), "[t]he credibility of witnesses is generally not an appropriate subject for expert testimony." *Id.* at 1470. There are several reasons for the prohibition against expert testimony on other witness' credibility. Such testimony: (1) "usurps a critical function of the jury"; (2) "is not helpful to the jury, which can make its own determination of credibility"; and (3) when provided by "impressively qualified experts on the credibility of other witnesses is prejudicial and unduly influences the jury." *Id.* (citations omitted).

*   *   *

It appears our sibling circuits that have considered this issue have uniformly agreed. *See Engesser v. Dooley*, 457 F.3d 731, 736 (8th Cir. 2006) ("An expert may not opine on another witness's credibility."); *Nimely v. City of New York*, 414 F.3d 381, 398 (2d Cir. 2005) ("[T]his court, echoed by our sister circuits, has consistently held that expert opinions that constitute evaluations of witness credibility, even when such evaluations are rooted in scientific or technical expertise, are inadmissible under Rule 702."); *United States v. Vest*, 116 F.3d 1179, 1185 (7th Cir.1997) ("Credibility is not a proper subject for expert testimony; the jury does not need an expert to tell it whom to believe, and the expert's stamp of approval on a particular witness' testimony may unduly influence the jury." (quotations omitted)); *United States v. Gonzalez-Maldonado*, 115 F.3d 9, 16 (1st Cir. 1997) ("An expert's opinion that another witness is lying or telling the truth is ordinarily inadmissible pursuant to Rule 702 because the opinion exceeds the scope of the expert's specialized knowledge and therefore merely informs the jury that it should reach a particular conclusion." (quotation omitted)); *United States v. Beasley*, 72 F.3d 1518, 1528 (11th Cir. 1996) ("Absent unusual circumstances, expert medical testimony concerning the truthfulness or credibility of a witness is inadmissible . . . because it invades the jury's province to make credibility determinations."); *United States v. Rivera*, 43 F.3d 1291, 1295 (9th Cir. 1995) ("[A]n expert witness is not permitted to testify specifically to a witness' credibility or to testify in such a manner as to improperly buttress a witness' credibility." (quotation and alteration omitted)); *United States v. Dorsey*, 45 F.3d 809, 815 (4th Cir. 1995) ("[E]xpert testimony can be properly excluded if it is introduced merely to cast doubt on the credibility of other eyewitnesses, since the evaluation of a witness's credibility is a determination usually within the jury's exclusive purview.").

*   *   *

III

For the foregoing reasons, we REVERSE and REMAND with instructions to VACATE Stanley Hill's convictions and sentence.

[E]   The Expert's Qualifications

After it is determined that the testimony of an expert witness could assist the finder of facts, the court must then determine whether the witness called possesses the qualifications necessary to provide that assistance as defined in Rule 702. This is a preliminary question of fact that the presiding judge will determine pursuant to Rule 104(a). The burden is on the proponent to establish the expert's qualifications. The proponent usually establishes a proffered expert's qualifications through the witness' own testimony, although the proponent is not limited to this form of evidence alone. In making this preliminary determination pursuant to Rule 104(a), the court, of course, is not bound by the rules of evidence and therefore may consider any information that is relevant to the issue, regardless of whether it is admissible.

After the witness relates her qualifications, and before the proponent elicits substantive testimony, the opponent may request, and the court will usually grant, an opportunity to conduct a preliminary cross-examination of the witness for the limited purpose of testing the foundation laid by the proponent. In addition to this cross-examination, the court may allow the opponent to present independent evidence to establish the proffered expert's lack of qualifications. This preliminary inquiry into an expert witness' qualifications is called *voir dire*.

After a party proffers a witness as an expert, it is incumbent upon the opponent to request, at that time, the right to conduct a *voir dire* examination to test the proposed expert's qualifications. Courts have held that, once the court has accepted the witness as an expert, the opponent may not thereafter raise the question of qualifications for purposes of challenging the admissibility of the expert's opinion. If the opponent, therefore, fails to challenge the expert's qualifications at *voir dire*, the court will deem the opponent to have waived the right to do so. Does this waiver, however, preclude the opponent from subsequently cross-examining the witness concerning her qualifications and from presenting evidence *to the jury* for the purpose of demonstrating that the "expert's" testimony is entitled to little weight?

In *Hall v. General Motors Corp.*, 647 F.2d 175 (D.C. Cir. 1980), the court held that the opponent's failure to object to a proffered expert's qualifications at *voir dire* waived the opponent's right to *any* further exploration of qualification during the expert witness' cross-examination. The court held that it was not error for the trial judge to restrict cross-examination to the basis of the expert's opinion because once a witness is offered and accepted as an expert, impeachment through cross-examination about the witness' basic qualifications is inappropriate.

Why is it inappropriate? If the admissibility of evidence and the weight that the finder of facts should give to it once admitted are separate questions, the first to be decided by the presiding judge and the second to be decided by the jury, how does it reasonably follow that waiving the presentation of evidence on the first precludes the presentation of evidence on the second? Is it unreasonable, illogical, or inappropriate for one to concede that a witness has sufficient qualification to be classified as an expert, but insufficient knowledge, experience, and credibility to be believed over the other experts presented during the trial? Fortunately, most courts do not follow this precedent.

When a court determines that a witness is qualified to give expert testimony, this is usually announced in open court upon proffer of the offering party. After demonstrating his expertise through the testimonial delineation of his credentials and experience, the proponent will likely say to the presiding judge, "Your honor, we would offer Dr. Jacobs as an expert in biophysical engineering." After entertaining objections and arguments by both sides, the judge usually announces a decision immediately, *e.g.*, finding that the witness is a qualified expert in the pertinent subject and allowing the examination to proceed.

However, there is no requirement that the presiding judge make such an explicit acknowledgment of the witness' expertise. In fact, the preferable procedure in a jury trial would be to avoid such acknowledgments, because they may influence the jury in its evaluation of the expert. *United States v. Bartley*, 855 F.2d 547, 552 (8th Cir. 1988). The judge's decision is implicit in either permitting the examination to go forward or prohibiting it.

In *Khairkhua*, the court considers the question of whether particular individuals are qualified to address areas of specialized knowledge — in this case, Afghan political and military affairs.

KHAIRKHWA v. OBAMA
United States District Court, District of Columbia
793 F. Supp. 2d 1 (2011)

MEMORANDUM OPINION

RICARDO M. URBINA, DISTRICT JUDGE.

I. INTRODUCTION

This matter comes before the court on the petition for a writ of habeas corpus filed by Khairulla Said Wali Khairkhwa (ISN 579) ("the petitioner"), an Afghan national detained at the United States Naval Station in Guantanamo Bay, Cuba ("GTMO"). The government contends that the petitioner, a former senior Taliban official, is lawfully detained because he was part of Taliban forces and purposefully and materially supported such forces in hostilities against the United States. The petitioner maintains that his detention is unlawful because he was merely a civilian administrator in the Taliban government with no involvement in the Taliban's military operations, and because he had disassociated himself from the Taliban by the time of his capture.

In March 2011, the court held a merits hearing to assess the lawfulness of the petitioner's detention. During the course of that hearing, the parties introduced dozens of exhibits from a variety of classified and public sources, including media reports, scholarly works, interrogation reports and declarations from intelligence analysts. The court also received live testimony and declarations from subject matter experts offered by the petitioner. At the conclusion of the hearing, both parties submitted detailed proposed findings of fact and conclusions of law encapsulating and amplifying the evidence and argument presented during the merits hearing.

Having carefully considered the parties' extensive presentations, the court reaches the following findings. The petitioner was, without question, a senior member of the Taliban both before and after the U.S.-led invasion of Afghanistan in October 2001. The petitioner served as a Taliban spokesperson, the Taliban's Acting Interior Minister, the Taliban Governor of Kabul and a member of the Taliban's highest governing body, the Supreme Shura. The petitioner was a close associate of Taliban leader Mullah Mohammed Omar, who appointed him Governor of the province of Herat in 1999. The petitioner held this office at the time the Taliban government fell to U.S. coalition forces in late 2001.

Although the petitioner contends that he had no military responsibilities in any of his posts within the Taliban, the record belies that contention. The petitioner has repeatedly admitted that after the terrorist attacks of September 11, 2001, he served as a member of a Taliban envoy that met clandestinely with senior Iranian officials to discuss Iran's offer to provide the Taliban with weapons and other military support in anticipation of imminent hostilities with U.S. coalition forces. The petitioner has also exhibited a detailed knowledge about sensitive military-related matters, such as the locations, personnel and resources of Taliban military installations, the relative capabilities of different weapons systems and the locations of weapons caches. Furthermore, the petitioner operated within the Taliban's formal command structure, providing material support to Taliban fighters both before and after the outset of hostilities with U.S. coalition forces. These facts are consistent with the Taliban's governance model, in which nearly all senior Taliban officials were tasked with both civilian and military responsibilities.

Despite the petitioner's efforts to portray himself as a reluctant, marginal figure within the Taliban, the record indicates that the petitioner rose to the highest level of the Taliban and had close ties to Mullah Omar, who repeatedly appointed the petitioner to sensitive, high-profile positions. Indeed, even after the U.S.-led invasion of Afghanistan, the petitioner remained within Mullah Omar's inner circle, despite the fact that Mullah Omar had limited his contacts to only his most trusted commanders.

The petitioner remained part of Taliban forces at the time of his capture in early 2002. Although the petitioner contacted individuals allied with the United States to discuss the possibility of surrendering himself to U.S. coalition forces, he never turned himself in and was ultimately captured at the home of a senior Taliban military commander.

In sum, based on a totality of the evidence, the court concludes that the government has proven by a preponderance of the evidence that the petitioner was part of Taliban forces at the time of his capture. The petitioner is therefore lawfully detained and his petition for a writ of habeas corpus must be denied.

II. BACKGROUND

A. Factual Overview

The following facts are undisputed. The petitioner was born in the Kandahar province of Afghanistan some time between 1967 and 1972. GE 91 (Joint Stipulation of Undisputed Facts) ¶ 10; GE 20 (ISN 579 FD-302 (July 2, 2002)) at 1; GE 44 (ISN 579 FD-302 (May 26, 2002)) at 1; GE 45 (ISN 579 FD-302 (May 13, 2002)) at 1; GE 70 (ISN 579 CSRT Summarized Statement (Nov. 8, 2004)) at 1–2. He is a Durrani Pashtu and a member of the Popalzai tribe. GE 91 ¶ 11. Following the Soviet invasion of Afghanistan in 1979, the petitioner relocated with his family to a refugee camp near Quetta, Pakistan. GE 20 at 1. The petitioner spent the bulk of his youth in Pakistan and was educated at different madrassas in that country. GE 91 ¶ 14; GE 43 (ISN 579 MFR (May 10, 2002)) at 1; GE 45 at 1.

In 1994, with the Soviets expelled from Afghanistan and various factions fighting for control over the country, the petitioner returned to Afghanistan. GE 91 ¶ 13. He moved to the village of Spin Boldak in Kandahar province, where he began working for the Taliban. Id. In Spin Boldak, the petitioner functioned primarily as a wayand, or spokesperson, serving as the Taliban's spokesman to media outlets such as the BBC and Voice of America. GE 20 at 1–2; GE 45 at 1. The petitioner also served as the Taliban's district administrator for Spin Boldak, the highest-ranking official in that city. GE 71 (ISN 579 ARB Statement (June 22, 2006)) at 3; Mar. 31 Tr. at 87.

The petitioner rose quickly through the Taliban ranks. In 1996, the petitioner was appointed Governor of Kabul, PE 110 ¶ 50, and shortly thereafter, became the Taliban's Acting Minister of the Interior, id.; GE 91 ¶ 16. By that time, the Taliban had seized control over southern and central Afghanistan, including Kabul, and were advancing on the Northern Alliance stronghold city of Mazar-e-Sharif. GE 91 ¶¶ 2–3. The Taliban attempted to seize the city in May and September 1997, but both assaults proved unsuccessful. Id. ¶ 3. The Taliban finally captured Mazar-e-Sharif in August 1998. Id. ¶ 4.

On October 26, 1999, the petitioner was appointed Governor of Herat, id. ¶ 17, the westernmost province in Afghanistan, GE 92. The petitioner held this post when U.S. coalition forces commenced Operation Enduring Freedom on October 7, 2001. See GE 91 ¶ 5. By mid-November 2001, U.S. coalition forces had pushed the Taliban out of Mazar-e-Sharif, Herat and Kabul. Id. ¶¶ 6–8. Kandahar fell in early December 2001. Id.

In late January or early February 2002, Pakistani authorities captured the petitioner in Chaman, Pakistan at the home of Abdul Manan Niazi, the former Taliban Governor of Kabul. Id. ¶ 18. The petitioner has been detained at GTMO since approximately March 2002.

*   *   *

D. Qualification of the Petitioner's Experts

During the merits hearing, the petitioner sought to introduce testimony from two individuals proffered as expert witnesses: Hekmat Karzai and Brian Williams. Karzai submitted a declaration on the petitioner's behalf, see generally PE 110 (Decl. of Hekmat Karzai), and testified at the merits hearing, see Mar. 31 Tr. at 45–152. Williams also offered a declaration on the petitioner's behalf, see generally PE 111A (Decl. of Brian Williams), though he did not testify at the merits hearing.

Following extensive voir dire by the government, the court concluded that Karzai was qualified to offer expert testimony on each of the matters addressed in his declaration. Mar. 31 Tr. at 92. The court also heard extensive argument from the parties regarding Williams's qualifications to offer expert testimony in this case, though it declined to rule on the matter during the hearing.

In the following sections, the court explains in greater detail the basis for its ruling on Karzai's qualifications and assesses the expert qualifications of Williams. The court begins by briefly recounting the general principles governing the qualification of expert witnesses.

1. Legal Standard for the Qualification of Expert Witnesses

Federal Rule of Evidence 702 provides that a witness must qualify as an expert to testify on matters that are scientific, technical or specialized in nature. See Fed. R. Evid. 702. The court must act as a "gatekeeper" and determine the admissibility of expert testimony and the qualifications of expert witnesses. *Meister v. Med. Eng'g Corp.*, 267 F.3d 1123, 1127 n. 9 (D.C. Cir. 2001) (quoting *Daubert v. Merrell Dow Pharm., Inc.*, 509 U.S. 579, 592 n. 10, 113 S. Ct. 2786, 125 L. Ed. 2d 469 (1993)). The trial court's gatekeeping obligation applies not only to scientific testimony but to all expert testimony. *Kumho Tire Co. v. Carmichael*, 526 U.S. 137, 148, 119 S. Ct. 1167, 143 L. Ed. 2d 238 (1999).In general, Rule 702 has been interpreted to favor admissibility. *See Daubert*, 509 U.S. at 587, 113 S. Ct. 2786; see also Fed. R. Evid. 702 advisory committee's note (2000) ("A review of the caselaw after *Daubert* shows that the rejection of expert testimony is the exception rather than the rule."). The adversarial system remains the "traditional and appropriate" mechanism for exposing "shaky but admissible evidence." Fed. R. Evid. 702 advisory committee's note (2000) (quoting *Daubert*, 509 U.S. at 596, 113 S. Ct. 2786). Nonetheless, the party presenting the expert bears the burden, by a "preponderance of proof," of establishing the qualifications of the proposed expert. *Meister*, 267 F.3d at 1127 n. 9.

Rule 702 does not specify any particular means for qualifying an expert, requiring only that the witness possess the "knowledge, skill, experience, training, or education" necessary to "assist" the trier of fact. Fed. R. Evid. 702. As the Supreme Court stated in *Daubert*, the trial court must determine whether the proposed expert possesses "a reliable basis in the knowledge and experience of [the relevant] discipline." 509 U.S. at 592, 113 S. Ct. 2786. In considering whether this standard is met, courts may consider the factors articulated in *Daubert*, such as (1) whether the expert's technique or theory can be or has been tested; (2) whether the technique or theory has been subject to peer review and publication; (3) the known or potential rate of error of the technique or theory when applied; (4) the existence and maintenance of standards and controls; and (5) whether the technique or theory has been generally accepted in the scientific community. *Id.*

The Supreme Court has, however, noted that the *Daubert* factors are not exclusive and may not apply in all cases. *Kumho Tire Co.*, 526 U.S. at 150–51, 119 S. Ct. 1167 (noting that Rule 702 envisions a "flexible" inquiry). In cases in which the *Daubert* factors do not apply, "reliability concerns may focus on personal knowledge or experience." *Groobert v. President & Dirs. of Georgetown Coll.*, 219 F. Supp. 2d 1, 6 (D.D.C. 2002) (citing *Kumho Tire Co.*, 526 U.S. at 149, 119 S. Ct. 1167). Formal education ordinarily suffices, and a person who holds a graduate degree typically qualifies as an expert in his or her field. *See, e.g., Lavespere v. Niagara Mach. & Tool Works, Inc.*, 910 F.2d 167, 176–77 (5th Cir. 1990); *Am. Gen. Life. Ins. Co. v. Schoenthal Family*, LLC, 555 F.3d 1331, 1338–39 (11th Cir. 2009).

There is, however, no requirement that an expert possess formal education, and an expert may be qualified on the basis of his or her practical experience. See, e.g., *Thomas v. Newton Int'l Enters.*, 42 F.3d 1266, 1269–70 (9th Cir. 1994) (concluding that a longshoreman with twenty-nine years of experience in various positions within the industry was qualified to testify as an expert about proper safety procedures). As noted in the advisory committee notes to Rule 702, "[i]f the witness is relying solely or primarily on experience, then the witness must explain how that experience leads to the conclusion reached, why that experience is a sufficient basis for the opinion, and how that experience is reliably applied to the facts." Fed. R. Evid. 702 advisory committee's note (2000).

The degree of "knowledge, skill, experience, training, or education" required to qualify an expert witness "is only that necessary to insure that the witness's testimony 'assist' the trier of fact." *See Mannino v. Int'l Mfg. Co.*, 650 F.2d 846, 851 (6th Cir. 1981) (noting that the weight of the evidence is a matter to be assessed by the trier of fact). "[I]t is not necessary that the witness be recognized as a leading authority in the field in question or even a member of a recognized professional community." 29 Fed. Prac. & Proc. (Evid.)) § 6265. "The 'assist' requirement is satisfied where expert testimony advances the trier of fact's understanding to any degree." *Id.*

2. Hekmat Karzai

Hekmat Karzai, one of the proposed experts on whom the petitioner relies, is the Director of the Centre for Conflict and Peace Studies, an independent research institute in Afghanistan dedicated to reducing the threat of political violence and fostering an environment of peace and stability in that nation. PE 110 ¶¶ 1–2. Karzai earned a master's degree in strategic studies, focusing on issues such as terrorism, militancy and insurgency, has authored scholarly works on the Taliban and its relationship with al-Qaida, has traveled extensively in the region and is personally acquainted with many former Taliban leaders as well as local Afghan officials. Id. ¶¶ 4–6; Mar. 31 Tr. at 46–49, 52. He is also a senior fellow at the Joint Special Operations University, Special Operations Command for the United States Military and regularly briefs senior U.S. commanders in Afghanistan. Mar. 31 Tr. at 46–49.

The petitioner offered Karzai to provide expert testimony on the following subjects: (1) background on the Taliban government and its relations with Iran; (2) a profile of Mullah Omar; and (3) the petitioner's background and his role within the Taliban government. PE 110 ¶ 7. Following a lengthy voir dire, the government conceded Karzai's qualifications to offer expert testimony on the first two of these issues. Mar. 31 Tr. at 89. The government objected, however, to Karzai offering expert testimony on the third issue, arguing that his views on the petitioner's roles within the Taliban were based more on ipse dixit than on rigorous analysis. *Id.* at 89–90. The government noted that Karzai had published no scholarly works about me petitioner and based his opinions about the petitioner primarily on his discussions with individuals associated with the petitioner rather than on any rigorous analytical inquiry. *Id.* at 90. In effect, the government argued, the petitioner was attempting to introduce hearsay evidence in the guise of expert testimony. *Id.* at 91.

The court overruled the government's objection based on the following considerations: having authored a master's thesis on the relationship between the Taliban and al-Qaida, as well as numerous scholarly works on the Taliban and Afghanistan, Karzai had amassed over a decade of experience conducting research on issues related to the Taliban and Afghanistan by the time he began researching the petitioner in 2006. *Id.* at 44–49, 86. Accordingly, Karzai plainly possessed the training and experience necessary to conduct research into the petitioner, a prominent and senior member of the Taliban government.

Indeed, it would appear that in a manner consistent with his training and experience, Karzai conducted a systematic inquiry into the petitioner. Karzai testified that he formed his opinions about the petitioner's background and posts within the Taliban by interviewing numerous people associated with him, including his family, those who worked with him in the Taliban government on a daily basis and current senior Afghan government officials. *Id.* at 83–85. He also consulted primary and secondary sources, such as local Afghan publications, for information regarding the petitioner's role within the Taliban. *Id.* at 84. Karzai testified that he sought out a variety of individuals with firsthand knowledge about the petitioner, speaking not only with individuals from Taliban-dominated southern Afghanistan, but also with individuals from both the Mazar-e-Sharif region in the north and Herat province in western Afghanistan. *Id.* at 89. Moreover, Karzai attempted to verify the information he obtained from any source by seeking corroboration through other sources. *Id.* at 86–87.

The government did not explain why Karzai's reliance on information that he obtained from these interviews precludes him from offering expert testimony, particularly in light of his efforts to cross-reference and corroborate this information. Although the government suggested that the rigor of Karzai's inquiry was undermined by his personal desire to see the petitioner freed, Mar. 31 Tr. at 90–91, in the court's view, this factor is relevant to the weight afforded to Karzai's testimony, not his expertise.

Accordingly, based on Karzai's knowledge, training and experience regarding the Taliban and his efforts to research the petitioner's background and roles within the Taliban, the court concluded during the merits hearing that Karzai was qualified to offer expert testimony on the petitioner's background and posts within the Taliban.

3. Brian Williams

Brian Williams is a professor of Islamic History at the University of Massachusetts–Dartmouth, where he has taught since 2001. PE 111A ¶ 1. He has a doctoral degree in Central Asian History, as well as a master's degree in Russian History and Central Eurasian Studies. *Id.* Williams has authored more than seventy articles on war and terrorism in Central Eurasia. *Id.* He has testified as an expert in other GTMO proceedings. *See, e.g., Khan,* 741 F. Supp. 2d at 8 (noting that Williams offered expert testimony on Afghan warlords).

In his declaration, Williams offers expert opinion testimony on the following four subjects: (1) the Taliban's conquest of Mazar-e-Sharif; (2) Iranian-Taliban cooperation against the United States; (3) intelligence sharing between the Taliban and Iran; and (4) al-Qaida bases located in Herat. See generally PE 111A. The government does not dispute Williams's qualifications to offer testimony on subjects one and four. Mar. 31 Tr. at 6. The government asserts, however, that Williams lacks the qualifications necessary to offer expert testimony on subjects two and three, both of which concern the relationship between the Taliban and Iran. *Id.* More specifically, the government contends that Williams has little expertise on Afghanistan or the Taliban, having focused the majority of his scholarly endeavors on the Russian Caucasus and Turkey, and that he has no specialized education or training on Iran. *Id.* at 6–21. The government also points to mistakes and inconsistencies in testimony offered by Williams in other GTMO proceedings as evidence of his lack of expertise. *Id.* at 22–30.

The court disagrees with the government's assessment of Williams's expertise. The government itself has previously relied on Williams as an expert on the Taliban. Williams authored a book published in 2001 by U.S. Army Publications entitled "Afghanistan 101: A Guide to the Afghan Theater of Operations," GE 100 ¶ 5, and has lectured on the Taliban and Afghanistan at the U.S. Special Operations Command at Macdill Air Force Base ("The Role of Foreign Fighters in the Taliban Insurgency"), Air Force Special Operations Command at Hurlburt Airfield ("Waging Counter-Insurgency in Afghanistan 1842–2008"), the Joint Information Operations Warfare Command at Lackland Air Force Base ("Background on Islam, Suicide Terrorism and Jihad in the Middle East") and the Central Intelligence Agency's Counter Terrorist Center ("Profiling Afghan Suicide Bombers"), GE 111B (Curriculum Vitae of Brian Williams) at 9–10. Williams has worked for a U.S. Army Information Operations team at NATO Headquarters in Kabul and wrote the Joint Information Operations Warfare Command's field manual on Afghanistan. PE 111A ¶ 2.

Williams has traveled to Afghanistan on four occasions since the fall of the Taliban government. *Id.* He has also authored articles discussing Afghanistan in the age of Taliban-rule that have been published in scholarly journals, as well as policy journals and other collections. PE 111B at 3–7. Furthermore, Williams has taught at least one course covering modern Afghan history, including the period of the Taliban, titled "Empires and Invasions: A History of Afghanistan from Genghis Khan to the War on Terror." GE 95 at 1.

Given his demonstrated scholarship on the history of the Taliban, as well as the government's own reliance on him as an expert on matters related to the Taliban, it is clear that Williams possesses the specialized knowledge needed to offer expert opinion testimony on the Taliban and Afghanistan. Indeed, as previously noted, the government has conceded that Williams is qualified to offer expert testimony about the battle for Mazar-e-Sharif during the rise of the Taliban and about the presence of al-Qaida bases in Herat province during the Taliban's rule over Afghanistan. *See* Mar. 31 Tr. at 6.

Such expertise could not be obtained without developing a specialized knowledge of the Taliban's relationships with its regional neighbors, including Iran. It is well-established that Iran, which shares a 400-mile border with Afghanistan, played a central role in Afghan affairs during the Taliban's rise to power, providing substantial military support to the Northern Alliance and other groups in their struggle for control of Afghanistan. *See, e.g.,* PE 75 (Thomas H. Johnson, Ismail Khan, Herat, and Iranian Influence, 3 Strategic Insights, no. 7, July 2004, at 1) at 3; PE 76 (Mohsen M. Milani, Iran's Policy Towards Afghanistan, 60 MIDDLE E.J., no. 2, Spring 2006, at 235) at 244 (noting that Iran provided key support to the Northern Alliance during the battle for Mazar-e-Sharif, in which the Taliban ultimately prevailed with the aid of Pakistan).

Although the fact that Williams has little demonstrated expertise in Iran is relevant to the weight that the court ascribes to his views on the relationship between the Taliban and Iran, it does not preclude him from offering expert testimony on the issue. Accordingly, the court concludes that Williams is qualified to offer expert opinion testimony on all of the issues for which he has been proffered

* * *

V. CONCLUSION

For the foregoing reasons, the court denies the petition for a writ of habeas corpus, An Order consistent with this Memorandum Opinion is issued separately and contemporaneously this 27th day of May, 2011.

EXERCISES

1. At Kevin's trial for bank robbery, the government seeks to introduce expert testimony that shoeprints found at the scene "could have been made" by the shoes that Kevin was wearing at the time of his arrest. Kevin's defense attorney objects on the ground that such testimony fails to meet the standard for admissibility prescribed in *Daubert*. The court agrees to conduct a *Daubert* hearing. As the prosecutor, what type of testimony should you elicit at the *Daubert* hearing?

2. Dorel, an experienced stucco business owner and operator, took delivery of a stucco application pump and the accompanying high-pressure hose directly from the manufacturing plant. The next day, less than 15 minutes into its first operation, the high-pressure hose dislodged and struck Dorel's legs, causing multiple bone fractures and extensive soft-tissue injuries. Dorel files a products liability suit against the manufacturer. Assume that you represent Dorel and the expense of litigation is not a concern. What type of experts (*e.g.*, area of expertise, qualifications) will you seek to hire to prove your case?

3.   The defendant was arrested for alleging engaging in a drug distribution conspiracy. At trial the government called the Drug Enforcement Agent who conducted the investigation to testify both as a lay witnesses (or fact witness) and as an expert witness. The Agent testified about facts he had obtained through the investigation. Then the government played several recorded phone conversations for the jury, and asked the Agent to give his expert opinion about the meaning of various terms used in the calls. Do you see any potential issues with allowing a witness to testify in this dual capacity?

Chapter 9

PRIVILEGES

§ 9.01 INTRODUCTION

"Privileged communications" are an exception to the general principle that the law is entitled to every man's evidence. Professor Wigmore has delineated four conditions that courts generally have considered fundamental to the establishment of any privilege:

(1) The communications must originate in a *confidence* they will not be disclosed.

(2) This element of *confidentiality* must be essential to the full and satisfactory maintenance of the relation between the parties.

(3) The *relation* must be one that in the opinion of the community ought to be sedulously *fostered*.

(4) The injury that would inure to the relation by the disclosure of the communications must be *greater than the benefit* thereby gained for the correct disposal of litigation.

8 Wigmore, Evidence § 2285 (McNaughton rev. 1961).

Since these conditions are fundamental to all privileges, their application has given rise to universal problems in interpreting the concept of confidentiality and in defining the limits of the protection through waiver. Illustrative are the spousal (husband-wife), physician-patient, and attorney-client privileges.[1] For brevity's sake, the material in this chapter focuses on the attorney-client privilege because it is the most complex of all contemporary privileges. The attorney-client privilege has given rise to the greatest number and most varied kinds of problems in its application, and is the privilege most essential for a practicing attorney to understand, because it is the privilege that he or she will encounter most frequently. Initially, however, the chapter surveys the spousal and physician-patient privileges. The chapter then draws parallels to these privileges during the more extended discussion of the attorney-client privilege.

---

[1] These three privileges, of course, represent only a fraction of the constitutional, common law, and statutory privileges that exist. Other privileges include: the Fifth Amendment privilege against compelled self-incrimination; a variety of governmental privileges for information collected and reported through different agencies, for national security secrets, for government deliberations and for police informers; and privileges for special relationships that society perceives as needing to be fostered: priest-penitent, clergyman-communicant, and journalist-informant.

§ 9.02 SPOUSAL PRIVILEGE

[A] Scope and Rationale

The concept of spousal privilege actually encompasses two separate privileges. The first privilege is an immunity, which, in the past, courts have considered a ground for witness incompetency. This privilege precludes a party from calling an individual as a witness against his or her spouse on any matter, regardless of how or when the spousal-witness acquired the information sought. The sole criterion for the application of this privilege is that the witness be married to the party against whom he or she is asked to testify when the testimony is sought. The purpose of this privilege is to protect the marital relationship. Courts believe that requiring one spouse to testify against the other would place too great a strain on the relationship.

The second spousal privilege is the "marital communications" privilege. This privilege protects communications between a man and woman who are lawfully married at the time the communications are made, if those communications are confidential (intended to be confidential and not knowingly made in the presence of others). Courts justify this privilege not only on the rationale of the spousal immunity described above, but also on the ground it is necessary to encourage confidential communications between spouses, as they foster the "harmony and sanctity of the marital relationship." *Trammel v. United States*, 445 U.S. 40, 44 (1980).

There is more agreement as to the individuals to whom the marital communications privilege runs than there is over whom the immunity covers, because, unlike the immunity, the marital communications privilege is based on the confidential nature of the communication involved. Because both parties are perceived as beneficiaries of the stable marital relationship, and therefore of the privilege that protects it, courts have held that either spouse may raise the privilege to exclude the testimony. A number of courts, however, have perceived the communicating spouse to be the holder of the privilege. Even under this more restricted view, where the testifying spouse was not the communicating spouse, courts have still accorded the testifying spouse the authority to exercise the privilege on behalf of the nontestifying spouse if, because the nontestifying spouse was absent from the proceeding, he or she was unable to protect his or her interests personally.

[B] Exceptions to Spousal Privilege

As courts have based both aspects of the spousal privilege on social policy, they also have recognized exceptions to the privilege on the same ground. Although these exceptions vary from one jurisdiction to another, they are all based on the belief that in certain situations the rationale for the spousal privilege is no longer applicable, or that the disclosure of the information that the privilege otherwise would have protected serves a greater good than the maintenance of confidentiality. Under the fourth condition identified by Professor Wigmore (*see* § 9.01), these exceptions are applicable in situations in which the benefit to be gained by the litigation's correct disposition is greater than the injury that might result to the marital relationship from disclosure. Such situations generally would include: civil actions between the spouses arising from the martial relationship itself, prosecutions for crimes committed by one spouse against the other or against the children of either, and prosecutions in which one spouse offers the other's communications in his or her defense.

Courts have recognized an additional exception to the spousal immunity for communications relating to joint criminal activity between the spouses. However, the courts have disagreed whether the exception applies to both the marital communications privilege and the spousal immunity. It is generally agreed that confidential marital communications enjoy a privileged status in order to protect marital privacy and foster frank communications between spouses. The spousal immunity, on the other hand, is perceived as protecting marital harmony. If spouses were required to testify against one another it would likely injure, if not destroy, any relationship the couple might have. Most courts have concluded that the public interest in discovering the truth about criminal activities outweighs the public interest in marital privacy, but not in marital harmony. Consequently, they have recognized the joint participation exception only with regard to the former: the marital communication privilege. *See In re Grand Jury Subpoena United States*, 755 F.2d 1022 (2d Cir. 1985); *United States v. Ammar*, 714 F.2d 238 (3d Cir. 1983).

Courts have increasingly overridden both the spousal immunity and marital communications privilege where the threat of the marriage's deterioration is absent. For example, when spouses are separated, even though not by judicial decree, and there is little hope of reconciliation, courts have held that society's need to obtain evidence outweighs the formality of the relationship. *See In re Witness Before Grand Jury*, 791 F.2d 234, 238–239 (2d Cir. 1986); *United States v. Byrd*, 750 F.2d 585 (7th Cir. 1984).

[C]　Spousal Privilege Under Federal Rules of Evidence

Under Rule 501 of the Federal Rules of Evidence, the principles of the common law govern privileges, except in actions in which the state law supplies the rule of decision. In such actions, state law also determines the privilege of a witness or party.

[*See* Fed. R. Evid. 501]

Congress adopted this general privilege rule instead of a number of specific proposed provisions that addressed individual privileges. These proposed rules only codified certain common-law privilege principles. Proposed Rule 505, for example, would have codified the spousal immunity privilege but not the marital communications privilege. Although not adopted, these rules and their accompanying Advisory Committee's Notes have been influential in the interpretation and development of the federal common law under Rule 501 in those actions in which federal law supplies the rule of decision. For the text of Proposed Rule 505 and its accompanying Advisory Committee Note, *see* Appendix B, in the separate supplement pamphlet accompanying this casebook.

The following opinion illustrates how federal courts have generally responded to both the spousal privilege and the marital communications privilege, and illustrates the application of a number of important concepts (*e.g.*, waiver, the crime/fraud exception, and negative inferences) to each.

IN RE RESERVE FUND SECURITIES AND DERIVATIVE LITIGATION EYEGLASSES
United States District Court, S.D. New York
275 F.R.D. 154 (2011)

MEMORANDUM OPINION & ORDER

PAUL G. GARDEPHE, DISTRICT JUDGE:

The Commission seeks an order compelling Defendants to produce approximately sixty emails between Bruce Bent II and his wife, Rebecca Bent, exchanged on September 15 and 16, 2008 (the "Bent emails"). Defendants contend that these emails are protected by the marital privilege. (Oct. 22, 2010 Joint Ltr. at 7) In a November 29, 2010 Order — familiarity with which is presumed — this Court reserved decision concerning the production of these emails and directed "the Commission and Defendants to make submissions . . . addressing this issue in greater detail and citing supporting legal authority." (Nov. 29, 2010 Order at 17) The parties have provided additional briefing, and the issue is ripe for resolution.

I. THE MARITAL COMMUNICATIONS PRIVILEGE

The law recognizes two types of marital privilege. The first is referred to as the "adverse spousal testimony" privilege and permits an individual to refuse to testify adversely against his or her spouse. *See Trammel v. United States*, 445 U.S. 40, 53, 100 S. Ct. 906, 63 L. Ed. 2d 186 (1980). "This privilege rests on the notion that a husband and wife should be able to trust each other completely, and that marriage is a sanctuary. The privilege is described as being 'broadly aimed at protecting marital harmony.'" *United States v. Premises Known as 281 Syosset Woodbury Rd., Woodbury, N.Y.*, 71 F.3d 1067, 1070 (2d Cir. 1995) (quoting *In re Grand Jury Subpoena United States*, 755 F.2d 1022, 1027 (2d Cir. 1985), *vacated on other grounds sub nom. United States v. Koecher*, 475 U.S. 133, 106 S. Ct. 1253, 89 L. Ed. 2d 103 (1986)).

The second type of marital privilege, referred to as the "marital communications privilege," protects private and confidential communications between spouses from disclosure. *See Blau v. United States*, 340 U.S. 332, 333, 71 S. Ct. 301, 95 L. Ed. 306 (1951); *Premises Known as 281 Syosset Woodbury Rd., Woodbury, N.Y.*, 71 F.3d at 1070. It provides that "[c]ommunications between the spouses, privately made, are generally assumed to have been intended to be confidential, and hence they are privileged . . . ." *Wolfle v. United States*, 291 U.S. 7, 14, 54 S. Ct. 279, 78 L. Ed. 617 (1934). The marital communications privilege is at issue here. There are three prerequisites for assertion of the marital communications privilege:

(1) a valid marriage at the time of the communication, *United States v. Lustig*, 555 F.2d 737, 747–48 (9th Cir. 1977) (privilege claim denied in part because common law marriage of defendant is not recognized as valid under state law), *cert. denied*, 434 U.S. 926, 98 S. Ct. 408, 54 L. Ed. 2d 285 (1977); (2) the privilege "applies only to utterances or expressions intended by one spouse to convey a message to the other," *id.* at 748; and (3) the communication must have been made in confidence, which is presumed, *Pereira v. United States*, 347 U.S. 1, 6, 74 S. Ct. 358, 98 L. Ed. 435 (1954).

United States v. Premises Known as 281 Syosset Woodbury Rd., 862 F. Supp. 847, 853–54 (E.D.N.Y. 1994).

"The basis of the immunity given to communications between husband and wife is the protection of marital confidences, regarded as so essential to the preservation of the marriage relationship as to outweigh the disadvantages to the administration of justice which the privilege entails. . . . " *Wolfle*, 291 U.S. at 14, 54 S. Ct. 279. "The confidential communications privilege . . . provides assurance that all private statements between spouses — aptly called the 'best solace of human existence,' — will be forever free from public exposure." *In re Witness Before Grand Jury*, 791 F.2d 234, 237 (2d Cir. 1986) (quoting *Trammel*, 445 U.S. at 51, 100 S. Ct. 906) (internal quotations omitted).

The marital communications privilege, however, like other evidentiary privileges, deprives "fact-finders of potentially useful information." *United States v. Etkin*, 2008 U.S. Dist. LEXIS 12834, [at *5] (S.D.N.Y. Feb. 20, 2008) (citing *In re Witness Before the Grand Jury*, 791 F.2d at 237); see *Trammel*, 445 U.S. at 50–51, 100 S. Ct. 906 (1980) ("Testimonial exclusionary rules and privileges contravene the fundamental principle that 'the public . . . has a right to every man's evidence.' " (quoting *United States v. Bryan*, 339 U.S. 323, 331, 70 S. Ct. 724, 94 L. Ed. 884 (1950))); *United States v. Int'l Bhd. of Teamsters, Chauffeurs, Warehousemen & Helpers of Am., AFL-CIO*, 119 F.3d 210, 214 (2d Cir. 1997) (an evidentiary privilege must be "strictly confined within the narrowest possible limits consistent with the logic of its principle" (internal quotations omitted)). "As such, [a privilege] must be strictly construed and accepted 'only to the very limited extent that permitting a refusal to testify or excluding relevant evidence has a public good transcending the normally predominant principle of utilizing all rational means for ascertaining truth.' " *Trammel*, 445 U.S. at 50, 100 S. Ct. 906 (citations omitted).

" 'The party asserting an evidentiary privilege, such as the marital communications privilege, bears the burden of establishing all of the essential elements involved.' " *United States v. Acker*, 52 F.3d 509, 514–15 (4th Cir. 1995) (quoting *United States v. White*, 950 F.2d 426, 430 (7th Cir. 1991)); *Mercator Corp. v. U.S. of Am. (In re Grand Jury Subpoenas Dated March 19, 2002 & August 2, 2002)*, 318 F.3d 379, 384 (2d Cir. 2003) ("It is, moreover, well established that the party invoking a privilege bears the burden of establishing its applicability to the case at hand." (citations omitted)); *Morganroth & Morganroth v. DeLorean*, 123 F.3d 374, 383 (6th Cir. 1997) ("As the trial judge correctly held, the person asserting the marital privilege has the burden of proving that a communication is a marital communication."); *United States v. Mardis*, 2011 U.S. Dist. LEXIS 2736, [at *24] (W.D. Tenn. Jan. 11, 2011) (" '[T]he person asserting the marital privilege has the burden of proving that a communication is a marital communication.'" (quoting *Morganroth & Morganroth v. DeLorean*, 123 F.3d 374, 383 (6th Cir. 1997))); *see also Chevron Corp. v. Donziger*, 783 F. Supp. 2d 713, 730, 2011 U.S. Dist. LEXIS 49220, at *46 (S.D.N.Y. May 9, 2011) ("As the party asserting privilege, the [plaintiffs] had the burden of establishing it."); *Seyler v. T-Systems N. Am., Inc.*, 771 F. Supp. 2d 284, 287 (S.D.N.Y. 2011) ("The party claiming the [attorney-client] privilege bears the burden of establishing it." (citations omitted)).

Here, the parties do not dispute that there was a "valid marriage" and that the emails were "utterances or expressions intended by one spouse to convey a message to the other." *See Premises Known as 281 Syosset Woodbury Rd.*, 862 F. Supp. at 854. Accordingly, only the third prerequisite for assertion of the marital communication privilege is at issue: whether the Bent email communications "were made in confidence." *Id.*

II. RMCI'S EMAIL POLICY

In September 2008, Bent II was the Vice Chairman, President, and part-owner of RMCI. (Cmplt. ¶¶ 22, 19) The emails in question were exchanged by Bent II and his wife on September 15 and 16, 2008 — the crucial two-day period following Lehman Brothers' September 14, 2008 bankruptcy announcement, during which a run on the Reserve Primary Fund ensued, leading to the Fund's collapse and this litigation. The emails were transmitted by Bent II using an RMCI computer and were stored on RMCI's server. (Jan. 12, 2011 SEC Ltr. at 4; Dec. 6, 2010 Def. Supp. Br. at 2; Oct. 22, 2010 Joint Ltr., Ex. E) It is undisputed that in September 2008, RMCI had in place a written "Email Policy" and that Bent II was aware of that policy. (Oct. 22, 2010 Joint Ltr., Ex. E; Dec. 6, 2010 Def. Supp. Br. 11)

The stated purpose of RMCI's email policy is to "promot[e] the use of e-mail as an efficient communication tool" and "to prevent unauthorized or inadvertent disclosure of sensitive company information via a forwarded or redirected email." (Oct. 22, 2010 Joint Ltr., Ex. E) To that end, the policy states that "Employees must exercise extreme caution when forwarding any email from inside the Reserve to any other email account. The email address you are forwarding to must be valid and verified. . . . Sensitive information . . . will not be forwarded via any means, unless that email is critical to business and is encrypted. . . ." (*Id.*) The policy also states that "Employees may use only the e-mail system provided by Reserve to communicate with clients and the public. Use of outside Internet service providers or Websites providing e-mail accounts while on Reserve's premises is prohibited." (*Id.*)

RMCI's email policy makes clear that RMCI's email system should be used only for business purposes: "Employees should limit their use of the e-mail resources to official business. . . ." To the extent that personal messages nonetheless appear in an employee's inbox, the policy directs them to delete such communications: "Employees should also remove personal and transitory messages from personal inboxes on a regular basis. . . ." (*Id.*)

RMCI's email policy also warns employees that their email communications are saved and are subject to disclosure, whether those communications are directed to clients or to the public at large:

Employees are reminded that client/public e-mail communications received by and sent from Reserve are automatically saved regardless of content. Since these communications, like written materials, may be subject to disclosure to regulatory agencies or the courts, you should carefully consider the content of any message you intend to transmit. . . .

(*Id.*)

The policy further states that while employee email will not be routinely monitored by RMCI, the company reserves the right to access employee email:

The e-mail system administrator will not routinely monitor employee's e-mail and will take reasonable precautions to protect the privacy of e-mail. However, the company reserves the right to access an employee's e-mail for a legitimate business reason, such as the need to access information when an employee is absent for an extended period of time, to diagnose and resolve technical problems involving system hardware, software or communications, or to investigate possible misuse of e-mail when a reasonable suspicion of abuse exists or in conjunction with an approved investigation.

(*Id.*)

DISCUSSION

I. REASONABLE EXPECTATION OF PRIVACY IN EMAILS SENT OVER AN EMPLOYER'S EMAIL SYSTEM

A. Applicable Law

Although communications between spouses are presumed to be confidential, see In re Witness Before Grand Jury, 791 F.2d at 239 (citing *Blau v. United States*, 340 U.S. at 333, 71 S. Ct. 301), "wherever a communication, because of its nature or the circumstances under which it was made, was obviously not intended to be confidential, it is not a privileged communication. And, when made in the presence of a third party, such communications are usually regarded as not privileged because not made in confidence." *Wolfle*, 291 U.S. at 14, 54 S. Ct. 279. "There can [be] no confidential communication where the spouses are on actual or constructive notice that their communications may be overheard, read, or otherwise monitored by third parties." *Etkin*, 2008 U.S. Dist. LEXIS 12834, [at *12] n. 5 (citing *United States v. Griffin*, 440 F.3d 1138 (9th Cir. 2006); *United States v. Madoch*, 149 F.3d 596 (7th Cir. 1998); *United States v. Harrelson*, 754 F.2d 1153 (5th Cir. 1985)). "Each case should be given an individualized look to see if the party requesting the protection of . . . privilege was reasonable in [his] actions." *Convertino v. U.S. Dep't of Justice*, 674 F. Supp. 2d 97, 110 (D.D.C. 2009) (citing *Curto v. Med. World Commc'ns, Inc.*, 2006 U.S. Dist. LEXIS 29387, 2006 WL 1318387, at *6 (E.D.N.Y. May 15, 2006)); *see also O'Connor v. Ortega*, 480 U.S. 709, 718, 107 S. Ct. 1492, 94 L. Ed. 2d 714 (1987) ("Given the great variety of work environments[,] . . . the question whether an employee has a reasonable expectation of privacy must be addressed on a case-by-case basis.").

To determine whether Bent II had a reasonable expectation of privacy in the emails he sent to his wife over RMCI's server, the Court must consider whether he was on actual or constructive notice that these communications could be "read[ ] or otherwise monitored by third parties." *See In re Asia Global Crossing, Ltd.*, 322 B.R. 247, 258–59 (Bankr. S.D.N.Y. 2005) ("[T]he question of privilege comes down to whether the intent to communicate in confidence was objectively reasonable. . . . Accordingly, the objective reasonableness of that intent will depend on the company's e-mail policies regarding use and monitoring, its access to the e-mail system, and the notice provided to the employees."). In *In re Asia Global Crossing, Ltd.*, the court set forth a four-factor test — which has been widely adopted — regarding the "reasonable expectation of privacy" determination in the context of email transmitted over and maintained on a company server:

> (1) does the corporation maintain a policy banning personal or other objectionable use, (2) does the company monitor the use of the employee's computer or e-mail, (3) do third parties have a right of access to the computer or e-mails, and (4) did the corporation notify the employee, or was the employee aware, of the use and monitoring policies?

In re Asia Global Crossing, Ltd., 322 B.R. at 257.

Because an employer's announced policies regarding the confidentiality and handling of email and other electronically stored information on company computers and servers are critically important in determining whether an employee has a reasonable expectation of privacy in such materials, the cases in this area tend to be highly fact-specific and the outcomes are largely determined by the particular policy language adopted by the employer. *See, e.g., Leventhal v. Knapek*, 266 F.3d 64, 73–74 (2d Cir. 2001) (State agency employee found to have reasonable expectation of privacy in personal computer files stored on his work computer where agency (1) had no policy regarding the confidentiality of personal email or other electronically stored information maintained on agency computers; (2) "did not prohibit the mere storage of personal materials in [agency] computer[s]"; (3) did not have a "general practice of routinely conducting searches of office computers"; and (4) had not "placed [the employee] on notice that he should have no expectation of privacy in the contents of his office computer"); *Muick v. Glenayre Elecs.*, 280 F.3d 741, 743 (7th Cir. 2002) ("[the employee] had no right of privacy in the computer that [the employer] had lent him for use in the workplace. . . . [Where an employer has] announced [a policy saying] that it could inspect the laptops that it furnished for the use of its employees, . . . this destroyed any reasonable expectation of privacy that [the employee] might have had and so scotches his claim."); *Miller v. Blattner*, 676 F. Supp. 2d 485, 497 (E.D. La. 2009) ("Where, as here, an employer has a rule prohibiting personal computer use and a published policy that emails on Allpax's computers were the property of Allpax, an employee cannot reasonably expect privacy in their prohibited communications."); *Etkin*, 2008 U.S. Dist. LEXIS 12834, [at *15–*16] ("employees do not have a reasonable expectation of privacy in the contents of their work computers when their employers communicate to them via a flash-screen warning a policy under which the employer may monitor or inspect the computers at any time" (citations omitted)); *Sims v. Lakeside School*, 2007 U.S. Dist. LEXIS 69568, [at *3] (W.D. Wash. Sept. 20, 2007) ("where an employer indicates that it can inspect laptops that it furnished for use of its employees, the employee does not have a reasonable expectation of privacy over the employer-furnished laptop" (citations omitted)); *Thygeson v. U.S. Bancorp*, 2004 U.S. Dist. LEXIS 18863, [at *72] (D. Or. Sept. 15, 2004) ("[W]hen, as here, an employer accesses its own computer network and has an explicit policy banning personal use of office computers and permitting monitoring, an employee has no reasonable expectation of privacy."); *Kelleher v. City of Reading*, 2002 U.S. Dist. LEXIS 9408, [at *24-*26] (E.D. Pa. May 29, 2002) (because employer's email system was to be used solely for official city business, employee had no reasonable expectation of privacy in email sent over employer's email system).B. Application of *Asia Global Crossing's* Four-Part Test

1. RMCI's Policy Regarding Personal Use

Under *Asia Global Crossing's* four-part test for determining whether an employee has a reasonable expectation of privacy in email stored on a company system, the first issue is whether "the corporation maintain[s] a policy banning personal or other objectionable use." See In re Asia Global Crossing, Ltd., 322 B.R. at 257. Here, RMCI's email policy clearly bans personal use of RMCI's email system:

> Employees should limit their use of the e-mail resources to official business . . . . Employees should . . . remove personal and transitory messages from personal inboxes on a regular basis. . . .

(Oct. 22, 2010 Joint Ltr., Ex. E (emphasis added))

Defendants' argument (Dec. 6, 2010 Def. Supp Br. at 8–9) that "should" — as used in RMCI's email policy — is precatory or aspirational is not persuasive. The dictionary tells us that "should" is "[u]sed to express duty or obligation." Webster's II New College Dictionary 1022 (2001); accord Webster's New Universal Unabridged Dictionary 1679 (2d ed. 1983) ("should" is "used to express . . . obligation, duty, propriety, necessity . . . ."); *see also Bord v. Rubin*, 1998 U.S. Dist. LEXIS 11364, [at *11] (S.D.N.Y. July 27, 1998) ("Grammatically speaking, 'should' is the past tense of 'shall' and therefore is defined as a verb meant 'to express duty or obligation.'" (citing Webster's II New Riverside University Dictionary 1078 (1984))); *cf. United States v. Anderson*, 798 F.2d 919, 924 (7th Cir. 1986) ("The common interpretation of the word 'should' is 'shall' and thus a straight-forward construction of [the code of ethics] reveals that it imposes a mandatory rule of conduct upon a judge.").

While "should" "has various shades of meaning" and "does not automatically denote . . . a mandatory . . . direction," and while "the meaning depends on the context in which the words are found," *Bord*, 1998 U.S. Dist. LEXIS 11364, [at *12] (citing *McDonnell Douglas Corp. v. Islamic Republic of Iran*, 758 F.2d 341, 347 (8th Cir. 1985) (noting that "[the] verb 'should' has various shades of meaning")), there is nothing in RMCI's email policy suggesting that "should" was intended to be precatory or aspirational.

Defendants' contention that the policy's direction that employees "remove personal . . . messages from personal inboxes on a regular basis" (Oct. 22, 2010 Joint Ltr., Ex. E) somehow authorizes employees — in contravention of the policy's preceding sentence — to use the RMCI system for personal emails (Dec. 6, 2010 Def. Supp. Br. at 8) is not convincing. While this provision acknowledges the possibility that employees may receive personal email from outsiders over RMCI's system, it does not undermine the mandatory nature of the preceding sentence. Indeed, it reaffirms the prohibition on personal use by instructing employees to regularly delete any personal messages they receive from their inboxes.

Defendants argue, however, that RMCI tacitly allowed employees "to send personal emails [over RMCI's system] and did not intervene," and that courts have considered not only an employer's written policy but "how an employer applies or enforces its email policy." (Dec. 6, 2010 Def. Supp. Br. at 9) Defendants rely on *DeGeer v. Gillis*, 2010 U.S. Dist. LEXIS 97457 . . . (N.D. Ill. Sept. 17, 2010), *Curto v. Med. World Commc'ns, Inc.*, 2006 U.S. Dist. LEXIS 29387 . . . (E.D.N.Y. May 15, 2006), and *United States v. Long*, 64 M.J. 57 (C.A.A.F. 2006), for the proposition that how an employer "applies" or "enforces" its email policy is a factor in determining whether an employee has a reasonable expectation of privacy in email transmitted over a company system. None of these cases suggests that RMCI's clear prohibition against personal use of its email system should be ignored.

DeGeer v. Gillis, 2010 U.S. Dist. LEXIS 97457 . . . (N.D. Ill. Sept. 17, 2010) provides no support for Defendants' arguments. In that case, the court considered whether plaintiff "waived the attorney-client privilege by communicating with his counsel over his work email address and on his [company-]supplied laptop." Noting that "the record does not contain [the company's] computer usage policy" and that the court could not "determine whether [the company] prohibited employees from using their company computers to conduct personal legal matters," and stating that "[t]here is no evidence with respect to whether DeGeer personally knew about a [company] computer usage policy," the court found no waiver. *Id.* Here, of course, there is evidence both that RMCI prohibited personal use and that Bent II was aware of this policy.

In *Curto v. Med. World Commc'ns, Inc.*, 2006 U.S. Dist. LEXIS 29387 . . . (E.D.N.Y. May 15, 2006), plaintiff's employer's email policy provided that "[e]mployees should not have an expectation of privacy in anything they create, store, send, or receive on the computer system. The computer system belongs to the company and may be used only for business purposes." Plaintiff — who worked at home — was issued laptop computers by her employer. The "laptops were not connected to [the company's] computer server and were not located in [the company's] offices." *Id.* at [*17]. Plaintiff's employment was terminated, and before returning both laptops, plaintiff deleted all personal files, including communications to counsel. *Id.* at [*3]. After she filed a lawsuit against her employer, the company did a forensic analysis of the laptops, and recovered emails between plaintiff and her counsel that had been sent by plaintiff "through her personal AOL account[,] which did not go through [her employer's] servers." *Id.* at [*9]. The court held that the attorney-client privilege had not been waived as to these communications. *Id.* at [*5].

Curto likewise provides little guidance here. That case turns on the question of whether plaintiff's inadvertent disclosure of attorney-client communications resulted in a waiver. *Id.* at [*9]. In finding that the privilege had not been waived, the court ruled that plaintiff — in deleting her personal files from the laptops — had taken reasonable steps to ensure the confidentiality of her attorney-client communications. *Id.* at [*9, 17]. Given that the laptops issued to plaintiff were not connected to her employer's computer system, it was not even clear in *Curto* that the employer's email policy applied. Finally, the *Curto* court was careful to say that its "holding is limited to the question of whether an employee's personal use of a company-owned computer in her home waives any applicable attorney-client privilege or work product immunity that may attach to the employee's computer files and/or e-mails. It does not purport to address an employee's right to privacy in an office computer in general." *Id.* at [*25] (emphasis added). Here, there is no question that RMCI's email policy applies and no dispute that Bent II sent the emails in question over his work email account and over RMCI's email system.

The *Curto* court did not address the cases holding that an employee has no expectation of privacy in workplace computer files where the employer explicitly informs the employee that no expectation of privacy exists, finding that all of these cases arose under the Fourth Amendment or common law, and not in the context of determining waiver of the attorney-client privilege. *Id.* at [*16]. To the extent that *Curto* suggests that the reasonable expectation of privacy cases are not relevant to a determination of whether the prerequisites for assertion of an evidentiary privilege exist, the case will not be followed here.

Finally, Defendants cite to *United States v. Long*, 64 M.J. 57 (C.A.A.F. 2006), a case from the U.S. Court of Appeals for the Armed Forces that is likewise not on point. The defendant in Long sought to suppress inculpatory emails she sent over the military's email servers. Her emails were retrieved by a network administrator at the request of law enforcement officers searching for evidence of Long's misconduct. *Id.* at 59. In concluding that defendant had a reasonable expectation of privacy concerning her emails, the court relied on the fact that the defendant "was authorized to use the government computer for personal use." *Id.* at 65; see also *id.* at 64 (noting that network administrator testified that "using the network to send personal e-mails . . . was considered authorized [use]"). Here, of course, RMCI's policy explicitly states that "[e]mployees should limit their use of [RMCI's] e-mail resources to official business. . . ." (Oct. 22, 2010 Joint Ltr., Ex. E)

In sum, because RMCI's email policy bans personal use of the RMCI email system, this factor weighs in favor of finding that Bent II had no reasonable expectation of privacy in the emails he sent to his wife over that system on September 15 and 16, 2008. Where an employer's policy bans personal use of the employer's email system, courts frequently find that employees have no reasonable expectation of privacy in email transmitted over that system. *See, e.g., Miller*, 676 F. Supp. 2d at 497 ("[where] an employer has a rule prohibiting personal computer use . . . employee[s] cannot reasonably expect privacy in their prohibited communications"); *Long v. Marubeni America Corp.*, 2006 U.S. Dist. LEXIS 76594, [at *8, 9] (S.D.N.Y. Oct. 19, 2006) (no attorney-client privilege or work product protection for emails exchanged over employer's email system where employer's policy prohibited personal use of email system); *Thygeson v. U.S. Bancorp*, 2004 U.S. Dist. LEXIS 18863, [at *14] (D. Or. Sept. 15, 2004) (where employee handbook states that "personal computers . . . including e-mail . . . are intended for Company business only . . . . [and] e-mail is the exclusive property of [the

Company] and is not intended for personal use," no reasonable expectation of privacy in email sent over employer's email system); *Kelleher v. City of Reading*, 2002 U.S. Dist. LEXIS 9408, [at *26] (E.D. Pa. 2002) (because employer's email system was to be used solely for official city business, employee had no reasonable expectation of privacy in email sent over employer's email system); *Scott v. Beth Israel Med. Ctr. Inc.*, 17 Misc.3d 934, 940, 847 N.Y.S.2d 436 (N.Y. Sup. Ct. 2007) (email sent over employer's email system not subject to attorney-client privilege where employer's policy states that email system "should be used for business purposes only").

2. Routine Monitoring of Employee Email

The second *Asia Global Crossing* factor is whether the employer monitors employee email. RMCI's email policy provides that the company will not "routinely monitor employee's e-mail and will take reasonable precautions to protect the privacy of e-mail." However, in its policy, RMCI "reserves the right to access an employee's e-mail for a legitimate business reason . . . or in conjunction with an approved investigation." (Oct. 22, 2010 Joint Ltr., Ex. E)

Where an employer reserves the right to access or inspect an employee's email or work computer, courts often find that the employee has no reasonable expectation of privacy. See *Scott*, 17 Misc.3d at 940, 847 N.Y.S.2d 436 (Finding that "[t]he second [*Global Crossing*] requirement [was] satisfied because [the company's] policy allows for monitoring. Although [the company] acknowledge[d] that it did not monitor [the employee's] e-mail, it retain[ed] the right to do so in the e-mail policy," which notified employees that the employer "reserves the right to access and disclose [information on its computers] at any time without prior notice."); see also *Muick v. Glenayre Elecs.*, 280 F.3d 741, 743 (7th Cir. 2002) ("[the employer] had announced that it could inspect the laptops that it furnished for the use of its employees, and this destroyed any reasonable expectation of privacy that [the employee] might have had and so scotches his claim"); *United States v. Angevine*, 281 F.3d 1130, 1135 (10th Cir. 2002) (no reasonable expectation of privacy where employer "reserve[d] the right to inspect electronic mail usage by any person at any time without prior notice"); *Thygeson*, 2004 U.S. Dist. LEXIS 18863, [at *69] (no reasonable expectation of privacy in computer files and email where employer had reserved right to monitor computer files and email); *Garrity v. John Hancock Mutual Life Ins. Co.*, 2002 U.S. Dist. LEXIS 8343, [at *2] (D. Mass. May 7, 2002) (no reasonable expectation of privacy where employer email policy states that "[i]t is not company policy to intentionally inspect E- mail usage" but warns that "there may be business or legal situations that necessitate company review of E-mail messages and other documents" and "management reserves the right to access all E-mail files").

Because RMCI expressly reserved the right to access and monitor its employees' emails, the second Asia Global Crossing factor weighs against finding a reasonable expectation of privacy.

3. Third Parties' Right of Access to Emails

The third *Asia Global Crossing* factor requires courts to consider whether, under the employer's email policy, third parties have a right of access to the employee's emails. Here, RMCI's policy explicitly warns employees that their email communications will be automatically saved and are subject to review by RMCI and disclosure to third parties:

> Employees are reminded that client/public e-mail communications received by and sent from Reserve are automatically saved regardless of content. Since these communications, like written materials, may be subject to disclosure to regulatory agencies or the courts, you should carefully consider the content of any message you intend to transmit. . . .

(Oct. 22, 2010 Joint Ltr., Ex. E (emphasis added))

This provision provides clear notice to RMCI employees that their communications over RMCI's email system may be disclosed to regulators and to the courts. In the heavily regulated industry in which RMCI operates — in which companies are required by law to preserve email communications for later use by regulators or other interested parties — it is not reasonable for those using a company's email system to believe that their emails sent over that system are private. See *Garrity*, 2002 U.S. Dist. LEXIS 8343, [at *4–5]; Angevine, 281 F.3d at 1135.

4. Notice to Employees of Employer's Email Policy

There is no issue here as to the final Asia Global Crossing factor: whether the employee was aware of the employer's email policy. Here, Defendants concede that "Mr. Bent was aware of the company's e-mail policy." (Dec. 6, 2010 Def. Supp. Br. at 11)

*   *   *

Application of the four *Asia Global Crossing* factors here indicates that Bent II did not have a reasonable expectation of privacy in emails he sent or received over RMCI's email system: RMCI banned personal use of its email system; RMCI reserved its right to access employee email; RMCI warned employees that email sent over RMCI's system might be subject to disclosure to regulators and the courts; and Bent II was aware of RMCI's email policy.

Because Bent II had no reasonable expectation of privacy in emails he sent over RMCI's system, they were not sent "in confidence" and are not protected by the marital communications privilege. *United States v. Premises Known as 281 Syosset Woodbury Rd.*, 862 F. Supp. at 853 (citing *Pereira v. United States*, 347 U.S. at 6, 74 S. Ct. 358).

CONCLUSION

For the reasons stated above, the Commission's request for an order compelling Defendants to produce emails exchanged between Bent II and his wife on September 15 and 16, 2008 is GRANTED.

SO ORDERED.

EXERCISE

Rick operates a lucrative methamphetamine distribution business by mailing drugs to customers through the postal service. On several occasions Rick's wife, Brenda, agrees to deliver the packages to the post office. Rick is very careful to make sure that no one overhears his conversations with Brenda. Eventually the couple is arrested and they proceed to a joint trial. Brenda wants to testify that she did not know the contents of the package, but that her husband frequently asked her to mail suspicious packages. Rick objects, arguing that under the marital privilege Brenda is prohibited from testifying against him. How should the court rule?

§ 9.03   PHYSICIAN-PATIENT PRIVILEGE

The rationale for this privilege is that protection for patient communications is necessary in order to ensure the patient's full disclosure to the physician. Federal courts have found this rationale to be tenuous, at best. They have concluded that the desire for adequate treatment is a sufficient incentive for the patient's complete disclosure. Consequently, the physician-patient privilege has not been part of the federal common law. Thus, under Rule 501, which directs that privileges be governed by the principles of the common law, interpreted in light of reason and experience, the privilege should continue to be part of state jurisprudence, but its status in federal courts is uncertain. Federal courts, of course, will continue to apply the privilege in diversity actions, in which state law controls the parties' rights.

Significantly, Congress would not have adopted the general physician-patient privilege even under the proposed specific privilege provisions. Under proposed Rule 504, Congress would have recognized a physician-patient privilege only for communications between a *psychotherapist* and his or her patient. As the Advisory Committee explained in its Note accompanying the proposed rule, its limited recognition of a physician-patient privilege was based on the belief that because of the unique nature of psychiatric consultation and treatment, and the often embarrassing nature of the information that a patient must disclose to obtain adequate treatment, a lack of psychiatric confidentiality would jeopardize the complete disclosures required. For the text of Proposed Rule 504 and its accompanying Note, see Appendix B, in the supplement pamphlet accompanying this casebook.

Whether this limited recognition of the physician-patient privilege in the proposed rules will result in the expansion of the federal common law under the "interpreted . . . in the light of reason and experience" language of Rule 501 is yet to be determined. In recognizing the psychotherapist-patient privilege in *Jaffee v. Redmond*, 518 U.S. 1, 10 (1996), the U.S. Supreme Court contrasted the increased need for the psychotherapist privilege over the physician-patient privilege:

> Treatment by a physician for physical ailments can often proceed success-fully on the basis of a physical examination, objective information supplied by the patient, and the results of diagnostic tests. Effective psychotherapy,

by contrast, depends upon an atmosphere of confidence and trust in which the patient is willing to make a frank and complete disclosure of facts, emotions, memories, and fears. Because of the sensitive nature of the problems for which individuals consults psychotherapists, disclosure of confidential communications made during counseling sessions may cause embarrassment or disgrace. For this reason, the mere possibility of disclosure may impede development of the confidential relationship necessary for successful treatment.

The following case illustrates the complex evidentiary issues that often arise in reviewing the physician/patient privilege.

IN RE SEALED GRAND JURY SUBPOENAS
United States District Court, W.D. Virginia
810 F. Supp. 2d 788 (2011)

MEMORANDUM OPINION

Pamela Meade Sargent, United States Magistrate Judge.

These grand jury matters are before the undersigned on the court's show cause orders directed to a District of Columbia psychiatrist and his practice, the motions of a the psychiatrist and his practice to vacate or modify these orders and the motions of the Government for the court to set out procedures for review of subpoenaed medical records to protect privileged material. Based on the arguments and representations of counsel, the court will vacate the show cause orders and order the production of the subpoenaed records.

I. Facts and Procedural Background

Earlier this year, this court issued subpoenas to testify before the grand jury to a Washington, D.C., psychiatrist, and to the custodian of records for his practice, also located in Washington, D.C. The witnesses were subpoenaed to appear before the grand jury in the Abingdon Division of the Western District of Virginia. The subpoenas also required the witnesses to bring the following patient records for 2521 named individuals and for each other patient to whom the psychiatrist had prescribed a Schedule II controlled substance at any time between December 31, 2008, and March 4, 2011: "all patient medical records and billing records including, but not limited to, claim forms, operative reports, charts and histories, test results, x-rays, billing statements, appointment logs, patient assessments and evaluations, patient consents, patient referral forms, prescription files, copies of prescriptions, payment receipts, insurance records, correspondence, explanation of benefits forms, and patient progress notes." In lieu of appearance, the subpoenas allowed the witnesses to provide the requested documents along with certificates of authenticity of business records to the U.S. Attorney's Office by a date earlier than the grand jury appearance date.

The Government subsequently moved the court to issue show cause orders against the psychiatrist and the records custodian based on their failure to either appear or produce the requested records. In its motions, the Government admitted that it had received a packet containing some responsive documents by overnight delivery on the date of the scheduled grand jury appearance. Many of the documents produced had information such as patient names redacted. The packet also contained a letter from counsel representing the psychiatrist. This letter stated that many responsive documents were not being provided to the Government because the psychiatrist asserted that they were protected from production under the federal psychotherapist-patient privilege or the District of Columbia physician-patient privilege. The letter also stated that many of the responsive documents had been seized by the Government during the execution of search warrants recently on the psychiatrist's residence and office. The letter further stated that additional documents would be produced on a rolling basis over the course of the next several weeks and that a privilege log would be provided at the conclusion of the production.

The court granted the Government's motions and issued show cause orders ordering the psychiatrist and a representative of the practice to appear before the court to show cause why they should not be held in contempt for failing to comply with the grand jury subpoenas. Subsequently, the psychiatrist and his practice moved the court to vacate or modify these show cause orders. A hearing on the show cause orders and motions to vacate or modify was held. At this hearing, counsel for the psychiatrist and his practice requested the court delay its ruling pending a decision from the D.C. District Court regarding the scope of the privilege issue raised in a motion to return the patient records seized in the searches of the psychiatrist's residence and office. The court denied this motion, but granted counsel additional time and set another hearing on the show cause orders and motions to vacate or modify.

At this hearing, the parties asked the court to delay ruling. The parties sought the delay to allow the parties time to negotiate an agreed procedure for review by a "filter team" to determine which of the seized records were protected from disclosure by privilege. The court set deadlines by which each party would file a proposal with the court and scheduled another hearing.

Prior to this hearing, the Government filed motions seeking a determination from the court as to the proper procedures to be established for review of the subpoenaed and seized records to protect privileged material. The motions seek to establish a "filter team" not involved in the underlying grand jury investigation in the Western District of Virginia to review the subpoenaed and seized documents to protect from production those records covered by the federal psychotherapist-patient privilege.

At the hearing, counsel informed the court that the D.C. District Court had decided to defer its decision pending resolution of the privilege issue in this court. According to counsel, the parties had reached no agreement on the scope of the applicable privilege at issue. The parties also disagreed as to the procedure to be put in place to review the seized documents for privileged materials. The parties asked this court to determine what, if any, privilege applied to the records sought and what procedure should be used to ensure that any privileged records were adequately protected. The Government also announced that it was willing to narrow the scope of the subpoenas to seek the records of only those patients specifically named in the subpoenas, all of whom, pharmacy records reflect, were prescribed Schedule II controlled substances by the psychiatrist. The Government also represents that each of these named patients either resides in the Western District of Virginia or had prescriptions from this psychiatrist filled at a pharmacy located in the Western District of Virginia.

Further, the Government submitted the affidavit attached to the applications for the warrants to search the psychiatrist's residence and office for in camera ex parte review by the court. While the court is unable to detail the facts set forth in this affidavit without jeopardizing the ongoing criminal investigation, suffice it to say that a federal magistrate found that this affidavit set forth adequate probable cause that violations of 21 U.S.C. §§ 841(a)(1) and 846 of the Controlled Substance Act had occurred and that evidence of those crimes could be found in the psychiatrist's residence and office. In particular, the search warrants provided for the seizure of the "[p]atient medical records and billing files . . . to include, but not limited to, claim forms, operative reports, charts and histories, test results, x-rays, billing statements, appointment logs, patient assessments and evaluations, patient consents, patient referral forms, prescription files, copies of prescriptions, payment receipts, insurance records, correspondence, explanation of benefits forms, and patient progress notes for patients that visited [the psychiatrist] for medical services" for 194 of the patients specifically named in these grand jury subpoenas.

Counsel for the psychiatrist and his practice assert that, to date, almost 17,000 pages of responsive documents have been provided to the Government pursuant to these grand jury subpoenas. The Government asserts that most of these documents have been redacted to the point that they are worthless to it in its grand jury investigation. The Government also asserts that no privilege log has been provided to date.

The motions are ripe for decision.

II. Analysis

The first issue the court must determine is what, if any, privilege applies to documents sought by these grand jury subpoenas. The psychiatrist and his practice assert that many of the requested records are protected from production by the federal psychotherapist-patient privilege, see *Jaffee v. Redmond*, 518 U.S. 1, 116 S. Ct. 1923, 135 L. Ed. 2d 337 (1996), and/or the D.C. physician-patient privilege found at District of Columbia Statute § 14-307. The Government argues that the D.C. physician-patient privilege does not apply to documents sought for production before a grand jury sitting in the Western District of Virginia. While the Government concedes that the federal psychotherapist-patient privilege recognized in *Jaffee* might apply to protect certain of the psychiatrist's records, the Government argues that this privilege would not protect the records of patients who saw the psychiatrist for pain management or the treatment of chronic pain rather than psychotherapy.

In federal court proceedings regarding federal law, including grand jury proceedings, questions of evidentiary privileges are determined by federal law. See Fed. R. Evid. 501, 1101(c), (d)(2); *United States v. Gillock*, 445 U.S. 360, 367–68, 100

S. Ct. 1185, 63 L. Ed. 2d 454 (1980). The law of evidentiary privileges under the federal common law is not static. "Federal Rule of Evidence 501 provides that privileges in federal court are to be 'governed by the principles of the common law as they may be interpreted by the courts of the United States in the light of reason and experience.'" *United States v. Dunford*, 148 F.3d 385, 390 (4th Cir. 1998). Federal law, to date, does not recognize a physician-patient privilege. See Whalen v. Roe, 429 U.S. 589, 601 n. 28, 97 S. Ct. 869, 51 L. Ed. 2d 64 (1977). Federal law does, however, recognize a psychotherapist-patient privilege. See *Jaffee*, 518 U.S. 1, 116 S. Ct. 1923.

In *Jaffee*, the Supreme Court held that confidential communications between a licensed psychotherapist and patient in the course of diagnosis and treatment are protected from compelled disclosure in discovery in a civil case. See *Jaffee*, 518 U.S. at 15, 116 S. Ct. 1923. The Court specifically rejected recognizing any "balancing component" whereby "the promise of confidentiality [is] contingent upon . . . the relative importance of the patient's interest in privacy and the evidentiary need for disclosure. . . ." *Jaffee*, 518 U.S. at 17, 116 S. Ct. 1923. The Court, however, refused to "define the details of [the] new privilege[ ]," leaving that to be developed on "a case-by-case basis." *Jaffee*, 518 U.S. at 18, 116 S. Ct. 1923. The Court further stated: "Because this is the first case in which we have recognized a psychotherapist privilege, it is neither necessary nor feasible to delineate its full contours in a way that would 'govern all conceivable future questions in this area.'" *Jaffee*, 518 U.S. at 18, 116 S. Ct. 1923 (quoting *Upjohn Co. v. United States*, 449 U.S. 383, 386, 101 S. Ct. 677, 66 L. Ed. 2d 584 (1981)).

Unlike *Jaffee*, this case involves the application of the psychotherapist-patient privilege in the criminal context. In particular, this case involves application of the privilege to prevent production of records in response to a grand jury investigation, which raises special considerations. As the Fourth Circuit explained in *In re: Grand Jury Proceedings # 5*, 401 F.3d 247, 250 (4th Cir. 2005):

Grand jury proceedings occupy an essential role in the federal criminal justice system. A grand jury serves the invaluable function of both "determining if there is probable cause to believe that a crime has been committed and of protecting citizens against unfounded criminal prosecutions." *Branzburg v. Hayes*, 408 U.S. 665, 686–87, 92 S. Ct. 2646, 33 L. Ed. 2d 626 (1972). To this end, a grand jury's "investigative powers are necessarily broad . . . [and its] authority to subpoena witnesses is not only historic, but essential to its task." *[Branzburg]* at 688[, 92 S. Ct. 2646] Thus, in the context of a grand jury subpoena, the longstanding principle that the public has a right to each person's evidence is particularly strong. *Id.* Absent a compelling reason, a court may not interfere with the grand jury process. *In re Weiss*, 596 F.2d 1185, 1186 (4th Cir. 1979).

A court will intervene, however, when a recognized privilege provides a legitimate ground for refusing to comply with a grand jury subpoena.

The Fourth Circuit also has stated that "[t]he subpoena power — the authority to command persons to appear and testify or to produce documents or things — is a longstanding and necessary adjunct to the governmental power of investigation and inquisition. . . ." *In re Subpoena Duces Tecum*, 228 F.3d 341, 346 (4th Cir. 2000); *see also, United States. v. Auster*, 517 F.3d 312, 319 (5th Cir. 2008) ("public interest at stake in a criminal trial of any sort is substantial, more so than in a civil case like *Jaffee*").

Based at least in part on the public's strong interest in investigating and prosecuting crime, the federal courts, including the Fourth Circuit, have recognized a "crime-fraud" exception to the attorney-client privilege. *See In re: Grand Jury Proceedings # 5*, 401 F.3d at 251. Under the crime-fraud exception, attorney-client communications are not protected by privilege if they were made for the purpose of committing or furthering a crime or fraud. *See In re: Grand Jury Proceedings # 5*, 401 F.3d at 251.

> The party asserting the crime-fraud exception . . . must make a prima facie showing to the court that the privileged communications fall within the exception. *Chaudhry v. Gallerizzo*, 174 F.3d 394, 403 (4th Cir. 1999). In satisfying the prima facie standard, proof either by a preponderance or beyond a reasonable doubt of the crime or fraud is not required. . . . Rather, the proof "must be such as to subject the opposing party to the risk of non-persuasion if the evidence as to the disputed fact is left unrebutted."
> . . .

In re: Grand Jury Proceedings # 5, 401 F.3d at 251.

Furthermore, at least one Circuit Court of Appeals has recognized the crime-fraud exception to the psychotherapist-patient privilege established by *Jaffee*. In fact, the First Circuit has held that the crime-fraud exception to the psychotherapist-patient privilege allowed enforcement of grand jury subpoenas directed at a grand jury target's psychiatrists. *See In re Grand Jury Proceedings* (Gregory P. Violette), 183 F.3d 71 (1st Cir. 1999). In *Violette*, the target was the subject of a federal grand jury investigation for possible bank fraud and other related charges. *See* 183 F.3d at 72. The Government alleged that *Violette* had made false statements to financial institutions for the purpose of obtaining loans and credit disability insurance and then had feigned an array of disabilities to certain health care providers, including his psychiatrist, to fraudulently induce payments by the credit disability insurance. *See Violette*, 183 F.3d at 72. The court held that the crime-fraud exception to the psychotherapist-patient privilege applied in the case because "communications that are intended to further a crime or fraud will rarely, if ever, be allied with bona fide psychotherapy and, thus, protecting such communications will not promote mental health." *Violette*, 183 F.3d at 77. The First Circuit emphasized, however, that the exception to the privilege applies "[o]nly when communications are intended directly to advance a particular criminal or fraudulent endeavor. . . ." *Violette*, 183 F.3d at 77. See *United States v. Mazzola*, 217 F.R.D. 84, 88 (D.Mass.2003) (federal psychotherapist privilege did not apply to prevent production of therapy records of important government witness in a criminal case); *see also Doe v. United States*, 711 F.2d 1187 (2nd Cir. 1983) (refusing to recognize psychotherapist-patient privilege to prevent production of psychiatrist's patient records in grand jury investigation of illegal drug distribution by the psychiatrist).

While the Supreme Court has not specifically recognized the crime-fraud exception to the psychotherapist-patient privilege, the Court in *Jaffee* recognized that "[a]lthough it would be premature to speculate about most future developments in the federal psychotherapist privilege, we do not doubt that there are situations in which the privilege must give way. . . ." 518 U.S. at 18 n. 19, [116 S. Ct. 1923]. The Supreme Court also historically has recognized that evidentiary privileges must be "strictly construed," and may be recognized "only to the very limited extent that . . . excluding relevant evidence has a public good transcending the normally predominant principle of utilizing all rational means for ascertaining truth." *Trammel v. United States*, 445 U.S. 40, 50, 100 S. Ct. 906, 63 L. Ed. 2d 186 (1980) (holding that, apart from confidential communications, witness spouse alone has privilege to refuse to testify adversely and may be neither compelled to testify nor foreclosed from testifying).

Based on the First Circuit's analysis in *Violette*, I am persuaded that the federal common law should recognize a crime-fraud exception to the psychotherapist-patient privilege. Based on the facts of this case, I find that this exception should apply to allow production of the records sought by these grand jury subpoenas. As explained by the First Circuit in *Violette*, it is questionable whether communications made with a psychotherapist in furtherance of a crime would be protected by privilege because they were not made in the course of "bona fide psychotherapy." *See Violette*, 183 F.3d at 77. Nonetheless, even if I assume that these records would be protected by the privilege, I find that the Government has made a sufficient prima facie showing that they should be produced under the crime-fraud exception. The Government voluntarily has limited the scope of its subpoenas to the records of the named individuals listed in the subpoenas. The Government has represented that the psychiatrist has prescribed a Scheduled II controlled substance to each of these individuals. Furthermore, the D.C. District Court has found that the government has established probable cause that violations of 21 U.S.C. §§ 841(a)(1) and 846 of the Controlled Substances Act have occurred and that evidence of those violations is contained in the medical records of these named patients. Also, these records are being gathered for use in a grand jury investigation, proceedings which are not open to public review. To hold that the records of a psychiatrist would be protected by the federal psychotherapist-patient privilege from production in response to a grand jury subpoena under these circumstances could result in a complete inability to investigate and, if necessary, prosecute psychiatrists for the illegal distribution of controlled substances. Therefore, I find that the records requested by these grand jury subpoenas are not protected from production by the federal psychotherapist-patient privilege.

I also reject the argument that the District of Columbia physician-patient privilege statute protects these records from production in response to these grand jury subpoenas. District of Columbia Statute § 14-307 states:

> (a) In the Federal courts in the District of Columbia and District of Columbia courts a physician or surgeon or mental health professional . . . may not be permitted, without the consent of the client, or of his legal representative, to disclose any information, confidential in its nature, that he has acquired in attending a client in a professional capacity and that was necessary to enable him to act in that capacity, whether the information was obtained from the client or from his family or from the person or persons in charge of him.

(b) This section does not apply to:

(1) evidence in a grand jury, delinquency, family, or domestic violence proceeding where a person is targeted for or charged with causing the death of or injuring a human being, or with attempting or threatening to kill or injure a human being, . . . and the disclosure is required in the interests of public justice; . . . .

D.C. Code § 14-307 (2011). Thus, the D.C. statute, on its face, states that it applies only in federal courts in the D.C. District and in D.C. courts. See *Doe v. Stephens*, 851 F.2d 1457, 1465 (D.C. Cir. 1988).

Based on my finding that the records sought by these grand jury subpoenas are not protected from production by privilege, it is not necessary to address the issue of whether a filter team should be used by the Government to review the subpoenaed records for privileged material and, if so, what procedures should be employed. Insofar as the Government may have improperly seized records protected by the psychotherapist-patient privilege pursuant to execution of search warrants issued by other districts, relief must be sought from the district court where the property was seized. See Fed. R. Crim. P. 41(g). While this opinion may be instructive to the parties as to the scope of the federal psychotherapist-patient privilege and the application of the crime-fraud exception, and may assist in their efforts to reach an agreement as to the disposition of the records seized in the search of the psychiatrist's residence and office, it is not controlling.

An appropriate order will be entered ordering the production of the records sought by these grand jury subpoenas as narrowed by the Government or, in the alternative, if the Government currently possesses these records, to allow their review.

EXERCISE

Hessam, a chemist with a history of mental health problems, voluntarily admitted himself to a hospital emergency room, concerned that he might harm himself or someone else. An ER nurse conducted an initial evaluation during which Hessam stated that he had cyanide in his apartment and that he might use it later to kill himself. The following day a clinical psychiatrist met with Hessam to perform a clinical examination. Hessam appeared more hostile and stated that not only did he still have suicidal thoughts, but also that he had thoughts of harming others affiliated with the government and that he had access to chemicals. The psychotherapist then notified the police as to Hessam's statements. Police searched Hessam's apartment, found the cyanide, and charged him with possessing a chemical weapon. At Hessam's trial the prosecution seeks to call both the ER nurse and the psychotherapist to testify against Hessam. Hessam objects, arguing that each man's testimony should be excluded under the psychotherapist-patient privilege. How should the trial court rule?

§ 9.04   ATTORNEY-CLIENT PRIVILEGE

[A]   Scope and Rationale

[1]   In General

The attorney-client privilege protects from disclosure communications from a client to an attorney that the client made in confidence for the purpose of obtaining legal advice or assistance. The rationale underlying this privilege is that guaranteeing the confidentiality of these communications will encourage the client to make complete disclosures to his or her attorney and this, in turn, will ensure a higher quality of legal advice and assistance. And through this advice the client can better understand his or her obligations and responsibilities under the law, which in turn will increase the law's effectiveness by increasing compliance with it. *See generally* RICE, ATTORNEY-CLIENT PRIVILEGE IN THE UNITED STATES, § 2.3 (West Group 2d ed. 1999).

The actual benefits that society has derived from the privilege's existence are entirely speculative. One cannot measure the extent to which the privilege actually encourages disclosures that a client would not otherwise have made absent the privilege's protections. Conversely, the detriment that the privilege has created — the loss of probative evidence — is apparent. Thus, courts have generally interpreted the privilege narrowly, imposing on the person claiming it the burden of establishing each of its elements. These elements require that:

(1)   the client consulted an attorney;

(2)   the consultation was for the purpose of obtaining legal advice or assistance;

(3)   the client intended that the communications be confidential; and

(4)   the requisite confidentiality has subsequently been maintained.

[2]   Confidential Communications from Client

[a]   Characteristics of Protected Communications

The loss of evidence due to the attorney-client privilege is not as great as it may initially appear. The privilege protects only a client's *communications* (oral or written) to his or her attorney if the client made these communications in confidence. It does not protect the knowledge and information that a client possesses and that happened to be in his or her communications with the attorney. Consequently, if a party seeks the *information* itself directly from the client rather than from the communications the client made to his or her attorney, the client must disclose the information sought. The client, for example, would have to respond fully to interrogatories or deposition questions regarding information he or she possessed, even though the client had previously communicated that information in confidence to his or her attorney. In this instance, the privilege would protect from disclosure only the fact that the client had disclosed the information to his or her attorney for the purpose of obtaining legal advice. The same is true of a client's written communications with his or her attorney.

If the client drafts a letter for the purpose of communicating with his or her attorney, the attorney-client privilege will protect that letter. If, however, a client gives a preexisting document or writing (or any tangible object for that matter) to the attorney to obtain advice, only the fact that the client gave the document to the attorney for the purpose of obtaining advice is protected, not the document or object itself. Consequently, if a party seeks to have the client produce the object in question, the client must retrieve it from the attorney and produce it. *See generally* RICE, ATTORNEY-CLIENT PRIVILEGE IN THE UNITED STATES, §§ 5:14, 5:19 (West Group 2d ed. 1999).

The attorney's possession and the circumstances of communications to the attorney do not change the status of a document or object. If it was not privileged in the client's hands before its transfer to the attorney, it does not acquire a privileged status by the transfer. This distinction is critical to the survival of the attorney-client privilege because without it parties could completely avoid discovery by the simple expedient of funneling all materials related to a cause of action to their attorneys. The preexisting documents, however, should not be discoverable directly from the attorney because the attorney's production of it would disclose not only the information but also the fact it was communicated to the attorney by the client. Judge Posner addressed this issue in the following case.

UNITED STATES v. WILLIAMS
United States Court of Appeals, Seventh Circuit
698 F.3d 374 (2012)

POSNER, CIRCUIT JUDGE.

Corvet Williams and Brian Austin were tried together for armed bank robbery and use of a firearm in a crime of violence, 18 U.S.C. §§ 2113(a), (d), 924(c)(1)(A), and were convicted by a jury. Their convictions were reversed, 576 F.3d 385 (2009), on a ground unrelated to the present appeals. They were retried, again convicted by a jury, and each sentenced to 684 months in prison. They appeal, challenging both their convictions and their sentences.

There were two robberies, two weeks apart, pretty obviously committed by the same two persons — so similar were the modus operandi of the robbers on the two occasions: two black men, one short and one tall, both brandishing pistols and wearing black gloves plus masks that covered the head completely except for eyes and mouth, with the shorter of the two men jumping over the teller counter to get the money while the taller pointed a silver-colored semi-automatic handgun held in his left hand at bank employees and customers, whom he had ordered to lie on the floor. And in each robbery the robbers had driven a stolen vehicle to the bank, left it with its motor running while they robbed the bank, and after the robbery driven away in another stolen vehicle, parked nearby.

* * *

Williams contends . . . that the government impermissibly bolstered its case by calling his original lawyer as a witness. The lawyer testified that Williams had mailed him an envelope marked "legal mail" (so that it would not be opened by the jail) that contained a sealed letter addressed to a cousin of Williams and a note asking the lawyer to forward the letter to Williams's family to give to the cousin. The lawyer was suspicious and read the letter. It instructed the cousin to provide an alibi for Williams by testifying that Williams had been involved in a marijuana deal on the day of the robbery. Realizing that Williams was trying to obstruct justice by asking the cousin to provide him with a false alibi, the lawyer did not forward the letter. Instead, with the judge's permission the lawyer withdrew as Williams's counsel, turned the letter over to the government, and agreed at the government's request to testify at Williams's trial. He testified that the letter was a "blatant attempt to get me involved in smuggling something out of the jail that in turn would be a potential instrument for obstruction." Williams, who like Austin had decided to testify, admitted on the stand that his aim in writing the letter had indeed been to induce his cousin to lie for him.

He argues that his lawyer did a terrible thing in turning against him as he did; indeed that the lawyer violated the Sixth Amendment right to effective assistance of counsel; and that the impact on the jury of the lawyer's testimony must have been devastating. These are separate points and we shall discuss them separately.

There was no violation of the lawyer-client privilege. In asking the lawyer to forward the letter Williams was not soliciting legal advice or providing information that the lawyer might use in crafting Williams's defense. "When information is transmitted to an attorney with the intent that the information will be transmitted to a third party . . . , such information is not confidential." *United States v. Lawless*, 709 F.2d 485, 487 (7th Cir. 1983). For "an individual cannot purchase anonymity by hiring a lawyer to deliver his money or his messages." *In re Grand Jury Subpoena*, 204 F.3d 516, 522 and n. 5 (4th Cir. 2000).

The ethical rule applicable when the lawyer turned against Williams was the rule of the Northern District of Illinois that permitted a lawyer to "reveal . . . the intention of a client to commit a crime," N.D. Ill. L.R. 83.51.6(c)(2), although it did not require him to do so unless "it appear[ed] necessary to prevent the client from committing an act that would result in death or serious bodily harm." *Id.* at 6(b). Oddly, the parties do not cite that rule, but instead the Northern District's current rule, adopted in 2011, which, we are surprised to discover, is less protective of public safety. It permits a lawyer to reveal information relating to the representation of a client *only* in specified circumstances, such as "to the extent the lawyer reasonably believes [that revelation is] necessary (1) to prevent reasonably certain death or substantial bodily harm; (2) to prevent the client from committing a crime or fraud that is reasonably certain to result in substantial injury to the financial interests or property of another and in furtherance of which the client has used or is using the lawyer's services; [or] (3) to prevent, mitigate or rectify substantial injury to the financial interests or property of another that is reasonably certain to result or has resulted from the client's commission of a crime or fraud in furtherance of which the client has used the lawyer's services." ABA Model Rule of Professional Conduct 1.6(b)(1)-(3). The new Northern District rule adopts the ABA Model Rules of Professional Conduct. N.D. Ill. L.R. 83.50. But the current rule is not applicable to this case. The old Northern District rule — the rule applicable to this case — placed no limitations on a lawyer's reporting the intention of his client to commit a crime.

And more than an *intention* was involved. Williams had already committed the crime of attempting to suborn perjury by preparing the letter to his cousin and asking the lawyer to forward it, and he intended the further crime of actually suborning perjury. An unfulfilled intention to commit or suborn (that is, get someone else to commit) perjury is not a crime, but the intention plus a significant step toward completion, which Williams took, is a crime. And there is more than just suborning perjury in this case, because the cousin would have committed perjury had he agreed to Williams's request, as would Williams had he testified to the false alibi. So we're really talking about three crimes, one completed, two intended: suborning perjury; perjury by Williams; and perjury by the cousin. (The lawyer would have suborned perjury too had he delivered the note to the cousin after reading it, but that was never in the cards.)

The literature on the ethical duties of lawyers counsels that a lawyer should attempt to dissuade his client from illegal conduct before disclosing his client's intentions to the court or to law enforcement authorities. But the literature phrases this as a recommendation rather than as a flat command, frequently hedging it with qualifications such as "ordinarily" and "practicable." See, e.g., *Restatement (Third) of Law Governing Lawyers* § 120, comment g (2000); 2 Geoffrey C. Hazard & W. William Hodes, *The Law of Lawyering* § 29.21 (3d ed. 2011); ABA Model Rule 1.6, comment 14; ABA Model Rule 3.3, comment 6. This makes sense in the usual case; the harm to the client's interests and to the attorney-client relationship from disclosure is great, and the benefit of disclosure in preventing criminal activity is usually small when the crime is perjury since the lawyer can refuse to introduce the perjured testimony. But this is not the usual case. Had Williams's lawyer merely refused to forward the letter, Williams might have found a different means of conveying his unlawful request to his family (maybe orally in jail to a visiting family) — perhaps with instructions to find someone other than the cousin to be the false alibi witness, someone the lawyer had never heard of and therefore would have no basis for refusing to call as a witness. Facing a possible sentence of more than 50 years for the bank robberies and having already attempted to suborn perjury, Williams was unlikely to hearken to an ethics lecture by his lawyer.

This was not a case in which a client tells the lawyer that he would like to give testimony that the lawyer knows is a lie, and the lawyer tells him he must not do so and is confident the client will obey. Williams took a substantial step toward procuring a false witness and having embarked on that course had other means of reaching his destination even if the lawyer prevented the cousin from testifying. In such a case a lawyer is allowed to exercise discretion concerning whether to withdraw from representing the defendant and report the defendant's crime of attempting to suborn perjury.

More important than what we think is that allowing the exercise of such discretion is consistent with the Northern District's (old) rule of lawyer conduct, the rule applicable to Williams's lawyer, which authorized the lawyer to "reveal . . . the intention of a client to commit a crime." Even ABA Model Rule of Professional Conduct 3.3(b), which the Northern District has now adopted, states, albeit in tension with the other one of the model rules that we quoted, that "a lawyer who represents a client in an adjudicative proceeding and who knows that a person intends to engage, is engaging or has engaged in criminal or fraudulent conduct related to the proceeding shall take reasonable remedial measures, including, if necessary, disclosure to the tribunal." And in *Nix v. Whiteside*, 475 U.S. 157, 169 (1986) (emphasis added), the Supreme Court said that "it is universally agreed that *at a minimum* the attorney's first duty when confronted with a proposal for perjurious testimony is to attempt to dissuade the client from the unlawful course of conduct." In other words, the lawyer's *minimum* duty to the court — to the law — is to try to dissuade his client from committing perjury. The maximum would be to withdraw and testify against him. And the Court in *Nix* (like the other authorities on professional ethics on which William does or could rely) was dealing with a case in which a crime (perjury) had merely been proposed, rather than, as in this case, with a crime (attempted subornation of perjury) that had already been committed.

That is not a trivial distinction. "In tort law, unsuccessful attempts do not give rise to liability . . . . The criminal law, because it aims at taking dangerous people out of circulation before they do harm, takes a different approach. A person who demonstrates by his conduct that he has the intention and capability of committing a crime is punishable even if his plan was thwarted." *United States v. Gladish*, 536 F.3d 646, 648-49 (7th Cir. 2008). Williams is differentnfrom the client who merely proposes perjury, because his substantial step towards the crime "makes it reasonably clear that had [he] not been interrupted or made a mistake . . . [he] would have completed the crime." *Id.*

The Supreme Court in *Bobby v. Van Hook*, 558 U.S. 4 (2009), criticized courts of appeals not only for relying on ABA guidelines that post-dated the relevant conduct but also for treating the guidelines "not merely as evidence of what reasonably diligent attorneys would do, but as inexorable commands." Lawyers enjoy a broad discretion in responding to litigation misconduct by their clients, and in the unusual circumstances of this case we do not think the lawyer acted unethically.

Even if he did, it would not follow that his testimony was inadmissible, unless otherwise barred by the Federal Rules of Evidence, for example because deemed unduly prejudicial in relation to its probative value. Fed. R. Evid. 401. Exclusionary rules, which protect the guilty, are no longer favored. "Suppression of evidence . . . has always been our last resort, not our first impulse. The exclusionary rule generates substantial social costs which sometimes include setting the guilty free and the dangerous at large." *Hudson v. Michigan*, 547 U.S. 586, 591 (2006); see also *Sanchez-Llamas v. Oregon*, 548 U.S. 331, 343–50 (2006); *Trammel v. United States*, 445 U.S. 40, 50–51 (1980). "Only communications subject to the attorney-client privilege cannot be disclosed under judicial compulsion," *Newman v. State*, 863 A.2d 321, 332 (Md. 2004) — and the privilege doesn't extend to a client's asking his lawyer to help him commit a crime. See also *United States v. Zolin*, 491 U.S. 554, 563 (1989); *In re Grand Jury*, 475 F.3d 1299, 1305–06 (D.C. Cir. 2007).

Rejection of an exclusionary rule does not mean that there is no remedy for misconduct by a lawyer. Defendant Williams — or for that matter a judge of this court — can complain to the local bar association about the conduct of his original lawyer. Lawyers are subject to professional discipline up to and including disbarment, and the threat of discipline should deter willful violations. The reason for an exclusionary rule is not to make the defendant whole by putting him back in the position that he would have occupied had it not been for the violation. Exclusionary rules exclude improperly obtained evidence that often is highly probative of guilt. That is true in this case. And rather than being a victim deserving a remedy, Williams is a confessed attempted suborner of perjury.

Exclusionary rules should be reserved for cases in which there is no alternative method of deterrence. Professional discipline is an alternative. True, one can imagine a case in which the defendant's former lawyer, having retired from practice and thus no longer being subject to professional discipline, offers to testify for the prosecution about client confidences. But in that case, either his testimony would be barred by attorney-client privilege or, if not, he could be compelled to testify under subpoena. ABA Model Rule 1.6, comment 13 ("lawyer may be ordered to reveal information relating to the representation of a client by a court").

In this case, the lawyer's testifying to his former client's effort to enlist him in suborning perjury could not have violated Williams's constitutional right to effective assistance of counsel. The lawyer was no longer Williams's counsel when he testified; he had withdrawn as counsel and his right to do so is not questioned. Williams does not accuse the lawyer who represented him at trial (his original lawyer having withdrawn by then) of having rendered ineffective assistance of counsel. We can't find any authority for holding that a lawyer's actions after withdrawing from a litigation can give rise to a claim of ineffective assistance by a party he formerly represented — especially since, as just noted, a lawyer may be ordered to reveal information relating to the representation of a client by a court. If we ordered a new trial, the government could subpoena the lawyer to testify again.

*   *   *

[b]   Expectation of Confidentiality

The issue of whether the client intended communications with his or her attorney to be confidential has not been a significant issue after it has been determined that legal advice or assistance was sought through the communications. Although courts state that the proponent must establish each element of the privilege and that they will not presume confidentiality by the mere existence of an attorney-client relationship (*see* RICE, ATTORNEY-CLIENT PRIVILEGE IN THE UNITED STATES, § 6:31 (West Group 2d ed. 1999)), their unstated practice is to infer an intention of confidentiality when the required purpose of the consultation is established and nothing in the communication's content or its distribution suggests otherwise. *See United States v. American Tel. & Tel.*, Special Masters' Guidelines for the Resolution of Privilege Claims, Guideline 6, Comment, 86 F.R.D. 603, 613 (1980).

There are instances, however, when courts have concluded that consultations were not intended to be confidential, even though for the purpose of obtaining legal advice. These instances generally include consultations with lawyers for the purpose of preparing materials that will be distributed to third parties. In tax consultations, for example, when the lawyer is retained to prepare returns, communications to the lawyer are presumed to be for the purpose of inclusion in those returns, thereby destroying any reasonable basis for an expectation of confidentiality. *See United States v. Lawless*, 709 F.2d 485, 487 (7th Cir. 1983). The burden is then on the taxpayer to establish his or her expectation of confidentiality in the communications because other advice or assistance was sought. Courts also have found no expectation of confidentiality when attorneys have been retained and communications made to them for the purpose of procuring a tax opinion for inclusion in coal-leasing promotional materials (*United States v. Jones*, 696 F.2d 1069 (4th Cir. 1982)), or even when they have been consulted for the purpose of preparing a prospectus for public distribution, even though the project was abandoned prior to publication. *In re Grand Jury Proceedings*, 727 F.2d 1352, 1356–1358 (4th Cir. 1984). Communications to a patent attorney for the purpose of preparing a patent application have received similar treatment. *See Jack Winter, Inc. v. Koratron Co.*, 54 F.R.D. 44, 46 (N.D. Cal. 1971).

In all of the above instances the attorneys are perceived as mere conduits through which disclosures are intended to be made by the client. Is this reasonable? If communications for the purpose of having a tax return or patent application filed are assumed not to be confidential, how are communications for the purpose of filing a law suit different?

Doesn't the reasoning of the tax and patent cases assume, without any basis in logic or practice, the client intends to relinquish all control of what is filed by the attorney when the client initiates the consultation? If one correctly acknowledges that such filings are not made without approval of the client, doesn't this destroy the basis for claiming there is no expectation of confidentiality? Since the client can change the filings or withdraw them altogether, there is little reason to assume that the client relinquishes expectations of confidentiality until he or she authorizes them to be filed. This has prompted some courts to hold that "a more realistic rule would be that the client intends that only as much of the information will be conveyed to the government as the attorney concludes should be, and ultimately is, sent to the government. In short, whatever is finally sent to the government is what matches the client's intent." *United States v. Schlegal*, 313 F. Supp. 177, 179 (N.D. Neb. 1970). *See also United States v. Willis*, 565 F. Supp. 1186, 1193 (S.D. Iowa 1983). For a persuasive explanation of why this "conduit" theory is flawed in the patent application context, see *Knogo Corp. v. United States*, 213 U.S.P.Q. 936, 940–941 (Ct. Cl. 1980).

[c]   Expansion of Circle of Confidentiality

Courts have expanded the privilege's scope to include confidential communications made by or to agents of both the client and the attorney. Consequently, confidential communications made to the attorney by a client's representative or to a range of agents who might be assisting the attorney, such as legal associates, investigators, or secretaries, will be within the privilege's protection. Courts have held that this agency expansion of the circle of confidentiality of the attorney-client privilege also applies to physicians who have assisted the attorney in advising the client. Consequently, as the court explains in the following case, even if the physician-patient privilege would not be applicable to a patient's communications because the consultation was not solely for the purpose of treatment, the client's communications to the physician could still be privileged as attorney-client communications.

IN RE KELLOGG BROWN & ROOT, INC.

United States Court of Appeals, District of Columbia Circuit
756 F.3d 754 (2014)

Avanaugh, Circuit Judge:

More than three decades ago, the Supreme Court held that the attorney-client privilege protects confidential employee communications made during a business's internal investigation led by company lawyers. See *Upjohn Co. v. United States*, 449 U.S. 383, 101 S. Ct. 677, 66 L. Ed. 2d 584 (1981). In this case, the District Court denied the protection of the privilege to a company that had conducted just such an internal investigation. The District Court's decision has generated substantial uncertainty about the scope of the attorney-client privilege in the business setting. We conclude that the District Court's decision is irreconcilable with Upjohn. We therefore grant KBR's petition for a writ of mandamus and vacate the District Court's March 6 document production order.

I

Harry Barko worked for KBR, a defense contractor. In 2005, he filed a False Claims Act complaint against KBR and KBR-related corporate entities, whom we will collectively refer to as KBR. In essence, Barko alleged that KBR and certain subcontractors defrauded the U.S. Government by inflating costs and accepting kickbacks while administering military contracts in wartime Iraq. During discovery, Barko sought documents related to KBR's prior internal investigation into the alleged fraud. KBR had conducted that internal investigation pursuant to its Code of Business Conduct, which is overseen by the company's Law Department.

KBR argued that the internal investigation had been conducted for the purpose of obtaining legal advice and that the internal investigation documents therefore were protected by the attorney-client privilege. Barko responded that the internal investigation documents were unprivileged business records that he was entitled to discover. *See generally* Fed.R.Civ.P. 26(b)(1).

After reviewing the disputed documents in camera, the District Court determined that the attorney-client privilege protection did not apply because, among other reasons, KBR had not shown that "the communication would not have been made 'but for' the fact that legal advice was sought." *United States ex rel. Barko v. Halliburton Co.*, — F.3d — , 37 F. Supp. 3d 1, 2014 U.S. Dist. LEXIS 36490, at [*5] (D.D.C. Mar. 6, 2014) (quoting *United States v. ISS Marine Services, Inc.*, 905 F. Supp. 2d 121, 128 (D.D.C. 2012)). KBR's internal investigation, the court concluded, was "undertaken pursuant to regulatory law and corporate policy rather than for the purpose of obtaining legal advice." Id. at — , 2014 U.S. Dist. LEXIS 36490, [at *8].

KBR vehemently opposed the ruling. The company asked the District Court to certify the privilege question to this Court for interlocutory appeal and to stay its order pending a petition for mandamus in this Court. The District Court denied those requests and ordered KBR to produce the disputed documents to Barko within a matter of days. *See United States ex rel. Barko v. Halliburton Co.*, 4 F. Supp. 3d 162, 2014 U.S. Dist. LEXIS 30866 (D.D.C. Mar. 11, 2014). KBR promptly filed a petition for a writ of mandamus in this Court. A number of business organizations and trade associations also objected to the District Court's decision and filed an amicus brief in support of KBR. We stayed the District Court's document production order and held oral argument on the mandamus petition.

The threshold question is whether the District Court's privilege ruling constituted legal error. If not, mandamus is of course inappropriate. If the District Court's ruling was erroneous, the remaining question is whether that error is the kind that justifies mandamus. *See Cheney v. U.S. District Court for the District of Columbia*, 542 U.S. 367, 380–81, 124 S. Ct. 2576, 159 L. Ed. 2d 459 (2004). We address those questions in turn.

II

We first consider whether the District Court's privilege ruling was legally erroneous. We conclude that it was.

Federal Rule of Evidence 501 provides that claims of privilege in federal courts are governed by the "common law — as interpreted by United States courts in the light of reason and experience." Fed. R. Evid. 501. The attorney-client privilege is the "oldest of the privileges for confidential communications known to the common law." *Upjohn Co. v. United States*, 449 U.S. 383, 389, 101 S. Ct. 677, 66 L. Ed. 2d 584 (1981). As relevant here, the privilege applies to a confidential communication between attorney and client if that communication was made for the purpose of obtaining or providing legal advice to the client. *See 1 Restatement (Third) Of The Law Governing Lawyers* §§ 68–72 (2000); In re Grand Jury, 475 F.3d 1299, 1304 (D.C. Cir. 2007); *In re Lindsey*, 158 F.3d 1263, 1270 (D.C. Cir.1998); *In re Sealed Case*, 737 F.2d 94, 98–99 (D.C. Cir. 1984); *see also Fisher v. United States*, 425 U.S. 391, 403, 96 S. Ct. 1569, 48 L. Ed. 2d 39 (1976) ("Confidential disclosures by a client to an attorney made in order to obtain legal assistance are privileged.").

In *Upjohn*, the Supreme Court held that the attorney-client privilege applies to corporations. The Court explained that the attorney-client privilege for business organizations was essential in light of "the vast and complicated array of regulatory legislation confronting the modern corporation," which required corporations to "constantly go to lawyers to find out how to obey the law, . . . particularly since compliance with the law in this area is hardly an instinctive matter." 449 U.S. at 392, 101 S. Ct. 677 (internal quotation marks and citation omitted). The Court stated, moreover, that the attorney-client privilege "exists to protect not only the giving of professional advice to those who can act on it but also the giving of information to the lawyer to enable him to give sound and informed advice." *Id.* at 390, 101 S. Ct. 677. That is so, the Court said, because the "first step in the resolution of any legal problem is ascertaining the factual background and sifting through the facts with an eye to the legally relevant." *Id.* at 390–91, 101 S. Ct. 677. In *Upjohn*, the communications were made by company employees to company attorneys during an attorney-led internal investigation that was undertaken to ensure the company's "compliance with the law." *Id.* at 392, 101 S. Ct. 677; *see id.* at 394, 101 S. Ct. 677. The Court ruled that the privilege applied to the internal investigation and covered the communications between company employees and company attorneys.

KBR's assertion of the privilege in this case is materially indistinguishable from Upjohn's assertion of the privilege in that case. As in *Upjohn*, KBR initiated an internal investigation to gather facts and ensure compliance with the law after being informed of potential misconduct. And as in Upjohn, KBR's investigation was conducted under the auspices of KBR's in-house legal department, acting in its legal capacity. The same considerations that led the Court in Upjohn to uphold the corporation's privilege claims apply here.

The District Court in this case initially distinguished *Upjohn* on a variety of grounds. But none of those purported distinctions takes this case out from under *Upjohn* 's umbrella.

First, the District Court stated that in *Upjohn* the internal investigation began after in-house counsel conferred with outside counsel, whereas here the investigation was conducted in-house without consultation with outside lawyers. But *Upjohn* does not hold or imply that the involvement of outside counsel is a necessary predicate for the privilege to apply. On the contrary, the general rule, which this Court has adopted, is that a lawyer's status as in-house counsel "does not dilute the privilege." *In re Sealed Case*, 737 F.2d at 99. As the Restatement's commentary points out, "Inside legal counsel to a corporation or similar organization . . . is fully empowered to engage in privileged communications." 1 Restatement § 72, cmt. c, at 551.

Second, the District Court noted that in Upjohn the interviews were conducted by attorneys, whereas here many of the interviews in KBR's investigation were conducted by non-attorneys. But the investigation here was conducted at the direction of the attorneys in KBR's Law Department. And communications made by and to non-attorneys serving as agents of attorneys in internal investigations are routinely protected by the attorney-client privilege. *See FTC v. TRW, Inc.*, 628 F.2d 207, 212 (D.C. Cir. 1980); *see also* 1 Paul R. Rice, Attorney-Client Privilege in the United States § 7:18, at 1230–31 (2013) ("If internal investigations are conducted by agents of the client at the behest of the attorney, they are protected by the attorney-client privilege to the same extent as they would be had they been conducted by the attorney who was consulted."). So that fact, too, is not a basis on which to distinguish *Upjohn*.

Third, the District Court pointed out that in *Upjohn* the interviewed employees were expressly informed that the purpose of the interview was to assist the company in obtaining legal advice, whereas here they were not. The District Court further stated that the confidentiality agreements signed by KBR employees did not mention that the purpose of KBR's investigation was to obtain legal advice. Yet nothing in Upjohn requires a company to use magic words to its employees in order to gain the benefit of the privilege for an internal investigation. And in any event, here as in Upjohn employees knew that the company's legal department was conducting an investigation of a sensitive nature and that the information they disclosed would be protected. *Cf. Upjohn*, 449 U.S. at 387, 101 S. Ct. 677 (Upjohn's managers were "instructed to treat the investigation as 'highly confidential' "). KBR employees were also told not to discuss their interviews "without the specific advance authorization of KBR General Counsel." *United States ex rel. Barko v.*

Halliburton Co., — F.3d —, — n. 33, 2014 U.S. Dist. LEXIS 36490, [at *11] n. 33 (D.D.C. Mar. 6, 2014).

In short, none of those three distinctions of *Upjohn* holds water as a basis for denying KBR's privilege claim.

More broadly and more importantly, the District Court also distinguished Upjohn on the ground that KBR's internal investigation was undertaken to comply with Department of Defense regulations that require defense contractors such as KBR to maintain compliance programs and conduct internal investigations into allegations of potential wrongdoing. The District Court therefore concluded that the purpose of KBR's internal investigation was to comply with those regulatory requirements rather than to obtain or provide legal advice. In our view, the District Court's analysis rested on a false dichotomy. So long as obtaining or providing legal advice was one of the significant purposes of the internal investigation, the attorney privilege applies, even if there were also other purposes for the investigation and even if the investigation was mandated by regulation rather than simply an exercise of company discretion.

The District Court began its analysis by reciting the "primary purpose" test, which many courts (including this one) have used to resolve privilege disputes when attorney-client communications may have had both legal and business purposes. See *id.* [at *7]; *see also In re Sealed Case*, 737 F.2d at 98–99. But in a key move, the District Court then said that the primary purpose of a communication is to obtain or provide legal advice only if the communication would not have been made "but for" the fact that legal advice was sought. 2014 U.S. Dist. LEXIS 36490, [at *7]. In other words, if there was any other purpose behind the communication, the attorney-client privilege apparently does not apply. The District Court went on to conclude that KBR's internal investigation was "undertaken pursuant to regulatory law and corporate policy rather than for the purpose of obtaining legal advice." *Id.* [at *8–*9]; see *id.* at *3 n. 28 (citing federal contracting regulations). Therefore, in the District Court's view, "the primary purpose of" the internal investigation "was to comply with federal defense contractor regulations, not to secure legal advice." *United States ex rel. Barko v. Halliburton Co.*, 4 F. Supp. 3d 162, 166, 2014 U.S. Dist. LEXIS 30866, [at *7] (D.D.C. Mar. 11, 2014); see id. ("Nothing suggests the reports were prepared to obtain legal advice. Instead, the reports were prepared to try to comply with KBR's obligation to report improper conduct to the Department of Defense.").

The District Court erred because it employed the wrong legal test. The but-for test articulated by the District Court is not appropriate for attorney-client privilege analysis. Under the District Court's approach, the attorney-client privilege apparently would not apply unless the sole purpose of the communication was to obtain or provide legal advice. That is not the law. We are aware of no Supreme Court or court of appeals decision that has adopted a test of this kind in this context. The District Court's novel approach to the attorney-client privilege would eliminate the attorney-client privilege for numerous communications that are made for both legal and business purposes and that heretofore have been covered by the attorney-client privilege. And the District Court's novel approach would eradicate the attorney-client privilege for internal investigations conducted by businesses that are required by law to maintain compliance programs, which is now the case in a significant swath of American industry. In turn, businesses would be less likely to disclose facts to their attorneys and to seek legal advice, which would "limit the valuable efforts of corporate counsel to ensure their client's compliance with the law." *Upjohn*, 449 U.S. at 392, 101 S. Ct. 677. We reject the District Court's but-for test as inconsistent with the principle of *Upjohn* and longstanding attorney-client privilege law.

Given the evident confusion in some cases, we also think it important to underscore that the primary purpose test, sensibly and properly applied, cannot and does not draw a rigid distinction between a legal purpose on the one hand and a business purpose on the other. After all, trying to find the one primary purpose for a communication motivated by two sometimes overlapping purposes (one legal and one business, for example) can be an inherently impossible task. It is often not useful or even feasible to try to determine whether the purpose was A or B when the purpose was A and B. It is thus not correct for a court to presume that a communication can have only one primary purpose. It is likewise not correct for a court to try to find the one primary purpose in cases where a given communication plainly has multiple purposes. Rather, it is clearer, more precise, and more predictable to articulate the test as follows: Was obtaining or providing legal advice a primary purpose of the communication, meaning one of the significant purposes of the communication? As the Reporter's Note to the Restatement says, "In general, American decisions agree that the privilege applies if one of the significant purposes of a client in communicating with a lawyer is that of obtaining legal assistance." 1 Restatement § 72, Reporter's Note, at 554. We agree with and adopt that formulation — "one of the significant purposes" — as an accurate and appropriate description of the primary purpose test. Sensibly and properly applied, the test boils down to whether obtaining or providing legal advice was one of the significant purposes of the attorney-client communication. In the context of an organization's internal investigation, if one of the significant purposes of the internal investigation was to obtain or provide legal advice, the privilege will apply. That is true regardless of whether an internal investigation was conducted pursuant to a company compliance program required by statute or regulation, or was otherwise conducted pursuant to company policy. Cf. Andy Liu et al., How To Protect Internal Investigation Materials from Disclosure, 56 Government Contractor ¶ 108 (Apr. 9, 2014) ("Helping a corporation comply with a statute or regulation — although required by law — does not transform quintessentially legal advice into business advice.").

In this case, there can be no serious dispute that one of the significant purposes of the KBR internal investigation was to obtain or provide legal advice. In denying KBR's privilege claim on the ground that the internal investigation was conducted in order to comply with regulatory requirements and corporate policy and not just to obtain or provide legal advice, the District Court applied the wrong legal test and clearly erred.

*   *   *

In reaching our decision here, we stress, as the Supreme Court did in *Upjohn*, that the attorney-client privilege "only protects disclosure of communications; it does not protect disclosure of the underlying facts by those who communicated with the attorney." *Upjohn Co. v. United States*, 449 U.S. 383, 395, 101 S. Ct. 677, 66 L. Ed. 2d 584 (1981). Barko was able to pursue the facts underlying KBR's investigation. But he was not entitled to KBR's own investigation files. As the Upjohn Court stated, quoting Justice Jackson, "Discovery was hardly intended to enable a learned profession to perform its functions . . . on wits borrowed from the adversary." *Id.* at 396, 101 S. Ct. 677 (quoting *Hickman v. Taylor*, 329 U.S. 495, 515, 67 S. Ct. 385, 91 L. Ed. 451 (1947) (Jackson, J., concurring)).

Although the attorney-client privilege covers only communications and not facts, we acknowledge that the privilege carries costs. The privilege means that potentially critical evidence may be withheld from the factfinder. Indeed, as the District Court here noted, that may be the end result in this case. But our legal system tolerates those costs because the privilege "is intended to encourage 'full and frank communication between attorneys and their clients and thereby promote broader public interests in the observance of law and the administration of justice.' " *Swidler & Berlin v. United States*, 524 U.S. 399, 403, 118 S. Ct. 2081, 141 L. Ed. 2d 379 (1998) (quoting Upjohn, 449 U.S. at 389, 101 S. Ct. 677).

So Ordered.

PSK, LLC v. HICKLAN
United States District Court, N.D. Iowa
2010 U.S. Dist. LEXIS 61784

I. INTRODUCTION

On the 16th day of June 2010, this matter came on for hearing on the Motion to Quash or Modify Subpoena and/or Motion for Protective Order (docket number 33) filed by the Plaintiff on May 14, 2010.

II. RELEVANT FACTS

Plaintiff PSK, L.L.C., d/b/a Overhead Door Company of Cedar Rapids and Iowa City ("PSK"), has been providing garage door installation and repair services since 1956. It is the exclusive distributor for Overhead Door Corporation ("OHD") in Benton, Cedar, Iowa, Johnson, Linn, and Jones counties.1 In approximately the spring of 2007, PSK "became concerned" regarding certain advertisements in local telephone directories, which it claims caused confusion in the marketplace. According to the affidavit of Martin Fauchier, general manager of PSK, "PSK believed the advertising was an intentional attempt to exploit our name and reputation."

Mr. Fauchier decided to contact OHD "to ask for assistance." According to Fauchier's affidavit, PSK "routinely turn[s] to Overhead Door Corp. for advice." Mr. Fauchier contacted Christine Johnson, a lawyer in OHD's legal department, "to ask what rights and/or remedies Overhead Door Company of Cedar Rapids and Iowa City might have against the businesses that we believe were infringing our rights." According to Mr. Fauchier, Ms. Johnson responded in an email with "her impressions, legal advice and recommendation."

PSK subsequently engaged the services of the law firm of Bradley & Riley "to review our rights and pursue a lawsuit." Daniel Slaughter, another in-house lawyer for OHD, "asked that he be allowed to review and edit the proposed Complaint, and also asked to review any subsequent Court documents before they were filed." A number of emails were then exchanged between Mr. Fauchier and lawyers for OHD. Other emails were exchanged between counsel at Bradley & Riley and in-house lawyers for OHD.

On or about April 27, 2010, Defendants Randy Hicklin and Danetta Hicklin ("the Hicklins") caused a subpoena to produce documents to be served on OHD.2 The subpoena asks that OHD provide "all documents" in four areas: (1) those pertaining to the Overhead Door Company of Cedar Rapids and Iowa City (PSK), (2) communications with distributors concerning OHD's use of the terms "overhead door" or "overhead," (3) communications with competitors regarding the use of the terms "overhead door" or "overhead," and (4) communications with the United States Patent and Trademark Office concerning OHD's trademark, trade name, or mark applications.

On April 30, 2010, PSK served the Hicklins with a privilege log, identifying emails which would otherwise be discoverable by the Hicklins, but which PSK claims are protected by the attorney-client and/or work product privilege.3 On May 11, 2010, counsel for OHD wrote to PSK's attorney and advised him that "Overhead Door Corporation disagrees with your designation of these materials as attorney-client privilege and/or work product." The letter stated OHD's intent to produce the emails, unless PSK pursued a court order to quash the subpoena. The instant motion to quash or for protective order soon followed.

III. ISSUE PRESENTED

The subpoena served by the Hicklins on OHD consists of four parts. The parties agreed at the hearing that only the first numbered paragraph is relevant to the instant motion.4 The amended privilege log contains 16 entries, but the Hicklins concede that the last 6 entries (identified as P-33–P-54), consisting of emails between Mr. Fauchier and Mr. Squires, are privileged communications. That is, the issue before the Court is whether the first ten entries on the amended privilege log are discoverable, or are otherwise protected by the attorney-client and/or work product privilege.

IV. DISCUSSION

PSK argues that emails exchanged between Mr. Fauchier and attorneys for OHD are protected by the attorney-client privilege. "The attorney-client privilege is the oldest of the privileges for confidential communications known to the common law." *Upjohn Company v. United States*, 449 U.S. 383, 389, 101 S. Ct. 677, 66 L. Ed. 2d 584 (1981). "Its purpose is to encourage full and frank communication between attorneys and their clients and thereby promote broader public interests in the observance of law and administration of justice." Id. It is apparently undisputed that Christine Johnson and Daniel Slaughter are attorneys-at-law. The fighting issue, however, is whether Mr. Fauchier's communications with OHD's counsel established an attorney-client relationship.

Accordingly, the Court must determine whether an attorney-client relationship existed between OHD's in-house counsel and PSK. At the outset, the Court notes that this is not a case where a corporation's employee contacts the corporation's in-house counsel seeking legal advice. *See, e.g., Upjohn v. United States*, 449 U.S. 383, 101 S. Ct. 677, 66 L. Ed. 2d 584 (1981). Nor is there any question that Mr. Fauchier was acting as a representative of PSK. *See In re Bieter Company*, 16 F.3d 929 (8th Cir. 1994). Rather, the issue is whether Mr. Fauchier, an employee of PSK, sought and received legal advice from Ms. Johnson and Mr. Slaughter, in-house counsel for OHD, thereby establishing an attorney-client relationship.

This case differs from the ordinary case, in the sense that the person ostensibly seeking legal advice did not contact a privately practicing attorney, but instead contacted in-house counsel with whom the person was familiar. The parties have not directed the Court to any cases directly on point, and the Court has found none. That is, the parties have not cited any case where an "outsider" established an attorney-client relationship with in-house counsel of an unrelated corporation; but neither have the parties found a case which holds that such a relationship cannot be established.

It seems apparent that there was no pre-existing attorney-client relationship between PSK and Ms. Johnson or Mr. Slaughter. While PSK is an authorized distributor for OHD's products, they are distinct companies. The distributor agreement establishes certain rights and responsibilities of the parties, but it clearly does not establish an attorney-client relationship between PSK and OHD's in-house counsel. Accordingly, the Court must determine whether Mr. Fauchier's emails to Ms. Johnson and Mr. Slaughter, and the responses received from counsel, established an attorney-client relationship.

In *Diversified Industries, Inc. v. Meredith*, 572 F.2d 596 (8th Cir. 1978), the Court set out "the conditions under which the attorney-client privilege is applicable":

> The privilege applies only if (1) the asserted holder of the privilege is or sought to become a client; (2) the person to whom the communication was made (a) is a member of the bar of a court, or his subordinate and (b) in connection with this communication is acting as a lawyer; (3) the communication relates to a fact of which the attorney was informed (a) by his client (b) without the presence of strangers (c) for the purpose of securing primarily either (i) an opinion on law or (ii) legal services or (iii) assistance in some legal proceeding, and not (d) for the purpose of committing a crime or tort; and (4) the privilege has been (a) claimed and (b) not waived by the client.

Id. at 601–02 (quoting *United States v. United Shoe Machinery Corp.*, 89 F. Supp. 357, 358–59 (D. Mass. 1950)).

The Court in Diversified Industries also offered the following "shorter definition of the privilege":

> Where legal advice of any kind is sought from a professional legal adviser in his capacity as such, the communications relevant to that purpose, made

in confidence by the client, are at his instance permanently protected from disclosure by himself or by the legal adviser except the protection be waived.

Id. at 602 (quoting *Wonneman v. Stratford Securities Co.*, 23 F.R.D. 281, 285 (S.D.N.Y. 1959)).

A. Emails in April and May 2007

On April 25, 2007, Mr. Fauchier sent an email to Terence Hobbs and Christine Johnson at OHD.5 According to Mr. Fauchier's affidavit, Christine Johnson is a lawyer in OHD's legal department. The record is silent, however, regarding what position Terence Hobbs may hold. Copies of the email were directed to Scott Farquhar, Kevin Leonard, and Deric Powell. According to Mr. Fauchier's supplemental affidavit, Mr. Farquhar is a representative of TMP Directional Marketing, which is "the agency designated by Overhead Door Corporation" for use by its distributors to obtain Yellow Pages placements. According to the amended privilege log, Mr. Leonard is associated with OHD, although the record is silent regarding what role he plays in that corporation. The email identifies Mr. Powell as PSK's "owner."

In his email, Mr. Fauchier asserts that a "scam compan[y] has moved into our area" and was misusing the word "OVERHEAD" in its advertising. Mr. Fauchier advises Mr. Hobbs and Ms. Johnson that "I plan on working with our State's Attorney General and the Better Business Bureau." Mr. Fauchier concludes: "Would be interested and much appreciative of any help you have to offer on the subject."

Later the same day, Mr. Farquhar responded to the email, acknowledging that it was "a growing problem" and stating that he "will discuss with corporate next week." In addition to the original recipients of the email, a copy of the reply was sent to Carolyn Arra. According to Mr. Fauchier's supplemental affidavit, Ms. Arra is also a representative from TMP Directional Marketing. Ms. Johnson responded to Mr. Farquhar's email, with copies to the other recipients, stating: "I will review our file because we may have some history with this group in a different market. I will let you know what we locate."

On May 8, 2007, Mr. Fauchier emailed Ms. Johnson and Mr. Farquhar again, with copies to the other recipients, asking if they had "any more information on the scammer service company." The email concludes: "Please forward your thoughts and position on this. We would like to have as much information as possible as we communicate with our state's attorney general." Ms. Johnson responded the same day, copying Mr. Powell, Mr. Leonard, and Mr. Hobbs, but not providing copies to Mr. Farquhar or Ms. Arra.

On May 10, 2007, Mr. Farquhar responded to Mr. Fauchier's email of May 8, 2007. Mr. Farquhar's response, together with the first four emails identified on Addendum A, constitute the email string which was previously provided to the Hicklins and attached to their response as Exhibit A. (Apparently, however, the Hicklins did not receive a copy of the fifth email, from Ms. Johnson to Mr. Fauchier, dated May 8, 2007.) Further email communication between PSK and OHD's in-house counsel did not occur for more than one year.

The party asserting the attorney-client privilege has the burden of showing the privilege is applicable. *Id.* at 609. Here, PSK bears the burden. The Court concludes that the communications set forth above do not prove that an attorney-client relationship was established between PSK and Ms. Johnson. In his initial letter, Mr. Fauchier advises Ms. Johnson and others that he "plan [s] on working with" the Attorney General and the Better Business Bureau. Mr. Fauchier does not seek any legal advice, but simply indicates that he "[w]ould be interested and much appreciative of any help you have to offer on the subject." Similarly, Ms. Johnson offers no legal advice. In her initial response of April 25, 2007, Ms. Johnson indicates she will "review our file" for any "history with this group." The Court has reviewed in camera Ms. Johnson's second response, dated May 8, 2007. She opines regarding the legal issues involved and also "encourages" PSK to employ certain language in its advertising. Ms. Johnson offers PSK no advice, however, regarding its legal remedies, if any.

Furthermore, the Court concludes that even if an attorney-client relationship existed between PSK and Ms. Johnson, any privilege relating to her May 8, 2007 email was waived by copies being provided to Kevin Leonard and Terence Hobbs. Voluntary disclosure of attorney-client communications waives the privilege. *United States v. Workman*, 138 F.3d 1261, 1263 (8th Cir. 1998). While PSK claims that it had an attorney-client relationship with Ms. Johnson, that attorney-client relationship would not extend to other employees at OHD. *WebXchange, Inc. v. Dell, Inc.*, 264 F.R.D. 123, 126 (D. Del. 2010) ("In the corporate context, 'the privilege is waived if the communications are disclosed to employees who did not need access to them.'") (quoting *SmithKline Beecham Corp. v. Apotex Corp.*, 232 F.R.D. 467, 476 (E.D. Pa. 2005)). PSK has failed to prove what role Mr. Hobbs played at OHD, or that his assistance was necessary for Ms. Johnson to provide legal assistance to PSK. Accordingly, even if an attorney-client relationship existed between PSK and Ms. Johnson, disclosure of a communication to others at OHD destroyed the privilege. *See In re Grand Jury Proceedings*, 2007 U.S. Dist. LEXIS 27912 (N.D. Iowa 2007) (Generally, a disclosure to a third party indicates that the communication between the attorney and client is not confidential or privileged.). Accordingly, the Court concludes that the emails identified as Document 760 on the Amended Privilege Log (and as numbers 1–6 on Addendum A) are not protected by the attorney-client privilege.

B. Emails in August and September 2008

On August 6, 2008, Mr. Fauchier renewed his email correspondence with Ms. Johnson. Mr. Fauchier states that "our lawyer now believes there is justification to take legal action on a local level," and advises Ms. Johnson that "it appears this is our only option." Copies of the email are directed to Mr. Farquhar, Ms. Arra, Mr. Powell, Beth Somplatsky-Martori and Michael Pugh. According to PSK's amended privilege log, Ms. Somplatsky-Martori is associated with OHD, while Mr. Pugh is associated with Bradley & Riley Law Firm.

Again, Mr. Fauchier does not seek legal advice from Ms. Johnson. In fact, in his email of August 6, 2008, Mr. Fauchier identifies "our lawyer" as Mr. Squires. As discussed above, even if an attorney-client relationship existed between PSK and Ms. Johnson, disclosure of the August 6, 2008 email to Mr. Farquhar, Ms. Arra, and Ms. Somplatsky-Martori destroyed any attorney-client privilege which may have otherwise attached.

The next email produced for in camera inspection is from Mr. Fauchier to Daniel Slaughter, another attorney at OHD. Apparently at Mr. Slaughter's request, on August 19, 2008, Mr. Fauchier provided information from two Cedar Rapids telephone directories. Additional requests and exchanges of information occurred on September 2 and 3, 2008. (These emails are identified as numbers 8 through 12 on Addendum A.) While Mr. Fauchier was providing information to Mr. Slaughter, it does not necessarily follow that an attorney-client relationship existed between PSK and Mr. Slaughter. In the designated emails, Mr. Fauchier does not seek legal advice, nor is any offered by Mr. Slaughter. Rather, it appears that the information was provided pursuant to the Distributor Agreement, which required PSK to advise OHD regarding its intention to pursue litigation. See Distributor Agreement, ¶ III(d) at 3 (docket number 34-1 at 6). This view is supported by the email from Mr. Fauchier to Mr. Slaughter, dated September 9, 2008, which states: "Can you please give us your position by weeks end." (emphasis added).

Even if an attorney-client relationship existed between PSK and Mr. Slaughter, potentially making the emails identified as numbers 8 through 13 protected by the attorney-client privilege, it would appear that the privilege was waived for those documents when they were attached to an email from Mr. Slaughter to Mr. Fauchier on September 12, 2008. (Identified as email number 14 on Addendum A). That is, on September 12, 2008, Mr. Slaughter sent an email to Mr. Fauchier, completing an email chain which started with Mr. Fauchier's email of August 19, 2008. The September 12, 2008 email, and thus all of the prior emails, were copied to Terence Hobbs. By disclosing the email to an OHD employee other than Ms. Johnson or Mr. Slaughter, the attorney-client privilege, if any, was waived.

Accordingly, the documents identified as P-55–P-59 and P-1–P-16 on the amended privilege log (and as email numbers 7-14 on Addendum A) are not privileged and must be disclosed.

C. Emails Between Mr. Squires and Mr. Slaughter

On October 14, 2008, PSK's attorney, Vernon P. Squires, exchanged emails with Daniel Slaughter regarding the proposed pleadings. Mr. Fauchier and Mr. Squires then exchanged emails regarding Mr. Slaughter's comments. (This email chain is identified on the amended privilege log as P-17–P-20, and on Addendum A to the instant Order as email numbers 15 through 19.) The emails between Mr. Fauchier and Mr. Squires are clearly protected by the attorney-client privilege. There is no doubt that Mr. Fauchier was acting on behalf of PSK, and Mr. Squires was acting as counsel for PSK. The Court must determine whether the emails exchanged between Mr. Squires and Mr. Slaughter on that date are protected by the work product privilege.

In the landmark case of *Hickman v. Taylor*, 329 U.S. 495, 67 S. Ct. 385, 91 L. Ed. 451 (1947), the Court held that communications which fall outside the scope of the attorney-client privilege may nonetheless be protected by the work product doctrine. Work product may consist of "raw factual information," or it may include the attorney's "mental impressions, conclusions, opinions or legal theories." *Baker v. General Motors Corp.*, 209 F.3d 1051, 1054 (8th Cir. 2000). Ordinarily, a party may not discover documents prepared in anticipation of litigation by another party unless the documents are otherwise discoverable and "the party shows that it has substantial need for the materials to prepare its case and cannot, without undue hardship, obtain their substantial equivalent by other means." Fed. R. Civ. P. 26(b)(3)(A). If the court orders discovery of those materials, however, it must protect against disclosure of "the mental impressions, conclusions, opinions, or legal theories" of the opposing party. Rule 26(b)(3)(B). *PepsiCo, Inc. v. Baird, Kurtz & Dobsen, LLP*, 305 F.3d 813, 817 (8th Cir. 2002). "[O]pinion work product enjoys almost absolute immunity and can be discovered only in very rare and extraordinary circumstances, such as when the material demonstrates that an attorney engaged in illegal conduct or fraud." *Baker*, 209 F.3d at 1054.

In the emails of October 14, 2008, counsel exchange their "mental impressions, conclusions, opinions, or legal theories." This disclosure by PSK was required by the distributor agreement. Nonetheless, the Court concludes that it is protected work product pursuant to Rule 26(b)(3). Therefore, email numbers 15 through 19 as identified on Addendum A, which constitute the email chain identified as P-17–P-20 on the amended privilege log, are not subject to discovery.

On October 16, 2008, Mr. Squires and Mr. Slaughter exchanged two additional emails, identified as email numbers 20 and 21 on Addendum A. (Copies of the earlier October 14 emails between counsel were attached and make up the email chain identified as P-21–P-27 on the amended privilege log.) Mr. Squires advises Mr. Slaughter of the manner in which PSK intends to proceed. The Court concludes that the exchanges are in anticipation of litigation and are protected by the work product privilege.

Finally, Mr. Squires and Mr. Slaughter exchange emails on October 21 and October 23, 2008. (Identified as email numbers 22 and 23 on Addendum A, and as P-28–P-32 on the amended privilege log.) Counsel exchanged information on the proposed complaint and the expected course of the litigation. The Court concludes that the work product privilege applies.

D. Emails Between Mr. Squires and Mr. Fauchier

The remaining emails identified on the amended privilege log are exchanges between Mr. Fauchier and Mr. Squires. They are identified on the amended privilege log as P-33 through P-54. At the time of hearing, counsel for PSK acknowledged that he was not pressing for disclosure of the emails between PSK and its counsel, dated August 3, 2009 to December 31, 2009.

E. Summary

In summary, the Court concludes that the email chains identified on the Amended Privilege Log as document number 760, P-55–P-59, and P-1–P-16 are not privileged and must be produced. That is, the Court concludes that the first seven entries on the amended privilege log (email numbers 1–14 on Addendum A to this Order) are not privileged and must be produced.

The Court further concludes that the next three entries on the Amended Privilege Log, identified as P-17–P-32, constitute privileged work product and are not discoverable. That is, that portion of the subpoena which would otherwise require OHD to produce the emails identified as numbers 15–16 and 20–23 on Addendum A will be quashed. (Email numbers 17–19 are also privileged, but it is the Court's understanding that they are not in OHD's possession and, therefore, are not subject to the subpoena.)

The Hicklins concede that the final six items listed on the amended privilege log, identified as P-33–P-54, are protected by the attorney-client privilege and not discoverable. (Furthermore, they are not in OHD's possession and not subject to the subpoena.)

V. ORDER

IT IS THEREFORE ORDERED that the motion to quash and/or for protective order (docket number 33) filed by the Plaintiff on May 14, 2010 is hereby GRANTED in part and DENIED in part, as set forth above.

[3] Relationship of Communication to Legal Advice

Once it has been established that consultations with an attorney were for the purpose of obtaining legal advice and were conducted in confidence, are all of the communications during those consultations privileged? The answer is no. However, there has been some confusion in the courts over which communications should be protected. In *Fisher v. United States*, 425 U.S. 391 (1976), the Supreme Court first announced that a client's communication would be protected only if it were "essential" to the legal advice sought. Prior to *Fisher*, the cases and secondary authorities did not support this proposition. The pre-*Fisher* standard required only that the communication *reasonably relate* (or reasonably be thought necessary) to the purpose of the consultation.

An absolute standard of necessity presumes an unrealistic level of sophistication and expertise on the part of clients which, in our complex legal environment, is inconsistent with the rationale of the privilege. The absolute standard would discourage the openness and candor the privilege should encourage. As explained by Judge Richey in *In re Ampicillin Antitrust Litigation*, 81 F.R.D. 377, 385 n.10 (D.D.C. 1978):

> [T]he Court does not intend to imply that a communication will only be protected if it, in fact, contains information necessary to the decision-making process for a particular legal problem, because such an *ex post facto* approach would discourage full disclosure by [the client or the client's agent] who may not know what information is necessary. What is meant is that communications made in *the reasonable belief that they contain such necessary information* will be protected. . . . [C]ommunications which contain no such reasonable belief . . . because of the nature of the information . . . will not be protected.

See also RICE, ATTORNEY-CLIENT PRIVILEGE IN THE UNITED STATES, § 6:14 (West Group 2d ed. 1999).

Are the client's communications of his or her identity or address protected? Are details of the attorney-client relationship (for example, fees and dates and times of meetings) protected? Generally, the identity of the client is not considered protected because it is not essential to the rendering of the legal advice that was sought or because there was no expectation by the client that his or her identity would be confidential. *See* Saltzburg, *Communications Falling Within the Attorney-Client Privilege*, 66 IOWA L. REV. 811, 820–28 (1981). The same is true of general details of the attorney-client relationship. *Id.* at 826–27.

The identity of the client and details of the client's meetings with legal counsel can be incriminating. Therefore, courts have recognized three exceptions to the general rule:

1. The first exception, commonly referred to as the "legal advice" exception, holds that such information is privileged when there is a strong possibility that disclosure would implicate the client in the very matter for which he or she sought legal advice in the first place.

2. The second exception holds that the fee or identity information is privileged if it provides the "last link" in a chain of incriminating evidence that could lead to the indictment of the attorney's client. . . .[7]

3. The third exception, the "communication rationale" exception, provides that information concerning fees or identity is privileged if disclosure would connect the client to an already disclosed and independently privileged exchange.

Developments in the Law — Privileged Communications, 98 HARV. L. REV. 1450, 1520–21 (1985).

Communications from the client must have been for the purpose of obtaining legal advice. Courts have consistently held that unintentional communications by the client during these consultations (for example, facts about the client that are visually apparent from the client's mere presence, like scars, race, weight, etc.) are not protected by the privilege. *See United States v. Pipkins*, 528 F.2d 559 (5th Cir.), *cert. denied*, 426 U.S. 952 (1976). *See generally* RICE, ATTORNEY-CLIENT PRIVILEGE IN THE UNITED STATES, §§ 6:15–6:16 (West Group 2d ed. 1999).

---

[7] This "last link" exception to the nonapplicability of the attorney-client privilege also has been recognized for communications from the attorney to the client, which otherwise would not be protected because they did not disclose confidential communications of the client. *See, e.g., In re Grand Jury Subpoena Bierman*, 765 F.2d 1014 (11th Cir. 1985), where the court held that an attorney need not disclose whether he had communicated to his client the trial court's order to surrender and begin serving his sentence because it would have provided a critical link in the government's case: proving that the defendant's failure to appear was willful. *But see Matter of Witnesses Before Special March 1980 Grand Jury*, 729 F.2d 489 (7th Cir. 1984).

[4]   Attorney-Client Privilege in Corporate Context

[a]   General Application of Privilege in Corporate Setting

The corporation is a non-personal entity created by the state through which many individuals represent the interests of many other individuals. Does the attorney-client privilege have any application in the corporate context?

Beyond *Upjohn*: The Attorney-Client Privilege in the Corporate Context

Michael L. Waldmana
28 Wm. & Mary L. Rev. 473 (1987)

I. INTRODUCTION

The federal courts have experienced great difficulty determining which employees in a corporation who reveal information to the corporation's lawyer are entitled to invoke the attorney-client privilege. In its first attempt at resolving this question, an equally divided Supreme Court merely affirmed the lower court's judgment without opinion. Rather than settle the differences among the circuit courts, the Supreme Court left the lower courts to continue interpreting the proper scope of the attorney-corporate client privilege without the benefit of the Supreme Court's guidance or reasoning.

In 1981, the Supreme Court was more successful. In *Upjohn Co. v. United States*, the Court unanimously rejected the "control group" test then favored generally in the federal courts. The Court ruled that limiting the privilege to those who control or take a substantial part in corporate decisions restricted the privilege too severely. Justice Rehnquist, writing for the Court, reasoned that the "control group" test hindered corporate attorneys' efforts to formulate sound legal advice and to ensure their clients' compliance with the law.

Besides striking down the "control group" test as improperly restrictive, however, the Upjohn opinion gave lower courts little guidance. Over a pointed concurrence from Chief Justice Burger, the Court explicitly declined to provide any rules or guidelines on the proper scope of the attorney-corporate client privilege. The Court again left lower courts to strike their own balance between the need to discover truth and the desire to preserve adequate legal representation in the corporate context. Since 1981, the lower courts have granted the privilege to corporate employees on a case-by-case basis whenever appropriate under "the principles of the common law as . . . interpreted . . . in light of reason and experience."

This Article examines some of the reasons why determining the proper scope of the attorney-client privilege in the corporate context has proved so nettlesome. Part II traces the historical development of the attorney-corporate client privilege in the courts. This historical analysis focuses on the initial challenges to extending the privilege to corporations and on the emergence in the 1960s and early 1970s of the two major tests, the "control group" test and the "subject matter" test. The development of these different tests highlights the different justifications for the attorney-client privilege and their applicability to the fiction of the corporate form. In Part III, a study of the Upjohn opinion explicates the current state of the case law. Part IV scrutinizes the policy assumptions underlying Upjohn and the visions of privilege law and corporations that Upjohn represents. Building on the theoretical and practical flaws in Upjohn outlined in Part IV, Part V presents new tests for the attorney-corporate client privilege. The tests offered in this final section are both consistent with the traditional purposes of general privilege law and calculated to overcome the present problems plaguing the privilege in the corporate context.

II. THE DEVELOPMENT OF THE PRIVILEGE IN THE CORPORATE CONTEXT: THE QUESTION PRESENTED

The privilege granted to employee communications with company lawyers grew out of the law's traditional deference to the attorney-client relationship. Wigmore traces the history of the attorney-client privilege "back to the reign of Elizabeth I, where the privilege already appears as unquestioned." Others have reached farther back, finding the notion that a lawyer cannot be a witness against his client deeply rooted in Roman law. The sanctity of communications between client and attorney has remained firmly established despite the preeminence since the late eighteenth century of "the judicial search for truth" and its demand for every man's evidence. Extension of the privilege to corporate clients, however, has strained this long-standing tradition. Courts developed the attorney-client privilege for the individual client. The rise of the corporate form destroyed the paradigm case of an individual seeking legal advice and created the problem of identifying the "client" for purposes of the privilege.

The corporate client differs from the individual client in important ways. The most obvious but critical difference is that corporations are inanimate, artificial entities created by the state; they lack the human qualities — the basic human dignity and rights — that our legal system recognizes and respects. Secondly, while attorneys generally can rely on the individual client as the sole source of information about the case, "the corporate client may have to summon a vast array of spokesmen — from upper management to 'blue collar' employees — in order to communicate such relevant information to counsel." This dispersal of information usually is matched by a dispersal of responsibility. The complexity of the modern corporation dictates that the tasks of supplying information, receiving legal advice, and acting on that advice be spread among a large number of employees at different levels of the corporation. These fundamental differences serve as grounds for attacking the extension of a broad privilege to corporate employees.

A. Radiant Burners: The Privilege Under Attack

Chief Judge Campbell of the United States District Court for the Northern District of Illinois launched the modern debate over the scope of the attorney-corporate client privilege in 1962. In *Radiant Burners, Inc. v. American Gas Association*, Judge Campbell "suggested to the profession and adopted as the law

. . . that a corporation is not entitled to make claim for the privilege." Stating that no previous court had decided the issue expressly, he ruled that letters from corporate officers and employees to the corporation's lawyers were not privileged and must be produced in discovery.

Judge Campbell isolated two reasons for not extending the attorney-client privilege to corporations. First, "the attorney-client privilege, analogous to the privilege against self-incrimination, is historically and fundamentally personal in nature." Campbell cited Supreme Court cases which had held that the fifth amendment privilege was inherently personal and therefore unavailable to corporations. He stated that the abhorrence with which the legal system views forcing individuals to choose between convicting themselves or lying, and forcing lawyers to choose between convicting their clients or lying, loses its force when extended to a corporation. The moral dilemma and personal anguish which accompany the disclosure of a client's confidences appear less distressing when the client is a corporate fiction, "a mere creature of the state and not a natural entity."

Second, Judge Campbell argued that the lack of confidentiality intrinsic in the corporate hierarchy would diminish the force of the privilege. Confidentiality, he noted, is "[o]ne of the fundamental, universally accepted and most generally stated common law elements" of any privilege. This fundamental element of privilege, Campbell wrote, is incompatible with the natural flow of information within a corporation. Officers, directors, supervisory personnel, office staff, other employees, and shareholders all have access to files and could possibly "profane " the confidence. Because the personal relationship and personal confidences of the individual client and his attorney do not characterize the attorney-corporate client relationship, a corporation should not be afforded the privilege.

Judge Campbell's decision, announced by a distinguished jurist in a huge utilities antitrust case, sparked a rash of commentary. One can understand the opinion's impact only when the opinion is considered in light of the long history of unquestioned acceptance of the privilege. As Judge Campbell noted, "the privilege had somewhat generally been taken for granted by the judiciary." Indeed, prior to Judge Campbell's decision courts made no distinction between individuals and corporations in applying the attorney-client privilege. The then-prevailing federal test for corporate officers and employees, enunciated in *United States v. United Shoe Machinery Corp.*, deviated little from the basic requirements for the attorney-client privilege that Wigmore delineated. The privilege protected information furnished to the attorney by any officer or employee if furnished in confidence and without the presence of third persons; the privilege left open only communications with persons outside the corporate organization.

The United States Court of Appeals for the Seventh Circuit authoritatively quashed Judge Campbell's attempt in *Radiant Burners* to eliminate the unlimited *United Shoe* privilege for corporate employees. Sitting en banc, the circuit court unanimously reversed; it held that "[a] corporation is entitled to the same treatment as any other 'client' — no more and no less." The opinion included a lengthy footnote listing dozens of federal, state, and English cases dating back to the early nineteenth century in which courts had applied the attorney-client privilege to corporations. The court described a number of these opinions in greater detail, placing particular weight on a 1915 Supreme Court decision, *United States v. Louisville & Nashville Railroad*, which permitted a railroad to assert the attorney-client privilege. With these cases as background, the court rejected Judge Campbell's emphasis on the personal character of the privilege: "We believe this is a misconception of the principle underlying the privilege. Our conclusion is that the privilege is that of a 'client' without regard to the noncorporate or corporate character of the client, designed to facilitate the workings of justice."

The court focused on utilitarian justifications for the privilege, stressing that the need to foster attorney effectiveness by encouraging full disclosure by clients is essential in both the individual and corporate contexts. The privilege's benefits — promoting free and open exchanges between attorney and client — play as necessary a part in the corporate context as they do for the individual client. The utilitarian justifications for the system, therefore, and not personal rights, formed the basis for the Seventh Circuit's solicitude toward the privilege. Although the court acknowledged that "several noted scholars" such as Dean McCormick and Professor Morgan had reached a contrary utilitarian balance in the attorney-corporate client area, the Seventh Circuit elected to "follow Wigmore" in recognizing and applying the privilege to corporate employees as well as to individuals.

Even though Judge Campbell's opinion in *Radiant Burners* was overturned on appeal and subsequent courts and legislatures have shown no inclination to embrace its holding, his opinion has had significant doctrinal consequences. In the short run, Judge Campbell's reexamination of the policies underlying the privilege led other federal judges to do the same. His incisive refutation of the confidentiality rationale weakened the justification for the privilege in the corporate context and made courts wary about unthinkingly applying the unlimited United Shoe approach. Although rejecting his conclusions, courts could not fail to be impressed by Judge Campbell's reasoning. As one judge stated, for example: "To the extent that the learned judge Campbell recognizes that application of the immunity to the corporation is problematical, I concur . . . . However, the proper approach lies in tailoring the ordinary rules to the peculiar cloth of this legal entity." Another judge began a leading case that revised the scope of the privilege by conceding that " Judge Campbell's opinion is supported by a good deal of history and sound logic, but the availability of the privilege to corporations has gone unchallenged so long and has been so generally accepted that I must recognize that it does exist."

Campbell's exposure of the difficulties in extending the privilege thus engendered a new skepticism toward the attorney-client privilege. That courts developed the narrow control group test less than a year after Judge Campbell's opinion appeared is far from coincidental.

Judge Campbell's long run doctrinal impact was to head off any attempt to justify the attorney-corporate client privilege in nonutilitarian terms. Individual autonomy and human dignity, rather than any beneficial effect on people's behavior or the administration of justice, underlie most privileges. Judge Campbell argued forcefully against the application of these privacy/rights-based justifications in the corporate context. The moral imperatives against disclosing intimacies and breaching confidences lack force when applied to a monolithic corporation. As one commentator noted, "the strongest of the nonutilitarian arguments . . . relies upon the existence of a personal relationship between the lawyer and her client and is therefore difficult to advance in relation to a corporate attorney-client privilege." By contrasting the inanimate, artificial corporation with the "fundamentally personal" nature of the attorney-client privilege, Judge Campbell forced the Seventh Circuit and future courts to fall back entirely on the Wigmorian utilitarian rationale. The total reliance on utilitarian justifications is, in part, a legacy of Judge Campbell's cogent attack on any privacy/rights-based justification for the attorney-client privilege in the corporate context.

B. The Control Group Test: Narrowing the Privilege

The control group test developed in response to Judge Campbell's trenchant analysis of the inapplicability of the attorney-client privilege in the corporate setting. Challenged by Campbell's reasoning, courts were forced to fall back on Wigmore's utilitarian rationale. Wigmore had described various preconditions for a privilege, stating, among other things, that "the injury that would inure to the relation by the disclosure of the communications must be greater than the benefit thereby gained for the correct disposal of the litigation," and that the privilege must be "strictly confined within the narrowest possible limits consistent with the logic of its principles." The result of the courts' new interest in Wigmore was the control group test, first enunciated in. The test was developed only months after Judge Campbell's decision, and it quickly gained acceptance around the country. The control group test enabled courts to extend the privilege to corporations, albeit in a sharply circumscribed form.

The control group test rejected the expansive United Shoe approach of privileging exchanges between any employee and the corporation's lawyers; instead, it required that the communicant be "in a position to control or even to take a substantial part in a decision about any action which the corporation may take upon the advice of the attorney," or that the communicant be a member of a group having such authority.

Courts developed the more limited control group test after expressing three concerns about a pure Wigmorian cost/benefit analysis of the attorney-corporate client privilege. The first concern, relied on explicitly in *City of Philadelphia*, was that extending the privilege to statements made by witnesses would be contrary to the Supreme Court's decision in *Hickman v. Taylor*. According to the court in City of Philadelphia, Hickman "settled . . . that a statement given by a witness to a lawyer who is collecting information in order to prepare for litigation pending against the lawyer's client is not privileged." Although Hickman protects attorneys' mental impressions and free exchanges between clients and lawyers, it makes clear that the preeminent need for full disclosure requires that all witnesses furnish relevant and material information to the court. To find that all employees are, by virtue of nothing more than their employee status, the "corporate client" would be to ignore the Supreme Court's teachings in *Hickman*. Given the structure of a modern corporation, employees with relevant information often more closely resemble accidental, unrelated witnesses than responsible, informed clients. Consequently, *City of Philadelphia* set out a more restrictive test which extended the privilege only to those "clients" who could act on the attorney's advice rather than those who merely supplied basic information.

The second and related concern was that corporations would manipulate an expansive attorney-corporate client privilege so as to privilege all embarrassing or incriminating documents. Images abounded of a corporation using the privilege "to funnel its papers and documents into the hands of its lawyers . . . [to] avoid disclosure" and using its corporate counsel as "the exclusive repository of unpleasant facts." Unlike an individual, a corporate client could structure its procedures so as to privilege much of its routine transactions through transmittal to counsel. As one court noted, "in the corporate context, given the large number of employees, frequent dealings with lawyers and masses of documents, the 'zone of silence grows large.'" The control group test met this concern by ensuring removal of routine intra-corporate communications from the privilege's protection.

The third concern involved the need for certainty in the identification of communications within the privilege's protection. The attorney-client privilege is supposed to induce a client to communicate more freely with his or her attorney, thereby promoting more effective legal representation. An uncertain privilege, however, will inhibit communications because clients will fear the eventual public disclosure of their conversations. A proper application of the privilege, therefore, requires a bright line in order to reassure attorneys and corporate managers of the secrecy of their communications. Proponents of the control group test believed it to be such a bright line, lauding it for its "predictability and ease of application." By limiting the privilege to the small group of senior managers who control decision making, the control group test allowed corporations to identify easily who could speak as the client.

C. The Subject Matter Test: The Need for Effective Advice

Until 1970, the control group test reigned supreme; all federal courts utilized the test, and the drafters recommended it in their original proposals for the Federal Rules of Evidence. The United States Court of Appeals for the Seventh Circuit first challenged this dominance in *Harper & Row Publishers, Inc. v. Decker* by adopting a broader test for determining the scope of the attorney-corporate client privilege. In Harper & Row, the court focused on the subject matter of the employee's communications rather than on the nature of the employee who was communicating the information. Under this "subject matter" test, an employee's communication to the corporation's attorney is privileged where the employee makes the communication at the direction of his superiors in the corporation and where the subject matter upon which the attorney's advice is sought by the corporation and dealt with in the communication is the performance by the employee of the duties of his employment.

Although the court's per curiam opinion was somewhat short on explanation, the reasoning behind a broader privilege was readily apparent. Opponents of the control group test argued that only by extending the privilege to low-level employees could attorneys advise their corporate clients adequately. To restrict the privilege to communications of top-level executives was to ignore "the realities of corporate life" because control group members often lack the information needed by attorneys to formulate sound legal advice. Because the critical flow of information often begins with the low-level employees who actually possess the hard facts, the control group test inhibited attorney communications with these knowledgeable employees. Under the control group test, an attorney is thus faced with a "Hobson's choice." If he interviews employees not having "the very highest authority," their communications to him will not be privileged. If, on the other hand, he interviews only those with "the very highest authority," he may find it extremely difficult, if not impossible, to determine what actually transpired.

The more expansive subject matter test was designed to avoid these dilemmas. The subject matter test as expounded by *Harper & Row* extends the privilege to all information employees convey, with the exception of information obtained "almost fortuitously" and not related to their on-the-job activity. The test's emphasis on ensuring effective legal advice won many adherents. After an equally divided Supreme Court summarily affirmed *Harper & Row*, the drafters removed the control group test from the proposed rules and left further development in the corporate client privilege area to the case law.

Federal courts in the 1970s usually adopted one of the two established tests, although some attempted variations or syntheses of these tests. For example, in *Duplan Corp. v. Deering Milliken, Inc.*, a district court held that communications must meet both the control group and subject matter tests in order to be privileged. In *In re Ampicillin Antitrust Litigation*, another district court attempted to modify the breadth of the *Harper & Row* test. The fear that the privilege would extend to routine reports and everyday exchanges led this district court to "focus on the relationship between the subject matter of the particular communication and the decisionmaking process regarding the corporation's legal problem," The privilege attached only if, among other things, the "communication of information . . . was reasonably believed to be necessary to the decision-making process concerning a problem on which legal advice was sought."

The best known variation on the subject matter test appeared in *Diversified Industries, Inc. v. Meredith.* In that case, the United States Court of Appeals for the Eighth Circuit modified the subject matter test along the lines suggested by Judge Weinstein in his treatise on evidence. In addition to requiring that the communication be made at the direction of superiors and that it cover information within the employee's duties, the court in *Diversified Industries* required that the communication be made for the purpose of obtaining legal services for the corporation and that it be kept confidential within the corporation. The court reasoned that these further requirements would restrict the privilege to legitimate attorney-client exchanges, rather than ordinary business records. Under the *Diversified Industries* test, the mere receipt of routine reports by corporate counsel would not make the communication privileged because such routine communications ordinarily are available widely and are not made for the purpose of securing legal advice. These modifications would "substantially limit whatever potential for abuse the *Harper & Row* subject matter test presents" and would "better protect the purpose underlying the attorney-client privilege." Some courts in the late 1970s nonetheless continued to view the control group test as "the rule most likely to obtain the greatest discovery, the rule more easily applied by the Court . . . the rule more likely to be recognized as reasonable by the parties, and the rule most consonant with the purposes of the attorney-client privilege."

III. *Upjohn Co. v. United States*: THE SUPREME COURT SPEAKS

Upjohn Co. v. United States presented the Supreme Court with an archetypical set of facts. In 1976, auditors alerted Upjohn to the possibility that certain of its subsidiaries were making improper payments to foreign government officials. Because of a heightened awareness in the post-Watergate era of the problems posed by secret domestic political contributions, corporate payoffs to foreign officials, and commercial bribery, Upjohn's general counsel launched an internal investigation. Corporate counsel sent out confidential questionnaires and conducted interviews with "all foreign general and area managers" as well as more than thirty other members of senior management. When the company voluntarily disclosed certain questionable payments to the Securities and Exchange Commission, the Internal Revenue Service issued a summons for the production of all documents gathered during Upjohn's internal investigation. Upjohn offered to make all of its officials available for interrogation but declined to produce the questionnaires and interview notes, claiming that the attorney-client privilege and attorney work product immunity protected the documents. The district court enforced the summons, and the company appealed.

The United States Court of Appeals for the Sixth Circuit affirmed the district court's order of production. In its opinion, the court propounded a classic defense of the control group test. The court first pointed out the problematic nature of extending to a corporation a privilege based partly on the "privacy" and "loyalty" of the "intimate relationship" between an individual and his lawyer. The court also questioned the efficacy of the subject matter test, worrying that the corporate counsel would become "the exclusive repository of unpleasant facts" and that "corporate managers would shield themselves from information about possibly illegal transactions." The court finally noted the severe burden that the questioning of large numbers of foreign citizens would entail for the IRS. Concluding that the subject matter test would inflict significant costs on the IRS investigation and create the potential for a broad "zone of silence," the court applied the narrower control group test. The court ruled that the communications by Upjohn employees could not meet this stricter test. Upjohn again appealed. Although Upjohn presented the Supreme Court with the same question that had deadlocked the Court a decade earlier and that had inspired a vociferous debate among the lower courts, the Court appeared to have little trouble reversing the Sixth Circuit. The Court unanimously and emphatically rejected the control group test, needing only eight pages of Justice Rehnquist's majority opinion to explain its position.

In the first part of the opinion, Justice Rehnquist established the purpose of the privilege: "to encourage full and frank communication between attorneys and their clients and thereby promote broader public interests in the observance of law and administration of justice." The Court cited privilege cases dating from 1888 to support its proposition that the historical justification for the attorney-client privilege had been to promote justice by encouraging full disclosure. The Court concluded that this reasoning applied equally when the client is a corporation.

Next, the Court held that the control group test failed to further the original aims of the attorney-client privilege. The Court explained that the control group test's emphasis on the employee's ability to act on legal advice from the counsel did not provide enough protection to encourage a flow of information to the lawyer. By restricting the privilege to a small group within the corporation, the control group test inhibited the flow of important information to the attorney. The Court opined that " middle-level — and indeed lower level — employees . . . have the relevant information needed by corporate counsel if he is adequately to advise the client with respect to such actual or potential legal difficulties." Without the vital facts possessed by noncontrol group employees, the corporation would be deprived of effective legal advice concerning "the vast and complicated array of regulatory legislation confronting it." The Court also criticized the control group test's "Hobson's choice" of either interviewing noncontrol group employees without the protection of the attorney-client privilege or not interviewing such employees and thus giving advice with only a partial understanding of the facts. Justice Rehnquist pointed out that even if the attorney could formulate a legal opinion without talking to low-level employees, "the control group test ma de it more difficult to convey full and frank legal advice" to the lower level employees who would put the policy into effect. The Court also criticized the control group test for its unpredictability. Noting that some degree of certainty is essential to encourage the free flow of information that the attorney-client privilege prizes, the Court stated that "disparate decisions in cases applying the control group test illustrate its unpredictability."

The final part of the Court's analysis applied the principles of the privilege to the facts in the case. The Court restated what it considered to be the salient facts: the communications were made by Upjohn employees to counsel at the direction of corporate superiors; Upjohn needed the communications as a basis for legal advice; the employees, because of a letter from an Upjohn senior manager, were "sufficiently aware" that they were being questioned so that the corporation could receive legal advice; the communications concerned matters within the scope of the employees' duties; and Upjohn kept the communications "highly confidential." Given these facts, the Court concluded that protecting the communications was "consistent with the underlying purposes of the attorney-client privilege."

Lest lower courts read his opinion as implicitly embracing the modified subject matter test of Diversified Industries, Justice Rehnquist emphasized that the Court was deciding one case only. The Court explicitly and repeatedly disavowed any attempt to promulgate rules or guidelines and never even mentioned the subject matter test by name. Although Chief Justice Burger urged the Court to adopt a modified subject matter test, and despite the test's place in the federal courts as the chief alternative to the control group test, the Court was content to hold that the control group test was too narrow to govern the development of the law of attorney-corporate client privilege. The Court left such future development to the wisdom of the lower courts, applying the principles of the common law.

IV. *Upjohn Co. v. United States*: THE SOUNDS OF SILENCE

After the epic battles fought in courtrooms and law reviews for almost twenty years, the Supreme Court's decision in *Upjohn* seemed almost anticlimatic. The opinion's conclusory tone and the Court's refusal to set out any definitive guidelines exacerbated this disappointment. Justice Rehnquist's discussion of the issue, meeting no dissent, was striking for its cursory treatment of the concerns of the lower courts and commentators. This section discusses some of the important issues that the Supreme Court brushed aside in its rush to invalidate the control group test.

First, the Supreme Court failed to address the legacy of Judge Campbell's *Radiant Burners* opinion. Although the circuit court's opinion in *Upjohn* had noted that the "privacy" and "intimate relationship" rationale underlying the attorney-client privilege was problematic when applied to corporations, the Supreme Court did not confront this threshold question. The Court made no attempt to justify its primary assumption that the attorney-client privilege should apply in the corporate context, but merely stated:

Admittedly complications in the application of the privilege arise when the client is a corporation, which in theory is an artificial creature of the law, and not an individual; but this Court has assumed that the privilege applies when the client is a corporation, . . . and the Government does not contest the general proposition.

Such cavalier treatment was unfortunate. A privacy/rights-based rationale historically has played an important role in justifying the attorney-client privilege. As Judge Campbell pointed out in Radiant Burners, the inapplicability of this rationale to the corporate context has significant implications. The Supreme Court had an obligation to confront these implications.

To the extent that the Court offered an explanation for its willingness to extend the protection of the attorney-client privilege to corporations, it relied on a "voluntary compliance" model. This model rested on the premise that a free flow of communications between corporate employees and attorneys would promote voluntary compliance with the law. The attorney, if given all relevant information, could inform corporate officers of their legal duties; these corporate officers, as law-abiding citizens, then would conform their behavior to their legal obligations. This model led the Court in *Upjohn* to bestow preeminent value upon fostering the flow of information between corporate clients and their attorneys. This justification seemed particularly suited to the facts in *Upjohn*, where the corporation aimed its investigation at achieving compliance with SEC and other federal regulations. Unfortunately, the Court never considered the darker side of corporate behavior. The Court singlemindedly concentrated on the benefits of the privilege and ignored the accompanying costs. For a decision based on the utilitarian cost/benefit balancing approach, this was a fundamental flaw.

By focusing on the benefits of the privilege, the Court missed the special costs inherent in applying the privilege to corporations. One such ignored cost is that the corporation is more likely than an individual client to manipulate the privilege to conceal information used for nonlegal purposes. The division of corporate responsibility that requires attorneys to go beyond the control group for vital information also requires the control group to look to lower levels in order to formulate business decisions. Employing lawyers to serve as the conduits keeps the information secret from potential legal adversaries while allowing management to take the necessary business actions. As communications move through the informational and decision-making structure, the motives for the communications can be mixed: the company may want its lawyers to gather information to aid in the preparation of legal advice, while it needs the information collected for more general business purposes. An expansive attorney-corporate client privilege may encourage corporations to conduct legal investigations into the details of any potentially embarrassing incident, not as a result of legal need, but because of the secrecy the privilege provides to business decisions.

The subject matter test, especially as modified by *Diversified Industries*, theoretically should exclude from the privilege all communications made for the purpose of obtaining nonlegal advice. In practice, however, courts are unable to discern whether the lawyer's role was solely, predominantly, or marginally for legal purposes. The pervasive involvement of in-house and regular counsel in corporate affairs makes such a distinction difficult to perceive; lawyers are involved intimately with company management and operations. The ease with which potential legal questions can be imaginatively created after the fact makes claims of legal purpose nearly unimpeachable. Every transaction from personnel changes to corporate contracts has some possible legal ramification. An expansive attorney-corporate client privilege thus might enable corporate management to institute needed business measures in secret, allow company lawyers to collect lucrative fees for their "legal" investigations, and force any eventual government or civil investigators to probe the slippery memories of any available employees they might discover.

The Court in *Upjohn* also ignored the special obstacles that the modern corporation poses to information gathering. Although the Court held that the privilege does not protect underlying facts, this concession provides cold comfort to litigants confronted with the byzantine, multilayered structure of many corporations. The Court itself recognized this dilemma in an earlier case, and refused to extend the fifth amendment to corporations:

The greater portion of evidence of wrongdoing by an organization or its representatives is usually to be found in the official records and documents of that organization. Were the cloak of the privilege to be thrown around these impersonal records and documents, effective enforcement of many federal and state laws would be impossible.

A litigant generally may discover information from an individual opponent as easily as from the opponent's attorney, but the corporate lawyer may serve as a nerve center for corporate information gathered from many sources, often from around the world. Without access to the corporate attorney's reports, an adversary must attempt to track down this widely dispersed information. Such tracking is a costly, difficult, and, especially if done years later when memories have faded or conformed, often fruitless task. Not only may the privilege force an adversary to duplicate the questioning of vast numbers of individuals scattered around the country or world, but it also may prevent the best evidence from ever coming to light. The "paper trail" can provide the most effective means of understanding and attacking a corporate action. As discussed earlier, however, the "paper trail" can be funnelled through an attorney and structured to fit the mold of an expansive attorney-corporate client privilege. With these contemporaneous records enveloped in "the zone of silence," the corporation may frequently prove a black hole from which no incriminating information will escape.

The Supreme Court's opinion in *Upjohn* also neglected the costs of allowing some measure of corporate misconduct to go unpunished. The Court envisioned voluntary compliance with government regulation, but much regulation of business is still founded upon the threat of judicial and administrative penalties. The IRS, for example, was unwilling to accept the voluntary disclosures of Upjohn and demanded further information on the corporation's activities. An expansive corporate client privilege can hamper effective law enforcement to an extent which outweighs the benefits of voluntary compliance. Nevertheless, after *Upjohn*, government agencies and prosecutors are limited in the information available to them in the discovery and prosecution of criminal behavior; the Supreme Court has determined that the voluntary compliance model is more efficacious than deterrent enforcement. The empirical data or logical basis for this decision remains illusive, however.

The Court's attitude toward unpunished corporate misconduct likely was influenced by its perception of the nature of these misdeeds. In the years immediately preceding *Upjohn*, the corporate activities under review were the post-Watergate problems of foreign payoffs and illegal campaign contributions. The Court understandably found such activities troubling but not of sufficient magnitude to justify restricting the traditionally protected activities of lawyers. Areas of corporate misconduct today appear qualitatively different, however. Today's corporate misdeeds — financial institutions laundering money for organized crime, fraudulent securities schemes on a huge scale, massive overcharges by defense contractors, and illegal handling and dumping of toxic materials — inflict a much higher cost on society. The *Upjohn* opinion's broad corporate privilege reflects an inadequate consideration of the potential for a new view of corporate criminality, which should lead to a greater stress on enforcement and a more restrictive privilege.

Finally, commentators have criticized *Upjohn* for its failure to provide the certainty needed to achieve the purposes of the privilege. The Court brought much of this criticism upon itself by an internal inconsistency in its opinion. In arguing that the control group test is inadequate due to its unpredictability, Justice Rehnquist stated:

[I]f the purpose of the attorney-client privilege is to be served, the attorney and client must be able to predict with some degree of certainty whether particular discussions will be protected. An uncertain privilege, or one which purports to be certain but results in widely varying applications by the Courts, is little better than no privilege at all.

In spite of this strong affirmation of the need for certainty, *Upjohn* failed to set forth any test or standard to guide corporations, attorneys, and courts. Instead, the Court left the development of the privilege to the vagaries of the common law, which inevitably will lead to "widely varying applications by the courts" which is "little better than no privilege at all." Even Justice Rehnquist conceded that the case-by-case approach might "to some slight extent undermine desirable certainty." In a concurrence which urged that the Court adopt a uniform standard, Chief Justice Burger noted sardonically that Justice Rehnquist's concession "neither minimizes the consequences of continuing uncertainty and confusion nor harmonizes the inherent dissonance of acknowledging that uncertainty while declining to clarify it within the frame of issues presented."

The Court's criticism of the control group test as inherently uncertain and unpredictable also is highly suspect. The Upjohn opinion first stated its conclusion that "the very terms of the [control group] test suggest the unpredictability of its application." To support this proposition, the Court then stated that "disparate decisions illustrate its unpredictability" and cited two cases: a 1967 Oklahoma case which included the leaders of a corporate research and development division as members of the control group, and a 1969 Pennsylvania case which excluded the research and development division heads from the control group. Two cases seem flimsy evidence on which to indict a test that had been applied countless times over twenty years. More significantly, the Court also failed to understand that these two decisions may well be consistent. The meaningful criteria are not the labels or titles used to designate various individuals, but those persons' actual duties and responsibilities. The "disparate decisions" may have been in fact the correct and predictable results of applying the control group test to the different organizational structures of different corporations.

Moreover, many courts and commentators dispute *Upjohn's* contention that the control group test is unpredictable in application. In most cases, determining whether an individual is a member of the senior management team is a clear cut decision. The United States Court of Appeals for the Third Circuit found that the control group test "draws as bright a line as any of the proposed approaches," and one commentator concluded that the test "provides an easily applicable bright line rule to facilitate judicial decisionmaking." The Illinois Supreme Court, in rejecting Upjohn and adopting the control group test to govern Illinois law, relied on the fact that "the control group test has been noted for its predictability and ease of application." The *Upjohn* opinion's criticism of the control group test's "unpredictability" and "uncertainty" is questionable, especially when the Court refused to set out an alternative test.

V. TOWARD A NEW TEST

As the Supreme Court demonstrated in *Upjohn*, cataloguing the shortcomings of proposed tests is relatively easy; the true challenge is developing an attorney-corporate client privilege test that will withstand such scrutiny. This section sets out two possible tests and argues that either test is superior to the subject matter test that courts have followed since *Upjohn*. The first proposal calls for a return to the control group standard. Although the control group test is, in itself, superior to the subject matter test, an unlimited privilege for all employee communications occurring after a lawsuit commences would further augment the control group test's advantages. Under the second proposal, courts which continue to follow the *Upjohn* opinion could qualify the absolute nature of the subject matter test by permitting a showing of special need to overcome the attorney-corporate client privilege. With such a test, courts would no longer lose the especially probative evidence that Upjohn presently shields.

A. A Representational Privilege

The Supreme Court in *Upjohn* failed to undertake a comprehensive examination of the costs and benefits associated with the more expansive privilege it established. A more thorough examination shows the merits of the control group test to be a close question which the Court wrongly decided. The costs incurred by the Court's voluntary compliance model are substantial. The specter of corporations cloaking incriminating records in the privilege is a troubling one. The often insurmountable problems posed when attempting to discover information from large corporations further warrant restricting the privilege. The Court also should have noted the ineffectiveness of voluntary compliance as opposed to the deterrent effect of enforcement, and should have been more concerned about the harms caused by corporate criminality. Moreover, whether a more expansive privilege actually will lead corporations to confide more readily in their attorneys or, rather, will induce corporate management to use the privilege improperly as protection for business decisions surely remains open to question.

The cost/benefit calculus tilts most strongly against an expansive privilege when one recognizes that the privacy/rights-based rationale does not apply in the corporate context. As a recent study of the theories of privilege demonstrates, this privacy/rights-based rationale not only has independent force in justifying a privilege but also plays an important role in bolstering the utilitarian justifications of a privilege. The utilitarian and privacy/rights-based justifications "can be incorporated within a broad utilitarian framework . . . which is consistent with non-utilitarian principles because it takes account of the relative weight of the various rights with which non-utilitarians are concerned." This collapsing of rationales, however, does not support the attorney-corporate client privilege because intimacy and privacy concerns are not present in the inanimate corporate form. Without the support of a strong privacy/rights-based rationale, an expansive privilege loses a key justification under this utilitarian analysis.

At a fundamental level, the Court in *Upjohn* took issue with what it perceived to be the control group test's approach to defining the privilege — namely, an attempt to identify those corporate actors who so personified the corporation as to be deemed the corporate "client." The Court maintained that by attempting to isolate and privilege those who "can be said to possess an identity analogous to the corporation as a whole," the control group test overlooked the very purpose of the privilege, which is to protect certain types of communications, not people. The Court apparently found the subject matter test better suited to ferret out those communications consistent with the purposes underlying the privilege because the test avoided the control group test's focus on which corporate employees resemble an individual client.

The Court, however, misperceived the nature of the control group test. The test does not seek to protect the individuals within the control group itself, but rather seeks to encourage the type of confidential, top-level communications that typically flow from such personnel. In this regard, it is significant to note that the modified subject matter test presented in *Diversified Industries* consists largely of background rules of privilege that apply even under the control group test. The requirements of confidentiality and a legal purpose are readily implied from Wigmore and *United Shoe*. The control group test therefore possesses the same functional concerns and minimal standards as the subject matter test, but the control group test also applies a stricter requirement concerning the nature of the employee's responsibilities. This further requirement serves as a proxy, narrowing the area of protected communications while allowing the judge to determine quickly which among the hundreds or even thousands of documents before him are likely to involve especially valuable communications that the privilege seeks to encourage.

The control group test prevents corporate officials from manipulating the privilege to suppress embarrassing documents or cloak nonlegal decisions in secrecy. By its restrictive nature, the control group test inevitably sacrifices some measure of useful communication between employees and their company's lawyers. Courts might achieve the advantages of the restrictive control group test with less loss of useful communications by allowing the privilege to cover any employee communications to the corporation's attorneys that take place after the initiation of a legal action.

Practical and theoretical considerations argue for an unlimited attorney-corporate client privilege only when the attorney is representing the corporation in pending litigation. The practical argument is relatively simple: the corporation is less likely to manipulate the privilege if the communications protected are generated in response to an existing lawsuit. One of the chief fears associated with an expansive privilege is that the corporation will structure normal business transactions and records through the lawyer in order to benefit from the privilege. Funneling documents through a lawyer will not avail the corporation under a control group test that expands only after legal representation has begun. The representational privilege will not shield normal business transactions and records because the corporation cannot "plan" an existing lawsuit. The "zone of silence" surrounding the primary events which usually will be the source of the lawsuit thereby remains small; only the later employee-attorney discussions about those events earn the privilege. These latter discussions might not have occurred absent the lawsuit, will be of less probative value than direct testimony, and presumably will inform the lawyer about the lawsuit rather than suppress unpleasant facts.

The control group test, if augmented by an unlimited representational privilege, not only prevents the suppression of valuable information but also reinforces the requirement that the privilege be used exclusively for legal advice. The requirement that the communications be for legal advice is present in the background rules of the privilege, and is emphasized in the modified subject matter test. Nonetheless, management officials may abuse the privilege by using confidential information they receive from lawyers for business decisions. If executives cannot initiate privileged communications through counsel, however, they will be less able to base necessary business decisions on secret data collected by lawyers. When a lawsuit is pending, communications between employees and corporate attorneys are more to likely serve a legitimate legal purpose. In this way, the control group test, expanded with an unlimited representational privilege, will ensure that legal investigations are not initiated solely for nonlegal purposes.

The right to an effective defense also suggests an unlimited representational privilege. The right to retain legal assistance is constitutionally mandated in both criminal and civil actions. The Supreme Court has stated that "the assistance of counsel is often a requisite to the very existence of a fair trial." This right to counsel includes the right to a confidential relationship with one's attorney. Uninhibited communication with employees aids the corporate counsel's preparation and is an important part of this relationship. The Court stated in another context:

Counsel is provided to assist the defendant in presenting his defense, but in order to do so effectively . . . may require the defendant to disclose embarrassing and intimate information to his attorney. In view of the importance of uninhibited communication between a defendant and his attorney, attorney-client communications generally are privileged.

The attorney-client privilege protects the right to counsel and the ability to present a full defense to unjust charges. Moreover, as Professor Nesson has illustrated, the privilege plays an important role in strengthening the legitimacy of the legal system. The privilege allows litigants to test fully their opponent's case, thus enhancing the credibility of the eventual verdict.

Although the Supreme Court in Upjohn stressed a corporation's need for legal advice in order to enable corporations to obey "the vast and complicated array of regulatory legislation confronting the modern corporation," a corporation's right to uninhibited communications is less compelling in the advice context. When a corporation seeks legal advice unrelated to litigation, it is attempting to push out on its own into the gray areas of the law. The corporation should bear the risks when it does so. That the law is "vast and complicated" certainly justifies a right to counsel but not necessarily a right to the privilege. An unlimited advice privilege serves to encourage marginal, possibly illegal, activity in the gray areas by shielding these questionable decisions from scrutiny. Such a privilege is especially undesirable because these communications occurring in the advice context between corporate managers and attorneys are likely to go to the heart of a later lawsuit. To extend a privilege to such advice thus would shield much probative evidence involving activities of marginal social utility.

B. A Qualified Privilege

This Article argues that adopting a control group test modified by an unlimited representational privilege would enable courts to protect only the attorney-corporate client communications most valuable to effective legal representation and would prevent widespread abuse. Courts can achieve much the same result, however, by adopting an expansive privilege and carving out exceptions for information which is especially probative and necessary to truth seeking. If the Supreme Court prefers the subject matter test, the attorney-corporate client privilege should be a qualified one which parties may overcome by a showing of special need for the protected communications. The correct balancing of costs and benefits necessitates that the privilege be subject to an exception that allows discovery of critical communications in those rare cases where no adequate substitute exists.

A qualified privilege would not be unprecedented. Although the attorney-corporate client privilege always has been assumed to be absolute, other related evidentiary privileges contain exceptions based on substantial need. The attorney work-product rule, for example, protects information gathered by an attorney in anticipation of litigation and rests, as does the attorney-corporate client privilege, on a desire to foster effective legal advice and representation. Work-product immunity is not absolute, though. A party can overcome the immunity "upon a showing that the party seeking discovery has substantial need of the materials in preparation of his case and that he is unable without undue hardship to obtain the substantial equivalent of the materials by other means." This Article suggests that courts should apply a similar exception to the attorney-corporate client privilege.

The presidential privilege presents another example of a qualified judicial privilege. The Supreme Court has noted that confidentiality of presidential communications deserves the greatest respect because such confidentiality is essential to fulfilling the awesome responsibilities of the presidency. In *United States v. Nixon*, however, the Court held that a claim of absolute privilege for presidential communications would not "prevail over the fundamental demands of due process of law in the fair administration of criminal justice." Faced with a showing of specific need in a criminal trial, the Court stated that even the presidential privilege must give way. Other privileges running in favor of the government, such as the informer's privilege, also have been qualified to accommodate defendants' due process rights.

Courts already have developed similar exceptions for certain specialized areas of the attorney-corporate client privilege. The prevailing rule today in shareholder derivative suits, for example, grants the corporation only a qualified privilege. In *Garner v. Wolfinbarger*, the United States Court of Appeals for the Fifth Circuit held that when stockholders sue a corporation for acting inimically to shareholder interest, "the availability of the privilege should be subject to the right of the stockholders to show cause why it should not be invoked in a particular instance." In balancing the interests of the shareholders, the corporation, and the general public, the court in *Garner* listed several indicia of "good cause," including the discovering party's need for the evidence, the information's availability from other sources, the claim's legitimacy and the risk of revealing corporate trade secrets. The crime/fraud exception is another instance where courts will override the attorney-corporate client privilege in the interest of social utility. In such cases courts will withdraw the privilege upon a prima facie showing that the client sought the lawyer's advice or representation for the purpose of furthering wrongful conduct.

The arguments against a qualified attorney-corporate client privilege center upon the need for certainty. In order to achieve the privilege's purpose of inducing open communication, the attorney and client must be assured of confidentiality. The goal of achieving certainty in the attorney-corporate client privilege, however, may be little more than wishful thinking. A variety of factors undermine the ideal of certainty regardless of which test courts use for the attorney-corporate client privilege.

Few would claim, for example, that either the subject matter test or the control group test is overly precise. The subject matter test, even in its modified form, requires that courts decide what "the scope of an employee's duties" includes, what "the direction of a superior" means, and what constitutes "legal advice." The control group test requires that courts identify those persons who "control or take a substantial part in a decision." These tests employ somewhat amorphous criteria at best. The variety of different state law tests for the attorney-corporate client privilege also prevents uniformity. Some states have maintained the control group test despite the Supreme Court's opinion in *Upjohn*. Most states have opted for a broader test, often echoing the unlimited *United Shoe* protections. The extent of the attorney-corporate client privilege, therefore, will depend largely on the jurisdiction in which the action is brought, especially because state rules of privilege govern federal court actions brought in diversity. These varying tests do not engender certainty and confidence among large national companies subject to multiple jurisdictions. Finally, corporate employees may be reluctant to reveal embarrassing or incriminating information to the corporate attorney out of fear that the company will decide not to assert the privilege and will elect to disclose the information. No test will provide the corporate executive in such a situation with the "certainty" needed to guarantee free attorney-client communication. Under these circumstances, the adoption of a qualified privilege would hardly have cataclysmic consequences on the goal of "certainty."

The facts of *Upjohn* illustrate some of the advantages of a qualified privilege. Upjohn wished to keep confidential the questionnaire responses and interview summaries of its foreign managers and senior executives. Under a qualified privilege, the IRS would have been required to show a "substantial need" to breach the privilege protecting those documents. The IRS would have had difficulty making such a showing because it had ready access to the American-based Upjohn employees. If an important Upjohn employee had died or become otherwise unavailable prior to direct examination, however, the need for his or her questionnaire responses might have warranted breaking through the privilege. Similarly, if the IRS could have shown that questioning foreign managers was impossible or prohibitively expensive and that their knowledge was indispensable, the Court might have overridden the privilege. Although courts will have to decide how high a standard of "substantial need" parties must meet, at least in extreme cases the qualified subject matter test would allow courts to overcome the privilege. In these rare instances of true substantial need, the benefits of fair adjudication clearly outweigh the marginal chill on future attorney-corporate client communications caused by overriding the privilege.

VI. CONCLUSION

Upjohn has been a growth industry for lawyers. The eagerness of corporations to avail themselves of the expansive attorney-client privilege has made for a troubling spectacle. Contrary to the rosy expectations expressed in Upjohn, corporations seem to be employing the privilege more to evade the law than to comply with it. Cases abound of corporations quickly switching the handling of embarrassing and potentially incriminating matters to lawyers for no other apparent reason than the advantage of the secrecy provided by the attorney-corporate client privilege. This Article questions the justifications for this phenomenon, arguing that the utilitarian balance struck by Upjohn was incomplete and one-sided. The control group test, particularly if augmented by an unlimited representational privilege, better accounts for the narrower set of benefits and the fuller range of costs associated with the attorney-client privilege in the corporate context. Alternatively, *Upjohn's* broad subject matter test might achieve this same balance if the privilege is a qualified one, capable of being overcome by a showing of substantial need. Although these proposed changes in the attorney-corporate client privilege would cut back on the lucrative opportunity that *Upjohn* created for lawyers, they would enhance the goals of truth seeking and a fair legal system.

[b]   Who Personifies the Corporate Client?

The attorney-client privilege is intended to encourage the client's full communication of all relevant facts to his or her attorney so the attorney can render the most effective legal advice possible. If the client is a corporation, whose communications with the attorney does the privilege protect? Inasmuch as only a small group within the corporation has the power to retain an attorney and seek legal advice, should the privilege's protection extend only to communications by those members of what might be called the "control group"? Or, is the power to retain legal service or act on the advice received irrelevant as to which communications the protection should apply? Should the source of information on which effective advice must be based be considered independent of the power to seek or act on that advice? Courts were embroiled in a debate over this issue for decades.

Before 1981, the two leading opinions in which the courts adopted different tests were *Philadelphia v. Westinghouse Electric Corp.*, 210 F. Supp. 483 (E.D. Pa. 1962), and *Harper & Row Publishers, Inc. v. Decker*, 423 F.2d 487 (7th Cir. 1970).

The court in *Westinghouse* adopted a "control group" test. Under this test, a person personifies the corporation — and the person's communications to the corporation's attorney are protected — if the person is an employee, of whatever rank, and is

> in a position to control or even to take a substantial part in a decision about any action the corporation may take on the advice of the attorney, or if he is an authorized member of a body or group which has that authority. . . . In all other cases the employee would be merely giving information to the lawyer to enable the latter to advise those in the corporation having the authority to act or refrain from acting on the advice.

Westinghouse, 210 F. Supp. at 485.

The court in *Harper & Row*, finding the *Westinghouse* "control group" test inadequate because it was too restrictive, set forth what subsequently became known as the "subject matter" test:

> We conclude that an employee of a corporation though not a member of its control group is sufficiently identified with the corporation so that his communication to the corporation's attorney is privileged where the employee makes the communication at the direction of his superiors in the corporation and where the subject matter upon which the attorney's advice is sought by the corporation and dealt with in the communication is the performance by the employee of the duties of his employment.

Harper & Row, 423 F.2d at 491–492.

The Supreme Court did not address this issue of who personifies the corporate client until 1981, in *Upjohn Co. v. United States*. In this opinion, excerpted below, the Court rejected the "control group" test enunciated in *Westinghouse* but, some commentators believe, still did not embrace the "subject matter" test announced in *Harper & Row*.

UPJOHN CO. v. UNITED STATES
United States Supreme Court
449 U.S. 383 (1981)

JUSTICE REHNQUIST delivered the opinion of the Court.

We granted certiorari in this case to address important questions concerning the scope of the attorney-client privilege in the corporate context and the applicability of the work-product doctrine in proceedings to enforce tax summonses. With respect to the privilege question the parties and various amici have described our task as one of choosing between two "tests" which have gained adherents in the courts of appeals. We are acutely aware, however, that we sit to decide concrete cases and not abstract propositions of law. We decline to lay down a broad rule or series of rules to govern all conceivable future questions in this area, even were we able to do so. We can and do, however, conclude that the attorney-client privilege protects the communications involved in this case from compelled disclosure and that the work-product doctrine does apply in tax summons enforcement proceedings.

I

Petitioner Upjohn manufactures and sells pharmaceuticals here and abroad. In January 1976 independent accountants conducting an audit of one of petitioner's foreign subsidiaries discovered that the subsidiary made payments to or for the benefit of foreign government officials in order to secure government business. The accountants so informed Mr. Gerard Thomas, petitioner's Vice President, Secretary, and General Counsel. Thomas is a member of the Michigan and New York Bars, and has been petitioner's General Counsel for 20 years. He consulted with outside counsel and R. T. Parfet, Jr., petitioner's Chairman of the Board. It was decided that the company would conduct an internal investigation of what were termed "questionable payments." As part of this investigation the attorneys prepared a letter containing a questionnaire which was sent to "All Foreign General and Area Managers" over the Chairman's signature. The letter began by noting recent disclosures that several American companies made "possible illegal" payments to foreign government officials and emphasized that the management needed full information concerning any such payments made by Upjohn. The letter indicated that the Chairman had asked Thomas, identified as "the company's General Counsel," "to conduct an investigation for the purpose of determining the nature and magnitude of any payments made by the Upjohn Company or any of its subsidiaries to any employee or official of foreign government." The questionnaire sought detailed information concerning such payments. Managers were instructed to treat the investigation as "highly confidential" and not to discuss it with anyone other than Upjohn employees who might be helpful in providing the requested information. Responses were to be sent directly to Thomas. Thomas and outside counsel also interviewed the recipients of the questionnaire and some 33 other Upjohn officers or employees as part of the investigation.

On March 26, 1976, the company voluntarily submitted a preliminary report to the Securities and Exchange Commission on Form 8-K disclosing certain question-able payments.[8] A copy of the report was simultaneously submitted to the Internal Revenue Service, which immediately began an investigation to determine the tax consequences of the payments. Special agents conducting the investigation were given lists by Upjohn of all those interviewed and all who had responded to the questionnaire. On November 23, 1976, the Service issued a summons pursuant to 26 USC § 7602 demanding production of:

> All files relative to the investigation conducted under the supervision of Gerard Thomas to identify payments to employees of foreign governments and any political contributions made by the Upjohn Company or any of its affiliates since January 1, 1971 and to determine whether any funds of the Upjohn Company had been improperly accounted for on the corporate books during the same period.
>
> The records should include but not be limited to written questionnaires sent to managers of the Upjohn Company's foreign affiliates, and memo-randums or notes of the interviews conducted in the United States and abroad with officers and employees of the Upjohn Company and its subsidiaries.

The company declined to produce the documents specified in the second paragraph on the grounds that they were protected from disclosure by the attorney-client privilege and constituted the work product of attorneys prepared in anticipation of litigation. On August 31, 1977, the United States filed a petition seeking enforcement of the summons . . . in the United States District Court for the Western District of Michigan. That court adopted the recommendation of a Magistrate who concluded that the summons should be enforced. Petitioner appealed to the Court of Appeals for the Sixth Circuit which rejected the Magistrate's finding of a waiver of the attorney-client privilege, 600 F.2d 1223, 1227, n.12, but agreed that the privilege did not apply "[t]o the extent that the communications were made by officers and agents not responsible for directing Upjohn's actions in response to legal advice . . . for the simple reason that the communications were not the 'client's.' " *Id.* at 1225. The court reasoned that accepting petitioner's claim for a broader application of the privilege would encourage upper-echelon management to ignore unpleasant facts and create too broad a "zone of silence." Noting that petitioner's counsel had interviewed officials such as the Chairman and President, the Court of Appeals remanded to the District Court so that a determination of who was within the "control group" could be made. In a concluding footnote the court stated that the work-product doctrine "is not applicable to administrative summonses issued under 26 USC § 7602." *Id.* at 1228, n.13.

II

Federal Rule of Evidence 501 provides that "the privilege of a witness . . . shall be governed by the principles of the common law as they may be interpreted by the

---

[8] (Courts original footnote 1.) On July 28, 1976, the company filed an amendment to this report disclosing further payments.

courts of the United States in light of reason and experience." The attorney-client privilege is the oldest of the privileges for confidential communications known to the common law. 8 J.WIGMORE, EVIDENCE § 2290 (McNaughton rev. 1961). Its purpose is to encourage full and frank communication between attorneys and their clients and thereby promote broader public interests in the observance of law and administration of justice. The privilege recognizes that sound legal advice or advocacy serves public ends and that such advice or advocacy depends upon the lawyer being fully informed by the client. As we stated last Term in *Trammel v. United States*, 445 U.S. 40, 51 (1980): "The lawyer-client privilege rests on the need for the advocate and counselor to know all that relates to the client's reasons for seeking representation if the professional mission is to be carried out." And in *Fisher v. United States*, 425 U.S. 391, 403 (1976), we recognized the purpose of the privilege to be "to encourage clients to make full disclosure to their attorneys." This rationale for the privilege has long been recognized by the Court. . . . Admittedly complications in the application of the privilege arise when the client is a corporation, which in theory is an artificial creature of the law, and not an individual; but this Court has assumed that the privilege applies when the client is a corporation, . . . and the Government does not contest the general proposition.

The Court of Appeals, however, considered the application of the privilege in the corporate context to present a "different problem," since the client was an inanimate entity and "only the senior management, guiding and integrating the several operations, . . . can be said to possess an identity analogous to the corporation as a whole." 600 F.2d, at 1226. The first case to articulate the so-called "control group test" adopted by the court below, *Philadelphia v. Westinghouse Electric Corp.* 210 F. Supp. 483, 485 (E.D. Pa.), petition for mandamus and prohibition denied sub. nom. *General Electric Co. v. Kirkpatrick*, 312 F.2d 742 (CA3 1962), *cert. denied*, 372 U.S. 943 (1963), reflected a similar conceptual approach:

> Keeping in mind that the question is, Is it the corporation which is seeking the lawyer's advice when the asserted privileged communication is made?, the most satisfactory solution, I think, is that if the employee making the communication, of whatever rank he may be, is in a position to control or even to take a substantial part in a decision about any action which the corporation may take upon the advice of the attorney, . . . then, in effect, *he is (or personifies) the corporation* when he makes his disclosure to the lawyer and the privilege would apply. (Emphasis supplied.)

Such a view, we think, overlooks the fact that the privilege exists to protect not only the giving of professional advice to those who can act on it but also the giving of information to the lawyer to enable him to give sound and informed advice. . . . The first step in the resolution of any legal problem is ascertaining the factual background and sifting through the facts with an eye to the legally relevant. See ABA Code of Professional Responsibility, Ethical Consideration 4-1:

> A lawyer should be fully informed of all the facts of the matter he is handling in order for his client to obtain the full advantage of our legal system. It is for the lawyer in the exercise of his independent professional judgment to separate the relevant and unimportant. The observance of the ethical obligation of a lawyer to hold inviolate the confidences and secrets

of his client not only facilitates the full development of facts essential to proper representation of the client but also encourages laymen to seek early legal assistance. . . .

In the case of the individual client the provider of information and the person who acts on the lawyer's advice are one and the same. In the corporate context, however, it will frequently be employees beyond the control group as defined by the court below — "officers and agents . . . responsible for directing [the company's] action in response to legal advice" — who will possess the information needed by the corporation lawyers. Middle-level — and indeed lower-level — employees can, by actions within the scope of their employment, embroil the corporation in serious legal difficulties, and it is only natural that these employees would have the relevant information needed by corporate counsel if he is adequately to advise the client with respect to such actual or potential difficulties. This fact was noted in *Diversified Industries, Inc. v. Meredith*, 572 F.2d 596 (8th Cir. 1978) (en banc):

> In a corporation, it may be necessary to glean information relevant to a legal problem from middle management or non-management personnel as well as from top executives. The attorney dealing with a complex legal problem "is thus faced with a 'Hobson's choice'. If he interviews employees not having 'the very highest authority', their communications to him will not be privileged. If, on the other hand, he interviews *only* those employees with 'the very highest authority', he may find extremely difficult, if not impossible, to determine what happened."

Id. at 608–609 (emphasis in original).

The control group test adopted by the court below thus frustrates the very purpose of the privilege by discouraging the communication of relevant information by employees of the client to attorneys seeking to render legal advice to the client corporation. The attorney's advice will also frequently be more significant to noncontrol group members than to those who officially sanction the advice, and the control group test makes it more difficult to convey full and frank legal advice to the employees who will put into effect the client corporation's policy. ("After the lawyer forms his or her opinion, it is of no immediate benefit to the Chairman of the Board or the President. It must be given to the corporate personnel who will apply it").

The narrow scope given the attorney-client privilege by the court below not only makes it difficult for corporate attorneys to formulate sound advice when their client is faced with a specific legal problem but also threatens to limit the valuable efforts of corporate counsel to ensure their client's compliance with the law. In light of the vast and complicated array of regulatory legislation confronting the modern corporation, corporations, unlike most individuals, "constantly go to lawyers to find out how to obey the law," . . . particularly since compliance with the law in this area is hardly an instinctive matter, ...[9] The test adopted by the court below is difficult

---

[9] (Court's original footnote 2.) The Government argues that the risk of civil or criminal liability suffices to ensure that corporations will seek legal advice in the absence of the protection of the privilege. This response ignores the fact that the depth and quality of any investigations to ensure compliance with the law would suffer, even were they undertaken. The response also proves too much, since it applies to all communications covered by the privilege: an individual trying to comply with the law or faced with a

to apply in practice, though no abstractly formulated and unvarying "test" will necessarily enable courts to decide questions such as this with mathematical precision. But if the purpose of the attorney-client privilege is to be served, the attorney and client must be able to predict with some degree of certainty whether particular discussions will be protected. An uncertain privilege, or one which purports to be certain but results in widely varying applications by the courts, is little better than no privilege at all. The very terms of the test adopted by the court below suggest the unpredictability of its application. The test restricts the availability of the privilege to those officers who play a "substantial role" in deciding and directing a corporation's legal response. Disparate decisions in cases applying this test illustrates its unpredictability. . . .

The communications at issue were made by Upjohn employees to counsel for Upjohn acting as such, at the direction of corporate superiors in order to secure legal advice from counsel. As the Magistrate found, "Mr. Thomas consulted with the Chairman of the Board and outside counsel and thereafter conducted a factual investigation to determine the nature and extent of the questionable payments *and to be in a position to give legal advice to the company with respect to the payments.*" (Emphasis supplied.) Information, not available from upper-echelon management, was needed to supply a basis for legal advice concerning compliance with securities and tax laws, foreign laws, currency regulations, duties to shareholders, and potential litigation in each of these areas. The communications concerned matters within the scope of the employees' corporate duties, and the employees themselves were sufficiently aware that they were being questioned in order that the corporation could obtain legal advice. The questionnaire identified Thomas as "the company's General Counsel" and referred in its opening sentence to the possible illegality of payments such as the ones on which information was sought. A statement of policy accompanying the questionnaire clearly indicated the legal implications of the investigation. The policy statement was issued "in order that there be no uncertainty in the future as to the policy with respect to the practices which are the subject of this investigation." It began "Upjohn will comply with all laws and regulations," and stated that commissions or payments "will not be used as a subterfuge for bribes or illegal payments" and that all payments must be "proper and legal." Any future agreements with foreign distributors or agents were to be approved "by a company attorney" and any questions concerning the policy were to be referred "to the company's General Counsel." This statement was issued to Upjohn employees worldwide, so that even those interviewees not receiving a questionnaire were aware of the legal implications of the interviews. Pursuant to explicit instruction from the Chairman of the Board, the communications were considered "highly confidential" when made, . . . and have been kept confidential by the company. Consistent with the underlying purposes of the attorney-client privilege, these communications must be protected against compelled disclosure.

The Court of Appeals declined to extend the attorney-client privilege beyond the limits of the control group test for fear that doing so would entail severe burdens on discovery and create a broad "zone of silence" over corporate affairs. Application of

---

legal problem also has strong incentive to disclose information to his lawyer, yet the common law has recognized the value of the privilege in further facilitating communications.

the attorney-client privilege to communications such as those involved here, however, puts the adversary in no worse position than if the communications had never taken place. The privilege only protects disclosure of communications; it does not protect disclosure of the underlying facts by those who communicated with the attorney:

> [T]he protection of the privilege extends only to *communications* and not to facts. A fact is one thing and a communication concerning that fact is an entirely different thing. The client cannot be compelled to answer the question, "What did you say or write to the attorney?" but may not refuse to disclose any relevant fact within his knowledge merely because he incorporated a statement of such fact into his communication to his attorney.

Philadelphia v. Westinghouse Electric Corp., 205 F. Supp. 830, 831 (E.D. Pa. 1962).

Here the Government was free to question the employees who communicated with Thomas and outside counsel. Upjohn has provided the IRS with a list of such employees, and the IRS has already interviewed some 25 of them. While it would probably be more convenient for the Government to secure the results of petitioner's internal investigation by simply subpoenaing the questionnaires and notes taken by petitioner's attorneys, such considerations of convenience do not overcome the policies served by the attorney-client privilege. As Justice Jackson noted in his concurring opinion in *Hickman v. Taylor*, 329 U.S., at 516, "Discovery was hardly intended to enable a learned profession to perform its functions . . . on wits borrowed from the adversary."

Needless to say, we decide only the case before us, and do not undertake to draft a set of rules which should govern challenges to investigatory subpoenas. Any such approach would violate the spirit of Federal Rule of Evidence 501. See S. Rep. No. 93-1277, p. 13 (1974) ("the recognition of a privilege based on a confidential relationship . . . should be determined on a case-by-case basis"). . . . While such a "case-by-case" basis may to some slight extent undermine desirable certainty in the boundaries of the attorney-client privilege, it obeys the spirit of the Rules. At the same time we conclude that the narrow "control group test" sanctioned by the Court of Appeals in this case cannot, consistent with "the principles of the common law as . . . interpreted . . . in the light of reason and experience," Fed. Rule Evid. 501, govern the development of the law in this area.

[c]   Maintenance of Confidentiality

However the courts define the group that personifies the corporation, the nature of large corporate enterprises is such that the preservation of confidentiality always poses a problem. As a consequence, courts have not been willing to presume that the corporation has maintained confidentiality. Rather, courts have imposed on the corporate client the burden of establishing it has properly maintained the requisite confidentiality. The corporation usually can satisfy this burden by demonstrating the existence of internal security practices that ensure the segregation of confidential documents and limited access on a need-to-know basis by authorized personnel. Absent evidence to the contrary, the court will presume the corporation followed such procedures for each communication for which the corporation has claimed a privilege. *See Diversified Industries, Inc. v. Meredith*, 572 F.2d 596, 609 (8th Cir. 1977) (en banc); *In re Grand Jury Proceedings Involving Berkley & Co.*, 466 F. Supp. 863 (D. Minn. 1979); *United States v. Kelsey-Hayes Wheel Co.*, 15 F.R.D. 461, 465 (E.D. Mich. 1954). The tenuous logic underlying the requirement of confidentiality is discussed in Paul R. Rice, *Attorney-Client Privilege: The Eroding Concept of Confidentiality Should Be Abolished*, 47 Duke L. Rev. 101 (1998).

[d] Stockholders' Right to Confidential Corporate Communications

A corporation is owned by its stockholders. What rights do those stockholders have to the privileged communications between the corporation's directors or employees and the attorneys the corporation has hired to obtain legal advice or assistance? In a stockholders' derivative action against corporate directors, for example, can the stockholders discover from the directors the latter's communications with the corporation's attorneys on matters that relate to the subject on which the action is based? The court in *Milroy v. Hanson* (excerpted below) provides the analysis that represents the majority rule.

MILROY v. HANSON
United States District Court, District of Nebraska
875 F. Supp. 646 (1995)

MEMORANDUM AND ORDER

Kopf, District Judge.

The interesting issue presented by this appeal (Filings 134, 136) from Magistrate Judge Piester's order (Filing 128) compelling production of documents is:

> whether a director of a corporation, who is also a minority stockholder, has the right to documents, which are otherwise presumably protected by the attorney-client privilege, when the corporation the director serves asserts the privilege against the director in the context of litigation brought by the director against the corporation and the remaining stockholders and directors wherein the director personally seeks from the defendant corporation and remaining defendants money damages and liquidation of the corporation.

Judge Piester held that the directors of the corporation were the "collective corporate 'client'" for purposes of the attorney-client privilege, (Filing 128, at 11), and the defendant corporation accordingly could not assert the attorney-client privilege against a director. Although I am reluctant to disagree with the magistrate judge's thoughtful opinion, I have concluded that Judge Piester erred as a matter of law when he reached this conclusion. Accordingly, I shall grant the appeal and remand the matter to Judge Piester for further consideration in accordance with this opinion. My reasons for this decision are set forth in the following portions of this memorandum.

I. BACKGROUND

Michael S. Milroy (Milroy) sued John G. Hanson, John F. Hanson, Jerry D. Hanson, and Jay Hanson (the "Hanson defendants"). Also named as a "nominal" defendant is Sixth Street Food Stores, Inc. ("Sixth Street"). Milroy is an attorney who resides in Arizona and practices at a large Arizona law firm.

Sixth Street is a closely held Nebraska corporation. It operates grocery stores in west-central Nebraska. At all material times, Milroy owned a minority interest in Sixth Street's stock, and he served and continues to serve as a member of the company's board of directors. At all material times, the Hanson defendants were majority stockholders in Sixth Street, owning the balance of the outstanding and issued stock. Some or all of the Hanson defendants constituted and continue to constitute a majority of Sixth Street's board of directors. There are no "outside" directors; thus, Milroy and some or all of the Hanson defendants constituted and continue to constitute the entire board of directors. Sometime prior to November, 1992, Milroy was treasurer of the corporation, but he has not served as a corporate officer since. All other significant corporate offices have always been and are now held by the Hanson defendants or some of them.

Milroy asserts three causes of action in his amended complaint. (Filing 29.) First, Milroy claims the Hanson defendants have abused the corporation and violated their fiduciary duty to him. Second, Milroy asserts a stockholder derivative suit on behalf of the corporation, claiming, among other things, that the Hanson defendants have wasted the assets of the corporation. Third, Milroy asserts a civil RICO action against the Hanson defendants, claiming they have operated Sixth Street as an unlawful enterprise. Milroy makes various claims for relief: he prays for monetary damages against all defendants, including the corporation; and he also requests that a judgment be entered against the corporation, ordering liquidation of corporate assets.

Milroy sought to obtain through discovery various documents held by either Sixth Street's outside accounting firm or Sixth Street's outside counsel. There has been no showing that Milroy was ever represented by Sixth Street's outside counsel. There has also been no showing that Milroy ever participated in any of the meetings, conferences, or discussions that gave rise to the assertion of the attorney-client privilege. There is no showing that Milroy has offered to review the documents solely in his fiduciary capacity as a director of Sixth Street or that he has otherwise agreed not to use the privileged material to further his personal interests in this litigation.

Although the company produced thousands of documents, Sixth Street has resisted the production of five documents held by its accountants and 96 documents held by its lawyers on the basis that these documents are protected by the attorney-client privilege. Sixth Street submitted to the court and all counsel so-called privilege logs and affidavits detailing the date each document was prepared, the party who prepared it, the subject matter of the document, the location of the document, the nature of any objection to production, and to whom the documents were distributed. (Filing 126.)

After Sixth Street refused to produce the requested documents, Milroy filed various motions to compel. (Filings 74–75.) Sixth Street responded by seeking a protective order. (Filing 79.)

Judge Piester ruled that Sixth Street could not assert the attorney-client privilege against Milroy, "assuming arguendo" that the "requirements of the attorney-client privilege have been satisfied" because Milroy, "as a director of Sixth Street, is a part of the collective corporate 'client' who holds and controls the corporation's attorney-client privilege, and thus the privilege cannot be invoked against him as it could against an outsider." (Filing 128, at 10.) Judge Piester relied primarily upon two cases for his conclusion: *Harris v. Wells*, 1990 U.S. Dist. LEXIS 13215, [at *9–*10] (D. Conn. 1990), and *Kirby v. Kirby*, [1987 Del. Ch. LEXIS 463] (Del. Ch. 1987). Judge Piester also found indirect support for his analysis in *Gottlieb v. Wiles*, 143 F.R.D. 241, 247 (D. Colo. 1992).

II. DISCUSSION

It is undisputed that corporations, like people, are entitled to the benefits of the attorney-client privilege under both federal law and Nebraska law. Compare *Commodity Futures Trading Comm. v. Weintraub*, 471 U.S. 343, 348–49, 105 S. Ct. 1986, 1990–91, 85 L. Ed. 2d 372 (1985) (citing *Upjohn Co. v. United States*, 449 U.S. 383, 101 S. Ct. 677, 66 L. Ed. 2d 584 (1981)) with Neb. Rev. Stat. § 27–503(1)(a) & (3) (Reissue 1989).

Milroy asks the court to adopt an exception to this general rule. He argues that the corporation should not be entitled to assert the privilege against him (1) because he is a director of the corporation and thus belongs to the entity which controls the corporation, or (2) because he is a stockholder who has initiated a stockholder derivative suit that presumably will benefit the corporation. I am not persuaded by either argument.

A. MILROY AS DIRECTOR

Since a corporation is not a natural person, its affairs are conducted in accordance with the laws that provide for the creation of corporations. *Weintraub*, 471 U.S. at 348 n. 4, 105 S. Ct. at 1991 n. 4. (discussing who could waive the privilege for a corporation and noting that "[s]tate corporation laws generally vest management authority in a corporation's board of directors"). In this case, the applicable law is Nebraska law. Under Nebraska law the affairs of a corporation are run by its board of directors. Neb. Rev. Stat. § 21-2035(1) (Reissue 1991) ("All corporate powers shall be exercised by or under the authority of and the business and affairs of a corporation shall be managed under the direction of a board of directors. . . ."). When there is a dispute between directors, under Nebraska law the majority decision of the directors governs what the corporation will or will not do. Neb. Rev. Stat. § 21-2040 (Reissue 1991). In this case, the majority of the directors of Sixth Street, who are all defendants herein, have determined (at least informally) to assert the attorney-client privilege against Milroy on behalf of the corporation.

Under normal circumstances, the majority decision of the board of directors would seem to end the matter because "for solvent corporations, the power to waive the corporate attorney-client privilege rests with the corporation's management and is normally exercised by its officers and directors." *Weintraub*, 471 U.S. at 348, 105 S. Ct. at 1991. It is "control" of the corporation which counts. The United States Supreme Court has recognized that "when control of a corporation passes to new management, the authority to assert and waive the corporation's attorney-client privilege passes as well." *Id.* at 349, 105 S. Ct. at 1991.

Therefore, since the majority decision of the board of directors of a Nebraska corporation "controls" the corporation under Nebraska law, it follows that an individual director is bound by the majority decision and cannot unilaterally waive or otherwise frustrate the corporation's attorney-client privilege if such an action conflicts with the majority decision of the board of directors.

However, Judge Piester reasoned that because Milroy was a member of the board of directors of Sixth Street at all pertinent times, Milroy essentially became the "client," albeit one part of "the collective corporate 'client.'" Thus, the judge reasoned that the privilege, belonging as it did to the client, could not be asserted against the "client." The cases relied upon by Judge Piester for this proposition are all based upon a Delaware chancery court's opinion known as *Kirby v. Kirby*, [1987 Del. Ch. LEXIS 463] (Del. Ch. 1987).

In *Kirby*, the court was confronted with a dispute between four siblings over control of a charitable foundation. Plaintiffs, three of the siblings, claimed to be among the directors of the foundation. They sued their brother Fred, admittedly a director, other defendants who claimed to be directors, and the F.M. Kirby Foundation. The foundation was a nonstock, nonprofit corporation. Plaintiffs sought to compel production of documents. The F.M. Kirby Foundation asserted the attorney-client privilege in response to the effort to compel production.

There were two periods of time at issue. *Id.* at 7. The first period of time was when the plaintiffs were admittedly directors of the corporation (prior to August 13, 1986), and the second period of time (after August 13, 1986) was when the plaintiffs ostensibly had been removed, unlawfully it was claimed, as directors. *Id.* Kirby thus involved documents produced both when plaintiffs were and were not directors.

With regard to the time period when the plaintiffs were directors, the issue pertinent to this case, the court reasoned that the "directors are all responsible for the proper management of the corporation, and it seems consistent with their joint obligations that they be treated as the 'joint client' when legal advice is rendered to the corporation through one of its officers or directors." *Id.* This proposition was stated without citation to any authority.

In *Harris v. Wells*, 1990 U.S. Dist. LEXIS 13215, 1990 WL 150445, at 4 (D. Conn. Sept. 5, 1990), another case relied upon by Judge Piester, the court was confronted with a suit involving a Delaware corporation. The facts of the case are not set forth with any clarity in the court's opinion, and "[f]amiliarity is presumed with the convoluted factual and procedural background behind these consolidated lawsuits . . . ." *Id.* at 1.

In any event, *Harris v. Wells* seems to involve a suit where one group of directors sued a corporation and a sole director. *Id.* at 3–4. The defendant director was also an attorney for the corporation. Plaintiffs, as directors, sought to compel production from the defendant director. *Id.* When this one director sought to assert the attorney-client privilege against the other directors, the court, relying upon *Kirby*, concluded that the sole director could not assert the privilege against the other plaintiff directors. *Id.* at 4.

Judge Piester also cited *Gottlieb v. Wiles*, 143 F.R.D. 241, 247 (D. Colo. 1992). In that case, a former director, who had previously been chief executive officer and chairman of the board, sought production of documents in a suit against the corporation he once served. Relying upon *Kirby*, the court found that the attorney-client privilege could not be asserted against the former director. The court reasoned that the situation in Gottlieb was analogous to a situation where parties with a common interest retain a single attorney but later become adverse. The court observed that neither party in that situation is permitted to assert the attorney-client privilege against the other. Thus, the *Gottlieb* court reasoned that the present board of directors should not be permitted to assert the privilege against a former member of the board.

With all due respect, cases like *Kirby*, *Harris*, and *Gottlieb* make a fundamental error by assuming that for a corporation there exists a "collective corporate 'client' " which may take a position adverse to "management" for purposes of the attorney-client privilege. There is but one client, and that client is the corporation. *Weintraub*, 471 U.S. at 348, 105 S. Ct. at 1990. This is true despite the fact that a corporation can only act through human beings. As the Supreme Court has stated, "for solvent corporations" the "authority to assert and waive the corporation's attorney-client privilege" rests with "management." *Weintraub*, 471 U.S. at 348–49, 105 S. Ct. at 1991 (emphasis added). A dissident director is by definition not "management" and, accordingly, has no authority to pierce or otherwise frustrate the attorney-client privilege when such action conflicts with the will of "management."

It is undisputed that as the majority of the board of directors, the Hanson defendants or some of them are "management." Accordingly, Milroy has no right to frustrate the attorney-client privilege in the face of opposition from Sixth Street's management. A number of cases have recognized this principle in a wide variety of circumstances. *See, e.g., In re Braniff, Inc.*, 153 B.R. 941, 945 (Bankr. M.D. Fla. 1993) (absent a specialized showing, former directors and officers were not entitled to documents when privilege asserted by corporation); *Tail of the Pup, Inc. v. Webb*, 528 So.2d 506 (Fla. Dist. Ct. App. 1988) (individual stockholder who was also officer and director had no authority to waive or assert the privilege against the wishes of the corporation's board of directors); *In re Estate of Weinberg*, 133 Misc. 2d 950, 509 N.Y.S.2d 240, 242–43 (1986), *aff'd sub nom., In re Beiny*, 132 A.D.2d 190, 522 N.Y.S.2d 511 (1987) (officer of a corporation had no claim to see corporation's privileged materials or to waive the privilege); *Hoiles v. Superior Ct.*, 157 Cal. App. 3d 1192, 204 Cal. Rptr. 111 (1984) (corporation's attorney-client privilege properly asserted against minority shareholder and director).

Five concluding comments are appropriate. I turn to those observations now.

First, both sides presented good policy arguments regarding the attorney-client privilege and why their respective positions should be adopted. However, those arguments are beside the point. The relevant substantive law defines how corporations function, and such law dictates who may assert, waive, or frustrate the privilege. Whether the purposes behind the attorney-client privilege would be enhanced or degraded by expanding or decreasing the class of individuals who can assert, waive, or frustrate the corporation's privilege is irrelevant because, as the Supreme Court noted in *Weintraub*, 471 U.S. at 348 n. 4, 105 S. Ct. at 1991 n. 4, for solvent corporations it is necessary to focus on "state corporation law" to answer the question. Simply put, once it is determined that a corporation has the attorney-client privilege, judicial policy choices regarding the attorney-client privilege cannot and should not trump the legislatively enacted substantive law of corporations regarding the rights of corporate "management."

Second, this is not a case predicated upon Nebraska corporate law regarding whether Milroy, as a member of Sixth Street's board of directors, has some right to examine corporate documents in his role as a corporate director. He has filed suit, in major part, to benefit himself. He does not contend that under Nebraska corporate law he has some entitlement to documents in his fiduciary role as a corporate director. Furthermore, he has made no showing that he wants the documents to fulfil his fiduciary duty to Sixth Street and all its shareholders, as opposed to using the documents to further his personal goals in this litigation. Accordingly, the attorney-client privilege is properly asserted against Milroy, notwithstanding his position as a director of the corporation. *Hoiles v. Superior Ct.*, 157 Cal. App. 3d at 1201–02, 204 Cal. Rptr. 111 (since shareholder had not brought underlying suit for breach of fiduciary duty and to dissolve closely held corporation in his capacity as a corporate director and had not requested information from corporate counsel on a fiduciary basis, attorney-client privilege was properly asserted).

Third, Judge Piester assumed, as do I, that the attorney-client privilege existed as to the specific documents at issue. Nothing I have said is intended to prohibit Judge Piester from determining on remand whether this assumption is valid.

Fourth, Milroy asserts the so-called crime-fraud exception to the attorney-client privilege. Judge Piester did not reach this issue, and neither do I. Judge Piester will be free to probe this issue upon remand.

Fifth, there is no claim by Milroy that he was as a matter of fact the "joint" client, together with Sixth Street, of outside counsel. For reasons articulated above, I am unwilling to analogize to the joint-client situation for purposes of determining who may assert, waive, or frustrate the corporation's privilege. However, should there be evidence that Milroy was in fact the joint client of outside counsel, an entirely different situation would be presented. Judge Piester is free to explore this question, if otherwise appropriate, upon remand.

In sum, when viewed from the perspective of the applicable substantive corporate law, Milroy, as a dissident director, has no right to waive or otherwise pierce Sixth Street's attorney-client privilege because he is not the "management" of the corporation and "management" of the corporation, as it has a right to do, asserts the privilege against him.

B. MILROY AS STOCKHOLDER

Relying upon *Garner v. Wolfinbarger*, 430 F.2d at 1100–04, Milroy asserts an alternative argument. He claims he ought to be entitled to the documents since he brought this action at least in part as a stockholder's derivative suit. Thus, Milroy believes that on balance his interest as a representative of all stockholders in the derivative suit outweighs the interests of the corporation in the privilege.

In *Garner*, the United States Court of Appeals for the Fifth Circuit ruled that in a stockholder class-action suit, the class representative could obtain documents over the corporation's claim of attorney-client privilege if the class showed "good cause." *Id.* at 1103. The "good cause" was measured by nine factors. *Id.* at 1104. The Garner court reasoned that when stockholders sue a corporation, it may be inappropriate to allow the attorney-client privilege to be asserted against the stockholders because in some circumstances such an assertion would amount to use of the privilege to harm the true owners of the privilege — the stockholders.

I will not follow Garner for two reasons.

First, Garner has not been adopted by the United States Court of Appeals for the Eighth Circuit. In fact, "Garner's continued vitality is suspect . . . even in federal courts." *Hoiles v. Superior Ct.*, 157 Cal. App. 3d at 1198–99, 204 Cal. Rptr. 111. Many commentators believe "*Garner* was wrong and . . . the attorney-client privilege in shareholder cases should apply just at it does in other litigation." Stephen A. Saltzburg, Corporate Attorney-Client Privilege in Shareholder Litigation and Similar Cases: Garner Revisited, 12 Hofstra L. Rev. 817, 840 (1984) (This and other like commentary is cited and discussed in Defs.' Reply Br. at 11–14.). But see Jack B. Weinstein et al., Weinstein's Evidence ¶ 503(b)[05], at 503-93–98 (1992) (approving Garner, but recognizing that the issue is "currently unresolved and troublesome").

In my opinion, *Garner*, adopted as it was prior to the Supreme Court's opinions in *Upjohn* and *Weintraub*, is problematic because (a) it is in effect a lower-court-created exception to the general rule announced by the Supreme Court in *Upjohn* and *Weintraub* that a corporation has the right to assert an attorney-client privilege, and (b) the *Garner* opinion does not focus on the critical issue of "management," as the Supreme Court did in *Weintraub*, and the relevant substantive law of corporations for purposes of determining who may assert, waive, or otherwise frustrate the attorney-client privilege for a solvent corporation. As a result, I am not inclined to adopt *Garner* without clear direction from the court of appeals.

Second, whatever the utility of the *Garner* rationale, it has no applicability where the plaintiff stockholder asserts claims primarily to benefit himself, particularly where such claims will undoubtedly harm all other stockholders if successful. *Cox v. Administrator U.S. Steel & Carnegie*, 17 F.3d 1386, 1415–16 (11th Cir.), modified on other grounds, 30 F.3d 1347 (11th Cir. 1994) (court declined to follow Garner because "[t]he plaintiffs . . . seek damages not on behalf of the Union [the defendant], but for their personal benefit at the expense of the Union and its other members"); *Weil v. Investment/Indicators, Research & Management, Inc.*, 647 F.2d 18, 23 (9th Cir. 1981) (because plaintiff sought "to recover damages from the corporation for herself and the members of her proposed class," the court concluded that "*Garner's* holding and policy rationale simply do not apply here").

While it is true that Milroy has asserted a stockholder derivative action in this case, such an assertion does not invoke the *Garner* policy rationale because Milroy's suit is intended primarily to benefit Milroy personally, to the detriment of all remaining stockholders who are defendants. Milroy specifically asserts two claims in his personal capacity, and those claims are directed at both the corporation and the remaining stockholders. Moreover, the derivative suit will not benefit other Sixth Street stockholders because all of the other stockholders are defendants. Thus, the *Garner* policy rationale, whatever its general appeal, is not applicable here.

In summary, Milroy is not entitled to the documents based upon the so-called Garner rule because that rule has not been adopted by the United States Court of Appeals for the Eighth Circuit and the rationale for application of the rule is not present because the plaintiff stockholder has sued primarily to benefit himself, to the detriment of all remaining stockholders.

Accordingly,

IT IS ORDERED that:

(1) The appeals (Filings 134, 136) are sustained, and the matter is remanded to United States Magistrate Judge David L. Piester for further proceedings;

(2) Sixth Street's motion for stay pending appeal (Filing 137) is denied as moot.

[B] Duration of Privilege

Once established, how long does the attorney-client privilege survive? It survives forever. Not only does it survive the termination of the attorney-client relationship, it also survives the death of the client. *Swidler & Berlin v. United States*, 524 U.S. 399 (1998). Aside from a waiver of the privilege, the only exception to this rule arises if there is litigation between the testator's heirs, legatees, devisees, or other parties to litigation concerning the validity or construction of the deceased client's will. In this limited situation, the courts have used the legal fiction that the testator would want the attorney to reveal the contents of the testator's prior confidential communications so that his or her intent can be effectuated through the will. *See Stegman v. Miller*, 515 S.W.2d 244 (Ky. Ct. App. 1974).

[C] Crime-Fraud Exception to Privilege

The Supreme Court addressed the fraud exception to the privilege concept in *Clark v. United States*, 289 U.S. 1 (1932). Although the particular issue in that case concerned the effect of fraud on the privilege applicable to jury deliberations, not the attorney-client privilege, the Court acknowledged that the effect was the same on both. Referring to the attorney-client privilege, the Court stated: "The privilege takes flight if the relation is abused. A client who consults an attorney for advice that will serve him in the commission of a fraud will have no help from the law. He must let the truth be told." *Id.* at 15. The Court then addressed the standard by which the proponent must establish the charge of fraud:

> There are early cases apparently to the effect that a mere charge of illegality, not supported by any evidence, will set the confidences free. . . . But this concept of the privilege is without support in later rulings. "It is obvious that it would be absurd to say that the privilege could be got rid of merely by making a charge of fraud." *O'Rourke v. Darbishire*, [1920] A.C. 581, 604. To drive the privilege away, there must be "something to give colour to the charge;" there must be "*prima facie* evidence that it has some foundation in fact." *Id.*; also pp. 614, 622, 631, 633. When that evidence is supplied, the seal of secrecy is broken. . . . Nor does the loss of the privilege depend upon the showing of a conspiracy, upon proof that client and attorney are involved in equal guilt. The attorney may be innocent, and still the guilty client must let the truth come out.

Clark, 289 U.S. at 15.

The following case further explains the operation and effect of this act of waiver.

UNITED STATES v. LENTZ
United States District Court, Eastern District of Virginia
419 F. Supp. 2d 820 (2005)

ELLIS, DISTRICT JUDGE.

In this remanded kidnapping for murder prosecution, the defendant seeks suppression of certain tape-recorded telephone communications between defendant Jay E. Lentz ("Lentz") and his attorney regarding a murder-for-hire plot to eliminate key witnesses and the prosecutor in defendant's case. At issue is (i) whether the tape recordings are protected by the attorney-client privilege and (ii) whether the tape recordings were illegally obtained in violation of defendant's Sixth Amendment rights.

I.

The facts relevant to this motion to suppress occurred following remand of this case for retrial and while Lentz was incarcerated at Northern Neck Regional Jail (NNRJ) awaiting the retrial. Yet, a brief synopsis of the underlying kidnapping for murder prosecution and the procedural history of this case provides the context essential to a full understanding of the questions presented.

Lentz is charged with kidnapping for murder in violation of 18 U.S.C. § 1201(a) for the disappearance and murder of his ex-wife, Doris Lentz ("Doris"). Because neither Doris' body nor a murder weapon were ever found, the government's case against Lentz in the first trial in June 2003 was largely circumstantial. In this regard, the government presented evidence at trial tending to show, inter alia, (i) that Lentz had physically and verbally abused Doris during their marriage; (ii) that, based on a prior arrangement between Doris and Lentz, Doris had gone to Lentz's house to pick up their daughter, Julia, on the day Doris disappeared; (iii) that Doris had told her mother, boyfriend, aunt, and friend that she was going to Lentz's house in Maryland to pick up Julia on the day she disappeared; (iv) that within days of Doris' disappearance, her car was found abandoned in a District of Columbia parking lot, unlocked, and with her purse and keys in plain view; (v) that there were blood stains in the car's interior, nearly all of which contained Doris' DNA; (vi) that one of the blood stains in Doris' car was a match for Lentz's DNA; and (vii) that the driver's seat of Doris' car had been adjusted to fit someone who (like Lentz) was much taller than Doris.

After two weeks of trial and approximately five days of jury deliberation, the jury convicted Lentz of kidnapping resulting in death in violation of 18 U.S.C. § 1801(a), but the district court then entered a judgment of acquittal on the ground that the government's evidence was insufficient to meet the holding element required by the statute. Because certain evidence not admitted at trial had found its way into the jury room, the district court also ordered a new trial. *See United States v. Lentz*, 275 F. Supp. 2d 723 (E.D. Va. 2003), *rev'd in part*, 383 F.3d 191 (4th Cir. 2004) (Memorandum Opinion). On appeal, the Fourth Circuit reversed the trial court's judgment of acquittal, but upheld the grant of a new trial. *See United States v. Lentz*, 383 F.3d 191, 195 (4th Cir. 2004) (*Lentz I*). Accordingly, the matter was remanded for a new trial to be conducted by a different district judge. See *id.* at 221. The matter is now here on remand for a retrial, which is now scheduled to commence on November 28, 2005.

During the interim between the remand of this case and the originally scheduled July 11 trial date, the case took a surprising twist. On May 19, 2005, the government, in an ex parte, under seal pleading, represented that it had information from inmate Christopher Jackmon ("Jackmon"), who was incarcerated with Lentz at NNRJ from late 2004 until early 2005, concerning Lentz's murder-for-hire plot. Specifically, Jackmon was prepared to testify that Lentz had discussed his case with him and ultimately had solicited Jackmon's help in a plot to kill (i) certain key prosecution witnesses Lentz believed had provided especially damaging testimony in his first trial; and (ii) one or both of the prosecutors in his case, namely Assistant United States Attorneys Steven D. Mellin and Patricia M. Haynes. Most relevant here, the government also represented that it had obtained tape recordings of three telephone conversations that occurred on January 10, 2005 between Lentz and his attorney, Frank Salvato, that the government believes corroborates Jackmon's story.

These three telephone calls occurred between 9:39 a.m. and 10:26 a.m. on January 10, 2005, and were placed by Lentz to his counsel from a telephone located in "C Pod," the pod that included Lentz's cell at NNRJ. The record convincingly establishes that during the period in question, all outgoing telephone calls from NNRJ were recorded and subject to monitoring by jail officials and that Lentz and his counsel knew this was so. At the pretrial evidentiary hearing on this issue, Major Ted Hull, the assistant superintendent for the NNRJ, testified (i) that all outgoing telephone calls placed by inmates at NNRJ are placed through the same telephone system; (ii) that all such calls are subject to monitoring and recording; and (iii) that prior to connecting each outgoing call, the system plays a pre-recorded message, heard by both parties, stating that the call is subject to monitoring and recording. Accordingly, NNRJ has a recording of all outgoing inmate calls, including those made by Lentz on the day in question and, prior to connecting the parties, both Lentz and his counsel received the pre-recorded message advising them that the call would be recorded and was subject to monitoring. Indeed, Lentz and his counsel essentially acknowledged as much during the course of their conversations.

The content of the three telephone calls at issue merits a brief description. During the first call, Lentz asked Mr. Salvato what he knew about "a guy named Ridley [who] got murdered at the Springfield Mall." When Mr. Salvato inquired why this murder was relevant to Lentz's case, Lentz explicitly refused to answer. Immediately following this exchange, Lentz began to press Mr. Salvato for details about Jackmon. In this regard, at one point Lentz explicitly stated to Mr. Salvato, "I'm asking you to certify some information. This is important." Presumably, what Lentz meant by this was that the purpose of his calls was to determine whether Jackmon had been telling Lentz the truth about being released from prison soon because a key witness in the case against Jackmon had been murdered. Lentz apparently believed that this murder was the handiwork of a "hit man" Jackmon had hired, and that the murder had taken place at Springfield Mall. During the third call, when Mr. Salvato inquired how Jackmon would be able to help Lentz, Lentz replied that Jackmon would be able to help Lentz secure a hit man "in case [Lentz] need[ed] something like that to happen in [his] case." The context of this statement leaves no doubt that the "something like that" to which Lentz referred was a murder-for-hire arrangement. Moreover, during these calls Lentz specifically directed Mr. Salvato not to call him by name, but to use an alias, "Bucks," instead. Over the course of these conversations, Mr. Salvato repeatedly asked Lentz if he was kidding about hiring a hit man. In response, Lentz stated that "[he doesn't] joke at 9 in the morning." Presumably to entice Mr. Salvato to empathize with him, Lentz stated that he was "sitting in the bowels of hell," that he was "at the end of his rope," and that "[he's] gotta do what [he's] gotta do to survive."

In sum, the three calls in question focus chiefly on whether Jackmon could be trusted regarding Lentz's possible use of a hit man to murder witnesses and perhaps a prosecutor prior to his forthcoming retrial. The contents of these calls, taken as a whole, invite the inference that Lentz was seriously considering a murder-for-hire plot, and was calling Mr. Salvato to inquire about Jackmon's reliability with respect to information Jackmon had provided Lentz about his own case.

On May 19, 2005, the government filed an ex parte, under seal motion seeking an order permitting the government team investigating the taped calls to disclose the transcripts of those calls as well as the recordings of the calls themselves, to both the prosecutors assigned to conduct the Lentz retrial and the team of prosecutors investigating the murder-for-hire plot. That motion was denied, and the government was directed instead to deliver promptly to defense counsel a copy of the government's under seal motion and its attachments, which included the telephone call transcripts. See *United States v. Lentz*, Case No. 1:01cr150 (E.D. Va. May 20, 2005) (Order). Lentz was then allowed a period of time to investigate the matter, after which he moved, by counsel, to suppress all transcripts and recordings of his telephone conversations with his attorney. In Lentz's view, the telephone calls and their contents (i) are protected by the attorney-client privilege; and (ii) were illegally obtained in violation of his Sixth Amendment rights. The issue, then, is whether either the attorney-client privilege or Lentz's Sixth Amendment right to counsel precludes the government from using the contents of these telephone conversations for any purpose, including offering them at the retrial as evidence of Lentz's consciousness of guilt with respect to Doris' murder.

II.

Few principles of law are as well-settled as the attorney-client privilege; it is a bedrock principle of the adversary system. In essence, the privilege's purpose is to encourage full and frank communication between attorneys and clients by according court-enforced protection against disclosure of such communications when the client invokes the privilege. The privilege recognizes that sound legal advice and informed advocacy serves the public interest, that such advice or advocacy depends upon the lawyer's being fully informed by the client, and that this occurs only where the client feels secure that communications with counsel will not be disclosed. *Upjohn Co. v. United States*, 449 U.S. 383, 389, 101 S. Ct. 677, 66 L. Ed. 2d 584 (1981). *See also Trammel v. United States*, 445 U.S. 40, 51, 100 S. Ct. 906, 63 L. Ed. 2d 186 (1980) ("The lawyer-client privilege rests on the need for the advocate and counselor to know all that relates to the client's reasons for seeking representation if the professional mission is to be carried out."); *Fisher v. United States*, 425 U.S. 391, 403, 96 S. Ct. 1569, 48 L. Ed. 2d 39 (1976) (stating that the attorney-client privilege encourages full disclosure by clients to their attorneys).

While recognizing the fundamental importance of the privilege, courts have nonetheless been careful not to stretch its application to circumstances beyond its rationale. This is so because the attorney-client privilege, like all privileges, "impedes [the] full and free discovery of the truth," and is "in derogation of the public's 'right to every man's evidence.' " *In re Grand Jury Proceedings*, 727 F.2d 1352, 1355 (4th Cir. 1984) (quoting *Weil v. Investment/Indicators, Research & Management, Inc.*, 647 F.2d 18, 24 (9th Cir. 1981)). Accordingly, courts carefully construe the privilege to apply only to those situations in which the party invoking the privilege consulted an attorney for the purpose of securing a legal opinion or services, and in connection with that consultation, communicated information intended to be kept confidential. *See In re Grand Jury Proceedings*, 727 F.2d at 1355; *United States v. Jones*, 696 F.2d 1069, 1072 (4th Cir. 1982). Thus, in this circuit and elsewhere, the boundaries of the attorney-client privilege are clearly demarcated and well-settled. The privilege applies only if:

> (1) the asserted holder of the privilege is or sought to become a client; (2) the person to whom the communication was made (a) is a member of the bar of a court, or his subordinate and (b) in connection with this communication is acting as a lawyer; (3) the communication relates to a fact of which the attorney was informed (a) by his client (b) without the presence of strangers (c) for the purpose of securing primarily either (i) an opinion on law or (ii) legal services or (iii) assistance in some legal proceeding, and not (d) for the purpose of committing a crime or tort; and (4) the privilege has been (a) claimed and (b) not waived by the client. *Jones*, 696 F.2d at 1072 (4th Cir. 1982).

And importantly, the burden is on the proponent of the attorney-client privilege to demonstrate its applicability. Specifically, the proponent must establish "not only that an attorney-client relationship existed, but also that the particular communications at issue are privileged and that the privilege was not waived." *In re Grand Jury Subpoena*, 341 F.3d 331, 335 (4th Cir. 2003). And, it is also well-settled that a client waives the attorney-client privilege by voluntarily disclosing otherwise privileged communications to a third party. In fact, this requirement of confidentiality is so central to any claim of privilege that the privilege may be lost even by an inadvertent disclosure to a third party. *See In re Grand Jury Proceedings*, 727 F.2d at 1356 (holding that the privilege is lost where the party did not take "reasonable steps to insure and maintain [the] confidentiality [of the communications.]"); *see also id.* (noting that the presence of eavesdroppers in certain circumstances may destroy the privilege). Waiver need not be explicit; the client waives the privilege by conduct "which implies a waiver of the privilege or a consent to disclosure." *U.S. v. Dakota*, 197 F.3d 821, 825 (6th Cir. 1999); *In re von Bulow*, 828 F.2d 94, 104 (2d Cir. 1987) (same). *See also Hanson v. U.S. Agency for Intern. Development*, 372 F.3d 286, 293–94 (4th Cir. 2004) ("A client can waive an attorney-client privilege expressly or through his own conduct.").

These principles, applied here, compel the conclusion that an inmate's telephone conversations with counsel are not protected by the attorney-client privilege where, as here, the inmate is notified at the outset that the calls are recorded and subject to monitoring. In these circumstances, Lentz could not reasonably have assumed that his conversations with Mr. Salvato would be confidential. His decision to proceed with the conversations, despite notification that the conversations were being recorded and were subject to monitoring, is no different from Lentz electing to proceed with these conversations notwithstanding the known presence of a third party within earshot of the conversation.

The Fourth Circuit has not yet squarely addressed the question whether inmates waive any privilege protection for telephone conversations when they choose to proceed with these conversations in the face of notice that the calls are being recorded and subject to monitoring. Significantly, however, the three circuits that have done so have uniformly held that such notice destroys any expectation of privilege. Particularly instructive in this regard is the Eight Circuit's opinion in *United States v. Hatcher*, in which the panel held that:

The presence of the prison recording device destroyed the attorney-client privilege. Because the inmates and their lawyers were aware that their conversations were being recorded, they could not reasonably expect that their conversations would remain private. The presence of the recording device was the functional equivalent of the presence of a third party. These conversations were not privileged. *Hatcher*, 323 F.3d at 674.

Similarly, Lentz here could not "reasonably expect that . . . [his] conversations would remain private." *Id.* It follows that Lentz's recorded conversations with his attorney, like the recorded conversations in Hatcher, were not privileged. Lentz attempts to distinguish Hatcher on the ground that the monitoring notice at NNRJ was not played before all calls and that, as a result, he reasonably believed that his calls to Mr. Salvato were confidential or protected by the privilege. This argument fails. Contrary to Lentz's argument, the record establishes that, with only one exception not relevant here, the NNRJ system automatically and unfailingly provided the recording and monitoring notice before each call was connected, and that this occurred with respect to the three calls at issue here. Thus, Lentz and Mr. Salvato received the notice before each of the three calls and Lentz's decision to proceed with the conversations under these circumstances constituted a waiver of the attorney-client privilege. *See U.S. v. Dakota*, 197 F.3d 821, 825 (6th Cir. 1999) (stating that client's waiver of privilege can be implied from conduct inconsistent with the assertion of that privilege); *In re von Bulow*, 828 F.2d 94, 104 (2d Cir. 1987) (same); *Hanson*, 372 F.3d at 293–94 (4th Cir. 2004) (same). Moreover, as noted previously, Lentz's concern that the calls might be recorded suggests that he did not, in fact, believe that the calls were privileged. If Lentz truly believed that his conversations with Mr. Salvato were privileged, then he would have been unconcerned about any possible recording, since it would be inadmissible.

In sum, then, the notice at the beginning of each call, as well as Lentz's statements during the calls, make clear that Lentz could not reasonably have expected the conversations to be confidential. Accordingly, the telephone calls between Lentz and Mr. Salvato are not privileged.

III.

A separate and independent ground for the result reached here is the well-established crime fraud exception to the attorney-client privilege. Thus, assuming, arguendo, that Lentz had a reasonable expectation that his conversations with Mr. Salvato would be confidential, they nonetheless would not be privileged because communications made for an unlawful purpose or to further an illegal scheme are not privileged. The crime-fraud exception applies only to communications about ongoing or future activities. Communications concerning past crimes or frauds are privileged unless the privilege has otherwise been waived. *In re Grand Jury Subpoena Duces Tecum*, 731 F.2d 1032, 1041 (2nd Cir. 1984) (stating that communications with respect to past frauds are privileged); *X Corp.*, 805 F. Supp. at 1307 (same).

The rationale for the crime-fraud exception is closely tied to the policies underlying the attorney-client privilege. Whereas confidentiality of communications facilitates the rendering of sound legal advice, which is to be encouraged, it cannot be said that advice in furtherance of a fraudulent or unlawful goal is sound, nor is it to be encouraged. Rather, advice in furtherance of such goals is anathema to our system of justice; hence, a client's communications seeking such advice are not worthy of protection. It is immaterial whether the attorney knew that the client was seeking his advice for illegal purposes or whether the attorney joined in, or, as here, counseled against the illegal activity. The attorney's knowledge and intent are not material to the operation of the crime fraud exception; only the client's knowledge and intent are material in this regard. It is similarly immaterial whether the defendant actually succeeded in completing the crime or fraud in question; rather, solicitation alone triggers the exception. *In re Grand Jury Subpoena Duces Tecum*, 731 F.2d 1032, 1039 (2d Cir. 1984) ("The crime or fraud need not have occurred for the exception to be applicable; it need only have been the objective of the client's communication.").

The party asserting the crime-fraud exception to the privilege-here, the government-bears the burden to establish a prima facie case that the communications in question fall outside the scope of the privilege. *In re Grand Jury Proceedings # 5*, 401 F.3d at 251; *Chaudhry v. Gallerizzo*, 174 F.3d 394, 403 (4th Cir. 1999). To overcome an established privilege using the crime-fraud exception, the government must show that the communications (i) were made for an unlawful purpose or to further an illegal scheme and (ii) reflect an ongoing or future unlawful or illegal scheme or activity. Importantly, the purported crime or fraud need not be proved either by a preponderance or beyond a reasonable doubt. Rather, the proof "must be such as to subject the opposing party to the risk of non-persuasion of the evidence as to the disputed fact is left unrebutted." *See Union Camp Corp.*, 385 F.2d at 144–45. Finally, when making its prima facie showing, the government is not limited to admissible evidence; it may rely on any relevant evidence, including hearsay, that has been lawfully obtained that is not otherwise privileged.

These principles, applied here, make clear that the government has made a prima facie showing that the crime-fraud exception applies to the conversations in question. In this case, the contents of the telephone calls, viewed as a whole, leave no doubt that Lentz's primary purpose in calling Mr. Salvato was to discuss Lentz's murder-for-hire plot. Specifically, Lentz sought to corroborate certain things that Jackmon had told him, including (i) whether Jackmon's release from prison was imminent and (ii) whether Jackmon's release was related to the murder of a witness in his case. When Mr. Salvato asked Lentz why this was relevant, Lentz replied that Jackmon might help him "in case [Lentz] needed something like that to happen on [his] case." The conversations in general, and this comment in particular, leave no doubt that Lentz's purpose in calling Mr. Salvato was to get information that would assist Lentz in the planning and carrying out the murder-for-hire plot.

In sum, then, Lentz called Mr. Salvato in order to assess the validity of what Jackmon had told him, which would in turn help Lentz decide whether he should continue to trust Jackmon and involve Jackmon in the planning and/or execution of Lentz's murder-for-hire plot. Accordingly, there can be little doubt that Lentz, in contacting Mr. Salvato, was seeking aid and information from his attorney to further his nascent murder-for-hire plot.

Given that the government has more than met its burden to show that the calls at issue fall within the crime-fraud exception, it falls to Lentz to rebut this showing. He has failed to do so; he offers no plausible justification or argument for why the conversations at issue should escape the crime-fraud exception to the privilege. Therefore, because the crime-fraud exception strips the conversations at issue of any privilege protection, the contents of the calls between Lentz and Mr. Salvato would not be protected by the privilege even had they been confidential.

IV.

Quite apart from Lentz's privilege claim, he advances two Sixth Amendment claims to prevent the government's disclosure and use of the recorded telephone conversations. First, Lentz claims that his statements during the telephone calls were improperly elicited by the government through its agent, Jackmon, in violation of Lentz's Sixth Amendment right to counsel. Second, he claims that the

NNRJ's policy of tape recording all outgoing calls constitutes a denial of his right to counsel, since the monitoring effectively prevented Lentz from conferring confidentially with his attorney. Both claims fail.

* * *

To be sure, telephone communications might well be more convenient for counsel, but NNRJ is not constitutionally compelled to provide Lentz with the most convenient or his preferred mode of conferring with his attorney. *See Bellamy v. McMickens*, 692 F. Supp. at 214 (noting that the government need not provide the best manner of access to counsel); *Aswegan*, 981 F.2d at 314 (same); *Dalsheim*, 558 F. Supp. at 675 (same). Instead, NNRJ officials must have discretion to strike a proper balance between providing reasonable avenues for inmate-attorney confidential communications and accommodating the important penological interests in detecting and thwarting inmate criminal conduct carried out in part by telephone calls. This record reflects that NNRJ has not abused its discretion in striking this balance, and the NNRJ policy of recording and monitoring all inmate telephone calls does not infringe Lentz's Sixth Amendment rights.

In sum, therefore, the record evidence does not support the conclusion that the telephone calls at issue on January 10, 2005 between Lentz and Mr. Salvato should be suppressed under either the attorney-client privilege or the Sixth Amendment right to counsel. Accordingly, defendant's motion to suppress the recordings of the telephone calls and to preclude their disclosure to the government's trial team must be denied, and the government may now disclose the recordings and the associated transcripts both to the team investigating the alleged murder-for-hire plot, and to the trial team. Importantly, however, all prosecutors on all three teams, as well as all defense counsel and defendant, are directed to treat as sealed all matters relating to the alleged murder-for-hire plot until further Order of the Court.

An appropriate Order will issue.

§ 9.05 WAIVER OF ATTORNEY-CLIENT PRIVILEGE

[A] Waiver Rule Summarized

The attorney-client privilege protects the confidentiality of a communication so long as the client does not:

(1) breach the confidentiality on which the privilege is premised through disclosure of the communication to third parties; or

(2) take action that is inconsistent with the confidentiality of the privilege by:

    (a) accusing the attorney of ineffective assistance, thereby forcing the attorney to disclose the confidential communications in order to defend herself against such a charge, or

    (b) making the confidential communications a material issue in a judicial proceeding by relying on it as a defense, for example by relying on the defense of advice of counsel to meet the charge of fraudulent intent.

[B]   Acts of Waiver

[1]   Allegations of Ineffective Assistance of Counsel

BITTAKER v. WHITFORD
United States Court of Appeals, Ninth Circuit
331 F.3d 715 (2003)

KOZINSKI, CIRCUIT JUDGE.

Lawrence Bittaker was convicted in California state court of multiple murders and was sentenced to death. After unsuccessfully exhausting his state remedies, In re Bittaker, No. S052371, 2000 Cal. LEXIS 9066 (Cal. Nov. 29, 2000); In re Bittaker, No. S058797, 2000 Cal. LEXIS 9067 (Cal. Nov. 29, 2000), Bittaker filed a federal habeas petition pursuant to 28 U.S.C. § 2254 raising a multitude of claims, including a variety of ineffective assistance of counsel claims. It has long been the rule in the federal courts that, where a habeas petitioner raises a claim of ineffective assistance of counsel, he waives the attorney-client privilege as to all communications with his allegedly ineffective lawyer. *See, e.g., Wharton v. Calderon*, 127 F.3d 1201, 1203 (9th Cir. 1997); *Tasby v. United States*, 504 F.2d 332, 336 (8th Cir. 1974); *Laughner v. United States*, 373 F.2d 326, 327 (5th Cir. 1967). The question presented to us is the scope of the habeas petitioner's waiver: Does it extend only to litigation of the federal habeas petition, or is the attorney-client privilege waived for all time and all purposes — including the possible retrial of the petitioner, should he succeed in setting aside his original conviction or sentence?

The district court entered a protective order precluding use of the privileged materials for any purpose other than litigating the federal habeas petition, and barring the Attorney General from turning them over to any other persons or offices, including, in particular, law enforcement or prosecutorial agencies. The state appeals this order, arguing that petitioner completely waived his privilege and the district court therefore had no authority to preclude dissemination of these non-privileged materials, or their use to re-prosecute petitioner.

The Merits

A.

The rule that a litigant waives the attorney-client privilege by putting the lawyer's performance at issue during the course of litigation dates back to at least *Hunt v. Blackburn*, 128 U.S. 464, 9 S. Ct. 125, 32 L. Ed. 488 (1888), where the Court stated: "When Mrs. Blackburn entered upon a line of defence which involved what transpired between herself and Mr. Weatherford [her lawyer], and respecting which she testified, she waived her right to object to his giving his own account of the matter." *Id.* at 470–71, 9 S.Ct. 125. The Court thought this proposition so self-evident it felt no need to support it with either citation to authority or further analysis. In the intervening years, courts and commentators have come to identify this simple rule as the fairness principle. *See, e.g., United States v. Amlani*, 169 F.3d 1189, 1196 (9th Cir. 1999); 8 John Henry Wigmore, Evidence in Trials at Common Law § 2327, at 636 (John T. McNaughton rev., 1961) [hereinafter Wigmore on Evidence]. The principle is often expressed in terms of preventing a party from using the privilege as both a shield and a sword. *See, e.g., Chevron Corp. v. Pennzoil Co.*, 974 F.2d 1156, 1162 (9th Cir. 1992) ("The privilege which protects attorney-client communications may not be used both as a sword and a shield."); 3 Jack B. Weinstein & Margaret A. Berger, Weinstein's Federal Evidence § 503.41[1], at 503-104.1 to .2 (Joseph M. McLaughlin ed., 2d ed. 2003) ("[T]he privilege may be found to have been waived by implication when a party takes a position in litigation that makes it unfair to protect that party's attorney-client communications. . . . The doctrine of waiver by implication reflects the position that the attorney-client privilege was intended as a shield, not a sword." (internal quotation marks omitted)). In practical terms, this means that parties in litigation may not abuse the privilege by asserting claims the opposing party cannot adequately dispute unless it has access to the privileged materials. The party asserting the claim is said to have implicitly waived the privilege. *See, e.g.*, Christopher B. Mueller & Laird C. Kirkpatrick, Evidence: Practice Under the Rules § 5.30, at 549 (2d ed. 1999) ("Substantial authority holds the attorney-client privilege to be impliedly waived where the client asserts a claim or defense that places at issue the nature of the privileged material.").

Such waivers by implication differ materially from the more traditional express waivers. An express waiver occurs when a party discloses privileged information to a third party who is not bound by the privilege, or otherwise shows disregard for the privilege by making the information public. See generally Mueller & Kirkpatrick § 5.28, at 530–33; Developments in the Law — Privileged Communications, 98 Harv. L. Rev. 1450, 1630 & n. 2 (1985) [hereinafter Privileged Communications]. Disclosures that effect an express waiver are typically within the full control of the party holding the privilege; courts have no role in encouraging or forcing the disclosure — they merely recognize the waiver after it has occurred. The cases upon which the state relies, *see, e.g., Permian Corp. v. United States*, 665 F.2d 1214, 1219–22 (D.C. Cir. 1981); *Westinghouse Elec. Corp. v. Republic of the Philippines*, 951 F.2d 1414, 1423–27 (3d Cir. 1991), fall into this category. These cases hold that, once documents have been turned over to another party voluntarily, the privilege is gone, and the litigant may not thereafter reassert it to block discovery of the information and related communications by his adversaries. *See also In re Sealed Case*, 676 F.2d 793, 809 (D.C. Cir. 1982). Because these express waiver cases do not involve the court-ordered disclosure of privileged information after "the client [has] assert[ed] a claim or defense that place[d] at issue the nature of the privileged material," Mueller & Kirkpatrick § 5.30, at 549, we do not find them particularly useful in ascertaining the scope of Bittaker's waiver of his attorney-client privilege under the fairness principle. *See In re von Bulow*, 828 F.2d 94, 101–02 (2d Cir. 1987) (declining to extend the fairness principle to disclosures made outside the course of judicial proceedings).

We look, instead, to the doctrine of implied waiver. "[T]he doctrine of implied waiver allocates control of the privilege between the judicial system and the party holding the privilege." Privileged Communications, 98 Harv. L. Rev. at 1630. The court imposing the waiver does not order disclosure of the materials categorically; rather, the court directs the party holding the privilege to produce the privileged materials if it wishes to go forward with its claims implicating them. The court thus gives the holder of the privilege a choice: If you want to litigate this claim, then you must waive your privilege to the extent necessary to give your opponent a fair opportunity to defend against it. *See, e.g., Amlani*, 169 F.3d at 1195 (holding that courts must evaluate "whether allowing the privilege would deny the opposing party access to information vital to its defense" (internal quotation marks omitted)); *Chevron*, 974 F.2d at 1162. Essentially, the court is striking a bargain with the holder of the privilege by letting him know how much of the privilege he must waive in order to proceed with his claim.

Three important implications flow from this regime. The first is that the court must impose a waiver no broader than needed to ensure the fairness of the proceedings before it. Because a waiver is required so as to be fair to the opposing side, the rationale only supports a waiver broad enough to serve that purpose. Courts, including ours, that have imposed waivers under the fairness principle have therefore closely tailored the scope of the waiver to the needs of the opposing party in litigating the claim in question. *See, e.g., Kerr v. U.S. Dist. Court*, 426 U.S. 394, 405, 96 S. Ct. 2119, 48 L. Ed. 2d 725 (1976) (recognizing the need to ensure that the "balance between petitioners' claim[ ] of . . . privilege and plaintiffs' asserted need for the documents is correctly struck"); *Amlani*, 169 F.3d at 1196 (holding that "only those documents or portions of documents relating to the [claim asserted by the client] [should be] disclosed"); *Greater Newburyport Clamshell Alliance v. Pub. Serv. Co.*, 838 F.2d 13, 22 (1st Cir. 1988) (holding that the client need reveal only information "for which defendants have so far shown a true need and without which they may be unfairly prejudiced in their defense"); *see also* Mueller & Kirkpatrick § 5.31, at 553 (suggesting that "in applying the doctrine of implied waiver by claim assertion, courts must be careful to target only" those privileged materials without which the adverse party would be unfairly prejudiced).

Second, the holder of the privilege may preserve the confidentiality of the privileged communications by choosing to abandon the claim that gives rise to the waiver condition. Cf. *Lyons v. Johnson*, 415 F.2d 540, 541–42 (9th Cir. 1969) (affirming dismissal of plaintiff's complaint after she persisted in hiding behind the privilege against self-incrimination by refusing to answer any deposition questions or to submit to discovery).

Finally, if a party complies with the court's conditions and turns over privileged materials, it is entitled to rely on the contours of the waiver the court imposes, so that it will not be unfairly surprised in the future by learning that it actually waived more than it bargained for in pressing its claims. *See Transamerica Computer Co. v. IBM Corp.*, 573 F.2d 646, 652 (9th Cir. 1978) (holding that, because the district court had made an explicit ruling "protecting and preserving all claims of privilege" to expedite the parties' discovery, "IBM did not waive its right to claim the privilege as to any documents produced after [the] date [of the order]"). It follows that the court imposing the waiver must be able to bind the party receiving the privileged materials to the court's limitations and conditions. *See id.* The party receiving and using privileged materials pursuant to a court-imposed waiver implicitly agrees to the conditions of the waiver; if it does not wish to be bound, it is free to reject the materials and litigate without them, but it must do so before any disclosure is made.

B.

With these considerations in mind, we turn to the question of the proper scope of the waiver in cases such as the one now before us. We start by noting that, in the federal habeas context, we must strike a delicate balance between the interests of the state and those of the federal government. *See Duckworth v. Eagan*, 492 U.S. 195, 211, 109 S. Ct. 2875, 106 L. Ed. 2d 166 (1989) (O'Connor, J., concurring) (noting that federal habeas review "has always been a flashpoint of tension in the delicate relationship of the federal and state courts"). The state, for its part, has established the attorney-client privilege, Cal. Evid. Code § 954, and has made it fully applicable to "all proceedings," id. § 910. The California Supreme Court has recently described the privilege as "fundamental to [its] legal system" and "a hallmark of [its] jurisprudence." *People v. Superior Court (Laff)*, 25 Cal. 4th 703, 715, 107 Cal. Rptr. 2d 323, 23 P.3d 563 (2001) (internal quotation marks omitted). The "lawyer-client privilege," as it's officially known in California, is "no mere peripheral evidentiary rule, but is held vital to the effective administration of justice." *Roberts v. City of Palmdale*, 5 Cal. 4th 363, 380, 20 Cal. Rptr. 2d 330, 853 P.2d 496 (1993). State law imposes upon every attorney the duty " '[t]o maintain inviolate the confidence, and at every peril to himself or herself to preserve the secrets, of his or her client.' " *Laff*, 25 Cal. 4th at 715, 107 Cal. Rptr. 2d 323, 23 P.3d 563 (quoting Cal. Bus. & Prof. Code § 6068(e)). Lawyers in California, as elsewhere, consider this duty central to the attorney-client relationship.

At the same time, Congress has given state prisoners the right to petition the federal courts for collateral review of their state convictions to ensure that state proceedings comply with constitutional requirements. 28 U.S.C. § 2254. In performing their constitutional duties, the federal courts have determined that claims of ineffective assistance of counsel cannot be fairly litigated unless the petitioner waives his privilege for purposes of resolving the dispute. *See, e.g., Wharton*, 127 F.3d at 1203. However sensible and necessary the waiver rule might be in practice, it nonetheless runs counter to the rationale behind the privilege and carries with it the potential of severely undermining the state's interest in maintaining the confidentiality of attorney-client communications. Claims of ineffective assistance of counsel are routinely raised in felony cases, particularly when a sentence of death has been imposed. If the federal courts were to require habeas petitioners to give up the privilege categorically and for all purposes, attorneys representing criminal defendants in state court would have to worry constantly about whether their casefiles and client conversations would someday fall into the hands of the prosecution. In addition, they would have to consider the very real possibility that they might be called to testify against their clients, not merely to defend their own professional conduct, but to help secure a conviction on retrial. A broad waiver rule would no doubt inhibit the kind of frank attorney-client communications and vigorous investigation of all possible defenses that the attorney-client and work product privileges are designed to promote.

Were such a broad waiver necessary to satisfy federal interests, the state's interest in protecting lawyer-client confidences might have to yield. But we can conceive of no federal interest in enlarging the scope of the waiver beyond what is needed to litigate the claim of ineffective assistance of counsel in federal court. A waiver that limits the use of privileged communications to adjudicating the ineffective assistance of counsel claim fully serves federal interests. *See Laughner,* 373 F.2d at 327. At the same time, a narrow waiver rule — one limited to the rationale undergirding it — will best preserve the state's vital interest in safeguarding the attorney-client privilege in criminal cases, thereby ensuring that the state's criminal lawyers continue to represent their clients zealously.

A narrow waiver rule is also consistent with the interests of the habeas petitioner in obtaining a fair adjudication of his petition and securing a retrial untainted by constitutional errors. Here, Bittaker is claiming that he was denied a constitutionally adequate criminal trial because he had ineffective counsel and for many other reasons as well. If he succeeds on any of these claims, it will mean that his trial was constitutionally defective. Extending the waiver to cover Bittaker's retrial would immediately and perversely skew the second trial in the prosecution's favor by handing to the state all the information in petitioner's first counsel's casefile. If a prisoner is successful in persuading a federal court to grant the writ, the court should aim to restore him to the position he would have occupied, had the first trial been constitutionally error-free. Giving the prosecution the advantage of obtaining the defense casefile — and possibly even forcing the first lawyer to testify against the client during the second trial — would assuredly not put the parties back at the same starting gate.

What's more, requiring the petitioner to enter such a broad waiver would force him to the painful choice of, on the one hand, asserting his ineffective assistance claim and risking a trial where the prosecution can use against him every statement he made to his first lawyer and, on the other hand, retaining the privilege but giving up his ineffective assistance claim. This would violate the spirit, and perhaps the letter, of *Simmons v. United States,* 390 U.S. 377, 394, 88 S. Ct. 967, 19 L. Ed. 2d 1247 (1968). It is no answer to say that Bittaker created this dilemma for himself — that he was the one who voluntarily "chose" to challenge his conviction on grounds of ineffective assistance. The Constitution guarantees Bittaker the right to effective assistance of counsel at trial, *Strickland v. Washington,* 466 U.S. 668, 686, 104 S. Ct. 2052, 80 L. Ed. 2d 674 (1984), and Congress has provided him an avenue to claim that his constitutional rights were violated, 28 U.S.C. § 2254. As one of our sister circuits has recognized in a different context, one may be "a 'voluntary' party only because there is no other means of protecting legal rights. . . . The scope of required disclosure should not be so broad as to effectively eliminate any incentive to vindicate [one's] constitutional right [s]. . . ." *Greater Newburyport Clamshell Alliance,* 838 F.2d at 21–22.

Nor would a narrowly tailored waiver unfairly prejudice the prosecution. State law precludes access to materials in the defense lawyer's casefile and commands the lawyer to stand mute if he has information damaging to his client. The fortuity that defendant's initial trial was constitutionally defective gives the prosecution no just claim to the lawyer's casefile or testimony. To the contrary, allowing the prosecution at retrial to use information gathered by the first defense lawyer — including defendant's statements to his lawyer — would give the prosecution a wholly gratuitous advantage. It is assuredly not consistent with the fairness principle to give one side of the dispute such a munificent windfall for use in proceedings unrelated to the matters litigated in federal court.

We are not alone in our concern about the effect of a broad waiver on the fairness of state criminal trials. In one case that has been brought to our attention, the California Supreme Court, during the course of a state habeas proceeding, entered an order very similar to the one here. While the order is not published, and therefore presumably not binding in future cases, it does seem to strike the same balance among the competing interests as we do. Significantly, the order specifically bars the use of privileged materials at petitioner's possible retrial. While we can only infer the court's rationale, we believe it must have been similar to our own.

C.

Relying on the majority's analysis in *Anderson v. Calderon*, 232 F.3d 1053, 1099–100 (9th Cir. 2000), the state argues that precluding the prosecution from using evidence found in defense counsel's casefile in subsequent state court proceedings "would constitute an unwarranted anticipatory interference with the prerogatives of the state courts" and "contravene basic principles of comity and federalism," in violation of *Younger v. Harris*, 401 U.S. 37, 43–54, 91 S. Ct. 746, 27 L. Ed. 2d 669 (1971), and its progeny. *Anderson*, 232 F.3d at 1099–100. But *Anderson* was decided on the mistaken premise that petitioner's waiver of the attorney-client privilege is governed by state law and therefore best determined by the state courts. *Id.* at 1100. For the reasons already explained, we hold that the scope of the implied waiver must be determined by the court imposing it as a condition for the fair adjudication of the issue before it. When that court is a federal court, the scope of the waiver is a matter of federal law. See Fed. R. Evid. 501; *Tennenbaum v. Deloitte & Touche*, 77 F.3d 337, 340 (9th Cir. 1996) (applying federal law on the question of waiver); Weil, 647 F.2d at 24 (same). After all, it is the federal courts that are inducing petitioner to waive his privilege, so the federal courts must be able to guarantee the integrity of the bargain if petitioner chooses to waive the privilege so he can litigate his ineffective assistance of counsel claim. *See generally* William W Schwarzer et al., California Practice Guide: Federal Civil Procedure Before Trial § 11:113.15, at 11–70 (2002) ("In appropriate circumstances, courts may grant a protective order restricting the use of any discovery to the present lawsuit. . . . A court may also limit dissemination of information obtained through discovery" by, among other things, "restricting disclosure.").

Nor do we believe that the protective order impinges on the dignity or authority of the state courts. The power of courts, state as well as federal, to delimit how parties may use information obtained through the court's power of compulsion is of long standing and well-accepted. *See, e.g., Degen v. United States*, 517 U.S. 820, 826, 116 S. Ct. 1777, 135 L. Ed. 2d 102 (1996) (noting that protective orders may be used "to prevent parties from using civil discovery to evade restrictions on discovery in criminal cases"); *E.I. DuPont De Nemours Powder Co. v. Masland*, 244 U.S. 100, 103, 37 S. Ct. 575, 61 L. Ed. 1016 (1917) ("It will be understood that if, in the opinion of the trial judge, it is or should become necessary to reveal the secrets to others, it will rest in the judge's discretion to determine whether, to whom, and under what precautions, the revelation should be made."); *Brown Bag Software v. Symantec*

Corp., 960 F.2d 1465, 1469, 1471–72 (9th Cir. 1992) (upholding a protective order that precluded plaintiff's in-house counsel from accessing defendant's trade secrets while providing the information to an independent consultant); *Covey Oil Co. v. Cont'l Oil Co.*, 340 F.2d 993 (10th Cir. 1965) (upholding a protective order that restricted access to sensitive documents to counsel and independent certified public accountants and prohibited use of the materials for competitive purposes), overruled on other grounds as stated in *FTC v. Alaska Land Leasing, Inc.*, 778 F.2d 577, 578 (10th Cir. 1985); *Chem. & Indus. Corp. v. Druffel*, 301 F.2d 126, 130 (6th Cir. 1962) (noting that the district court may enter a protective order prohibiting public disclosure of information obtained through discovery); *see also* 8 Charles Alan Wright, Arthur R. Miller & Richard L. Marcus, Federal Practice and Procedure § 2043, at 566 (2d ed. 1994) (listing examples of protective orders "limiting the persons who are to have access to the information disclosed and the use to which these persons may put the information"). Courts could not function effectively in cases involving sensitive information — trade secrets, medical files and minors, among many others — if they lacked the power to limit the use parties could make of sensitive information obtained from the opposing party by invoking the court's authority.

The courts of California remain free, of course, to determine whether Bittaker waived his attorney-client privilege on some basis other than his disclosure of privileged information during the course of the federal litigation. In addition, if the district attorney is able to obtain the privileged materials through a source other than the Attorney General's office, he would be free to present them to the state court and seek a ruling on their admissibility. The district court's order simply precludes a party before it from misusing materials it obtained for a limited purpose by invoking the court's power of compulsion. We are confident that the state courts will not feel in the least uncomfortable because a party may not use confidential information it secured by invoking our power and authority, just as we would respect a similar order limiting the use of privileged materials obtained during the course of state court litigation. This is comity, not encroachment.

We are comforted in our conclusion by the fact that the parties have failed to bring to our attention — and we have been unable to find — very many cases where the prosecution has even attempted to use privileged information obtained as a result of federal discovery procedures in a defendant's retrial. Except for a small handful of cases from our own court, all originating in California, see *Osband*, 290 F.3d at 1042–43; *Anderson*, 232 F.3d at 1099–100; *McDowell v. Calderon*, 197 F.3d 1253, 1255–56 (9th Cir. 1999) (en banc) (per curiam), the only case we have found that even remotely raises this possibility is *United States v. Suarez*, 820 F.2d 1158 (11th Cir. 1987). In *Suarez*, the defendant sought to withdraw his guilty plea, claiming that he was misinformed by his lawyer. The lawyer testified, and the plea was set aside. At trial, the same lawyer testified about Suarez's reaction — how his " 'attitude completely changed' when he heard [an][audio]tape containing his voice." *Id.* at 1159. This testimony supported the prosecution's theory that defendant was involved in secretly recorded meetings involving the charged offenses.

We are somewhat surprised by the result in *Suarez*, but note that this holding has not been replicated in the Eleventh Circuit or any other federal court in the intervening fifteen years. In any event, *Suarez's* two cautionary passages —

explaining what issues the court there did not consider — distinguish the case from ours. First, in footnote 3, *Suarez* explicitly notes that the court did not consider the argument that the waiver of the privilege was limited to the suppression hearing, because counsel had not attempted to limit the scope of the waiver. *Id.* at 1160 n. 3. While it is not clear to us that counsel is required to utter magic words to demarcate the scope of the waiver, what matters for our purposes is that Suarez simply did not consider the limited waiver argument. Second, in the penultimate paragraph, the *Suarez* court tells us unequivocally that it did not consider Simmons because that argument had not been timely raised. *Id.* at 1161. We are reasonably confident that, had the *Suarez* court considered these arguments, it would have reached a different conclusion.

D.

We turn, finally, to the question of enforcement. As is evident, the narrow waiver rule we adopt today is not self-enforcing. That is to say, unlike the usual situation where those given access to confidential materials have an independent ethical, and perhaps legal, obligation to maintain that confidence (such as the ethical constraints on lawyers, doctors and the clergy), those who are given access to confidential attorney-client materials under our limited waiver rule have no such obligation or incentive. Given this absence of external constraints (external to the case), district courts have the obligation, whenever they permit discovery of attorney-client materials as relevant to the defense of ineffective assistance of counsel claims in habeas cases, to ensure that the party given such access does not disclose these materials, except to the extent necessary in the habeas proceeding, i.e., to ensure that such a party's actions do not result in a rupture of the privilege.

Fortunately, district courts have ample tools at their disposal to ensure compliance with any limitations they impose on the dissemination of confidential materials. Parties in habeas cases, unlike those in ordinary civil cases, have no right to discovery. *Campbell v. Blodgett*, 982 F.2d 1356, 1358 (9th Cir. 1993) ("[T]here simply is no federal right, constitutional or otherwise, to discovery in habeas proceedings as a general matter." (citing *Harris v. Nelson*, 394 U.S. 286, 296, 89 S. Ct. 1082, 22 L. Ed. 2d 281 (1969))). In a habeas case, discovery under the Federal Rules of Civil Procedure is available "if, and to the extent that, the judge in the exercise of his discretion and for good cause shown grants leave to do so, but not otherwise." Rules Governing Section 2254 Cases in the United States District Courts [hereinafter Habeas Rules], Rule 6(a); *see Bracy v. Gramley*, 520 U.S. 899, 904, 117 S. Ct. 1793, 138 L. Ed. 2d 97 (1997). If a district court exercises its discretion to allow such discovery "to the extent that . . . good cause [is] shown," it must ensure compliance with the fairness principle. To that end, it must enter appropriate orders clearly delineating the contours of the limited waiver before the commencement of discovery, and strictly police those limits thereafter.

The district court was entirely justified in entering the protective order that is the subject of this appeal; indeed, it would have abused its discretion had it done otherwise. The portion of *Anderson v. Calderon*, 232 F.3d 1053, that reached a contrary conclusion is overruled. On remand, the district court remains free to modify the order as it deems appropriate to fully protect petitioner's rights.

AFFIRMED.

[2]   Disclosure to Third Parties

[a]   In General

Disclosures to third parties of confidential communications between an attorney and his or her client have given rise to a variety of results on the waiver question because of the myriad circumstances surrounding those communications. As a general rule, the courts have acknowledged that because of the confidentiality requirement, once disclosure has occurred (regardless of whether it is the result of the intentional or inadvertent acts of the client or the attorney), the privilege disappears. Practice, however, has not always been consistent with the theory. Rather, courts have shown a marked tendency to excuse inadvertent disclosures and disclosures expressly made "without prejudice."

This topic of disclosure gives rise to two general issues. First, what level of disclosure will result in a waiver of the privilege? Second, must the client be responsible for the disclosure before a waiver can occur?

[b]   What Level of Disclosure Waives Privilege?

Courts determine whether a particular disclosure has destroyed the confidentiality forming the basis of the attorney-client privilege, and hence the privilege itself, primarily on the basis of four somewhat overlapping factors:

(1)   the nature of the disclosure: whether it indicates that the client no longer considers the communications involved confidential;

(2)   the extent to which the disclosure reveals the substantive content of the protected communication;

(3)   the extent to which the client benefits from the portion of the communication disclosed, thereby creating unfairness for those against whom the benefits or advantage were gained by nondisclosure of the remaining portions; and

(4)   the court's perception of the concept of confidentiality: whether it is a rigid, tightly-held circle encompassing only the attorney, the client and their agents, or a flexible circle that can be expanded to include others to whom disclosures have been made.

For example, if a client were to reveal, in her testimony or through disclosure of a letter to her attorney, that an attorney-client relationship existed and that advice was sought on particular occasions, this would not waive the confidentiality of the communications involved in those consultations. It is likely the client would not destroy the confidentiality of these communications even if she revealed the general nature of the advice sought, i.e., whether it was advice concerning business or domestic matters. As the particularity of the description of the nature of the advice increases, however, so does the likelihood of waiver, particularly if the client gains an advantage through her description. For example, if the client used the fact that she sought advice on a particular matter as evidence of her good faith regarding the matter on which subsequent action was taken, this additional advantage the client obtained as a result of merely describing her attorney consultation may result in a waiver that would not have been found solely on the basis of what she disclosed through her description.

The quintessential example of waiver through the client's demonstrating that she does not value the communication's confidentiality occurs when the client communicates with the attorney in the presence of third parties. Such communication will not waive the privilege's protection if the court deems the third parties necessary agents of either the client or attorney.

Disclosing *facts* communicated to the attorney, without disclosing that the communication actually occurred, will not waive the privilege that attaches to the *communication*. For example, if a client testified to the facts surrounding a business transaction that is the subject of an antitrust action, her testimony would not waive the privilege applicable to the communications with her attorney on the same facts when advice was sought. The privilege survives only if the client does not disclose that those facts to which she testified were the subject of the consultations with her attorney.

The courts' understanding of the concept of confidentiality is important to a determination of the privilege's continued existence after disclosures have been made under extenuating circumstances. These extenuating circumstances are discussed in the next section, addressing the conduct that can result in the expiration of the privilege.

[c]   Whose Conduct May Result in Waiver or Destruction of Privilege?

[i]   Voluntary Disclosures by Client

The attorney-client privilege is premised on the need for confidentiality in the client's communications with the attorney. When the client voluntarily destroys the confidentiality by disclosing the substance of those communications, the client waives the privilege. This is true whether the client is an individual or a corporation. In the corporate context the question of client waiver is complicated by the fact that the corporation can act only through its authorized agents. In *Upjohn* (excerpted at § [A][5][b], *above*), the Supreme Court acknowledged that employees from many levels of the corporate hierarchy can create a confidential attorney-client relationship for the corporation. Who among those having power to create the privilege also has the power to waive it? This question was addressed by the Supreme Court in *Commodity Futures Trading Comm'n v. Weintraub*, 471 U.S. 343 (1985), set out below.

COMMODITY FUTURES TRADING COMMISSION v.
WEINTRAUB

United States Supreme Court
471 U.S. 343 (1985)

JUSTICE MARSHALL delivered the opinion of the Court.

The question here is whether the trustee of a corporation in bankruptcy has the power to waive the debtor corporation's attorney-client privilege with respect to communications that took place before the filing of the petition in bankruptcy.

I

The case arises out of a formal investigation by petitioner Commodity Futures Trading Commission to determine whether Chicago Discount Commodity Brokers (CDCB), or persons associated with that firm, violated the Commodity Exchange Act. . . . CDCB was a discount commodity brokerage house registered with the Commission as a futures commission merchant. On October 27, 1980, the Commission filed a complaint against CDCB in the United States District Court for the Northern District of Illinois alleging violations of the Act. That same day, respondent Frank McGhee, acting as sole director and officer of CDCB, entered into a consent decree with the Commission, which provided for the appointment of a receiver and for the receiver to file a petition for liquidation under Chapter 7 of the Bankruptcy Reform Act of 1978 (Bankruptcy Code). The District Court appointed John K. Notz, Jr., as receiver.

Notz then filed a voluntary petition in bankruptcy on behalf of CDCB. He sought relief under Subchapter IV of Chapter 7 of the Bankruptcy Code, which provides for the liquidation of bankrupt commodity brokers. . . . The bankruptcy court appointed Notz as interim trustee and, later, as permanent trustee.

As part of its investigation of CDCB, the Commission served a subpoena *duces tecum* upon CDCB's former counsel, respondent Gary Weintraub. The Commission sought Weintraub's testimony about various CDCB matters, including suspected misappropriation of customer funds by CDCB's officers and employees, and other fraudulent activities. Weintraub appeared for his deposition and responded to numerous inquiries but refused to answer 23 questions, asserting CDCB's attorney-client privilege. The Commission then moved to compel answers to those questions. It argued that Weintraub's assertion of the attorney-client privilege was inappropriate because the privilege could not be used to "thwart legitimate access to information sought in an administrative investigation."

Even though the Commission argued in its motion that the matters on which Weintraub refused to testify were not protected by CDCB's attorney-client privilege, it also asked Notz to waive that privilege. In a letter to Notz, the Commission maintained that CDCB's former officers, directors, and employees no longer had the authority to assert the privilege. According to the Commission, that power was vested in Notz as the then-interim trustee. In response to the Commission's request, Notz waived "any interest I have in the attorney-client privilege possessed by that debtor for any communications or information occurring or arising on or before October 27, 1980" — the date of Notz's appointment as receiver.

On April 26, 1982, a United States Magistrate ordered Weintraub to testify. The Magistrate found that Weintraub had the power to assert CDCB's privilege. He added, however, that Notz was "successor in interest of all assets, rights, and privileges of CDCB, including the attorney-client privilege at issue herein," and that Notz's waiver was therefore valid. The District Court upheld the Magistrate's order on June 9. Thereafter, Frank McGhee and his brother, respondent Andrew McGhee, intervened and argued that Notz could not validly waive the privilege over their objection. The District Court rejected this argument and, on July 27, entered a new order requiring Weintraub to testify without asserting an attorney-client privilege on behalf of CDCB.

The McGhees appealed from the District Court's order of July 27, and the Court of Appeals for the Seventh Circuit reversed. 722 F.2d 338 (1984). It held that a bankruptcy trustee does not have the power to waive a corporate-debtor's attorney-client privilege with respect to communications that occurred before the filing of the bankruptcy petition. The court recognized that two other Circuits had addressed the question and had come to the opposite conclusion. . . . We granted certiorari to resolve the conflict. We now reverse the Court of Appeals.

II

It is by now well established, and undisputed by the parties to this case, that the attorney-client privilege attaches to corporations as well as to individuals. *Upjohn Co. v. United States*, 449 U.S. 383 (1981). Both for corporations and individuals, the attorney-client privilege serves the function of promoting full and frank communications between attorneys and their clients. It thereby encourages observance of the law and aids in the administration of justice. . . .

The administration of the attorney-client privilege in the case of corporations, however, presents special problems. As an inanimate entity, a corporation must act through agents. A corporation cannot speak directly to its lawyers. Similarly, it cannot directly waive the privilege when disclosure is in its best interest. Each of these actions must necessarily be undertaken by individuals empowered to act on behalf of the corporation. In *Upjohn Co.*, we considered whether the privilege covers only communications between counsel and top management, and decided that, under certain circumstances, communications between counsel and lower-level employees are also covered. Here, we face the related question of which corporate actors are empowered to waive the corporation's privilege.

The parties in this case agree that, for solvent corporations, the power to waive the corporate attorney-client privilege rests with the corporation's management and is normally exercised by its officers and directors. The managers, of course, must exercise the privilege in a manner consistent with their fiduciary duty to act in the best interests of the corporation and not of themselves as individuals. . . .

The parties also agree that when control of a corporation passes to new management, the authority to assert and waive the corporation's attorney-client privilege passes as well. New managers installed as a result of a takeover, merger, loss of confidence by shareholders, or simply normal succession, may waive the attorney-client privilege with respect to communications made by former officers and directors. Displaced managers may not assert the privilege over the wishes of current managers, even as to statements that the former might have made to counsel concerning matters within the scope of their corporate duties. . . .

The dispute in this case centers on the control of the attorney-client privilege of a corporation in bankruptcy. The Government maintains that the power to exercise that privilege with respect to prebankruptcy communications passes to the bankruptcy trustee. In contrast, respondents maintain that this power remains with the debtor's directors.

III

[Initially the Court examined the Bankruptcy Code but found no guidance other than the legislative history that indicated Congress had not intended to limit the trustee's ability to obtain corporate information.]

IV

In light of the lack of direct guidance from the Code, we turn to consider the roles played by the various actors of a corporation in bankruptcy to determine which is most analogous to the role played by the management of a solvent corporation. . . . Because the attorney-client privilege is controlled, outside of bankruptcy, by a corporation's management, the actor whose duties most closely resemble those of management should control the privilege in bankruptcy, unless such a result interferes with policies underlying the bankruptcy laws.

A

The powers and duties of a bankruptcy trustee are extensive. Upon the commencement of a case in bankruptcy, all corporate property passes to an estate represented by the trustee. . . . The trustee is "accountable for all property received" . . . and has the duty to maximize the value of the estate. . . . He is directed to investigate the debtor's financial affairs . . . and is empowered to sue officers, directors, and other insiders to recover, on behalf of the estate, fraudulent or preferential transfers of the debtor's property. . . . Subject to court approval, he may use, sell, or lease property of the estate.

Moreover, in reorganization, the trustee has the power to "operate the debtor's business" unless the court orders otherwise. Even in liquidation, the court "may authorize the trustee to operate the business" for a limited period of time. In the course of operating the debtor's business, the trustee "may enter into transactions, including the sale or lease of property of the estate" without court approval.

As even this brief and incomplete list should indicate, the Bankruptcy Code gives the trustee wide-ranging management authority over the debtor. . . . In contrast, the powers of the debtor's directors are severely limited. Their role is to turn over the corporation's property to the trustee and to provide certain information to the trustee and to the creditors. Congress contemplated that when a trustee is appointed, he assumes control of the business, and the debtor's directors are "completely ousted."

In light of the Code's allocation of responsibilities, it is clear that the trustee plays the role most closely analogous to that of a solvent corporation's management. Given that the debtor's directors retain virtually no management powers, they should not exercise the traditional management function of controlling the corporation's attorney-client privilege, unless a contrary arrangement would be inconsistent with policies of the bankruptcy laws.

B

We find no federal interests that would be impaired by the trustee's control of the corporation's attorney-client privilege with respect to pre-bankruptcy communications. On the other hand, the rule suggested by respondents — that the debtor's directors have this power — would frustrate an important goal of the bankruptcy laws. In seeking to maximize the value of the estate, the trustee must investigate the conduct of prior management to uncover and assert causes of action against the debtor's officers and directors. It would often be extremely difficult to conduct this inquiry if the former management were allowed to control the corporation's attorney-client privilege and therefore to control access to the corporation's legal files. To the extent that management had wrongfully diverted or appropriated corporate assets, it could use the privilege as a shield against the trustee's efforts to identify those assets. The Code's goal of uncovering insider fraud would be substantially defeated if the debtor's directors were to retain the one management power that might effectively thwart an investigation into their own conduct. . . .

Respondents contend that the trustee can adequately investigate fraud without controlling the corporation's attorney-client privilege. They point out that the privilege does not shield the disclosure of communications relating to the planning or commission of ongoing fraud, crimes, and ordinary torts. . . . The problem, however, is making the threshold showing of fraud necessary to defeat the privilege. . . . Without control over the privilege, the trustee might not be able to discover hidden assets or looting schemes, and therefore might not be able to make the necessary showing.

In summary, we conclude that vesting in the trustee control of the corporation's attorney-client privilege most closely comports with the allocation of the waiver power to management outside of bankruptcy without in any way obstructing the careful design of the Bankruptcy Code.

* * *

[R]espondents maintain that the result we reach today would also apply to *individuals* in bankruptcy, a result that respondents find "unpalatable." But our holding today has no bearing on the problem of individual bankruptcy, which we have no reason to address in this case. As we have stated, a corporation, as an inanimate entity, must act through agents. When the corporation is solvent, the agent that controls the corporate attorney-client privilege is the corporation's management. Under our holding today, this power passes to the trustee because the trustee's functions are more closely analogous to those of management outside of bankruptcy than are the functions of the debtor's directors. An individual, in contrast, can act for himself; there is no "management" that controls a solvent individual's attorney-client privilege. If control over that privilege passes to a trustee, it must be under some theory different from the one that we embrace in this case.

[R]espondents [also] argue that giving the trustee control over the attorney-client privilege will have an undesirable chilling effect on attorney-client communications. According to respondents, corporate managers will be wary of speaking freely with corporate counsel if their communications might subsequently be disclosed due to bankruptcy. But the chilling effect is no greater here than in the case of a solvent corporation, where individual officers and directors always run the risk that successor management might waive the corporation's attorney-client privilege with respect to prior management's communications with counsel.

Respondents also maintain that the result we reach discriminates against insolvent corporations. According to respondents, to prevent the debtor's directors from controlling the privilege amounts to "economic discrimination" given that directors, as representatives of the shareholders, control the privilege for solvent corporations. Respondents' argument misses the point that, by definition, corporations in bankruptcy are treated differently from solvent corporations. "Insolvency is a most important and material fact, not only with individuals but with corporations, and with the latter as with the former the mere fact of its existence may change radically and materially its rights and obligations." Respondents do not explain why we should be particularly concerned about differential treatment in this context.

Finally, respondents maintain that upholding trustee waivers would create a disincentive for debtors to invoke the protections of bankruptcy and provide an incentive for creditors to file for involuntary bankruptcy. According to respondents, "[i]njection of such considerations into bankruptcy would skew the application of the bankruptcy laws in a manner not contemplated by Congress." The law creates numerous incentives, both for and against the filing of bankruptcy petitions. Respondents do not explain why our holding creates incentives that are inconsistent with congressional intent, and we do not believe that it does.

VII

For the foregoing reasons, we hold that the trustee of a corporation in bankruptcy has the power to waive the corporation's attorney-client privilege with respect to prebankruptcy communications. We therefore conclude that Notz, in his capacity as trustee, properly waived CDCB's privilege in this case. The judgment of the Court of Appeals for the Seventh Circuit is accordingly reversed.

It is so ordered.

[ii]   Breaches of Confidentiality by Attorney

If the client instructed the attorney to disclose to a third party the substance of a confidential communication, the attorney's act would be considered that of the client and any applicable privilege would be waived. Even when such disclosures have occurred without the client's expressed consent, courts still have found a waiver, but have done so by finding an implied authority from the client for the attorney's action. Some courts have justified this finding of implicit authority on the fact the attorney made the disclosures in question for the client's benefit. *See Sprader v. Mueller*, 127 N.W.2d 176 (Minn. 1963) (disclosure of privileged communications to county prosecutor in order to spare client from an interview and to gain additional information that prosecutor controlled was for client's benefit and waived attorney-client privilege); *Klang v. Shell Oil Co.*, 17 Cal. App. 3d 933 (1971) (disclosure of information about automobile accident to police officer in order to prevent filing of criminal charges against client was for client's benefit and constituted waiver of attorney-client privilege). Other courts have followed the lead of *In re Grand Jury Investigation of Ocean Transp.*, excerpted below, and have reasoned the attorney has authority to waive the client's privilege based on the nature of the agency relationship.

IN RE GRAND JURY INVESTIGATION OF OCEAN TRANSPORTATION
United States Court of Appeals, District of Columbia Circuit
604 F.2d 672 (1979)

PER CURIAM:

The District Court denied a motion of Sea-Land Services, Inc. ("Sea-Land") for the return of various documents which Sea-Land alleges are protected by the attorney-client privilege but which were inadvertently disclosed to the Antitrust Division of the United States Department of Justice in the course of responding to a grand jury *duces tecum* subpoena. Sea-Land appeals. In response, the government questions this Court's jurisdiction and asserts that, in any event, the District Court's order must be sustained because any privilege that existed as to these documents has been effectively waived. Accepting jurisdiction, we affirm.

* * *

II

A brief recital of the facts is all that is necessary. It is undisputed that the United States has acted from the outset in complete good faith. Upon receipt of the subpoena in August 1976, Sea-Land instructed its counsel ("original counsel") to withhold from production all documents which were felt might be covered by the attorney-client privilege. On September 30, 1976, said counsel responded to the subpoena and turned over two groups of documents which Sea-Land's current counsel are now claiming were protected by the privilege.

One group need not detain us any further. For whatever reason, original counsel did not mark these papers as potentially privileged and voluntarily turned them over. This must be deemed a complete waiver. Original counsel's responsibility was to determine the privileged status of Sea-Land's documents. Its decisions in this regard were binding on its client. Privilege claims cannot be reopened by retaining new counsel who read the privilege rules more broadly than did their predecessor.

The second group of documents was marked by original counsel with a "P." When the Antitrust Division received them it thought something might be amiss and promptly asked original counsel whether the set had been disclosed by mistake. Counsel investigated and explicitly, even though mistakenly, advised that the documents were intended to be disclosed and that no privilege was accordingly claimed. It was not until March 1977 that original counsel discovered their mistake, so advised the Antitrust Division, and indicated that a formal demand for return would be forthcoming. No such demand was made, however, until early 1978 after new counsel had been retained by Sea-Land. Sea-Land itself was first advised of the inadvertent disclosure in December of 1977. Since September 1976, the documents have been copied, digested, and analyzed by the Antitrust Division, as well as periodically used in connection with the grand jury investigation. Several witnesses have been asked questions concerning the documents, including Mr. Halloran, a high official of Sea-Land who was represented by personal counsel and testified with respect to the documents pursuant to a related order of the District Court.

Assuming that these documents were in fact privileged prior to their disclosure to the Government — an issue not before this Court — it is clear that the mantle of confidentiality which once protected the documents has been so irretrievably breached that an effective waiver of the privilege has been accomplished. Because of the privilege's adverse effect on the full disclosure of the truth, it must be narrowly construed. . . . An intent to waive one's privilege is not necessary for such a waiver to occur. . . . "A privileged person would seldom be found to waive, if his intention not to abandon could alone control the situation. There is always the objective consideration that when his conduct touches a certain point of disclosure, fairness requires that his privilege shall cease whether he intended that result or not." 8 WIGMORE, EVIDENCE § 2327 (McNaughton rev. 1961). Moreover, "[a]ll involuntary disclosures, in particular, through the loss or theft of documents from the attorney's possession are not protected by the privilege, on the principle . . . that the law . . . leaves to the client and attorney to take measures of caution sufficient to prevent being overheard by third persons. The risk of insufficient precautions is upon the client." 8 WIGMORE, EVIDENCE § 2325 (McNaughton rev. 1961). . . . Perhaps this latter rule should not be strictly applied to all cases of unknown or inadvertent disclosure; this, however, is not a case where any such exception would be appropriate. Here, the disclosure cannot be viewed as having been inadvertent in all respects. Original counsel knew that some papers marked "P" had been divulged. This production was brought to their attention on at least one occasion; each time, however, said counsel declined to assert the privilege. Similarly, the Government cannot be said in any way to have "compelled" Sea-Land or original counsel to produce privileged documents; and there certainly was here an adequate opportunity in September 1976 to claim the privilege. . . .

To be sure, in the final analysis, the privilege is for the client, not the attorney, to assert. . . . Original counsel, however, acted as Sea-Land's agent in determining which documents would be produced pursuant to the subpoena and which documents would be withheld under the attorney-client privilege. Original counsel acted within the scope of authority conferred upon it, and Sea-Land may not now be heard to complain about how that authority was exercised.

Most importantly, it would be unfair and unrealistic now to permit the privilege's assertion as to these documents which have been thoroughly examined and used by the Government for several years. . . . The Government attorneys' minds cannot be expunged, the grand jury is familiar with the documents, and various witnesses' testimony regarding the papers has been heard. This is not a case of mere inadvertence where the breach of confidentiality can be easily remedied. Here, the disclosure cannot be cured simply by a return of the documents. The privilege has been permanently destroyed.

Affirmed.

[iii]   Involuntary Disclosures

Courts' insistence on responsibility, and disregard for the actual status of the confidentiality on which the privilege is based, is most apparent when either the attorney or the client makes disclosures *involuntarily*; for example, pursuant to court order. In such circumstances, both the litigants and the courts seem to have universally accepted, without question, that disclosures compelled in one case do not constitute a waiver for all litigation thereafter, *see Transamerica Computer Co. v. International Business Machines Corp.*, 573 F.2d 646, 650–51 (9th Cir. 1978). Technically it may be true that a "waiver," as such, may not have occurred (using that term in the sense of a voluntary relinquishment), but to hold that the disclosure has not destroyed the circle of confidentiality, and therefore the basis of the privilege, is difficult to understand. It cannot be disputed there has been a "relinquishment" of the privilege relative to the party of whom disclosure has been required. The practical effect of allowing the privilege to survive against other individuals after its relinquishment to some is that the privilege's circle of confidentiality is being expanded to include the party of whom disclosure was required. Once it has been decided that this is theoretically permissible, the next logical question is why this same result cannot be achieved through voluntary disclosures by the client? In fact, courts have begun to protect such disclosures if done in response to subpoenas, *United States v. Wrinkle, Inc.*, Trade Cas. ¶ 67,873 (S.D. Ohio 1954); at the "suggestion" of the court, *Duplan Corp. v. Deering Milliken, Inc.*, 397 F. Supp. 1146 (D.S.C. 1975); in cooperation with regulatory agencies, *Teachers Ins. & Annuity Ass'n of Am. v. Shamrock Broadcasting Co.*, 521 F. Supp. 638, 641 (S.D.N.Y. 1981); and in an accelerated pretrial discovery program in which inadvertent disclosures would be inevitable, *see Transamerica Computer, above* (court equated accelerated discovery program and massive volume of documents and inadvertent disclosures that it would spawn with involuntary or compelled disclosure).

This expansion of the circle of confidentiality to include persons to whom forced disclosures have been made raises the prospect of a concept of "limited waiver," which will be discussed in the next section, in which the consequences of "waiver" are addressed.

[C] Consequences of Waiver

[1] In General

Once there has been a disclosure of a privileged communication beyond the circle of confidentiality between the attorney and client, what is the scope of the resulting "waiver" or "relinquishment" in terms of subject matter and the persons or entities to which it may apply?

[2] "Subject Matter" Waiver

If a court finds that a party has waived the attorney-client privilege, what is the scope of that waiver? For example, if waiver occurs through disclosure to third parties, is the waiver limited to the communications that were disclosed or does its scope extend to all communications on the topic involved in that disclosure? As the court explained in *Duplan Corp. v. Deering Milliken, Inc.*, 397 F. Supp. 1146 (D.S.C. 1975), the waiver extends "to all communications between the same attorney and the same client on the same subject."

This conclusion reflects courts' commonly accepted view that the concept of "selective waiver" within a subject area is untenable because it is unfair. A client should not be allowed to use his communications with his attorney as a sword when they happen to be favorable to his case, while simultaneously using the attorney-client privilege to shield unfavorable communications. Generally, courts construe waivers as narrowly as possible, consistent with the principle of fairness to the adversary in the particular context in which the issue is raised. For example, if the client had consulted with the attorney on the legal implications of defects in a particular product that was being marketed, waiver would likely be limited to other communications relating to defects in the same product. However, if this communication were disclosed for the purpose of demonstrating lack of knowledge of similar defects in other products or other product defects that were inquired about (because the custom of the company is to seek legal advice on all potential defects, and the failure to mention others in this letter is circumstantial evidence of a lack of knowledge about them), it would be patently unfair to limit the scope of the waiver to the subject of the letter since it is being used for such a broader purpose.

The following opinion illustrates how the circumstances of the waiver may prompt drastically different decisions on its scope. At one extreme, courts have limited the waiver to the particular document through which the waiver has occurred (in effect rejecting a subject matter waiver). At the other extreme, courts have not only found a subject matter waiver, but have expanded its scope by enlarging the time frame within which the subject matter waiver is applicable.

CENTER PARTNERS, LTD. v. GROWTH HEAD GP, LLC
Supreme Court of Illinois
981 N.E.2d 345 (2012)

JUSTICE GARMAN delivered the judgment of the court, with opinion.

Defendants appeal from a circuit court of Cook County order that granted plaintiffs' motion to compel the production of certain documents containing privileged attorney-client communications. Defendants refused to comply with the court's order to compel production of documents and were found in contempt. Defendants appealed pursuant to Supreme Court Rule 304(b)(5) (eff. Feb. 26, 2010). The appellate court affirmed the granting of the motion to compel. 2011 IL App (1st) 110381, 957 N.E.2d 496, 354 Ill. Dec. 180. Defendants have appealed to this court, arguing the subject matter waiver doctrine should not apply to compel production of undisclosed, privileged communications where the disclosed communications were extrajudicial in nature and were not used to gain an advantage in litigation. This court granted leave to appeal. Ill. S. Ct. R. 315 (eff. Feb. 26, 2010). We have allowed the Illinois State Bar Association, Association of Corporate Counsel, Association of Corporate Counsel Chicago Chapter, the International Association of Defense Counsel, and Illinois Association of Defense Counsel to file amicus curiae briefs pursuant to Supreme Court Rule 345 (Ill. S. Ct. R. 345) (eff. Sept. 20, 2010). For the following reasons, we reverse the judgments of the appellate and circuit courts and remand the cause to the circuit court.

BACKGROUND

Defendants are independent real estate companies that own and operate retail shopping malls throughout the United States. In late 2001 and early 2002, defendants Westfield, Rouse, and Simon negotiated to jointly purchase the assets of a Dutch company, Rodamco North America, N.V. (Rodamco). Among the assets purchased with the acquisition of Rodamco was Urban Shopping Centers, L.P. (Urban), an Illinois limited partnership that owns high-end retail shopping centers across the United States. Defendants acquired a large majority interest in Urban, including full ownership of Head Acquisitions, L.P. (Head), Urban's general partner. Plaintiffs are minority limited partners in Urban.

The Business Negotiations

Defendants entered into a purchase agreement with Rodamco in January 2002. On the same day, defendants entered into a separate joint purchase agreement with one another that concerned the allocation of Rodamco's assets and the share of the purchase price each of them would pay. The purchase of Rodamco closed in May 2002. When the purchase closed, defendants executed an amended Head partnership agreement that included provisions allocating control over Urban's numerous mall interests amongst themselves. Plaintiffs were not a party to the Rodamco purchase transaction or to the negotiations leading up to it.

During the course of the negotiations leading up to the purchase of Rodamco, defendants discussed legal issues in negotiating the transaction's terms. They also disclosed to each other some of their attorneys' views about the legal implications of the transaction, the legal importance of the documents under negotiation, and the rights and obligations of the parties to the transaction. Defendants also shared with one another some documents that concerned the legal and financial terms of the transaction. Additionally, defendants' attorneys discussed with one another the terms for a new partnership agreement concerning Urban's mall interests. In these discussions, attorneys for Westfield, Rouse, and Simon shared with each other their legal concerns and legal conclusions about the structure of a new partnership agreement and how it would operate. This new partnership arrangement has been referred to in this litigation as the "synthetic partnership."

The Underlying Lawsuit

Plaintiffs first brought suit in 2004, alleging that, since purchasing Head, defendants had breached alleged fiduciary and contractual duties they owed to Urban and plaintiffs (as limited partners of Urban). Plaintiffs alleged that defendants' division of responsibility for Urban's mall interests under the "synthetic partnership" was a breach of defendants' alleged duties and deprived Urban of sufficient corporate opportunities.

At the heart of plaintiffs' claim is the Urban partnership agreement. Urban was founded to hold, manage, and grow a portfolio of shopping centers then owned by JMB Realty Corporation. In 1993 Urban went public, and by 2000 had become an industry leader in operating, managing, and developing regional malls. In late 2000 Rodamco bought Urban's outstanding shares and took the entity private. Plaintiffs continued to own units as Urban's limited partners. Head, a Rodamco subsidiary, became Urban's new general partner. Rodamco negotiated a partnership agreement with Urban's limited partners (including plaintiffs). The Urban partnership agreement defines the rights, obligations, and liabilities of Head as general partner, as well as the rights and responsibilities of the limited partners. It is plaintiffs' contention that the "[a]greement reflects an intent to grow Urban through the acquisition and development of additional properties." The agreement does not permit Head or its affiliates to compete with Urban in business opportunities, such as acquiring additional real estate, attracting joint venture partners to acquire properties, or developing properties.

Plaintiffs alleged that defendants received legal advice on how to structure a "synthetic partnership," so as to evade the contractual terms and avoid the legal and fiduciary obligations they owed as Urban's general partner. Plaintiffs claimed defendants allocated Urban's properties among themselves, stopped growing Urban's business through acquisitions or ground-up developments, disregarded partnership agreement terms, and stole Urban's opportunities for themselves.

The Motions to Compel

In 2008 plaintiffs filed their first motion to compel the production of privileged communications. Plaintiffs noted that, on the privilege log filed by defendants, one defendant had purposely disclosed privileged documents to another defendant.

Plaintiffs sought the compelled production of documents that defendants had shared among themselves. Defendants objected, arguing that the sought-after documents were protected by the common interest doctrine, and were thus privileged. The circuit court, on December 10, 2008, granted plaintiffs' motion to compel, finding that certain documents containing legal advice could be produced on the ground that defendants had waived any assertion of privilege by sharing the information amongst themselves. The court, however, was careful to limit its order to only those documents that had been disclosed. The court wrote:

> "Further, with regard to the documents to be produced as identified on Appendix B, defendants may redact the contents of any email in an email string if that communication with defendant's counsel was not circulated to any other defendant or third party."

Following the production of the documents, the parties conducted further discovery, including depositions of defendants' executives. In March 2009 plaintiffs filed a second motion to compel, arguing, specifically, that defendant Westfield improperly directed Westfield witness Mark Stefanek, Westfield's chief financial officer, not to testify about matters as to which he had waived the attorney-client privilege. Plaintiffs claimed that Westfield attorneys permitted Stefanek to testify to the actual legal advice received from counsel, but then refused to allow him to testify about the rationale and other details of the legal advice. Plaintiffs argued that this "selective and offensive invocation of the attorney-client privilege waive[d] the privilege regarding the subject matter about which he voluntarily testified — his belief that Westfield had no duty to consider new business opportunities for Urban." The circuit court denied the motion.

Plaintiffs filed a third motion to compel, the motion at issue in this appeal, in April 2010, seeking over 1,500 documents identified in defendants' privilege logs. In the third motion to compel, plaintiffs accused defendants of breaching their fiduciary duties to Urban by usurping business opportunities, in violation of the Urban partnership agreement. Plaintiffs alleged that, during depositions, defendants' witnesses confirmed that during the business negotiations in 2001–02 each defendant's individual counsel attended negotiating sessions and discussed with nonclients legal advice regarding: (1) acquisition structure and use of a "synthetic partnership" to avoid certain partnership obligations; and (2) liability and obligations as Urban's general partner, including continuing obligations to acquire and develop additional properties through Urban. Plaintiffs specifically pointed to the deposition testimony of defendants' witnesses, including arguments concerning the testimony of Stefanek that had been raised in the prior motion to compel, to support compelled production of the requested documents.

Plaintiffs first contended that Anthony Deering, defendant Rouse's former chief executive officer, testified to privileged attorney-client discussions during his deposition. During the January 12, 2010, deposition, plaintiffs' attorney asked Deering if he ever conferred with anyone at Rouse as to whether Rouse had a duty to consider putting new acquisitions within Urban. Rouse's deposition counsel objected, as it called for a legal conclusion, and cautioned Deering not to disclose any attorney-client communications about that issue he may have had at the time. Deering could otherwise answer the question. Deering testified that he had consultations with the other defendants' officers and outside counsel about structuring the partnership. Plaintiffs' attorney asked Deering if he had received legal advice, to which Deering responded "yes." At that point, one of Rouse's attorneys intervened, and informed Deering that any communication his attorneys had with him, in the presence of Simon and Westfield, could be disclosed. However, the Rouse attorney instructed Deering that any legal advice his attorney gave to him in private should not be disclosed. Plaintiffs' attorney then asked Deering what the legal rationale was for Deering's conclusion that Rouse had no duty, after the transaction was complete, to put new acquisitions within Urban. Rouse's attorney again cautioned Deering that it was acceptable to disclose communications he had with his attorney when people from Simon and Westfield were present, but private, privileged communications should not be disclosed. Deering answered plaintiffs' question, saying that his attorney did not give a synopsis of why the synthetic partnership structure worked, but did outline the structure and assured defendants that it would be acceptable and sustainable. Plaintiffs' attorney later again asked Deering what the basis was for his understanding that, after the closing of the Rodamco transaction, Rouse did not feel it had a duty to put new acquisitions within Urban. After again being warned by counsel to be cognizant of not disclosing attorney-client communications, Deering testified that the synthetic partnership insulated Rouse from having to do anything extraordinary in terms of presenting corporate opportunities, acquisitions or any other deals to Urban. That understanding was based on advice given to him at the time by Rouse's attorney, and was given in front of representatives from Simon and Westfield.

Plaintiffs next cited to the testimony of Robert Minutoli, a former Rouse vice president. Minutoli confirmed during the January 28, 2010, deposition that he discussed the substance of legal advice he received with representatives from Simon and Westfield concerning the synthetic partnership. Minutoli was warned by his counsel not to discuss anything that was covered by attorney-client privilege. Plaintiffs' attorney asked if he could recall any aspects of the rationale for the advice that defendants could buy the Urban partnership yet leave behind certain provisions of the partnership agreement with a liquidating entity. After objections from Rouse's counsel, Minutoli answered that it was his recollection that Rouse was in full compliance with the partnership agreement.

Plaintiffs, in the third motion to compel, also cited to the January 7, 2009, deposition testimony of Westfield chief financial officer Mark Stefanek. Plaintiffs' attorney asked Stefanek what basis he had for believing there was no duty to consider business opportunities for Urban. Over the objection of counsel, Stefanek answered his belief was based on legal advice from Westfield's attorneys. Plaintiffs' counsel then asked what the basis was for Westfield's attorneys' legal advice that Westfield had no duty to put any new business opportunities before Urban. Westfield's attorney at the deposition objected and instructed Stefanek not to answer. The following exchange then occurred:

"[Plaintiffs' counsel]: Well, he's already testified to the legal advice. I take it you are waiving, right, privilege?

[Westfield's counsel]: No, we are not waiving.

[Plaintiffs' counsel]: Well, you let him testify to the legal advice.

[Westfield's counsel]:   I have — you — I have given my instruction. You can proceed."

Plaintiffs' counsel then told Stefanek that he was only asking his basis for his belief as a businessman, not legal advice. Stefanek testified that he believed that, while Westfield had a duty on behalf of Urban to consider new business opportunities for Urban in the form of existing redevelopments on existing Urban properties, it did not have a duty to consider new acquisitions on behalf of Urban. Plaintiffs' counsel then asked if this understanding was based on legal advice from Westfield's counsel, to which Westfield's deposition counsel objected. Later in the deposition, plaintiffs' counsel asked the same question, to which there was another objection. Plaintiffs' attorney later asked Stefanek if it was "logical" to think that legal advice was shared between defendants, leading to this exchange:

"[Stefanek]:   Well, we all signed it, so it would seem pretty logical that — you know, that — that anything significant would have been discussed with everybody, yes.

[Plaintiffs' attorney]:   Again, I think that's — there's been a waiver in light of the court's prior ruling on that, [Westfield's attorney], and did you want to reconsider your advice to instruct him not to answer that?

[Westfield's attorney]:   What's your question?

[Plaintiffs' attorney]:   I would like to know what the legal advice was.

[Westfield's attorney]:   If — if — as the — what — if — do you mind asking the foundational question, whether he knows what the legal advice that was shared was?

[Plaintiffs' attorney]:   You received legal advice on why Simon, Rouse and Westfield believed they could exclude certain provisions of the Urban partnership agreement. Correct?

[Stefanek]:   I received advice what — based on why we could.

[Plaintiffs' attorney]:   Okay. And you believe that it's logical that advice was shared with the other partners, Simon and — Rouse? Is that correct?

[Stefanek]:   Seems logical that it would be, yes."

In the third motion to compel plaintiffs argued that defendants could not have it both ways, and having disclosed legal advice on these subjects with each other outside of any confidential relationship in 2001–02, they could not in litigation object that advice on those same subjects is privileged. Plaintiffs also accused defendants of disclosing "tid-bits" to plaintiffs that "act as a sword, while asserting privilege as a shield as to other materials on these same subjects." Plaintiffs contended that any privilege regarding legal advice on the Rodamco acquisition structure and the "synthetic partnership" had been waived when Rouse's witnesses testified that the structure was created by Rouse attorneys who relayed their legal analyses and conclusions to Simon and Westfield and their attorneys. Plaintiffs requested the production of all documents relating to the Rodamco acquisition structure and "synthetic partnership." Plaintiffs also claimed that the attorney-client privilege regarding legal advice on obligations and liabilities to Urban's general partners had been waived, since witnesses for defendants testified defendants and their attorneys freely shared legal advice on this subject matter with each other. Plaintiffs requested the production of all documents defendants had withheld regarding the Urban partnership agreement.

Defendants argued in response that they had not intentionally waived the attorney-client privilege by asserting the advice of counsel as a defense or otherwise placing privileged communications at issue in the litigation, and that the disclosure of even privileged attorney-client communications in a business negotiation does not as a matter of law result in a "subject matter waiver" of all other undisclosed communication a party has with its attorney. The circuit court asked defendants to submit the documents requested by plaintiffs for an in camera review, informing the parties it could not make a decision on the motion to compel without first looking at the requested documents. In October 2010, the circuit court granted the motion to compel, finding that since "[d]efendants had shared privileged communications it follows that the subject of those communications is susceptible to discovery." The court rejected defendants' motion to reconsider. Defendant Westfield's counsel advised the circuit court that Westfield would not produce the documents to plaintiffs and asked to be held in "friendly contempt." The court entered a contempt order against Westfield. Westfield and Rouse appealed separately from the court's order compelling disclosure of the requested documents and communications.

The Appellate Court Ruling

The appellate court affirmed the circuit court's ruling on the motion to compel. The appellate court held that when, in 2001 and 2002, defendants "disclosed privileged attorney-client communications among one another regarding the purchase of Rodamco and specifically the acquisition of Head, those disclosures resulted in a subject-matter waiver of all privileged communications regarding the purchase." 2011 IL App (1st) 110381, ¶ 15, 354 Ill. Dec. 180, 957 N.E.2d 496. Concerning defendants' argument that prior Illinois cases on subject matter waiver were inapplicable to the instant case because those disclosures occurred in the context of litigation rather than a business transaction, the court wrote, "[W]e find no reason to distinguish between a waiver occurring during the course of litigation or during a business negotiation." 2011 IL App (1st) 100381, ¶ 16, 354 Ill. Dec. 180, 957 N.E.2d 496. The appellate court also rejected defendants' arguments that the scope of the waiver was excessive, concluding that, because defendants have the burden of proving the existence of the privilege, defendants had the burden of pointing out the excessive rulings, with specificity as to each document, and they had not done so.

ANALYSIS

On appeal, defendants contend that the subject matter waiver doctrine only applies when privileged attorney-client communications are disclosed during litigation for the purpose of achieving an advantage in that litigation. Defendants argue that, in the instant case, the privileged communications were disclosed only during business negotiations, and thus the subject matter waiver does not apply to compel production of undisclosed, privileged attorney-client communications. Plaintiffs respond that subject matter waiver applies when certain previously privileged communications are disclosed, regardless of whether the disclosure occurred during litigation or in an extrajudicial context. In the alternative, plaintiffs argue that defendants, during their deposition testimony, disclosed privileged communications so as to gain a tactical advantage in this litigation, justifying application of the subject matter waiver doctrine.

I. Application of the Subject Matter Waiver Doctrine to Extrajudicial Disclosures

The first question this court must answer is whether, as a matter of law, the subject matter waiver doctrine applies to the disclosure of privileged statements made outside of a litigation or judicial setting, i.e., in an "extrajudicial" setting. Illinois courts have not previously been confronted with the question of extending the subject matter waiver doctrine to extrajudicial settings. Therefore, the question is one of first impression in this court.

The issue of whether the subject matter waiver doctrine extends to extrajudicial disclosures is a question of law concerning the application of privilege rules in discovery, and thus is reviewed de novo. *Norskog v. Pfiel*, 197 Ill. 2d 60, 71, 755 N.E.2d 1, 257 Ill. Dec. 899 (2001) ("In this appeal, we are deciding whether disclosure of mental health information is prohibited by a statutory discovery privilege and whether any exception to the privilege applies. These are matters of law subject to de novo review.").

A. The Attorney-Client Privilege in Illinois

Before directly addressing the application of subject matter waiver in extrajudicial settings, some discussion of the attorney-client privilege is necessary. Our court rules govern disclosure of privileged material and work product during discovery. *Waste Management, Inc. v. International Surplus Lines Insurance Co.*, 144 Ill. 2d 178, 189, 161 Ill. Dec. 774, 579 N.E.2d 322 (1991). Supreme Court Rule 201(b)(2) states:

> "(2) Privilege and Work Product. All matters that are privileged against disclosure on the trial, including privileged communications between a party or his agent and the attorney for the party, are privileged against disclosure through any discovery procedure. Material prepared by or for a party in preparation for trial is subject to discovery only if it does not contain or disclose the theories, mental impressions, or litigation plans of the party's attorney. The court may apportion the cost involved in originally securing the discoverable material, including when appropriate a reasonable attorney's fee, in such manner as is just." Ill. S. Ct. R. 201(b)(2) (eff. July 1, 2002).

Where legal advice of any kind is sought from a lawyer in his or her capacity as a lawyer, the communications relating to that purpose, made in confidence by the client, are protected from disclosure by the client or lawyer, unless the protection is waived. *Fischel & Kahn, Ltd. v. van Straaten Gallery, Inc.*, 189 Ill. 2d 579, 584,

244 Ill. Dec. 941, 727 N.E.2d 240 (2000); *People v. Simms*, 192 Ill. 2d 348, 381, 249 Ill. Dec. 654, 736 N.E.2d 1092 (2000); *People v. Adam*, 51 Ill. 2d 46, 48, 280 N.E.2d 205 (1972); 8 John Henry Wigmore, Evidence § 2292 (McNaughton rev. ed. 1961). "The attorney-client privilege is an 'evidentiary privilege [which] provides limited protection to communications from the client by prohibiting their unauthorized disclosure in judicial proceedings.' " *In re Marriage of Decker*, 153 Ill. 2d 298, 312, 180 Ill. Dec. 17, 606 N.E.2d 1094 (1992) (quoting Annotated Model Rules of Professional Conduct R. 1.6, at 90 (2d ed.1992)). The privilege is one of the oldest privileges for confidential communications known to the common law and "has been described as being essential 'to the proper functioning of our adversary system of justice.' " *Decker*, 153 Ill. 2d at 312–13, 180 Ill. Dec. 17, 606 N.E.2d 1094 (quoting *United States v. Zolin*, 491 U.S. 554, 562, 109 S. Ct. 2619, 105 L. Ed. 2d 469 (1989)). The privilege is based upon the confidential nature of the communications between the lawyer and client. *Simms*, 192 Ill. 2d at 381, 249 Ill. Dec. 654, 736 N.E.2d 1092.

> " 'The purpose of the attorney-client privilege is to encourage and promote full and frank consultation between a client and legal advisor by removing the fear of compelled disclosure of information.' " *Waste Management*, 144 Ill. 2d at 190, 161 Ill. Dec. 774, 579 N.E.2d 322 (quoting *Consolidation Coal Co. v. Bucyrus-Erie Co.*, 89 Ill. 2d 103, 117–18, 432 N.E.2d 250, 59 Ill. Dec. 666 (1982)). "Moreover, '[t]he [attorney-client] privilege recognizes that sound legal advice or advocacy serves public ends and that such advice or advocacy depends upon the lawyer being fully informed by the client.' " *Fischel & Kahn*, 189 Ill. 2d at 585, 244 Ill. Dec. 941, 727 N.E.2d 240 (2000) (quoting *Upjohn Co. v. United States*, 449 U.S. 383, 389, 101 S. Ct. 677, 66 L. Ed. 2d 584 (1981)).

Illinois adheres "to a strong policy of encouraging disclosure, with an eye toward ascertaining that truth which is essential to the proper disposition of a lawsuit." *Waste Management*, 144 Ill. 2d at 190, 161 Ill. Dec. 774, 579 N.E.2d 322. The privilege is to be strictly confined within its narrowest limits and limited solely to those communications which the claimant either expressly made confidential or which he could reasonably believe under the circumstances would be understood by the attorney as such. Waste Management, 144 Ill. 2d at 190, 161 Ill. Dec. 774, 579 N.E.2d 322.

B. Subject-Matter Waiver

1. Waiver in General

Among the exceptions to the attorney-client privilege is the concept of "waiver." The attorney-client privilege belongs to the client, rather than the attorney, although the attorney asserts the privilege on behalf of the client. *Decker*, 153 Ill. 2d at 313, 180 Ill. Dec. 17, 606 N.E.2d 1094. Only the client may waive the privilege. *Decker*, 153 Ill. 2d at 313, 180 Ill. Dec. 17, 606 N.E.2d 1094. The attorney, although presumed to have authority to waive the privilege on the client's behalf, may not do so over the client's objection. Richard O. Lempert et al., A Modern Approach to Evidence 884–85 (3d ed. 2000). "Any disclosure by the client is inherently inconsistent with the policy behind the privilege of facilitating a confidential attorney-client relationship and, therefore, must result in a waiver of the privilege." *Profit Management Development, Inc., v. Jacobson, Brandvik & Anderson, Ltd.,* 309 Ill. App. 3d 289, 299, 721 N.E.2d 826, 242 Ill. Dec. 547 (1999). Thus, for example, the attorney-client privilege may be waived by the client when the client voluntarily testifies to the privileged matter (*Profit Management*, 309 Ill. App. 3d at 299, 242 Ill. Dec. 547, 721 N.E.2d 826), or when the client voluntarily injects into the case either a factual or legal issue, the truthful resolution of which requires examination of confidential communications, such as legal malpractice actions (*Fischel & Kahn*, 189 Ill. 2d at 585, 244 Ill. Dec. 941, 727 N.E.2d 240 (2000); *Lama v. Preskill*, 353 Ill. App. 3d 300, 305, 288 Ill. Dec. 755, 818 N.E.2d 443 (2004)). The basic, well-settled rule is that when a client discloses to a third-party a privileged communication, that particular communication is no longer privileged and is discoverable or admissible in litigation. Michael H. Graham, Evidence: An Introductory Problem Approach 563 (2002)("The holder of the privilege against disclosure of the confidential matter or communication waives the privilege if he or his predecessor while holder of the privilege voluntarily discloses or consents to disclosure of any significant part of the matter or communication * * *.").

2. The Subject Matter Waiver Doctrine

The type of waiver at issue in the present case is known as "subject matter waiver." According to Wigmore, "[t]he client's offer of his own or the attorney's testimony as to a specific communication to the attorney is a waiver as to all other communications to the attorney on the same matter." (Emphasis in original.) 8 John Henry Wigmore, Evidence § 2327, at 638 (McNaughton rev. ed. 1961). Further, a client's offer of his own or his "attorney's testimony as to a part of any communication to the attorney is a waiver as to the whole of that communication, on the analogy of the principle of completeness." (Emphasis in original.) 8 John Henry Wigmore, Evidence § 2327, at 638 (McNaughton rev. ed. 1961); *In re Sealed Case*, 676 F.2d 793, 809 (D.C. Cir. 1982) ("[A]ny voluntary disclosure by the client to a third party breaches the confidentiality of the attorney-client relationship and therefore waives the privilege, not only as to the specific communication disclosed but often as to all other communications relating to the same subject matter.").

Illinois has long recognized the doctrine of subject matter waiver, with this court holding that when a client voluntarily testifies and waives the privilege, such waiver "extends no further than the subject-matter concerning which testimony had been given by the client." (Emphasis added.) *People v. Gerold*, 265 Ill. 448, 481, 107 N.E. 165 (1914). Our appellate court has refined and elaborated on subject matter waiver:

> "Although voluntary disclosure of confidential information does not effec-
> tively waive an attorney-client privilege as to all other non-disclosed
> communications that may have taken place [citation], where a client reveals
> portions of her conversation with her attorney, those revelations amount to
> a waiver of the attorney-client privilege as to the remainder of the
> conversation or communication about the same subject matter." *In re
> Grand Jury January 246*, 272 Ill. App. 3d 991, 997, 209 Ill. Dec. 518, 651
> N.E.2d 696 (1995) (citing *People v. O'Banner*, 215 Ill. App. 3d 778, 793, 159
> Ill. Dec. 201, 575 N.E.2d 1261 (1991)).

The purpose behind the doctrine of subject matter waiver is to prevent partial or selective disclosure of favorable material while sequestering the unfavorable. *Graco Children's Products, Inc. v. Dressler, Goldsmith, Shore & Milnamow, Ltd.*, 1995 U.S. Dist. LEXIS 8157, [*20–*24] (N.D. Ill. June 14, 1995). "This is so because the privilege of secret consultation is intended only as an incidental means of defense, and not as an independent means of attack, and to use it in the latter character is to abandon it in the former." 8 John Henry Wigmore, Evidence § 2327, at 638 (McNaughton rev. ed. 1961). Courts have characterized this reasoning as the "sword" and the "shield" approach, in that a litigant should not be able to disclose portions of privileged communications with his attorney to gain a tactical advantage in litigation (the sword), and then claim the privilege when the opposing party attempts to discover the undisclosed portion of the communication or communications relating to the same subject matter. *In re EchoStar Communications Corp.*, 448 F.3d 1294, 1303 (Fed. Cir. 2006) ("The overarching goal of waiver in such a case is to prevent a party from using the advice he received as both a sword, by waiving privilege to favorable advice, and a shield, by asserting privilege to unfavorable advice."); *In re Keeper of the Records (Grand Jury Subpoena Addressed to XYZ Corp.)*, 348 F.3d 16, 24 (1st Cir. 2003) ("Implying a subject matter waiver in such a case ensures fairness because it disables litigants from using the attorney-client privilege as both a sword and a shield.").

The Supreme Court of Delaware articulated the importance of fairness to the subject matter waiver doctrine thusly:

> "The purpose underlying the rule of partial disclosure is one of fairness to discourage the use of the privilege as a litigation weapon in the interest of fairness A party should not be permitted to assert the privilege to prevent an inquiry by an opposing party where the professional advice, itself, is tendered as a defense or explanation for disputed conduct. [Citation.] VLI introduced portions of the advice of its new patent counsel in support of its claim that the disclosures concerning the prospect of the patent reinstatement were adequate given the uncertainty surrounding that issue. It would be manifestly unfair to permit selective utilization of these portions and at the same time assert the attorney-client privilege to shield any inquiry into the totality of counsel's advice and its factual basis. [Citation.]" *Zirn v. VLI Corp.*, 621 A.2d 773, 781–82 (Del.1993).

See also Sylgab Steel & Wire Corp. v. Imoco-Gateway Corp., 62 F.R.D. 454, 457 (N.D. Ill. 1974) ("[W]hen a party's conduct reaches a certain point of disclosure fairness requires that the privilege should cease whether the party intended that result or not. A party cannot be allowed, after disclosing as much as he pleases, to withhold the remainder.").

3. Application of the Subject Matter Waiver Doctrine to Extrajudicial Settings

The issue for the court to decide in this case is whether the subject matter waiver doctrine extends to disclosures of privileged communications made in an extrajudicial setting. Defendants argue that the purpose of the doctrine would be defeated if the court applied it to disclosures made outside of litigation, since the purpose of the doctrine is prevent a party from using the privilege as a weapon to gain tactical advantage in litigation. Further, defendants claim extending subject matter waiver outside of litigation would hamper attorneys' ability to provide legal advice to clients during business transactions and other matters. Plaintiffs respond that some courts have found subject matter waiver extends to extrajudicial disclosures, and that such an extension would be in keeping with this state's policy of open disclosure and search for the truth.

First, both parties would concede that the vast majority of cases to apply the subject matter waiver doctrine have done so in the context of judicial disclosures. This court could find no Illinois state case, and the parties could point to none, that applied the doctrine to a disclosure made in an extrajudicial setting. Illinois cases have applied subject matter waiver in the context of litigation. In *Gerold*, the disclosures giving rise to subject matter waiver occurred during court testimony in a criminal case. *Gerold*, 265 Ill. at 481, 107 N.E. 165. In *Newton v. Meissner*, 76 Ill. App. 3d 479, 499, 31 Ill. Dec. 864, 394 N.E.2d 1241 (1979), the plaintiff voluntarily testified on cross-examination at trial that she told her attorney (at the time) that she had no recollection of the accident, thus waiving the privilege and opening the door for her former attorney to testify concerning that particular matter. In *In re Grand Jury January 246*, the court found subject matter waiver where a witness testified in her deposition that her attorneys had discussed "financial options" with her in her lawsuit against a congressman. *In re Grand Jury January 246*, 272 Ill. App. 3d at 996–97, 209 Ill. Dec. 518, 651 N.E.2d 696. In O'Banner, subject matter waiver applied when the defendant took the stand and testified as to portions of conversations with his attorney. O'Banner, 215 Ill. App. 3d at 793, 159 Ill. Dec. 201, 575 N.E.2d 1261. Thus, the issue of whether subject matter waiver extends to extrajudicial disclosures is one of first impression in Illinois.

The extension of subject matter waiver to extrajudicial disclosures, however, has been addressed in the federal courts. Two federal appellate courts, in *In re von Bulow*, 828 F.2d 94 (2d Cir. 1987), and *In re Keeper of the Records (Grand Jury Subpoena Addressed to XYZ Corp.)*, 348 F.3d 16 (1st Cir. 2003), have examined the issue and determined that subject matter waiver should not extend to extrajudicial disclosures.

In *In re von Bulow*, the plaintiffs attempted to claim subject matter waiver based on extrajudicial disclosures made in a book written by Claus von Bulow and his attorney Alan Dershowitz about Von Bulow's prosecution for the murder of his wife. The plaintiffs had filed a civil suit against Von Bulow over his wife's murder. After the civil suit commenced, Von Bulow and Dershowitz published a book chronicling Von Bulow's first trial, successful appeal, and eventual acquittal at a second trial. The plaintiffs moved to compel discovery of certain discussions between Von Bulow and Dershowitz based on the alleged waiver of attorney-client privilege with respect to communications related in the book. The trial court found Von Bulow waived the privilege via the publishing of the book, and extended waiver to: (1) the contents of the published conversations; (2) all communications between Von Bulow and Dershowitz relating to the published conversations; and (3) all communications between Von Bulow and any defense attorney relating to the published conversations. *von Bulow*, 828 F.2d at 100.

On review, the reviewing court found Von Bulow had waived the privilege.

However, the court refused to extend subject matter waiver when "the privilege-holder or his attorney [have] made extrajudicial disclosures, and those disclosures have not subsequently been placed at issue during litigation." *von Bulow*, 828 F.2d at 102. First, as to unpublished contents of the published conversations, the appellate court noted that the cases relied on by the trial court finding implied waivers on account of fairness involved material issues raised by a client's assertion during the course of a judicial proceeding. *von Bulow*, 828 F.2d at 102. The court concluded that, under the fairness doctrine, extrajudicial disclosures of an attorney-client communication, not subsequently used by the client in a judicial proceeding to his adversary's prejudice, do not waive the privilege as to the undisclosed portions of the communication. *von Bulow*, 828 F.2d at 102.

Next, concerning communications between Von Bulow and Dershowitz that had the same subject matter as those disclosed in the book, the court noted that subject matter waiver "has been invoked most often where the privilege-holder has attempted to use the privilege as both 'a sword' and 'a shield' or where the attacking party has been prejudiced at trial." *von Bulow*, 828 F.2d at 103. The court held that subject matter waiver did not apply to extrajudicial disclosures, concluding:

> "[W]here, as here, disclosures of privileged information are made extrajudicially and without prejudice to the opposing party, there exists no reason in logic or equity to broaden the waiver beyond those matters actually revealed. Matters actually disclosed in public lose their privileged status because they obviously are no longer confidential. The cat is let out of the bag, so to speak. But related matters not so disclosed remain confidential. Although it is true that disclosures in the public arena may be 'one-sided' or 'misleading', so long as such disclosures are and remain extrajudicial, there is no legal prejudice that warrants a broad court-imposed subject matter waiver. The reason is that disclosures made in public rather than in court — even if selective — create no risk of legal prejudice until put at issue in the litigation by the privilege-holder. Therefore, insofar as the district court broadened petitioner's waiver to include related conversations on the same subject it was in error." (Emphases in original.) *von Bulow*, 828 F.2d at 103.

A subsequent federal appellate court opinion, *In re Keeper of the Records*, reaffirmed the holding of von Bulow. In *In re Keeper of the Records*, XYZ Corporation made a decision to recall a medical device. XYZ conducted a conference call with its co-venturer Smallco to discuss the recall. The participants in the discussion included two officers of XYZ, outside counsel for XYZ, the principals of Smallco, and Smallco's medical advisor. During the conference call, XYZ's outside counsel advocated for XYZ's position in the face of strong counterarguments from the Smallco representatives. The federal government soon commenced an investigation of XYZ and, as part of that investigation, filed a motion to compel the production of certain documents. The government argued that XYZ had waived the attorney-client privilege during its conference call with Smallco because XYZ's outside counsel had given legal advice in the presence of third parties and had disclosed legal advice previously provided to XYZ, thus effecting a waiver of attorney-client privilege as to all communications on the same subject matter. The trial court agreed and granted the motion.

On appeal, the reviewing court agreed with the trial court that any previously privileged information actually revealed during the call lost any veneer of privilege. However, the court rejected any application of subject matter waiver to the extrajudicial conference call. The court noted that:

> "Virtually every reported instance of an implied waiver extending to an entire subject matter involves a judicial disclosure, that is, a disclosure made in the course of a judicial proceeding. *See von Bulow*, 828 F.2d at 103 (collecting cases). This uniformity is not mere happenstance; it exists because such a limitation makes eminently good sense. Accordingly, we hold, as a matter of first impression in this circuit, that the extrajudicial disclosure of attorney-client communications, not thereafter used by the client to gain adversarial advantage in judicial proceedings, cannot work an implied waiver of all confidential communications on the same subject matter." *In re Keeper of the Records*, 348 F.3d at 24.

The court went on to explain the rationale behind its holding, noting "[t]here is a qualitative difference between offering testimony at trial or asserting an advice of counsel defense in litigation, on the one hand, and engaging in negotiations with business associates, on the other hand." *In re Keeper of the Records*, 348 F.3d at 24. The court found that in the litigation setting, the likelihood of prejudice loomed large so that once a litigant put privileged communications at issue, only the revelation of all related exchanges allowed the truth-seeking process to function unimpeded. *In re Keeper of the Records*, 348 F.3d at 24. In the business negotiation setting, however, concerns of prejudice are absent, as the introduction of a party's attorney into the proceedings does nothing to cause prejudice to the opposition or subvert the truth-seeking process. *In re Keeper of the Records*, 348 F.3d at 24.

In support of their argument that subject matter waiver should apply to extrajudicial disclosures, plaintiffs cite to *Flagstar Bank, FSB v. Freestar Bank, N.A.*, 2009 U.S. Dist. LEXIS 76842 (N.D. Ill. Aug. 25, 2009). In Flagstar, the plaintiff asserted the defendant waived the attorney-client privilege when the defendant disclosed a certain document to a third party, apparently outside the context of litigation or judicial proceedings. Specifically, the disclosure at issue concerned a letter authored by the defendant's attorney and forwarded to the defendant's president, who in turn sent the letter to an employee of a company the defendant hired for marketing services. Flagstar, 2009 U.S. Dist. LEXIS 76842, [at *14]. The court found the letter was not privileged, as it was disclosed to a third party who was not acting in a legal capacity for the defendant. The court found that disclosing the letter "effectuated a waiver of the attorney client privilege as to that document and to any other documents of the same subject matter." Flagstar, 2009 U.S. Dist. LEXIS 76842, [at *18].

Plaintiffs further cite to *In re OM Group Securities Litigation*, 226 F.R.D. 579 (N.D. Ohio 2005), as an example of a court applying subject matter waiver to purely extrajudicial disclosures. In OM Group, a plaintiff shareholder sued defendant corporation in a shareholder action. The defendant corporation's audit committee was conducting an investigation of defendant. The audit committee's counsel, and a forensic accounting firm hired by counsel, gave a power point presentation to the corporation's board of directors regarding the findings of the ongoing investigation.

The plaintiff shareholder filed a motion to compel production of documents underlying the presentation. After being provided the power point presentation itself, along with two spreadsheets regarding the investigation, defendant refused to provide any of the requested underlying documents. The plaintiff argued that the defendants waived any privilege over the documents containing the same subject matter as the presentation. The defendants argued that the scope of any waiver should be narrowly construed because they would not gain an unfair tactical advantage by the power point presentation and the two spreadsheets.

The court ordered the production of the underlying documents, finding they were within the scope and subject matter of the audit committee's intentional disclosure. *OM Group*, 226 F.R.D. at 593. The court rejected the defendants' pledge that they would not use the underlying documents for a tactical advantage in the litigation, reasoning:

> "Defendants attempt to restrict application of the fairness doctrine solely to whether they would gain a tactical advantage in litigation by not disclosing the underlying documents. The Court does not interpret the fairness doctrine so narrowly. The Court must consider, not only whether there is a tactical benefit, but whether it is fair to uphold the privilege considering the nature of the disclosure." *OM Group*, 226 F.R.D. at 593.

Plaintiff also points to a comment from the Restatement (Third) of The Law Governing Lawyers, stating "[w]ith respect to out-of-court partial disclosures, the substantial majority of decisions announces a broad and almost automatic subject-matter-waiver rule." Restatement (Third) of The Law Governing Lawyers § 79, Reporters Notes cmt. f (2000). The comment cites to several federal court cases in support. In *In re Sealed Case*, 877 F.2d 976 (D.C.Cir.1989), a company that had contracted with the Department of Defense was being audited by the Defense Contract Audit Agency (DCAA). During the audit, an internal company document containing legal advice was disclosed to the DCAA. While acknowledging that "a waiver of the privilege in an attorney-client communication extends 'to all other communications relating to the same subject matter,'" the court remanded the cause to the lower court for a determination of how broadly to apply the waiver. *In re Sealed Case*, 877 F.2d at 980–81 (quoting *In re Sealed Case*, 676 F.2d 793, 809 (D.C. Cir. 1982)).

In *In re Martin Marietta Corp.*, 856 F.2d 619, 623 (4th Cir. 1988), the court allowed in all privileged communications relating to a position paper sent by a company facing indictment to the United States Attorney. The position paper contained legal arguments on why the company should not be indicted. In *AMCA International Corp. v. Phipard*, 107 F.R.D. 39 (D. Mass. 1985), the plaintiff sent a memorandum to the defendant containing legal advice the plaintiff had received regarding a new formula for calculating royalties for the defendant (it is not clear from the written opinion if this was before or after initiation of litigation). The defendant argued that the disclosure of the memorandum operated as a waiver of the privilege not only as to the document but to all documents relating to the same subject matter. The court held the release of the memorandum served as a waiver of the privilege as to a partial group of documents which related to the same subject matter, but would not extend the waiver to all prior and subsequent communications between plaintiff and its counsel on the interpretation of the contracts at issue. AMCA, 107 F.R.D. at 44.

Finally, in *Smith v. Alyeska Pipeline Service Co.*, 538 F. Supp. 977 (D. Del. 1982), the court ordered production of 36 documents exchanged between the plaintiff and his attorney relating to an infringement case. The court found that the plaintiff had waived the privilege when plaintiff's attorney, acting on behalf of plaintiff, sent an opinion letter to the defendant concerning the same subject matter as that contained in the 36 privileged documents. The disclosure was apparently made in an extrajudicial context.

We find the line of cases declining to extend subject matter waiver to extrajudicial disclosures more persuasive. First, limiting application of subject matter waiver to disclosures made in litigation better serves the purpose of the doctrine. The purpose of the doctrine is to prevent a party from strategically and selectively disclosing partial attorney-client communications with his attorney to use as a sword, and then invoking the privilege as a shield to other communications so as to gain a tactical advantage in litigation. See *In re Keeper of the Records*, 348 F.3d at 24. Expanding the doctrine to cover extrajudicial disclosures that are not made for tactical advantage in litigation would necessarily broaden the scope of the doctrine's purpose. When a partial disclosure is made in the litigation context, the apparent prejudice that could result to the opposing party is obvious: a party has injected into the litigation communications with his attorney which may aid in the party's prosecution or defense of a claim, yet the party can also frustrate the truth-seeking process by claiming privilege when the opposition seeks to discover the full context of the confidential communications. Such an abuse of the judicial process should be looked upon with disfavor, and the doctrine of subject matter waiver ensures that the full context of the partial disclosure is discoverable so the court may fulfill its truth-seeking function and extend fairness to the opposing party. That same purpose is not served, however, when the doctrine is expanded to cover disclosures made before litigation is initiated or, in many cases, even contemplated.

Next, the cases cited in support of limiting the doctrine to the context of litigation are more thorough and persuasive than those cited in opposition. As discussed above, both *In re Keeper of the Records* and *von Bulow* contain detailed and thorough reasoning as to why the subject matter waiver doctrine should not be extended to purely extrajudicial disclosures. See *In re Keeper of the Records*, 348 F.3d at 24–26; *von Bulow*, 828 F.2d at 101–03. In contrast, *Flagstar* and the cases cited in the Restatement (Third) of The Law Governing Lawyers do not contain any reasoning or explanation for why subject matter waiver should extend to purely extrajudicial disclosures. We acknowledge that in those cases the courts did apply subject matter waiver to what appear to be extrajudicial disclosures. However, as those cases do not contain any reasoning or justification for extension of the subject matter waiver doctrine, we do not find them as persuasive as the more complete analyses found in *In re Keeper of the Records* and *von Bulow*.

Further, we reject the analysis of the court in *OM Group*. The *OM Group* court explicitly declined to decide whether the defendants gained a tactical advantage in litigation through its extrajudicial partial disclosures, instead relying solely on fairness to apply subject matter waiver. *OM Group*, 226 F.R.D. at 593. The purpose behind subject matter waiver is to prevent the disclosing party from using the privilege as a sword and a shield in litigation, i.e., to prevent one party from gaining a tactical advantage in litigation over another party through selective use of the privilege. "Fairness" should not be separated from the "tactical advantage" aspect of subject matter waiver's purpose. The *OM Group* analysis is incomplete.

Finally, we believe limiting subject matter waiver to the context of judicial disclosures to be sound policy. "[A] rule that would allow broad subject matter waivers to be implied from such communications would provide perverse incentives: parties would leave attorneys out of commercial negotiations for fear that their inclusion would later force wholesale disclosure of confidential information." *In re Keeper of the Records*, 348 F.3d at 24. We agree with the *In re Keeper of the Records* court that such a consequence would strike at the heart of the attorney-client relationship and could deprive clients of counsel at times when such counsel is most valuable.

While we do not limit our holding only to advice given in business transactions, we recognize that the present case involves a business transaction and business negotiations would be uniquely burdened by extending subject matter waiver. We find informative the analysis of the court in *Hewlett-Packard Co. v. Bausch & Lomb Inc.*:

> "This court also is concerned about the effect that finding waiver too freely might have on the sort of business transaction in which defendant and GEC were involved. Holding that this kind of disclosure constitutes a waiver could make it appreciably more difficult to negotiate sales of businesses and products that arguably involve interests protected by laws relating to intellectual property. Unless it serves some significant interest courts should not create procedural doctrine that restricts communication between buyers and sellers, erects barriers to business deals, and increases the risk that prospective buyers will not have access to important information that could play key roles in assessing the value of the business or product they are considering buying. Legal doctrine that impedes frank communication between buyers and sellers also sets the stage for more lawsuits, as buyers are more likely to be unpleasantly surprised by what they receive. By refusing to find waiver in these settings courts create an environment in which businesses can share more freely information that is relevant to their transactions. This policy lubricates business deals and encourages more openness in transactions of this nature." *Hewlett-Packard Co. v. Bausch & Lomb Inc.*, 115 F.R.D. 308, 311 (N.D. Cal. 1987).

It is of no matter if disclosure made during a business negotiation is done to gain a tactical advantage during the business negotiation. Such a disclosure during a business negotiation is not in the province of this court, but is between the two entities engaging in the negotiation, unless a law or Illinois legal ethics rule was broken. Further, to address a point raised at oral argument, if a disclosure is made during a business negotiation to gain a later tactical advantage in anticipated litigation, subject matter waiver would still apply if such a disclosure is later used by the disclosing party at any point during the litigation to gain a tactical advantage. *See In re Keeper of the Records*, 348 F.3d at 25 ("[I]f confidential information is revealed in an extrajudicial context and later reused in a judicial setting, the circumstances of the initial disclosure will not immunize the client against a claim of waiver."). However, if the disclosure is not later reused during litigation, subject matter waiver would not apply, regardless of whether there was some hidden intent on the part of the disclosing party to gain some sort of advantage in later litigation. To apply subject matter waiver in such a manner would require determining the intent of the disclosing party, and would be pure speculation on the court's part as to why the disclosure was made. Further, if the disclosure is not later used in litigation, it would not serve the purpose of the subject matter waiver doctrine. We hold that subject matter waiver does not apply to the extrajudicial disclosure of attorney-client communications not thereafter used by the client to gain an adversarial advantage in litigation. *See In re Keeper of the Records*, 348 F.3d at 24.

II. Whether Defendants' Statements During Discovery Depositions Placed Disclosures at Issue in Litigation

Plaintiffs contend, in the alternative, that even if this court holds that subject matter waiver does not apply to extrajudicial disclosures, the doctrine would still apply in this case because defendants are using the legal advice they received to advance their defense in the underlying lawsuit. Specifically, plaintiffs argue that defendants' witnesses (Rouse's officers Deering and Minutoli and Westfield executive Stefanek), during deposition testimony, disclosed privileged communications in order to gain a tactical advantage in the litigation. Defendants respond that plaintiffs' alternative argument is completely unsupported by the record.

While privileged extrajudicial disclosures are not subject to subject matter waiver, if those same privileged communications are later reused in a judicial setting, the circumstances of the initial disclosure will not immunize the client against a claim of waiver. *See In re Keeper of the Records*, 348 F.3d at 25. Thus, if defendants have introduced into the litigation privileged communications to be used as a sword for tactical advantage, those communications, and undisclosed communications of the same subject matter, are discoverable. Whether the attorney-client privilege or any exception thereto exists is reviewed de novo. *Norskog*, 197 Ill. 2d at 71, 257 Ill. Dec. 899, 755 N.E.2d 1; *Fox Moraine, LLC v. United City of Yorkville*, 2011 IL App (2d) 100017, ¶ 63, 356 Ill. Dec. 21, 960 N.E.2d 1144.

In general, " '[w]aiver' means the voluntary relinquishment of a known right" and arises from an affirmative, consensual act consisting of an intentional relinquishment of a known right. *Maniez v. Citibank, F.S.B.*, 404 Ill. App. 3d 941, 947, 344 Ill. Dec. 531, 937 N.E.2d 237 (2010). A waiver by a client of the attorney-client privilege can be either express or implied. *Lama v. Preskill*, 353 Ill. App. 3d 300, 305, 288 Ill. Dec. 755, 818 N.E.2d 443 (2004). A clear example of an express waiver is when a client voluntarily testifies about privileged communications. *See Profit Management*, 309 Ill. App. 3d at 299, 242 Ill. Dec. 547, 721 N.E.2d 826. The client may also waive the privilege by expressly agreeing to do so or by failing to assert the privilege when privileged information is requested. Richard O. Lempert et al., A Modern Approach to Evidence 885 (3d ed. 2000). An implied waiver may be found when the client asserts claims or defenses that put his or her communications with the legal advisor at issue in the litigation. *Profit Management*, 309 Ill. App. 3d at

300, 242 Ill. Dec. 547, 721 N.E.2d 826. However, a party can preserve the privilege when it attempts to limit disclosure. *See In re Continental Illinois Securities Litigation*, 732 F.2d 1302, 1314 (7th Cir. 1984). Generally, failure to assert the privilege prior to turning over the privileged documents constitutes a voluntary waiver. *See Maryville Academy v. Loeb Rhoades & Co.*, 559 F. Supp. 7, 8–9 (N.D. Ill. 1982). The determination of whether a party has waived the privilege must be made on a case-by-case basis. *Ritacca v. Abbott Laboratories*, 203 F.R.D. 332, 335 (N.D. Ill. 2001).

If waiver is found, the next step is to determine the scope of the waiver and whether the waiver applies to all of the communications relating to the same subject matter. *Rowe International Corp. v. Ecast, Inc.*, 241 F.R.D. 296, 301 (N.D. Ill. 2007). " '[T]here is no bright line test for determining what constitutes the subject matter of a waiver, rather courts weigh the circumstances of the disclosure, the nature of the legal advice sought and the prejudice to the parties of permitting or prohibiting further disclosures.' " *Rowe*, 241 F.R.D. at 301 (quoting *Fort James Corp. v. Solo Cup Co.*, 412 F.3d 1340, 1349–50 (Fed. Cir. 2005)).

We will examine the deposition testimony of Deering, Minutoli, and Stefanek cited by plaintiffs in turn to determine first if waiver occurred and, if so, the scope of the waiver and the waiver's subject matter. We find that Deering and Minutoli, in their depositions, did not voluntarily waive the privilege as to legal advice received from counsel and shared with third parties. The cited deposition testimony of Deering and Minutoli concern the third-party disclosures made by defendants to each other during the 2001–02 business negotiations. First, we note that the testimony was elicited after repeated questioning by plaintiffs' attorney. Next, and most important, the testimony occurred after the circuit court granted plaintiffs' motion to compel and ordered the production of documents containing or discussing the shared communications. Defendants had contested that motion to compel and invoked the privilege. Following the court's order on the motion to compel, it is apparent that defendants were operating under the assumption that the court had deemed the privilege waived for documents and communications containing legal advice that were shared among defendants. Thus, defendant Rouse did not voluntarily waive the privilege during the depositions. *See Regan v. Garfield Ridge Trust & Savings Bank*, 220 Ill. App. 3d 1078, 1090–91, 163 Ill. Dec. 605, 581 N.E.2d 759 (1991)(privilege not waived where former attorney called to testify by client and reveals no privileged communications during direct examination and, during cross examination attorney properly invokes the privilege during questioning); *Profit Management*, 309 Ill. App. 3d at 300, 242 Ill. Dec. 547, 721 N.E.2d 826 ("The plaintiffs further waived the privilege when they did not object to the material in federal court on the basis of its confidential nature.").

Plaintiffs also contend that Stefanek, Westfield's chief financial officer, waived the privilege as to attorney-client communications discussed openly among defendants. Again, for the same reasons discussed above, we do not find Stefanek's testimony to have waived the privilege. Attorney-client communications shared among defendants had already been deemed waived by the circuit court in its December 10, 2008, order. Defendants had objected to the motion to compel, invoking the privilege. When Stefanek was deposed on January 7, 2009, a month after the order, the transcript reveals Stefanek, Westfield's attorney and plaintiffs' attorney were operating under the assumption that any privilege as to the shared communications had been deemed waived, pursuant to the order of the circuit court. This is particularly illustrated in the following exchange after plaintiffs' counsel asked whether Stefanek's understanding of the synthetic partnership was based on legal advice received from counsel:

"[Stefanek]:   Well, we all signed it, so it would seem pretty logical that — you know, that — that anything significant would have been discussed with everybody, yes.

[Plaintiffs' attorney]:   Again, I think that's — there's been a waiver in light of the court's prior ruling on that, [Westfield's attorney], and did you want to reconsider your advice to instruct him not to answer that?

[Westfield's attorney]:   What's your question?

[Plaintiffs' attorney]:   I would like to know what the legal advice was.

[Westfield's attorney]:   If — if — as the — what — if — do you mind asking the foundational question, whether he knows what the legal advice that was shared was?

[Plaintiffs' attorney]:   You received legal advice on why Simon, Rouse and Westfield believed they could exclude certain provisions of the Urban partnership agreement. Correct?

[Stefanek]:   based on why we could." (Emphasis added.)

Clearly, the parties assumed that waiver had occurred, based on the court's ruling regarding the extrajudicial third-party disclosures made by defendants to each other during the 2001–02 business negotiations. By sharing information with each other, defendants, during the 2001–02 negotiations, had waived the attorney-client privilege with respect to documents and communications containing legal advice disclosed to third parties. However, for the reasons stated above in discussing Deering's and Minutoli's testimony, Stefanek did not waive the privilege during the deposition as to the shared communications.

Plaintiffs further argue that Stefanek waived the privilege as to certain advice he received from Westfield's attorneys about the structure of the partnership, outside of the shared communications covered by the circuit court's December 10, 2008, order. During the deposition, plaintiffs' attorney asked Stefanek what the basis was "for [Stefanek's] awareness that there was no duty to consider new business opportunities for Urban." Westfield's attorney immediately objected, stating "[s]ame objection; same instruction." Stefanek then answered that the basis was legal advice given by Westfield attorney Peter Schwartz sometime during the acquisition of Rodamco. Plaintiffs' attorney then asked Stefanek the basis for Schwartz's legal advice. Westfield's attorney again objected and instructed Stefanek not to answer the question. The following exchange then occurred:

"[Plaintiffs' attorney]:   Well, he's already testified to the legal advice. I take it you are waiving, right, privilege?

[Westfield's attorney]:   No, we are not waiving.

[Plaintiffs' attorney]:　Well, you let him testify to the legal advice.

[Westfield's attorney]:　I have — you — I have given my instruction. You can proceed.

[Plaintiffs' attorney]:　I just want you to know that we are going to move to compel because you can't have it both ways. You can't have him testifying to legal advice and then say that you are not waiving. So this will be a motion—

[Westfield's attorney]:　He's—

[Plaintiffs' attorney]:　— to compel. I just want to meet and confer on that now. So—

[Westfield's attorney]:　Proceed with your questioning.

[Plaintiffs' attorney]:　Okay. That's fine. So you are going to continue to stand on that instruction?

[Westfield's attorney]:　Yeah. I am instructing him not to — not to reveal attorney-client advice.

[Plaintiffs' attorney]:　All right."

Plaintiffs' attorney asked again about the basis for the legal advice. Westfield's attorney interjected, instructing Stefanek not to provide the content of the communication. When plaintiffs' counsel asked what the rationale for the legal advice was, Westfield's attorney stated, "I object it is — Instruct not to answer."

Based on the transcript excerpt provided in the record, we do not find that defendant Westfield waived the privilege through Stefanek's testimony. The record reveals that, while Stefanek did testify to legal advice received from Westfield's attorneys about the synthetic partnership, he did not testify as to the actual content and basis of the legal advice. *See United States v. O'Malley*, 786 F.2d 786, 794 (7th Cir. 1986) (a client does not waive the attorney-client privilege merely by disclosing a subject which he had discussed with his attorney, but rather, in order to waive the privilege the client must disclose the communication with the attorney itself). Further, and most importantly, the record shows that Westfield's attorney at the deposition repeatedly objected to plaintiffs' attorney's line of questioning regarding legal advice. Westfield's attorney indicated that he was standing on his instruction to Stefanek "not to reveal attorney-client advice." Under such circumstances and facts, it is apparent that defendant Westfield invoked the privilege during the deposition, and thus did not waive it with regard to Stefanek's testimony.

Plaintiffs finally argue that defendants have necessarily put the legal advice received from counsel "at issue," and thus effected an implied waiver by using legal advice as a defense in support of defendants' claims of "good faith" in constructing the synthetic partnership. *See Lama*, 353 Ill. App. 3d at 305, 288 Ill. Dec. 755, 818 N.E.2d 443. Plaintiffs claim they would suffer prejudice if defendants' witnesses are permitted to testify about their reliance on legal advice, but plaintiffs are precluded from obtaining discovery on the subject matter at issue. However, based on the record before this court, we see no evidence that defendants have claimed reliance, or are planning to claim reliance, on legal advice in its defense of this case. Outside of the deposition testimony, plaintiffs' have not pointed this court to any legal filings by defendants where defendants utilize legal advice as a defense. If any party has injected defendants' lawyers' legal advice into this case, it is plaintiffs. Plaintiffs have filed three motions to compel seeking privileged documents and communications. During depositions, it was plaintiffs' attorney who asked defendants' witnesses questions relating to legal advice the witnesses received. Plaintiffs have already received, following the granting of their motion to compel, documents where defendants waived the privilege by disclosing privileged communications with one another. We cannot say that defendants impliedly waived the privilege by putting "at issue" their attorney-client communications. If, on remand, defendants do inject their attorney-client communications into the litigation, the circuit court may revisit the issue. Upon the record provided to this court in this appeal, however, we do not find any waiver by defendants during the litigation.

CONCLUSION

In conclusion, we hold that subject matter waiver does not apply to disclosures made in an extrajudicial context when those disclosures are not thereafter used by the client to gain a tactical advantage in litigation. Further, the cited deposition testimony of defendants' corporate officers did not waive the attorney-client privilege so as to allow application of subject matter waiver to certain attorney-client communications. For the foregoing reasons, the appellate and circuit courts' judgments are reversed. The cause is remanded to the circuit court for proceedings consistent with this order.

Judgments reversed.

Cause remanded.

IN RE ECHOSTAR COMMUNICATIONS CORPORATION
United States Court of Appeals for the Federal Circuit
448 F.3d 1294 (Fed. Cir. 2006)

ON PETITION FOR WRIT OF MANDAMUS

ORDER

*   *   *

I

TiVo sued EchoStar for infringement of its U.S. Patent No. 6,233,389 ("the '389 patent"). In response to the allegation of willful infringement, EchoStar asserted the defense of reliance on advice of counsel. Prior to the filing of the action, EchoStar relied on advice of in-house counsel. After the action was filed, EchoStar obtained additional legal advice from Merchant & Gould but elected not to rely on it. Presumably to explore further EchoStar's state of mind in determining that it did not infringe the patent, TiVo sought production of documents in the possession of EchoStar and Merchant & Gould. The district court held that by relying on advice of in-house counsel EchoStar waived its attorney-client privilege and attorney work-product immunity relating to advice of any counsel regarding infringement, including Merchant & Gould. The district court indicated that the scope of the waiver included communications made either before or after the filing of the complaint and any work product, whether or not the product was communicated to EchoStar. The district court also held that EchoStar could redact information related only to trial preparation or information unrelated to infringement. EchoStar produced communications, including two infringement opinions from Merchant & Gould, but did not produce any work product related to the Merchant & Gould opinions.

Thereafter, the parties sought clarification of the district court's order. TiVo argued that the district court should order EchoStar to produce all Merchant & Gould documents that relate to the advice-of-counsel defense, even if EchoStar was not in possession of the documents because they were never communicated to EchoStar. EchoStar argued that it should only be required to produce documents that were provided to it by Merchant & Gould.

On October 5, 2005, the district court issued an order that clarified its previous order and stated that the waiver of immunity extended to all work product of Merchant & Gould, whether or not communicated to EchoStar. The district court determined that the documents could be relevant or lead to the discovery of admissible evidence because they might contain information that was conveyed to EchoStar, even if the documents were not themselves conveyed to EchoStar. EchoStar petitions this court for a writ of mandamus with respect to the Merchant & Gould documents not provided to EchoStar, challenging the district court's rulings. Merchant & Gould moves for leave to intervene in EchoStar's petition and submits its own petition for a writ of mandamus.

II

The remedy of mandamus is available in extraordinary situations to correct a clear abuse of discretion or usurpation of judicial power. . . . A party seeking a writ bears the burden of proving that it has no other means of obtaining the relief desired, . . . and that the right to issuance of the writ is "clear and indisputable," *Allied Chem. Corp. v. Daiflon, Inc.*, 449 U.S. 33, 35, 101 S. Ct. 188, 66 L. Ed. 2d 193 (1980). A writ of mandamus may be sought when the challenged order turns on questions of privilege. . . .

EchoStar argues that a writ of mandamus should issue, among other reasons, because the district court erred in determining that (1) the attorney-client privilege had been waived and (2) the waiver of any privilege extended to work-product that was not communicated to EchoStar because, inter alia, the documents are not relevant to whether EchoStar had a good faith belief that it did not infringe. Merchant & Gould also argues that the district court erred in requiring the production of documents that Merchant & Gould did not provide to EchoStar because any such documents could not be relevant to whether EchoStar reasonably had a good faith belief that it did not infringe, based upon advice from counsel.

In response, TiVo argues, inter alia, that (1) EchoStar is not entitled to a writ of mandamus because it has complied, in large part, with the district court orders it now challenges, (2) the attorney-client privilege was waived when EchoStar asserted a defense of reliance on advice of in-house counsel, (3) the relevance of the Merchant & Gould documents can be determined when they are offered as evidence, and (4) even though the Merchant & Gould documents may not have been provided to EchoStar, they may contain information that was otherwise conveyed to EchoStar.

Regarding TiVo's first argument, that EchoStar is not entitled to mandamus because it has complied in large part with the order, we do not believe it is a requirement that a party refuse to comply at all with an order, if it seeks to challenge only a part of the order. Such a rule would encourage parties not to comply with district court orders that, in large part, they do not challenge, so that they could preserve a challenge only to the portions that they believe are erroneous. EchoStar cannot undo the disclosures it has made to TiVo, but it can challenge the portions of the order that require additional disclosures.

We now turn to the more substantive arguments underlying this petition.

III

In this petition, we apply our own law, rather than the law of the regional circuit. This case involves the extent to which a party waives its attorney-client privilege and work-product immunity when it asserts the advice-of-counsel defense in response to a charge of willful patent infringement. "Federal Circuit law applies when deciding whether particular written or other materials are discoverable in a patent case, if those materials relate to an issue of substantive patent law." . . . A remedy for willful patent infringement is specifically provided for in the Patent Act, see 35 U.S.C. §§ 284–285; therefore, questions of privilege and discoverability that arise from assertion of the advice-of-counsel defense necessarily involve issues of substantive patent law . . . .

A

EchoStar first challenges the district court's holding that EchoStar waived the attorney-client privilege when it asserted its defense in response to the charge of willful infringement. The attorney-client privilege protects disclosure of communications between a client and his attorney. . . .

Once a party announces that it will rely on advice of counsel, for example, in response to an assertion of willful infringement, the attorney-client privilege is waived. "The widely applied standard for determining the scope of a waiver of attorney-client privilege is that the waiver applies to all other communications relating to the same subject matter." . . .

EchoStar argues that it did not assert the advice-of-counsel defense because it intended to rely only on an "in-house investigation supervised by in-house counsel." The district court held that the opinion formed by in-house counsel and conveyed to EchoStar executives, although not a traditional opinion of counsel, constituted a legal opinion. We see no error in the district court's determination.

EchoStar summarily asserts that "an internal investigation involving in-house engineers and in-house counsel is simply a different subject matter from legal opinions commissioned at a later date from outside lawyers." This argument is without merit. Whether counsel is employed by the client or hired by outside contract, the offered advice or opinion is advice of counsel or an opinion of counsel. Use of in-house counsel may affect the strength of the defense, but it does not affect the legal nature of the advice. . . .

Thus, when EchoStar chose to rely on the advice of in-house counsel, it waived the attorney-client privilege with regard to any attorney-client communications relating to the same subject matter, including communications with counsel other than in-house counsel, which would include communications with Merchant & Gould. . . .

B

EchoStar next asserts that the district court's order cast too wide a net by including within the waiver's scope documents that were never communicated from Merchant & Gould (the attorney) to EchoStar (the client). The district court stated:

> EchoStar had the benefit of choice, as explained by the Federal Circuit in Knorr-Bremse Systeme Fuer Nutzfahrzeuge GmbH v. Dana Corp., of whether to introduce [in-house counsel's] opinion. But once EchoStar chose to introduce the opinion, it opened to inspection all related advice sought and developed regarding EchoStar's potential infringement of the '389 patent. Regardless of when the opinions or materials were transcribed or communicated to EchoStar, such information necessarily relates to the opinion being offered by [in-house counsel] and goes to show EchoStar's state of mind with respect to willful infringement. This is particularly true where, as is the case here, EchoStar's willfulness witness was privy to the substance of the willfulness opinions developed by outside counsel both pre-and post-filing. . . .

. . . Noting that district courts had ruled differently on whether the waiver of work-product protection covered documents that were not disclosed to the client, the district court discussed the reasons for requiring production of uncommunicated work product:

> Still, other courts have mandated production of all material regardless of whether they were disclosed, maintaining that the discovery of such information is necessary to uncover what the client was actually told by opinion counsel. . . . In *Novartis*, the court stated, "it is critical for the patentee to have a full opportunity to probe, not only the state of mind of the infringer, but also the mind of the infringer's lawyer upon which the infringer so firmly relied." . . . The rationale behind this approach is that, by imposing broad waiver, the advice of counsel defense will only be invoked by "infringers who prudently and sincerely sought competent advice from competent counsel . . ." and "moreover, focusing on the infringer's waiver rather than state of mind may reduce the chances of legal gamesmanship creeping into the practice of rendering infringement and validity opinions."

. . . "If negative information was important enough to reduce to a memorandum, there is a reasonable possibility that the information was conveyed in some form or fashion to the client." . . .

* * *

In a subsequent order, the district court further explained why the scope of the waiver should include work product that was not disclosed to EchoStar:

Were discovery of "uncommunicated" materials not allowed, accused infringers could easily shield themselves from disclosing any unfavorable analysis by simply requesting that their opinion counsel not send it. This would be unfair.

* * *

We review the district court's determination as to the scope of the waiver for an abuse of discretion. . . . EchoStar asserts that to apply the broad scope employed by the district court to the waiver of both attorney-client privilege and work-product doctrine was an abuse of discretion. We agree.

The attorney-client privilege and the work-product doctrine, though related, are two distinct concepts and waiver of one does not necessarily waive the other. . . . In general, a party may obtain discovery of any matter that (1) is "not privileged" and (2) "is relevant to the claim or defense of any party." Fed. R. Civ. P. 26(b)(1). Among other things, attorney-client communications are designated as "privileged." . . . "The attorney-client privilege protects the confidentiality of communications between attorney and client made for the purpose of obtaining legal advice." . . . We recognize the privilege in order to promote full and frank communication between a client and his attorney so that the client can make well-informed legal decisions and conform his activities to the law. . . . The client can waive the attorney-client privilege when, for instance, it uses the advice to establish a defense. . . . However, selective waiver of the privilege may lead to the inequitable result that the waiving party could waive its privilege for favorable advice while asserting its privilege on unfavorable advice. . . . In such a case, the party uses the attorney-client privilege as both a sword and a shield. . . . To prevent such abuses, we recognize that when a party defends its actions by disclosing an attorney-client communication, it waives the attorney-client privilege as to all such communications regarding the same subject matter. . . .

In contrast to the attorney-client privilege, the work-product doctrine, or work-product immunity as it is also called, can protect "documents and tangible things" prepared in anticipation of litigation that are both non-privileged and relevant. Fed. R. Civ. P. 26(b)(3). Unlike the attorney-client privilege, which protects all communication whether written or oral, work-product immunity protects documents and tangible things, such as memorandums, letters, and e-mails. . . . We recognize work-product immunity because it promotes a fair and efficient adversarial system by protecting "the attorney's thought processes and legal recommendations" from the prying eyes of his or her opponent. . . . Essentially, the work-product doctrine encourages attorneys to write down their thoughts and opinions with the knowledge that their opponents will not rob them of the fruits of their labor. . . .

[Un]like the attorney-client privilege, however, the work-product doctrine is not absolute. . . . First, a party may discover certain types of work product if they have "substantial need of the materials in the preparation of the party's case and that the party is unable without undue hardship to obtain the substantial equivalent . . . by other means." Rule 26(b)(3). This rule, however, only allows discovery of "factual" or "non-opinion" work product and requires a court to "protect against the disclosure of the mental impressions, conclusions, opinions, or legal theories of an attorney or other representative." . . .

Second, a party may discover work product if the party waives its immunity. . . . However, work product waiver is not a broad waiver of all work product related to the same subject matter like the attorney-client privilege. . . . Instead, work-product waiver only extends to "factual" or "non-opinion" work product concerning the same subject matter as the disclosed work product. . . .

We recognize that the line between "factual" work product and "opinion" work product is not always distinct, especially when, as here, an attorney's opinion may itself be "factual" work product. When faced with the distinction between where that line lies, however, a district court should balance the policies to prevent sword-and-shield litigation tactics with the policy to protect work product.

That being said, we recognize at least three categories of work product that are potentially relevant to the advice-of-counsel defense here. They include: (1) documents that embody a communication between the attorney and client concerning the subject matter of the case, such as a traditional opinion letter; (2) documents analyzing the law, facts, trial strategy, and so forth that reflect the attorney's mental impressions but were not given to the client; and (3) documents that discuss a communication between attorney and client concerning the subject matter of the case but are not themselves communications to or from the client. . . . As to the first category, we already noted in section A that when a party relies on the advice-of-counsel as a defense to willful infringement the party waives its attorney-client privilege for all communications between the attorney and client, including any documentary communications such as opinion letters and memoranda. . . .[16] As to the other two categories, scholars have noted that our prior opinions do not clearly define the scope of the work-product waiver. As a result, the district courts that have addressed this issue are split on just how far to extend that scope. Compare Thorn EMI, 837 F. Supp. at 621–623 and *Steelcase, Inc. v. Haworth, Inc.*, 954 F. Supp. 1195, 1198–99 (W. D. Mich. 1997) with *Mushroom Assoc. v. Monterey Mushrooms, Inc.*, 24 U.S.P.Q. 2d 1767, 1992 U.S. Dist. LEXIS 19664 (N. D. Cal.

---

[16] EchoStar contends that waiver of opinions does not extend to advice and work product given after litigation began. While this may be true when the work product is never communicated to the client, it is not the case when the advice is relevant to ongoing willful infringement, so long as that ongoing infringement is at issue in the litigation. See *Akeva LLC*, 243 F. Supp. 2d at 423 ("Once a party asserts the defense of advice of counsel, this opens to inspection the advice received during the entire course of the alleged infringement."); see also *Crystal Semiconductor Corp. v. Tritech Microelectronics Int'l, Inc.*, 246 F.3d 1336, 1351–1353 (Fed. Cir. 2001) (noting that an infringer may continue its infringement after notification of the patent by filing suit and that the infringer has a duty of due care to avoid infringement after such notification).

1992); *FMT Corp. v. Nissei ASB Co.*, 24 U.S.P.Q. 2d 1073, 1992 U.S. Dist. LEXIS 21500 (N. D. Ga. 1992); and *Handgards, Inc. v. Johnson & Johnson*, 413 F. Supp. 926 (N. D. Cal. 1976). As we discuss in more detail below, we conclude that waiver extends to the third category but does not extend so far as the second.

By asserting the advice-of-counsel defense to a charge of willful infringement, the accused infringer and his or her attorney do not give their opponent unfettered discretion to rummage through all of their files and pillage all of their litigation strategies. . . . Work-product waiver extends only so far as to inform the court of the infringer's state of mind. Counsel's opinion is not important for its legal correctness. It is important to the inquiry whether it is "thorough enough, as combined with other factors, to instill a belief in the infringer that a court might reasonably hold the patent is invalid, not infringed, or unenforceable." . . . It is what the alleged infringer knew or believed, and by contradistinction not what other items counsel may have prepared but did not communicate to the client, that informs the court of an infringer's willfulness.

The overarching goal of waiver in such a case is to prevent a party from using the advice he received as both a sword, by waiving privilege to favorable advice, and a shield, by asserting privilege to unfavorable advice. . . . To the extent the work-product immunity could have such an effect, it is waived.

The second category of work product, which is never communicated to the client, is not discoverable. Under Rule 26(b)(3), this so-called "opinion" work product deserves the highest protection from disclosure. . . . While an accused infringer may waive the immunity for work product that embodies an opinion in letters and memorandum communicated to the client, he does not waive the attorney's own analysis and debate over what advice will be given. . . . Upon waiver of attorney-client privilege, communicative documents, such as opinion letters, become evidence of a non-privileged, relevant fact, namely what was communicated to the client, . . . however, counsel's legal opinions and mental impressions that were not communicated do not acquire such factual characteristics and are, therefore, not within the scope of the waiver.

> There is relatively little danger that a litigant will attempt to use a pure mental impression or legal theory as a sword and as a shield in the trial of a case so as to distort the factfinding process. Thus, the protection of lawyers from the broad repercussions of subject matter waiver in this context strengthens the adversary process, and, unlike the selective disclosure of evidence, may ultimately and ideally further the search for the truth.

. . . Thus, if a legal opinion or mental impression was never communicated to the client, then it provides little if any assistance to the court in determining whether the accused knew it was infringing, and any relative value is outweighed by the policies supporting the work-product doctrine.

The third category of work product material falls admittedly somewhere interstitially between the first and second. In some instances there may be documents in the attorney's file that reference and/or describe a communication between the attorney and client, but were not themselves actually communicated to the client. For example, if an attorney writes a memorandum or an e-mail to his associate referencing a phone call with the client, in which he indicates that he discussed the client's potential infringement, then such a memorandum is discoverable. Unlike work product that was uncommunicated, this work product references a specific communication to the client. Though it is not a communication to the client directly nor does it contain a substantive reference to what was communicated, it will aid the parties in determining what communications were made to the client and protect against intentional or unintentional withholding of attorney-client communications from the court.

Still, we must emphasize that such communications may contain work product of the second kind — legal analysis that was not communicated. In those situations, the parties should take special care to redact such information, and if necessary the district court may review such material in camera. . . .

Therefore, when an alleged infringer asserts its advice-of-counsel defense regarding willful infringement of a particular patent, it waives its immunity for any document or opinion that embodies or discusses a communication to or from it concerning whether that patent is valid, enforceable, and infringed by the accused. This waiver of both the attorney-client privilege and the work-product immunity includes not only any letters, memorandum, conversation, or the like between the attorney and his or her client, but also includes, when appropriate, any documents referencing a communication between attorney and client.

Here, Merchant & Gould work product that was not communicated to EchoStar or does not reflect a communication is not within the scope of EchoStar's waiver because it obviously played no part in EchoStar's belief as to infringement of the '389 patent. . . . It may very well be true, as TiVo suggests, that at times some parties would communicate draft opinion letters or the contents thereof to the client confidentially in order to avoid disclosing that communication during potential discovery if and when the attorney-client privilege is waived, but we cannot eviscerate the legitimate policies of the work-product doctrine and chill the principles of our adversary system as a whole on account of the possibility that, from time to time, there may be occurrences of ethical transgressions.

In sum, the advice-of-counsel defense to willfulness requires the court to decide, inter alia, whether counsel's opinion was thorough enough to "instill a belief in the infringer that a court might reasonably hold the patent is invalid, not infringed, or unenforceable." . . . If a Merchant & Gould document was not communicated to EchoStar or if a Merchant & Gould document does not reference a communication between Merchant & Gould and EchoStar, its relevant value is outweighed by the policies of the work-product doctrine. Thus, it was an abuse of discretion for the district court to determine that the scope of the waiver of privilege extended to such documents.

Some courts have construed *EchoStar* quite broadly. *See, e.g., Informatica v. Business Objects Data Integration, Inc.* 454 F. Supp. 2d 957 (N.D. Cal. 2006), *aff'd,* 2006 U.S. Dist. LEXIS 58976 (N.D. Cal. Aug. 9, 2006):

This Court finds that, by asserting advice of counsel as a defense to a charge of willful infringement of Informatica's patents, BODI waived privilege for both pre-and post-filing pertinent attorney-client communications and work product. Under the analysis in *Echostar*, it is immaterial whether BODI's opinion counsel and trial counsel are from the same firm, different firms or are even the same. What matters is that: 1. BODI relies on advice of counsel as a defense to Informatica's charge that it willfully infringed Informatica's patents; 2. Therefore, BODI waives privilege for communications with counsel on the subject of the opinion or advice on which it relies as well as work product on that subject communicated to BODI or which refers to communications on that subject; 3. Informatica alleges that BODI continues to infringe Informatica's patents; 4. Therefore Informatica is entitled to information subject to waiver which BODI received even after Informatica filed its complaint; 5. The categories of information which BODI must turn over the Informatica include (a) attorney-client communications with any counsel on the subject of the opinion or advice on which BODI relies; (b) work product communicated to BODI on that same subject; (c) work product which reflects any communication on that subject.").

But see, Ampex Corp. v. Eastman Kodak Co., 2006 U.S. Dist. LEXIS 48702 (D. Del. July 17, 2006) where the court declined to order discovery of opinions of trial counsel received by the client on the same subject matter after the initiation of the infringement action. The court noted that the trial counsel's pretrial infringement opinion was the opinion relied upon in *Echostar*, whereas a different lawyer's opinion was relied upon in the case at hand. The court was of the view that extending the waiver to a different trial counsel's opinion on the same subject would "demolish" the practical significance of the attorney-client privilege. *See generally* P.R. RICE, ATTORNEY-CLIENT PRIVILEGE IN THE UNITED STATES, § 9:96, Time-frame of Waiver, (Thomson West 2d ed. 1999).

Relative to the scope of waiver under the various standards of waiver, Federal Rule of Evidence 502 has been adopted:

Rule 502 Attorney-Client Privilege and Work Product; Limitations on Waiver

(a) Disclosure Made in a Federal Proceeding or to a Federal Office or Agency; Scope of a Waiver — When the disclosure is made in a Federal proceeding or to a Federal office or agency and waives the attorney-client privilege or work-product protection, the waiver extends to an undisclosed communication or information in a Federal or State proceeding only if:

(1) the waiver is intentional;

(2) the disclosed and undisclosed communications or information concern the same subject matter; and

(3) they ought in fairness to be considered together.

New Rule 502(a) appears to provide no new standards for defining the scope of waiver.

[3] "Limited Waiver"

The court in *Duplan Corp. v. Deering Milliken, Inc.*, 397 F. Supp. 1146 (D.S.C. 1975), after correctly holding that waiver results from disclosure to third parties, regardless of whether that disclosure was the result of the intentional or inadvertent acts of either the client or the client's attorney, and regardless of whether express limitations were placed on the disclosures, held that if disclosures are made at the direction, or even suggestion, of the court, such cooperation is impliedly coercive and therefore will not be construed as a waiver, because to do so would discourage parties' voluntary cooperation. Is such a result consistent with the philosophy of the attorney-client privilege and the circle of confidentiality on which it is based? In a previous decision in *In re Penn Central Commercial Paper Litigation*, 61 F.R.D. 453, 463–464 (S.D.N.Y. 1973), Judge Edelstein held that it was not. With regard to the disclosures made by a party's attorney during his voluntary appearance in a nonpublic SEC investigation, the judge ruled that a transcript of the attorney's testimony had to be disclosed, stating:

> The court finds that the attorney-client privilege was waived by the appearance of Williams [the attorney] before the SEC. The weight of authority unequivocally contradicts the position on nonwaiver asserted by defendant. It is hornbook law that the voluntary disclosure of a communication, otherwise subject to a claim of privilege, effectively waives the privilege. . . . This view is universally shared by both the courts and leading commentators. The theoretical predicate underlying all recognized privileges is that secrecy and confidentiality are necessary to promote the relationship fostered by the privilege. Once the secrecy or confidentiality is destroyed by a voluntary disclosure to a third party, the rationale for granting the privilege in the first instance no longer applies.

> In the case at bar it was acknowledged that Williams' client voluntarily waived the attorney-client privilege with respect to Williams' appearance before the SEC. No claim was made either by counsel to defendant herein, or by counsel for Williams that this waiver was not voluntary or that it was made without opportunity to claim the privilege. Accordingly, the court must reject defendant's contention that the kind of disclosure that we are confronted with — i.e., one made during a nonpublic SEC investigation — does not effect a waiver of the attorney-client privilege.

> Defendant's public policy argument must also be rejected. Although it is probably correct to assume that a witness would be less likely to cooperate with authorities if his testimony, given in a nonpublic proceeding, is subject to discovery in later civil litigation, this factor alone is an inadequate basis for a court to break new legal ground against the overwhelming weight of authority. Moreover, it is well settled that a claim of privilege cannot be selectively waived. To allow Williams to assert the attorney-client privilege in the instant litigation would permit selective waiver of the privilege. Consequently, defendant's argument that First Boston did not waive the

privilege except for purposes of the SEC proceeding is unpersuasive.

Id. at 463–464.

Most courts, however, have not adopted Judge Edelstein's position. In *Diversified Indus., Inc. v. Meredith*, 572 F.2d 596 (8th Cir. 1977) (*en banc*), for example, the court held that the voluntary surrender to the SEC of documents relating to the results of internal corporate investigations of alleged bribery activities in foreign countries resulted in a waiver of the attorney-client privilege, but only as to the SEC.

> We finally address the issue whether Diversified waived its attorney-client privilege with respect to the privileged materials by voluntarily surrendering them to the SEC pursuant to an agency subpoena. As Diversified disclosed these documents in a separate and non-public SEC investigation we conclude that only a limited waiver of the privilege occurred. . . . To hold otherwise may have the effect of thwarting the developing procedure of corporations to employ independent outside counsel to investigate and advise them in order to protect stockholders, potential stockholders, and customers.

Id. at 611. Although this opinion appeared to turn on the necessity of encouraging internal corporate investigations, its principal concern was to encourage corporations' cooperation with law enforcement agencies through their voluntary disclosure of the results of their internal investigations.

The court in *Teachers Ins. & Annuity Ass'n of Am. v. Shamrock Broadcasting Co.*, 521 F. Supp. 638 (S.D.N.Y. 1981), reached a similar result. In *Teachers Insurance*, the court adopted the concept of limited waiver but limited its application to disclosures made to the SEC with an express reservation of the claim of privilege. The court did not adequately explain, however, why the express reservation should be central to the waiver question.

Judge Edelstein's view found support in *Permian Corp. v. United States*, 665 F.2d 1214 (D.C. Cir. 1981), in which the court explicitly rejected the concept of limited waiver. The court concluded that Occidental, Permian's parent company, had destroyed the confidential status of certain attorney-client communications by permitting their disclosure to the SEC staff. Addressing the concept of "limited waiver," the court stated:

> Occidental asks this court to create an exception to the traditional standard for waiver by adopting the "limited waiver" theory of *Diversified Industries, Inc. v. Meredith*, 572 F.2d 596 (8th Cir. 1977) (en banc). . . .
>
> First, we cannot see how the availability of a "limited waiver" would serve the interests underlying the common law privilege for confidential communications between attorney and client. As the Supreme Court has recently reiterated, "[t]he privilege recognizes that sound legal advice or advocacy serves public ends and that such advice or advocacy depends upon the lawyer being fully informed by the client"; the attorney's "assistance can only be safely and readily availed of when free from the consequences or the apprehension of disclosure." *Upjohn Co. v. United States*, 449 U.S.

383 (1981) (quoting *Hunt v. Blackburn*, 128 U.S. 464, 470 (1888)). The privilege depends on the assumption that full and frank communication will be fostered by the assurance of confidentiality, and the justification for granting the privilege "ceases when the client does not appear to have been desirous of secrecy." 8 J. Wigmore, EVIDENCE § 2311, at 599 (McNaughton rev. 1961). The Eighth Circuit's "limited waiver" rule has little to do with this confidential link between the client and his or her legal advisor. Voluntary cooperation with government investigations may be a laudable activity, but it is hard to understand how such conduct improves the attorney-client relationship. If the client feels the need to keep his communications with his attorney confidential, he is free to do so under the traditional rule by consistently asserting the privilege, even when the discovery request comes from a "friendly" agency.

Because the attorney-client privilege inhibits the truth-finding process, it has been narrowly construed, . . . and courts have been vigilant to prevent litigants from converting the privilege into a tool for selective disclosure. . . . The client cannot be permitted to pick and choose among his opponents, waiving the privilege for some and resurrecting the claim of confidentiality to obstruct others, or to invoke the privilege as to communications whose confidentiality he has already compromised for his own benefit. . . . In the present case, Occidental has been willing to sacrifice confidentiality in order to expedite approval of the exchange offer, and now asserts that the secrecy of the attorney-client relationship precludes disclosure of the same documents in other administrative litigation.[18] The attorney-client privilege is not designed for such tactical employment.

Finally, we reject the argument that some public policy imperative inherent in the SEC's regulatory program requires that the traditional waiver doctrine be overridden. Occidental insists that this court should respect the attempts that Occidental and the SEC made to "accommodate[] each other's interest — a mutual interest — in the integrity of the Commission's investigatory and registration processes." . . . Important though the SEC's mission may be, we are aware of no congressional directive or judicially-recognized priority system that places a higher value on cooperation with the SEC than on cooperation with other regulatory agencies, including the Department of Energy. At least one district court has viewed the "limited waiver" doctrine as extending beyond SEC inquiries to Internal Revenue Service and grand jury investigations; . . . we agree that the doctrine's rationale would dictate a wide scope of application for the "limited waiver." It is apparent that such a doctrine would enable litigants to pick and choose among regulatory agencies in disclosing and withholding communications of tarnished confidentiality for their own purposes. We believe that the attorney-client privilege should be available only at the traditional price: a litigant who wishes to assert confidentiality must maintain genuine confidentiality.

---

[18] (Court's original footnote 14.) It is true that Occidental's waiver of the privilege with respect to the SEC is implied from its conduct, not express, but both forms are equally binding. . . .

Id. at 1220–1222.

Courts have recognized the concept of limited waiver in the context of disclosures to the SEC, grand juries, and the IRS. Consistent throughout these opinions is the perceived public need to encourage cooperation with governmental investigations. Is this goal an appropriate consideration in the determination of the scope or duration of the attorney-client privilege? One writer has concluded that it is not. "[T]he goal of furthering cooperation with government agencies is unrelated to the goal underlying the privilege itself — that of furthering legal consultation." Comment, *Stuffing the Rabbit Back into the Hat: Limited Waiver of the Attorney-Client Privilege in an Administrative Agency Investigation,* 130 U. PA. L. REV. 1198, 1227 (1982). Undoubtedly, furthering cooperation with the Government is unrelated to the goal of furthering legal consultation. However, as long as pursuit of cooperation is not inconsistent with the goal of furthering legal consultation and is not otherwise unfair to an adversary, why should this fact justify rejecting the concept of limited waiver? *See generally* RICE, ATTORNEY-CLIENT PRIVILEGE IN THE UNITED STATES, §§ 9:86–9:87 (West Group 2d ed. 1999).

The limited waiver concept allows the client to expand the circle of confidentiality beyond that which has classically defined the attorney-client privilege. Is this desirable? What are the consequences of such an expansion? On its face it does not appear to be undesirable. In substance, however, the court would be destroying the standard by which courts have determined whether the client intended his or her communications to be confidential — the relationship between those privy to the communications and the legal advice sought through those communications.

If we accept the client's right to expand the circle of confidentiality, is there any basis on which a court could limit it to governmental investigations? Is it not in the best interest of public policy to encourage cooperation among all adversaries, private as well as public, in the disclosure of relevant evidence?

For a view favoring the limited waiver concept, see Block & Barton, *Waiver of the Attorney-Client Privilege by Disclosure to the SEC,* 1982 LITIGATION 170.

Although not recognized as such, a number of courts have adopted the concept of limited waiver through their use of protective orders under Rule 26(c) of the Federal Rules of Civil Procedure. To accommodate the serious possibility of waiver-of-privilege claims through inadvertent disclosures of documents in expedited pretrial discovery programs that involve large numbers of documents, courts have issued protective orders. Those orders allow parties to withdraw from the discovery process and the possession of their adversaries documents that have been disclosed without adequate screening to determine whether disclosure should have been opposed on privilege grounds. Such disclosures can be made without prejudice to the subsequent claim of immunity from discovery. In addition, such orders have provided that by designating documents *"Protected — U.S. v. AT&T",* for example, such documents may be used only in that litigation, inspected only by designated persons working with the opposing side, and that all documents and copies of them must be returned to the disclosing party at the termination of the litigation. *See* Pretrial Order No. 7, Protective Order, *United States v. American Telephone & Telegraph Co.,* Civil Action No. 74-1698 (Dec. 15, 1976). Such orders are effective in the action in which they are issued, but it has yet to be determined whether these special exceptions to the waiver principle will be binding in subsequent litigation. Could a subsequent judge reasonably interpret the inadvertent disclosures as waivers because they breached the circle of confidentiality that is central to the privilege? The practical consequence of a refusal to honor these protective orders, of course, would be increased delays and inefficiencies in the pretrial discovery process. *See* RICE, ATTORNEY-CLIENT PRIVILEGE IN THE UNITED STATES, §§ 9:88–9:92 (West Group 2d ed. 1999).

[D] Special Waiver Issues

[1] Disclosure Among Codefendants and Co-Counsel

A variation of the problem of disclosure of communications to third parties arises when codefendants discuss matters of common interest in the presence of co-counsel. *See generally* RICE, ATTORNEY-CLIENT PRIVILEGE IN THE UNITED STATES, §§ 4:35–4:38 (West Group 2d ed. 1999). As explained in *United States v. Stepney*, excerpted below, the courts have long recognized a common-defense rule that serves to extend the protection of the attorney-client privilege to these communications.

UNITED STATES v. STEPNEY

United States District Court, N.D. California
246 F. Supp. 2d 1069 (2003)

MEMORANDUM AND ORDER
re Joint Defense Agreements

PATEL, CHIEF JUDGE.

Defendants have been charged with conspiracy and numerous violations of federal drug and weapons laws. In a previous order, this court required that all joint defense agreements be put into writing and submitted to the court. Counsel for defendants submitted proposed joint defense agreements for in camera review. Having reviewed the proposed joint defense agreements and having heard arguments from defendants on this matter, and for the reasons stated below, the court issues the following order.

BACKGROUND

Defendants are charged with participation in the criminal enterprises of a street gang in the Hunter's Point area of San Francisco. In a series of three indictments, the government has charged a total of nearly thirty defendants with over seventy substantive counts relating to the operation of the gang over a period of several years. The number of defendants and the separate crimes charged render this case extraordinarily factually complex. Defense counsel report that they have already received discovery of over 20,000 pages of police reports, FBI memos, and other law enforcement materials.

In an effort to prepare coherent defenses efficiently, various defense counsel have sought to enter into joint defense agreements that would allow defendants to share factual investigations and legal work product. Out of concern for the Sixth Amendment rights of the defendants and the integrity of the proceedings, at the parties' initial appearance on October 15, 2001, the court ordered that any joint defense agreements be committed to writing and provided to the court for in camera review. Oct. 15, 2001 Reporter's Transcript at 11:11–19. No joint defense agreements were ever filed with the court pursuant to this order.

More than a year after the court's initial order, the attorney for one defendant moved to withdraw his representation on the grounds that he had entered into a joint defense agreement with another defendant who he had since come to believe was cooperating with the prosecution. Although the attorney seeking to withdraw did not believe that he had obtained confidential information from the cooperating defendant, he did believe that the joint defense agreement had created an implied attorney-client relationship that included a duty of loyalty. The attorney maintained that this duty of loyalty would prevent him from cross-examining the cooperating defendant, should he testify at trial.

The court denied the motion to withdraw after conducting a colloquy in which the cooperating defendant waived any attorney-client privilege with respect to information received by the moving attorney. The court also ruled that joint defense agreements do not create in one attorney a duty of loyalty toward the defendant with whom he collaborates. In an order dated November 22, 2002, the court set forth requirements that future joint defense agreements: (1) be in writing; (2) contain a full description of the extent of the privilege shared; (3) contain workable withdrawal provisions; and (4) be signed not only by the attorneys but also by the clients who hold the privileges at issue. Order re Motion To Withdraw, Nov. 22, 2002, at 2.

At the following status conference, the court ordered that a proposed joint defense agreement be submitted to the court for in camera review. Defense counsel submitted two proposed agreements, which the court discussed with defense attorneys at an in camera status conference on January 13, 2003.1 One proposed agreement, entitled "Joint Defense Agreement Extending Attorney-Client Privileges" (hereinafter "Joint Defense Agreement"), discusses the duties of confidentiality and loyalty each attorney who signs the agreement will owe to each client who signs. The other, entitled "Joint Defense Agreement re Work Product" (hereinafter "Work Product Agreement"), addresses the confidential sharing of legal research and discovery analysis among the lawyers for the various defendants.

DISCUSSION

I. The Joint Defense Privilege Generally

The joint defense privilege is commonly described as an extension of the attorney-client privilege. *See, e.g., In re Santa Fe Intern. Corp.*, 272 F.3d 705, 719 (5th Cir. 2001); *United States v. Evans*, 113 F.3d 1457, 1467 (7th Cir. 1997); *United States v. Aramony*, 88 F.3d 1369, 1392 (4th Cir. 1996), cert. denied, 520 U.S. 1239,

117 S. Ct. 1842, 137 L. Ed. 2d 1046 (1997). *United States v. Schwimmer*, 892 F.2d 237, 243 (2d Cir. 1989); *Waller v. Financial Corp. of Am.*, 828 F.2d 579, 583 n. 7 (9th Cir. 1987). Scholarly commentators have uniformly argued that the joint defense privilege differs sufficiently from the attorney-client privilege in both purpose and scope that the two should be viewed as entirely separate doctrines. *See, e.g.*, Deborah Stavile Bartel, Reconceptualizing the Joint Defense Doctrine, 65 Fordham L. Rev. 871 (1996); Craig S. Lerner, Conspirators' Privilege and Innocents' Refuge: A New Approach to Joint Defense Agreements, 77 Notre Dame L. Rev. 1449 (2002); Susan K. Rushing, Note: Separating the Joint-Defense Doctrine From the Attorney-Client Privilege, 68 Tex. L. Rev. 1273 (1990). To inform the analysis of the proposed joint defense agreements, the court must first examine in detail the nature of the joint defense privilege.

1. Protections for Attorney-Client Communications

"The attorney-client privilege is an evidentiary rule designed to prevent the forced disclosure in a judicial proceeding of certain confidential communications between a client and a lawyer." *United States v. Rogers*, 751 F.2d 1074, 1077 (9th Cir. 1985), quoted in *Wharton v. Calderon*, 127 F.3d 1201, 1205 (9th Cir. 1997). The purpose of the privilege is to encourage "full and frank communication between attorneys and their clients and thereby promote broader public interests in the observance of law and administration of justice." *Upjohn Co. v. United States*, 449 U.S. 383, 389, 101 S. Ct. 677, 66 L. Ed. 2d 584 (1981); *see also Hunt v. Blackburn*, 128 U.S. 464, 470, 9 S. Ct. 125, 32 L. Ed. 488 (1888) (grounding the privilege "in the interest and administration of justice, of the aid of persons having knowledge of the law and skilled in its practice, which assistance can only be safely and readily availed of when free from the consequences or the apprehension of disclosure").

The attorney-client privilege limits only the power of a court to compel disclosure of attorney-client communications or otherwise admit the communications themselves into evidence. Outside the courtroom, the privilege does not provide grounds for sanctioning an attorney's voluntary disclosure of confidential communications to third parties. *Wharton*, 127 F.3d at 1205–06 (attorney-client privilege could not provide grounds to bar respondents from informally communicating with petitioner's former attorneys). This is not to say that attorneys may freely reveal their clients' confidences should they so desire. Mechanisms other than the attorney-client privilege protect against voluntary disclosure of confidential communications by counsel. The ethical rules governing attorneys require that all information pertaining to a client's case be kept confidential. Cal. Bus. & Prof.Code § 6068(e) (setting forth attorney's duty "[t]o maintain inviolate the confidence, and at every peril to himself or herself to preserve the secrets, of his or her client"); Model Rules of Prof'l Conduct, R. 1.6 (3d ed. 1999). The comment to Model Rule of 1.6 discusses the relationship between the attorney-client privilege and the ethical duty of confidentiality:

> The principle of confidentiality is given effect in two related bodies of law, the attorney-client privilege (which includes the work product doctrine) in the law of evidence and the rule of confidentiality established in professional ethics. The attorney-client privilege applies in judicial and other

proceedings in which a lawyer may be called as a witness or otherwise required to produce evidence concerning a client. The rule of client-lawyer confidentiality applies in situations other than those where evidence is sought from the lawyer through compulsion of law. The confidentiality rule applies not merely to matters communicated in confidence by the client but also to all information relating to the representation, whatever its source.

Id., R. 1.6 cmt. The ethical duty of confidentiality may be enforced by more than just sanctions against an offending attorney. In a criminal case, where an attorney violates this ethical duty by revealing a client's confidences to the government, a court may suppress the resulting evidence. *Rogers*, 751 F.2d at 1078–79. Prosecutors may also be subject to sanctions where they have induced an attorney to violate her duty of confidentiality. Model Rules of Prof'l Conduct, R. 8.4(a).

In criminal cases, the Constitution also protects confidential attorney-client communications from the eyes and ears of the government. An intrusion by the government into an attorney-client relationship in order to obtain confidential information may be deemed a violation of a defendant's Sixth Amendment right to effective assistance of counsel or Fifth Amendment due process rights. *See, e.g., United States v. Haynes*, 216 F.3d 789, 796 (9th Cir. 2000), *cert. denied*, 531 U.S. 1078, 121 S. Ct. 776, 148 L. Ed. 2d 674 (2001) (deliberate intrusion into attorney-client relationship may violate Fifth Amendment); *United States v. Aulicino*, 44 F.3d 1102, 1117 (2d Cir. 1995) (unintentional interference with attorney-client relationship may violate defendant's Sixth Amendment rights where government gains confidential information and prejudice results). In such a situation, a court may suppress evidence gathered as a result of the communication or, in egregious cases where the prejudice cannot otherwise be cured, dismiss the indictment. *Haynes*, 216 F.3d at 796; *United States v. Marshank*, 777 F. Supp. 1507, 1521–22 (N.D. Cal. 1991).

These three doctrines — the evidentiary rule of attorney-client privilege, the ethical duty of confidentiality imposed on attorneys, and the ethical and constitutional requirements that the government not intrude upon the attorney-client relationship — serve the common end of keeping communications between attorney and client from disclosure either to adversaries or the finder of fact, thus encouraging the full and frank communications between attorney and client that are required for the adversarial system to function.

2. The Evolution of the Joint Defense Privilege

The joint defense privilege initially arose as an extension of the attorney-client privilege against court-ordered disclosure against confidential communications. Ordinarily, the attorney-client privilege will be deemed waived where a client discloses the contents of an otherwise privileged communication to a third party or where the communication occurs in the presence of third parties. *United States v. Gann*, 732 F.2d 714, 723 (9th Cir.), *cert. denied*, 469 U.S. 1034, 105 S. Ct. 505, 83 L. Ed. 2d 397 (1984) (privilege waived when communication made in presence of third party); *Weil v. Investment/Indicators, Research and Management, Inc.*, 647 F.2d 18, 24 (9th Cir. 1981) (subsequent disclosure of content of communication waives privilege). The joint defense privilege was adopted as an exception to this waiver rule, under which communications between a client and his own lawyer remain protected by the attorney-client privilege when disclosed to co-defendants or their counsel for purposes of a common defense. *Hunydee v. United States*, 355 F.2d 183, 185 (9th Cir. 1965); *Continental Oil Co. v. United States*, 330 F.2d 347, 350 (9th Cir. 1964); *Chahoon v. Virginia*, 62 Va. 822 (1871); *see also Waller*, 828 F.2d at 583 n. 7.

Although established as an evidentiary rule which bound courts from compelling disclosure of certain evidence, the joint defense privilege was soon applied as an ethical doctrine which imposed on counsel a limited duty of confidentiality toward their client's co-defendants regarding information obtained in furtherance of a common defense.2 In particular, courts have ruled that an attorney may be disqualified if her client's interests require that she cross-examine (or oppose in a subsequent action) another member of a joint defense agreement about whom she has learned confidential information. *See generally*, Arnold Rochvarg, Joint Defense Agreements and Disqualification of Co-Defendant's Counsel, 22 Am. J. Trial Advoc. 311 (1998); *Bartel, supra.*

In the first case to raise the issue, *Wilson P. Abraham Constr. Corp. v. Armco Steel Corp.*, 559 F.2d 250, 253 (5th Cir. 1977), the Fifth Circuit addressed a motion to disqualify plaintiff's counsel brought by defendants in a civil antitrust action. In a prior criminal action against various steel mills for price fixing in which Armco had been charged, plaintiff's attorney had represented another steel company also named as a defendant. In this capacity, he had conferred with representatives of other indicted companies, including Armco, at meetings designed to develop a joint defense. In its motion, Armco maintained that the attorney's obligation to maintain the confidences learned through the previous joint defense effort conflicted with his client's present interests and warranted his disqualification. The Fifth circuit agreed, finding:

> Just as an attorney would not be allowed to proceed against his former client in a cause of action substantially related to the matters in which he previously represented that client, an attorney should also not be allowed to proceed against a co-defendant of a former client wherein the subject matter of the present controversy is substantially related to the matters in which the attorney was previously involved, and wherein confidential exchanges of information took place between the various co-defendants in preparation of a joint defense.

Id. at 253.

Despite the analogy to attorney-client relationships, the Abraham Construction court did not treat the attorney's participation in a joint defense agreement as identical to formal representation of a client. Had plaintiff's attorney actually represented Armco, he would have been disqualified automatically on the irrebuttable presumption that he had gained confidences during the prior representation on a related matter. *In re Yarn Processing Patent Validity Litigation*, 530 F.2d 83, 89 (5th Cir. 1976); *accord Trone v. Smith*, 621 F.2d 994, 998 (9th Cir. 1980); *Elan Transdermal Ltd. v. Cygnus Therapeutic Sys.*, 809 F. Supp. 1383, 1388 (N.D. Cal. 1992). Finding that there had been "no direct attorney-client relationship," the court refused to presume that plaintiff's attorney had obtained confidential information in the course of the joint defense. The court instead placed the burden on the party moving for disqualification to prove that the plaintiff's attorney had actually been privy to confidential information. *Abraham Constr.*, 559 F.2d at 253.Subsequent courts have followed suit in requiring a showing that the attorney actually obtained confidences before disqualifying counsel. See, *e.g., Fred Weber, Inc. v. Shell Oil Co.*, 566 F.2d 602, 608, 610 (8th Cir. 1977), *cert. denied*, 436 U.S. 905, 98 S. Ct. 2235, 56 L. Ed. 2d 403 (1978), overruled on other grounds by *In re Multipiece Rim Products Liability Litigation*, 612 F.2d 377, 378 (8th Cir. 1980); *Essex Chemical Corp. v. Hartford Accident & Indemnity Co.*, 993 F. Supp. 241, 251–52 (D.N.J. 1998); *GTE North, Inc. v. Apache Products Co.*, 914 F. Supp. 1575, 1580 (N.D. Ill. 1996); *see generally Rochvarg, supra*. While a joint defense agreement does impose a duty of confidentiality, that duty is limited in that the showing required to establish a conflict of interest arising from prior participation in a joint defense agreement is significantly higher than that required to make out a conflict based on former representation of a client.

Finally, a few courts have assumed that the prosecution in a criminal case could violate a defendant's constitutional rights by receiving information from cooperating co-defendants (or their attorneys) that was obtained through a joint defense agreement. *See Aulicino*, 44 F.3d at 1117 (attendance at joint defense meeting of defendant in negotiations to cooperate with government does not require hearing on Sixth Amendment violation without showing that cooperating defendant had provided privileged information); *United States v. Hsia*, 81 F. Supp. 2d. 7, 16–20 (D.D.C. 2000) (even knowing intrusion into the attorney-client relationship during plea negotiation with co-defendant's attorney does not constitute violation without showing that communications actually passed to government).

II. The Court's Power to Inquire into Joint Defense Agreements

As a threshold matter, defendants object to the court's inquiries into joint defense agreements prior to any controversy arising that would require such disclosure. Defendants assert that there is no authority for requiring advance disclosure of joint defense agreements and that such disclosures inhibit their ability to represent their clients effectively. Defendants also object to the court's requirement that the joint defense agreements be committed to writing. The court therefore begins by addressing how its inherent supervisory powers permit inquiry into the circumstances of representation and imposition of procedural requirements on joint defense agreements in order to safeguard defendants' Sixth Amendment rights to conflict-free counsel.

"Under their supervisory power, courts have substantial authority to oversee their own affairs to ensure that justice is done." *United States v. Simpson*, 927 F.2d 1088, 1089 (9th Cir. 1991). A court may exercise its supervisory powers to implement a remedy for the violation of a recognized statutory or constitutional right, or may take preemptive steps to avoid such violations by imposing procedural rules not specifically required by the Constitution or Congress. *United States v. Hasting*, 461 U.S. 499, 505, 103 S. Ct. 1974, 76 L. Ed. 2d 96 (1983); *Simpson*, 927 F.2d at 1090.

These supervisory powers unquestionably allow courts to require disclosure of the precise nature of a criminal defendant's representation to ensure that no conflict of interest exists that would deprive a defendant of his Sixth Amendment right to effective assistance of counsel. Courts have routinely intervened — prior to any controversy arising — where the circumstances of a criminal defendant's representation raises the potential for conflict of interest during the course of the proceedings, even before intervention is required by statutory or constitutional rule. *See Bucuvalas v. United States*, 98 F.3d 652, 655 (1st Cir.1996) (exercising supervisory power to require that federal district courts inquire into representation of multiple defendants by a single attorney); *Henderson v. Smith*, 903 F.2d 534, 537 (8th Cir.) (grounding requirements on inquiry into multiple representation in supervisory powers), *cert. denied*, 498 U.S. 989, 111 S. Ct. 529, 112 L. Ed. 2d 539 (1990); *Ford v. United States*, 379 F.2d 123, 125–26 (D.C. Cir. 1967) (same).

Indeed, the Supreme Court has recently considered under what circumstances the Sixth Amendment requires a trial court to inquire into potential conflicts that are brought to its attention. *See Mickens v. Taylor*, 535 U.S. 162, 122 S. Ct. 1237, 152 L. Ed. 2d 291 (2002) (addressing whether state trial court had duty to inquire into potential conflict of interest arising from representation of defendant accused of killing attorney's client). The Supreme Court has long held that in cases of joint representation of multiple defendants by a single attorney, where a trial court knows or should know about a particular conflict of interest, that court has a constitutional duty to explore the conflict further and to ensure that defendant's Sixth Amendment rights have been adequately protected or knowingly waived. *See Cuyler v. Sullivan*, 446 U.S. 335, 344–47, 100 S. Ct. 1708, 64 L. Ed. 2d 333 (1980). Congress has seen fit to exceed the constitutional minimum and mandate exploration of potential conflicts by federal trial courts in every instance of multiple representation. Fed. R. Crim. P. 44(c)(2). These decisions by the Court and Congress to require inquiry under certain circumstances presuppose that trial courts possess the power to investigate such potential conflicts in the first place.

As discussed above, joint defense agreements impose an ethical duty of confidentiality on participating attorneys, presenting the potential for conflicts of interest that might lead to the withdrawal or disqualification of a defense attorney late in the proceedings or the reversal of conviction on appeal. *See, e.g., United States v. Henke*, 222 F.3d 633, 643 (9th Cir. 2000) (reversing defendants' convictions where trial court improperly denied defense counsel's motion to withdraw on the eve of trial). When a party to a joint defense agreement decides to cooperate with the government, the potential for disclosure of confidential information also threatens other defendants' Sixth Amendment rights. *See Aulicino, supra; Hsia, supra.* "Federal courts have an independent interest in ensuring that criminal trials are conducted within the ethical standards of the profession and that legal proceedings appear fair to all who observe them." *Wheat v. United States*, 486 U.S. 153, 160, 108 S. Ct. 1692, 100 L. Ed. 2d 140 (1988). Courts also "[have] an independent interest in protecting a fairly-rendered verdict from trial tactics that may be designed to generate issues on appeal." *United States v. Moscony*, 927 F.2d 742 (3d Cir.), *cert. denied*, 501 U.S. 1211, 111 S. Ct. 2812, 115 L. Ed. 2d 984 (1991). Given the high potential for mischief, courts are well justified in inquiring into joint defense agreements before problems arise.

The present case appears particularly likely to lead to conflicts caused by cooperation between defendants. Here, there are a large number of defendants, some of whom may not have known each other prior to their first appearance before this court. The charges span a variety of incidents over several distinct periods of time and allege roles of varying degrees of culpability. The interests of any two defendants are less likely to coincide precisely than in the case of two defendants accused of essentially equal participation in a single crime. Where defendants do not have cohesive interests, the potential for conflict is, by definition, greater — as is the potential for cooperating with the government.

In addition to the lack of cohesion obvious from the face of the indictment, the unfolding of the present proceedings has provided further evidence that the defendants' interests are not generally united. A significant number of the defendants in this case have in fact entered guilty pleas and cooperated with the government. One of the cooperating defendants has been murdered and another has received threats. Whether or not these actions can be attributed to any defendants in this case, they have proven intimidating to other defendants seeking to plead guilty or cooperate with the government. These circumstances illustrate that defendants interests are not cohesive, indicating a far greater likelihood of conflict than in a case with fewer defendants and a more unified defense.

The threat that these agreements might pose to defendants' Sixth Amendment rights — and to the integrity of the proceedings — warrants the minimal disclosures that the court has thus far required and the restrictions imposed by this court. The court appreciates defendants' concern that disclosing who among them have signed a joint defense agreement might give the government insight into the trial strategies of various defendants. Defendants have not, however, asserted any legal grounds to prevent disclosure of joint defense agreements to the court. To the extent that joint defense agreements simply set forth the existence of attorney-client relationships — implied or otherwise — between various attorneys and defendants, the contents of such agreements do not fall within the attorney-client privilege. *United States v. Bauer*, 132 F.3d 504, 508–09 (9th Cir. 1997) (attorney-client privilege does not cover the identity of an attorney's client); *see also Hsia*, 81 F.Supp.2d at 11 n. 3 (expressing doubt that "either the existence or the terms of a [joint defense agreement] are privileged"). The court has nonetheless conducted its inquiry into joint defense agreements in camera in order to avoid offering the prosecution any hint of defense strategies.

Once disclosed to the court, a joint defense agreement may indicate a potential for future conflicts of interest that warrants further action. The present case certainly calls for inquiry. As set forth below, the proposed joint defense agreement has heightened the court's concern that potential conflicts might arise in this particular case, or that the defendants have been substantially misinformed of their rights under the joint defense privilege. The court now turns to these areas of concern.

III. Problems with the Proposed Joint Defense Agreements

The proposed Joint Defense Agreement submitted by counsel contemplates "open and candid exchange of investigation leads and legal theories of defense." The agreement suggests that any defendant who is a party to the case will "meet to discuss the case and . . . candidly and openly address all charges and possible defenses." It provides in unqualified terms that "all counsel who sign this agreement will owe all defendants who sign this agreement a duty of confidentiality." It also provides that each attorney will owe each defendant a duty of loyalty. The agreement notes that individuals may withdraw from the agreement by notifying all remaining members, but that withdrawal does not relieve a party of the duties created by the agreement.

The proposed agreement submitted by defendants is problematic in at least two material respects. First, the proposed agreement purports to create a duty of loyalty on the part of signing attorneys that extends to all signing defendants. The proposed defense agreement also does not contain workable withdrawal provisions that adequately avoid the possibility of disqualification on the eve of trial, or even during trial.

A. Ethical Obligations Imposed by the Privilege

The proposed joint defense agreement explicitly imposes on signing attorneys not only a duty of confidentiality, but a separate general duty of loyalty to all signing defendants. Such a duty has no foundation in law and, if recognized, would offer little chance of a trial unmarred by conflict of interest and disqualification.

Joint defense agreements are not contracts which create whatever rights the signatories chose, but are written notice of defendants' invocation of privileges set forth in common law.5 Joint defense agreements therefore cannot extend greater protections than the legal privileges on which they rest. A joint defense agreement which purports to do so does not accurately set forth the protections which would be given to defendants who sign. In the present case, unless the joint defense privilege recognized in this Circuit imposes a duty of loyalty on attorneys who are parties to a joint defense agreement, the duty of loyalty set forth in the proposed agreement would have no effect other than misinforming defendants of the actual scope of their rights.

Courts have consistently viewed the obligations created by joint defense agreements as distinct from those created by actual attorney-client relationships. *Abraham Constr.*, 559 F.2d at 253; *see also Weber*, 566 F.2d at 607–10; *GTE North*, 914 F. Supp. at 1580. As discussed above, courts have also consistently ruled that where an attorney represents a client whose interests diverge from a party with whom the attorney has previously participated in a joint defense agreement, no conflict of interest arises unless the attorney actually obtained relevant confidential information. This position is inconsistent with a general duty of loyalty owed to former clients, which would automatically preclude an attorney from subsequently representing a client with an adverse interest. Model Rules of Prof'l Conduct, R. 1.9.

To support the proposed imposition of a general duty of loyalty, defendants rely exclusively on the Ninth Circuit's opinion in *United States v. Henke*, 222 F.3d 633 (9th Cir. 2000) (per curiam), which states that a joint defense agreement "establishes an implied attorney-client relationship with the co-defendant," *id.* at 637. Defendants' argument rests on the conclusion that by referring to an "implied attorney-client relationship," the Ninth Circuit implicitly expanded the joint defense privilege beyond the recognized protection against disclosure of confidential information learned through a joint defense agreement to impose on each attorney an additional general duty of loyalty to her client's co-defendants. Defendants have cited no legal authority suggesting that joint defense agreements entail a duty of loyalty.

In *Henke*, three co-defendants participated in joint defense meetings in which confidential information was discussed. *Id.* On the eve of trial, one defendant pleaded guilty and agreed to testify for the government. Counsel for the other two defendants each moved to withdraw on the grounds that the duty of confidentiality prevented them from cross-examining the former co-defendant and impeaching him with prior statements made in confidence. *Id.* The cooperating co-defendant filed papers expressly stating that he did not waive the attorney-client privilege and would take legal action if the remaining defense counsel disclosed confidential information, even in an ex parte motion to withdraw. *Id.* at 638.

The conflict addressed by the Henke court resulted from the attorney's duty to protect specific confidential information revealed during the course of a joint defense meeting, not from a broader duty of loyalty owed to the cooperating witness. Although the Henke court referred to joint defense agreements in terms of an "implied attorney-client relationship," the court's analysis focused exclusively on confidential information. Accepting that the cooperating witness had made statements at joint defense meetings which would contradict his testimony, the court noted that the remaining defense attorneys could neither introduce those statements nor seek out further evidence to support those statements without using the witness's confidences against him. Id. at 637–38. In finding a conflict, the court did not rest on the attorneys' adverse position to the former party to the joint defense agreement, but relied instead on the fact that the defense attorneys would use or divulge specific pieces of privileged information.

Admittedly, there is a significant difference between the disclosure of confidential information and the use of confidential information without disclosure. Both the common law doctrine of attorney-client privilege and the ethical duty of confidentiality address only the disclosure of confidential information and not the use of confidential information, without disclosure, in a manner adverse to the client's interests. See 8 Wigmore, Evidence § 2292 (attorney-client privilege); Model Rules of Prof'l Conduct, R. 1.6 (duty of confidentiality). Any obligation on the part of an attorney not to use confidential information against a client arises from separate duties. See ABA Model Rules of Prof'l Conduct, R. 1.9(c) ("A lawyer who has formerly represented a client in a matter . . . shall not thereafter (1) use information relating to the representation to the disadvantage of the client . . . ."). An attorney might use information gained in confidence to structure an investigation for facts with which she could discredit the cooperating witness without ever disclosing the information and running afoul of either the attorney-client privilege or the duty of confidentiality.

The *Henke* court suggests that the duty to protect confidential information divulged under a joint defense agreement may extend beyond the duty not to disclose and include a duty not to use the information gained in a manner adverse to the interests of the client. *See, e.g. Henke*, 222 F.3d at 637–38 ("Had [the attorneys] pursued the material discrepancy in some other way, a discrepancy they learned about in confidence, they could have been charged with using it against their one-time client . . . ."). This position is entirely consistent with the rule for disqualification established in *Abraham Construction* and followed by other courts: disqualification is proper where a party seeking disqualification can show that an attorney for another defendant actually obtained relevant confidential information through a joint defense agreement. Indeed, the *Henke* court unambiguously adopted the standard set forth in *Abraham Construction* by quoting that decision at length. *See Henke*, 222 F.3d at 637 (quoting *Abraham Constr.*, 559 F.2d at 253).

For the *Henke* court, a conflict of interest only arose where the attorney possessed relevant confidential information. Even the possession of some confidential information by an attorney would not require disqualification unless the defense of her client required disclosure or use of that information:

> There may be cases in which defense counsel's possession of information about a former co-defendant/government witness learned through joint defense meetings will not impair defense counsel's ability to represent the defendant or breach the duty of confidentiality to the former co-defendant. Here, however, counsel told the district court that this was not a situation where they could avoid reliance on the privileged information and still fully uphold their ethical duty to represent their clients.

Henke, 222 F.3d at 638.

In distinguishing cases based on reliance on protected information, the *Henke* court specifically noted that joint defense meetings in and of themselves are not disqualifying. *Id.* at 638. This refusal to extend a per se rule would not be possible if a general duty of loyalty existed to a cooperating former co-defendant, because the interests of the testifying witness in cooperating effectively would always be adverse to the interests of the remaining defendants in preventing or minimizing the witness's testimony.

Finally, the court notes that the cases on which the Henke court relied to reach its conclusion do not suggest a general duty of loyalty or a full attorney-client relationship between an attorney and all co-defendants who are party to a joint defense agreement. See *Abraham Const.*, 559 F.2d at 253 (finding that in the context of a common defense, "there is no presumption that confidential information was exchanged as there was no direct attorney-client relationship. [The attorney] should not be disqualified unless the trial court should determine that [he] was actually privy to confidential information."). These cases address only whether the protections for confidential information are waived when the information is shared with co-defendants or their counsel who are parties to a joint defense arrangement. *See Waller v. Financial Corp. of America*, 828 F.2d 579, 583 n. 7 (9th Cir. 1987) (describing the joint defense privilege as "an extension of the attorney-client privilege" under which "communications by a client to his own lawyer remain privileged when the lawyer subsequently shares them with co-defendants for purpose of a common defense"); *United States v. McPartlin*, 595 F.2d 1321, 1326 (7th Cir.) (finding that statements of a former co-defendant remain protected by attorney-client privilege because waiver of the privilege is not inferred from the disclosure in confidence to a co-party's attorney for a common purpose), *cert. denied*, 444 U.S. 833, 100 S. Ct. 65, 62 L. Ed. 2d 43 (1979); *Abraham Constr.*, 559

F.2d at 253 (finding that in a joint defense arrangement, "the counsel of each defendant is, in effect, the counsel of all for the purposes of invoking the attorney-client privilege in order to shield mutually shared confidences"). The court finds no cases recognizing joint defense agreements as creating either a true attorney-client relationship or a general duty of loyalty.

There is good reason for the law to refrain from imposing on attorneys a duty of loyalty to their clients' co-defendants. A duty of loyalty between parties to a joint defense agreement would create a minefield of potential conflicts. Should any defendant that signed the agreement decide to cooperate with the government and testify in the prosecution's case-in-chief, an attorney for a non-cooperating defendant would be put in the position of cross-examining a witness to whom she owed a duty of loyalty on behalf of her own client, to whom she also would owe a duty of loyalty. This would create a conflict of interest which would require withdrawal. *See Moscony*, 927 F.2d at 750 ("Conflicts of interest arise whenever an attorney's loyalties are divided, and an attorney who cross-examines former clients inherently encounters divided loyalties.") (citations omitted). Thus, the existence of a duty of loyalty would require that the attorneys for all noncooperating defendants withdraw from the case in the event that any one participating defendant decided to testify for the government.

A duty of loyalty would even require withdrawal where a defendant sought to put on a defense that in any way conflicted with the defenses of the other defendants participating in a joint defense agreement. An attorney with a duty of loyalty to defendants other than her client could not shift blame to other defendants or introduce any evidence which undercut their defenses. Nor could an attorney cross-examine a defendant who testified on his own behalf.

As these scenarios illustrate, a joint defense agreement that imposes a duty of loyalty to all members of the joint defense agreement eliminates the utility of employing separate counsel for each defendant and (for purposes of conflict analysis) effectively creates a situation in which all signing defendants are represented jointly by a team of all signing attorneys. The court certainly could not permit joint representation of defendants with such disjointed *1084 interests as those in the present case. Fed. R. Crim. P. 44(c)(2).

Disqualification of attorneys late in the proceedings benefits no one — it deprives defendants of counsel whom they know and trust and perhaps even chose; it forces delays while new counsel become acquainted with the case, which harm defendants, the prosecution, and the court. In the present case, where certain attorneys have acted as lead counsel for large groups of defendants on major issues, disqualification could prejudice all defendants, not simply those who are parties to the joint defense agreement. The potential for disqualification arising from joint defense agreements can be "used as a weapon in the hands of aggressive prosecutors" that discourages formation of the agreements. Bartel, supra, at 872–73; see also Anderson, supra (addressing prosecutor's motion to disqualify based on defense attorney's participation in joint defense agreement with cooperating witness). To avoid these problems, many defense attorneys draft joint defense agreements that explicitly disclaim any attempt to create an attorney-client relationship. Lerner, supra, at 1507–08 & n. 246; Joint Defense Agreement, Am. Law Institute-Am. Bar Ass'n,

Trial Evidence in the Federal Courts: Problems and Solutions, at 35 (1999) (providing that the agreement should not be read "to create an attorney-client relationship between any attorney and anyone other than the client of that attorney").

Because neither precedent nor sound policy supports imposing on attorneys who sign a joint defense agreement a general duty of loyalty to all participating defendants, the court finds the provisions of the proposed Joint Defense Agreement that purport to create a duty of loyalty unacceptable. Should defendants wish to enter into representation in which attorneys owe multiple defendants a general duty of loyalty, they would need to obtain approval of the court pursuant to Federal Rule of Criminal Procedure 44(c)(2).8

B. Withdrawal Provisions

The proposed joint defense agreement provides that any member may withdraw from the agreement by giving notice to all other members. At the hearing on the proposed agreements, defense counsel suggested that signing defendants were willing accept the risk of conflict created by a withdrawing defendant by accepting the risk that counsel might be disqualified. Ordinarily, defendants seeking to enter into representation which holds potential conflicts of interest accept risks by waiving their rights to assert the conflict, rather than by steeling themselves to assert it as defense counsel suggests. The situation created by the joint defense agreement is no exception.

A first question arising as to the nature of an appropriate waiver is at what point in the proceedings defendants should waive their rights in order to avoid conflicts. Given the highly divergent interests of defendants in the present case, the court is entitled to require that waiver provisions be included in the joint defense agreement, so that defendants who participate *1085 are fully apprised of the potential for conflict and understand the consequences both of entering into the joint defense agreement and of withdrawing from it. The alternative — deferring action on waiver until one defendant decides to testify — fails to avoid the danger of disqualification entirely.

A second and more complicated question is what sort of waiver provisions would avoid the threat of conflict while adequately protecting defendants' right to cooperate on a joint defense. Defendants could conceivably waive potential conflicts through provisions in the joint defense agreement in one of two ways. One court has allowed defendants to waive potential conflict by agreeing in advance that no attorney will use any information obtained by reason of the confidentiality in cross-examining defendants. *United States v. Anderson*, 790 F. Supp. 231, 232 (W.D. Wash. 1992). This method of waiving conflict, however, stands in tension with the general principle that where an attorney has actually obtained confidential information relevant to her representation of a client, the law presumes that she cannot avoid relying on the information — however indirectly or unintentionally — in forming legal advice and trial strategy. *See Henke*, 222 F.3d at 637–38 ("Had [the attorneys] pursued the material discrepancy in some other way, a discrepancy they learned about in confidence, they could have been charged with using it against their one-time client . . . ."). Because the cross-examining attorney still holds relevant confidences of the witness, it is not clear that she can truly operate free from conflict. The solution also compromises one defendant's right to a fully zealous attorney for another defendant's decision to testify. The waiver is less informed, as each defendant must waive the right to use the others' confidences before knowing what those confidences are.

The better form of waiver is suggested by the American Law Institute-American Bar Association in their model joint defense agreement, which provides:

> Nothing contained herein shall be deemed to create an attorney-client relationship between any attorney and anyone other than the client of that attorney and the fact that any attorney has entered this Agreement shall not be used as a basis for seeking to disqualify any counsel from representing any other party in this or any other proceeding; and no attorney who has entered into this Agreement shall be disqualified from examining or cross-examining any client who testifies at any proceeding, whether under a grant of immunity or otherwise, because of such attorney's participation in this Agreement; and the signatories and their clients further agree that a signatory attorney examining or cross-examining any client who testifies at any proceeding, whether under a grant of immunity or otherwise, may use any Defense Material or other information contributed by such client during the joint defense; and it is herein represented that each undersigned counsel to this Agreement has specifically advised his or her respective client of this clause and that such client has agreed to its provisions.

Joint Defense Agreement, Am. Law Institute-Am. Bar Ass'n, Trial Evidence in the Federal Courts: Problems and Solutions, at 35 (1999). Under this regime, all defendants have waived any duty of confidentiality for purposes of cross-examining testifying defendants, and generally an attorney can cross-examine using any and all materials, free from any conflicts of interest. This form of waiver also places the loss of the benefits of the joint defense agreement only on the defendant who makes the choice to testify. Defendants who testify for the government under a grant of immunity lose nothing by this waiver. Those that testify on their own behalf have already made the decision to waive their Fifth Amendment right against self-incrimination and to admit evidence through their cross-examination that would otherwise be inadmissible.

The conditional waiver of confidentiality also provides notice to defendants that their confidences may be used in cross-examination, so that each defendant can choose with suitable caution what to reveal to the joint defense group. Although a limitation on confidentiality between a defendant and his own attorney would pose a severe threat to the true attorney-client relationship, making each defendant somewhat more guarded about the disclosures he makes to the joint defense effort does not significantly intrude on the function of joint defense agreements. The attorney-client privilege protects "full and frank" communication because the attorney serves as the client's liaison to the legal system. Without a skilled attorney, fully apprised of her client's situation, our adversarial system could not function. Any secret a client keeps from his own counsel compromises his counsel's ability to represent him effectively and undermines the purpose of the attorney-client privilege.

Joint defense agreements, however, serve a different purpose. Each defendant entering a joint defense agreement already has a representative, fully and confidentially informed of the client's situation. The joint defense privilege allows defendants to share information so as to avoid unnecessarily inconsistent defenses that undermine the credibility of the defense as a whole. *Bartel, supra,* at 873, 881. In criminal cases where discovery is limited, such collaboration is necessary to assure a fair trial in the face of the prosecution's informational advantage gained through the power to gather evidence by searches and seizures. Co-defendants may eliminate inconsistent defenses without the same degree of disclosure that would be required for an attorney to adequately represent her client. The legitimate value of joint defense agreements will not be significantly diminished by including a limited waiver of confidentiality by testifying defendants for purposes of cross-examination only.

CONCLUSION

For the foregoing reasons, the Court rules as follows:

(1) Any joint defense agreement entered into by defendants must be committed to writing, signed by defendants and their attorneys, and submitted in camera to the court for review prior to going into effect.

(2) Each joint defense agreement submitted must explicitly state that it does not create an attorney-client relationship between an attorney and any defendant other than the client of that attorney. No joint defense agreement may purport to create a duty of loyalty.

(3) Each joint defense agreement must contain provisions conditionally waiving confidentiality by providing that a signatory attorney cross-examining any defendant who testifies at any proceeding, whether under a grant of immunity or otherwise, may use any material or other information contributed by such client during the joint defense.

(4) Each joint defense agreement must explicitly allow withdrawal upon notice to the other defendants.

IT IS SO ORDERED.

[2] Joint Representation in One Case, Adversaries in Another

If a single attorney represents two clients and those clients ultimately become adversaries over the matter about which they initially sought joint representation, may either party rely on the attorney-client privilege to withhold from the other prior communications with the shared attorney? *See* RICE, ATTORNEY-CLIENT PRIVILEGE IN THE UNITED STATES, § 4:33 (West Group 2d ed. 1999). As reflected in the case of *Truck Ins. Exchange v. St. Paul Fire & Marine Ins. Co.*, below, in this situation neither party may assert the privilege against the other.

TRUCK INSURANCE EXCHANGE v. ST. PAUL FIRE & MARINE INSURANCE CO.

United State District Court, Eastern District of Pennsylvania
66 F.R.D. 129 (1975)

Memorandum and Order

BRODERICK, DISTRICT JUDGE.

Currently before this Court is Plaintiff's Motion for a Protective Order seeking to bar the production of the records and files of Charles Bogdanoff, Esq., and the deposition of Mr. Bogdanoff. Oral argument was held on November 22, 1974.

This action was commenced by the plaintiff, Truck Insurance Exchange, in an effort to recover by way of indemnity and/or contribution against the defendant, St. Paul Fire and Marine Insurance Company (St. Paul), the amounts it paid on behalf of American Security Van Lines (American Security), in settlement of a verdict obtained by Lt. James A. Zimble in a negligence action against American Security. Truck Insurance Exchange also seeks reimbursement for the attorney's fees it paid to Charles Bogdanoff, Esq., to defend the suit brought by Lt. Zimble against American Security. It is the contention of Truck Insurance Exchange that St. Paul was actually the insurer of American Security and that St. Paul should have defended American Security in the suit brought against it by Lt. Zimble. Truck Insurance Exchange further argues that as a consequence of its insurance contract, St. Paul is liable for the amounts Truck Insurance Exchange paid on behalf of American Security in settlement of the underlying lawsuit and the fees it paid Mr. Bogdanoff to defend American Security.

On August 1, 1970, Lt. James A. Zimble was struck and injured in Needles, Arizona, by a truck being operated by American Security. A lawsuit was subsequently filed by Lt. Zimble against American Security in the United States District Court for the Eastern District of Pennsylvania which was settled after a verdict in favor of the plaintiff. This action was defended by Charles Bogdanoff, Esq., of Philadelphia at the request of Truck Insurance Exchange, the insurance carrier for American Security. The truck which struck Lt. Zimble was leased by American Security from Morgan Van and Storage (Morgan) in July of 1970. Morgan agreed in its lease with American Security to indemnify the lessee against any loss or damage resulting from the negligence of any driver furnished by the lessor Morgan. It is unclear whether the driver of the truck which struck Lt. Zimble was an employee of Morgan. It is uncontested, however, that Morgan was an insured of the defendant St. Paul. This fact became known to the plaintiff, Truck Insurance Exchange, at some point during the litigation brought by Lt. Zimble, and Truck Insurance Exchange made a demand upon the defendant St. Paul to take over the defense of American Security on the ground that St. Paul insured Morgan who had agreed to indemnify American Security. In this lawsuit, plaintiff Truck Insurance Exchange seeks to recover from the defendant St. Paul the amounts it paid to Lt. Zimble in settlement of the underlying lawsuit and to Mr. Bogdanoff for attorney's fees.

Defendant St. Paul contends it has no enforceable insurance contract with

American Security under which it can be held liable. In the alternative, defendant St. Paul contends that even if there is an enforceable insurance contract, it is exempt from liability because the plaintiff Truck Insurance Exchange did not give it timely notice. St. Paul also questions the reasonableness of the settlement made with Lt. Zimble and the amount of fees paid to Mr. Bogdanoff. In connection with its defense of this action, St. Paul seeks the file and the deposition of Charles Bogdanoff, Esq.

Plaintiff Truck Insurance Exchange contends that the information sought from Mr. Bogdanoff is protected by the common law privilege between attorney and client. . . .

The cases and the Proposed Rules of Evidence are uniform in holding . . . that when a lawyer represents two clients in a matter of common interest, the privilege cannot be claimed by one client as to communications made by him to the attorney when offered in an action between the clients. Rule 503(d)(5) of the Proposed Rules of Evidence. . . . In such a case either party may waive the privilege and the communication can be compelled.

In *Shapiro v. Allstate Insurance Company*, 44 F.R.D. 429 (E.D. Pa. 1968), the plaintiff sued his insurance company claiming bad faith on its part in handling a prior tort action brought against the plaintiff which resulted in a verdict greatly in excess of the liability insurance coverage provided the plaintiff by the defendant insurance company. The defendant insurance company claimed that the attorney-client privilege precluded it from turning over certain relevant documents requested by the plaintiff. My learned colleague, Judge Fullam, in holding the attorney-client privilege inapplicable under such facts, stated:

> [T]he legal relationship between the insurance company and its policy-holder is essentially one of indemnity; but insofar as the conduct of litigation is concerned, it is an agency relationship. . . . All of the cases cited in this opinion are uniform in holding that, in its conduct of the litigation and in its handling of settlement negotiations, the insurance company acts in a fiduciary capacity vis-a-vis its assured, and is obliged to act in the utmost good faith, without allowing its own interests to predominate over those of the assured.

It thus seems clear that, in relation to counsel retained to defend the claim, the insurance company and the policy-holder are in privity. Counsel represents both, and, at least in the situation where the policy-holder does not have separate representation, there can be no privilege on the part of the company to require the lawyer to withhold information from his other client, the policy-holder. In short, I am satisfied that, with respect to all matters from the beginning of the litigation until the termination of the attorney-client relationship between the assured and the attorney, there can be no attorney-client privilege which would prevent disclosure to the policy-holder.

This reasoning is persuasive under the facts of this case. The plaintiff, Truck Insurance Exchange, is claiming that the defendant, St. Paul, was the insurer of American Security in the underlying lawsuit and that since it was acting on behalf of St. Paul, Truck Insurance Exchange has a right to recover whatever it paid on behalf of St. Paul. If the plaintiff's allegation proves correct, Mr. Bogdanoff, the attorney who defended the underlying action brought by Lt. Zimble, was the attorney representing both the plaintiff, Truck Insurance Exchange, and the defendant, St. Paul. Therefore, neither client can claim the attorney-client privilege when waived by the other and the privilege is inapplicable to the facts of this case.

* * *

[3] Inadvertent Disclosure

In pretrial discovery, particularly in this computer age in which massive numbers of documents are involved in the production process, mistakes are inevitable. These mistakes often involve the production of communications that are protected by the attorney-client privilege. Without an appreciation that documents being given to the opposing party are protected by the privilege, the producing party breaches their confidentiality through their disclosure. When this is subsequently discovered, the producing party requests their returned. In the past, this breach of confidentiality destroyed the privilege. This result was consistent with the way courts responded to the theft of privileged communications. The reason for the destruction was irrelevant. Since the foundation upon which the privilege was built no longer existed, the privilege could no longer exist.

Over time, courts began to ignore the element of confidentiality, and focus solely on the issue of waiver — adopting what could appropriately be called an 'Oops' Rule. When the client acted in good faith (used reasonable efforts to guard against such mistaken disclosures), did not consciously produce the privileged communications (and therefore did not intend to effect a waiver), made no adversarial gains from its production, and timely discovered the mistake and notified the opposing party (so that the opposing party should not have relied on the communications in the preparation of that party's case), courts excused the mistake. They refused to find a waiver, required the party who mistakenly received the communications to either return or destroy them, and prohibited the receiving party from using their content in the preparation of its case. The most frequently quoted statement of factors that court consider in assessing inadvertence appears in *Lois Sportwear, U.S.A. v. Levi Strauss & Co.*, 104 F.R.D. 103, 105 (S.D.N.Y. 1985):

> The elements which go into [the determination of whether the release of documents is a waiver or an excusable mistake] include [1] the reasonableness of the precautions to prevent inadvertent disclosure, [2] the time taken to rectify the error, [3] the scope of the discovery and [4] the extent of the disclosure. There is, of course, an overreaching issue of fairness and the protection of an appropriate privilege which, of course, must be judged against the care or negligence with which the privilege is guarded. . . .

The following opinion in *United States v. Citgo Petroleum Corp.* illustrates how the concept has been employed.

UNITED STATES OF AMERICA v.
CITGO PETROLEUM CORPORATION
2007 U.S. Dist. LEXIS 27986 (S.D. Tex. Apr. 16, 2007)

Opinion By: John D. Rainey

MEMORANDUM OPINION & ORDER

Factual Background

Citgo became the subject of a criminal environmental investigation by the Department of Justice and the federal grand jury in early 2003. The investigation centered around Citgo's alleged mismanagement of its benzene waste operations at its Corpus Christi refinery in violation of the Clean Air Act. . . . In response to several grand jury subpoenas *duces tecum* issued to Citgo, it produced thousands of documents, including privileged documents.

Citgo first learned of the inadvertently disclosed documents on December 15, 2005 when the Government subpoenaed Citgo's Senior Counsel claiming Citgo had waived its privilege. The Government provided Citgo's counsel at the time, Terence Lynam, with the documents upon which it based its waiver argument. In response, Lynam wrote a detailed letter on December 28, 2005 explaining that the documents either were not privileged or were inadvertently disclosed and requested their return. The Government refused. Citgo filed its motion to compel the return of the documents on March 1, 2007.

In its motion in limine, the Government cited six documents upon which it rests its claim for waiver of privilege. These documents include: (1) a report prepared by David Monfore which was solicited by Citgo's Senior Counsel, Dana Burch; (2) an email and slides prepared by Dana Burch for the purpose of briefing Citgo senior management on the status of benzene compliance at the refinery; (3) the handwritten notes of a meeting between outside counsel, Susan Harris, and Citgo's environmental personnel; (4) a list of questions prepared by Susan Harris to determine Citgo's compliance with Subpart FF at all of its refineries; (5) briefing documents prepared by ERM, an outside consultant, concerning compliance with Subpart FF at the Corpus Christi refinery; and (6) a draft TAB (i.e. total annual benzene) report for the operating year 2001 showing TAB calculations lower than those totals submitted to the Texas Commission on Environmental Quality. All the documents cited above were marked privileged and confidential. The Government contends these documents contained the advice of Citgo's counsel relating to compliance with the federal regulations governing management of benzene, and therefore Citgo has waived its privilege by disclosing these documents.

In response to the Government's motion in limine, Citgo explained from the beginning of the investigation in early 2003 it produced thousands of documents in response to grand jury

> subpoenas. Several of the documents relating to internal audits may have
> been labeled "privileged," however, Citgo thoroughly reviewed them and

either redacted the privileged information and provided a corresponding privilege log or determined they in fact were not privileged. Citgo denies that all the documents upon which the Government bases its waiver argument are privileged. Citgo maintains that only four documents were inadvertently disclosed or had not been redacted. Citgo argues that its communications with the Government and the privilege log demonstrate that it never waived any privileges.

Discussion

*   *   *

In determining whether an inadvertent disclosure waives the attorney-client privilege, courts must consider the circumstances surrounding the disclosure on a case-by-case basis. Alldread v. City of Grenada, 988 F.2d 1425, 1434 (5th Cir. 1993). The court should consider several factors, none of which are dispositive: (1) the reasonableness of precautions taken to prevent disclosure; (2) the amount of time taken to remedy the error; (3) the scope of the discovery; (4) the extent of the disclosure; and (5) the overriding issue of fairness. . . .

The work product protection can also be waived. The work-product doctrine protects documents prepared in anticipation of litigation, including a "lawyer's research, analysis of legal theories, mental impressions, notes, and memoranda of witnesses' statements. . . . For a document to be prepared in "anticipation of litigation," litigation does not necessarily have to be imminent, but "the primary motivating purpose behind the creation of the document [must be] to aid in possible future litigation." . . . Excluded from work product protection are "materials assembled in the ordinary course of business or pursuant to public requirements unrelated to litigation." FED. R. Civ. P. 26(b)(3).

"[B]ecause the work product privilege looks to the vitality of the adversary system rather than simply seeking to preserve confidentiality, it is not automatically waived by the disclosure to a third party." . . . Waiver of work product protection only results if the work product is disclosed to an adversary. . . . To waive work product protection, the disclosure must be inconsistent with maintaining the secrecy of an attorney's trial preparation.

The issue presented to this Court is whether Citgo's inadvertent disclosure of privileged documents warrants a full subject matter waiver of its privilege as it relates to Citgo's compliance with benzene regulations. The Government claims Citgo waived its work product and attorney-client privileges relating to "all information on the issue of benzene waste management" 4 by producing several documents containing privileged information. Citgo argues a full subject matter waiver is inappropriate because only four documents out of thousands were inadvertently produced pursuant to the grand jury subpoenas. Citgo requests the return of the four privileged documents and argues that the Government has mischaracterized several of the documents it claims are privileged and therefore cannot base its waiver argument on those documents. Specifically, Citgo asserts that many of the documents cited by the Government were not privileged because they were related to the audits and compliance activities Citgo created in the ordinary course of business. Citgo also posits further reasons why the Government's waiver argument should fail, namely that it waited almost two years after the disclosure of the privileged documents before asserting waiver, and it violated its ethical obligations by failing to notify Citgo promptly once it discovered the privileged nature of the documents.

The positions of the parties on the status of the privileged nature of these documents presents almost a reversal of roles from the usual privilege disputes. The burden of demonstrating whether a document is privileged is placed on the holder of the privilege. However, in this case, the Government is asserting the privilege for several documents where Citgo disclaims privilege. Of course, the Government takes this position in order to bolster its waiver argument. Because of this unique situation, the Court will not discuss the privileged nature of all the documents cited by the Government, but will only address the four inadvertently produced documents. Both parties have effectively agreed that at least portions of the inadvertently disclosed documents are privileged. The following four documents are the inadvertently disclosed privileged documents:

(1) Handwritten notes. Notes of meeting between outside counsel, Susan Harris, and Citgo's environmental office on October 1, 1999 (Bates Nos. CEP209769(9)–209774(9)). Citgo maintains that these notes were inadvertently disclosed and are privileged because they refer to communications with Susan Harris, which should have been redacted.

(2) Attorney Questions. Typewritten questions prepared by Susan Harris for a meeting with senior management titled "Citgo Benzene Waste NESHAPS Issues" (Bates Nos. CEP209775(9)–209777(9)). The document also includes some handwritten notations. Citgo denies that the handwritten notes are privileged.

(3) Sidley Memo. An environmental management systems review conducted by Sidley & Austin (Bates Nos. Cit.Cor000905–00911). The document was on Sidley & Austin letterhead and was solicited by Citgo in order to respond to the Texas Natural Resources Conservation Commission's Notice of Enforcement.

(4) A near verbatim copy of the Sidley Memo contained in an undated draft of its 2001 HS &E Excellence Review report (Bates Nos. Cit.Cor01349–01356).

A. Waiver of Privilege

The Court must consider the *Alldread* factors to determine first if Citgo's inadvertent disclosures constitute a waiver of privilege. Evidence of multiple disclosures on multiple occasions leads the Court to believe that Citgo did not take reasonable precautions to prevent disclosure. This factor weighs against Citgo. While Citgo maintains that it thoroughly reviewed the documents before producing them, several facts surrounding the disclosures demonstrate that Citgo did not take reasonable precautions to preserve the confidentiality of the documents. First, Terence Lynam, Citgo's counsel during the grand jury investigation explained in his affidavit that it was Citgo's practice to label documents related to internal environmental audits "privileged" — whether they were privileged or not — because the legal department provided assistance with the audits. This practice of "mislabeling" documents likely led to the inadvertent disclosure in this case. Although Citgo disclaims the importance of the privilege labels, marking a document "privileged" indicates that the document is worthy of close scrutiny. The failure of Citgo to carefully review these documents labeled "privilege" supports the finding that Citgo did not act reasonably to prevent disclosure. Further, each document produced in response to the grand jury subpoenas was Bates stamped. Presumably, these documents were subjected to some form of review, but obviously the steps taken were not adequate to prevent the privileged documents from being disclosed. Citgo, under the direction of current counsel, also reproduced the same documents on a disk to the Government during discovery. Before copying the disk for the Government, Citgo had another opportunity to withhold the documents they claimed were privileged. Moreover, allowing not one, but two versions of the Sidley Memo to be disclosed evidences the carelessness on Citgo's part in properly preserving its privilege. The multiple disclosures, by different law firms, at different times, before and after the Government's claim of waiver demonstrates the lack of reasonable efforts expended by Citgo to protect the confidentiality of these documents.

The amount of time taken to remedy the error also does not weigh in favor of Citgo. The first inadvertent disclosure occurred around July, 2003 during the grand jury investigation. Had the Government not presented its waiver argument in December, 2005, Citgo would have never known it inadvertently disclosed the documents. Citgo did promptly request the return of the documents at that point in December, 2005. However, despite the Government's repeated refusals to return the documents, it still took Citgo over a year to seek relief from the Court. Citgo's failure to take steps to effectuate the return of the documents until March, 2007 dooms its late attempt to assert the privilege.

Next, there is no question that the scope of the discovery was voluminous. There have been thousands, and perhaps hundreds of thousands, documents produced in this case. Citgo's "lost in the shuffle" argument would have greater weight had it not twice disclosed the privilege documents in different forms at different times. And while thousands of documents were produced, the number of documents produced that were labeled "privileged" was far less. A Government investigator estimated that of 27 file drawers of documents retained by the Government in this case from Citgo, only one and a half file drawers contained documents labeled "privileged." The Court does not discount that the overall scope of discovery was voluminous in this case, but when considering only those documents labeled "privileged," the extent of the disclosure is far more significant than Citgo would like to lead this Court to believe.

Finally, the overriding issue of fairness does not save Citgo from waiver. Citgo argues a waiver should not be found in this case because the Government violated its ethical duties when it did not timely notify Citgo that it had potentially privileged documents. Citgo also claims the Government's waiver argument is untimely because it waited for almost two years after the documents were disclosed to seek a waiver. While the Court does not believe the Government handled its obligations with the utmost timeliness and candor, the Court cannot ignore the fact that Citgo failed to preserve its privilege. It was Citgo's burden to maintain the confidentiality of the privilege documents, and in that respect it failed. The Government's behavior will not exonerate Citgo's failures. Further, the essential function of the privilege, which is to protect a client's confidence, has been lost, leaving the privilege with no legitimate function to perform. After considering the *Alldread* factors, the Court finds that Citgo has waived its privilege by inadvertently disclosing privileged material to the Government. The Court will not relieve Citgo of the consequences of their carelessness because "the circumstances surrounding the disclosure do not clearly demonstrate that continued protection is warranted." . . .

B. Scope of Waiver

Generally, the "disclosure of any significant portion of a confidential communication waives the privilege as to the whole." . . . This general principle has applied to circumstances in which the holder of the privilege voluntarily discusses privileged communications with a third party or selectively discloses privileged information for its tactical benefit. For example, in [*Nguyen v. Excel Corp.*, 197 F.3d 200 (5th Cir. 1999)], the executives (i.e. the holder of the privilege) voluntarily testified about attorney-client communications and the legal research undertaken by their attorneys in order to advance its defense that it had a good faith belief in the legality of its practices in a Fair Labor Standards Act suit. . . . The Fifth Circuit held the defendant employer, through its executives, had waived its attorney-client privilege by selectively disclosing portions of privileged communications. . . . Thus, a broad subject matter waiver is often justified on the grounds that such waiver is warranted if the holder of the privilege relies on the advice of counsel as part of its defense or claim, or selectively discloses portions of privileged communications in their own self-interest, or by some other means intentionally waives privilege. . . .

The primary distinction between this case and the cases permitting broad subject matter waiver is the inadvertent nature of Citgo's disclosure. Overall the treatment of the inadvertent and scope of waiver issues should be analyzed in terms of fairness and the "principal concern is selective use of privileged material to garble the truth, which mandates giving the opponent access to related privileged material to set the record straight." . . . Citgo was not attempting to make strategic use of this information and has gained no tactical advantage by disclosing this privileged information. In those contexts where privileged information is selectively disclosed for strategic reasons or as part of a claim or defense, it absolutely would prejudice the opposing party to not have full access to all the privileged communications on the same subject. However, the Government in this case will suffer no prejudice by only having access to the specific documents disclosed. The Court believes this ruling strikes the appropriate balance between condemning Citgo's carelessness with respect to preserving the confidentiality of these specific documents and upholding the important and valued policies underlying the attorney-client privilege. Therefore, the Court finds the inadvertent disclosure of the four privileged documents does not waive the privilege with respect to the entire subject matter of the representation, i.e. all issues related to benzene waste management.

Conclusion

For the reasons set forth above, the Government's Motion in Limine is granted in part and Citgo's Motion to Compel (Dkt. # 136) is denied.

It is so ORDERED.

———

This "Oops" Rule has been widely recognized in both state and federal courts. The concept has frequently been incorporated into pretrial Protective Order. *See* P.R. RICE, ATTORNEY-CLIENT PRIVILEGE IN THE UNITED STATES, §§ 9:71–78 (Thomson West 2nd ed. 1999) and P.R. RICE, ATTORNEY-CLIENT PRIVILEGE: STATE LAW, §§ 9:71–78 (Rice Publishing 2008). The most notable holdout in this rush to ignore the absence of confidentiality and excuse inadvertent, albeit intentional, disclosures has been the D.C. Circuit. *In re Sealed Case*, 877 F.2d 976, 980 (D.C. Cir. 1989).

> Even assuming Company's disclosure was due to "bureaucratic error," which we take to be a euphemism that necessarily implied human error, that unfortunate lapse simply reveals that someone in the company and thereby Company itself (since it can only act through its employees) was careless with the confidentiality of its privileged communications. Normally the amount of care taken to ensure confidentiality reflects the importance of that confidentiality to the holder of the privilege. To hold, as we do, that an inadvertent disclosure will waive the privilege imposes a self-governing restraint on the freedom with which organizations such as corporations, unions, and the like label documents related to communications with counsel as privileged. To readily do so creates a greater risk of "inadvertent" disclosure by someone and thereby the danger that the "waiver" will extend to all related matters, perhaps causing grave injury to the organization. But that is as it should be. Otherwise, there is a temptation to seek artificially to expand the content of privileged matter. In other words, if a client wishes to preserve the privilege, it must treat the confidentiality of attorney-client communications like jewels — if not crown jewels. Short of court-compelled disclosures . . . or other equally extraordinary circumstances [e.g., communications acquired by third parties despite all possible precautions] we will not distinguish between various degrees of "voluntariness" in waivers of the attorney-client privilege.

Without addressing the inconsistency between the inadvertence rule and the requirement of confidentiality, or the initial extension of the privilege protection to corporate entities who are usually the clients seeking to take advantage of this exception to waiver, the concept of inadvertence has been adopted in proposed revisions to Rule 502(b).

———

Fed. R. Civ., P. 26(b)(5)(B) provides:

Rule 26 Duty to Disclose; General Provisions Governing Discovery

* * *

(b) DISCOVERY SCOPE AND LIMITS.

*   *   *

(5) *Claiming Privilege or Protecting Trial-Preparation Materials.*

*   *   *

(B) *Information Produced.* If information produced in discovery is subject to a claim of privilege or of protection as trial-preparation material, the party making the claim may notify any party that received the information of the claim and the basis for it. After being notified, a party must promptly return, sequester, or destroy the specified information and any copies it has; must not use or disclose the information until the claim is resolved; must take reasonable steps to retrieve the information if the party disclosed it before being notified; and may promptly present the information to the court under seal for a determination of the claim. The producing party must preserve the information until the claim is resolved.

§ 9.06 NEW PRIVILEGE RULES RECOGNIZED UNDER AUTHORITY GRANTED IN RULE 501 ("IN LIGHT OF REASON AND EXPERIENCE")

Federal Rule of Evidence 501 states, in part, that privileges "shall be governed by principles of the common law as they may be interpreted . . . in light of reason and experience." The Supreme Court has stated the purpose of Rule 501 is to "provide the courts with the flexibility to develop rules of privilege on a case-by-case basis . . . and to leave the door open to change." *Trammel v. United States*, 445 U.S. 40, 47 (1980). Exercising this flexibility, courts have recognized new privileges in a number of different contexts in which the confidentiality of communications has been found to be essential to certain relationships that are important to the functioning of valuable societal institutions, and the benefits of this encouragement outweigh the potential benefit to the judicial system of compelled disclosure.

Academic freedom privilege

In *EEOC v. University of Notre Dame du Lac*, 715 F.2d 331 (7th Cir. 1983), the court recognized an academic freedom privilege that protected from disclosure the names and identities of persons participating in a peer review process through which tenure decisions were made. The court concluded the protection was "essential to the proper functioning of the faculty tenure review process," which is critical to the integrity and excellence of our academic institutions. *But see Parvarandeh v. Goins*, 124 F.R.D. 169 (E.D. Tenn. 1988) (rejecting academic freedom privilege with extended discussion of conflicting case law); *EEOC v. Franklin & Marshall College*, 775 F.2d 110 (3d Cir. 1985) (rejecting academic freedom privilege). The court in *Franklin & Marshall* concluded that either an absolute or qualified privilege that permits schools to avoid a thorough investigation "would allow the institutions to hide evidence of discrimination behind a wall of secrecy." *Id.* at 115. "In the face of the clear mandate from Congress which identified and recognized the threat of unchecked discrimination in education, . . . we have no choice but to trust that the honesty and integrity of the tenure reviewers in evaluation decisions will overcome feelings of discomfort and embarrassment and will outlast the demise of absolute confidentiality." *Id.*

Parent-child privilege

In *In re Agosto*, 553 F. Supp. 1298 (D. Nev. 1983), the court recognized a parent-child privilege. In a particularly thorough and persuasive opinion, Chief Judge Claiborne concluded the courts must protect and foster the privacy of the parent-child relationship, no less than the privacy of the husband-wife relationship, because it is fundamental to the integrity, stability, and supportive structure of the family unit. The court held that this privilege not only protects communications between the parent and child, it also precluded the government from calling the child as a witness to testify against a parent. There are convincing parallels that can be drawn between the spousal privilege and a parent-child privilege; however, the vast majority of federal courts that have addressed the question have refused to extend the protection to the parent-child context. *See United States v. Ismail*, 756 F.2d 1253 (6th Cir. 1985). Despite the judicial reluctance to apply the parent-child privilege, scholars continue to urge its acceptance based on the theory of a constitutional right of privacy between parents and their children. *See* Schlueter, *The Parent-Child Privilege: A Response Calls for Adoption*, 19 St. Mary's L.J. 35 (1987); Watts, *The Parent-Child Privilege: Hardly a New or Revolutionary Concept*, 28 Wm. & Mary L. Rev. 583 (1987).

Deliberative process privilege

In *Resolution Trust Corp. v. Diamond*, 137 F.R.D. 634 (S.D.N.Y. 1991), the court recognized a deliberative-process privilege but rejected a claim by the Resolution Trust Corporation, an organ of the Federal Government. The court held that to qualify under the deliberative-process privilege, the sheltered communication must relate to the formulation of new policy by a government agency and must occur before the policy decision becomes final. The materials in question were generated by attorneys as afterthoughts to the corporation's previously formulated regulatory policy. The court stated, "the circumstances of this case suggest that the decision to assert the privilege was made not by agency policy makers in consideration of the agency's interest in deliberative confidentiality, but by its outside counsel as a matter of litigation strategy." *Id.* at 641.

Self-critical analysis privilege

Somewhat akin to the government deliberative privilege in the private context is the "self-critical analysis privilege," initially recognized in *Bredice v. Doctor's Hosp., Inc.*, 50 F.R.D. 249 (D.D.C. 1970), *aff'd without opinion*, 479 F.2d 920 (1973), and subsequently adopted by a number of both federal and state courts and applied in many different contexts. *See Reichhold Chems. v. Textron, Inc.*, 157 F.R.D. 522, 524–525 (N.D. Fla. 1994), and cases discussed therein. The rationale has been that such critical self-evaluation fosters the compelling public interest in observance of the law. *See Granger v. National R.R. Passenger Corp.*, 116 F.R.D. 507, 508 (E.D. Pa. 1987). In lieu of this privilege, courts might provide the same protection for self-analysis through the privilege for subsequent remedial measures in Rule 407 of the Federal Rules of Evidence. *See Capellupo v. FMC Corp.*, 126 F.R.D. 545 (D. Minn. 1988). A few courts have rejected the privilege in the belief it is not necessary to the free flow of critical information within an organization. *See Williams v. Vulcan-Hart Corp.*, 136 F.R.D. 457, 459 (W.D. Ky. 1991); *Wei v. Bodner*, 127 F.R.D. 91, 100–101 (D.N.J. 1989); *Witten v. A.H. Smith & Co.*, 100 F.R.D. 446, 449–454 (D. Md. 1984).

EXERCISE

Jeffrey, a former CIA agent, is alleged to have disclosed classified information about a covert CIA operation to James, for publication in a book written by James, in violation of the Espionage Act. The government has subpoenaed James to testify at Jeffrey's criminal trial. The government intends on asking James who provided James with the details for James' book. James refuses to testify, arguing that under the journalist-source privilege, he cannot be compelled to identify his source. Is James correct?

Chapter 10

SHORTCUTS TO PROOF

§ 10.01 PRESUMPTIONS

[A] In General

[1] Characteristics of a True Presumption

A presumption has two principle characteristics: it is *mandatory* and it is *rebuttable*. It is mandatory because the finder of facts has no discretion but to find the presumed fact, Fact B, to be true if it finds the primary or basic fact, Fact A, to have been established, provided (and this is a critical qualification that will be discussed below) the presumed fact has not been successfully rebutted. Without evidence rebutting the presumption, the presiding judge will instruct the jury at the end of the trial, "If you find Fact A, you *must* find Fact B."

This mandatory characteristic distinguishes the presumption from simple logical inferences (which often form the basis for presumptions). An inference simply permits a conclusion on the basis of the logical deduction that the presumption compels. For example, if the presumption of receipt by the addressee were not recognized for properly mailed letters, the jurors would not be instructed that they must find Fact B if they found Fact A. Instead, the fact that the letter was properly mailed would give rise to the logical inference that the letter was actually received — thereby *permitting* the conclusion that the presumption would compel. Thus, if judges were permitted to comment on the evidence (which is not true in most states), they could suggest to the jurors that if they found Fact A to be true, they *may* also find Fact B to be true. Otherwise, the judge may not mention an inference to the jury.

Presumptions are rebuttable because the facts presumed to be true are not always true. If the opponent were precluded from refuting these presumed facts, the presumptions would effectively be converted into rules of law that eliminate the presumed facts as elements of the causes of action or defenses. For example, with the presumption regarding the receipt of properly mailed letters, if the addressee were not permitted to rebut the presumption of receipt, the statutory requirement of notice could be converted from one of actual notice to one of constructive notice through reasonable efforts to apprise, because proof of "proper" mailing would always suffice. With the social policy presumption that a child born to a married woman is legitimate, if legitimacy were not rebuttable, marriage would be converted into a substantive rule of law establishing the husband's absolute responsibility for offspring born during the marriage. Because presumptions must be rebuttable, so called "conclusive presumptions," such as the presumption that a child under the age of seven cannot commit a crime, are not presumptions at all. They are simply rules of law that conclusively establish certain facts in a cause of action.

[2] Rebutting Presumptions

The presumed fact, Fact B, arises because the proponent has proven Fact A, the basic or primary fact. In response to the presumption, the opponent can offer evidence to disprove either the primary fact or the presumed fact. Technically, the opponent can rebut the presumption only by offering evidence to disprove the presumed fact (non-B evidence). Evidence that disproves the primary fact (non-A evidence) only addresses whether the presumption arises in the first instance. In the context of the presumption concerning the receipt of a properly mailed letter, for example, if the opponent responded only with evidence to disprove that the letter was properly mailed (*i.e.*, evidence that the letter was not properly addressed, stamped, or deposited in a proper receptacle), and not with evidence to disprove the addressee's actual receipt of the letter, the only issue for the finder of facts to resolve would be whether the proponent had established Fact A (proper mailing). Consequently, the judge would instruct the jury that if it found from the evidence presented that the letter was properly mailed to Frank Johnson, it *must* find that Johnson received it, because the law recognizes a presumption that an addressee received a properly mailed letter.[1]

In the above hypothetical, it is highly unlikely that Johnson would contest the question of receipt of notice with only non-A evidence. If he failed to receive the notice, even if it were properly mailed, he would also offer his own testimony to that effect.[2] This would constitute non-B evidence — *true* rebuttal evidence — because it refutes the presumed fact.

This presentation of rebuttal evidence gives rise to several questions that the courts have answered with varying degrees of clarity. What quantum of proof must the opponent present to rebut the presumption? Once rebutted, what happens to the presumption? How should the judge instruct the jury once the opponent has presented rebuttal evidence? The answers to these questions turn on the function that the presumption is intended to serve — an issue that has been the subject of continual debate.

---

[1] Conversely, the judge would instruct the jury that, if it found that the letter had *not been mailed at all*, it must find that Johnson had not received it and that Johnson had not, therefore, received proper notice of his default. The judge would not give such an instruction, however, if the jury found that the bank had mailed the notice but had mailed it improperly, because improper mailing can still result in the letter's delivery.

[2] A time when such direct evidence of nondelivery might not be presented in opposition to the presumption is if Frank Johnson is unavailable. For example, if the notice had been sent and allegedly received when Frank Johnson was alive but the action is against his estate, he obviously could not be called to refute the presumption. In such a case, other non-B evidence would have to be offered, such as the absence of a listing of the receipt of such notice in an incoming mail register that Johnson had maintained.

[3]   Effect of Evidence Rebutting the Presumption

[a]   Two Basic Theories

The effect of rebuttal evidence on the presumption is directly tied to the presumption's perceived function. Two basic theories have emerged. The first view is attributed to its early proponent, Professor James B. Thayer. *See* J. Thayer, PRELIMINARY TREATISE ON EVIDENCE AT THE COMMON LAW 353–389 (1898). This view was later advocated by Professor Wigmore. *See* 9 J. WIGMORE, EVIDENCE § 2491 (Chadbourn rev. 1961). This view is discussed in § [b], below.

Professor Morgan proposed the second view, *see* Morgan, *Instructing the Jury upon Presumptions and Burdens of Proof*, 47 HARV. L. REV. 59 (1933); E. Morgan, BASIC PROBLEMS OF EVIDENCE 34–44 (1962), which Professor McCormick later adopted, *see* MCCORMICK ON EVIDENCE, § 338 (4th ed. 1992). As noted in the opinion in *Texas Dept. of Community Affairs v. Burdine, below* § 10.01[A][4][a], the Thayer approach has proven to be the most popular view. Morgan's approach is discussed in § [c], below.

[b]   The Thayer/Wigmore View

According to the Thayer/Wigmore view, the presumption establishes a prima facie case for the existence of the presumed fact, thereby shifting to the opposition the burden of going forward with evidence to contradict that fact. If the opponent does not respond to this shifted burden, the court must find in favor of the party for whom the presumption was created. If the opponent responds with evidence to disprove the presumed fact — rebuttal evidence — the presumption is destroyed, because it has served its sole function under this view. It has forced the opposing party to come forward with rebuttal evidence. This view has come to be known as the "bursting bubble" theory.

Courts have differed considerably in deciding precisely how much rebuttal evidence the opposition must present to satisfy its burden of production and thereby destroy the presumption. Some courts have suggested that *any evidence* will suffice. Many courts have simply characterized a need for *some evidence*, without characterizing or quantifying it. Others have required *any credible evidence*. Most courts, however, believe that these standards are so lax they render the shifted burden of production virtually meaningless. These courts have held that rebuttal is achieved only if *sufficient evidence* is produced *upon which a reasonable person could find* that the presumed fact is not true.

Typical of the kind of evidence that courts have found to be inadequate to meet this burden of production was the evidence offered in *Matter of Emerald Oil Co.*, 695 F.2d 833 (5th Cir. 1983). In *Emerald*, a trustee in bankruptcy sued the creditor to avoid the transfer of funds under the Bankruptcy Act on the ground that it was a preferential transfer because it was made while the debtor was insolvent. To establish the debtor's insolvency, the trustee relied upon section 547(f) of the Bankruptcy Code, which provided that, in proceedings to avoid a preferential transfer, "the debtor is presumed to have been insolvent on and during the 90 days immediately preceding the date of the filing of the petition [in bankruptcy]." To rebut the presumption, the creditor presented the testimony of a certified public accountant who offered the opinion that certain assets of the debtor (ongoing drilling contracts) may have been undervalued because the trustee's accountant may have improperly employed the "percentage of completion of ongoing contracts" method of accounting. This opinion was based neither on an examination of the debtor's records nor on an inspection of the working papers of the trustee's accountant, who had conducted an extensive audit of the failing business. Because the witness did not testify that the assets of the debtor's business exceeded its liabilities on the date in question but only that the analysis of the other accountant *may* have been improper, the court held that the testimony constituted nothing more than speculation about a potential error and, therefore, "did not constitute any evidence sufficient to cast doubt on the statutory presumption of insolvency." *Id.* at 838.

As previously indicated, once the presiding judge finds that the opponent has satisfied its burden, the presumption bursts like a bubble and is destroyed. If the presumption has been destroyed, the answer to the question, "How should the judge instruct the jury regarding the presumption?" is apparent: the judge should not mention it in the instructions because there is nothing to mention. The presumption logically cannot, and therefore should not, have any effect on the jury deliberations. The following Supreme Court opinion in *Texas Department of Community Affairs v. Burdine* demonstrates the operation of this "bursting bubble" theory.

TEXAS DEPARTMENT OF COMMUNITY AFFAIRS v. BURDINE
United States Supreme Court
450 U.S. 248 (1981)

JUSTICE POWELL delivered the opinion of the Court.

This case requires us to address again the nature of the evidentiary burden placed upon the defendant in an employment discrimination suit brought under Title VII of the Civil Rights Act of 1964, 42 U.S.C. § 2000e *et seq.* The narrow question presented is whether, after the plaintiff has proved a prima facie case of discriminatory treatment, the burden shifts to the defendant to persuade the court by a preponderance of the evidence that legitimate, non-discriminatory reasons for the challenged employment action existed.

I

Petitioner, the Texas Department of Community Affairs (TDCA), hired respondent, a female, in January 1972, for the position of accounting clerk in the Public Service Careers Division (PSC). PSC provided training and employment opportunities in the public sector for unskilled workers. When hired, respondent possessed several years' experience in employment training. She was promoted to Field Services Coordinator in July 1972. Her supervisor resigned in November of that year, and respondent was assigned additional duties. Although she applied for the supervisor's position of Project Director, the position remained vacant for six months.

PSC was funded completely by the United States Department of Labor. The Department was seriously concerned about inefficiencies at PSC. In February 1973, the Department notified the Executive Director of TDCA, B.R. Fuller, that it would terminate PSC the following month. TDCA officials, assisted by respondent, persuaded the Department to continue funding the program, conditioned upon PSC's reforming its operations. Among the agreed conditions were the appointment of a permanent Project Director and a complete reorganization of the PSC staff.

After consulting with personnel within TDCA, Fuller hired a male from another division of the agency as Project Director. In reducing the PSC staff, he fired respondent along with two other employees, and retained another male, Walz, as the only professional employee in the division. It is undisputed that respondent had maintained her application for the position of Project Director and had requested to remain with TDCA. Respondent soon was rehired by TDCA and assigned to another division of the agency. She received the exact salary paid to the Project Director at PSC, and the subsequent promotions she has received have kept her salary and responsibility commensurate with what she would have received had she been appointed Project Director.

Respondent filed this suit in the United States District Court for the Western District of Texas. She alleged that the failure to promote and the subsequent decision to terminate her had been predicated on gender discrimination in violation of Title VII. After a bench trial, the District Court held that neither decision was based on gender discrimination. The court relied on the testimony of Fuller that the employment decisions necessitated by the commands of the Department of Labor were based on consultation among trusted advisers and a nondiscriminatory evaluation of the relative qualifications of the individuals involved. He testified that the three individuals terminated did not work well together, and that TDCA thought that eliminating this problem would improve PSC's efficiency. The court accepted this explanation as rational and, in effect, found no evidence that the decisions not to promote and to terminate respondent were prompted by gender discrimination.

The Court of Appeals for the Fifth Circuit reversed in part. . . . The court held that the District Court's "implicit evidentiary finding" that the male hired as Project Director was better qualified for that position than respondent was not clearly erroneous. Accordingly, the court affirmed the District Court's finding that respondent was not discriminated against when she was not promoted. The Court of Appeals, however, reversed the District Court's finding that Fuller's testimony sufficiently had rebutted respondent's prima facie case of gender discrimination in the decision to terminate her employment at PSC. The court reaffirmed its previously announced views that the defendant in a Title VII case bears the burden of proving by a preponderance of the evidence the existence of legitimate nondiscriminatory reasons for the employment action and that the defendant also must prove by objective evidence that those hired or promoted were better qualified than the plaintiff. The court found that Fuller's testimony did not carry either of these evidentiary burdens. It, therefore, reversed the judgment of the District

Court and remanded the case for computation of backpay. Because the decision of the Court of Appeals as to the burden of proof borne by the defendant conflicts with interpretations of our precedents adopted by other Courts of Appeals, we granted certiorari. . . . We now vacate the Fifth Circuit's decision and remand for application of the correct standard.

II

In *McDonnell Douglas Corp. v. Green*, 411 U.S. 792 (1973), we set forth the basic allocation of burdens and order of presentation of proof in a Title VII case alleging discriminatory treatment. First, the plaintiff has the burden of proving by the preponderance of the evidence a prima facie case of discrimination. Second, if the plaintiff succeeds in proving the prima facie case, the burden shifts to the defendant "to articulate some legitimate, nondiscriminatory reason for the employee's rejection." *Id.* at 802. Third, should the defendant carry this burden, the plaintiff must then have an opportunity to prove by a preponderance of the evidence that the legitimate reasons offered by the defendant were not its true reasons, but were a pretext for discrimination. *Id.* at 804.

The nature of the burden that shifts to the defendant should be understood in light of the plaintiff's ultimate and intermediate burdens. The ultimate burden of persuading the trier of fact that the defendant intentionally discriminated against the plaintiff remains at all times with the plaintiff. . . . The *McDonnell Douglas* division of intermediate evidentiary burdens serves to bring the litigants and the court expeditiously and fairly to this ultimate question.

The burden of establishing a prima facie case of disparate treatment is not onerous. The plaintiff must prove by a preponderance of the evidence that she applied for an available position for which she was qualified, but was rejected under circumstances which gave rise to an inference of unlawful discrimination. The prima facie case serves an important function in the litigation: it eliminates the most common nondiscriminatory reasons for the plaintiff's rejection. . . . As the Court explained in *Furnco Construction Corp. v. Waters*, 438 U.S. 567, 577 (1978), the prima facie case "raises an inference of discrimination only because we presume these acts, if otherwise unexplained, are more likely than not based on the consideration of impermissible factors." Establishment of the prima facie case in effect creates a presumption that the employer unlawfully discriminated against the employee. If the trier of fact believes the plaintiff's evidence, and if the employer is silent in the face of the presumption, the court must enter judgment for the plaintiff because no issue of fact remains in the case.[3]

The burden that shifts to the defendant, therefore, is to rebut the presumption of discrimination by producing evidence that the plaintiff was rejected, or someone else was preferred, for a legitimate, nondiscriminatory reason. The defendant need

---

[3] (Court's original footnote 7.) The phrase "prima facie case" not only may denote the establishment of a legally mandatory, rebuttable presumption, but also may be used by courts to describe the plaintiff's burden of producing enough evidence to permit the trier of fact to infer the fact at issue. . . . *McDonnell Douglas* should have made it apparent that in the Title VII context we use "prima facie case" in the former sense.

not persuade the court that it was actually motivated by the proffered reasons. . . . It is sufficient if the defendant's evidence raises a genuine issue of fact as to whether it discriminated against the plaintiff.[4] To accomplish this, the defendant must clearly set forth, through the introduction of admissible evidence, the reasons for the plaintiff's rejection.[5] The explanation provided must be legally sufficient to justify a judgment for the defendant. If the defendant carries this burden of production, the presumption raised by the prima facie case is rebutted,[6] and the factual inquiry proceeds to a new level of specificity. Placing this burden of production on the defendant thus serves simultaneously to meet the plaintiff's prima facie case by presenting a legitimate reason for the action and to frame the factual issue with sufficient clarity so that the plaintiff will have a full and fair opportunity to demonstrate pretext. The sufficiency of the defendant's evidence should be evaluated by the extent to which it fulfills these functions.

The plaintiff retains the burden of persuasion. She now must have the opportunity to demonstrate that the proffered reason was not the true reason for the employment decision. This burden now merges with the ultimate burden of persuading the court that she has been the victim of intentional discrimination. She may succeed in this either directly by persuading the court that a discriminatory reason more likely motivated the employer or indirectly by showing that the employer's proffered explanation is unworthy of credence . . . .

* * *

IV

In summary, the Court of Appeals erred by requiring the defendant to prove by a preponderance of the evidence the existence of nondiscriminatory reasons for terminating the respondent and that the person retained in her stead had superior objective qualifications for the position. When the plaintiff has proved a prima facie case of discrimination, the defendant bears only the burden of explaining clearly the

---

[4] (Court's original footnote 8.) This evidentiary relationship between the presumption created by a prima facie case and the consequential burden of production placed on the defendant is a traditional feature of the common law. "The word 'presumption' properly used refers only to a device for allocating the production burden." F. James & G. Hazard, CIVIL PROCEDURE § 7.9, p. 255 (2d ed. 1977) (footnote omitted). *See* Fed. R. Evid. 301. *See generally* 9 J. WIGMORE, EVIDENCE § 2491 (3d ed. 1940). . . . Usually, assessing the burden of production helps the judge determine whether the litigants have created an issue of fact to be decided by the jury. In a Title VII case, the allocation of burdens and the creation of a presumption by the establishment of a prima facie case is intended progressively to sharpen the inquiry into the elusive factual question of intentional discrimination.

[5] (Court's original footnote 9.) An articulation not admitted into evidence will not suffice. Thus, the defendant cannot meet its burden merely through an answer to the complaint or by argument of counsel.

[6] (Court's original footnote 10.) *See generally* J. Thayer, PRELIMINARY TREATISE ON EVIDENCE 346 (1898). In saying that the presumption drops from the case, we do not imply that the trier of fact no longer may consider evidence previously introduced by the plaintiff to establish a prima facie case. A satisfactory explanation by the defendant destroys the legally mandatory inference of discrimination arising from the plaintiff's initial evidence. Nonetheless, this evidence and inferences properly drawn therefrom may be considered by the trier of fact on the issue of whether the defendant's explanation is pretextual. Indeed, there may be some cases where the plaintiff's initial evidence, combined with the effective cross-examination of the defendant, will suffice to discredit the defendant's explanation.

nondiscriminatory reasons for its actions. The judgment of the Court of Appeals is vacated, and the case is remanded for further proceedings consistent with this opinion.

It is so ordered.

[c]   The Morgan/McCormick View

Professor Morgan proposed that a presumption should shift to the party against whom it operates the burden of *persuasion* on the presumed fact as well as the burden of producing evidence. For example, with the presumption of receipt of a properly mailed letter, Morgan's view would shift the burden to the addressee to persuade the finder of facts that he did not receive the letter. Morgan considered the policies underlying presumptions as requiring more than mere production of some evidence to contradict the presumed fact.

He set forth two reasons why the presumption should shift the burden of persuasion on the presumed fact. First, Morgan stated that this shift is what many courts in effect accomplish anyway, by continuing to mention the presumption and telling the jury to find the presumed fact unless the opponent disproves it by evidence of equal weight. Second, he noted that the reasons for creating presumptions, and for allocating burdens of persuasion on particular issues, are the same: probability, fairness, and social policy. Thus, he argued that the initial assignment of burdens, based on the nature of the cause of action stated in the pleadings, should be fine-tuned throughout the trial on the basis of the same policy considerations that arise from the evidence relied upon at the trial.

Under Morgan's view of presumptions, the introduction of evidence to disprove the presumed fact, non-B evidence, would have no effect on the presumption. Such evidence would only serve to satisfy the burden of persuasion that had shifted to the opposing party when the presumption arose. Theoretically, there would be no rebuttal of the presumption, because it would no longer be rebuttable in the sense that it could be destroyed and the action would proceed as if it never existed. Instead, under the Morgan view, the amount of evidence that the opponent must produce in response to the presumption will be whatever is sufficient to convince the finder of facts, by the level of persuasiveness applicable to that issue prior to its shift to the opposing side, that the proposition presumed to be true is, in fact, not true.

Relative to the final question — how the judge should instruct the jury about the presumption — the answer is always the same regardless of whether non-B evidence has been introduced. Under the Morgan view, the judge will instruct the jury that the law presumes Fact B to be true from proof of Fact A. If the jury finds that the proponent has produced evidence that establishes Fact A, it must also find Fact B to be true unless the opposing party convinces it of the nonexistence of that fact, usually by a preponderance of the evidence.

[4] Conflicting Presumptions

How should courts resolve factual issues in the face of presumptions that compel opposite conclusions? For example, a party who claimed that a certain document was properly filed with a government agency within a certain time frame could rely on having properly mailed it as giving rise to the presumption of the Government's receipt. On the other hand, if the Government claims that it did not receive the document until later in the month, it could rely on the date stamped on the face of the document by a receiving clerk upon delivery, if placing such a stamp were part of the clerk's regular responsibilities, and that would, in turn, give rise to the presumption that the government employee properly performed his duties. If the court follows the "bursting bubble" theory of presumptions, which only requires the opponent to come forward with some rebuttal evidence, should the court consider the primary facts establishing each conflicting presumption as rebuttal evidence that destroys the other presumption, thereby leaving the resolution of the issue to the logical inferences arising from the underlying facts? Or should the court attempt to resolve the conflict, by examining the compelling nature of the logic and policies that underlie each presumption and giving legal effect to the stronger of the two?

Courts have split on this question. Some courts have even adopted a third approach of creating still another presumption to take the place of the two that conflict. In substance, are these approaches different from one another? In theory they probably are not. Regardless of whether a court considers the presumptions destroyed, and, therefore, resorts to the strength of the logical inferences created by the underlying facts of each, or weighs the compelling nature of each and chooses the stronger of the two, the focus will be on the same thing: the logically compelling nature of the underlying facts. Similarly, the nature of the new presumption that the court might create would necessarily be based on the compelling nature of the facts underlying the presumptions that were replaced.

The practical difference will be in who decides the question. If the question is viewed as a factual issue after the presumptions have been destroyed, the jury will make the determination. If the question is the survival of the stronger presumption, either in its existing form or in the form of a new third presumption, the judge will make the decision. If the judge is also the finder of facts in a nonjury proceeding or on a motion for summary judgment in any kind of proceeding, the approaches, for all practical purposes, are the same. The following opinion in *Legille v. Dann* is typical of how courts approach this problem.

LEGILLE v. DANN
United States Court of Appeals, D.C. Circuit
544 F.2d 1 (1976)

SPOTTSWOOD W. ROBINSON, III, CIRCUIT JUDGE:

An application for a United States patent filed within twelve months after filing of an application for a foreign patent on the same invention is statutorily accorded the filing date of the foreign application and the effect thereof. If, however, the interval between the filings exceeds twelve months, patent protection in the United

States may not be available. The practice of the Patent Office, unchallenged in this litigation, is to file the duplicating United States application upon receipt.

This appeal, by the Commissioner of Patents, brings to this court a controversy as to the filing date properly to be given four applications domestically mailed to the Patent Office in time for normal delivery before expiration of the twelve-month period but allegedly received thereafter. On cross-motions for summary judgment, the District Court, utilizing the familiar presumption of regularity of the mails, ruled in favor of the applicants. Our examination of the record, however, discloses potential evidence capable of dispelling the presumption and generating an issue of fact as to the date on which the applications arrived. We accordingly reverse the judgment and remand the case for trial.

I

From affidavits submitted in support of the motions for summary judgment, we reconstruct the facts apparently undisputed. On March 1, 1973, appellees' attorney mailed from East Hartford, Connecticut, to the Patent Office in Washington, D.C., a package containing four patent applications. Each of the applications had previously been filed in the Grand Duchy of Luxembourg, three on March 6, 1972, and the fourth on the following August 11. The package was marked "Airmail," bore sufficient airmail postage and was properly addressed. Delivery of air mail from East Hartford to Washington at that time was normally two days.

The applications were date-stamped "March 8, 1973," by the Patent Office. Each of the four applications was assigned that filing date on the ground that the stamped date was the date of receipt by the Patent Office. If the action of the Patent Office is to stand, three of appellees' applications, on which Luxembourg patents had been granted, fail in this country.

Appellees petitioned the Commissioner of Patents to reassign the filing date. The petition was denied. Appellees then sued in the District Court for a judgment directing the Commissioner to accord the applications a filing date not later than March 6, 1973. Both sides moved for summary judgment on the basis of the pleadings and affidavits respectively submitted. Not surprisingly, none of the affidavits reflected any direct evidence of the date on which the applications were actually delivered to the Patent Office.

The District Court correctly identified the central issue: "whether there exists a genuine issue of fact as to when these applications were received by the Patent Office." By the court's appraisal, appellees' suit was "predicated upon the legal presumption that postal employees discharge their duties in a proper manner and that properly addressed, stamped and deposited mail is presumed to reach the addressee in due course and without unusual delay, unless evidence to the contrary is proven." The court believed, however, that the Commissioner's position rested "primarily upon a presumption of procedural regularity based upon the normal manner, custom, practice and habit established for the handling of incoming mail at the Patent Office and upon the absence of evidence showing that the subject applications were not handled routinely in accordance with those established procedures." On this analysis, the court "concluded that the presumption relied upon by the [Commissioner] is insufficient to overcome the strong presumption that mails, properly addressed, having fully prepaid postage, and deposited in the proper receptacles, will be received by the addressee in the ordinary course of the mails." "This latter presumption," the court held, "can only be rebutted by proof of specific facts and not by invoking another presumption"; "the negative evidence in this case detailing the manner, custom, practice and habit of handling incoming mail by the Patent Office fails to overcome or rebut the strong presumption that the applications were timely delivered in the regular course of the mails to the Patent Office." In sum,

> [appellees] rely upon the strong presumption of the regularity of the mails to show that, in the normal course of postal business, these applications would be delivered within two days from March 1, 1973. [The Commissioner] does not show nor offer to show by way of any positive evidence that the presumption is inapplicable in this case. On the contrary, he relies on negative evidence as to custom, habit and usual procedure to create a conflicting presumption that the agency's business and procedure were followed in this case. Under the circumstances of this case, this Court holds, as a matter of law, that this presumption is insufficient to rebut or overcome the presumption of the regularity of the mails.

II

Proof that mail matter is properly addressed, stamped and deposited in an appropriate receptacle has long been accepted as evidence of delivery to the addressee. On proof of the foundation facts, innumerable cases recognize a presumption to that effect. Some presume more specifically that the delivery occurred in due course of the mails. The cases concede, however, that the presumption is rebuttable. We think the District Court erred in adhering to the presumption in the face of the evidentiary showing which the Commissioner was prepared to make.

Rebuttable presumptions are rules of law attaching to proven evidentiary facts certain procedural consequences as to the opponent's duty to come forward with other evidence. In the instant case, the presumption would normally mean no more than proof of proper airmailing of appellees' applications required a finding, in the absence of countervailing evidence, that they arrived at the Patent Office within the usual delivery time. There is abundant authority undergirding the proposition that, as a presumption, it did not remain viable in the face of antithetical evidence. As Dean Wigmore has explained, "the peculiar effect of a presumption 'of law' (that is, the real presumption) is merely to invoke a rule of law compelling the [trier of fact] to reach a conclusion in the absence of evidence to the contrary from the opponent. If the opponent does offer evidence to the contrary (sufficient to satisfy the judge's requirement of some evidence), the presumption disappears as a rule of law, and the case is in the [factfinder's] hands free from any rule." As more poetically the explanation has been put, "[p]resumptions . . . may be looked on as the bats of the law, flitting in the twilight, but disappearing in the sunshine of actual facts."

We are aware of the fact that this view of presumptions — the so-called "bursting bubble" theory — has not won universal acclaim. Nonetheless, it is the prevailing view, to which jurists preponderantly have subscribed; it is the view of the Supreme Court, and of this court as well. It is also the approach taken by the Model Code of Evidence and, very importantly, by the newly-adopted Federal Rules of Evidence. These considerations hardly leave us free to assume a contrary position. Beyond that, we perceive no legal or practical justification for preferring either of the two involved presumptions over the other.[7] In light of the Commissioner's showing on the motions for summary judgment, then, we conclude that the District Court should have declined a summary disposition in favor of a trial.

III

Conservatively estimated, the Patent Office receives through the mails an average of at least 100,000 items per month. The procedures utilized for the handling of that volume of mail were meticulously described in an affidavit by an official of the Patent Office, whose principal duties included superintendence of incoming mail. Ordinary mail — other than special delivery, registered and certified — arrives at the Patent Office in bags, which are date-marked if the items contained were placed by the postal service in the Patent Office pouch earlier than the date of delivery of the bags. A number of readers open the wrappers, compare the contents against any included listing — such as a letter of transmittal or a return postcard — and note any discrepancy, and apply to at least the principal included paper a stamp recording thereon the receipt date and the reader's identification number. Another employee then applies to the separate papers the official mail-room stamp, which likewise records the date; the two stamps are used in order to minimize the chance of error. The date recorded in each instance is the date on which the Patent Office actually receives the particular bag of mail, or a previous date when the bag is so marked. From every indication, the affidavit avers, appellees' applications were not delivered to the Patent Office until March 8, 1973.

We cannot agree with the District Court that an evidentiary presentation of this caliber would do no more than raise "a presumption of procedural regularity" in the Patent Office. Certainly it would accomplish that much; it would cast upon appellees the burden of producing contradictory evidence, but its effect would not be exhausted at that point. The facts giving rise to the presumption would also have evidentiary force, and as evidence would command the respect normally accorded proof of any fact.[8] In other words, the evidence reflected by the affidavit, beyond creation of a presumption of regularity in date-stamping incoming mail, would have

---

[7] (Court's original footnote 39.) The presumption of due delivery of the mails is predicated upon the fixed methods and systematic operation of the postal service . . . . The presumption of regularity of the Patent Office's handling of incoming mail, . . . rests on exactly the same phenomena. In sum, both presumptions have a common origin in regularity of action . . . . We see nothing suggesting that the methodology buttressing the one is any more or less foolproof than that underpinning the other. We are mindful that some presumptions are founded in part upon exceptionally strong and visible policies, which have been said to persist despite proof rebutting the factual basis for the presumption . . . . The answer here is that from aught that appears the policy reflections are in equilibrium.

[8] (Court's original footnote 53.) *Stone v. Stone*, 136 F.2d 761, 763, 78 U.S. App. D.C. 5, 7 (1943) (while presumption that public officer properly performs official duties disappears upon introduction of substantial countervailing evidence, "the basic fact that public officials usually do their duty . . . has and continues to have, throughout the action, that quality and quantity of probative value to which it is

probative value on the issue of date of receipt of appellees' applications; and even if the presumption were dispelled, that evidence would be entitled to consideration, along with appellees' own evidence, when a resolution of the issue is undertaken.[9] And, clearly, a fact-finder convinced of the integrity of the Patent Office's mail-handling procedures would inexorably be led to the conclusion that appellees' applications simply did not arrive until the date which was stamped on them.[10]

In the final analysis, the District Court's misstep was the treatment of the parties' opposing affidavits as a contest postulating a question of law as to the relative strength of the two presumptions[11] rather than as a prelude to conflicting evidence necessitating a trial. Viewed as the mere procedural devices we hold that they are, presumptions are incapable of waging war among themselves.[12] Even

---

entitled, entirely apart from any presumption; just as is true of any other fact which is based upon common experience.") . . . .

[9] (Court's original footnote 54.) And, of course, proven facts sufficient to raise initially a presumption of arrival in due course of the mails are entitled to like value as evidence tending to show such an arrival.

[10] (Court's original footnote 55.) In *Wolfgang v. Burrows*, 181 F.2d 630, 631, 86 U.S. App. D.C. 340, 341 (1950), we held that a presumption — there of ownership — "must be countervailed by substantial evidence . . . . The countervailing evidence must, if believed by the trier of the fact issues, establish facts from which reasonable minds can draw but one inference" (citations omitted). By our assessment, the evidence with which the Commissioner is armed amply meets the test. It delineates standard operations, engaging a substantial body of personnel, by which the large volume of Patent Office mail is receipt-dated. Should that evidence be accepted by the trier of fact as satisfactory proof of what the process purports to be — a process reliably recording the date of receipt of each item of mail — the only conclusion rationally possible is that appellees' applications did not reach the Patent Office prior to the date recorded. Should, on the other hand, the finding be that in the instant situation the postal system lived up to the promise of delivery in due course, the conclusion that appellees' applications arrived within the statutory period would be inevitable.

[11] (Court's original footnote 56.) . . . What seems wholly an issue of fact — the actual date of receipt of the applications by the Patent Office — cannot properly be treated as an issue of law. Our disposition poses no dilemma for the parties or the factfinder. The key, we think, is our treatment of the parties' opposing factual presentations ultimately as conflicting evidence rather than simply as presumptions competing for supremacy. The parties would submit their evidence, and findings would be rendered according to the preponderance — the greater persuasive power. Initially the evidence would be gauged for its direct import; basically, the details of the mailing of the applications and those of the receipting of mail in the Patent Office. Assuming satisfaction in these respects, it seems apparent that the conclusion on the pivotal issue — as to whether the applications arrived in due course of the mails or instead on the receipt-date stamped on them — would depend upon a conviction as to the more reliable functioning, in the circumstances of the case, of the two business operations in question — the handling of the mails on the one hand and the date-stamping of Patent Office mail on the other.

The District Court did not have this role when it decided the case on cross-motions for summary judgment. By the same token, it could not have derived from a mere reading of the parties' opposing affidavits the benefits normally accruing from a trial featuring the affidavits as live witnesses. And lest it be forgotten, in the context of a trial there would be ample opportunity for each side to conduct all relevant probes into the factual positions of the other.

[12] (Court's original footnote 58.) "[P]resumptions do not conflict. The evidentiary facts, free from any rule of law as to the duty of producing evidence, may tend to opposite inferences, which may be said to conflict. But the rule of law which prescribes this duty of production either is or is not at a given time upon a given party. If it is, and he removes it by producing contrary evidence, then that presumption, as a rule of law, is satisfied and disappears; he may then by his evidence succeed in creating another presumption which now puts the same duty upon the other party, who may in turn be able to dispose of it satisfactorily. But the same duty cannot at the same time exist for both parties, and thus in strictness the presumptions raising the duty cannot conflict. There may be successive shiftings of the duty, by

more importantly, the court's disposition of the case on a legal ruling disregarded the divergent inferences which the evidentiary tenders warranted, and consequently the inappropriateness of a resolution of the opposing claims by summary judgment. As only recently we said, "[t]he court's function is not to resolve any factual issue, but to ascertain whether any exists, and all doubts in that regard must be resolved against summary judgment." Here the District Court was presented with an issue of material fact as to the date on which appellees' applications were received by the Patent Office, and summary judgment was not in order.

The judgment appealed from is accordingly reversed, and the case is remanded to the District Court for further proceedings. The cross-motions for summary judgment will be denied, and the case will be set down for trial on the merits in regular course.

So ordered.

Fahy, Senior Circuit Judge (dissenting):

I am in essential agreement with Judge Waddy of the District Court. The evidence reflected in the affidavit relied upon by the Patent Office in my opinion is not sufficient to overcome the strong presumption arising from the evidence reflected in the affidavits filed by appellee — a presumption of law that the applications were received by the Patent Office in regular course of the mails, that is, not later than March 6, 1973:

> Where, as in this case, matter is transmitted by the United States mails, properly addressed and postage fully prepaid, there is a strong presumption that it will be received by the addressee in the ordinary course of the mails . . . . While the presumption is a rebuttable one it is a very strong presumption and can only be rebutted by specific facts and not by invoking another presumption . . . .

In *Charlson Realty Company v. United States*, 384 F.2d 434, 181 Ct.Cl. 262 (1967), the Court of Claims considered at length the relative weight of this mail presumption compared with a file-stamped date of receipt. In the opinion of Judge Skelton, for himself, Chief Judge Cowen and Senior Judge Jones, the latter also concurring separately, it is stated:

> The evidence as to the habit and custom of the court's officers and employees in handling the mail is negative evidence and has no appreciable value in proving the omission or commission of a specific act at a particular time when there is a presumption to the contrary as in this case. . . .
>
> . . . [T]o overcome the strong presumption of the arrival of a letter in due course of the mails, the countervailing evidence must show the contrary to be true by direct and positive proof of affirmative facts.

Id. at 444–445.

---

means of presumptions successively invoked by each; but it is not the one presumption that overturns the other, for the mere introduction of sufficient evidence would have the same effect in stopping the operation of the presumption as a rule of law.' 9 J. Wigmore, Evidence § 2493 at 292 (3d ed. 1940).

Judge Nichols concurred, placing his position upon his view of the intent of Congress in the situation presented.

* * *

There are cases, as the court's opinion again demonstrates, in which the facts which give rise to the mail presumption are considered simply as part of the total evidentiary situation bearing upon the issue of the time of receipt of a mailed paper. The opinion of the court in the present case so considers the facts reflected in the respective affidavits. But the authorities relied upon for submitting to the fact-finder in this manner the issue referred to are not in my view helpful in the situation before us now. The agency of the Government here involved contemplates the use of the mails for the conduct of business with it, as appellees did. The applications were air-mailed at Hartford, Connecticut, March 2, in ample time to be received by the Patent Office by March 6, giving rise to the strong presumption that they actually were so received, a presumption not lightly to be rebutted. The inadequacy of the evidence reflected in the Patent Office affidavit to accomplish rebuttal I think is demonstrable, even if it be assumed that the procedures detailed in the affidavit did more than raise a competing presumption and constituted affirmative evidence the applications were not physically received at the Patent Office building until March 8; for Rule 6(b) of the Rules of Practice and Procedure in Patent Cases, 37 C.F.R. § 1.6(b) (1974), states:

> Mail placed in the Patent Office pouch up to midnight on weekdays, excepting Saturdays and holidays, by the Post Office at Washington, D.C., serving the Patent Office, is considered as having been received in the Patent Office on the day it was so placed in the pouch.

The affidavit relied on by the Patent Office does not reflect evidence indicating when these applications were placed in the Patent Office pouch at the Washington, D.C., Post Office serving the Patent Office. Giving the affidavit an interpretation favorable to appellant it can be read to indicate that some bags or pouches are marked with the date that they are readied at the Post Office to go to the Patent Office if that date is different from the date of physical delivery to the Patent Office. Under this reading, other bags when received at the Patent Office are unmarked. More importantly, the practice and custom set forth in the affidavit of the Patent Office shows nothing as to the time the particular applications in suit were placed in the Patent Office pouch at the Washington Post Office, and thus received under Rule 6(b). The affidavit shows only that they were stamped "March 8" at the Patent Office. Their actual movement or location at any time prior thereto is not indicated by the Patent Office affidavit.

The case was in the above posture when the parties submitted it to the District Court for decision on cross-motions for summary judgment. Since the strong presumption available to appellees was not rebutted by the evidence reflected in the affidavit relied upon by the appellant the motion of appellees was properly granted by the court. No genuine issue of material fact required its denial and appellees were entitled to judgment as a matter of law. Rule 56(d), Fed.R.Civ.P. I would affirm and, accordingly,

I respectfully dissent.

[5]   Presumptions Against Criminal Defendants

It has generally been accepted that there are *no true presumptions* in criminal actions relative to the prosecution's case *against* the *criminal defendant.* Presumptions would violate defendants' Sixth Amendment right to trial by jury and due process rights under the Fifth or Fourteenth Amendment to have the prosecution establish, beyond a reasonable doubt, every fact necessary to prove the elements of the offenses charged. *See In re Winship*, 397 U.S. 358 (1970). The trial judge may not enter a directed verdict against the defendant if the defendant fails to come forward with evidence to meet the presumed fact. Moreover, until recent decisions from the Supreme Court (which will be discussed below), it has also been accepted that the trial judge may not instruct the jury that it must find certain facts to be true from proof of other facts. Although judges have not used conclusive presumptions in jury instructions, trial judges have still instructed jurors that if they find Fact A (the basic fact) to have been established, they also *may* find Fact B (the presumed fact) to be true. Not being mandatory in its effect, the presumption is nothing more than a permissible inference, and the instruction on it is the equivalent of judicial comment on the evidence. This parallel with judicial comment is particularly appropriate after the Supreme Court's opinion in *Ulster County Court v. Allen.*

ULSTER COUNTY COURT v. ALLEN
United States Supreme Court
442 U.S. 140 (1979)

Mr. Justice Stevens delivered the opinion of the Court.

A New York statute provides that, with certain exceptions, the presence of a firearm in an automobile is presumptive evidence of its illegal possession by all persons then occupying the vehicle. The United States Court of Appeals for the Second Circuit held that respondents may challenge the constitutionality of this statute in a federal habeas corpus proceeding and that the statute is "unconstitutional on its face." . . . We granted certiorari to review these holdings and also to consider whether the statute is constitutional in its application to respondents. . . .

Four persons, three adult males (respondents) and a 16-year-old girl (Jane Doe, who is not a respondent here), were jointly tried on charges that they possessed two loaded handguns, a loaded machinegun, and over a pound of heroin found in a Chevrolet in which they were riding when it was stopped for speeding on the New York Thruway shortly after noon on March 28, 1973. The two large-caliber handguns, which together with their ammunition weighed approximately six pounds, were seen through the window of the car by the investigating police officer. They were positioned crosswise in an open handbag on either the front floor or the front seat of the car on the passenger side where Jane Doe was sitting. Jane Doe admitted that the handbag was hers. The machinegun and the heroin were discovered in the trunk after the police pried it open. The car had been borrowed from the driver's brother earlier that day; the key to the trunk could not be found in the car or on the person of any of its occupants, although there was testimony that two of the occupants had placed something in the trunk before embarking in the borrowed car. The jury convicted all four of possession of the handguns and acquitted them of possession of the contents of the trunk.

Counsel for all four defendants objected to the introduction into evidence of the two handguns, the machinegun, and the drugs, arguing that the State had not adequately demonstrated a connection between their clients and the contraband. The trial court overruled the objection, relying on the presumption of possession created by the New York statute. Because that presumption does not apply if a weapon is found "upon the person" of one of the occupants of the car, the three male defendants also moved to dismiss the charges relating to the handguns on the ground that the guns were found on the person of Jane Doe. Respondents made this motion both at the close of the prosecution's case and at the close of all evidence. The trial judge twice denied it, concluding that the applicability of the "on the person" exception was a question of fact for the jury.

At the close of the trial, the judge instructed the jurors that they were entitled to infer possession from the defendants' presence in the car. He did not make any reference to the "on the person" exception in his explanation of the statutory presumption, nor did any of the defendants object to this omission or request alternative or additional instructions on the subject.

Defendants filed a post-trial motion in which they challenged the constitutionality of the New York statute as applied in this case. The challenge was made in support of their argument that the evidence, apart from the presumption, was insufficient to sustain the convictions. The motion was denied, and the convictions were affirmed by the Appellate Division without opinion.

* * *

Respondents filed a petition for a writ of habeas corpus in the United States District Court for the Southern District of New York contending that they were denied due process of law by the application of the statutory presumption of possession. The District Court issued the writ, holding that respondents had not "deliberately bypassed" their federal claim by their actions at trial and that the mere presence of two guns in a woman's handbag in a car could not reasonably give rise to the inference that they were in the possession of three other persons in the car.

The Court of Appeals for the Second Circuit affirmed . . . without deciding whether the presumption was constitutional as applied in this case. It concluded that the statute is unconstitutional on its face because the "presumption obviously sweeps within its compass (1) many occupants who may not know they are riding with a gun (which may be out of their sight), and (2) many who may be aware of the presence of the gun but not permitted access to it."

* * *

Inferences and presumptions are a staple of our adversary system of factfinding. It is often necessary for the trier of fact to determine the existence of an element of the crime — that is, an "ultimate" or "elemental" fact — from the existence of one or more "evidentiary" or "basic" facts. . . . The value of these evidentiary devices, and their validity under the Due Process Clause, vary from case to case, however, depending on the strength of the connection between the particular basic and elemental facts involved and on the degree to which the device curtails the factfinder's freedom to assess the evidence independently. Nonetheless, in criminal cases, the ultimate test of any device's constitutional validity in a given case remains constant: the device must not undermine the factfinder's responsibility at trial, based on evidence adduced by the State, to find the ultimate facts beyond a reasonable doubt. *See In re Winship*, 397 U.S. 358, 364.

The most common evidentiary device is the entirely permissive inference or presumption, which allows — but does not require — the trier of fact to infer the elemental fact from proof by the prosecutor of the basic one and that places no burden of any kind on the defendant. . . . In that situation the basic fact may constitute prima facie evidence of the elemental fact . . . . When reviewing this type of device, the Court has required the party challenging it to demonstrate its invalidity as applied to him. . . . Because this permissive presumption leaves the trier of fact free to credit or reject the inference and does not shift the burden of proof, it affects the application of the "beyond a reasonable doubt" standard only if, under the facts of the case, there is no rational way the trier could make the connection permitted by the inference. For only in that situation is there any risk that an explanation of the permissible inference to a jury, or its use by a jury, has caused the presumptively rational factfinder to make an erroneous factual determination.

A mandatory presumption is a far more troublesome evidentiary device. For it may affect not only the strength of the "no reasonable doubt" burden but also the placement of that burden; it tells the trier that he or they must find the elemental fact upon proof of the basic fact, at least unless the defendant has come forward with some evidence to rebut the presumed connection between the two facts. . . .[13]

---

[13]   (Court's original footnote 16.) This class of more or less mandatory presumptions can be subdivided into two parts: presumptions that merely shift the burden of production to the defendant, following the satisfaction of which the ultimate burden of persuasion returns to the prosecution; and presumptions that entirely shift the burden of proof to the defendant. The mandatory presumptions examined by our cases have almost uniformly fit into the former subclass, in that they never totally removed the ultimate burden of proof beyond a reasonable doubt from the prosecution. . . .

To the extent that a presumption imposes an extremely low burden of production — *e.g.*, being satisfied by "any" evidence — it may well be that its impact is no greater than that of a permissive inference, and it may be proper to analyze it as such. *See generally Mullaney v. Wilbur*, 421 U.S. 684.

In deciding what type of inference or presumption is involved in a case, the jury instructions will generally be controlling, although their interpretation may require recourse to the statute involved and the cases decided under it. *Turner v. United States* provides a useful illustration of the different types of presumptions. It analyzes the constitutionality of two different presumption statutes (one mandatory and one permissive) as they apply to the basic fact of possession of both heroin and cocaine, and the presumed facts of importation and distribution of narcotic drugs. The jury was charged essentially in the terms of the two statutes.

The importance of focusing attention on the precise presentation of the presumption to the jury and the scope of that presumption is illustrated by a comparison of *United States v. Gainey*, 380 U.S. 63, with *United States v. Romano*. Both cases involved statutory presumptions based on proof that the defendant was present at the site of an illegal still. In *Gainey* the Court sustained a conviction "for carrying on" the business of the distillery in violation of 26 U.S.C. § 5601(a)(4) [26 U.S.C.S. § 5601(a)(4)], whereas in *Romano*, the Court set aside a conviction for being in "possession, or custody, or . . . control" of such

In this situation, the Court has generally examined the presumption on its face to determine the extent to which the basic and elemental facts coincide. . . . To the extent that the trier of fact is forced to abide by the presumption, and may not reject it based on an independent evaluation of the particular facts presented by the State, the analysis of the presumption's constitutional validity is logically divorced from those facts and based on the presumption's accuracy in the run of cases. It is for this reason that the Court has held it irrelevant in analyzing a mandatory presumption, but not in analyzing a purely permissive one, that there is ample evidence in the record other than the presumption to support a conviction. . . .

Without determining whether the presumption in this case was mandatory, the Court of Appeals analyzed it on its face as if it were. In fact, it was not, as the New York Court of Appeals had earlier pointed out.

The trial judge's instructions make it clear that the presumption was merely a part of the prosecution's case, that it gave rise to a permissive inference available only in certain circumstances, rather than a mandatory conclusion of possession, and that it could be ignored by the jury even if there was no affirmative proof offered by defendants in rebuttal. The judge explained that possession could be actual or constructive, but that constructive possession could not exist without the intent and ability to exercise control or dominion over the weapons. He also carefully instructed the jury that there is a mandatory presumption of innocence in favor of the defendants that controls unless it, as the exclusive trier of fact, is satisfied beyond a reasonable doubt that the defendants possessed the handguns in the manner described by the judge. In short, the instructions plainly directed the jury to consider all the circumstances tending to support or contradict the inference that all four occupants of the car had possession of the two loaded handguns and to decide the matter for itself without regard to how much evidence the defendants introduced.

Our cases considering the validity of permissive statutory presumptions such as the one involved here have rested on an evaluation of the presumption as applied to the record before the Court. None suggests that a court should pass on the

---

a distillery in violation of § 560l(a)(1). The difference in outcome was attributable to two important differences between the cases. Because the statute involved in *Gainey* was a sweeping prohibition of almost any activity associated with the still, whereas the *Romano* statute involved only one narrow aspect of the total undertaking, there was a much higher probability that mere presence could support an inference of guilt in the former case than in the latter.

Of perhaps greater importance, however, was the difference between the trial judge's instructions to the jury in the two cases. In *Gainey*, the judge had explained that the presumption was permissive; it did not require the jury to convict the defendant even if it was convinced that he was present at the site. On the contrary, the instructions made it clear that presence was only "a circumstance to be considered along with all the other circumstances in the case." As we emphasized, the "jury was thus specifically told that the statutory inference was not conclusive." 380 U.S., at 69–70. In *Romano*, the trial judge told the jury that the defendant's presence at the still "shall be deemed sufficient evidence to authorize conviction." 382 U.S., at 138. Although there was other evidence of guilt, that instruction authorized conviction even if the jury disbelieved all of the testimony except the proof of presence at the site. This Court's holding that the statutory presumption could not support the *Romano* conviction was thus dependent, in part, on the specific instructions given by the trial judge. Under those instructions it was necessary to decide whether, regardless of the specific circumstances of the particular case, the statutory presumption adequately supported the guilty verdict.

constitutionality of this kind of statute "on its face." It was error for the Court of Appeals to make such a determination in this case.

III

As applied to the facts of this case, the presumption of possession is entirely rational. Notwithstanding the Court of Appeals' analysis, respondents were not "hitch-hikers or other casual passengers," and the guns were neither "a few inches in length" nor "out of [respondents'] sight." . . . The argument against possession by any of the respondents was predicated solely on the fact that the guns were in Jane Doe's pocketbook. But several circumstances — which, not surprisingly, her counsel repeatedly emphasized in his questions and his argument — made it highly improbable that she was the sole custodian of those weapons.

Even if it was reasonable to conclude that she had placed the guns in her purse before the car was stopped by police, the facts strongly suggest that Jane Doe was not the only person able to exercise dominion over them. The two guns were too large to be concealed in her handbag. The bag was consequently open, and part of one of the guns was in plain view, within easy access of the driver of the car and even, perhaps, of the other two respondents who were riding in the rear seat.

Moreover, it is highly improbable that the loaded guns belonged to Jane Doe or that she was solely responsible for their being in her purse. As a 16-year-old girl in the company of three adult men she was the least likely of the four to be carrying one, let alone two, heavy handguns. It is far more probable that she relied on the pocketknife found in her brassiere for any necessary self-protection. Under these circumstances, it was not unreasonable for her counsel to argue and for the jury to infer that when the car was halted for speeding, the other passengers in the car anticipated the risk of a search and attempted to conceal their weapons in a pocketbook in the front seat. The inference is surely more likely than the notion that these weapons were the sole property of the 16-year-old girl.

Under these circumstances, the jury would have been entirely reasonable in rejecting the suggestion — which, incidentally, defense counsel did not even advance in their closing arguments to the jury — that the handguns were in the sole possession of Jane Doe. Assuming that the jury did reject it, the case is tantamount to one in which the guns were lying on the floor or the seat of the car in the plain view of the three other occupants of the automobile. In such a case, it is surely rational to infer that each of the respondents was fully aware of the presence of the guns and had both the ability and the intent to exercise dominion and control over the weapons. The application of the statutory presumption in this case therefore comports with the standard laid down in *Tot v. United States*, 319 U.S., at 467, and restated in *Leary v. United States*, 395 U.S., at 36. For there is a "rational connection" between the basic facts that the prosecution proved and the ultimate fact presumed, and the latter is "more likely than not to flow from" the former.

Respondents argue, however, that the validity of the New York presumption must be judged by a "reasonable doubt" test rather than the "more likely than not" standard employed in *Leary*.[14] Under the more stringent test, it is argued that a statutory presumption must be rejected unless the evidence necessary to invoke the inference is sufficient for a rational jury to find the inferred fact beyond a reasonable doubt . . . . Respondents' argument again overlooks the distinction between a permissive presumption on which the prosecution is entitled to rely as one not necessarily sufficient part of its proof and a mandatory presumption which the jury must accept even if it is the sole evidence of an element of the offense.[15]

In the later situation, since the prosecution bears the burden of establishing guilt, it may not rest its case entirely on a presumption unless the fact proved is sufficient to support the inference of guilt beyond a reasonable doubt. But in the former situation, the prosecution may rely on all of the evidence in the record to meet the reasonable-doubt standard. There is no more reason to require a permissive statutory presumption to meet a reasonable-doubt standard before it may be permitted to play any part in a trial than there is to require that degree of probative force for other relevant evidence before it may be admitted. As long as it is clear that the presumption is not the sole and sufficient basis for a finding of guilt, it need only satisfy the test described in *Leary*.

The permissive presumption, as used in this case, satisfied the *Leary* test. And, as already noted, the New York Court of Appeals has concluded that the record as a whole was sufficient to establish guilt beyond a reasonable doubt.

The judgment is reversed.

So ordered.

MR. CHIEF JUSTICE BURGER, concurring. [Opinion omitted].

MR. JUSTICE POWELL, with whom MR. JUSTICE BRENNAN, MR. JUSTICE STEWART, and MR. JUSTICE MARSHALL join, dissenting.

I agree with the Court that there is no procedural bar to our considering the underlying constitutional question presented by this case. I am not in agreement, however, with the Court's conclusion that the presumption as charged to the jury in this case meets the constitutional requirements of due process as set forth in our prior decisions. On the contrary, an individual's mere presence in an automobile

---

[14] (Court's original footnote 28.) "The upshot of *Tot* . . . is, we think, that a criminal statutory presumption must be regarded as 'irrational' or 'arbitrary,' and hence unconstitutional, unless it can at least be said with substantial assurance that the presumed fact is more likely than not to flow from the proved fact on which it is made to depend." 395 U.S., at 36.

[15] (Court's original footnote 29.) The dissenting argument rests on the assumption that "the jury [may have] rejected all of the prosecution's evidence concerning the location and origin of the guns." . . . Even if that assumption were plausible, the jury was plainly told that it was free to disregard the presumption. But the dissent's assumption is not plausible; for if the jury rejected the testimony describing where the guns were found, it would necessarily also have rejected the only evidence in the record proving that the guns were found in the car. The conclusion that the jury attached significance to the particular location of the handguns follows inexorably from the acquittal on the charge of possession of the machinegun and heroin in the trunk.

where there is a handgun does not even make it "more likely than not" that the individual possesses the weapon.

I

In the criminal law, presumptions are used to encourage the jury to find certain facts, with respect to which no direct evidence is presented, solely because other facts have been proved. . . . The purpose of such presumptions is plain: Like certain other jury instructions, they provide guidance for jurors' thinking in considering the evidence laid before them. Once in a juryroom, jurors necessarily draw inferences from the evidence — both direct and circumstantial. Through the use of presumptions, certain inferences are commended to the attention of jurors by legislatures or courts.

Legitimate guidance of a jury's deliberations is an indispensable part of our criminal justice system. Nonetheless, the use of presumptions in criminal cases poses at least two distinct perils for defendants' constitutional rights. The Court accurately identifies the first of these as being the danger of interference with "the factfinder's responsibility at trial, based on evidence adduced by the State, to find the ultimate facts beyond a reasonable doubt." . . . If the jury is instructed that it must infer some ultimate fact (that is, some element of the offense) from proof of other facts unless the defendant disproves the ultimate fact by a preponderance of the evidence, then the presumption shifts the burden of proof to the defendant concerning the element thus inferred.[16]

But I do not agree with the Court's conclusion that the only constitutional difficulty with presumptions lies in the danger of lessening the burden of proof the prosecution must bear. As the Court notes, the presumptions thus far reviewed by the Court have not shifted the burden of persuasion, . . . instead, they either have required only that the defendant produce some evidence to rebut the inference suggested by the prosecution's evidence, . . . or merely have been suggestions to the jury that it would be sensible to draw certain conclusions on the basis of the evidence presented.[17] . . . Evolving from our decisions, therefore, is a second standard for judging the constitutionality of criminal presumptions which is based — not on the constitutional requirement that the State be put to its proof — but rather on the due process rule that when the jury is encouraged to make factual inferences, those inferences must reflect some valid general observation about the

---

[16] (Court's original footnote 2.) The Court suggests that presumptions that shift the burden of persuasion to the defendant in this way can be upheld provided that "the fact proved is sufficient to support the inference of guilt beyond a reasonable doubt." . . . As the present case involves no shifting of the burden of persuasion, the constitutional restrictions on such presumptions are not before us, and I express no views on them.

It may well be that even those presumptions that do not shift the burden of persuasion cannot be used to prove an element of the offense, if the facts proved would not permit a reasonable mind to find the presumed fact beyond a reasonable doubt. My conclusion in Part II, infra, makes it unnecessary for me to address this concern here.

[17] (Court's original footnote 3.) The Court suggests as the touchstone for its analysis a distinction between "mandatory" and "permissive" presumptions. . . . I have found no recognition in the Court's prior decisions that this distinction is important in analyzing presumptions used in criminal cases. . . .

natural connection between events as they occur in our society.

This due process rule was first articulated by the Court in *Tot v. United States*, [319 U.S. 463], in which the Court reviewed the constitutionality of § 2(f) of the Federal Firearms Act. That statute provided in part that "possession of a firearm or ammunition by any . . . person [who has been convicted of a crime of violence] shall be presumptive evidence that such firearm or ammunition was shipped or transported [in interstate or foreign commerce]." As the Court interpreted the presumption, it placed upon a defendant only the obligation of presenting some exculpatory evidence concerning the origins of a firearm or ammunition, once the Government proved that the defendant had possessed the weapon and had been convicted of a crime of violence. Noting that juries must be permitted to infer from one fact the existence of another essential to guilt, "if reason and experience support the inference," 319 U.S. at 467, the Court concluded that under some circumstances juries may be guided in making these inferences by legislative or common-law presumptions, even though they may be based "upon a view of relation broader than that a jury might take in a specific case," *id.*, at 468 . . . .

Subsequently, in *Leary v. United States*, 395 U.S. 6 (1969), the Court reaffirmed and refined the due process requirement of *Tot* that inferences specifically commended to the attention of jurors must reflect generally accepted connections between related events. At issue in *Leary* was the constitutionality of a federal statute making it a crime to receive, conceal, buy, or sell marijuana illegally brought into the United States, knowing it to have been illegally imported. The statute provided that mere possession of marijuana "shall be deemed sufficient evidence to authorize conviction unless the defendant explains his possession to the satisfaction of the jury." After reviewing the Court's decisions in *Tot v. United States*, and other criminal presumption cases, Mr. Justice Harlan, writing for the Court, concluded "that a criminal statutory presumption must be regarded as 'irrational' or 'arbitrary,' and hence unconstitutional, unless it can at least be said with substantial assurance that the presumed fact is more likely than not to flow from the proved fact on which it is made to depend." 395 U.S., at 36. The Court invalidated the statute, finding there to be insufficient basis in fact for the conclusion that those who possess marijuana are more likely than not to know that it was imported illegally.

* * *

In sum, our decisions uniformly have recognized that due process requires more than merely that the prosecution be put to its proof.[18] In addition, the Constitution restricts the court in its charge to the jury by requiring that, when particular factual inferences are recommended to the jury, those factual inferences be accurate reflections of what history, common sense, and experience tell us about the relations between events in our society. Generally, this due process rule has been articulated as requiring that the truth of the inferred fact be more likely than not whenever the premise for the inference is true. Thus, to be constitutional a presumption must be at least more likely than not true.

---

[18] (Court's original footnote 6.) The Court apparently disagrees, contending that "the factfinder's responsibility . . . to find the ultimate facts beyond a reasonable doubt" is the only constitutional restraint upon the use of criminal presumptions at trial. . . .

II

In the present case, the jury was told:

> Our Penal Law also provides that the presence in an automobile of any machine gun or of any handgun or firearm which is loaded is presumptive evidence of their unlawful possession. In other words, [under] these presumptions or this latter presumption upon proof of the presence of the machine gun and the hand weapons, you may infer and draw a conclusion that such prohibited weapon was possessed by each of the defendants who occupied the automobile at the time when such instruments were found. The presumption or presumptions is effective only so long as there is no substantial evidence contradicting the conclusion flowing from the presumption, and the presumption is said to disappear when such contradictory evidence is adduced.

Undeniably, the presumption charged in this case encouraged the jury to draw a particular factual inference regardless of any other evidence presented: to infer that respondents possessed the weapons found in the automobile "upon proof of the presence of the machine gun and the hand weapon" and proof that respondents "occupied the automobile at the time such instruments were found." I believe that the presumption thus charged was unconstitutional because it did not fairly reflect what common sense and experience tell us about passengers in automobiles and the possession of handguns. People present in automobiles where there are weapons simply are not "more likely than not" the possessors of those weapons.

Under New York law, "to possess" is "to have physical possession or otherwise to exercise dominion or control over tangible property." . . . Plainly, the mere presence of an individual in an automobile — without more — does not indicate that he exercises "dominion or control over" everything within it. As the Court of Appeals noted, there are countless situations in which individuals are invited as guests into vehicles the contents of which they know nothing about, much less have control over. Similarly, those who invite others into their automobile do not generally search them to determine what they may have on their person; nor do they insist that any handguns be identified and placed within reach of the occupants of the automobile. Indeed, handguns are particularly susceptible to concealment and therefore are less likely than are other objects to be observed by those in an automobile.

* * *

As I understand it, the Court today does not contend that in general those who are present in automobiles are more likely than not to possess any gun contained within their vehicles. It argues, however, that the nature of the presumption here involved requires that we look, not only to the immediate facts upon which the jury was encouraged to base its inference, but to the other facts "proved" by the prosecution as well. The Court suggests that this is the proper approach when reviewing what it calls "permissive" presumptions because the jury was urged "to consider all the circumstances tending to support or contradict the inference." . . .

It seems to me that the Court mischaracterizes the function of the presumption charged in this case. As it acknowledges was the case in *Romano, below,* the "instruction authorized conviction even if the jury disbelieved all of the testimony except the proof of presence" in the automobile.[19] The Court nevertheless relies on all of the evidence introduced by the prosecution and argues that the "permissive" presumption could not have prejudiced defendants. The possibility that the jury disbelieved all of this evidence, and relied on the presumption, is simply ignored.

I agree that the circumstances relied upon by the Court in determining the plausibility of the presumption charged in this case would have made it reasonable for the jury to "infer that each of the respondents was fully aware of the presence of the guns and had both the ability and the intent to exercise dominion and control over the weapons." But the jury was told that it could conclude that respondents possessed the weapons found therein from proof of the mere fact of respondents' presence in the automobile. For all we know, the jury rejected all of the prosecution's evidence concerning the location and origin of the guns, and based its conclusion that respondents possessed the weapons solely upon its belief that respondents had been present in the automobile.[20] For purposes of reviewing the constitutionality of the presumption at issue here, we must assume that this was the case.

The Court's novel approach in this case appears to contradict prior decisions of this Court reviewing such presumptions. Under the Court's analysis, whenever it is determined that an inference is "permissive," the only question is whether, in light of all of the evidence adduced at trial, the inference recommended to the jury is a reasonable one. The Court has never suggested that the inquiry into the rational basis of a permissible inference may be circumvented in this manner. Quite the contrary, the Court has required that the "evidence *necessary to invoke the inference* [be] sufficient for a rational juror to find the inferred fact . . . ." *Barnes v. United States,* 412 U.S., at 843 (emphasis supplied) . . . . Under the presumption charged in this case, the only evidence necessary to invoke the inference was the presence of the weapons in the automobile with respondents — an inference that is plainly irrational.

---

[19] (Court's original footnote 7.) In commending the presumption to the jury, the court gave no instruction that would have required a finding of possession to be based on anything more than mere presence in the automobile. Thus, the jury was not instructed that it should infer that respondents possessed the handguns only if it found that the guns were too large to be concealed in Jane Doe's handbag; that the guns accordingly were in the plain view of respondents; that the weapons were within "easy access of the driver of the car and even, perhaps, of the other two respondents who were riding in the rear seat;" that it was unlikely that Jane Doe was solely responsible for the placement of the weapons in her purse; or that the case was "tantamount to one in which the guns were lying on the floor or the seat of the car in the plain view of the three other occupants of the automobile."

[20] (Court's original footnote 8.) The Court is therefore mistaken in its conclusion that, because "respondents were not 'hitch-hikers or other casual passengers,' and the guns were neither 'a few inches in length' nor 'out of [respondents'] sight,'" reference to these possibilities is inappropriate in considering the constitutionality of the presumption as charged in this case. . . . To be sure, respondents' challenge is to the presumption as charged to the jury in this case. But in assessing its application here, we are not free, as the Court apparently believes, to disregard the possibility that the jury may have disbelieved all other evidence supporting an inference of possession. The jury may have concluded that respondents — like hitchhikers — had only an incidental relationship to the auto in which they were traveling, or that, contrary to some of the testimony at trial, the weapons were indeed out of respondents' sight.

In sum, it seems to me that the Court today ignores the teaching of our prior decisions. By speculating about what the jury may have done with the factual inference thrust upon it, the Court in effect assumes away the inference altogether, constructing a rule that permits the use of any inference — no matter how irrational in itself — provided that otherwise there is sufficient evidence in the record to support a finding of guilt. Applying this novel analysis to the present case, the Court upholds the use of a presumption that it makes no effort to defend in isolation. In substance, the court — applying an unarticulated harmless-error standard — simply finds that the respondents were guilty as charged. They may well have been, but rather than acknowledging this rationale, the Court seems to have made new law with respect to presumptions that could seriously jeopardize a defendant's right to a fair trial. Accordingly, I dissent.

[6]   Constitutionality of Presumptions

In *Michael H. v. Gerald D.*, the United States Supreme Court found that a party negatively impacted by a presumption is not denied due process because the presumption is conclusive or irrebuttable.

MICHAEL H. v. GERALD D.
United States Supreme Court
491 U.S. 110 (1989)

JUSTICE SCALIA announced the judgment of the Court and delivered an opinion, in which THE CHIEF JUSTICE joins, and in all but footnote 6 of which JUSTICE O'CONNOR and JUSTICE KENNEDY join.

Under California law, a child born to a married woman living with her husband is presumed to be a child of the marriage. Cal. Evid. Code Ann. § 621 (West Supp. 1989). The presumption of legitimacy may be rebutted only by the husband or wife, and then only in limited circumstances. *Ibid.* The instant appeal presents the claim that this presumption infringes upon the due process rights of a man who wishes to establish his paternity of a child born to the wife of another man, and the claim that it infringes upon the constitutional right of the child to maintain a relationship with her natural father.

I

The facts of this case are, we must hope, extraordinary. On May 9, 1976, in Las Vegas, Nevada, Carole D., an international model, and Gerald D., a top executive in a French oil company, were married. The couple established a home in Playa del Rey, California, in which they resided as husband and wife when one or the other was not out of the country on business. In the summer of 1978, Carole became involved in an adulterous affair with a neighbor, Michael H. In September 1980, she conceived a child, Victoria D., who was born on May 11, 1981. Gerald was listed as father on the birth certificate and has always held Victoria out to the world as his daughter. Soon after delivery of the child, however, Carole informed Michael that she believed he might be the father.

In the first three years of her life, Victoria remained always with Carole, but found herself within a variety of quasi-family units. In October 1981, Gerald moved to New York City to pursue his business interests, but Carole chose to remain in California. At the end of that month, Carole and Michael had blood tests of themselves and Victoria, which showed a 98.07% probability that Michael was Victoria's father. In January 1982, Carole visited Michael in St. Thomas, where his primary business interests were based. There Michael held Victoria out as his child. In March, however, Carole left Michael and returned to California, where she took up residence with yet another man, Scott K. Later that spring, and again in the summer, Carole and Victoria spent time with Gerald in New York City, as well as on vacation in Europe. In the fall, they returned to Scott in California.

In November 1982, rebuffed in his attempts to visit Victoria, Michael filed a filiation action in California Superior Court to establish his paternity and right to visitation. In March 1983, the court appointed an attorney and guardian ad litem to represent Victoria's interests. Victoria then filed a cross-complaint asserting that if she had more than one psychological or de facto father, she was entitled to maintain her filial relationship, with all of the attendant rights, duties, and obligations, with both. In May 1983, Carole filed a motion for summary judgment. During this period, from March through July 1983, Carole was again living with Gerald in New York. In August, however, she returned to California, became involved once again with Michael, and instructed her attorneys to remove the summary judgment motion from the calendar.

For the ensuing eight months, when Michael was not in St. Thomas he lived with Carole and Victoria in Carole's apartment in Los Angeles and held Victoria out as his daughter. In April 1984, Carole and Michael signed a stipulation that Michael was Victoria's natural father. Carole left Michael the next month, however, and instructed her attorneys not to file the stipulation. In June 1984, Carole reconciled with Gerald and joined him in New York, where they now live with Victoria and two other children since born into the marriage.

In May 1984, Michael and Victoria, through her guardian ad litem, sought visitation rights for Michael pendente lite. To assist in determining whether visitation would be in Victoria's best interests, the Superior Court appointed a psychologist to evaluate Victoria, Gerald, Michael, and Carole. The psychologist recommended that Carole retain sole custody, but that Michael be allowed continued contact with Victoria pursuant to a restricted visitation schedule. The court concurred and ordered that Michael be provided with limited visitation privileges pendente lite.

On October 19, 1984, Gerald, who had intervened in the action, moved for summary judgment on the ground that under Cal.Evid.Code § 621 there were no triable issues of fact as to Victoria's paternity. This law provides that "the issue of a wife cohabiting with her husband, who is not impotent or sterile, is conclusively presumed to be a child of the marriage." Cal. Evid. Code Ann. § 621(a) (West Supp.1989). The presumption may be rebutted by blood tests, but only if a motion for such tests is made, within two years from the date of the child's birth, either by the husband or, if the natural father has filed an affidavit acknowledging paternity, by the wife. §§ 621(c) and (d).

On January 28, 1985, having found that affidavits submitted by Carole and Gerald sufficed to demonstrate that the two were cohabiting at conception and birth and that Gerald was neither sterile nor impotent, the Superior Court granted Gerald's motion for summary judgment, rejecting Michael's and Victoria's challenges to the constitutionality of § 621. The court also denied their motions for continued visitation pending the appeal under Cal. Civ. Code § 4601, which provides that a court may, in its discretion, grant "reasonable visitation rights . . . to any . . . person having an interest in the welfare of the child." Cal. Civ. Code Ann. § 4601 (West Supp. 1989). It found that allowing such visitation would "violat[e] the intention of the Legislature by impugning the integrity of the family unit." Supp. App. to Juris. Statement A-91.

On appeal, Michael asserted, inter alia, that the Superior Court's application of § 621 had violated his procedural and substantive due process rights. Victoria also raised a due process challenge to the statute, seeking to preserve her de facto relationship with Michael as well as with Gerald. She contended, in addition, that as § 621 allows the husband and, at least to a limited extent, the mother, but not the child, to rebut the presumption of legitimacy, it violates the child's right to equal protection. Finally, she asserted a right to continued visitation with Michael under § 4601. After submission of briefs and a hearing, the California Court of Appeal affirmed the judgment of the Superior Court and upheld the constitutionality of the statute. 191 Cal. App. 3d 995, 236 Cal. Rptr. 810 (1987). It interpreted that judgment, moreover, as having denied permanent visitation rights under § 4601, regarding that as the implication of the Superior Court's reliance upon § 621 and upon an earlier California case, *Vincent B. v. Joan R.*, 126 Cal. App. 3d 619, 179 Cal. Rptr. 9 (1981), *appeal dism'd*, 459 U.S. 807, 103 S. Ct. 31, 74 L. Ed. 2d 45 (1982), which had held that once an assertion of biological paternity is "determined to be legally impossible" under § 621, visitation against the wishes of the mother should be denied under § 4601. 126 Cal. App. 3d, at 627–628, 179 Cal. Rptr., at 13.

The Court of Appeal denied Michael's and Victoria's petitions for rehearing, and, on July 30, 1987, the California Supreme Court denied discretionary review. On February 29, 1988, we noted probable jurisdiction of the present appeal. 485 U.S. 903, 108 S. Ct. 1072, 99 L. Ed. 2d 232. Before us, Michael and Victoria both raise equal protection and due process challenges. We do not reach Michael's equal protection claim, however, as it was neither raised nor passed upon below. See *Bankers Life & Casualty Co. v. Crenshaw*, 486 U.S. 71, 108 S. Ct. 1645, 100 L. Ed. 2d 62 (1988).

II

The California statute that is the subject of this litigation is, in substance, more than a century old. California Code of Civ.Proc. § 1962(5), enacted in 1872, provided that "[t]he issue of a wife cohabiting with her husband, who is not impotent, is indisputably presumed to be legitimate." In 1955, the legislature amended the statute by adding the preface: "Notwithstanding any other provision of law." 1955 Cal. Stats., ch. 948, p. 1835, § 3. In 1965, when California's Evidence Code was adopted, the statute was codified as § 621, with no substantive change except replacement of the word "indisputably" with "conclusively," 1965 Cal. Stats., ch. 299,

§ 2, pp. 1297, 1308. When California adopted the Uniform Parentage Act, 1975 Cal. Stats., ch. 1244, § 11, pp. 3196–3201, codified at Cal. Civ. Code Ann. § 7000 et seq. (West 1983), it amended § 621 by replacing the word "legitimate" with the phrase "a child of the marriage" and by adding nonsterility to nonimpotence and cohabitation as a predicate for the presumption. 1975 Cal. Stats., ch. 1244, § 13, p. 3202. In 1980, the legislature again amended the statute to provide the husband an opportunity to introduce blood-test evidence in rebuttal of the presumption, 1980 Cal. Stats., ch. 1310, p. 4433; and in 1981 amended it to provide the mother such an opportunity, 1981 Cal. Stats., ch. 1180, p. 4761. In their present form, the substantive provisions of the statute are as follows:

"§ 621. Child of the marriage; notice of motion for blood tests

"(a) Except as provided in subdivision (b), the issue of a wife cohabiting with her husband, who is not impotent or sterile, is conclusively presumed to be a child of the marriage.

"(b) Notwithstanding the provisions of subdivision (a), if the court finds that the conclusions of all the experts, as disclosed by the evidence based upon blood tests performed pursuant to Chapter 2 (commencing with Section 890) of Division 7 are that the husband is not the father of the child, the question of paternity of the husband shall be resolved accordingly.

"(c) The notice of motion for blood tests under subdivision (b) may be raised by the husband not later than two years from the child's date of birth.

"(d) The notice of motion for blood tests under subdivision (b) may be raised by the mother of the child not later than two years from the child's date of birth if the child's biological father has filed an affidavit with the court acknowledging paternity of the child.

"(e) The provisions of subdivision (b) shall not apply to any case coming within the provisions of Section 7005 of the Civil Code [dealing with artificial insemination] or to any case in which the wife, with the consent of the husband, conceived by means of a surgical procedure."

III

We address first the claims of Michael. At the outset, it is necessary to clarify what he sought and what he was denied. California law, like nature itself, makes no provision for dual fatherhood. Michael was seeking to be declared the father of Victoria. The immediate benefit he evidently sought to obtain from that status was visitation rights. See Cal. Civ. Code Ann. § 4601 (West 1983) (parent has statutory right to visitation "unless it is shown that such visitation would be detrimental to the best interests of the child"). But if Michael were successful in being declared the father, other rights would follow — most importantly, the right to be considered as the parent who should have custody, Cal. Civ. Code Ann. § 4600 (West 1983), a status which "embrace[s] the sum of parental rights with respect to the rearing of a child, including the child's care; the right to the child's services and earnings; the right to direct the child's activities; the right to make decisions regarding the control, education, and health of the child; and the right, as well as the duty, to prepare the child for additional obligations, which includes the teaching of moral standards, religious beliefs, and elements of good citizenship." 4 California Family Law § 60.02[1][b] (C. Markey ed. 1987) (footnotes omitted). All parental rights, including visitation, were automatically denied by denying Michael status as the father. While Cal. Civ. Code Ann. § 4601 places it within the discretionary power of a court to award visitation rights to a nonparent, the Superior Court here, affirmed by the Court of Appeal, held that California law denies visitation, against the wishes of the mother, to a putative father who has been prevented by § 621 from establishing his paternity. See 191 Cal. App. 3d, at 1013, 236 Cal. Rptr., at 821, citing *Vincent B. v. Joan R.*, 126 Cal. App. 3d, at 627–628 179 Cal.Rptr., at 13.

Michael raises two related challenges to the constitutionality of § 621. First, he asserts that requirements of procedural due process prevent the State from terminating his liberty interest in his relationship with his child without affording him an opportunity to demonstrate his paternity in an evidentiary hearing. We believe this claim derives from a fundamental misconception of the nature of the California statute. While § 621 is phrased in terms of a presumption, that rule of evidence is the implementation of a substantive rule of law. California declares it to be, except in limited circumstances, irrelevant for paternity purposes whether a child conceived during, and born into, an existing marriage was begotten by someone other than the husband and had a prior relationship with him. As the Court of Appeal phrased it:

> " 'The conclusive presumption is actually a substantive rule of law based upon a determination by the Legislature as a matter of overriding social policy, that given a certain relationship between the husband and wife, the husband is to be held responsible for the child, and that the integrity of the family unit should not be impugned.' " 191 Cal. App. 3d, at 1005, 236 Cal. Rptr., at 816, quoting *Vincent B. v. Joan R.*, supra, 126 Cal. App. 3d, at 623, 179 Cal. Rptr., at 10.

Of course the conclusive presumption not only expresses the State's substantive policy but also furthers it, excluding inquiries into the child's paternity that would be destructive of family integrity and privacy.

This Court has struck down as illegitimate certain "irrebuttable presumptions." See, e.g., *Stanley v. Illinois*, 405 U.S. 645, 92 S. Ct. 1208, 31 L. Ed. 2d 551 (1972); *Vlandis v. Kline*, 412 U.S. 441, 93 S. Ct. 2230, 37 L. Ed. 2d 63 (1973); *Cleveland Board of Education v. LaFleur*, 414 U.S. 632, 94 S. Ct. 791, 39 L. Ed. 2d 52 (1974). Those holdings did not, however, rest upon procedural due process. A conclusive presumption does, of course, foreclose the person against whom it is invoked from demonstrating, in a particularized proceeding, that applying the presumption to him will in fact not further the lawful governmental policy the presumption is designed to effectuate. But the same can be said of any legal rule that establishes general classifications, whether framed in terms of a presumption or not. In this respect there is no difference between a rule which says that the marital husband shall be irrebuttably presumed to be the father, and a rule which says that the adulterous natural father shall not be recognized as the legal father. Both rules deny someone in Michael's situation a hearing on whether, in the particular circumstances of his case, California's policies would best be served by giving him parental 1 rights. Thus, as many commentators have observed, see, e.g., Bezanson, Some Thoughts on the Emerging Irrebuttable Presumption Doctrine, 7 Ind. L. Rev. 644 (1974); Nowak, Realigning the Standards of Review Under the Equal Protection Guarantee — Prohibited, Neutral, and Permissive Classifications, 62 Geo. L.J. 1071, 1102–1106 (1974); Note, Irrebuttable Presumptions: An Illusory Analysis, 27 Stan. L. Rev. 449 (1975); Note, The Irrebuttable Presumption Doctrine in the Supreme Court, 87 Harv.L.Rev. 1534 (1974), our "irrebuttable presumption" cases must ultimately be analyzed as calling into question not the adequacy of procedures but — like our cases involving classifications framed in other terms, see, e.g., *Craig v. Boren*, 429 U.S. 190, 97 S. Ct. 451, 50 L. Ed. 2d 397 (1976); *Carrington v. Rash*, 380 U.S. 89, 85 S. Ct. 775, 13 L. Ed. 2d 675 (1965) — the adequacy of the "fit" between the classification and the policy that the classification serves. See *LaFleur, supra*, 414 U.S., at 652, 94 S. Ct., at 802 (Powell, J., concurring in result); *Vlandis, supra*, 412 U.S., at 456–459, 93 S. Ct., at 2238–2240 (White, J., concurring), 466–469, 93 S.Ct., at 2243–2245 (Rehnquist, J., dissenting); *Weinberger v. Salfi*, 422 U.S. 749, 95 S. Ct. 2457, 45 L. Ed. 2d 522 (1975). We therefore reject Michael's procedural due process challenge and proceed to his substantive claim.

Michael contends as a matter of substantive due process that, because he has established a parental relationship with Victoria, protection of Gerald's and Carole's marital union is an insufficient state interest to support termination of that relationship. This argument is, of course, predicated on the assertion that Michael has a constitutionally protected liberty interest in his relationship with Victoria.

It is an established part of our constitutional jurisprudence that the term "liberty" in the Due Process Clause extends beyond freedom from physical restraint. See, e.g., *Pierce v. Society of Sisters*, 268 U.S. 510, 45 S. Ct. 571, 69 L. Ed. 1070 (1925); *Meyer v. Nebraska*, 262 U.S. 390, 43 S. Ct. 625, 67 L. Ed. 1042 (1923). Without that core textual meaning as a limitation, defining the scope of the Due Process Clause "has at times been a treacherous field for this Court," giving "reason for concern lest the only limits to . . . judicial intervention become the predilections of those who happen at the time to be Members of this Court." *Moore v. East Cleveland*, 431 U.S. 494, 502, 97 S. Ct. 1932, 1937, 52 L. Ed. 2d 531 (1977). The need for restraint has been cogently expressed by Justice White:

> "That the Court has ample precedent for the creation of new constitutional rights should not lead it to repeat the process at will. The Judiciary, including this Court, is the most vulnerable and comes nearest to illegitimacy when it deals with judge-made constitutional law having little or no cognizable roots in the language or even the design of the Constitution. Realizing that the present construction of the Due Process Clause represents a major judicial gloss on its terms, as well as on the anticipation of the Framers . . . , the Court should be extremely reluctant to breathe still further substantive content into the Due Process Clause so as to strike down legislation adopted by a State or city to promote its welfare. Whenever the Judiciary does so, it unavoidably pre-empts for itself another part of the governance of the country without express constitutional authority." *Moore, supra*, at 544, 97 S. Ct., at 1958 (dissenting opinion).

In an attempt to limit and guide interpretation of the Clause, we have insisted not merely that the interest denominated as a "liberty" be "fundamental" (a concept that, in isolation, is hard to objectify), but also that it be an interest traditionally protected by our society.2 As we have put it, the Due Process Clause affords only those protections "so rooted in the traditions and conscience of our people as to be ranked as fundamental." *Snyder v. Massachusetts*, 291 U.S. 97, 105, 54 S. Ct. 330, 332, 78 L.Ed. 674 (1934) (Cardozo, J.). Our cases reflect "continual insistence upon respect for the teachings of history [and] solid recognition of the basic values that underlie our society . . . ." *Griswold v. Connecticut*, 381 U.S. 479, 501, 85 S. Ct. 1678, 1690, 14 L. Ed. 2d 510 (1965) (Harlan, J., concurring in judgment).

This insistence that the asserted liberty interest be rooted in history and tradition is evident, as elsewhere, in our cases according constitutional protection to certain parental rights. Michael reads the landmark case of *Stanley v. Illinois*, 405 U.S. 645, 92 S. Ct. 1208, 31 L. Ed. 2d 551 (1972), and the subsequent cases of Quilloin v. Walcott, 434 U.S. 246, 98 S. Ct. 549, 54 L. Ed. 2d 511 (1978), *Caban v. Mohammed*, 441 U.S. 380, 99 S. Ct. 1760, 60 L. Ed. 2d 297 (1979), and *Lehr v. Robertson*, 463 U.S. 248, 103 S. Ct. 2985, 77 L. Ed. 2d 614 (1983), as establishing that a liberty interest is created by biological fatherhood plus an established parental relationship — factors that exist in the present case as well. We think that distorts the rationale of those cases. As we view them, they rest not upon such isolated factors but upon the historic respect — indeed, sanctity would not be too strong a term — traditionally accorded to the relationships that develop within the unitary family. See *Stanley, supra,* 405 U.S., at 651, 92 S. Ct., at 1212; *Quilloin, supra,* 434 U.S., at 254–255, 98 S.Ct., at 554–555; *Caban, supra,* 441 U.S., at 389, 99 S. Ct., at 1766; *Lehr, supra,* 463 U.S., at 261, 103 S. Ct., at 2993. In *Stanley,* for example, we forbade the destruction of such a family when, upon the death of the mother, the State had sought to remove children from the custody of a father who had lived with and supported them and their mother for 18 years. As Justice Powell stated for the plurality in *Moore v. East Cleveland, supra,* 431 U.S., at 503, 97 S. Ct., at 1938: "Our decisions establish that the Constitution protects the sanctity of the family precisely because the institution of the family is deeply rooted in this Nation's history and tradition."

Thus, the legal issue in the present case reduces to whether the relationship between persons in the situation of Michael and Victoria has been treated as a protected family unit under the historic practices of our society, or whether on any other basis it has been accorded special protection. We think it impossible to find that it has. In fact, quite to the contrary, our traditions have protected the marital family (Gerald, Carole, and the child they acknowledge to be theirs) against the sort of claim Michael asserts.

The presumption of legitimacy was a fundamental principle of the common law. H. Nicholas, Adulturine Bastardy 1 (1836). Traditionally, that presumption could be rebutted only by proof that a husband was incapable of procreation or had had no access to his wife during the relevant period. Id., at 9–10 (citing Bracton, De Legibus et Consuetudinibus Angliae, bk. i, ch. 9, p. 6; bk. ii, ch. 29, p. 63, ch. 32, p. 70 (1569)). As explained by Blackstone, nonaccess could only be proved "if the husband be out of the kingdom of England (or, as the law somewhat loosely phrases it, extra quatuor maria [beyond the four seas]) for above nine months . . . ." 1

Blackstone's Commentaries 456 (J. Chitty ed. 1826). And, under the common law both in England and here, "neither husband nor wife [could] be a witness to prove access or nonaccess." J. Schouler, Law of the Domestic Relations § 225, p. 306 (3d ed. 1882); R. Graveson & F. Crane, A Century of Family Law: 1857–1957, p. 158 (1957). The primary policy rationale underlying the common law's severe restrictions on rebuttal of the presumption appears to have been an aversion to declaring children illegitimate, see Schouler, supra, § 225, at 306–307; M. Grossberg, Governing the Hearth 201 (1985), thereby depriving them of rights of inheritance and succession, 2 J. Kent, Commentaries on American Law, and likely making them wards of the state. A secondary policy concern was the interest in promoting the "peace and tranquillity of States and families," Schouler, *supra*, § 225, at 304, quoting Boullenois, Traité des Status, bk. 1, p. 62, a goal that is obviously impaired by facilitating suits against husband and wife asserting that their children are illegitimate. Even though, as bastardy laws became less harsh, "[j]udges in both [England and the United States] gradually widened the acceptable range of evidence that could be offered by spouses, and placed restraints on the 'four seas rule' . . . [,] the law retained a strong bias against ruling the children of married women illegitimate." Grossberg, *supra*, at 202.

We have found nothing in the older sources, nor in the older cases, addressing specifically the power of the natural father to assert parental rights over a child born into a woman's existing marriage with another man. Since it is Michael's burden to establish that such a power (at least where the natural father has established a relationship with the child) is so deeply embedded within our traditions as to be a fundamental right, the lack of evidence alone might defeat his case. But the evidence shows that even in modern times — when, as we have noted, the rigid protection of the marital family has in other respects been relaxed — the ability of a person in Michael's position to claim paternity has not been generally acknowledged. For example, a 1957 annotation on the subject: " Who may dispute presumption of legitimacy of child conceived or born during wedlock," 53 A.L.R.2d 572, shows three States (including California) with statutes limiting standing to the husband or wife and their descendants, one State (Louisiana) with a statute limiting it to the husband, two States (Florida and Texas) with judicial decisions limiting standing to the husband, and two States (Illinois and New York) with judicial decisions denying standing even to the mother. Not a single decision is set forth specifically according standing to the natural father, and "express indications of the nonexistence of any . . . limitation" upon standing were found only "in a few jurisdictions." *Id.*, at 579.

Moreover, even if it were clear that one in Michael's position generally possesses, and has generally always possessed, standing to challenge the marital child's legitimacy, that would still not establish Michael's case. As noted earlier, what is at issue here is not entitlement to a state pronouncement that Victoria was begotten by Michael. It is no conceivable denial of constitutional right for a State to decline to declare facts unless some legal consequence hinges upon the requested declaration. What Michael asserts here is a right to have himself declared the natural father and thereby to obtain parental prerogatives. What he must establish, therefore, is not that our society has traditionally allowed a natural father in his circumstances to establish paternity, but that it has traditionally accorded such a father parental rights, or at least has not traditionally denied them. Even if the law in all States had always been that the entire world could challenge the marital presumption and obtain a declaration as to who was the natural father, that would not advance Michael's claim. Thus, it is ultimately irrelevant, even for purposes of determining current social attitudes towards the alleged substantive right Michael asserts, that the present law in a number of States appears to allow the natural father — including the natural father who has not established a relationship with the child — the theoretical power to rebut the marital presumption, see Note, Rebutting the Marital Presumption: A Developed Relationship Test, 88 Colum. L. Rev. 369, 373 (1988). What counts is whether the States in fact award substantive parental rights to the natural father of a child conceived within, and born into, an extant marital union that wishes to embrace the child. We are not aware of a single case, old or new, that has done so. This is not the stuff of which fundamental rights qualifying as liberty interests are made.

In *Lehr v. Robertson*, a case involving a natural father's attempt to block his child's adoption by the unwed mother's new husband, we observed that "[t]he significance of the biological connection is that it offers the natural father an opportunity that no other male possesses to develop a relationship with his offspring," 463 U.S., at 262, 103 S. Ct., at 2993, and we assumed that the Constitution might require some protection of that opportunity, *id.*, at 262–265, 103 S. Ct., at 2993–2995. Where, however, the child is born into an extant marital family, the natural father's unique opportunity conflicts with the similarly unique opportunity of the husband of the marriage; and it is not unconstitutional for the State to give categorical preference to the latter. In *Lehr* we quoted approvingly from Justice Stewart's dissent in *Caban v. Mohammed*, 441 U.S., at 397, 99 S. Ct., at 1770, to the effect that although " '[i]n some circumstances the actual relationship between father and child may suffice to create in the unwed father parental interests comparable to those of the married father,' " " 'the absence of a legal tie with the mother may in such circumstances appropriately place a limit on whatever substantive constitutional claims might otherwise exist.' " 463 U.S., at 260, n. 16, 103 S. Ct., at 2993, n. 16. In accord with our traditions, a limit is also imposed by the circumstance that the mother is, at the time of the child's conception and birth, married to, and cohabitating with, another man, both of whom wish to raise the child as the offspring of their union. It is a question of legislative policy and not constitutional law whether California will allow the presumed parenthood of a couple desiring to retain a child conceived within and born into their marriage to be rebutted. We do not accept Justice Brennan's criticism that this result "squashes" the liberty that consists of "the freedom not to conform." *Post*, at 2351. It seems to us that reflects the erroneous view that there is only one side to this controversy — that one disposition can expand a "liberty" of sorts without contracting an equivalent "liberty" on the other side. Such a happy choice is rarely available. Here, to provide protection to an adulterous natural father is to deny protection to a marital father, and vice versa. If Michael has a "freedom not to conform" (whatever that means), Gerald must equivalently have a "freedom to conform." One of them will pay a price for asserting that "freedom" — Michael by being unable to act as father of the child he has adulterously begotten, or Gerald by being unable to preserve the integrity of the traditional family unit he and Victoria have established. Our disposition does not choose between these two "freedoms," but leaves that to the people of California. Justice Brennan's approach chooses one of them as the constitutional imperative, on no apparent basis except that the unconventional is to be preferred.

IV

We have never had occasion to decide whether a child has a liberty interest, symmetrical with that of her parent, in maintaining her filial relationship. We need not do so here because, even assuming that such a right exists, Victoria's claim must fail. Victoria's due process challenge is, if anything, weaker than Michael's. Her basic claim is not that California has erred in preventing her from establishing that Michael, not Gerald, should stand as her legal father. Rather, she claims a due process right to maintain filial relationships with both Michael and Gerald. This assertion merits little discussion, for, whatever the merits of the guardian ad litem's belief that such an arrangement can be of great psychological benefit to a child, the claim that a State must recognize multiple fatherhood has no support in the history or traditions of this country. Moreover, even if we were to construe Victoria's argument as forwarding the lesser proposition that, whatever her status vis-à-vis Gerald, she has a liberty interest in maintaining a filial relationship with her natural father, Michael, we find that, at best, her claim is the obverse of Michael's and fails for the same reasons.

Victoria claims in addition that her equal protection rights have been violated because, unlike her mother and presumed father, she had no opportunity to rebut the presumption of her legitimacy. We find this argument wholly without merit. We reject, at the outset, Victoria's suggestion that her equal protection challenge must be assessed under a standard of strict scrutiny because, in denying her the right to maintain a filial relationship with Michael, the State is discriminating against her on the basis of her illegitimacy. See *Gomez v. Perez*, 409 U.S. 535, 538, 93 S. Ct. 872, 875, 35 L. Ed. 2d 56 (1973). Illegitimacy is a legal construct, not a natural trait. Under California law, Victoria is not illegitimate, and she is treated in the same manner as all other legitimate children: she is entitled to maintain a filial relationship with her legal parents.

We apply, therefore, the ordinary "rational relationship" test to Victoria's equal protection challenge. The primary rationale underlying § 621's limitation on those who may rebut the presumption of legitimacy is a concern that allowing persons other than the husband or wife to do so may undermine the integrity of the marital union. When the husband or wife contests the legitimacy of their child, the stability of the marriage has already been shaken. In contrast, allowing a claim of illegitimacy to be pressed by the child — or, more accurately, by a court-appointed guardian ad litem — may well disrupt an otherwise peaceful union. Since it pursues a legitimate end by rational means, California's decision to treat Victoria differently from her parents is not a denial of equal protection.

The judgment of the California Court of Appeal is Affirmed.

[7] Is the Constitutional Requirement of a Rational Connection Applicable to Presumptions in Civil Cases?

The standard by which courts measure the constitutionality of the use of presumptions in civil actions is unclear. In 1910, the Supreme Court announced a "rational connection" test for evaluating the constitutionality of civil presumptions. In *Mobile, Jackson & Kansas City Railroad Co. v. Turnipseed*, 219 U.S. 35 (1910), the Court upheld a presumption of negligence on the part of the railroad or its servants where there was proof of injury from the running of the locomotive or cars of such company, because there was a rational connection between the fact proved and the fact presumed. The Court stated:

> That a legislative presumption of one fact from evidence of another may not constitute a denial of due process of law or a denial of the equal protection of the law, it is only essential that there shall be some rational connection between the fact proved and the ultimate fact presumed, and that the inference of one fact from proof of another shall not be so unreasonable as to be a purely arbitrary mandate.

Id. at 43. The Court concluded that "[i]t is not an unreasonable inference that a derailment of railway cars is due to some negligence, either in construction or maintenance of the track or trains, or some carelessness in operation." *Id.* at 44. It was not clear whether the Court's decision was influenced by the fact that the presumption in *Turnipseed* only shifted to the railroad company the burden of going forward with *some* evidence to disprove negligence, but did not shift the burden of persuasion. Nineteen years later, however, the Supreme Court appears to have attributed central importance to the fact that the presumption in *Turnipseed* shifted only the burden of going forward. Thus, in *Western & A.R.R. Co. v. Henderson*, 279 U.S. 639 (1929), the Court held the same kind of presumption of negligence to be unconstitutional because the Court interpreted it as shifting the burden of persuasion.

> Upon the mere fact of collision and resulting death, the statute is held to raise a presumption that defendant and its employees were negligent in each of the particulars alleged, and that every act or omission in plaintiff's specifications of negligence was the proximate cause of the death, and it makes defendant liable unless it showed due care in respect of every matter alleged against it. And, by authorizing the jury, in the absence of evidence, to find negligence in the operation of the engine and train, the court necessarily permitted the presumption to be considered and weighed as evidence against the testimony of defendant's witnesses tending affirmatively to prove such operation was not negligent in any respect.

*   *   *

> Legislation declaring that proof of one fact or group of facts shall constitute prima facie evidence of an ultimate fact in issue is valid if there is a rational connection between what is proved and what is to be inferred. A prima facie presumption casts upon the person against whom it is applied the duty of going forward with his evidence on the particular point to which

the presumption relates. A statute creating a presumption that is arbitrary, or that operates to deny a fair opportunity to repel it, violates the due process clause of the Fourteenth Amendment. Legislative fiat may not take the place of fact in the judicial determination of issues involving life, liberty, or property. . . .

The mere fact of collision between a railway train and a vehicle at a highway grade crossing furnishes no basis for any inference as to whether the accident was caused by negligence of the railway company, or of the traveler on the highway, or of both, or without fault of any one. Reasoning does not lead from the occurrence back to its cause.

Id. at 641–642.

When the Advisory Committee proposed the adoption of the Morgan view of presumptions in Rule 301, its Note accompanying the proposed rule resolved the apparent inconsistency between *Turnipseed* and *Henderson*, and the question concerning the constitutional validity of presumptions that shift the burden of persuasion:

In the opinion of the Advisory Committee, no constitutional infirmity attends [the Morgan] view of presumptions. In *Mobile, J. & K.C.R. Co. v. Turnipseed*, 219 U.S. 35 (1910), the Court upheld a Mississippi statute which provided that in actions against railroads proof of injury inflicted by the running of trains should be prima facie evidence of negligence by the railroad. The injury in the case had resulted from a derailment. The opinion made the points (1) that the only effect of the statute was to impose on the railroad the duty of producing some evidence to the contrary, (2) that an inference may be supplied by law if there is a rational connection between the fact proved and the fact presumed, as long as the opposite party is not precluded from presenting his evidence to the contrary, and (3) that considerations of public policy arising from the character of the business justified the application in question. Nineteen years later, in *Western & Atlantic R. Co. v. Henderson*, 279 U.S. 639 (1929), the Court overturned a Georgia statute making railroads liable for damages done by trains, unless the railroad made it appear that reasonable care had been used, the presumption being against the railroad. The declaration alleged the death of plaintiff's husband from a grade crossing collision, due to specified acts of negligence by defendant. The jury was instructed that proof of the injury raised a presumption of negligence; the burden shifted to the railroad to prove ordinary care; and unless it did so, they should find for plaintiff. The instruction was held erroneous in an opinion stating (1) that there was no rational connection between the mere fact of collision and negligence on the part of anyone, and (2) that the statute was different from that in *Turnipseed* in imposing a burden upon the railroad. The reader is left in a state of some confusion. Is the difference between a derailment and a grade crossing collision of no significance? Would the *Turnipseed* presumption have been bad if it had imposed a burden of persuasion on defendant, although that would in nowise have impaired its "rational connection"? If

Henderson forbids imposing a burden of persuasion on defendants, what happens to affirmative defenses?

Two factors serve to explain *Henderson*. The first was that it was common ground that negligence was indispensable to liability. Plaintiff thought so, drafted her complaint accordingly, and relied upon the presumption. But how in logic could the same presumption establish her alternative grounds of negligence that the engineer was so blind he could not see decedent's truck and that he failed to stop after he saw it? Second, take away the basic assumption of no liability without fault, as *Turnipseed* intimated might be done ("considerations of public policy arising out of the character of the business"), and the structure of the decision in *Henderson* fails. No question of logic would have arisen if the statute had simply said: a prima facie case of liability is made by proof of injury by a train; lack of negligence is an affirmative defense, to be pleaded and proved as other affirmative defenses. The problem would be one of economic due process only. While it seems likely that the Supreme court of 1929 would have voted that due process was denied, that result today would be unlikely. See, for example, the shift in the direction of absolute liability in the consumer cases. Prosser, *The Assault Upon the Citadel (Strict Liability to the Consumer)*, 69 Yale L. J. 1099 (1960).

Any doubt as to the constitutional permissibility of a presumption imposing a burden of persuasion of the nonexistence of the presumed fact in civil cases is laid to rest by *Dick v. New York Life Ins. Co.*, 359 U.S. 437 (1959). The Court unhesitatingly applied the North Dakota rule that the presumption against suicide imposed on defendant the burden of proving that the death of insured, under an accidental death clause, was due to suicide.

Advisory Committee Note to Rule 301, 56 F.R.D. 183, 208–209 (1972).

If, contrary to the opinion of the Advisory Committee, the Supreme Court's perception of the requirements of substantive due process did not change from 1910 to 1929, could *Turnipseed* and *Henderson* reasonably be interpreted as establishing a variable probability test for the constitutionality of presumptions that is dependent upon the presumption's effect — whether it merely shifts the burden of going forward with evidence and is easily destroyed by the introduction of some rebuttal testimony, or whether it shifts the burden of persuasion and is given the effect of evidence to be weighed by the jury? The former would require, in the language of *Turnipseed*, only "*some* rational connection," so that the presumed fact can be said to be more than a purely arbitrary mandate. The latter would require an undefined, but greater, level of probability. The Court has given no indication since *Henderson*, however, that the level of probability or connection required is dependent upon the presumption's effect.

The precedential value of both *Turnipseed* and *Henderson* for the logical connection test that the Court employed is questionable. Strictly construed, that test would preclude presumptions based on grounds other than probability (such as social policy, convenience, and access to proof). This exclusion would be inconsistent with the state's power to establish, alter, and eliminate claims and defenses so long as the Government's actions are rationally related to legitimate governmental ends.

Despite protestations from a number of commentators, the courts, including the Supreme Court, have continued to employ the rational connection test in the civil context. *See Barry v. Barchi*, 443 U.S. 55 (1979) (upholding a presumption that the trainer of a horse is responsible for the horse's ingestion of drugs prior to a race); *United States Steel Corp. v. Oravetz*, 686 F.2d 197 (3d Cir. 1982) (upholding a rational presumption of eligibility for black lung benefits after 25 years of service in the mines). The Supreme Court has also continued to cite with approval its opinion in *Turnipseed*, and the rational connection test recognized in that opinion. *See Usery v. Turner Elkhorn Mining Co.*, 428 U.S. 1, 28 (1976). Because of the Court's continued use of the rational connection terminology, it is difficult to determine whether the Court has moved away from a strict rational *connection* requirement that turns solely on probability, to something more akin to a rational *basis* test to look to whether there is an *acceptable reason in either policy or logic* for the presumption that has been created and the burden that it assigned.

[B] Federal Rules of Evidence — Rule 301: Presumptions in General in Civil Actions and Proceedings

[1] What Presumptions?

Article III of the Federal Rules of Evidence recognizes no specific presumptions. Does this mean that all common law presumptions are silently perpetuated or abolished? If abolished, then Article III would only define the purpose of statutory presumptions for which a different purpose has not been specified in the statute. This question is explored in the following excerpt:

Paul R. Rice,
Electronic Evidence: Law and Practice
(ABA 2004)[21]

While many judges find it convenient and fair to employ presumptions to compel what logic may permit, federal judges will encounter significant problems under Article III of the Federal Rules of Evidence. That Article has adopted the most restrictive and least useful theory about the effect of presumptions — the "bursting bubble" theory. This, coupled with the fact that it fails to recognize a single presumption, and provides no guidance on the status of previously existing common law presumptions, creates a significant question about whether any common law presumptions have survived codification. Given the inherent complexities of presumptions . . . Article III has helped to make this evidentiary principle one of the most confusing, misunderstood, and ignored areas of evidence law. . . .

---

[21] Copyright © 2004. Reprinted by permission.

These rules [in Article III] address only the *effect* of presumptions in civil actions. Rule 301 provides that "a presumption imposes on the party against whom it is directed the *burden of going forward with evidence* to rebut or meet the presumption. . . ." (Emphasis added.) Unlike the Evidence Code of California, . . . not a single presumption is delineated. . . . This raises the question, what has survived codification?

There is no clear answer to this question, and it is only the first of a series of unresolved issues. If common law presumptions have survived, can courts still modify them for use in the Internet age, as they would have under the common law? Can courts create new presumptions without going through the cumbersome Congressional legislative or quasi-legislative Advisory Committee processes?

The Evidence Code supercedes the common law rules of evidence. Because the Evidence Code recognizes *no specific presumptions*, it is possible that no common law presumptions continue to exist.

It is provided in Fed. R. Evid. 102 that the "rules shall be construed to secure fairness in administration, elimination of unjustifiable expense and delay, and promotion of growth and development of the law of evidence to the end that the truth may be ascertained and proceedings justly determined." This rule does not perpetuate common law evidentiary rules unless they are essential to, and thus implicit in, the rules that have been codified. Which rules, if any, would sponsor the recognition and creation of presumptions?

To interpret Article III as abolishing all common law presumptions would be significant, but it would not be irrational or render the provisions of Article III meaningless. It would merely leave the codified provisions in control a fewer statutory presumptions that do not expressly reject the 'bursting bubble' approach. Rule 301 would still have a purpose. Elsewhere in the Evidence Code, when Congress intended common law rules to be perpetuated, for instance, in Article V, Privileges, the perpetuation was *explicit*. Therefore, neither logic nor legislative intent demands an interpretation of the Evidence Code that preserves all common law presumptions.

The most compelling justification for judicial recognition of presumptions may be the inherent power of judges to comment on the evidence. If courts are empowered to suggest to the jury logical inferences and conclusions that can be drawn from the evidence that has been heard,[22] it

---

[22] (Original footnote 22) A judge's power to comment on the evidence descended from English common law. "In the courts of the United States, as in those of England, from which our practice was derived, the judge, in submitting a case to the jury, may, at his discretion, whenever he thinks it necessary to assist them in arriving at a just conclusion, comment upon the evidence, call their attention to parts of it which he thinks important, and express his opinion upon the facts; and the expression of such an opinion, when no rule of law is incorrectly stated, and all matters of fact are ultimately submitted to the determination of the jury, cannot be reviewed on writ of error." *Vicksburg & M.R. Co. v. Putnam*, 118 U.S. 545, 553 (1886). At least one scholar suggests that the devices of presumptions and judicial comments on the evidence act as "functional equivalents." "When a judge instructs a jury that it may

would not be too great a stretch to conclude that they can convert such comments into a presumption that compels the conclusion. The reply doctrine provides a helpful example. If an e-mail message is shown to have been in response to a prior e-mail message, and it incorporates a reference to the prior message (or with e-mail, it attaches to the prior message), the strong logical inference is that the response was from the person to whom the initial message was sent. This inference likely would carry the day unless refuted by the opposing party, especially if federal trial judges chose to exercise their power to encourage it. A presumption would compel what otherwise may be inevitable.

Article III is in dire need of attention. One simple fix is for Congress or the Advisory Committee on the Federal Rules of Evidence to adopt the language of Rule 501 governing privileges. If, like privileges, presumptions were "governed by the principles of the common law as they may be interpreted by the courts in light of reason and experience," the problems of (1) whether common law presumptions have survived codification, and (2) whether new presumptions, or amendments to old presumptions, can be created by the courts, would be resolved. Both Congress and the Judicial Conference could leave the resolution of these matters to those who are most familiar with them because they have to employ them, the trial judges. This also would leave to trial judges the more controversial question about the nature of the presumption: whether it is simply a procedural device that shifts to the opposing party only the burden of coming forward with evidence (current practice), or one that shifts to the opposing party the burden of persuasion (the alternative that gives the presumption greater force and effect).

[2] Rule 301 Does Not Cover Criminal Actions and Actions Controlled by State Law, and Does Not Apply Where "Otherwise Provided"

The terms of Rule 301 do not govern the use of presumptions in criminal prosecutions, or at least presumptions used against the defendant in criminal cases, see [A][7], above, and civil actions "otherwise provided for by Act of Congress or by these rules . . . ."

[See Fed. R. Evid. 301, 302]

Civil diversity and pendent jurisdiction cases, therefore, in which state law controls the outcome, must be added to the proceedings in which Rule 301 does not

presume the existence of certain unproved incriminating facts from the proof at trial of other less incriminating facts, or suggests by comment that the jury may draw various reasonable inferences, the effect is to increase the weight of the evidence presented by the prosecution." Ronald J. Allen, *Structuring Jury Decisionmaking in Criminal Cases: A Unified Constitutional Approach to Evidentiary Devices*, 94 Harv. L. Rev. 321, 322, 330 (1980) (following an "unbroken line of cases" in which the Supreme Court has upheld authority of trial judges to comment on evidence); *see also* Charles R. Nesson, *Rationality, Presumptions, and Judicial Comment: A Response to Professor Allen*, 94 Harv. L. Rev. 1574, 1588–89 (1980).

compel the use of the Thayer-Wigmore approach to presumptions. In addition to recognizing exceptions based on other provisions within the Federal Rules of Evidence, Rule 301 exempts proceedings in which Congress otherwise has provided.

Congress obviously included this "otherwise provided" provision within the rules to accommodate those of the view that there can be no single rule controlling the use of presumptions because presumptions are created for different purposes in different contexts. The provision, however, has destroyed any hopes that Rule 301 could achieve uniformity and consistency in the use of presumptions. Instead, courts have construed the provision as requiring a determination whether Congress' intention was, in fact, to "otherwise provide" by examining both the express terms of each statute, rule, or regulation creating a presumption, and the implicit policies being furthered in the legislative scheme in which each presumption is being used, Not surprisingly, as many judges are predisposed to the Morgan-McCormick approach to presumptions, courts have found a legislative intent to shift burdens of persuasion, as opposed to mere burdens of production, in a number of instances. This has further diminished the value of Rule 301 and perpetuated the confusion and inconsistencies in the use of presumptions that preceded the rule's adoption. The following cases illustrate how the courts have applied this "otherwise provided" provision.

In *Solder Removal Co. v. United States International Trade Commission*, 582 F.2d 628 (C.C.P.A. 1978), the court found that Congress intended the presumption of a patent's validity to shift the burden of proving the patent's invalidity to the one challenging it. It found this intent in the explicit terms of the statute creating the presumption. Although the first sentence of 35 U.S.C. § 282 states only that "A patent shall be presumed valid," the last sentence provides, "The burden of establishing invalidity of a patent or any claim therefore shall rest on the party asserting it."

With less explicit direction, the court in *Alabama By-Products Corp. v. Killingsworth*, 733 F.2d 1151 (11th Cir. 1984), arrived at the same conclusion relative to an administrative regulation establishing a presumption of total disability when a coal miner with ten years of experience presented a chest X-ray that established a diagnosis of pneumoconiosis ("black lung"). The court concluded that the regulation shifted the burden of persuasion to the employer to disprove total disability, because another subdivision of the regulation, which addressed the presumption's rebuttal, stated that the presumption was rebutted if the evidence "established" specifically delineated conditions. The court reasoned: " 'Establish' is clearly synonymous with 'prove.' Furthermore, under [the rebuttal provision,] the factfinder must consider 'all relevant medical evidence' to determine if the presumption has been rebutted, thus indicating that the factfinder must consider evidence introduced by both sides and that the operator [employer] must persuade the factfinder." *Id.* at 1514.

Similarly, in *Plough, Inc. v. Mason and Dixon Lines*, 630 F.2d 468 (6th Cir. 1980), the court held that the Carmack Amendment to the Interstate Commerce Act, 49 U.S.C. § 20(11), impliedly created a presumption of negligence on the part of common carriers for damage to goods while in their possession because it imposed liability unless the carrier could "show" that the damage resulted from one of four delineated causes. The court found that the statute not only created a presumption of negligence but shifted the burden of persuasion to the carrier to prove lack of negligence. The court believed that the tenor of the statute's language compelled this result, which was justified because the shipper has no control over the goods after they have been delivered to the carrier, has no way of observing how they were handled and would have an intolerable task if required to bear the burden of persuasion on the issue of negligence.

This evaluation of legislative intent has not been limited to presumptions created in legislative enactment. In *National Labor Relations Board v. Tahoe Nugget, Inc.*, 584 F.2d 293 (9th Cir. 1978), the court considered the nonstatutory presumption of continued majority support by employees for a union that once demonstrated that support, and found that the presumption was intended to shift the burden of persuasion (disproving the majority support) to an employer who refuses to bargain with the union. The court did so by examining the goals of the National Labor Relations Act, the needs of a system of collective bargaining that depends upon the good faith of its participants, and precedent.

> The employers argue that placing on them the burden of refuting the presumption of majority status is unfair because the Union has superior access to the information regarding Union support. The effect, respondents conclude, is that they are forced to assume the risk of erroneous determinations. We agree: the employer usually does have inferior access to the relevant information and may risk further penalty in garnering additional data. Yet we think the burden is fair.

> In refusing to bargain because of an alleged decline in union adherents, the employer is acting as vicarious champion of its employees, a role no one has asked it to assume. The employees were free to petition for decertification; here, they never did. Respondents were also free to petition for an election, the preferred method for resolving majority disputes, but neither did until much later. When the employer chooses to unilaterally disrupt an established bargaining relationship without an election, the threat to industrial peace must be counterbalanced by good cause. When the employer has doubts, the goal of the Act would be better served by filing an election petition. Requiring the employer to show that his refusal to bargain was reasonable fairly allocates the burdens and concomitant risks.

Id. at 301–302.

Does Rule 301 authorize courts to ignore the Thayer-Wigmore theory that Congress adopted by allowing *common law* presumptions to shift the burden of persuasion because they are unrelated to any legislative scheme and congressional intent? Consider *James v. River Parishes Co., Inc.*, 686 F.2d 1129 (5th Cir. 1982), in which the court concluded that a common-law presumption of negligence in securing a vessel that breaks loose from its moorings shifted the burden of persuasion to the vessel's custodian to establish a lack of negligence.

> While we have not deemed drifting to be conclusive evidence of negligence, we have noted, in a case involving a drifting vessel, that "where

a collision occurs between a moving vessel and a moored vessel, a presumption of fault is raised against the offending vessel, which presumption must be rebutted by a preponderance of the evidence." . . . If the drifting or moving vessel offers as a defense that the collision was an unavoidable accident . . . , "[t]he burden of proving inevitable accident of Act of God rests heavily upon the vessel asserting such defense." The vessel must show that the accident could not have been prevented by "human skill and precaution and a proper display of nautical skills[.]"

Accordingly we now make explicit what we believe to be the correct rubric: When a drifting vessel causes damage, an inference arises as a matter of law that the vessel was adrift through negligence. Such an inference is called a presumption. The custodian of the drifting vessel bears the burden of disproving fault by a preponderance of the evidence. In other words, he bears the risk of non-persuasion. This inference or presumption of negligence is a rule of law based on the logical deduction that a vessel found floating loose was improperly moored. . . . It is not governed by Rule 301 of the Federal Rules of Evidence. The weight and effect of such a presumption is determined, as a matter of substantive law, in the light of the considerations that prompted its adoption. Judge Weinstein and Professor Berger have commented in their treatise on the Federal Rules of Evidence: "That the federal courts may need to create and modify presumptions in enforcing federal substantive law seems clear." 1 J. Weinstein, EVIDENCE ¶ 301[02] (1981).

Here, of course, we neither create nor modify a presumption but merely apply a rule that long antedated adoption of the Federal Rules of Evidence. In doing so, we act in conformity to the traditional responsibility of the federal courts to enunciate and develop the substantive principles of admiralty and maritime law. . . . The allocation of burdens we apply today has been fashioned by the federal courts under the authority of Article III of the Constitution. In addition to the factors we have discussed that make this allocation of burdens logical, we would be reluctant to hold that adoption of the Rules of Evidence altered such a substantive principle.

Id. at 1132–1133.

Was the court's reasoning in *James* persuasive? If the courts are empowered to override Rule 301 whenever they deem it appropriate, of what value is the rule? Consider Judge Garwood's dissenting opinion in *James*:

I respectfully dissent. The trial court, like the majority, decided this case under what I consider the erroneous view that C & R had the burden of persuasion on the issue of whether the adrift condition of the barges was due to its negligence. This is contrary to the provision of Rule 301 of the Federal Rules of Evidence, that presumptions do not effect a shifting of the burden of persuasion.

The fact that C & R's barges were adrift gave rise to a presumption that this was due to C & R's negligence. Under Rule 301, the effect of the presumption was to cast on C & R the burden of producing evidence that such condition did not result from its own negligence. I believe C & R met this burden by evidence that the barges were properly moored. However, this evidence was not conclusive. Nor does the production of such evidence operate to "burst the bubble" of a presumption. Accordingly, despite C & R's evidence, there remained for consideration by the trier of fact what the majority accurately describes as "the logical deduction that a vessel found floating loose was improperly moored." In this posture of the case, the trial court, as fact finder, was free to find, in accordance with the presumption and on the basis of the referenced "logical deduction," that C & R was negligent. But the trial court was not *required* to so find. And, such a finding should not have been made unless the trial court was affirmatively persuaded on consideration of the evidence as a whole, including both the "logical deduction" and C & R's testimony, that C & R was in fact negligent. Since it is evident from the trial court's memorandum opinion that it cast the ultimate burden of persuasion on C & R, and ruled against it because it had failed to convince the trial court it was free from negligence, I believe the case should be remanded for findings on this issue under the correct standard.

The language of Rule 301 reflects that it is to apply in all civil actions, except where otherwise specified by the Rules or an Act of Congress. Certainly this includes admiralty cases. *See* Rule 1101(b). It is true that for some purposes the burden of persuasion may be regarded as substantive, rather than a procedural, matter. The significance of this is, I believe, implicitly recognized in Rule 302, which provides that state law will control the effect of presumptions concerning claims or defenses established by state law. Accordingly, the drafters of the Federal Rules of Evidence appear to have contemplated that Rule 301 would govern in numerous other instances where the application of the burden of persuasion might properly be characterized as "substantive." There is nothing in the language of Rule 301, or elsewhere in the Federal Rules of Evidence, to indicate that Rule 301 was intended to apply only to those specific presumptions expressly recognized or provided for in the Federal Rules of Evidence. Rather, the intent seems to have been to create a uniform rule for civil cases respecting the effect, on the burden of producing evidence and the burden of persuasion, of all nonconclusive presumptions, except as otherwise might be provided in the Rules of Evidence themselves or in an Act of Congress. I do not reach the question of whether it was the intention of Congress to prevent the courts in civil cases from ever applying different judge-made rules regarding the shifting of the burden of persuasion, or the extent of Congress' constitutional power in that regard. Simply as a matter of policy, and in the interests of uniformity, it seems to me to be preferable to follow the provisions of Rule 301, absent some most compelling reason to the contrary. Finding none such here, I believe Rule 301 should have been applied in the instant case. The decisions of the Supreme Court and of this Court relied on by the majority which speak to the issue of the burden of persuasion were decided before adoption of the Federal Rules of Evidence, and hence are not controlling on this question.

Id. at 1133–1134.

[3]   Use of Presumptions Against Prosecution in Criminal Cases: What Rule Controls Their Admissibility?

Rule 301, by its literal terms, only applies to civil cases. Moreover, the due process right to be proven guilty beyond a reasonable doubt and the Sixth Amendment right to trial by jury only apply to the criminal defendant and, therefore, only limit the *prosecution's* use of presumptions against criminal defendants. Consequently, the question arises as to what controls the use of presumptions by defendants against the prosecution? Courts can take either of two approaches.

The first approach would be to construe Rule 301 as applying to defendants' use of presumptions in criminal cases, regardless of the rule's explicit restriction to civil actions. This approach is based on the argument that Congress' intention in limiting Rule 301 to civil cases was solely to avoid the constitutional problems that arise in criminal cases. Because those constitutional problems exist with regard only to presumptions used against the defendant, Congress obviously did not intend to restrict Rule 301 solely to civil actions.

Two facts support this reasoning. First, there are several instances in the rules where Congress, concerned about the rights of criminal defendants, imposed limitations in criminal cases generally, making the limitations applicable to both the Government and the defendant, or, instead, imposed limitations that applied to both civil and criminal defendants. In Rule 803(8)(B), for example, Congress was concerned about the prosecution's use of the hearsay exception for public records to admit police reports against criminal defendants instead of calling the police officer as a witness. The fear was that this practice would violate the defendant's Sixth Amendment right of confrontation. To address the problem, Congress made police reports inadmissible in "criminal cases." By the literal terms of this limitation, the defendant could not use the police officer's report against the Government, just as the Government could not use the report against him. Again in Rule 609, which addresses the admissibility of prior convictions for impeachment purposes, Congress was concerned with the fair treatment of the criminal defendant, and the dilemma that the criminal defendant often faces in determining whether to testify. On the one hand, the jury reasons that a criminal defendant who does not take the witness stand has something to hide; on the other hand, if the defendant does testify, the jurors may be unfairly influenced in their determination of culpability if the Government is allowed to impeach the defendant with evidence of prior convictions. To address this problem, Congress restricted the admissibility of felony convictions for impeachment purposes to those convictions that the trial judge determined had a probative value that outweighed their prejudicial effect "*to the defendant.*" By its literal terms, the provision favored both *civil and criminal defendants* — a result Congress obviously did not intend. In neither of the above instances, however, have the courts interpreted or applied the provision in a manner that its literal terms would compel. Instead, courts have restricted each rule's applicability to the Government's use of prohibited evidence against criminal defendants.

[4] Instructing the Jury on the Rebutted Presumption

Because Rule 301 has adopted the Thayer-Wigmore theory of presumptions, the introduction of rebuttal evidence (evidence to contradict the presumed fact) bursts the presumption bubble, thereby destroying it. Having forced the opponent to come forward with rebuttal evidence, the presumption has served its purpose, and, therefore, it disappears. Consequently, after that point there is no presumption about which to instruct the jury. Therefore, any instruction that mentions the term presumption or suggests that the jury *must* find the presumed fact from proof of the basic fact would be erroneous.

Acknowledging this result, the Report of the Senate Committee on the Judiciary states that the court still "may instruct the jury that they may infer the existence of the presumed fact from proof of the basic facts giving rise to the presumption." This statement is correct only to the extent that the presumption was based on a logical inference of the existence of the presumed fact from the basic fact, rather than public policy. Instructions on the logical inferences that can be drawn from the evidence that has been presented at the trial is appropriate only to the extent that judicial comment on the evidence is permissible. Such comment is acceptable to the extent logic permits.

EXERCISES

1. A federal bail statute imposes a rebuttable presumption favoring pretrial detention for defendants accused of certain violent crimes. In order to rebut the presumption, the defendant must come forward with evidence that he does not pose a danger to the community or a risk of flight. What factors do you think the trial judge should consider when evaluating whether the presumptions of dangerousness and flight have been rebutted?

2. What is the purpose or policy reason behind the court's adoption of these presumptions?

   a. In estate litigation, after seven years an individual who disappears without a trace is presumed dead.

   b. In immigration proceedings, where service of a notice of a deportation proceeding is sent by certified mail through the United States Postal Service and there is proof of attempted delivery and notification of certified mail, a presumption of effective service and receipt arises.

   c. In a products liability action brought against a product manufacturer, there is a rebuttable presumption that the manufacturer is not liable for any injury to a claimant caused by the design of a product if the manufacturer establishes that the product's design complied with mandatory federal safety standards or regulations.

§ 10.02   JUDICIAL NOTICE

[A]   In General

[1]   Purpose and Effect of Judicial Notice

Judicial notice is the judicial practice of accepting certain facts as established without demanding a showing of evidentiary support at the proceeding. Its purposes are to promote trial efficiency by eliminating unnecessary evidence and to prevent flagrant error by directing the jury to find certain facts that logic and experience dictate are true. Like presumptions, judicial notice is a shortcut to proof. Unlike presumptions, however, this shortcut is based on the nature of the fact noticed, and generally is not rebuttable or contestable. Once a court takes judicial notice of a fact, that fact is conclusively established.

Historically, courts have divided judicial notice into two categories: judicial notice of facts and judicial notice of law. The latter classification is actually a form of factual notice — noticing the fact of what the law is.

[2]   Judicial Notice of Fact

[a]   Facts Subject to Judicial Notice

Certain facts are so commonly known and well understood by reasonably intelligent people that their truth is literally indisputable. Consequently, courts take judicial notice of those facts without evidentiary support. The nature of the facts falling within this classification is not absolute as illustrated and explained in the case of *Williams v. Commonwealth*.

WILLIAMS v. COMMONWEALTH
Virginia Supreme Court
771 S.E.2d 675 (2015)

Opinion by CHIEF JUSTICE DONALD W. LEMONS.

In this appeal, we consider whether the Court of Appeals erred by "inferring" that the trial court took judicial notice that the situs of an offense was within its territorial jurisdiction. We also consider under what circumstances an appellate court may properly take judicial notice of a fact not clearly noticed in the trial court. Finally, we decide whether the evidence was sufficient to prove venue in this case.

I. Facts and Proceedings

The appellant, Tony Williams ("Williams"), was tried in the Circuit Court of the City of Norfolk ("trial court") and convicted of possession with intent to distribute cocaine (third offense) in violation of Code § 18.2-248. At trial, Norfolk Police Investigator Issoufou Boubacar ("Investigator Boubacar") testified that he was working as an undercover narcotics officer on the night of March 1, 2013, when he came into contact with Williams in the 1700 block of O'Keefe Street, which he testified is located in the City of Norfolk. Investigator Boubacar told Williams he wanted to buy "hard" cocaine, and Williams "agreed to assist . . . in buying [the] crack cocaine."

Williams got into Investigator Boubacar's vehicle and instructed him "to drive to the 800 block of Fremont Street." Investigator Boubacar testified that the two men "drove over there." Once they arrived, Investigator Boubacar told Williams he wanted to buy 20 dollars' worth of cocaine and gave Williams 20 dollars of "Norfolk City recorded money."

Investigator Boubacar watched Williams get out of the vehicle and meet another man to make the purchase. Williams and the other individual were approximately 10 to 15 feet away from Investigator Boubacar during the transaction. When Williams returned to the vehicle, he handed Investigator Boubacar "two plastic [bags] containing [an] off-white hard substance," which later testing confirmed to be approximately 0.2 grams of cocaine, a Schedule II controlled substance. Williams then instructed Investigator Boubacar to return to the 1700 block of O'Keefe Street. When Investigator Boubacar and Williams returned to that location, an arrest team took Williams into custody.

At the conclusion of the Commonwealth's evidence, Williams moved to strike on two grounds: (1) that the Commonwealth failed to present sufficient evidence to establish chain of custody and (2) that the Commonwealth failed to prove venue.[3] Williams argued that the Commonwealth failed to establish venue because, while Investigator Boubacar testified that the initial place of meeting — the 1700 block of O'Keefe Street — was in Norfolk, the Commonwealth never proved that the 800 block of Fremont Street was also located within the corporate limits of the City of Norfolk. Williams maintains that the evidence established that all the elements of the offense were committed in the 800 block of Fremont Street, therefore, the evidence was insufficient to prove venue.

The Commonwealth responded by arguing that Investigator Boubacar's testimony was sufficient for the trial court to take judicial notice of venue, stating, "I think it's reasonable for the Court to take judicial notice that [Investigator Boubacar and Williams] were still within the City of Norfolk" when the drug transaction took place because Investigator Boubacar had testified "to initially coming into contact with the defendant in the City of Norfolk on O'Keefe Street, and . . . to the relatively short drive to Fremont Street." The trial court overruled both motions to strike at the conclusion of the parties' arguments, stating, "I overrule the motions," without commenting on judicial notice.

Williams presented no evidence and renewed his motions to strike, which the trial court again denied. The court immediately thereafter found the defendant guilty of the offense and ordered a presentence report. On August 16, 2013, following presentation of the presentence report, the trial court sentenced Williams to ten years' imprisonment, and an additional one year suspended conditioned on one year of post-release supervision.

Williams appealed to the Court of Appeals and assigned error to the trial court's finding that the Commonwealth presented sufficient evidence to establish venue. In a published opinion, the Court of Appeals affirmed Williams' conviction, holding that it could infer that the trial court had taken judicial notice of the fact that the 800 block of Fremont Street is located within the corporate limits of the City of Norfolk and, therefore, the evidence was sufficient to prove venue. *Williams v. Commonwealth*, 758 S.E.2d 553, 557 (2014). The Court of Appeals held that while the trial court never explicitly stated that it was taking judicial notice of the fact that the 800 block of Fremont Street was in Norfolk, in overruling Williams' motion to strike on venue, the Commonwealth specifically requested the trial court to do so and, therefore, it "can be safely inferred" that the trial court took judicial notice of that fact. *Id.* at 557.

Williams appealed the judgment of the Court of Appeals to this Court, and we awarded an appeal on the following assignments of error:

1. The Court of Appeals erred in ruling that the trial court had taken judicial notice that the situs of the possession with intent to distribute was within the City of Norfolk and therefore within the territorial jurisdiction of the Court.

2. The Court of Appeals erred in finding that the trial court had venue over the offense of conviction because the evidence of record did not establish a strong presumption that the offense was committed within the territorial jurisdiction of the trial court.

II. Analysis

A. Venue and Judicial Notice

The burden is on the Commonwealth to establish venue. *Ware v. Commonwealth*, 201 S.E.2d 791, 793 (1974). A criminal charge cannot be sustained unless the evidence furnishes the foundation for a "strong presumption" that the offense was committed within the territorial jurisdiction of the court. *Harding v. Commonwealth*, 110 S.E. 376, 378 (1922); *Butler v. Commonwealth*, 81 Va. 159, 163 (1885). "The taking of judicial notice is generally within the discretion of the trial court." *Ryan v. Commonwealth*, 247 S.E.2d 698, 703 (1978). However, the question whether the Court of Appeals erred by inferring that the trial court took judicial notice that the situs of the offense was within the corporate limits of the City of Norfolk is a mixed question of law and fact, which this Court reviews de novo. *See Commonwealth v. Morris*, 705 S.E.2d 503, 505 (2011) ("We review questions of law de novo, including those situations where there is a mixed question of law and fact") (internal quotation marks and citation omitted).

"Judicial notice is a short cut to avoid the necessity for the formal introduction of evidence in certain cases where there is no need for such evidence." *Williams v. Commonwealth*, 56 S.E.2d 537, 542 (1949). Whether a trial court will exercise its discretion to take judicial notice of a fact "depends partly on the nature of the subject, the issue, the apparent justice of the case, partly on the information of the court and the means of information at hand, and partly on the judicial disposition." *Randall v. Commonwealth*, 31 S.E.2d 571, 572 (1944).

It is well-established that a trial court may take "judicial notice of geographical

facts that are matters of common knowledge, or shown by maps in common use."
McClain v. Commonwealth,, 55 S.E.2d 49, 52 (1949). Such notice may supplement
other facts proved to establish venue, or in some circumstances, "the judge may, by
judicial notice, dispense with proof" of venue. *See Randall*, 31 S.E.2d at 573 (holding
that a trial court did not abuse its discretion in taking judicial notice of the fact that
the halfway house referred to in evidence was located in York County, because the
trial court's "certificate [was] a statement that its location in that county was a
matter of wide public knowledge" within the limits of that court's territorial
jurisdiction).

i. Taking Judicial Notice in Trial Court

In *Keesee v. Commonwealth*, 217 S.E.2d 808 (1975), the evidence at trial proved
that all of the offenses took place at "'Hill's Department Store' and on its adjacent
parking lot" but no evidence was offered to prove that "Hill's Department Store"
was located in the City of Lynchburg. 217 S.E.2d at 809–10. We recognized that
geographical facts that are matters of common knowledge in a jurisdiction can be
judicially noticed, but stated that in this case "the record fail[ed] to show that the
trial court took judicial notice of the location of the store property." *Id.* at 810.
Because the record failed to show that judicial notice of the store's location had been
taken by the trial court, the evidence was insufficient to establish venue, and the
conviction was reversed and remanded. *Id.*

As the Court of Appeals has correctly observed, *Keesee* stands for the proposition
that

> [while] a trial court need not intone the words "judicial notice" in order to
> notice a fact, the evidence, the arguments of the parties and the statements
> of the trial court must demonstrate clearly that the trial court has taken
> judicial notice of the fact before a party may rely upon such notice on
> appeal.

Edmonds v. Commonwealth, 597 S.E.2d 210, 212 (2004) (quoting *Dillard v.
Commonwealth*, 504 S.E.2d 411, 414 (1998)); *see also Sutherland v. Commonwealth*,
368 S.E.2d 295, 298 (1988).

Turning to the record in this case, the Commonwealth argued to the trial court:

> Investigator Boubacar did testify initially to coming into contact with the
> defendant in the City of Norfolk on O'Keefe Street, and I believe testified
> to the relatively short drive to Fremont Street. *Based on that, Your Honor,*
> I think it's reasonable for the Court to take judicial notice that they were
> still within the City of Norfolk.

(Emphasis added.) While the Commonwealth asked the trial court to take judicial
notice "that [Investigator Boubacar and Williams] were still in the City of Norfolk"
when the offense occurred, the Commonwealth did not argue that the location of the
800 block of Fremont Street was a matter of common knowledge, nor did the
Commonwealth request that the trial court take judicial notice that the address was
located within the corporate limits of the City of Norfolk by reference to a map of
common use. The Commonwealth argued that the evidence already in the record

was sufficient for the trial court to find that venue had been established.

Because the trial court subsequently denied the motion to strike the evidence on venue without commenting on the issue of judicial notice, we are unable to discern whether the trial court decided to take judicial notice of the location of the offense, or whether the trial court simply accepted the Commonwealth's sufficiency argument on the issue of venue, based upon the evidence adduced from testimony.

Additionally, because the trial court did not indicate that it was taking judicial notice of the fact that the 800 block of Fremont Street was within its territorial jurisdiction, it deprived Williams of the opportunity to object to the trial court's action or dispute the accuracy of any "facts" noticed prior to the trial court's ruling on his motion. *See* Va. R. Evid. 2:201(c) (a party is entitled upon request "to an opportunity to be heard as to the propriety of taking judicial notice"). *Cf. State Farm Mut. Auto. Ins. Co. v. Powell*, 318 S.E.2d 393, 395 (1984) (holding that the trial court erred in taking judicial notice sua sponte of certain facts that were not included in the parties' stipulation because "State Farm had no prior opportunity to be heard either to dispute the 'facts' or to object to the court's action"). Therefore, we hold that the Court of Appeals erred in inferring that the trial court had taken judicial notice that the situs of the offense was located within its territorial jurisdiction.

ii. Taking Judicial Notice in Appellate Court

While we have determined that we cannot hold that the trial court took judicial notice that the situs of the offense was within the City of Norfolk, that does not end our analysis. The Court of Appeals also observed in a footnote, and the Commonwealth has argued on appeal to this Court, that an appellate court also "has the discretionary power to take judicial notice of the official municipal street maps of the City of Norfolk." *Williams*, 758 S.E.2d at 557 n. 6.

Rule 2:201(b) states: "Judicial notice may be taken at any stage of the proceeding." We have recognized that appellate courts may take judicial notice of geographical facts that are so well known that they are matters of common knowledge in the Commonwealth. *See, e.g., Buttery v. Robbins*, 14 S.E.2d 544, 546 (1941) (taking judicial notice that the "Skyline Drive is in the Shenandoah National Park" because "[t]hat is a matter of common knowledge"). However, as we stated in *Keesee*, there is a range of procedural postures in which issues arise, and the existence of differing records, and hence some geographical facts will not be the subject of judicial notice on appeal. *See* 217 S.E.2d at 810 (reversing conviction because the record did not show that the location of "Hill's Department Store" was a "matter of common knowledge susceptible of being judicially noticed"). We have also declined to take judicial notice of certain documents when they were not relied upon in the trial court. *See Commonwealth v. Woodward*, 452 S.E.2d 656, 657 (1995).

The fact that the 800 block of Fremont Street is in the City of Norfolk is not a matter of common knowledge susceptible of being judicially noticed by this Court. While it is true that a street address is a geographical fact that is typically ascertainable by reference to a map of common use, no map was proffered or referenced in the trial court. In this case we will not exercise our discretion to take judicial notice.

B. Sufficiency of the Evidence

On appeal, we review "whether the evidence, when viewed in the light most favorable to the Commonwealth, is sufficient to support the [trial court's] venue findings." *Cheng v. Commonwealth*, 393 S.E.2d 599, 604 (1990).

Code § 19.2–244 provides that "the prosecution of a criminal case shall be had in the county or city in which the offense was committed." As noted earlier, the Commonwealth has the burden "to prove venue by evidence which is either direct or circumstantial." *Pollard v. Commonwealth*, 261 S.E.2d 328, 330 (1980). Such evidence, when viewed in the light most favorable to the Commonwealth, must give rise to a "'strong presumption' that the offense was committed within the jurisdiction of the court." *Meeks v. Commonwealth*, 651 S.E.2d 637, 639 (2007) (quoting *Cheng*, 393 S.E.2d at 604).

"The failure to clearly prove venue is usually due to inadvertence, flowing naturally from the familiarity of court, counsel, witnesses, and jurors with the locality of the crime"; therefore; this Court "will generally and properly lay hold of and accept as sufficient any evidence in the case, direct or otherwise, from which the fact may be reasonably inferred." *Randall*, 31 S.E.2d at 573 (quoting *West v. Commonwealth*, 99 S.E. 654, 654–55 (1919) and *Byrd v. Commonwealth*, 98 S.E. 632, 634 (1919)).

Neither the allegation of venue set forth in the indictment, nor the fact that the Norfolk police conducted the investigation in this case, standing alone, may support an inference that the crime took place within the trial court's territorial jurisdiction. *See Keesee*, 217 S.E.2d at 810 ("The mere fact that the local police department was involved in the investigation of the crimes and that warrants recited proper venue, standing alone as they do here, will not suffice.").

The Commonwealth failed to present evidence concerning whether the 800 block of Fremont Street, where Williams possessed and sold the crack cocaine, is located within the City of Norfolk. Although the Commonwealth argued to the trial court that Investigator Boubacar had "testified to the relatively short drive to Fremont Street" from O'Keefe Street, the evidence does not support this argument. Investigator Boubacar testified that he met Williams in the 1700 block of O'Keefe Street, in the City of Norfolk; that he and Williams "drove over there," — referring to the 800 block of Fremont Street; and that after the transaction was completed they returned to the 1700 block of O'Keefe Street, where an arrest team took Williams into custody. Williams' signed confession introduced into evidence only indicates that he met Investigator Boubacar in the 1700 block of O'Keefe Street and does not mention the 800 block of Fremont Street or whether the crime occurred within the City of Norfolk. Nothing in the record indicates the distance between the two locations, the route of travel, or even the duration of the entire encounter.

Even with all reasonable inferences drawn in the light most favorable to the Commonwealth, we hold that this evidence was insufficient to create a "strong presumption" that the offense was committed in the City of Norfolk. Therefore, the

Commonwealth failed to meet its burden of proof regarding venue in this case.

III. Conclusion

The record does not clearly reflect that the trial court took judicial notice that the situs of the offense was within the corporate limits of the City of Norfolk, and absent such judicial notice, the evidence was insufficient to prove venue. Therefore, we will reverse the judgment of the Court of Appeals.

However, "[p]roof of venue . . . is not regarded as material, so far as the merits of the prosecution are concerned, and so the allegation of venue is not a part of the crime." *Randall*, 31 S.E.2d at 573. Because failure to offer proof establishing proper venue "did not stem from evidentiary insufficiency with respect to the guilt or innocence of the defendant," *Pollard*, 261 S.E.2d at 330, we will remand the case to the Court of Appeals with directions that it remand the case to the circuit court for a new trial, if the Commonwealth be so advised.

Reversed and remanded.

JUSTICE POWELL, with whom JUSTICE McCLANAHAN joins, dissenting.

I respectfully disagree with the majority's conclusion that the Court of Appeals erred by "inferring" that the trial court took judicial notice that the situs of the offense was within the City of Norfolk. In my opinion, the trial court implicitly took judicial notice of venue by overruling Williams' motion to strike the Commonwealth's evidence after the Commonwealth stated the trial court could and should take judicial notice that the 800 block of Fremont Street is located within the boundaries of the City of Norfolk.

As the majority recognizes, the trial court did not need to explicitly state it was taking judicial notice of the location of Fremont Street.

> "[A] trial court need not intone the words 'judicial notice' in order to notice a fact, [however] the evidence, the arguments of the parties and the statements of the trial court must demonstrate clearly that the trial court has taken judicial notice of the fact before a party may rely upon such notice on appeal."

Edmonds v. Commonwealth, 597 S.E.2d 210, 212 (2004) (emphasis omitted) (quoting *Dillard v. Commonwealth*, 504 S.E.2d 411, 414 (1998)). Here the evidence, the arguments of counsel, and the statements of the trial court all clearly demonstrate that the trial court took judicial notice of the location of the 800 block of Fremont Street. Therefore, I would affirm the judgment of the Court of Appeals.

The evidence in this case shows that Norfolk Police Investigator Boubacar met Williams on O'Keefe Street in the City of Norfolk and arranged the drug deal. The deal itself occurred on the 800 block of Fremont Street. Williams was indicted in the City of Norfolk. The trial court did not question whether the 800 block of Fremont Street was outside of the City of Norfolk once Williams raised the venue issue. The addition of the street name draws a distinction between evidence that is insufficient to support the inference, and evidence that is sufficient for that purpose.

Indeed, our jurisprudence clearly supports a finding that the evidence is sufficient to support an inference when the street name is provided, coupled with the often pronounced legal principle that

> [a] trial court may take judicial notice of those facts that are either (1) so "generally known" within the jurisdiction or (2) so "easily ascertainable" by reference to reliable sources that reasonably informed people in the community would not regard them as reasonably subject to dispute.

Taylor v. Commonwealth, 502 S.E.2d 113, 116, (1998) (quoting *Ryan v. Commonwealth*, 247 S.E.2d 698, 703 (1978)) (citing 2 McCormick on Evidence § 328 (John William Strong ed., 4th ed.1992); Charles E. Friend, The Law of Evidence in Virginia, § 19–2 (3d ed.1988)).

In *West v. Commonwealth*, 99 S.E. 654 (1919), we stated:

> [i]n the case at bar there is no direct proof that the crime was committed at Petersburg, but the following circumstances fully warrant the inference that it did take place there: The indictment charged that the property was stolen in the city of Petersburg, and belonged either to E.A. Robertson or to his wife. The case was tried at Petersburg, and the witness Worrell testified that he was employed as a detective with "the local police force," went with Wilkerson, another police officer, to investigate the case, found the stolen property at the prisoner's home, then went to the home of Mrs. Robertson and brought her to the prisoner's home to identify the property. Wilkerson testified "that he was employed as a detective with the local police department, and went to see Mrs. E.A. Robertson in response to a telephone call from her advising him that certain articles were missing from her home, and went with the officer, Worrell, to the home of Frances West and found the alleged stolen articles there; that he remained at her home while Officer Worrell went to get Mrs. Robertson to identify the various stolen articles." C.E. Perkinson testified "that he was employed as a detective with the local police department, and assisted in the investigation of the West case." E.A. Robertson and wife testified that the property was stolen from their home on Sycamore street.

Id. at 655. From these facts, this Court upheld a finding of venue stating,

> [t]he record in this case shows that the court, counsel, jurors and witnesses must necessarily have been familiar with the location of the Robertson home on Sycamore street.

Id. at 655. The Court also noted that the facts in *West* "raise[d] a violent presumption that the Robertson house was within the local jurisdiction of the court, and we do not feel warranted in reversing the judgment upon this point." *Id.*

A review of the evidence in *West* demonstrates that in addition to testimony regarding the location charged in the indictment and the fact that police officers from the relevant jurisdiction investigated the crime, the only other fact related to the issue of venue was a street name.

Keesee v. Commonwealth, 217 S.E.2d 808 (1975), provides additional support for the proposition that evidence of venue set forth in the indictment and evidence that the local police department conducted the investigation, coupled with a street name and the fact that a trial court may take judicial notice of facts that are "generally known" or "easily ascertainable" are sufficient to establish venue. *Ryan*, 247 S.E.2d at 703. In finding the facts establishing that the local police department investigated the crime, the car was towed to the local impound lot, and the warrants identified the city and the name of the establishment were insufficient, we specifically stated, "[t]he record fails to reveal *even* the street on which the store is located." *Keesee*, 217 S.E.2d at 810 (emphasis added). The clear implication was that this fact would have made a difference to the Court's decision.

Similarly, in *Hart v. Commonwealth*, 109 S.E. 582 (1921), emphasis was placed upon the fact that the victim lived "on a certain road," was "going along said road from her home toward her place of work . . . , and that the point in the road at which she was assaulted was on the side of the road 'coming to Staunton.'" *Id.* at 584. The Court found that "when the facts proved . . . are considered along with the fact of which the court will take judicial notice . . . it appears that the venue has been proved by the Commonwealth beyond any reasonable doubt." *Id.* at 586. The Court also noted that

> it is a geographical fact, shown by any map in common use, and thus a matter of common knowledge, that the city of Staunton is located within the county of Augusta, and is so located therein that the county of Augusta surrounds, and, beyond all question, extends for a distance of over fifteen miles to the west of the corporate limits of the city of Staunton. The court will, therefore, take judicial notice of that fact.

Id. at 584–85. Therefore, the evidence supports a finding that the trial court took judicial notice of venue and properly did so.

Likewise, in the instant case, the arguments of the parties and the statements of the trial court demonstrate that the trial court took judicial notice of the fact of venue. At the conclusion of the Commonwealth's case, Williams made a motion to strike on two bases, venue and chain of custody. In response to the venue argument, the Commonwealth made one assertion, that the trial court should take judicial notice of the location of the 800 block of Fremont Street. With only one argument raised regarding venue and one response given, the trial court's response was, "I overrule the motions." As the Court of Appeals found, the only logical conclusion is that the trial court, in response to the venue challenge, actually took judicial notice that the 800 block of Fremont Street is in Norfolk.

State Farm Mutual Automobile Insurance Co. v. Powell, 318 S.E.2d 393 (1984) is inapposite because in that case, the trial court took judicial notice of certain facts sua sponte, thereby depriving the defendant of the opportunity to be heard and to object. *Id.* at 395. Here, Williams was heard and indeed raised the issue of venue. The Commonwealth's only response was to ask the trial court to take judicial notice of the fact of venue. After overruling Williams' motion, the trial court asked, "Anything else, Mr. Pollack?" to which Williams' counsel responded, "No, Your Honor." Clearly, Williams had an opportunity to be heard, to dispute the facts, and to object.

Therefore, the evidence indicates that the trial court took judicial notice of the fact of venue and that based on our precedent, it properly did so. *See Hart*, 109 S.E. at 584–86; *West*, 99 S.E. at 655. I would therefore find that the Court of Appeals did not err in affirming the trial court's judgment and would decline to address Williams' second assignment of error as moot.

[b]   Indisputable Facts

[i]   Commonly Known Facts

Some facts are universal truths commonly known by everyone, such as the facts that the sun rises in the east and sets in the west, and that people are mortal and eventually die. Such facts are judicially noticed by all courts. As *Williams* illustrated, however, a fact need not be of universal notoriety to be the subject of judicial notice. It can be distinctly local in character. It need only be commonly known in the local community where the court is sitting. The character of Mission Street in *Varcoe* was such a fact. Other examples of locally known facts include: that pine trees will not grow where cypress trees grow, *see Fox v. City of West Palm Beach*, 383 F.2d 189, 194–195, n.2 (5th Cir. 1967); and that a particular lake is a navigable waterway, *see Smith v. Hustler, Inc.*, 514 F. Supp. 1265, 1268 (W.D. La. 1981). Obviously, therefore, facts that are the proper subject of judicial notice will vary from one jurisdiction to the next.

An important theoretical qualification of this category of judicially noticeable facts is that the judge's knowledge cannot be equated with that of the community generally. The presiding judge's knowledge does not provide the assurance of indisputability that justifies short-circuiting the adversarial process. Therefore, the judge may not render a decision on the basis of facts that the judge acquired as a practicing attorney. *See Fox v. City of West Palm Beach*, 383 F.2d 189 (5th Cir. 1967). Similarly, a judge may not elect to believe one witness over another simply because the judge has personal knowledge of the needs and motives of the witness whose testimony the judge believed. *See Government of the Virgin Islands v. Gereau*, 523 F.2d 140 (3d Cir. 1975). As Professor Wigmore explained:

> There is a real but elusive line between the judge's *personal knowledge* as a private man and these matters of which he takes judicial notice as a judge. The latter does not necessarily include the former; as a judge, indeed, he may have to ignore what he knows as a man, and contrariwise.

*   *   *

> It is therefore plainly accepted that the judge is not to use from the bench, under the guise of judicial knowledge, that which he knows *only as an individual* observer outside the court. The former is in truth "known" to him merely in the fictional sense that it is known and notorious to all men, and the dilemma is only the result of using the term "knowledge" in two senses. Where to draw the line between knowledge by notoriety and knowledge by personal observation may sometimes be difficult, but the principle is plain.

9 J. WIGMORE, EVIDENCE § 2569, at 722–723 (Chadbourn rev. 1981).

Conversely, of course, it is inappropriate for a judge to refuse to take judicial notice of facts merely because the judge is not personally familiar with them. If certain facts are shown to be commonly accepted status, the judge's previous unawareness of them is simply irrelevant.

Realistically, the presiding judges' special knowledge or ignorance will inevitably influence their decisions on judicial notice because people perceive themselves as being both knowledgable and well-informed. Thus, most judges will define what is commonly known and accepted as true by what they know.

A number of facts of which courts have taken judicial notice include those which, although once commonly known, can no longer be recalled with accuracy. These include such historical facts as the day of the week on which a particular date occurred or the identity of one who has held a particular public office at a give time. Because witnesses could refresh their memories by reference to unimpeachable sources (calendars, for example, for the day of the week, and official state publications for an officeholder's identity), courts initially took judicial notice of such facts under the rubric of common knowledge. Over time, however, this charade was seen for what it was — a legal fiction — and courts came to recognize a second category of indisputable facts: those that could be established with accuracy from unimpeachable sources.

[ii]   Facts That Are Easily Verifiable from Unimpeachable Sources

Courts have concluded that it is a waste of judicial time to require proof of facts that can be established with accuracy from unimpeachable and authoritative sources. This category of facts is potentially very broad, because courts have not established guidelines for determining what constitutes a competent or authoritative source. For example, in *B.V.D. Licensing Corp. v. Body Action Design, Inc.*, 846 F.2d 727, 728 (Fed. Cir. 1988), the court took judicial notice of the fact that "B.V.D." referred to underwear. The court relied on an entry in Webster's Third New International Dictionary (1971) that read "B.V.D. . . . *trademark* — used for underwear." Therefore, the matter is wholly within the trial court's discretion. Historically, courts have tended to limit this category of facts to matters that can be established by reference to easily accessible sources — such as almanacs, dictionaries, encyclopedias, maps, and other common reference materials.

To varying degrees, although with less frequency than might be expected, courts have also taken judicial notice of public records. Courts are generally willing to notice matters of record in the case before the court. However, trial judge's willingness to take judicial notice diminishes as the difficulty of obtaining access to the records from other proceedings increases. For example, a number of courts have noticed facts of record in other judicial proceedings involving the same parties in the same jurisdiction, *see In re Clausen*, 289 N.W.2d 153 (Minn. 1980) (taking judicial notice of records from the criminal and juvenile divisions of the same court), but have refused notice facts of unrelated cases within the same jurisdiction. This unwillingness is more pronounced for facts from cases from other jurisdictions. The same hesitation exists regarding facts from other governmental entities.

Courts have also judicially noticed scientific facts, even though the facts are neither commonly known nor as readily verifiable from common reference sources as other judicially noticed facts. If the accuracy and reliability of a scientific principle has been repeatedly established in judicial proceedings, a time comes (which cannot be accurately defined) when the presiding judge will no longer require a factual demonstration. In effect, the judge will rely on personal knowledge of the principle that was acquired from the prior demonstrations (a basis which, standing alone, would be an insufficient justification for taking judicial notice) and will refer to sources that the judge has come to know are authoritative and unimpeachable. This manner of taking judicial notice is illustrated in the following case, *Hollingr v. Shoppers Paradise of New Jersey, Inc.*, in which the court took judicial notice of the fact that one cannot contract trichinosis from properly cooked pork.

HOLLINGER v.
SHOPPERS PARADISE OF NEW JERSEY, INC.
Superior Court of New Jersey
340 A.2d 687 (1975)

Rosenberg, J.S.C.

This matter involves various claims for damages suffered by plaintiffs when they allegedly contracted trichinosis from pork sold by defendant Shoppers Paradise of New Jersey, Inc.1 Trial was held on March 18 to 24, 1975. At the close of plaintiffs' case Shoppers Paradise moved for involuntary dismissal of the claims against it under R. 4:37-2(b), upon which motion the court reserved decision. At the conclusion of its case Shoppers Paradise renewed its application for involuntary dismissal and defendants Windish and Dubuque Packing Co. moved under R. 4:37-2(c) to dismiss the claims for contribution asserted against them by Shoppers Paradise. After argument all motions for dismissal were granted. An order of dismissal as to all defendants encompassing these rulings was entered on April 7, 1975. Plaintiffs appeal this order in a notice of appeal served April 28, 1975. This supplemental opinion is filed in response to that notice pursuant to R. 2:5-1(b) to aid the appellate court in its determinations.

The principal facts of this case do not appear to be in dispute. On October 9, 1971 Mrs. Hollinger purchased a raw pork roast, which was sliced into a quantity of pork chops, at the Shoppers Paradise store located at Route 46 in Fairfield, New Jersey. Some of these chops were prepared by Mrs. Hollinger and consumed by her, her husband and their four children on October 10, 1971. Within sometime thereafter (the precise period is unclear) all the family members experienced some muscle pain, nausea and diarrhea; in the case of Mrs. Hollinger the symptoms were aggravated and included chest pains, heavy perspiration, skin rash and swelling of various parts of the body. This led to her hospitalization, where it was determined that she suffered from a parasitic infection diagnosed as trichinosis. Both Mr. Hollinger and the children were tested for this condition, with the results indicating no trace of the disease in Mr. Hollinger but mild cases in the children; at present, with the exception of muscle pain in one of the children, there is no indication of either the symptoms of the illness or the presence of trichinae parasites in Mr. Hollinger or the children. Although her condition has improved, Mrs. Hollinger still complains of muscle aches, chest pains, headaches and a spotting of the skin. Blood tests indicate that she continues to suffer from trichinosis.

An understanding of the nature and characteristics of the disease is helpful in analyzing the issues raised in this case. Under Evid. R. 9(2)(e) the court takes judicial notice of facts contained in two United States Department of Agriculture (U.S.D.A.) publications: 'Facts About Trichinosis,' Agriculture Research Bulletin ARS 91-72 (April 1969), and 'Trichinosis,' Leaflet No. 428, U.S.D.A. (revised September 1968). The disease is caused by parasitic worms called trichinae (Trichinella spiralis) and may infect humans eating raw or under-cooked pork in which the parasite is encysted. On ingestion of contaminated meat the parasites travel into the intestinal tract where they reproduce and move through the bloodstream to invade the voluntary muscles, growing and eventually becoming encysted therein. When the parasites reach the intestines they may cause upset stomach, vomiting, diarrhea and other symptoms of intestinal disorder. During the period of migration and encystment the host may have muscular pain, rising fever, headaches and prostration. When the larvae reach the muscles, swelling of the face and other parts of the body, sore eyes, hemorrhaging under the skin, sore throat, headache, fever and difficulty breathing commonly are experienced. After encystment these symptoms gradually may disappear although muscle stiffness can linger in severe cases. Most patients suffering from the disease recover with proper treatment.

Stringent control over the feeding of hogs and meat inspection procedures which assure that pork used in products customarily eaten without further cooking has been treated so as to kill trichinae have helped reduce the extent of the disease from an estimated incidence of about 16% Of the population during the 1930's and early 1940's to approximately 4 to 5% In recent years. Despite these gains in disease control, there is no completely effective method for detecting trichinae in raw pork. As a result the U.S.D.A. does not require inspection of unprocessed meat sold for human consumption. However, it is a known scientific fact that heating raw pork above a temperature of 137 F. will destroy the parasite and render the meat safe to eat. Thorough cooking is the only means of insuring that raw pork is completely free of trichinae.

*   *   *

Two reasonable inferences which could be drawn from the sale of the pork chops to Mrs. Hollinger and the subsequent illness of her and her family are that the meat was unfit for consumption and that this unfitness proximately caused plaintiffs' injuries. However, to infer that the product was unfit upon reviewing the consequences of its use is not to say that it was not Reasonably fit at the time of sale for its ordinary and intended purpose. Raw pork is a unique product in that it may contain an inherent defect (trichinae) which is undetectable by the seller but curable through preparation by the consumer. The fact that there is a danger of illness as a consequence of eating uncooked or underdone pork is a matter of common knowledge which courts in other jurisdictions have recognized and of which this court takes notice. Evid.R. 9(2)(d); *Silverman v. Swift & Co.*, 141 Conn. 450, 107 A.2d 277 (Sup. Ct. Err. 1954); *Meyer v. Greenwood*, 125 Ind. App. 288, 124 N.E.2d 870 (App. Ct. 1955); *Adams v. Scheib*, 408 Pa. 452, 184 A.2d 700 (Sup. Ct. 1962). It follows that the ordinary and intended purpose for raw pork is consumption after Proper cooking by the consumer and that if the chops in question were reasonably fit at the time of sale for such use Shoppers Paradise may avoid a finding of strict liability or breach of warranty.

On direct examination Mrs. Hollinger was asked how she cooked the pork chops served on October 10, 1971. Her testimony indicates the method and degree of preparation:

Q. Now, will you tell me exactly in what manner you prepared the pork chops for that day. Explain exactly what you did on Sunday with regard to those pork chops * * *

A. * * * I salted, peppered them put garlic on. And I prepared them and I fried them in a cast-iron skillet * * * I had four pork chops at one time in the skillet which fitted on the bottom, and they were browned on one side. I turned them over, browned the other side for 15 minutes, 10 to 15 minutes approximately, each side. I took them out and then I browned the other three, did the same thing, browned them on both sides * * * in oil * * * then I browned some diced onions. When they were brown, I added the pork chops back into the skillet and added water to cover the pork chops and put a cover on and boiled them for an hour and ten minutes.

Q. What kind of stove do you have?

A. Gas stove.

Q. Gas. How would you describe how the flame was on the stove that day?

A. It was medium.

Q. Was the water bubbling?

A. Yes, it was boiling.

Q. Did the water boil over?

A. No.

Q. Now, at the end of this hour and ten minute period, you say you took the — what did you say? At the end of the hour and ten minutes, what did you do with the pork chops?

A. I tested them first with the fork and they were very nice and tender, and I removed them from the heat and I served them.

Q. When you say you tested them with the fork, what did you do with the fork?

A. I stuck the fork in it and they were beautifully, perfectly cooked because I made pork chops many times before.

Q.   When you say 'beautifully, perfectly cooked' what was the color inside?

A.   It was a gray, whatever, or browned. It was browned. It was brownish, whatever—

Q.   Well, was there—

A.   Well, the pork chops fell apart. This is how soft they were. How can I — they were browned and I had gravy over it so they were — the pork chops were brown from frying them and with the gravy — with the gravy over it, with the fried onions, so it makes it brownish.

It is apparent that if plaintiffs contracted trichinosis from the pork chops despite this seemingly thorough cooking, all the meat was not exposed to the minimum temperature of 137 F. necessary to destroy the trichinae. This necessarily leads to the question of whether the pork in fact was properly cooked by Mrs. Hollinger before consumption which, in turn, depends on how the term 'properly cooked' is defined. A question of first impression in New Jersey, its resolution determines whether Shoppers Paradise might be held liable for sale of a product not reasonably fit for its ordinary and intended purpose.

Although our courts have not previously dealt with this problem, courts in other jurisdictions have considered situations similar to the one posed here. In *Holt v. Mann*, 294 Mass. 21, 200 N.E. 403 (Sup. Jud. Ct. 1936), plaintiff contracted trichinosis from eating ham. The court determined that whether the meat was properly cooked was a jury question and the standard to which the consumer should be held is one of 'ordinary household cooking.' 294 Mass. at 24, 200 N.E. at 405. It went on to express its reasoning:

> It is true according to the evidence, that trichinae are killed by exposure to heat of one hundred thirty-seven degrees Fahrenheit. But in ordinary household cooking it is not easy to be sure that every part of a ham will be heated to so high a degree. It could have been found that the ham was cooked as thoroughly as could be expected in a family, but without killing trichinae with which it was infested. The ham could have been found not 'reasonably fit' for the purpose for which it was bought. (294 Mass. at 24, 200 N.E. at 405)

This approach was reaffirmed in Massachusetts in *Arena v. John P. Squire Co.*, 321 Mass. 423, 73 N.E.2d 836 (Sup. Jud. Ct. 1947), and adopted in *Connecticut, Silverman v. Swift & Co.*, *supra*, 141 Conn. 450, 107 A.2d 277; Indiana, *Meyer v. Greenwood*, *supra*, 125 Ind. App. 288, 124 N.E.2d 870; Maryland, *Vaccarino v. Cozzubo*, 181 Md. 614, 31 A.2d 316 (1943); and Pennsylvania, *Adams v. Schieb*, *supra*, 408 Pa. 452, 184 A.2d 700.

The so-called 'Massachusetts rule' expressed above has been explicitly rejected in two jurisdictions. Illinois' courts have held that proper cooking of raw pork means that the meat has been heated to the temperature of 137 F. *Zorger v. Hillman's*, *supra*, 287 Ill. App. 357, 4 N.E.2d 900; *Nicketta v. National Tea Co.*, 338 Ill. App. 159, 87 N.E.2d 30 (App. Ct. 1949). Language used by the court in *Nicketta* is particularly expressive of the Illinois view: Plaintiffs allege that the only obligation which exists between a purchaser of fresh pork and a retail seller is that there is an implied warranty that the pork will be fit, wholesome and proper for human consumption after proper cooking. They also allege that they purchased the pork from the defendant; that it was properly cooked; that they ate it; and that they acquired or became infested with trichinosis. They alleged a factual impossibility, a fact irrefutable by a well established scientific rule, of which it was the duty of the trial court to take judicial notice, namely, that a human being cannot acquire trichinosis from eating pork which has been properly cooked. (338 Ill. App. at 168, 87 N.E.2d at 34). See also, *Golaris v. Jewel Tea Co.*, 22 F.R.D. 16 (D.C.N.D. Ill. 1958). This same position was endorsed by the Supreme Judicial Court of Maine in *Kobeckis v. Budzko*, Me., 225 A.2d 418 (1967):

> The phrases 'ordinary domestic cooking,' etc., cited above are no real guide in the cooking of pork and pork products as a premise upon which to found a complaint for breach of implied warranty. As of this date, authoritative sources are uniform in saying that raising the pork or pork product to a temperature of 137 Fahrenheit kills trichinae and 'proper' cooking as used in this case means raising the temperature throughout the meat or meat product to a minimum of 137 Fahrenheit. (Me., 225 A.2d at 424)

A necessary implication to be drawn from this approach is that a consumer who prepares raw pork for consumption and thereafter contracts trichinosis from it has not properly cooked the meat. Since the product thus cannot be shown to be unfit for its ordinary and intended purpose, I.e. eating after proper cooking, recovery for breach of warranty (or strict liability) is impossible. See *Frumer & Friedman, supra*, s 25.04(2).

It is the view of this court that as between these two rules the latter is the more sound. To require proper cooking of raw pork by the consumer to eliminate trichinae and then to hold that such cooking need not in fact make the meat safe is anomalous; if not a 'factual impossibility,' as observed in *Nicketta, supra*, this approach at least invites an illogical result. An even more compelling reason for adopting the minority rule is that it is compatible with the doctrine of strict liability developed by our courts.

> Since the landmark case of *Henningsen v. Bloomfield Motors, Inc.*, 32 N.J. 358, 161 A.2d 69 (1960), New Jersey has been in the forefront of jurisdictions extending protection to consumers by imposing strict liability in tort. The doctrine expressly has been extended to the manufacturer and/or seller of automobiles, *Henningsen, supra; Scanlon v. Gen. Motors Corp., supra*, 65 N.J. 582, 326 A.2d 673; *Moraca v. Ford Motor Co.*, 66 N.J. 454, 332 A.2d 599 (1975); motorcycles, *Sabloff v. Yamaha Motor Co., Ltd.*, 113 N.J. Super. 279, 273 A.2d 606 (App. Div. 1971), aff'd 59 N.J. 365, 283 A.2d 321 (1971); carpeting, *Santor v. A. & M. Karagheusian, Inc., supra*, 44 N.J. 52, 207 A.2d 305; grinding discs, *Jakubowski v. Minn. Mining & Manufacturing*, 80 N.J. Super. 184, 193 A.2d 275 (App. Div. 1963), rev'd on other grounds, 42 N.J. 177, 199 A.2d 826 (1964); mass-produced houses, *Schipper v. Levitt & Sons, Inc.*, 44 N.J. 70, 207 A.2d 314 (1965); cafeteria food, *Sofman v. Denham Food Service, Inc., supra*, 37 N.J. 304, 181 A.2d 168; a power punch press, *Bexiga v. Havir Mfg. Corp.*, 60 N.J. 402, 290 A.2d 281 (1972); *Finnegan v. Havir Mfg. Corp.*, 60 N.J. 413, 290 A.2d 286 (1972);

carbonated beverage bottles, *Corbin v. Camden Coca-Cola Bottling Co.*, *supra*, 60 N.J. 425, 290 A.2d 441; permanent hair wave solution, *Newmark v. Gimbel's Inc.*, *supra*, 54 N.J. 585, 258 A.2d 697; and water meters, *Rosenau v. New Brunswick, etc.*, 51 N.J. 130, 238 A.2d 169 (1968); it also applies to lessors of rented motor vehicles and trailers, *Cintrone v. Hertz Truck Leasing, etc.*, 45 N.J. 434, 212 A.2d 769 (1965); *Ettin v. Ava Truck Leasing, Inc.*, 53 N.J. 463, 251 A.2d 278 (1969). Recovery is based on considerations of policy rather than actionable conduct by the defendant. These considerations are identified in *Cintrone, supra:*Warranties of fitness are regarded by law as an incident of a transaction because One party to the relationship is in a better position than the other to know and control the condition of the chattel transferred and To distribute the losses which may occur because of a dangerous condition the chattel possesses. These factors make it likely that the party acquiring possession of the article will assume it is in a safe condition for use and therefore refrain from taking precautionary measures himself. 2 Harper & James, Torts, s 28.19 (1956). * * * (45 N.J. at 446, 212 A.2d at 775; emphasis supplied)

In the case of raw pork the factual premise upon which the first policy consideration rests is not present. Because of the character of the product it is impossible for the seller to detect the presence of the latent defect. In this sense the situation is analogous to that posed by the presence of serum hepatitis in whole blood. In the recent case of *Brody v. Overlook Hosp.*, 127 N.J. Super. 331, 317 A.2d 392 (App. Div. 1974), aff'd 66 N.J. 448, 332 A.2d 596 (1975), the court was unwilling to impose strict liability upon a blood bank for the death of plaintiff's decedent caused by a transfusion of blood containing hepatitis. The decision was based largely on the fact that no method existed whereby the blood could be tested for serum hepatitis virus prior to transfusion. *Id.* at 336, 317 A.2d 392. The same result was reached in *Jackson v. Muhlenberg Hosp.*, 96 N.J. Super. 314, 232 A.2d 879 (Law Div. 1967), rev'd on other grounds, 53 N.J. 138, 249 A.2d 65 (1969), where it was concluded that 'The Unavoidable presence of hepatitis virus in the blood furnished does not give rise to strict liability for the resultant harm.' *Id.* at 333, 232 A.2d at 890 (emphasis supplied). Shoppers Paradise is in much the same position as to the trichinous pork chops as Overlook and Muhlenberg Hospitals were as to the contaminated blood; as in the blood cases the policy justification is not here present upon which strict liability may be predicated.

One significant way in which this case is distinguishable from the blood cases is that here a cure exists for the latent defect in the product. In both Jackson and Brody the court found support for the nonapplication of strict liability in Restatement, Torts 2d, s 402A, comment (k), dealing with 'unavoidable unsafe products,' which are characterized as 'products which, in the present state of human knowledge, are quite incapable of being made safe for their intended use, The courts endorsed the reasoning of the Restatement in concluding that blood properly prepared and accompanied by proper directions and warnings is not unreasonably dangerous in light of its utility, and the seller therefore 'is not be held to strict liability for unfortunate consequences attending their (sic) use, merely because he has undertaken to supply the public with an apparently useful and desirable product, attended with a known but apparently reasonable risk.' Restatement, *supra*; *Brody v. Overlook*, *supra*, 127 N.J. Super. at 339, 317 A.2d 392. Since the presence of trichinae in raw pork can be cured But only by the consumer, the rationale for absolving the helpless seller from strict liability for damages caused by the parasite is even more compelling than in the case of a product where no cure is known. To put it another way, where the user of the product is contributorily negligent for failing to make the product safe, the seller should not be held to a strict liability standard. Contributory negligence is a good defense to strict liability unless considerations of policy and justice make it inapplicable. *Bexiga v. Havir Mfg. Corp.*, *supra*, 60 N.J. at 412, 290 A.2d 281; *Cintrone v. Hertz Truck Leasing, etc.*, *supra*, 45 N.J. at 457–459, 212 A.2d 769; *Ettin v. Ava Truck Leasing, Inc.*, *supra*, 53 N.J. at 471–474, 251 A.2d 278; *Maiorino v. Weco Products Co.*, 45 N.J. 570, 214 A.2d 18 (1965). Here, because of the unique character of raw pork, considerations of policy and justice compel a finding of contributory negligence as a matter of law. Since the inherent danger in uncooked or underdone pork is a fact of common knowledge chargeable to the consumer, he can neither assume that the seller has taken action to cure the defect nor avoid responsibility for failing to take such action himself.

The other policy ground upon which the cases base strict liability is one of 'risk distribution' which suggests that the seller should bear the cost of damages arising from the product because he is better able to spread the risks by procuring liability insurance or impleading other potentially culpable parties (manufacturer, wholeasler, distributor, etc.). Such a rationale is arbitrary in that it fails to account for the specific characteristics of the product in question and the relationship between the particular consumer and seller from which the action for strict liability arises. For this reason the 'loss spreading' theory has been given relatively little weight when compared to other policy considerations; 'it plays 'only the part of a make weight argument',' *Magrine v. Krasnica*, 94 N.J. Super. 228, 239, 227 A.2d 539, 546 (Cty. Ct. 1967); *Brody v. Overlook Hosp.*, *supra*, 127 N.J. Super. at 341, 317 A.2d 392. In light of the more compelling considerations of knowledge and curability of the defect discussed above, the 'risk distribution' theory does not provide a sufficient basis upon which to hold the defendant strictly liable.

For the foregoing reasons it is the opinion of the court that the policies compelling application of strict liability are not applicable in the case of a consumer contracting trichinosis from pork chops. This is consistent with the holding that Mrs. Hollinger failed to properly cook the meat served on October 10, 1971 and leads to the conclusion that plaintiffs have failed to prove as a matter of law that defendant sold a product not reasonably fit for its ordinary and intended purpose. For these reasons the motion of Shoppers Paradise for dismissal of the complaint is granted.

[c]　　　Legislative Facts — Facts upon Which the Law Is Interpreted and Applied

Professor Davis coined the label "legislative facts" to distinguish facts that influence or control the creation, revision, interpretation or application of legal principles from the adjudicative facts of a particular case to which the law is applied. *See* Davis, *An Approach to Problems of Evidence in the Administrative*

Process, 55 Harv. L. Rev. 364, 402–403 (1942). Courts have imposed different and more stringent rules on the taking of judicial notice of adjudicative facts than of legislative facts. Explaining this distinction in treatment, Professor Davis later wrote:

> When a court . . . finds facts concerning the immediate parties — who did what, where, when, how, and with what motive or intent — the court or agency is performing an adjudicative function, and the facts so determined are conveniently called adjudicative facts. When a court or an agency develops law or policy, it is acting legislatively; the courts have created the common law through judicial legislation, and the facts which inform the tribunal's legislative judgment are called legislative facts.
>
> Stated in other terms, the adjudicative facts are those to which the law is applied in the process of adjudication. They are the facts that normally go to the jury in a jury case. They relate to the parties, their activities, their properties, their businesses. Legislative facts are those which help the tribunal to determine the content of law and policy and to exercise its judgment or discretion in determining what course of action to take. Legislative facts are ordinarily general and do not concern the immediate parties. In the great mass of cases decided by courts and by agencies, the legislative element is either absent, unimportant, or interstitial, because in most cases the applicable law and policy have been previously established. But whenever a tribunal is engaged in the creation of law or of policy, it may need to resort to legislative facts, whether or not those facts have been developed on the record.
>
> The exceedingly practical difference between legislative and adjudicative facts is that, apart from facts properly noticed, the tribunal's findings of adjudicative facts must be supported by evidence, but findings or assumptions of legislative facts need not, frequently are not, and sometimes cannot be supported by evidence.

Davis, *Judicial Notice*, 55 Colum. L. Rev. 945, 952 (1955).

Adjudicative facts are the facts to which the law is applied. Legislative facts are the facts by which the law is interpreted. Regardless of the nature of the facts — whether social, economic, political, or scientific — a fact is legislative if used to interpret or determine the statute's validity or to extend or restrict a rule of law, whether statutory, constitutional or common-law in origin. *See* McCormick on Evidence, § 331 (4th ed. 1992). Contrary to what the label might suggest, "legislative facts" are limited neither to facts developed or relied upon by a legislature in formulating statutory provisions, nor to laws created by legislation. Legislative facts include all facts relevant to the interpretation of law (in the broadest sense of that term) and the assessment of its meaning and purpose.

Every level of the judicial process must occasionally take judicial notice of legislative facts, as part of the responsibility of correctly interpreting the applicable law. There are numerous examples of instances where courts have taken judicial notice of legislative facts. Several of these instances involve the United States Supreme Court. In *Brown v. Board of Educ.*, 347 U.S. 483 (1953), for example, in considering whether the segregation of black and white children in public schools violated the black children's equal protection rights, the Court concluded that such segregation was unconstitutional after taking judicial notice of the fact that segregating black children "generates a feeling of inferiority as to their status in the community that may affect their hearts and minds in a way unlikely ever to be undone." In *Trammel v. United States*, 445 U.S. 40 (1979), the Court considered the scope of the spousal privilege, which allows one spouse to preclude the other from testifying against him. The spousal privilege was designed to foster the harmony and sanctity of the marriage relationship. After concluding (or taking judicial notice of the fact) that "[w]hen one spouse is willing to testify against the other in a criminal proceeding — whatever the motivation — their relationship is almost certainly in disrepair; there is probably little in the way of marital harmony for the privilege to preserve," the Court held that the privilege should be modified so that the witness-spouse alone has the privilege to refuse to testify adversely. In upholding a law that prohibited women from working more than ten hours per day, the Court in *Muller v. Oregon*, 208 U.S. 412 (1908), took "judicial cognizance of all matters of general knowledge," which included the facts that "[t]he two sexes differ in structure of body, in the functions to be performed by each, in the amount of physical strength, in the capacity for long continued labor, particularly when done standing, the influence of vigorous health upon the future well-being of the race, the self-reliance which enables one to assert full rights, and in the capacity to maintain the struggle for subsistence." *Id.* at 423.

One important aspect of legislative facts that should be apparent from the above examples is that they need not be indisputable for a court to take notice of them. Legislative facts need only be acceptably sound to be judicially noticed. In *Brown*, for example, it was by no means undisputed in 1953 among noted sociologists and psychologists that segregation had the effect on blacks that the Court noticed as a legislative fact. Similarly, even in 1908, it was hardly a universally accepted fact that women had less capacity for long-continued labor than men.

Unlike adjudicative facts, there are no restrictions on the sources that judges may consult for instruction and guidance about legislative facts. A court may judicially notice adjudicative facts only if the facts can be accurately verified from unimpeachable or *authoritative sources*. The judge may discover legislative facts from any source that the judge chooses to consult. Moreover, because legislative facts relate only generally to the cause of action, it is not essential that the court notify the litigants that it is considering taking judicial notice of these facts; nor need the parties be given an opportunity to be heard. The court's failure to give the parties notice and an opportunity to be heard will not impinge upon the fairness or accuracy of its conclusion. The parties are deemed to be no more qualified to know the facts, to have no better access to those facts, and to be no more capable of ascertaining the facts than the judges and their staffs.

Although the courts' power to judicially notice legislative facts is exceptionally broad, it is not without limitations. In *Minnesota v. Clover Leaf Creamery Co.*, 449 U.S. 456 (1981), the Supreme Court held that when courts determine the constitutionality of legislation under the "rational relationship" test — determining whether a statute is rationally related to its articulated objectives (as opposed to the "strict scrutiny" employed when fundamental interests and suspect classifications are involved, *see Brown v. Board of Educ., below*) — it is impermissible for them to take notice of legislative facts different from those noted by the legislature where there is a rational basis for the legislature's findings. So long as the facts noticed by the legislature are at least debatable, the constitutionality of the legislation must be determined on the basis of those facts. *Id.* at 464. The courts may not substitute their evaluation of legislative facts for that of the legislature under this limited standard of review.[24]

Davis' legislative-adjudicative fact distinction was not generally adopted in our common-law jurisprudence. Nevertheless, the labels accurately categorized facts that courts treated differently. Since adoption of the Federal Rules of Evidence, however, this distinction has become more significant, because Congress adopted it in Rule 201 of the Federal Rules of Evidence as the basis for limiting the scope of that rule.

[3] Judicial Notice of Law

How does the plaintiff establish the controlling law in the cause of action.

Over time, most states extended this practice to the general laws of sister states because those laws were readily accessible through published codes, even though they were not as familiar to the presiding judge as the law of the forum. Although this relieved the parties of the obligation of proving the laws, many jurisdictions still required that they be specifically pleaded for both notice and convenience purposes. Most jurisdictions, however, required only that the pleadings put the opponent on notice of the foreign laws on which the pleading party would rely. In the federal courts, the judge was required to take judicial notice of both federal laws and the laws of all state jurisdictions without either plea or proof. *See Lamar v. Micou*, 114 U.S. 218, 223 (1885).

In contrast to most state and federal laws, judges will not normally take judicial notice of private laws (private acts of the legislature through which special rights and privileges are granted to particular individuals) or of provisions of municipal codes, generally because of their limited accessibility. The same is generally true of the laws of foreign countries. In each of these instances, the laws must still be specifically pleaded and proven.

If required to do so, a party can establish foreign law in a number of ways; the proving party may choose the method of proof. Treated like any issue of fact that must be pleaded and proven, the foreign law can be established through expert

---

[24] In *Clover Leaf* the State had enacted a statute banning the retail sale of milk in plastic, nonreturnable, nonrefillable containers but permitted the continued sale in other types of nonreturnable, nonrefillable containers. The state's objectives were to promote resource conservation, ease solid waste disposal problems, and conserve energy. Plastic containers were singled out because it was concluded, on the basis of several reputable studies, that (1) the use of plastic milk containers was less energy efficient; (2) plastic milk bottle production consumed nonrenewable petroleum resources as opposed to renewable wood product paperboard containers; and (3) plastic milk bottles created disposal problems because they occupied a greater volume in sanitary landfills than did other nonreturnable milk containers. The Court held that because the results of these studies supported the legislature's findings and were consistent with its stated objectives, the courts could not review the legislation on the basis of other factual assumptions.

testimony (whether the expert is retained privately or court-appointed) or learned treatises, or by calling upon the proper foreign officials to certify and hence authenticate the text of the foreign law.

[4]   Distinction Between Legislative and Adjudicative Facts

[a]   General Principles Applied by Courts

Rule 201 and its procedural rights apply only to judicial notice of adjudicative facts. Consequently, the distinction between legislative and adjudicative facts has become an important preliminary issue that the court must resolve before taking judicial notice of any fact. The following case presents a discussion of the nature of this preliminary issue and the difficult problems that courts will encounter in resolving it.

UNITED STATES v. BELLO
United States Court of Appeals, First Circuit
194 F.3d 18 (1999)

LIPEZ, CIRCUIT JUDGE.

Jesús Bello appeals his conviction and sentence for assaulting a fellow prisoner in the Metropolitan Detention Center in Guaynabo, Puerto Rico ("MDC-Guaynabo") in violation of 18 U.S.C. § 113(a)(6). Bello claims that the court erred in taking judicial notice of the jurisdictional element of the offense, namely, that MDC-Guaynabo was within the territorial jurisdiction of the United States. He also claims that the court erred in refusing to instruct the jury on his defenses of self-defense and duress, and in telling the jurors outside of the presence of counsel, in response to a jury inquiry, that self-defense was not applicable in this case. In challenging his sentence, he claims that the court mistakenly believed that it lacked the legal authority to grant a downward departure on grounds of coercion or duress, and that the court erred in refusing to grant a reduction in offense level for acceptance of responsibility. We affirm.

I.

Factual background

At the time of the events in question, Bello was a prisoner confined at MDC-Guaynabo where he worked as a food service orderly, serving food to other prisoners. In this capacity, he was responsible for ensuring that food was distributed to all inmates. The victim of Bello's assault, Domingo Santana-Rosa, was also a prisoner in MDC-Guaynabo. Bello testified that Santana frequently sneaked into the food service line and requested seconds even when all other prisoners had not yet eaten. According to Bello, at around 5:00 PM on July 23, 1996, he refused to serve Santana a second helping at dinner because five other inmates had yet to eat. Santana then told Bello that he and another inmate were "going to crack open

[Bello's] head." After making the threat, Santana sat down with several other inmates, including one "Porra." Porra later advised Bello that Santana planned to attack him while Bello was working out in the recreational yard of the prison. Bello testified that he did not report the threat to prison authorities because he feared the repercussions of being labeled a "snitch" by his peers.

On July 25, 1996, at around 11:30 AM, Santana was playing dominoes with other inmates in the recreational yard. Bello noticed Santana's presence, and he became alarmed when he further noticed that the table for playing dominoes, which was ordinarily in the prison's game room, had been moved into the yard where it now stood only a few feet away from where Bello intended to exercise. Bello grabbed a push broom from the corner of the yard and hit the wall of the yard with its handle, stating that it was a good stick for playing baseball. At that point Santana first noticed Bello's presence in the yard, but he continued playing dominoes. Bello removed the handle from the push broom and kept the head. He walked towards Santana and, once behind him, Bello hit him in the back of the head with the push broom head. Santana collapsed, unconscious, and was taken to the hospital where he was operated on to relieve an epidural hematoma (a blood clot under the skull). Santana survived and regained consciousness six days later. The entire incident was captured on videotape.

Bello was indicted on one count of assault within the jurisdiction of the United States (as defined in 18 U.S.C. § 7(3)), in violation of 18 U.S.C. § 113(a)(6). Pursuant to Fed.R.Evid. 201 ("Rule 201"), the government filed a pretrial motion requesting that the court take judicial notice that MDC-Guaynabo is located within Fort Buchanan, a military base on lands "reserved or acquired for the use of the United States, and under the exclusive or concurrent jurisdiction thereof," and thus is within the "special maritime or territorial jurisdiction of the United States." The pretrial motion was accompanied by documentation1 tending to prove the requisite elements. The court deferred making a ruling on the motion until trial.

At trial, the government presented before the jury the testimony of Alma López, the legal advisor to the warden of MDC-Guaynabo, who stated that the land on which the prison was located was owned by the federal Bureau of Prisons and was formerly part of Fort Buchanan, but was transferred to the Bureau by the Department of Defense. After cross-examining López, defense counsel objected to the court taking judicial notice of the fact that MDC Guaynabo is under the exclusive jurisdiction of the United States. Because López was not in a position to authenticate the documentation submitted with the pretrial motion, the documents were not admitted into evidence. However, the court examined the documents outside the presence of the jury and concluded that it could take judicial notice (based on both the testimony in evidence and the documents) that the MDC-Guaynabo facility was within the jurisdiction of the United States. The court announced to the jury that it was taking judicial notice of this jurisdictional fact, but informed them that they were "not required to accept as conclusive any fact that the Court has judicially noticed." The jury was similarly instructed before it retired to deliberate.

The court denied Bello's request to instruct the jury on his defenses of duress and self-defense, ruling that there were no facts which justified such instructions.

During deliberations, the jury requested clarification on the meaning of self-defense. The court responded by informing the jurors that self-defense was not applicable to this case. The jury found Bello guilty of assault.

The court subsequently denied an oral motion by Bello to set aside the verdict on the ground that there was insufficient proof of the jurisdictional element of which the court took judicial notice. Bello then filed a motion for a new trial, arguing that the court erred in failing to instruct on self-defense. The court denied the motion.

Bello was subsequently sentenced to a term of imprisonment of 120 months, 60 months of which was to be served concurrently with the remainder of a previous federal criminal sentence. A supervised release term of 3 years and a special monetary assessment of $100 were also imposed. This appeal ensued.

II.

Judicial notice

Bello argues that the court improperly took judicial notice that the assault occurred "within the special maritime and territorial jurisdiction of the United States." In so doing, the Court took judicial notice of an element of the offense for which Bello was convicted. That fact lends particular significance to the judicial notice issue.

Since the government petitioned, and the trial court ruled, pursuant to Rule 201, we address the conformity of the court's judicial notice determination with that rule. Rule 201 provides in relevant part:

(a) Scope of rule. This rule governs only judicial notice of adjudicative facts.

(b) Kinds of facts. A judicially noticed fact must be one not subject to reasonable dispute in that it is either (1) generally known within the territorial jurisdiction of the trial court or (2) capable of accurate and ready determination by resort to sources whose accuracy cannot reasonably be questioned.

*   *   *

(g) Instructing jury. In a civil action or proceeding, the court shall instruct the jury to accept as conclusive any fact judicially noticed. In a criminal case, the court shall instruct the jury that it may, but is not required to, accept as conclusive any fact judicially noticed.

Fed. R. Evid. 201. By its terms, Rule 201 applies only to adjudicative facts, and the parties and the court assumed that the jurisdictional element at issue here involved an adjudicative rather than a legislative fact. They assumed correctly. Whether a fact is adjudicative or legislative depends not on the nature of the fact — e.g., who owns the land — but rather on the use made of it (i.e., whether it is a fact germane to what happened in the case or a fact useful in formulating common law policy or interpreting a statute) and the same fact can play either role depending on context. See Fed. R. Evid. 201, Advisory Committee's note ("Adjudicative facts are simply the facts of the particular case. Legislative facts, on the other hand, are those which have relevance to legal reasoning and the lawmaking process . . . ."). Where the prison sits is an element of the offense and unquestionably an adjudicative fact, and we review the trial court's decision to take judicial notice under Rule 201 for abuse of discretion. See *United States v. Chapel*, 41 F.3d 1338, 1342 (9th Cir.1994); see also *Taylor v. Charter Medical Corp.*, 162 F.3d 827, 829 (5th Cir.1998) (applying abuse of discretion standard to refusal to take judicial notice).

MDC-Guaynabo's location within the jurisdiction of the United States is the "kind of fact" judicially recognizable under Rule 201(b). To qualify for judicial notice, a fact "must be one not subject to dispute in that it is either (1) generally known within the territorial jurisdiction of the trial court or (2) capable of accurate and ready determination by resort to sources whose accuracy cannot reasonably be questioned." The Advisory Committee's note to Rule 201 explains:

> The usual method of establishing adjudicative facts is through the introduction of evidence, ordinarily consisting of testimony of the witnesses. If particular facts are outside the area of reasonable controversy, this process is dispensed with as unnecessary. A high degree of indisputability is an essential prerequisite.

Rule 201, Advisory Committee's note (emphasis provided).

The trial court based judicial notice on both prongs of Rule 201(b), finding that MDC-Guaynabo's presence within the jurisdiction of the United States is of such common knowledge and can be so accurately and readily determined that it cannot reasonably be disputed. By "generally known" Rule 201(b)(1) "must refer to facts which exist in the unaided memory of the populace; if the fact is one that a reasonable person would not know from memory but would know where to find, it falls within subdivision (2)," not (1). 21 Wright & Graham, Federal Practice and Procedure § 5105, at 407 (1977). Although the label "federal penitentiary" might suggest to the average person that MDC-Guaynabo is under the jurisdiction of the United States, it is unlikely that the "reasonable person" has any familiarity with MDC-Guaynabo at all, let alone its jurisdictional status. Hence, Rule 201(b)(1) cannot supply a basis for judicially noticing the jurisdictional fact in this case.

However, judicial notice was proper pursuant to Rule 201(b)(2), based on "sources whose accuracy cannot reasonably be questioned." Indeed, "[g]eography has long been peculiarly susceptible to judicial notice for the obvious reason that geographic locations are facts which are not generally controversial and thus it is within the general definition contained in Fed. R. Evid. 201(b) . . . ." *United States v. Piggie*, 622 F.2d 486, 488 (10th Cir.1980); see also *United States v. Blunt*, 558 F.2d 1245, 1247 (6th Cir.1977). Moreover, "official government maps have long been held proper subjects of judicial notice." *Government of Canal Zone v. Burjan*, 596 F.2d 690, 694 (5th Cir.1979). The government submitted to the court official government maps, letters from Army officials, and various legislative acts of Puerto Rico, all tending to show that MDC-Guaynabo was within the jurisdiction of the United States. Although the defense cross-examined López, the legal advisor to the warden of MDC-Guaynabo, suggesting some "dispute" over López's testimony, it is clear from the record that the trial court based its decision to take judicial notice largely on the maps and other documents submitted by the government whose accuracy was not questioned by the defense. To be sure, the trial court's decision to judicially recognize a fact upon which testimony had already been presented and subjected to cross-examination before the jury was unusual. Nonetheless, the existence of independent and undisputed documentary evidence in the form of government maps, official letters, and public laws provided a sufficient basis for judicial notice under Rule 201(b)(2), irrespective of López's testimony.

Concluding that the trial court properly exercised its discretion in taking judicial notice of the jurisdictional fact, we must decide next whether the trial court correctly adhered to Rule 201's procedures for instructing the jury. Rule 201(g) provides that: "In a civil action or proceeding, the court shall instruct the jury to accept as conclusive any fact judicially noticed. In a criminal case, the court shall instruct the jury that it may, but is not required to, accept as conclusive any fact judicially noticed." Fed.R.Evid. 201(g). "Congress intended to . . . create one kind of judicial notice for criminal cases and another for civil cases." 21 Wright & Graham, Federal Practice and Procedure § 5111, at 274 (1999 Supp.). "In a criminal case, Rule 201(g) treats judicial notice like a presumption; it relieves one party of the need to produce evidence but does not prevent the other party from contesting" the noticed fact with evidence and argument to the jury. Id. at 534.

The instruction offered by the court was as follows:

> Even though no evidence has been introduced about it in your presence, I believe that the fact that the Metropolitan Detention Center is within a land reserved for the use of the United States and under its exclusive jurisdiction . . . is of such common knowledge and can be so accurately and readily determined from the Metropolitan Detention Center officials that it cannot reasonably be disputed. You may, therefore, reasonably treat this fact as proven even though no evidence has been presented on this point before you.

> As with any fact presented in the case, however, the final decision whether or not to accept it is for you to make and you are not required to agree with me.

This instruction was based on a nearly identical instruction from the Eighth Circuit, Model Crim. Jury Instr. 8th Cir. § 2.04 (1989); see also 1 Weinstein's Federal Evidence § 201.34[3] (1999) (quoting Federal Judicial Center Pattern Criminal Jury Instructions, no. 7 (commentary), which is itself based on one of the few opinions treating the application of Rule 201(g), *United States v. Deckard*, 816 F.2d 426, 428 (8th Cir.1987)). As in *Deckard*, "[h]ere the trial court meticulously followed the command of Rule 201(g). After having instructed the jury generally on presumption of innocence and burden of proof," 816 F.2d at 428, the court issued an instruction that complied entirely with the dictates of the rule.

Of course, compliance with Rule 201 does not establish that application of Rule 201 in this case was constitutional. The Sixth Amendment of the Constitution guarantees to a criminal defendant the opportunity for a jury to decide guilt or innocence. See *Duncan v. Louisiana*, 391 U.S. 145, 149, 88 S. Ct. 1444, 20 L. Ed. 2d 491 (1968). "A necessary corollary is the right to have one's guilt determined only upon proof beyond the jury's reasonable a charged crime." *United States v. Mentz*,

840 F.2d 315, 319 (6th Cir.1988); see also *Moore v. United States*, 429 U.S. 20, 22, 97 S. Ct. 29, 50 L. Ed. 2d 25 (1976) (per curiam). "[A] judge may not direct a verdict of guilty no matter how conclusive the evidence." *United Bhd. of Carpenters and Joiners v. United States*, 330 U.S. 395, 408, *United States v. Argentine*, 814 F.2d 783, 788 (1st Cir.1987). "A plea of not guilty places all issues in dispute, even the most patent truths." *Mentz*, 840 F.2d at 320 (internal quotation marks omitted).

Nonetheless, there is widespread agreement that Rule 201(g), which makes judicial notice non-conclusive in criminal cases, adequately safeguards the criminal defendant's Sixth Amendment right to a trial by jury. In rejecting a version of 201(g) that would have made judicial notice conclusive in both civil and criminal cases, Congress emphasized that while a "mandatory instruction to a jury in a criminal case to accept as conclusive any fact judicially noticed is inappropriate because contrary to the spirit of the Sixth Amendment right to a jury trial . . . a discretionary instruction in criminal trials," is constitutional. H.R. Rep. 93–650, at 6–7 (1973), U.S. Code Cong. & Admin. News at 7075, 7079–80. Commenting on the original draft of Rule 201 which made the judicial notice non-conclusive in criminal cases (the version ultimately adopted by Congress), the Advisory Committee noted:

> The considerations which underlie the general rule that a verdict cannot be directed against the accused in a criminal case seem to foreclose the judge's directing the jury on the basis of judicial notice to accept as conclusive any adjudicative facts in the case. However, this view presents no obstacle to the judge's advising the jury as to a matter judicially noticed, if he instructs them that it need not be taken as conclusive.

Weinstein's Federal Evidence § 201App.01[3] (quoting Fed. R. Evid. 201 Advisory Committee's note (March 1969 draft)).

Moreover, the few courts that have considered the constitutionality of Rule 201 have reached similar conclusions. In *Mentz*, the Sixth Circuit ruled that "[a] trial court commits constitutional error when it takes judicial notice of facts constituting an essential element of the crime charged, but fails to instruct the jury according to rule 201(g)." 840 F.2d at 322 (emphasis provided). Similarly, in *United States v. Jones*, 580 F.2d 219, 223–24 (6th Cir.1978), the court concluded that Rule 201(g) preserves the jury's "traditional prerogative." More generally, numerous Courts of Appeals have upheld judicial notice that a location is within the jurisdiction of the United States. See *Hernandez-Fundora*, 58 F.3d at 811 (2d Cir.) (federal penitentiary); Bowers, 660 F.2d at 531 (5th Cir.) (federal penitentiary); *Piggie*, 622 F.2d at 487–90 (10th Cir.) (federal penitentiary); *United States v. Lavender*, 602 F.2d 639, 641 (4th Cir.1979) (federal highway); *Blunt*, 558 F.2d at 1247 (6th Cir.) (federal penitentiary); *United States v. Hughes*, 542 F.2d 246, 248 n. 1 (5th Cir.1976) (military base); *United States v. Anderson*, 528 F.2d 590, 591–92 (5th Cir.1976) (per curiam) (federal penitentiary); *United States v. Benson*, 495 F.2d 475, 481 (5th Cir.1974) (military base); *United States v. Miller*, 499 F.2d 736, 739–40 (10th Cir.1974) (federal penitentiary); *Hayes v. United States*, 367 F.2d 216, 218 (10th Cir.1966) (federal penitentiary). Accordingly, we conclude that the trial court did not err by taking judicial notice that MDC-Guaynabo was within the "special maritime and territorial jurisdiction of the United States."

* * *

Affirmed.

[b]   Do Courts Distort Legislative-Adjudicative Fact Distinction in Criminal Cases to Avoid the Effect of Rule 201(g)?

Rule 201(g) makes all judicially noticed facts permissive, rather than mandatory, in criminal cases. However, Rule 201 addresses only adjudicative facts. Thus, if a court can classify a fact as nonadjudicative, it can take judicial notice of that fact free from the limitations of Rule 201(g). The court can then instruct the jury that it *must* find the noticed fact, thereby making the notice conclusive of that fact.

Did the trial court correctly distinguish between adjudicative and nonadjudicative facts in *United States v. Bowers*, 660 F.2d 527 (5th Cir. 1981), in which it took judicial notice of the fact that Fort Benning, Georgia, is on land which is property of the United States and, therefore, under the jurisdiction of the United States and instructed the jury that it was required to accept this fact as true? The appellate court upheld this action, concluding that such a jurisdictional fact is legislative rather than adjudicative. Changing the focus of the meaning of legislative facts somewhat, the court defined them as " 'established truths, facts, or pronouncements that do not change from case to case but apply universally, while adjudicative facts are those developed in a particular case.' " *Id.* at 531. According to the court in *Bowers*, only the fact that the defendant committed the offense on the property of Fort Benning was an adjudicative fact. *See also United States v. Hernandez-Fundora*, 58 F.3d 802 809–810 (2d Cir. 1995) (trial court charged the jury that "[T]he Government must prove the alleged assault took place within the special maritime and territorial jurisdiction of the United States. This simply means that the alleged assault must have occurred in any lands reserved or acquired for the use of the United States and under the exclusive or concurrent jurisdiction thereof. I charge you now that [Raybrook] is a place that falls within the territorial jurisdiction of the United States. Therefore, if you find beyond a reasonable doubt that the act[] alleged occurred at [Raybrook], the sixth element of the offense has been met"; appellate court affirmed this handling of the jurisdictional issue); *United States v. Warren*, 984 F.2d 325, 327 (9th Cir. 1993) (the existence of federal jurisdiction over a geographic area is a legal question, while the locus of the offense within that area is a factual question for the jury); *United States v. Blunt*, 558 F.2d 1245 (6th Cir. 1977) (permitting trial court to take judicial notice that crime committed within a federal correction institution occurred within the territorial jurisdiction of the United States); *United States v. Jones*, 480 F.2d 1135, 1139 (2d Cir. 1973) (defendant was charged with theft within territorial jurisdiction of the United States — a Veterans Administration hospital; trial court instructed jury that the hospital was within the special territorial jurisdiction of the United States, and that the jury should determine whether the theft occurred at the hospital; "the court's instruction correctly left the factual element — the locus of the crime — to the jury, while reserving the question of law — whether the federal government had accepted jurisdiction — to itself").

By refocusing the definition of a legislative fact on its nature (being an established truth), rather than on the purpose for which courts use it (to interpret the law), the courts have blurred the distinction between indisputable facts and legislative facts. Under this new definition, for example, if it were proven that the defendant possessed a pistol that was loaded, it would be a legislative fact that the object was a deadly weapon. Such an interpretation would also permit the court to take judicial notice and thereby preclude the jury from deciding that cocaine is a controlled substance under the applicable criminal statutes. *See United States v. Berrojo*, 628 F.2d 368, 370 (5th Cir. 1980).

The same problem with the permissive mandate of Rule 201(g) in criminal cases arises when appellate courts consider taking judicial notice pursuant to Rule 201(f). Because there is no jury to instruct at that level, the taking of judicial notice is, in effect, a fait accompli. Thus, it is mandatory for all practical purposes because there is no one to reject or override it. To circumvent the Sixth Amendment right to trial by jury, and Rule 201(g), appellate courts have judicially noticed venue and jurisdictional facts by construing them as nonadjudicative facts that need not be proven as elements of the offense beyond a reasonable doubt. For example, in *Government of the Canal Zone v. Burjan*, 596 F.2d 690 (5th Cir. 1979), the court held that proving that the described place of the offense was within the Canal Zone was unnecessary because the court could take judicial notice of that fact. The description of the place was sufficient to allow the court to determine that the location was not reasonably subject to dispute.

Have these courts correctly interpreted what constitutes a legislative fact? Professor Saltzburg argues that they have, suggesting that the courts are recognizing "a sound distinction between adjudicative facts and the legal significance of those facts." SALTZBURG, ABA LITIGATION SECTION, EMERGING PROBLEMS UNDER THE FEDERAL RULES OF EVIDENCE, at 36 (1983).

[5] Verified Facts — Rule 201 Is Not Intended to Make Judge an Expert Witness

Congress did not intend Rule 201(b)(2) to place judges in the role of expert witnesses by permitting them to take judicial notice of scientific facts that other expert witnesses have contested or would contest during the trial. This is illustrated in the following cases.

In *Prestige Homes, Inc. v. Legouffe*, 658 P.2d 850 (Colo. 1983), the referee of a worker's compensation claim denied benefits because the claimant had failed to establish a causal link between his heart attack and an industrial accident in which he had been shocked by a 220-volt power line. The evidence showed that he suffered from a disease that impaired the proper functioning of his heart and the expert testimony at the hearing on the issue of causation was in conflict. After the denial of his claim, Legouffe appealed and the Colorado Court of Appeals reversed, taking judicial notice of certain scientific propositions found in medical treatises.[27] The court concluded that one of the doctors' opinions on which the referee and Workman's Compensation Commission had relied had been based upon an erroneous assumption of scientific fact and therefore could not serve as a basis for the

---

[27] The Colorado evidence rule on judicial notice was identical to Rule 201 of the Federal Rules of Evidence.

referee's conclusion that no causal connection had been shown. Reversing this action by the Court of Appeals, the Colorado Supreme Court stated:

> The court of appeals relied on medical treatises not offered or admitted into evidence, and not cited by either Dr. Lissauer or Dr. Mutz, for its finding that an electric shock caused by contact with a 220 volt power line can cause serious injury without leaving a visible burn mark. The court in effect assumed the role of an expert medical witness by discrediting the opinion of Dr. Mutz based on independent research and interpretation of medical texts which properly should be interpreted only by experts in the appropriate field. . . . To accept the court's substitution of its own fact findings for those of the referee in this instance would expand the judicial notice rule far beyond its intended scope. The court compared the type of facts judicially noticed here with the simple mathematical calculations based on distance and speed in *Winterberg v. Thomas, supra*, The conclusions to be drawn from the scientific propositions cited by the court of appeals, however, are clearly not indisputable, as shown by the conflicting testimony in the present case. Dr. Lissauer and Dr. Mutz, both certified as experts in the field of cardiology, had different opinions about the effects of a 220 volt shock on the human body. Dr. Lissauer stated that, although he could not express an opinion as to the significance of external burns, in his experience he had observed a patient with severe heart damage from electrocution without external burns. Dr. Mutz, on the other hand, expressed his opinion, without citing specific cases, that the lack of visible burn marks on the hands reflects that the shock did not directly damage Legouffe's heart.

> Even if the proposition that a 220 volt shock could cause serious injury without burn marks were widely recognized within the relevant community, the fact that two medical experts have a reasonable dispute over the conclusion to be reached from that proposition — namely, whether Legouffe's heart attack was caused by the shock in this case — makes the court of appeals' disregard of the referee's finding clearly erroneous. As we stated in *Anderson v. Lett*:

>> Courts cannot indulge in arbitrary deductions from scientific laws as applied to evidence except where the conclusions reached are so irrefutable that no room is left for the entertainment by reasonable minds of any other conclusion.

>> . . . Mutz' medical conclusion that Legouffe's heart attack could not have been caused by the shock is entirely consistent with the factual proposition stated by the court of appeals that "serious injury" can result from a 220 volt shock without external burns. The court of appeals has supplied its own conclusion from a scientific proposition that does not compel that conclusion.

Id. at 853–854.

Rule 201 permits courts to take judicial notice of medical and scientific facts, through reliance upon authoritative treatises, only if those facts are not subject to reasonable dispute. Similar to facts that are within the general common knowledge of the community, "judicial notice applies to self-evident truths that no reasonable person could question, truisms that approach platitudes or banalities." *Hardy v. Johns-Manville Sales Corp.*, 681 F.2d 334, 347 (5th Cir. 1982). In *Hardy*, the court disapproved of the trial court taking judicial notice of the fact that asbestos causes cancer.

[6] Parties Have Right to be Heard, No Right to Prior Notification; How Important Is Prior Notification?

As previously noted, Rule 201(e) affords parties a right to be heard on questions of whether a court should take judicial notice of adjudicative facts. It does not, however, require the court to notify the parties that the court is considering questions of judicial notice. When the court is contemplating such action on the basis of a motion by one of the parties, notification would be automatic. Notification problems only exist when the court is taking judicial notice *sua sponte*. In such situations there is no mechanism by or through which notification would be provided.

Why did Congress not provide a means for giving notice in these situations? It certainly was not an oversight on the part of the Advisory Committee and Congress, because the Advisory Committee's Note expressly acknowledges that there may be instances in which party will receive no advance notice at all. *See* Advisory Committee Notice to Rule 201, 56 F.R.D. 183, 206 (1972).

There are several probable reasons for the omission of a notification require-ment. First, Congress may have assumed, with some justification, that most judicially noticed facts would be of a nonadjudicative or legislative nature (therefore not covered by the rule). Moreover, most of the adjudicative facts that courts would notice under the rule will result from requests by the parties; thus, regular motion practice procedures would result in the notification of the opposing side. Those few instances in which a court will notice adjudicative facts *sua sponte* will likely involve facts so indisputable that it would be a waste of time to require that notice be given in each instance. Finally, the rule recognizes a party's right to be heard after the court takes judicial notice of a fact. Thus, no fairness to the parties is sacrificed for the sake of judicial efficiency.

Delayed notification proved to be pivotal in the court's refusal to take judicial notice in *Knop v. Johnson*, 667 F. Supp. 467 (W.D. Mich. 1987). Five days before the end of the trial, the defendants asked the court to take judicial notice of state and federal court records concerning lawsuits brought by other inmates on the issue of access to courts. Defendants contended that the records in those cases impeached the plaintiff's testimony and proved that inmates were provided with adequate access to the courts. The court found the late timing of the request to be inexcusable and concluded that noticing such records would be unfair at such a late point in the trial because it would effectively preclude the plaintiffs from presenting rebuttal evidence.

Regardless of whether prior notice of the trial court's intention to take judicial notice was given to a party, no claim of error will be reviewed by an appellate court unless the opposing party moves for a hearing on the issue at trial. *See Nationalist Movement v. City of Cumming*, 913 F.2d 885 (11th Cir. 1990), *aff'd sub nom. Forsyth County v. Nationalist Movement*, 505 U.S. 123 (1992).

[7] Taking Judicial Notice After Trial — Fairness Limits Court's Power to Judicially Notice Facts Under Rule 201(f)

Although Rule 201(f) sanctions, without reservation, the taking of judicial notice at any stage of the judicial process, considerations of fairness may discourage courts from judicially noticing some facts after trial. For example, in *Colonial Leasing Co. of New England, Inc. v. Logistics Control Group International*, 762 F.2d 454 (5th Cir. 1985), the defendant declined to produce evidence at the trial, relying on the plaintiff's failure to establish a prima facie case. The appellate court held it to be error when the trial judge, after the jury had been discharged, took judicial notice of the only fact necessary to complete the plaintiff's prima facie proof, because it deprived the defendant of the opportunity to adduce evidence on a critical fact placed in issue by the court's action. *Id.* at 461.

[8] Tension Between Power of Appellate Courts to Take Judicial Notice and Requirement of Rule 201(g) That Judicial Notice in Criminal Cases Be Permissive

[a] Does Rule 201(g) Limit Power of Appellate Courts to Take Judicial Notice in Criminal Trials?

Because of the criminal defendant's Sixth Amendment rights to confrontation and to trial by jury, Congress revised proposed rule 201(g), which directed that jury instructions on all judicially noticed facts be stated in mandatory terms, to require that the effect of judicially noticed facts in criminal cases be permissive only. The jury would have the right to reject the noticed facts, even if the fact could not reasonably be disputed. Doesn't this provision create a conflict with subsection 201(f), which allows appellate courts to take judicial notice of adjudicative facts? If the defendant has exercised the right to a jury trial, will not judicial notice at the appellate level be in conflict with that right, and with the directive of subsection (g) which sprang from it? The following opinion in *United States v. Jones* offers one solution to this obvious conflict.

UNITED STATES v. JONES
United States Court of Appeals, Sixth Circuit
580 F.2d 219 (1978)

ENGEL, CIRCUIT JUDGE.

Appellee William Allen Jones, Jr., was convicted by a district court jury of illegally intercepting telephone conversations of his estranged wife and of using the contents of the intercepted communications, in violation of 18 U.S.C. §§ 2511(1)(a) and (d) (1976). The proofs at trial showed only that the telephone which Jones had tapped was furnished by South Central Bell Telephone Company. Other than this fact, the government offered no evidence to show that South Central Bell was at the time a "person engaged as a common carrier in providing or operating . . . facilities for the transmission of interstate or foreign communications." 18 U.S.C. § 2510(1). . . .

Following the jury verdict of guilty on three of the five counts of the indictment, Jones' counsel moved the court for a new trial on the ground that the government had altogether failed to prove that the wire communication which the defendant tapped came within the definition of Section 2510. Upon a careful review of the evidence, United States District Judge Frank Wilson agreed and entered a judgment of acquittal. The government has appealed.

It is not seriously disputed that an essential element of the crimes charged, and one which the government was obligated to prove beyond a reasonable doubt, was that the conversation which was tapped was a "wire communication" as defined in the Act. Instead, the issue is whether the abbreviated proof offered by the government was minimally sufficient for the *prima facie* case which the government was obligated to place before the jury. In other words, was the proof that the tapped telephone was installed and furnished by "South Central Bell Telephone Company," without more, sufficient to enable the jury to find as a matter of fact that South Central Bell was a common carrier which provided facilities for the transmission of interstate or foreign communications? The government contends that, construing that evidence in the light most favorable to it, these facts could be permissibly inferred by the jury without any other proof.

The government's argument is essentially twofold. First, it urges that South Central Bell's status may reasonably be characterized as a fact within the common knowledge of the jury and that no further record evidence was necessary. Failing that, the government urges that such a fact is the proper subject of judicial notice which may be taken at any stage of the proceeding, including appeal, under Federal Rule of Evidence 201(f).

The government's first argument finds some support in Wigmore. 9 WIGMORE ON EVIDENCE § 2570, at 524–43 (3d ed. 1940). Similarly, the legislative history of the Federal Rules of Evidence indicates that, even in criminal cases, "matters falling within the common fund of information supposed to be possessed by jurors need not be proved." Advisory Committee Note to Federal Rule of Evidence 201(g) (1969 draft), *quoted,* 1 WEINSTEIN'S EVIDENCE 201–2 (1977). As that Note further indicates, however, such matters "are not, properly speaking, adjudicative facts but an aspect of legal reasoning." *Id.* Thus, while the jury may properly rely upon its own knowledge and experience in evaluating evidence and drawing inferences from that evidence, there must be sufficient record evidence to permit the jury to consult its general knowledge in deciding the existence of the fact.

While Wigmore notes that "[t]he range of [a jury's] general knowledge is not precisely definable." WIGMORE, *supra*, § 2570, at 546, "the scope of this doctrine is narrow; it is strictly limited to a few matters of elemental experience in human nature, commercial affairs, and everyday life." *Id.* at 544. This category of fact is not so much a matter of noticing facts outside the record as it is a matter of the communication value of the words used, which can only be understood in the light of the common experience of those who employ them. . . .

While the issue is not without difficulty, we are satisfied that South Central Bell's status as a "common carrier . . . providing . . . facilities for the transmission of interstate . . . communication" is a fact which, if to be established without direct or circumstantial proof, must be governed by the judicial notice provisions of the Federal Rules of Evidence.

The government did not at any time during the jury trial specifically request the district court to take judicial notice of the status of South Central Bell. Nevertheless, it relies upon the provisions of Rule 201(f) which state that "[j]udicial notice may be taken at any stage of the proceeding." It is true that the Advisory Committee Note to 201(f) indicates that judicial notice is appropriate "in the trial court *or on appeal.*" (Emphasis added). . . . It is also true that the language of 201(f) does not distinguish between judicial notice in civil or criminal cases. There is, however, a critical difference in the manner in which the judicially noticed fact is to be submitted to the jury in civil and criminal proceedings:

> Instructing jury. In a civil action or proceeding, the court shall instruct the jury to accept as conclusive any fact judicially noticed. In a criminal case, the court shall instruct the jury that it may, but is not required to, accept as conclusive any fact judicially noticed.

Fed. R. Evid. 201(g). Thus, under subsection (g) judicial notice of a fact in a civil case is conclusive while in a criminal trial the jury is not bound to accept the judicially noticed fact and may disregard it if it so chooses.

It is apparent from the legislative history that the congressional choice of language in Rule 201 was deliberate. In adopting the present language, Congress rejected a draft of subsection (g) proposed by the Supreme Court, which read:

> The judge shall instruct the jury to accept as established any facts judicially noticed.

The House Report explained its reason for the change:

> Rule 201(g) as received from the Supreme Court provided that when judicial notice of a fact is taken, the court shall instruct the jury to accept that fact as established. Being of the view that mandatory instruction to a jury in a criminal case to accept as conclusive any fact judicially noticed is inappropriate because contrary to the spirit of the Sixth Amendment right to a jury trial, the Committee adopted the 1969 Advisory Committee draft of this subsection, allowing a mandatory instruction in civil actions and

proceedings and a discretionary instruction in criminal cases.

. . . Congress intended to preserve the jury's traditional prerogative to ignore even uncontroverted facts in reaching a verdict. The legislature was concerned that the Supreme Court's rule violated the spirit, if not the letter, of the constitutional right to a jury trial by effectively permitting a partial directed verdict as to facts in a criminal case.

As enacted by Congress, Rule 201(g) plainly contemplates that the jury in a criminal case shall pass upon facts which are judicially noticed. This it could not do if this notice were taken for the first time after it had been discharged and the case was on appeal. We, therefore, hold that Rule 201(f), authorizing judicial notice at the appellate level, must yield in the face of the express congressional intent manifested in 201(g) for criminal jury trials. To the extent that the earlier practice may have been otherwise, we conceive that it has been altered by the enactment of Rule 201.

Accordingly, the judgment of the district court is affirmed.

[b]   Does Mandatory Jury Instruction by Trial Court, or Taking of Judicial Notice by Appellate Court, Violate Criminal Defendant's Right to Trial by Jury?

Rule 201(g) requires the judge in criminal cases to instruct the jury about judicially noticed facts in a permissive form, rather than a mandatory or conclusive form. This limitation aside, does the Sixth Amendment right to trial by jury require that the jury must be given the opportunity to decide all factual questions, including the power to arbitrarily reject all evidence offered in support of those facts, regardless of their uncontestable nature? Must the jury's power of nullification necessarily extend to each fact essential to the substantiation of the charges that have been made, or is it sufficient that the jury has the power to reject a finding of guilt that otherwise has been established? Consider the opinion of the court in *Gold v. United States.*

GOLD v. UNITED STATES
United States Court of Appeals, Ninth Circuit
378 F.2d 588 (1967)

MADDEN, JUDGE:.

Appellant Gold was convicted of knowingly using a common carrier for the carriage in interstate commerce of obscene film in violation of 18 U.S.C. section 1462 and of conspiring to commit that offense in violation of 18 U.S.C. section 371. Appellants Fusco and Halbett were convicted only of the conspiracy charge. We affirm.

Evidence presented to the jury showed that special agents of the Federal Bureau of Investigation maintained a surveillance during business hours of the premises of the Eastern Film Laboratories in Henderson, Nevada, for several days in October and November, 1965. During this time the special agents observed appellants Gold and Halbett entering and leaving the premises on various occasions.

On November 3, 1965, appellants Gold and Halbett arrived at the film laboratory in a Cadillac automobile. At approximately 2:40 p.m. they were observed loading five cartons into the Cadillac. After the cartons were loaded, Gold and Halbett were seen driving off together. At approximately 3:20 p.m. the vehicle and Gold alone were observed at the United Airlines freight dock at McCarran Field, Las Vegas, Nevada. Gold was then observed to deliver the five cartons to a United Airlines employee, who completed the air waybill. Gold paid the freight charge in cash and departed.

The waybill was made up from information supplied in part by Gold and indicated that the cartons contained "electronic controls." The shipping document and labels on the cartons themselves indicated that the shipper was Pont Distributors of 1020 South First Street, Las Vegas. A government agent had previously determined that 1020 South First Street was a nonexistent address, and the agent had been unable to identify any company by the name of Pont Distributors.

After the shipment had been delivered to United Airlines and appellant Gold had departed, the airlines customer service manager was contacted by the government agents and informed that the agents had reason to believe that the description on the air waybill of the contents of the packages was inaccurate and that the address of the shipper was nonexistent. The agents then left the manager's office. Though the manger asked them, they did not reveal what they suspected the true contents of the packages to be.

Sometime thereafter the manager decided to investigate further and directed a freight supervisor to take the shipment to the air freight room. There the supervisor and the manager opened one of the packages and discovered film containers. The manager looked at some of the film and subsequently notified the government agents. The agents returned and viewed the films with a projector. They advised the manager to keep the shipment locked in his office, and they returned the next morning with a warrant and seized the packages.

*   *   *

At the close of the government's case, the court, in response to the request of government counsel, took judicial notice of the fact that United Airlines is a common carrier engaged in interstate commerce, and so instructed the jury. Appellant Gold assigns this ruling as error. Gold does not contend that a carrier's status as a common carrier is not an appropriate subject of judicial notice. He did not at trial and does not here challenge the testimony of the United Airlines' employees who testified to the airline's interstate, common carrier operations. Rather he bases his objection upon the broad proposition that a court cannot, in a criminal case, take judicial notice of a fact which constitutes an element of the crime charged. He contends that the government's burden of proving every element of the crime charged cannot be fulfilled by the court's taking judicial notice of an element of the crime.

If the appellant's broad proposition is valid, it would mean that in a criminal case in a federal court in which there is a constitutional right to a jury trial, even the most obvious and indisputable facts, such as, for example, the fact that 12 o'clock midnight is in the nighttime, would have to be formally proved, at the risk that the failure to do so would require a reversal of an otherwise valid conviction. It would mean, at least, that the trial judge could not instruct the jury that midnight is in the nighttime.

In the case of *State v. Duranleau*, 99 N.H. 30, 104 A.2d 519 (1954), Chief Justice Kenison, for the Supreme Court of New Hampshire, said, at page 522:

> Many years ago it was stated that "judges are not necessarily to be ignorant in court of what everyone else, and they themselves out of Court, are familiar with. . . ."

In the New Hampshire case the court reversed the conviction because the fact of which the trial judge took judicial notice and so instructed the jury was not indisputable, and the appellate record did not show that the defendant was afforded an opportunity to dispute it.

The instant case presents no such problem as that involved in the New Hampshire case. The government, on the record, requested the court to take judicial notice that United Airlines is a common carrier engaged in interstate commerce. The appellant objected, and the court at first denied the government's request. Later the court advised the parties that it had decided to grant the request. The appellant did not, of course, offer or request an opportunity to offer evidence that United Airlines is not a common carrier engaged in the interstate commerce. Equally of course, the appellant does not here request a reversal for the purpose of affording him such an opportunity. He requests a reversal so that the case may be tried again upon the same uncontradicted evidence of the government as to the status of the carrier, but without the court's judicial notice of the indisputable fact and its instruction to the jury that the fact existed.

Such a reversal would be completely formalistic and useless and is not required in order to preserve the right to trial by jury. The defendant in a criminal case has a constitutional right that the jury, regardless of the evidence against him, may acquit him. But he does not have the right that the jury should be free, in its deliberations, to decide that the earth is flat.

In *Rosen v. United States*, 161 U.S. 29 (1896), a case involving a prosecution for mailing obscene matter, the Court said:

> It has long been the settled doctrine of this court that the evidence before the jury, if clear and uncontradicted upon any issue made by the parties, presented a question of law, in respect of which the court could, without usurping the functions of the jury, instruct them as to the principles applicable to the case made by such evidence.

The court, in *Rosen*, further said that if the trial court had instructed the jury that the material was obscene, "no error would have been committed," since the material was before the court and was obviously obscene.

In *Rosen*, the Court treated a question of fact, the obscenity of the material, which was obvious and uncontradicted, as a "question of law" and therefore a proper subject of a binding instruction. The Court would not have approved a directed verdict of guilty, yet it said that a binding instruction as to one element of the crime would have been proper.

In the case of *Dennis v. United States*, 341 U.S. 494, 513, the Court had under consideration the propriety of the trial court's instruction to the jury that the court took judicial notice that a certain element of the crimes existed, and that the jury must take its existence as a fact. The crimes charged were violations of the conspiracy provisions of the Smith Act, which made advocacy of the overthrow of the government unlawful. The trial court had recognized that, in addition to the specific acts of advocacy, etc., specified in the statute, it was necessary, in order not to run afoul of the freedom of speech guarantee of the First Amendment, that there be a "clear and present danger" that the advocacy described in the statute might result in overthrow of the government. The existence of "clear and present danger" was, therefore, an element of the crime. Judge Medina, in the district court, instructed the jury:

> . . . I find as a matter of law that there is sufficient danger of a substantive evil that the Congress had a right to prevent, to justify the application of the statute under the First Amendment of the Constitution.
>
> This is a matter of law about which you have no concern. It is a finding on a matter of law which I deem essential to support my ruling that the case should be submitted to you to pass upon the guilt or innocence of the defendants.

The defendants in *Dennis* were convicted. In the Supreme Court of the United States they attacked the constitutionality, under the constitutional guarantee of trial by jury, of the trial court's binding instruction on clear and present danger.

The Supreme Court rejected the attack. Chief Justice Vinson said, for the Court:

> When facts are found that establish the violation of a statute, the protection against conviction afforded by the First Amendment is a matter of law. The doctrine that there must be a clear and present danger of a substantive evil that Congress has a right to prevent is a judicial rule to be applied as a matter of law by the courts. The guilt is established by proof of facts. Whether the First Amendment protects the activity which constitutes the violation of the statute must depend upon a judicial determination of the scope of the First Amendment *applied to the circumstances of the case.* (Italics added.)

"The circumstances of the case," referred to in the last phrase in the foregoing quotation, are facts. As Mr. Justice Douglas points out in his dissenting opinion, with which Mr. Justice Black agreed, there was no evidence in the record as to the strength of the Communist party in the United States, the positions of Communists in industry and government, the extent to which they have infiltrated the police, the armed services, transportation, stevedoring, power plants, munitions works and other critical places.

It is apparent that the trial judge, in taking judicial notice that a clear and present danger existed, must have had in mind a considerable congeries of facts which led him to that conclusion which seemed to him so obviously right that to require evidence of those facts would be a sheer waste of time, a futile formality. The Supreme Court agreed with the trial judge, and approved his binding instruction because it related to "a matter of law." It is perhaps of significance that Judge Medina, in his instruction quoted herein above, referred to it as a "Finding," which suggests that it was based upon facts.

In the instant case, the status of United Airlines as a common carrier engaged in the interstate transportation of goods is indisputable and undisputed. Whether we approve the trial court's instruction that it was so engaged as a proper exercise of judicial notice or, as the Supreme Court did in *Rosen, below,* and *Dennis, below,* as ruling upon a matter of law, we arrive at the same conclusion. The giving of the instruction was not error.

* * *

The judgments against the appellants are affirmed.

[9] Effect of Taking Judicial Notice

The effect of taking judicial notice is only a problem with adjudicative facts — facts upon which the resolution of particular claim and defenses will turn — because the jury usually resolves these factual questions. If the court intervenes in the jury's fact-finding process, the court must instruct the jury regarding the effect of the court's action.

The ramifications of taking judicial notice of a fact can be appreciated only if we understand the doctrine's perceived purpose and the importance of establishing the truth of the fact before judicially noticing it. One view, espoused by Professor Morgan and adopted in many, if not most, jurisdictions, is that the primary purpose of judicial notice is to "prevent a party from presenting a moot issue or inducing a false result by disputing what in the existing state of society is demonstrably indisputable among reasonable men." Morgan, *Judicial Notice*, 57 HARV. L. REV. 269, 273 (1944). Under this view, because the standard for taking judicial notice is the facts' indisputable nature, the taking of judicial notice is conclusive of those facts. The parties could present conflicting evidence to the presiding judge while the judge is considering the preliminary question of whether a fact is indisputable. However, once judges have determined that judicial notice is appropriate because no reasonable dispute exists, no contradictory evidence will thereafter be admissible, and they will instruct the jury to accept the fact as true. Under this view, the truth of the noticed fact may not be challenged because logically such evidence would be both unnecessary and irrelevant if the presiding judge correctly decided the judicial notice question.

Professors Thayer and Wigmore advocated a different view of the effect of judicial notice. *See* J. THAYER, PRELIMINARY TREATISE ON THE LAW OF EVIDENCE AT COMMON LAW, Chap. 7 (1898); 9 WIGMORE, EVIDENCE §§ 2565–2583 (Chadbourn rev. 1981). They argued that courts should use judicial notice primarily as a time-saving device in situations in which facts, although disputable, are unlikely to be disputed. Thayer and Wigmore contended that judicial notice is a procedural mechanism for establishing a *prima facie* case for the existence of a particular fact, thereby shifting the burden of going forward (if not the burden of persuasion) to the

25

opposing side. Having this effect, judicial notice operates much like the Thayer-Wigmore type presumption, which shifts to the opposing side the burden of going forward with evidence to rebut the presumed fact. As Professor Thayer explained:

> Taking judicial notice does not import that the matter is indisputable. It is not necessarily anything more than a *prima facie* recognition leaving the matter still open to controversy. . . . In very many cases . . . taking judicial notice of a fact is merely presuming it, *i.e.*, assuming it until there shall be reason to think otherwise.

J. THAYER, A PRELIMINARY TREATISE ON THE LAW OF EVIDENCE AT COMMON LAW, 308–309 (1898). *See* § 10.01[A][5][b].

Is a theory of judicial notice that is based on parallels between judicial notice and presumptions wise, in light of the significant problems that courts have encountered in applying the prevailing Thayer-Wigmore "bursting bubble" presumption theory? Would this not open another legal Pandora's box? Professor Morgan argued that it would.

> [I]f judicially noticed matter is subject to rebuttal by evidence, it cannot be long before members of the bar will be demanding rulings as to the exact effect of judicially noticing a matter. If the matter is subject to judicial notice, the court may, by universally declared authority, seek information from any and all sources which it deems reliable. Must these sources be disclosed to counsel and the authors of the material relied on be produced for cross-examination? Is the court to be subject to cross-examination as to the extent of its search for relevant data and the validity of its deductions? How much evidence is required to make the contrary of the judicially noticed matter an open question for the trier of fact? How much will entirely nullify the *prima facie* effect of judicial notice? In a jury case may the judge reveal to the jury either the data which has caused him to deem the matter a proper subject of judicial notice or the fact that the matter is within the field of judicial notice? Must he reveal this? In either case, what instruction must he give as to this aspect of the case? Does the party disputing judicially noticed matter have only the burden of producing evidence, or the burden of persuasion also, or something less or something more? If rebuttable judicial notice is not just another name for a presumption, how does it differ from a presumption? If it is a presumption, is it a species of presumption which requires special treatment?

Morgan, *Judicial Notice*, 57 HARV. L. REV. 269, 286 (1944).

If the courts have failed to provide consistent and definitive answers to these questions relative to presumptions, is it likely that the courts will also be unable to resolve these questions for judicial notice under the Thayer-Wigmore approach?

As previously noted, Professors Thayer and Wigmore do not completely disagree with Professor Morgan. Professor McNaughton explains the extent of their disagreement below:

> There is no difference of opinion as to matters of law. Where judicial notice of law is proper, it is agreed that a judge is not obliged to receive

formal evidence to rebut his taking of judicial notice of any matter (legislative facts) helpful in determining the tenor of that law. Even with respect to matters of fact, the disagreement is not pervasive. There is no dissent from the proposition that judicial notice of the rarely mentioned matters of fact relating to judge-imposed sentences is not rebuttable by formal evidence. There may even be no disagreement as to the rebuttability of "jury notice" of the vague and almost indefinable matters of belief used peripherally in the reasoning process, but this point has not been emphasized and is therefore unclear. The real difference between these authorities is limited to rebuttability of judicial notice where it is applied to other matters of fact. Disregarding for the moment "jury-notice" facts and "judge-sentencing" facts, it can be said that the dispute relates to the rebuttability of judicial notice of "adjudicative facts."

McNaughton, *Judicial Notice — Excerpts Relating to the Morgan-Wigmore Controversy*, 14 VAND. L. REV. 779, 794–795 (1961).

The Morgan view of judicial notice, which deems noticed facts to be conclusive and unimpeachable, renders the effect of taking judicial notice the same as the court's having directed a verdict on those noticed facts.

It is unclear which of the two views predominates under the common law. As Professor McNaughton explains, "[t]he cases and statutes are in cloudy confusion." *Id.* at 795–796.

[10] Procedural Aspects of Judicial Notice

Generally, there are no established procedures for the taking of judicial notice. A court can take notice at any level of the judicial process, from the resolution of pretrial motions, throughout trial, and on appeal. Notice can be taken upon request by a party or upon the court's own motion (*sua sponte*). Whenever notice is taken, there have generally been no requirements that the court either inform the parties on the taking of notice or give them an opportunity to be heard on the nature of what the court should notice. There seems to be a rough consensus, however, that the court should afford an opportunity to be heard if the court contemplates taking judicial notice of facts that directly relate to the basis for the cause of action — adjudicative facts. *See* McCORMICK ON EVIDENCE, § 333 (4th ed. 1992).

If the court takes judicial notice on motion by a party, the opposition will be notified and an opportunity to be heard will likely be afforded, particularly if requested by one of the parties. The most difficult question of procedural niceties arises if the court takes judicial notice *sua sponte*. The facts noticed in this manner will usually be of a legislative rather than an adjudicative nature. Often, if the parties do not indicate in their oral and written presentations to the court that a factual or policy issue is material to the disposition of the claims in the litigation, the court, most frequently at the appellate level, will simply announce its decision and disclose the facts that it has independently investigated and found to be true. After the announcement of the decision, of course, the adversely affected party may request that the court reconsider the factual questions and give the requesting party an opportunity to address the issue. Such reconsideration, however, is completely discretionary and the courts are not inclined to grant it. The rationale for not establishing a general requirement of prior notification before the taking of judicial notice of legislative facts has been the fear that it might unnecessarily inhibit judges from enlightening themselves by noticing those extrajudicial materials. This, in turn, would impede the law's development and directly affect the quality of justice.

Inasmuch as there is no formal notice of nonadjudicative or interpretive facts that form the basis of a judge's or juror's understanding of testimony and reasoning, there are no established procedures for the court to follow in taking such notice. Even if there were established procedures, they would likely be of little consequence because the courts seldom recognize this kind of judicial notice.

In those instances in which courts consciously take judicial notice, their discretionary decision to notify the parties and give them an opportunity to be heard will likely turn on the following variables: "(a) whether the facts are close to the center of the controversy between the parties or whether they are background facts at or near the periphery, (b) whether they are adjudicative or legislative facts, and (c) the degree of certainty or doubt — whether the facts are certainly indisputable, probably indisputable, probably debatable or certainly debatable." Davis, *Judicial Notice*, 55 COLUM. L. REV. 945, 977 (1955).

Consistent with the court's power to take judicial notice at any stage of the judicial process, parties can make a request for such notice at any time. Such requests can be made prior to trial through a motion *in limine*, so that factual issues can be eliminated from the trial, thereby diminishing trial preparation effects and costs. Parties typically anticipate, however, having to present evidence to satisfy all elements of their claims or defenses, preparing for trial without exploring, or even considering, this potential shortcut to proof. Parties usually make a request for judicial notice as a case-saving maneuver at the end of a trial or on appeal, when it has become apparent that the moving party has forgotten or been unable to present evidence to satisfy its burden of persuasion.

If a court does give the parties the opportunity to be heard on the question of judicial notice, this opportunity may take many forms, because there are no limits on the kinds of materials upon which the judge may rely in taking judicial notice, and the rules of evidence do not limit the judge in deciding preliminary questions of fact. Information sufficient to convince a judge to notice or refrain from noticing a fact can be supplied through any means — testimony, affidavits, learned treatises, etc. At the appellate level, the parties often supply this information through copious appendices to briefs in which a broad range of materials are incorporated. The prototype of such a brief is the "Brandeis brief" — the brief submitted by Louis Brandeis in *Muller v. Oregon*, 205 U.S. 412 (1908), in which he was defending the constitutionality of the Oregon statute that regulated the working hours of women. Virtually his entire brief was devoted to the presentation of social and economic data, upon which evidence had not been presented in the lower court, that Brandeis had collected to demonstrate the nature and dimension of the problem that the statute was designed to address.

EXERCISES

1. Dippin' Dots markets and sells a brightly-colored flash-frozen ice cream product consisting of free flowing small spheres or beads of ice cream. Dippin' Dots filed a federal trade dress infringement suit against Frosty Bites, a company that sold a very similar product. To survive summary judgement Dippin' Dots must establish that the physical appearance of its product is unique and entitled to federal protection. At a hearing the judge, *sua sponte*, asks both parties if they have any objection to her taking judicial notice that chocolate ice cream is, generally speaking, brown, vanilla is white, strawberry is pink, and so on. May the judge take judicial notice of this fact? Does it matter that the fact is central to the court's trade dress infringement analysis?

2. Is it proper for a judge to grant judicial notice:

    a. that census data establishes that many young black men live in the area where the armed robbery occurred?

    b. that ice hockey is a very rough physical contact sport?

    c. that there is bound to be danger to sports players who happen to be on a one-eyed player's blind side, no matter how well his mask may protect his one good eye?

    d. of the proper method for canning baked beans in New England?

    e. that bingo is a largely senior citizen pastime?

    f. that credit cards play a vital role in modern American society?

    g. that most establishments that sell beer also sell tobacco products?

    h. that calendars have long been affixed to walls by means of a punched hole at the top of the calendar?

[11] Rule 803(18) — Learned Treatises

The learned treatise exception to the hearsay rule is the only exception that *explicitly* recognizes judicial notice as a means of satisfying the factual foundation for admissibility. It specifies that certain kinds of treatises may be established as reliable authority either by expert testimony "or by judicial notice."

This does not preclude courts from using judicial notice with other hearsay exceptions. Its application, of course, is inherently limited by the nature of the statements and documents that are addressed in the other exceptions — not being within the common knowledge of the general community or subject to accurate verification from unimpeachable sources. Exceptions with foundation requirements that a court could judicially notice as facts readily verifiable might include public records (particularly records of the court taking the judicial notice), and certain market reports, and commercial publications.

TABLE OF CASES

[References are to pages]

[References are to pages]

[References are to pages]

[References are to pages]

[References are to pages]

N

[References are to pages]

[References are to pages]

[References are to pages]

[References are to pages]

[References are to pages]

X

Y

Z

INDEX

[References are to sections.]

[References are to sections.]

[References are to sections.]

[References are to sections.]

[References are to sections.]

[References are to sections.]